Object-Oriented Analysis and Design

with the Unified Process

Object-Oriented Analysis and Design with the Unified Process
John W. Satzinger, Robert B. Jackson, Stephen D. Burd

ISBN-10: 81-315-0269-4
ISBN-13: 978-81-315-0269-3

Cengage Learning India Private Limited
418 F.I.E. Patparganj
New Delhi-110092

Tel: 91-11- 43641111
Fax: 91-11- 43641100

Cengage Learning products are represented in Canada by Nelson Education, Ltd.

For product information, visit www.cengage.co.in

Printed in India by Yash Printographics, Noida
Fourth Indian Reprint 2011

Object-Oriented Analysis and Design

with the Unified Process

John W. Satzinger
Southwest Missouri State University

Robert B. Jackson
Brigham Young University

Stephen D. Burd
University of New Mexico

COURSE TECHNOLOGY
CENGAGE Learning™

Dedication

To JoAnn, Brian, and Kevin and to Arnold and LaVone —JWS
To Anabel and my children for their continued support —RBJ
To Dee, Amelia, and Alex —SDB

BRIEF CONTENTS

PART 1	**SYSTEM DEVELOPMENT AND THE UNIFIED PROCESS**	**1**
chapter 1	The World of the Modern Systems Analyst	2
chapter 2	Object-Oriented Development and the Unified Process	36
chapter 3	Project Management and the Inception Phase	78
PART 2	**MODELING AND THE REQUIREMENTS DISCIPLINE**	**123**
chapter 4	The Requirements Discipline	124
chapter 5	Use Cases and Domain Classes	164
chapter 6	Use Case Modeling and Detailed Requirements	210
PART 3	**THE DESIGN DISCIPLINE**	**259**
chapter 7	Design Activities and Environments	260
chapter 8	Use Case Realization: The Design Discipline within UP Iterations	292
chapter 9	Advanced Topics in Object-Oriented Design	358
chapter 10	Designing the Data Access Layer	396
chapter 11	Designing the User-Interface Layer	440
chapter 12	Designing System Interfaces, Controls, and Security	486
PART 4	**IMPLEMENTATION, TESTING, AND DEPLOYMENT DISCIPLINES**	**529**
chapter 13	Making the System Operational	530
chapter 14	Current Trends in System Development	574

CONTENTS

PART 1 SYSTEM DEVELOPMENT AND THE UNIFIED PROCESS 1

chapter 1 **The World of the Modern Systems Analyst** 2

A Systems Analyst at Consolidated Refineries 3
Overview 3
The Analyst as a Business Problem Solver 4
Systems That Solve Business Problems 6
Required Skills of the Systems Analyst 10
The Environment Surrounding the Analyst 13
The Analyst's Role in Strategic Planning 15
Rocky Mountain Outfitters and Its Strategic Information Systems Plan 18
The Analyst as a System Developer (the Heart of the Course) 27
Summary 30
Key Terms 30
Review Questions 31
Thinking Critically 31
Experiential Exercises 32
Case Studies 32
Further Resources 35

chapter 2 **Object-Oriented Development and the Unified Process** 36

Development Approaches at Ajax Corporation, Consolidated Concepts, and Pinnacle Manufacturing 37
Overview 37
The Systems Development Life Cycle 38
Methodologies, Models, Tools, and Techniques 47
The Unified Process as a System Development Methodology 50
The UP Disciplines 55
Overview of Object-Oriented Concepts 60
Tools to Support System Development 68
Summary 74
Key Terms 74
Review Questions 75
Thinking Critically 75
Experiential Exercises 76
Case Studies 76
Further Resources 77

CONTENTS

chapter 3 **Project Management and the Inception Phase** 78

Blue Sky Mutual Funds: A New Development Approach 79
Overview 79
Project Management 80
The Unified Process and the Inception Phase 86
Completing the Inception Phase 114
Project Monitoring and Control 114
Summary 116
Key Terms 116
Review Questions 117
Thinking Critically 117
Experiential Exercises 119
Case Studies 120
Further Resources 121

PART 2 MODELING AND THE REQUIREMENTS DISCIPLINE 123

chapter 4 **The Requirements Discipline** 124

Mountain States Motor Sports 125
Overview 125
The Requirements Discipline in More Detail 126
System Requirements 129
Models and Modeling 131
Techniques for Information Gathering 135
Validating the Requirements 153
Summary 159
Key Terms 159
Review Questions 160
Thinking Critically 160
Experiential Exercises 161
Case Studies 162
Further Resources 163

chapter 5 **Use Cases and Domain Classes** 164

Waiters on Call Meal-Delivery System 165
Overview 165
Events and Use Cases 166
Problem Domain Classes 178

CONTENTS

The Class Diagram 185
Locations and the CRUD Matrix 197
Use Cases, the Domain Model, and Iteration Planning 201
Summary 202
Key Terms 202
Review Questions 203
Thinking Critically 203
Experiential Exercises 205
Case Studies 206
Further Resources 209

chapter 6 **Use Case Modeling and Detailed Requirements** **210**

Electronics Unlimited, Inc.: Integrating the Supply Chain 211
Overview 211
Detailed Object-Oriented Requirements Definitions 212
System Processes—A Use Case/Scenario View 214
Identifying Inputs and Outputs—The System Sequence Diagram 226
Identifying Object Behavior—The Statechart Diagram 237
Integrating Object-Oriented Models 246
Summary 249
Key Terms 249
Review Questions 250
Thinking Critically 250
Experiential Exercises 254
Case Studies 255
Further Resources 258

PART 3 THE DESIGN DISCIPLINE 259

chapter 7 **Design Activities and Environments** **260**

Fairchild Pharmaceuticals: Finalizing Architectural Design for a Production System 261
Overview 261
Moving from Business Modeling to Requirements to Design 262
Understanding the Elements of Design 263
Design Discipline Activities 263
Project Management—Coordinating the Project 267
Deployment Environment 270
Software Architecture 277
Network Design 283
Summary 287
Key Terms 287
Review Questions 288
Thinking Critically 288
Experiential Exercises 289
Case Studies 289
Further Resources 291

CONTENTS

chapter 8	**Use Case Realization: The Design Discipline within UP Iterations**	**292**
	New Capital Bank: Part 1	293
	Overview	293
	Object-Oriented Design—The Bridge between Requirements and Implementation	294
	Design Classes and Design Class Diagrams	302
	Interaction Diagrams—Realizing Use Cases and Defining Methods	312
	Designing with Sequence Diagrams	315
	Designing with Communication Diagrams	334
	Updating the Design Class Diagram	337
	Package Diagrams—Structuring the Major Components	339
	Implementation Issues for Three-Layer Design	342
	Summary	345
	Key Terms	345
	Review Questions	346
	Thinking Critically	347
	Experiential Exercises	353
	Case Studies	353
	Further Resources	357
chapter 9	**Advanced Topics in Object-Oriented Design**	**358**
	New Capital Bank: Part 2	359
	Overview	359
	Modeling System Behavior and Method Logic with Design Statecharts	360
	Design Principles and Design Patterns	366
	Designing Enterprise-Level Systems	376
	Summary	389
	Key Terms	389
	Review Questions	390
	Thinking Critically	390
	Experiential Exercises	393
	Case Studies	394
	Further Resources	395
chapter 10	**Designing the Data Access Layer**	**396**
	Nationwide Books: Designing a New Database	397
	Overview	397
	Databases and Database Management Systems	398
	Object-Oriented Databases	400
	Relational Databases	407
	Object-Relational Interaction	420
	Distributed Databases	423
	Database Design within the UP	431
	Summary	434
	Key Terms	434
	Review Questions	435
	Thinking Critically	436
	Experiential Exercises	437
	Case Studies	437
	Further Resources	439

chapter 11 **Designing the User-Interface Layer** 440

Interface Design at Aviation Electronics 441
Overview 441
Identifying and Classifying Inputs and Outputs 442
Understanding the User Interface 444
Guidelines for Designing User Interfaces 453
Documenting Dialog Designs 457
Guidelines for Designing Windows and Browser Forms 464
Guidelines for Designing Web Sites 469
Designing Dialogs for Rocky Mountain Outfitters 471
Summary 479
Key Terms 479
Review Questions 480
Thinking Critically 480
Experiential Exercises 481
Case Studies 482
Further Resources 485

chapter 12 **Designing System Interfaces, Controls, and Security** 486

Downslope Ski Company: Designing a Secure Supplier System Interface 487
Overview 487
Identifying System Interfaces 488
Designing System Inputs 492
Designing System Outputs 497
Designing Integrity Controls 506
Designing Security Controls 513
Summary 522
Key Terms 522
Review Questions 523
Thinking Critically 523
Experiential Exercises 525
Case Studies 525
Further Resources 527

PART 4 **IMPLEMENTATION, TESTING, AND DEPLOYMENT DISCIPLINES** 529

chapter 13 **Making the System Operational** 530

Tri-State Heating Oil: Juggling Priorities to Begin Operation 531
Overview 531
Implementation 532
Testing 533
Configuration and Change Management 540
Deployment 547
Planning and Managing Implementation, Testing, and Deployment 553
Putting It All together—RMO Revisited 565
Summary 569

Key Terms 569
Review Questions 570
Thinking Critically 570
Experiential Exercises 571
Case Studies 571
Further Resources 573

chapter 14 **Current Trends in System Development** **574**

Valley Regional Hospital: Measuring a Project's Progress 575
Overview 575
Software Principles and Practices 576
Adaptive Approaches to Development 580
Model-Driven Architecture—Generalizing Solutions 594
Frameworks and Components 598
Summary 606
Key Terms 607
Review Questions 607
Thinking Critically 607
Experiential Exercises 608
Case Studies 609
Further Resources 611

The following appendices are available on the student Companion Web Site www.course.com/OOAD:

appendix A **Principles of Project Management**
appendix B **Developing a Project Schedule with PERT/CPM Charts**
appendix C **Calculating Net Present Value, Payback Period, and Return on Investment**
appendix D **Presenting the Results to Management**
appendix E **Guide to Microsoft Project 2003**

FEATURES

Object-Oriented Analysis and Design with the Unified Process was written and developed with both instructor and student needs in mind. Here is just a sample of the unique and exciting features that help bring the field of object-oriented analysis and design and the Unified Process to life.

By 2005, RMO had grown to become a significant regional sports clothing distributor in the Rocky Mountain and Western states. The states of Arizona, New Mexico, Colorado, Utah, Wyoming, Idaho, Oregon, Washington, Nevada, and the eastern edge of California had seen tremendous growth in recreation activities. Along with the increased interest in outdoor sports, the market for both winter and summer sports clothes had exploded. Skiing, snowboarding, mountain biking, water-skiing, jet skiing, river running, jogging, hiking, ATV biking, camping, mountain climbing, and rappelling had all seen a tremendous increase in interest in these states. Of course, people needed appropriate sports clothes for their activities. So, RMO expanded its line of sportswear to respond to this market. It also added a line of casual and active wear to round out its offerings to the expanding market of active people. The current RMO catalog offers an extensive selection (see Figure 1-9).

FIGURE 1-9 Current RMO catalog cover (Spring 2006)

Rocky Mountain Outfitters now employs more than 600 people most $100 million annually in sales. The mail-order operation is st of revenue, at $60 million. In-store retail sales remained a modest p with sales of $2.5 million at the Park City retail store and $5 millio opened Denver store. In the early 1990s, the Blankenses added a ph tion that now accounts for $30 million in sales. To the customer, th ural extension, but to RMO, it meant considerable changes in trans systems to handle the phone orders.

RMO STRATEGIC ISSUES

Rocky Mountain Outfitters was also one of the first sports clothing vide a Web site featuring its products. The site originally gave RMO ence to enhance its image and to allow potential customers to requ of the catalog. It also served as a portal to which were linked all sor sports Web sites. The first RMO Web site enhancement added more

CHAPTER 1 THE WORLD OF THE MODERN SYSTEMS ANALYST

① The text uses an **integrated case study** of moderate complexity—Rocky Mountain Outfitters (RMO)—to illustrate key concepts and techniques. Details about the RMO case are integrated directly into each chapter to make a point or to illustrate a concept—just-in-time examples—rather than isolating the case study in separate sections of the chapters.

[4] Retail store system (RSS): Replace the existing retail store system with a system that can integrate with the customer support system. Package solution.
[5] Accounting/finance: Purchase a package solution, definitely an intranet application, to maximize employee access to financial data for planning and control.
[6] Human resources: Purchase a package solution, definitely an intranet application, to maximize employee access to human resource (HR) forms, procedures, and benefits information.

The timetable for implementing the application architecture plan is shown in Figure 1-13. Key components of the supply chain management system, particularly inventory management components, must be defined before the customer support system project can be started. The customer support system project must be started as soon as possible, however, as it is the core system supporting customer relationship management.

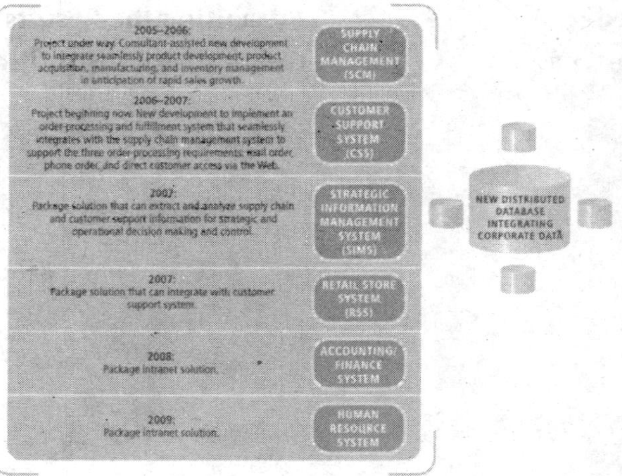

FIGURE 1-13 The timetable for RMO's application architecture plan

CHAPTER 1 THE WORLD OF THE MODERN SYSTEMS ANALYST 25

② An overview of the **strategic systems plan for RMO** is presented in Chapter 1 to place the project in context. The planned system architecture provides for rich examples—a client/server Windows-based component, as well as a Web-based, e-commerce component with direct customer interaction via the Internet. The Unified Process and UML 2.0 are used for all RMO development projects (naturally, tailored to the needs of each project).

FEATURES

③ The new **customer support system (CSS)** is the system development project used throughout the text for examples and explanations. It is strategically important to RMO, and the company must integrate the new system with legacy systems and other planned systems. It will be designed and implemented using **object-oriented techniques and tools**.

④ The **Unified Process (UP)** system development methodology is used for the RMO CSS project and integrated into the text in every chapter. The development project is an iterative and adaptive approach that uses the UP life cycle.

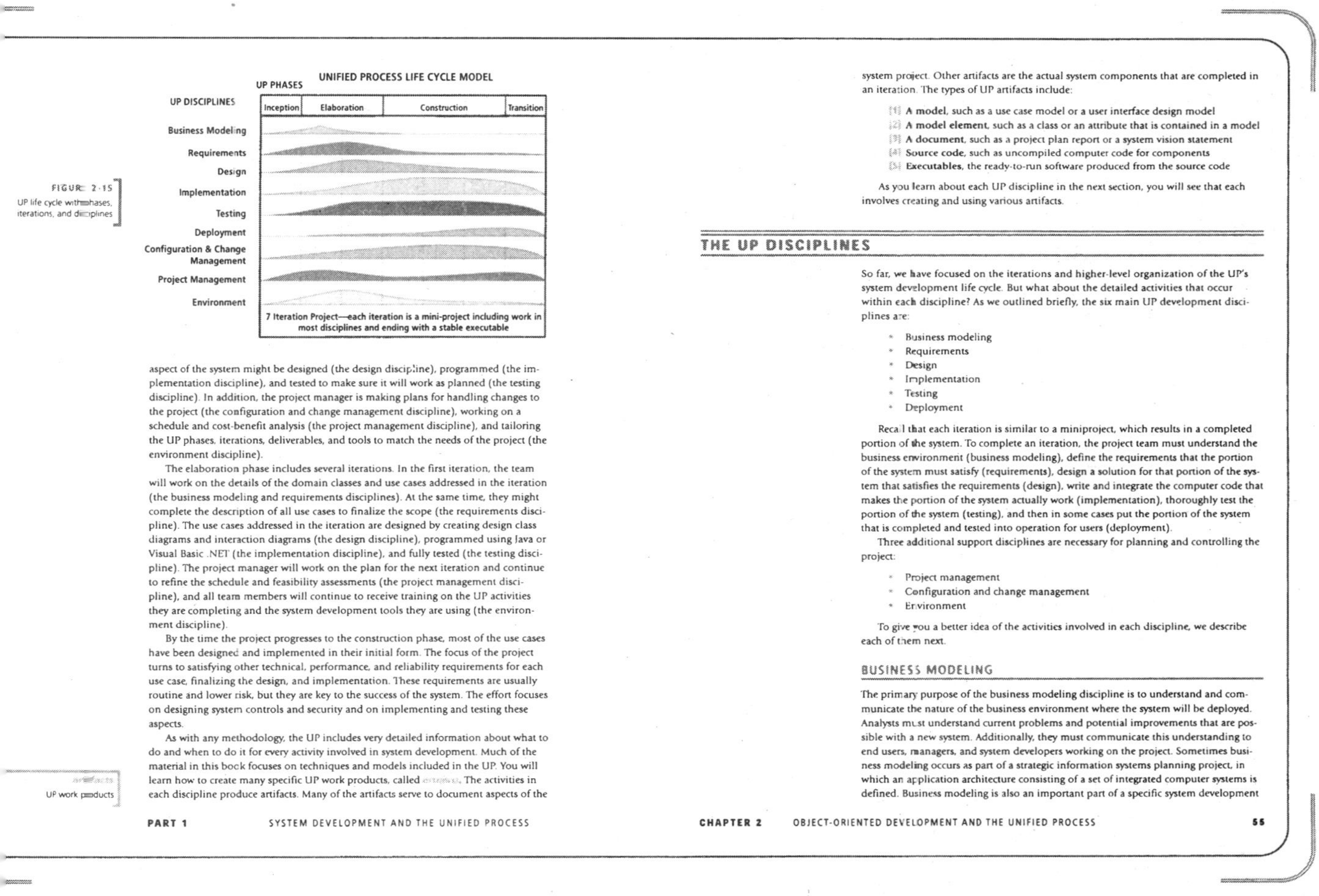

UNIFIED PROCESS LIFE CYCLE MODEL

UP PHASES: Inception | Elaboration | Construction | Transition

UP DISCIPLINES: Business Modeling, Requirements, Design, Implementation, Testing, Deployment, Configuration & Change Management, Project Management, Environment

7 Iteration Project—each iteration is a mini-project including work in most disciplines and ending with a stable executable

FIGURE 2-15
UP life cycle with phases, iterations, and disciplines

aspect of the system might be designed (the design discipline), programmed (the implementation discipline), and tested to make sure it will work as planned (the testing discipline). In addition, the project manager is making plans for handling changes to the project (the configuration and change management discipline), working on a schedule and cost-benefit analysis (the project management discipline), and tailoring the UP phases, iterations, deliverables, and tools to match the needs of the project (the environment discipline).

The elaboration phase includes several iterations. In the first iteration, the team will work on the details of the domain classes and use cases addressed in the iteration (the business modeling and requirements disciplines). At the same time, they might complete the description of all use cases to finalize the scope (the requirements discipline). The use cases addressed in the iteration are designed by creating design class diagrams and interaction diagrams (the design discipline), programmed using Java or Visual Basic .NET (the implementation discipline), and fully tested (the testing discipline). The project manager will work on the plan for the next iteration and continue to refine the schedule and feasibility assessments (the project management discipline), and all team members will continue to receive training on the UP activities they are completing and the system development tools they are using (the environment discipline).

By the time the project progresses to the construction phase, most of the use cases have been designed and implemented in their initial form. The focus of the project turns to satisfying other technical, performance, and reliability requirements for each use case, finalizing the design, and implementation. These requirements are usually routine and lower risk, but they are key to the success of the system. The effort focuses on designing system controls and security and on implementing and testing these aspects.

As with any methodology, the UP includes very detailed information about what to do and when to do it for every activity involved in system development. Much of the material in this book focuses on techniques and models included in the UP. You will learn how to create many specific UP work products, called artifacts. The activities in each discipline produce artifacts. Many of the artifacts serve to document aspects of the

artifacts
UP work products

PART 1 SYSTEM DEVELOPMENT AND THE UNIFIED PROCESS

system project. Other artifacts are the actual system components that are completed in an iteration. The types of UP artifacts include:

1. **A model**, such as a use case model or a user interface design model
2. **A model element**, such as a class or an attribute that is contained in a model
3. **A document**, such as a project plan report or a system vision statement
4. **Source code**, such as uncompiled computer code for components
5. **Executables**, the ready-to-run software produced from the source code

As you learn about each UP discipline in the next section, you will see that each involves creating and using various artifacts.

THE UP DISCIPLINES

So far, we have focused on the iterations and higher-level organization of the UP's system development life cycle. But what about the detailed activities that occur within each discipline? As we outlined briefly, the six main UP development disciplines are:

- Business modeling
- Requirements
- Design
- Implementation
- Testing
- Deployment

Recall that each iteration is similar to a miniproject, which results in a completed portion of the system. To complete an iteration, the project team must understand the business environment (business modeling), define the requirements that the portion of the system must satisfy (requirements), design a solution for that portion of the system that satisfies the requirements (design), write and integrate the computer code that makes the portion of the system actually work (implementation), thoroughly test the portion of the system (testing), and then in some cases put the portion of the system that is completed and tested into operation for users (deployment).

Three additional support disciplines are necessary for planning and controlling the project:

- Project management
- Configuration and change management
- Environment

To give you a better idea of the activities involved in each discipline, we describe each of them next.

BUSINESS MODELING

The primary purpose of the business modeling discipline is to understand and communicate the nature of the business environment where the system will be deployed. Analysts must understand current problems and potential improvements that are possible with a new system. Additionally, they must communicate this understanding to end users, managers, and system developers working on the project. Sometimes business modeling occurs as part of a strategic information systems planning project, in which an application architecture consisting of a set of integrated computer systems is defined. Business modeling is also an important part of a specific system development

CHAPTER 2 OBJECT-ORIENTED DEVELOPMENT AND THE UNIFIED PROCESS 55

⑤ All nine **UP disciplines** are covered, with the most emphasis placed on the requirements discipline, the design discipline, and the project management discipline.

FEATURES

① Project management aspects of the case are reinforced throughout by use of **RMO memos** describing the status of the development project in every chapter.

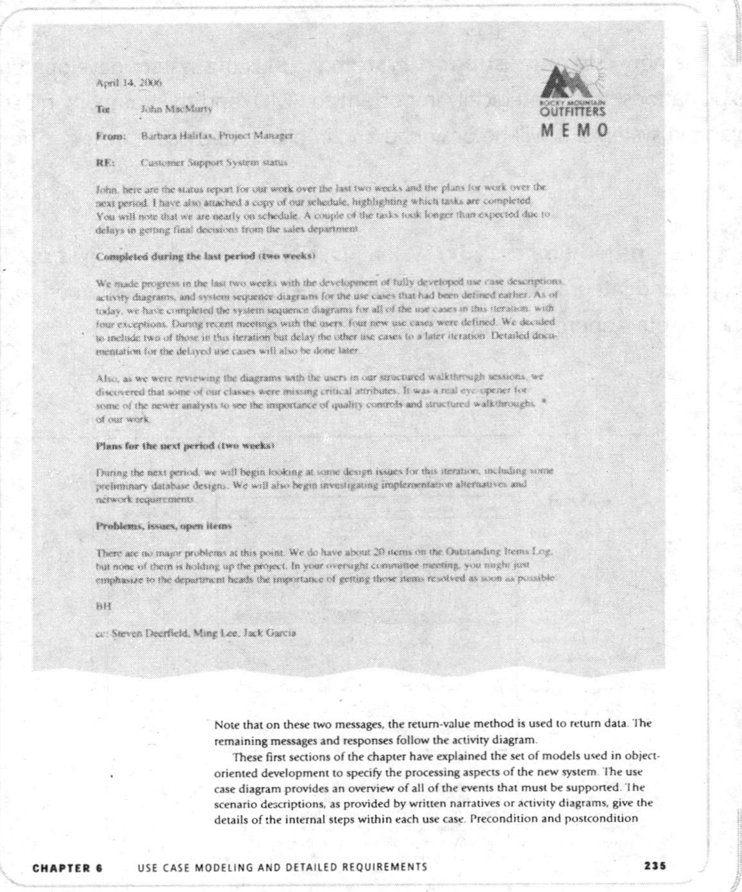

April 14, 2006

To: John MacMurty

From: Barbara Halifax, Project Manager

RE: Customer Support System status

ROCKY MOUNTAIN OUTFITTERS MEMO

John, here are the status report for our work over the last two weeks and the plans for work over the next period. I have also attached a copy of our schedule, highlighting which tasks are completed. You will note that we are nearly on schedule. A couple of the tasks took longer than expected due to delays in getting final decisions from the sales department.

Completed during the last period (two weeks)

We made progress in the last two weeks with the development of fully developed use case descriptions, activity diagrams, and system sequence diagrams for the use cases that had been defined earlier. As of today, we have completed the system sequence diagrams for all of the use cases in this iteration, with four exceptions. During recent meetings with the users, four new use cases were defined. We decided to include two of those in this iteration but delay the other use cases to a later iteration. Detailed documentation for the delayed use cases will also be done later.

Also, as we were reviewing the diagrams with the users in our structured walkthrough sessions, we discovered that some of our classes were missing critical attributes. It was a real eye-opener for some of the newer analysts to see the importance of quality controls and structured walkthroughs of our work.

Plans for the next period (two weeks)

During the next period, we will begin looking at some design issues for this iteration, including some preliminary database designs. We will also begin investigating implementation alternatives and network requirements.

Problems, issues, open items

There are no major problems at this point. We do have about 20 items on the Outstanding Items Log, but none of them is holding up the project. In your oversight committee meeting, you might just emphasize to the department heads the importance of getting those items resolved as soon as possible.

BH

cc: Steven Deerfield, Ming Lee, Jack Garcia

Note that on these two messages, the return-value method is used to return data. The remaining messages and responses follow the activity diagram.

These first sections of the chapter have explained the set of models used in object-oriented development to specify the processing aspects of the new system. The use case diagram provides an overview of all of the events that must be supported. The scenario descriptions, as provided by written narratives or activity diagrams, give the details of the internal steps within each use case. Precondition and postcondition

CHAPTER 6 USE CASE MODELING AND DETAILED REQUIREMENTS 235

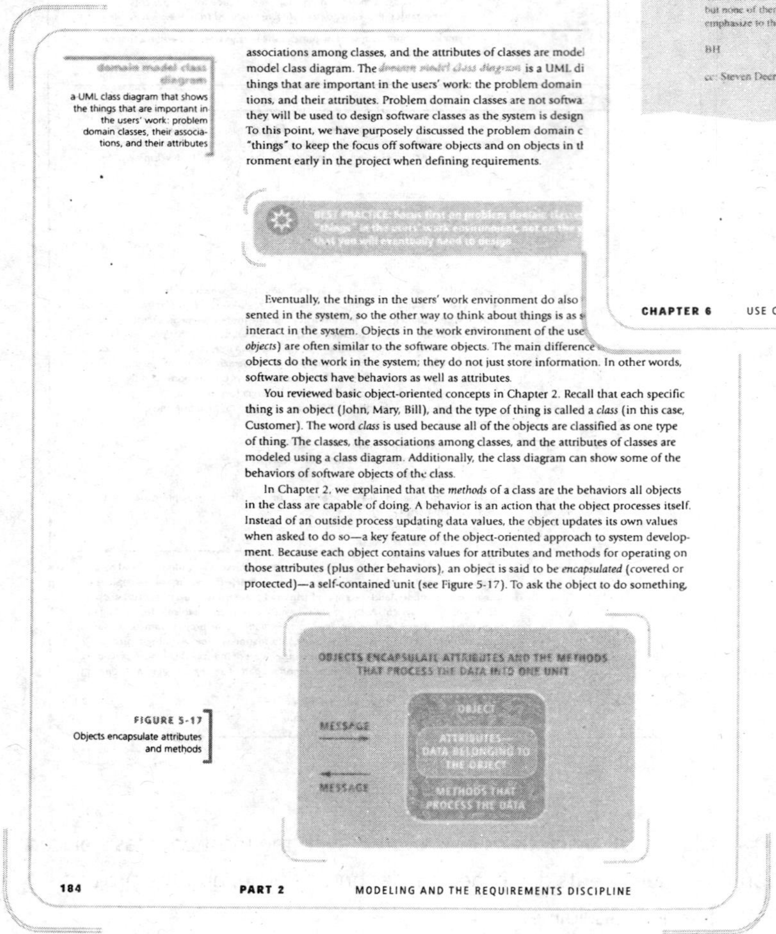

domain model class diagram
a UML class diagram that shows the things that are important in the users' work: problem domain classes, their associations, and their attributes

associations among classes, and the attributes of classes are model
model class diagram. The domain model class diagram is a UML di
things that are important in the users' work: the problem domain
tions, and their attributes. Problem domain classes are not softwa
they will be used to design software classes as the system is design
To this point, we have purposely discussed the problem domain c
"things" to keep the focus off software objects and on objects in tl
ronment early in the project when defining requirements.

Eventually, the things in the users' work environment do also
sented in the system, so the other way to think about things is as s
interact in the system. Objects in the work environment of the use
objects) are often similar to the software objects. The main difference
objects do the work in the system; they do not just store information. In other words, software objects have behaviors as well as attributes.

You reviewed basic object-oriented concepts in Chapter 2. Recall that each specific thing is an object (John, Mary, Bill), and the type of thing is called a *class* (in this case, Customer). The word *class* is used because all of the objects are classified as one type of thing. The classes, the associations among classes, and the attributes of classes are modeled using a class diagram. Additionally, the class diagram can show some of the behaviors of software objects of the class.

In Chapter 2, we explained that the *methods* of a class are the behaviors all objects in the class are capable of doing. A behavior is an action that the object processes itself. Instead of an outside process updating data values, the object updates its own values when asked to do so—a key feature of the object-oriented approach to system development. Because each object contains values for attributes and methods for operating on those attributes (plus other behaviors), an object is said to be *encapsulated* (covered or protected)—a self-contained unit (see Figure 5-17). To ask the object to do something,

FIGURE 5-17
Objects encapsulate attributes and methods

184 PART 2 MODELING AND THE REQUIREMENTS DISCIPLINE

② Every chapter highlights **best practices** applicable to system development concepts in the chapter.

③ Every chapter follows up on the RMO case details by adding an end-of-chapter case study named **Rethinking Rocky Mountain Outfitters**. Each case extends an example in the chapter or poses additional questions to consider about the RMO development project.

RETHINKING ROCKY MOUNTAIN OUTFITTERS

Barbara Halifax wrote her boss that she was moving ahead with the customer support system project, using the Unified Process as the development methodology for RMO. She is still considering how to best tailor the methodology to the project. Additionally, she is still planning how to best introduce the details of the methodology to her project team. Most of the team members have had initial training on the UP, UML, and OO development, but it is still difficult to put a new methodology into practice on a real project.

Consider the nine UP disciplines as a framework for planning the detailed training that members of the project team will need. Look at the specific activities for each discipline.

[1] For each activity, list the CIS or MIS courses at your university that teach the techniques and models related to the activity. Also, for each activity, list supporting business courses at your university that cover related concepts and techniques.

[2] From your investigations, what is the body of knowledge required to fully understand and use the UP on a real project?

FOCUSING ON RELIABLE PHARMACEUTICAL SERVICE

In Chapter 1, you generated some ideas related to Reliable Pharmaceutical Service's five-year information systems plan. Management has placed a high priority on developing a Web-based application to connect client facilities with Reliable. Before the Web component can be implemented, though, Reliable must automate more of the basic information it handles about patients, health-care facilities, and prescriptions.

Next, Reliable must develop an initial informational Web site, which will ultimately evolve into an extranet through which Reliable will share information and link its processes closely with its clients and suppliers. One significant requirement of the extranet is compliance with the Health Insurance Portability and Accountability Act of 1996, better known as HIPAA. HIPAA requires health-care providers and their contractors to protect patient data from unauthorized disclosure. Ensuring compliance with HIPAA will require careful attention to extranet security.

Once basic processes are automated and the extranet Web site is in place, the system will enable clients to add patient information and place orders through the Web. The system should streamline processes for both Reliable and its clients. It should also provide useful query and patient management capabilities to distinguish Reliable's services from those of its competitors, possibly including drug interaction and overdose warnings, automated validation of prescriptions with insurance reimbursement policies, and drug and patient cost data and summaries.

[1] One approach to system development that Reliable might take is to start one large project that uses a predictive approach to the SDLC, to thoroughly plan the project, analyze all requirements in detail, design every component, and then implement the entire system, with all phases completed sequentially. What are some of the risks of taking this approach? What planning and management difficulties would this approach entail?

[2] Another approach to system development might be to start with the first required component and get it workin... other projects could be undertaken to work on the ... fied capabilities. What are some of the risks of ... approach? What planning and management diffic... this approach entail?

[3] A third approach to system development might ... one large project that will use an adaptive and iterat... to the SDLC, such as the Unified Process. Briefly d... you would include in each iteration. Describe how ... development might apply to this project. How woul... approach decrease project risks compared wi... approach? How might it decrease risks compared ... ond approach? What are some risks the iterati... might add to the project?

FURTHER RESOURCES

Scott W. Ambler, *Agile Modeling: Effective Practices for Extreme Programming and the Unified Process*. Wiley Computer Publi...

D. E. Avison and G. Fitzgerald, *Information Systems Development: Methodologies, Techniques and Tools* (2nd ed.). McGraw-H...

Kent Beck, *Extreme Programming Explained: Embrace Change*. Addison-Wesley Publishing Company, 2000.

Ivar Jacobson, Grady Booch, and James Rumbaugh, *The Rational Unified Process*. Addison-Wesley, 1999.

Craig Larman, *Applying UML and Patterns: An Introduction to Object-Oriented Analysis and Designs* (2nd ed.). Prentice-Hall, ...

John Satzinger and Tore Orvik, *The Object-Oriented Approach: Concepts, System Development, and Modeling with UM...* Course Technology, 2001.

CHAPTER 2 OBJECT-ORIENTED DEVELOPMENT AND THE UNIFIED PROCESS

⑥ **Margin definitions** of key terms are placed in the text when the term is first used.

⑦ Each chapter includes extensive **figures and illustrations** designed to clarify and summarize key points and to provide examples of models and other deliverables produced by an analyst.

④ Also, a case study named **Focusing on Reliable Pharmaceutical Service** is included at the end of every chapter to provide additional experience with problem-solving techniques and issues addressed in the chapter. Reliable is a smaller company than RMO, and its strategic information system plan and specific system development project provide a different perspective of object-oriented analysis and design.

⑤ Every chapter includes a list of **additional resources** that can be reviewed for further information about course topics. Here we see references to leading-edge developers Scott Ambler, Kent Beck, Grady Booch, James Rumbaugh, Ivar Jacobson, and Craig Larman, for example, whose innovative ideas are reflected throughout this text.

to complete. A requirements model does not need to indicate how the system is actually implemented, so the model should omit the implementation details.

system controls checks or safety procedures put in place to protect the integrity of the system

Most of these events involve **system controls**, which are checks or safety procedures put in place to protect the integrity of the system. Logging on to a system is required because of system security controls, for example. Other controls, such as backing up the data every day, protect the integrity of the database. Both of these controls are important to the system, and they will certainly be added to the system. But spending time on these controls during early iterations—when the focus is on the users' requirements—only adds unnecessary complexity to the requirements model details. Users are not typically very concerned about system controls; they trust IS staff to take care of such details. Usually, system controls are part of the routine design details that are addressed in later iterations in the construction phase of the UP life cycle.

perfect technology assumption the assumption that events should be included during early iterations only if the system would be required to respond under perfect conditions

One technique used to help decide which events apply to controls is to assume that technology is perfect. The **perfect technology assumption** states that events should be included during the definition of requirements only if the system would be required to respond under perfect conditions—that is, with equipment never breaking down, with unlimited capacity for processing and storage, and with people operating the system who are completely honest and never make mistakes. By pretending that technology is perfect, analysts can eliminate events such as *Time to back up the database*, because they can assume that the disk will never crash. Again, during later iterations, the project team adds these controls because technology is obviously not perfect. Figure 5-7 lists some examples of events that can be deferred until the later iterations.

Don't worry too much about these until the UP construction iterations

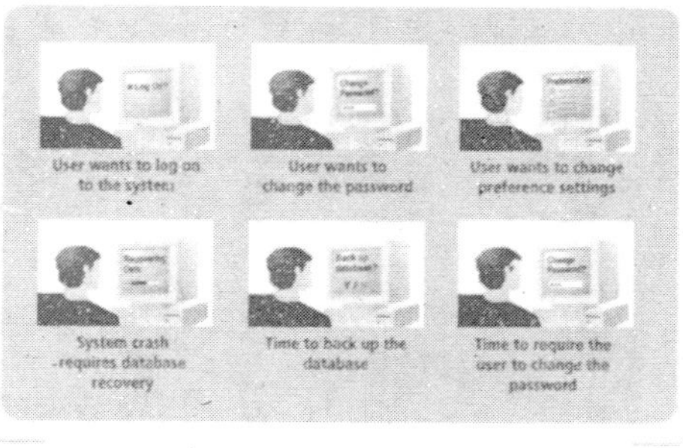

FIGURE 5-7 Events deferred until later iterations

EVENTS IN THE ROCKY MOUNTAIN OUTFITTERS CASE

The Rocky Mountain Outfitters customer support system involves a variety of events, many of them similar to those just discussed. A list of the external events is shown in Figure 5-8. Some of the most important external events involve customers: *Customer wants to check item availability, Customer places an order, Customer changes or cancels an order*. Other external events involve RMO departments: *Shipping fulfills order, Marketing wants to send promotional material to customers, Merchandising updates catalog*. The analyst

CHAPTER 5 USE CASES AND DOMAIN CLASSES 173

FEATURES

① Each chapter begins with a list of **learning objectives** and **chapter outline.**

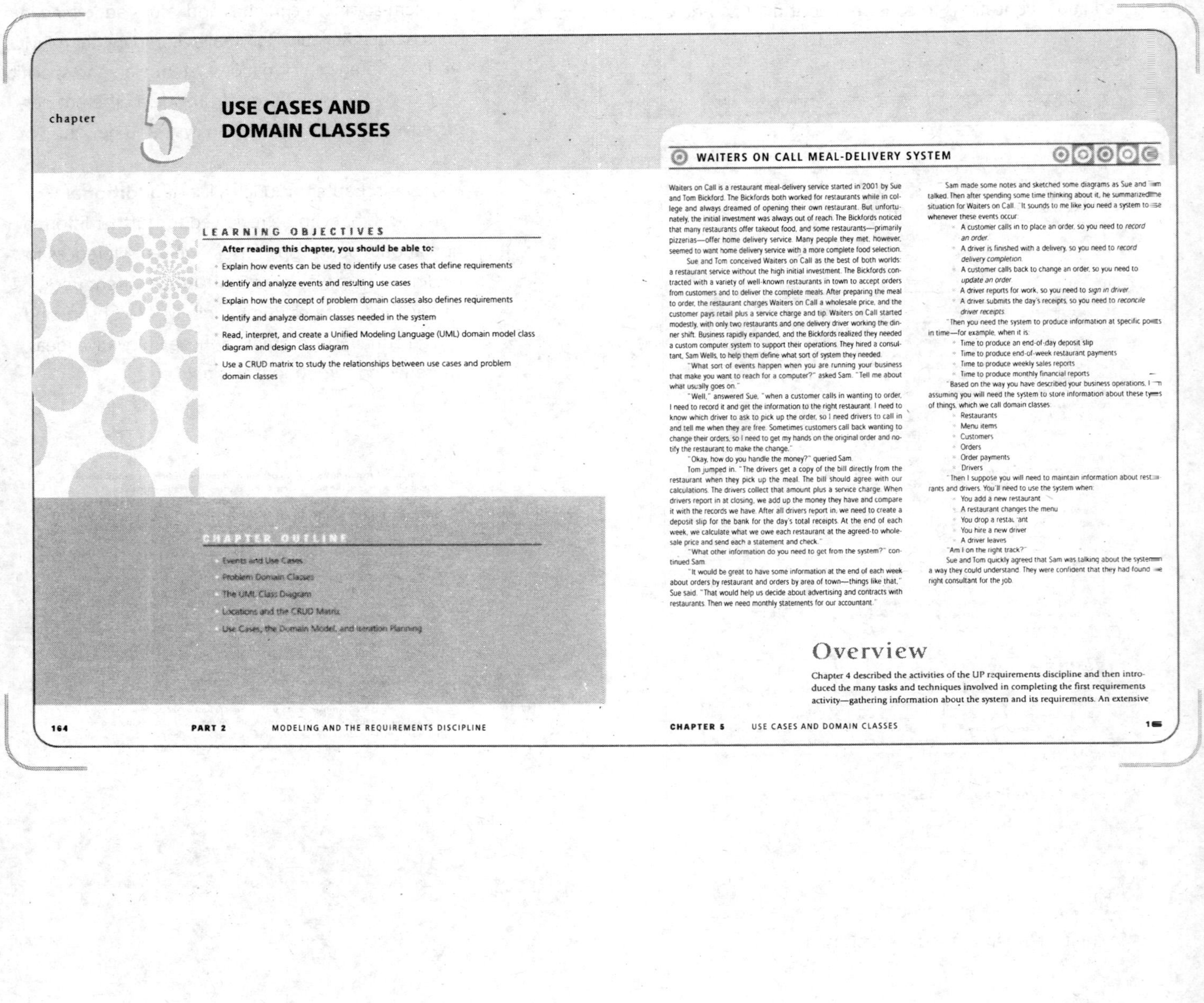

chapter 5

USE CASES AND DOMAIN CLASSES

LEARNING OBJECTIVES

After reading this chapter, you should be able to:

- Explain how events can be used to identify use cases that define requirements
- Identify and analyze events and resulting use cases
- Explain how the concept of problem domain classes also defines requirements
- Identify and analyze domain classes needed in the system
- Read, interpret, and create a Unified Modeling Language (UML) domain model class diagram and design class diagram
- Use a CRUD matrix to study the relationships between use cases and problem domain classes

CHAPTER OUTLINE

- Events and Use Cases
- Problem Domain Classes
- The UML Class Diagram
- Locations and the CRUD Matrix
- Use Cases, the Domain Model, and Iteration Planning

WAITERS ON CALL MEAL-DELIVERY SYSTEM

Waiters on Call is a restaurant meal-delivery service started in 2001 by Sue and Tom Bickford. The Bickfords both worked for restaurants while in college and always dreamed of opening their own restaurant. But unfortunately, the initial investment was always out of reach. The Bickfords noticed that many restaurants offer takeout food, and some restaurants—primarily pizzerias—offer home delivery service. Many people they met, however, seemed to want home delivery service with a more complete food selection.

Sue and Tom conceived Waiters on Call as the best of both worlds: a restaurant service without the high initial investment. The Bickfords contracted with a variety of well-known restaurants in town to accept orders from customers and to deliver the complete meals. After preparing the meal to order, the restaurant charges Waiters on Call a wholesale price, and the customer pays retail plus a service charge and tip. Waiters on Call started modestly, with only two restaurants and one delivery driver working the dinner shift. Business rapidly expanded, and the Bickfords realized they needed a custom computer system to support their operations. They hired a consultant, Sam Wells, to help them define what sort of system they needed.

"What sort of events happen when you are running your business that make you want to reach for a computer?" asked Sam. "Tell me about what usually goes on."

"Well," answered Sue, "when a customer calls in wanting to order, I need to record it and get the information to the right restaurant. I need to know which driver to ask to pick up the order, so I need drivers to call in and tell me when they are free. Sometimes customers call back wanting to change their orders, so I need to get my hands on the original order and notify the restaurant to make the change."

"Okay, how do you handle the money?" queried Sam.

Tom jumped in. "The drivers get a copy of the bill directly from the restaurant when they pick up the meal. The bill should agree with our calculations. The drivers collect that amount plus a service charge. When drivers report in at closing, we add up the money they have and compare it with the records we have. After all drivers report in, we need to create a deposit slip for the bank for the day's total receipts. At the end of each week, we calculate what we owe each restaurant at the agreed-to wholesale price and send each a statement and check."

"What other information do you need to get from the system?" continued Sam.

"It would be great to have some information at the end of each week about orders by restaurant and orders by area of town—things like that," Sue said. "That would help us decide about advertising and contracts with restaurants. Then we need monthly statements for our accountant."

Sam made some notes and sketched some diagrams as Sue and Tom talked. Then after spending some time thinking about it, he summarized the situation for Waiters on Call. "It sounds to me like you need a system to use whenever these events occur:

- A customer calls in to place an order, so you need to *record an order.*
- A driver is finished with a delivery, so you need to *record delivery completion.*
- A customer calls back to change an order, so you need to *update an order.*
- A driver reports for work, so you need to *sign in driver.*
- A driver submits the day's receipts, so you need to *reconcile driver receipts.*

"Then you need the system to produce information at specific points in time—for example, when it is:

- Time to produce an end-of-day deposit slip
- Time to produce end-of-week restaurant payments
- Time to produce weekly sales reports
- Time to produce monthly financial reports

"Based on the way you have described your business operations, I am assuming you will need the system to store information about these types of things, which we call domain classes:

- Restaurants
- Menu items
- Customers
- Orders
- Order payments
- Drivers

"Then I suppose you will need to maintain information about restaurants and drivers. You'll need to use the system when:

- You add a new restaurant
- A restaurant changes the menu
- You drop a restaurant
- You hire a new driver
- A driver leaves

"Am I on the right track?"

Sue and Tom quickly agreed that Sam was talking about the system in a way they could understand. They were confident that they had found the right consultant for the job.

Overview

Chapter 4 described the activities of the UP requirements discipline and then introduced the many tasks and techniques involved in completing the first requirements activity—gathering information about the system and its requirements. An extensive

② Short stand-alone **opening case studies** describe a real-world situation relevant to the material in each chapter. A variety of companies and situations is included to provide the reader with a broad view of the problems and opportunities found in the real world.

③ Accurate and detailed UML 2.0 diagrams are used throughout the text to model requirements and designs. Students are taught to create UML models and apply design principles and design patterns to their models.

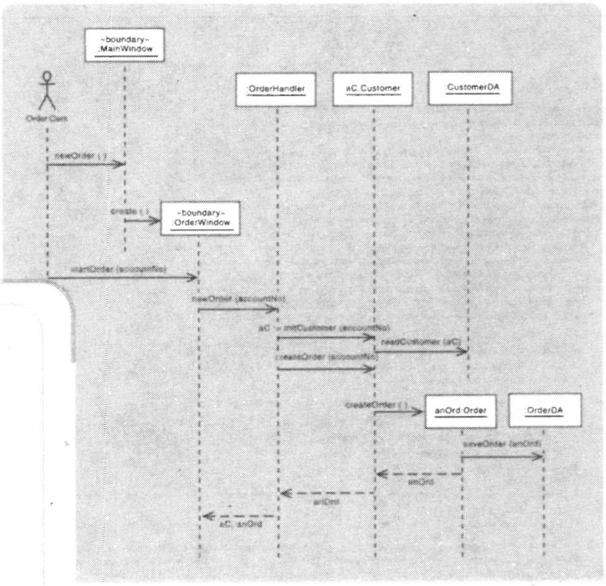

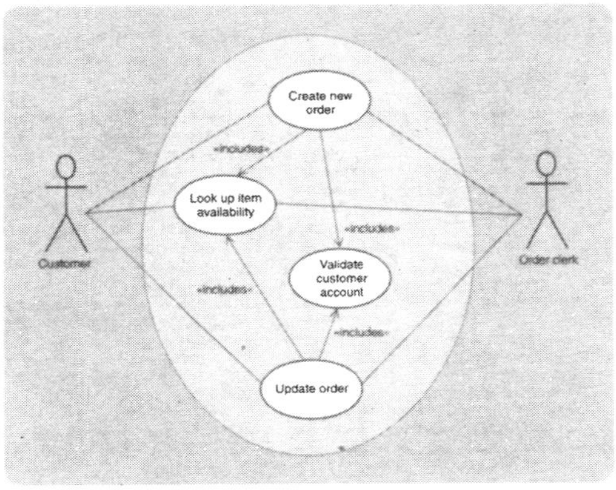

FIGURE 6-6
An example of the Order-entry subsystem with «includes» use cases

Analysts also make adjustments by splitting a single event into multiple use cases. Additional use cases are usually identified either (1) when they contain the «includes» relationship and two use cases can be developed from one large use case, or (2) when another use case is defined from recognizing a common subroutine, as discussed previously.

As you move from the business events to the use case diagram, pay careful attention to temporal and state events. For example, when identifying business events, we might define *Produce monthly payroll* as a temporal event. However, the monthly payroll, even though it is always produced at the end of the month, is initiated by a manager actor. So in the use case diagram, it is connected to the manager and is not shown as a temporal event. Other temporal or state events may not have an obvious actor. However, temporal and state events are important use cases that the system must support, so they must be included in the system requirements. In use case diagrams, analysts often connect these business events to an administrator actor that might invoke them as a "special" procedure. For example, a state event might be to order more inventory when a reorder point is reached. However, a manager could also initiate a "special" procedure to order inventory, and that event requires the same use case—*Order inventory*. So, *Order inventory* should be included in the use case diagram.

The process for moving from the business events to defining use cases requires two steps, done in iteration:

1. Identify the actors for each use case. Remember that the system boundary defines the automated system, so the actors you identify must actually contact the system—that is, have hands. As you identify the actors of the system,

CHAPTER 6 USE CASE MODELING AND DETAILED REQUIREMENTS 219

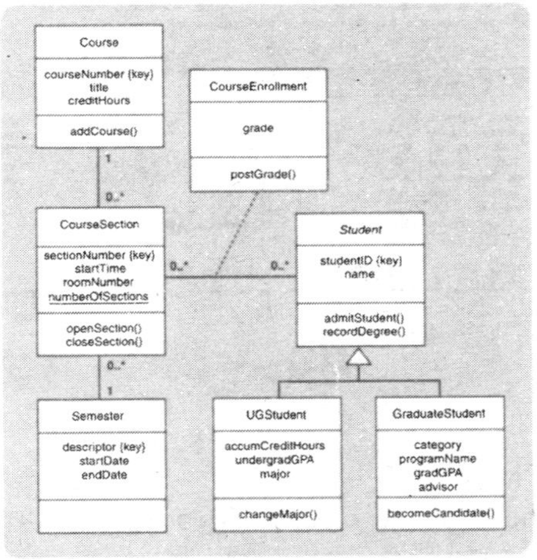

FIGURE 5-30
...ded course enrollment ...ign class diagram (with methods)

item is for a specific inventory item, meaning a specific size and color of shirt. An inventory item should have an attribute for quantity on hand of items in that size and color. Since there are many colors and sizes (each with its own quantity), each inventory item is associated with a product item that describes the item generically (vendor, gender, description).

An earlier version of the model showed that each product item is contained in one or more catalogs, and each catalog contains one or more product items, a many-to-many association. Therefore, this model adds an *association class* named CatalogProduct between Catalog and ProductItem because the association has some attributes that need to be remembered, specifically the regular and special prices. Each catalog can list a different price for the same product item (ski pants might be cheaper in the spring catalog).

The class diagram for Rocky Mountain Outfitters also has information about shipments. Since this diagram includes requirements for orders, not retail sales, each order item is eventually part of a shipment. A shipment may contain many order items. Each shipment is shipped by one shipper.

A generalization/specialization hierarchy is included to show that an order can be any one of three types—Web order, telephone order, or mail order—as discussed previously. Note that all types of orders share the attributes listed for Order, but each special

CHAPTER 5 USE CASES AND DOMAIN CLASSES 195

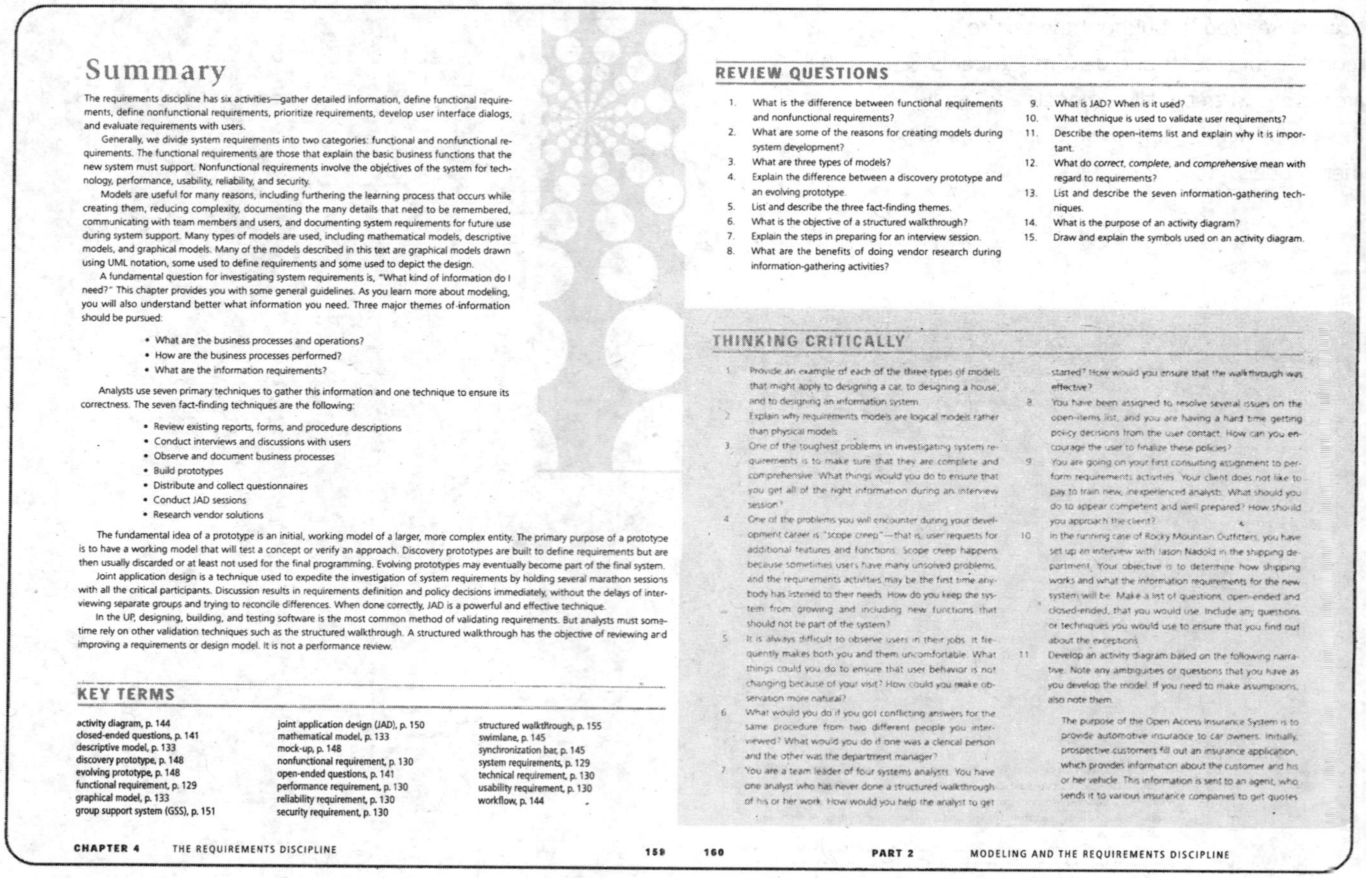

Summary

The requirements discipline has six activities—gather detailed information, define functional requirements, define nonfunctional requirements, prioritize requirements, develop user interface dialogs, and evaluate requirements with users.

Generally, we divide system requirements into two categories: functional and nonfunctional requirements. The functional requirements are those that explain the basic business functions that the new system must support. Nonfunctional requirements involve the objectives of the system for technology, performance, usability, reliability, and security.

Models are useful for many reasons, including furthering the learning process that occurs while creating them, reducing complexity, documenting the many details that need to be remembered, communicating with team members and users, and documenting system requirements for future use during system support. Many types of models are used, including mathematical models, descriptive models, and graphical models. Many of the models described in this text are graphical models drawn using UML notation, some used to define requirements and some used to depict the design.

A fundamental question for investigating system requirements is, "What kind of information do I need?" This chapter provides you with some general guidelines. As you learn more about modeling, you will also understand better what information you need. Three major themes of information should be pursued:

- What are the business processes and operations?
- How are the business processes performed?
- What are the information requirements?

Analysts use seven primary techniques to gather this information and one technique to ensure its correctness. The seven fact-finding techniques are the following:

- Review existing reports, forms, and procedure descriptions
- Conduct interviews and discussions with users
- Observe and document business processes
- Build prototypes
- Distribute and collect questionnaires
- Conduct JAD sessions
- Research vendor solutions

The fundamental idea of a prototype is an initial, working model of a larger, more complex entity. The primary purpose of a prototype is to have a working model that will test a concept or verify an approach. Discovery prototypes are built to define requirements but are then usually discarded or at least not used for the final programming. Evolving prototypes may eventually become part of the final system.

Joint application design is a technique used to expedite the investigation of system requirements by holding several marathon sessions with all the critical participants. Discussion results in requirements definition and policy decisions immediately, without the delays of interviewing separate groups and trying to reconcile differences. When done correctly, JAD is a powerful and effective technique.

In the UP, designing, building, and testing software is the most common method of validating requirements. But analysts must sometime rely on other validation techniques such as the structured walkthrough. A structured walkthrough has the objective of reviewing and improving a requirements or design model. It is not a performance review.

KEY TERMS

activity diagram, p. 144
closed-ended questions, p. 141
descriptive model, p. 133
discovery prototype, p. 148
evolving prototype, p. 148
functional requirement, p. 129
graphical model, p. 133
group support system (GSS), p. 151
joint application design (JAD), p. 150
mathematical model, p. 133
mock-up, p. 148
nonfunctional requirement, p. 130
open-ended questions, p. 141
performance requirement, p. 130
reliability requirement, p. 130
security requirement, p. 130
structured walkthrough, p. 155
swimlane, p. 145
synchronization bar, p. 145
system requirements, p. 129
technical requirement, p. 130
usability requirement, p. 130
workflow, p. 144

CHAPTER 4 THE REQUIREMENTS DISCIPLINE 159

REVIEW QUESTIONS

1. What is the difference between functional requirements and nonfunctional requirements?
2. What are some of the reasons for creating models during system development?
3. What are three types of models?
4. Explain the difference between a discovery prototype and an evolving prototype.
5. List and describe the three fact-finding themes.
6. What is the objective of a structured walkthrough?
7. Explain the steps in preparing for an interview session.
8. What are the benefits of doing vendor research during information-gathering activities?
9. What is JAD? When is it used?
10. What technique is used to validate user requirements?
11. Describe the open-items list and explain why it is important.
12. What do *correct*, *complete*, and *comprehensive* mean with regard to requirements?
13. List and describe the seven information-gathering techniques.
14. What is the purpose of an activity diagram?
15. Draw and explain the symbols used on an activity diagram.

THINKING CRITICALLY

1. Provide an example of each of the three types of models that might apply to designing a car, to designing a house, and to designing an information system.
2. Explain why requirements models are logical models rather than physical models.
3. One of the toughest problems in investigating system requirements is to make sure that they are complete and comprehensive. What things would you do to ensure that you get all of the right information during an interview session?
4. One of the problems you will encounter during your development career is "scope creep"—that is, user requests for additional features and functions. Scope creep happens because sometimes users have many unsolved problems, and the requirements activities may be the first time anybody has listened to their needs. How do you keep the system from growing and including new functions that should not be part of the system?
5. It is always difficult to observe users in their jobs. It frequently makes both you and them uncomfortable. What things could you do to ensure that user behavior is not changing because of your visit? How could you make observation more natural?
6. What would you do if you got conflicting answers for the same procedure from two different people you interviewed? What would you do if one was a clerical person and the other was the department manager?
7. You are a team leader of four systems analysts. You have one analyst who has never done a structured walkthrough of his or her work. How would you help the analyst to get started? How would you ensure that the walkthrough was effective?
8. You have been assigned to resolve several issues on the open-items list, and you are having a hard time getting policy decisions from the user contact. How can you encourage the user to finalize these policies?
9. You are going on your first consulting assignment to perform requirements activities. Your client does not like to pay to train new, inexperienced analysts. What should you do to appear competent and well prepared? How should you approach the client?
10. In the running case of Rocky Mountain Outfitters, you have set up an interview with Jason Nadold in the shipping department. Your objective is to determine how shipping works and what the information requirements for the new system will be. Make a list of questions, open-ended and closed-ended, that you would use. Include any questions or techniques you would use to ensure that you find out about the exceptions.
11. Develop an activity diagram based on the following narrative. Note any ambiguities or questions that you have as you develop the model. If you need to make assumptions, also note them.

   The purpose of the Open Access Insurance System is to provide automotive insurance to car owners. Initially, prospective customers fill out an insurance application, which provides information about the customer and his or her vehicle. This information is sent to an agent, who sends it to various insurance companies to get quotes

160 PART 2 MODELING AND THE REQUIREMENTS DISCIPLINE

① End-of-chapter material includes a **detailed summary** and an **indexed list of key terms**.

② Each chapter also includes ample **review questions** and problems and exercises to get the student **thinking critically**.

③ Also, a collection of **experiential exercises** involving additional research or problem solving is provided for each chapter.

④ An assortment of end-of-chapter **case studies** invites students to practice completing analysis and design tasks related to the chapter topics.

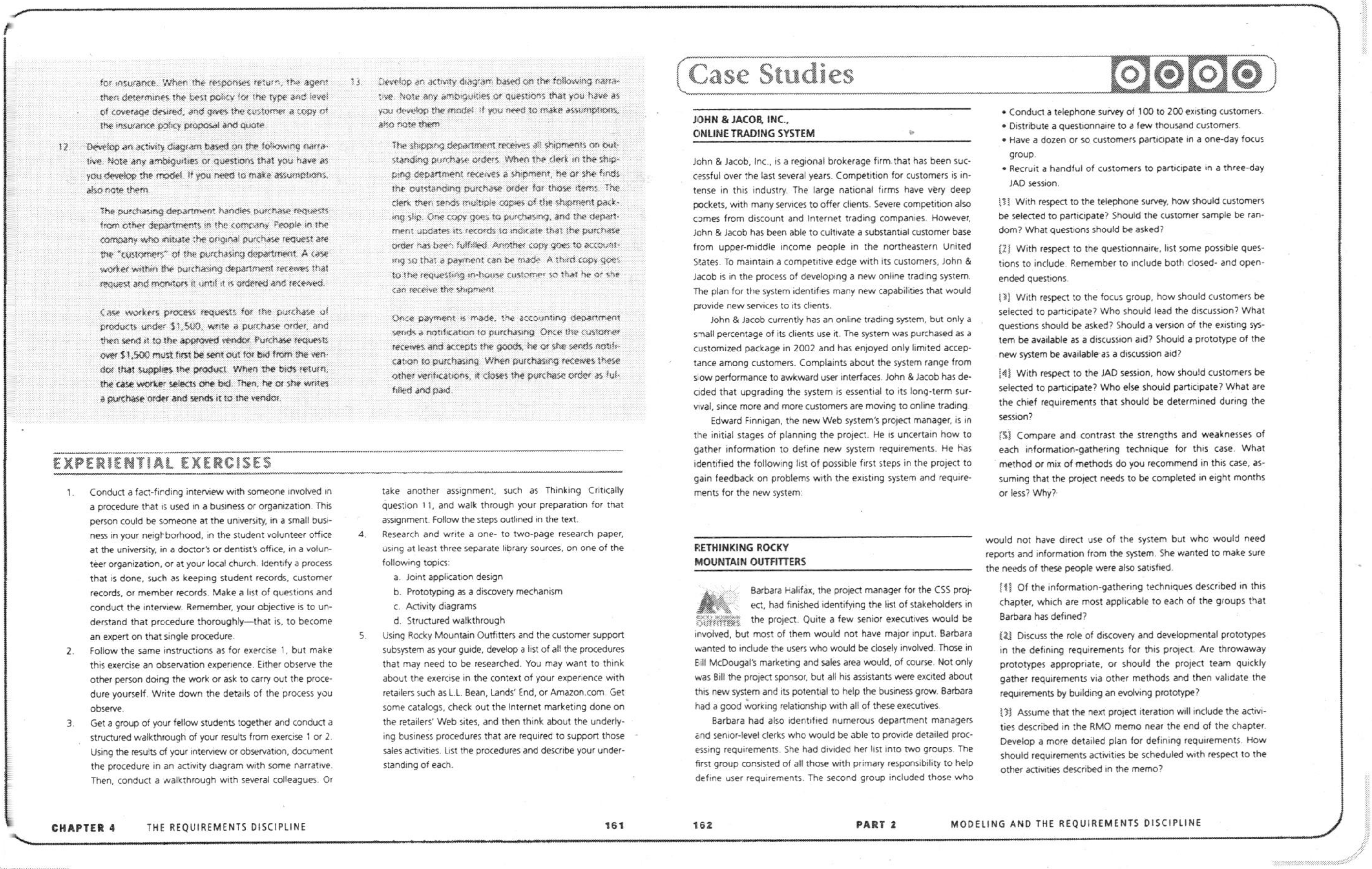

for insurance. When the responses return, the agent then determines the best policy for the type and level of coverage desired, and gives the customer a copy of the insurance policy proposal and quote.

12. Develop an activity diagram based on the following narrative. Note any ambiguities or questions that you have as you develop the model. If you need to make assumptions, also note them.

    The purchasing department handles purchase requests from other departments in the company. People in the company who initiate the original purchase request are the "customers" of the purchasing department. A case worker within the purchasing department receives that request and monitors it until it is ordered and received.

    Case workers process requests for the purchase of products under $1,500, write a purchase order, and then send it to the approved vendor. Purchase requests over $1,500 must first be sent out for bid from the vendor that supplies the product. When the bids return, the case worker selects one bid. Then, he or she writes a purchase order and sends it to the vendor.

13. Develop an activity diagram based on the following narrative. Note any ambiguities or questions that you have as you develop the model. If you need to make assumptions, also note them.

    The shipping department receives all shipments on outstanding purchase orders. When the clerk in the shipping department receives a shipment, he or she finds the outstanding purchase order for those items. The clerk then sends multiple copies of the shipment packing slip. One copy goes to purchasing, and the department updates its records to indicate that the purchase order has been fulfilled. Another copy goes to accounting so that a payment can be made. A third copy goes to the requesting in-house customer so that he or she can receive the shipment.

    Once payment is made, the accounting department sends a notification to purchasing. Once the customer receives and accepts the goods, he or she sends notification to purchasing. When purchasing receives these other verifications, it closes the purchase order as fulfilled and paid.

EXPERIENTIAL EXERCISES

1. Conduct a fact-finding interview with someone involved in a procedure that is used in a business or organization. This person could be someone at the university, in a small business in your neighborhood, in the student volunteer office at the university, in a doctor's or dentist's office, in a volunteer organization, or at your local church. Identify a process that is done, such as keeping student records, customer records, or member records. Make a list of questions and conduct the interview. Remember, your objective is to understand that procedure thoroughly—that is, to become an expert on that single procedure.
2. Follow the same instructions as for exercise 1, but make this exercise an observation experience. Either observe the other person doing the work or ask to carry out the procedure yourself. Write down the details of the process you observe.
3. Get a group of your fellow students together and conduct a structured walkthrough of your results from exercise 1 or 2. Using the results of your interview or observation, document the procedure in an activity diagram with some narrative. Then, conduct a walkthrough with several colleagues. Or take another assignment, such as Thinking Critically question 11, and walk through your preparation for that assignment. Follow the steps outlined in the text.
4. Research and write a one- to two-page research paper, using at least three separate library sources, on one of the following topics:
   a. Joint application design
   b. Prototyping as a discovery mechanism
   c. Activity diagrams
   d. Structured walkthrough
5. Using Rocky Mountain Outfitters and the customer support subsystem as your guide, develop a list of all the procedures that may need to be researched. You may want to think about the exercise in the context of your experience with retailers such as L.L. Bean, Lands' End, or Amazon.com. Get some catalogs, check out the Internet marketing done on the retailers' Web sites, and then think about the underlying business procedures that are required to support those sales activities. List the procedures and describe your understanding of each.

CHAPTER 4 THE REQUIREMENTS DISCIPLINE 161

Case Studies

JOHN & JACOB, INC., ONLINE TRADING SYSTEM

John & Jacob, Inc., is a regional brokerage firm that has been successful over the last several years. Competition for customers is intense in this industry. The large national firms have very deep pockets, with many services to offer clients. Severe competition also comes from discount and Internet trading companies. However, John & Jacob has been able to cultivate a substantial customer base from upper-middle income people in the northeastern United States. To maintain a competitive edge with its customers, John & Jacob is in the process of developing a new online trading system. The plan for the system identifies many new capabilities that would provide new services to its clients.

John & Jacob currently has an online trading system, but only a small percentage of its clients use it. The system was purchased as a customized package in 2002 and has enjoyed only limited acceptance among customers. Complaints about the system range from slow performance to awkward user interfaces. John & Jacob has decided that upgrading the system is essential to its long-term survival, since more and more customers are moving to online trading.

Edward Finnigan, the new Web system's project manager, is in the initial stages of planning the project. He is uncertain how to gather information to define new system requirements. He has identified the following list of possible first steps in the project to gain feedback on problems with the existing system and requirements for the new system:

- Conduct a telephone survey of 100 to 200 existing customers.
- Distribute a questionnaire to a few thousand customers.
- Have a dozen or so customers participate in a one-day focus group.
- Recruit a handful of customers to participate in a three-day JAD session.

[1] With respect to the telephone survey, how should customers be selected to participate? Should the customer sample be random? What questions should be asked?

[2] With respect to the questionnaire, list some possible questions to include. Remember to include both closed- and open-ended questions.

[3] With respect to the focus group, how should customers be selected to participate? Who should lead the discussion? What questions should be asked? Should a version of the existing system be available as a discussion aid? Should a prototype of the new system be available as a discussion aid?

[4] With respect to the JAD session, how should customers be selected to participate? Who else should participate? What are the chief requirements that should be determined during the session?

[5] Compare and contrast the strengths and weaknesses of each information-gathering technique for this case. What method or mix of methods do you recommend in this case, assuming that the project needs to be completed in eight months or less? Why?

RETHINKING ROCKY MOUNTAIN OUTFITTERS

Barbara Halifax, the project manager for the CSS project, had finished identifying the list of stakeholders in the project. Quite a few senior executives would be involved, but most of them would not have major input. Barbara wanted to include the users who would be closely involved. Those in Bill McDougal's marketing and sales area would, of course. Not only was Bill the project sponsor, but all his assistants were excited about this new system and its potential to help the business grow. Barbara had a good working relationship with all of these executives.

Barbara had also identified numerous department managers and senior-level clerks who would be able to provide detailed processing requirements. She had divided her list into two groups. The first group consisted of all those with primary responsibility to help define user requirements. The second group included those who would not have direct use of the system but who would need reports and information from the system. She wanted to make sure the needs of these people were also satisfied.

[1] Of the information-gathering techniques described in this chapter, which are most applicable to each of the groups that Barbara has defined?

[2] Discuss the role of discovery and developmental prototypes in the defining requirements for this project. Are throwaway prototypes appropriate, or should the project team quickly gather requirements via other methods and then validate the requirements by building an evolving prototype?

[3] Assume that the next project iteration will include the activities described in the RMO memo near the end of the chapter. Develop a more detailed plan for defining requirements. How should requirements activities be scheduled with respect to the other activities described in the memo?

162 PART 2 MODELING AND THE REQUIREMENTS DISCIPLINE

PREFACE

We are delighted to present *Object-Oriented Analysis and Design with the Unified Process*. This text is our very latest book on systems analysis and design—one that is exclusively object oriented and use case driven, with in-depth coverage of object-oriented (OO) software design and design patterns, compliant with UML 2.0 modeling standards, and supported by an agile version of the Unified Process (UP) as the system development methodology. This text is designed for use in undergraduate and graduate courses that teach the OO approach to business systems analysis and design and that demand coverage of the very latest agile and model-driven approaches to development.

This is the sixth book title we have collectively published with Course Technology over the last nine years, all of which address leading-edge information technology topics and object-oriented development. So, our approach to teaching object orientation and OO analysis and design has been classroom tested and refined over many years, and our previous OO books have proven themselves in classrooms and training facilities around the world on six continents. There are no compromises here—this text is for the OO pure of heart (and those who want to be). But it is written for the information systems (CIS/MIS) major with a business systems focus.

EXCLUSIVE COVERAGE OF THE OO APPROACH AND UML 2.0

The OO approach presented in this text is grounded in the Unified Modeling Language (UML 2.0) from the Object Management Group, as originated by Grady Booch, James Rumbaugh, and Ivar Jacobson. A model-driven approach to analysis starts with use cases and scenarios and then defines problem domain classes involved in the users' work. We explain requirements modeling with use case diagrams, use case descriptions, activity diagrams, and system sequence diagrams. Design models are also discussed in detail, with particular attention to detailed sequence diagrams, design class diagrams, and package diagrams. Design principles and design patterns are discussed throughout the text. Our database design chapter covers two approaches to object persistence—a hybrid approach using relational database management and a pure approach using object database management systems (ODBMS). Our user-interface design chapter applies guidelines from the field of human-computer interaction and shows how UML diagrams can be used to design the user-interface layer in three-layer design architectures. Our system interface chapter addresses security and system controls in the context of three-layer design. These design discipline topics are fully integrated into the OO approach.

FULL INTEGRATION OF THE UNIFIED PROCESS (UP)

System development practitioners have shown great interest in agile and iterative system development methodologies over the last few years. The very latest, de facto standard methodology is called *the Unified Process* (*UP*). It is iterative, use case driven, and object oriented. The UP was developed by Grady Booch, James Rumbaugh, and Ivar Jacobson, the same three system development methodologists who originated UML. Finally, the analysis and design field has a practical and useful approach to the system development life cycle that can be applied to real development projects. The UP defines four life cycle phases—inception, elaboration, construction, and transition—that draw on nine system development "disciplines" for iterative development. Unlike other texts that introduce the UP but then revert to the older sequential life cycle, our text fully integrates the UP and its nine disciplines throughout—from cover to cover.

REAL DEPTH IN OO SOFTWARE DESIGN

This text also delves deeply into the details of OO software design. Unlike texts that discuss analysis techniques and use cases and then skip over the design details, this text builds directly on use case descriptions to define object interactions using sequence diagrams. Design class diagrams are derived from the domain model and sequence diagrams, which reveal the required class methods. As design of each use case proceeds, a three-layer architecture emerges, which can be directly implemented with code. Students with an OO programming background can see the value of the design models and develop an appreciation of the OO analysis and design techniques very quickly. This link between analysis, design, and code is key to learning OO development and the UP.

EMPHASIS ON DESIGN PRINCIPLES AND DESIGN PATTERNS

To create an efficient and maintainable design, today's developers look for and use design principles and guidelines. Once the design is complete, developers search for criteria to use to evaluate the design's quality. This text emphasizes OO design principles that have been adapted from traditional software design—modular design with low coupling and high cohesion, for example. But OO designers have also defined and cataloged a growing set of design patterns, which are design solutions that can be applied to common technical problems. Rather than continually reinventing the wheel, designers look for patterns that address the problem they face, and then they apply a design pattern to their problem. The development and refinement of design patterns helps to continuously improve the software design discipline, resulting in better design solutions and more effective system developers. Teaching these patterns has become at least as important as teaching programming language syntax, and this text presents both an overview of patterns and in-depth coverage of several fundamental patterns.

DETAILED EXAMPLES AND HANDS-ON APPROACH

To become proficient system developers, students need to hone their critical problem-solving skills. The examples shown in each chapter go beyond simple cases to show how more complex situations are handled with OO development. We don't just describe solutions; instead, we show step-by-step procedures to follow to create solutions. This hands-on approach to problem solving is required for students to actually learn the techniques. We also include a running case on Rocky Mountain Outfitters that is integrated right into each chapter, showing solutions to part of the company's needed system. End-of-chapter exercises then build on those concepts, allowing students to complete solutions for additional parts of the system. We also include a second end-of-chapter running case on Reliable Pharmaceutical Service, a smaller firm than Rocky

Mountain Outfitters, which allows students to apply their problem-solving skills to another scenario. The emphasis remains focused on doing OO analysis and design rather than just reading about it.

EMERGING CONCEPTS AND TECHNIQUES

In response to the realities of system development today, we include emerging concepts and techniques that lend flexibility and choice to analysts. First, system development and the system development life cycle (SDLC) must be tailored to each project, ranging on a spectrum from purely predictive to completely adaptive. The agile approach to the Unified Process presented in this text is located near the midpoint of this scale. The text does not ignore situations in which projects are fairly predictable and can be managed sequentially. Yet most projects are less predictable and more risky, demanding an iterative and adaptive approach to development. This text reflects that reality. We also introduce additional highly adaptive approaches, including Extreme Programming (XP), Agile Modeling, and Scrum. Component-based development and Model-Driven Architecture (MDA) are also covered.

PROJECT MANAGEMENT COVERAGE AND SOFTWARE TOOLS

Many undergraduate programs depend on the systems analysis and design course to teach project management principles. To satisfy this need, we continue to cover project management by taking a two-pronged approach. First, a fairly extensive treatment of project management concepts and principles as they apply to the UP inception phase is provided. Additional background on project management is included in an appendix on the book's Web site. This information is based on the Project Management Body of Knowledge (PMBOK) as developed by the Project Management Institute—the primary professional organization for project managers in the United States. Second, specific project management techniques, skills, and tasks are included and highlighted throughout chapters of the book. This integration teaches students how to apply specific project management tasks to the various phases of the UP systems development life cycle and the activities of the UP disciplines. In addition, we now include a 120-day trial version of Microsoft Project 2003 Professional in the back of every book so that students can obtain hands-on experience with this important tool.

ORGANIZATION

The text is organized into four parts, containing fourteen chapters, and fits several course sequences and emphases. Instructors can use the text in a course that emphasizes the Unified Process and OO analysis in depth. Alternatively, OO design can also be covered in great depth. Some courses survey the entire UP life cycle and all nine disciplines. Others might use the text for a two-course sequence, first covering system development in depth, and then including prototyping and coding of OO software in a second detailed design course. Instructors will find that there are many ways this text can be effectively used.

PART 1: SYSTEM DEVELOPMENT AND THE UNIFIED PROCESS

Chapter 1 discusses the work of a modern systems analyst, including a streamlined discussion of systems and the role of the systems analyst as a problem solver in a modern business organization. The strategic information systems plan for Rocky Mountain Outfitters is discussed, and the customer support system project is identified as the planned project ready to start development using OO analysis and design and the Unified Process. Chapter 2 then asks, Now that we have a project, what do we have to do to get this system built? That is, what are the methodologies, models, tools, and techniques that can be used to develop systems? The system development life cycle (SDLC) and both predictive and adaptive variations are introduced. The Unified Process life cycle and the UP as a comprehensive system development methodology are presented. Chapter 2 concludes with a review of OO concepts and some examples of software tools to support developers. Chapter 3 moves right to the heart of the course—the system development project—introduced while describing the inception phase of the Unified Process, the business modeling discipline, and the project management discipline. Students are drawn quickly into the RMO project so that the material has a meaningful context.

PART 2: MODELING AND THE REQUIREMENTS DISCIPLINE

Part 2 moves ahead with defining the requirements for the system. The requirements discipline is described in detail, and information-gathering and requirements modeling techniques are taught in three chapters. Requirements models are developed in the context of the iterative Unified Process, in which requirements, design, implementation, and testing are completed for a set of use cases in each iteration. Chapter 4 describes the activities of the requirements discipline in detail, covering models and modeling and functional versus nonfunctional requirements. Then it focuses on investigating requirements, including gathering information and interviewing system owners and users. Chapter 5 covers two key concepts that are the foundation of functional requirements: use cases and domain classes. System decomposition into use cases and domain modeling using the UML class diagram are demonstrated in depth. Chapter 6 continues the discussion of use cases begun in Chapter 5, showing how to create the use case model of the system requirements. Use case descriptions are developed, activity diagrams are drawn, and system sequence diagrams are created to define input and output messaging requirements. Finally, object states and state transitions are explored to help uncover additional functional requirements, modeled using the UML statechart diagram.

PART 3: THE DESIGN DISCIPLINE

Chapter 7 introduces system design and the UP design discipline. The activities of the design discipline are described, again in the context of iterative development in which requirements, design, implementation, and testing are completed for a few use cases in each iteration. Details of the technological environment that affect design are reviewed, including networks, client/server architecture, and three-layer design. Chapters 8 and 9 address object-oriented software design. Chapter 8 teaches students how to design the interaction details for each use case—use case realization. Implementation issues for the three-layer design architecture are also discussed. Chapter 9 discusses more advanced design patterns and design principles, including OO design for enterprise-level and

Web-based systems. Additionally, state transitions and the statechart diagram at the design level are discussed in detail. Software design is not the only activity of the design discipline. Chapter 10 covers the data access layer—using a relational hybrid approach and object-oriented databases. Chapter 11 covers the user-interface layer, discussing human-computer interaction and general principles and concepts of dialog design in addition to using UML diagrams to model the dialog. Chapter 12 discusses system interfaces, with particular attention to system controls and system security.

PART 4: IMPLEMENTATION, TESTING, AND DEPLOYMENT DISCIPLINES

Chapter 13 describes additional UP disciplines that are required to bring a system into being. These disciplines include implementation, testing, deployment, and configuration and change management. The fact that we cover several disciplines in a single chapter does not mean that they are simple or unimportant. Rather, they are complex disciplines that students will learn in detail in other courses. Our purpose in covering them in this chapter is to round out our discussion of the UP and to show how all of the disciplines interrelate. Chapter 14 discusses the very latest concepts and techniques behind what is referred to as Agile Development. The Unified Process, the Extreme Programming (XP) methodology, and the Scrum methodology all contribute to this approach. Additionally, an important new approach called Model-Driven Architecture (MDA) is introduced.

ONLINE APPENDICES AT THE STUDENT COMPANION WEB SITE

Don't forget to locate the five appendices at the Student Companion Web Site. The appendices cover project management; development of a schedule with PERT/CPM charts; calculation of net present value, payback period, and return on investment; presentation basics; and MS Project. We have placed these appendices on the Web to provide more flexibility in the use of the text and to allow us to cover additional material that may be of interest to students and their instructors.

STUDENT COMPANION WEB SITE

We have created an exciting online companion, at *www.course.com/OOAD*, for students to utilize as they work through the book. This Web resource includes a number of interesting and helpful features for practice and further learning. Instructors and students should make sure to check the site at the start of their course to take advantage of further resources added to the site.

- **Practice Quizzes.** Brand new quizzes, created specifically for this text, allow users to test themselves on the content of each chapter and immediately see what questions were answered right and wrong. For each question answered incorrectly, users are provided with the correct answer and the page in the text where that information is covered. Special testing software randomly compiles a selection of questions from a large database, so quizzes can be taken multiple times on a given chapter, with some new questions included each time.
- **Case Project.** An additional case project, similar in scope and complexity to the Reliable Pharmaceuticals case found in the book is offered, giving students

the opportunity to sharpen their skills. It contains installments for each chapter and the corresponding solutions.

- **PowerPoint Slides.** Students can view the book's PowerPoint presentations, which cover the key points from each chapter. These presentations are a useful study tool.
- **Online Appendices.** Students can access the following appendices on the site:
  - Appendix A, Principles of Project Management
  - Appendix B, Developing a Project Schedule with PERT/CPM Charts
  - Appendix C, Calculating Net Present Value, Payback Period, and Return on Investment
  - Appendix D, Presenting the Results to Management
  - Appendix, Guide to Microsoft Project 2003
- **Useful Web Links.** The site offers a repository of links to various Web sites where students can find more information about systems analysis and design in industry, possible careers, and other interesting resources for further learning.

INSTRUCTOR SUPPORT

Object-Oriented Analysis and Design with the Unified Process includes teaching tools to support instructors in the classroom. The ancillaries that accompany the textbook include an Instructor's Manual, Solutions, Test Banks and Test Engine, Distance Learning content, and PowerPoint presentations. Please contact your Course Technology sales representative to request the Teaching Tools CD-ROM, if you have not already received it. Or go to the Web page for this book at www.course.com to download many of these items.

THE INSTRUCTOR'S MANUAL

The Instructor's Manual includes suggestions and strategies for using the text, including course outlines for instructors emphasizing the object-oriented approach, as well as for those teaching graduate courses on analysis and design.

SOLUTIONS

We provide instructors with answers to review questions and suggested solutions to chapter exercises and cases.

EXAMVIEW®

This objective-based test generator lets the instructor create paper, LAN, or Web-based tests from test banks designed specifically for this Course Technology text. Instructors can use the QuickTest Wizard to create tests in fewer than five minutes by taking advantage of Course Technology's question banks or create customized exams.

DISTANCE LEARNING CONTENT

Course Technology, the premiere innovator in management information systems publishing, is proud to present online courses in WebCT and Blackboard, to provide the most complete and dynamic learning experience possible.

- **Blackboard and WebCT Level 1 Online Content.** If you use Blackboard or WebCT, the test bank for this textbook is available at no cost in a simple, ready-to-use format. Go to www.course.com and search for this textbook to download the test bank.

- **Blackboard and WebCT Level 2 Online Content.** Blackboard Level 2 and WebCT Level 2 are also available for *Object-Oriented Analysis and Design with the Unified Process*. Level 2 offers course management and access to a Web site that is fully populated with content for this book. Students purchase the Blackboard User Guide or the WebCT User Guide. The User Guides include a password that allows student access to Level 2.

For more information on how to bring distance learning to their course, instructors should contact their Course Technology sales representative.

POWERPOINT PRESENTATIONS

Microsoft PowerPoint slides are included for each chapter. Instructors might use the slides in a variety of ways, including their use as teaching aids during classroom presentations or as printed handouts for classroom distribution. Instructors can add their own slides for additional topics introduced to the class.

FIGURE FILES

Figure Files allow instructors to create their own presentations using figures taken directly from the text.

SOFTWARE BUNDLING OPTIONS

Many instructors like to include software for students to use for exercises and course projects, and this text offers many bundling possibilities. Some instructors like to emphasize CASE tools, and Course Technology can bundle several popular CASE tools with the text, including Embarcadero Describe. In addition, we offer Microsoft Visio, Microsoft Project 2003, and Edge Diagrammer. Instructors can contact their Course Technology representative for the latest information.

FEEDBACK

We value your opinion. Please email any feedback about this book to the Course Technology MIS Team at .mis@thomson.com.

CREDITS AND ACKNOWLEDGMENTS

First and foremost we wish to thank our developmental editor, Karen Hill of Elm Street Publishing Services, who guided us through the development of this text. She collected and digested the comments and reactions of reviewers, provided guidance and design for the features and chapter pedagogy, suggested improvements and refinements to the organization and content, read each draft of each chapter from the perspective of the student to help us be consistent and clear, and edited the chapters to provide a consistent style. We could not have completed the book without her help, and we appreciate her willingness to adjust her schedule to allow us to move ahead with the project. Thanks also to the management of Elm Street Publishing Services for hosting our authors' and editor meeting during an unusually cold Chicago winter week.

We are also grateful for the forward thinking and support of Course Technology executive editor Mac Mendelsohn and senior acquisitions editor Maureen Martin. We were also very fortunate to have senior product manager Eunice Yeates-Fogle placed in charge of managing the project. She was instrumental in helping us create a workable schedule and for making countless adjustments, solving numerous problems, and helping in so many ways as we went along. We also want to thank production editor Summer Hughes for all of her careful checking and double-checking during the production process.

Many other people at Course Technology have also contributed so much to our work on this book. Jennifer Locke was instrumental in turning the original idea for an analysis and design book into the successful series we have today. Barrie Tysko was actively involved in the development of so many of the features and ideas for the book that we can't even begin to count them all. We are grateful to both of them and wish them well in their current endeavors.

Many other colleagues and friends at SMSU, Brigham Young University, the University of New Mexico, and elsewhere contributed to and supported our work in one way or another. We also gained much from the feedback of participants in our 2003 AMCIS conference tutorial on OOA&D and our 2003 ISECON workshop on OO and the Unified Process. Special thanks also go to Lavette Teague, Lorne Olfman, and Paul Gray for guidance and inspiration.

Last, but certainly not least, we want to thank all of the reviewers who worked so hard for us, beginning with an initial proposal and continuing all the way through to the completion of the first, second, and third editions of our analysis and design text and now the first edition of this OO analysis and design text. We were lucky enough to have reviewers with broad perspectives, in-depth knowledge, and diverse preferences. We listened very carefully, and the text is much better as a result of their input. We particularly wish to thank Rob Anson for his thoughtful and always helpful insights and examples. The reviewers who have worked so hard for us include:

Rob Anson, *Boise State University*
Marsha Baddeley, *Niagara College*
Teri Barnes, *DeVry Institute—Phoenix*
Robert Beatty, *University of Wisconsin—Milwaukee*
Anthony Cameron, *Fayetteville Technical Community College*
Genard Catalano, *Columbia College*
Paul H. Cheney, *University of Central Florida*
Jung Choi, *Wright State University*
Jon D. Clark, *Colorado State University*
Lawrence E. Domine, *Milwaukee Area Technical College*
Sam S. Gill, *San Francisco State University*
Jeff Hedrington, *University of Phoenix*
Ellen D. Hoadley, *Loyola College in Maryland*
Norman Jobes, *Conestoga College, Waterloo, Ontario*
Gerald Karush, *Southern New Hampshire University*
Robert Keim, *Arizona State University*
Rajiv Kishore, *The State University of New York, Buffalo*
Rebecca Koop, *Wright State University*
Hsiang-Jui Kung, *Georgia Southern University*
James E. LaBarre, *University of Wisconsin—Eau Claire*

Tsun-Yin Law, *Seneca College*
David Little, *High Point University*
George M. Marakas, *Indiana University*
Roger McHaney, *Kansas State University*
Cindi A. Nadelman, *New England College*
Bruce Neubauer, *Pittsburgh State University*
Michael Nicholas, *Davenport University—Grand Rapids*
George Pennells
Julian-Mark Pettigrew
Mary Prescott, *University of South Florida*
Alex Ramirez, *Carleton University*
Eliot Rich, *The State University of New York,* Albany
Robert Saldarini, *Bergen Community College*
Laurie Schatzberg, *University of New Mexico*
Deborah Stockbridge, *Quincy College*
Jean Smith, *Technical College of the Lowcountry*
Peter Tarasewich, *Northeastern University*
Craig VanLengen, *Northern Arizona University*
Bruce Vanstone, *Bond University*
Terence M. Waterman, *Golden Gate University*

All of us involved in the development of this text wish you all the best as you take on the challenge of *Object-Oriented Analysis and Design with the Unified Process.*

—John Satzinger
—Bob Jackson
—Steve Burd

PART 1

SYSTEM DEVELOPMENT AND THE UNIFIED PROCESS

CHAPTER 1
The World of the Modern Systems Analyst

CHAPTER 2
Object-Oriented Development and the Unified Process

CHAPTER 3
Project Management and the Inception Phase

chapter 1

THE WORLD OF THE MODERN SYSTEMS ANALYST

LEARNING OBJECTIVES

After reading this chapter, you should be able to:

- Explain the key role of a systems analyst in business
- Describe the various types of systems an analyst might work on
- Explain the importance of technical, people, and business skills for an analyst
- Explain why ethical behavior is crucial for a systems analyst's career
- Describe the many types of technology an analyst needs to understand
- Describe various job titles and places of employment where analysis and design work is done
- Discuss the analyst's role in strategic planning for an organization
- Describe the analyst's role in a system development project

CHAPTER OUTLINE

- The Analyst as a Business Problem Solver
- Systems That Solve Business Problems
- Required Skills of the Systems Analyst
- The Environment Surrounding the Analyst
- The Analyst's Role in Strategic Planning
- Rocky Mountain Outfitters and Its Strategic Information Systems Plan
- The Analyst as a System Developer (the Heart of the Course)

A SYSTEMS ANALYST AT CONSOLIDATED REFINERIES

Mary Wright thought back about her two-year career as a programmer analyst. She had been asked to talk to visiting computer information system (CIS) students about life on the job. "It seems like yesterday that I finally graduated from college and loaded up a U-Haul to start my new job at Consolidated," she began.

Consolidated Refineries is an independent petroleum-refining company in west Texas. Consolidated buys crude oil from freelance petroleum producers and refines it into gasoline and other petroleum products for sale to independent distributors. Demand for refined petroleum products had been increasing rapidly, and Consolidated was producing at maximum capacity. Capacity planning systems and refining operations systems were particularly important computer information systems for Consolidated, since careful planning and process monitoring resulted in increased production at reduced costs. This increasing demand, and other competitive changes in the energy industry, made information systems particularly important to Consolidated.

Mary continued her informal talk to visiting students. "At first I did programming, mainly fixing things that end users wanted done. I completed some training on Java and object-oriented enterprise development to round out my experience. I was able to apply my skills in object-oriented programming, UML, and the Unified Process from day one. In other words, the job was pretty much what I had expected at first," she continued, "until everything went crazy over the IPCS project."

The Integrated Process Control System (IPCS) project had been part of the company's information systems plan drawn up the year before. Edward King, the CEO of Consolidated Refineries, pushed for more strategic planning overall at the company from the beginning, including drawing up a five-year strategic plan for information systems. In that plan, all major systems projects were slated to use Unified Process as the development approach. The IPCS development project was scheduled to begin in the third or fourth year of the plan, but suddenly priorities changed. Demand for petroleum products had never been higher, and supplies of crude oil were becoming scarce. At the same time, political pressure was making price increases an unpopular option.

Something had to be done to increase production and reduce costs. It would be years before an additional refinery could be built, and additional crude oil supplies from new oil fields were years away. The only option for Consolidated's growth and increased profits was to do a better job with the plants and supplies they had. So, top executives decided to make a major commitment to implementing the IPCS project, with the goal of radically improving capacity planning and process monitoring. Everyone at Consolidated also wanted access to this information anywhere and anytime.

"It seemed like the IPCS project was the only thing the company cared about," continued Mary. "I was assigned to the project as the junior analyst assisting the project manager, so I got in on everything. Suddenly I was in meeting after meeting, and I had to digest all kinds of information about refining and distribution, as if I were a petroleum engineer. I met with production supervisors, suppliers, and marketing managers to learn about the oil business, just as if I were taking business school courses. I traveled all over to visit oil fields and pipelines (including a four-day trip to Alaska on about two days' notice)! I interviewed technology vendors' representatives and consultants who specialized in capacity planning and process control systems. I've been spending a lot of time at my computer, too, writing reports, use case descriptions, letters, and memos—not programming!

"We have been working on the project for seven months now, and every time I turn around, Mr. King, our CEO, is saying something about how important the IPCS project is to the future of the company. He repeats the story to employees and to the stockholders. Mr. King attends many of our status meetings, and he even sat next to me the day I presented a list of key requirements for the system to the top management team.

"This is not at all the way I thought it would be."

Overview

As Mary Wright's story about Consolidated Refineries illustrates, information systems with strategic value are now developed using object-oriented technology and an approach to system development called the *Unified Process*. Most of the activities and tasks completed by a system developer, even a new graduate like Mary, involve much more than programming. It is really more about understanding the business and its goals and strategies, defining requirements for information systems that support those goals and strategies, and supporting the business. It's not at all the way most college students imagine it to be.

Information systems are crucial to the success of modern business organizations, and new systems are constantly being developed to make businesses more competitive. People today are attracted to information systems careers because information technology can have a dramatic impact on productivity and profits. Most of you regularly use the latest technologies for online purchases and reservations, online auctions and customer support, and e-mail and wireless messaging. But it is not the technology itself that increases productivity and profits; it is the people who develop information system solutions that harness the power of the technology that makes these benefits possible. The challenges are great because more and more people expect to have information systems that provide access to information anywhere and anytime.

The key to successful system development is thorough systems analysis and design to understand what the business requires from the information system. *Systems analysis* means understanding and specifying in detail what the information system should do. *Systems design* means specifying in detail how the many components of the information system should be physically implemented. This text is about systems analysis and design techniques used by a *systems analyst*, a business professional who develops information systems. It focuses specifically on what is often called *object-oriented analysis* and *object-oriented design*.

systems analysis
the process of understanding and specifying in detail what the information system should do

systems design
the process of specifying in detail how the many components of the information system should be physically implemented

systems analyst
a business professional who uses analysis and design techniques to solve business problems using information technology

This chapter describes the world of the systems analyst—the nature of the work, the knowledge and skills that are important, and the types of systems and special projects an analyst works on. First, the analyst's work is described as problem solving for an organization, so the problem-solving process the analyst follows is described. Next, since most problems an analyst works on are solved in part by an information system, it is important to review the types of information systems that businesses use. A systems analyst is a business professional who requires extensive technical, business, and people knowledge and skills, so these skills are reviewed. Then the types of technology used for information systems and the variety of workplaces and positions where analysis work is done are surveyed. Sometimes an analyst works on special projects such as strategic planning, business process reengineering, and enterprise resource planning.

Finally, this chapter introduces Rocky Mountain Outfitters (RMO), a regional sports clothing distributor headquartered in Park City, Utah. RMO is following a strategic information systems plan that calls for a series of information system development and integration projects over the next several years. The project that RMO is about to launch is a system development project for a new customer support system that will integrate phone orders, mail orders, and direct customer orders via the Internet. RMO plans to use object-oriented system development and the Unified Process exclusively on the project. The Rocky Mountain Outfitters case is used throughout the text to illustrate object-oriented analysis and object-oriented design techniques in detail.

THE ANALYST AS A BUSINESS PROBLEM SOLVER

Systems analysis and design is, first and foremost, a practical field grounded in both time-tested and rapidly evolving knowledge and techniques. A number of newer object-oriented analysis and design techniques have been developed recently and require study and mastery. Analysts must certainly know about computers and computer programs, particularly object-oriented programming. They possess special skills and develop expertise in computer technology. But they must also bring to the job a fundamental curiosity to explore how things are done and the determination to make them work better.

Developing information systems is not just about writing programs. Information systems are developed to solve problems for organizations, as the opening case study demonstrated, and a systems analyst is often thought of as a problem solver rather than a programmer. So, what kinds of problems does an analyst typically solve?

FIGURE 1-1
The analyst's approach to problem solving

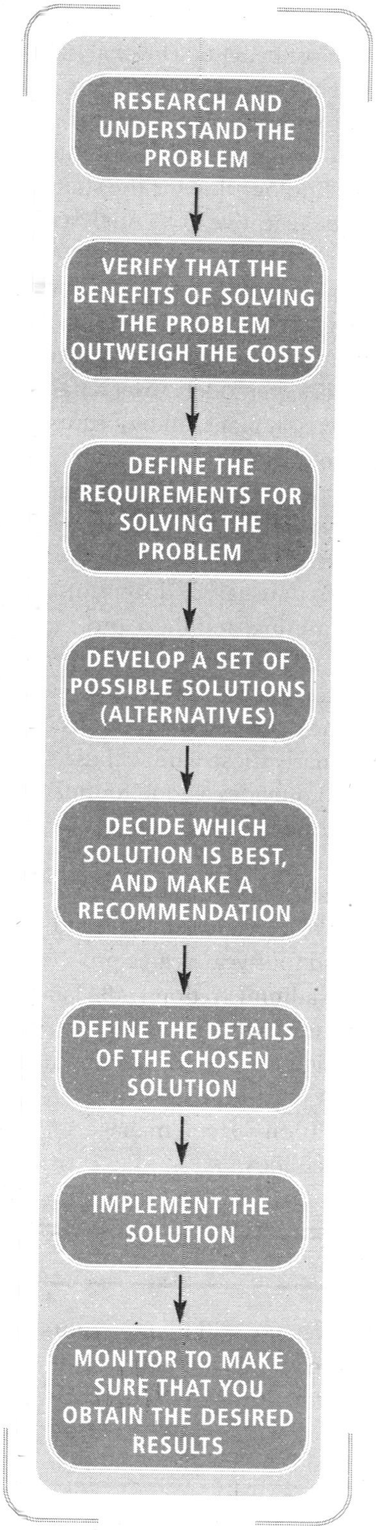

- Customers want to order products anytime of the day or night. So, the problem is how to process those orders round the clock without adding to the selling cost.
- Production needs to plan very carefully the amount of each type of product to produce each week. So, the problem is how to estimate the dozens of parameters that affect production and then allow planners to explore different scenarios before committing to a specific plan.
- Suppliers want to minimize their inventory holding costs by shipping parts used in the manufacturing process in smaller daily batches. So, the problem is how to order in smaller lots and accept daily shipments to take advantage of supplier discounts.
- Marketing wants to anticipate customer needs better by tracking purchasing patterns and buyer trends. So, the problem is how to collect and analyze information on customer behavior that marketing can put to use.
- Management continually wants to know the current financial picture of the company, including profit and loss, cash flow, and stock market forecasts. So, the problem is how to collect, analyze, and present all of the financial information management wants.
- Employees demand more flexibility in their benefits programs, and management wants to build loyalty and morale. So, the problem is how to process transactions for flexible health plans, wellness programs, employee investment options, retirement accounts, and other benefit programs offered to employees.

Information system developers work on problems such as these—and many more. Some of these problems are large and strategically important. Some are much smaller, affecting fewer people, but important in their own way. All programming eventually done for the information system that solves the business problem is important, but solving each of these problems involves more than programming.

How does an analyst solve problems? Systems analysis and design focuses on understanding the business problem and outlining the approach to be taken to solve it. Figure 1-1 shows a general approach to problem solving that can be adapted to solving business problems using information technology. Obviously, part of the solution is a new information system, but that is just part of the story.

The analyst must first understand the problem and learn everything possible about it—who is involved, what business processes come into play, what other systems would be affected when solving this problem. Then the analyst needs to confirm for management that the benefits of solving the problem outweigh the costs. Sometimes it would cost a fortune to solve the problem, so it might not be worth solving.

If solving the problem is feasible, the analyst defines in detail what is required to solve it—what specific objectives must be satisfied, what data need to be stored and used, what processing must be done to the data, what outputs must be produced. *What* needs to be done must be defined first. *How* it will be done is not important yet.

Once requirements are identified, the analyst develops a set of possible solutions. Each possible solution (an alternative) needs to be thought through carefully. Usually, an information system alternative is defined as a set of choices about physical components that make up an information system—*how* it will be done. Many choices must be made, and the choices involve questions such as these:

- What are the needed components?
- What technology should be used to build the different components?
- Where are the components located?
- How will components communicate over networks?
- How are components configured into a system?

- How will people interact with the system?
- Which components are custom-made and which are purchased from vendors?
- Who should build the custom-made components?
- Who should assemble and support the components?

Many different alternatives must be considered, and the challenge involves selecting the best—that is, the solution with the fewest risks and most benefits. The analyst needs to consider whether alternatives for solving the problem are cost-effective, but those alternatives also must be consistent with the corporate strategic plan. Does the alternative contribute to the basic goals and objectives of the organization? Will it integrate seamlessly with other planned systems? Does it use technology that fits the strategic direction that management has defined? Will end users be receptive to it? Analysts must consider many factors and make tough decisions.

Once the systems analyst has determined, in consultation with management, which alternative is best for the organization, the details must be worked out. Here the analyst is concerned with creating a blueprint (detailed requirements models and detailed design models) for how the new system will work. Systems design models cover databases, user interfaces, networks, operating procedures, conversion plans, and, of course, software classes. The project team typically works on a single subset of the system requirements at a time. Once the models of the subset are complete, the actual construction of that part of the system can begin, including the programming and testing.

An information system can cost a lot of money to build and install, perhaps millions of dollars. So detailed plans must be drawn up. It is not unusual for dozens of programmers to work on programs to get a system up and running, and those programmers need to know exactly what the system is to accomplish—thus, detailed specifications are required. We present in this text the tools and techniques that an analyst uses during object-oriented system development to create the detailed specifications.

This text is written for potential systems analysts, particularly those who will use object-oriented analysis and design techniques. The text also provides a good foundation for others who will become involved with a business problem that could be solved with the help of an information system. Managers throughout business must become more and more knowledgeable about how to use information technology to solve business problems. Many general business students take a systems analysis and design course to round out their background in two-year and four-year degree programs. Many graduate programs, such as master of business administration (MBA) and master of accountancy (M.Acc.) programs, have technology tracks that include courses that use this book. Remember that systems analysis and design work is not just about developing systems; it is really about solving business problems using information technology. So even though they will never build an information system, managers need to gain expertise in these concepts to be effective in their jobs.

SYSTEMS THAT SOLVE BUSINESS PROBLEMS

system
a collection of interrelated components that function together to achieve some outcome

We described the systems analyst as a business problem solver. We said that the solution to the problem is usually an information system. Before we talk about how you learn to be a systems analyst, let's quickly review some information systems concepts.

INFORMATION SYSTEMS

A *system* is a collection of interrelated components that function together to achieve

information system
a collection of interrelated components that collect, process, store, and provide as output the information needed to complete business tasks

subsystem
a system that is part of a larger system

supersystem
a larger system that contains other systems

functional decomposition
dividing a system into components based on subsystems that in turn are further divided into subsystems

some outcome. An *information system* is a collection of interrelated components that collect, process, store, and provide as output the information needed to complete a business task. Completing a business task is usually the "problem" we talked about earlier.

A payroll system, for example, collects information on employees and their work, processes and stores that information, and then produces paychecks and payroll reports (among other things) for the organization. A sales management system collects information about customers, sales, products, and inventory levels, and then processes and stores the information. Then information is provided to manufacturing so the department can schedule production.

What are the interrelated components of an information system? There are several ways to think about components. Any system can have subsystems. A *subsystem* is a system that is part of another system. So, the subsystems might be one way to think about the components. For example, a customer support system might have an order-entry subsystem that creates new orders for customers. Another subsystem might handle fulfilling the order, including shipping and back orders. A third subsystem might maintain the product catalog database. The view of a system as a collection of subsystems is very useful to the analyst. These subsystems are interrelated components that function together.

Every system, in turn, is part of a larger system, called a *supersystem*. So, the customer support system is really just a subsystem of the production system. The production system includes other subsystems, such as inventory management and manufacturing. Figure 1-2 shows how one system can be divided, or decomposed, into subsystems, which in turn can be further decomposed into subsystems. This approach to dividing a system into components is referred to as *functional decomposition*.

Another way to think about the components of a system is to list the parts that interact. For example, an information system includes hardware, software, inputs, outputs, data, people, and procedures. This view is also very useful to the analyst. The

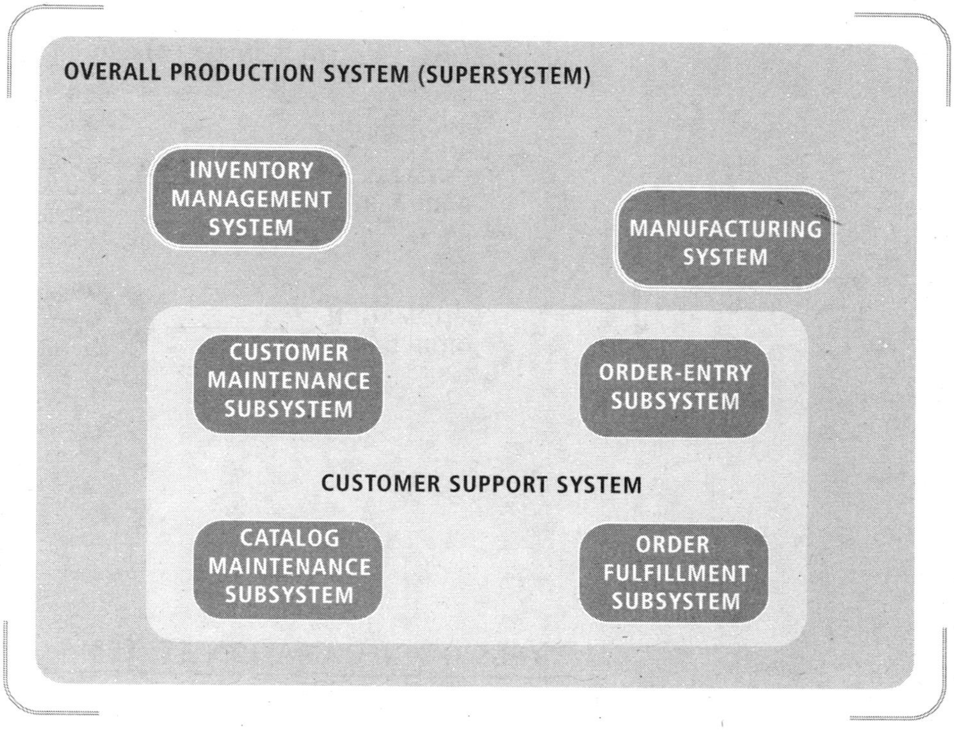

FIGURE 1-2
Information systems and subsystems

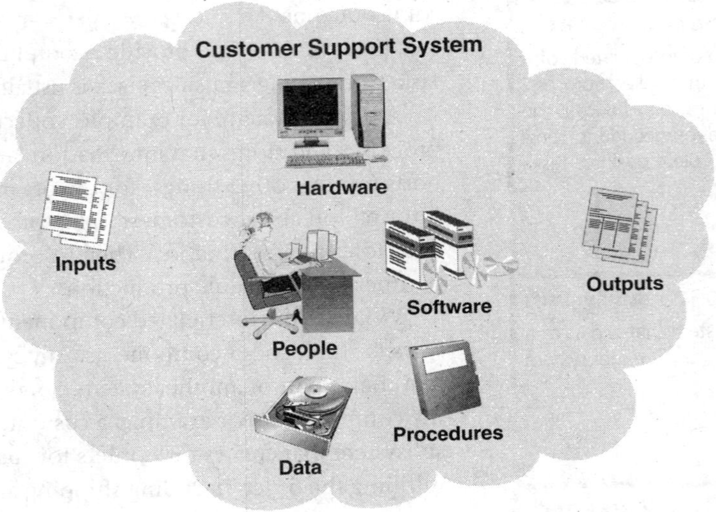

FIGURE 1-3
Information systems and component parts

hardware, software, inputs, outputs, data, people, and procedures are interrelated components that function together in a system, as shown in Figure 1-3.

system boundary
the separation between a system and its environment that inputs and outputs must cross

automation boundary
the separation between the automated part of a system and the manual part of a system

Every system has a boundary between it and its environment. Any inputs or outputs must cross the *system boundary*. Defining what these inputs and outputs are is an important part of systems analysis and design. In an information system, people are also key components, and these people do some of the work accomplished by the system. So there is another boundary that is important to a systems analyst—the *automation boundary*. On one side of the automation boundary is the automated part of the system, where work is done by computers. On the other side is the manual part of the system, where work is done by people (see Figure 1-4).

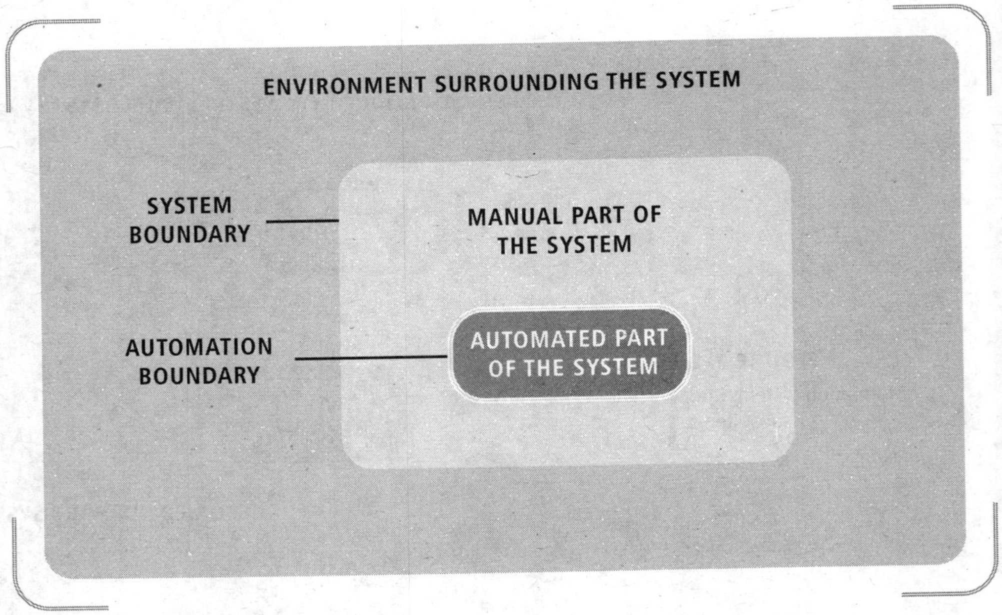

FIGURE 1-4
The system boundary versus the automation boundary

TYPES OF INFORMATION SYSTEMS

Because organizations perform many different types of activities, there are many different types of information systems. All of these information systems can be innovative

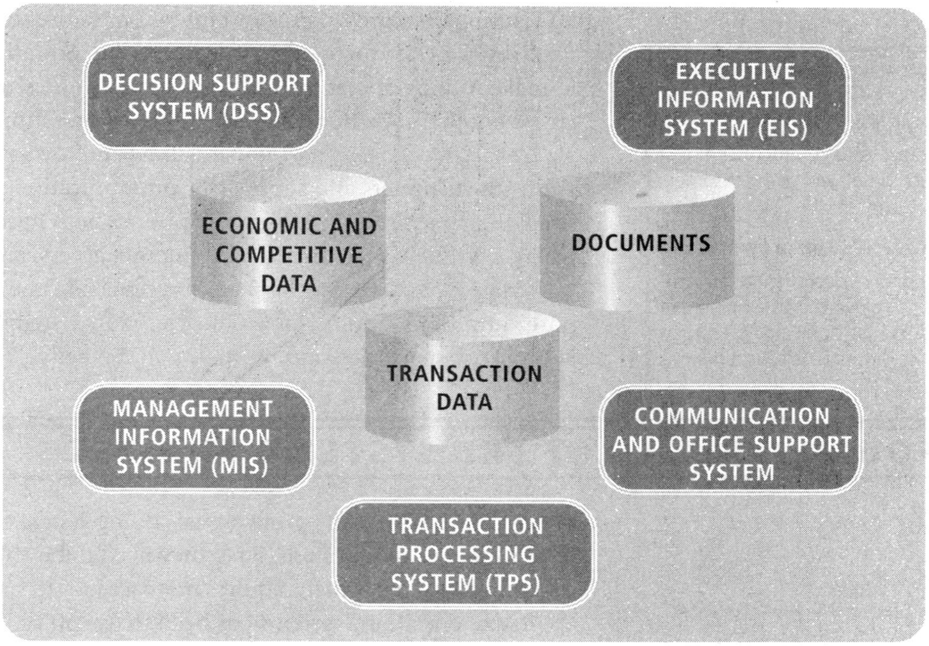

FIGURE 1-5
Types of information systems

and use the latest technologies. The types of systems found in most businesses include transaction processing systems, management information systems, executive information systems, decision support systems, communication support systems, and office support systems (see Figure 1-5). You learned about these types of systems in your introductory information systems course, so we will briefly review only the most common ones here.

transaction processing systems (TPS)
information systems that capture and record information about the transactions that affect the organization

Transaction processing systems (TPS) capture and record information about the transactions that affect the organization. A transaction occurs each time a sale is made, each time supplies are ordered, and each time an interest payment is made. Usually these transactions create credit or debit entries in accounting ledgers. They eventually end up on accounting statements used for financial accounting purposes, such as the income statement. Transaction processing systems were among the first to be automated by computers. Newer transaction processing systems use state-of-the-art technology and present some of the greatest challenges to information systems developers. They also present some of the greatest competitive advantages and returns on investments for companies. Business-to-consumer (B2C) and business-to-business (B2B) e-commerce systems are the latest challenges in transaction processing. Newer transaction processing systems are often called *online transaction processing systems*—OLTP.

management information systems (MIS)
information systems that take information captured by transaction processing systems and produce reports that management needs for planning and control

executive information systems (EIS)
information systems for executives to use for monitoring the competitive environment and for strategic planning

decision support systems (DSS)
support systems that allow a user to explore the impact of available options or decisions

Management information systems (MIS) are systems that take information captured by transaction processing systems and produce reports that management needs for planning and controlling the business. Management information systems are possible because the information has been captured by the transaction processing systems and placed in organizational databases.

Executive information systems (EIS) provide information for executives to use for monitoring the competitive environment and for strategic planning. Some of the information comes from the organizational databases, but much of the information comes from external sources—news about competitors, stock market reports, economic forecasts, and so on.

Decision support systems (DSS) allow a user to explore the impact of available options or decisions. Sometimes this process is referred to as "what if" analysis, because the user asks the system to answer questions such as, "What if sales dip below $100 million during the third quarter and interest rates rise to 7.5 percent?" Financial projections made by the DSS can then explore the results. Some decision support systems are used to make routine operational decisions, such as how many rental cars to move from one city to another for a holiday weekend based on estimated business travel patterns.

communication support systems
support systems that allow employees to communicate with each other and with customers and suppliers

office support systems
support systems that help employees create and share documents, including reports, proposals, and memos

Communication support systems allow employees to communicate with each other and with customers and suppliers. Communication support now includes wireless personal digital assistants (PDAs), cell phones with messaging and PDA features, anywhere anytime e-mail, broadband Internet access, and desktop video conferencing.

Office support systems help employees create and share documents, including reports, proposals, and memos. Office support systems also help maintain information about work schedules, appointments, and meetings.

REQUIRED SKILLS OF THE SYSTEMS ANALYST

Systems analysts (or any professionals doing systems analysis and design work) need a great variety of special skills. First, they need to be able to understand how to build information systems, which requires quite a bit of technical knowledge. The most recent approach to building systems has been to use object-oriented technologies. Then, as discussed previously, they have to understand the business they are working for and the ways the business uses each of the types of systems. Finally, the analysts need to understand quite a bit about people and the way they work, since people will use the information systems. These three types of knowledge and skills are summarized in Figure 1-6.

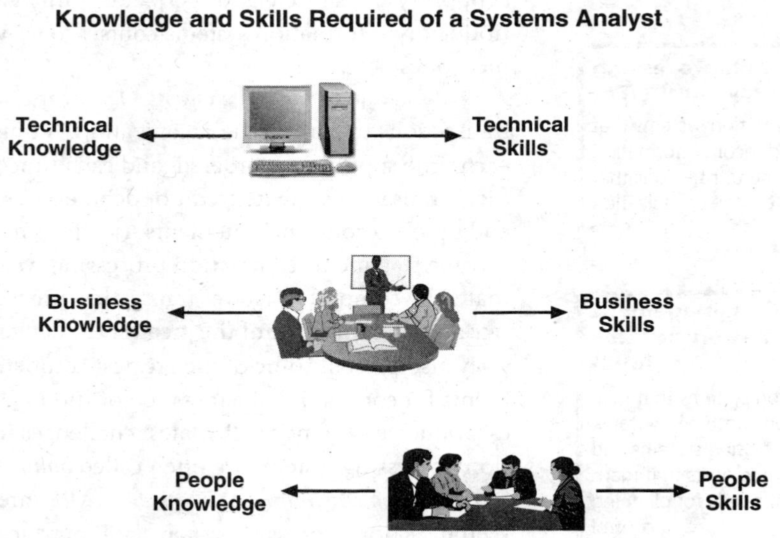

FIGURE 1-6
Required skills of the systems analyst

TECHNICAL KNOWLEDGE AND SKILLS

It should not be surprising that a systems analyst needs technical expertise. Even if an analyst is not involved in programming duties, it is still crucial to have an understanding of different types of technology—what they are used for, how they work, and how they are evolving. No one person can be an expert in all types of technology; technical specialists can provide the details. But a systems analyst should understand the fundamentals about:

- Computers and how they work
- Devices that interact with computers, including input devices, storage devices, and output devices
- Communications networks and protocols that connect computers
- Databases and database management systems
- Object-oriented programming languages and class libraries
- Operating systems and utilities

tools
software products used to develop analysis and design specifications and completed system components

A systems analyst also needs to know a lot about tools and techniques for developing systems. *Tools* are software products that help professionals develop analysis and design specifications and completed system components. Some tools used in system development include the following:

- Integrated development environments (IDEs) for specific programming languages, such as Sun ONE Studio for Java or Microsoft Visual Studio .NET for VB .NET and C# .NET
- Computer-aided system engineering (CASE) tools that store information about system specifications created by analysts and that also generate program code, such as Rational XDE Modeler, Borland Together, or Embarcadero Describe
- Program code generators, testing tools, configuration management tools, software library management tools, documentation support tools, project management tools, and so on

techniques
strategies for completing specific system development activities

Techniques are used to complete specific system development activities. How do you plan and manage a system development project? How do you define requirements? How do you design object interactions using design principles and best practices? How do you complete implementation and testing? How do you install and support a new information system? Much of this text explains how to use specific techniques for project planning, defining requirements, and designing objects and interactions. But it also covers some aspects of implementation and support. Some examples of techniques include:

- Project planning techniques
- Cost/benefit analysis techniques
- Interviewing techniques
- Requirements modeling techniques
- Architectural analysis techniques
- Network configuration techniques
- Database design techniques

BUSINESS KNOWLEDGE AND SKILLS

Other knowledge and skills that are crucial for an analyst include those that apply to understanding business organizations in general. After all, the problem to be solved is a business problem. What does the analyst need to know? The following are examples:

- What business functions do organizations perform?
- How are organizations structured?
- How are organizations managed?
- What type of work goes on in organizations—for example, finance, manufacturing, marketing, customer service, and so on?

Systems analysts benefit from a fairly broad understanding of businesses in general, so they typically study business administration in college. In fact, computer information systems (CIS) or management information systems (MIS) majors are often included in the college of business for that reason. The accounting, marketing, management, and operations courses taken in a CIS or MIS degree program serve the very important purpose of preparing the graduate for the workplace.

Systems analysts also need to understand the type of organization for which they work. Some analysts specialize in a specific industry for their entire career—perhaps in manufacturing, retailing, financial services, or aerospace. The reason for this business focus is simple: It takes a long time to understand the problems of a specific industry. An analyst with deep understanding of a specific industry can solve complex problems for companies in the industry.

Familiarity with a specific company is also important for someone providing guidance on system needs and changes. Often, just knowing the people who work for a company and understanding subtleties of the company culture can make a big difference in the effectiveness of an analyst. It takes years of experience working for a company to really understand what is going on. The more an analyst knows about how an organization works, the more effective he or she can be. Some specifics the analyst needs to know about the company include the following:

- What the specific organization does
- What makes it successful
- What its strategies and plans are
- What its traditions and values are

BEST PRACTICE: Be sure you understand the organization, its culture, its mission, and its objectives before jumping to conclusions about system solutions.

PEOPLE KNOWLEDGE AND SKILLS

Because analysts usually work on development teams with other employees, systems analysts need to understand a lot about people and possess many people skills. An analyst spends a great deal of time working with people, trying to understand their perspectives on the problems they are trying to solve. It is critical that the analyst understand how people:

- Think
- Learn
- React to change
- Communicate
- Work (in a variety of jobs and levels)

Analysts must understand how people think so that they can better anticipate the way people will want to interact with the computer system, for example, to have the computer appear to anticipate their actions. How people learn is important when designing training materials and system help, since people must learn to use a new system. When a new system is implemented, it can change the way people do their jobs, and they must be prepared for the change and helped to see the benefits of the change. An analyst must use a variety of people skills to get the required information and to influence and motivate people to cooperate. These types of skills include interpersonal skills and communication skills. Finally, since the information systems are designed to support the work of people, it is necessary to understand the work that people perform in a variety of jobs and at a variety of levels, ranging from clerical and factory workers to managers and executives. Because analysts come into contact with so many people throughout an organization, they have a unique opportunity to influence the organization as a whole.

A FEW WORDS ABOUT INTEGRITY AND ETHICS

One aspect of a career in information systems that students often underestimate is the importance of personal integrity and ethics. A systems analyst is asked to look into problems that involve information in many different parts of an organization. Especially if it involves individuals, the information might be very private, such as salary, health, and job performance. The analyst must have the integrity to keep this information private.

But the problems the analyst works on can also involve confidential corporate information, including proprietary information about products or planned products, strategic plans or tactics, and even top-secret information involving government military contracts. Sometimes a company's security processes or specific security systems can be involved in the analyst's work.

Some system developers work for consulting firms that are called in to work on specific problems for clients. They are expected to uphold the highest ethical standards when it comes to private proprietary information they might encounter on the job. Any appearance of impropriety can ruin an analyst's career.

THE ENVIRONMENT SURROUNDING THE ANALYST

TYPES OF TECHNOLOGY ENCOUNTERED

Most students have used and are familiar with personal computers. In many university MIS or CIS degree programs, students complete modest course projects using Java or Visual Basic .NET that run on PCs. But not all businesses function with desktop systems, and sometimes students don't recognize how different the large-scale systems are that they will work on when they are out in the real world.

Many basic systems now are run with personal computers on desktops, but behind the scenes, these computers may be connected to data centers through very complex networks. When a company talks about an online order-processing application, it might involve a system with thousands of users spread over hundreds of locations. The database might contain hundreds of tables with millions of records in each table. The system might have taken years to complete, costing millions of dollars. If the system fails for even an hour, the company could lose millions of dollars in sales. Such a system is critical for the business, so the programmers and analysts who work to support and maintain it work in round-the-clock shifts, often wearing pagers in case of a problem. The importance of these systems to business cannot be overstated.

Different configurations of information systems that future analysts may encounter, which are discussed in later chapters, include the following:

- Desktop systems
- Networked desktop systems that share data
- Client/server systems
- Large-scale centralized mainframe systems
- Systems using Internet, intranet, and extranet technology

Just as an organization's business environment continually changes, so does the technology used for its information systems. Enterprise-level systems increasingly require flexible development environments provided by Web-based technology so that employees and customers can get access to systems and data anywhere and anytime. The rapid change in technology often drives needed changes. Thus, it is important for all people involved in information system development to upgrade their knowledge and skills continually. Those who don't will be left behind.

BEST PRACTICE: In the information systems field, you need to be prepared to constantly upgrade your knowledge and skills.

TYPICAL JOB TITLES AND PLACES OF EMPLOYMENT

We have discussed the work of a systems analyst in terms of problem solving and system development. But it is important to recognize that many different people do systems analysis and design work. Not all have the job title of systems analyst. Sometimes analysis and design work is done by end users assigned to the project to provide expertise. Often analysis and design work is combined with other tasks (such as programming or end-user support). A recent graduate employed as a programmer analyst will typically work on system maintenance and support projects doing programming. Even so, maintenance programming requires analysis of the requirements for the change, design of the solution, and implementation of the change. In this regard, even beginning programmers are involved in analysis and design.

Here are some job titles you may encounter:

- Programmer analyst
- Business systems analyst
- System liaison
- End-user analyst
- Business consultant
- Systems consultant
- System support analyst
- Systems designer
- Software engineer
- System architect
- Webmaster
- Web developer

Sometimes systems analysts might also be called *project leaders* or *project managers*. Be prepared to hear all kinds of titles for people who are involved in analysis and design work.

People who do analysis and design work are also found at organizations of all sizes—small businesses, medium-sized regional businesses, national *Fortune* 500 businesses, and multinational corporations. The type of technology used and the nature of the projects differ quite a bit, based on the size of the organization. In addition, some businesses have very centralized information systems departments or divisions, while others have smaller information systems units that serve specialized parts of the organization. And the size of the organization may not always correspond to the size of the systems the analyst works on. So some analysts work at smaller companies with a large-company feel, and others work at a large company with a small-company feel.

But not all analysts work directly for the company with the problem to solve. Analysis and design work for a company is accomplished in many different work arrangements, including:

- Programmer analysts working for the company (part of the time is spent in analysis and design work)
- Systems analysts (who specialize in analysis and design) working for the company
- Independent contractors (who work as analysts or programmer analysts) working as needed under the direction of company managers
- Outsource provider employees (who work on- or off-site) working on a project under contract for the company
- Consultants (who are employed by a consulting firm) working on a specific project for the company
- Software development firm employees (who work on developing and supporting software packages purchased by the company)
- Application service provider (ASP) employees (who work on developing and supporting ASP system solutions contracted for by the company)

Analysis and design work is also done in other situations. Naturally, companies such as Microsoft, Sun Microsystems, and IBM hire software developers to create or adapt software packages such as Office XP and operating systems such as Windows XP. These developers do analysis and design work, too, but the problem to be solved is generally different. Computer science graduates are more likely to work on new versions of Windows or Office, which use their technical skills to best advantage. In this text, though, we assume the analyst is working on information systems that solve business problems, not on operating systems or software packages.

THE ANALYST'S ROLE IN STRATEGIC PLANNING

We have described a systems analyst as someone who solves specific business problems by developing or maintaining information systems. The analyst might also be involved with senior managers on strategic management problems—that is, problems involving the future of the organization and plans and processes to ensure its survival and growth. Sometimes an analyst only a few years out of college can be summoned to meet with top-level executives and even be asked to present recommendations to achieve corporate goals. How might this happen?

SPECIAL PROJECTS

First, the analyst might be working to solve a problem that affects executives, such as designing an executive information system. The analyst might interview the executives to find out what information they need to do their work. An analyst may be asked to spend a day with an executive or even travel with an executive to get a feel for the nature of the executive's work. Then the analyst might develop and demonstrate prototypes of the system to get more insight into the needs of executives.

business process reengineering
a technique that seeks to alter the nature of the work done in a business function with the objective of radically improving performance

Another situation that could involve an analyst in strategic management problems is a business process reengineering study. *Business process reengineering* seeks to alter radically the nature of the work done in a business function. The objective is radical improvement in performance, not just incremental improvement. Therefore, the analyst might be asked to participate in a study that carefully examines existing business processes and procedures and then to propose information system solutions that can have a radical impact. Many tools and techniques of analysis and design are used to analyze business processes, redesign them, and then provide computer support to make them work.

STRATEGIC PLANNING

strategic planning
a process during which executives try to answer questions about the company, such as where the business is now, where they want the business to be, and what they have to do to get there

Most business organizations invest considerable time and energy in completing strategic plans that typically cover five or more years. During the *strategic planning* process, executives ask themselves such fundamental questions about the company as where the business is now, where they want the business to be, and what they have to do to get there. A typical strategic planning process can take months or even years, and often plans are continually updated. Many people from throughout the organization are involved, all completing forecasts and analyses, which are combined into the overall strategic plan. Once a strategic plan is set, it drives all of the organization's processes, so all areas of the organization must participate and coordinate their activities. Therefore, a marketing strategic plan and a production strategic plan must fit within the overall strategic plan.

INFORMATION SYSTEMS STRATEGIC PLANNING

information systems strategic plan
the plan defining the technology and applications that the information systems function needs to support the organization's strategic plan

One major component of the strategic plan is the *information systems strategic plan*. Today, information systems are so tightly integrated with an organization that nearly any planned change calls for new or improved information systems. Beyond that, the information systems themselves often drive the strategic plan. For example, after some chaotic early years involving the Internet, many new Internet-based companies have survived (such as Amazon.com and eBay), and many other companies have altered their business processes and developed new markets in which to compete. In other cases, the opportunities presented by new information systems technology have led to new products and markets with more subtle impacts. Information systems and the possibilities that they present play a large role in the strategic plans of most organizations.

Information systems strategic planning sometimes involves the whole organization. Usually at the recommendation of the chief information systems executive, top management will authorize a major project to plan the information systems for the entire organization. Unlike ongoing planning, a specific information systems strategic planning project might be authorized every five years or so, depending on the changes in the industry or company.

In developing the information systems strategic plan, members of the staff look at the organization overall to anticipate problems rather than react to systems problems as they come up. Several techniques help the organization complete an information systems strategic planning project. A consulting firm is often hired to help with the project. Consultants can offer experience with strategic planning techniques and can train managers and analysts to complete the plan.

Usually managers and staff from all areas of the organization are involved, but the project team is generally led by information systems managers with the assistance of consultants. Systems analysts often become involved in collecting information and interviewing people.

application architecture plan
a description of the integrated information systems that the organization needs to carry out its business functions

Many documents and existing systems are reviewed. Then the team tries to create a model of the entire organization—to map the business functions it performs. Another model, one that shows the types of data the entire organization creates and uses, is also developed. The team examines all of the locations where functions are performed and data are created and used. From these models, the team puts together the *application architecture plan*, a list of integrated information systems necessary for the organization to carry out its business functions. Then, given the existing systems and other factors, the team outlines the sequence needed to implement the required systems.

technology architecture plan
a description of the hardware, software, and communications networks required to implement planned information systems

Given the list of information systems needed, the team defines the *technology architecture plan*—that is, the types of hardware, software, and communications networks required to implement all of the planned systems. The team must look at trends in technology and make commitments to specific technologies and possibly even technology vendors. The components of the information systems strategic plan are shown in Figure 1-7.

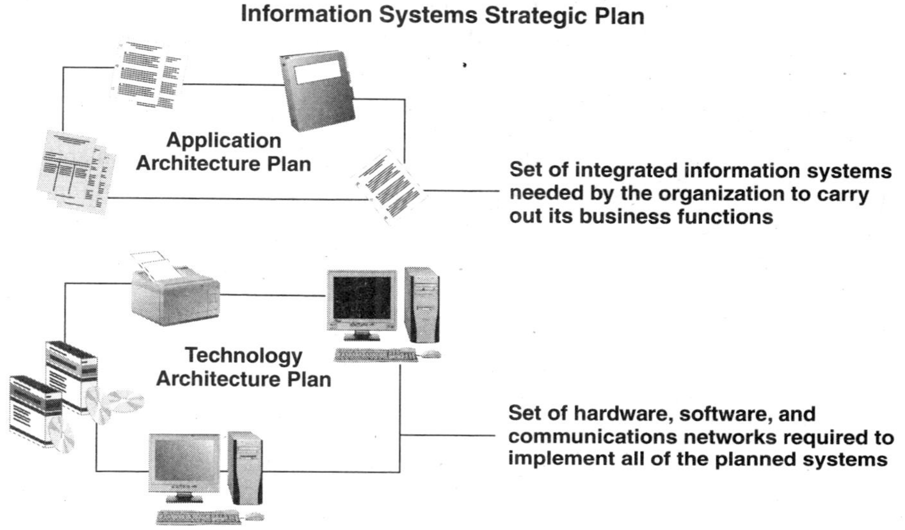

FIGURE 1-7
Components of an information systems strategic plan

In the ideal world, a comprehensive information systems planning project solves all of the problems that information systems managers face. Unfortunately, the world continues to change at such a rate that plans must be continually updated. Unplanned information system projects come up all the time, and priorities must be continually evaluated.

ENTERPRISE RESOURCE PLANNING

enterprise resource planning (ERP)
a process in which an organization commits to using an integrated set of software packages for key information systems

An increasing number of organizations are addressing their information systems requirements using an approach called *enterprise resource planning (ERP)*, which commits to using an integrated set of software packages for key information systems. Software vendors such as SAP and PeopleSoft offer comprehensive packages for companies in specific industries. To adopt an ERP solution, the company must carefully study its existing processes and information needs and then determine which ERP vendor provides the best match. ERP systems are so complex that an organization must often commit nearly everyone in the information systems department and throughout the organization to research options. They are also very expensive, in initial cost and in support cost. Much change is involved, for management and for staff. And once the decision is made to adopt an ERP system, it is very difficult to return to the old ways of doing business—and the old systems. An analyst involved in an ERP project will have to draw heavily on technical, business, and people skills and can play a key role in the project.

ROCKY MOUNTAIN OUTFITTERS AND ITS STRATEGIC INFORMATION SYSTEMS PLAN

To demonstrate the important object-oriented systems analysis and design techniques in this text, we follow a system development project for a company named Rocky Mountain Outfitters (RMO). RMO is a sports clothing manufacturer and distributor that is about to begin development of a new customer support system. The company is using object-oriented development exclusively for this project. You will encounter RMO customer support system examples in all chapters of this book. For now, try to get a feel for the nature of the business, the approach the company took to define the information systems strategic plan, and the basic objectives of the customer support system that is part of the plan.

INTRODUCING ROCKY MOUNTAIN OUTFITTERS (RMO)

RMO started in 1978 as the dream of John and Liz Blankens of Park City, Utah. Liz had always been interested in fashion and clothing and had worked her way through college by designing, sewing, and selling winter sports clothes to the local ski shops in Park City. She continued with this side business even after she graduated, and soon it was taking all of her time.

Liz had been dating John Blankens since they met at a fashion merchandising convention. John had worked for several years for a retail department store chain after college and had just completed his MBA. Together they decided to try to expand Liz's business into retailing to reach a larger customer base. Also, around this time they married.

The first step in their expansion involved direct mail-order sales to customers, using a small catalog (see Figure 1-8). Liz immediately had to expand the manufacturing operations by adding a designer and production supervisor. As interest in the catalog increased, the Blankenses sought out additional lines of clothing and accessories to sell along with their own product lines. They also opened a retail store in Park City.

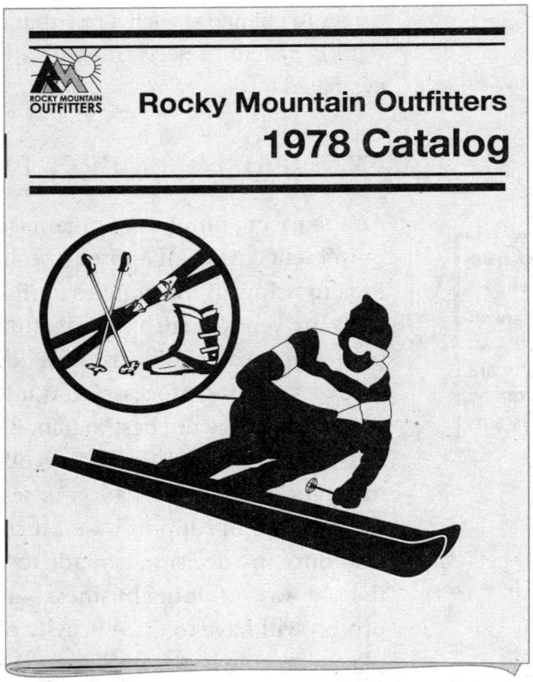

FIGURE 1-8
Early RMO catalog cover (Spring 1978)

By 2005, RMO had grown to become a significant regional sports clothing distributor in the Rocky Mountain and Western states. The states of Arizona, New Mexico, Colorado, Utah, Wyoming, Idaho, Oregon, Washington, Nevada, and the eastern edge of California had seen tremendous growth in recreation activities. Along with the increased interest in outdoor sports, the market for both winter and summer sports clothes had exploded. Skiing, snowboarding, mountain biking, water-skiing, jet skiing, river running, jogging, hiking, ATV biking, camping, mountain climbing, and rappelling had all seen a tremendous increase in interest in these states. Of course, people needed appropriate sports clothes for their activities. So, RMO expanded its line of sportswear to respond to this market. It also added a line of casual and active wear to round out its offerings to the expanding market of active people. The current RMO catalog offers an extensive selection (see Figure 1-9).

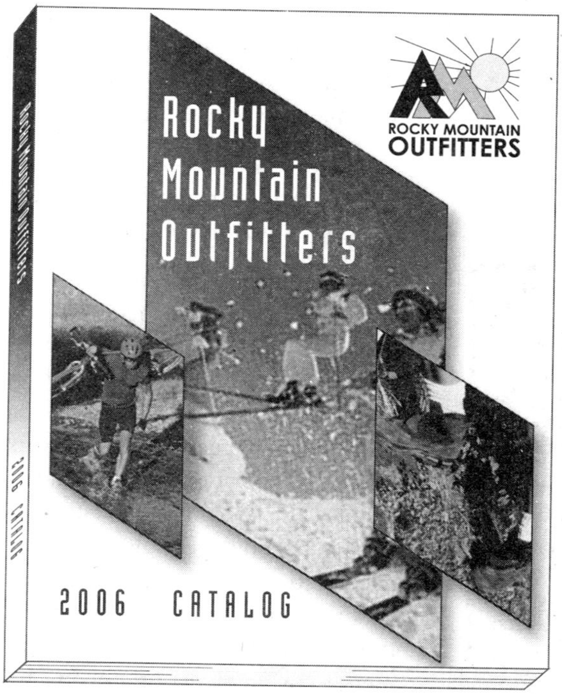

FIGURE 1-9
Current RMO catalog cover
(Spring 2006)

Rocky Mountain Outfitters now employs more than 600 people and produces almost $100 million annually in sales. The mail-order operation is still the major source of revenue, at $60 million. In-store retail sales remained a modest part of the business, with sales of $2.5 million at the Park City retail store and $5 million at the recently opened Denver store. In the early 1990s, the Blankenses added a phone-order operation that now accounts for $30 million in sales. To the customer, this service was a natural extension, but to RMO, it meant considerable changes in transaction processing systems to handle the phone orders.

RMO STRATEGIC ISSUES

Rocky Mountain Outfitters was also one of the first sports clothing distributors to provide a Web site featuring its products. The site originally gave RMO a simple Web presence to enhance its image and to allow potential customers to request a copy of the catalog. It also served as a portal to which were linked all sorts of outdoor sports Web sites. The first RMO Web site enhancement added more specific product information, including weekly specials that could be ordered by phone. Eventually, nearly all product offerings were included in an online catalog posted at the Web site. But orders could only be placed by mail or by phone.

John and Liz had considered making a major commitment to business-to-consumer (B2C) e-commerce in 2002. But Liz worried about the risk of sudden and potentially explosive growth. She had seen many small manufacturers and distributors jump into online order processing without being able to support the sales properly. Inventory shortages, unreliable service, poorly handled returns, and even occasional double billing had ruined some successful and well-respected brick-and-mortar companies overnight. Liz was determined that RMO would not make the same mistake.

John and Liz could see the potential of e-commerce, but they wanted to be careful to do it right, not just tack it on as an afterthought. The Blankenses had always planned carefully, and they also knew that the role of information technology in their business would continue to grow in strategic importance. Therefore, they decided to think carefully about their entire information technology infrastructure and create a strategic information systems plan. A consulting firm was brought in to help with the strategic information systems planning process.

The consulting firm recommended focusing on two key strategic thrusts:

- Supply chain management
- Customer relationship management

supply chain management (SCM)
a process that seamlessly integrates product development, product acquisition, manufacturing, and inventory management

customer relationship management (CRM)
processes that support marketing, sales, and service operations involving direct and indirect customer interaction

Supply chain management (SCM) concerns processes that seamlessly integrate product development, product acquisition, manufacturing, and inventory management. *Customer relationship management (CRM)* concerns processes that support marketing, sales, and service operations involving direct and indirect customer interaction. Both of these strategies help businesses—especially retailers such as RMO—provide products and services to customers while promoting efficient operations.

The information systems strategic plan included an application architecture plan, detailing the information systems development projects that the company needed to complete, and a technology architecture plan, detailing the technology infrastructure needed to support the systems. Both components of the plan were based on the supply chain management objectives and the customer relationship management objectives RMO defined for the next five years. Another key aspect of the planning was a commitment to using object-oriented technology and newer object-oriented development techniques for system development projects.

BEST PRACTICE: Most business executives understand that information systems are strategically important, and they usually have excellent ideas and insights. Be sure to ask for their input.

The next section provides some additional background on RMO and summarizes the overall information systems plan it is currently following. In subsequent chapters of this book, we will focus on one of the crucial information systems that is part of the plan—the customer support system.

RMO'S ORGANIZATIONAL STRUCTURE AND LOCATIONS

Rocky Mountain Outfitters is still managed on a daily basis by John and Liz Blankens. John is president, and Liz is vice president of merchandising and distribution (see Figure 1-10). Other top managers include William McDougal, vice president of marketing and

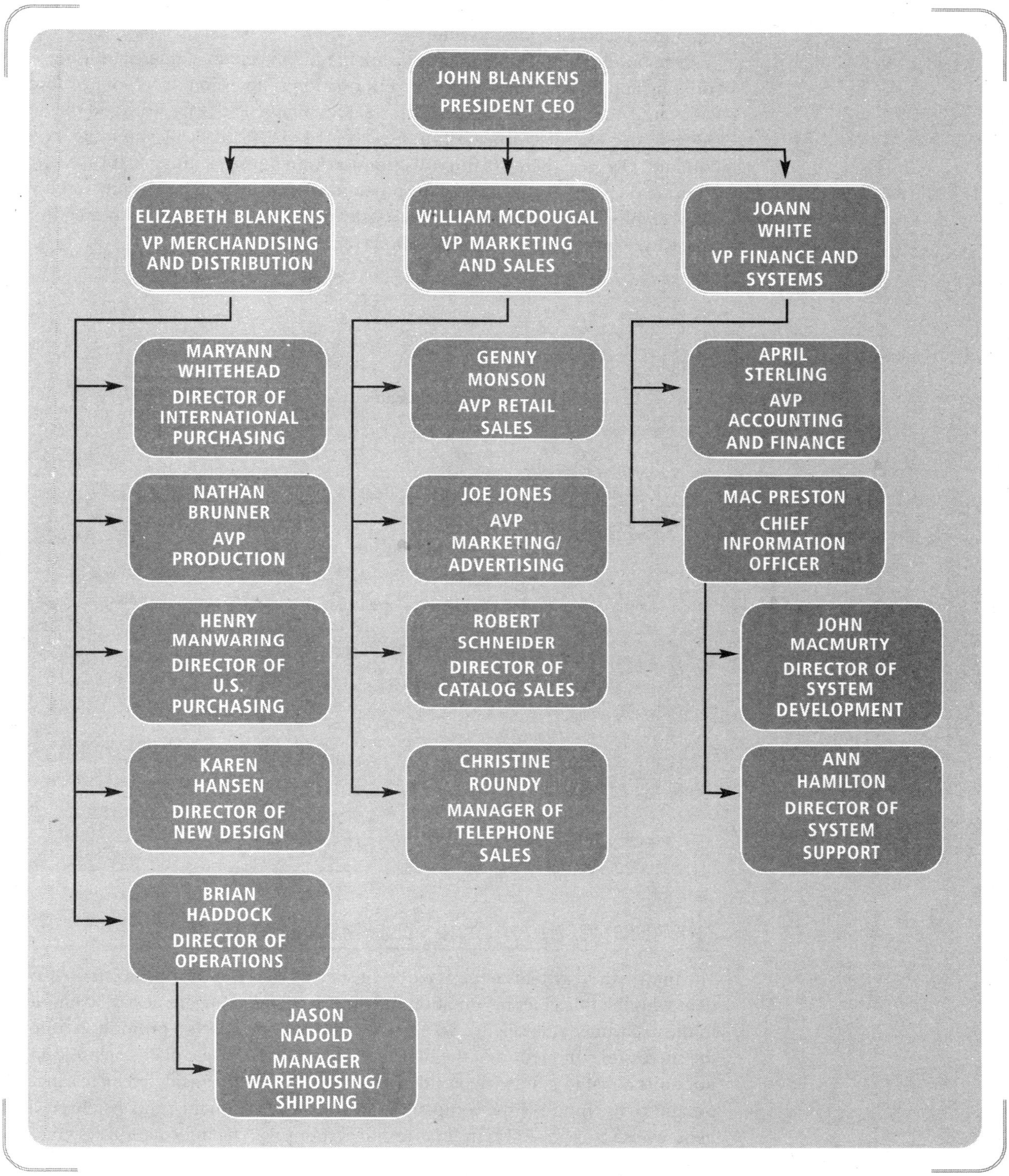

FIGURE 1-10
Rocky Mountain Outfitters' organizational structure

sales, and JoAnn White, vice president of finance and systems. The information systems department reports to JoAnn White.

One hundred thirteen employees work in human resources, merchandising, accounting and finance, marketing, and information systems in the corporate offices in Park City, Utah. There are two retail stores: the original Park City store and the newer Denver store. Manufacturing facilities are located in Salt Lake City and more recently Portland, Oregon. There are three distribution/warehouse facilities: Salt Lake City, Albuquerque, and Portland. All mail-order processing is done in a facility in Provo, Utah, employing 58 people. The phone-sales center, employing 20, is located in Salt Lake City. Figure 1-11 shows the locations of these facilities.

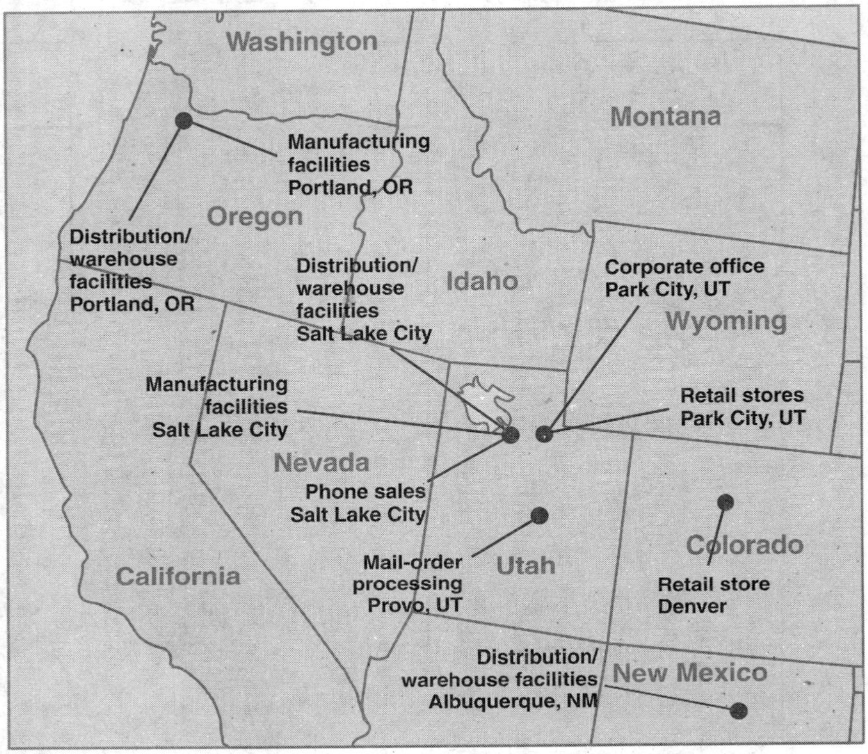

FIGURE 1-11
Rocky Mountain Outfitters' locations

THE RMO INFORMATION SYSTEMS DEPARTMENT

The information systems department is headed by Mac Preston, an assistant vice president with the title chief information officer (CIO), and there are nearly 50 employees in the department (see Figure 1-12). Mac's title of CIO reflects a promotion following the successful completion of the information systems strategic planning project. He is not quite equal to a full vice president, but his position is considered increasingly important to the future of the company. Mac reports to the finance and systems vice president, whose background is in finance and accounting. The information systems department will eventually report directly to the CEO if Mac has success implementing the new strategic information systems plan.

Mac organized information systems into two areas—system support and system development. Ann Hamilton is director of system support. System support involves such functions as telecommunications, database administration, operations, and user support. John MacMurty is director of system development. System development includes four project managers, six systems analysts, ten programmer analysts, and a couple of clerical support employees.

FIGURE 1-12
RMO information systems department staffing

IS staffing

Chief information officer

- Secretary (1)

Director of system support

- Managers (4)
- Telecom analysts (2)
- Database analysts (2)
- Operations (6)
- User support (4)
- Secretarial/clerical (2)
- Off-site operations (4)

Director of system development

- Project managers (4)
- Systems analysts (6)
- Programmer analysts (10)
- Secretarial/clerical (2)

EXISTING RMO SYSTEMS

Most of the computer technology and information systems staff at RMO is located at the data center in Park City. A small mainframe computer runs the inventory, mail-order, accounting, and human resource functions by connecting to the distribution and mail-order sites by dedicated telecommunication links. The manufacturing sites have dial-up capability to the mainframe.

Office functions at the home office, distribution sites, and manufacturing sites are supported by local area networks with file servers. Retail stores run a point-of-sale software package with a local server and dial-up batch updates to the inventory system on the mainframe. The phone-sales center has a small local area network with a client/server order-processing application running under Windows. Batch inventory updates are made to the mainframe. The RMO informational Web site is hosted by an Internet service provider (ISP) that maintains the Web content off-site.

The existing information systems and their technology are organized as follows:

- **Merchandising/Distribution.** A mainframe application developed in-house using COBOL/CICS with some DB2 relational database and VSAM files. Implemented 12 years ago.
- **Mail Order.** A mainframe application developed in-house using COBOL. Mail-order clerks in Provo use dedicated terminals. The application is fast and efficient but unsuitable for handling phone orders. Implemented 14 years ago.
- **Phone Order.** A modest Windows application developed using Visual Basic and Oracle as a quick solution to customer demand for phone orders. It is a multiuser file-server design that is not integrated well with merchandising/distribution and has reached capacity. Implemented six years ago.
- **Retail Store Systems.** A retail store package with point-of-sale processing and overnight batch inventory update with the mainframe. Implemented eight years ago.

- **Office Systems.** A local area network with office software, Internet access, and e-mail services in the Park City offices and other sites. Implemented three years ago.
- **Human Resources.** An application developed in-house for payroll and benefits running on the mainframe. Implemented 13 years ago.
- **Accounting/Finance.** A mainframe package from a leading accounting package vendor. Implemented 10 years ago.
- **RMO Informational Web site.** A static site with catalog information and other links. Implemented and hosted by an ISP three years ago.

THE INFORMATION SYSTEMS STRATEGIC PLAN

The information systems strategic plan developed with the help of the consultants includes the technology architecture plan and the application architecture plan. The planning team looked closely at existing systems and at the business objectives of RMO. As initially proposed, supply chain management and customer relationship management provided a vision for the plan. These ideas support the strategic objectives of RMO to build more direct customer relationships and to expand the marketing presence beyond the Western states.

The main features of the plans include the following:

TECHNOLOGY ARCHITECTURE PLAN

[1] Distribute business applications across multiple locations and computer systems, reserving the mainframe for Web server, database, and telecommunications functions to allow incremental and rapid growth in capacity.

[2] Deploy new systems (including the supply chain management systems and customer support system) using scalable object-oriented technology such as .NET or Sun J2EE.

[3] Move toward conducting strategic business processes via the Internet, first supporting supply chain management, next supporting direct customer ordering on a new, dynamic Web site, and finally supporting additional customer relationship management (CRM) functions that link internal systems and databases.

[4] Anticipate the eventual move toward Web-based intranet solutions for business functions such as human resources, accounting, finance, and information management.

APPLICATION ARCHITECTURE PLAN

[1] Supply chain management (SCM): Implement systems that seamlessly integrate product development, product acquisition, manufacturing, and inventory management in anticipation of rapid sales growth. Custom development with support of consultants.

[2] Customer support system (CSS): Implement an order-processing and fulfillment system that seamlessly integrates with the supply chain management systems to support the three order-processing requirements: mail order, phone order, and direct customer access via the Web. Custom in-house development.

[3] Strategic information management system (SIMS): Implement an information system that can extract and analyze supply chain and customer support information for strategic and operational decision making and control. Package solution.

[4] Retail store system (RSS): Replace the existing retail store system with a system that can integrate with the customer support system. Package solution.

[5] Accounting/finance: Purchase a package solution, definitely an intranet application, to maximize employee access to financial data for planning and control.

[6] Human resources: Purchase a package solution, definitely an intranet application, to maximize employee access to human resource (HR) forms, procedures, and benefits information.

The timetable for implementing the application architecture plan is shown in Figure 1-13. Key components of the supply chain management system, particularly inventory management components, must be defined before the customer support system project can be started. The customer support system project must be started as soon as possible, however, as it is the core system supporting customer relationship management.

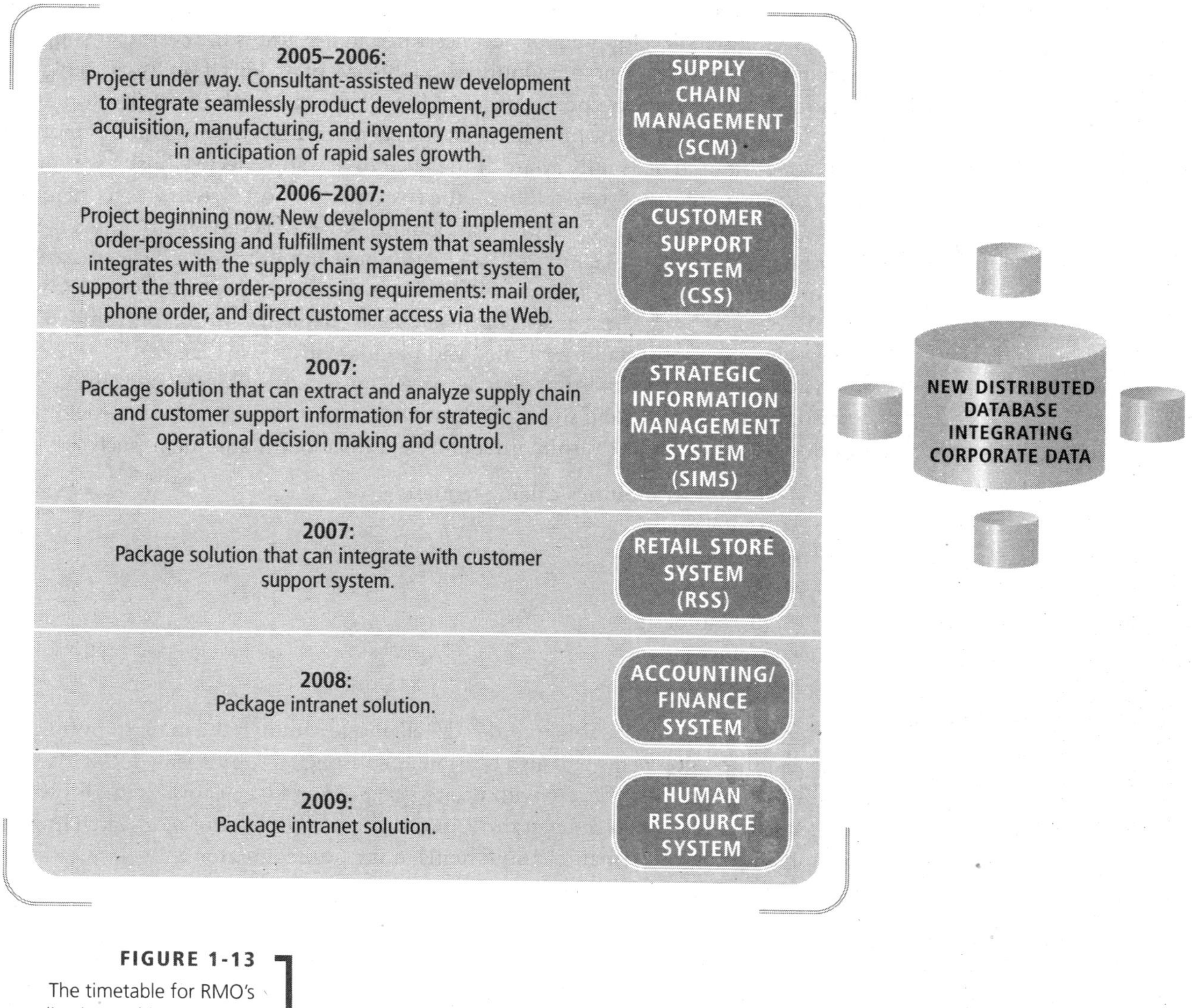

FIGURE 1-13
The timetable for RMO's application architecture plan

The supply chain management (SCM) system and the customer support system (CSS) require custom software development. Custom development is advisable when the system must match very specific company requirements. Consultants have been called in to help define requirements and develop the integration plan for supply chain management. Several leading consulting firms specialize in supply chain management.

The customer support system will probably be developed in-house by the information systems staff, although final decisions about the implementation approach will be deferred until a more complete project proposal is completed.

The other systems in the plan will probably be software package solutions selected from among the best-rated software currently available. Package solutions are desirable for standard business systems such as accounting and human resources. The key requirement is that any package must integrate seamlessly with other RMO systems and use intranet technology.

THE CUSTOMER SUPPORT SYSTEM

The RMO system development project described in this text is the customer support system (CSS). Rocky Mountain Outfitters has always prided itself on its customer orientation. One of the core competencies of RMO has been its ability to develop and maintain customer loyalty. John Blankens has kept himself current on important business concepts, and he is fully aware of the need to develop effective business processes with a customer focus. So even though the customer support system was to include all of the required sales and marketing components, he wants everyone to understand that its primary objective is to support RMO's customers. John's long-held view regarding customers has become popular recently with consultants and software vendors, who call the approach *customer relationship management* (defined earlier). John smiled approvingly as the consultants explained CRM to his staff.

The application architecture plan detailed some specific objectives for the customer support system. The system should include all functions associated with providing products for the customer, from order entry to arrival of the shipment, such as:

- Customer inquiries/catalog requests
- Order entry
- Order tracking
- Shipping
- Back-ordering
- Returns
- Sales analysis

Customers should be able to order by telephone, through the mail, or over the Internet. All catalog items will also be available through a sophisticated RMO Web catalog, which must be consistent with printed catalogs so that customers can browse the printed catalog and then order at the RMO Web site, if they choose, or search the Web site for additional information about items in the printed catalog.

Order-entry processing needs to support the graphical, self-help style of the Web interface, as well as a streamlined, rapid-response Windows interface required for phone-sales representatives and mail-order clerks. Returns, back orders, and order status also need to be accessible both on the Web and to RMO employees at their desks.

Although some objectives are defined for the system, a complete requirements analysis will define the system in detail. These objectives only form some guidelines to keep in mind as the project gets under way.

THE ANALYST AS A SYSTEM DEVELOPER (THE HEART OF THE COURSE)

We have discussed many roles that a systems analyst can play in an organization, including strategic planning and helping identify the major information systems projects that the business will pursue. However, the main job of an analyst is working on a specific information systems development project. This text is about planning and executing an information systems project—in other words, working as a system developer. The text is organized around this theme. In this section, we provide an overview of the text—a preview of what system development involves—as exemplified by the development process ahead for Barbara Halifax, who is in charge of the RMO customer support system project that is about to start (see Barbara's memo).

ROCKY MOUNTAIN OUTFITTERS

MEMO

February 4, 2006

To: John Blankens, President

From: Barbara Halifax, System Development Project Manager

RE: Customer Support System (CSS) Project

John MacMurty suggested I write you a brief note to let you know how excited and proud I am to be in charge of the customer support system (CSS) project. I enjoyed working with you and other RMO staff of the strategic information system plan last year, and I know I have you to thank for putting in a good word for me with Mac Preston (and with John) for this important assignment. It is particularly exciting to be able to approach this project using object-oriented analysis and design techniques. As you know, all of us in systems have invested a lot of time learning about UML Modeling and the United Process approach to system development.

With the SCM system now well under way, we are all ready to begin the CSS project. I have reviewed all of our planning documents and have met regularly with Jack Garcia about the SCM system. Everything I see in the IS trade press concerning the integrated supplier and customer systems continues to confirm our assumptions about the need for these projects. My next step is to begin detailed project planning now that it is time to begin the CSS project formally. There are some new procedures to follow now that we are using the Unified Process.

Naturally, I'll be writing my regular status reports to John MacMurty, but please let us know if you have any questions or ideas you might want to share with us. I know how important the CSS project is to RMO, and I share your commitment to providing unparalleled customer support with this new system.

Thanks for the opportunity!

BH

cc: Mac Preston, John MacMurty

PART 1: SYSTEM DEVELOPMENT AND THE UNIFIED PROCESS

The first part of the text describes the work of the systems analyst who is involved in a system development project. This chapter (Chapter 1) describes the nature of the analyst's work in terms of types of problems solved, the required skills, possible job titles, and the places where an analyst might work. We hope it is clear so far that the analyst does much more than think about and write programs. The rest of the text is organized around the problem-solving approach we described at the beginning of the chapter.

Not only does the analyst get involved with business problems, but he or she can work on very high-level strategic issues and with people at all levels of the organization, relatively early in his or her career. In this chapter we also described Rocky Mountain Outfitters and its strategic information systems plan. The rest of the text will focus on one of the planned new systems—the customer support system—and its development.

Chapter 2 focuses on the overall approach used to develop an object-oriented system, called the *Unified Process* (*UP*). The Unified Process defines phases the project goes through from start to finish, and each phase requires one or more cycles, or iterations, of development work that completes part of the information system. Each iteration is essentially a miniproject, in which the general problem-solving approach discussed earlier in this chapter is used to define the requirements, design the solution, and implement and test the system components. The Unified Process also defines a set of nine disciplines the developers draw on to complete each iteration. The Unified Process is an example of a system development methodology, and the UP disciplines specify a variety of tools, techniques, and models that should be used to complete system development tasks. The chapter concludes with a discussion of the object-oriented approach and describes some tools used to support the work of the developer using the Unified Process.

Chapter 3 gets to the heart of the system development project by describing how a project is planned and managed when using the Unified Process. The first phase of the Unified Process is called the *Inception Phase*, and includes much of the project planning. Project management is one of the Unified Process's disciplines, and Chapter 3 describes models, tools, and techniques for project management, such as feasibility studies, project scheduling, and project staffing. An information systems project is just like any other project in these respects. It is important for an analyst to understand the role of project management in the Unified Process. Two additional Unified Process disciplines are also discussed: *business modeling* and *environment*.

PART 2: BUSINESS MODELING AND THE REQUIREMENTS DISCIPLINE

Chapters 4 through 6 cover what is often called *object-oriented analysis* in detail, although current terminology refers to this work as the the *requirements discipline*. Because the Unified Process suggests using several iterations for each phase, each iteration involves business modeling, requirements, design, and implementation work. Therefore, we will continually remind readers that although the book covers object-oriented analysis in this part and then object-oriented design in the next part, we are really discussing the work that goes on in any given iteration. The project does not complete all analysis work before beginning all of the design work, as has been the case in earlier approaches to system development. Chapter 4 discusses the activities of the requirements discipline and then focuses on the techniques for gathering information about the problem that the new system is to solve. The concept of models and modeling to record the detailed requirements for the system in a useful form is also introduced. Techniques such as interviewing, prototyping, joint application development meetings, and walkthroughs are introduced to help the analyst communicate with everyone involved.

Chapter 5 discusses two key concepts that are particularly useful for defining requirements: (1) use cases, which define the situations where the system needs to be used, and (2) problem domain classes—things that are part of the users' work environment. These two concepts, use cases and problem domain classes, are critical to object-oriented system development. Business events are used to identify use cases, and the class diagram is introduced as a model of domain classes.

Chapter 6 continues the discussion of modeling system requirements by introducing and explaining the use case model, which focuses on users and their interactions with the system. The Unified Process is use case driven, meaning that the work in each iteration addresses only a few of the use cases that are identified early in the project. Use case diagrams show the set of use cases and the users involved, called *actors*. Use case descriptions, activity diagrams, and system sequence diagrams define the requirements for each use case in detail. We will again remind readers that each iteration goes on to design and implement the software.

PART 3: THE DESIGN DISCIPLINE

Chapters 7 through 12 cover system design issues. Chapter 7 provides an overview of the activities of the design discipline that are examined in more detail in this part. The technical environment is also discussed. Chapter 8 describes the design activity that specifies the object interactions for each use case. This chapter goes deep into three-layer design architecture and draws on design patterns that are used to design object-oriented software. Sequence diagrams and design class diagrams are used extensively. Chapter 9 discusses advanced design principles and design patterns and demonstrates detailed analyses of object states modeled using statecharts.

Chapter 10 describes the issues involved when designing the database for the system, using either a relational database, an object-oriented database, or a hybrid approach that combines relational databases with object technology. Chapter 11 discusses the user interface to the system, providing an overview of the field of human-computer interaction (HCI) and guidelines for developing user-friendly systems. The chapter covers Windows graphical user interfaces and browser-based interfaces used in Web development. Chapter 12 covers the design of system interfaces, system controls, and security. System interfaces include output design of various types of reports that are typically produced online and on paper as well as other automated system-to-system interfaces that are increasingly important.

PART 4: IMPLEMENTATION, TEST, AND DEPLOYMENT DISCIPLINES

Chapter 13 describes the activities of the additional Unified Process development disciplines: implementation, test, and deployment. In addition, the configuration and change management support discipline is discussed. These activities are also completed for each iteration, but the focus of this book is more on project management, requirements, and design, so we do not go into as much detail about these disciplines.

Chapter 14 covers a selection of important emerging topics and technologies. There are variations to the Unified Process, and many current trends emphasize agility in development. Additionally, component-based development and object frameworks are discussed.

Summary

A systems analyst is someone who solves business problems using information systems technology. Object-oriented technology and an approach to system development called the *Unified Process* are the current focus of most projects. Problem solving means looking into the problem in great detail, understanding the problem, and designing and implementing a solution. Information systems are usually part of the solution, and information systems development is much more than writing programs.

A system is a collection of interrelated components that function together to achieve some outcome. Information systems, like other systems, contain components, and an information systems outcome is the solution to a business problem. Information systems components can be thought of as subsystems that interact or as hardware, software, inputs, outputs, data, people, and procedures. Many different types of systems exist to solve organizational problems. These systems include transaction processing systems, management information systems, executive information systems, decision support systems, communication support systems, and office support systems.

A systems analyst needs broad knowledge and a variety of skills, including technical, business, and people knowledge and skills. Integrity and ethical behavior are crucial to the success of the analyst. Analysts encounter a variety of technologies that often change rapidly. Systems analysis and design work is done by people with a variety of job titles, such as systems analyst but also programmer analyst, systems consultant, systems engineer, and Web developer, among others. Analysts also work for consulting firms, as independent contractors, and for companies that produce software packages.

A systems analyst can become involved in strategic planning by working with executives on special projects, by helping with business process reengineering projects, and by working on company strategic plans. Analysts also assist businesses in their efforts to select and implement enterprise resource planning systems. Sometimes an information systems strategic planning project is conducted for the entire organization, and analysts often are involved. The Rocky Mountain Outfitters information systems strategic planning project described in this chapter is an example.

Usually the systems analyst works on a system development project, one that solves a business problem identified by strategic planning. That is the emphasis in the rest of this text: how the analyst works on a system development project, completing project planning and conducting many project iterations that complete part of the final system. The analyst defines requirements, designs software, writes code, and completes extensive testing in each iteration. The Rocky Mountain Outfitters customer support system project is used to illustrate the system development process.

KEY TERMS

application architecture plan, p. 16
automation boundary, p. 8
business process reengineering, p. 15
communication support systems, p. 10
customer relationship management (CRM), p. 20
decision support systems (DSS), p. 9
enterprise resource planning (ERP), p. 17
executive information systems (EIS), p. 9
functional decomposition, p. 7
information system, p. 7
information systems strategic plan, p. 16
management information systems (MIS), p. 9
office support systems, p. 10
strategic planning, p. 16
subsystem, p. 7
supersystem, p. 7
supply chain management (SCM), p. 20
system, p. 6
system boundary, p. 8
systems analysis, p. 4
systems analyst, p. 4
systems design, p. 4
techniques, p. 11
technology architecture plan, p. 17
tools, p. 11
transaction processing systems (TPS), p. 9

REVIEW QUESTIONS

1. Give an example of a business problem.
2. What are the main steps followed when solving a problem?
3. Define *system*.
4. Define *information system*.
5. What are the types of information systems found in most organizations?
6. List the six fundamental technologies an analyst needs to understand.
7. List three types of tools the analyst needs to use to develop systems.
8. List five types of techniques used during system development.
9. What are some of the things an analyst needs to understand about businesses and organizations in general?
10. What are some of the things an analyst needs to understand about people?
11. What are some of the types of technology an analyst might encounter?
12. List 10 job titles that involve analysis and design work.
13. How might an analyst become involved with executives and strategic planning relatively early in his or her career?
14. Why are iterations an important part of the Unified Process?

THINKING CRITICALLY

1. Describe a business problem your university has that you would like to see solved. How can information technology help solve it?
2. Describe how you would go about solving a problem you face. Is the approach taken by a systems analyst, as described in the text, any different?
3. Many different types of information systems were described in this chapter. Give an example of each type of system that might be used by a university.
4. What is the difference between technical skills and business skills? Explain how a computer science graduate might be strong in one area and weak in another. Discuss how the preparation for a CIS or MIS degree is different from preparation to be a computer science graduate.
5. Explain why an analyst needs to understand how people think, how they learn, how they react to change, how they communicate, and how they work.
6. Who needs greater integrity to be successful, a salesperson or a systems analyst? Or does every working professional need integrity and ethical behavior to be successful? Discuss.
7. Explain why developing an information system requires different skills for a client/server system than for a large-scale centralized mainframe architecture.
8. How might working for a consulting firm for a variety of companies make it difficult for the consultant to understand the business problem a particular company faces? What might be easier for the consultant to understand about a business problem?
9. Explain why a strategic information systems planning project must involve people outside the information systems department. Why would a consulting firm be called in to help organize the project?
10. Explain why a commitment to enterprise resource planning (ERP) would be so difficult to undo once it has been made.

EXPERIENTIAL EXERCISES

1. It is important to understand the nature of the business you work for as an analyst. Contact some information systems developers and ask them about their employers. Do they seem to know a lot about the nature of the business? What types of courses did they take to prepare themselves (for example, banking courses, insurance courses, retail management courses, hospital administration courses, manufacturing technology courses)? Do they plan to take additional courses? If so, which?
2. Think about the type of position you want (working for a specific company, working for a consulting firm, or working for a software package vendor). Do some research on each job by looking at companies' recruiting brochures or Web sites. What do they indicate are the key skills they look for in a new hire? Are there any noticeable differences between consulting firms and the other organizations?
3. You have read an overview of the Rocky Mountain Outfitters' strategic information systems plan, including the technology architecture plan and the application architecture plan. Research system planning at your university. Is there a plan for how information technology will be used over the next few years? If so, describe some of the key provisions of the technology architecture plan and the application architecture plan.

Case Studies

ASSOCIATION FOR INFORMATION TECHNOLOGY PROFESSIONALS MEETING

"I'll tell you exactly what I look for when I interview a new college grad," Alice Adams volunteered. Alice, a system development manager at a local bank, was talking with several professional acquaintances at a monthly dinner meeting of the Association for Information Technology Professionals (AITP). AITP provides opportunities for information systems professionals to get together occasionally and share experiences. Usually a few dozen professionals from information systems departments at a variety of companies attend the monthly meetings.

"When I interview students, I look for problem-solving skills," continued Alice. "Every student I interview claims to know all about Java and .NET and Dreamweaver and XYZ or whatever the latest development package is," claimed Alice. "But I always ask students one thing: 'How do you generally approach solving problems?' And then I want to know if they have even thought much about banks like mine and financial services generally, so I ask, 'What would you say are the greatest problems facing the banking industry these days?'"

Jim Parsons, a database administrator for the local hospital, laughed. "Yes, I know what you mean. It really impresses me if they seem to appreciate how a hospital functions, what the problems are for us—how information technology can help solve some of our problems. It is the ability to see the big picture that really gets my attention."

"Yeah, I'm with you," added Sam Young, the manager of marketing systems for a retail store chain. "I am not that impressed with the specific technical skills an applicant has. I assume they have the aptitude and some skills. I do want to know how well they can communicate. I do want to know how much they know about the nature of our business. I do want to know how interested they are in retail stores and the problems we face."

"Exactly," confirmed Alice.

[1] Do you agree with Alice and the others about the importance of problem-solving skills? Industry-specific insight? Communication skills? Discuss.

[2] Should you research how a hospital is managed before interviewing for a position with an information systems manager at a hospital? Discuss.

[3] Do you think it really makes a difference whether you work for a bank, a hospital, or a retail chain in terms of your career? Or is an information systems job going to be the same no matter where you work? Discuss.

RETHINKING ROCKY MOUNTAIN OUTFITTERS

RMO's strategic information systems plan calls for building a new supply chain management (SCM) system prior to building the customer support system (CSS). John Blankens has stated often that customer orientation is the key to success. If that is so, why not build the CSS first, so customers can immediately benefit from improved customer ordering and fulfillment? Wouldn't that increase sales and profits faster? RMO already has factories that produce many items RMO sells, and RMO has longstanding relationships with suppliers around the globe. The product catalog is well established, and the business has existing customers who appear eager and willing to shop online. Why wait? Perhaps John Blankens has made a mistake in planning.

[1] What are some of the reasons that RMO decided to build the supply chain management system prior to the customer support system?

[2] What are some of the consequences to RMO if it is wrong to wait to build the customer support system?

[3] What are some of the consequences to RMO if the owners change their minds and start with the customer support system before building the supply chain management system?

[4] What are some other changes that you might make to the RMO strategic information systems plan (both the application architecture plan and the technology architecture plan)? Discuss.

FOCUSING ON RELIABLE PHARMACEUTICAL SERVICE

The Reliable Pharmaceutical Service is a privately held company incorporated in 1975 in Albuquerque, New Mexico. It provides pharmacy services to health-care delivery organizations that are too small to have their own in-house pharmacy. Reliable grew rapidly in its first decade, and by the late 1980s its clients included two dozen nursing homes, three residential rehabilitation facilities, two small psychiatric hospitals, and four small specialty medical hospitals. In 1990, Reliable expanded its Albuquerque service area to include Santa Fe and started two new service areas in Las Cruces and Gallup.

Reliable accepts pharmacy orders for patients in client facilities and delivers the orders in locked cases every 12 hours. In the Albuquerque and Santa Fe service area, Reliable employs approximately 12 delivery personnel, 20 pharmacist's assistants (PAs), 6 licensed pharmacists, and 10 office and clerical staff. Another 15 employees work in the Las Cruces and Gallup service areas. The management team includes another six people, mainly company owners.

Personnel at each health-care facility submit patient prescription orders by telephone. Many prescriptions are standing orders, which are filled during every delivery cycle until specifically canceled. Orders are logged into a computer as they are received. At the start of each 12-hour shift, the computer generates case manifests for each floor or wing of each client facility. A case manifest identifies each patient and the drugs he or she has been prescribed, including when and how often the drugs should be administered. The shift supervisor assigns the case manifests to pharmacists who, in turn, assign tasks to pharmacy assistants (PAs). Pharmacists supervise and coordinate the PAs' work.

All drugs for a single patient are collected in one plastic drawer of a locking case. Each case is marked with the institution's name, floor number, and wing number (if applicable). Each drawer is marked with the patient's name and room number. Dividers are inserted within a drawer to separate multiple prescriptions for the same patient. When all of the individual components of an order have been assembled, a pharmacist makes a final check of the contents, signs each page of the manifest, and places two copies of the manifest in the bottom of the case, one copy in a file cabinet in the assembly area, and the final copy in a mail basket for billing. When all of the cases have been assembled, they are loaded onto a truck and delivered to the health-care facilities.

Order-entry, billing, and inventory-management procedures are a hodgepodge of manual and computer-assisted methods. Reliable uses a combination of Excel spreadsheets, an Access database, and antiquated custom-developed billing software running on personal computers. Pharmacy assistants use the custom-developed billing software to enter orders received by telephone and to produce case manifests. The system has become increasingly unwieldy as facility contracts and Medicare and Medicaid reimbursement procedures have become more complex. Some costs are billed to the health-care facilities, some to insurance companies, some to Medicare and Medicaid, and some directly to patients. The company that developed and maintained the billing software has gone out of business, and the office staff has had to work around software shortcomings and limitations with cumbersome procedures. Inventory management is done manually.

In 1999 Reliable's revenues leveled off at $40 million, and profits plateaued at $5.5 million. By 2003, revenue was declining approximately 4 percent per year, and profit was declining at over 8 percent per year. Several reasons for the decline included the following:

- Price controls in both Medicare and Medicaid reimbursements and contracts with facilities managed by health maintenance organizations (HMOs) and large national health-care companies
- Increasing competition from national retail pharmacy chains such as Walgreens and in-house pharmacies at large local hospitals
- Inefficient operating procedures, which haven't received a comprehensive review or overhaul in almost two decades

Reliable's management team spent most of the last year developing a strategic plan, the key element of which is a major effort to streamline operations to improve service and reduce costs. Managers see this effort as their only hope of surviving in a future dominated by large health-care companies that can dictate price and outsource pharmaceutical services to whomever they choose. They plan a significant expansion into neighboring states after the system is up and running, to recoup its costs and increase economies of scale.

Reliable is much smaller than Rocky Mountain Outfitters, the company discussed in this chapter. But the organization still requires an integrated set of information systems to support its operations and management. We will include a case study at the end of each chapter that applies chapter concepts to Reliable Pharmaceutical Service.

[1] How many information systems staff members do you think Reliable can reasonably afford to employ? What mix of skills would they require? How flexible would they have to be in terms of the work they do each day?

[2] What impact would Web technology have on the way Reliable deploys its systems? Would the Web change the way Reliable does business?

[3] Create an "application architecture plan" and a "technology architecture plan" for Reliable Pharmaceutical Service to follow for the next five years. What system projects come first in your plan? What system projects come later?

FURTHER RESOURCES

Effy Oz, *Management Information Systems* (4th ed.). Course Technology, 2004.
Kathy Schwalbe, *Information Technology Project Management* (3d ed.). Course Technology, 2004.
Ralph M. Stair and George W. Reynolds, *Principles of Information Systems* (7th ed.). Course Technology, 2005.

chapter 2

OBJECT-ORIENTED DEVELOPMENT AND THE UNIFIED PROCESS

LEARNING OBJECTIVES

After reading this chapter, you should be able to:

- Explain the purpose and various phases of the traditional systems development life cycle (SDLC)
- Explain when to use an adaptive approach to the SDLC in place of the more predictive traditional SDLC
- Describe how the more adaptive Unified Process (UP) life cycle uses iterative and incremental development
- Explain the differences between a model, a tool, a technique, and a methodology
- Describe the Unified Process as a comprehensive system development methodology that combines proven best practices with the iterative UP life cycle
- Describe the disciplines used in a UP development project
- Describe the key features of the object-oriented approach
- Explain how automated tools are used in system development

CHAPTER OUTLINE

- The Systems Development Life Cycle
- Methodologies, Models, Tools, and Techniques
- The Unified Process as a System Development Methodology
- The UP Disciplines
- Overview of Object-Oriented Concepts
- Tools to Support System Development

DEVELOPMENT APPROACHES AT AJAX CORPORATION, CONSOLIDATED CONCEPTS, AND PINNACLE MANUFACTURING

Kim, Mary, and Bob, two graduating seniors and a junior applying for an internship, were discussing their recent interviews at different companies that recruited computer information system (CIS) majors on their campus. All agreed that they had learned a lot by visiting the companies, but they also all felt somewhat overwhelmed at first.

"At first I wasn't sure I knew what they were talking about," Kim cautiously volunteered. During her on-campus interview, Kim had impressed Ajax Corporation with her knowledge of object-oriented modeling. When she visited the Ajax home office data center for the second interview, the interviewers spent quite a lot of time describing the company's system development methodology.

"A few people said to forget everything I learned in school," continued Kim. Ajax Corporation had purchased a complete development methodology called *IM One* from a small consulting firm. Most employees agreed it worked fairly well. The people who had worked for Ajax for quite a while thought *IM One* was unique, and they were very proud of it. They had invested a lot of time and money learning and adapting to it.

"Well, that got my attention when they said to forget what I learned in school," noted Kim, "but then they started telling me about their SDLC phases, about iterations, about development disciplines, about use cases, and things like that." Kim had recognized that many of the key concepts in the *IM One* methodology were fairly standard models and techniques from the Unified Process system development methodology but packaged under a different name.

"I know what you mean," said Mary, a very talented programmer who knew just about every new programming language available but hadn't yet completed her analysis and design course. "Consolidated Concepts went on and on about things like OMG, UML, and UP and some people named Booch, Rumbaugh, and Jacobson. But then it turned out that they were using the object-oriented approach to develop systems, and they liked the fact that I knew Java and VB .NET. No problem once I got past all of the terminology they used. I just haven't studied analysis and design yet, so they said they'd send me out for training on Rational XDE, a CASE tool for the object-oriented approach, to get me started."

Bob had a different story. "A few people said analysis and design were no longer a big deal. I'm thinking, 'Knowing that would have saved me some time in school.'" Bob had visited Pinnacle Manufacturing, which had a small system development group supporting manufacturing and inventory control. "They said they try to just jump in and get to the code as soon as possible. Little documentation. Not much of a project plan. Then they showed me some books on their desks, and it looked like they had been doing a lot of reading about analysis and design. I could see they were using eXtreme Programming and agile modeling techniques and focusing only on best practices needed for their small projects. It turns out they just organize their work differently by looking at risk and building prototypes. I recognized some sketches of class diagrams and sequence diagrams on the boss's whiteboard, so I felt fairly comfortable."

Kim, Mary, and Bob all agreed that there was much to learn in these work environments but also that many different terms and points of view are used to describe the same key concepts and techniques they learned in school. They were all glad they focused on the fundamentals in their CIS classes and that they had been exposed to some leading-edge concepts and techniques like UML, the Unified Process, and some of the lighter, more agile methodologies.

Overview

As the experiences of Kim, Mary, and Bob demonstrate, today's businesses and their employees are extremely interested in object-oriented system development—and specifically in object-oriented analysis and design techniques based on the Unified Process (UP). Project managers rely on a variety of aids to help them with every step of the development process. The traditional systems development life cycle (SDLC) introduced in this chapter provides a backdrop for understanding the predictive approach to system development. The more recent Unified Process life cycle uses iterative and incremental development practices that have proven to be useful when an adaptive approach is required. But within that framework, the system developer relies on many more concepts, including methodologies, models, tools, and techniques. It is very important for you to understand what these concepts are before exploring system development in any detail.

This chapter also introduces the Unified Process as a comprehensive system development methodology. It includes guidelines for completing every step in the system development process, and it defines six system development disciplines that system developers need to master. The development disciplines include business modeling, requirements, design, implementation, testing, and deployment. Additional support disciplines must also be mastered, most importantly project management. The Unified Process and these disciplines are emphasized throughout this text.

Because this text emphasizes object-oriented (OO) development, object-oriented concepts are briefly reviewed in this chapter. You probably first learned about object-oriented development in a programming course, so most of these concepts should be familiar to you. We will discuss them throughout the text. One of the benefits of object-oriented development is that the same concepts used in OO programming are used to define the requirements and specify the design of the software. In other words, what you learned in OO programming should be useful to you when learning OO analysis and OO design, and what you learn in analysis and design should be useful to you when programming.

Finally, system developers need computer support tools to complete work tasks, including drawing tools and specially designed computer-aided system engineering (CASE) tools. This chapter presents some examples of these software tools.

At Rocky Mountain Outfitters, one of Barbara Halifax's initial jobs as the project manager for the customer support system project is to make decisions about how best to apply the Unified Process to the development project.

THE SYSTEMS DEVELOPMENT LIFE CYCLE

project
a planned undertaking that has a beginning and an end and that produces a desired result or product

Chapter 1 explained that systems analysts solve business problems. For problem-solving work to be productive, it needs to be organized and goal oriented. Analysts achieve these results by organizing the work into projects. A *project* is a planned undertaking that has a beginning and an end and that produces a desired result or product. The term *system development project* describes a planned undertaking that produces a new information system. Some system development projects are very large, requiring thousands of hours of work by many people and spanning several calendar years. In the RMO case study introduced in Chapter 1, the system being developed will be a moderately sized computer-based information system, requiring a moderately sized project lasting less than a year. Many system development projects are smaller, lasting a month or two. For a system development project to be successful, the people developing the system must have a detailed plan to follow. Success depends heavily on having a plan that includes an organized, methodical sequence of tasks and activities that culminate with an information system that is reliable, robust, and efficient.

One of the key, fundamental concepts in information system development is the systems development life cycle. Businesses and organizations use information systems to support all the many, varied processes that a business needs to carry out its functions. As explained in Chapter 1, there are many different kinds of information systems, and each has its own focus and purpose in supporting business processes. Each one of these information systems has a life of its own, and we, as system developers, refer to this idea as the *life cycle of a system*. During the life of an information system, it is first conceived as an idea; then it is designed, built, and deployed during a development project; and finally it is put into production and used to support the business. However, even during its productive use, a system is still a dynamic, living entity that is updated, modified, and repaired during smaller upgrading projects. This entire process of building, deploying, using, and updating an information system is called

systems development life cycle (SDLC)
the entire process of building, deploying, using, and updating an information system

the *systems development life cycle*, or *SDLC*. As noted previously, several different projects may be required during the life of a system to develop the original system and upgrade it later. In this chapter, and in fact in most of this textbook, we will focus on the initial development project and not on the support projects. In other words, our primary concern is getting the system developed and deployed the very first time.

In today's diverse environment of building and deploying information systems, many different versions or approaches to developing systems are still in use. All of these approaches are based on different SDLCs. As you might suppose, some approaches have been in use for a long time and have varying rates of success. In our dynamic, ever-changing world of information technology, new, unique approaches to building systems have emerged, which also have varying success rates. Although it might be impossible to find a single, comprehensive classification system for all of the approaches, one useful technique is to categorize SDLC approaches according to whether they are more predictive or adaptive. These two classifications represent the end points of a continuum from completely predictive to completely adaptive (see Figure 2-1).

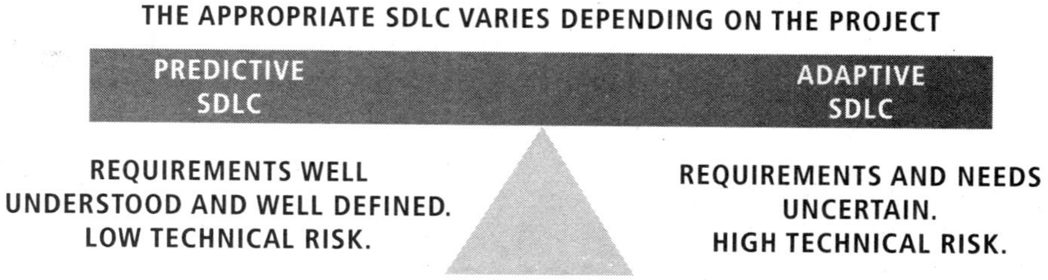

FIGURE 2-1
Predictive versus adaptive approaches to the SDLC

predictive approach
an SDLC approach that assumes the development project can be planned and organized in advance and that the new information system can be developed according to the plan

adaptive approach
an SDLC approach that is more flexible, assuming that the project cannot be planned out completely in advance but must be modified as it progresses

A *predictive approach* to the SDLC is an approach that assumes that the development project can be planned and organized in advance and that the new information system can be developed according to the plan. Predictive SDLCs are useful for building systems that are well understood and defined. For example, a company may want to convert its old, mainframe inventory system to a newer networked client/server system. In this type of project, the staff already understands the requirements very well, and nothing different needs to be done. So the project can typically be planned carefully, and the system can be built according to the specifications.

At the other end of the scale, an *adaptive approach* to the SDLC is used when the exact requirements of a system or needs of users are not well understood. In this situation, the project cannot be planned completely in advance. Possibly some requirements of the system have yet to be determined, after some preliminary development work. Developers should still be able to build the solution, but they must be flexible and adapt the project as it progresses.

In practice, any project could have—and most do have—both predictive and adaptive elements. That is why Figure 2-1 shows the characteristics as end points on a sliding scale—not as two mutually exclusive categories. The predictive approaches are more traditional and were invented during the 1970s, '80s, and '90s. Many of the newer, adaptive approaches have evolved along with the object-oriented approach and were created during the 1990s and into the twenty-first century. Let's first look at some of the more predictive approaches and then examine some of the newer adaptive approaches.

BEST PRACTICE: Recognize that any specific project you work on will have some predictive and some adaptive elements.

THE TRADITIONAL PREDICTIVE SDLC APPROACHES

The development of a new information system requires several different, but related, activities. One group of activities must focus on understanding the business problem that needs to be solved and defining the business requirements. We refer to this set of activities as *analysis activities*. In other words, the intent is to understand exactly what the system must do to support the business processes. A second group of activities is focused on designing the new system. Those activities, called *design activities*, use the requirements that were defined earlier and develop the program structure and algorithms for the new system. Yet another group of activities is necessary to build the system. We call those activities *implementation activities*. Included in implementation are programming, testing, and installing the system for the business users. Because this approach is a predictive approach, we also have a group of activities that plan, organize, and schedule the project, usually called *planning activities*.

These four groups of activities—planning, analysis, design, and implementation—are sometimes referred to as *phases*, and together they comprise the elements of the project to develop a new system. Another phase, called the *support phase*, includes the activities needed to upgrade and maintain the system after it has been deployed. The support phase is part of the overall SDLC, but it is not normally considered to be part of the initial development project. Figure 2-2 illustrates the five phases of a traditional SDLC.

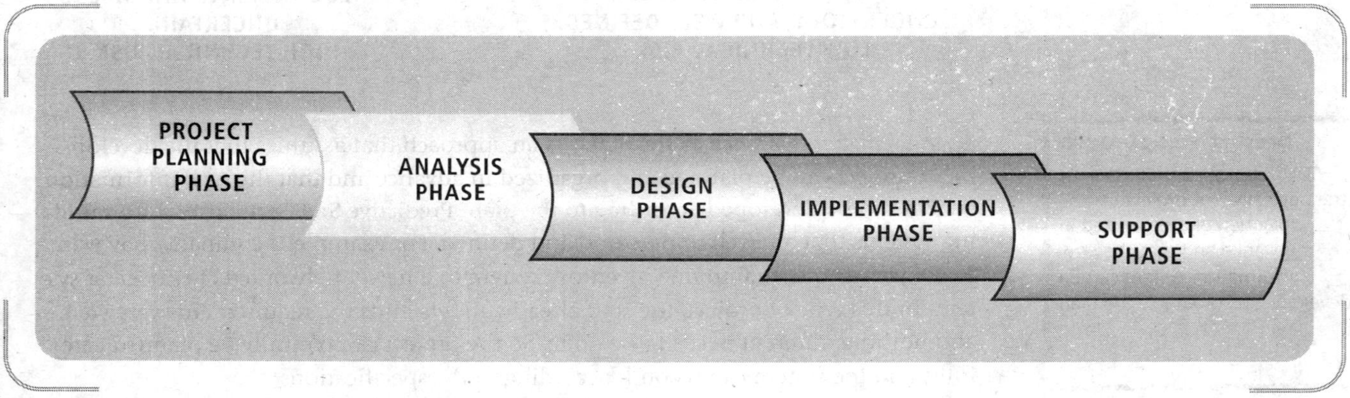

FIGURE 2-2
Traditional information systems development phases

The five phases are quite similar to the steps in the general problem-solving approach outlined in Chapter 1. First, the organization recognizes it has a problem to solve (project planning). Next, the project team investigates and thoroughly understands the problem and the requirements for a solution (analysis). Once the problem is understood, a solution is specified in detail (design). The system that solves the problem is then built and installed (implementation). As long as the system is being used by the organization, it is maintained and enhanced to make sure it continues to provide the intended benefits (support) (see Figure 2-3).

waterfall approach
an SDLC approach that assumes the various phases of a project can be completed sequentially—one phase leads (falls) into the next phase

The SDLC approach that is farthest to the left on the predictive/adaptive scale—that is, most predictive—is called a *waterfall approach*. As shown in Figure 2-4, the *waterfall approach* assumes that the various phases of a project can be carried out and completed entirely sequentially. A detailed plan is first developed, then the requirements are thoroughly specified, then the system is designed down to the last algorithm, then it is programmed, tested, and installed. Once a project drops over the waterfall into the next phase, there is no going back. In practice, the waterfall approach requires rigid planning and final decision making at each step of the development project. You can probably guess that a pure waterfall approach did not work very well. Developers, being

SDLC PHASE	OBJECTIVE
Project Planning	To identify the scope of the new system, ensure that the project is feasible, and develop a schedule, resource plan, and budget for the remainder of the project
Analysis	To understand and document in detail the business needs and the processing requirements of the new system
Design	To design the solution system based on the requirements defined and decisions made during analysis
Implementation	To build, test, and install a reliable information system with trained users ready to benefit as expected from use of the system
Support	To keep the system running productively initially and during the many years of the system's lifetime

FIGURE 2-3
SDLC phases and objectives

human, have never been able to complete a phase without making mistakes or leaving out important components that had to be added later. Even though we do not use the waterfall approach in its purest form anymore, it still provides a valuable foundation for development. No matter what system is being developed, we still need to include planning activities, analysis activities, design activities, and implementation activities. We just cannot do them in pure waterfall steps.

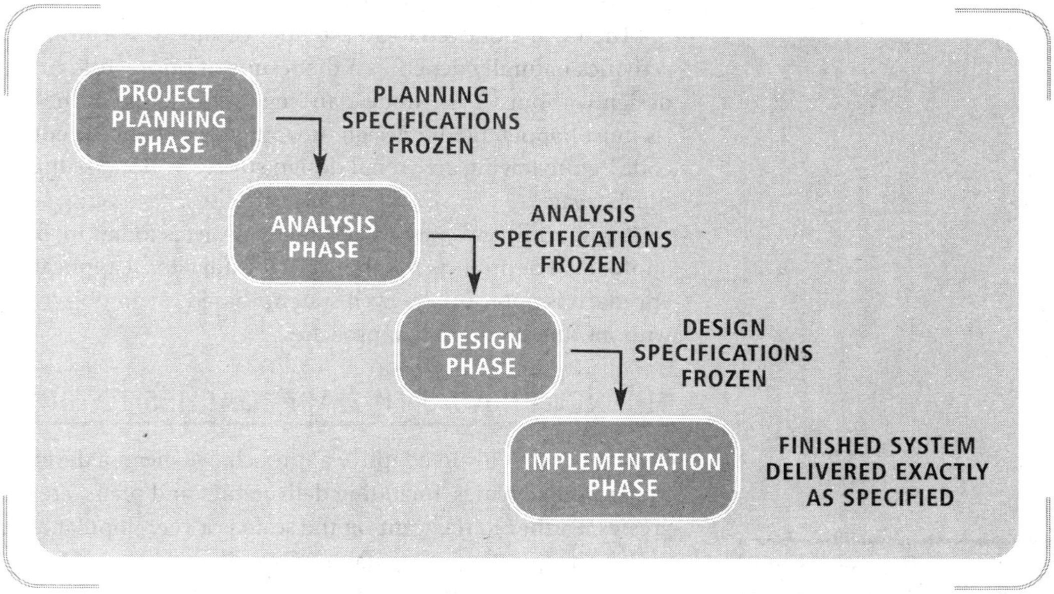

FIGURE 2-4
The waterfall approach to the SDLC

Moving to the right on the predictive/adaptive scale, we find modified waterfall approaches. In these approaches, we still want to be predictive—that is, still develop a fairly thorough plan—but we recognize that the phases of projects must overlap, influencing and depending on each other. Some analysis must be done before the design can start, but during the design, we discover that we need more detail in the requirements, or even that some of the requirements cannot be met in the manner originally requested. Figure 2-5 illustrates how these activities can overlap.

Another reason phases overlap is efficiency. While the team members are analyzing needs, they may be thinking about and designing various forms or reports. To help them understand the needs of the users, they may want to design some of the final system. But when they do early design, they will frequently throw some components away and save others for later inclusion in the final system. In addition, many components

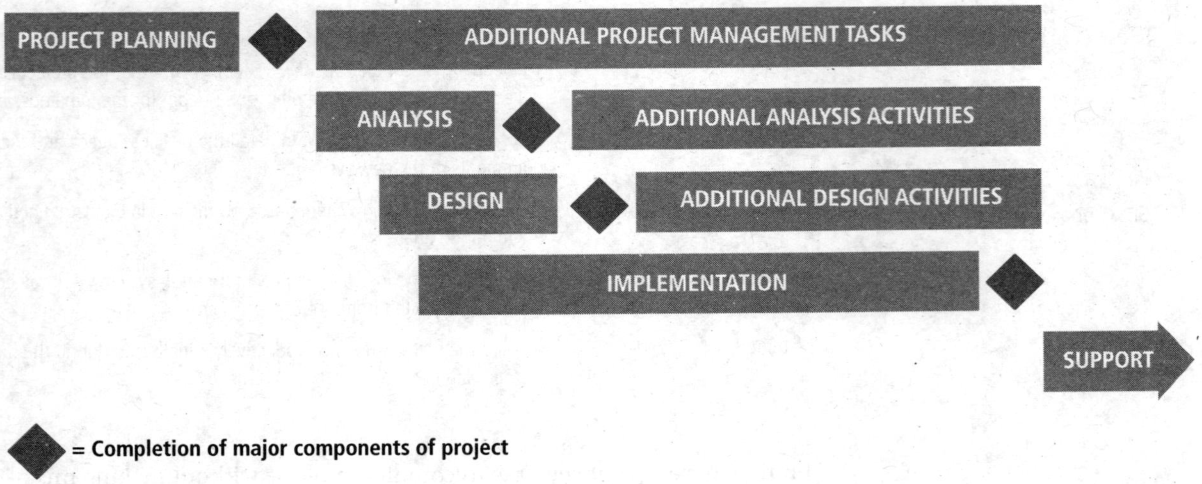

FIGURE 2-5
The overlap of system development activities

of a computer system are interdependent, which requires analysts to do both analysis and some design at the same time.

Then why not overlap all activities completely? The answer is dependency. Some activities naturally depend on the results of prior work. Analysts cannot go very far into design without a basic understanding of the nature of the problem. Thus, some analysis must happen before design. It would also be inefficient for them to write program code before having an overall design structure, because they would have to throw too much away.

Many company systems and many projects today are based on a modified waterfall approach. For projects that build well-understood applications, a modified waterfall approach is appropriate. Even systems based on an object-oriented approach are built with modified waterfall approaches.

THE NEWER ADAPTIVE APPROACHES TO THE SDLC

Remember that by an adaptive approach, we mean a development approach in which the project activities, including deliverables and plans, are adjusted as the project progresses. Farther to the right on the scale is a very popular approach called the *spiral model*. The *spiral model* contains many adaptive elements, and it is generally considered to be the first adaptive approach to system development. The life cycle is shown as a spiral, starting in the center and working its way outward, over and over again, until the project is complete. This model looks very different from the static waterfall approach and sets the tone for the project to be managed differently. Figure 2-6 shows the spiral model graphically.

spiral model
an adaptive SDLC approach that cycles over and over again through development activities until a project is complete

There are many different ways of implementing a spiral model approach. The example in Figure 2-6 begins with an initial planning phase, as shown in the center of the figure. The purpose of the initial planning phase is to gather just enough information to begin developing an initial prototype. Planning phase activities include a feasibility study, a high-level user requirements survey, generation of implementation alternatives, and choice of an overall design and implementation strategy.

After the initial planning is completed, work begins in earnest on the first prototype (the blue ring in the figure). A *prototype* is a preliminary working model of a larger system. For each prototype, the development process follows a sequential path through

prototype
a preliminary working model showing some aspect of a larger system

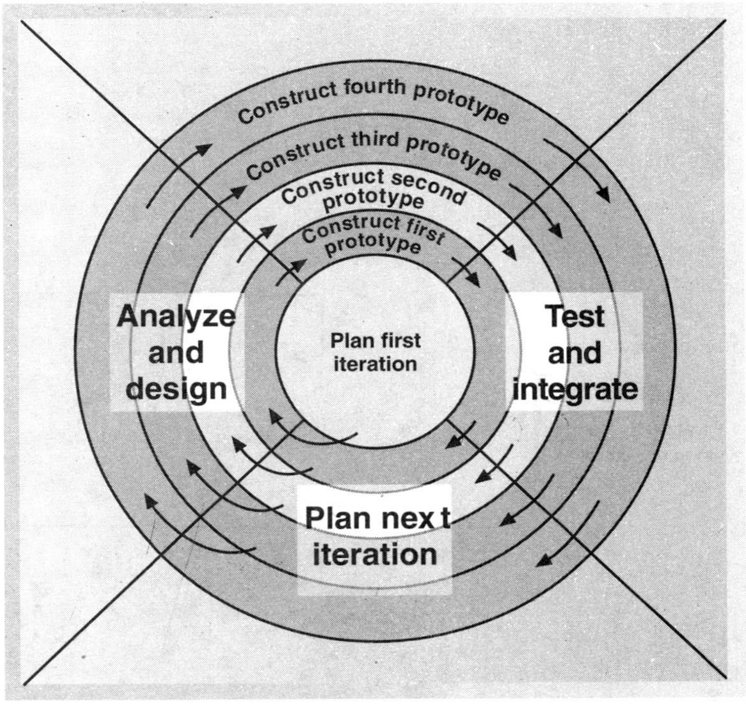

FIGURE 2-6
The spiral life cycle model

analysis, design, construction, testing, integration with previous prototype components, and planning for the next prototype. When planning for the next prototype is completed, the cycle of activities begins again. Although the figure shows four prototypes, the spiral model approach can be adapted for any number of prototypes.

A key concept in the spiral model approach is the focus on *risk*. Although there are many ways to choose what to focus on in each iteration, the spiral model recommends identifying risk factors that must be studied and mitigated. The part of the system that appears to have the greatest risk should be addressed in the first iteration. Sometimes the greatest risk is not one subsystem or one set of system functions; rather, the greatest risk might be the technological feasibility of new technology. If so, the first iteration might focus on a prototype that proves the technology will work as planned. Then the second iteration might begin work on a prototype that addresses risk associated with the system requirements or other issues. Another time, the greatest risk might be user acceptance of change. So the first iteration might focus on producing a prototype to show the users that their working lives will be enriched by the new system.

iteration
system development process in which work activities—analysis, design, implementation—are done once, then again, and yet again on different system components; they are repeated until the system is closer to what is ultimately needed

Figure 2-6, which shows the spiral model, uses the term *iteration*. In problem solving, iterations are used to divide a very large, complex problem into smaller, more easily managed problems. Each small problem is solved in turn until the large problem is solved. System development uses iteration for the same purpose. We take a large system and figure out some way to partition it, or divide it into smaller components. Then we plan, analyze, design, and implement each smaller component. Of course, we also add an integration step to combine the smaller components into a total solution. This approach is frequently called an *iterative approach* to the SDLC. Many of the more popular adaptive approaches today use iteration as a fundamental element of the approach. Figure 2-7 illustrates how an iterative approach works.

Iteration means that work activities—analysis, design, implementation—are done once, then again, and yet again; they are repeated. With each iteration, the developers refine the result so that it is closer to what is ultimately needed. Iteration assumes that no one gets the right result the first time. With an information system, you need to do

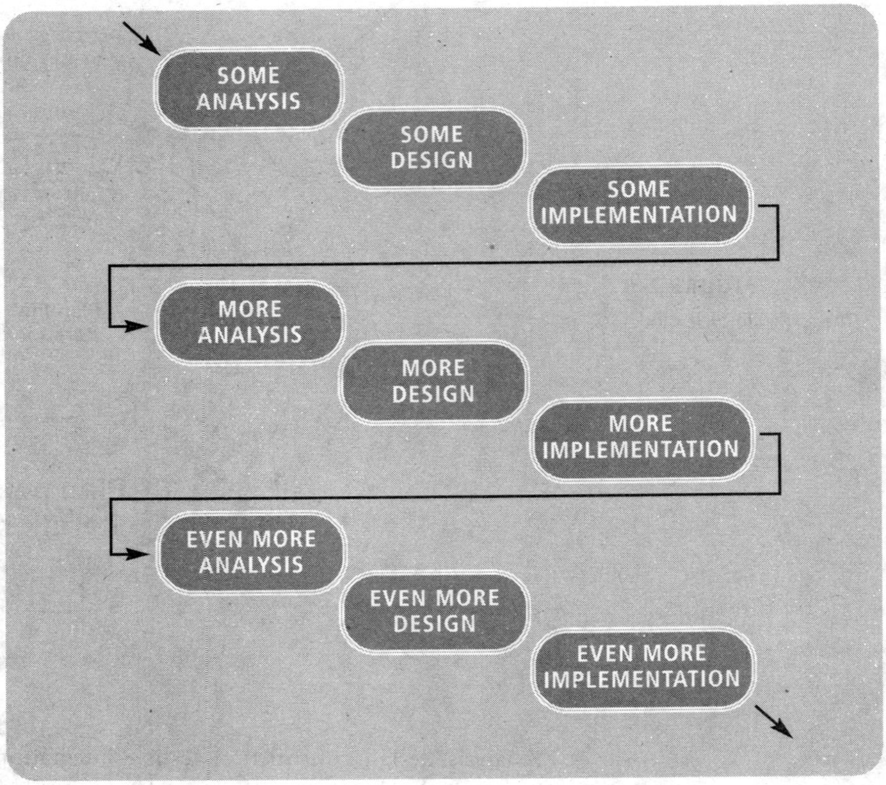

FIGURE 2-7
Iteration of system development activities

some analysis and then some design before you really know whether the system will work and accomplish its goals. Then you do more analysis and design to make improvements. In this view, it is not realistic to complete analysis (define all of the requirements) before starting work on the design. Similarly, completing the design is very difficult unless you know how the implementation will work (particularly with constantly changing technology). So you complete some design, then some implementation, and the iteration process continues—more analysis, more design, and more implementation. Naturally, the approach to iteration or the amount of iteration depends on the complexity of the project.

There are several ways to define each iteration. One approach is to define the key functions that the system must include and then implement those key functions in the first iteration. Once they are completed, the next set of required, but less crucial, system functions are implemented. Finally, optional system functions, those that would be "nice to have," are implemented in the last iteration. Another approach is to focus on one subsystem at a time. The first subsystem implemented contains the core functions and data on which the other subsystems depend. Then the next iteration includes an additional subsystem, and so on.

Sometimes iterations are defined according to the complexity or risk of certain components. Often the most complex or risky parts of the system are addressed first because, if you find out early whether they can be handled as planned, you can still change plans. Other times, some of the simplest parts are handled first to get as much of the system finished as quickly as possible. How the iterations are defined depends on many factors and might be different with every project you encounter. Most adaptive approaches suggest tackling the toughest problems with the highest risk first.

BEST PRACTICE: Address the aspects of the project that pose the greatest risk in early project iterations.

incremental development
a development approach that completes parts of a system in several iterations and then puts them into operation for users

A related approach, which is a type of iterative approach, is called *incremental development*. With this approach, you complete parts of the system in a few iterations and then put the system into operation for users. This approach gets part of the system into users' hands as early as possible so they can benefit from it. Then you complete a few more iterations to develop another part of the system, integrate it with the first part, and again put it into operation. Finally, you complete the last part and integrate it with the rest. Today, much of system development uses varying degrees of iteration. The object-oriented approach is always described as highly iterative.

THE UNIFIED PROCESS LIFE CYCLE

Because of the need for iterations in system development—each containing analysis, design, and implementation activities—a new system development life cycle model has been developed to make it easier to plan and manage iterations. The Unified Process life cycle includes phases through which the project moves over time, but each life cycle phase includes one or more iterations involving analysis, design, and implementation for part of the system. At the end of each iteration, the project team using the UP life cycle has completed some working software that has been tested and reviewed with system users. The four phases of the UP life cycle are named *inception*, *elaboration*, *construction*, and *transition*, as shown in Figure 2-8.

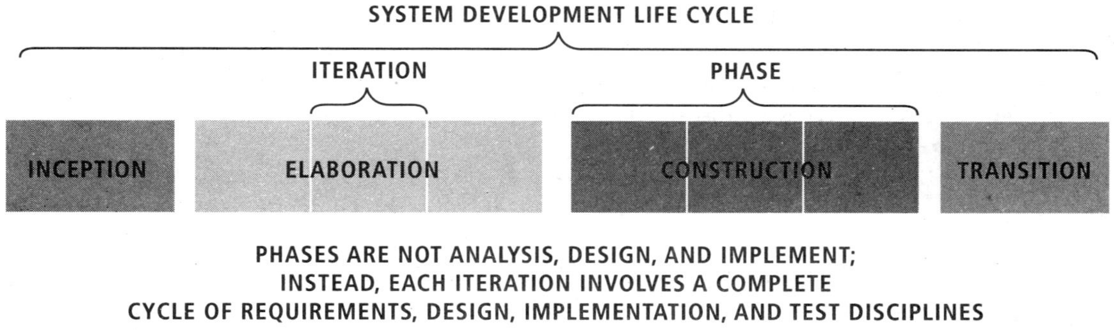

FIGURE 2-8
The Unified Process system development life cycle

Even though the project team completes some working software in each iteration, the sequential phases of the UP life cycle describe the *emphasis* or *objectives* of the project team and their activities at any point in time (see Figure 2-9). Therefore, the four phases do provide a project management framework for planning and tracking the project over time. It is possible to plan the project so that the elaboration phase begins on a specific date and ends on a specific date. Within the phase, however, several iterations are planned to allow flexibility. Similarly, the construction phase can begin on a specific date, again assuming that many changes will have occurred up to that point.

The emphases or objectives of the project team in each of the four phases are described briefly in the following sections. This adaptive life cycle is part of a comprehensive system development methodology called the *Unified Process*, which is discussed in more detail later in this chapter.

UP PHASE	OBJECTIVE
Inception	Develop an approximate vision of the system, make the business case, define the scope, and produce rough estimates for cost and schedule.
Elaboration	Refine the vision, identify and describe all requirements, finalize the scope, design and implement the core architecture and functions, resolve high risks, and produce realistic estimates for cost and schedule.
Construction	Iteratively implement the remaining lower-risk, predictable, and easier elements and prepare for deployment.
Transition	Complete the beta test and deployment so users have a working system and are ready to benefit as expected.

FIGURE 2-9
UP phases and objectives

BEST PRACTICE: Be sure not to confuse the UP phases with the waterfall approach to the SDLC. Elaboration is not at all like the traditional analysis phase.

INCEPTION PHASE

As in any project planning phase, in the inception phase the project manager develops and refines a vision for the new system to show how it will improve operations and solve existing problems. The project manager makes the business case for the new system, meaning that the benefits of the new system must outweigh the cost of development. The scope of the system must also be defined so that it is clear what the project will accomplish. Defining the scope includes identifying many of the key requirements for the system.

The inception phase is usually completed in one iteration, and as with any iteration, parts of the actual system might be designed, implemented, and tested. Usually any work on the system itself must demonstrate that the system vision matches user expectations or that the technology to be used will work as planned. Sometimes prototypes are discarded after proving that point.

ELABORATION PHASE

The elaboration phase usually involves several iterations, and early iterations typically complete the identification and definition of all of the system requirements. Since the UP is an adaptive approach to development, the requirements are expected to evolve and change once work starts on the project.

Elaboration phase iterations also complete the analysis, design, and implementation of the core architecture of the system. Usually the aspects of the system that pose the greatest risk are identified and implemented first. Until developers know exactly how the highest-risk aspects of the project will work out, they cannot have a firm idea of the amount of effort required to complete the project. By the end of the elaboration phase, the project manager should have more realistic estimates for a project's cost and schedule, and the business case for the project can be confirmed. Remember that the design, implementation, and testing of key parts of the system are completed during the elaboration phase. The elaboration phase is not at all the same as the traditional SDLC's analysis phase.

CONSTRUCTION PHASE

The construction phase involves several iterations that continue the design and implementation of the system. The core architecture and highest-risk aspects of the system are already complete. Now the focus of the work turns to the routine and predictable parts of the system. These parts might include detailing the system controls such as data validation, fine-tuning the user interface's design, finishing routine data maintenance functions, and completing the help and user preference functions. The team also begins to plan for deployment of the system.

TRANSITION PHASE

During the transition phase, one or more final iterations involve the final user-acceptance and beta tests, and the system is made ready for operation. Once the system is in operation, it will need to be supported and maintained.

Now that you have an overview of the basic development approaches and the UP life cycle that we will use throughout this text, we turn next to the ways developers accomplish their activities: methodologies, models, tools, and techniques.

METHODOLOGIES, MODELS, TOOLS, AND TECHNIQUES

Systems analysts have a variety of aids at their disposal to help them complete activities and tasks in system development beyond a systems development life cycle. These include methodologies, models, tools, and techniques. The following sections discuss each of these aids.

METHODOLOGIES AND SYSTEM DEVELOPMENT PROCESSES

system development methodology
guidelines to follow for completing every activity in systems development, including specific models, tools, and techniques

A *system development methodology* provides guidelines to follow for completing every activity in system development, including specific models, tools, and techniques. Some methodologies are homegrown, developed by systems professionals in the company based on their experience. Some methodologies are purchased from consulting firms or other vendors. The Unified Process introduced earlier is an example of a methodology. The term *process* is a synonym for methodology, meaning the complete process followed when developing an information system.

Some methodologies (whether homegrown or purchased) contain written documentation that can fill a bookcase. The documentation defines everything the developers might need to produce at any point in the project, including how documentation should look and what reports to management should contain. Other methodologies are much more informal—one document will contain general descriptions of what should be done. Most people want a methodology to be flexible, so that it can be adapted to many different types of projects and systems.

Because a methodology contains instructions about how to use models, tools, and techniques, you must understand what models, tools, and techniques are.

MODELS

model
a representation of an important aspect of the real world

Anytime people need to record or communicate information, in any context, it is very useful to create a model—and a model in information system development has the same purpose as any other model. A *model* is a representation of an important aspect of the real world. Sometimes the term *abstraction* is used because we abstract (separate out) an aspect of particular importance to us. Consider a model of an airplane. To talk about the aerodynamics of the airplane, it is useful to have a small model that shows the plane's overall shape in three dimensions. Sometimes a drawing showing the cross-sectional details of the wing of the plane is what is needed. Other times, a list of mathematical characteristics of the plane might be necessary to understand how the plane will behave. All of them are models of the same plane.

Some models are physically similar to the real product, some models are graphical representations of important details, and still others are abstract mathematical notations. Each emphasizes a different type of information. In airplane design, aerospace engineers use lots of different models. Learning to be an aerospace engineer involves learning how to create and use all of the models. It is the same for an information system developer, although models for information systems are not yet as precise as aerospace models. An information system is much less tangible than an airplane—you can't really see, hold, or touch it. Therefore, the models of the information system can seem much less tangible, too.

What sort of models do developers make of aspects of an information system? Models used in system development include representations of inputs, outputs, processes, data, objects, object interactions, locations, networks, and devices, among other things. Most of the models are graphical models, which are drawn representations that employ agreed-upon symbols and conventions. These are often called *diagrams* and *charts*. Much of this text describes how to read and create a variety of models that represent an information system.

Unified Modeling Language (UML)
a standard set of model constructs and notations developed specifically for object-oriented development

The diagrams created to show system models are drawn according to the notation defined by the *Unified Modeling Language (UML)*. UML is a standard set of model constructs and notations developed specifically for object-oriented development. By using UML, analysts and end users are able to depict and understand a variety of specific diagrams used in a system development project. Prior to UML, there was no standard, so diagrams could be confusing. As a result, they were often misinterpreted, leading to errors and rework. The development of UML is credited to Grady Booch, James Rumbaugh, and Ivar Jacobson of Rational Software, now part of IBM. The standard was drawn on ideas and examples from many system development methodologists, and after several revisions, UML was accepted as a standard by the Object Management Group (OMG). More details about UML and OMG can be found on the OMG Web site at www.omg.org.

Another kind of model important to develop and use is a project-planning model, such as PERT or Gantt charts, which are shown in Chapter 3. These models represent the system development project itself, highlighting its tasks and task completion dates. Another model related to project management is a chart showing all of the people assigned to the project. Figure 2-10 lists some models used in system development.

FIGURE 2-10
Some models used in system development

Models of system components using UML

- Use case diagram
- Class diagram
- Activity diagram
- Sequence diagram
- Communication diagram
- Package diagram

Models used to manage development process

- PERT chart
- Gantt chart
- Organization hierarchy chart
- Financial analysis models (net present value, return on investment)

TOOLS

tool
software support that helps create models or other components required in the project

As we discussed in Chapter 1, a *tool* in the context of system development is software that helps create models or other components required in a development project. Tools may be simple drawing programs for creating diagrams. They might include a database application that stores information about the project, such as class definitions or written descriptions of specifications. A project management software tool, such as Microsoft Project (described in Chapter 3), is another example of a tool used to create models. The project management tool creates a model of the project tasks and task dependencies.

Tools have been specifically designed to help system developers. Programmers should be familiar with integrated development environments (IDEs) that include many tools to help with programming tasks—smart editors, context-sensitive help, and debugging tools. Some tools can generate program code for the developer. Some tools reverse-engineer old programs—generating a model from the code so that the developer can figure out what the program does, in case the documentation is missing (or was never done).

CASE tool
a computer-aided system engineering tool that helps a systems analyst complete development tasks

The most comprehensive tool available for system developers is called a *CASE tool*. *CASE* stands for computer-aided system engineering. CASE tools are described in more detail later in this chapter. Basically, they help the analyst create the important system models and automatically check the models for completeness and compatibility with other system models. Finally, the CASE tools can generate program code based on the models. Figure 2-11 lists types of tools used in system development.

FIGURE 2-11
Some tools used in system development

- Project management application
- Drawing/graphics application
- Word processor/text editor
- Computer-aided system engineering (CASE) tool
- Integrated development environment (IDE)
- Database management application
- Reverse-engineering tool
- Code generator tool
- Automated testing tool

TECHNIQUES

technique
a collection of guidelines that help an analyst complete a system development activity or task

best practices
generally accepted approaches for completing a system development task that have been proven over time to be effective

As we also discussed in Chapter 1, a *technique* in system development is a collection of guidelines that help an analyst complete a system development activity or task. A technique often includes step-by-step instructions for creating a model, or it might include more general advice for collecting information from system users. Some examples include domain-modeling techniques, use case modeling techniques, software-testing techniques, user interviewing techniques, and relational database design techniques.

Figure 2-12 lists some techniques commonly used in system development. Many of these techniques are based on generally accepted approaches for best completing the work, known as *best practices*. Best practices have been proven over time to be effective, and analysts try to identify the best practice to use when faced with a system development task.

FIGURE 2-12
Some techniques used in system development

- Strategic planning techniques
- Project scheduling techniques
- Cost-benefit analysis techniques
- User interviewing techniques
- Domain-modeling techniques
- Use case modeling techniques
- User interface design techniques
- Software-testing techniques
- Relational database design techniques
- Security design techniques

How do all these components fit together? A *methodology* includes a collection of *techniques* that are used to complete activities of the system development project. The activities include completion of a variety of *models* as well as other documents and deliverables. Like any other professionals, system developers use software *tools* to help them complete their activities. Figure 2-13 shows the relationships among the components of a methodology.

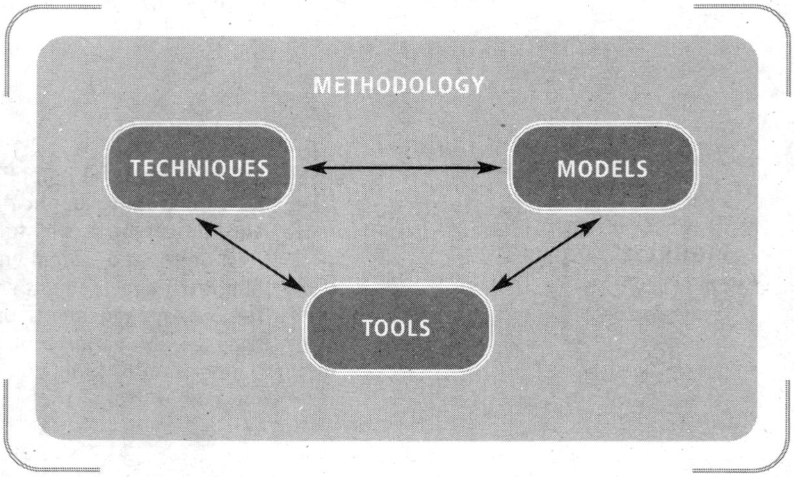

FIGURE 2-13
Relationships of models, tools, and techniques in a system development methodology

THE UNIFIED PROCESS AS A SYSTEM DEVELOPMENT METHODOLOGY

Unified Process (UP)
an object-oriented system development methodology originally developed by Grady Booch, James Rumbaugh, and Ivar Jacobson

You have learned that some companies obtain complete system development methodologies from consulting firms, either by purchasing rights to the methodology or by contracting for extensive training services from the consulting firm to learn the methodology. The *Unified Process (UP)* is an object-oriented system development methodology originally offered by Rational Software, which is now part of IBM. Developed by Grady Booch, James Rumbaugh, and Ivar Jacobson—the three pioneers who are also behind the success of the Unified Modeling Language (UML)—the UP is their attempt to define a complete methodology that, in addition to providing several unique features, uses UML for system models and the UP system development life cycle described earlier. In the UP, the term development *process* is synonymous with development *methodology*.

The UP is now the most influential system development methodology for object-oriented development, and there are many variations in use. The original UP defined an elaborate set of activities and deliverables for every step of the development process. More recent versions use a streamlined approach to the UP, with fewer activities and deliverables, simplifying the methodology. These "lighter" UP variations are often referred to as *agile development*. Consistent with the spirit of adaptive approaches to development, the UP should be tailored to the needs of the specific organization and system project. These agile approaches are discussed in detail in Chapter 14.

As part of her responsibility as project manager for the new customer support system for Rocky Mountain Outfitters, Barbara Halifax has to make decisions about the methodology to use to develop the system, and she has chosen a "lighter" UP variation for the customer support system project (see Barbara's memo).

ROCKY MOUNTAIN OUTFITTERS

MEMO

February 14, 2006

To: John MacMurty, CIO

From: Barbara Halifax, System Development Project Manager

RE: Customer Support System Project Update

John, this is just a brief note to let you know I am working on scheduling and staffing for the project, and as such, we need to make some decisions about tailoring the new system development methodology we are using. The Unified Process allows much flexibility in scheduling and defining required deliverables and artifacts. In terms of scheduling, we are moving ahead with what is called a "lightweight" or "agile" version of the UP, probably looking at about eight iterations in total.

I'm actually working in the UP environment discipline right now, defining how we will tailor the UP to our project, checking up on the tools we are using, and selecting a few more people to send out for their advanced design discipline training. My next step is to get more familiar with the project management discipline as we launch the project and formally begin the inception phase.

So far so good with the UP. I really think the way each UP discipline is defined is helping me sort through all the issues that will demand my attention throughout this project. That's it for now. Let me know if you have any questions or concerns.

BH

cc: Steven Deerfield, Ming Lee, Jack Garcia

The UP life cycle, UML models, tools, and techniques are designed to reinforce some examples of best practices of system development that are common to many system development methodologies:

[1] **Develop iteratively:** Divide the project into a series of miniprojects, each completed by an iteration that builds part of the working software.

[2] **Define and manage system requirements:** Define the requirements overall early in the project, but then finalize and refine the details of the requirements as the project progresses through each iteration.

[3] **Use component architectures:** Define a software architecture that allows the system to be built using well-defined components, and design and implement the system to achieve a component architecture.

[4] **Create visual models:** Use UML diagrams to complete models of requirements and designs of system components to help the team visualize and then communicate the requirements and designs as the system is built.

[5] **Verify quality:** Test the system early and continually, starting by defining test cases based on the system requirements and then completing unit tests, integration tests, usability tests, and user acceptance tests in each iteration.

[6] **Control changes:** Document the request for any change and the decision to make any change, and make sure the correct version of any model or component is identified and used as the project moves forward.

The UP also introduced an additional best practice that has become a de facto standard in both predictive and adaptive approaches to development: The project should be *use case driven,* meaning that use cases provide the foundation for defining functional requirements and designs throughout the project. A *use case* is an activity the system carries out, usually in response to a request by a user. Each use case is defined in detail to specify functional requirements. Then the software needed for each use case is designed, implemented, and tested. Usually, one iteration in the project addresses a few use cases at a time, so use cases also provide the framework for planning the iterations. Once all use cases are implemented and integrated into one complete system, the system is available for final testing and deployment.

use case
an activity the system carries out, usually in response to a request by a user

BEST PRACTICE: Plan and manage every project so it is use case driven, meaning use cases are always the focus when defining system requirements and designing, implementing, and testing the system.

As discussed previously, the UP introduced a new adaptive approach to the systems development life cycle that incorporates iterations and phases, called the *UP life cycle.* The UP defines four life cycle phases: inception, elaboration, construction, and transition (seen previously in Figure 2-8). Each UP iteration is use case driven, defines and manages requirements, uses component architectures, creates visual models, verifies quality, and controls change. The details of the UP methodology provide many guidelines and steps to follow to apply these best practices. For example, use cases are identified, described, designed, implemented, and tested throughout the project.

As we mentioned earlier, the four UP phases define the project sequentially by indicating the emphasis of the project team at any point in time. To make iterative development manageable, the UP defines disciplines within each phase. A *discipline* is a set of functionally related activities that together contribute to one aspect of the development project. They include business modeling, requirements modeling, design,

discipline
a set of functionally related activities that together contribute to one aspect of a UP development project

implementation, testing, deployment, project management, configuration and change management, and environment. We discuss each of the disciplines in more detail in the next section. Each iteration involves activities from all disciplines.

Figure 2-14 shows how the UP disciplines are involved in each iteration, which is typically planned to span four weeks. The size of the shaded area under the curve for each discipline indicates the relative amount of work included in each discipline during the iteration. The amount and nature of the work differs from iteration to iteration. For example, in iteration 2 much of the effort focuses on business modeling and defining requirements, with much less effort focused on implementation and deployment. In iteration 5, very little effort is focused on requirements, with much more effort focused on implementation, testing, and deployment. But most iterations involve work in all disciplines.

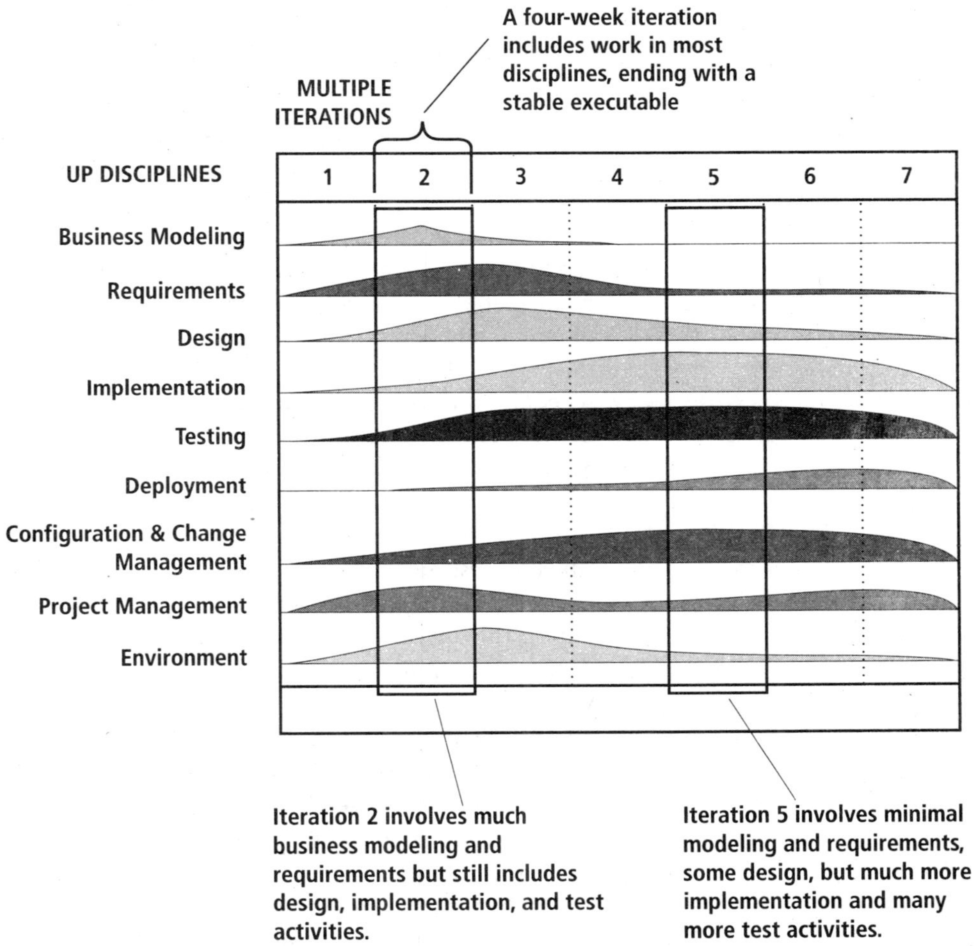

FIGURE 2-14
UP disciplines used in varying amounts in each iteration

Figure 2-15 shows the entire UP life cycle with phases, iterations, and disciplines. We will refer to this figure throughout this book whenever we are discussing the UP. This figure includes all of the key UP life cycle features and is useful for understanding how a typical information system development project is managed.

For example, in the inception phase there is one iteration. During the inception phase iteration, the project manager might complete a model showing some aspect of the system environment (the business modeling discipline). The scope of the system is delineated by defining many of the key requirements of the system and listing use cases (the requirements discipline). To prove technological feasibility, some technical

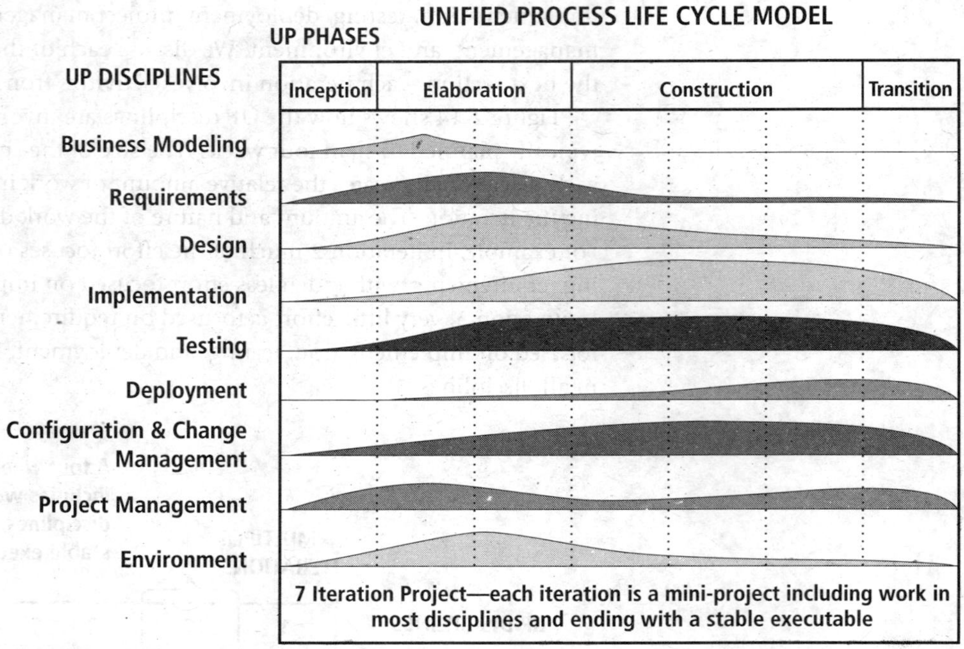

FIGURE 2-15
UP life cycle with phases, iterations, and disciplines

aspect of the system might be designed (the design discipline), programmed (the implementation discipline), and tested to make sure it will work as planned (the testing discipline). In addition, the project manager is making plans for handling changes to the project (the configuration and change management discipline), working on a schedule and cost-benefit analysis (the project management discipline), and tailoring the UP phases, iterations, deliverables, and tools to match the needs of the project (the environment discipline).

The elaboration phase includes several iterations. In the first iteration, the team will work on the details of the domain classes and use cases addressed in the iteration (the business modeling and requirements disciplines). At the same time, they might complete the description of all use cases to finalize the scope (the requirements discipline). The use cases addressed in the iteration are designed by creating design class diagrams and interaction diagrams (the design discipline), programmed using Java or Visual Basic .NET (the implementation discipline), and fully tested (the testing discipline). The project manager will work on the plan for the next iteration and continue to refine the schedule and feasibility assessments (the project management discipline), and all team members will continue to receive training on the UP activities they are completing and the system development tools they are using (the environment discipline).

By the time the project progresses to the construction phase, most of the use cases have been designed and implemented in their initial form. The focus of the project turns to satisfying other technical, performance, and reliability requirements for each use case, finalizing the design, and implementation. These requirements are usually routine and lower risk, but they are key to the success of the system. The effort focuses on designing system controls and security and on implementing and testing these aspects.

artifacts
UP work products

As with any methodology, the UP includes very detailed information about what to do and when to do it for every activity involved in system development. Much of the material in this book focuses on techniques and models included in the UP. You will learn how to create many specific UP work products, called *artifacts*. The activities in each discipline produce artifacts. Many of the artifacts serve to document aspects of the system project. Other artifacts are the actual system components that are completed in an iteration. The types of UP artifacts include:

[1] **A model**, such as a use case model or a user interface design model
[2] **A model element**, such as a class or an attribute that is contained in a model
[3] **A document**, such as a project plan report or a system vision statement
[4] **Source code**, such as uncompiled computer code for components
[5] **Executables**, the ready-to-run software produced from the source code

As you learn about each UP discipline in the next section, you will see that each involves creating and using various artifacts.

THE UP DISCIPLINES

So far, we have focused on the iterations and higher-level organization of the UP's system development life cycle. But what about the detailed activities that occur within each discipline? As we outlined briefly, the six main UP development disciplines are:

- Business modeling
- Requirements
- Design
- Implementation
- Testing
- Deployment

Recall that each iteration is similar to a miniproject, which results in a completed portion of the system. To complete an iteration, the project team must understand the business environment (business modeling), define the requirements that the portion of the system must satisfy (requirements), design a solution for that portion of the system that satisfies the requirements (design), write and integrate the computer code that makes the portion of the system actually work (implementation), thoroughly test the portion of the system (testing), and then in some cases put the portion of the system that is completed and tested into operation for users (deployment).

Three additional support disciplines are necessary for planning and controlling the project:

- Project management
- Configuration and change management
- Environment

To give you a better idea of the activities involved in each discipline, we describe each of them next.

BUSINESS MODELING

The primary purpose of the business modeling discipline is to understand and communicate the nature of the business environment where the system will be deployed. Analysts must understand current problems and potential improvements that are possible with a new system. Additionally, they must communicate this understanding to end users, managers, and system developers working on the project. Sometimes business modeling occurs as part of a strategic information systems planning project, in which an application architecture consisting of a set of integrated computer systems is defined. Business modeling is also an important part of a specific system development project, particularly in early UP project iterations where the new system is defined. Three major activities are part of business modeling:

- Understand the business environment
- Create the system vision
- Create business models

Understanding the business environment requires research on the problem the system must solve. It is important to identify and understand who all of the people affected by the new system (the stakeholders) are. No system exists in a vacuum, so it is also important to identify and understand all of the other information systems that will be affected by the new system. Finally, the new system project will have to fit within the existing technological architecture and conform to the organization's information systems standards.

Business modeling also involves creating the vision of what the new system will be. Creating a vision involves defining system objectives, listing system capabilities, and identifying and documenting the primary business benefits.

Models can be created to show important aspects of the business environment and the new system vision. Some useful models are organizational charts, location layout diagrams, existing computing infrastructure charts and schematics, and charts of existing systems and databases. Additionally, UML diagrams can be used to document aspects of the environment or new system vision by modeling workflows, business objects, and essential use cases the system must support.

REQUIREMENTS

The primary objective of the requirements discipline is to understand and document the business needs and the processing requirements for the new system. Defining requirements is essentially a discovery process, that is, discovering what the users require. Therefore, the key words that drive the activities of the requirements discipline are *discovery* and *understanding*. The requirements discipline, along with some aspects of business modeling, is closest to what has traditionally been called *systems analysis*. The activities include:

- Gather detailed information
- Define functional requirements
- Define nonfunctional requirements
- Prioritize requirements
- Develop user interface dialogs
- Evaluate requirements with users

problem domain
the area of the user's business that needs an information system solution

Gathering information is a fundamental part of defining requirements. The analyst meets with users to learn as much as possible about the *problem domain*—the area of the user's business that needs an information system solution and that is being researched. The analysts obtain information about the problem domain by observing the users as they do their work; by interviewing and asking questions of the users; by reading existing documents about procedures, business rules, and job responsibilities; and by reviewing existing automated systems. In addition to gathering information from the users of the system, the analysts should consult other interested parties. They may include middle managers, senior executives, and at times even external customers. Gathering information is the core activity for discovery and understanding.

But it is not sufficient simply to gather information. Analysts must review, analyze, and structure the information they have obtained to develop an overall understanding of the new system's functional requirements. The functional requirements are the activities that the system must perform—that is, the business uses (use cases) for the system. Detailed use case descriptions of users interacting with the system are written, and UML diagrams are drawn showing the problem domain and user interactions. Nonfunctional requirements must also be defined in detail. They include requirements related to technology, performance expectations, usability, reliability, and security.

It is very important when using an iterative approach to carefully define the priority level for each requirement so that the most important requirements are included. Low-priority requirements might be addressed in later iterations or included in a plan for a later release. Additionally, it is important to control the changes that are requested by users during the project.

As we mentioned previously, the UP is use case driven, so the functional requirements for each use case are very tightly integrated with the requirements for user-computer interaction. Therefore, it is important to begin defining the approach to be used for the user-computer dialog for each use case. In a technique called *storyboarding*, sketches of screens are drawn and arranged in a sequence to illustrate how the user will actually use the computer for each use case. Finally, the requirements, as discovered and understood by the project team, must be continually reviewed with users to ensure accuracy.

DESIGN

The objective of the design discipline is to design the solution system based on the previously defined requirements. High-level design consists of developing an architectural structure for software components, databases, the user interface, and the operating environment. Low-level design entails developing the detailed classes, methods, and structures that are required for software development. Six major activities are included in the design discipline:

- Design the support services architecture and deployment environment
- Design the software architecture
- Design use case realizations
- Design the database
- Design the system and user interfaces
- Design the system security and controls

Design activities are closely interrelated and generally are done with substantial overlap in each iteration. Designing the support services and deployment environment involves network and connectivity issues. The network consists of computer equipment, connections, and operating system platforms that will house the new information system. Most systems today are being installed in network and client/server environments. So, design includes configuring these environments to provide the level of service the system requires. Additionally, components such as Web services, security layers, and data access protocols must be designed.

Designing the software architecture involves packaging the software into subsystems or components. Also, the multilayer architecture to be used must be defined and established—user interface, problem domain, and data access layers, for example. Based on the architectural layers, each use case must be designed in detail. The design of the software that implements each use case is referred to as *use case realization*. UML design class diagrams and interaction diagrams are used to document the design. The design of this software represents the major design effort. You will learn the details of use case realization in Chapter 8.

Databases and information files are an integral part of information systems used for business. Domain class diagrams developed in the requirements discipline are used to design the database that will support the system. At times, the database for a specific system must also be integrated with information databases of other systems already in use.

The user interface is another critical component of any new system. Storyboards for each dialog are developed as part of the requirements discipline, and during design the details of the user interface that implements the storyboards are defined. Also, online and printed reports and forms must be designed. Most information systems communicate with other existing systems, so the design of these system interfaces must also be completed.

Finally, every system must have sufficient controls to protect the integrity of the data and application programs. Because of the highly competitive nature of the global economy and the risks associated with technology and security, every new system must include adequate mechanisms to protect the assets of the organization. These controls should be included in the new system when it is designed, not after it is constructed.

Remember, each iteration addresses only part of the system, perhaps a subset of use cases. Early iterations emphasize packaging and architecture of the software and many of the network and support services. Early iterations also focus on use case realization, database design, and user interface design for the initial use cases. In contrast, construction iterations focus on finalizing the software design, perhaps focusing on security and controls and on integrating the components of the application.

IMPLEMENTATION

The implementation discipline involves actually building or acquiring needed system components. The activities of implementation include:

- Build software components
- Acquire software components
- Integrate software components

The software can be written using various techniques. For example, the problem domain software classes that interact in a use case realization might be coded first. User interface and data access classes might be coded separately, even by separate teams. Some components are obtained from class libraries or vendor sources. These components must be acquired and integrated with custom components to complete parts of the system. During any iteration, the new system components must be integrated with already completed system components, so coding, acquiring components, and writing code to integrate components occur continually.

TESTING

The testing discipline has been acknowledged as one of the most important disciplines in system development. Very early in the project, test cases are defined based on use cases. When working with users to define the initial requirements, analysts should ask the users to generate test cases and sample data that they can use later to evaluate the system under actual conditions. You can see in Figure 2-15 that the testing discipline is involved even in the inception phase for this reason. As the project proceeds, testing involves the following activities:

- Define and conduct unit testing
- Define and conduct integration testing
- Define and conduct usability testing
- Define and conduct user acceptance testing

Unit tests verify the functionality of a software component to ensure it works properly. For example, when writing code for one software class, a programmer must test the methods of the class. As more functionality is added to the class, such as validation and exception handling, more unit tests are conducted on the class. Integration testing verifies that components work together. Obviously, as each iteration adds more software components to the system, more and more integration testing is required.

Usability testing focuses on testing the ease of use and usefulness of the user interface design. Usability testing can begin in early iterations as dialogs and storyboards are developed and then proceed as the interfaces are designed and implemented. User acceptance testing has traditionally meant the final approval of the system—when it is completed and ready to deploy. In adaptive approaches such as the UP, acceptance testing can occur throughout the project as the system is built.

DEPLOYMENT

The deployment discipline refers to the activities required to make the system operational. Any hardware and system software needed for the system must be assembled. The final components must be packaged and installed. Users of all types must be trained. Finally, data that must be included in the system files and databases must be obtained, converted from the original source into the format required by the new system, and initialized. The activities include:

- Acquire hardware and system software
- Package and install components
- Train users
- Convert and initialize data

Deployment activities can occur in any iteration, although they tend to be more prominent in preparation for the transition phase.

PROJECT MANAGEMENT

The six disciplines just discussed are directly related to the development process. A UP project also requires the use of additional disciplines to support the development team. Project management is the most important and involves the most effort. Much of the project planning occurs in the inception phase, but project management activities continue throughout the project. Project management is discussed in detail in Chapter 3. The activities of the project management discipline include:

- Finalize the system and project scope
- Develop the project and iteration schedule
- Identify project risks and confirm the project's feasibility
- Monitor and control the project's plan, schedule, internal and external communications, and risks and outstanding issues

CONFIGURATION AND CHANGE MANAGEMENT

As the project progresses, many changes occur in the requirements, design, source code, and executables. It is crucial to have plans and procedures for tracking any changes and for identifying current versions of any component. Additionally, as changes to components are made, the models and other documents that describe the components must be updated. In adaptive approaches such as the UP, configuration and change management is an ongoing concern. The two activities in this discipline are:

- Develop change control procedures
- Manage models and software components

ENVIRONMENT

A final discipline involves managing the development environment used by the project team. The development environment includes the available facilities, the design of the workspace, and other arrangements for team members to communicate and interact. Additionally, the development tools to be used must be identified, acquired, and installed. Also, team members must be trained on use of the development tools.

The Unified Process as a system development methodology must be tailored to the development team and specific project. Choices must be made about which deliverables to produce and the formality to be used. Sometimes a project requires formal reporting and controls. Other times, it can be less formal. The UP should always be tailored to the project. The activities of the environment discipline include:

- Select and configure the development tools
- Tailor the UP development process
- Provide technical support services

Now that you have an understanding of the six UP development disciplines and the three UP support disciplines, we review some basic concepts of the object-oriented approach to system development, the approach underlying the Unified Process.

OVERVIEW OF OBJECT-ORIENTED CONCEPTS

object-oriented approach
a system development approach that views an information system as a collection of interacting objects that work together to accomplish tasks

object
a thing in the computer system that can respond to messages

The *object-oriented approach* to system development views an information system as a collection of interacting objects that work together to accomplish tasks. Conceptually, there are no separate processes or programs; there are no separate data entities or files. The system in operation consists of objects. An *object* is a thing in the computer system that is capable of responding to messages.

The object-oriented approach began with the development of the Simula programming language in Norway in the 1960s. Simula was used to create computer simulations involving "objects" such as ships, buoys, and tides in fjords. It is very difficult to write procedural programs that simulate ship movement, but a new way of programming simplified the problem. In the 1970s, the Smalltalk language was developed to solve the problem of creating graphical user interfaces that involved "objects" such as pull-down menus, buttons, check boxes, and dialog boxes. Other object-oriented languages include C++ and, more recently, Java, C#, and Visual Basic .NET. These languages focus on writing definitions of the types of objects needed in a system, and as a result, all parts of a system can be thought of as objects, not just the graphical user interface.

object-oriented analysis (OOA)
defining all of the types of objects that do the work in a system and showing what user interactions are required to complete tasks

object-oriented design (OOD)
defining all of the types of objects necessary to communicate with people and devices in the system, showing how the objects interact to complete tasks, and refining the definition of each type of object so it can be implemented with a specific language or environment

Because the object-oriented approach views information systems as collections of interacting objects, *object-oriented analysis (OOA)* defines all of the types of objects that the user needs to work with and shows what user interactions are required to complete tasks. *Object-oriented design (OOD)* defines all of the additional types of objects necessary to communicate with people and devices in the system, shows how the objects interact to complete tasks, and refines the definition of each type of object so it can be implemented with a specific language or environment. *Object-oriented programming (OOP)* consists of writing statements in a programming language to define what each type of object does.

RECOGNIZING THE BENEFITS OF OO DEVELOPMENT

The object-oriented approach was originally found to be useful in computer simulations and for graphical user interfaces, but why is it now being used in more conventional

object-oriented programming (OOP)
writing statements in a programming language to define what each type of object does, including the messages that the objects send to each other

naturalness
characteristic of the object-oriented approach that describes its match with the way people usually think about their world—that is, it conforms with people's tendency to talk about their work and discuss system requirements in terms of classes of objects

information system development? The two main reasons are the benefits of naturalness and reuse.

OBJECTS ARE MORE NATURAL

Naturalness of the object-oriented approach refers to the fact that people usually think about their world in terms of objects, so when people talk about their work and discuss system requirements, they tend to define the classes of objects involved. So, the object-oriented approach mirrors, or matches, human beings' typical way of viewing their world. Additionally, OOA, OOD, and OOP all involve modeling classes of objects, so the focus remains on objects throughout the development process.

Some experienced system developers continue to avoid OO development, arguing that it is really not as natural as procedural programming. In fact, many experienced developers have had difficulty learning the OO approach. Because procedural programming was the first approach to programming they learned, it might seem more natural to them now. But for most people, including those new to programming, procedural programming is very difficult. Few people can think through and write complex procedural code. For most new programmers learning about system development, the OO approach does seem fairly natural. In addition, object-orientation is natural to system users. They can easily discuss the objects involved in their work. Classes, classification, and generalization/specialization hierarchies are the natural way people organize their knowledge.

CLASSES OF OBJECTS CAN BE REUSED

reuse
benefit of the object-oriented approach that allows classes and objects to be invented once and used many times

In addition to naturalness, the ability to reuse classes and objects is another benefit of object-oriented development. *Reuse* means that classes and objects can be invented once and used many times. Once a developer defines a class, such as the Customer class, it can be reused in many other systems that have customer objects. If the new system has a special type of customer, the existing Customer class can be extended to a new subclass by inheriting all that a customer is and then adding the new characteristics. Classes can be reused in this manner during analysis, design, or programming.

When programming, developers do not have to see the source code for the class that is being reused, even if they are defining a new class that inherits from it. This simplifies development. Object-oriented programming languages come with class libraries that contain predefined classes most programmers need, for example, the .NET framework class library and the Java SDK. User interface classes such as buttons, labels, text boxes, and check boxes come in .NET and Java class libraries. As a programmer, you do not need to create these classes from scratch. Instead, you use the class to create objects you need for your user interface. Other useful classes are also included in class libraries, such as those used to connect to databases or networks and to hold collections of objects.

UNDERSTANDING OBJECT-ORIENTED CONCEPTS

As discussed previously, object-oriented development assumes a system is a collection of objects that interact to accomplish tasks. To understand and discuss OOA and OOD, you should be familiar with the key concepts that apply to objects and OO development, shown in Figure 2-16. These concepts are briefly introduced in this section and are explained and demonstrated more completely throughout the book.

OBJECTS, ATTRIBUTES, AND METHODS

An *object* in a computer system is like an object in the real world—it is a thing that has attributes and behaviors. A computer system can have many types of objects, such as

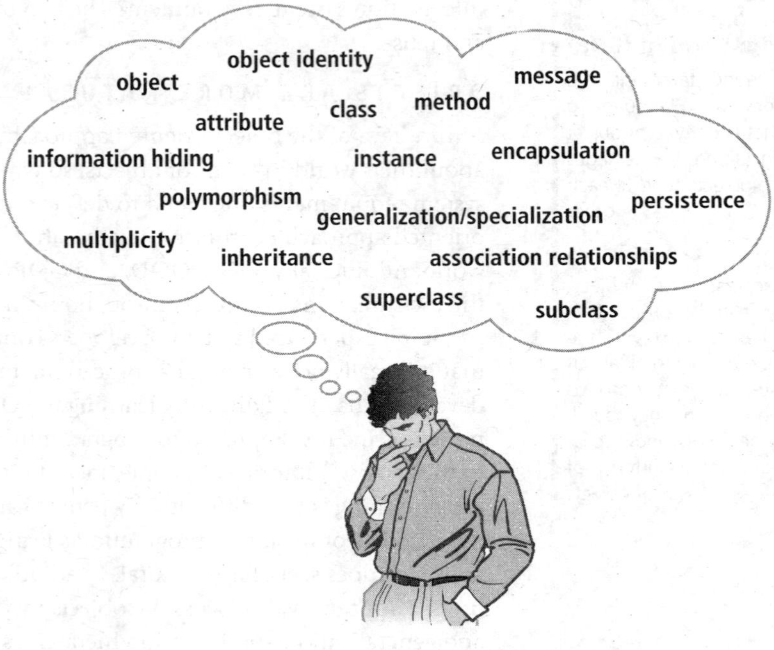

FIGURE 2-16
Key OO concepts

user interface (UI) objects that make up the user interface and the system and problem domain objects that are the focus of the users' task environment. A *user interface object* uses graphics, such as a button or label, to represent part of a system. A user interface object has *attributes*, which are characteristics that have values: the size, shape, color, location, and caption of a button or label, for example. A form or window on a screen has attributes, such as height and width, border style, and background color. These user interface objects also have behaviors, or *methods*, which describe what an object can do. For example, a button can be clicked, a label can display text, and a form or window can change size and appear or disappear. Figure 2-17 lists some UI objects with their attributes and methods.

user interface object
an object the user interacts with while using the system, such as a button, menu item, text box, or label

attributes
object characteristics that have values, such as the size, shape, color, location, and caption of a button or label or the name, address, and phone number of a customer

methods
behaviors or operations that describe what an object is capable of doing

UI OBJECTS	ATTRIBUTES	METHODS
Button	size, shape, color, location, caption	click, enable, disable, hide, show
Label	size, shape, color, location, text	see text, get text, hide, show
Form	width, height, border style, background color	change size, minimize, maximize, appear, disappear

FIGURE 2-17
Attributes and methods of UI objects

UI objects are the easiest to understand because users (and developers) can see them and interact with them directly. But OO systems contain other types of objects, called *problem domain objects*, which are specific to a business application. For example, a business system that processes orders includes customer objects, order objects, and product objects. Like UI objects, problem domain objects also have attributes and methods, as shown in Figure 2-18. The attributes are similar to the attributes of data entities used in relational database design: each customer has a name, address, and phone number, for example. But in OO development, these objects also have methods, giving problem domain objects the ability to perform tasks. For example, the methods of each customer include the ability to set name and address, give the values of name and address, and add a new order for the customer. The methods of an order might be to set the order date, calculate an order amount, and add a product to the order.

problem domain objects
objects that are specific to a business application—for example, customer objects, order objects, and product objects in an order-processing system

PROBLEM DOMAIN OBJECTS

	ATTRIBUTES	METHODS
Customer	name, address, phone number	set name, set address, add new order for customer
Order	order number, date, amount	set order date, calculate order amount, add product to order, schedule order shipment
Product	product number, description, price	add to order, set discription, get price

FIGURE 2-18
Attributes and methods in problem domain objects

CLASSES AND INSTANCES

An order-processing system has many customer objects, one for each real-world customer (see Figure 2-19). All of the customer objects are *classified* as a type of thing—a customer—so in OO development, you refer to the customer class when you are talking about all of the customer objects. The *class* defines what all objects of the class represent. When you are talking about computer programming and objects, you can refer to the objects as *instances* of the class. When an object is created for the class, it is common to say the class is *instantiated*. Therefore, the terms *instance* and *object* are often used interchangeably.

class
a type or classification to which all similar objects belong

instance
a synonym for object

OBJECT INTERACTIONS AND MESSAGES

Objects interact by sending *messages* to each other, asking other objects to invoke, or carry out, one of their methods. In other words, a user interface object such as a form with buttons and text boxes might send a message asking a class to create a new instance of itself, such as the order class creating a new instance for order 134. The new order instance might send a message to the customer object Susan, informing that customer there is a new order.

messages
communications between objects in which one object asks another object to invoke, or carry out, one of its methods

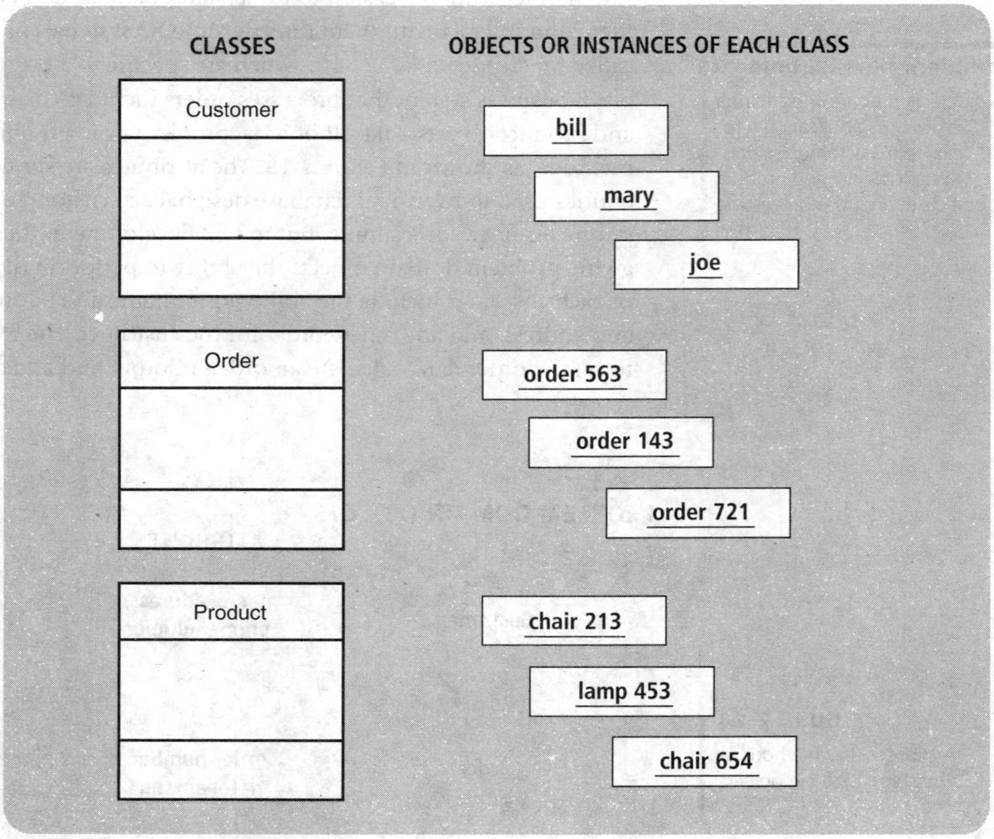

FIGURE 2-19
Class versus objects or instances of the class

Figure 2-20 shows an order-processing system containing customer Susan and order 134 and other interacting objects. The user interacts with UI objects to carry out the use case for adding a new order. The UI objects interact with problem domain objects by sending messages.

The order-processing system works as follows:

[1] The user types information about the order in text boxes or selects items in list boxes, and then clicks the button. The user is sending a message to the system asking it to create a new order for Susan Franks for an executive desk and a chair.

[2] The button knows that when it is clicked, it should get information from the text boxes and list boxes and send a message to the Order class, asking it to add a new order object. When the new order object is created, it knows to assign itself a new order number and get today's date. It also knows to take the customer and project information it receives from the button and send some messages to other objects. These are the responsibilities any new order object has.

[3] The new order object 134 finds an available executive desk object that is not yet sold and sends a message to it, asking it to add itself to the order. Executive desk 19874 does so and sends information back about its number and price.

[4] Order object 134 next finds an available chair object that is not yet sold and sends a message to it, asking it to add itself to the order. Chair 76532 does so and sends information back about its number and price.

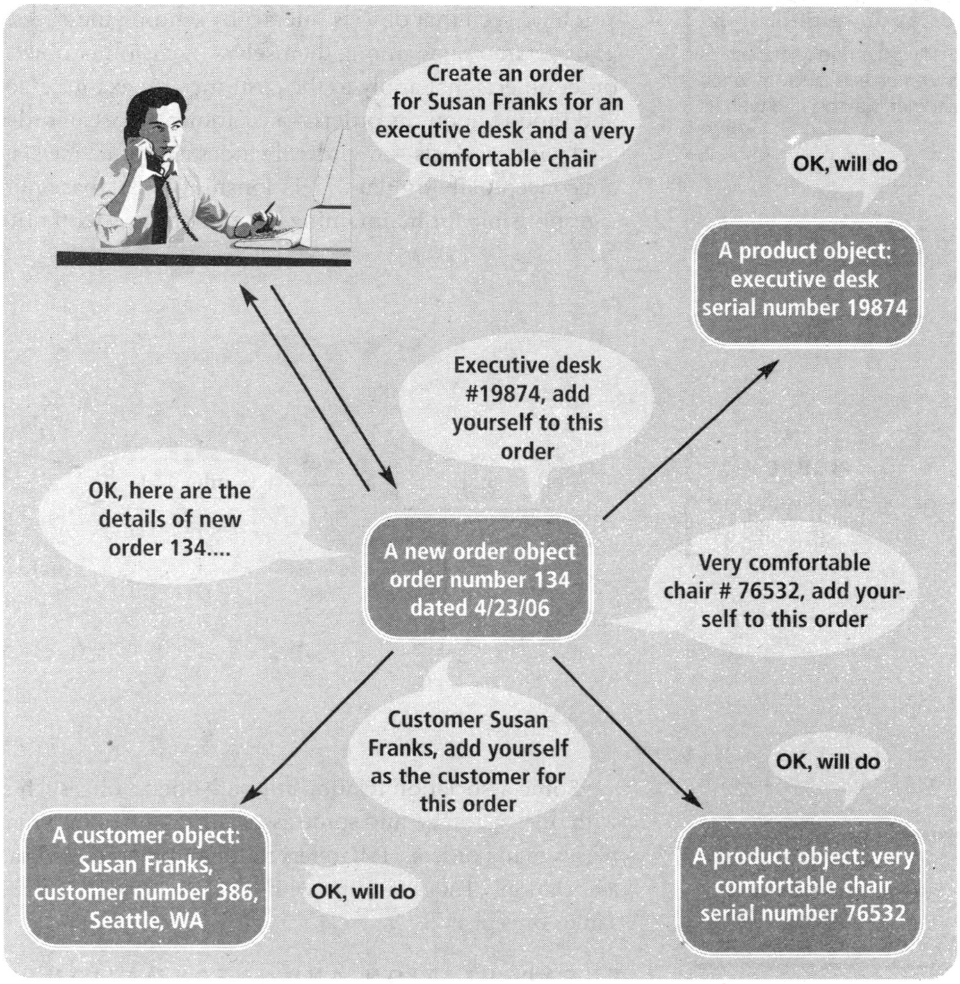

FIGURE 2-20
Order-processing system where objects interact by sending messages

[5] Order object 134 now finds the customer object 386 representing customer Susan Franks and sends it a message, asking it to add itself as the customer for the order. It does so and sends back information about the name and address for shipping.

[6] Now that order 134 has all the information it needs to finalize the processing, it calculates the total cost, shipping, and taxes and sends a message summarizing all the desk, chair, and customer details back to the user to confirm the processing is complete. These details are displayed on the user interface form in labels.

Notice that each object in the system has responsibilities and knows how to carry them out. Each object also retains a memory of the transaction because it remembers values of its attributes and interactions with other objects. Therefore, if a sales representative later asked the customer object Susan Franks to summarize all of her orders, the customer object would find the first order, ask it for its order number and date, and then ask it for each product's details. That order object would find the first product and ask it for its details. Then it would find the second product and ask it for its details. The order would then return all the information to customer object Susan Franks, who would find the next order and ask it for details. Eventually, customer Susan Franks would have all the information about all of her orders and return it to the sales representative.

association relationships naturally occurring relationships between objects, such as when a customer is associated with its orders

ASSOCIATIONS AND MULTIPLICITY

You have seen that objects interact by sending messages, but they also maintain *association relationships* among themselves. A customer object maintains associations with order objects that apply to the customer, for example, so the customer object can find and inquire about its orders—a customer places an order. Each order object is associated with products—an order includes a product (see Figure 2-21). Object associations are conceptually similar to relationships in database modeling, except that each object is responsible for maintaining its relationships with other objects.

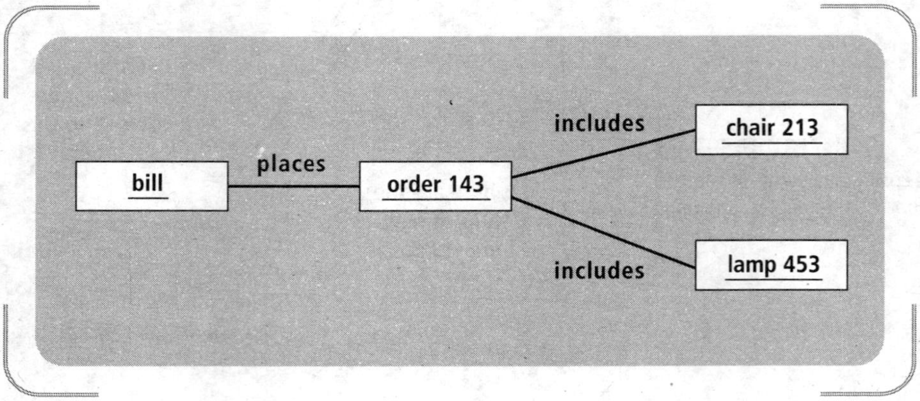

FIGURE 2-21 Associating objects with other objects

Some association relationships are one-to-one, such as when one order is associated with one customer, and some associations are one-to-many, such as when one customer places many orders. UML refers to the number of associations as the *multiplicity* of the association. (Those familiar with database modeling use the term *cardinality* for the same concept.)

multiplicity the number of associations between objects

ENCAPSULATION AND INFORMATION HIDING

encapsulation combining attributes and methods into one unit and hiding its internal structure of objects

information hiding a characteristic of object-oriented development in which data associated with an object are not visible to the outside world

identity a unique reference to an object that allows another object to find it and send it a message

persistent objects objects that a system remembers and that are available for use over time

inheritance a concept in which one class of objects shares some characteristics of another class

In Figure 2-20, the objects Customer 386 and Order 134 both have attributes and methods, giving them the ability to respond to messages. *Encapsulation* means that an object has attributes and methods combined into one unit. Combining attributes and methods means you do not need to know the internal structure of the object to send messages to it. You only need to know what an object can do for you. Encapsulation hides the internal structure of objects, also protecting them from corruption. This is what is meant by *information hiding* in OO, another key concept.

Each object also has a unique *identity*, meaning you can find it, or refer to it, and send it a message. You need to know an object's identity before you can ask the object to do something for you, such as adding a chair to an order. The object's identity is usually stored as a memory address. The system uses a specific object like Customer 386 over a period of time, so it requires some mechanism for keeping it available. *Persistent objects* are those that are available for use over time. If a system uses thousands of customer objects, each with its own orders, the system must be able to remember all of them.

INHERITANCE AND POLYMORPHISM

Probably the most-often-used concept when discussing objects and classes is the concept of *inheritance*, whereby one class of objects takes on characteristics of another class and extends them. For example, an object belonging to the Customer class might also be something more general, such as a person. Therefore, if the Person class is already defined, the Customer class can be defined by extending the Person class to take on more specific attributes and methods required of a customer.

superclass
a general class in a generalization/specialization hierarchy, which can be extended by a subclass

subclass
a specialized class in a generalization/specialization hierarchy, which contains additional attributes and methods distinguishing it from a more general class that it extends

For example, the Person class might have attributes for name and address. The Customer class is a special type of person with additional attributes for shipping address and credit-card information. Similarly, a SalesClerk object is also a person, so the SalesClerk class can also be defined by extending the Person class. For example, a salesclerk has additional attributes for job title and pay rate. The Person class is a *superclass*, and both Customer and SalesClerk are *subclasses*. This relationship is shown in Figure 2-22.

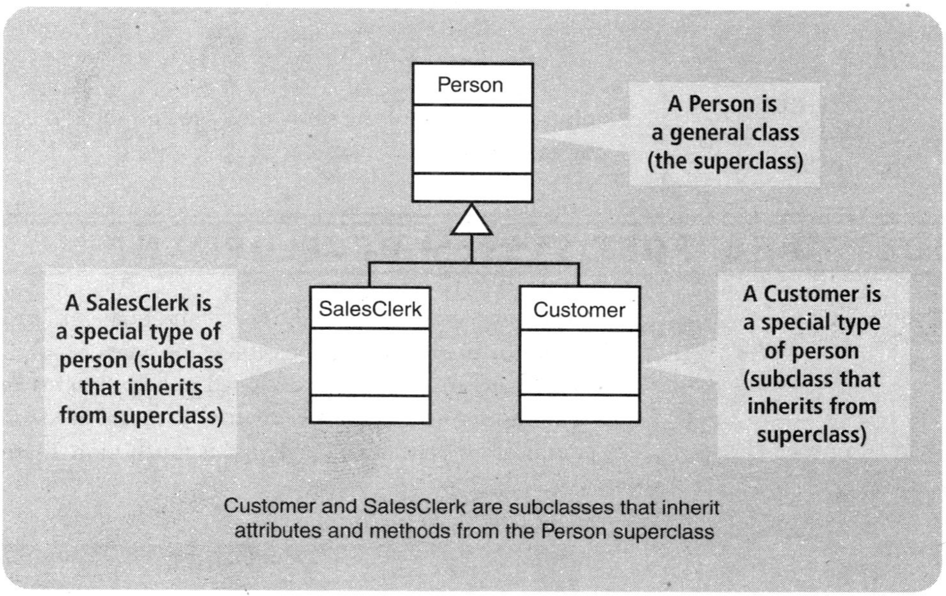

FIGURE 2-22
Superclass and subclasses

Classifying objects helps to identify special types of problem domain objects, which provide more specific information about the requirements for the system. The result of extending general classes into more specific subclasses is referred to as a *generalization/specialization hierarchy*, sometimes called an *inheritance hierarchy*.

generalization/specialization hierarchy
a classification system that structures or ranks classes from the more general superclass to the more specialized subclasses; also called *inheritance hierarchy*

polymorphism
a characteristic of objects that allows them to respond differently to the same message

Attributes are not the only characteristics inherited from a superclass. Subclasses also inherit methods and association relationships. A final key concept that is related to generalization/specialization hierarchies and inheritance of methods is *polymorphism*, which means "many forms." In OO development, polymorphism refers to the way different objects can respond in their own way to the same message. For example, a dialog box, a network connection, and a document might each receive a message to *close*. Each knows how to close and does so in its own way when asked. The sender of the message does not need to know what type of object it is or how it does it; the sender only needs to know that the object responds to the *close* message. Classes are polymorphic if their instances can respond to the same message.

For example, a bank has several types of bank accounts, including money market accounts and passbook accounts. Both types of accounts calculate interest, but they follow different rules for interest. The sender of the message *calculateInterest* does not need to know what type of account it is, only that it calculates interest when asked (see Figure 2-23). It greatly simplifies processing when all bank account

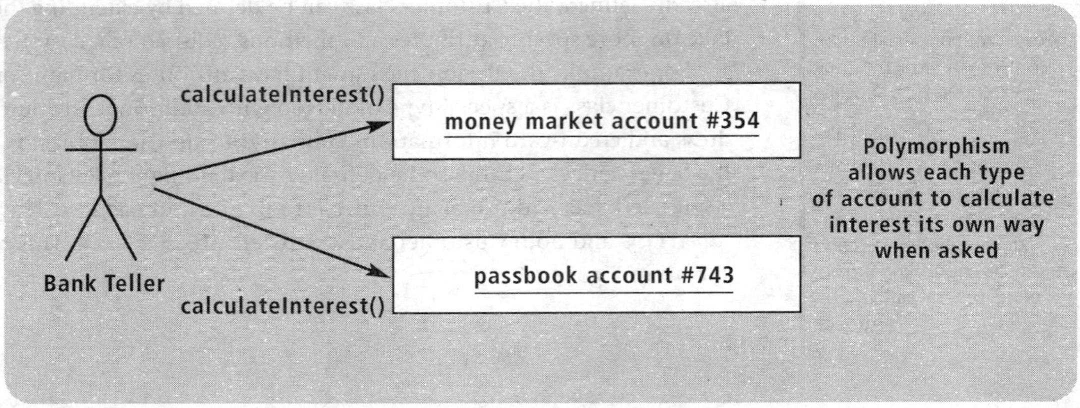

FIGURE 2-23
Polymorphism for two different types of bank accounts

objects can be sent the same message and the job is done correctly and completely by each object.

TOOLS TO SUPPORT SYSTEM DEVELOPMENT

Automated tools improve the speed and quality of system development work, so they should be used whenever possible. One type of tool discussed earlier is a CASE tool. CASE tools are specifically designed to help systems analysts complete system development tasks. Analysts use a CASE tool to create models of the system, many of them graphical models. But a CASE tool is much more than a drawing tool.

> **BEST PRACTICE: Use automated tools whenever possible, but remember that sketches on napkins or envelopes are often enough for a small team on a small project. Don't let the tool create more problems than it solves.**

CHARACTERISTICS OF CASE TOOLS

repository
a database of information about the system used by a CASE tool, including models, descriptions, and references that link the various models

A CASE tool contains a database of information about the project, called a *repository*. The repository stores information about the system, including models, descriptions, and references that link the various models. The CASE tool can check the models to make sure they are complete and follow the correct diagramming rules. The CASE tool also can check one model against another to make sure they are consistent. If you consider how much time an analyst spends creating models, checking them, revising them, and then making sure they all fit together, it is apparent how much help a CASE tool can provide. Figure 2-24 shows CASE tool capabilities surrounding the repository. If system information is stored in a repository, the development team can use the information in a variety of ways. Every time a team member adds information about the system, it is immediately available for everyone else.

Some CASE tools are designed to be as flexible as possible, allowing analysts to use any development approach they desire. Other CASE tools are designed for very specific methodologies. Not all of these tools are called *CASE tools* by their vendors. For many developers and managers, CASE tools failed to meet expectations and fell into disuse.

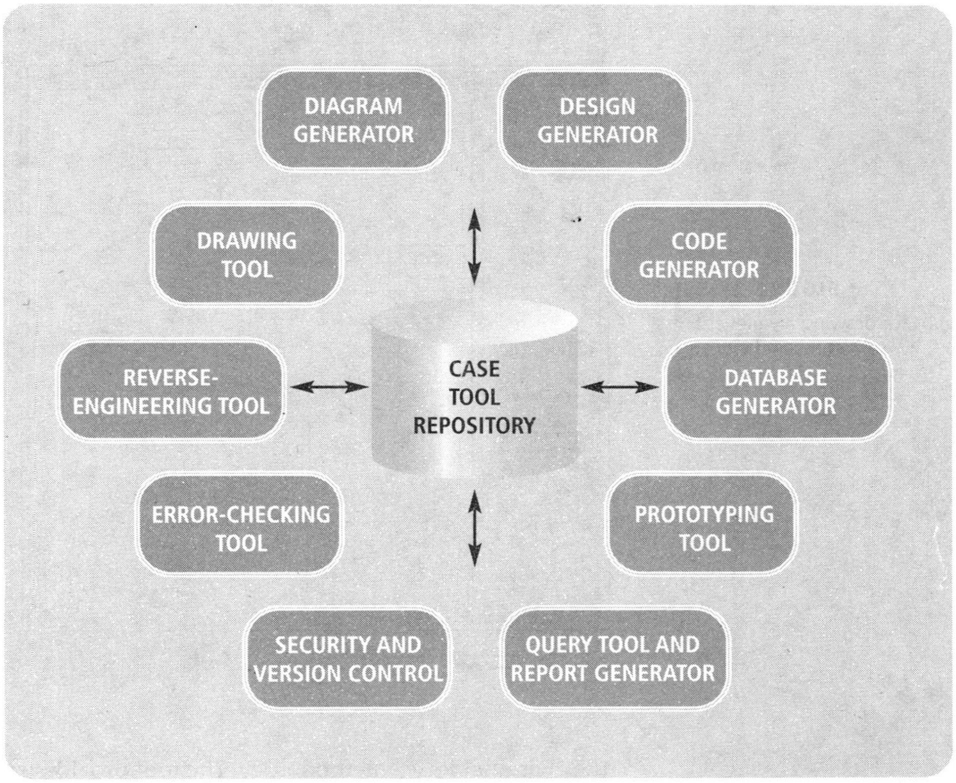

FIGURE 2-24
A CASE tool repository contains all information about the system

Vendors today refer to their tools as *visual modeling tools, integrated application development tools,* or *round-trip engineering tools.*

MICROSOFT VISIO

Although not really a CASE tool, Visio is a drawing tool that analysts use to create just about any system model they might need. Visio comes with a collection of drawing templates that include symbols used in a variety of business and engineering applications. Software and system development templates provide symbols for UML diagrams and others found throughout this text. The templates provide a limited repository for storing definitions and descriptions of diagram elements, but Visio does not provide a complete repository for a system development project. Many system developers prefer the flexibility that Visio offers for drawing any diagram needed, however.

Figure 2-25 shows Visio displaying two drawings. One drawing shows several UML diagrams: a class diagram, a use case diagram, and a sequence diagram. The other drawing shows computer and networking symbols that can be used for designing a network.

RATIONAL ROSE

Rational Rose is a well-known tool from Rational Software, now part of IBM (www.ibm.com), that specifically supports the object-oriented approach. Rational Rose is referred to as a *visual modeling tool* rather than a CASE tool. Rational Rose can be used with the Unified Process or with any methodology that uses UML diagrams, and because Rational Rose has been so influential, many developers refer to the UP as

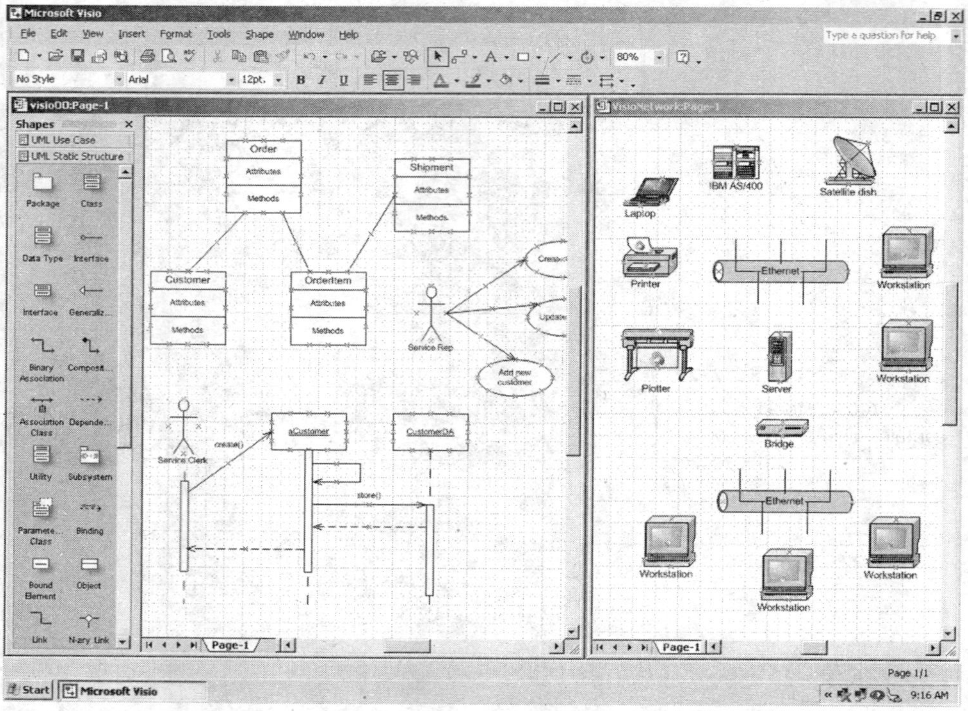

FIGURE 2-25
Visio for drawing a variety of diagrams and charts

the "Rational Rose" methodology. The tool provides reverse-engineering and code-generating capability, as well as a repository, and can be integrated with additional tools to provide a complete development environment. Rational Software also has other system modeling tools that are tightly integrated with specific IDEs, including Visual Studio .NET (discussed later). Figure 2-26 shows Rational Rose displaying some UML models.

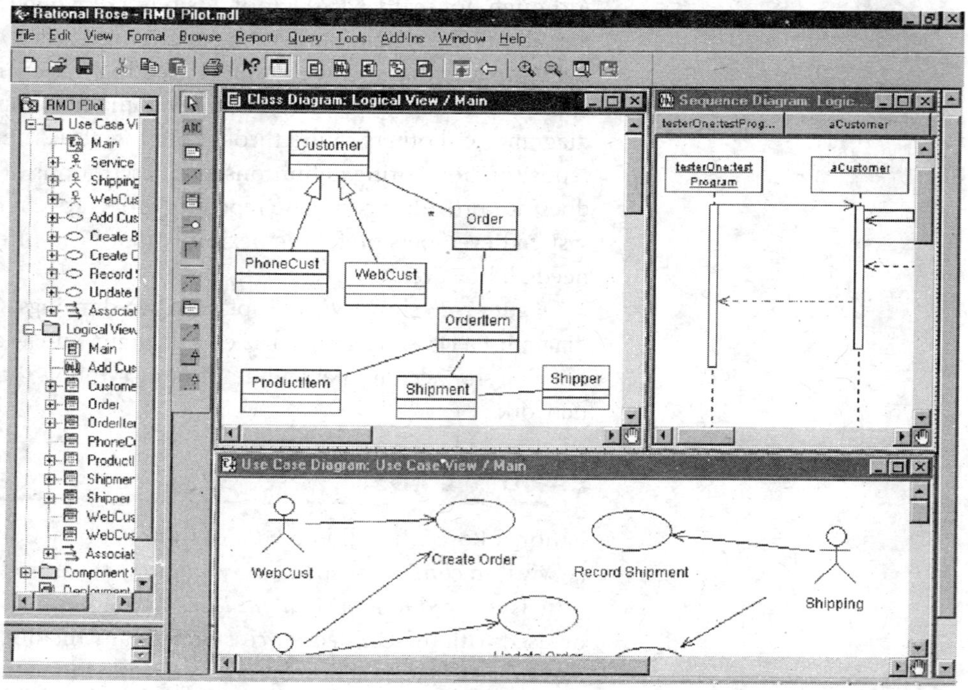

FIGURE 2-26
Visual modeling tool Rational Rose displaying UML diagrams

TOGETHER

round-trip engineering
automating the process of synchronizing graphical models with program code so changes to code automatically update the models and changes to models automatically update the code

A recent advance in automated tools is the concept of *round-trip engineering*. Because system development can be so iterative, particularly in the object-oriented approach, it is important to synchronize the graphical models (such as class diagrams) continually with generated program code. For example, if the analyst changes the program code, he or she must also update the class diagram. Likewise, changing the class diagram means updating the program code. Unlike CASE tools that generate code from the graphical models, newer tools automate the process of synchronization in both directions (in a round trip).

Peter Coad and TogetherSoft, now part of Borland (www.borland.com), pioneered round-trip engineering with the tool named *Together*. Together uses UML diagrams with several different OO programming languages to provide round-trip engineering support. Figure 2-27 shows Together with a class diagram and synchronized Java code. If the developer prefers to write the code to define the class, the class diagram is updated automatically. If the developer prefers to draw the class diagram first, the code to define the class is updated.

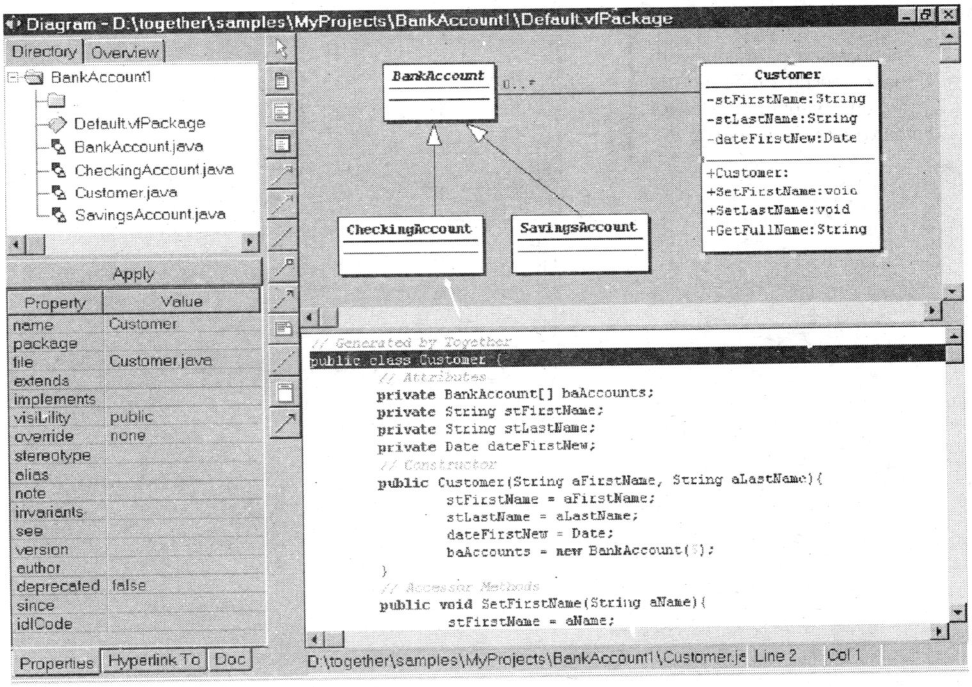

FIGURE 2-27
The round-trip engineering tool Together, showing a class diagram with synchronized Java source code

EMBARCADERO DESCRIBE

Another product that includes both visual modeling and round-trip engineering features is Embarcadero Describe (www.embarcadero.com). The Enterprise edition of Describe features flexible UML modeling capabilities for requirements and design, including round-trip engineering with Java (see Figure 2-28). Describe Developer can integrate with several Java development tools.

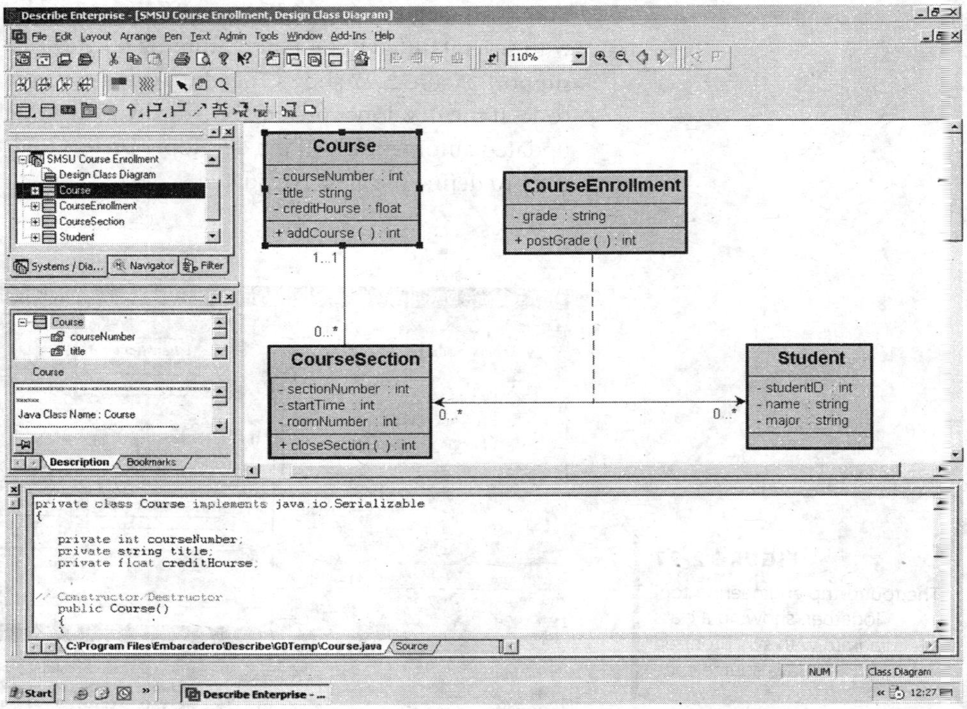

FIGURE 2-28

Embarcadero Describe with visual modeling and round-trip engineering. *Courtesy of Embarcadero Technologies, Inc.*

RATIONAL XDE PROFESSIONAL

The latest approach to system modeling tools combines a full-featured modeling and round-trip engineering tool with the integrated development environment (IDE) of another vendor, where program code is generated and refined. Rational XDE Professional, shown in Figure 2-29, is integrated with the Microsoft Visual Studio .NET IDE, allowing round-trip engineering and code generation to become part of the IDE used by the developer. The developer no longer has a CASE tool and a separate IDE. All the support functionality the developer needs is included in one integrated tool.

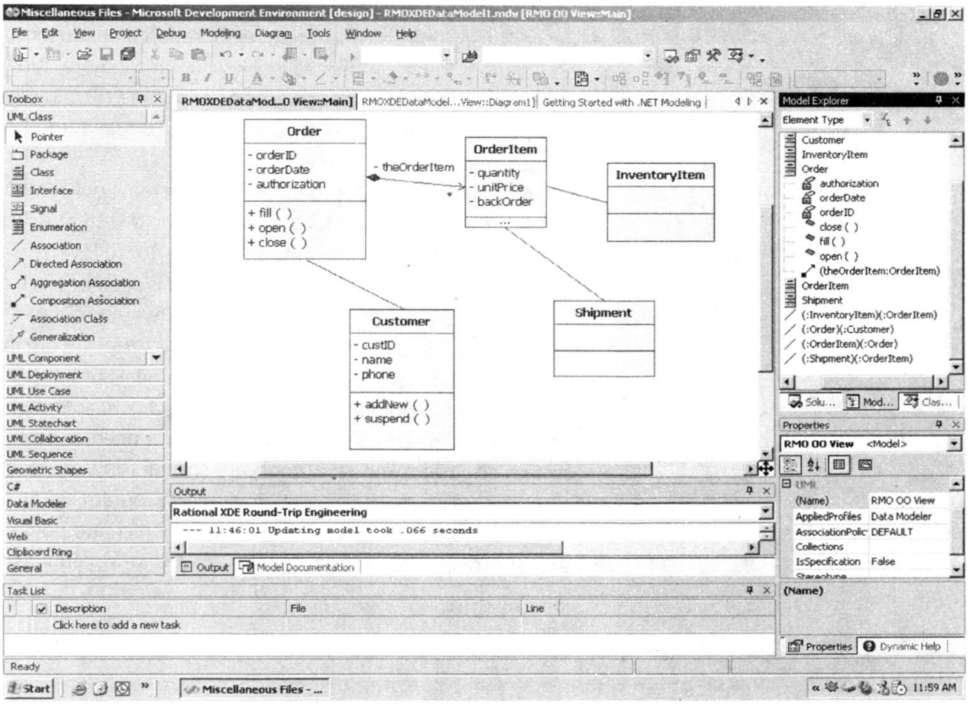

FIGURE 2-29

Rational XDE Professional is integrated with Visual Studio .NET

Summary

System development projects are organized around the systems development life cycle (SDLC), which includes a set of activities that must be completed for any system development project. Predictive approaches to the SDLC are used when the requirements and technology are well understood in advance, allowing the project to be planned and carried out using sequential phases. System developers learn the SDLC phases and activities sequentially, according to a waterfall approach; in practice, however, the phases overlap and many activities are completed in parallel. Adaptive approaches to the SDLC are used when the requirements are uncertain or technology is rapidly changing, requiring the project plan to change and adapt over time. The spiral model is an example of an adaptive approach to the SDLC, and it introduced iteration, completing parts of the system in a series of smaller cycles.

The most commonly used adaptive SDLC is the Unified Process life cycle model. The UP life cycle includes four phases—inception, elaboration, construction, and transition—that allow the project to be planned. But each phase involves one or more iterations during which working software is completed, and each iteration involves work in nine UP disciplines, which are business modeling, requirements, design, implementation, testing, deployment, project management, configuration and change management, and environment.

All development approaches use a systems development life cycle to manage the project, plus models, techniques, and tools that make up a system development methodology. A system development methodology provides guidelines to follow for completing every activity in the SDLC. Sometimes the term development *process* is used in place of development *methodology*.

The Unified Process from Rational Software (now part of IBM) is a comprehensive system development methodology that uses the UP life cycle, UP disciplines, iterations, and other best practices. This text emphasizes the techniques and models of the UP. This text will also focus on object-oriented development exclusively, so object-oriented concepts such as object, class, methods, encapsulation, associations, inheritance, and polymorphism need to be reviewed by most students. Computer-aided system engineering (CASE) tools are special tools designed to help analysts complete development tasks, including modeling and generating program statements directly from the models. This chapter discussed some examples of CASE tools, which are now referred to as integrated application development tools, visual modeling tools, or round-trip engineering tools.

KEY TERMS

adaptive approach, p. 39
artifacts, p. 54
association relationships, p. 66
attributes, p. 62
best practices, p. 49
CASE tool, p. 49
class, p. 63
discipline, p. 52
encapsulation, p. 66
generalization/specialization hierarchy, p. 67
identity, p. 66
incremental development, p. 45
information hiding, p. 66
inheritance, p. 66
instance, p. 63
iteration, p. 43
messages, p. 63
methods, p. 62
model, p. 47
multiplicity, p. 66
naturalness, p. 61
object, p. 60
object-oriented analysis (OOA), p. 60
object-oriented approach, p. 60
object-oriented design (OOD), p. 60
object-oriented programming (OOP), p. 61
persistent objects, p. 66
polymorphism, p. 67
predictive approach, p. 39
problem domain, p. 56
problem domain objects, p. 63
project, p. 38
prototype, p. 42
repository, p. 68
reuse, p. 61
round-trip engineering, p. 71
spiral model, p. 42
subclass, p. 67
superclass, p. 67
system development methodology, p. 47
systems development life cycle (SDLC), p. 39
technique, p. 49
tool, p. 49
Unified Modeling Language (UML), p. 48
Unified Process (UP), p. 50
use case, p. 52
user interface object, p. 62
waterfail approach, p. 40

REVIEW QUESTIONS

1. What are the five phases of the traditional SDLC?
2. How is the traditional SDLC based on the problem-solving approach described in Chapter 1?
3. Explain what is meant by a waterfall life cycle approach.
4. What concept suggests repeating activities over and over until you achieve your objective?
5. What concept suggests completing part of the system and putting it into operation before continuing with the rest of the system?
6. What type of project is right for a predictive approach to the SDLC?
7. What type of project requires a more adaptive approach to the SDLC?
8. How does the spiral model show each iteration in the project?
9. When are the riskier aspects of the project addressed when using the spiral model?
10. What are the four phases of the UP life cycle?
11. What are the objectives of each UP phase?
12. What is the difference between a model and a tool?
13. What is the Unified Modeling Language?
14. What is the difference between a technique and a methodology?
15. Differentiate between the UP life cycle and the complete UP methodology.
16. Who are the three people who developed both UML and the UP?
17. What are some of the best practices supported by the UP methodology?
18. Explain how the UP is use case driven.
19. What are artifacts, and what are the five types of artifacts?
20. What are the six UP development disciplines?
21. What are the three UP support disciplines?
22. What are CASE tools? Why are they used?
23. What are some newer terms used to describe CASE tools?

THINKING CRITICALLY

1. Write a one-page paper that distinguishes among the fundamental purposes of the traditional analysis phase, the design phase, and the implementation phase. Explain how each phase includes work in one or more of the UP disciplines.
2. Describe a system project that might have three subsystems. Discuss how three iterations might be used for the project.
3. Why might it make sense to learn UP disciplines and activities sequentially, as in the waterfall approach, even though in practice iterations are used in nearly all development projects?
4. List some of the models that architects create to show different aspects of a house they are designing. Explain why several models are needed.
5. What models might an automotive designer use to show different aspects of a car?
6. Sketch the layout of your room at home. Now write a description of the layout of your room. Are these both models of your room? Which is more accurate? More detailed? Easier to follow for someone unfamiliar with your room?
7. Describe a "technique" you use to help you complete the activity "Get to class on time." What are some "tools" you use with the technique?
8. Describe a "technique" you use to make sure you get assignments done on time. What are some "tools" you use with the technique?
9. What are some other techniques you use to help you complete activities in your life?

EXPERIENTIAL EXERCISES

1. Go to the campus placement office and gather some information on companies that recruit information systems graduates on your campus. Try to find any information about the approach they use to develop systems. Is their SDLC described? Do they mention the UP? Do any mention a CASE tool or round-trip engineering tools? Visit the company Web sites and see whether you can find any more information.
2. Visit the Web sites for a few leading information systems consulting firms. Try to find information about the approach they use to develop systems. Are their SDLCs described? Do their sites mention any CASE tools?
3. Visit the Rational Web site (www-306.ibm.com/software/rational/) and explore what it says about the Unified Process (which it calls RUP). Find and review the site's version of the UP life cycle model. Find and review its description of the UP disciplines. Find and review its system development tools, including Rational XDE. What other types of tools are offered, and what disciplines do they support?

Case Studies

A "COLLEGE EDUCATION COMPLETION" METHODOLOGY

Like many readers of this book, you are probably a college student working on a degree. Think of completing college as a project—a big project, lasting many years and costing more than you might want to admit. Some students do a better job managing the college completion project than others. Many fail entirely (certainly not you), and most students probably complete college late and way over budget (again, certainly not you).

As with any other project, to be successful, you should follow some sort of "college education completion" methodology. That is, you should follow a comprehensive set of guidelines for completing activities and tasks from the beginning of planning for college through to the successful completion.

[1] What might be the phases of your personal college education completion life cycle?

[2] What are some of the activities of each phase?

[3] What are some techniques you use to help complete the activities? What models might you create during the process of completing college? Differentiate models you create that get you through college from those that help you plan and control the process of completing college.

[4] In what ways is college completion an iterative process? To what extent has your college "project" been predictive or adaptive?

[5] What are some of the tools you use to help you complete the models?

FACTORY SYSTEM DEVELOPMENT PROJECT

Sally Jones is assigned to manage a new system development project that will automate some of the work being done in her company's factory. It is fairly clear what the company needs: to automate the tracking of the work in progress and the finished goods inventory. What is less clear is the impact of any automated system on the factory workers. Sally has several concerns: How might a new system affect the workers? Will they need a lot of training? Will working with a new system slow down their work or interfere with the way they now work? How receptive will the workers be to the changes the new system will surely bring to the shop floor?

At the same time, Sally recognizes that the factory workers themselves might have some good ideas about what will work and what won't, especially concerning (1) which technology is more likely to survive in the factory environment and (2) what sort of user interface will work best for the workers. Sally doesn't know much about factory operations, although she does understand inventory accounting.

[1] Is the proposed system an accounting system? A factory operations system? Or both?

[2] Which approach might be more appropriate for this project, a predictive approach or an adaptive approach? Discuss.

[3] Which activities of the UP disciplines discussed in this chapter should involve factory workers and factory management?

RETHINKING ROCKY MOUNTAIN OUTFITTERS

Barbara Halifax wrote her boss that she was moving ahead with the customer support system project, using the Unified Process as the development methodology for RMO. She is still considering how to best tailor the methodology to the project. Additionally, she is still planning how to best introduce the details of the methodology to her project team. Most of the team members have had initial training on the UP, UML, and OO development, but it is still difficult to put a new methodology into practice on a real project.

Consider the nine UP disciplines as a framework for planning the detailed training that members of the project team will need. Look at the specific activities for each discipline.

[1] For each activity, list the CIS or MIS courses at your university that teach the techniques and models related to the activity. Also, for each activity, list supporting business courses at your university that cover related concepts and techniques.

[2] From your investigations, what is the body of knowledge required to fully understand and use the UP on a real project?

FOCUSING ON RELIABLE PHARMACEUTICAL SERVICE

In Chapter 1, you generated some ideas related to Reliable Pharmaceutical Service's five-year information systems plan. Management has placed a high priority on developing a Web-based application to connect client facilities with Reliable. Before the Web component can be implemented, though, Reliable must automate more of the basic information it handles about patients, health-care facilities, and prescriptions.

Next, Reliable must develop an initial informational Web site, which will ultimately evolve into an extranet through which Reliable will share information and link its processes closely with its clients and suppliers. One significant requirement of the extranet is compliance with the Health Insurance Portability and Accountability Act of 1996, better known as HIPAA. HIPAA requires health-care providers and their contractors to protect patient data from unauthorized disclosure. Ensuring compliance with HIPAA will require careful attention to extranet security.

Once basic processes are automated and the extranet Web site is in place, the system will enable clients to add patient information and place orders through the Web. The system should streamline processes for both Reliable and its clients. It should also provide useful query and patient management capabilities to distinguish Reliable's services from those of its competitors, possibly including drug interaction and overdose warnings, automated validation of prescriptions with insurance reimbursement policies, and drug and patient cost data and summaries.

[1] One approach to system development that Reliable might take is to start one large project that uses a predictive approach to the SDLC, to thoroughly plan the project, analyze all requirements in detail, design every component, and then implement the entire system, with all phases completed sequentially. What are some of the risks of taking this approach? What planning and management difficulties would this approach entail?

[2] Another approach to system development might be to start with the first required component and get it working. Later, other projects could be undertaken to work on the other identified capabilities. What are some of the risks of taking this approach? What planning and management difficulties would this approach entail?

[3] A third approach to system development might be to define one large project that will use an adaptive and iterative approach to the SDLC, such as the Unified Process. Briefly describe what you would include in each iteration. Describe how incremental development might apply to this project. How would an iterative approach decrease project risks compared with the first approach? How might it decrease risks compared with the second approach? What are some risks the iterative approach might add to the project?

FURTHER RESOURCES

Scott W. Ambler, *Agile Modeling: Effective Practices for Extreme Programming and the Unified Process.* Wiley Computer Publishing, 2002.

D. E. Avison and G. Fitzgerald, *Information Systems Development: Methodologies, Techniques and Tools* (2nd ed.). McGraw-Hill, 1995.

Kent Beck, *Extreme Programming Explained: Embrace Change*. Addison-Wesley Publishing Company, 2000.

Ivar Jacobson, Grady Booch, and James Rumbaugh, *The Rational Unified Process*. Addison-Wesley, 1999.

Craig Larman,. *Applying UML and Patterns: An Introduction to Object-Oriented Analysis and Designs* (2nd ed.). Prentice-Hall, 2002.

John Satzinger and Tore Orvik, *The Object-Oriented Approach: Concepts, System Development, and Modeling with UML* (2nd ed.). Course Technology, 2001.

chapter 3

PROJECT MANAGEMENT AND THE INCEPTION PHASE

LEARNING OBJECTIVES

After reading the chapter, you should be able to:

- Explain the elements of project management and the responsibilities of a project manager
- Describe how the UP disciplines of business modeling and environment relate to the inception phase
- Describe the project management activities that are done during the inception phase
- Develop a project schedule using a work breakdown structure (WBS) and PERT and Gantt charts
- Use Microsoft Project to build the project schedule
- Perform a risk analysis of potential project risks
- Develop a cost/benefit analysis using net present value calculations
- List the key deliverables and activities of the end of the inception phase
- Discuss three techniques for monitoring and controlling a system development project

CHAPTER OUTLINE

- Project Management
- The Unified Process and the Inception Phase
- Completing the Inception Phase
- Project Monitoring and Control

BLUE SKY MUTUAL FUNDS: A NEW DEVELOPMENT APPROACH

"There are some things I like about this new approach, but other things worry me." Jim Williams, vice president of finance for Blue Sky Mutual Funds, was speaking to Gary Johnson, director of information technology.

"This idea of 'growing' the system through several iterations makes a lot of sense to me. It is always hard for my people to know exactly what they need a new information system to do and what will work best for the company. So if they can get their hands on the system early, they can begin acceptance testing and trying it out to see whether it addresses their needs in the best way. Let me see if I understand the big picture, though. Your development team and my investment advisors decide on a few core processes that the system needs to support, and then your team designs and builds a system to support those core business processes. You do that in a miniproject of about six weeks. Then you continue adding more functionality via several miniprojects until the system is complete and functioning well. Is that right?" Jim was becoming more enthusiastic about this new approach to system development.

Gary answered, "Yes, that is the basic idea. We call this approach the 'Unified Process for system development.' It consists of several different iterations, which you have called miniprojects. For the first few iterations, we make sure we understand your users' needs and the business processes that the system must support. Then for the last few iterations, we make the system robust and complete—with all the service functions, such as security support and high-volume capability. Your users need to understand that the first few versions of the system are not complete and may not be completely robust. But the early versions will give them something to work with and try out. We also need good feedback from their acceptance testing so that the system will be thoroughly tested by the time we are through."

"Right. I think I understand. I know my people will like not having to think about everything they need at the beginning, without trying something out. As I said earlier, I like this approach. However, the part I don't like is that you say it is harder to give me a firm time schedule and project cost. That is the part that worries me. In the past, two of the major tools we have used to monitor a project's progress have been the schedule and the budget. Do you mean that now we won't have a schedule and you want an open budget?" Jim began to frown.

Gary responded, "It's not as bad as it first sounds. This approach to system development is referred to as an 'adaptive' approach. By that we mean that, since the system is growing, the project is also somewhat more open-ended. The project manager will still build a schedule and estimate the project costs, but since the system is growing, she normally will not try to identify and freeze all the required functionality for several iterations. Since the scope of the system is continually being refined over the first few iterations, we do have the risk of 'scope creep.' That is one of the biggest risks with adaptive approaches to development. You and I should meet with the project manager fairly frequently to ensure that the scope is controlled and the project does not get out of control. The positive side is that, since we are building the most important things first, and because we have a new version every month or so, we can stop adding functionality at the end of any iteration. After that, the project should need only two or three more iterations to finish and put the system into production."

"Okay. You have convinced me to try this new approach. However, let's treat this project as a pilot and see how it works. If it is successful, then we will consider using the UP on our other projects." Jim and Gary agreed that a pilot was the best way to get started. Gary then headed off to meet with the project manager and get the project started.

Overview

In Chapter 2 you learned about the Unified Process (UP) as an adaptive system development methodology. In this chapter, we delve deeper into the UP, showing how to use it in the context of a real development project. The UP is a development methodology composed of phases and disciplines. These phases and disciplines become the framework around which a company can define and execute a project. So we identify and describe the details of how the UP can be applied to a specific project.

The first section of this chapter introduces and explains general project management concepts. Project management is a support discipline in the UP, but one that is critical to system development. More and more system developers are finding that project management skills are essential for success in their careers as members of an IT organization. Project management is a broad subject with an extensive body of knowledge. In this chapter we introduce the most important project management concepts to provide you with a solid foundation. The first section starts by establishing the context of projects and project management. It next explores reasons why some software development projects are successful and others are not. Good project managers have a set of skills that enable them to lead and manage complicated projects. So we identify and discuss those skills next. The section concludes with a brief discussion of the principal project management knowledge areas. Since each project management area is extensive, we have provided additional materials on the book's Web site for those wanting more in-depth coverage. We suggest you review that material to deepen your understanding of project management issues and skills.

The second major section of the chapter explores how UP projects are conducted and how project management skills apply to a development project using the UP. As with all projects, a lot of project planning is conducted at the beginning of a development project. In the UP, much of that is done during the inception phase. We look carefully at the inception phase of a project and study the detailed project management activities that must be done. The objective of this part of the chapter is for you to understand all the project management tasks that are done during inception.

The chapter closes with a short section on the project management issues related to monitoring and controlling projects. Also, throughout the book, we raise project management issues as they apply to a specific chapter's topics. Here, we provide an overview of monitoring and controlling to introduce the concept.

PROJECT MANAGEMENT

Chapter 2 identified project management as one of the most important support disciplines of the UP. In this chapter, we look first at project management in a broader context—as a requirement for managing all types of projects.

The development of a new software system, the enhancement or upgrade of an existing system, or even the integration and deployment of a software package into an existing environment are all brought about during a development project. As we discussed in Chapter 1, a *project* is a planned undertaking with a beginning and an end that produces a predetermined result or product and is usually constrained by a schedule and resources. This definition is quite broad and, in fact, fits many different activities within and outside a business context. Information systems projects are usually quite complex endeavors with many people and tasks that all must be organized and coordinated. Whatever its objective, each project is unique; no two are exactly alike. Different products are produced, different activities are required for varying schedules, and different resources are used. This fact is one reason that projects are so difficult to control—each involves new activities that have never been done exactly the same way before.

PROJECT SUCCESS FACTORS

System development projects are projects whose end result is the deployment of a new computer software system. Projects can range from the deployment of a simple Web site to the implementation of a high-volume, real-time, interactive business application with massive amounts of data. The inherent complexities of computer systems make development projects very difficult. The combination of sophisticated business needs and changing technology, along with the need to integrate operating systems, support programs, and new systems, results in a process that is extremely difficult to understand, control, and manage. Developing technology solutions is much more than sitting down and writing new computer code.

Historically, the success rate of system development projects has not been very good. The dubious success rate spurred research into the underlying causes for success and failure. In 1994, the Standish Group began studying system development projects and found that nearly 32 percent of all development projects were canceled before they were completed. In addition, more than half of computer system projects cost almost double the original budget. Less than half (about 42 percent) had the same scope and functionality as originally proposed. In fact, many systems were implemented with only a portion of the original requirements satisfied. Depending on company size, completely successful projects (on time, on budget, with full functionality) ranged from only 9 percent to about 16 percent. As of 2000, the percentage of successful system development projects was still a dismal 28 percent, with 72 percent canceled or completed late, over budget, or with limited functionality. Clearly, system development is a difficult activity requiring very careful planning, control, and execution.

The reasons that projects do not fulfill desired objectives vary. Research done by the Standish Group has discovered that projects fail, or are only partially successful, due to the following reasons:

- Incomplete or changing system requirements
- Limited user involvement
- Lack of executive support
- Lack of technical support
- Poor project planning
- Unclear objectives
- Lack of required resources

Other studies of successful projects help to highlight the reasons that projects succeed. Some reasons for success are the following:

- Clear system requirement definitions
- Substantial user involvement
- Support from upper management
- Thorough and detailed project plans
- Realistic work schedules and milestones

The success factors are, in most cases, just the reverse of those for failures. Note that reasons such as "the technology is too complex" do not appear in the failure list. What this omission indicates is that projects fail most frequently because project management has failed. Successful projects result from strong project management that ensures that the necessary elements are part of the project.

The obvious question then is, "How can we improve the project success rate?" The companies that have better success rates have attacked the problem from three different perspectives. First, they incorporate good principles of project management into their projects. They identify best practices in project management, and they train their project managers on those principles. In this chapter, and throughout the book, you will learn many principles of good project management. Second, they adopt a standard development methodology. In many cases, the development methodology they use is an adaptation of a standard methodology. Current trends indicate that iterative, evolutionary approaches help to improve project success. Chapter 2 introduced you to various development methodologies and indicated that newer adaptive approaches seemed to increase success. One of the primary benefits that you will gain from this book and your course is an understanding of how the Unified Process works and how it is applied in system development. Third, successful companies pay particular attention to the factors that influence project success. The organization becomes focused on instituting characteristics of successful projects, and all team members and stakeholders work to incorporate best practices.

THE ROLE OF THE PROJECT MANAGER

project management organizing and directing other people to achieve a planned result within a predetermined schedule and budget

Project management is organizing and directing other people to achieve a planned result within a predetermined schedule and budget. At the beginning of a project, a detailed plan is developed to specify the activities that must take place, the deliverables that must be produced, and the resources that are needed. So, project management can also be defined as the set of processes used to plan the project and then to monitor and control it.

The project manager is the most important element in the definition and execution of project management tasks. The success, or failure, of a given project is directly related to the skills and abilities of the project manager. The project success factors identified earlier are, for the most part, under the control of the project manager, and he or she must ensure that sufficient attention is given to those project details. A project manager has both internal and external responsibilities.

From the internal perspective, the project manager serves as the director and locus of control for the project team and all of the project activities. The project manager establishes the team infrastructure so that the work of the project can be accomplished. The following list identifies a few of these responsibilities:

- Identify project tasks and build a work breakdown structure
- Develop the project schedule
- Recruit and train team members
- Assign team members to tasks
- Coordinate activities of team members and subteams
- Assess project risks
- Monitor and control project deliverables and milestones
- Verify the quality of project deliverables

From an external perspective, the project manager is the focal point or main contact for the project. He or she must represent the needs of the project and the team to the outside world. Some of the major external responsibilities include:

- Report project status and progress
- Establish the working relationships with those providing the system requirements (i.e., the users)
- Work with the client (the project's sponsor) and other stakeholders
- Identify resource needs and obtain resources

Obviously, the project manager does not always perform all the tasks to carry out these responsibilities. Other team members assist the manager. However, the primary responsibility for the project rests with the project manager.

In looking at businesses and organizations around the world and the way that projects are handled, we see that the role of the project manager and careers in project management vary tremendously. Figure 3-1 illustrates some of the different positions project managers hold. In some companies, the role of project manager is that of a coordinator without direct "line" (reporting) authority. At the other end of the spectrum, where IT projects can be big, the project manager may be a very experienced developer with both management skills and a solid understanding of the range of technical issues. In those situations, the role of the project manager is very much a "line" position with appropriate responsibility and authority.

Many career paths lead to project management. In some companies, the project coordination role is done by recent college graduates. Other companies recognize the value of a person with very strong organizational and people skills, who understands the technology but does not want a highly technical career. Those companies provide

TITLE	POWER/ AUTHORITY	ORGANIZATION STRUCTURE	DESCRIPTION OF DUTIES
Project coordinator or project leader	Limited	Projects may be run within departments, or projects may have a strong "lead developer" that controls the development of the end product.	Develops the plans. Coordinates activities. Keeps people informed of status and progress. Does not have "line" authority on the product deliverables.
Project manager, project officer, or team leader	Moderate	Projects are run within an IT department, but other business functions are independent.	May have both project management duties and some technical duties. Projects are generally medium sized. Clients may share in project responsibility.
Project manager or program manager	High to almost total	Project organization is a prime, high-profile part of the company. Company is organized around projects, or there is a large and powerful IT department.	Usually has extensive experience in technical issues as well as project management. Involved in both management decisions and technical issues. Frequently has support staff to do paperwork. Projects can be big.

FIGURE 3-1
Various roles of project managers

opportunities for employees to gain experience on projects, but primarily from the management and business skills perspective. In these companies, the career path to project management is primarily through experience as a project coordinator managing smaller projects. Other companies take a "lead engineer" approach to project management, in which a person must thoroughly understand the technology to manage a project. These companies believe that project management requires someone with strong development skills to understand the technical issues and to manage other developers.

Chapter 1 identified several different types of skills that are important for a systems developer. Included in the list are technical knowledge and skills, business knowledge and skills, and people knowledge and skills. But all system developers must also have project management knowledge and skills, for two reasons. First, even though each project has a designated project manager, all team members help develop project management tasks, such as developing the project schedule. Every member of a project team contributes to planning, organizing, and controlling the work of the team. Second, many system developers eventually want to progress in their career by taking on more project management responsibilities. Learning and applying good principles of project management to your own work, to the work of a small team, and eventually to an entire project can help you advance. Developing good project management skills does not happen by accident, however. It requires you to focus on the important skills and make a conscientious effort to understand and learn them.

We turn now to a description of nine critical knowledge areas of project management. These nine areas provide, in effect, a checklist of topics that a project manager should include in her planning as she leads a project.

PROJECT MANAGEMENT KNOWLEDGE AREAS

The Project Management Institute (PMI) is a professional organization that promotes project management, primarily within the United States but also throughout the world. In addition, professional organizations in other countries promote project management. If you are interested in strengthening your project management skills, then you should consider joining one of these organizations, obtaining their materials and participating in training. The PMI has a well-respected and rigorous certification program. In fact, many corporations today encourage project managers to become certified, and industry articles frequently indicate that project management is one of the most important skills required in IT today.

As part of its mission, the PMI has defined a body of knowledge (BOK) for project management. This body of knowledge, referred to as the PMBOK, is a widely accepted foundation of information that every project manager should know. The PMBOK has been organized into nine different knowledge areas. Although these nine areas do not represent all there is to know about project management, they provide an excellent foundation.

- **Project Scope Management.** Defining and controlling the functions that are to be included in the system as well as the scope of the work to be done by the project team
- **Project Time Management.** Building a detailed schedule of all project tasks and then monitoring the progress of the project against defined milestones
- **Project Cost Management.** Calculating the initial cost/benefit analysis and its later updates and monitoring expenditures as the project progresses
- **Project Quality Management.** Establishing a total plan for ensuring quality, which includes quality control activities for every phase of the project
- **Project Human Resources Management.** Recruiting and hiring project team members; training, motivating, and team building; and implementing related activities to ensure a happy, productive team
- **Project Communications Management.** Identifying all stakeholders and the key communications to each; also establishing all communications mechanisms and schedules
- **Project Risk Management.** Identifying and reviewing throughout the project all potential risks for failure and developing plans to reduce these risks
- **Project Procurement Management.** Developing requests for proposals, evaluating bids, writing contracts, and then monitoring vendor performance
- **Project Integration Management.** Integrating all the other knowledge areas into one seamless whole.

Additional details of each of these knowledge areas are provided in Appendix A on the book's Web site. Other textbooks that focus exclusively on project management, several of which are listed in the references at the end of the chapter, also provide in-depth discussion and specific techniques that apply to each knowledge area. As we move through various iterations of the UP, we will also indicate how to apply the principles of the various knowledge areas to the activities associated with that iteration.

As you progress in your career, you would be wise to keep a record of project management skills you observe in others, as well as those you learn by your own experience. One place to start is with the set of skills for a systems analyst described in Chapter 1. However, good project management requires more than just those skills. A good project manager knows how to develop a plan, execute it, anticipate problems, and make adjustments for variances. Project management skills *can* be learned. Those who aspire to managing projects are proactive in self-improvement and learn the necessary skills. Build on what you learn in this textbook and continue to practice and hone your project management skills.

Next we discuss the ways project management skills relate to the Unified Process in general and the inception phase in particular.

PROJECT MANAGEMENT WITHIN THE UNIFIED PROCESS

Project management is also an integral part of the Unified Process. One of the support business disciplines defined for the UP is project management. We hope you recognize from the previous discussion that project management is, in fact, the most important business discipline for successful UP projects. Figure 3-2, which is similar to Figure 2-14, depicts the UP phases and business disciplines. In this figure, a project with a single inception phase iteration is illustrated. As indicated by the area under the project management curve, a large amount of effort is expended in project management tasks during the inception phase. At the beginning of a project, a lot of project definition and planning must always be done. Hence, major project management effort is required to get a project started. In the iterations immediately following inception, additional project management tasks are necessary to refine and solidify the project plans.

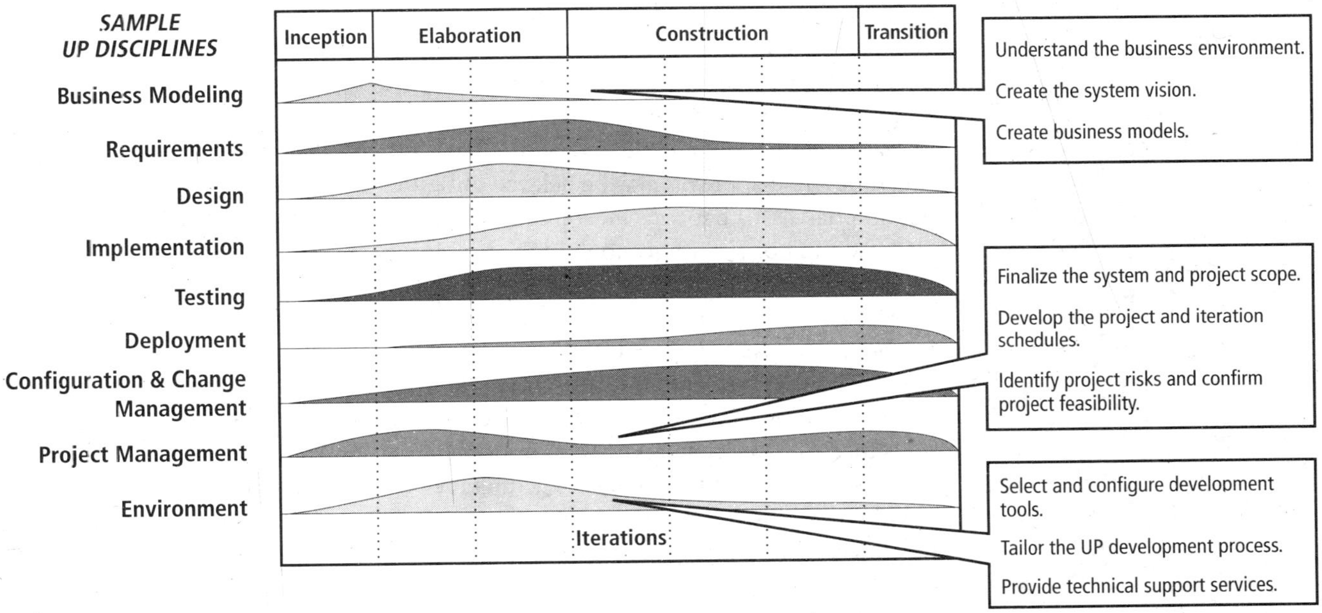

FIGURE 3-2
UP phases and iterations with business disciplines

Our definition of a project—with a beginning and end and with a schedule to produce a deliverable—applies not only to the overall development effort but also to individual iterations. Each iteration is, in essence, a miniproject with a beginning, an end, a schedule, and a deliverable. In many cases, the deliverable will be an ever-growing set of functions within the new system. One way of thinking about the UP's iterative approach to development is that the system evolves and grows with each iteration.

Referring back to Figure 3-2, you will notice that two other disciplines have heavy involvement during the inception phase: business modeling and environment. Additional disciplines, such as requirements and design, may also begin during the inception phase. In the next section, we will discuss in detail the three business disciplines of business modeling, environment, and project management. Since so much of the project management activities depend heavily on understanding the business and environment, we discuss those first. We conclude with a detailed discussion of project management tasks during inception.

Requirements definition also begins during the inception phase. However, it also extends heavily throughout the elaboration phase and includes substantial technical details about model building. Hence, we defer the discussion of the requirements discipline until Chapters 4, 5, and beyond. You should remember, however, that frequently some requirements tasks also begin during the inception phase.

THE UNIFIED PROCESS AND THE INCEPTION PHASE

The inception phase of the UP has the following objectives:

- Identify the business need for the project
- Establish the vision for the solution
- Identify the scope of the new system and the project
- Develop preliminary schedules and cost estimates
- Develop the business case for the project

The end result of this phase is to have a set of documents that establish the vision, scope, business case, schedule, and direction for the rest of the project. For many projects a single iteration can complete the inception phase. For large projects, two iterations may be required. Typically, final project approval occurs at the end of the inception phase. In other instances, the project may already be approved based on preliminary information, and the inception phase finalizes the plans and scope. However, sometimes final approval may be delayed until the first or second iteration of the elaboration phase. This happens most frequently when the system being implemented is very new and not well understood in the beginning.

Because every project is unique, every inception iteration is unique. Some inception iterations are very formal, with rigorous requirements for documentation, approval, cost/benefit analysis, and so forth. Others are quite informal, with approval requiring no more than a "yes, let's do it" from a key sponsor. In this chapter we present a project midway between those two extremes—one that is not highly structured but is more rigorous than one that requires only an informal approval. First, we briefly introduce business modeling in the context of getting the project approved. Later, we discuss a typical set of activities that would be appropriate for the environment discipline and the project management discipline.

BUSINESS MODELING AND THE INCEPTION PHASE

The primary purpose of the business modeling discipline is to ensure that the system developers thoroughly understand the needs of the business and that the solution system will, in fact, address the correct issues of the business. The business modeling discipline is tightly integrated with requirements definition, and in some versions of the UP, it is integrated with and part of requirements. However, it is so critically important for system developers to take the time and expend the effort necessary to have a deep understanding of the business that we choose to maintain it as a separate discipline in the UP. The requirements discipline is discussed in depth in the following chapters (Chapter 4, 5, and 6), and even though business modeling is not discussed, you should remember that it is an important aspect of requirements definition.

So what is meant by business modeling? Business modeling includes all the activities that help the system developer understand the business environment that the new system will support. It includes tasks to understand the business strategy, the competitive market, the business processes, the particular business need that must be addressed, the desires of the system users and other interested stakeholders, and so forth.

Business modeling may be done informally, with simple descriptions of the business. Alternatively, a more formal approach may be used with diagrams and charts of business processes, workflows, and the operating environment.

Business modeling begins in the inception phase. As you saw in Figure 2-14, business modeling activities are heaviest in the first few iterations of the UP. During the inception phase, it is most important that a clear vision of the new system and the overall scope be defined. The following activities, as listed in Chapter 2, are business modeling activities used routinely during inception.

- Understand the business environment
  - Describe the problem or need
  - Consider needed interfaces to other systems
  - Evaluate existing architecture and system constraints or standards
  - Analyze the various system stakeholders
- Create the system vision
  - Generate a list of primary business benefits
  - Create a list of system objectives
  - Develop a list of system capabilities
- Create business models
  - Identify business events
  - Model business processes and workflows
  - Define information and data flow models

UNDERSTANDING THE BUSINESS ENVIRONMENT

The object of this activity is to understand the context in which a project must operate. One of the first documents the team produces is a statement of the business problem that needs to be solved, because the reason for a project is to provide a solution to a business problem. If that is not clear from the start, a wrong solution might be provided. Figure 3-3 illustrates a narrative description of the business problem for the Rocky Mountain Outfitters (RMO) customer support system done by Barbara Halifax's team. Note that it provides enough background information so that someone who is not familiar with the business situation will understand why this project is important.

The next two parts of understanding the business environment—considering needed interfaces to other systems and evaluating existing architecture—are technical issues that determine constraints for the proposed system. In most cases a new system will be part of an integrated processing environment. Frequently, it will have to accept input data from and provide outputs to existing systems. Although the details of how all that works can be left to a later, more detailed iteration, it is a good practice to note that such interfaces are needed and to identify what they are.

The new system also is part of a complete IT environment that supports the entire organization. In some situations, a new environment will be developed for the new system. Usually, however, the new system must fit within the existing environment and be consistent with the strategic architectural plan. In some cases the organization may have a combination of environments, such as both Novell and Windows network operating systems and possibly Apache (Java) and Microsoft Internet servers. The project team must assess the complexity of the target deployment environment and make some preliminary decisions. More details about the various alternatives for deploying systems are provided in Chapter 13. During project inception, these preliminary decisions and any constraints should be noted and documented as part of the project's charter.

Customer Support System: Background and Problem Definition

Catalog sales began as a small experiment that soon developed into a rapidly growing division of the company. At first, sales started out slowly. However, during the two-year period from 2002 through 2003, volumes increased rapidly. The sales environment around the world was changing, with more and more people using the Internet to find and purchase items. Over that period, we added more and more items to the online catalog. By 2004, every item in the RMO line of goods could be purchased through brick-and-mortar stores, catalog telephone orders, or Internet online purchases. Support was initially provided by manual procedures, with some simple off-the-shelf programs to assist in order taking and fulfillment. During 2003, as volumes increased, more and more support was required to keep the system operational.

At the end of 2003, a major IT strategic initiative began. As a result of this effort, two major system development projects were begun. The objective of the first system was to support back-office processes such as inventory purchasing and control. This system, called the Supply Chain Management System (SCM), began early in 2004 and appears to be progressing on schedule.

The objective of the second major system is to integrate all front-office sales and customer-related activities. Currently, the company has three separate sales systems; they are not integrated. The three systems are the retail store system, the catalog sales system, and an Internet portal and Web-based system. Temporary programs have been developed in each of these three systems to access inventory information from the new SCM system and to feed sales information to the SCM system. However, there is no integrated database of sales figures. Other temporary programs have been written to produce combined sales activity and to feed information to the accounting systems. There are no systems in place that give current, accurate information about what products are selling most rapidly. There are no historical data that can be used to forecast future trends or needs. There is no way to analyze purchasing patterns or to do promotions of specific items to targeted customers.

There is a need for a comprehensive sales and customer support system to provide integrated support for all sales channels. To operate at high levels of efficiency and to take advantage of market opportunities, the company needs a new comprehensive system that is tightly integrated with the SCM system. This new system will be called the customer support system (CSS).

FIGURE 3-3
Sample statement of business need for the RMO customer support system

The other major task in this activity is to perform a stakeholder analysis. Stakeholders are the people who have some interest in the development of the new system. For most projects three categories of stakeholders should be considered:

- Users: Both internal and external
- Sponsors: The clients who oversee and approve the project
- Support staff: Technical staff

internal users
people inside the company who will use the system to do their work

external users
people outside the company who use the system, such as Internet customers or approved suppliers

Users are the people who will actually be using the system to do their work. *Internal users* are employees inside the company. There are several different kinds of internal users. Some need access to all system functions to perform the various business processes. Others, especially middle and upper managers, may only use the system to gather general information or to receive reports from it. In addition to the internal users, systems also have *external users*, people outside the organization who access the system. For example, if a system supports Internet e-commerce activities, then online shoppers will be using the system. Trusted suppliers may also have access. To ensure that a system meets an organization's needs, developers must include external users in the requirements definition. It is sometimes hard to involve external users in the requirements definition for the new system, but the new system must be user-friendly to these critical users. So, the project team needs to be sure to involve some representatives of this class of users.

sponsor
a person or group who has authorized and funded a development project, also called a *client*

The *sponsor* of a project is a person or group who has authorized the project and funded it, also called a project's *client*. You will remember from the earlier discussion of project success factors that one of the criteria for a successful project is to have the support of upper management. It is critical that the project team understand the desires and needs of the project sponsor.

The support staff includes the people who will have responsibility for the system after it goes into operation—in other words, the system support people such as network and operating environment technicians and other operations staff. Their input during the project definition activities will make sure that the system can be deployed effectively on the organization's existing computers and networks.

A stakeholder analysis consists of identifying all of the stakeholders who have an interest in the system, and determining each one's interest level, the information they need to provide during the project, and the information that should be provided back to them.

THE STAKEHOLDERS FOR ROCKY MOUNTAIN OUTFITTERS

An important part of investigating system requirements is to identify all of the stakeholders. The set of requirements is incomplete if users (internal and external), sponsors, or important technical staff are not consulted as information is being gathered.

The project sponsor is one of the most critical people to identify, and developers need to ensure that he or she is committed to the project. As discussed earlier, one of the most important factors for project success is a strong, committed project sponsor. In RMO's case, there is a strong project sponsor—the vice president of marketing and sales, William McDougal. More than anybody else in the company, he needs the new customer support system (CSS) to accomplish his strategic goals for the company. Other executive stakeholders in the company are John and Liz Blankens. As owners, they have a special interest in the success of this project. However, front-line sponsorship rests in Mr. McDougal.

At RMO, operational users of the new order-processing system include inside sales representatives who take orders over the phone and clerks who process mail orders. They all have different views about what the system should do for them. Sales representatives talk about looking up product information for customers and confirming availability and shipping dates. Mail-order clerks talk about scanning order information into the system to eliminate typing. The warehouse workers who put the shipments together need information about orders that have been shipped, orders to be shipped, and back orders, as well as their normal operational screens that allow them to put orders together into shipments with printed bills of lading.

Other executives of the company are also interested in various reports and information that they can extract from the system. Finally, since this system will involve new technology—the Internet and distributed systems—very heavy involvement is required by the technical staff. Consequently, many stakeholders will have input into the types of information that can be extracted from the system.

Figure 3-4 illustrates, from the upper-level RMO organization chart, people who will be involved. The orange positions indicate the executives and middle managers who will be involved as stakeholders. The project manager will build a list of all users who need to be involved in requirements definition. This organization chart is just the beginning. Other department managers and key employees will also be added.

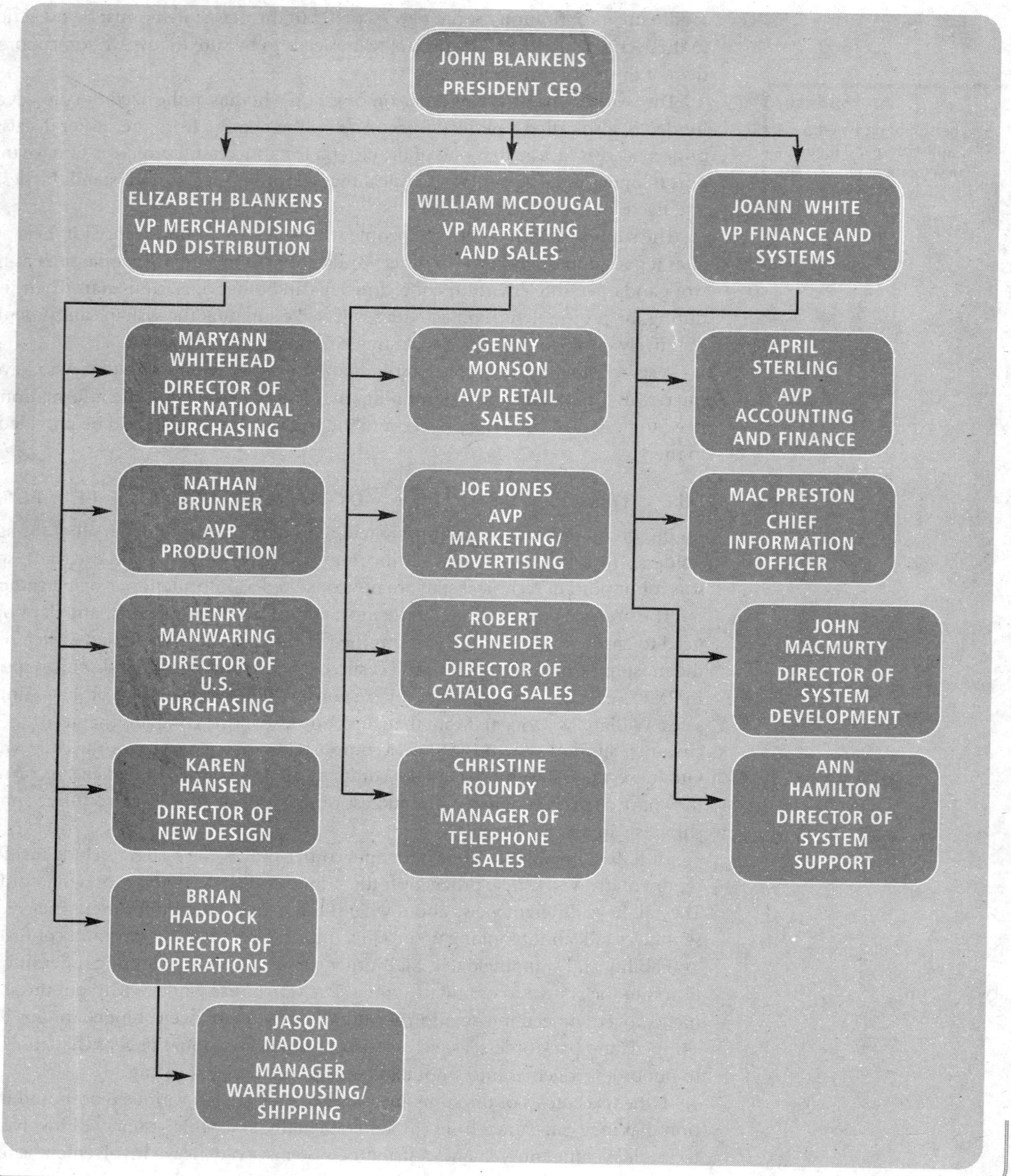

FIGURE 3-4
RMO stakeholders—sponsor and users

A detailed understanding of the needs of each of these stakeholders can be developed using a stakeholder analysis form. Figure 3-5 is a partially completed stakeholder analysis form that illustrates each stakeholder, types of information and level of interest for each, and any special information needs.

Stakeholder Category	*Stakeholder Name*	*Project Role*	*Schedule Focus*	*Cost Focus*	*Product Focus*	*Reporting Frequency*	*Special Information Needs*
Executive	John Blankens		High	Medium	Low	Monthly	
	Elizabeth Blankens	Steering Committee	High	High	Medium	Monthly	
Sponsor	William McDougal	Steering Committee	High	High	High	Biweekly	Progress Report
Middle management	Genny Monson	Requirements Definition	Medium	Low	High	Monthly	
	Joe Jones	Requirements Definition	Low	Low	High	Monthly	
	Robert Schneider	Requirements Definition	Medium	Low	High	Monthly	
	Christine Roundy	Requirements Definition	Medium	Low	High	Monthly	
	Mac Preston	Steering Committee	Medium	Medium	Low	Monthly	
Technical support groups	Ann Hamilton	Steering Committee	Medium	Low	Low		
Business users	Brian Haddock	Requirements Definition	Low	Low	High		
	Jason Nadold	Requirements Definition	Low	Low	High		
External stakeholders	? to be found						

FIGURE 3-5
Sample stakeholder analysis form for RMO

At this point, it is better to err on the side of including too many stakeholders than to miss important sources of requirements. One of the key problems in the CSS project is how to involve external users. Barbara Halifax sent John MacMurty a memo updating him on her progress in identifying the CSS stakeholders and her upcoming plans for gathering information (see Barbara's memo on page 92).

CREATING THE SYSTEM VISION

The purpose of creating a system vision is to ensure that there is a clear understanding of how a development project and the new system contribute to the strategic direction of the organization. One of the key success factors of system projects is that there be a clear vision. Everyone needs to understand why the project has been initiated and what contribution it is expected to make to the organization. So, not only is it important to have a clear vision, that vision must be communicated to the team and to other stakeholders.

Now that the project manager and team have defined and documented the business need or problem, the next step is to describe how the project and the new system will solve that business need. Usually the major objectives of the project can be identified with a few bullet points.

business benefits
improvements or benefits that will accrue to the company as a result of the project and its deliverables

One of the first steps in this process is to make a list of the business benefits. *Business benefits* are the improvements or benefits that will accrue to the company as a result of the project and its deliverables. The project manager should remember two key points when identifying business benefits. First, the benefits directly affect the sponsor, not the development team. So, a team should not try to invent benefits or

ROCKY MOUNTAIN OUTFITTERS

MEMO

March 10, 2006

To: John MacMurty

From: Barbara Halifax

RE: Customer Support System Update

As we begin the fact-finding activities of the project, I wanted to let you know where we are in the development of an interview schedule and questions. As you can see from the attached organization chart, we have identified the senior managers who should be included in our fact-finding interviews. Please let me know if we have missed anybody who should be included.

We have also worked with the department managers to put together a list of people who will be interviewed in each of the various departments. In some departments, the manager wanted us to have group interviews and have several users participate using a more collaborative workgroup style. I think this will work well because it will help us get final decisions quickly.

We do have one major question, however. How do we identify external users, such as Web customers, and how do we get them involved? Do you think RMO would be willing to provide some incentive to a couple of customers to help out—maybe a $100 shopping spree or something?

Finally, you should know that we have already collected copies of all the existing forms and reports. We used the existing documents to help us in developing a set of questions to help us get started. Since we want to encourage the users to "think outside the box," we will probably not use the forms in the interviews but only as a source for ideas and questions.

BH

cc: Steven Deerfield, Ming Lee

persuade the client of what they are. Instead, the team should work with the client to help identify benefits, but they should ultimately be identified by the project's sponsor. The second issue is that these benefits should be concrete—related to a dollar value for the organization. For example, the new system may permit a new product to be sold or a new market to be opened up.

Once the sponsor and the team have identified the business benefits, the project team needs to analyze those benefits and determine the major objectives of the system—its components. We call this the list of *system capabilities*, a fairly short, high-level list of functions that the system must have, to achieve the objectives of the project and produce the defined business benefits. System capabilities are defined in terms of what the system will do or have. For example, the system may need to support a comprehensive purchasing history for each customer to support target marketing activities. Defining these system capabilities will help establish the scope of the project and lay the foundation for later development of the project plan.

system capabilities
a fairly short, high-level list of functions that the system must contain to achieve the objectives of the project and produce the defined business benefits

Figure 3-6 is a sample document for the RMO customer support system, which lists its objectives, business benefits, and system capabilities. Other documents, such as the

System Objective

The objective of the new customer support system (CSS) is to provide a complete, comprehensive, integrated, high-volume "front-end" sales and customer support system.

Business Benefits

The primary business benefit to be obtained from the new system is for RMO to maintain its leadership position in the sportswear industry. More immediate benefits will:

- Reduce errors caused by manual processing of orders
- Expedite order fulfillment due to more rapid order processing
- Maintain or reduce staffing levels in mail-order and phone-order processing
- Dramatically increase Internet sales through a highly interactive Web site
- Increase inventory turnover by tracking sales of popular items and slow movers
- Increase level of customer loyalty through extensive customer support and information
- Increase efficiencies in inventory and supply chain management

System Capabilities

To obtain the business benefits listed, the customer support system shall include the following capabilities:

- Be a high-support system with online customer, order, back order, and returns information
- Support traditional telephone and mail catalog sales with rapid-entry screens
- Include Internet customer and catalog sale capability, including purchase and order tracking
- Support and integrate with store "brick-and-mortar" sales
- Maintain adequate database and history information to support market analysis
- Provide a history of customer transactions for customer query
- Be able to handle substantial increases in volume (300 percent or more) without degradation
- Support 24-hour shipment of new orders
- Coordinate order shipment from multiple warehouses
- Maintain sales history to support analysis of sales and forecasting of market demand
- Integrate with the supply chain management system to tightly control inventory purchases and stocking

FIGURE 3-6
Objectives, business benefits, and system capabilities of the RMO customer support system

project charter
a set of documents that define the need, objective, benefits, and scope of the new system

statement of business need and stakeholder analysis form, are attached to this form to provide a complete package that will serve as a project charter. The *project charter* is a set of documents that define the need, objective, benefits, and scope of the new system.

In Figure 3-6, the objective statement is a brief statement of what is required to satisfy or resolve the business need. Its purpose is to help provide an overall vision of what needs to be done. The next component, the business benefits, describes in more detail the benefits that the company expects to derive from the successful deployment of the system. The items listed in the business benefits always have an implied dollar benefit. It should be clear to someone reading them that there is a direct benefit to the bottom line of the organization. The system capabilities, on the other hand, are expressed as functions that the system will perform. In some instances there may be a one-to-one correspondence between a business benefit and a system capability. This list should not be too detailed. Its purpose is to provide an overall vision of the new system and its functionality.

CREATING BUSINESS MODELS

As indicated earlier, creating the business models is closely tied with defining the system requirements. A more detailed description of model building, and of the way to build different types of models, is provided in the chapters immediately following. The format and rigor of the models will vary from project to project. Smaller projects tend to use less formal techniques. Remember that business modeling is not an end in itself. We follow the UP guidelines provided in Chapter 2 to build only the models that are useful and necessary and that provide information for later deliverables. But the design of a system depends on the business process it supports, so it makes sense to understand that process and to document it in some form. Most businesses and systems are so complex that it is unreasonable to expect the developers to remember all the details of all the business processes in their heads.

Many different areas of the business must be understood and modeled to develop a comprehensive solution system. Each project is different, and the areas that need clarification change depending on the situation. However, three major areas normally require business models: business events, business processes, and information repositories and flows.

The first area, business events, describes all of the things that are necessary to carry out the objectives of the business. As you will see in later chapters, such models as the event table and use case diagrams are effective models that help you understand and describe business events.

The second area, business processes, describes the detailed steps that are carried out by the employees of the company. Sometimes these workflows can get very detailed and complex. Analysts need to take care that describing the processes does not become an end in itself. The focus of documenting the processes should be limited to only those steps that affect the system support.

Finally, since almost every business information system is a repository for information about the business and its operations, another model describes the information in the organization. This includes both permanently stored information and the transient information that moves within the various departments of the organization.

ENVIRONMENT AND THE INCEPTION PHASE

The environment discipline includes all the issues related to the development environment for the project. This discipline focuses on the infrastructure of the development project and the support required by the development team. As outlined in Chapter 2, the following activities are included:

- Select and configure the development tools
- Tailor the UP development process
- Provide technical support services

As explained previously, a preliminary analysis of the target deployment environment is done in conjunction with business modeling. For this activity, the development environment needs to be delineated. A programming language and related tools are identified. For many projects, the environment and tools are already defined, especially when the project fits into a larger existing system. But sometimes, the project departs from the past environment. When this is so, the team may spend considerable time researching and testing the best tools. Normally, each developer needs a set of tools to document and carry out his or her tasks. These tools include those used for analysis, modeling, and requirements documenting and range from tools that will help in the creation of UML models to those that are useful in documenting data field requirements. Developers also need programming and code-generation tools. Most programming today is done with integrated development environment (IDE) tools. Other important tools will include testing tools, documentation tools, and source code control tools.

In some cases, integrated tools, such as advanced computer-aided system engineering (CASE) tools, can support all activities of requirements, design, programming, and testing. In other situations, companies may utilize a suite of different tools that work together. In any event, careful consideration should be given to the tools developers need so that they can be productive and work efficiently.

The second area that needs to be considered in setting up the environment is the development methodology itself. The Unified Process provides a general framework for developing systems, but there are many different variations on and approaches to that framework. For example, some of the newer adaptive systems development (ASD) approaches are based on ideas of the UP but also modify it substantially. As mentioned earlier, some variations of adaptive approaches—including agile development, Extreme Programming and Scrum—all have unique characteristics.

One aspect to be considered is the level of rigor needed for the project. Smaller projects tend to be somewhat informal, with verbal status reports and infrequent meetings. Larger, more complex projects with many stakeholders will require much more formal, or rigorous, processes to monitor and control the project. In such projects, it may be prudent—and necessary—to use formalized techniques, with written status reports, detailed project schedules, and formal milestones. Figure 3-7 provides a list that may be used to help define the rigor of a project. The set of criteria defined in the left column can be used to indicate how complex the project is. Your company may have reporting and control procedures at different levels to monitor and track projects at different levels of complexity.

CRITERIA TO JUDGE RIGOR OF THE PROJECT MANAGEMENT	LOW RIGOR NEEDED	MEDIUM RIGOR NEEDED	HIGH RIGOR NEEDED
Strategically important	No	No	Yes
Technically complex	No	Some	Yes
New technologies needed	No	Yes	Yes
Organizational complexity	Low	Med	High
Number of people on team	<4	5–8	>8
Dollar estimate of project (U.S.$)	<$50,000	$50,000–$250,000	>$250,000
Length of time to complete	<3 months	3–4 months	>6 months
Overall project rigor	Low	Medium	High

FIGURE 3-7
Sample criteria for defining the rigor of project controls

A final area of establishing the development environment is to identify what kind of technical support services the team may need. For smaller systems and projects, technical support may be minimal. However, today many companies are building systems with teams that are diverse and geographically dispersed—even including offshore team members. Special technical support may be needed to facilitate working in such complicated team structures. Special hardware and software components may also be needed.

PROJECT MANAGEMENT AND THE INCEPTION PHASE

Project management is one of the key disciplines of the inception phase. Activities associated with business modeling and the environment provide much of the detailed information that the development team uses to finalize the project's scope and plans.

Thus, the project management discipline integrates the other activities. During the inception phase, the initiating and planning processes are the primary focus. The following list identifies the main activities involved in initiating and planning the project:

- Finalize the system and project scope
- Develop the project and iteration schedules
  - Develop the work breakdown structure (WBS), including intermediate deliverables
  - Develop the schedule
  - Develop resource requirements and the staffing plan
- Identify project risks and confirm project feasibility
  - Assess the risks to the project (risk management)
  - Determine the organizational/cultural feasibility
  - Evaluate the technological feasibility
  - Determine the schedule feasibility
  - Assess the resource feasibility
  - Determine the economic feasibility (cost/benefit analysis)

FINALIZING THE SYSTEM AND PROJECT SCOPE

The activities associated with business modeling discussed previously—defining the business environment and creating the system vision—lay the foundation for finalizing the project's scope. This key project management activity has the objective of ensuring that the scope of the new system and the project to develop it are well defined.

Note that we distinguish between system scope and project scope. The system scope defines what is going to be built, and the project scope describes how it is going to be built. For example, maybe the project is to develop a new inventory management system. The system scope will define the capabilities that need to be included in the new system. The project scope might describe whether the project will include staff training and data conversion. Project scope also defines how much acceptance testing will be required, as well as other quality control checks. As shown in Figure 3-8, we can consider the system scope to be a component of a larger project scope.

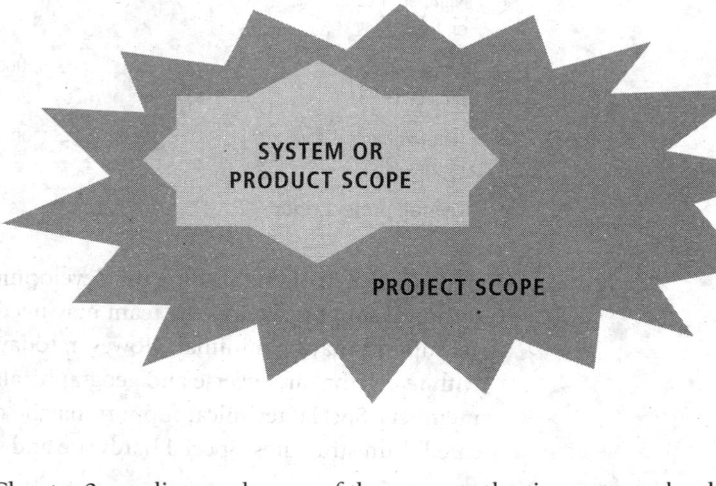

FIGURE 3-8
System scope and project scope

In Chapter 2, we discussed some of the current adaptive systems development (ASD) approaches to building software systems. With the ASD approaches' emphasis on speed and iterations, you may wonder how important defining the scope is. At one extreme you could say, "Just let the project happen, and we will identify what we need as we go," but this view is dangerous. Every project has a limited budget and time constraints. One of the benefits of determining the scope is that we can prioritize the system capabilities to maximize the business benefits. If the scope is not identified, we may spend all of our time and money on functions that do not provide the needed capabilities. We can also identify criteria to know when we are finished with the project.

scope creep
the addition of new functions to the scope of a system that cause the project to increase in size

A major problem causing projects to fail is a phenomenon called *scope creep*, which is the addition of new functions to a system after the project is under way. It has always been a concern with predictive system development, whereby we try to precisely define the scope at the beginning of the project. But with the adaptive approach, since the scope is more flexible, scope creep can become a very serious problem. The user and the development team are often tempted to "add this one little feature," but doing so can cause serious delays and reversals in a project.

System scope can be defined in several ways. In fact, we began developing the system scope during business modeling, when we defined the business benefits, the system objectives, and the system capabilities. The points on those lists describe what the system is expected to accomplish and the capabilities necessary to meet the objectives.

essential use case model
a model that is often built during the inception phase to define the most critical functions the system must perform to respond to a business event

Many times project teams build some preliminary models to help delineate the scope of a system. One model that is often built during the inception phase is the *essential use case model*. A use case is a brief statement of what the system must do to respond to a business event. The essential use cases are those that are most critical to a business. An example might be to "Create a new customer order." The business event is that the customer wants to buy something, so the system must respond by creating an order. We describe how to identify and build a use case model in detail in Chapter 6. At this point in the project, the essential use case model is used as you would a table of contents—to list the use cases that will be needed in the new system. Figure 3-9 illustrates a sample essential use case list for RMO. Obviously, the essential use case model must be consistent with the system objectives and the list of system capabilities identified earlier. The essential use case list is attached to the project charter and becomes another document in that package.

Look up item availability
Create new order
Update order
Ship an order
Return an item
Back-order an item
Create new customer
Maintain customer account
Create a new catalog
Update a catalog
Create special promotion
Send promotion materials

FIGURE 3-9
Sample essential use case list for RMO

Project scope is defined using a work breakdown structure, which is explained in the next section.

DEVELOPING THE PROJECT AND ITERATION SCHEDULE

Once the system scope and project scope are set, the development team needs to set a schedule for the entire project and for the iterations. The tasks involved in scheduling include the following:

- Develop the work breakdown structure (WBS), including intermediate deliverables

- Develop the schedule
- Develop resource requirements and the staffing plan

Project schedules vary substantially, especially in the newer adaptive approaches to system development. Since an adaptive approach is flexible, includes iterations, and allows changes as the project progresses, project managers build detailed schedules only for the current and the next iteration. Later iterations are left open, with only a few major activities defined. In fact, with an adaptive approach, the project team may not even know how many iterations will be needed to complete the project. One of the difficulties of this approach is answering questions from the project's sponsor, such as "How much will it cost?" and "How long will it take?" It is a tough balancing act for the project manager to provide an approximation of time and budget while maintaining a flexible approach to development.

work breakdown structure (WBS)
the hierarchy of phases, activities, and tasks of a project; one method to estimate and schedule the tasks of a project

The first step in building a project schedule is to develop a *work breakdown structure*, or *WBS*. Building a WBS is an important technique used in project management. In essence, the WBS identifies every piece of work—every task—that must be done. In other words, a WBS lists all the activities and tasks to be completed in the project or portion of the project. We use the terms *task* to represent the smallest piece of work and *activity* to represent a larger piece of work that is made up of individual tasks. All core members of the project team should help create the WBS. The quality of the WBS can easily make or break the schedule. If it is poorly done—not identifying many required tasks—then the project will certainly take longer than estimated. For that reason, a good project manager always ensures that the WBS is thorough and complete.

For an iterative approach to development, the WBS can be built iteration by iteration. One of the advantages of an iterative approach is that many of the activities in the iterations are very similar. The team just concentrates on building a different set of use cases during each iteration. To simplify the process, in the example that follows, we focus on building a WBS and then a schedule for a single iteration. The principles for building a schedule for an entire project are the same.

Developing the WBS

There are two general approaches for building a WBS: (1) by deliverable and (2) by a sequential timeline. The first approach identifies every deliverable, both intermediate and final, that must be developed during the time period. Then the WBS identifies every task that is necessary to create that deliverable. For example, if the project is to build a house, one of the intermediate deliverables would be to install all of the electrical wiring. The tasks for that deliverable, then, relate to hiring an electrical contractor, drilling holes, running wires, connecting junction boxes, connecting fixtures, and so forth. The second approach—the sequential timeline approach—works through the normal sequence of activities that are required for the final deliverable. For our example of building a house, the sequential timeline approach yields tasks such as surveying the property, digging the foundation, pouring the foundation, framing the walls, and so forth.

The four most effective techniques for identifying the tasks of the WBS are:

- **Top-down:** Identifying major activities first and then listing internal tasks
- **Bottom-up:** Listing all the tasks you can think of and organizing them later
- **Template:** Using a standard template of tasks for projects that are fairly standard
- **Analogy:** Finding a similar, or analogous, project that is finished and copying its tasks

When it is possible, teams try to use the template or analogy approach. Otherwise, a combination of the top-down and bottom-up approaches can be used to brainstorm a good list of tasks. Figure 3-10 is a sample WBS for RMO, which focuses primarily on the inception phase. This WBS is based on the CSS project's deliverables. Barbara Halifax and her CSS team used a top-down approach by first identifying the deliverables that are required during the inception phase. Next, they identified all the tasks that are required to produce each deliverable. Finally, they just brainstormed in a bottom-up fashion to try to identify any other tasks that they thought might have to be done. They did this using a blank wall and large Post-it notes so that they could move tasks around and reorganize them.

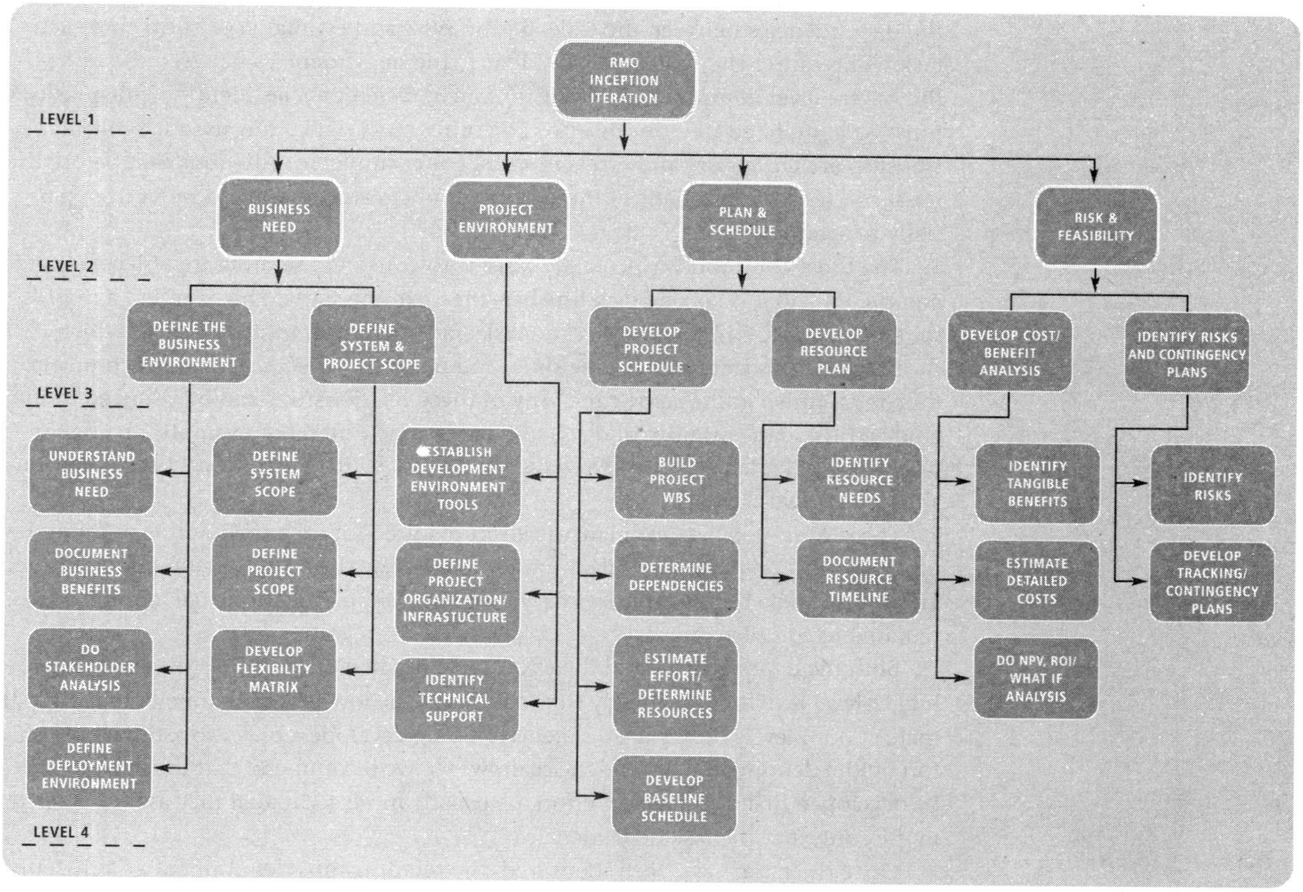

FIGURE 3-10
WBS for the inception iteration of RMO's customer support system

As you look at this WBS you should notice that even though the CSS staff built it for RMO, it appears to be rather generic. You could use the WBS as a sample or template for other projects. In reality, there will be many other individual tasks that are unique to each project being planned. For example, specific tasks for the CSS could be "Sign off business benefits with Mr. William McDougal, V.P. Sales," or "Review business need of e-commerce sales."

Several formats can be used to document the WBS. The one shown in Figure 3-10 is a hierarchy chart. On the left of the figure are several levels of the WBS. The top level is the overall iteration. Since this WBS is based on the deliverables for the iteration, the second level lists the major deliverables. The third level denotes major activities, and the fourth level contains the individual tasks. It is not necessary to take all the branches to the same level of detail. Some deliverables may only require a single activity, while others may need to be expanded to several more layers.

When developing a WBS, new analysts frequently ask, "How detailed should the individual tasks be?" A few guidelines can help answer that question:

[1] There should be a way to recognize when the task is complete.

[2] The definition of the task should be clear enough so that someone can estimate the effort required to complete it.

[3] As a general rule for software projects, the effort should take from 2 to 10 working days.

Developing the Schedule

A project schedule lists all of the activities and tasks of the projects and the order in which they must be completed. To build the schedule, the project team must identify dependencies between the tasks on the WBS and estimate the effort that each task will require. The first step is to identify the dependencies between the tasks—the lowest-level items on each vertical branch. Dependencies identify which tasks must be completed first or must precede other tasks. The terms used for this relationship are *predecessor* and *successor tasks*. For example, it is obvious that before the team can test a component of the system, it must be programmed, or at least partially programmed.

The most common way to relate tasks is to consider the order in which they are completed—that is, as one task finishes, the next one starts. This is called a *finish-start relationship*. Other ways to relate tasks include *start-start relationships*, which means that tasks start at the same time, and *finish-finish relationships*, which means they must finish at the same time. Any of these relationships can be adjusted to include a timespan (number of days) and lead or lag times. For example, an analyst may decide that task B starts two days after task A starts. This is a start-start relationship with a two-day lag.

The second step is to estimate the effort required for each task. At this point in the process of building the schedule, we want to estimate the actual person-effort required. The effort can be in hours or days or weeks, but it should be the actual amount of work required to complete the task.

Both the dependencies and the effort are estimated on the lowest-level tasks. The higher-level activities are merely summations of the low-level task times. Trying to estimate at both levels causes inconsistencies. Some developers prefer to estimate the effort before defining the dependencies; however, we recommend that the dependencies be developed first. Estimates of effort are usually more accurate if they are considered in the context of the task dependencies.

Once the tasks have been identified, the relationships determined, and the effort estimated, you can begin building the schedule. Today, we use a project scheduling tool such as Microsoft Project to build schedules. Even though MS Project is a fairly sophisticated scheduling tool, it is quite simple to begin using it. Of course, to understand the more advanced features of MS Project does require some time and study.

You can use the scheduling tool to help document your work as you define the relationships and effort. We distinguish between the first three tasks and building the schedule only because those first three are "human brain" tasks that must be done by the project planner. Building the schedule itself can be done by the tool.

Entering the WBS into MS Project

In this section, we provide a brief introduction to MS Project. For more detailed instructions, please refer to this book's Web site, which contains an appendix titled "Guide to Microsoft Project 2003" (www.course.com/ooad). Two types of charts are

PERT/CPM chart
a chart for scheduling a project based on individual tasks or activities and their dependencies

Gantt chart
a bar chart that represents the tasks and activities of the project schedule and tracks the current date and tasks completed

used to show a project schedule, a *PERT/CPM chart* and a *Gantt chart*. Both charts show essentially the same information, but in different formats. Each has its own strengths and weaknesses.

To begin entering your project into MS Project, you create a new project. Click on File | New and then enter the date you want the project to start. The first view you will see is the Gantt Chart data-entry view. Normally, the page has three panes open: an icon menu pane on the left, the task data-entry pane in the middle, and a calendar bar chart pane on the right. In the middle panel we begin by entering the name of each task in the column titled "Task Name." The easiest way is to look at your WBS diagram beginning at the top and going top to bottom down each leg from left to right. Enter all the activities and tasks, including the top-level activities. If your WBS reflects a left-to-right sequence of tasks, then the Gantt chart will also group the tasks by the order they are executed. The only critical issue at this point is to make sure the lower-level tasks are positioned directly below their higher-level activity.

Once all of the tasks are entered, you should begin at the lowest level, in this case level 4, and select all of the tasks listed below a given activity. Once they are selected, click on the right arrow, which is the second (from the left) icon located on the second task bar. This "demotes" all of those tasks so that they are subtasks to the activity. Continue to do this process for all lowest-level tasks. Next, select both third- and fourth-level tasks that are associated with a single second-level activity. Demote the entire group of third- and fourth-level tasks. Notice that the relationship between the third level and the fourth level remains.

Figure 3-11 illustrates this process. In the figure, you can see where the indentation scheme has been completed for all sublevels beneath the activity "Business Need" (line 2). In fact, they have also been demoted beneath "Inception Iteration" (line 1). Also shown is the selection of the lowest-level tasks beneath "Develop Project Schedule" (line 17) in preparation for demoting those tasks.

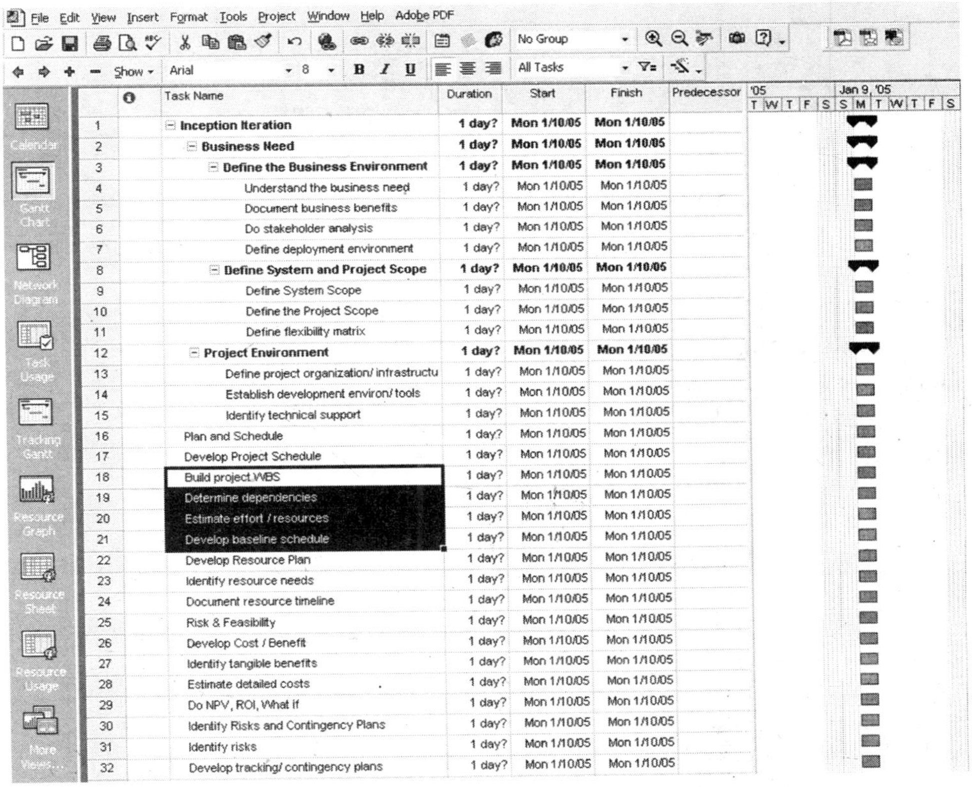

	Task Name	Duration	Start	Finish	Predecessor
1	Inception Iteration	1 day?	Mon 1/10/05	Mon 1/10/05	
2	Business Need	1 day?	Mon 1/10/05	Mon 1/10/05	
3	Define the Business Environment	1 day?	Mon 1/10/05	Mon 1/10/05	
4	Understand the business need	1 day?	Mon 1/10/05	Mon 1/10/05	
5	Document business benefits	1 day?	Mon 1/10/05	Mon 1/10/05	
6	Do stakeholder analysis	1 day?	Mon 1/10/05	Mon 1/10/05	
7	Define deployment environment	1 day?	Mon 1/10/05	Mon 1/10/05	
8	Define System and Project Scope	1 day?	Mon 1/10/05	Mon 1/10/05	
9	Define System Scope	1 day?	Mon 1/10/05	Mon 1/10/05	
10	Define the Project Scope	1 day?	Mon 1/10/05	Mon 1/10/05	
11	Define flexibility matrix	1 day?	Mon 1/10/05	Mon 1/10/05	
12	Project Environment	1 day?	Mon 1/10/05	Mon 1/10/05	
13	Define project organization/ infrastructu	1 day?	Mon 1/10/05	Mon 1/10/05	
14	Establish development environ/ tools	1 day?	Mon 1/10/05	Mon 1/10/05	
15	Identify technical support	1 day?	Mon 1/10/05	Mon 1/10/05	
16	Plan and Schedule	1 day?	Mon 1/10/05	Mon 1/10/05	
17	Develop Project Schedule	1 day?	Mon 1/10/05	Mon 1/10/05	
18	Build project WBS	1 day?	Mon 1/10/05	Mon 1/10/05	
19	Determine dependencies	1 day?	Mon 1/10/05	Mon 1/10/05	
20	Estimate effort / resources	1 day?	Mon 1/10/05	Mon 1/10/05	
21	Develop baseline schedule	1 day?	Mon 1/10/05	Mon 1/10/05	
22	Develop Resource Plan	1 day?	Mon 1/10/05	Mon 1/10/05	
23	Identify resource needs	1 day?	Mon 1/10/05	Mon 1/10/05	
24	Document resource timeline	1 day?	Mon 1/10/05	Mon 1/10/05	
25	Risk & Feasibility	1 day?	Mon 1/10/05	Mon 1/10/05	
26	Develop Cost / Benefit	1 day?	Mon 1/10/05	Mon 1/10/05	
27	Identify tangible benefits	1 day?	Mon 1/10/05	Mon 1/10/05	
28	Estimate detailed costs	1 day?	Mon 1/10/05	Mon 1/10/05	
29	Do NPV, ROI, What if	1 day?	Mon 1/10/05	Mon 1/10/05	
30	Identify Risks and Contingency Plans	1 day?	Mon 1/10/05	Mon 1/10/05	
31	Identify risks	1 day?	Mon 1/10/05	Mon 1/10/05	
32	Develop tracking/ contingency plans	1 day?	Mon 1/10/05	Mon 1/10/05	

FIGURE 3-11
Entering the WBS into MS Project

Notice that each line in the schedule is assigned a line number. This numbering is fixed by MS Project, and you cannot change it. Also, notice that MS Project uses the word *duration* instead of *effort* to measure the size of the task. Duration is the length of time the task takes, and it is related to effort by the following equation:

$$\text{Duration} \times \text{Persons} = \text{Effort}$$

The default duration is one day.

You should first enter your effort estimates in the Duration column. You may need to modify them later, when you enter resources. Also notice that there is a column to denote predecessor tasks. You enter the line number (task ID) for the predecessor task(s) in that column. As you enter predecessors and durations, Project automatically builds the Gantt chart on the right pane of the window. Notice that the defaults show all the tasks beginning on the first day of the project with a duration of one day.

Once you have entered all the tasks and identified the correct hierarchy relationships, you can enter the durations and the predecessors. Enter durations and predecessor only for the lowest-level tasks. MS Project will calculate the total duration, with beginning and ending dates, for all of the summary-level activities. You can enter this information right on the data-entry view, as shown in Figure 3-11. Another way to do this is to go to Window | Split. The lower half of the screen splits and presents a form that you can use to enter effort, predecessor, resource, and other information about each task. Whichever task is highlighted on the data-entry panel is the one shown in the split window.

Once you have entered the desired information, click OK to apply the changes. You can also navigate up and down the task list with the Previous and Next buttons on the split window. Figure 3-12 shows the Gantt chart with a split window. In this case, the split window is showing a drop-down box of all the tasks, to allow you to

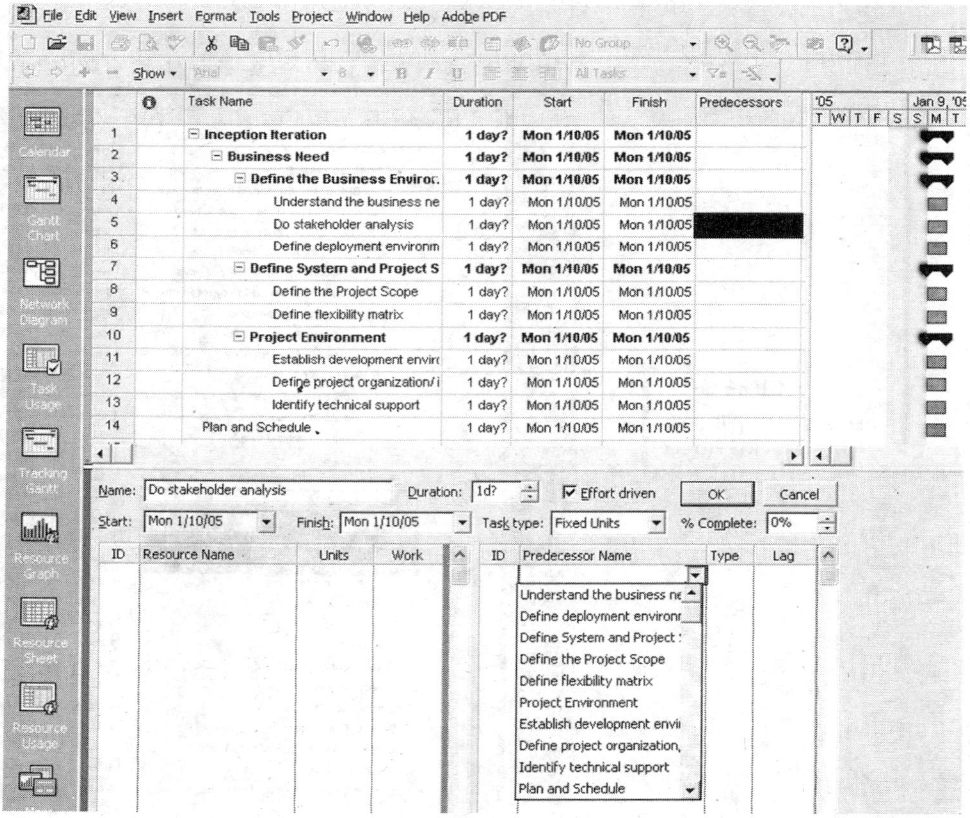

FIGURE 3-12
Using a split window to update task information

choose one or more as the predecessor task(s). At the top of the split window is a box in which to enter the duration. Once you have entered the information for predecessors and duration, click the OK button to apply the update. After the update has been applied, the OK and Cancel buttons change to Previous and Next to allow you to navigate to other tasks.

As you enter the predecessor and duration information, MS Project updates the bars on the Gantt chart to reflect the actual project schedule. Figure 3-13 shows the updated Gantt chart, which reflects the actual schedule. Of course, this is an estimated schedule—in other words, it is the plan. The actual project will most likely not unfold exactly this way. When you save your work in MS Project, you will be asked if you want to save it with a baseline. Most often, you will not want to save a baseline yet. The baseline is an indication that your planned schedule is now firm and that you want to freeze the estimate so that you can begin to actually track the project. Saving the schedule as a baseline is usually the last thing a planner does before beginning to track progress. In most cases since the schedule is an estimate, it will be refined several times before it is ready to be saved as a baseline.

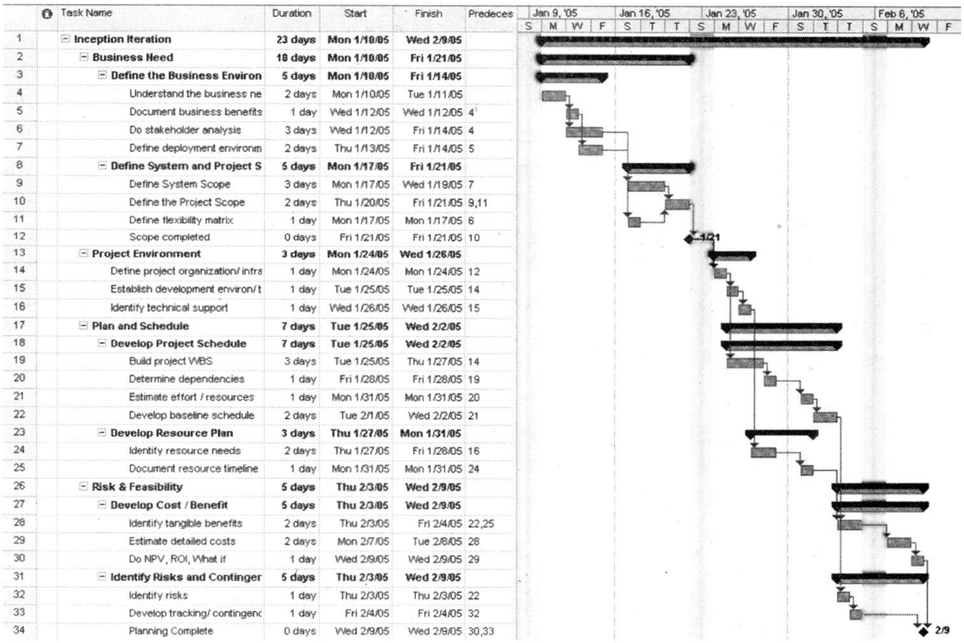

	Task Name	Duration	Start	Finish	Predeces
1	**Inception Iteration**	**23 days**	**Mon 1/10/05**	**Wed 2/9/05**	
2	**Business Need**	**10 days**	**Mon 1/10/05**	**Fri 1/21/05**	
3	**Define the Business Environ**	**5 days**	**Mon 1/10/05**	**Fri 1/14/05**	
4	Understand the business ne	2 days	Mon 1/10/05	Tue 1/11/05	
5	Document business benefits	1 day	Wed 1/12/05	Wed 1/12/05	4
6	Do stakeholder analysis	3 days	Wed 1/12/05	Fri 1/14/05	4
7	Define deployment environm	2 days	Thu 1/13/05	Fri 1/14/05	5
8	**Define System and Project S**	**5 days**	**Mon 1/17/05**	**Fri 1/21/05**	
9	Define System Scope	3 days	Mon 1/17/05	Wed 1/19/05	7
10	Define the Project Scope	2 days	Thu 1/20/05	Fri 1/21/05	9,11
11	Define flexibility matrix	1 day	Mon 1/17/05	Mon 1/17/05	6
12	Scope completed	0 days	Fri 1/21/05	Fri 1/21/05	10
13	**Project Environment**	**3 days**	**Mon 1/24/05**	**Wed 1/26/05**	
14	Define project organization/ infra	1 day	Mon 1/24/05	Mon 1/24/05	12
15	Establish development environ/ t	1 day	Tue 1/25/05	Tue 1/25/05	14
16	Identify technical support	1 day	Wed 1/26/05	Wed 1/26/05	15
17	**Plan and Schedule**	**7 days**	**Tue 1/25/05**	**Wed 2/2/05**	
18	**Develop Project Schedule**	**7 days**	**Tue 1/25/05**	**Wed 2/2/05**	
19	Build project WBS	3 days	Tue 1/25/05	Thu 1/27/05	14
20	Determine dependencies	1 day	Fri 1/28/05	Fri 1/28/05	19
21	Estimate effort / resources	1 day	Mon 1/31/05	Mon 1/31/05	20
22	Develop baseline schedule	2 days	Tue 2/1/05	Wed 2/2/05	21
23	**Develop Resource Plan**	**3 days**	**Thu 1/27/05**	**Mon 1/31/05**	
24	Identify resource needs	2 days	Thu 1/27/05	Fri 1/28/05	16
25	Document resource timeline	1 day	Mon 1/31/05	Mon 1/31/05	24
26	**Risk & Feasibility**	**5 days**	**Thu 2/3/05**	**Wed 2/9/05**	
27	**Develop Cost / Benefit**	**5 days**	**Thu 2/3/05**	**Wed 2/9/05**	
28	Identify tangible benefits	2 days	Thu 2/3/05	Fri 2/4/05	22,25
29	Estimate detailed costs	2 days	Mon 2/7/05	Tue 2/8/05	28
30	Do NPV, ROI, What if	1 day	Wed 2/9/05	Wed 2/9/05	29
31	**Identify Risks and Continger**	**5 days**	**Thu 2/3/05**	**Wed 2/9/05**	
32	Identify risks	1 day	Thu 2/3/05	Thu 2/3/05	22
33	Develop tracking/ contingenc	1 day	Fri 2/4/05	Fri 2/4/05	32
34	Planning Complete	0 days	Wed 2/9/05	Wed 2/9/05	30,33

FIGURE 3-13
Gantt chart of RMO's inception iteration

Let's review the Gantt chart in Figure 3-13. In this figure, only the data-entry pane (on the left) and the bar chart pane (on the right) are visible. In the data-entry pane, the indentation indicates the summary activities from the detailed tasks. On the right, the summary bars also have a different bar representation with a black roof on the bar. The duration of the summary tasks is automatically derived from the sum of the detailed tasks. The dates are also calculated automatically by MS Project.

critical path
a sequence of tasks that cannot be delayed without causing the project to be completed late

You will notice that some task bars are shown in red and others are shown in blue. The red tasks are on the critical path of the project. The *critical path* is the sequence of tasks that determine the length of the project. The critical path indicates the earliest that the project can be completed. Another important characteristic of the critical path is that if any of the tasks on the critical path are delayed, or take longer than expected to finish, then the entire project is delayed. This fact is important for a project manager, because he or she should watch the tasks on the critical path very carefully and take special steps to see that they are not delayed.

The tasks shown with the blue bars are those that are not on the critical path. Each of those tasks has some slack time. *Slack time*, or *float* as it is sometimes called, is the amount of time any task can be delayed and still not have a negative impact on the completion date of the project. For example, look at task number 9 and task number 11. Both of the tasks run in parallel, with task 9 requiring 3 days and task 11 requiring 1 day. Task number 10 cannot start until both finish. Hence, task 10 cannot start until 3 days after task 9 starts. So task 11, requiring 1 day to complete, has 2 days of slack time, or float.

slack time, or float
the amount of time any task can be delayed without having a negative impact on the completion date of the project

Another important concept from this diagram is the idea of a milestone. A *milestone* is a precise point on the project schedule that indicates a specific completion point. Often, a milestone is accompanied by a deliverable or end product. Milestones provide checkpoints for project managers to verify the progress of the project. In Figure 3-13, there are two milestones, task 12, in the middle of the project, and task 34, indicating the completion of the iteration. In MS Project, milestones are created by entering a duration of zero days.

milestone
a precise point on the project schedule that indicates a specific completion point

So far, we have been dealing with Gantt charts in MS Project. The other type of chart that is sometimes used to show and manage a schedule is a PERT/CPM chart. MS Project calls its version of the PERT/CPM chart a *network diagram*. A network diagram is a collection of nodes, with arrows connecting the nodes. The arrows indicate valid paths through the network. This definition fits the concept of a schedule, which is a set of tasks (the nodes) that must be completed in some sequence (indicated by the arrows). Figure 3-14 is a snapshot from MS Project of a portion of the schedule. The advantage of a network diagram is that it is very easy to see the predecessor and successor relationships. In other words, it provides an easy-to-read graphical view of the sequence of the tasks. Many project managers use the network diagram to double-check the schedule to see that it makes sense and that it has no errors. Notice in Figure 3-14 that some tasks are red, while others are blue. Again, the colors represent critical path tasks versus noncritical-path tasks.

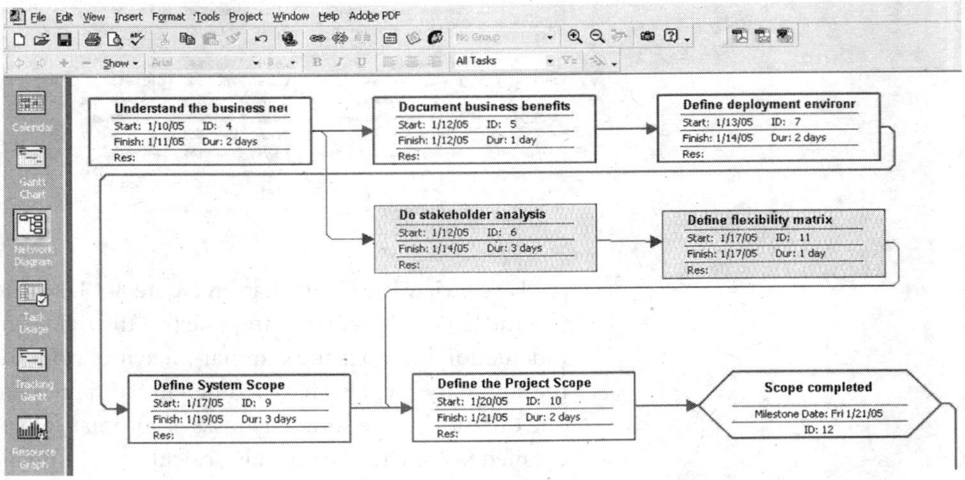

FIGURE 3-14
Network diagram of RMO's inception iteration schedule

Develop the Resource Requirements and the Staffing Plan

Another important activity that planners must complete as part of developing the project's schedule is to develop a resource and staffing plan. As the project manager and one or two other experienced developers work to create the WBS and estimate the effort required for each task, they normally also try to identify the specific resources needed to complete the task. The core team members usually carry out much of the inception iteration, since most of the tasks are project management activities. Even though, for our learning example, we only show the inception iteration, later iterations are also planned to the extent that they can be.

There are several ways to enter the resource information into MS Project. The first step is to identify the specific resources for the project by using the Resource Sheet view, as shown in Figure 3-15. In this figure, we have indicated a project manager for 100 percent availability and have even assigned him a rate for the project. We have also indicated that senior analysts will be part of the project and have noted that there will be two of them—for a total of 200 percent availability and a rate of $50 per hour. (These rates may seem high, but we are taking into account benefits and perhaps even "consulting rate" charges.) Resources can be identified by type, as we have done here, or even by specific names of persons. Usually it is better just to identify types of resources needed.

FIGURE 3-15
Resource sheet showing two resources

	❶	Resource Name	Type	Material Label	Initials	Group	Max. Units	Std. Rate	Ovt. Rate	Cost/Use	Accrue At	Base Calendar
1		Project Manager	Work		P		100%	$75.00/hr	$75.00/hr	$0.00	Prorated	Standard
2		Senior Analyst	Work		S		200%	$50.00/hr	$60.00/hr	$0.00	Prorated	Standard

The second step is to assign these resources to the tasks. The way we prefer is to use the split window approach, as explained earlier. You select a task, then use the drop-down box under the Resource Name column. Select the resource and indicate how long that resource will be available for that task. Figure 3-16 illustrates entering the resources for task 7, Define deployment environment. Notice that we have assigned one and one-half senior analysts to this task.

FIGURE 3-16
Entering resources for the scheduled tasks

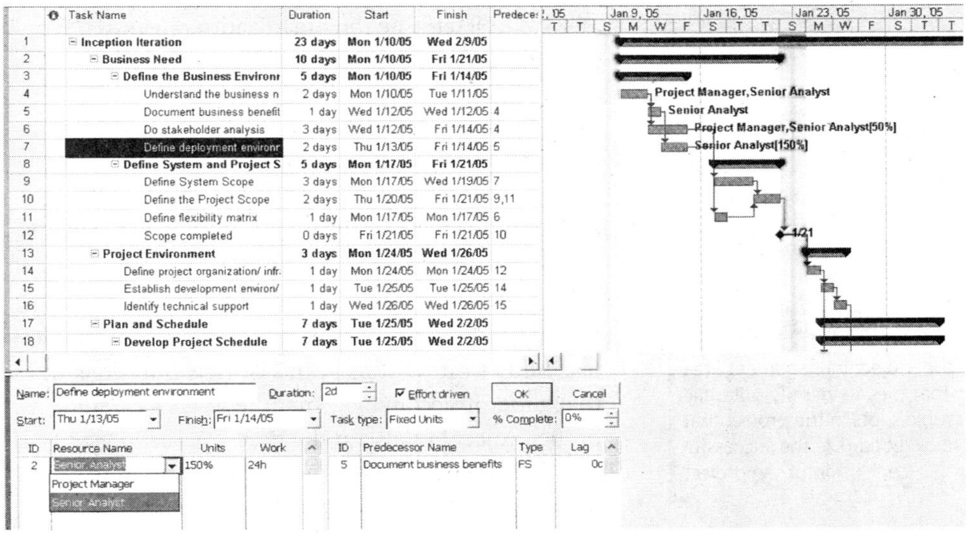

There is one caveat that you need to bear in mind when entering resources. Remember the equation

$$\text{Duration} \times \text{Persons} = \text{Effort}$$

The first time you enter the resources through this split window, MS Project ignores that equation and leaves the duration as you originally estimated it. However, after the first time, MS Project applies that equation every time you modify or change the resources. The Effort driven check box in the split window indicates to MS Project that the effort should remain constant. So, referring to this equation, if you change the number of resources or the availability of the resources, MS Project will change the task duration so that the effort remains a constant. You can turn this feature off by unchecking the Effort driven check box.

We have provided this very brief introduction to MS Project to illustrate how to use a tool in the development of the WBS and the project schedule. Obviously, MS Project has many more features that you will need to learn if you want to use its full capabilities. The "Guide to Microsoft Project 2003" appendix on the book's Web site provides a more detailed tutorial on its use (www.course.com/ooad).

IDENTIFY PROJECT RISKS AND CONFIRM PROJECT FEASIBILITY

Project feasibility analysis is an activity that verifies whether a project may be started and successfully completed. Since, by definition, a project is a unique endeavor, every project has unique challenges that affect its feasibility. As we learned early in the chapter, information system projects do not have a very good track record of success. Even well-planned projects sometimes go awry and get into trouble.

The objective in assessing feasibility is to determine whether a development project has a reasonable chance of success. Feasibility analysis essentially identifies all the risks of failure. The project team assesses the original assumptions and identifies other risks that could jeopardize the project's success. The team first identifies those risks and then, if necessary, establishes plans and procedures to ensure that those risks do not interfere with the success of the project. However, if the team suspects there are serious risks that could jeopardize the project, members must discover and evaluate them as soon as possible. Generally, the team performs these activities when confirming a project's feasibility:

- Assess the risk to the project (risk management)
- Determine the organizational/cultural feasibility
- Evaluate the technological feasibility
- Determine the schedule feasibility
- Assess the resource feasibility
- Determine the economic feasibility (cost/benefit analysis)

Assessing the Risks to the Project (Risk Management)

risk management
the project management area that tries to identify potential trouble spots in the project that may jeopardize the successful conclusion of the project

Feasibility analysis also includes risk management. *Risk management* is the project management area that is forward-looking and tries to identify potential trouble spots that may jeopardize the success of the project. Sometimes project managers look at the feasibility from various points of view but forget to identify specific risks. We believe that good project management requires a careful look not only at the overall feasibility of the project but also at the risks. We first present a simple technique for identifying and assessing risks. Then we explain various areas that should be considered for project feasibility and risk management.

Risk management is done throughout the life of the project. During a project's initiation, the primary activity of risk management is to identify potential risks and assess their potential for negative impact. There are no quick and easy ways to identify all of the risks that a project might face. We have found that the best way to identify risks is simply to have a brainstorming session. The core team members should be the primary participants in this session. In addition to team members, selected stakeholders might also participate. The best people to include in the sessions are those who are experienced and have worked on previous projects. As with any brainstorming session, participants should let the ideas flow freely before judging and eliminating the bad ones.

After the potential risks have been identified, the team can use a simple matrix to analyze the potential for harm to the project. Figure 3-17 is an example of a simple table that illustrates the technique. The left column is the final list of identified risks. The second column, entitled "Potential Impact on Project" is an assessment of how badly the project will be affected if the risk materializes. The team makes a subjective judgment of three possible values: High, Medium, or Low. The next column indicates how likely it is that the negative event will really happen. Instead of making some sophisticated probability calculation, again just estimate High, Medium, or Low.

FIGURE 3-17
Simplified risk analysis

RISK DESCRIPTION	POTENTIAL IMPACT ON PROJECT (HIGH, MEDIUM, LOW)	LIKELIHOOD OF OCCURRENCE (HIGH, MEDIUM, LOW)	DIFFICULTY OF TIMELY ANTICIPATION (HARD, MEDIUM, EASY)	OVERALL THREAT (HIGH, MEDIUM, LOW)
Critical team member (expert) not available	High	Medium	Medium	High
Changing legal requirements	High	Low	Hard	Low
Organization employees not computer savvy	Medium	Medium	Easy	Medium

The next column records the evaluation of how hard or easy it is to predict that the negative event will happen, and whether that prediction can be made in time to take corrective action. For example, the first risk is that a critical expert will not be available to the team. If the project manager finds out on the day the team member is supposed to start work that he or she is not available, that risk is obviously hard to predict and can have a very negative impact on the project. If the project manager expects to have a month's warning that the resource is not going to be available, then the negative event is easy to predict, and some other contingency can be arranged. Evaluate the risks in this column by Hard, Medium, and Easy.

Finally, given the values in the middle three columns, the team assigns an overall evaluation to each risk. The project manager uses this information to watch and track the potential risks and is often able either to prevent the negative event from happening or to have a backup plan ready when it does occur.

Determining Organizational and Cultural Feasibility

Each company has its own culture, and any new system must be accommodated within that culture. A new system may depart so dramatically from existing norms that it cannot be successfully deployed. The analysts involved with feasibility analysis should evaluate organizational and cultural issues to identify potential risks for the new system. Such issues might include the following:

- A low level of computer competency among employees
- Substantial computer phobia
- A perceived loss of control by staff or management
- Potential shifting of political and organizational power due to the new system
- Fear of change of job responsibilities

- Fear of loss of employment due to increased automation
- Reversal of long-standing work procedures

It is not possible to enumerate all the potential organizational and cultural risks that exist. The project management team needs to be very sensitive to reluctance within the organization to identify and resolve these risks. The question to ask for organizational/cultural feasibility is, "What items might prevent the effective utilization of the new system and result in the loss of business benefits?"

After identifying the risks, the project management team can take positive steps to counter them. For example, the team can hold additional training sessions to teach new procedures and provide increased computer skills. Higher levels of user involvement in the development of the new system will tend to increase user enthusiasm and commitment.

Evaluating the Technological Feasibility

Generally, a new system brings new technology into the company. At times, the new system stretches the state of the art of the technology. Other projects utilize existing technology but combine it into new, untested configurations. Finally, even existing technology can pose challenges if there is a lack of expertise within the company. If an outside vendor is providing new systems capabilities, the client organization usually assumes that the vendor is expert in the area in which it provides service. However, even an outside vendor is subject to the risk that the requested level of technology is too complicated.

The project management team needs to assess very carefully the proposed technological requirements and available expertise. When these risks are identified, the solutions are usually fairly straightforward. The solutions to technological risks include providing additional training, hiring consultants, or hiring more experienced employees. In some cases, the scope and approach of the project may need to be changed to ameliorate technological risk. The important point is that a realistic assessment will identify technological risks early, making it possible to implement corrective measures.

Determining the Schedule Feasibility

The development of a project schedule always involves high risk. Every schedule requires the project management team to make many assumptions and estimates without adequate information. For example, the needs, and hence the scope, of the new system may not be well known, the estimated time to research and finalize requirements must be estimated, and the availability and capability of team members could be questionable. Adaptive development projects are especially susceptible to schedule risks. By its nature, the practice of allowing the project to be modified as it progresses makes these projects difficult to manage. Even though it may make sense to let the project use an adaptive approach, business needs and deadlines must still be met.

Another frequent risk in the development of the schedule occurs when upper management indicates that the new system must be deployed within a certain time. Sometimes there is an important need for defining a fixed deadline, such as RMO needing to complete the CSS in time for online ordering for the holidays. Similarly, universities require the completion of new systems before key dates in the university schedule. For example, if a new admissions system is not completed before the admissions season, then it might as well wait another full year. In cases such as these, schedule feasibility can be the most important feasibility factor to consider.

If the deadline appears arbitrary or unrealistic, teams tend to build the schedule to show that it can be done. Unfortunately, this practice usually spells disaster. The project team should build the schedule without any preconceived notion of required completion dates. Once the schedule is completed, then comparisons can be made to see whether timetables coincide. If not, then the team can take corrective measures, such as reducing the scope of the project, to increase the probability of the project's on-time completion.

One of the objectives of defining milestones during the project schedule is to permit the project manager to assess the ongoing risk of the schedule's slipping. If the team begins to miss milestones, then the manager can possibly implement corrective measures early. Contingency plans can be developed and carried out to reduce the risk of further slippage.

Allocating adequate personnel with the right experience and expertise to a project is always a problem. Any complex project may incur overruns and schedule extensions. It may be difficult to identify the sources of these risks, but a conscious effort to identify them will at least highlight areas of weakness. Long projects are especially subject to difficulties with resource allocation and to schedule slippage. Solutions can involve contingency plans in case in-house resources are not available.

Assessing the Resource Feasibility

The project management team must assess the availability of resources for the project. The primary resource consists of the members of the team. Development projects require the involvement of systems analysts, system technicians, and users. Required people may not be available to the team at the necessary times. An additional risk is that the people who are assigned may not have the necessary skills for the project. Once the team is functioning, team members may have to leave the team. This threat can happen either when staff are transferred internally within the organization, if other special projects arise, or when qualified team members are hired away by other organizations. Although the project manager usually does not like to think about these possibilities, skilled people are in short supply and sometimes do leave projects.

The other resources required for a successful project include adequate computer resources, physical facilities, and support staff. Generally, these resources can be made available, but the schedule can be affected if delays in the availability of these resources occur.

Determining the Economic Feasibility

The test for economic feasibility consists of two questions: (1) Is the anticipated value of the benefits greater than projected costs of development? and (2) Does the organization have adequate cash flow to fund the project during the development period? Frequently, the justification for the development of a new system is that it will increase income, either through cost savings or by increased revenues. A determination of the economic feasibility of the project always is conducted through the use of a cost/benefit analysis. A *cost/benefit analysis* is a comparison of the costs of development versus the anticipated financial benefits of the new system.

cost/benefit analysis
a comparison of the costs of development versus the anticipated financial benefits of the new system

Economic feasibility is an especially hard challenge for adaptive projects. How does the project manager predict the cost of the project if the schedule is subject to change based on the direction of the project over time? However, senior executives, who are in charge of allocating scarce investment dollars, will always ask the questions, "How long will it take?" and "How much will it cost?" Project managers must provide some estimate of the projected cost of the development.

Developing a cost/benefit analysis is a three-step process. The first step is to estimate the anticipated development and operational costs. Development costs are those that are incurred during the development of the new system. Operational costs are those that will be incurred after the system is put into production. The second step is to estimate the anticipated financial benefits. Financial benefits are the expected annual savings or increases in revenue derived from the installation of the new system. The third step, the cost/benefit analysis, is calculated based on the detailed estimates of costs and benefits. The most frequent error that inexperienced analysts make during cost/benefit analysis is to try to do the calculations before thoroughly defining costs and benefits. A cost/benefit analysis that does not have thorough and complete supporting detail is valueless.

Although the project manager has final responsibility for estimating the costs of development, senior-level analysts always assist with the calculations. Generally, project costs fall into the following categories:

- Salaries and wages
- Equipment and installation
- Software and licenses
- Consulting fees and payments to third parties
- Training
- Facilities
- Utilities and tools
- Support staff
- Travel and miscellaneous

Salaries and wages are calculated based on the staffing requirements for the project. Fortunately, MS Project can calculate these amounts for you based on your schedule. If the project manager is able to develop a complete schedule that covers all the potential iterations of the project, then he or she can use the total cost provided by MS Project. With resources assigned to the various tasks and costs associated with each resource, MS Project calculates the cost of each task. Figure 3-18 is a snapshot of MS Project with cost figures included. The Cost column is not one of the default columns. It can be eas-

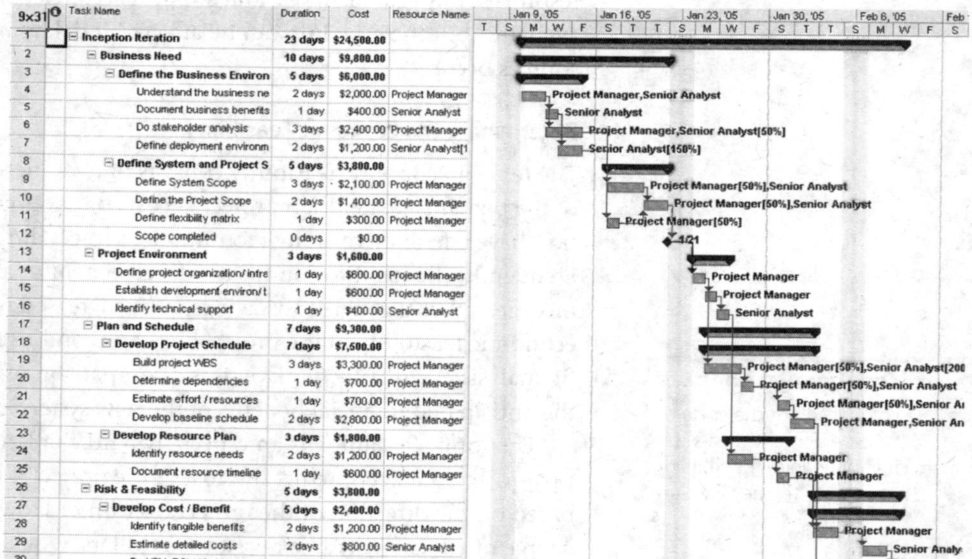

9x31	Task Name	Duration	Cost	Resource Name
1	**Inception Iteration**	**23 days**	**$24,500.00**	
2	**Business Need**	**10 days**	**$9,800.00**	
3	**Define the Business Environ**	**5 days**	**$6,000.00**	
4	Understand the business ne	2 days	$2,000.00	Project Manager
5	Document business benefits	1 day	$400.00	Senior Analyst
6	Do stakeholder analysis	3 days	$2,400.00	Project Manager
7	Define deployment environm	2 days	$1,200.00	Senior Analyst[1
8	**Define System and Project S**	**5 days**	**$3,800.00**	
9	Define System Scope	3 days	$2,100.00	Project Manager
10	Define the Project Scope	2 days	$1,400.00	Project Manager
11	Define flexibility matrix	1 day	$300.00	Project Manager
12	Scope completed	0 days	$0.00	
13	**Project Environment**	**3 days**	**$1,600.00**	
14	Define project organization/ infra	1 day	$600.00	Project Manager
15	Establish development environ/ t	1 day	$600.00	Project Manager
16	Identify technical support	1 day	$400.00	Senior Analyst
17	**Plan and Schedule**	**7 days**	**$9,300.00**	
18	**Develop Project Schedule**	**7 days**	**$7,500.00**	
19	Build project WBS	3 days	$3,300.00	Project Manager
20	Determine dependencies	1 day	$700.00	Project Manager
21	Estimate effort / resources	1 day	$700.00	Project Manager
22	Develop baseline schedule	2 days	$2,800.00	Project Manager
23	**Develop Resource Plan**	**3 days**	**$1,800.00**	
24	Identify resource needs	2 days	$1,200.00	Project Manager
25	Document resource timeline	1 day	$600.00	Project Manager
26	**Risk & Feasibility**	**5 days**	**$3,800.00**	
27	**Develop Cost / Benefit**	**5 days**	**$2,400.00**	
28	Identify tangible benefits	2 days	$1,200.00	Project Manager
29	Estimate detailed costs	2 days	$800.00	Senior Analyst
30	Do NPV, ROI, What if	1 day	$400.00	Senior Analyst
31	**Identify Risks and Continger**	**5 days**	**$1,400.00**	
32	Identify risks	1 day	$700.00	Project Manager
33	Develop tracking/ contingenc	1 day	$700.00	Project Manager
34	Planning Complete	0 days	$0.00	

FIGURE 3-18
MS Project showing project labor costs

ily added to the view, however, by using the Insert | column menu item. Remember that Figure 3-18 is a schedule only for the inception phase iteration, and there are only three people on the project. In this example, the total labor cost for the project manager and two systems analysts is $24,500. Figure 3-18 also shows how MS Project documents the assignment of resources to the tasks.

To estimate the total cost for the project, an estimate should be done for each category. If there is enough detail to build a preliminary schedule for the entire project, then labor costs can be extracted from the schedule on MS Project. Otherwise, a rough estimate can be made by multiplying the total size of the team times the anticipated length of the project and the daily rate for each type of team member. Each of the other categories of costs requires detailed calculations on usage to determine the estimated costs. The project manager can make detailed estimates of equipment, software licenses, training costs, and so forth. These details are then combined to provide an estimate of the total costs of development. Figure 3-19 is a summary table of all of the costs for the entire project. Each line in the summary table must be supported with details. As indicated earlier, estimating both the schedule and costs may be more difficult for adaptive approaches. However, in most cases, the sponsor and other funding clients will require an estimate.

FIGURE 3-19
Detailed est mates of project costs

EXPENSE CATEGORY	AMOUNT
Salaries/wages	$496,000.00
Equipment/installation	$385,000.00
Training	$78,000.00
Facilities	$57,000.00
Utilities	$152,000.00
Support staff	$38,000.00
Travel/miscellaneous	$112,000.00
Licenses	$18,000.00
Total	$1,336,000.00

Once the new system is up and running, normal operating costs are incurred every year. The calculation of the cost and benefit of the new system must also account for these annual operating costs. Generally, analysts do not include the normal costs of running the business in this cost. Only the costs that are directly related to the new system and its maintenance are included. The following list identifies the major categories of costs that might be allocated to the operation of the new system:

- Connectivity
- Equipment maintenance
- Costs to upgrade software licenses
- Computer operations
- Programming support
- Amortization of equipment
- Training and ongoing assistance (the help desk)
- Supplies

Figure 3-20 is a summary of the annual operating costs for RMO. As with the development costs, each entry in the table should be supported with detailed calculations.

This figure represents only the costs that are anticipated for the RMO system. Other organizations may have a different set of operating costs.

FIGURE 3-20
Summary of annual operating costs for RMO

RECURRING EXPENSE	AMOUNT
Connectivity	$60,000.00
Equipment maintenance	$40,000.00
Programming	$65,000.00
Help desk	$28,000.00
Amortization	$48,000.00
Total recurring costs	$241,000.00

The project manager and members of the project team can determine most of the development and operational costs. However, users and the project's sponsor receive the benefits of the system. Consequently, they must determine the value of the anticipated benefits. Members of the project team can and do assist, but they should never attempt to determine the value of benefits by themselves.

Benefits usually come from two major sources: decreased costs and increased revenues. Cost savings or decreases in expenses come from increased efficiency in company operations. Areas in which to look for reduced costs include the following:

- Reducing staff by automating manual functions or increasing efficiency
- Decreasing operating expenses such as shipping charges for "emergency shipments"
- Reducing error rates through automated editing or validation
- Achieving quicker processing and turnaround of documents or transactions
- Capturing lost discounts on money management
- Reducing bad accounts or bad credit losses
- Reducing inventory or merchandise losses through tighter controls
- Collecting receivables (accounts receivable) more rapidly

This list is just a sample of the myriad benefits that can accrue. Unlike development costs, there are no "standard" benefits. Each project is different, and the anticipated benefits are different. Figure 3-21 is an example of the benefits that RMO expects from the implementation of the new customer support system.

FIGURE 3-21
Sample benefits for RMO

BENEFIT/COST SAVING	AMOUNT	COMMENTS
Increased efficiency in mail-order department	$125,000.00	5 people @ $25,000
Increased efficiency in phone-order department	$25,000.00	1 person @ $25,000
Increased efficiency in warehouse/shipping	$87,000.00	
Increased earnings due to Web presence	$500,000.00	Increasing at 50%/year
Other savings (inventory, supplies, etc.)	$152,000.00	
Total annual benefits	$889,000.00	

net present value (NPV)
the present value of dollar benefits and costs for an investment such as a new system

Companies use a combination of methods to measure the overall benefit of a new system. One popular approach is to determine the *net present value (NPV)* of the new system. The two concepts behind net present value are (1) that all benefits and costs are calculated in terms of today's dollars (present value) and (2) that benefits and costs are combined to give a net value. The future streams of benefits and costs are netted together and then discounted by a factor for each year in the future. The discount factor is like an interest rate, except that it is used to bring future values back to current values. Appendix C on the book's Web site provides detailed instructions (using RMO's customer support system as the example) on how to calculate the various economic feasibility measures. You should read Appendix C after completing this text section, to ensure that you understand the details.

Figure 3-22 shows a copy of the RMO net present value calculation done in Appendix C (Figure C-1). In this case, the new system gives an NPV of $3,873,334 over a five-year period using a discount rate of 10 percent.

	RMO COST/BENEFIT ANALYSIS	YEAR 0	YEAR 1	YEAR 2	YEAR 3	YEAR 4	YEAR 5	TOTAL
1	Value of benefits		$889,000	$1,139,000	$1,514,000	$2,077,000	$2,927,000	
2	Discount factor (10%)	1.0000	0.9091	0.8264	0.7513	0.6830	0.6209	
3	Present value of benefits		$808,190	$941,270	$1,137,468	$1,418,591	$1,817,374	$6,122,893
4	Development costs	$(1,336,000)						$(1,336,000)
5	Ongoing costs		$(241,000)	$(241,000)	$(241,000)	$(241,000)	$(241,000)	
6	Discount factor (10%)	1.0000	0.9091	0.8264	0.7513	0.6830	0.6209	
7	Present value of costs		$(219,093)	$(199,162)	$(181,063)	$(164,603)	$(149,637)	$(913,559)
8	PV of net of benefits and costs	$(1,336,000)	$589,097	$742,107	$956,405	$1,253,988	$1,667,737	
9	Cumulative NPV	$(1,336,000)	$(746,903)	$(4,769)	$951,609	$2,205,597	$3,873,334	
10	Payback period		2 years + 4796 / (4796 + 951,609) = 2 + .005 or 2 years and 2 days					
11	5-year return on investment		(6,122,893 - (1,336,000 + 913,559)) / (1,336,000 + 913,559) = 172.18%					

FIGURE 3-22
Net present value, payback period, and return on investment for RMO

payback period
the point at which the increased cash flow (benefits) exactly pays off the costs of development and operation; sometimes called the *breakeven point*

Another method that organizations use to determine whether an investment will be beneficial is determining the *payback period*. The payback period, sometimes called the *breakeven point*, is the point at which the increased cash flow (benefits) exactly pays off the costs of development and operation. Appendix C on the book's Web site provides the detailed equations necessary for this calculation. Figure 3-22 illustrates the calculations for the payback period. A running accumulated net value is calculated year by year. The year when this value goes positive is the year in which payback occurs. In the RMO example, this payback happens within the third year.

COMPLETING THE INCEPTION PHASE

The inception phase of a project typically lasts about a month, so the inception iteration schedule shown in Figure 3-13 is a fairly typical schedule. Inception activities establish the foundation for the rest of the project. The scope and essential use case list provide a basis for defining the activities of the elaboration phase. The key deliverables of inception can be summarized in the following list:

- Project charter package
- Essential use case list
- Project schedule
- Cost/benefit analysis
- Project feasibility and risk analysis

These deliverables provide both the justification for the project and enough of a plan to proceed into the next iterations. Even though the UP development approach is an adaptive methodology, the schedule and activities should be defined as closely as possible.

The project's sponsor and upper management often expect a presentation at the end of the inception phase. Also, they usually expect a report of the findings of inception. By the end of the inception phase, the project team should be able to describe with adequate supporting detail the general scope of the new system and the approach to developing it. Hence, another responsibility of the project manager and the team is to present the results to the sponsor. Appendix D on the book's Web site provides guidelines on how to develop and present a good report. As indicated in Chapter 1, one of the most important skills of a good systems analyst and project manager is the ability to communicate well, both in written form and presentations.

The final activity of the inception phase is to launch the next iteration of the project. By this time, a detailed WBS and schedule for the second iteration should have been developed. One of the potential difficulties at this stage of the project may be the need to add more staff to the project team. The project manager will need to have arranged for the addition of these new team members. There will normally be an orientation period to get these new members of the team up to speed on the project. The project manager may need to conduct some additional training as the team gets more involved in the technical aspects of actually developing the solution. At this point in the project, coordination is key because of the many details necessary to keep the team on track. A project can be delayed by several days if the project manager is not organized, or if he or she does not provide clear direction to the team. With clear direction, however, the inception phase ends on time, and the team makes a smooth transition into the first elaboration iteration.

PROJECT MONITORING AND CONTROL

Project monitoring and control begins during the inception phase and continues throughout the project. As we saw in the development of the project schedule, iterative projects under the UP follow an adaptive development model. The schedule is flexible and is modified during the life of the project. We also saw that each iteration is like a miniproject, with its own schedule, resources, and deliverables. So, each iteration in an adaptive approach needs to be controlled. Project milestones and completion points must be established and monitored. Corrective actions must be taken from time to time to keep the project progressing at an acceptable rate.

Projects are monitored and controlled with respect to three areas:

- Manage and control the project plan, including the schedule and deliverables
- Manage and control internal and external communications
- Manage and control the risks and outstanding issues

During the inception phase, an overall project schedule is developed. At the conclusion of the inception phase, a detailed project schedule for the next iteration is developed. The schedules of later iterations remain fairly vague. During the life of the project, one of the concluding activities of each iteration is to refine and flesh out details for the next iteration's schedule. The amount of flexibility in the schedule depends heavily on the complexity of the project and the needs of the sponsoring organization. Generally, a completely open schedule cannot be tolerated. A completely inflexible schedule is also not a good alternative.

During an iteration, the project schedule is used to track progress. Status reports and progress reports are collected, and the completion of tasks and milestones can be compared with expected end dates. If the project gets off schedule, then the project manager must identify the causes and take corrective action to get the project back on schedule, or at least stay current with upcoming target dates.

Many experts today indicate that project communications management may be the most important area of project management. The project manager is the focal point for almost all of a project's communications. He or she is the gateway through which internal project and status information is communicated to external stakeholders. The project manager is also a critical element for internal project communications. Not only does the project manager receive much of the communication, but he or she also is responsible for establishing the infrastructure for all project communication.

There are two types of information within a development project: project-related information and system- or deliverable-related information. Project-related information includes plans and schedules, status and progress reports, and outstanding issues lists. The project manager is directly involved in all aspects of project-related information. System-related information consists of documents, such as requirements, design models, architectural decisions, and computer code. This information is composed of the intermediate deliverables that are produced as part of the project team's activities. The project manager may not be directly involved in producing this information, but he or she must establish the infrastructure and rules for capturing, storing, and disseminating this information.

The final area of project management at the end of inception is the tracking and control of risks and outstanding issues. As roadblocks or problems are encountered during the life of the project, if they cannot be resolved immediately, the project manager places them on a list or a log of open issues. Generally, a description of the issue and the date it was identified are noted. In most cases, a person is assigned responsibility to resolve or at least monitor the issue, and a required resolution date is identified. Then periodically, such as weekly, the status of each open item is checked. There may be several open issues logs. Some may be handled directly by the project manager, while other, more technical issues, may be managed by the technical leaders of the project.

Summary

The development of a new software system is a difficult endeavor with less than optimal success rates. Many of the difficulties with troubled projects can be tied to inadequate understanding of the user's requirements and lack of strong executive support. These problems are frequently caused by inexperienced and unqualified project managers. One solution to poor project success rates is to train and improve the management skill level of project managers.

Project management processes are the activities that are directly related to managing and controlling a project. These processes are usually categorized as initiating processes, planning processes, monitoring and controlling processes, and closing processes.

The project manager plays a pivotal role in the success of any project. He or she is the focal point for internal activities within the project team as well as the liaison between the team and the rest of the organization. Some of the more important responsibilities of the project manager include building the project schedule, assigning tasks to team members, coordinating the activities of the project, assessing project risks, tracking the progress of the project, and ensuring a high-quality result.

The Project Management Institute, a professional organization for project managers, has defined a project management body of knowledge, which is divided into nine major areas. This body of knowledge identifies areas of expertise that project managers must develop. The nine areas consist of integration management, scope management, time management, cost management, quality management, communication management, human resources management, risk management, and procurement management.

The Unified Process (UP) is a formal methodology for software development. The basic premise of the UP is that software should be developed in an iterative approach—that is, the new software system grows and evolves. First, a small, immature version is developed, and then it is enhanced until the full-featured system is finalized. Each iteration is, in essence, a miniproject that can be managed using project management techniques. During the life of a project, as the system grows, the focus of the iterations changes. At the start of the project, the first iteration, called the *inception iteration*, is focused on defining the scope of the new system. Next, the iterations focus on defining the user's requirements; this is referred to as the *elaboration phase*. The iterations then must focus on building a reliable, robust system. This set of iterations is called the *construction phase*. Finally, a few iterations may be required to test and deploy the system. This last phase is called the *transition phase*.

In addition to the iterations, the UP describes different types of development activities, called *disciplines*. These activities consist of business modeling, requirements, design, implementation, testing, deployment, project management, configuration and change management, and environment.

Since the focus of the inception phase is to get the project started, the three business disciplines that are the most prevalent during inception are (1) business modeling, to understand the business needs, (2) environment, to configure the development tools for the team, and (3) project management, to plan and schedule the rest of the project. Most of the effort required during the inception phase consists of tasks to develop a work breakdown structure and build the project schedule.

Other project management tasks include staffing the project, assessing project risks and feasibility, and calculating the cost/benefit analysis.

After the project begins and during later project iterations, the project manager must track and control the project. Project tracking and control focuses on three major areas: monitoring and controlling the schedule, tracking outstanding issues and problems, and ensuring that all project team members and other stakeholders are kept informed.

KEY TERMS

business benefits, p. 91
cost/benefit analysis, p. 109
critical path, p. 103
essential use case model, p. 97
external users, p. 88
Gantt chart, p. 101
internal users, p. 88
milestone, p. 104
net present value (NPV), p. 113
payback period, p. 113
PERT/CPM chart, p. 101
project charter, p. 93
project management, p. 82
risk management, p. 106
scope creep, p. 97
slack time, or float, p. 104
sponsor, p. 89
system capabilities, p. 92
work breakdown structure (WBS), p. 98

REVIEW QUESTIONS

1. Identify five or six primary reasons why software projects get in trouble.
2. Explain each of the four types of project management processes.
3. Identify five or six major responsibilities of a project manager.
4. List the nine areas of the project management body of knowledge.
5. What are the four phases of the UP? Explain the purpose of the phases and the objective of each phase.
6. List and explain the primary types of stakeholders who should be considered during project inception.
7. What is meant by the "business modeling" discipline? What is its objective during inception?
8. What is meant by the "environment" discipline? What three environment tasks are usually done during the inception iteration?
9. What are the three primary tasks of the project management discipline that relate to the inception phase? Briefly explain each.
10. Discuss the difference between the system scope and the project scope. Why is it important to consider each separately?
11. What is a WBS? What are some of the common techniques used to develop a WBS? Why is it important in planning a project?
12. Explain the concept of the critical path. Define *slack time*. How does slack time relate to the critical path?
13. What are the two most common views of a project schedule in MS Project—that is, what are the names of the diagrams showing the schedule? How do they differ?
14. Project risk analysis can be done using a simple matrix. Explain the matrix and how it is used to determine the severity of project risks.
15. What are five primary areas of project feasibility that should be evaluated?
16. Explain what is meant by organizational and cultural feasibility.
17. What is the NPV, and what purpose does it serve in the initiation of a project?
18. Explain in your own words how to calculate the NPV. What are the NPV's components, and how are they combined to determine the NPV?
19. In addition to prototypes of the new system, what are the five primary deliverables of the inception phase?
20. What are the three areas that require monitoring and controlling during the life of a project?

THINKING CRITICALLY

1. Given the following narrative, make a list of expected business benefits:

   Especially for You Jewelers is a small jewelry company in a college town. Over the last couple of years, Especially for You has experienced a tremendous increase in its business. However, its financial performance has not kept pace with its growth. The current system, which is partially manual and partially automated, does not track accounts receivable sufficiently, and Especially for You is having difficulty determining why the receivables are so high. In addition, Especially for You runs frequent specials to attract customers. It has no idea whether these specials are profitable or whether the benefit, if there is one, comes from associated sales. Especially for You also wants to increase repeat sales to existing customers, and thus needs to develop a customer database. The jewelry company wants to install a new direct sales and accounting system to help solve these problems.

2. Given the following narrative, make a list of system capabilities:

   The new direct sales and accounting system for Especially for You Jewelers is an important element in the future growth and success of the jewelry company. The direct sales portion of the system needs to track every sale and be able to link to the inventory system for cost data to provide a daily profit and loss report. The customer database needs to be able to produce purchase histories to assist management in preparing special mailings and special sales to existing customers. Detailed credit balances and aged accounts for each customer would help solve the problem with the high balance of accounts receivable. Special notice letters and credit history reports would help management reduce accounts receivable.

3. Build a Gantt chart using MS Project based on the table in Figure 3-23. Enter the tasks, dependencies, and durations. Print out both the PERT chart and the Gantt chart.

   Following is a list of tasks for a student to have an international experience by attending a university abroad. You can build schedules for several versions of this set of tasks. For the first version, assume that all predecessor tasks must finish before the succeeding task can begin (the simplest version). For a second version, identify several tasks that can begin a few days before the end of the predecessor task. For a third version, modify the second version so that some tasks can begin a few days after the beginning of a predecessor task. Also, insert a few overview tasks such as Application tasks, Preparation tasks, Travel tasks, and Arrival tasks. Be sure to state your assumptions for each version.

4. Develop a work breakdown structure based on the following narrative. The WBS should cover all aspects of the move, from the beginning of the project (now) to the end, when all employees are moved into their new offices. Use the same format as shown in Figure 3-23 (Problem 3), following these guidelines:
   - Include dependencies
   - Include effort (work) estimates
   - Have about 30 to 40 detailed tasks
   - Cover a period from at least two months to a maximum of six months

   You are an employee of a small company that has outgrown its facility. Your company is a Web development and hosting company, so you have technical network administrators, developers, and a couple of people handling marketing and sales. Your company has 10 employees total.

   The president of your company has found and purchased a single-story building nearby, and the company is going to move into it. The building will need some internal modifications to make it suitable. The president has asked you to take charge of the move. Your assignment is to (1) get the building ready, (2) arrange for the move, and (3) carry out the move.

   The building is nearly finished, so the job should not be too difficult (no construction is necessary, just some refurbishing). The building has several offices as well as a larger area that needs to be set up as cubicles.

   You and the president are walking through the building, and he is telling you what he would like.

   "Let's use the offices as they are. We will need a front reception desk to give a nice appearance for visiting customers. The office in the back corner should be okay for our computer servers. Let's put the salespeople in these offices along the east wall. We are short a few offices, so let's put up a few cubicles in the large room for our junior developers.

TASK ID	DESCRIPTION	DURATION (DAYS)	PREDECESSOR
1	Obtain forms from the international exchange office	1	None
2	Fill out and send in the foreign university application	3	1
3	Receive approval from the foreign university	21	2
4	Apply for scholarship	3	2
5	Receive notice of approval for scholarship	30	4
6	Arrange financing	5	3, 5
7	Arrange for housing in dormitory	25	6
8	Obtain a passport and the required visa	35	6
9	Send in preregistration forms to the university	2	8
10	Make travel arrangements	1	7, 9
11	Determine clothing requirements and go shopping	10	10
12	Pack and make final arrangements to leave	3	11
13	Travel	1	12
14	Move into the dormitory	1	13
15	Finalize registration for classes and other university paperwork	2	14
16	Begin classes	1	15

FIGURE 3-23
WBS task list for attending a university abroad

"Of course, we will need to get everybody connected to our system, and I think Ethernet would be faster than wireless for us. And we all need to have phones.

"Let's plan the move for a long weekend, like a Thursday, Friday, and Saturday. Of course, we need to be careful not to shut down the clients we are already hosting.

"Will you put together a schedule for the move for our employees and set up instructions for all the employees so they know how they are supposed to get ready for the move? Thanks."

5. Enter your WBS from Problem 3 into MS Project. First enter the tasks, dependencies, and durations. Then add some appropriate human resources for the project and assign them to the various tasks. Write a paragraph on your experience using MS Project.
6. Using the simplified risk analysis approach described in the chapter, do a risk analysis of the company move described in Problem 4. Include in your analysis possible risks associated with the schedule, human resources, organization and cultural issues, equipment and materials, and any other potential problem areas.
7. Develop an NPV spreadsheet similar to Figure 3-22 in the chapter. Use the following table (Figure 3-24) of benefits, costs, and discount factors (8 percent). The development costs for the system were $225,000.

YEAR	ANTICIPATED ANNUAL BENEFITS	EXPECTED ANNUAL OPERATING COSTS	DISCOUNT FACTORS AT 8 PERCENT
1	$55,000	$5,000	.9259
2	$60,000	$5,000	.8573
3	$70,000	$5,500	.7938
4	$75,000	$5,500	.7349
5	$80,000	$7,000	.6805
6	$80,000	$7,000	.6301
7	$80,000	$7,000	.5833
8	$80,000	$8,000	.5401

FIGURE 3-24
Benefits, costs, and discount factors for calculating NPV

EXPERIENTIAL EXERCISES

1. Investigate the role of the project manager vis-à-vis the role of the lead engineer. Be sure to investigate if and when it makes sense to have both roles reside in one person, and if and when it makes sense to separate those roles. What are the impacts (pros and cons) of each alternative? You can also investigate various alternatives to this theme:
   - The authority or power of the project manager versus the technical lead
   - The influence of the organization structure (project-oriented versus matrix) on the project
   - Career paths leading to project management ("professional" managers versus experience as technical leads)

   This assignment may be done either as a library research project or by interviewing project managers in various companies. Your instructor will identify which approach you should take. Write a two-page research paper based on your findings.
2. Investigate the impact of various software development methodologies on the way an IT project is organized, planned, and managed (that is, the impact on project management). Of particular interest might be a comparison of traditional predictive project development approaches such as the waterfall, modified waterfall, and spiral approach with some of the newer adaptive approaches such as Extreme Programming (XP) or the Unified Process (UP). Any other "new" approach (for example, agile development) could also be included in your investigation. Write a two-page research paper based on your findings.
3. Find a project manager in an IT department of a local company or in your university and ask him or her what kind of project management training or support the organization provides.
4. Using both library and Internet research sources, research the concept of a Project Management Office (PMO). Find out what the objective of a PMO is, how it is organized, and what kinds of activities are done by the members of a PMO. If possible, find a local company that has a PMO and interview the director of the PMO to find out how it works in the company and what benefits it provides to project managers.
5. Go to the CompTIA (www.compTIA.com) Web site and find the requirements for the project manager exam (IT Project+). Write a one-page summary of the expertise and knowledge required to pass the exam.

Case Studies

CUSTOM LOAD TRUCKING

It was time for Stewart Stockton's annual performance review. As Monica Gibbons, an assistant vice president of information systems, prepared for the interview, she reviewed Stewart's assignments over the last year and his performance. Stewart was one of the up-and-coming systems analysts in the company, and she wanted to be sure to give him solid advice on how to advance his career. She knew, for example, that he had a strong desire to become a project manager and accept increasing levels of responsibility. His desire was certainly in agreement with the needs of the company.

Custom Load Trucking (CLT) is a nationwide trucking firm that specializes in rapid movement of high-technology equipment. With the rapid growth of the communications and computer industries, CLT was feeling more and more pressure from its clients to be able to move its loads more rapidly and precisely. Several new information systems were planned that would enable CLT to schedule and track shipments and trucks almost to the minute. However, trucking is not necessarily a high-interest industry for information systems experts. With the shortage in the job market, CLT decided not to try to hire project managers for these new projects, but to build strong project managers from within the organization.

As Monica reviewed Stewart's record, she found that he had done an excellent job as a team leader on his last project. His last assignment was as a combination team leader/systems analyst on a four-person team. He was involved in systems analysis, design, and programming, and he also managed the work of the other three team members. He assisted in the development of the project schedule and was able to keep his team right on schedule. It also appeared that the quality of his team's work was as good as, if not better than, that of other teams on the project. She wondered what advice she should give him to help him advance his career. She was also wondering if now was the time to give him his own project.

[1] Do you think the decision by CLT to build its own project managers from the existing employee base is a good one? What advice would you give to CLT to make sure that it has strong project management skills in the company?

[2] What kind of criteria would you develop for Monica to use to measure whether Stewart (or any other potential project manager) is ready for project management responsibility?

[3] How would you structure the job for new project managers to ensure, or at least promote, a high level of success?

[4] If you were Monica, what kind of advice would you give to Stewart about managing his career and attaining his immediate goal to become a project manager?

RETHINKING ROCKY MOUNTAIN OUTFITTERS

As Barbara Halifax made preparations to start the project for the customer support system (CSS), she found that she felt a little apprehensive about exactly what she needed to accomplish for the inception phase of the project. The first iteration of the project was supposed to last about four weeks. Its objective was to get the project initiated properly. But she still wondered exactly what she needed to do. She decided that maybe the best way to start was to develop a work breakdown structure and schedule just for the inception iteration itself.

She thought that one good way to develop a WBS would be to first define the deliverables that she needed at the end of the inception phase and then identify the tasks necessary to develop those deliverables. She thought, "I think I will focus on two types of deliverables. I know that many of the outputs of the inception iteration are project management artifacts, such as a schedule and cost/benefit analysis. So, first I will make a list of those items. In addition, we will want to begin understanding the requirements of the new system itself, such as what system capabilities must be included in the system, and maybe develop some working prototypes. So, next I will make a list of the deliverables that I expect to have that are directly related to the new system."

[1] Develop a list of the project management artifacts that you should have at the end of the inception phase. Use the nine PMBOK areas as your guide. For example, under time management, a project schedule is an appropriate deliverable for the inception phase.

[2] Develop a list of the system-oriented artifacts that you might expect to have at the end of the inception iteration. For example, perhaps Barbara should expect to have a first-cut list of the major business processes that the system must support.

[3] Develop a WBS that lists all of the tasks for the inception iteration.

[4] Enter the WBS tasks into MS Project.

FOCUSING ON RELIABLE PHARMACEUTICAL SERVICE

Reliable PHARMACEUTICALS In Chapter 1 you learned about the basic business processes that need to be supported by Reliable Pharmaceutical's new system. In Chapter 2, you discussed the company's desire to make the system available to nursing homes through a Web portal that would allow clients to add patient and prescription information via the Internet. Of course, one of the issues to be addressed was ensuring conformance with the Health Insurance Portability and Accountability Act (HIPAA) requirements on patient privacy.

Reliable's executives, along with the director of IT, decided that there were two viable alternatives for developing the new system. One alternative was to develop an in-house system first, for use by Reliable employees, and then in a later project add the Web portal with update capability. This approach would require three projects, one for the internal system, one for an information Web site, and a final project to add a Web portal to the internal system. Although this approach entails three projects, the projects would each be relatively small. A second approach would be to initiate a large project that would integrate an internal system with a front-end Web portal that has both information and update capability.

[1] Discuss the relative merits of each of the two approaches. What advantages or benefits do you see with each approach? What are the risks and disadvantages of each? Which approach would you recommend?

[2] Assume the first approach was chosen, and you were selected as the project manager for a project to develop an internal system. You are planning to use the UP iterative approach. Develop a WBS for the inception phase. Think about all of the project management knowledge areas and the inception phase deliverables that you need to produce.

[3] Enter the WBS into MS Project. Identify and assign resources to the tasks, and estimate the cost for the inception phase.

[4] Assume the second approach was chosen and the entire system was to be developed at one time. Using the simplified risk management approach presented in the chapter, do a risk analysis for the project.

FURTHER RESOURCES

Ivar Jacobson, Grady Booch, and James Rumbaugh, *The Unified Software Development Process*. Addison-Wesley, 1999.

Philippe Kruchten, *The Rational Unified Process: An Introduction* (2nd ed.). Addison-Wesley, 2000.

Jack R. Meredith and Samuel J. Mantel Jr., *Project Management: A Managerial Approach* (6th ed.). John Wiley and Sons, Inc., 2004.

Joseph Phillips, *IT Project Management: On Track from Start to Finish*. McGraw-Hill, 2002.

Project Management Institute, *A Guide to the Project Management Body of Knowledge*. Project Management Institute, 2000.

Walker Royce, *Software Project Management: A Unified Framework*. Addison-Wesley, 1998.

Kathy Schwalbe, *Information Technology Project Management* (3rd ed.). Course Technology, 2004.

PART 2 MODELING AND THE REQUIREMENTS DISCIPLINE

CHAPTER 4
The Requirements Discipline

CHAPTER 5
Use Cases and Domain Classes

CHAPTER 6
Use Case Modeling and Detailed Requirements

chapter 4

THE REQUIREMENTS DISCIPLINE

LEARNING OBJECTIVES

After reading this chapter, you should be able to:

- Describe the activities of the requirements discipline
- Describe the difference between functional and nonfunctional system requirements
- Describe the kind of information that is required to develop system requirements
- Explain the many reasons for creating information system models
- Determine system requirements through review of documentation, interviews, observation, prototypes, questionnaires, vendor research, and joint application design sessions
- Discuss the need for validation of system requirements to ensure accuracy and completeness and the use of a structured walkthrough
- Discuss the need for validation of system requirements to ensure accuracy and completeness and the use of a structured walkthrough

CHAPTER OUTLINE

- The Requirements Discipline in More Detail
- System Requirements
- Models and Modeling
- Techniques for Information Gathering
- Validating the Requirements

MOUNTAIN STATES MOTOR SPORTS

Amanda Lamy, president and majority stockholder of Mountain States Motor Sports (MSMS), is an avid motorcycle enthusiast and businesswoman. Headquartered in Denver, MSMS is a retailer of motorized sporting vehicles, including boats, jet skis, all-terrain vehicles, and motorcycles. The company has 47 stores located in nearly every state west of the Mississippi and two Canadian provinces.

Over the last decade the market for motorcycles in general—and custom-built bikes in particular—had boomed. Amanda owned three custom bikes herself and decided a year ago that the time was ripe for MSMS to expand into that market. She began seeking business acquisitions or partnerships with custom motorcycle manufacturers throughout the West.

Amanda finalized a partnership agreement with Abeyta's Custom Choppers (ACC) in Tucson just over a month ago. Other acquisitions and partnerships are planned in the near future. The partnership gave MSMS exclusive rights to distribute ACC's custom bikes and gave ACC funds to enlarge and modernize its production facility and a percentage of all retail sales. As part of the modernization, MSMS would build ACC a new information system and would also use that system in other custom bike shops.

MSMS and ACC faced a significant dilemma in developing the new information system. MSMS had no experience in manufacturing, and ACC's current accounting and production control systems were a hodgepodge of manual procedures and automated support, primarily through Microsoft Excel spreadsheets. The business experts had little computer knowledge or experience, and the in-house computer experts at MSMS had no understanding of the business for which they would be building a new system. Buying a system off the shelf was not an option. The market was too small; no vendors served it.

After conferring with an experienced software development consulting firm, MSMS decided to conduct a joint application development (JAD) session over a three-day period. Participants in the session included the owner, accountant, and a salesperson from ACC, Amanda, her chief information officer, her vice president for operations, and a handful of MSMS programmers and developers. Participants from the consulting firm included the session leader, a developer with experience in custom and small lot production control systems, a technical support staff member, and an administrative assistant. The session was conducted at the consulting company's offices in a computerized meeting room with dedicated servers for prototype development and deployment, and appropriate CASE and related tools. All participants stayed in a nearby hotel to maximize available working hours.

The session got off to a rocky start. ACC's representatives lacked computer experience, and they were uncomfortable in the heavily automated meeting room and uncertain they could accomplish the task at hand. Most of the first morning was spent acclimating ACC representatives and other participants to the process. Through the skills of the session leader, who assigned an MSMS staff member to perform all "hands on" computer tasks for ACC personnel for the entire session, camaraderie developed among participants during the first morning and over an extended lunch.

Once everyone was comfortable, work proceeded in earnest. On the first day, the participants specified the overall scope and major functions of the system and described the interaction between ACC's and MSMS's accounting functions in detail. Graphical models of the interactions were generated as simple block diagrams. On the second day, attention turned to marketing and production. In the morning, the team created storyboards to describe how a salesperson in an MSMS store would display options for custom bikes as a prelude for creating a detailed order. While most of the participants ate lunch, two MSMS developers scanned pictures of customized bikes to mock up a user interface for an online design program.

In the afternoon, the mock-up was expanded into a more complete order-entry system, which captured most of the details that ACC would need, in order to schedule and complete production. During the second evening, MSMS developers worked late into the night to flesh out the prototype. On the third morning, participants evaluated the prototype and made suggestions for further enhancements and improvements. They devoted the remainder of the morning and most of the afternoon to developing requirements and design criteria for a production management system encompassing scheduling, parts management, and accounting for time and materials. The session concluded with a one-hour review of all the requirements that had been specified and the design decisions that had been made, followed by development of an open items list and a rough schedule and budget for the project.

The JAD session marked the start of the first iteration of the new system development project. The remainder of that iteration expanded on the work of the JAD session and addressed the more important items on the open items list. This project was unusual due to the team's up-front uncertainty over many important aspects of the new system, including the business case, system scope, and detailed requirements. For this project, performing most of the business modeling and other inception phase activities would have been impossible without first defining many of the detailed system requirements. Although some of the requirements defined in the JAD session were modified in later iterations, many of the requirements were incorporated into the system with little change. Most importantly, the session provided a "running start" for the entire project.

Overview

In Chapter 2, you learned that system development consists of four phases—inception, elaboration, construction, and transition—with activities grouped into disciplines including business modeling, requirements, design, implementation, testing, deployment, project management, configuration and change management, and environment. Chapter 3 discussed how the inception phase defines the vision, scope, business case, schedule, and direction for a system development project. This chapter focuses on the activities of the requirements discipline, which is most heavily concentrated in the elaboration phase.

The requirements discipline is primarily about building models. You were introduced to some models in Chapter 3. This chapter and those that follow will introduce you to many other model types and their development and validation techniques. Building and validating requirements models is based on many fact-finding and investigation techniques, which are also described in this chapter. Analysts interact extensively with users to elicit accurate information about requirements and to document and validate requirements models.

As fact finding and investigation proceed, you learn the details of business processes and daily operations. In fact, the objective is to try to become as knowledgeable about how the business operates as the users you interview. Why become an expert? Because only then can you ensure that the system meets the needs of the business. As an analyst, you bring a fresh perspective to the problem and possess a unique set of skills that you can employ to identify new and better ways to accomplish business objectives with information technology. Many current users are so used to the way they have been performing their tasks that they cannot envision better, more advanced ways to achieve results. Your technical knowledge combined with your newly acquired problem domain knowledge can bring unique solutions to business processes—and make a difference in the organization.

An additional benefit to becoming an expert in the problem domain is that you build credibility with the users. Your suggestions will carry more weight because they will meet users' specific needs. During the development of a new system, you will have many suggestions and recommendations about daily business procedures, which usually require major changes in user activities. If you can "walk the walk and talk the talk" of the users' business operations, then they are much more likely to accept your recommendations. Otherwise, you may be viewed as an outsider who really does not understand their problems.

The sections that follow first give an overview of the requirements discipline. They define system requirements and explore the different types of requirements that analysts encounter. Then they explain several techniques analysts use to learn about the business processes and to gather information, using both traditional and newer accelerated methods. The chapter ends with a discussion of validating requirements models.

THE REQUIREMENTS DISCIPLINE IN MORE DETAIL

Figure 4-1 lists the activities of the requirements discipline, as first described in Chapter 2. The activities are discussed in more detail here and in subsequent chapters. In business modeling, the emphasis is on defining the context within which the system will operate and the business objectives the system will achieve. In the requirements discipline, the focus shifts to the internal details of the system—from *what* the business objectives are to *how* those objectives will be achieved. During the requirements discipline, the analyst defines in great detail what the information system needs to accomplish to provide the organization with the desired benefits.

The transition from business modeling to requirements definition is not necessarily linear. To firmly establish the system vision, analysts often must define the details of the requirements. For example, the system vision often includes initial specifications of important use cases and may include other requirements models, such as an initial

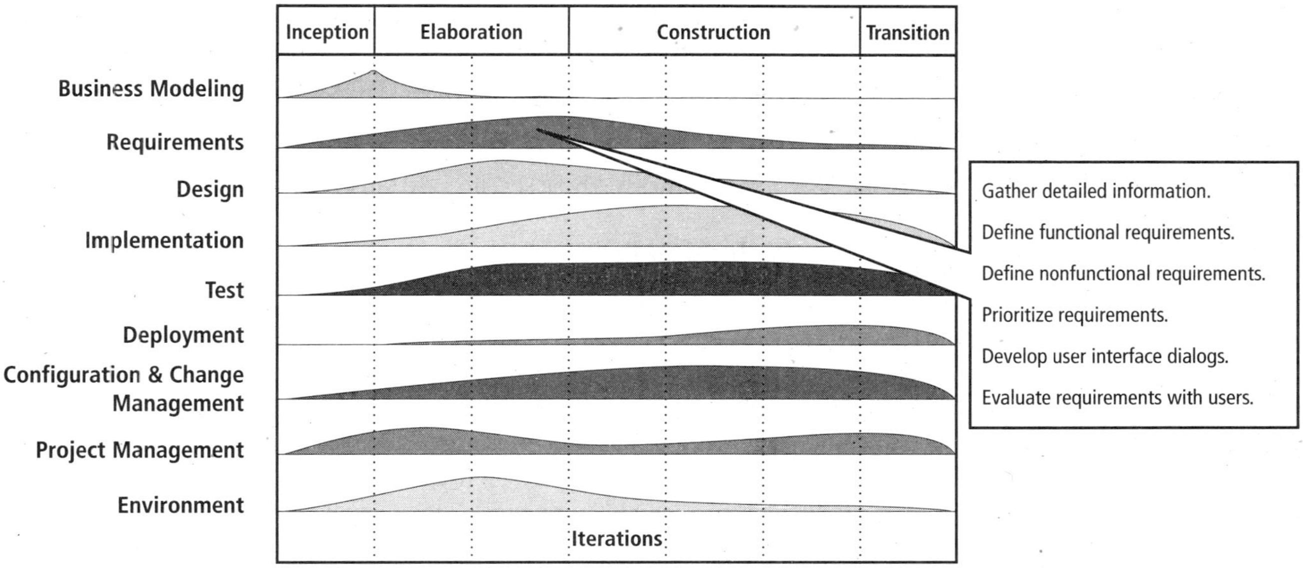

FIGURE 4-1
Activities of the requirements discipline

domain class diagram or an interaction diagram showing a key interface to another system. Those models are then refined and fully specified in later iterations.

Unlike business modeling activities, activities of the requirements discipline are usually spread over many iterations to avoid a shortcoming of sequential approaches to system development sometimes called *analysis paralysis*, the inability to begin modeling the system because the entire project is overwhelming. The UP breaks a system into manageable pieces, and an iteration includes requirements, design, implementation, testing, and other activities for a particular subset of the system. The output of the iteration is working software, although that software is often incomplete and is modified or expanded in later iterations. Combining requirements activities with related activities from other disciplines enables the requirements to be validated immediately. As the end users sign off on the software, the requirements that led to its construction are assumed to be correct.

GATHER DETAILED INFORMATION

The requirements discipline involves gathering a considerable amount of information. Systems analysts obtain some information from people who will be using the system, either by interviewing them or by watching them work. They obtain other information by reviewing planning documents and policy statements. Documentation from the existing system should also be studied carefully. Analysts can obtain additional information by looking at what other companies (particularly vendors) have done when faced with a similar business need. In short, analysts need to talk to nearly everyone who will use the new system or has used similar systems, and they must read nearly everything available about the existing system.

Beginning analysts often underestimate how much there is to learn about the work the user performs. The analyst must become an expert in the business area the system will support. For example, if you are implementing an order-entry system, you need to become an expert on the way orders are processed (including accounting). If you are implementing a loan-processing system, you need to become an expert on the rules used for approving credit. If you work for a bank, you need to think of yourself as a banker. The most successful analysts become very involved with their organization's main business.

Analysts also need to collect technical information. They try to understand the existing system by identifying and understanding activities of all current and future users, by identifying all present and future locations where work occurs, and by identifying all system interfaces with other systems, both inside and outside the organization. Beyond that, analysts need to identify software packages that might be used to satisfy the system requirements. These specifics are discussed later in the chapter.

DEFINE REQUIREMENTS

As all of the necessary information is gathered, it is very important to record it. Most of this information describes functional requirements—what the system is required to do. Some information describes nonfunctional requirements—for example, facts about needed system performance or the expected number of transactions. Defining functional requirements is not just a matter of writing down facts and figures. Instead, many different types of models are created to help record and communicate what is required.

The modeling process is a learning process for an analyst. As a model is developed, the analyst learns more and more about the system. Modeling continues while information is gathered, and the analyst continually reviews the models with the end users to verify that each model is complete and correct. In addition, the analyst studies each model, adds to it, rearranges it, and then checks how well it fits with other models being created. Just when the analyst is fairly sure the system requirements are fully specified, an additional piece of information surfaces, requiring yet more changes, and refinement begins again. Modeling can continue for quite some time, and it does not always have a defined end. The uncertainty involved makes some programmers uncomfortable, but it is unavoidable.

The specific models created depend on the system being developed. The UP provides a set of possible model types but does not require analysts to use all of them. Object-oriented requirements models almost always include class diagrams and use case diagrams. Other requirements models that may be developed include activity diagrams, location diagrams, interaction diagrams, and user interface storyboards. Because there are so many kinds of requirements models, no single chapter can describe them all. We describe most of the models in this chapter and the following two chapters. User interface models are further discussed in Chapter 11.

PRIORITIZE REQUIREMENTS

Once the system requirements are well understood and detailed models of the requirements are completed, it is important to establish which of the functional and nonfunctional requirements are most crucial for the system. Sometimes users suggest additional system functions that are desirable but not essential. However, users and analysts need to ask themselves which functions are truly important and which are fairly important but not absolutely required. Again, an analyst who understands the organization and the work done by the users will have more insight for answering these questions.

Why prioritize the functions requested by the users? Resources are always limited, and the analyst must always be prepared to justify the scope of the system. Therefore, it is important to know what is absolutely required. Unless the analyst carefully evaluates priorities, system requirements tend to expand as users make more suggestions (a phenomenon called *scope creep*).

DEVELOP USER INTERFACE DIALOGS

When a new system is replacing an old system that does similar work, users are usually quite sure about their requirements and the desired form of the user interface. But many system development projects break new ground by automating functions that were previously performed manually or by implementing functions that weren't performed in the past. In either case, users tend to be uncertain of many aspects of system requirements. Models such as use cases, activity diagrams, and interaction diagrams can be developed based on user input, but it is often difficult for users to interpret and validate such abstract models.

In comparison, user validation of an interface is much simpler and more reliable because the user can see and feel the system. To most users, the user interface *is* the system. Thus, developing user interface dialogs is a powerful method of eliciting and documenting requirements. Analysts can develop user interfaces as paper models such as storyboards (covered in more detail in Chapter 11), or they can develop user interface prototypes, using a CASE tool or other development tool. A prototype interface can serve as both a requirement and a starting point for developing a portion of the system. In other words, a user interface prototype developed in an early iteration can be expanded in later iterations to become a fully functioning part of the system.

EVALUATE REQUIREMENTS WITH USERS

Ideally, the activities of evaluating requirements with users and documenting the requirements are fully integrated. But in practice, users generally have other responsibilities besides developing a new system. So, analysts usually use an iterative process, in which they elicit user input, work alone to model requirements, return to the user for additional input or validation, then work alone to incorporate the new input and refine the models. The process may repeat many times until an acceptable requirements model is developed.

Evaluating a requirement or requirements model is not always a discrete or well-defined activity. Many alternatives exist for the final design and implementation of a system. So, it is very important to define carefully and then evaluate all of the possibilities. When requirements are prioritized, the analyst can generate several alternatives by eliminating some of the less important requirements. In addition, technology also raises several alternatives for the system. Beyond those considerations, decisions such as whether to build the system using in-house development staff or a consulting firm affect the outcome. Furthermore, one or more off-the-shelf software packages could possibly satisfy all of the requirements.

Requirements evaluation also incorporates validation—that is, determining the accuracy and correctness of requirements. In the UP, building and testing software that incorporates requirements is the preferred validation method. But various constraints may limit the analysts' ability to use this validation method. Validation is further discussed at the end of this chapter.

SYSTEM REQUIREMENTS

system requirements
specifications that define the functions to be provided by a system

functional requirement
a system requirement that describes an activity or process that the system must perform

System requirements are all of the capabilities that the new system must have and the constraints that the new system must meet. Generally, analysts divide system requirements into two categories: functional and nonfunctional requirements. *Functional requirements* are the activities that the system must perform—that is, the business uses to which the system will be applied. They are usually related directly to use cases. For example, if you are developing a payroll system, the required use cases might include functions such as "write paychecks," "calculate commission amounts," "calculate payroll taxes," "maintain employee-dependent information," and "report year-end tax deductions to the IRS." The new system must handle all these functions. Identifying and describing all of these use cases requires a substantial amount of time and effort because the functions and their relationships can be very complex.

Functional requirements are based on the procedures and rules that the organization uses to run its business. Sometimes they are well documented and easy to identify and describe. An example might be, "All new employees must fill out a W-4 form to enter information about their dependents in the payroll system." Other business rules might be more obtuse or difficult to find. An example from Rocky Mountain Outfitters might be that "an additional 2 percent commission rate is paid to order takers on telephone sales for 'special promotions' that are added to the order." These special promotions are unadvertised specials that are sold by the telephone order clerk—thus the special commission rate. Discovering rules such as this is critical to the final design of the system. If this rule weren't discovered, you might design a system that allows only fixed commission rates and discover much later that your design could not accommodate this rule.

nonfunctional requirement
a characteristic of the system other than activities it must perform or support

technical requirement
a system requirement that describes an operational characteristic related to an organization's environment, hardware, and software

Nonfunctional requirements are characteristics of the system other than activities it must perform or support. There are many different types of nonfunctional requirements, including the following:

- *Technical requirements* describe operational characteristics related to the environment, hardware, and software of the organization. For example, the client components of a new system might be required to operate on portable and desktop PCs running the Windows operating system and using Internet Explorer. The server components might have to be written in Java and communicate with one another using a component interaction standard such as CORBA (Common Object Request Broker Architecture) or SOAP (Simple Object Access Protocol).
- *Performance requirements* describe operational characteristics related to measures of workload, such as throughput and response time. For example, the client portion of a system might be required to have one-half-second response time on all screens, and the server components might need to support 100 simultaneous client sessions (with the same response time).
- *Usability requirements* describe operational characteristics related to users, such as the user interface, related work procedures, online help, and documentation. For example, a Web-based interface might be required to follow organization-wide graphic design guidelines such as menu placement and format, color schemes, use of the organization's logo, and required legal disclaimers.
- *Reliability requirements* describe the dependability of a system—how often a system exhibits behaviors such as service outages and incorrect processing and how it detects and recovers from those problems. Reliability requirements are sometimes considered a subset of performance requirements.
- *Security requirements* describe which users can perform which system functions under what conditions. For example, access to certain system outputs may be limited to managers at a certain level or employees of a specific department. Some access may be authorized from home and some only from within the organization's local network. Security requirements may also apply to areas such as network communications and data storage. For example, an organization might require encryption of all data transmitted over the Internet and control of all database server access through use of a username and password.

performance requirement
a system requirement that describes an operational characteristic related to workload measures, such as throughput and response time

usability requirement
a system requirement that describes an operational characteristic related to users, such as the user interface, work procedures, online help, and documentation

reliability requirement
a system requirement that describes the dependability of a system, accounting for such events as service outages, incorrect processing, and error detection and recovery

security requirement
a system requirement that describes user access to certain functions and the conditions under which access is granted

Both functional and nonfunctional system requirements are needed for a complete definition of a new system. Functional requirements are most often documented in graphical and textual models, as described in this chapter and the following two chapters. Nonfunctional requirements are usually documented in narrative descriptions that accompany the models.

MODELS AND MODELING

As we discussed in Chapter 2, a model is a representation of some aspect of the system being built. Because a system is so complex, an analyst creates a variety of models to encompass the detailed information that he or she collected and digested (see Figure 4-2). The UML activity diagram, described in detail later in this chapter, is one type of model that focuses on both user and system activities. Also, the analyst uses many different types of models to show the system at different levels of detail (or levels of abstraction), including a high-level overview as well as detailed views of certain aspects of the system. Some models show different parts of the problem and solution; for example, one model might show inputs, another the data stored. Some models show the same problem and solution from different perspectives; one model might show how objects interact from the perspective of outside actors, and another how objects interact in terms of sequencing.

FIGURE 4-2
An analyst needs a collection of models to understand system requirements

THE PURPOSE OF MODELS

Some developers think of a model as documentation produced after the requirements and design work is done. But actually, the process of creating a model helps an analyst clarify and refine requirements and design details. The analyst learns as he or she completes and then studies parts of the model. Analysts also raise questions while creating a model and answer them as the modeling process continues. New pieces are added; the consequences of changes are evaluated and again questioned. In this respect, the modeling process itself provides direct benefits to the analyst. The technique used to create the model is valuable in itself, even if the analyst never shows a particular model to anyone else. But usually models are shared with others as requirements and design activities progress.

Another key reason that modeling is important in system development is the complexity of describing information systems. Information systems are very complex, and parts of the systems are intangible. Models of the various parts help simplify the analyst's efforts and focus them on a few aspects of the system at a time. The reason that an analyst uses so many different models is that each relates to different aspects of the system. In fact, some of the models created by the analyst may serve only to integrate these aspects—showing how the other models fit together.

Because of the amount of information gathered and digested and the length of time each analyst spends on a project, analysts need to review the models frequently to help them recall details of work previously completed. People can retain only a limited amount of information, so we all need memory aids. Models provide a way of storing information for later use in a form that can be readily digested.

The support for communication is one of the most often cited reasons for creating the models. Given that the analyst learns while working through the modeling process and that the collection of models reduces the complexity of the information system, the models also serve a critical role in supporting communication among project team members and with system users. If one team member is working on models of inputs and outputs, and another team member is working on models of the object interactions that convert the inputs to outputs, then they need to communicate and coordinate to make sure these models fit together. The second team member needs to see what outputs are desired before modeling the interactions that create them. At the same time, both team members need to know what the problem domain classes are required to remember about the inputs and outputs. Models support essential communication and teamwork among the project team members.

Models also assist in communication with the system users and foster understanding. Typically, an analyst reviews the models with a variety of users to get feedback on the analyst's understanding of the system requirements. Users need to see clear and complete models to comprehend what the analyst is proposing. Additionally, the analyst sometimes works with users to develop the models, so the modeling process helps users better understand the possibilities that the new system can offer. Users also need to communicate among themselves using the models. And the analyst and the users together can use models to describe system capabilities to managers who are responsible for approving the system.

Finally, the requirements models produced by the analyst are used as documentation for future development teams when they maintain or enhance the system. Considering the amount of resources invested in a new system, it is critical for the development team to leave behind a clear record of what was created. An important activity during deployment is to package the documentation accurately, completely, and in a form that future developers can use. Much of the documentation consists of the models created throughout the project. Figure 4-3 summarizes the reasons modeling is important to system development.

FIGURE 4-3
Reasons for modeling

- Learning from the modeling process
- Reducing complexity by abstraction
- Remembering all of the details
- Communicating with other development team members
- Communication with a variety of users and stakeholders
- Documenting what was done for future maintenance/enhancement

Although this book emphasizes models and techniques for creating models, it is important to remember that system projects vary in the number of models required and in their formality. Smaller, simpler system projects will not need models showing every system detail, particularly when the project team has experience with the type of system being built. Sometimes the key models are created informally in a few hours. Although models are often created using powerful CASE tools and visual modeling tools, as discussed in Chapter 2, useful and important models are sometimes drawn quickly over lunch on a paper napkin or in an airport waiting room on the back of an envelope! As with any development activity, an iterative approach is used for creating requirements and design models. The first draft of a model has some but not all details worked out. The next iteration might fill in more details or correct previous misconceptions.

TYPES OF MODELS

Analysts use many different types of models when developing information systems. The type of model used depends on the nature of the information being represented. Models can be categorized into three general types: mathematical models, descriptive models, and graphical models.

MATHEMATICAL MODELS

mathematical model
a series of formulas that describe technical aspects of a system

A *mathematical model* is a series of formulas that describe technical aspects of a system. Mathematical models are used for precise aspects of the system that can be best represented by using formulas or mathematical notation, such as equations that represent network throughput requirements or a function expressing the response time required for a query. These models are examples of *technical* requirements. Additionally, scientific and engineering applications tend to compute results using elaborate mathematical algorithms. The mathematical notation is the most appropriate way to represent these *functional* requirements, and it is also the most natural way for scientific and engineering users to express those requirements. An analyst working on scientific and engineering applications had better be comfortable with math.

But mathematical notation is also sometimes efficient for simpler requirements for business systems. For example, in a payroll application, it is reasonable to model gross pay as regular pay plus overtime pay. A reorder point for inventory, a discount price for a product, or a salary adjustment for a promotion might be modeled with a simple formula.

DESCRIPTIVE MODELS

descriptive model
narrative memos, reports, or lists that describe some aspect of a system

Not all requirements can be precisely defined with mathematics. For these requirements, analysts use *descriptive models*, which can be narrative memos, reports, or lists. Figure 4-4 provides examples of descriptive models for RMO's customer support system. Initial interviews with users might require the analyst to jot down notes in a narrative form, such as the description of the phone-order process obtained from phone-order representatives. Sometimes users describe what they do in reports or memos to the analysts. The analyst might convert these narrative descriptions to a graphical modeling notation while compiling all of the information.

Sometimes a narrative description is the best form to use for recording information. Use case descriptions are often written out as one or two short paragraphs of text. More detailed use case descriptions are lists of steps required in processing between the actor and the system. Many useful models of information systems involve simple lists, such as lists of features, inputs, outputs, events, or users. Lists are a form of descriptive or narrative model that are concise, specific, and useful. Figure 4-4 contains a simple list of inputs to the customer support system.

GRAPHICAL MODELS

graphical model
diagrams and schematic representations of some aspect of a system

Probably the most useful models created by the analyst are graphical models. *Graphical models* include diagrams and schematic representations of some aspect of a system.

A narrative description of processing requirements as verbalized by an RMO phone-order representative:

"When customers call in, I first ask if they have ordered by phone with us before, and I try to get them to tell me their customer ID number that they can find on the mailing label on the catalog. Or, if they seem puzzled about the customer number, I need to look them up by name and go through a process of elimination, looking at all of the Smiths in Dayton, for example, until I get the right one. Next, I ask what catalog they are looking at, which sometimes is out of date. If that is the case, then I explain that many items are still offered, but that the prices might be different. Naturally, they point to a page number, which doesn't help me because of the different catalogs, but I get them to tell me the product ID somehow...."

List of inputs for the RMO customer support system:

Item inquiry
New order
Order change request
Order status inquiry
Order fulfillment notice
Back-order notice
Order return notice
Catalog request
Customer account update notice
Promotion package details
Customer charge adjustment
Catalog update details
Special promotion details
New catalog details

FIGURE 4-4
Some descriptive models

Graphical models make it easy to understand complex relationships that are too difficult to follow when described verbally. Recall the old saying that a picture is worth a thousand words. In system development, a carefully constructed graphical model might be worth a million words!

Some graphical models actually look similar to a real-world part of the system, such as a screen design or a report layout design. But for most of the analyst's work, the graphical models use symbols to represent more abstract things, such as external agents, processes, data, objects, messages, and connections. The key graphical models used for the requirements discipline tend to represent the more abstract aspects of a system. The more concrete models of screen designs and report layouts are outputs of design discipline activities.

A variety of graphical models is used. Each model highlights (or abstracts) important details of some aspect of the information system. Each type of model should ideally use unique and standardized symbols to represent pieces of information. That way, whoever looks at a model can understand it. The Unified Modeling Language (UML) now provides diagramming standards for models used in the object-oriented approach.

OVERVIEW OF MODELS USED IN REQUIREMENTS AND DESIGN

The requirements discipline activity named *Define functional requirements* involves creating a variety of models. They are referred to as *logical models* because they define in great detail what is required without committing to one specific technology. Analysts create many types of logical models to define system requirements.

Many models are also created by the design discipline. Design models are physical models because they show how some aspect of the system will be implemented with specific technology. Some of these models are extensions of requirements models or derive directly from the requirements models. Some models (for example, the class diagram) are used for requirements and design. Figure 4-5 shows some of the UML diagrams used in system development. Additional models are also used that are not strictly UML diagrams, such as event lists, event tables, use case descriptions, screen layouts, report layouts, location diagrams, and various charts and matrices, as shown in Figure 4-6.

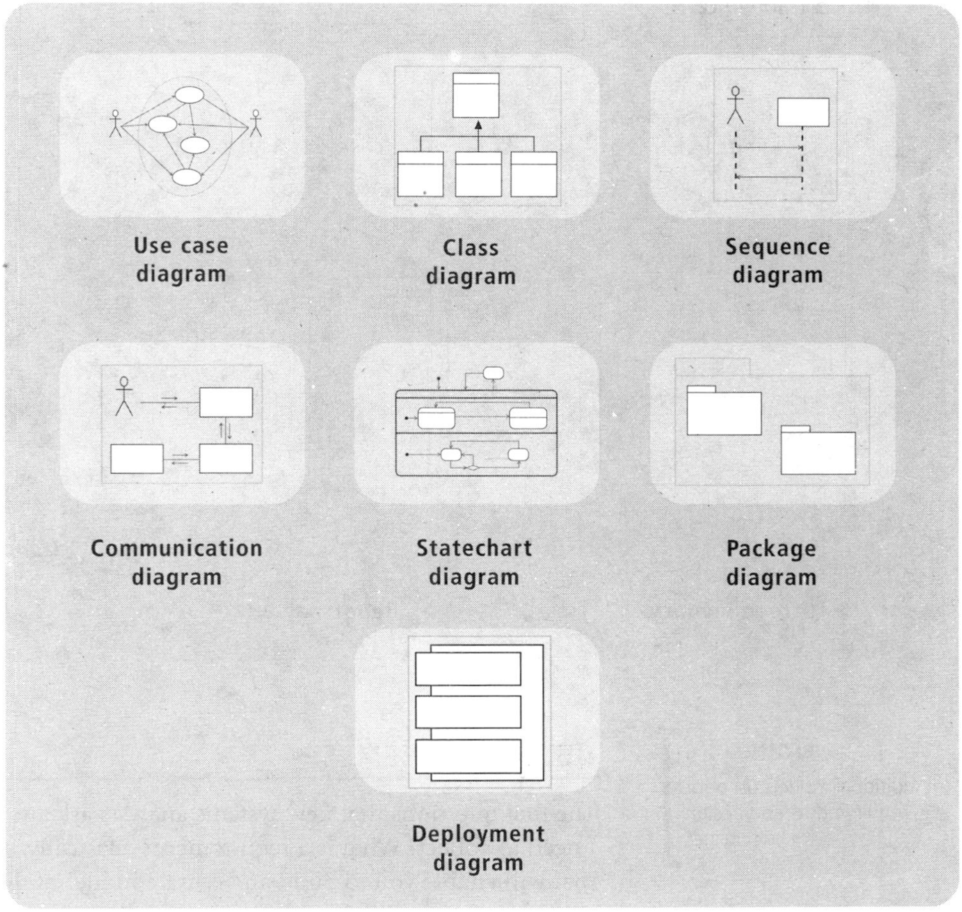

FIGURE 4-5
UML diagrams used for modeling

This chapter and the next two chapters describe various requirements models, including event lists, use cases, event tables, class diagrams, and CRUD matrices. Although there are many differences in the content and presentation of different model types, the techniques used to gather information to build the models are similar. These techniques are described in the next section.

TECHNIQUES FOR INFORMATION GATHERING

The following sections describe various information-gathering techniques analysts use to build models and define requirements. Most are useful in both the business modeling and requirements disciplines. Figure 4-7 summarizes the techniques and their contributions to the requirements discipline.

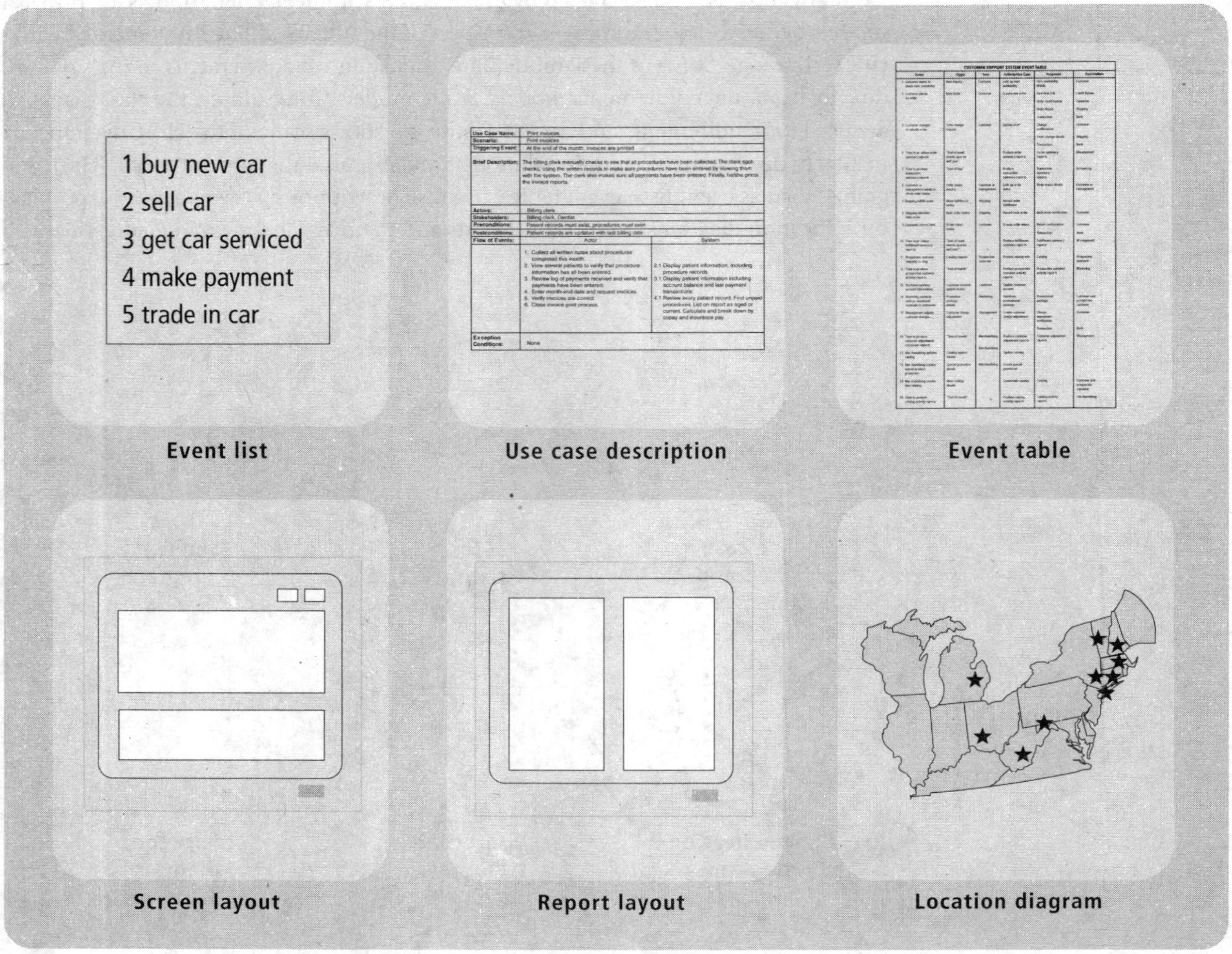

FIGURE 4-6
Additional models used for requirements and design disciplines

QUESTION THEMES

The first questions that new systems analysts ask are, "What kind of information do I need to collect? What is a requirement?" Basically, you want to obtain information that will enable you to build an accurate model of the new business system. As shown in Figure 4-8, three major themes should guide you as you pursue your investigation.

WHAT ARE THE BUSINESS PROCESSES?

In the first question—What do you do?—the focus is on understanding the business functions. This question is the first step in being able to walk the walk—understanding exactly what a system must do for users. The analyst must obtain a comprehensive list of all the business processes. In most cases, the users provide answers in terms of the current system, so the analyst must discern carefully which of those functions are fundamental—which will remain and which may possibly be eliminated with an improved system. For example, sales clerks may indicate that the first thing they do when a customer places an order is to check the customer's credit history. In the new system, sales clerks may never need to perform that function; the system might perform the check automatically. The function remains a system requirement, but the method of carrying out the function moves from the clerks to the computer system.

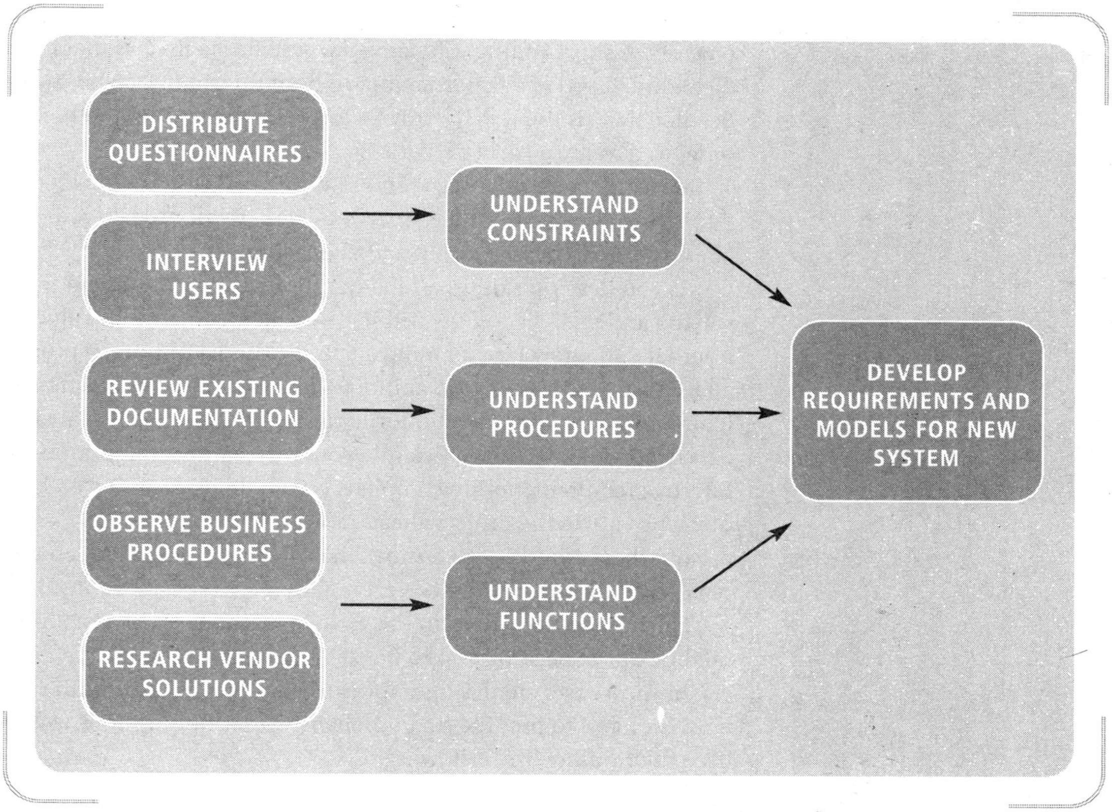

FIGURE 4-7
The relationship between information gathering and model building

FIGURE 4-8
Sample themes for defining requirements

THEME	QUESTIONS TO USERS
What are the business operations and processes?	What do you do?
How should those operations be performed?	How do you do it? What steps do you follow?
What information is needed to perform those operations?	What information do you use? What forms or reports do you use?

HOW IS THE BUSINESS PROCESS PERFORMED?

The second question—How should it be done?—moves the discussion from the current system to the new system. The focus is on how the new system should support the function rather than on how it does now. Thus, the first two questions go hand in hand; they discover the need and begin to define the system requirement in terms of the new system. The users most frequently talk about the current system, but it is critical for the systems analyst to go beyond the current process. He or she must be able to help the user visualize new and more efficient approaches to performing the business processes made possible by the new technology.

WHAT INFORMATION IS REQUIRED?

The final question—What information is needed?—elaborates the second question by defining specific information that the new system must provide. The answers to the second and third questions form the basis for the definition of the system requirements. One of the shortcomings of many new systems analysts is that they do not identify all of the required pieces of information. In both this question and the previous one, "detail, detail, detail" is the watchword. An analyst must understand the nitty-gritty detail in order to develop a correct solution.

Focusing on these three themes helps an analyst ask intelligent, meaningful questions in an investigation. Later, as you learn about models, you will be able to formulate additional meaningful, detailed questions to ask.

As you develop skill in asking questions and building models, your problem-solving and analytical skills will increase. Remember, your value as a systems analyst is not that you know how to build a specific model or how to program in a specific language. Your value is in your ability to analyze and solve business information problems—to gather the correct information. Fundamental to that skill is not only how effectively but also how efficiently you can identify and capture these business rules. Effective requirements are complete, comprehensive, and correct. An efficient analyst is one who moves the project ahead rapidly with minimal intrusion on users' time and use of other resources, yet ensures that the information gathered will produce complete, comprehensive, and correct requirements specifications.

The next sections present the various methods of information gathering. All these methods have been proven to be effective, although some are more efficient than others. In most cases, analysts combine methods to increase both their effectiveness and efficiency and to provide a comprehensive fact-finding approach. The most widely used methods are the following:

- Review existing reports, forms, and procedure descriptions
- Conduct interviews and discussions with users
- Observe and document business processes
- Build prototypes
- Distribute and collect questionnaires
- Conduct joint application design (JAD) sessions
- Research vendor solutions

REVIEW EXISTING REPORTS, FORMS, AND PROCEDURE DESCRIPTIONS

This step should probably be the first in fact-finding activities. There are two sources of information for existing procedures and forms. One source is external to the organization—at industry-wide professional organizations and at other companies. It may not be easy to obtain information from other companies, but they are a potential source of important information. Sometimes, industry journals and magazines report the findings or "best practices" studies. The project team would be negligent in its duties if its members were not familiar with best practice information. Also, with systems crossing organization boundaries more and more, external sources are an important source of system requirements.

The second source of reports, forms, and procedures is the existing business documents and procedure descriptions within the organization. This internal review serves two purposes. First, it is a good way to get a preliminary understanding of the processes. Often new systems analysts need to learn about the industry or the specific application that they are studying. A preliminary review of existing documentation will bring them up to speed fairly rapidly.

To begin the process, the analysts ask users to provide copies of the forms and reports that they currently are using. They also request copies of procedural manuals and work descriptions. Reviewing these materials provides an understanding of the business functions and forms the basis for developing detailed interview questions.

The second way to use documents and reports is in the interviews themselves. Forms and reports can serve as visual aids for the interview and as the working documents for discussion (see Figure 4-9). Discussion can center on the use of each form, its objective, its distribution, and its information content. The discussion should also include specific business events that initiate the use of the form. Several different business events might require the same form, and specific information about each event and business process is critical. It is also always helpful to have forms that have been filled out with real information to ensure that the analyst obtains a correct understanding of the fields and data content.

Rocky Mountain Outfitters—Customer Order Form

ROCKY MOUNTAIN OUTFITTERS

Name and address of person placing order.
(Please verify your mailing address and make correction below.)
Order Date ___/___/___

Name

Address Apt. No

City State Zip

Phone: Day ( ) Evening ( )

Gift Order or Ship To: (Use only if different from address at left.)

Name

Address Apt. No

City State Zip

Gift ☐ Address for this Shipment Only ☐ Permanent Change of Address ☐

Gift Card Message

Delivery Phone ( )

Item No.	Description	Style	Color	Size	Sleeve Length	Qty	Monogram	Style	Price Each	Total

Method of Payment

Check/Money Order ☐ Gift Certificate(s) ☐ AMOUNT ENCLOSED $____

American Express ☐ MasterCard ☐ VISA ☐ Other ☐

Account Number

MO YR ___/___ Expiration Date

Signature

MERCHANDISE TOTAL ____

Regular FedEx shipping $4.50 per U.S. delivery address ____
(Items are sent within 24 hours for delivery in 2 to 4 days)

Please add $4.50 per each additional U.S. delivery address ____

FedEx Standard Overnight Service ____

Any additional freight charges ____

International Shipping (see shipping information on back) ____

FIGURE 4-9
A sample order form for Rocky Mountain Outfitters

Reviewing the documentation of existing procedures helps identify business rules that may not come up in the interviews. Written procedures also help analysts discover discrepancies and redundancies in the business processes. However, procedure manuals frequently are not kept up to date, and they commonly include errors. To ensure that the assumptions and business rules that derive from the existing documentation are correct, analysts should review them with the users.

CONDUCT INTERVIEWS AND DISCUSSIONS WITH USERS

Interviewing stakeholders is by far the most effective way to understand business functions and business rules. It is also the most time-consuming and resource-expensive option. In this method, systems analysts meet with individuals or groups of users. A list of detailed questions is prepared, and discussion continues until all the processing requirements are understood and documented by the project team. Obviously, this process may take some time, so it usually requires multiple sessions with each of the users or user groups.

To conduct effective interviews, analysts need to organize in three areas: (1) preparing for the interview, (2) conducting the interview, and (3) following up the interview. Figure 4-10 is a sample checklist that summarizes the major points to be covered and is useful for preparing for and conducting an interview.

Checklist for Conducting an Interview

Before

- ☐ Establish the objective for the interview
- ☐ Determine correct user(s) to be involved
- ☐ Determine project team members to participate
- ☐ Build a list of questions and issues to be discussed
- ☐ Review related documents and materials
- ☐ Set the time and location
- ☐ Inform all participants of objective, time, and location

During

- ☐ Dress appropriately
- ☐ Arrive on time
- ☐ Look for exception and error conditions
- ☐ Probe for details
- ☐ Take thorough notes
- ☐ Identify and document unanswered items or open questions

After

- ☐ Review notes for accuracy, completeness, and understanding
- ☐ Transfer information to appropriate models and documents
- ☐ Identify areas needing further clarification
- ☐ Send thank-you notes if appropriate

FIGURE 4-10
A sample checklist to prepare for user interviews

PREPARING FOR THE INTERVIEW

Every successful interview requires preparation. The very first, and most important, step in preparing for an interview is to establish the objective of the interview. In other words, what do you want to accomplish with this interview? Write down the objective so that it is firmly established in your mind. The second step is to determine which users should be involved in the interview. Frequently, the first two steps are so intertwined that both are done together. Even if you don't do anything else to prepare for your interviews, you must at least complete these two steps. The objective and the participants drive everything else in the interview.

The interview participants include both users and project members. Generally, at least two project members are involved in every interview. The two project members help each other during the interview and compare notes afterward to ensure accuracy. The number of users varies depending on the objective of the interview. A small number of users is generally best when the interview objective is narrow or of a fact-finding nature. In such cases, interviewing more than three users at a time tends to cause unnecessarily long discussions. Larger groups are better if the objective is something more open-ended, such as exploring new process alternatives. Larger groups are often better for generating and evaluating new ideas. However, it can be difficult to manage a large group meeting to ensure high-quality input from all participants. Professional facilitators and formal discovery techniques such as joint application design (discussed later in this chapter) may be employed if the objective is complex or critical and the group is large.

BEST PRACTICE: Make sure at least two project members participate in user interviews.

open-ended questions
questions that require discussion and do not necessarily have a simple, short answer

closed-ended questions
questions that have a simple, definitive answer

The third step is to prepare detailed questions to be used in the interview. Write down a list of specific questions, and prepare notes based on the forms or reports received earlier. Usually you should prepare a list of questions that are consistent with the objective of the interview. Both open-ended questions and closed-ended questions are appropriate. *Open-ended questions* are questions that require discussion and explanation, such as, "How do you do this function?" *Closed-ended questions* are questions that have simple, definitive answers, such as, "How many forms a day do you process?" Closed-ended questions are used to get specific facts. Generally, open-ended questions help you get the discussion started and encourage the user to explain all the details of the business process and the rules.

The last step is to make the final interview arrangements and to communicate those arrangements to all participants. A specific time and location should be established. If possible, a quiet location should be chosen to avoid interruptions. Each participant should know the objective of the meeting and, when appropriate, should have a chance to preview the questions or materials to be reviewed. Interviews consume a substantial amount of time, and they can be made more efficient if each participant knows beforehand what is to be accomplished.

CONDUCTING THE INTERVIEW

New systems analysts are usually quite nervous about conducting interviews. However, remember that, in most cases, the users are excited about getting a better system to help them do their jobs. Practicing good manners usually ensures that the interview will go well. Here are a few guidelines:

Dress appropriately. Dress at least as well as the best-dressed user. In many corporate settings, such as banks or insurance companies with managers present, business suits are appropriate. In factory or manufacturing settings, work dress may be appropriate. The objective in dressing is to project competence and professionalism without intimidating the user.

Arrive on time. If anything, be a little early. If the session is in a conference room, ensure that it is set up appropriately. For a large group or a long session, plan for refreshment breaks.

Limit the time of the interview. Both the preparation and the interview itself affect the time required for the interview. As you set the objective and develop questions, plan for about an hour and a half. If the interview will require more time to cover the questions, it is usually better to break off the discussion and schedule another session. (Other techniques that we discuss later have all-day sessions.) The users have other responsibilities, and the systems analysts can absorb only so much information at one time. It is better to have several shorter interviews than one long marathon. A series of interviews provides you with an opportunity to absorb the material and to go back to get clarification later. Both the analysts and the users will have better attitudes with several shorter interviews.

Look for exception and error conditions. Look for opportunities to ask "what if" questions. "What if it doesn't arrive?" "What if the signature is missing?" "What if the balance is incorrect?" "What if two order forms are exactly the same?" The essence of good systems analysis is understanding all of the "what ifs." Make a conscious effort to identify all of the exception conditions and ask about them. More than any other skill, the ability to think of the exceptions will strengthen the skill of discovering the detailed business rules. It is a hard skill to teach from a textbook; experience will hone this skill. You will teach yourself this skill by conscientiously practicing it.

Probe for details. In addition to looking for exception conditions, the analyst must probe to ensure a complete understanding of all procedures and rules. One of the most difficult skills to learn as a new systems analyst is getting enough details. Frequently, it is easy to get a general overview of how a process works. But do not be afraid to keep asking detailed questions until you thoroughly understand how it works and what information is used. You cannot effectively elicit and document requirements by glossing over the details.

Take careful notes. It is a good idea to take handwritten notes. Usually, tape recorders make users nervous. Note taking, on the other hand, signals that you think the information you are obtaining is important, and the user is complimented. If two analysts conduct each interview, they can compare notes later. Identify and document in your notes any unanswered questions or outstanding issues that were not resolved. A good set of notes provides the basis for building the requirements models, as well as the basis for the next interview session.

Figure 4-11 is a sample agenda for an interview session. Obviously, you do not need to conform exactly to a particular agenda. However, as with the interview checklist shown in Figure 4-10, this figure will help prod your memory on issues and items that should be discussed in an interview. Make a copy and use it. As you develop your own style, you can modify the checklist for the way you like to work.

FOLLOWING UP THE INTERVIEW

Follow-up is an important part of each interview. The first task is to absorb, understand, and document the information that you obtained. Generally, analysts document the details of the interview by constructing models of the business processes and writing textual descriptions of nonfunctional requirements. These tasks should be completed as soon as possible after the interview and the results distributed to the interview participants for validation. If the modeling methods are complex or unfamiliar to the users, the analyst should schedule follow-up meetings to explain and verify the models, as described in the last section of this chapter.

During the interview, you probably asked some "what if" questions that the users could not answer. Because these are usually policy questions raised by the new system, management has probably not considered them before. It is extremely important that these questions not get lost or forgotten. Figure 4-12 is a sample form with representative questions from Rocky Mountain Outfitters. If several teams are working, a combined list can be maintained. Other columns that might be added to the list are an explanation of the resolution to the problem and the date resolved.

BEST PRACTICE: Maintain an open-items list for unresolved problems and questions.

Finally, make a list of new questions based on areas that need further elaboration or that are missing information. This list will prepare you for the next interview.

OBSERVE AND DOCUMENT BUSINESS PROCESSES

Along with interviews, another extremely useful information-gathering method is to observe users directly at their job sites and to document the processes you observe.

Discussion and Interview Agenda

Setting

Objective of Interview
Determine processing rules for sales commission rates

Date, Time, and Location
April 21, 2006, at 9:00 a.m. in William McDougal's office

User Participants (names and titles/positions)
William McDougal, vice president of marketing and sales, and several of his staff

Project Team Participants
Mary Ellen Green and Jim Williams

Interview/Discussion

1. *Who is eligible for sales commissions?*
2. *What is the basis for commissions? What rates are paid?*
3. *How is commission for returns handled?*
4. *Are there special incentives? Contests? Programs based on time?*
5. *Is there a variable scale for commissions? Are there quotas?*
6. *What are the exceptions?*

Follow-Up

Important decisions or answers to questions
See attached write-up on commission policies

Open items not resolved with assignments for solution
See Item numbers 2 and 3 on open items list

Date and time of next meeting or follow-up session
April 28, 2006, at 9:00 a.m.

FIGURE 4-11
Sample interview session agenda

This firsthand experience is invaluable to understanding exactly what occurs in business processes.

OBSERVING

The old adage that a picture is worth a thousand words is also true with systems analysis—in this case, a moving picture. More than any other activity, observing the business processes in action will help you understand the business functions. However, while observing existing processes, you must also be able to visualize the new system's associated business processes. That is, as you observe the current business processes to understand the fundamental business needs, you should never forget that the processes could, and often should, change to be more efficient. Don't get locked into believing there is only one way of performing the process.

You can observe the work in several ways, from a quick walkthrough of the office or plant to doing the work yourself. A quick walkthrough gives a general understanding of the layout of the office, the need for and use of computer equipment, and the general workflow. Spending several hours observing a user actually doing his or her job

ID	ISSUE TITLE	DATE IDENTIFIED	TARGET END DATE	RESPONSIBLE PROJECT PERSON	USER CONTACT	COMMENTS
1	Partial Shipments	6-12-2006	7-15-2006	Jim Williams	Jason Nadold	Ship partials or wait for full shipment?
2	Return and Commissions	2-27-2006	3-27-2006	Jim Williams	William McDougal	Are commissions recouped on returns?
3	Extra Commissions	2-27-2006	3-13-2006	Mary Ellen Green	William McDougal	How to handle commissions on special promotions?

OUTSTANDING ISSUES CONTROL TABLE

FIGURE 4-12
A sample open-items list

provides an understanding of the details of actually using the computer system and carrying out business functions. By being trained as a user and actually doing the job, you can discover the difficulties of learning new procedures, the importance of a system that is easy to use, and the stumbling blocks and bottlenecks of existing procedures and information sources.

It is not necessary to observe all processes at the same level of detail. A quick walk-through may be sufficient for one process, while another process that is critical or more difficult to understand might require an extended observation period. If you remember that the objective is a complete understanding of the business processes and rules, then you can assess where to spend your time to gain that thorough understanding. As with interviewing, it is usually better if two analysts combine their efforts in observing procedures.

Observation often makes the users nervous, so you need to be as unobtrusive as possible. There are several ways to put users at ease, such as working with a user or observing several users at once. Common sense and sensitivity to the needs and feelings of the users will usually result in a positive experience.

DOCUMENTING WITH ACTIVITY DIAGRAMS

As you gather information about business processes, primarily by interviewing the users and by observing the processes, you will need to document your results. One effective way to capture this information is through the use of diagrams. Eventually, you may want to use diagrams to describe the workflows of the new system, but for now, let's just focus on how we would document the current business workflows.

workflow
a sequence of steps to process a business transaction

A *workflow* is the sequence of processing steps that completely handles one business transaction or customer request. Workflows may be simple or complex. Complex workflows may be composed of dozens or hundreds of processing steps and may include participants from different parts of an organization. As an analyst, you may try to depend only on your memory to remember and understand the workflow (a bad idea), you may write it down in a long description, or you can document it with a diagram. The advantages of a simple diagram are that you can visualize it better, and you can review it with the users to make sure it is correct. One of the major benefits of using diagrams and models is that they become a powerful communication mechanism among the project team and the users.

No single method is usually employed to model workflows. Methodologies commonly used include flowcharts and activity diagrams. Flowcharts and activity charts are specifically designed to represent control flow among processing steps. Many analysts use a type of workflow diagram called an *activity diagram*. An *activity diagram* is simply a workflow diagram that describes the various user (or system) activities, the person who does each activity, and the sequential flow of these activities.

activity diagram
a type of workflow diagram that describes the user activities and their sequential flow

Figure 4-13 shows the basic symbols used in an activity diagram. The ovals represent the individual activities in a workflow. The connecting arrows represent the

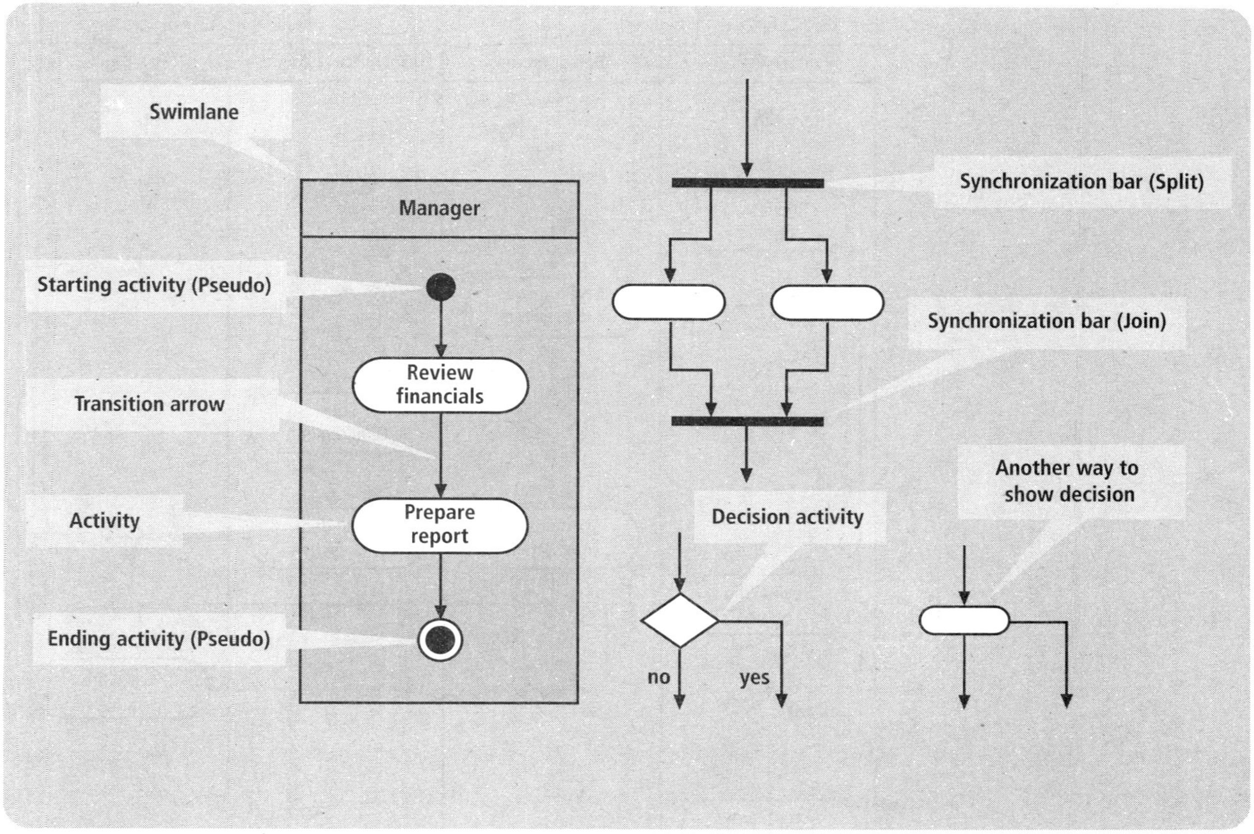

FIGURE 4-13
Activity diagram symbols

synchronization bar
a symbol used in an activity diagram to control the splitting or uniting of sequential paths

swimlane
a rectangular area on an activity diagram representing the activities done by a single agent

sequence among the activities. The black circles are used to denote the beginning and ending of the workflow. The diamond is a decision point at which the flow of the process will either follow one path or the other path. The heavy solid line is a *synchronization bar*, which either splits the path into multiple concurrent paths or recombines concurrent paths. The *swimlane* represents an agent who performs the activities. Since, in a workflow, it is common to have different agents (that is, people) performing different steps of the workflow process, the swimlane symbol divides the workflow activities into groups, showing which agent performs which activity.

Figure 4-14 is an actual activity diagram for a workflow. This workflow represents a customer requesting a quote from a salesperson. If it is a simple request, the salesperson can enter the data and create the quote. If it is complex, the salesperson requests assistance from a technical expert to generate the quote. In both cases, the computer system calculates the details of the quote.

Suppose in this case that you have interviewed the salesperson and observed the generation of a quote. Looking at Figure 4-14, you can see how the workflow progresses. The customer initiates the first step by requesting a quote. The salesperson performs the next step in the workflow. She writes down the details of the quote request and then decides whether she can do it herself or whether she needs help. If she does not need help, then the salesperson enters the information into the computer system. If the salesperson needs help, then the technical expert performs the next step. The expert reviews the quote request to make sure that the requested components can be integrated into a functioning computer system. The activity of checking the request is fairly complex, and you could in fact break it down into more detailed steps if desired.

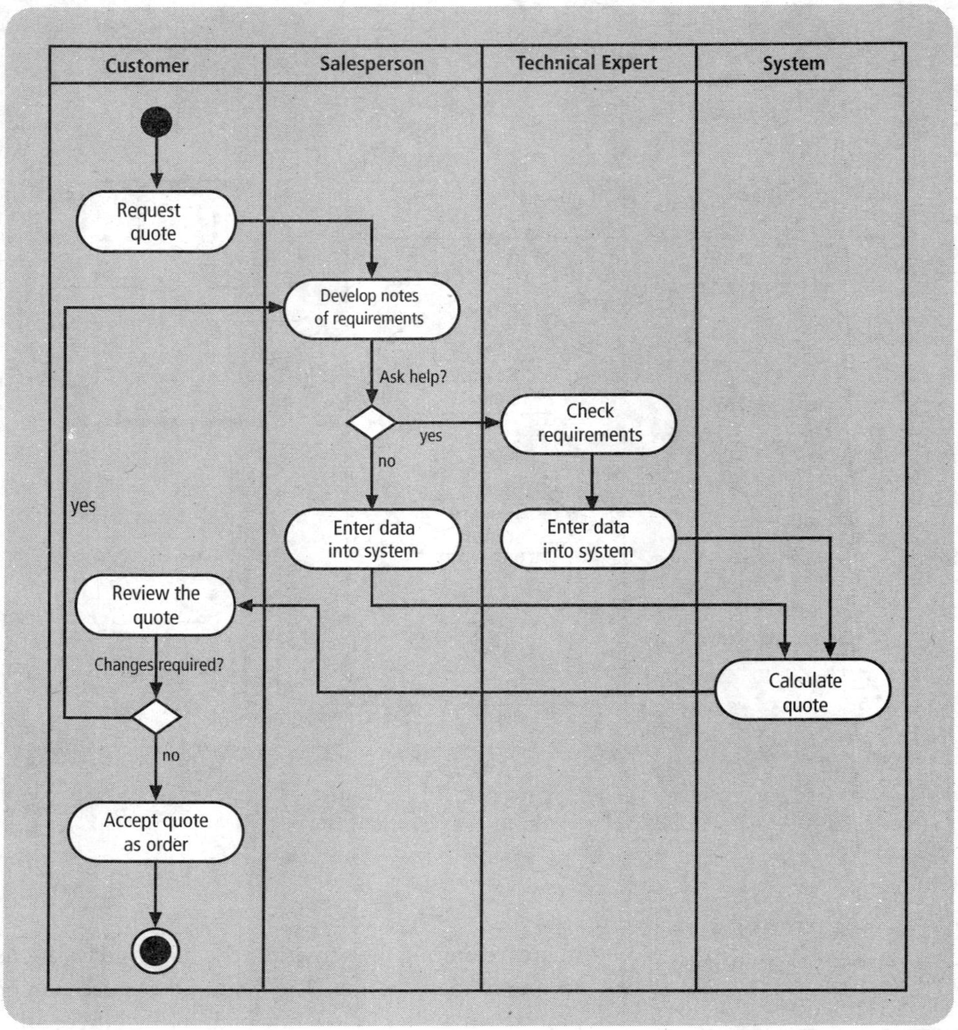

FIGURE 4-14
A simple activity diagram to demonstrate a workflow

For now, let's leave the diagram at this level of detail. The expert then enters the information into the system. At this point, the computer system generates the detailed quote. Notice that no matter which path is taken, they both result in this common activity. Finally, the customer reviews the quote and decides whether it needs changes or is acceptable. In this simple case, the customer always does buy something, so this workflow is obviously not completely accurate.

Notice that an activity diagram focuses on the sequence of activities. This diagram is straightforward and quite easy to understand. In fact, one of the strengths of using activity diagrams to document workflows is that users also find them very easy to understand. You can use graphical representations such as this diagram to review your understanding of the particular workflow procedure with the user.

Figure 4-15 illustrates another workflow. This diagram demonstrates some new concepts. Let's assume that the customer from the previous example did want to proceed with an order. This next figure shows the workflow that is required to get the order scheduled for production. The salesperson sends the printed quote, which has now become an order, to engineering. This example emphasizes the fact that a document is being transmitted. To indicate that a document is being passed, you place the

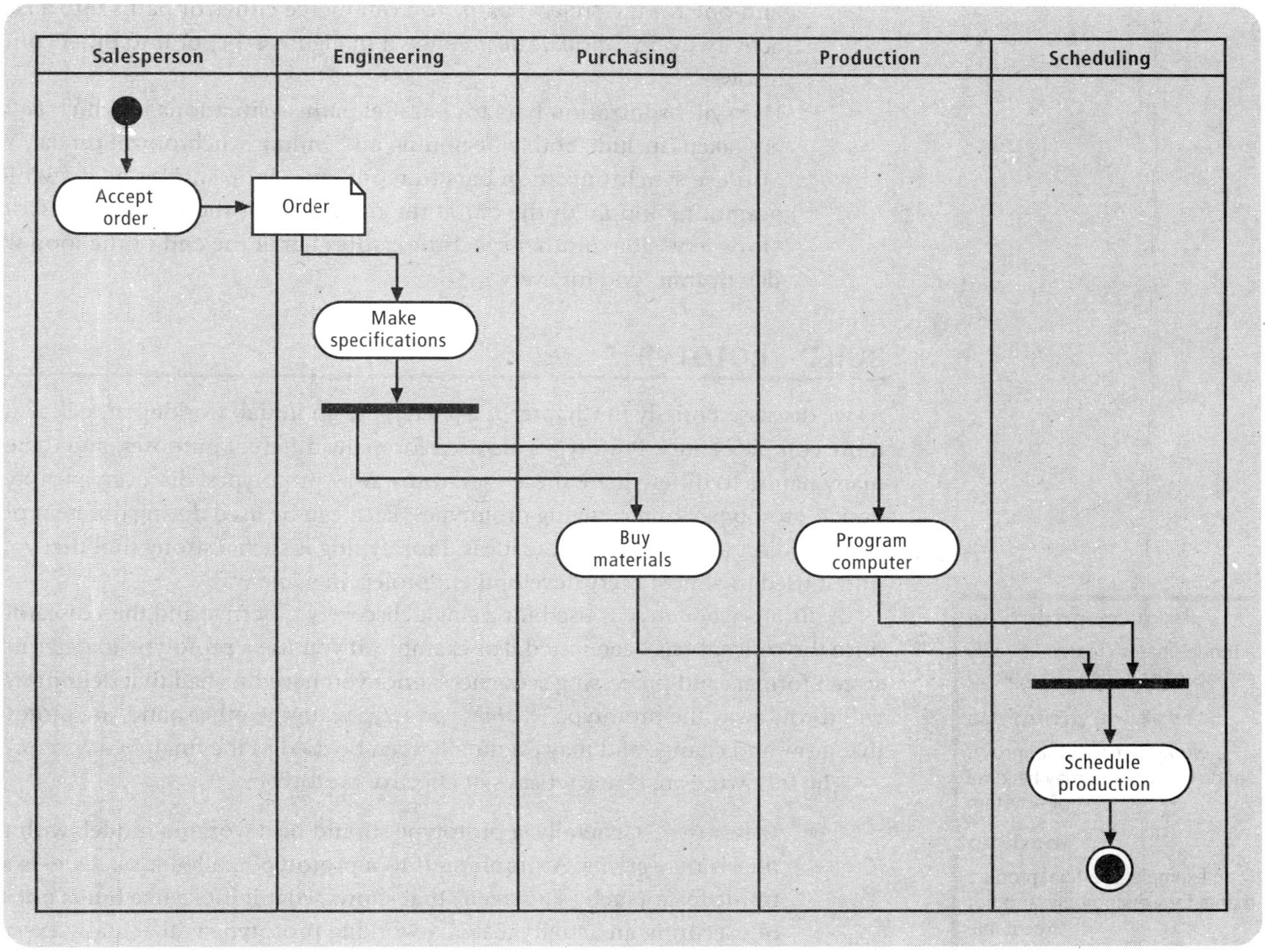

FIGURE 4-15
An activity diagram showing concurrent paths

document symbol at the end of the connecting arrow, and the arrow now becomes a conduit for transmitting a document, not just a flow of activities. After engineering develops the specifications, two concurrent activities happen: purchasing orders the materials, and production writes the program for the automated milling machines. These two activities are completely independent and can occur at the same time. Notice that one synchronization bar splits the path into two concurrent paths, and another synchronization bar reconnects them. Finally, scheduling puts the order on the production schedule.

Creating activity diagrams to document workflows is straightforward. The first step is to identify the agents to create the appropriate swimlanes. Next, just follow the various steps of the workflow and make appropriate ovals for the activities. Connect the activity ovals with arrows to show the direction of the workflow. Here are a couple of simple guidelines:

- Use a decision symbol to represent an either/or situation—one path *or* the other path, but not both. As a shorthand notation, you can merge an activity (using an oval) and a decision (using a diamond) into a single oval with two exit arrows, as indicated on the right in Figure 4-13. This notation represents a decision (either/or) activity. Wherever you have an activity that says "verify" or "check," you will probably require a decision—one for the "accept" path and one for the "reject" path. You can merge either/or paths into a common activity (as in *Calculate quote*, shown in Figure 4-14) or into other connecting arrows.

- Use synchronization bars for parallel paths—situations in which *both* paths are taken. Include both a beginning and ending synchronization bar. You can also use synchronization bars to represent a loop such as a "do while" programming loop. Put the bar at the beginning of the loop and describe it as "for every." Put another synchronization bar at the end of the loop with the description "end for every."

BUILD PROTOTYPES

As we discussed briefly in Chapter 2, a *prototype* is an initial, working model of a larger, more complex entity. Prototypes are used for many different purposes, and there are many names to differentiate these uses: throwaway prototypes, discovery prototypes, design prototypes, and evolving prototypes. Each can be used during different phases of the project to test and validate ideas. Prototyping is such a strong tool that you will find it used in almost every development project in some way.

discovery prototype
a model that is created to verify a concept and then is discarded

evolving prototype
a working model that grows and changes and may become part of a system

mock-up
an example of a final product that is for viewing only, and not executable

A *discovery prototype* is used for a single discovery objective and then discarded once the concept has been tested. For example, if you use a prototype to determine screen formats and processing sequences, once you have finished that definition, you will throw away the prototype. *Evolving prototypes*, on the other hand, are prototypes that grow and change and may eventually even be used as the final, live system.

The following are characteristics of effective prototypes:

- **Operative.** Generally, a prototype should be a working model, with the emphasis on *working*. A simple start to a prototype, called a *mock-up*, is an electronic form (such as a screen) that shows what it looks like but is not capable of executing an activity. Later, a working prototype will actually execute and provide both "look and feel" characteristics but may lack some functionality.
- **Focused.** To test a specific concept or verify an approach, a prototype should be focused on a single objective. Extraneous execution capability, not part of the specific objective, should be excluded. Although it may be possible to combine several simple prototypes into a larger prototype, the focused objective still applies. Later, the project team can combine prototypes to test the integration of several components.
- **Quick.** Tools, such as CASE tools, are needed to develop a prototype so that it can be built and modified quickly. Since a prototype's purpose is to validate an approach, if the approach is wrong, then the tools must be available to modify and test quickly to determine the correct approach.

Integrating prototyping activities in the project is fairly simple. The important point to keep in mind is to have an overall philosophy and purpose for building prototypes and to maintain a consistent focus across all the prototypes that are built.

DISTRIBUTE AND COLLECT QUESTIONNAIRES

Questionnaires have a limited and specific use in information gathering. The benefit of a questionnaire is that it enables the project team to collect information from a large number of users. Even if they are widely distributed geographically, they can still help define requirements through questionnaires.

Frequently, the project team can use a questionnaire to obtain preliminary insight on the information needs of the various stakeholders. That insight enables analysts to determine the areas that need further research with other techniques such as document reviews, interviews, and observation. Questionnaires are also helpful to answer quantitative questions such as "What forms are used to enter new customer information?" and "On average, how long does it take to enter one standard order?" Finally, questionnaires can be used to determine the users' opinions about various aspects of the system. As explained in the section on preparing for an interview, such questions as "On a scale of 1 to 7, how important is it to be able to access a customer's past purchase history?" are often called *closed-ended questions*, because they direct the person answering the question to provide a direct response to only that question. They do not invite discussion or elaboration. The strength of closed-ended questions, however, is that the answers are always limited to the set of choices. The project team can tabulate the answers to determine averages or trends.

Figure 4-16 is a sample questionnaire showing three types of questions. The first part has closed-ended questions to determine quantitative information. The second part consists of opinion questions, in which respondents are asked whether they agree or disagree with the statement. Both types of questions are useful for tabulating and determining quantitative averages. The final part requests an explanation of a procedure or problem. Questions such as these are good as a preliminary investigation to help direct further fact-finding activities.

Questionnaires are not well suited to helping you learn about processes, workflows, or techniques. The questions identified earlier, such as, "How do you do this process?" are best answered using interviews or observation. As we discussed earlier, questions that encourage discussion and elaboration are called *open-ended questions*. Although a questionnaire can contain a very limited number of open-ended questions, stakeholders frequently do not return questionnaires that contain many open-ended questions.

BEST PRACTICE: Limit the number of open-ended questions on a questionnaire.

CONDUCT JOINT APPLICATION DESIGN SESSIONS

Because the UP is an adaptive development methodology, flexibility is key to information gathering for the requirements discipline. Rather than relying solely on time-consuming interviews or static, scheduled questionnaires, analysts using the UP frequently turn to other techniques to expedite the flow of information. The normal interview and discussion approach, as explained earlier, requires a substantial amount of time. The analysts first meet with the users, then document the discussion by writing notes and building models, and then review and revise the models. Unresolved issues are placed on an open-items list and may require several additional meetings and reviews to be finalized. This process can extend from several weeks to months, depending on the size of the system and the availability of user and project team resources.

BEST PRACTICE: A JAD session speeds up the process of defining requirements.

RMO Questionnaire

This questionnaire is being sent to all telephone-order sales personnel. As you know, RMO is developing a new customer support system for order taking and customer service.

The purpose of this questionnaire is to obtain preliminary information to assist in defining the requirements for the new system. Follow-up discussions will be held to permit everybody to elaborate on the system requirements.

Part I. Answer these questions based on a typical four-hour shift.

1. How many phone calls do you receive?____________________
2. How many phone calls are necessary to place an order for a product?____________________
3. How many phone calls are for information about RMO products, that is, questions only?____________
4. Estimate how many times during a shift customers request items that are out of stock.____________
5. Of those out-of-stock requests, what percentage of the time does the customer desire to put the item on back order?____________%
6. How many times does a customer try to order from an expired catalog?____________________
7. How many times does a customer cancel an order in the middle of the conversation?____________
8. How many times does an order get denied due to bad credit?____________________

Part II. Circle the appropriate number on the scale from 1 to 7 based on how strongly you agree or disagree with the statement.

Question	Strongly Agree				Strongly Disagree		
It would help me do my job better to have longer descriptions of products available while talking to a customer	1	2	3	4	5	6	7
It would help me do my job better if I had the past purchase history of the customer available.	1	2	3	4	5	6	7
I could provide better service to the customer if I had information about accessories that were appropriate for the items ordered.	1	2	3	4	5	6	7
The computer response time is slow and causes difficulties in responding to customer requests.	1	2	3	4	5	6	7

Part III. Please enter your opinions and comments.

Please briefly identify the problems with the current system that you would like to see resolved in a new system.

____

____

____

FIGURE 4-16
A sample questionnaire

joint application design (JAD)
a technique to define requirements or design a system in a single session by having all necessary people participate

Joint application design (JAD) is a technique that expedites the investigation of system requirements. The objective of JAD is to compress all of these activities into a shorter series of JAD sessions with users and project team members. An individual JAD session may last from a single day to a week. During the session, all of the fact-finding, model-building, policy decisions, and verification activities are completed for a particular aspect of the system. If the system is small, the entire system may be specified during the JAD session. The critical factor in a successful JAD session is to have all of the important stakeholders present and available to contribute and make decisions. The actual participants vary depending on the objective of the specific JAD session. Those who are involved may include the following:

- **The JAD Session Leader.** One of the more important members of the group, the session leader is a person who is experienced or has been trained in understanding group dynamics and in facilitating group discussion. Normally, a JAD session involves quite a few people. Each session has a detailed agenda with specific objectives that must be met, and the discussion must progress toward meeting those objectives. Maintaining focus requires someone with skills and experience to keep people on task tactfully. Often it is tempting to appoint one of the systems analysts as the session leader. However, experience indicates that successful JAD sessions are conducted by someone who is trained to lead group decision making.

- **Users.** Earlier, this chapter identified various classes of users. It is important to have all of the appropriate users in the JAD sessions. Frequently, as requirements are discovered, managers must make policy decisions. If managers are not available in the sessions to make those decisions, then progress is halted. Because of business pressures, it may be difficult for top executives to be present during the entire session. In that case, arrangements should be made for executives to visit the session once or twice a day to become involved in those policy discussions.
- **Technical Staff.** A representative from the technical support staff should also be present in the JAD session. There are always questions and decisions about technical issues that need to be answered. For example, participants may need details of computer and network configurations, operating environments, and security issues.
- **Project Team Members.** Both systems analysts and user experts from the project team should be involved in JAD sessions. These members assist in the discussion, clarify points, control the level of detail needed, build models, document the results, and generally see that the system requirements are defined to the necessary level of detail. The session leader is a facilitator, but often the leader is not the expert on how much detail and definition is required. Members of the project team are the experts on ensuring that the objectives are completely satisfied.

JAD sessions are usually conducted in special rooms with supporting facilities. First, since the process is so intense, it is important to be away from the normal day-to-day interruptions. Sometimes an off-site location may be necessary, or notification that interruptions are not welcome may be posted. On the other hand, it is usually helpful to have telephone access to executives and technical staff who are not involved in the meetings but who may be invited from time to time to finalize policy or technical decisions.

Resources in the JAD session room should include computer and transparency projectors, a blackboard or whiteboard, flip charts, and adequate workspace for the participants. JAD sessions are work sessions, and all the necessary work paraphernalia should be provided.

JAD sessions require computer-based support to increase their efficiency. Discussion and documentation can be enhanced if participants have personal or laptop computers connected in a network. Then as requirements are documented with narrative descriptions or models, or even as some simple discovery prototypes are built, they can be made available to everybody. Often a CASE tool is provided on the computers to assist in visualization of screen and report layouts and file design. The CASE tool also provides a central repository for all the requirements developed during the session.

group support system (GSS)
a computer system that enables multiple people to participate with comments at the same time, each user on his or her own computer

Group support systems (GSSs), which also run on the network of computers, allow all participants to post comments (anonymously, if desired) in a common working chat room. This approach helps participants who may be shy in group discussions to become more active and contribute to the group decisions. GSSs also enable the team to store final requirements as decisions are made. Normally JAD sessions are conducted with everyone in the same room. However, GSSs on wider networks provide the opportunity for virtual meetings with participants at geographically dispersed locations.

Figure 4-17 shows an example of a conference room with electronic support. Such a room might be available in larger companies that have development projects in progress more frequently. The room shown in Figure 4-17 has workstations available to develop model diagrams and prototypes during the JAD sessions.

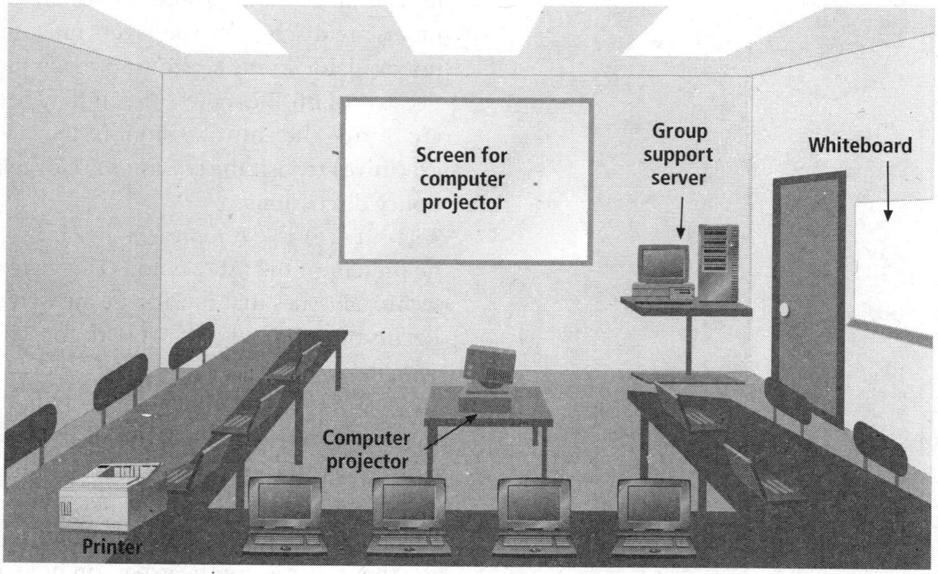

FIGURE 4-17
A JAD facility

One of the dangers of JAD is the risk involved in expediting decisions. Since the objective of JAD is to come to a conclusion quickly on policy decisions and requirements details, sometimes decisions are not optimal. At times, details are inappropriately defined or missed altogether. However, JAD sessions have been largely successful in reducing project development efforts and shortening the schedule.

RESEARCH VENDOR SOLUTIONS

Many of the problems and opportunities that companies want to address with new information systems have already been solved by other companies. In many instances, consulting firms have experience with the same problems, and sometimes software firms already have packaged solutions for a particular business need. Directories, such as *Data Sources*, also list literally thousands of hardware, software, consulting, and solution developers. It makes sense to learn about and capitalize on this existing knowledge.

There are three advantages and one danger in exploring existing solutions. First, researching alternate solutions will frequently help users generate new ideas of how to better perform their business functions. Seeing how someone else did them, and applying that idea to the culture and structure of the existing organization, will often provide viable alternate solutions for the business need.

Second, some of these solutions are in fact excellent and state of the art. Without this research, the development team may create a system that is obsolete even before it is conceptualized. Companies need solutions that not only solve basic business problems but also are up to date with current competitive practices.

Third, it is often cheaper and less risky to buy a solution rather than to build it. If the solution meets the needs of the company and can be purchased, then that is usually a safer, quicker, and less expensive route. There are many ways to buy solutions. Early in the development project, you want to research other alternatives but not make a final decision until you have investigated all the alternatives.

The danger, or caveat, in this process is that sometimes the users, and even the systems analysts, want to buy one of the alternatives immediately. But if a solution, such as a packaged software system, is purchased too early in the process, the company's needs may not be thoroughly investigated. That is like buying a suit without knowing what size it is. Too many companies have bought a system only to find out later that it only supports half the functions that were needed. Don't fall into this dangerous pit.

The first difficulty in researching vendor alternatives is simply to find out who has solutions that fit the business need. Many of the large software and hardware companies, such as Oracle, IBM, Microsoft, and Computer Associates, have specific solution systems. There are also directories of system solutions—of software, hardware, and developer companies. As mentioned earlier, *Data Sources* is one of the better ones. You can also search the Internet to find more directories. Sometimes these directories can be found in the library—a company technical library, the city library, or a nearby university library.

Other places to look are in trade journals for the industry. For example, the retail industry has several trade journals. System providers frequently advertise in these journals and at trade shows. Another method is word of mouth from other companies in the industry. Generally, users will have friends who work in competing companies. These people are sometimes aware of specific vendors that have helped solve their own business needs. Although companies compete fiercely on the sales and marketing end, it is not unusual for them to belong to a common trade organization that helps to share knowledge about the industry, including knowledge about system solutions.

Once a list of possible providers has been developed, the next step is to research the details of each solution. It is easy to get the sales and marketing literature, but it is more difficult to get specifics of the system. Techniques that may be useful are (1) technical specifications, (2) a demo or trial system, (3) references of existing clients who would let you observe their system, (4) an on-site visit, and (5) a printout of the screens and reports.

The final step is to review the details of the information received. Depending on the information obtained, it can be reviewed solely by the project team or with the users. In many cases, a review with key users is the most beneficial for understanding and identifying various approaches to addressing the business need. In any event, researching the solutions that have already been developed is an effective early step in understanding the business and identifying possible courses of action.

Now that you have learned about information-gathering techniques and ways to elicit requirements from the users, you need to find out how to make sure the information you gathered is correct. To evaluate the requirements, you use validation techniques, discussed next.

VALIDATING THE REQUIREMENTS

All too frequently, when systems analysts think they understand what the users need, they have failed to capture some very important subtleties about the business processes. Obviously, correcting such a mistake after the system has been deployed is very expensive. So how does an analyst determine whether documented requirements are correct before proceeding with other development activities? There are two basic approaches to answering that question, and those approaches are directly related to the continuum of predictive versus adaptive development, which was discussed in Chapter 2.

Under predictive development, requirements are assumed to be stable and easily determined. Thus, it is feasible and economically efficient for an analyst to fully specify and validate them before proceeding with any further development activities. The basic idea is to ensure that the software is built only once, based on known and stable requirements.

With adaptive development, requirements are assumed to be difficult to document and subject to change as development proceeds. So, fully documenting and validating requirements prior to design and construction is not feasible. The only way to truly validate requirements is to build a prototype or full-scale system that embodies the requirements and have users evaluate the system to determine whether it meets their needs.

As discussed in Chapter 2, the current trend is toward adaptive development, and that trend is fully embodied in the UP. In particular, the UP specifies development in short iterations, with each iteration combining activities from many disciplines to produce working software. That software can then be validated by the testing discipline's activities. Barbara Halifax followed this approach when developing the iteration plan for the customer support system, which she outlined in her memo to John MacMurty (see Barbara's memo). In short, within the UP, the most common requirements-validation technique is designing, building, and testing the corresponding parts of the system. Testing as a means of requirements validation is discussed further in Chapter 13.

BEST PRACTICE: Validate requirements by designing, building, and testing corresponding parts of the system.

Although building and testing software is the most commonly employed validation technique, it is not always appropriate or economically feasible. Often, nonfunctional system requirements and requirements concerned with infrastructure are too complex or expensive to warrant multiple iterations of building and testing. Acquiring and configuring infrastructure components such as servers, networks, and related system software is expensive and time-consuming. So, when analysts are dealing with requirements related to infrastructure, they commonly invest greater effort up front—typically in the first or second iteration—to specify and evaluate requirements, to ensure that their organizations are acquiring and configuring the right components. In this case, the time and expense of paper-based validation substantially reduces the risk of very expensive mistakes.

In some projects, other types of requirements, including functional requirements, may require an analyst to use other validation techniques before or instead of building prototypes or a testable system subset. For example, when analysts are designing software to support executive decision making, they must validate the system through user testing—in other words, have the executives spend a substantial amount of time trying out the system and providing feedback. Given the six- and seven-figure salaries of many executives, multiple iterations of user testing are probably not economically feasible. Thus, analysts need to expend extra effort to validate requirements before building testable software, so that they can minimize the amount of hands-on testing time for the executives. Other projects may face similar

February 15, 2006

To: John MacMurty

From: Barbara Halifax

RE: Customer support system update

ROCKY MOUNTAIN OUTFITTERS MEMO

We're planning the next iteration of the CSS project, and I wanted to inform you of the details. We now have a broad overview of the full system scope and have specified some requirements for the *Create new order* use case. The team has decided that the best step to take next is to make that use case and several related ones the focus of the next iteration.

So far, we've spent quite a bit of time talking to users and customers to outline the business case and customer needs. As part of that process, we developed storyboards for the user interface, a rough first-cut class diagram, and a few use case and sequence diagrams. In the old days, we'd have spent another month or two drilling down to the lowest level of detail in all of our requirements and design models. But since part of the project charter is full adoption of iterative development and the UP, now's the time to carve off a chunk of the system and push it through to construction and testing.

Customer order processing is the logical place to start since it's the heart of the system. It also has several high-risk aspects, including continued uncertainty about the exact user interface, performance, and security. Tackling it first will force us to resolve the uncertainties and will expose many issues that need to be addressed in later iterations. We'll work on both the Web-based and telephone sales user interfaces simultaneously, since they'll use the same back-end software and servers. The end result of the iteration will be a working prototype deployed in a fully functional test environment.

Here's a summary of the major tasks to be completed in the next iteration:

- Document the essential use cases *Look up item availability*, *Create new order*, *Update order*, and *Create new customer*—create or refine any needed requirements and design models
- Design the business classes and user interfaces, get user feedback, and revise as necessary
- Develop the database schema, implement a test database on a spare server, and create the interface between the business classes and the DBMS
- Bring test servers for Web services and application support online
- Deploy the software on our network and begin performance testing

Thanks, and take care.

BH

cc: Steven Deerfield, Ming Lee, Jack Garcia

challenges when users are unavailable because of other commitments, geographic distance, or any other obstacles.

Various techniques can be used to validate requirements without building and testing prototypes. To check internal consistency, analysts build models and verify that they are mathematically consistent. You will learn more about that in the next two chapters as each model is described in detail. One generic technique can be applied to a variety of model types.

structured walkthrough
a review of the findings from your investigation and of the models built based on those findings

A *structured walkthrough*, sometimes just called a *walkthrough*, is a review of the findings from your investigation and of the models built based on those findings. A walkthrough is considered structured because analysts have formalized the review process into a set procedure. The objective of a structured walkthrough is to find errors and problems. Its purpose is to ensure that the model is correct. The fundamental concept is one of documenting the requirements as you understand them and then reviewing them for any errors, omissions, inconsistencies, or problems. A review of the findings can be done informally with colleagues on the project team, but a structured walkthrough must be more formal.

It is important to note one critical point: A structured walkthrough is not a performance review. Managers should be involved only if they were involved in the original fact finding and thus are required for verification or validation. The review is of an analyst's work, not of the person.

WHAT AND WHEN

The first item to be reviewed during a structured walkthrough is the documentation that was developed during business modeling or requirements discipline activities. It can be a narrative describing a process, a flowchart showing a workflow, or a model diagram documenting an entire procedure. Normally, it is better to conduct several smaller walkthroughs that review three to six pages of documentation than to cover 30 pages of details. Any written work that is a fairly independent package can be reviewed in a walkthrough. Walkthroughs can be held regularly (for example, every week) or as needed. The frequency of the walkthroughs is not as critical as the timing—a walkthrough should be scheduled as soon as possible after the documents have been created.

WHO

The two main parties involved in walkthroughs are the person or persons who need their work reviewed and the group who reviews it. For verification—that is, internal consistency and correctness—it is best to have other experienced analysts involved in the walkthrough. They look for inconsistencies and problems. For validation—that is, ensuring that the system satisfies all the needs of the various stakeholders—the appropriate stakeholders should be involved. The nature of the work to be reviewed dictates who the reviewers should be. If it is a diagram showing a business process, then the users who supplied the original definition should be involved. If it is a technical specification of design details, then the technical staff should be involved in the review. At times, the reviewers may be members of the project team. In other instances, they are external users or technical staff. Those who can validate the correctness of the work are the people who should be invited.

HOW

As with an interview, a structured walkthrough requires preparation, execution, and follow-up.

PREPARATION

The analyst whose work is being reviewed gets the material ready for review. Next, he or she identifies the appropriate participants and provides them with copies of the material. Finally, the analyst schedules a time and place for the walkthrough and notifies all participants.

EXECUTION

During the walkthrough, the analyst presents the material point by point. If it is an activity diagram, he or she walks through the flow, explaining each component. One effective technique is to define a sample test case and process it through the defined flow. The reviewers look for inconsistencies or problems and point them out. A *librarian*, a helper for the presenter, documents the comments made by the reviewers. Presenters should never be their own librarians because they should not be distracted from explaining the documentation. To ensure accuracy, someone else should record the errors, comments, and suggestions.

BEST PRACTICE: In a structured walkthrough, have a nonparticipant act as librarian to record all errors, comments, and suggestions.

Corrections and solutions to problems are not made during the walkthrough. At most, some suggested solutions may be provided, but the documentation should not be corrected during the walkthrough. Since presenters are commonly a little nervous, it is unfair to ask them to make wise decisions on the spur of the moment. If a misunderstanding of the user requirements is uncovered, a brief review may be in order. However, if an error is fairly complex, it is better to schedule an additional interview to clarify the misunderstanding. The walkthrough should not get bogged down and become a fact-finding session. The reviewer should only provide feedback, and the presenter can integrate it into the material later, when he or she has the entire set of comments and can give the corrections his or her undivided attention and best effort, without interruptions or further criticism.

FOLLOW-UP

Follow-up consists of making the required corrections. If the reviewed material has major errors and problems, an additional walkthrough may be necessary. Otherwise, the corrections are made, and the project continues to the next activities.

Figure 4-18 is a sample review form that was used in one of the review sessions at Rocky Mountain Outfitters, for the sales commission rates and rules. Not shown are several attached sheets, including a couple of activity diagrams of procedures. The material reviewed in this case is simply a list of business rules for commission rates. The reviewers are senior managers from the user community. Since sales commission business rules are critical, and these managers make the policy decisions on commissions, they are the obvious choices to review the rules as uncovered in discussions and interview sessions.

Walkthrough Control Sheet

Project Control Information

Project: *Online Catalog System, Customer Support Subsystem*

Segment of project being reviewed: *Review of business rules for sales commission rates*

Team leader: *Mary Ellen Green*

Author of work: *Jim Williams*

Walkthrough Details

Date, time, and location
April 10, 2006, 10:00 a.m. MIS conference room.

Description of materials being reviewed:
This is a review of the business rules before they are integrated into the diagrams and models. There is a short flowchart attached showing the flow of the commission process. There is another flowchart showing the process to set commission rates. We will also review outstanding issues to ensure that all understand the policy decisions that must be made.

Participating reviewers:
William McDougal, Genny Monson, Robert Schneider

Results of Walkthrough

_______XX__Accept. sign-offs:____
___________Minor revisions. Description of revisions:

___________Rework and schedule new walkthrough. Description of required rework:
Excellent and thorough. No rework required.

FIGURE 4-18
A structured walkthrough evaluation form

Summary

The requirements discipline has six activities—gather detailed information, define functional requirements, define nonfunctional requirements, prioritize requirements, develop user interface dialogs, and evaluate requirements with users.

Generally, we divide system requirements into two categories: functional and nonfunctional requirements. The functional requirements are those that explain the basic business functions that the new system must support. Nonfunctional requirements involve the objectives of the system for technology, performance, usability, reliability, and security.

Models are useful for many reasons, including furthering the learning process that occurs while creating them, reducing complexity, documenting the many details that need to be remembered, communicating with team members and users, and documenting system requirements for future use during system support. Many types of models are used, including mathematical models, descriptive models, and graphical models. Many of the models described in this text are graphical models drawn using UML notation, some used to define requirements and some used to depict the design.

A fundamental question for investigating system requirements is, "What kind of information do I need?" This chapter provides you with some general guidelines. As you learn more about modeling, you will also understand better what information you need. Three major themes of information should be pursued:

- What are the business processes and operations?
- How are the business processes performed?
- What are the information requirements?

Analysts use seven primary techniques to gather this information and one technique to ensure its correctness. The seven fact-finding techniques are the following:

- Review existing reports, forms, and procedure descriptions
- Conduct interviews and discussions with users
- Observe and document business processes
- Build prototypes
- Distribute and collect questionnaires
- Conduct JAD sessions
- Research vendor solutions

The fundamental idea of a prototype is an initial, working model of a larger, more complex entity. The primary purpose of a prototype is to have a working model that will test a concept or verify an approach. Discovery prototypes are built to define requirements but are then usually discarded or at least not used for the final programming. Evolving prototypes may eventually become part of the final system.

Joint application design is a technique used to expedite the investigation of system requirements by holding several marathon sessions with all the critical participants. Discussion results in requirements definition and policy decisions immediately, without the delays of interviewing separate groups and trying to reconcile differences. When done correctly, JAD is a powerful and effective technique.

In the UP, designing, building, and testing software is the most common method of validating requirements. But analysts must sometime rely on other validation techniques such as the structured walkthrough. A structured walkthrough has the objective of reviewing and improving a requirements or design model. It is not a performance review.

KEY TERMS

activity diagram, p. 144
closed-ended questions, p. 141
descriptive model, p. 133
discovery prototype, p. 148
evolving prototype, p. 148
functional requirement, p. 129
graphical model, p. 133
group support system (GSS), p. 151
joint application design (JAD), p. 150
mathematical model, p. 133
mock-up, p. 148
nonfunctional requirement, p. 130
open-ended questions, p. 141
performance requirement, p. 130
reliability requirement, p. 130
security requirement, p. 130
structured walkthrough, p. 155
swimlane, p. 145
synchronization bar, p. 145
system requirements, p. 129
technical requirement, p. 130
usability requirement, p. 130
workflow, p. 144

REVIEW QUESTIONS

1. What is the difference between functional requirements and nonfunctional requirements?
2. What are some of the reasons for creating models during system development?
3. What are three types of models?
4. Explain the difference between a discovery prototype and an evolving prototype.
5. List and describe the three fact-finding themes.
6. What is the objective of a structured walkthrough?
7. Explain the steps in preparing for an interview session.
8. What are the benefits of doing vendor research during information-gathering activities?
9. What is JAD? When is it used?
10. What technique is used to validate user requirements?
11. Describe the open-items list and explain why it is important.
12. What do *correct*, *complete*, and *comprehensive* mean with regard to requirements?
13. List and describe the seven information-gathering techniques.
14. What is the purpose of an activity diagram?
15. Draw and explain the symbols used on an activity diagram.

THINKING CRITICALLY

1. Provide an example of each of the three types of models that might apply to designing a car, to designing a house, and to designing an information system.
2. Explain why requirements models are logical models rather than physical models.
3. One of the toughest problems in investigating system requirements is to make sure that they are complete and comprehensive. What things would you do to ensure that you get all of the right information during an interview session?
4. One of the problems you will encounter during your development career is "scope creep"—that is, user requests for additional features and functions. Scope creep happens because sometimes users have many unsolved problems, and the requirements activities may be the first time anybody has listened to their needs. How do you keep the system from growing and including new functions that should not be part of the system?
5. It is always difficult to observe users in their jobs. It frequently makes both you and them uncomfortable. What things could you do to ensure that user behavior is not changing because of your visit? How could you make observation more natural?
6. What would you do if you got conflicting answers for the same procedure from two different people you interviewed? What would you do if one was a clerical person and the other was the department manager?
7. You are a team leader of four systems analysts. You have one analyst who has never done a structured walkthrough of his or her work. How would you help the analyst to get started? How would you ensure that the walkthrough was effective?
8. You have been assigned to resolve several issues on the open-items list, and you are having a hard time getting policy decisions from the user contact. How can you encourage the user to finalize these policies?
9. You are going on your first consulting assignment to perform requirements activities. Your client does not like to pay to train new, inexperienced analysts. What should you do to appear competent and well prepared? How should you approach the client?
10. In the running case of Rocky Mountain Outfitters, you have set up an interview with Jason Nadold in the shipping department. Your objective is to determine how shipping works and what the information requirements for the new system will be. Make a list of questions, open-ended and closed-ended, that you would use. Include any questions or techniques you would use to ensure that you find out about the exceptions.
11. Develop an activity diagram based on the following narrative. Note any ambiguities or questions that you have as you develop the model. If you need to make assumptions, also note them.

    The purpose of the Open Access Insurance System is to provide automotive insurance to car owners. Initially, prospective customers fill out an insurance application, which provides information about the customer and his or her vehicle. This information is sent to an agent, who sends it to various insurance companies to get quotes for insurance. When the responses return, the agent then determines the best policy for the type and level of coverage desired, and gives the customer a copy of the insurance policy proposal and quote.

12. Develop an activity diagram based on the following narrative. Note any ambiguities or questions that you have as you develop the model. If you need to make assumptions, also note them.

    The purchasing department handles purchase requests from other departments in the company. People in the company who initiate the original purchase request are the "customers" of the purchasing department. A case worker within the purchasing department receives that request and monitors it until it is ordered and received.

    Case workers process requests for the purchase of products under $1,500, write a purchase order, and then send it to the approved vendor. Purchase requests over $1,500 must first be sent out for bid from the vendor that supplies the product. When the bids return, the case worker selects one bid. Then, he or she writes a purchase order and sends it to the vendor.

13. Develop an activity diagram based on the following narrative. Note any ambiguities or questions that you have as you develop the model. If you need to make assumptions, also note them.

    The shipping department receives all shipments on outstanding purchase orders. When the clerk in the shipping department receives a shipment, he or she finds the outstanding purchase order for those items. The clerk then sends multiple copies of the shipment packing slip. One copy goes to purchasing, and the department updates its records to indicate that the purchase order has been fulfilled. Another copy goes to accounting so that a payment can be made. A third copy goes to the requesting in-house customer so that he or she can receive the shipment.

    Once payment is made, the accounting department sends a notification to purchasing. Once the customer receives and accepts the goods, he or she sends notification to purchasing. When purchasing receives these other verifications, it closes the purchase order as fulfilled and paid.

EXPERIENTIAL EXERCISES

1. Conduct a fact-finding interview with someone involved in a procedure that is used in a business or organization. This person could be someone at the university, in a small business in your neighborhood, in the student volunteer office at the university, in a doctor's or dentist's office, in a volunteer organization, or at your local church. Identify a process that is done, such as keeping student records, customer records, or member records. Make a list of questions and conduct the interview. Remember, your objective is to understand that procedure thoroughly—that is, to become an expert on that single procedure.
2. Follow the same instructions as for exercise 1, but make this exercise an observation experience. Either observe the other person doing the work or ask to carry out the procedure yourself. Write down the details of the process you observe.
3. Get a group of your fellow students together and conduct a structured walkthrough of your results from exercise 1 or 2. Using the results of your interview or observation, document the procedure in an activity diagram with some narrative. Then, conduct a walkthrough with several colleagues. Or take another assignment, such as Thinking Critically question 11, and walk through your preparation for that assignment. Follow the steps outlined in the text.
4. Research and write a one- to two-page research paper, using at least three separate library sources, on one of the following topics:
   a. Joint application design
   b. Prototyping as a discovery mechanism
   c. Activity diagrams
   d. Structured walkthrough
5. Using Rocky Mountain Outfitters and the customer support subsystem as your guide, develop a list of all the procedures that may need to be researched. You may want to think about the exercise in the context of your experience with retailers such as L.L. Bean, Lands' End, or Amazon.com. Get some catalogs, check out the Internet marketing done on the retailers' Web sites, and then think about the underlying business procedures that are required to support those sales activities. List the procedures and describe your understanding of each.

Case Studies

JOHN & JACOB, INC., ONLINE TRADING SYSTEM

John & Jacob, Inc., is a regional brokerage firm that has been successful over the last several years. Competition for customers is intense in this industry. The large national firms have very deep pockets, with many services to offer clients. Severe competition also comes from discount and Internet trading companies. However, John & Jacob has been able to cultivate a substantial customer base from upper-middle income people in the northeastern United States. To maintain a competitive edge with its customers, John & Jacob is in the process of developing a new online trading system. The plan for the system identifies many new capabilities that would provide new services to its clients.

John & Jacob currently has an online trading system, but only a small percentage of its clients use it. The system was purchased as a customized package in 2002 and has enjoyed only limited acceptance among customers. Complaints about the system range from slow performance to awkward user interfaces. John & Jacob has decided that upgrading the system is essential to its long-term survival, since more and more customers are moving to online trading.

Edward Finnigan, the new Web system's project manager, is in the initial stages of planning the project. He is uncertain how to gather information to define new system requirements. He has identified the following list of possible first steps in the project to gain feedback on problems with the existing system and requirements for the new system:

- Conduct a telephone survey of 100 to 200 existing customers.
- Distribute a questionnaire to a few thousand customers.
- Have a dozen or so customers participate in a one-day focus group.
- Recruit a handful of customers to participate in a three-day JAD session.

[1] With respect to the telephone survey, how should customers be selected to participate? Should the customer sample be random? What questions should be asked?

[2] With respect to the questionnaire, list some possible questions to include. Remember to include both closed- and open-ended questions.

[3] With respect to the focus group, how should customers be selected to participate? Who should lead the discussion? What questions should be asked? Should a version of the existing system be available as a discussion aid? Should a prototype of the new system be available as a discussion aid?

[4] With respect to the JAD session, how should customers be selected to participate? Who else should participate? What are the chief requirements that should be determined during the session?

[5] Compare and contrast the strengths and weaknesses of each information-gathering technique for this case. What method or mix of methods do you recommend in this case, assuming that the project needs to be completed in eight months or less? Why?

RETHINKING ROCKY MOUNTAIN OUTFITTERS

Barbara Halifax, the project manager for the CSS project, had finished identifying the list of stakeholders in the project. Quite a few senior executives would be involved, but most of them would not have major input. Barbara wanted to include the users who would be closely involved. Those in Bill McDougal's marketing and sales area would, of course. Not only was Bill the project sponsor, but all his assistants were excited about this new system and its potential to help the business grow. Barbara had a good working relationship with all of these executives.

Barbara had also identified numerous department managers and senior-level clerks who would be able to provide detailed processing requirements. She had divided her list into two groups. The first group consisted of all those with primary responsibility to help define user requirements. The second group included those who would not have direct use of the system but who would need reports and information from the system. She wanted to make sure the needs of these people were also satisfied.

[1] Of the information-gathering techniques described in this chapter, which are most applicable to each of the groups that Barbara has defined?

[2] Discuss the role of discovery and developmental prototypes in the defining requirements for this project. Are throwaway prototypes appropriate, or should the project team quickly gather requirements via other methods and then validate the requirements by building an evolving prototype?

[3] Assume that the next project iteration will include the activities described in the RMO memo near the end of the chapter. Develop a more detailed plan for defining requirements. How should requirements activities be scheduled with respect to the other activities described in the memo?

FOCUSING ON RELIABLE PHARMACEUTICAL SERVICE

Reliable PHARMACEUTICALS Reliable Pharmaceutical Service plans to develop an extranet that enables its client health-care facilities to order drugs and supplies as if they were ordering from an internal pharmacy. The extranet should enable Reliable's suppliers to function as if they were part of Reliable's internal organization. These views of the final system have significant implications for defining system requirements and for gathering information about those requirements.

[1] What information-gathering methods are most appropriate for learning about requirements from Reliable's own management staff and other employees? From client health-care organizations? From suppliers?

[2] Should patients in client health-care facilities participate in the information-gathering process? If so, why, and in what ways should they participate?

[3] With respect to gathering information from suppliers and clients, how deeply within those organizations should systems analysts look when defining requirements? How might Reliable deal with supplier and client reluctance to provide detailed information on their internal operations?

[4] For which user community or communities (internal, supplier, or client) are discovery prototypes likely to be most beneficial? Why?

FURTHER RESOURCES

Vangalur S. Alagar, *Specification of Software Systems*. Springer-Verlag, 1998.

Soren Lauesen, *Software Requirements: Styles and Techniques*. Addison-Wesley, 2002.

Stan Magee, *Guide to Software Engineering Standards and Specifications*. Artech House, 1997.

Suzanne Robertson and James Robertson, *Mastering the Requirements Process*. Addison-Wesley, 2000.

Karl Wiegers, *Software Requirements*. Microsoft Press, 1999.

Jane Wood, *Joint Application Development*. John Wiley & Sons, 1995.

Ralph Young, *Effective Requirements Practices*. Addison-Wesley, 2001.

chapter 5

USE CASES AND DOMAIN CLASSES

LEARNING OBJECTIVES

After reading this chapter, you should be able to:

- Explain how events can be used to identify use cases that define requirements
- Identify and analyze events and resulting use cases
- Explain how the concept of problem domain classes also defines requirements
- Identify and analyze domain classes needed in the system
- Read, interpret, and create a Unified Modeling Language (UML) domain model class diagram and design class diagram
- Use a CRUD matrix to study the relationships between use cases and problem domain classes

CHAPTER OUTLINE

- Events and Use Cases
- Problem Domain Classes
- The UML Class Diagram
- Locations and the CRUD Matrix
- Use Cases, the Domain Model, and Iteration Planning

WAITERS ON CALL MEAL-DELIVERY SYSTEM

Waiters on Call is a restaurant meal-delivery service started in 2001 by Sue and Tom Bickford. The Bickfords both worked for restaurants while in college and always dreamed of opening their own restaurant. But unfortunately, the initial investment was always out of reach. The Bickfords noticed that many restaurants offer takeout food, and some restaurants—primarily pizzerias—offer home delivery service. Many people they met, however, seemed to want home delivery service with a more complete food selection.

Sue and Tom conceived Waiters on Call as the best of both worlds: a restaurant service without the high initial investment. The Bickfords contracted with a variety of well-known restaurants in town to accept orders from customers and to deliver the complete meals. After preparing the meal to order, the restaurant charges Waiters on Call a wholesale price, and the customer pays retail plus a service charge and tip. Waiters on Call started modestly, with only two restaurants and one delivery driver working the dinner shift. Business rapidly expanded, and the Bickfords realized they needed a custom computer system to support their operations. They hired a consultant, Sam Wells, to help them define what sort of system they needed.

"What sort of events happen when you are running your business that make you want to reach for a computer?" asked Sam. "Tell me about what usually goes on."

"Well," answered Sue, "when a customer calls in wanting to order, I need to record it and get the information to the right restaurant. I need to know which driver to ask to pick up the order, so I need drivers to call in and tell me when they are free. Sometimes customers call back wanting to change their orders, so I need to get my hands on the original order and notify the restaurant to make the change."

"Okay, how do you handle the money?" queried Sam.

Tom jumped in. "The drivers get a copy of the bill directly from the restaurant when they pick up the meal. The bill should agree with our calculations. The drivers collect that amount plus a service charge. When drivers report in at closing, we add up the money they have and compare it with the records we have. After all drivers report in, we need to create a deposit slip for the bank for the day's total receipts. At the end of each week, we calculate what we owe each restaurant at the agreed-to wholesale price and send each a statement and check."

"What other information do you need to get from the system?" continued Sam.

"It would be great to have some information at the end of each week about orders by restaurant and orders by area of town—things like that," Sue said. "That would help us decide about advertising and contracts with restaurants. Then we need monthly statements for our accountant."

Sam made some notes and sketched some diagrams as Sue and Tom talked. Then after spending some time thinking about it, he summarized the situation for Waiters on Call. "It sounds to me like you need a system to use whenever these events occur:

- A customer calls in to place an order, so you need to *record an order.*
- A driver is finished with a delivery, so you need to *record delivery completion.*
- A customer calls back to change an order, so you need to *update an order.*
- A driver reports for work, so you need to *sign in driver.*
- A driver submits the day's receipts, so you need to *reconcile driver receipts.*

"Then you need the system to produce information at specific points in time—for example, when it is:

- Time to produce an end-of-day deposit slip
- Time to produce end-of-week restaurant payments
- Time to produce weekly sales reports
- Time to produce monthly financial reports

"Based on the way you have described your business operations, I am assuming you will need the system to store information about these types of things, which we call domain classes:

- Restaurants
- Menu items
- Customers
- Orders
- Order payments
- Drivers

"Then I suppose you will need to maintain information about restaurants and drivers. You'll need to use the system when:

- You add a new restaurant
- A restaurant changes the menu
- You drop a restaurant
- You hire a new driver
- A driver leaves

"Am I on the right track?"

Sue and Tom quickly agreed that Sam was talking about the system in a way they could understand. They were confident that they had found the right consultant for the job.

Overview

Chapter 4 described the activities of the UP requirements discipline and then introduced the many tasks and techniques involved in completing the first requirements activity—gathering information about the system and its requirements. An extensive amount of information is required to properly define the system's functional and nonfunctional requirements, and models are used to help record and communicate information. This chapter, along with Chapter 6, presents techniques for documenting the functional requirements by creating a variety of models. These models are created in the requirements discipline activity we have named *Define functional requirements.*

We focus on two key concepts that help define functional requirements in the UP: use cases and problem domain classes. This chapter focuses on identifying use cases, which are later modeled in detail in Chapter 6. This chapter also focuses on identifying domain classes and completing the domain model using UML class diagram notation, which is also introduced. Keep in mind, though, that in any given system development project, most of the use cases and most of the problem domain classes are identified in early project iterations, beginning with the inception phase. The final details are worked out for each use case during several iterations in the elaboration phase, which also involve design and implementation.

EVENTS AND USE CASES

Chapter 4 discussed the importance of modeling in system development. We build on that discussion here to explain the specifics of modeling an information system's functional requirements. Virtually all approaches to system development begin the modeling process with the concept of a *use case*. As described in Chapter 2, a use case is an activity the system carries out, usually in response to a request by a user. In the inception phase of any project, analysts identify many of the key use cases. By the end of the elaboration phase, they should have identified all use cases and described them in detail.

Several techniques are recommended for identifying use cases. One approach is to list all users and think through what they need the system to do for their jobs. By focusing on one type of user at a time, the analyst can systematically address the problem of identifying use cases. Another approach is to start with the existing system and list all system functions that are currently included, adding any new functionality requested by users. A third approach is to talk to all users to get them to describe their goals in using the system.

Figure 5-1 lists a few Rocky Mountain Outfitter users (also called *actors*) and some of their work goals for the customer support system. By asking users about their goals, an analyst can focus on new or promising processes rather than just automating existing procedures. Many analysts find this approach useful for getting an initial list of use cases. However, the most comprehensive set of guidelines for identifying use cases is called the *event decomposition technique*, which you will learn how to do later in this chapter.

No matter which approach is used to identify use cases, it is important to identify them at the right level of analysis. For example, one analyst might identify a use case as

FIGURE 5-1
Identifying use cases by focusing on users and their goals

USER/ACTOR	USER GOAL
Order clerk	Look up item availability Create new order Update order
Shipping clerk	Record order fulfillment Record back order
Merchandising manager	Create special promotion Produce catalog activity report

typing in a customer name on a form. A second analyst might identify a use case as the entire process of adding a new customer. A third analyst might even define a use case as working with customers all day, which could include adding new customers, updating customer records, deleting customers, following up on late-paying customers, or contacting former customers. The first example is too low level to be useful. The second example defines a complete user goal, which is the right level of analysis for a use case. But working with customers all day is too broad to be useful.

elementary business processes (EBPs)
tasks that are performed by one person in one place, in response to a business event, that add measurable business value and leave the system and its data in a consistent state

The appropriate level of analysis for identifying use cases is one that focuses on *elementary business processes (EBPs)*. An EBP is a task performed by one person in one place, in response to a business event, which adds measurable business value and leaves the system and its data in a consistent state (see the Larman 2002 text in the "Further Resources" section at the end of the chapter for additional discussion of EBPs). In Figure 5-1 some of the RMO customer support system goals that become use cases are *Create new order*, *Record shipment*, *Create special promotion*, and so forth. These use cases are good examples of elementary business processes. Each is performed by one user in a set time and place, and once it is completed, the system and its data are in a consistent state.

BEST PRACTICE: Try to use several approaches for identifying use cases, and then cross-check to be sure no use cases have been overlooked.

event
an occurrence at a specific time and place that can be described and is worth remembering

Note that each EBP (and so each use case) occurs in response to a business event. An *event* occurs at a specific time and place, can be described, and should be remembered by the system. Events drive or trigger all processing that a system does, so listing events and analyzing events makes sense when you need to define system requirements by identifying use cases.

EVENT DECOMPOSITION

event decomposition
a technique analysts use to identify use cases by first focusing on the events a system must respond to and then looking at how a system responds

In determining what the use cases for a system are, analysts focus on *event decomposition*, a technique that first focuses on the events a system needs to respond to and then looks at how a system must respond—the system's use cases. When defining the requirements for a system, it is useful to begin by asking, "What events occur that will require the system to respond?" By asking about the events that affect the system, you direct your attention to the external environment and look at the system as a black box. This initial view helps keep your focus on a high-level view of the system (looking at the scope) rather than on the inner workings of the system. It also focuses your attention on the system's interfaces to outside people and other systems. End users, those who will actually use the system, can readily describe system needs in terms of events that affect their work. So, the external focus on events is appropriate when working with users. Finally, focusing on events gives you a way to divide (or decompose) the system requirements into use cases so you can study each separately.

Some events important to a charge account processing system for a store are shown in Figure 5-2. The system requirements are decomposed into use cases based on six events. A customer triggers three events: makes a charge, pays a bill, or changes address. The system responds with three use cases: process a charge, record a payment, or maintain customer data. Three other events are triggered inside the system by time: time to send out monthly statements, time to send late notices, and time to produce end-of-week summary reports. The system responds with use cases that carry out what it is time to do: produce monthly statements, send late notices, and produce summary reports. Describing this system in terms of events keeps the focus of the charge account system on the business requirements and the elementary business processes. Then the next step is to divide the work among developers; one analyst might focus on the events triggered by people, and another analyst might focus on events triggered internally. The system is decomposed in a way that allows it to be understood in detail. The result is a list of use cases triggered by business events at the right level of analysis.

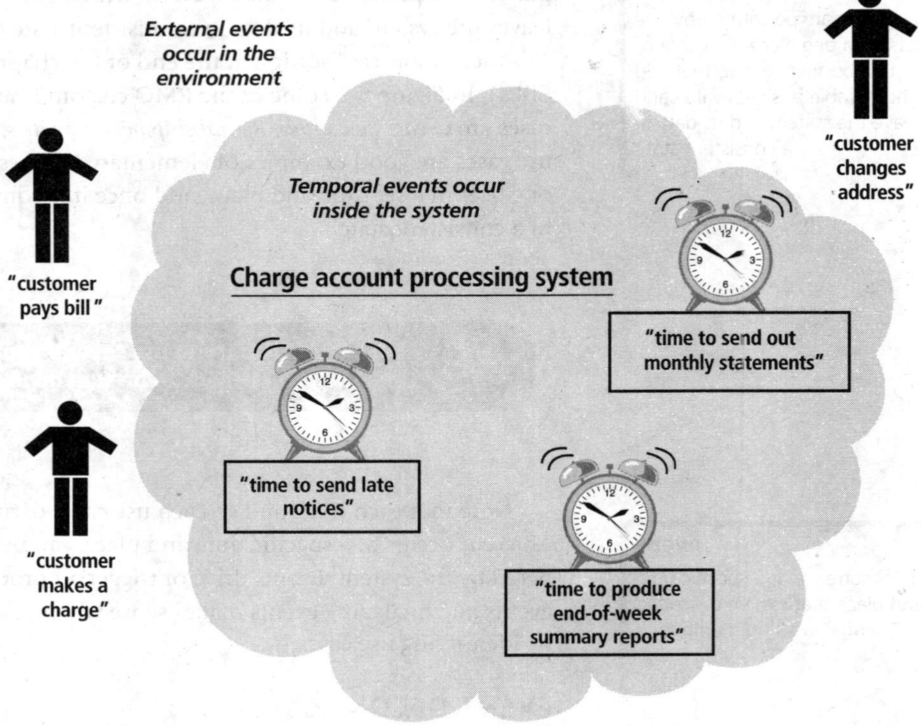

FIGURE 5-2
Events affecting a charge account processing system that lead to use cases

The importance of the concept of events for defining system requirements was first emphasized for modern structured analysis when this concept was adapted to real-time systems in the early 1980s. Real-time systems are required to react immediately to events in the environment. Early examples of real-time systems included control systems such as manufacturing process control or avionics guidance systems. For example, in process control, if a vat of chemicals is full, then the system needs to turn off the fill valve. The relevant event is "vat is full," and the system needs to respond to that event immediately. In an airplane guidance system, if the plane's altitude drops below 5,000 feet, then the system needs to turn on the low-altitude alarm.

Most information systems now being developed are so interactive that they can be thought of as real-time systems (in fact, people expect a real-time response to almost everything). So, use cases for business systems are now identified by using the event decomposition approach.

TYPES OF EVENTS

There are three types of events to consider: external events, temporal events, and state events. The analyst begins by trying to identify and list as many of these events as possible, refining the list while talking with system users.

EXTERNAL EVENTS

external event
an event that occurs outside the system, usually initiated by an external agent or actor

An *external event* is an event that occurs outside the system, usually initiated by an external agent. An external agent is a person or organizational unit that supplies or receives data from the system, not necessarily the system user. To identify the key external events, the analyst first tries to identify all of the external agents that might want something from the system. A classic example of an external agent is a customer. The customer may want to place an order for one or more products. This event is of fundamental importance to an order-processing system such as the one needed by Rocky Mountain Outfitters. But other events are associated with a customer. Sometimes a customer wants to return an ordered product, or a customer needs to pay the invoice for an order. External events such as these are the types that the analyst looks for because they begin to define what the system needs to be able to do. They are events that lead to important transactions or use cases that the system must process.

When describing external events, analysts need to name the event so that the external agent is clearly defined. The description should also include the action that the external agent wants to pursue. So, the event *Customer places an order* describes the external agent (a customer) and the action that the customer wants to take (to place an order for some products) that directly affects the system. Again, if the system is an order-processing system, it needs to process the order for the customer.

Important external events can also result from the wants and needs of people or organizational units inside the company—for example, management requests for information. A typical event in an order-processing system might be *Management checks order status*. Perhaps managers want to follow up on an order for a key customer, and the system must routinely provide that information.

Another type of external event occurs when external entities provide new information that the system simply needs to store for later use. For example, a regular customer reports a change in address, phone, or employer. Usually one event for each type of external agent can be described to handle updates to data, such as *Customer updates account information*. Figure 5-3 provides a checklist to help in identifying external events.

FIGURE 5-3
External event checklist

External Events to Look for Include:
✓External agent wants something resulting in a transaction
✓External agent wants some information
✓Data changed need to be updated
✓Management wants some information

TEMPORAL EVENTS

temporal event
an event that occurs as a result of reaching a point in time

A second type of event is a *temporal event*, an event that occurs as a result of reaching a point in time. Many information systems produce outputs at defined intervals, such as payroll systems that produce a paycheck every two weeks (or each month). Sometimes the outputs are reports that management wants to receive regularly, such as performance reports or exception reports. These events are different from external events in that the system should automatically produce the required output without being told to do so. In other words, no external agent is making demands, but the system is supposed to generate needed information or other outputs when they are needed.

The analyst begins identifying temporal events by asking about the specific deadlines that the system must accommodate. What outputs are produced at that deadline? What other processing might be required at that deadline? The analyst usually identifies these events by defining what the system needs to produce at that time. The payroll example discussed previously might be named *Time to produce biweekly payroll*. The event defining the need for a monthly summary report might be named *Time to produce monthly sales summary report*. Figure 5-4 provides a checklist to use in identifying temporal events.

FIGURE 5-4
Temporal event checklist

Temporal Events to Look for Include:
- ✓Internal outputs needed
  - ✓Management reports (summary or exception)
  - ✓Operational reports (detailed transactions)
  - ✓Internal statements and documents (including payroll)
- ✓External outputs needed
  - ✓Statements, status reports, bills, reminders

Temporal events do not have to occur on a fixed date. They can occur after a defined period of time has elapsed. For example, a bill might be given to a customer when a sale has occurred. If the bill has not been paid within 15 days, the system might send a late notice. The temporal event, *Time to send late notice*, might be defined as a point 15 days after the billing date.

STATE EVENTS

state event
an event that occurs when something happens inside the system that triggers the need for processing

A third type of event is a *state event*, an event that occurs when something happens inside the system that triggers the need for processing. For example, if the sale of a product results in an adjustment to an inventory record and the inventory in stock drops below a reorder point, it is necessary to reorder. The state event might be named *Reorder point reached*. Often state events occur as a consequence of external events. Sometimes they are similar to temporal events, except that the point in time cannot be defined. The reorder event might be named *Time to reorder inventory*, which sounds like a temporal event.

IDENTIFYING EVENTS

It is not always easy to define the events that affect a system and require a use case. But some guidelines can help an analyst think through the process.

EVENTS VERSUS PRIOR CONDITIONS AND RESPONSES

It is sometimes difficult to distinguish between an event and part of a sequence of prior conditions that leads up to the event. Consider an example of a customer buying a shirt from a retail store (see Figure 5-5). From the customer's perspective, this purchase involves a long sequence of events. The first event might be that a customer wants to get dressed. Then the customer wants to wear a striped shirt. Next, his striped shirt appears to be worn out. Then the customer decides to drive to the mall. Then he decides to go into Sears. Then he tries on a striped shirt. Then the customer decides to leave Sears and go to Wal-Mart to try on a shirt. Finally, the customer wants to purchase the shirt. The analyst has to think through such a sequence to arrive at the point where an event directly affects the system. In this case, the system is not affected until the customer is in the store, has a shirt in hand ready to purchase, and says, "I want to buy this shirt."

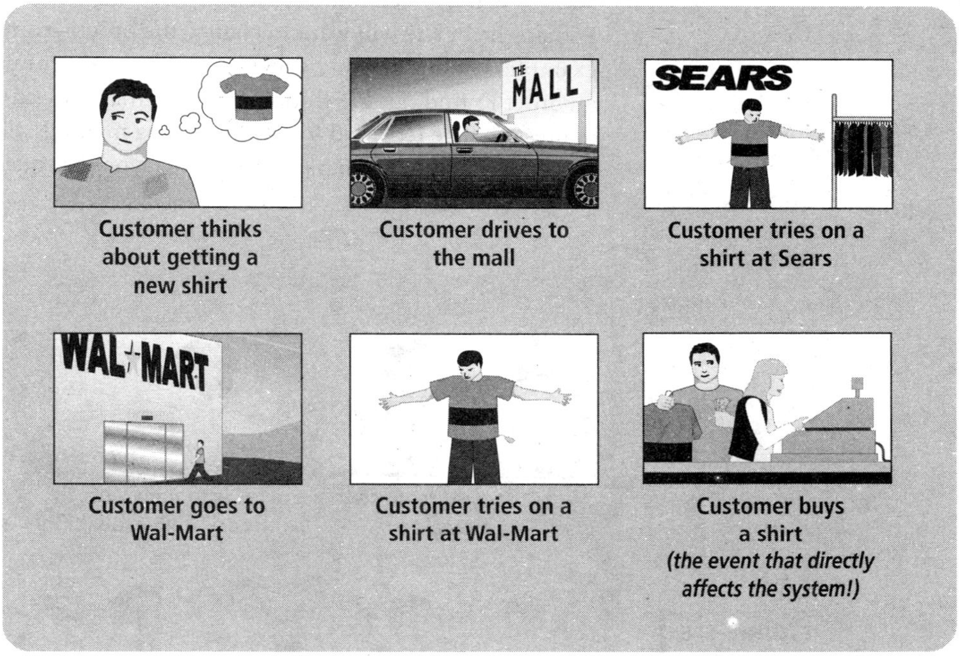

FIGURE 5-5
Sequence of actions that leads up to only one event affecting the system

In other situations, it is not easy to distinguish between an external event and the system's response. For example, when the customer buys the shirt, the system requests a credit card number, and the customer supplies the credit card. Is the act of supplying the credit card an event? In this case, no. It is part of the interaction that occurs during the original transaction, a step in the use case.

The way to determine whether an occurrence is an event or part of the interaction following the event is by asking whether any long pauses or intervals occur—that is, can the system transaction be completed without interruption, or is the system at rest again waiting for the next transaction? Once the customer wants to buy the shirt, the process continues until the transaction is complete. There are no significant stops once the transaction begins. Once the transaction is complete, the system is at rest, waiting for the next transaction to begin. In terms of the elementary business process (EBP) definition, the system is in a consistent state again.

On the other hand, separate events occur when the customer buys the shirt using his store credit card account. When the customer pays the bill at the end of the month, is that processing part of the interaction involving the purchase? In this case, no. The system records the transaction and then does other things. It does not halt all processes to wait for the payment. A separate event occurs later that results in sending the customer a bill (this is a temporal event: *Time to send monthly bills*). Eventually, another external event occurs (*Customer pays the bill*).

THE SEQUENCE OF EVENTS: TRACING A TRANSACTION'S LIFE CYCLE

It is often useful in identifying events to trace the sequence of events that might occur for a specific external agent. In the case of Rocky Mountain Outfitters' new customer support system, the analyst might think through all of the possible transactions that could result from one new customer (see Figure 5-6). First, the customer wants a catalog or asks for some information about item availability, resulting in a name and address being added to the database. Next, the customer might want to place an order. Perhaps he or she will want to change the order—correcting the size of the shirt, for example—or buy another shirt. Next, the customer might want to check the status of an order to find out the shipping date. Perhaps the customer has moved and wants an address change recorded for future catalog mailings. Finally, the customer might want to return an item. Thinking through this type of sequence can help identify events.

FIGURE 5-6
The sequence of "transactions" for one specific customer resulting in many events

TECHNOLOGY-DEPENDENT EVENTS AND SYSTEM CONTROLS

Sometimes the analyst is concerned about events that are important to the system but do not directly concern users or transactions. Such events typically involve design choices or system controls. When defining requirements, the analyst should temporarily ignore these events. They are important for the design discipline, however.

Events that affect design issues include external events that involve actually using the physical system, such as logging on. Although important to the final operation of the system, such a detail of implementation should be deferred. At this stage, the analyst should focus only on the functional requirements—the work that the system needs to complete. A requirements model does not need to indicate how the system is actually implemented, so the model should omit the implementation details.

system controls
checks or safety procedures put in place to protect the integrity of the system

Most of these events involve *system controls*, which are checks or safety procedures put in place to protect the integrity of the system. Logging on to a system is required because of system security controls, for example. Other controls, such as backing up the data every day, protect the integrity of the database. Both of these controls are important to the system, and they will certainly be added to the system. But spending time on these controls during early iterations—when the focus is on the users' requirements—only adds unnecessary complexity to the requirements model details. Users are not typically very concerned about system controls; they trust IS staff to take care of such details. Usually, system controls are part of the routine design details that are addressed in later iterations in the construction phase of the UP life cycle.

perfect technology assumption
the assumption that events should be included during early iterations only if the system would be required to respond under perfect conditions

One technique used to help decide which events apply to controls is to assume that technology is perfect. The *perfect technology assumption* states that events should be included during the definition of requirements only if the system would be required to respond under perfect conditions—that is, with equipment never breaking down, with unlimited capacity for processing and storage, and with people operating the system who are completely honest and never make mistakes. By pretending that technology is perfect, analysts can eliminate events such as *Time to back up the database*, because they can assume that the disk will never crash. Again, during later iterations, the project team adds these controls because technology is obviously not perfect. Figure 5-7 lists some examples of events that can be deferred until the later iterations.

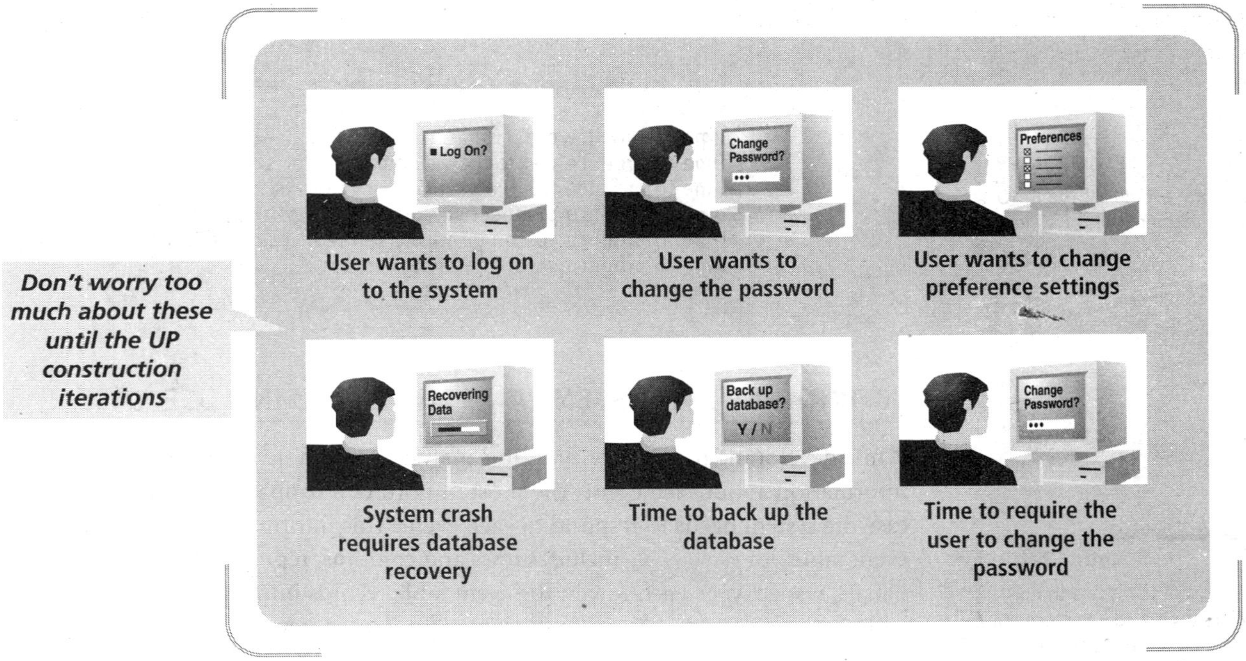

FIGURE 5-7
Events deferred until later iterations

EVENTS IN THE ROCKY MOUNTAIN OUTFITTERS CASE

The Rocky Mountain Outfitters customer support system involves a variety of events, many of them similar to those just discussed. A list of the external events is shown in Figure 5-8. Some of the most important external events involve customers: *Customer wants to check item availability, Customer places an order, Customer changes or cancels an order*. Other external events involve RMO departments: *Shipping fulfills order, Marketing wants to send promotional material to customers, Merchandising updates catalog*. The analyst

Customer wants to check item availability
Customer places an order
Customer changes or cancels order
Customer or management wants to check order status
Shipping fulfills order
Shipping identifies back order
Customer returns item (defective, changed mind, full or partial returns)
Prospective customer requests catalog
Customer updates account information
Marketing wants to send promotional materials to customers
Management adjusts customer charges (correct errors, make concessions)
Merchandising updates catalog (add, change, delete, change prices)
Merchandising creates special product promotion
Merchandising creates new catalog

FIGURE 5-8
External events for the RMO customer support system

can develop this list of external events by looking at all of the people and organizational units that want the system to do something for them.

The customer support system also includes quite a few temporal events, shown in Figure 5-9. Many of these produce periodic reports for organizational units: *Time to produce order summary reports, Time to produce fulfillment summary reports, Time to produce catalog activity reports*. The analyst can develop the list of temporal events by looking for all of the regular reports and statements that the system must produce at certain times.

Time to produce order summary reports
Time to produce transaction summary reports
Time to produce fulfillment summary reports
Time to produce prospective customer activity reports
Time to produce customer adjustment/concession reports
Time to produce catalog activity reports

FIGURE 5-9
Temporal events for the RMO customer support system

LOOKING AT EACH EVENT AND THE RESULTING USE CASE

event table
a catalog of use cases that lists events in rows and key pieces of information about each event in columns

While developing the list of events, the analyst should note for later use any additional information about each event. The most important information to identify is the use case the system needs to respond to each event. This information can be entered in an event table. An *event table* includes rows and columns, representing events and their details, respectively. Each row in the event table records information about one event and its use case. Each column in the table represents a key piece of information about that event and use case. The information about an event *Customer wants to check item availability* is shown in Figure 5-10. Note that the resulting use case is named *Look up item availability*.

BEST PRACTICE: Use an event table as a catalog of information about the use cases that make up the functional requirements of the system.

The event that causes the system to do something.

Source: For an external event, the external agent is the source of the data entering the system.

Response: What output (if any) is produced by the system?

Event	Trigger	Source	Use Case	Response	Destination
Customer wants to check item availability	Item inquiry	Customer	Look up item availability	Item availability details	Customer

Trigger: How does the system know the event occurred? For external events, the trigger is data entering the system. For temporal events, it is a definition of the point in time that triggers the system processing.

Use Case: What does the system do when the event occurs? The use case is what is important to define for functional requirements.

Destination: What external agent gets the output produced?

FIGURE 5-10
Information about each event and the resulting use case in an event table

trigger
a signal that tells the system that an event has occurred, either the arrival of data needing processing or a point in time

source
an external agent that supplies data to the system

Information in the event table documents important aspects of the event and the resulting use case. First, for each event, how does the system know the event has occurred? A signal that tells the system an event has occurred is called the *trigger*. For an external event, the trigger is the arrival of data that the system must process. For example, when a customer places an order, the new order details are provided as input. The *source* of the data is also important to know. In this case, the source of the new order details is the customer—an external agent. For a temporal event, the trigger is a point in time. For example, at the end of each business day, the system knows it is time to produce transaction summary reports.

Next, what does the system do when the event occurs? What the system does (the reaction to the event) is the *use case*. When a customer places an order, the system is used to carry out the use case *Create a new order*. When it is time to produce transaction summary reports, the system is used to carry out the use case *Produce transaction summary reports*.

response
an output, produced by the system, that goes to a destination

destination
an external agent that receives data from the system

Finally, what response does the use case produce? A *response* is an output from the system. When the system produces transaction summary reports, those reports are the outputs. One use case can generate several responses. For example, when the system creates a new order, an order confirmation goes to the customer, order details go to shipping, and a record of the transaction goes to the bank. The *destination* is the place where any response (output) is sent, again an external agent. Sometimes a use case generates no response at all. For example, if the customer wants to update account information, the information is recorded in the database, but no output needs to be produced. Recording information in the database is part of the use case.

The list of events—together with the trigger, source, use case, response(s), and destination(s) for each event—can be placed in an event table so that the analyst can keep track of them for later use. An event table is a convenient way to record key information about the requirements for the information system. The event table for the RMO customer support system is shown in Figure 5-11. The event table will later be used in Chapter 6 to identify use cases that need to be described in more detail. Barbara Halifax summarized her team's use case identification using the CSS event table in her status memo to John MacMurty (see Barbara's memo). She also discussed the need to identify and model domain classes as an important requirements step, which we discuss next.

CUSTOMER SUPPORT SYSTEM EVENT TABLE

EVENT	TRIGGER	SOURCE	USE CASE	RESPONSE	DESTINATION
1. Customer wants to check item availability	Item inquiry	Customer	Look up item availability	Item availability details	Customer
2. Customer places an order	New order	Customer	Create new order	Real-time link Order confirmation Order details Transaction	Credit bureau Customer Shipping Bank
3. Customer changes or cancels order	Order change request	Customer	Update order	Change confirmation Order change details Transaction	Customer Shipping Bank
4. Time to produce order summary reports	"End of week, month, quarter, and year"		Produce order summary reports	Order summary reports	Management
5. Time to produce transaction summary reports	"End of day"		Produce transaction summary reports	Transaction summary reports	Accounting
6. Customer or management wants to check order status	Order status inquiry	Customer or management	Look up order status	Order status details	Customer or management
7. Shipping fulfills order	Order fulfillment notice	Shipping	Record order fulfillment		
8. Shipping identifies back order	Back-order notice	Shipping	Record back order	Back-order notification	Customer
9. Customer returns item	Order return notice	Customer	Create order return	Return confirmation Transaction	Customer Bank
10. Time to produce fulfillment summary reports	"End of week month, quarter, and year"		Produce fulfillment summary reports	Fulfillment summary reports	Management
11. Prospective customer requests catalog	Catalog request	Prospective customer	Provide catalog info	Catalog	Prospective customer
12. Time to produce prospective customer activity reports	"End of month"		Produce prospective customer activity reports	Prospective customer activity reports	Marketing
13. Customer updates account information	Customer account update notice	Customer	Update customer account		
14. Marketing wants to send promotional materials to customers	Promotion package details	Marketing	Distribute promotional package	Promotional package	Customer and prospective customer
15. Management adjusts customer charges	Customer charge adjustment	Management	Create customer charge adjustment	Charge adjustment notification Transaction	Customer Bank
16. Time to produce customer adjustment/ concession reports	"End of month"		Produce customer adjustment reports	Customer adjustment reports	Management

(continued)

FIGURE 5-11
The complete event table for the RMO customer support system

Figure 5-11 continued

EVENT	TRIGGER	SOURCE	USE CASE	RESPONSE	DESTINATION
17. Merchandising updates catalog	Catalog update details	Merchandising	Update catalog		
18. Merchandising creates special product promotion	Special promotion details	Merchandising	Create special promotion		
19. Merchandising creates new catalog	New catalog details	Merchandising	Create new catalog	Catalog	Customer and prospective customer
20. Time to produce catalog activity reports	"End of month"		Produce catalog activity reports	Catalog activity reports	Merchandising

ROCKY MOUNTAIN OUTFITTERS
MEMO

March 20, 2006

To: John MacMurty

From: Barbara Halifax

RE: Customer Support System Project Update

John, I just wanted to report briefly that we are on track with identifying most of the functional requirements and domain classes for the CSS project. We are currently sorting through all of the information we have collected and finalizing the list of use cases for the system. We identified elementary business processes based on external and temporal events and mapped them against specific goals users had identified. The complete event table catalogs information on each event, its use case, and the source and destination of data. The list of use cases is the most important artifact now because we will begin to describe each use case in more detail.

We have also identified most of the domain classes for the system. Key attributes, associations, and hierarchies for each class are included in our first domain model class diagram. I'll bring the domain class diagram with me to the Friday status meeting. It is just a first step. We will convert the domain model class diagram to a design class diagram later, as we begin designing some of the use case realizations.

We will continue to work on the details of the requirements in the first few iterations of the project as we design and implement some software, but right now the use cases and domain classes have been identified and the scope seems to be holding as expected.

BH

cc: Steven Deerfield, Ming Lee, Jack Garcia

PROBLEM DOMAIN CLASSES

Another key concept used to define system requirements involves understanding and modeling things the users work with in the problem domain. As we discussed in Chapter 2, the problem domain contains things users deal with when they do their work—products, orders, invoices, and customers—that need to be part of the system. For example, an information system needs to store information about customers and products, so it is important for the analyst to identify lots of information about them. Often these things are similar to the external agents that provide information to or receive information from the system. For example, a customer external agent places an order, but the system also needs to store information about the customer. In other cases, these things in the system are distinct from external agents. For example, there is no external agent named *product*, but the system needs to store information about products.

These things make up the data about which the system stores information. The type of data that needs to be stored is definitely a key aspect of the requirements for any information system. In the object-oriented approach, these things also become the objects that interact in the system. Identifying and understanding these things in the users' problem domain are both key initial steps when defining requirements.

TYPES OF THINGS

As with events, an analyst should ask the users to discuss the types of things that they work with routinely. The analyst can ask about several types of things to help identify them. Many things are tangible and therefore more easily identified, but others are intangible. Different types of things are important to different users, so it is important to include information from all types of users.

Figure 5-12 shows some types of things to consider. Tangible things are often the most obvious, such as an airplane, book, or vehicle. In the Rocky Mountain Outfitters

FIGURE 5-12
Types of things

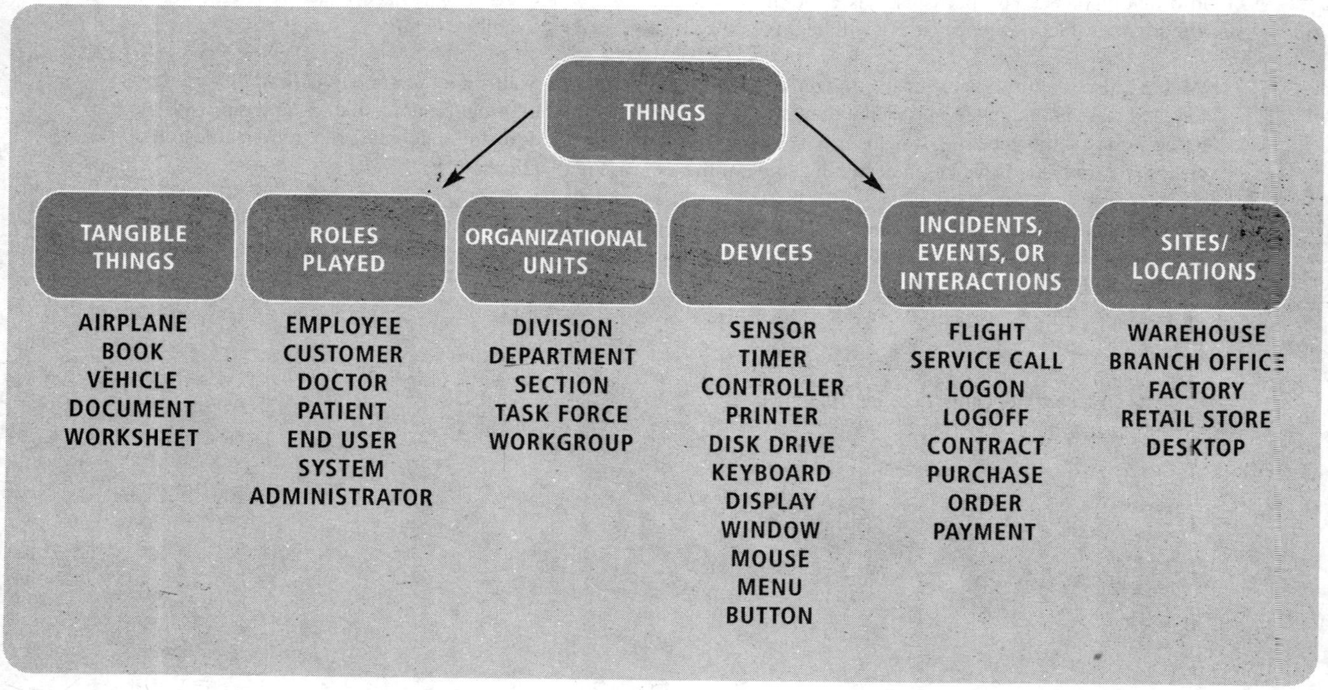

case, a catalog and an item in the catalog are tangible things of importance. Another common type of thing in an information system is a role played by a person, such as employee, customer, doctor, or patient. A customer is obviously a very important role a person plays in the Rocky Mountain Outfitters case.

Other types of things can include organizational units, such as a division, department, or workgroup. Similarly, sites or locations might be important in a particular system, such as a warehouse, a store, or a branch office. Finally, information about an incident or interaction of importance can be considered a thing—information about an order, a service call, a contract, or an airplane flight. An order, a shipment, and a return are important incidents in the Rocky Mountain Outfitters case. Sometimes these incidents are thought of as relationships between things. For example, an order is a relationship between a customer and an item of inventory.

The analyst identifies these types of things by thinking about each event in the event table and asking questions. For example, for each event, what types of things are affected that the system needs to know about and store information about? When a customer places an order, the system needs to store information about the customer, the items ordered, and the details of the order itself, such as the date and payment terms.

PROCEDURE FOR DEVELOPING AN INITIAL LIST OF THINGS

The general guidelines just discussed reveal that analysts can use many sources of information to develop an initial list of things about which the system needs to store information. A useful procedure to follow is to begin by listing all of the *nouns* that users mention when talking about the system. Consider the events, the use cases, the external agents, and the triggers and responses from the event table as potential things, for example. Then add to the list any additional nouns that appear in information about the existing system or that come up in discussions with stakeholders.

Step One. Using the event table and information about each event, identify all of the nouns.

For the RMO customer support system, the nouns include RMO, customer, product item, order, confirmation, transaction, shipping, bank, change request, summary report, management, transaction report, accounting, back order, back-order notification, return, return confirmation, fulfillment reports, prospective customer, catalog, marketing, customer account, promotional materials, charge adjustment, catalog details, merchandising, and catalog activity reports.

Step Two. Using other information from existing systems, current procedures, and current reports or forms, add items or categories of information needed.

For the RMO customer support system, these items might include more detailed information, such as price, size, color, style, season, inventory quantity, payment method, shipping address, and so forth. Some of these items might be additional categories, and some might be more specific pieces of information about things you have already identified (called *attributes*).

Step Three. Refine the list and record assumptions or issues to explore.

As this list of nouns builds, it will be necessary to refine it. Ask these questions about each noun to try to decide whether you should *include* it:

- Is it a unique thing the system needs to know about?
- Is it inside the scope of the system I am working on?
- Does the system need to remember more than one of these items?

Ask these questions about each noun to decide whether you should *exclude* it:

- Is it really just a synonym for some other thing I have identified?

- Is it really just an output of the system produced from other information I have identified?
- Is it really just an input that results in recording some other information I have identified?

Ask these questions about each noun to decide whether you should *research* it:

- Is it likely to be a specific piece of information (attribute) about some other thing I have identified?
- Is it something that I might need if assumptions change?

Figure 5-13 lists some of the nouns from the RMO customer support system event table and other sources, with some notes about each one.

IDENTIFIED NOUN	NOTES ON INCLUDING NOUN AS A THING TO STORE
Accounting	We know who they are. No need to store it.
Back order	A special type of order? Or a value of order status? Research.
Back-order information	An output that can be produced from other information.
Bank	Only one of them. No need to store.
Catalog	Yes, need to recall them, for different seasons and years. Include.
Catalog activity reports	An output that can be produced from other information. Not stored.
Catalog details	Same as catalog? Or the same as product items in the catalog? Research.
Change request	An input resulting in remembering changes to an order.
Charge adjustment	An input resulting in a transaction.
Color	One piece of information about a product item.
Confirmation	An output produced from other information. Not stored.
Credit card information	Part of an order? Or part of customer information? Research.
Customer	Yes, a key thing with lots of details required. Include.
Customer account	Possibly required if an RMO payment plan is included. Research.
Fulfillment reports	An output produced from information about shipments. Not stored.
Inventory quantity	One piece of information about a product item. Research.
Product item	Yes, what RMO includes in a catalog and sells. Include.
Management	We know who they are. No need to store.
Marketing	We know who they are. No need to store.
Merchandising	We know who they are. No need to store.
Order	Yes, a key system responsibility. Include.
Payment method	Part of an order. Research.
Price	Part of a product item. Research.
Promotional materials	An output? Or documents stored outside the scope? Research.
Prospective customer	Possibly same as customer. Research.
Return	Yes, the opposite of an order. Include.
Return confirmation	An output produced from information about a return. Not stored.
RMO	There is only one of these! No need to store.
Season	Part of a catalog? Or is there more to it? Research.
Shipment	Yes, a key thing to track. Include.

(continued)

FIGURE 5-13
Partial list of "things" based on nouns for RMO

Figure 5-13 continued

IDENTIFIED NOUN	NOTES ON INCLUDING NOUN AS A THING TO STORE
Shipper	Yes, they vary and we need to track the order. Include.
Shipping	Our department. No need to store.
Shipping address	Part of customer? Or order? Or shipment? Research.
Size	Part of a product item. Research.
Style	Part of a product item. Research.
Summary report	An output produced from other information. Not stored.
Transaction	Yes, each one is important and must be remembered. Include.
Transaction report	An output produced from transaction information. Not stored.

ASSOCIATIONS AMONG THINGS

After recording and refining the list of things, the analyst researches and records additional information. Many important relationships among things are important to the system. As we discussed in Chapter 2, an *association* is a naturally occurring relationship among specific things—for example, an order is placed by a customer and an employee works in a department (see Figure 5-14). *Is placed by* and *works in* are two associations that naturally occur between specific things. Information systems need to store information about employees and about departments, but equally important is storing information about the specific associations—John works in the accounting department, and Mary works in the marketing department, for example. Similarly, it is quite important to store the fact that Order 1043 for a shirt was placed by John Smith.

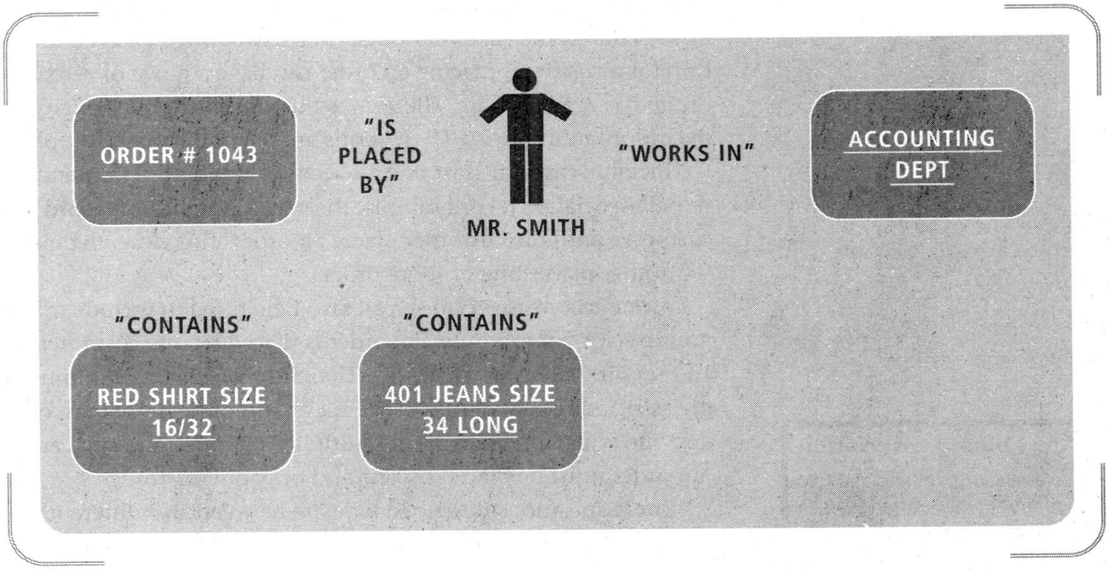

FIGURE 5-14
Associations naturally occur between things

Associations between things apply in two directions. For example, *a customer places an order* describes the association in one direction. Similarly, *an order is placed by a customer* describes the association in the other direction. It is important to understand the associations in both directions because sometimes it might seem more important for the system to record the association in one direction than in the other. For example, Rocky Mountain Outfitters definitely needs to know what items a customer ordered so the shipment can be prepared. However, it might not be apparent initially that the company needs to know all of the customers who have ordered a particular item. What if the company needs to notify all customers who ordered a defective or recalled product? Knowing this information would be very important, but the operational users might not immediately recognize that fact.

It is also important to understand the nature of each association in terms of the number of associations for each thing. For example, a customer might place many different orders, but an order is placed by only one customer. As we mentioned in Chapter 2, the number of associations that occur is referred to as the *multiplicity* of the association. Multiplicity can be one to one or one to many. Again, multiplicity is established for each direction of the association. Figure 5-15 lists examples of multiplicity for an order.

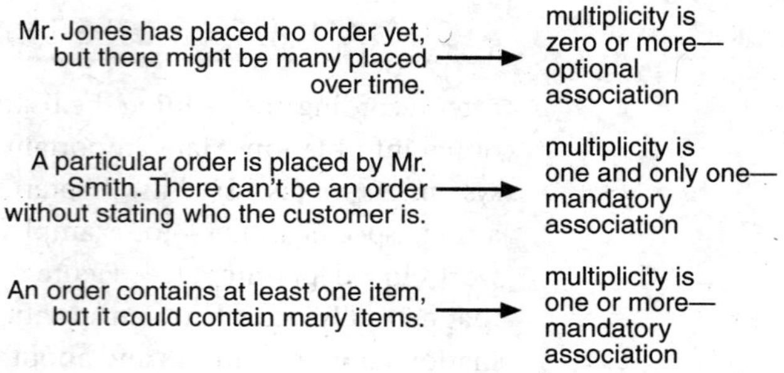

FIGURE 5-15
Multiplicity of relationships

Sometimes it is important to describe not just the multiplicity but also the range of possible values of the multiplicity (the minimum and maximum multiplicity). For example, a particular customer might not ever place an order. In this case, there are zero associations. Alternatively, the customer may place one order, meaning one association exists. Finally, the customer might place two, three, or even more orders. The association for a customer placing an order can have a range of zero, one, or more, usually indicated as zero or more. The zero is the minimum multiplicity, and "many" is the maximum multiplicity. These terms are referred to as "multiplicity constraints."

In some cases, at least one association is required (a mandatory as opposed to optional association). For example, the system might not record any information about a customer until the customer places an order. Therefore, the multiplicity would read "customer places one or more orders."

A one-to-one association can also be refined to include minimum and maximum multiplicity. For example, the order is placed by one customer—it is impossible to have an order if there is no customer. Therefore, one is the minimum multiplicity, making the association mandatory. Since there cannot be more than one customer for each order, one is also the maximum multiplicity. Sometimes such an association is read as "an order must be placed by one and only one customer."

binary association
a relationship between two different types of things, such as a customer and an order

unary (recursive) association
a relationship between two things of the same type, such as one person being married to another person

ternary association
a relationship among three different types of things

The associations described here are between two different types of things—for example, a customer and an order. These are called *binary associations*. Sometimes an association is between two things of the same type. For example, the association *is married to* is between two people. This type of association is called a *unary association* (sometimes called a *recursive association*). Another example of a unary association is an organizational hierarchy in which one organizational unit reports to another organizational unit—the packing department reports to shipping, which reports to distribution, which reports to marketing.

An association can also be among three different types of things, which is called a *ternary association*, or among any number of different types of things, which is called

n-ary association
a relationship among *n* (any number of) different types of things

an *n-ary association*. One particular order, for example, might be associated with a specific customer plus a specific sales representative, requiring a ternary association.

Storing information about the associations is just as important as storing information about the specific things. It is important to have information on the name and address of each customer, but it is equally important (or perhaps more so) to know what items each customer has ordered.

BEST PRACTICE: Initially, focus on identifying each "thing" in the problem domain, but also be sure to focus on associations among them, which are often just as important to the system users.

ATTRIBUTES OF THINGS

identifier (key)
an attribute that uniquely identifies a thing

compound attribute
an attribute that contains a collection of related attributes

Most information systems store and use specific pieces of information about each thing, as discussed in Figure 5-13 earlier. The specific pieces of information are called *attributes*. As we discussed in Chapter 2, a customer has a name, a phone number, a credit limit, and so on. Each of these details is an attribute. The analyst needs to identify the attributes of each thing that the system needs to know. One attribute may be used to identify a specific thing, such as a Social Security number for an employee or an order number for a purchase. The attribute that uniquely identifies the thing is called an *identifier*, or *key*. Sometimes the identifier is already established (a Social Security number, vehicle ID number, or product ID number). Sometimes the system needs to assign a specific identifier (an invoice number or transaction number).

A system may need to know many similar attributes. For example, a customer has several names—a first name, a middle name, a last name, and possibly a nickname. A *compound attribute* is an attribute that contains a collection of related attributes, so an analyst may choose one compound attribute to represent all of these names, perhaps naming it *Customer full name*. A customer might also have several phone numbers—a home phone number, office phone number, fax phone number, and cellular phone number. The analyst might start out by describing the most important attributes but later add to the list. Attribute lists can get quite long. Some examples of attributes of a customer and the values of attributes for specific customers are shown in Figure 5-16.

FIGURE 5-16
Attributes and values

ALL CUSTOMERS HAVE THESE ATTRIBUTES:	EACH CUSTOMER HAS A VALUE FOR EACH ATTRIBUTE:		
Customer ID	101	102	103
First name	John	Mary	Bill
Last name	Smith	Jones	Casper
Home phone	555-9182	423-1298	874-1297
Work phone	555-3425	423-3419	874-8546

CLASSES AND OBJECTS

When describing things important to a system, so far we have mainly used examples of things the system needs to store information about. In the object-oriented approach to system development, these things are called *problem domain classes*. The classes, the

domain model class diagram
a UML class diagram that shows the things that are important in the users' work: problem domain classes, their associations, and their attributes

associations among classes, and the attributes of classes are modeled using a domain model class diagram. The *domain model class diagram* is a UML diagram that shows the things that are important in the users' work: the problem domain classes, their associations, and their attributes. Problem domain classes are not software classes, although they will be used to design software classes as the system is designed and implemented. To this point, we have purposely discussed the problem domain classes more as "things" to keep the focus off software objects and on objects in the users' work environment early in the project when defining requirements.

BEST PRACTICE: Focus first on problem domain classes that are "things" in the users' work environment, not on the software classes that you will eventually need to design.

Eventually, the things in the users' work environment do also need to be represented in the system, so the other way to think about things is as software objects that interact in the system. Objects in the work environment of the user (*problem domain objects*) are often similar to the software objects. The main difference is that software objects do the work in the system; they do not just store information. In other words, software objects have behaviors as well as attributes.

You reviewed basic object-oriented concepts in Chapter 2. Recall that each specific thing is an object (John, Mary, Bill), and the type of thing is called a *class* (in this case, Customer). The word *class* is used because all of the objects are classified as one type of thing. The classes, the associations among classes, and the attributes of classes are modeled using a class diagram. Additionally, the class diagram can show some of the behaviors of software objects of the class.

In Chapter 2, we explained that the *methods* of a class are the behaviors all objects in the class are capable of doing. A behavior is an action that the object processes itself. Instead of an outside process updating data values, the object updates its own values when asked to do so—a key feature of the object-oriented approach to system development. Because each object contains values for attributes and methods for operating on those attributes (plus other behaviors), an object is said to be *encapsulated* (covered or protected)—a self-contained unit (see Figure 5-17). To ask the object to do something,

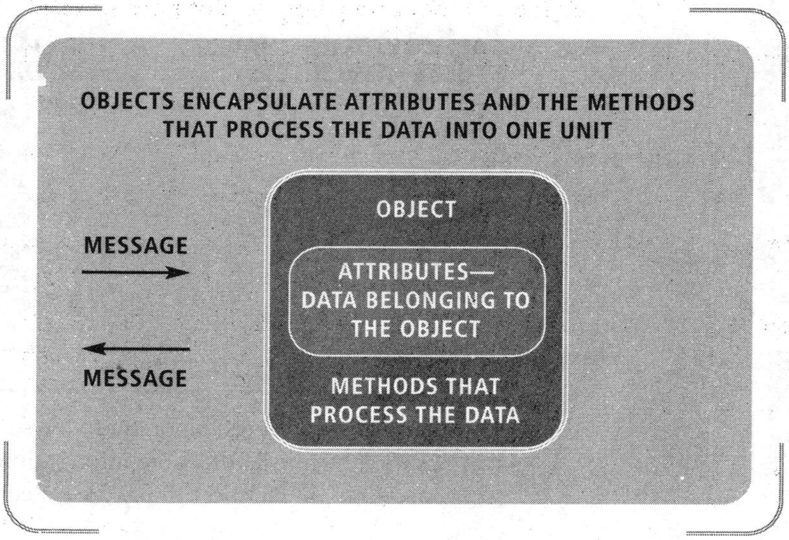

FIGURE 5-17
Objects encapsulate attributes and methods

another object sends it a message. One object can send another object a message, or an object can send the user a message. The information system as a whole becomes a collection of interacting objects, as described in Chapter 2.

Next we discuss two uses of the UML class diagram: as a domain model and as a software design model.

THE UML CLASS DIAGRAM

As just discussed, the diagram used to define the problem domain classes is called a UML class diagram. We saw some brief examples of class diagrams in Chapter 2 when we discussed generalization/specialization hierarchies and inheritance. In this section, you will learn more about the class diagram notation. The UML class diagram notation is used for both the domain model class diagram and the design class diagram.

DOMAIN MODEL CLASS DIAGRAM NOTATION

On the class diagram, rectangles represent classes, and the lines connecting the rectangles show the associations among classes. Figure 5-18 shows an example of a symbol for one class: Customer. The class symbol is a rectangle with three sections. The top section contains the name of the class, the middle section lists the attributes of the class, and the bottom section lists the important methods of the class. Methods are not shown on a domain model class diagram. In fact, the class symbol is often shown with only two sections to indicate that it is a domain model.

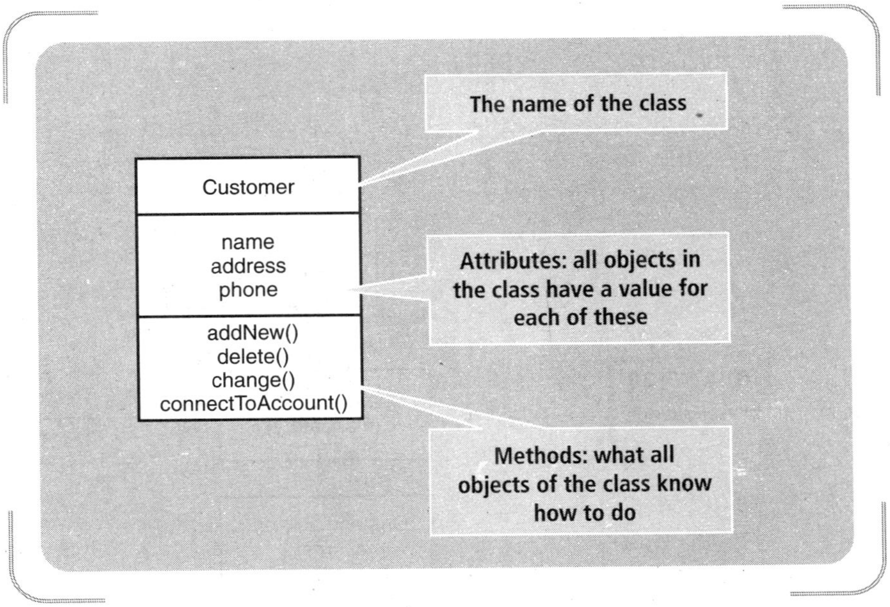

FIGURE 5-18
The UML class symbol with three sections for name, attributes, and methods

Figure 5-19 shows an example of a simplified domain model class diagram with two classes, Customer and Order. Here the class symbol includes only two sections. UML requires class names to be capitalized. In the diagram notation, we see that each Customer can place many Orders, and each Order is placed by one Customer; the association can be described on the diagram for clarity, but it is optional. The multiplicity is one to many in one direction and one to one in the other direction. The multiplicity notation, shown as an asterisk on the line next to the Order class, indicates "many" orders. See Figure 5-20 for a summary of multiplicity notation. The model in Figure 5-19 actually says that a Customer places a minimum of zero and a maximum of many Orders. Reading in the other direction, the model says an Order is placed by at least one and only one Customer. This notation expresses precise details about the system. The constraints reflect the business policies that users or management has defined, and the analyst must discover what those policies are. The analyst does not determine the constraints; users or management does.

FIGURE 5-19
A simple domain class diagram but with no attributes shown

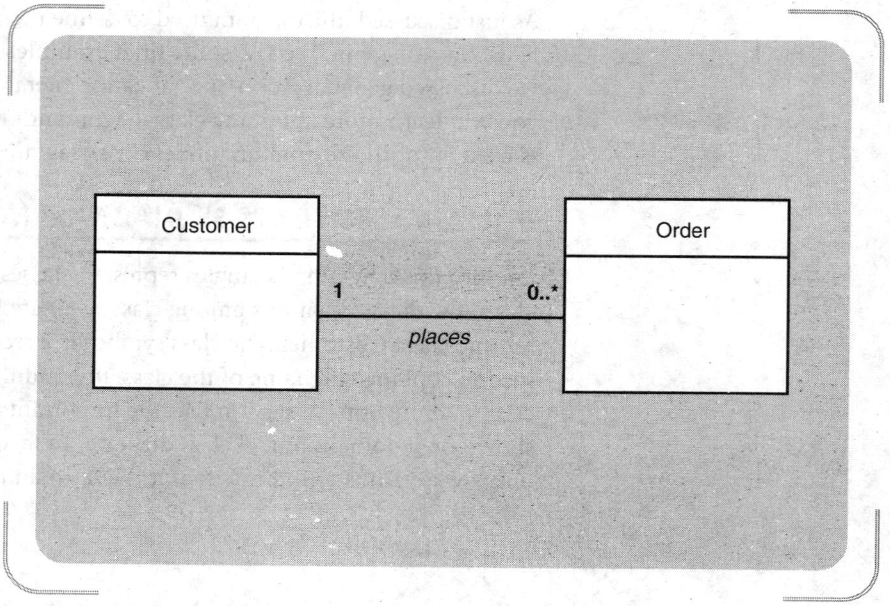

FIGURE 5-20
Multiplicity of associations

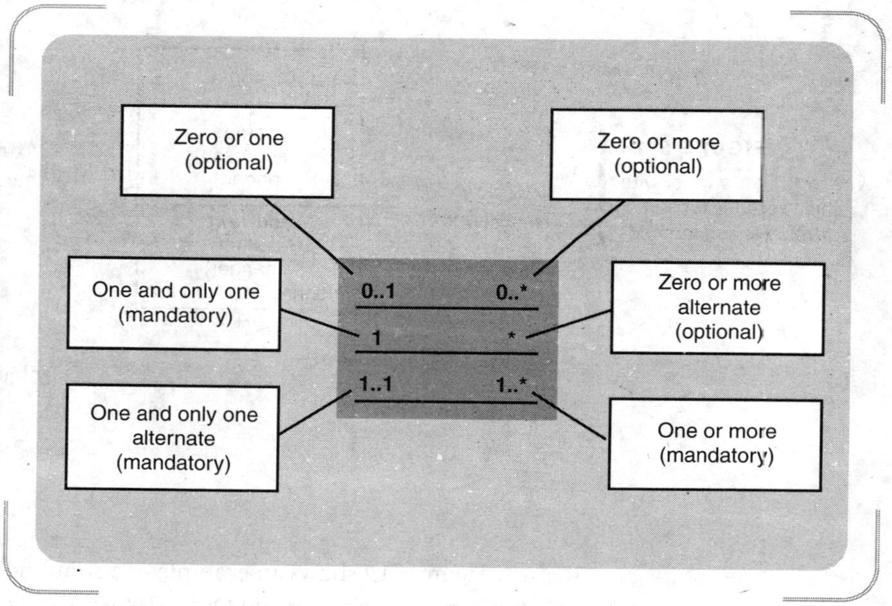

Figure 5-21 shows the model expanded to include the OrderItems—one or more specific items included in an order. Each order contains a minimum of one and a maximum of many items because there would not be an order without at least one item. For example, an order might include a shirt, a pair of shoes, and a belt, and each of these items is associated with the order. This example also shows some additional UML class notation: an attribute begins with a lowercase letter. A Customer has a customer number (custNumber), a name (name), a billing address (billAddress), and several phone numbers (homePhone, officePhone). Each Order has an orderID, orderDate, and amount. Each OrderItem has an itemID, quantity, and price. The attributes of the class are listed below the class name in the lower compartment of the class symbol, usually with the key identifier listed first.

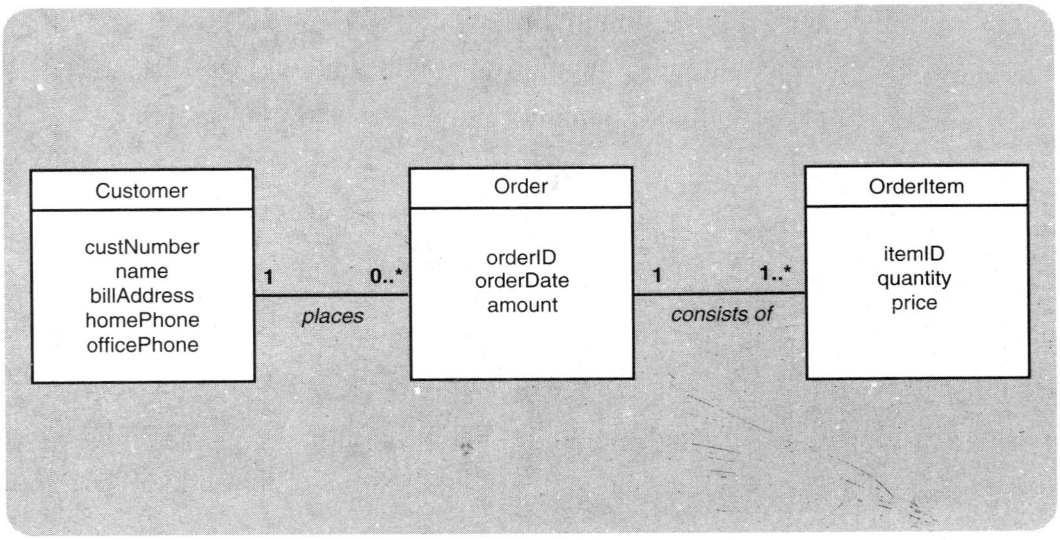

FIGURE 5-21
An expanded domain model class diagram showing attributes

Figure 5-22 shows how the actual objects in some transactions might look. John is a customer who has placed two orders. The first order, placed on February 4, was for two shirts and one belt. The second order, placed on March 29, was for one pair of boots and two pairs of sandals. Mary is a customer who has not yet placed an order. Recall that a customer might place zero or more orders. Therefore, Mary is not associated with any orders. Finally, Sara placed an order on March 30 for three pairs of sandals.

While working on the model, the analyst often refines the domain model class diagram. One example of refinement is analyzing many-to-many associations. Figure 5-23 shows an example of a many-to-many association—with the asterisk symbol at each end of the association line. At a university, courses are offered as course sections, and a student enrolls in many course sections. Each course section contains many students. Therefore, the association between course section and student is many to many. Many-to-many associations occur naturally, and they can be modeled as shown, with the asterisk on both ends of the association line.

On closer analysis, however, analysts often discover that many-to-many associations involve additional data that must be recorded. For example, in the class diagram in Figure 5-23, where is the grade that each student receives for the course recorded? This is important data, and although the model indicates which course section a student took, the model does not have a place for the grade. The solution is to add a class to represent the association between student and course section, called an *association class*. The association class is given the missing attribute. Figure 5-24 shows the expanded class diagram with an association class named Course Enrollment, which has an attribute for the student's grade. An association class is connected to the many-to-many association with a dashed line.

association class
a class that represents a many-to-many relationship between two other classes

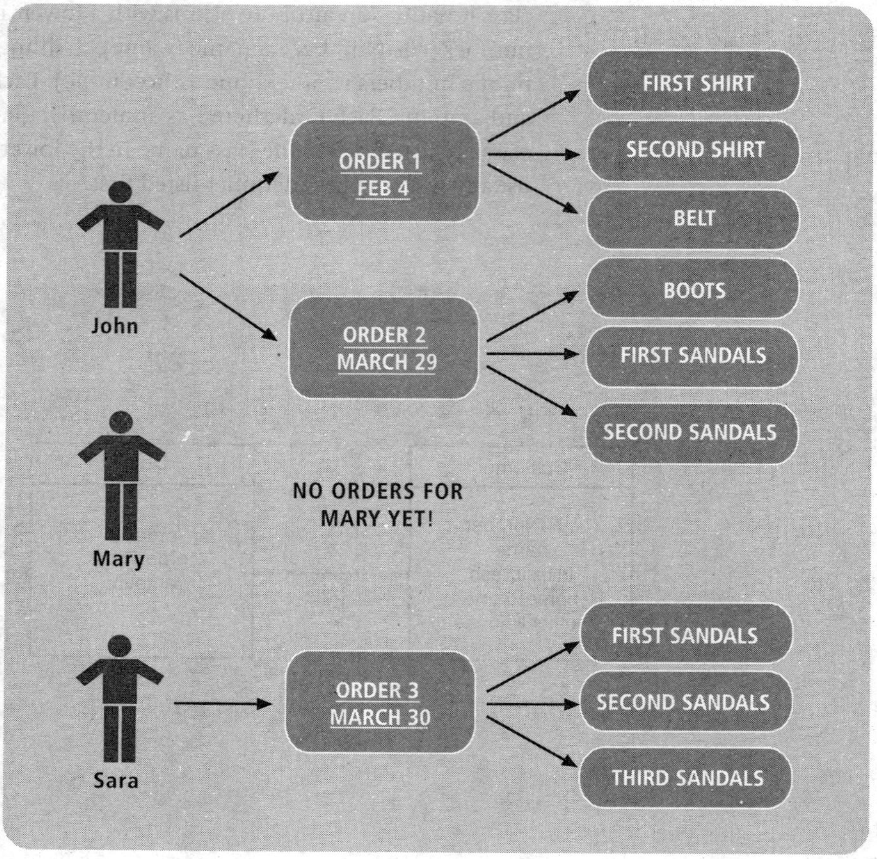

FIGURE 5-22
Customers, orders, and order items consistent with the expanded domain model class diagram

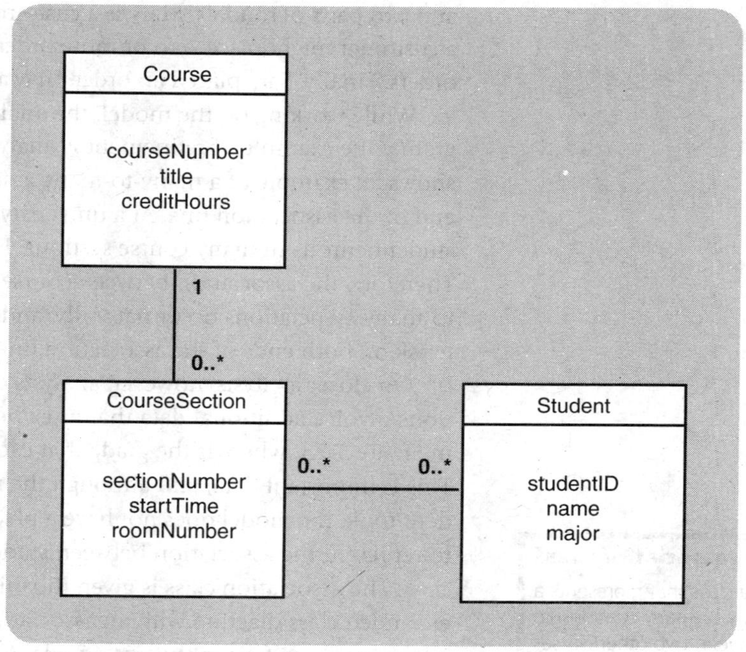

FIGURE 5-23
A university course enrollment domain model class diagram with a many-to-many association

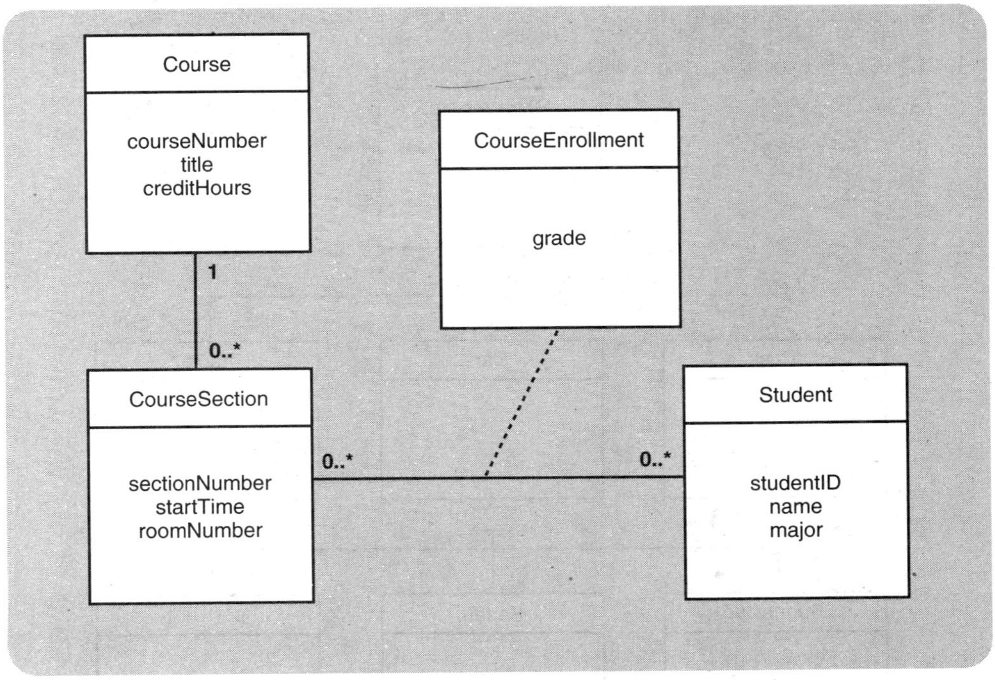

FIGURE 5-24
A refined university course enrollment domain model class diagram with an association class

Reading the associations in Figure 5-24 from left to right, the class diagram says that one course section has many course enrollments, each with its own grade, and each course enrollment applies to one specific student. Reading from right to left, it says one student has many course enrollments, each with its own grade, and each course enrollment applies to one specific course section. A system implemented on the basis of this domain model will be able to produce grade lists showing all students and their grades in each course section, as well as grade transcripts showing all grades earned by each student.

HIERARCHIES IN CLASS DIAGRAM NOTATION

There are two additional ways that people structure their understanding of problem domain classes in the real world: generalization/specialization hierarchies and whole-part hierarchies. We discuss their UML notation next.

GENERALIZATION/SPECIALIZATION NOTATION

As we discussed in Chapter 2, *generalization/specialization hierarchies* are based on the idea that people classify things in terms of similarities and differences. Generalizations are judgments that group similar types of things; for example, there are many types of motor vehicles—cars, trucks, tractors, and so forth. All motor vehicles share certain general characteristics, so a motor vehicle is a more general class. Specializations are judgments that categorize different types of things—for example, special types of cars include sports cars, sedans, and sport utility vehicles. These types of cars are similar in some ways, yet different in other ways. Therefore, a sports car is a special type of car.

A generalization/specialization hierarchy is used to structure or rank these things from the more general to the more special. As discussed in Chapter 2, classification refers to defining classes of things. Each class of thing in the hierarchy might have a more general class above it, called a *superclass*. At the same time, a class might have a more specialized class below it, called a *subclass*. In Figure 5-25, a car has three

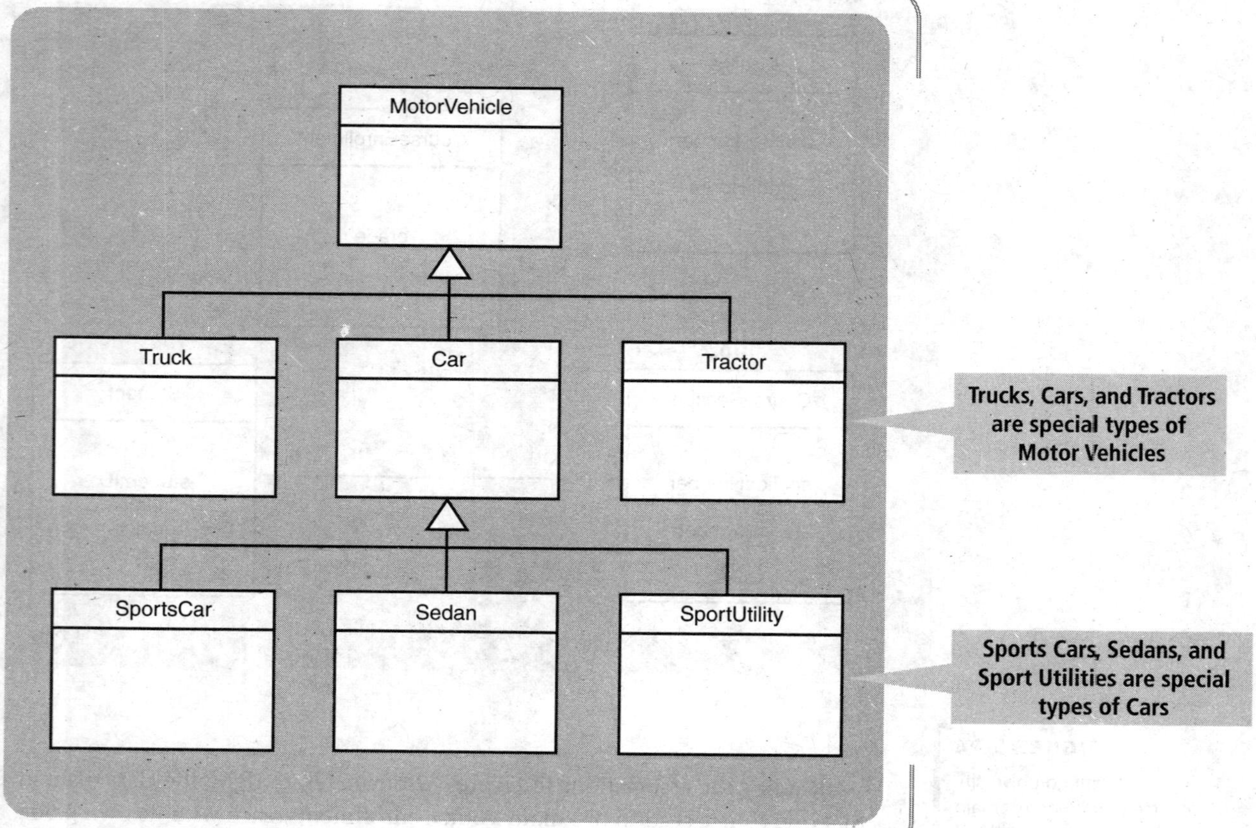

FIGURE 5-25
A generalization/specialization hierarchy notation for motor vehicles

subclasses and one superclass (MotorVehicle). The UML class diagram notation for a superclass and subclass is a small triangle on the line that points to the superclass.

People learn by refining the classifications they make about a field of knowledge. A knowledgeable banker can talk at length about special types of loans and deposit accounts. A knowledgeable merchandiser such as John Blankens at Rocky Mountain Outfitters can talk at length about special types of outdoor activities and clothes. Therefore, when an analyst asks users about their work, he or she is trying to understand the knowledge the user has about the work, which the analyst can then represent on a generalization/specialization hierarchy. At some level, the motivation for the new customer support system at RMO started with John's recognition that Rocky Mountain Outfitters might handle many special types of orders with a new system (Web orders, telephone orders, and mail orders). These special types of orders are shown in Figure 5-26.

Inheritance allows subclasses to share characteristics of their superclass. Returning to Figure 5-25, a car is everything any other motor vehicle is but also something special. A sports car is everything any other car is plus something special. In this way, the subclass "inherits" characteristics. In the object-oriented approach, inheritance is a key concept that is possible because of generalization/specialization hierarchies. Sometimes these hierarchies are referred to as *inheritance hierarchies*.

WHOLE-PART HIERARCHY NOTATION

Another way that people structure information about things is by defining them in terms of their parts. For example, learning about a computer system might involve recognizing that the computer is actually a collection of parts—processor, main memory,

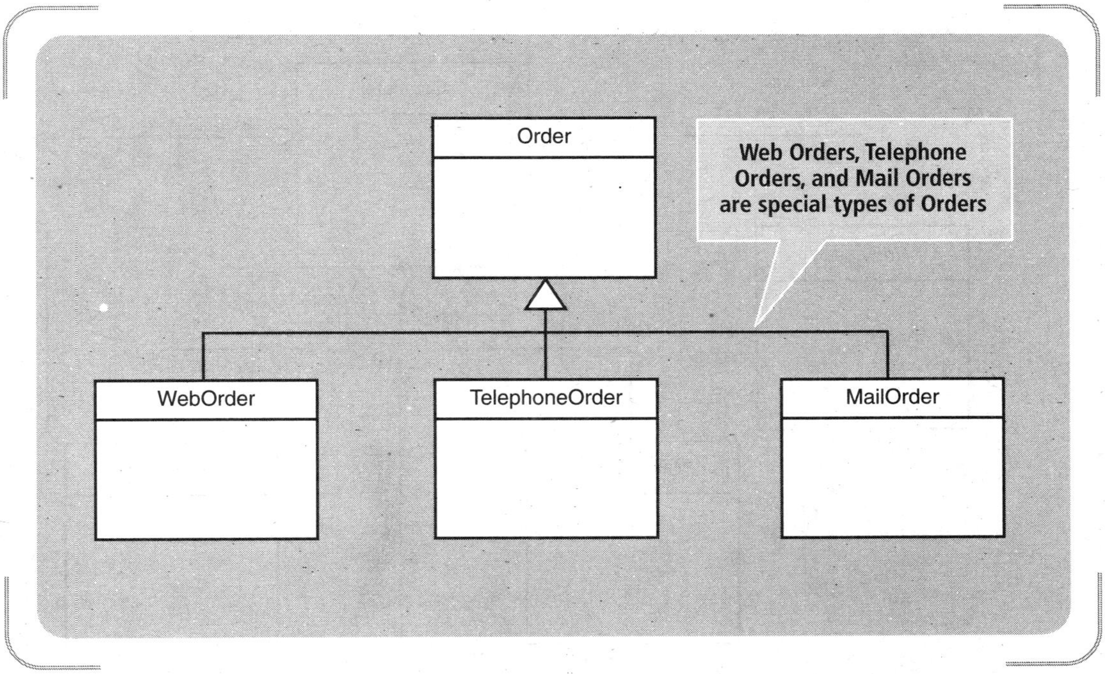

FIGURE 5-26
A generalization/specialization hierarchy for orders

whole-part hierarchies
hierarchies that structure classes according to their associated components

aggregation
whole-part relationship between an object and its parts in which the parts can exist separately

composition
whole-part relationship in which the parts cannot be dissociated from the object

keyboard, disk storage, and monitor. A keyboard is not a special type of computer; it is part of a computer. Yet, it is also something entirely separate in its own right. *Whole-part hierarchies* capture the relationships that people identify when they learn to make associations between an object and its components.

There are two types of whole-part hierarchies: aggregation and composition. The term *aggregation* is used to describe a whole-part association between the aggregate (whole) and its components (parts) in which the parts can exist separately. Figure 5-27 demonstrates the concept of aggregation in a computer system, using the diamond symbol to represent aggregation. The term *composition* is used to describe whole-part associations that are even stronger, in which the parts, once associated, can no longer exist separately. The diamond symbol is filled in to represent composition (not shown).

Whole-part hierarchies, both aggregation and composition, serve mainly to allow the analyst to express subtle distinctions about associations among classes. As with any association relationship, multiplicity can apply—for example, when a computer has one or more disk storage devices.

DESIGN CLASS DIAGRAM NOTATION

The UML class diagram examples we have seen so far are domain model class diagrams. The design class diagram is used to represent software classes that are included in the new system. You will learn about the process of converting the domain model class diagram to a design class diagram in Chapter 8. The design class diagram shows more about the actual design of the software. The class diagram in Figure 5-28 includes some methods to reinforce the idea that the software classes have both attributes and methods.

Figure 5-28 shows part of a design class diagram for a system that maintains bank accounts and that includes the Customer software class. This diagram does not show the methods of the Customer class because they are fairly standard. Any class is assumed to know how to add a new instance, update values, and report information about itself. The Account class lists a couple of methods because they are unique to bank accounts and central to the processing of the system. They include makeDeposit( ) and makeWithdrawal( ).

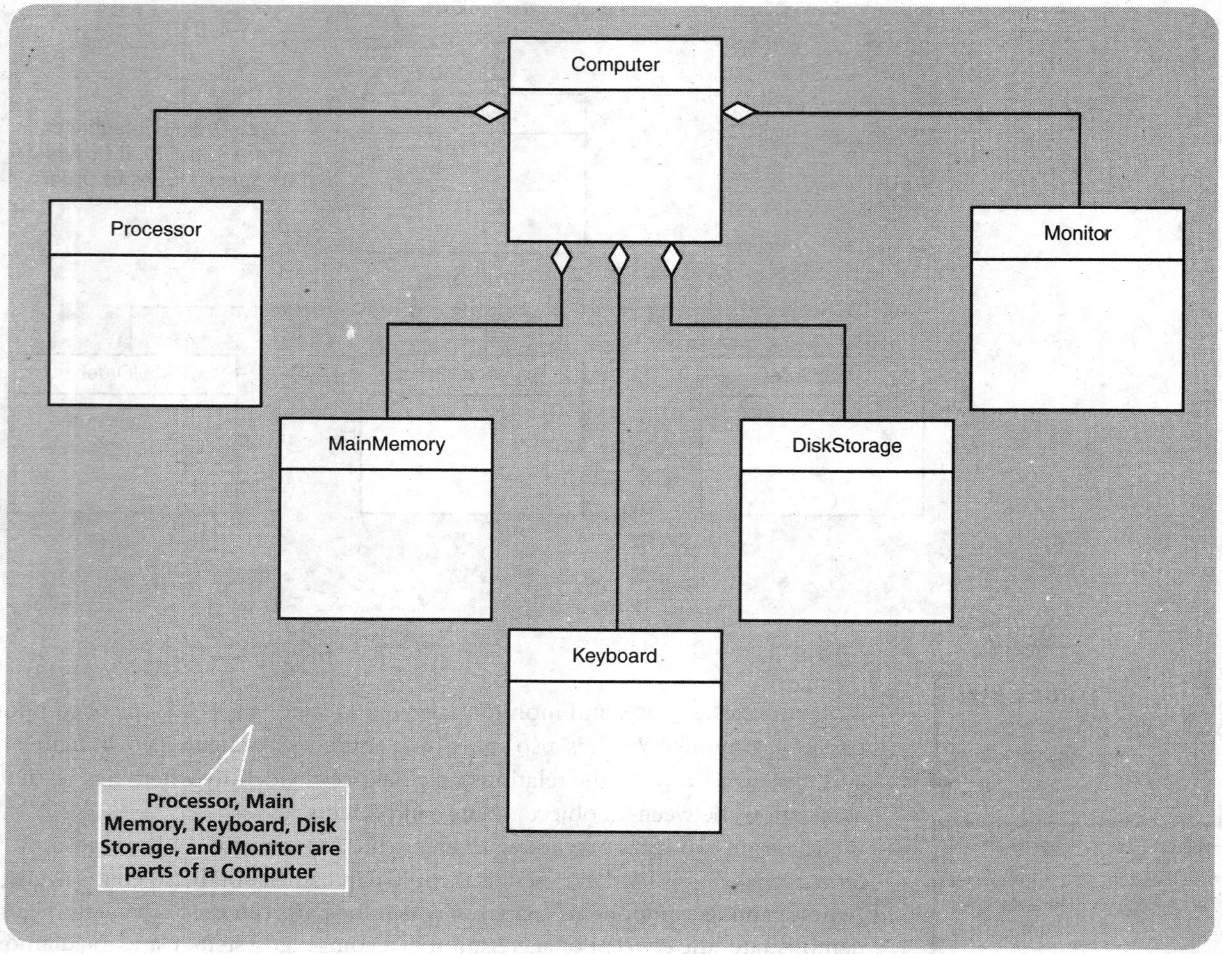

FIGURE 5-27 Whole-part (aggregation) associations between a computer and its parts

The bank account system includes a generalization/specialization hierarchy: Account is the superclass, and SavingsAccount and CheckingAccount are two subclasses. The triangle symbol drawn on a line connecting the classes indicates inheritance. The subclasses inherit attributes and behaviors from the superclass. Therefore, a CheckingAccount inherits the two methods plus all of the attributes from Account. Similarly, SavingsAccount inherits the same methods and attributes. But SavingsAccount also knows how to calculate interest; CheckingAccount does not. The result is that some attributes and methods are common to both types of accounts, but other attributes and methods are not.

In this example, inheritance means that when a SavingsAccount object is created (or instantiated), it will require values for four attributes, but a CheckingAccount object will require values for five attributes. The CheckingAccount object can be asked to make a deposit, as can the SavingsAccount object. The SavingsAccount object can be asked to calculate interest, but the CheckingAccount object cannot. Each object, or instance, maintains information and can be asked to invoke one of its methods.

The Customer class and the Account class have an association. Each customer can have zero or more accounts. Note that the diagram indicates the minimum and maximum multiplicity on the line connecting the classes. The asterisk means "many," so the multiplicity between Customer and Account is a minimum of zero and a maximum of many (0..* usually just shown as *). To indicate a mandatory relationship, the diagram would have to be changed to indicate a minimum of 1 and a maximum of many (1..*).

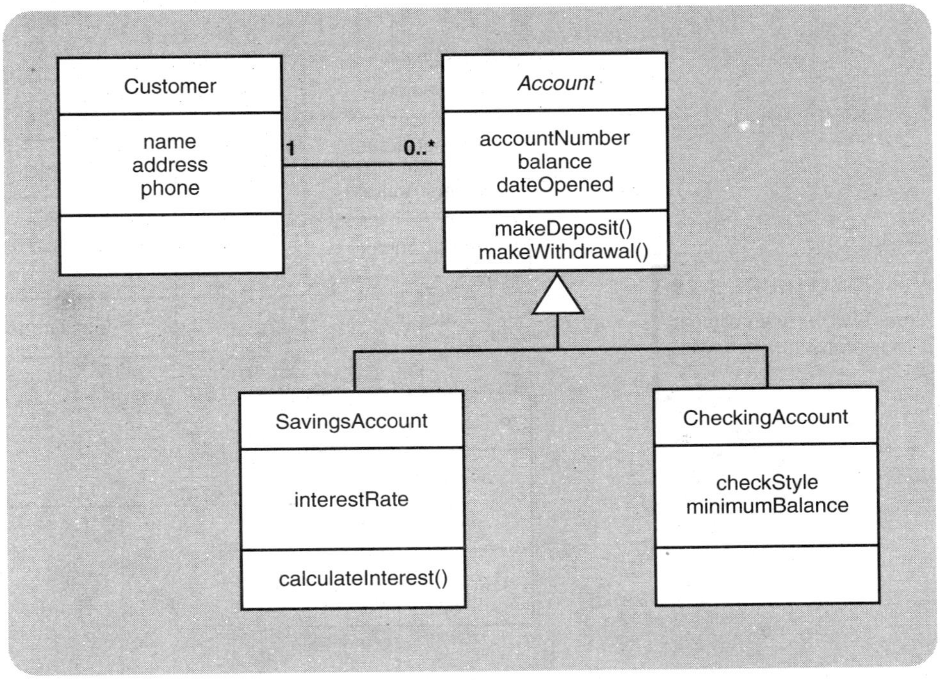

FIGURE 5-28
A bank account system design class diagram (with methods)

Each account is owned by one and only one customer in this example (1). The diagram could be changed to indicate an optional one-to-one association as a minimum of zero and a maximum of 1 (0..1).

Note also that the SavingsAccount and CheckingAccount classes inherit the association with Customer, so a customer is actually associated with a checking account or savings account, as appropriate. In fact, the bank does not offer anything like the simple Account class; the class exists only to allow special types of accounts to inherit attributes, methods, and associations. The Account class is an *abstract class*, a class that cannot be instantiated. On the class diagram, an abstract class has its name in italics, as in Figure 5-28. CheckingAccount, SavingsAccount, and Customer are examples of *concrete classes* that can be instantiated.

abstract class
a class that cannot be instantiated (no objects can be created), existing only to allow subclasses to inherit its attributes, methods, and associations

concrete class
a class that can be instantiated (objects can be created)

Figure 5-29 shows the course enrollment example as a design class diagram with methods. Course has a method to add a course. Course sections can be opened for enrollment and later closed. A student can be admitted and later receive a degree. Once the semester is over, a course enrollment can post a grade.

No generalization/specialization is shown in this example, but there could be special types of students (undergraduate and graduate) or special types of courses (credit and noncredit) in a university enrollment system. Figure 5-30 shows an expanded version of the course enrollment example. Semester is added, because a course section is offered in one specific semester. The diagram also shows generalization/specialization from Student to UnderGraduateStudent and GraduateStudent. For example, every object that is an UnderGraduateStudent is a special type of Student. The specialization classes inherit all of the attributes, associations, and methods of the generalization class. Student is now in italics because it is an abstract class.

Some additional notation on attributes is also shown. When modeling classes, it is often important to identify the primary key field or fields. In UML, properties of attributes are shown with curly braces, as shown by the courseNumber {key} in the Course class. Other classes have keys also. The attribute <u>numberOfSections</u> is underlined to

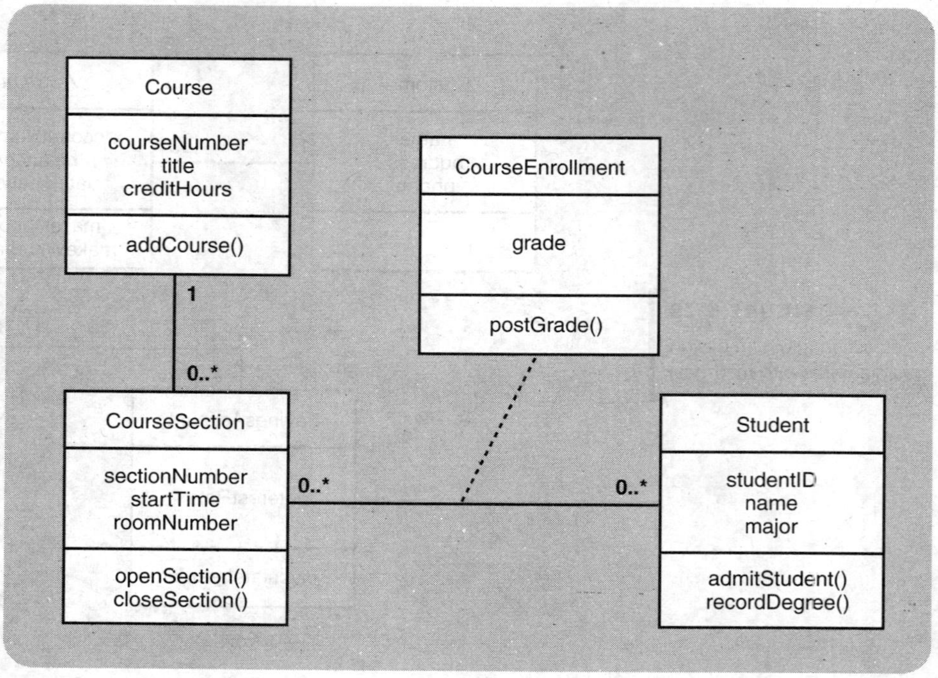

FIGURE 5-29
University course enrollment design class diagram (with methods)

indicate that it is a class-level attribute. Usually, an attribute has a unique value for each object. However, a class-level attribute has one value that applies to all objects of the class. In Java it is implemented as a static attribute, and in VB .NET it is implemented as a shared attribute. In this example, the system needs to store one value representing the number of course sections that are offered. Each time an additional section is added, the value is increased by one.

Some additional common class diagram notation conventions are useful. A class-level method (static method or shared method) is also underlined (not shown in Figure 5-30). Some attributes are calculated values. An attribute preceded by a forward slash (/) means the attribute is calculated rather than stored. For example, the numberOfSections class attribute might be better implemented as a calculated value, so it would be shown underlined as /numberOfSections. There are many more details of class diagramming that you will study as part of the design discipline, in Chapter 8. Remember that the requirements are modeled using the domain class diagram, without showing methods. The design class diagram shows methods and other software-specific details. We show the more complete UML class diagram notation here to document most of the important class diagram notation in one place.

THE ROCKY MOUNTAIN OUTFITTERS DOMAIN CLASS DIAGRAM

Returning to the requirements model for the customer support system project, the Rocky Mountain Outfitters domain class diagram is a variation of the customer and order example already described. Most of the classes are from the list of nouns developed in Figure 5-13. Figure 5-31 shows a fairly complete version of the RMO domain class diagram, showing attributes. Since it is a domain model class diagram, no methods are shown. The diagram shows only the problem domain classes the users deal with in their work, not software classes.

Each customer can place zero or more orders. Each order can have one or more order items, meaning the order might be for one shirt and two sweaters. Each order

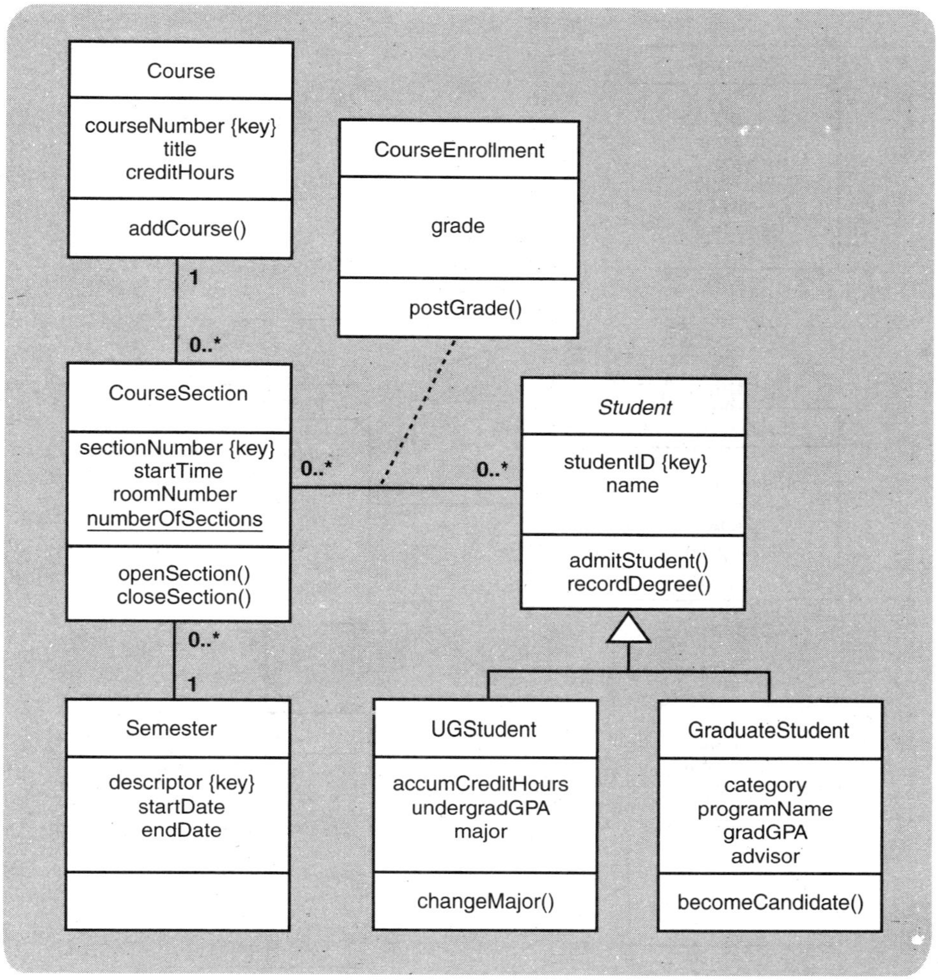

FIGURE 5-30
Expanded course enrollment design class diagram (with methods)

item is for a specific inventory item, meaning a specific size and color of shirt. An inventory item should have an attribute for quantity on hand of items in that size and color. Since there are many colors and sizes (each with its own quantity), each inventory item is associated with a product item that describes the item generically (vendor, gender, description).

An earlier version of the model showed that each product item is contained in one or more catalogs, and each catalog contains one or more product items, a many-to-many association. Therefore, this model adds an *association class* named CatalogProduct between Catalog and ProductItem because the association has some attributes that need to be remembered, specifically the regular and special prices. Each catalog can list a different price for the same product item (ski pants might be cheaper in the spring catalog).

The class diagram for Rocky Mountain Outfitters also has information about shipments. Since this diagram includes requirements for orders, not retail sales, each order item is eventually part of a shipment. A shipment may contain many order items. Each shipment is shipped by one shipper.

A generalization/specialization hierarchy is included to show that an order can be any one of three types—Web order, telephone order, or mail order—as discussed previously. Note that all types of orders share the attributes listed for Order, but each special

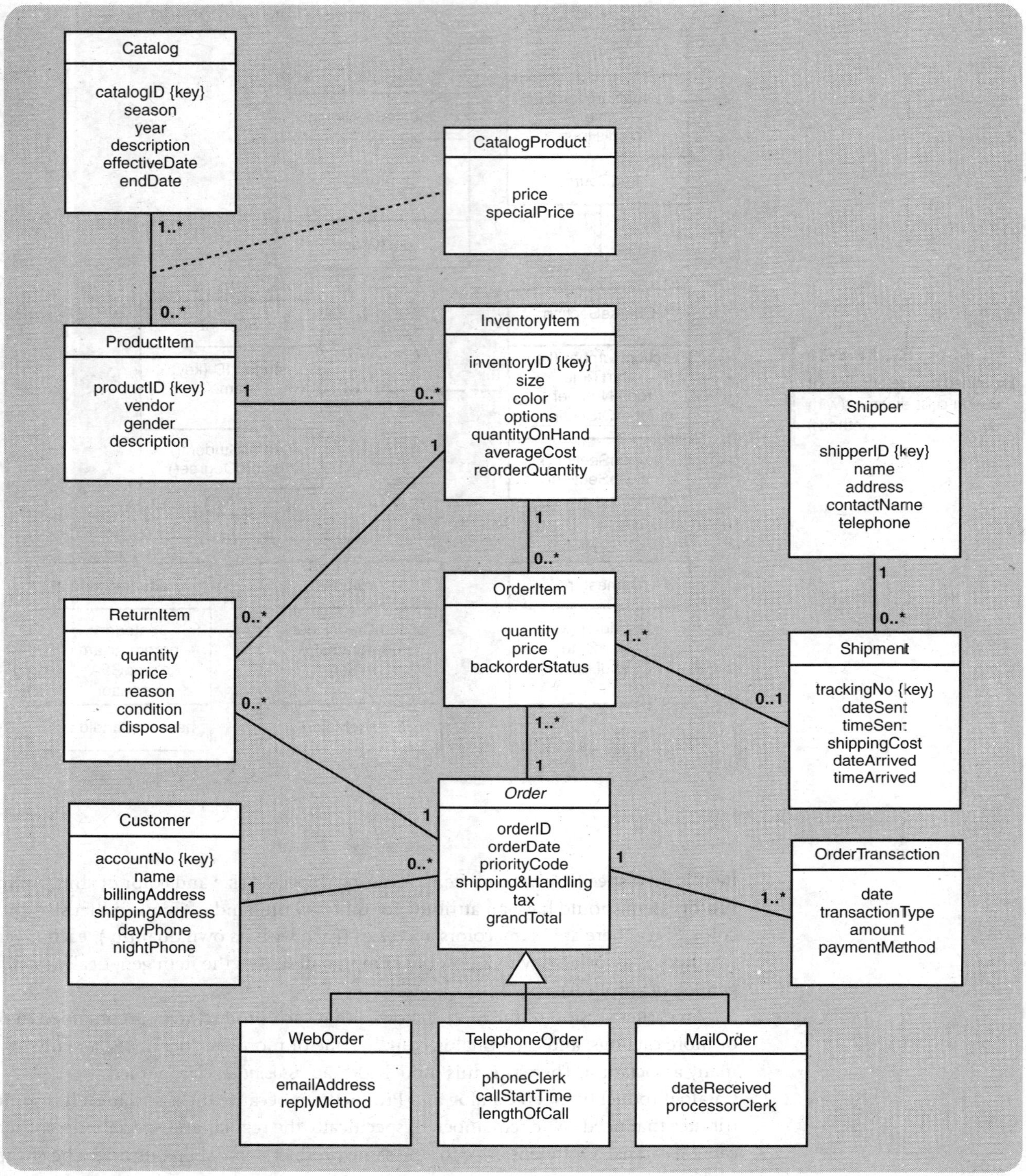

FIGURE 5-31
Rocky Mountain Outfitters domain model class diagram

type of order has some additional attributes. Order is an abstract class (the name is in italics), since any order must be one of the three special types.

No whole-part associations (aggregation or composition) are shown, although it might be argued that an OrderTransaction is part of an Order or that a ProductItem is part of a Catalog. It does not make much difference in this example because whole-part and association relationships are similar when they are implemented. Many analysts choose not to indicate aggregation or composition on class diagrams for business systems.

The class diagram shown in Figure 5-31 contains a lot of very specific information about the requirements for the system. Be sure that you can trace through all of the associations shown, and try to describe a specific object of each class involved in one specific order. Draw a sketch similar to that shown in Figure 5-22 to show some actual objects this class diagram describes.

Once it is developed, a model like this class diagram needs to be walked through carefully, as you would walk through the logic of a program. Being able to walk through and "debug" any model is a very important skill in system development, as discussed in Chapter 4.

To test your understanding of the diagram, consider whether one order might have items shipped by different shippers. Is it possible, given the requirements shown in this diagram? The answer is yes. Operationally, some order items might be back ordered, so when they are finally shipped, they are part of a different shipment. A different shipper could handle this shipment.

Other requirements shown in the model include one or more order transactions for each order. An order transaction is a record of a payment or a refund for the order. One order transaction is created when the customer initially pays for the order. Later, though, the customer might add another item to the order, generating an additional charge. This involves a second order transaction. Finally, the customer might return an item, requiring a refund and a third order transaction.

LOCATIONS AND THE CRUD MATRIX

Issues such as processing locations and networks are often ignored during early iterations of the project if they do not involve much risk. However, a great deal of information about use cases, domain classes, locations, and user distribution is eventually needed during later iterations. Examples include:

- Number of locations of users
- Processing and data access requirements of users at specific locations
- Volume and timing of processing and data access requests

This information is needed to make initial design decisions such as the distribution of computer systems, application software, and database components. It is also needed to determine required network capacity among user and processing locations. Analysts find it useful to create several tables, or matrices, that describe the relationships among use cases and locations, and use cases and problem domain classes. Examples include tables that describe which use case initially captures information about a domain class and which use cases later use that domain class.

Many analysts gather and summarize location information early in the project. The first step in gathering location information is to identify and describe the locations where work is being or will be performed. Possible locations include business offices, warehouses, and manufacturing facilities, and less obvious locations such as customer or supplier offices, employee homes, hotel rooms, and automobiles. All of these

location diagram
a diagram or map that identifies all of the processing locations of a system

locations should be listed, and a *location diagram* should be drawn to summarize the locations graphically. A location diagram for Rocky Mountain Outfitters is shown in Figure 5-32. The location diagram shows the analyst what network connections might be required, but it also has the added benefit of reminding everyone that users at all locations should be consulted about the system.

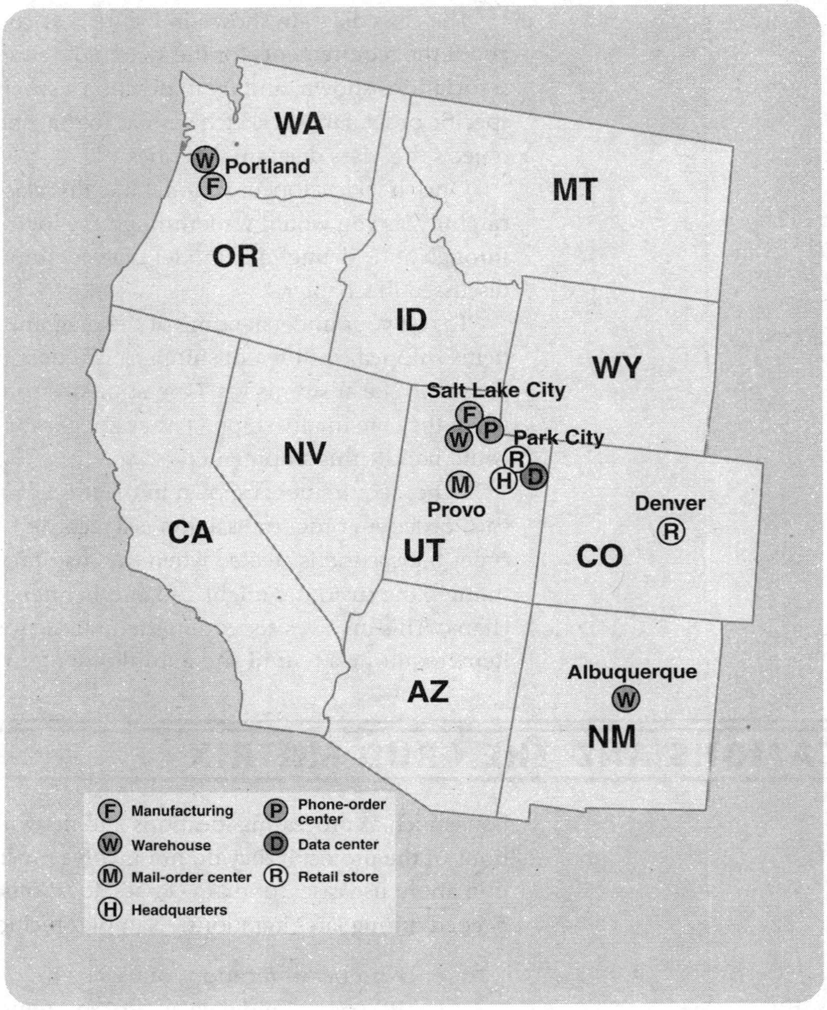

FIGURE 5-32
The Rocky Mountain Outfitters location diagram

use case–location matrix
a table that describes the relationship among use cases and the locations in which they are performed

The next step is to list the use cases that are performed by users at each location. Using the event table, the analyst can list where each use case is performed. Figure 5-33 shows a *use case–location matrix* that summarizes this information. Each row is a system use case, and each column represents a location. Many use cases are performed at multiple locations.

Recall that Rocky Mountain Outfitters also has a system project under way for the supply chain management (SCM) system. The SCM system will involve many use cases at the manufacturing facilities, but the customer support system will not. Additionally, RMO has a plan for integrating the system at the retail stores with the SCM system, but not with the customer support system. Therefore, these locations are not shown on the use case–location matrix.

USE CASE	LOCATION				
	Corporate Offices (Park City)	**Distribution warehouses** (Salt Lake City, Albuquerque. Portland)	**Mail-order** (Provo)	**Phone sales** (Salt Lake City)	**Customer direct interaction** (Anticipated)
Look up item availability	X	X	X	X	X
Create new order			X	X	X
Update order				X	X
Look up order status	X	X		X	X
Record order fulfillment		X			
Record back order		X			
Create order return		X			
Provide catalog info			X	X	X
Update customer account	X		X	X	X
Distribute promotional package	X				
Create customer charge adjustment	X				
Update catalog	X				
Create special promotion	X				
Create new catalog	X				

FIGURE 5-33
Use case–location matrix for the Rocky Mountain Outfitters customer support system

use case–domain class matrix
a table that shows which use case requires access to each domain class

CRUD
acronym of create, read, update, and delete

Other matrices can be created to highlight access requirements. One approach is to list use cases and domain classes in a *use case–domain class matrix*. This matrix shows which use case requires access to each domain class. This information will be needed when designing the object interactions for each use case. Creating a matrix to summarize this information can be useful.

Figure 5-34 shows a use case–domain class matrix for Rocky Mountain Outfitters. The cells of the matrix show additional information to clarify what the use case does to the domain class. The letter *C* means the use case creates new data, *R* means the use case reads data, *U* means the use case updates data, and *D* means the use case might delete data. The acronym *CRUD* (create, read, update, and delete) is often used to describe this type of matrix.

The RMO CRUD matrix shown in Figure 5-34 also serves an additional purpose when initially identifying use case and domain classes. An additional use case identification technique is to cross-check each domain class to verify that there are use cases that are responsible for creating, updating, and deleting each domain class. If the analyst does not find a use case that updates the domain class, then perhaps he or she has overlooked a necessary use case. Similarly, if no use case reads data about the domain class, perhaps a use case has been overlooked.

USE CASES	DOMAIN CLASSES										
	Catalog	Customer	Inventory Item	Order	Order Item	Order Transaction	Package	Product Item	Return Item	Shipment	Shipper
Look up item availability			R								
Create new order		CRU	RU	C	C	C	R	R		C	R
Update order		RU	RU	RUD	RUD	RUD	R	R		CRUD	R
Look up order status		R		R	R	R				R	R
Record order fulfillment					RU					RU	
Record back order					RU					CRU	
Create order return		CRU		RU		C			C		
Provide catalog info	R		R				R	R			
Update account customer		CRUD									
Distribute promotional package	R	R	R				R	R			
Create customer charge adjustment		RU				CRUD					
Update catalog	RU		R				RU	R			
Create special promotion	R		R				R	R			
Create new catalog	C		R				CRU	R			

C = Creates new data, R = Reads existing data, U = Updates existing data, D = Deletes existing data

FIGURE 5-34
Use case–problem domain class matrix for the Rocky Mountain Outfitters customer support system

USE CASES, THE DOMAIN MODEL, AND ITERATION PLANNING

Now that use cases are identified and the initial domain model class diagram is complete, RMO analysts will address some of the use cases and some of the classes in each project iteration. As discussed in Chapter 2, the issues that present the greatest risk are usually addressed in the early iterations. For example, the use cases that involve the core architecture might be selected and implemented to establish that the core architecture will work as planned. At other times, the processing requirements of some use case might be more complex, adding uncertainty to the project. These complex use cases might be studied and solved first.

Most of the use cases are identified and some of the initial domain model is completed during the inception phase of the UP life cycle. In the first iteration of the elaboration phase, the first set of use cases is described in more detail. In the next chapter, you will learn how to describe use cases in detail to create a use case model. In the first elaboration phase iteration, the project team would describe a subset of use cases in detail and then design, implement, and test the software for those use cases. In each subsequent iteration, additional use cases would be described in detail, designed, implemented, tested, and integrated with previously completed software. By the time the project reaches the construction phase, all use cases have been described in detail and key features have been implemented. Attention turns to finishing and fine-tuning each use case realization by, for example, adding system controls.

Summary

This chapter is the first of two chapters that present techniques for modeling a system's functional requirements, highlighting the tasks that are completed during the requirements discipline activity named *Define functional requirements*. Models of various aspects of the system are created to document the requirements. Use cases and problem domain classes in the user's work environment are key concepts common to defining requirements in all approaches to system development.

A key early step in the modeling process is to identify the use cases required in the system. To identify use cases at the right level of analysis, it is useful to identify elementary business processes (EBPs) by listing the events that require a response from the system. An event is something that can be described that occurs at a specific time and place and that is worth remembering. External events occur outside the system, usually triggered by someone who interacts with the system. Temporal events occur at a defined point in time, such as the end of a work day or the end of every month. State events occur according to an internal system change. Information about each event is recorded in an event table, which lists the event, the trigger for the event, the source of the trigger, the use case that the system must carry out, the response produced as system output, and the destination for the response.

The other key concept involves the things users deal with when doing their work—such as products, orders, invoices, and customers—that the system needs to remember. There are many naturally occurring associations among things in the users' work environment: A customer places an order, and an order requires an invoice. Multiplicity of an association refers to the number of associations involved: A customer might place many orders, and each order is placed by one customer. Attributes are specific pieces of information about a thing, such as a name and an address for a customer. When defining requirements, analysts using the object-oriented approach model these things as objects belonging to a problem domain class. These classes are based on real-world concepts in the users' work environment. They are not software classes. When the object-oriented approach describes the software classes during design, the classes have attributes as well as behaviors (called *methods*).

The object-oriented approach uses the UML class diagram to show the classes, attributes, and methods of the class, and associations among classes. The domain model class diagram is used to show domain classes in the users' work environment. The design class diagram is used to model software classes. Two additional concepts are used in class diagram notation: generalization/specialization hierarchies, which allow inheritance from a superclass to a subclass, and whole-part hierarchies, which allow a collection of objects to be associated as a whole and its parts.

A few additional models that are not UML diagrams are used to define requirements. The first is a location diagram, which can resemble a map. Matrices are also useful to show which location requires each use case and which use case uses which problem domain classes. The CRUD matrix is useful for cross-checking that all of the required use cases have been identified. The next chapter discusses use cases in more detail.

KEY TERMS

abstract class, p. 193
aggregation, p. 191
association class, p. 187
binary association, p. 182
composition, p. 191
compound attribute, p. 183
concrete class, p. 193
CRUD, p. 199
destination, p. 175
domain model class diagram, p. 184
elementary business processes (EBPs), p. 167
event, p. 167
event decomposition, p. 167
event table, p. 174
external event, p. 169
identifier (key), p. 183
location diagram, p. 198
n-ary association, p. 183
perfect technology assumption, p. 173
response, p. 175
source, p. 175
state event, p. 170
system controls, p. 173
temporal event, p. 169
ternary association, p. 182
trigger, p. 175
unary (recursive) association, p. 182
use case–domain class matrix, p. 199
use case–location matrix, p. 198
whole-part hierarchies, p. 191

REVIEW QUESTIONS

1. What are the two key concepts used to begin defining system requirements?
2. What are three general approaches to identifying use cases?
3. What is an elementary business process (EBP)?
4. What is an event, and how does it help identify a use case?
5. What are the three types of events?
6. Which type of event results in data entering the system?
7. Which type of event occurs at a defined point in time?
8. Which type of event does not result in data entering the system but always results in an output?
9. What type of event would be named *Employee quits job*?
10. What type of event would be named *Time to produce paychecks*?
11. What are some examples of system controls?
12. What does the perfect technology assumption state?
13. What are the columns in an event table?
14. What is a trigger? A source? A use case? A response? A destination?
15. What is a "thing" in the problem domain of the user called?
16. What is an association?
17. What is multiplicity of an association?
18. What are unary, binary, and *n*-ary associations?
19. What are attributes and compound attributes?
20. What is an association class?
21. What are the symbols shown in a class diagram?
22. What is encapsulated along with the values of attributes in an object?
23. How is a generalization/specialization hierarchy noted on a class diagram?
24. From what type of class do subclasses inherit?
25. What are two types of whole-part hierarchies?
26. What three pieces of information about a class are put in the three parts of the class symbol?
27. What is the difference between an abstract and a concrete class?
28. How is an association class shown on a class diagram?
29. What type of classes are shown in a domain model class diagram?
30. How does a design class diagram differ from a domain model class diagram?
31. Why is it important to know about locations and which use a use case?
32. What is shown on a CRUD matrix?

THINKING CRITICALLY

1. Review the external event checklist in Figure 5-3, and think about a university course registration system. What is an example of an event of each type in the checklist? Name each event using the guidelines for naming an external event.
2. Review the temporal event checklist in Figure 5-4. Would a student grade report be an internal or external output? Would a class list for the instructor be an internal or external output? What are some other internal and external outputs for a course registration system? Using the guidelines for naming temporal events, what would you name the events that trigger these outputs?
3. In a course registration system, for the event *Student registers for classes*, create an event table entry listing the event, trigger, source, use case, response(s), and destination(s). For the event *Time to produce grade reports*, create another event table entry.
4. Consider the following sequence of actions taken by a customer at a bank. Which action is the event the analyst should define for a bank account transaction processing system? (1) Kevin gets a check from Grandma for his birthday. (2) Kevin wants a car. (3) Kevin decides to save his money. (4) Kevin goes to the bank. (5) Kevin waits in line. (6) Kevin makes a deposit in his savings account. (7) Kevin grabs the deposit receipt. (8) Kevin asks for a brochure on auto loans.
5. Consider the perfect technology assumption, which states that events should be included during analysis only if the system would be required to respond under perfect

conditions. Could any of the events in the event table for Rocky Mountain Outfitters be eliminated based on this assumption? Explain. Why are events such as *User logs on to system* and *Time to back up the data* required only under imperfect conditions?

6. Draw a class diagram, including minimum and maximum multiplicity for the following: The system stores information about two things: cars and owners. A car has attributes for make, model, and year. The owner has attributes for name and address. Assume that a car must be owned by one owner, and an owner can own many cars but that an owner might not own any cars (perhaps she just sold them all, but you still want a record of her in the system).
7. Extend the class diagram from the last problem to include subclasses for sports car, sedan, and minivan with appropriate attributes.
8. Consider the class diagram shown in Figure 5-24, the refined class diagram showing course enrollment with an association class. Does this model allow a student to enroll in more than one course section at a time? Does the model allow a course section to contain more than one student? Does the model allow a student to enroll in several sections of the same course and get a grade for each enrollment? Does the model store information about all grades earned by all students in all sections?
9. Again consider the class diagram shown in Figure 5-24. Add the following to the diagram and list any assumptions you had to make. A faculty member usually teaches many course sections, but in some semesters a faculty member may not teach any. Each course section must have at least one faculty member teaching it, but sometimes teams teach course sections. Furthermore, to make sure that all course sections are similar, one faculty member is assigned as course coordinator to oversee the course, and each faculty member can be coordinator of many courses.
10. If the class diagram you drew in exercise 9 showed a many-to-many association between faculty member and course section, a further look at the association might reveal the need to store some additional information. What might this information include? (Hint: Does the instructor have specific office hours for each course section? Do you give an instructor some sort of evaluation for each course section?) Expand the class diagram to allow the system to store this additional information.
11. Consider a system that needs to store information about computers in a computer lab at a university—information such as the features and location of each computer. What are the things that might be included in a model? What are some of the associations among these things? What are some of the attributes of these things? Draw a domain class diagram for this system.
12. Refer to the class diagram for bank accounts in Figure 5-28. Expand the model to show that there are special types of customers—personal and commercial. All customers have a name and mailing address. Commercial customers have additional attributes for credit rating, contact person, and contact person phone. Personal customers have attributes for home phone and work phone. Additionally, expand the model to show that the bank has multiple branches, and each account is serviced by one branch. Naturally, each branch has many accounts.
13. Consider the class diagram for Rocky Mountain Outfitters shown in Figure 5-31. If a Web order is created, how many attributes does it have? If a telephone order is created, how many attributes does it have? If an existing customer places a phone order for one item, how many new objects are created for this transaction?
14. A product item for RMO is not the same as an inventory item. A product item is something such as a men's leather hunting jacket supplied by Leather 'R' Us. An inventory item is a specific size and color of the jacket—such as a size medium brown leather hunting jacket. If RMO adds a new jacket to its catalog, and six sizes and three colors are available in inventory, how many objects need to be added as a result?

15. Consider the following class diagram showing college, department, and faculty members.
  a. What kind of associations are shown in the model?
  b. How many attributes does a "faculty member" have? Which (if any) have been inherited from another class?
  c. If you add information about one college, one department, and four faculty members, how many objects do you add to the system?
  d. Can a faculty member work in more than one department at the same time? Explain.
  e. Can a faculty member work in two departments at the same time, if one department is in the College of Business and the other department is in the College of Arts and Sciences? Explain.

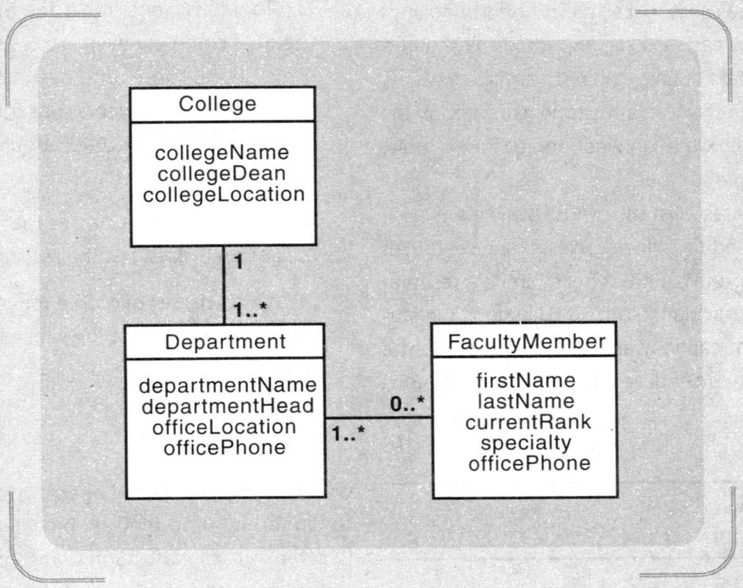

EXPERIENTIAL EXERCISES

1. Set up a meeting with a librarian. During your meeting, ask the librarian to describe the situations that come up in the library to which the book checkout system needs to respond. List these external events. Now ask about points in time, or deadlines, that require the system to produce a statement, notice, report, or other output. List these temporal events. Does it seem natural for the librarian to describe the system in this way? Name each use case the system carries out in response to each event. Similarly, ask the librarian to describe the things about which the system needs to store information. See whether you can get the librarian to list the important attributes and describe associations among things. Does it seem natural for the librarian to describe these things? Create a domain model class diagram based on what you learn.
2. Visit a restaurant or the college food service and talk to a server (or talk with a friend who is a food server). Ask about the external events, temporal events, and domain classes, as you did in exercise 1. What are the events for order processing at a restaurant? Complete an event table and a domain model class diagram.
3. Review the procedures for course registration at your university and talk with the staff in advising, in registration, and in your major department. Think about the sequence that goes on over an entire semester. What are the events that students trigger? What are the events that your major department triggers? What are the temporal events that result in information going to students? What are the temporal events that result in information going to instructors or departments?
4. Again review information about your own university. Create generalization/specialization hierarchies using the class diagram notation for (1) types of faculty, (2) types of students, (3) types of courses, (4) types of financial aid, and (5) types of housing. Include attributes for the superclass and the subclasses in each case.

Case Studies

SPRING BREAKS 'R' US TRAVEL SERVICE BOOKING SYSTEM

Spring Breaks 'R' Us Travel Service (SBRU) books spring-break trips at resorts for college students. During the fall, resorts submit availability information to SBRU indicating rooms, room capacity, and room rates for each week of the spring-break season. Each resort offers bookings for a different number of weeks each season, and rooms have different rates depending on the week. Usually, the resorts make a variety of rooms with different capacities available so students can book the right size room. Couples can book a two-person room, for example, and four people can book a room for four.

In December, SBRU generates a list of resorts, available weeks, and room rates that is distributed to college campus representatives all over the country. When a group of students submits a reservation request for a week at a particular resort, SBRU assigns the students to a room with sufficient capacity and sends each student a confirmation notice. When the cutoff date for a week arrives, SBRU sends each resort a list of students booked in each room for the following week. When the students arrive at the resort, they pay the resort directly for the room. Resorts send commission checks directly to the SBRU accounting system, which is separate from the booking system. When spring break is over, students return to their schools and hit the books.

[1] To what events must the SBRU booking system respond? Create a complete event table listing the event, trigger, source, use case, response, and destination for each event. Be sure to consider only the events that trigger processing in the booking system, not the SBRU accounting system or the systems operated by the resorts.

[2] List the domain classes that are mentioned. List the attributes of each class. List the associations among classes.

[3] Which classes might be refined into a generalization/specialization hierarchy? List the superclass and any subclasses for each of them.

THE REAL ESTATE MULTIPLE LISTING SERVICE SYSTEM

The Real Estate Multiple Listing Service system supplies information that local real estate agents use to help them sell houses to their customers. During the month, agents list houses for sale (listings) by contracting with homeowners. The agent works for a real estate office, which sends information on the listing to the multiple listing service. Therefore, any agent in the community can get information on the listing.

Information on a listing includes the address, year built, square feet, number of bedrooms, number of bathrooms, owner name, owner phone number, asking price, and status code. At any time during the month, an agent might directly contact the multiple listing service to request information on listings that match customer requirements. Information on the house, on the agent who listed the house, and on the real estate office the agent works for is provided. For example, an agent might want to call the listing agent to ask additional questions or call the homeowner directly to make an appointment to show the house. Twice each month (on the 15th and 30th), the multiple listing service produces a listing book that contains information on all listings. These books are sent to all of the real estate agents even though the information is available online. Many real estate agents want the books (which are easier to flip through), so they are provided even though the information is often out of date. Sometimes agents and owners decide to change information about a listing, by reducing the price, correcting previous information on the house, or indicating that the house is sold, for example. The real estate office sends in these change requests to the multiple listing service when the agent asks the office to do so.

[1] To what events must the multiple listing service system respond? Create a complete event table listing the event, trigger, source, use case, response, and destination for each event.

[2] Draw a domain class diagram to represent the requirements for the multiple listing service system, including the attributes mentioned. Does your model include classes for offer, buyer, and closing? If so, reconsider. Include information that the multiple listing service needs to store, which might be different from information the real estate office needs to store.

[3] Draw an expanded class diagram that shows that different types of listings have different attributes. The description in the case assumes all listings are for single-family houses. What about multifamily listings or commercial property listings?

THE STATE PATROL TICKET PROCESSING SYSTEM

The purpose of the State Patrol ticket processing system is to record driver violations, to keep records of the fines paid by drivers when they plead guilty or are found guilty of moving violations by the courts, and to notify the court that a warrant for arrest should be issued when such fines are not paid in a timely manner. A separate State Patrol system records accidents and verification of financial responsibility (insurance). Yet a third system produces driving record reports from the ticket and accident records for insurance companies. Finally, a fourth system issues, renews, or suspends drivers' licenses. These four systems are obviously integrated in that they share access to the same database, but otherwise, they are operated separately by different departments of the State Patrol. State Patrol operations (what the officers do) are entirely separate.

The portion of the database used with the ticket-processing system involves driver data, ticket data, officer data, and court data. Driver data, officer data, and court data are used by the system. The system creates and maintains ticket data. Driver attributes include license number, name, address, date of birth, date licensed, and so on. Ticket attributes include ticket number (each is unique and preprinted on each sheet of the officer's ticket book), location, ticket type, ticket date, ticket time, plea, trial date, verdict, fine amount, and date paid. Court and officer data include the name and address of each, respectively. Each driver may have zero or more tickets, and each ticket applies to only one driver. Officers write quite a few tickets.

When an officer gives a ticket to a driver, a copy of the ticket is turned in and entered into the system. A new ticket record is created, and relationships to the correct driver, officer, and court are established in the database. If the driver pleads guilty, he or she mails in the fine in a preprinted envelope with the ticket number on it. In some cases, the driver claims innocence and wants a court date. When the envelope is returned without a check and the trial request box has an "X" in it, the system notes the plea on the ticket record, looks up driver, ticket, and officer information, and sends a ticket details report to the appropriate court. A trial date questionnaire form is also produced at the same time and is mailed to the driver. The instructions on the questionnaire tell the driver to fill in convenient dates and mail the questionnaire directly to the court. Upon receiving this information, the court schedules a trial date and notifies the driver of the date and time.

When the trial is completed, the court sends the verdict to the ticketing system. The verdict and trial date are recorded for the ticket. If the verdict is innocent, the system that produces driving record reports for insurance companies will ignore the ticket. If the verdict is guilty, the court gives the driver another envelope with the ticket number on it for mailing in the fine.

If the driver fails to pay the fine within the required period, the ticket-processing system produces a warrant request notice and sends it to the court. This happens if the driver does not return the original envelope within two weeks or does not return the court-supplied envelope within two weeks of the trial date. What happens then is in the hands of the court. Sometimes the court requests that the driver's license be suspended, and the system that processes drivers' licenses handles the suspension.

[1] To what events must the ticket-processing system respond? Create a complete event table listing the event, trigger, source, use case, response, and destination for each event.

[2] Draw a class diagram to represent the domain model for the ticket-processing system, including the attributes mentioned. Explain why it is important to understand how the system is integrated with other State Patrol systems.

[3] Draw a class diagram to extend the domain model that assumes there are different types of drivers. Classifications of types of drivers vary by state. Some states have restricted licenses for minors, for example, and special licenses for commercial vehicle operators. Research your state's requirements, and create a generalization/specialization hierarchy for the class Driver, showing the different attributes each special type of driver might have. Consider the same issues for types of tickets. Include some special types of tickets in a generalization/specialization hierarchy in the class diagram.

RETHINKING ROCKY MOUNTAIN OUTFITTERS

ROCKY MOUNTAIN OUTFITTERS

When listing nouns and making some decisions about the initial list of things (see Figure 5-13), the RMO team decided to research Customer Account as a possible domain class if the system included an RMO payment plan (similar to a company charge account plan). Many retail store chains have their own charge accounts for the convenience of the customer—to increase sales to the customer and to better track customer purchase behavior.

Consider the implications to the system if management decided to incorporate an RMO charge account and payment plan as part of the customer support system.

[1] Discuss the implications that such a change would have on the scope of the project. How might this new capability change the list of stakeholders the team would involve when collecting information and defining the requirements? Would the change have any effect on other RMO systems or system projects planned or under way? Would the change have any effect on the project plan originally developed by Barbara Halifax? In other words, is this a minor change or a major change?

[2] What events need to be added to the event table? Complete the event table entries for these additional events. What use cases for existing events might be changed because of a charge account and payment plan? Explain.

[3] What are some additional things and associations among things that the system would be required to store because of the charge account and payment plan? Modify the class diagram to reflect these charges.

FOCUSING ON RELIABLE PHARMACEUTICAL SERVICE

Reliable PHARMACEUTICALS In Chapter 1 you learned about the background and prescription-processing operations for Reliable Pharmaceutical Service. As discussed in this chapter, defining the requirements for the new system starts by taking the information gathered about the needed system and then focusing on the events that require system processing and on the things about which the system needs to store information. The full system would involve many events and domain classes. In this chapter's case exercise, we focus on only a subset of events for the system and a subset of domain classes. Later chapters' exercises will add to the scope and complexity of the requirements for Reliable.

[1] Create an event table that lists information about system requirements based on the following specific system processing: When a nursing home needs to fill prescriptions for its patients, it provides order details to Reliable. Reliable immediately records information about the order and prescriptions. Prescription orders come in from all of Reliable's nursing-home clients throughout the day. At the start of each 12-hour shift, Reliable prepares a case manifest, detailing all recent orders, which is given to one of the pharmacists. When the pharmacist has assembled the orders for each client, the pharmacist records the order fulfillment. (Review the Reliable case description at the end of Chapter 1 for more details.) In addition, the system needs to add or update patient information, add or update drug inventory information, produce purchase orders to replenish the drug inventory, record inventory adjustments, and generate various management reports. For now, ignore any billing, payments, or insurance processing.

[2] Create a domain class diagram that shows the requirements for the following portion of the system. Add a few attributes to each class and show minimum and maximum multiplicity. Be sure to identify any association classes and use the correct notation. To process the prescription order, Reliable needs to know about the patients, the nursing home, and the nursing-home unit where each patient resides. Each nursing home has at least one, but possibly many, units. A patient is assigned to a specific unit. An order consists of one or more prescriptions, each for one specific drug and for one specific patient. An order, therefore, consists of prescriptions for more than one patient. Careful tracking and record keeping is obviously crucial. Additionally, each patient has many prescriptions. One pharmacist fills each order.

[3] How important is it to understand that each order includes prescriptions for more than one patient? Is this the type of information that is difficult to sort out at first? Did you see the implications initially, or did you have to work through the model until it made sense to you? Discuss.

FURTHER RESOURCES

Grady Booch, Ivar Jacobson, and James Rumbaugh, *The Unified Modeling Language User Guide*. Addison-Wesley, 1999.

Peter Coad, David North, and Mark Mayfield, *Object Models, Strategies, Patterns, and Applications* (2nd ed.). Prentice Hall, 1997.

Craig Larman, *Applying UML and Patterns: An Introduction to Object-Oriented Analysis and Designs* (2nd ed.). Prentice Hall, 2002.

Stephen McMenamin and John Palmer, *Essential Systems Analysis*. Prentice Hall, 1984.

John Satzinger and Tore Orvik, *The Object-Oriented Approach: Concepts, System Development, and Modeling with UML* (2nd ed.). Course Technology, 2001.

chapter 6

USE CASE MODELING AND DETAILED REQUIREMENTS

LEARNING OBJECTIVES

After reading this chapter, you should be able to:

- Develop use case diagrams
- Write use case and scenario descriptions
- Develop activity diagrams and system sequence diagrams
- Develop statechart diagrams to model object behavior
- Explain how UML diagrams work together to define functional requirements for the object-oriented approach

CHAPTER OUTLINE

- Detailed Object-Oriented Requirements Definitions
- System Processes—A Use Case/Scenario View
- Identifying Inputs and Outputs—The System Sequence Diagram
- Identifying Object Behavior—The Statechart Diagram
- Integrating Object-Oriented Models

ELECTRONICS UNLIMITED, INC.: INTEGRATING THE SUPPLY CHAIN

Electronics Unlimited is a warehousing distributor that buys electronic equipment from various suppliers and sells it to retailers throughout the United States and Canada. It has operations and warehouses in Los Angeles, Houston, Baltimore, Atlanta, New York, Denver, and Minneapolis. Its customers range from large nationwide retailers, such as Target, to medium-sized independent electronics stores.

Many of the larger retailers are moving toward integrated supply chains. Information systems used to be focused on processing internal data; however, today these retail chains want suppliers to become part of a totally integrated supply chain system. In other words, the systems need to communicate between companies to make the supply chain more efficient.

To maintain its position as a leading wholesale distributor, Electronics Unlimited has to convert its system to link with both its suppliers—the manufacturers of the electronic equipment—and its customers—the retailers. Since this system is to be adapted to the Web, it must be developed with object-oriented components. Object-oriented techniques facilitate system-to-system interfaces by using predefined components and objects to communicate across systems. Fortunately, many of the system development staff have recently begun learning about object-oriented development and are eager to apply the techniques and models to a system development project.

William Jones is explaining object-oriented development to the group of systems analysts who are being trained in this approach. "We're developing most of our new systems using object-oriented principles. The complexity of the new system, along with the need to communicate over the Internet, makes the object-oriented approach a natural way to develop requirements. It takes a little different thought process than you may be used to, but the object-oriented models track very closely with the new object-oriented programming languages."

William continued, "This way of thinking about a system in terms of objects is very interesting. It also is consistent with the object-oriented programming techniques you learned in your programming classes. You probably first learned to think about objects when you developed screens for the user interface. All of the controls on the screen, such as buttons, text boxes, and drop-down boxes, are objects. Each has its own set of trigger events that activate its program functions.

"Now you just extend that same thought process so that you think of things like purchase orders and employees as objects, too. We call them *problem domain objects* or sometimes *business objects* to differentiate them from screen objects such as windows and buttons. One of the first steps of business modeling is to identify all of these problem domain objects. These objects are critical both for the design of the database and for program structure. In this case, since our system must support internal users as well as communicate with external systems, the correct definition of the problem domain objects is one of the most important steps. Each one of these business objects becomes a problem domain programming class for the new system.

"Another major goal of developing the requirements is to define all of the processes for the new system. We do this by defining 'use cases.' Use cases become critically important to understanding what the system must do. They are also important because they drive much of the detailed definition and model building, both for the requirements and for the design."

"How do we define the use cases?" one of the analysts asked.

"You continue with your fact-finding activities and build a scenario for each business process. These scenarios are documented in the use case definitions and coordinated with the definition of the problem domain classes. The details of these two kinds of descriptions provide a thorough understanding of how the system will support the business functions. And, since we will be using the Unified Process, which is an iterative approach to developing this system, our accurate definition of the use cases and business objects will drive the work we do in the other iterations.

"The new system is going to be quite complex. However, with the techniques included in the Unified Process and the object-oriented approach to development, we should be able to divide the work in a way that makes it manageable."

Overview

This chapter continues the discussion of the business modeling and requirements disciplines that was begun in Chapter 4. Chapter 5 expanded on the idea of requirements modeling by introducing the basics of use cases and domain models. In this chapter, we "peel the onion" and examine these concepts even further. You will learn how to refine use cases with more detail by describing the processes inside a use case—that is, determine what must happen for the system to carry out and complete a use case.

The basic objective of requirements definition is understanding—understanding users' needs, understanding how the business processes are carried out, and understanding how the system will be used to support those business processes. The first step in understanding the requirements is discovery. In Chapter 4, you learned several fact-finding and discovery techniques for modeling the business processes. In Chapter 5, you learned more about discovery—how to find use cases and domain classes In this chapter, we take you to the next level, extending discovery to real understanding so that you will understand the details of the business processes and the way the computer must support those processes.

In this chapter you learn how to understand and define the requirements for a new system, using object-oriented analysis models and techniques. You should be aware that the line between object-oriented analysis and object-oriented design is somewhat fuzzy because the models that are built to define requirements during analysis are refined and extended to produce a systems design. However, in this chapter, as in the previous chapters, we focus primarily on understanding. In later chapters, we show you how to move to design by using techniques to modify and extend these models into an architectural design for the new system.

DETAILED OBJECT-ORIENTED REQUIREMENTS DEFINITIONS

As we discussed in Chapter 5, one of the great benefits of using models to document requirements is that it helps you, as the system developer, to think clearly and carefully about the details of the processing and information needs of the stakeholders. You learned in the last chapter how the information in the business events and the domain classes is related. In fact, you learned how a CRUD analysis helps you ensure that the set of models you develop is consistent. As you read this chapter and work the exercises associated with it, you should pay careful attention to how the models require you to search out and understand users' needs. Because of the benefit derived from developing models, object-oriented system requirements use modeling extensively.

New developers frequently ask which to define first, the processes or the classes of objects. In reality, these two aspects are closely related and are usually defined together. Experienced developers often move back and forth between identifying classes and business processes, and they make several passes before completing a set of requirements. Do not be discouraged if you find yourself changing your diagrams and models as you work to define requirements.

The object-oriented approach requires several interrelated models to create a complete set of specifications. It may seem complex at first to have so many different types of diagrams, but as you use them, you will learn to appreciate how they all fit together like a puzzle, to produce a complete specification. Essentially, the object-oriented methodology takes a "divide and conquer" approach to understanding complex systems. Each model describes a different aspect of the system, so you only focus on one aspect at a time. But you must learn all the different models and the way they fit together. Later, at the end of the chapter, we discuss how all of the diagrams unite to form a complete view of a system's functional requirements. As a beginner with UML, you should concentrate now on learning each new model and understanding its role in specifying the total system.

As shown in Figure 6-1, to capture system requirements, analysts use a collection of models based on use cases with the object-oriented approach. Four models—use case diagrams, use case descriptions, activity diagrams, and system sequence diagrams—are used to describe the system use cases from various points of view. This approach to defining system requirements is often referred to as "use case driven." The basic approach is to take each use case, one by one, and extend the requirements in more detail. The other model identified in Figure 6-1 is a statechart diagram. A statechart diagram is not use case driven but object driven. We now explain the basic purpose of each of these models.

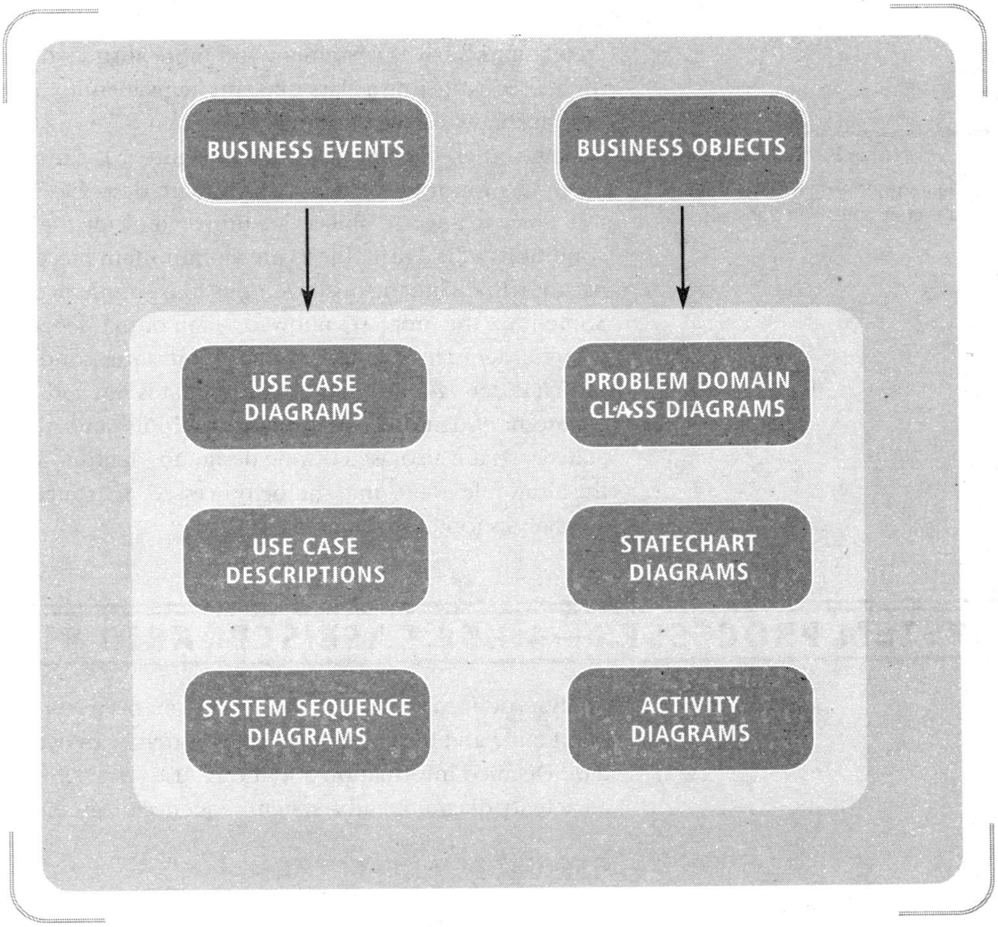

FIGURE 6-1
Requirements diagrams with UML models

use case diagram
a diagram showing the various user roles and the way those users interact with the system

The *use case diagram* serves as a kind of table of contents for the business events activities that must be supported by the system. It is used to identify the "uses," or use cases, of the new system—in other words, to identify how the system will be used and which actors will be involved in which use cases. As discussed in Chapter 5, the use case diagram can be derived directly from the event table, from the column titled "Use Case." A use case diagram is a convenient way to document the system events. Sometimes a single, comprehensive diagram is used to identify all use cases for an entire system. At other times, a set of narrower use case diagrams is used.

Each use case must also be described in detail. One way is to write out a narrative description of the steps that the user and the system do together to complete the use case. Each use case can also be defined using diagrams. As you learned in Chapter 4, activity diagrams can be used to describe any business processes done by people in an organization. However, they are also used to describe processes that include both manual and automated system activities.

system sequence diagram
a diagram showing the sequence of messages between an external actor and the system during a use case or scenario

System sequence diagrams (SSDs) are used to define the inputs and outputs and the sequential order of the inputs and outputs. SSDs are used in conjunction with detailed descriptions or with activity diagrams to show processing steps and interactions between the actors and the system. In a sequence diagram, these information flows in and out of a system are called *messages*.

You learned about classes of objects and the class diagram in Chapter 5. Class diagrams are used to identify the real-world "things" that determine the structure of the programming classes (and also the database structure). In the object-oriented view of systems, everything is considered an object. In Chapter 5, we explained that the objects identified belong to problem domain classes and that these classes consist of both concrete things, such as customers, and more abstract things, such as orders or airplane flights. Constructing a class diagram helps identify information about the real-world objects that will be part of the new system.

statechart diagram
a diagram showing the life of an object in states and transitions

One other diagram identified in Figure 6-1 is the statechart diagram. A *statechart diagram*, or more simply just a statechart, describes the collection of states of each object. Since real-world objects are mirrored inside the computer system, often the status conditions of the real objects are an important piece of information that an analyst can use to help define the business rules to be implemented in the computer system. Sometimes the processes allowed for an object depend on its status. For example, a customer order may have several important status conditions that control the processing of that order—for example, an order that is not complete should not be shipped. A statechart identifies these status conditions and specifies the processes allowed. Statecharts are also used during design to identify various states of the system itself and the allowable events that can be processed. So, statecharts can be considered either as an analysis tool or a design tool.

SYSTEM PROCESSES—A USE CASE/SCENARIO VIEW

Analysts define use cases at two levels—an overview level and a detailed level. The event table and the use case diagrams provide an overview of all the use cases for a system. Detailed information about each use case is described with a use case description, an activity diagram, and a system sequence diagram, or a combination of these models.

USE CASES AND ACTORS

In Chapter 5, you learned to develop an event table and identify use cases by analyzing the business and the business processes. Part of this analysis is to identify the source of the event. The source is the person or thing that initiates the business event. It is usually also the thing that initiates the trigger for the event. In use case analysis, we identify another entity, called the *actor*, which is similar to the source for an event, but has a slightly different definition. The actor is the person or thing that actually touches or interacts with the system.

An actor is always outside the automation boundary of the system but may be part of the manual portion of the system. In this respect, an actor is not always the same as the source of the event in the event table. A source of an event is the initiating person, such as a customer, and is always external to the system, including the manual system. In contrast, an actor in use case analysis is the person who is actually interacting with the computer system itself. For example, when a sales clerk takes an order from a customer over the phone, the sales clerk is the actor who is interacting with the system. By defining actors that way—as those who interact with the system—we can more precisely define the exact interactions to which the automated system must respond. This tighter focus helps define the specific requirements of the automated system itself—to refine them as we move from the event table to the use case details. One way to help identify actors at the right level of detail is to assume that actors must have hands.

BEST PRACTICE: Be sure that actors have direct contact with the automated system.

Thinking of actors as having hands encourages us to define actors as those who actually touch the automated system. But remember that some actors are not people. They can also be other systems or other devices that receive services from the system.

Another way to think of an actor is as a role. For example, in the RMO case, the use case *Create new order* might involve an order clerk talking to the customer on the phone. Or, the customer might be the actor if the customer places the order directly, through the Internet. One final way to think about an actor and a use case is that a use case is a goal that the actor wants to achieve. One way to state this goal is to say, "The order clerk uses the system to create a new order." Notice that in this sentence both the actor—the *order clerk*—and the use case—*Create new order*—are identified. In fact, stating the use cases in sentence form is a good technique for understanding the relationship between use cases and actors. Notice that the focus is on the automated system—on the activities that the *system* must perform to create an order.

THE USE CASE DIAGRAM

Figure 6-2 shows how a use case is documented in a use case diagram. A simple stick figure is used to represent an actor. The stick figure is given a name that characterizes the role the actor is playing. The use case itself is symbolized by an oval with the name of the use case inside. The connecting lines between actors and use cases indicate which actors utilize which use cases. Although hands are not part of the standard UML notation, the actor in this figure is drawn with hands to help you remember that this actor must have direct access to the automated system.

Actors can also be other systems that interface directly with the system being developed. In that case, you can illustrate the actor either with an appropriately named stick figure—that is, with a name such as *Purchasing subsystem*—or with a rectangle. However, the hands metaphor still applies, in that you only want to include actors that have a direct interface or contact with the main system. Again, we show hands on Figures 6-2 and 6-3 to reinforce this point. Remember that this is not part of the standard UML notation, so we drop it for later examples.

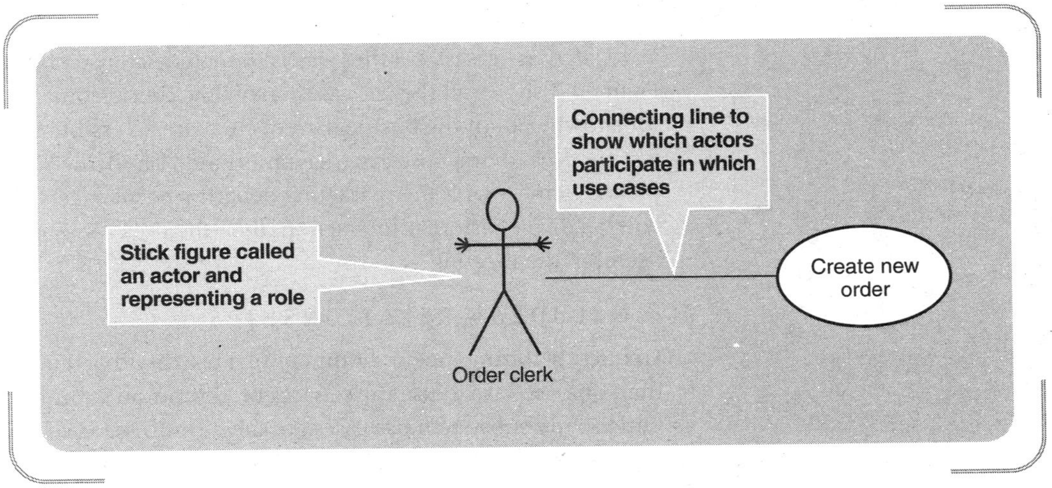

FIGURE 6-2
A simple use case with an actor

AUTOMATION BOUNDARY AND ORGANIZATION

Figure 6-3 expands the use case given in Figure 6-2 to include additional use cases and additional actors. In this instance, both the order clerk and the customer are allowed to access the system directly. As indicated by the relationship lines, each actor can use every use case. A boundary line is also drawn around the entire set of use cases.

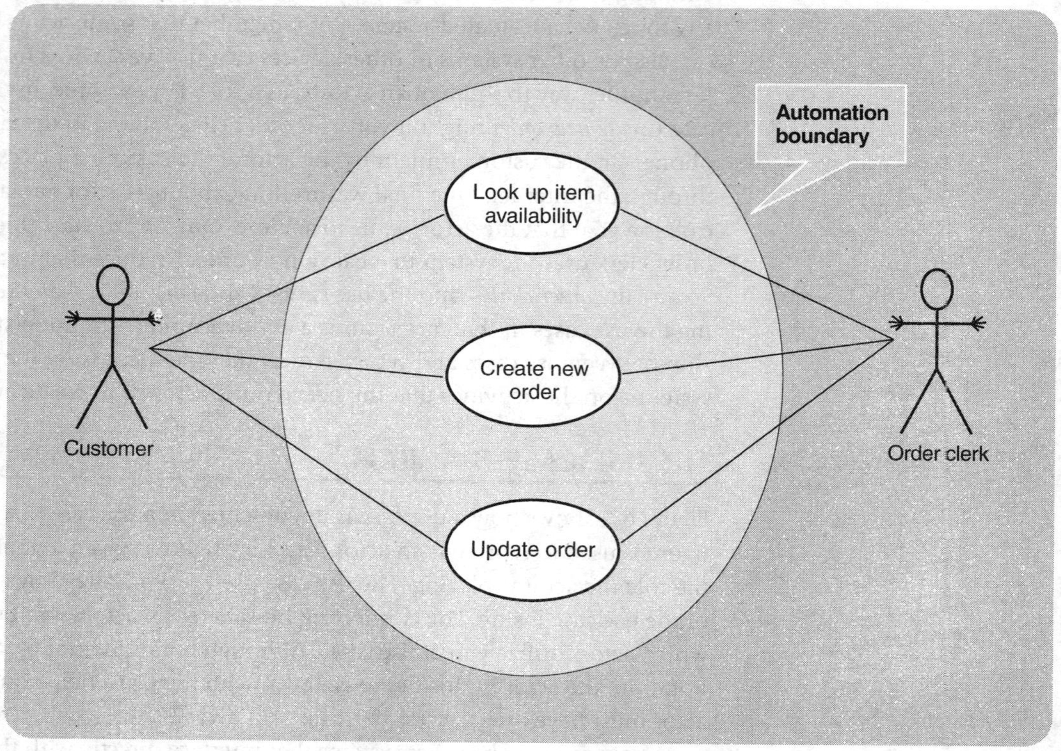

FIGURE 6-3
A use case diagram of the Order-entry subsystem for RMO, showing a system boundary

This boundary is the *automation boundary*. It denotes the boundary between the environment, where the actors reside, and the internal components of the computer system.

There are various ways to organize the use cases to depict different points of view. One is to organize the use cases by subsystem. Figure 6-3 is a partial use case diagram for one such subsystem, namely, the Order-entry subsystem. Figure 6-4 expands that figure to show all the subsystems for RMO's customer support system with some of the associated use cases. Another way is to include all use cases that involve a specific actor. Figure 6-5 shows all the use cases involving the Customer actor. This diagram is useful for showing all of the business events that are accessible through the Internet. An analyst chooses to draw use case diagrams based on the needs of the project team. If the plan is to meet with the marketing department managers to discuss all use cases involving direct customer interaction, then the use case diagram in Figure 6-5 will be very useful in the meeting.

«INCLUDES» RELATIONSHIPS

Frequently during the development of a use case diagram, it is reasonable for more than one use case to use the services of a common subroutine. For example, two of the Order-entry subsystem use cases are *Create new order* and *Update order*. Each of these use cases may need to validate the customer account. A common subroutine may be defined to carry out this function, and it becomes an additional use case. Figure 6-6 shows the additional use case, named *Validate customer account*, which is used by both the other use cases. The relationship between these use cases is denoted by the connecting line with the arrow. The direction of the arrow indicates which use case is included as a part of the major use case. The relationship is read *Create new order «includes» Validate customer account*. Sometimes this relationship is referred to as the «includes» relationship, or sometimes as the «uses» relationship.

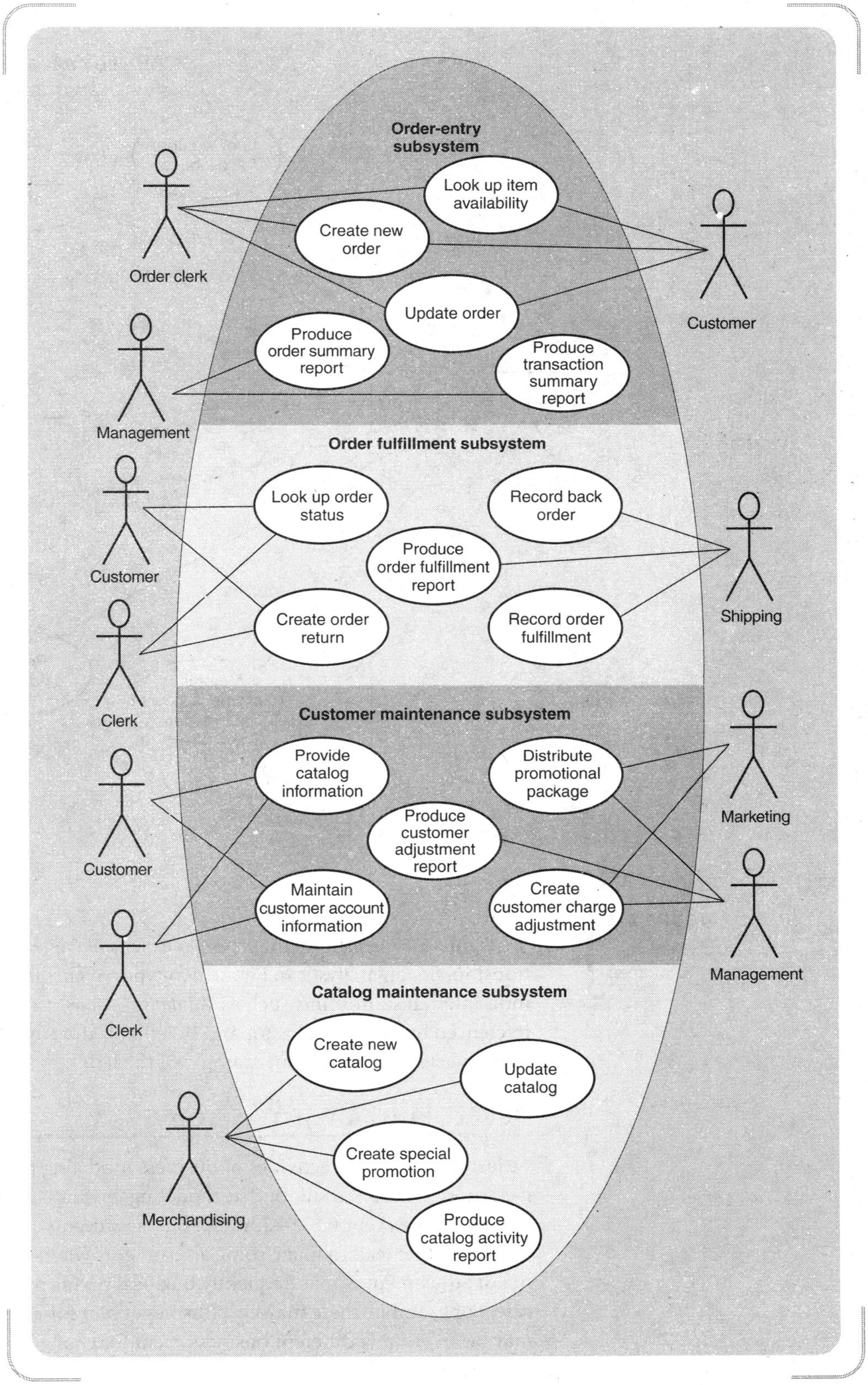

FIGURE 6-4
A use case diagram of the customer support system (by subsystem)

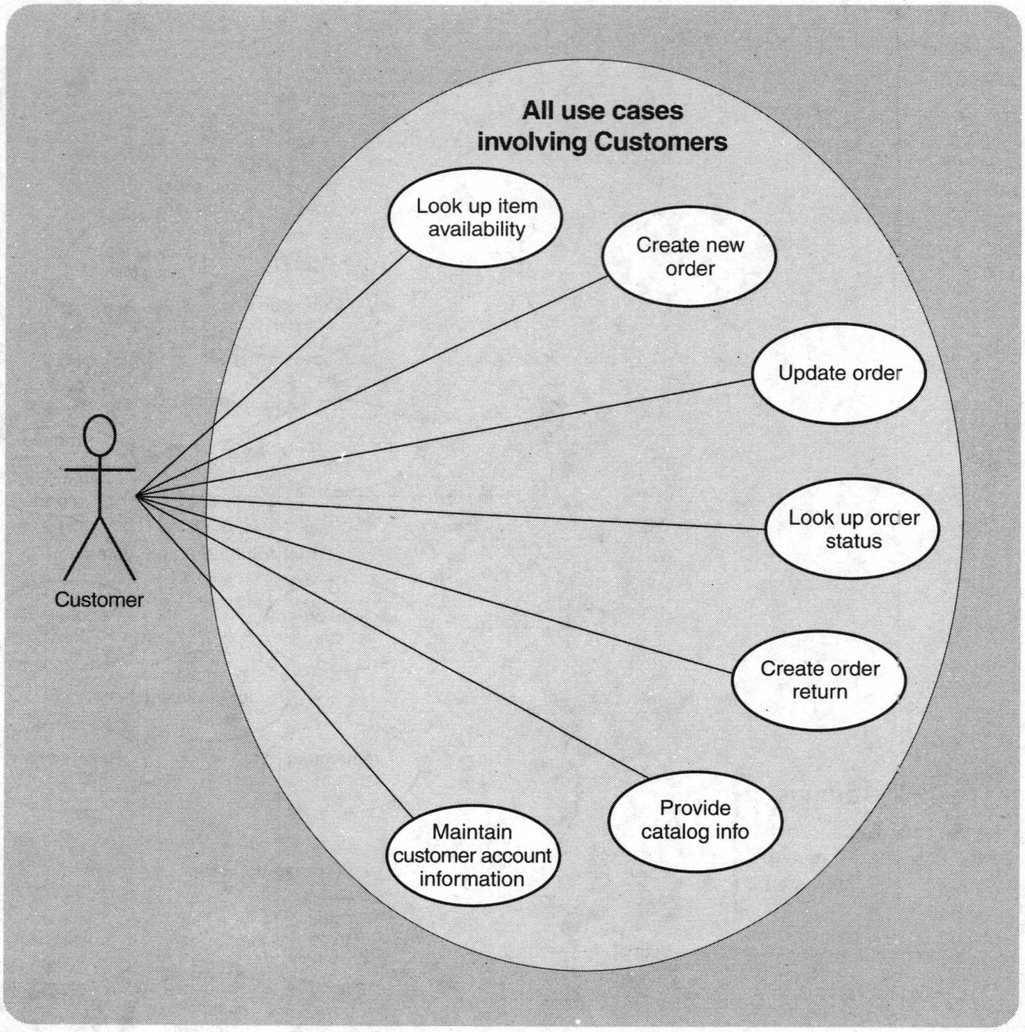

FIGURE 6-5
All use cases involving Customers

Figure 6-6 also shows that *Look up item availability* can be part of an «includes» relationship. So, an analyst can define two types of «includes» use cases: one that is a common internal subroutine, such as *Validate customer account,* and is not directly referenced by an external actor and one that is directly referenced by external actors. *Look up item availability* is an example of the latter.

DEVELOPING A USE CASE DIAGRAM

As just discussed, the activities of business modeling help analysts understand the business processes. As a result of that modeling, business events are identified and documented in the event table. Although business events are used to identify the use cases, analysts often need to make some adjustments when building a use case diagram. One major adjustment is that frequently business events may be combined into a single use case. For example, there may be a business event for adding a new customer, and there may be an entirely different business event for changing customer information. In fact, from the perspective of the business, these two processes may be done in different departments. However, from the automated system's point of view, these two events can be supported by a single use case—*Maintain customer information.*

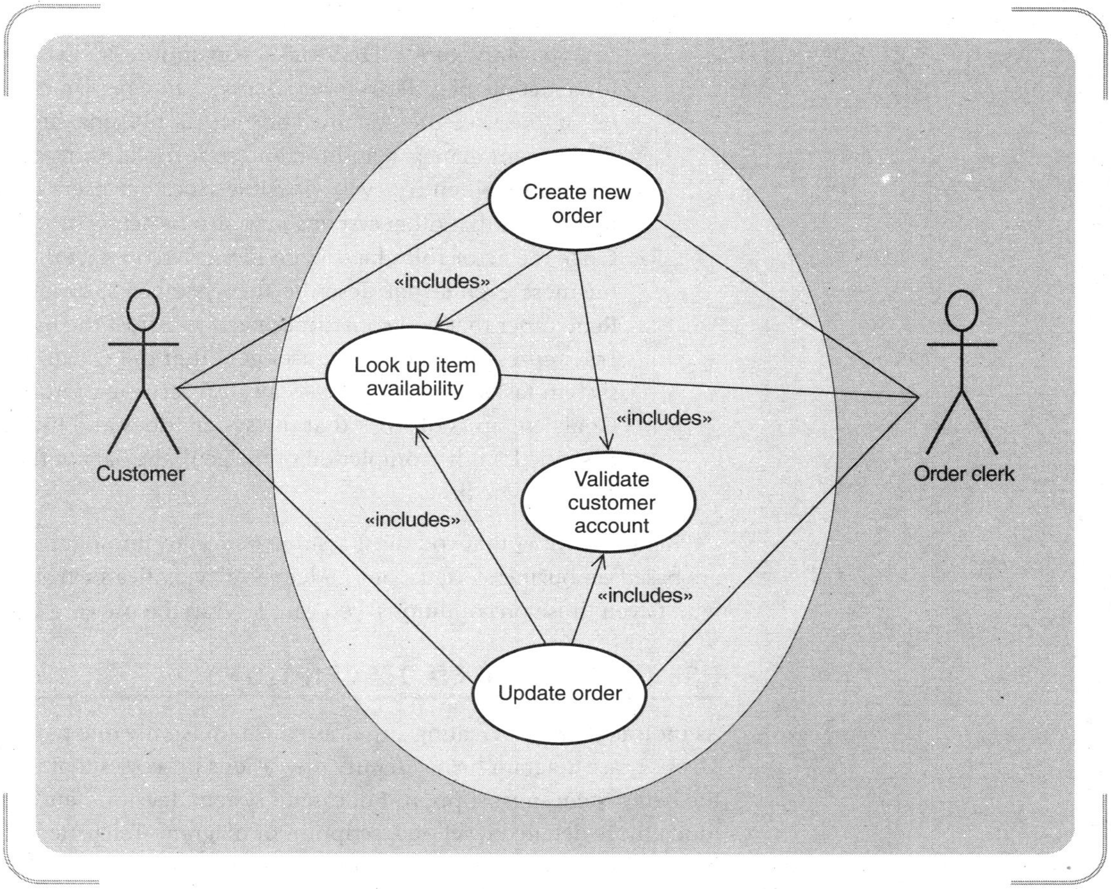

FIGURE 6-6
An example of the Order-entry subsystem with «includes» use cases

Analysts also make adjustments by splitting a single event into multiple use cases. Additional use cases are usually identified either (1) when they contain the «includes» relationship and two use cases can be developed from one large use case, or (2) when another use case is defined from recognizing a common subroutine, as discussed previously.

As you move from the business events to the use case diagram, pay careful attention to temporal and state events. For example, when identifying business events, we might define *Produce monthly payroll* as a temporal event. However, the monthly payroll, even though it is always produced at the end of the month, is initiated by a manager actor. So in the use case diagram, it is connected to the manager and is not shown as a temporal event. Other temporal or state events may not have an obvious actor. However, temporal and state events are important use cases that the system must support, so they must be included in the system requirements. In use case diagrams, analysts often connect these business events to an administrator actor that might invoke them as a "special" procedure. For example, a state event might be to order more inventory when a reorder point is reached. However, a manager could also initiate a "special" procedure to order inventory, and that event requires the same use case—*Order inventory*. So, *Order inventory* should be included in the use case diagram.

The process for moving from the business events to defining use cases requires two steps, done in iteration:

[1] Identify the actors for each use case. Remember that the system boundary defines the automated system, so the actors you identify must actually contact the system—that is, have hands. As you identify the actors of the system,

note that actors are actually roles played by users. Instead of listing the actors as Bob, Mary, or Mr. Hendricks, you should identify the specific roles that these people play. Remember that the same person may play various roles as he or she uses the system. Those roles become such titles as order clerk, department manager, auditor, and so forth. It is important to be comprehensive and to identify every possible role that users of the system will play. Remember that other systems may also be actors of a system.

[2] Once the actor roles have been identified, extract the information from the business events that describe the system response to the business event. Remember that you sometimes need to adjust the use cases so that each use case represents a common user goal that the system will support. Goals are system tasks such as "process a sale," "accept a return," or "ship an order." Goals are units of work that the system does and that can be identified and described. At the completion of the goal, the data of the system should be stable for some time.

Also remember that you must assume perfect technology. Be sure that the use cases are based on business events, not on technical activities such as logging on to the system. Given those preconditions, you can develop the use case diagram.

USE CASE DETAILED DESCRIPTIONS

As indicated earlier, creating a use case diagram is only one part of use case analysis. The use case diagram helps identify the various processes that users perform and that the new system must support. But careful system development requires us to go to a much more detailed level of description or diagram. To create a comprehensive, robust system that truly meets users' needs, we must understand all of the detailed steps. Internally, a use case includes a whole sequence of steps to complete a business process, and frequently, several variations of the business steps exist within a single use case. The use case *Create new order* will have a separate flow of activities for each actor that invokes the use case. The processes for an order clerk creating a new order over the telephone may be quite different from the processes for a customer creating an order over the Internet. Each flow of activities is a valid sequence for the *Create new order* use case. These different flows of activities are called *scenarios*, or sometimes *use case instances*. Thus, a scenario is a unique set of internal activities within a use case and represents a unique path through the use case.

scenario, or use case instance
a particular sequence of steps within a use case; a use case may have several different scenarios

Analysts elaborate a use case with various diagrams and descriptions. One of the more useful diagramming techniques for documenting a use case is an activity diagram, discussed later. Activity diagrams were first introduced in Chapter 4. Many analysts prefer to write narrative descriptions of use cases. Typically, use case descriptions are written at three separate levels of detail: brief description, intermediate description, and fully developed description. Written descriptions and activity diagrams can be used in any combination, depending on an analyst's needs.

BRIEF DESCRIPTION

A brief description can be used for very simple use cases, especially when the system to be developed is also a small, well-understood application. A simple use case would normally have a single scenario and very few, if any, exception conditions. A brief description used in conjunction with an activity diagram adequately describes a simple use case. Figure 6-7 provides a brief description of the *Create new order* use case. Generally, a use case such as *Create new order* is complex enough that either an intermediate or fully developed description is developed. We illustrate those descriptions next.

FIGURE 6-7
Brief description of *Create new order* use case

***Create new order* description**
When the customer calls to order, the order clerk and system verify customer information, create a new order, add items to the order, verify payment, create the order transaction, and finalize the order.

INTERMEDIATE DESCRIPTION

The intermediate-level use case description expands the brief description to include the internal flow of activities for the use case. If there are multiple scenarios, then each flow of activities is described individually. Exception conditions can be documented, if they are needed. Figures 6-8 and 6-9 show intermediate descriptions that document the two scenarios of *Order clerk creates telephone order* and *Customer creates Web order*. These two scenarios were identified earlier as separate workflows for the *Create new order* use case. Notice that each describes what the user and the system need to carry out the processing for the scenario. Exception conditions are also listed. Each step is identified with a number to make it easier to read. In many ways, this description resembles a type of writing called *structured English*, which can include sequence, decision, and repetition blocks.

Flow of activities for scenario of *Order Clerk creates telephone order*

Main Flow:

1. Customer calls RMO and gets order clerk.
2. Order clerk verifies customer information. If a new customer, invoke *Maintain customer account information* use case to add a new customer.
3. Clerk initiates the creation of a new order.
4. Customer requests an item be added to the order.
5. Clerk verifies the item and adds it to the order.
6. Repeat steps 4 and 5 until all items are added to the order.
7. Customer indicates end of order; clerk enters end of order; system computes totals.
8. Customer submits payment; clerk enters amount; system verifies payment.
9. System finalizes order.

Exception Conditions:

1. If an item is not in stock, then customer can
   a. choose not to purchase item, or
   b. request item be added as a back-ordered item.
2. If customer payment is rejected due to bad-credit verification, then
   a. order is canceled, or
   b. order is put on hold until check is received.

FIGURE 6-8
Intermediate description of the telephone order scenario for *Create new order*

FULLY DEVELOPED DESCRIPTION

The fully developed description is the most formal method for documenting a use case. Even though it takes a little more work to define all the components at this level, it is the preferred method of describing the internal flow of activities for a use case. One of the major difficulties that software developers have is struggling to obtain a deep understanding of the users' needs. But if you create a fully developed use case description, you increase the probability that you thoroughly understand the business processes and the ways the system must support them. Figure 6-10 is an example of a fully developed use case description of the telephone order scenario of the *Create new order* use case, and Figure 6-11 shows the Web order scenario for the same use case.

Flow of activities for scenario of *Customer creates Web order*
Main Flow: 1. Customer connects to the RMO home page and then links to the order page. 2. If this is a new customer, then customer links to the customer account page and adds the appropriate information to establish a customer account. 2a. If existing customer, customer logs in. 3. The system starts a new order and displays the catalog frame. 4. Customer searches the catalog. 5. When customer finds the correct item, he/she requests it be added to the order; the system adds it to the shopping cart. 6. Customer repeats steps 4 and 5. 7. Customer requests end of order; system displays a summary of the ordered items. 8. Customer makes any changes. 9. Customer requests payment screen; system displays payment screen. 9a. Customer enters payment information; system displays summary information and sends confirmation e-mail. 10. System finalizes order.
Exception Conditions: 1. If existing customer forgets password, then a. customer can invoke forgotten password processing, or b. customer can create a new customer account. 2. If customer payment is rejected due to bad-credit verification, then a. customer can cancel the order, or b. order is put on hold until check is received.

FIGURE 6-9
Intermediate description of the Web order scenario for *Create new order*

Figures 6-10 and 6-11 can also serve as a standard template for documenting a fully developed description for other scenarios and use cases. The first and second compartments are used to identify the use cases and scenarios within use cases, if needed, that are being documented. In larger or more formal projects, a unique identifier can also be added for the use case, with an extension identifying the particular scenario. Sometimes the name of the system developer who produced the form is also added.

The third compartment identifies the trigger that initiates the use case. This trigger is the same as that described in the event table, as explained in Chapter 5. There are two points of view from which to describe a trigger. One is to identify the business event that initiates the process. For example, in Figure 6-10 the *Create new order* process is started by a customer's telephoning RMO. This point of view is centered on the outside world. A second point of view of a trigger is as an activity that causes the automated system to first recognize that the use case has begun. From the second viewpoint, the trigger could be described as "The clerk enters a request for a new order." Since at this point in the development of the new system the objective is to understand the business need, the better viewpoint is the first—identifying the external event that initiates the entire process.

The fourth compartment is a brief description of the use case or scenario. Analysts may just duplicate the brief description they constructed earlier here. The fifth compartment identifies the actor or actors. This compartment duplicates some of the information that is contained in the use case diagram itself. The sixth compartment identifies other use cases and the way they are related to this use case, for example, the «includes» relationship we discussed earlier. Other, more advanced relationships can also be identified. The important point, however, is to add a cross-reference to other use cases to understand all aspects of the users' requirements.

The Stakeholders compartment identifies interested parties—other than specific actors. They may be users who do not actually invoke the use case but who have an interest in results produced from the use case. For example, in Figures 6-10 and 6-11, no one in the marketing department actually creates new orders, but marketers do perform

Use Case Name:	Create new order	
Scenario:	Create new telephone order	
Triggering Event:	Customer telephones RMO to purchase items from the catalog.	
Brief Description:	When customer calls to order, the order clerk and system verify customer information, create a new order, add items to the order, verify payment, create the order transaction, and finalize the order.	
Actors:	Telephone sales clerk	
Related Use Cases:	Includes: *Check item availability*	
Stakeholders:	Sales department: to provide primary definition Shipping department: to verify that information content is adequate for fulfillment Marketing department: to collect customer statistics for studies of buying patterns	
Preconditions:	Customer must exist. Catalog, Products, and Inventory items must exist for requested items.	
Postconditions:	Order and order line items must be created. Order transaction must be created for the order payment. Inventory items must have the quantity on hand updated. The order must be related (associated) to a customer.	
Flow of Events:	**Actor**	**System**
	1. Sales clerk answers telephone and connects to a customer.	
	2. Clerk verifies customer information.	
	3. Clerk initiates the creation of a new order.	3.1 Create a new order.
	4. Customer requests an item be added to the order.	
	5. Clerk verifies the item (*Check item availability* use case).	5.1 Display item information.
	6. Clerk adds item to the order.	6.1 Add an order item.
	7. Repeat steps 4, 5, and 6 until all items are added to the order.	
	8. Customer indicates end of order; clerk enters end of order.	8.1 Complete order. 8.2 Compute totals.
	9. Customer submits payment; clerk enters amount.	9.1 Verify payment. 9.2 Create order transaction. 9.3 Finalize order.
Exception Conditions:	2.1 If customer does not exist, then the clerk pauses this use case and invokes *Maintain customer information* use case. 2.2 If customer has a credit hold, then clerk transfers the customer to a customer service representative. 4.1 If an item is not in stock, then customer can a. choose not to purchase item, or b. request item be added as a back-ordered item. 9.1 If customer payment is rejected due to bad-credit verification, then a. order is canceled, or b. order is put on hold until check is received.	

FIGURE 6-10
Fully developed description of the telephone order scenario for *Create new order*

statistical analysis of the orders that were entered. So, they have an interest in the data that are captured and stored from the *Create new order* use case. Considering all stakeholders is an important step for system developers to ensure that they have understood all requirements.

The next two compartments provide critical information about the state of the system before and after the use case executes, called *preconditions* and *postconditions.*

Use Case Name:	Create new order	
Scenario:	Create new Web order	
Triggering Event:	Customer logs on to the RMO Web site and requests to purchase an item.	
Brief Description:	Customer logs in and requests the new order form. The customer searches the catalog online and purchases items from the catalog. The system adds the purchased items to the order. At the end, the customer enters credit card information.	
Actors:	Customer	
Related Use Cases:	Includes: *Register new customer, Check item availability*	
Stakeholders:	Sales department: to provide primary definition Shipping department: to verify that information content is adequate for fulfillment Marketing department: to collect customer statistics for studies of buying patterns	
Preconditions:	Catalog, Products, and Inventory items must exist for requested items.	
Postconditions:	Order and order line items must be created. Order transaction must be created for the order payment. Inventory items must have the quantity on hand updated. The order must be related (associated) to a customer.	
Flow of Events:	**Actor**	**System**
	1. Customer connects to the RMO home page and then links to the order page.	
	2. If this is a new customer, then customer links to the customer account page and adds the appropriate information to establish a customer account. 2a. If existing customer, customer logs in.	2.1 Create new customer record. 2a.1 Validate customer account. 2.2 Create a new shopping cart order; display order form with catalog frame.
	3. Customer searches catalog.	3.1 Display products from catalog based on searches and selections.
	4. When customer finds the correct item, he/she requests it be added to the order.	4.1 Add item to shopping cart order.
	5. Repeat steps 3 and 4.	
	6. Customer requests end of order.	6.1 Display shopping cart items, with totals and amounts due; edit and submit buttons.
	7. Customer makes any changes.	
	8. Customer requests payment screen.	8.1 Display payment details screen.
	9. Customer enters payment information.	9.1 Accept payment, finalize order, send confirmation e-mail.
Exception Conditions:	4.1 If an item is not in stock, then customer can a. choose not to purchase item, or b. request item be added as a back-ordered item. 8.1 If customer payment is rejected due to bad-credit verification, then a. order is canceled, or b. order is put on hold until check is received.	

FIGURE 6-11
Fully developed description of the Web order scenario for *Create new order*

Preconditions state what conditions must be true before a use case begins. In other words, a precondition identifies what the state of the system must be for the use case to begin, including what objects must already exist, what information must be available, and even what the condition of the actor is prior to beginning the use case.

precondition
a set of criteria that must be true prior to the initiation of a use case

postcondition
a set of criteria that must be true upon completion of the execution of a use case

A *postcondition* identifies what must be true upon completion of the use case. The same items that are used to describe the precondition should be included in the statement of the postcondition. For example, during the processing of a use case that updates various financial accounts, some accounts will be out of balance. So, a postcondition for that use case would be that the updates should be complete for all accounts and that they should all be in balance.

For simplicity, we suggest that you keep the definitions of pre- and postconditions fairly basic. We also assume perfect technology, such as that the system is up and running, the user is logged on, the database connection is active, and so forth. Preconditions usually include the following:

- What objects must exist in the system (or the database)
- What specific relationships must exist between objects, and which are important
- What specific values should be identified

For example, for some companies, an order cannot be created unless the customer exists and has a good credit rating. For other companies, adding a new customer may be part of the larger use case of creating a new order (an example of the «includes» relationship). Depending on the companies' policies, the preconditions for the use case will be different, but they should be specifically defined.

Use the same three guidelines for preconditions to define the postconditions: concentrate on what objects must exist, what relationships must exist, and what values are important. In addition, be sure to include one other element—identify which objects were updated or modified.

The final two compartments in the template describe the detailed flow of activities of the use case. In this instance, we have shown a two-column version, identifying the steps performed by the actor and the responses required by the system. The item numbering helps identify the sequence of the steps. Some developers prefer a one-column version, as shown in the intermediate description (see Figures 6-8 and 6-9). Alternate activities and exception conditions are described in the final compartment. The numbering of exception conditions also helps tie the exceptions with specific steps in the use case description.

One very important consideration, and one with which new developers sometimes struggle, is to identify the scope of a use case. A use case—and its business event—begins with the system in a stable state and does not end until the system is again stable. For example, in creating a new order, the use case would not logically end with simply creating an order; items must be added to it. An order with no items is not logically at a stable point. Sometimes this is easy to understand, but at other times the distinction can be more subtle. For example, is accepting a payment part of the order use case or part of another use case such as *Enter payment*? To answer that question, you need to go back to the business event and ask, "Can the order be completed without a payment?" In some cases, such as a cash payment at a grocery store, the payment is part of the same business event. For other cases, such as a purchase on credit at a furniture store, invoicing and making payments are separate use cases. However, the scope of a use case begins when the system is at a stable point and ends when it is again stable. Your definitions of pre- and postconditions will help you think this through correctly.

BEST PRACTICE: Pre- and postconditions are critical to understanding the processing done for a use case.

ACTIVITY DIAGRAM DESCRIPTION

The other way to document a use case scenario is with an activity diagram. In Chapter 4, you learned that an activity diagram is an easily understood diagram used to document the workflows of business processes. Activity diagrams are a standard type of UML diagram. Analysts also use activity diagrams to document the flow of activities for each use case scenario.

Figures 6-12 and 6-13 are the activity diagrams that document the same two scenarios shown in Figures 6-10 and 6-11. In Figure 6-12 the customer telephones the order clerk, who in turn uses the system. Since the purpose of a use case is to specify the interaction of an actor (with hands) with the system, the figure includes swimlanes for the Order Clerk and the Computer System. However, to aid in understanding the total flow of activities for the scenario, the Customer—the one who initiates the steps—is also included. Note that the Customer swimlane is an optional addition in Figure 6-12 that simply aids in understanding the total workflow. In Figure 6-13 with the Web order scenario, the customer is the actor who interacts with the computer system, so only two swimlanes are required to describe the steps in the scenario.

An activity diagram can be used to support any level of use case description. As you can see, activity diagrams are similar to the two-column description in the fully developed narrative description. The benefit of creating an activity diagram is that it is more visual and so can help both the user and the developer as they work together to fully document the use case.

As a quick glance at Figures 6-12 and 6-13 demonstrates, the two scenarios of the *Create new order* use case are quite different. Even though the scenarios carry out the same basic function, the set of screens and options on the screens may be quite different for each. Activity diagrams are also helpful in developing system sequence diagrams, as explained in the next section.

IDENTIFYING INPUTS AND OUTPUTS—THE SYSTEM SEQUENCE DIAGRAM

In the object-oriented approach, the flow of information is achieved through sending messages either to and from actors, or back and forth between internal objects. A system sequence diagram (SSD) is used to describe this flow of information into and out of the automated system. So, an SSD documents the inputs and the outputs and identifies the interaction between actors and the system. An SSD is a type of *interaction diagram*. In the following sections, and in industry practice, we often use the terms *interaction* and *message* interchangeably.

interaction diagram
either a communication diagram or a sequence diagram that shows the interactions between objects

SSD NOTATION

Figure 6-14 shows a generic SSD. As with a use case diagram, the stick figure represents an actor—a person (or role) that interacts with the system. In a use case diagram, the actor "uses" the system, but the emphasis in an SSD is on how the actor "interacts" with the system by entering input data and receiving output data. The idea is the same with both diagrams; the level of detail is different.

The box labeled :System is an object that represents the entire automated system. In SSDs and all interaction diagrams, instead of using class notation, analysts use object notation. Object notation indicates that the box refers to an individual object and not to the class of all similar objects. The notation is simply a rectangle with the name of the object underlined. The colon before the underlined class name is a frequently used, but optional, part of the object notation. In an interaction diagram, the messages are

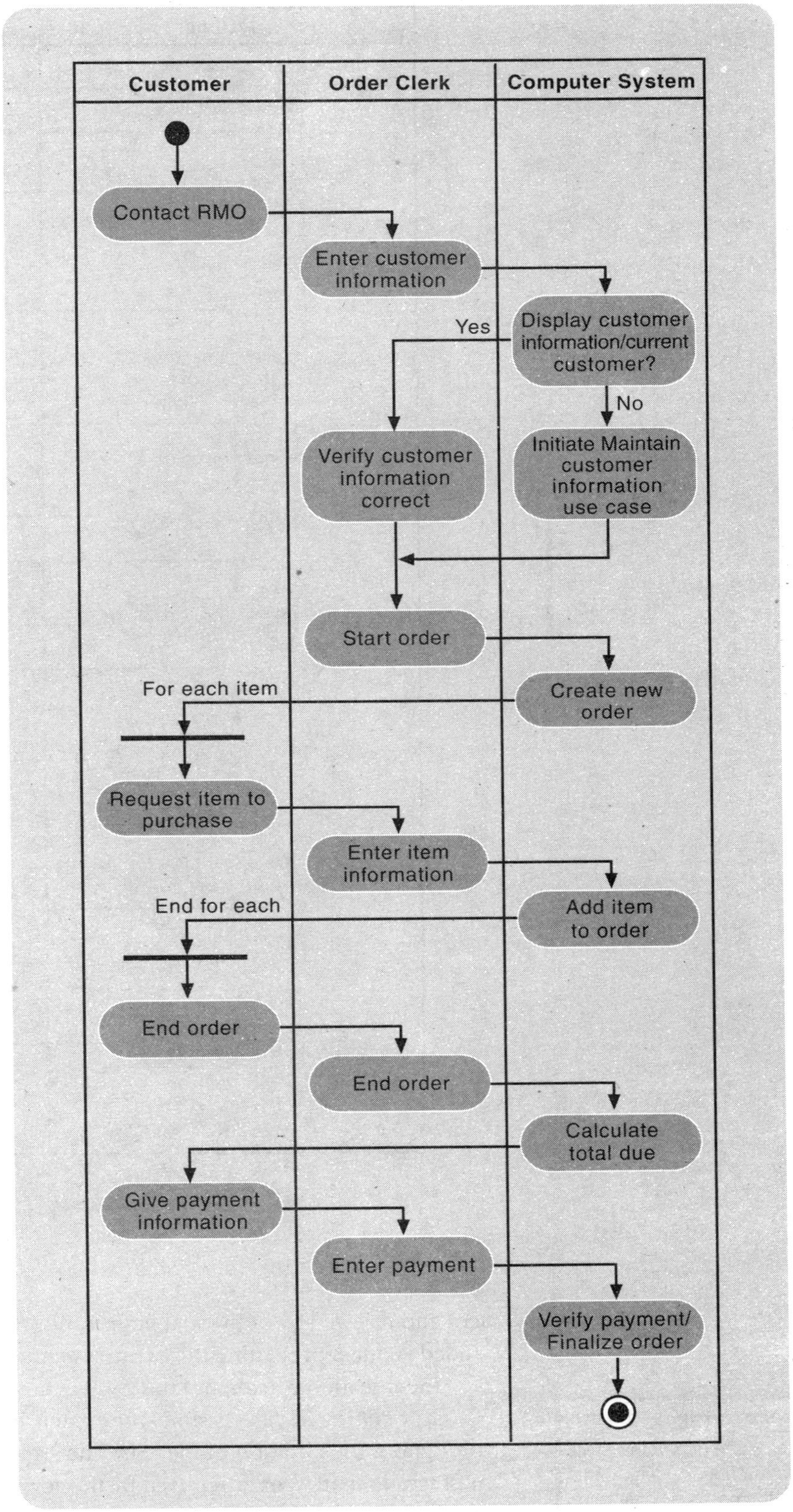

FIGURE 6-12
Activity diagram of the telephone order scenario

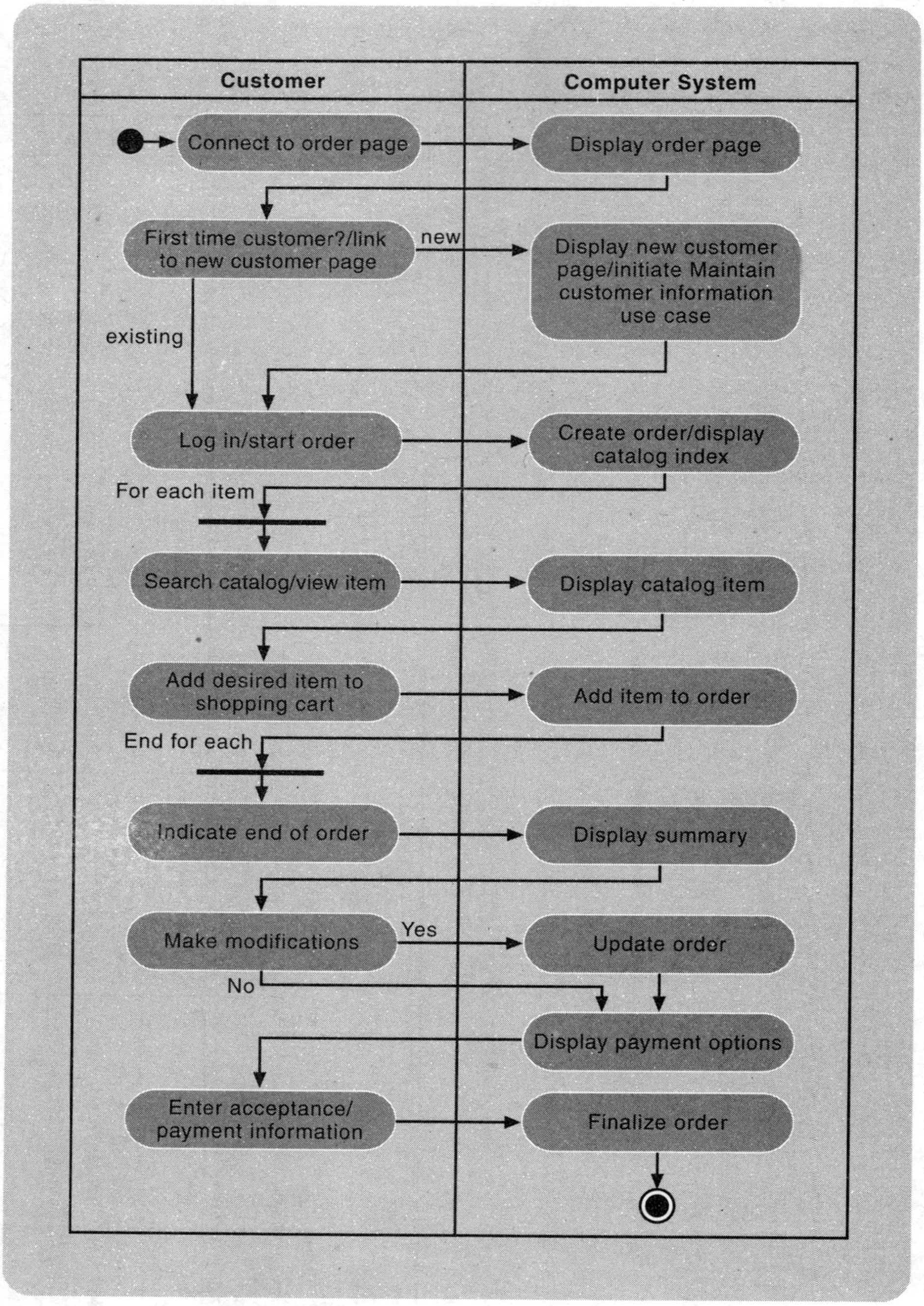

FIGURE 6-13
Activity diagram of the Web order scenario

sent and received by individual objects, not by a class. In an SSD, the only object included is one representing the entire system.

lifeline, or object lifeline
the vertical line under an object on a sequence diagram to show the passage of time for the object

Underneath the actor and the <u>:System</u> are vertical dashed lines called *lifelines*. A *lifeline*, or *object lifeline*, is simply the extension of that object, either actor or object, throughout the duration of the SSD. The arrows between the lifelines represent the messages that are sent or received by the actor or the system. Each arrow has an origin and a destination. The origin of the message is the actor or object that sends it, as indicated by the lifeline at the arrow's tail. Similarly, the destination actor or object of a message is indicated by the lifeline that is touched by the arrowhead. The purpose of

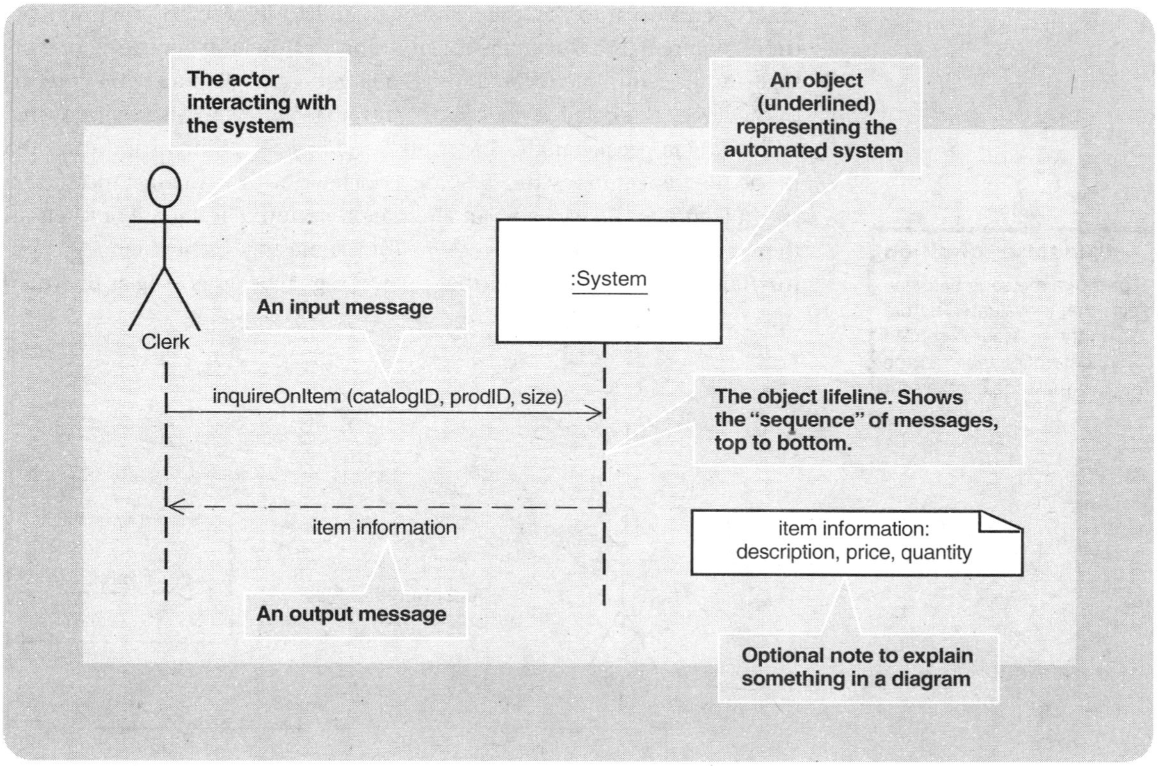

FIGURE 6-14
Sample system sequence diagram (SSD)

lifelines is to indicate the sequence of the messages sent and received by the actor and object. The sequence of messages is read from top to bottom in the diagram.

A message is labeled to describe both the message's purpose and any input data being sent. The syntax of the message label has several options; the simplest forms are shown in Figure 6-14. Remember that the arrows are used to represent both a message and input data. But what is meant by the term *message* here? In a sequence diagram, a message is considered to be an action that is invoked on the destination object, much like a command. Notice in Figure 6-14 that the input message is called inquireOnItem. The clerk is sending a request, or a message to the system, to find an item. The input data that are sent with the message are contained within the parentheses, and in this case they are data to identify the particular item. The syntax is simply the name of the message followed by the input parameters in parentheses. This form of syntax is attached to a solid arrow.

The return message has a slightly different format and meaning. Notice that the arrow is a dashed arrow. A dashed arrow is used to indicate a response or an answer and, as shown in the figure, immediately follows the initiating message. The format of the label is also different. Since it is a response, only the data that are sent on the response are noted. There is no message requesting a service, only the data being returned. In this case, a valid response might be a list of all the information returned—such as description, price, and quantity of an item. However, an abbreviated version is also satisfactory. In this case the information returned is named item information. Additional documentation is required to show the details. In Figure 6-14 this additional information is shown as a note. A note can be added to any UML diagram to add explanations. The details of item information could also be documented in supporting narratives or even simply referenced by the attributes in the Customer class.

Frequently, the same message is sent multiple times. For example, when an actor enters items on an order, the message to add an item to an order may be sent multiple times. Figure 6-15a illustrates the notation to show this repeating operation. The message and its return are located inside a larger rectangle. In a smaller rectangle at the top of the large rectangle is the descriptive text to control the behavior of the messages within the larger rectangle. The condition Loop for all items indicates that the messages in the box repeat many times or are associated with many instances.

In Figure 6-15b we show an alternate notation. The square brackets and text inside them are called a *true/false condition* for the messages. The asterisk (*) preceding the true/false condition indicates that the message repeats as long as the true/false condition

true/false condition
part of a message between objects that is evaluated before the message is sent to determine whether the message can be sent

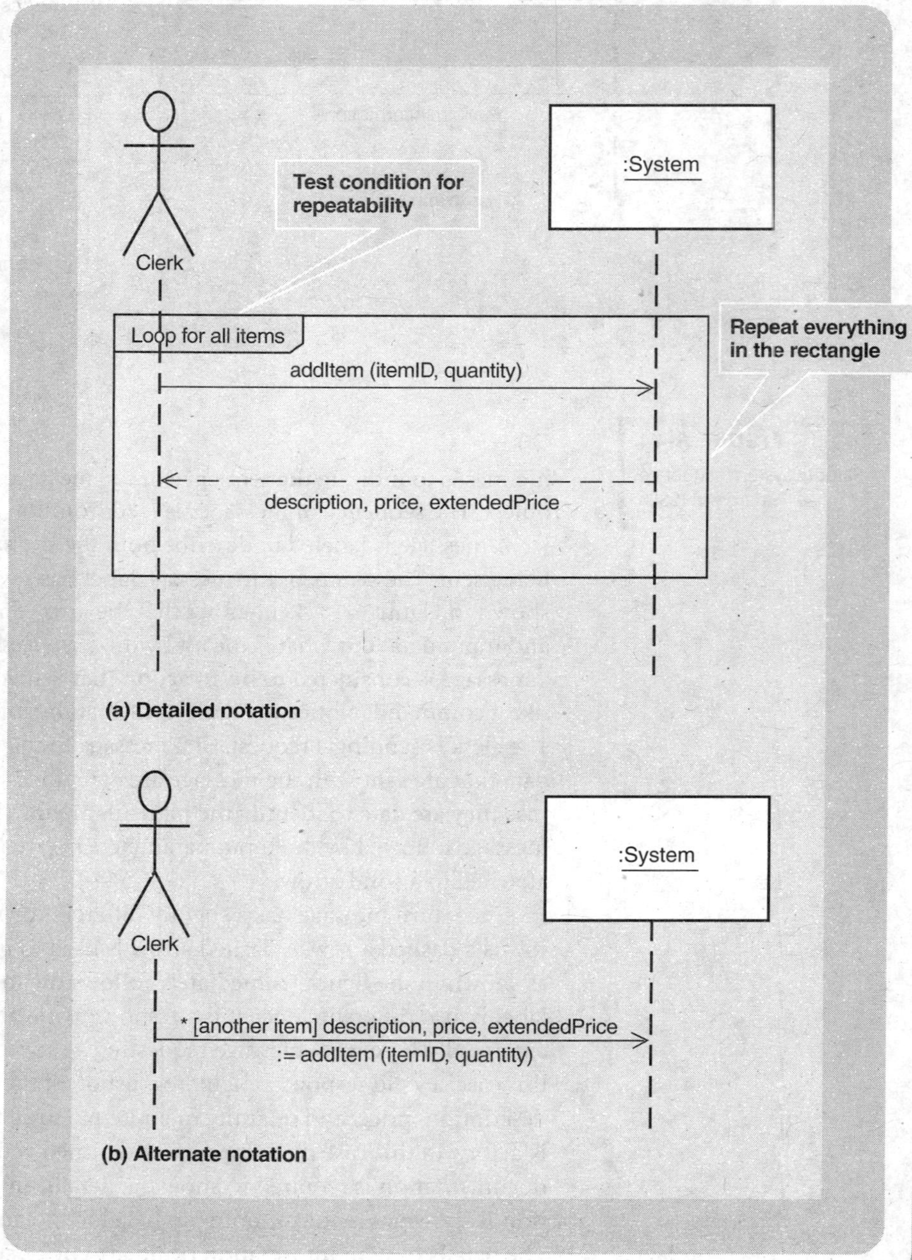

FIGURE 6-15
Repeating message
(a) Detailed notation
(b) Alternate notation

evaluates to true. Analysts use this abbreviated notation for several reasons. First, a message and the returned data can be shown in one step. Note that the return data are identified as a return value on the left side of an assignment operator—the := sign. This alternative simply shows a value that is returned. Second, the true/false condition is placed on the message itself. Note that in this example, the true/false condition is used for the control of the loop. True/false conditions are also used to evaluate any type of test that determines whether a message is sent. For example, [credit card payment] might be used to control whether a message is sent to the system to verify a credit card number. Finally, the asterisk is also placed on the message itself. So, for simple repeating messages, the alternate notation is shorter. However, if several messages are included within the repeat or there are multiple messages, each with its own true/false condition, then the more detailed notation is more explicit and precise.

The complete notation for a message is the following:

** [true/false condition] return-value := message-name (parameter-list)*

Any part of the message may be omitted. In brief, the notation components are the following:

- An asterisk (*) indicates repeat or looping of the message.
- Brackets [ ] indicate a true/false condition. It is a test for that message only. If it evaluates to true, the message is sent. If it evaluates to false, the message is not sent.
- Message-name is the description of the requested service. It is omitted on dashed-line return messages, which only show the return data parameters.
- Parameter-list (with parentheses on initiating messages and without parentheses on return messages) shows the data that are passed with the message.
- Return-value on the same line as the message (requires :=) is used to describe data being returned from the destination object to the source object in response to the message.

BEST PRACTICE: Develop SSDs carefully and correctly. They become critical components for detailed design and user interface design.

DEVELOPING A SYSTEM SEQUENCE DIAGRAM

An SSD is normally used in conjunction with the use case descriptions to help document the details of a single use case or scenario within a use case. To develop an SSD, you will need to have a detailed description of the use case, either in the fully developed form, as shown in Figures 6-10 or 6-11, or as activity diagrams, as shown in Figures 6-12 and 6-13. These two models identify the series of activities within a use case, but they do not explicitly identify the inputs and outputs. An SSD will do so. One advantage of using activity diagrams is that it is easy to identify when an input or output occurs. Inputs and outputs occur whenever an arrow in an activity diagram goes from an external actor to the computer system. Figure 6-16 is a simplified version of Figure 6-12 for the telephone order scenario of the RMO *Create new order* use case. Obviously, the simplified version has many things missing, but it allows us to focus here on the process and on the basics of SSD development, without having to consider all of the complexity of the real world.

In this simplified activity diagram, there are three swimlanes: the Customer, the Order Clerk, and the Computer System. Before beginning the SSD, you must first determine the system boundary. In this instance, the system boundary coincides with the

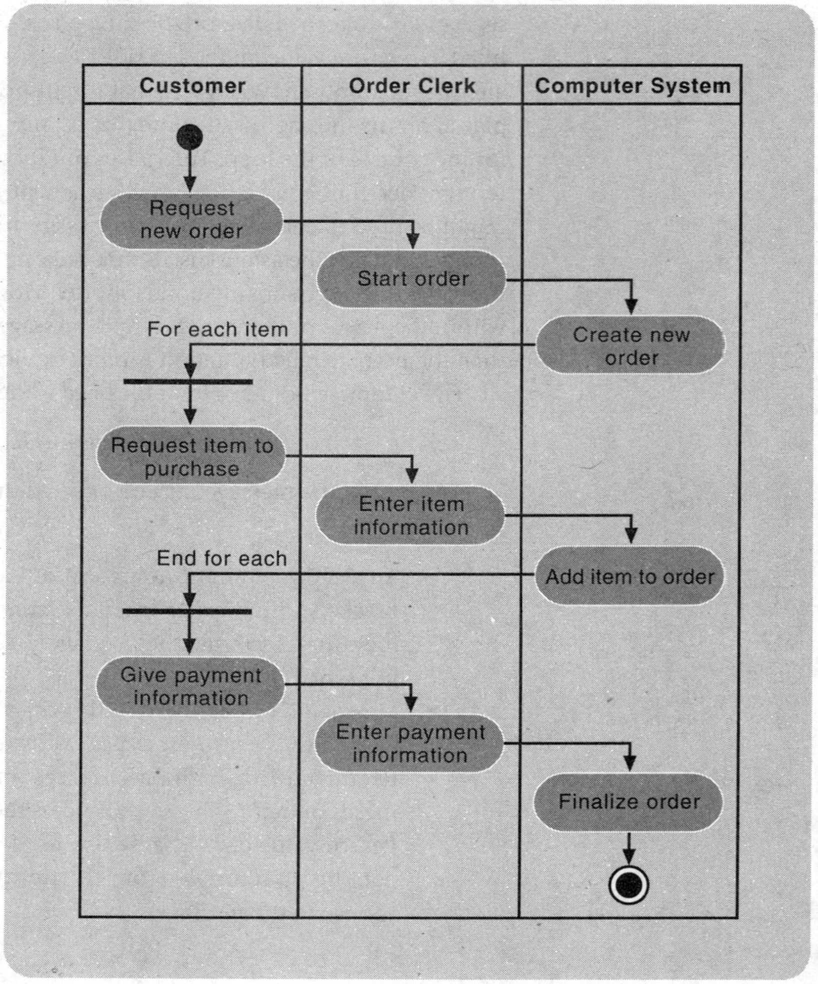

FIGURE 6-16
A simplified activity diagram of the telephone order scenario

vertical line between the Order Clerk swimlane and the Computer System swimlane. Since the purpose of the SSD is to describe the inputs to and outputs from the automated computer system, in the SSD only the Order Clerk and the Computer System will be included. It is not wrong to include both actors in the SSD, but it is more focused to show only the system and the actor who sends the inputs and receives the outputs.

The development of an SSD based on an activity diagram can be divided into four steps:

[1] **Identify the input messages.** In Figure 6-16 there are three locations with a workflow arrow crossing the boundary line between the clerk and the system. At each location where the workflow crosses the automation boundary, input data are required; therefore, a message is needed.

[2] **Describe the message from the external actor to the system, using the message notation described earlier.** In most cases, you will need a message name that describes the service requested from the system and the input parameters being passed. Figure 6-17, the SSD for the *Create new order* use case, illustrates the three messages. Notice that the names of the messages reflect the services that the actor is requesting of the system, startOrder, addItem, and completeOrder. Other names could also have been used. For example, instead of addItem, the name could be enterItemInformation.

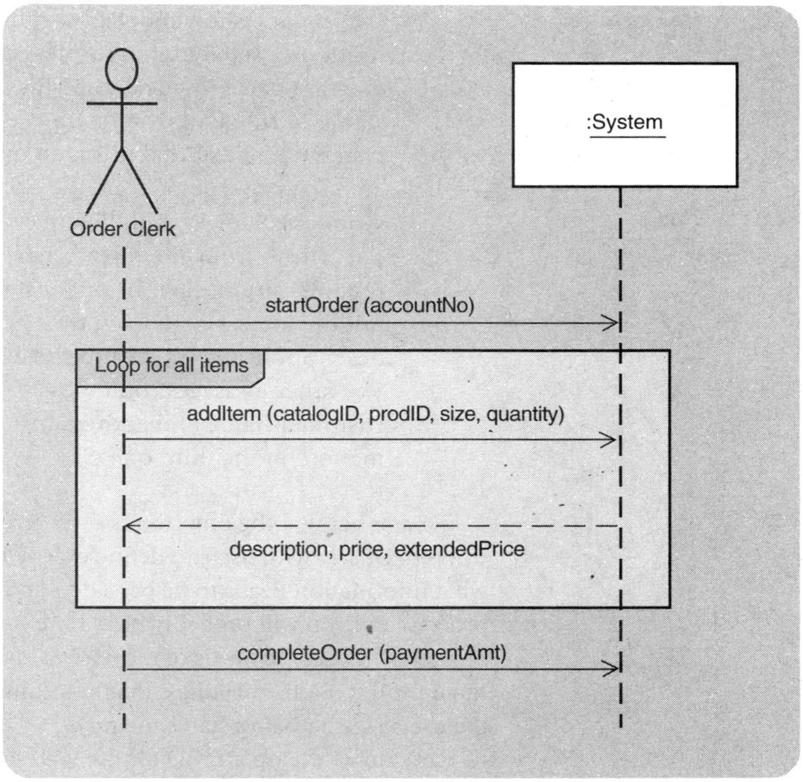

FIGURE 6-17
An SSD of the simplified telephone order scenario for the *Create new order* use case

The other information required is the parameter list for each message. Determining exactly which data items must be passed in is more difficult. In fact, developers frequently find that determining the data parameters requires several iterations before a correct, complete list is obtained. The important principle for identifying data parameters is to base the list on the class diagram. In other words, the appropriate attributes from the classes are listed as parameters. Looking at the attributes with an understanding of what the system needs to do will help you find the right attributes.

In the example of the first message, startOrder, the precondition for this use case states that a customer should exist. A postcondition is that the order must be connected to the customer. So, for this simplified version of the use case, the first message passes in the accountNo, which is the identifier in the customer class. (Refer to the RMO class diagram shown in Figure 5-31 to find the attributes for each class.) Other than the accountNo, no other parameters are needed for the system to locate the existing customer details.

In the second message, addItem, parameters are needed to identify the item from the catalog and the quantity to be purchased. The parameters catalogID, prodID, and size are used to describe the inventory item that will be added to the order. The quantity field, of course, simply identifies how many.

The third message, based on the activity diagram, enters the payment amount. This parameter corresponds to the amount attribute in the OrderTransaction class.

[1] **Identify and add any special conditions on the input messages, including iteration and true/false conditions.** In this instance, we have the test condition box Loop for all items to indicate repetition.

[2] **Identify and add the output return messages.** Remember, there are two options for showing return information: a return value on the message itself, or a separate return message with a dashed-line arrow. The activity diagram can provide some clues about return messages, but there is no standard rule that when a transition arrow in the workflow goes from the system to an external actor, an output always occurs. In Figure 6-16 there are two arrows going from the Computer System swimlane to the Customer swimlane. However, in Figure 6-17, only one output message is required. The arrow from the Create new order activity in Figure 6-16 does not require output data. In this instance the only output identified is on the middle message showing the details of the item added to the order—the description, the price, and the extended price (the price times quantity). The other messages could possibly have shown output information such as customer name and address for the first input message, and order confirmation for the third one.

Remember that the objective is discovery and understanding, so you should be working closely with users to define exactly how the workflow proceeds and exactly what information needs to be passed in and is provided as output. This is an iterative process, and you will probably need to refine these diagrams several times before they accurately reflect the needs of the users. During Rocky Mountain Outfitters' development project, Barbara Halifax, the project manager, has reviewed many diagrams with the users (see Barbara's status memo).

Let's now develop an SSD for the Web scenario of *Create new order*. Not only is this example more complex, but it also highlights how to develop the requirements for deploying Web-based systems. Refer back to Figure 6-13 for the activity diagram of a Web order. Notice that this workflow is fairly complex.

Figure 6-18 is the completed SSD for the Web-based scenario. In Figure 6-13, the workflow crosses the automated system boundary from the Customer to the Computer System eight times, some of which are optional flows. The first message, with its response message, begins the use case by requesting the new order page (requestNewOrder). The system does not need input data to perform the processes requested by these two messages, so no input parameters are required. The next input message is a request for the new customer page (newCustomerPage). On this message, there is a true/false condition to test whether this is a new customer. Thus, the message only fires if the new customer condition evaluates to true. Since the objective of a sequence diagram is only to show the messages and not to show processing logic, there is no message to show the branching out to another use case; a simple note is added to remind the developers about that jump.

The third message just allows the user to actually start an order (beginOrder). The message shows that the customer account number is an input parameter. When the user interface is actually developed, this information may already be in the system, since it may be on the screen from adding a new customer. However, showing it as an input parameter will tell the developers that it has to be available, either received from the user or captured from another page.

The next process is one of adding items to the order. The activity diagram in Figure 6-13 shows a loop to add items. That is captured by the iteration box. However, one of the activities in the workflow says *Search catalog/view item*. Even though a loop is not explicitly shown, a search normally implies a loop of some type. So, on the input message to view a product on Figure 6-18, an asterisk has been added for iteration. The iteration box and the asterisk on the input message create a nested loop condition.

April 14, 2006

To: John MacMurty

From: Barbara Halifax, Project Manager

RE: Customer Support System status

ROCKY MOUNTAIN OUTFITTERS
MEMO

John, here are the status report for our work over the last two weeks and the plans for work over the next period. I have also attached a copy of our schedule, highlighting which tasks are completed. You will note that we are nearly on schedule. A couple of the tasks took longer than expected due to delays in getting final decisions from the sales department.

Completed during the last period (two weeks)

We made progress in the last two weeks with the development of fully developed use case descriptions, activity diagrams, and system sequence diagrams for the use cases that had been defined earlier. As of today, we have completed the system sequence diagrams for all of the use cases in this iteration, with four exceptions. During recent meetings with the users, four new use cases were defined. We decided to include two of those in this iteration but delay the other use cases to a later iteration. Detailed documentation for the delayed use cases will also be done later.

Also, as we were reviewing the diagrams with the users in our structured walkthrough sessions, we discovered that some of our classes were missing critical attributes. It was a real eye-opener for some of the newer analysts to see the importance of quality controls and structured walkthroughs of our work.

Plans for the next period (two weeks)

During the next period, we will begin looking at some design issues for this iteration, including some preliminary database designs. We will also begin investigating implementation alternatives and network requirements.

Problems, issues, open items

There are no major problems at this point. We do have about 20 items on the Outstanding Items Log, but none of them is holding up the project. In your oversight committee meeting, you might just emphasize to the department heads the importance of getting those items resolved as soon as possible.

BH

cc: Steven Deerfield, Ming Lee, Jack Garcia

Note that on these two messages, the return-value method is used to return data. The remaining messages and responses follow the activity diagram.

These first sections of the chapter have explained the set of models used in object-oriented development to specify the processing aspects of the new system. The use case diagram provides an overview of all of the events that must be supported. The scenario descriptions, as provided by written narratives or activity diagrams, give the details of the internal steps within each use case. Precondition and postcondition

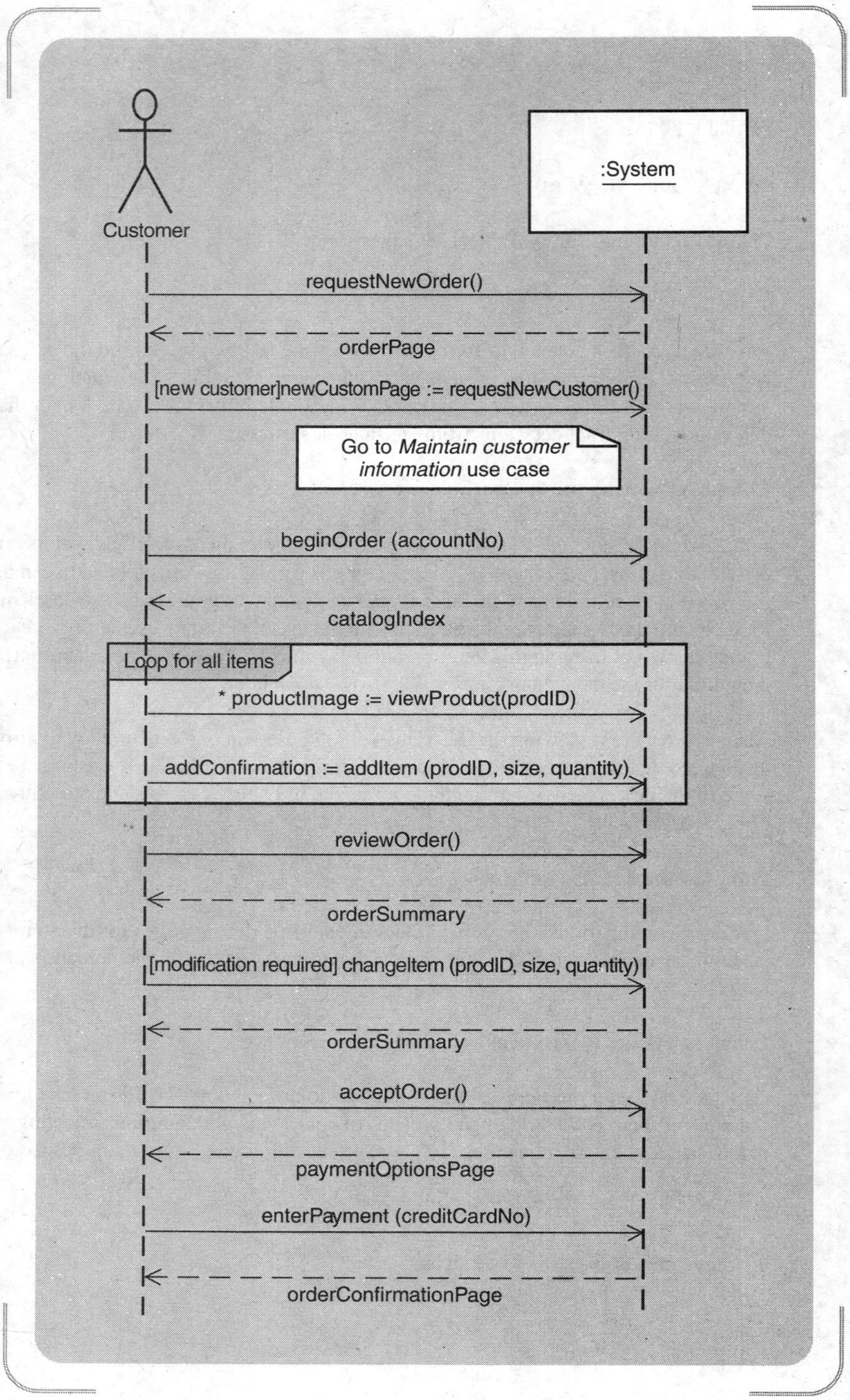

FIGURE 6-18 An SSD of the Web order scenario for the *Create new order* use case

statements help define the context for the use case—that is, what must exist before and after processing. Finally, the system sequence diagram describes the inputs and outputs that occur within a use case. Together, these models provide a comprehensive description of the processing requirements for the system and give the foundation for system design.

Now that the use cases have been explained, let's find out how to capture important object status information.

IDENTIFYING OBJECT BEHAVIOR—THE STATECHART DIAGRAM

Sometimes it is important for a computer system to maintain information about the current status of problem domain objects. For example, for a customer order, a customer might want to know whether the order is complete and whether it has been shipped. A manager might also ask about an order and may want to know not only whether it was shipped but also whether it has been paid for. All of those status conditions can be described in a statechart as different states of an Order object. In other words, a state in a statechart for a problem domain object is similar to a status condition for that object. These status conditions, and hence the statechart, span many business events, such as creating a new order and shipping an order. A statechart can be developed for any problem domain classes that have complex behavior or status conditions that need to be tracked. Not all classes will require a statechart, however. If an object in the problem domain class does not have status conditions that must control the processing that is allowed for that object, a statechart is probably not necessary. For example, in the RMO class diagram, a class such as Order may need a statechart. However, a class such as OrderTransaction probably does not. An order transaction is created when the payment is made and then just sits there; it does not need to track other conditions.

A statechart diagram is composed of ovals representing statuses of an object and arrows representing its transitions. Figure 6-19 illustrates a simple statechart for a printer. Since it is a little easier to learn about statecharts by using tangible items, we start with

FIGURE 6-19
Simple statechart for a printer

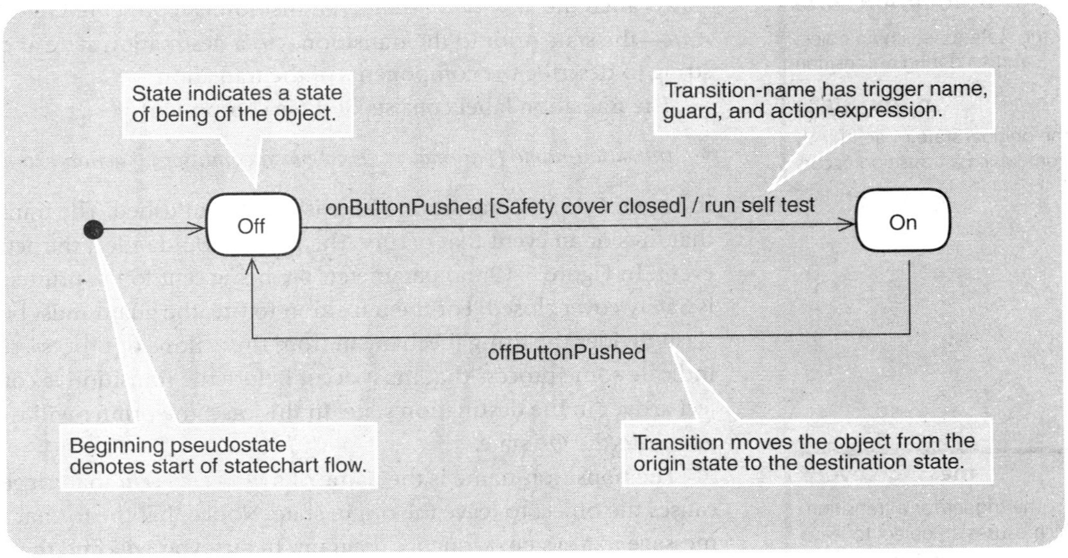

a few examples of computer hardware. Once the basics are explained, we will illustrate modeling of software objects in the problem domain. The starting point of a statechart is a black dot, which is called a *pseudostate*. The first oval after the black dot is the first state of the printer. In this case, the printer begins in the *Off* state. A state is represented by a rectangle with rounded corners (almost like an oval, but more squared), with the name of the state placed inside.

pseudostate
the starting point of a statechart, indicated by a black dot

state
a condition during an object's life when it satisfies some criterion, performs some action, or waits for an event

Defined precisely, a *state* of an object is a condition that occurs during its life when it satisfies some criterion, performs some action, or waits for an event. Each unique state has a unique name. A state is a semipermanent condition of an object, such as *On, Working*, or *Loading equipment*. States are described as semipermanent conditions because external events can interrupt them. An object remains in a state until some event causes it to move to another state.

The naming convention for status conditions helps identify valid states. A state may have a name of a simple condition such as *On* or *In repair*. Other states are more active, with names consisting of gerunds or verb phrases such as *Being shipped* or *Working*. For example, a specific Order object comes into existence when a customer orders something. Right after it is created, the object is in a state such as *Adding new order items*, then a state of *Waiting for items to be shipped*, and finally a state of *Order completed* when all items have been shipped. If you find yourself trying to use a noun to name a state, you probably have an incorrect idea about states or object classes. Rethink your analysis and describe only states of being of the object itself. Another way to help identify states is to think about status conditions that may need to be reported to management or to customers. A status condition such as *Shipped* for an order is something a customer may want to know.

transition
the movement of an object from one state to another state

As shown in Figure 6-19, the arrow leaving the *Off* state is called a *transition*. The firing of the transition causes the object to leave the *Off* state and make a transition to the *On* state. A *transition* is the movement of an object from one state to another state. It is the mechanism that causes an object to leave a state and change to a new state. Remember that states are semipermanent conditions. They are semipermanent because transitions interrupt them and cause them to end. Generally, transitions are considered to be short in duration, compared with states, and cannot be interrupted. In other words, once a transition begins, it runs to completion by taking the object to the new state, called the *destination state*. A transition is represented by an arrow from an *origin state*—the state prior to the transition—to a destination state and is labeled with a string to describe the components of the transition.

destination state
the state to which an object moves during a transition

origin state
the original state of an object, from which a transition occurs

The transition label consists of three components:

transition-name (parameters, ...) [guard-condition] / action-expression

In Figure 6-19, the transition-name is onButtonPushed. The transition is like a trigger that fires or an event that occurs. The name should reflect the action of a triggering event. In Figure 6-19, no parameters are being sent to the printer. The guard-condition is Safety cover closed. For the transition to fire, the guard must be true. The forward slash divides the firing mechanism from the actions or processes. Action-expressions indicate some process that must occur before the transition is completed and the object arrives in the destination state. In this case, the printer will run a self-test before it goes into the *On* state.

message event
the trigger for a transition, which causes an object to leave its original state

The transition-name is the name of a *message event* that triggers the transition and causes the object to leave the origin state. Notice that the format is very similar to a message in a system sequence diagram. In fact, you will find that the message names and transition-names use almost the same syntax. One other relationship exists between the messages and the transitions; transitions are caused by messages coming to the object. The parameter portion of the message name comes directly from the message parameters.

guard-condition
a true/false test to see whether a transition can fire

The *guard-condition* is a qualifier or test on the transition, and it is simply a true/false condition that must be satisfied before the transition can fire. For a transition to fire, first the trigger must occur, and then the guard must evaluate to true. Sometimes a transition has only a guard-condition and no triggering event. In that case, the trigger is constantly firing, and whenever the guard becomes true, the transition occurs.

Recall from the discussion of sequence diagrams that messages have a similar test, which is called a *true/false condition*. This true/false condition is a test on the sending side of the message, and before a message can be sent, the true/false condition must be true. In contrast, the guard-condition is on the receiving side of the message. The message may be received, but the transition fires only if the guard-condition is also true. This combination of tests, messages, and transitions provides tremendous flexibility in defining complex behavior.

action-expression
a description of the activities to be performed

The *action-expression* is a procedural expression that executes when the transition fires. In other words, it describes the action to be performed. Any of the three components—transition-name, guard-condition, or action-expression—may be empty. If either the transition-name or the guard-condition is empty, then it automatically evaluates to true. Either of them may also be complex, with AND and OR connectives.

NESTED STATES AND CONCURRENCY

concurrency, or concurrent states
the condition of being in more than one state at a time

path
a sequential set of connected states and transitions

composite state
a state containing multiple levels and transitions

Before moving into how to develop statecharts for business software objects, we present two related advanced concepts used in statechart modeling—nested states and concurrent states. The behavior of objects in the world, both system objects and physical objects, is more complex than simply being in one state at a time. The condition of being in more than one state at a time is called *concurrency*, or *concurrent states*. One way to show this is with a synchronization bar and concurrent paths, just as was done in activity diagrams (see Figure 4-15). A *path* is a sequential set of connected states and transitions. Another way to show concurrent states is to have states nested inside other, higher-level, states. These higher-level states are called *composite states*.

A *composite state* represents a higher level of abstraction and can contain nested states and transition paths. For example, in the previous printer example, we may want to identify an *On* state. But while the printer is on, it may also be idle or working. To show these two states, we draw lower-level statecharts within the *On* state. The rounded rectangle for the *On* state is divided into two compartments. The top compartment contains the name, and the lower compartment contains the nested states and transition paths. Figure 6-20 illustrates the notation for composite states. When the printer enters the *On* state, it automatically begins at the nested black dot and moves to the

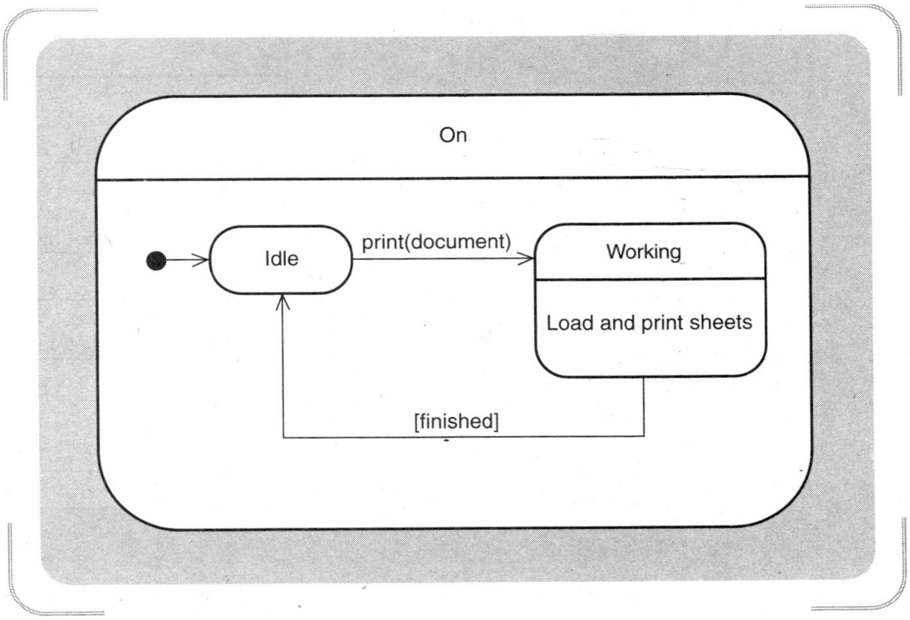

FIGURE 6-20
Sample composite states for the printer object

Idle state. So, the printer is in both the *On* state and the *Idle* state. When the print message is received, the printer makes the transition to the *Working* state but also remains in the *On* state. Some new notation is also introduced for the *Working* state. In this instance, the lower compartment contains the action-expressions, that is, the activities that occur while the printer is in the *Working* state.

Object behavior is frequently even more complex than that expressed with simple nested states. Perhaps an object has entire sets of states and transitions—multiple paths—that are active concurrently. To document concurrent behavior of a single object, we draw a composite state with the lower portion divided into multiple compartments, one for each concurrent path of behavior. For example, imagine a printer that has an input bin to hold the paper. This printer also cycles between two states in its work cycle of *Idle* and *Working*. We may want to describe two separate paths, one representing the states of the input paper tray and the other the states of the printing mechanism. The first path will have states of *Empty*, *Full*, and *Low*. The second path will contain the two states *Idle* and *Working*. These two paths are independent—the movement between states in one compartment is completely independent of movement between states in the other compartment.

The notation for composite states with nested paths can be expanded to represent multiple concurrent paths. Figure 6-21 extends the printer example from Figure 6-20. In this example, there are two concurrent paths within the composite state. The upper concurrent path represents the paper tray part of the printer. The two paths are completely independent, and the printer moves through the states and transitions in each path independently. When the Off button is pushed, the printer leaves the *On* state. Obviously, when the printer leaves the *On* state, it also leaves all of the paths in the nested states. It does not matter whether the printer is in a state or in the middle of a transition. When the Off button is pushed, all activity is stopped, and the printer exits the *On* state. Now that you know the basic notation of statecharts, we turn next to how to develop a statechart.

FIGURE 6-21
Concurrent paths for a printer in the *On* state

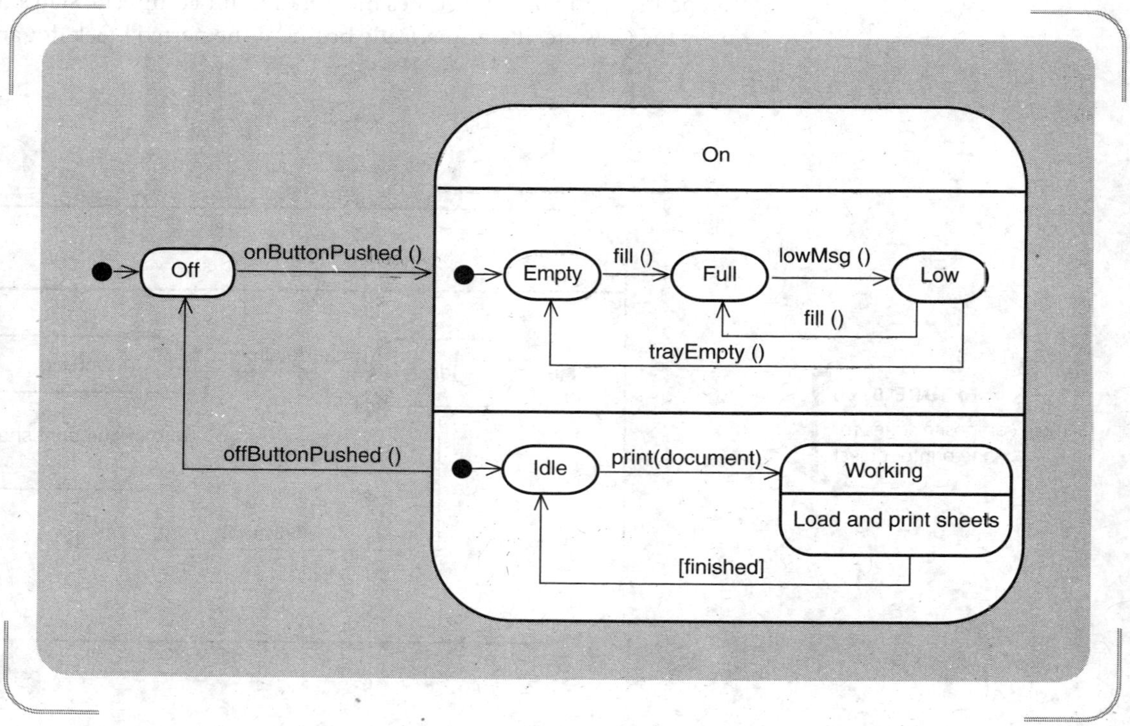

RULES FOR DEVELOPING STATECHARTS

Statechart development follows a set of rules. The rules help you to develop statecharts for classes in the problem domain. Usually the primary challenge in building a statechart is to identify the right states for the object. It may be helpful to pretend that you are the object itself. It is easy to pretend to be a customer, but a little more difficult to say, "I am an order," or, "I am a shipment. How do I come into existence? What states am I in?" However, if you can begin to think this way, it will help you develop statechart diagrams.

The other major area of difficulty for new analysts is to identify and handle composite states with nested threads. Usually, the primary cause of this difficulty is a lack of experience in thinking about concurrent behavior. The best solution is to remember that developing statecharts is an iterative behavior, more so than developing any other type of diagram. Analysts seldom get a statechart right the first time. They always draw it and then refine it again and again. Also, remember that when you are defining requirements, you are only getting a general idea of the behavior of an object. During design, as you build detailed sequence diagrams, you will have an opportunity to refine and correct important statecharts.

Finally, don't forget to ask about an exception condition—especially when you see the words *verify* or *check*. Normally, there will be two transitions out of states that verify something—one for acceptance and one for rejection.

Here is a list of steps that will help you get started in developing statecharts:

[1] **Review the class diagram and select the classes that will require statecharts.** Remember, we normally include only those that have various status conditions that are important to track in the system. Then begin with the classes that appear to have the simplest statecharts, such as the OrderItem class.

[2] **For each selected class in the group, make a list of all the status conditions you can identify.** At this point, simply brainstorm. If you are working in a team, have a brainstorming session with the whole team. Remember that you are defining states of being of the software classes. However, these states must also reflect the states for the real-world objects that are represented in software. Sometimes it is helpful to think of the physical object, identify states of the physical object, then translate those that are appropriate into corresponding system states or status conditions. It is also helpful to think of the life of the object. How does it come into existence in the system? When and how is it deleted from the system? Does it have active states? Does it have inactive states? Does it have states in which it is waiting? Think of activities done to the object or by the object. Often, the object will be in a particular state as these actions are occurring.

[3] **Begin building statechart fragments by identifying the transitions that cause an object to leave the identified state.** For example, if an Order is in a state of *Ready to be shipped*, then a transition such as beginShipping will cause the Order to leave that state.

[4] **Sequence these state-transition combinations in the correct order.** Then aggregate these combinations into larger fragments. As the fragments are being aggregated into larger paths, it is natural to begin to look for a natural life cycle for the object. Continue to build longer paths in the statechart by combining the fragments.

[5] **Review the paths and look for independent, concurrent paths.** When an item can be in two states concurrently, there are two possibilities. The two states may be on independent paths, as in the printer example of *Working* and *Full*. This occurs when the states and paths are independent, and one can

change without affecting the other. Alternately, one state may be a composite state, so that the two states should be nested, one inside the other. One way to identify a candidate for a composite state is to determine if it is concurrent with several other states, and these other states depend on the original state. For example, the *On* state has several other states and paths that can occur while the printer is in the *On* state, and those states depend on the printer being in the *On* state.

[6] **Look for additional transitions.** Often, during a first iteration, several of the possible combinations of state-transition-state are missed. One method to identify them is to take every paired combination of states and ask whether there is a valid transition between the states. Test for transitions in both directions.

[7] **Expand each transition with the appropriate message event, guard-condition, and action-expression.** Include with each state appropriate action-expressions. Much of this may have been done as the statechart fragments were being built.

[8] **Review and test each statechart.** We test statecharts by "desk-checking" them. Review each of your statecharts by doing the following:

a. Make sure your states are really states of the object in the class. Ensure that the names of states truly describe states of being of the object.
b. Follow the life cycle of an object from its coming into existence to its being deleted from the system. Be sure that all possible combinations are covered and that the paths on the statechart are accurate.
c. Be sure your diagram covers all exception conditions as well as the normal expected flow of behavior.
d. Look again for concurrent behavior (multiple paths) and the possibility of nested paths (complex states).

DEVELOPING RMO STATECHARTS

Let's practice these steps by developing two statecharts for RMO. Step 1 is to review the domain class diagram and select the classes that may have status conditions that need to be tracked. In this case, we select the Order and OrderItem classes. We assume that customers will want to know the status of their orders and the status of individual items on the order. Other classes that are candidates for statecharts are InventoryItem, to track in-stock or out-of-stock items; Shipment, to track arrivals; and possibly Customer, to track active and inactive customers. For our purposes here, we focus on the Order and OrderItem classes. We use the OrderItem class because it is simpler, and it is always best to start with the simplest class. Also, it is a dependent class—it depends on Order. Finally, it is best to use a bottom-up approach, starting with the lower items on a hierarchy, which usually have less ripple effect.

DEVELOPING THE ORDERITEM STATECHART

Start by identifying the possible status conditions that may be of interest. Some necessary status conditions are *Ready to be shipped, On back order*, and *Shipped*. An interesting question comes to mind at this point: Can an order item be partially shipped? In other words, if the customer ordered ten of a single item, but there are only five in inventory, should RMO ship those five and put the other five on back order? You should see the ramifications of this decision. The system and the database would need to be designed to track and monitor detailed information to support this capability. The domain class diagram for RMO (see Figure 5-31) indicates that an order item can be associated with either zero (not yet shipped) shipments or one (totally shipped) shipment. Based on the current specification, the definition does not allow partial shipments of order items.

This is just another example of the benefit of building models. Had we not been developing the statechart model, this question might never have been asked. The development of detailed models and diagrams is one of the most important activities that a system developer can perform. It forces analysts to ask fundamental questions. Sometimes new system developers think that model development is a waste of time, especially for small systems. However, truly understanding the users' needs before writing the program always saves time in the long run.

The next step is to identify exit transitions for each of the status conditions. Figure 6-22 is a table showing the states that have been defined and the exit transitions for each of those states. One additional state has been added to the list, *Newly added*, which covers the condition that occurs when an item has been added to the order, but the order is not complete or paid for, so the item is not ready for shipping.

FIGURE 6-22
States and exit transitions for OrderItem

STATE	TRANSITION CAUSING EXIT FROM STATE
Newly added	finishedAdding
Ready to ship	shipItem
On back order	itemArrived
Shipped	No exit transition defined

The fourth step is to combine the state-transition pairs into fragments and to build a statechart with the states in the correct sequence. Figure 6-23 illustrates the partially completed statechart. The flow from beginning to end for OrderItem is quite obvious. However, at least one transition seems to be missing. There should be some path to allow entry into the *On back order* state, so we recognize that this first-cut statechart needs some refinement. We will fix that in a moment.

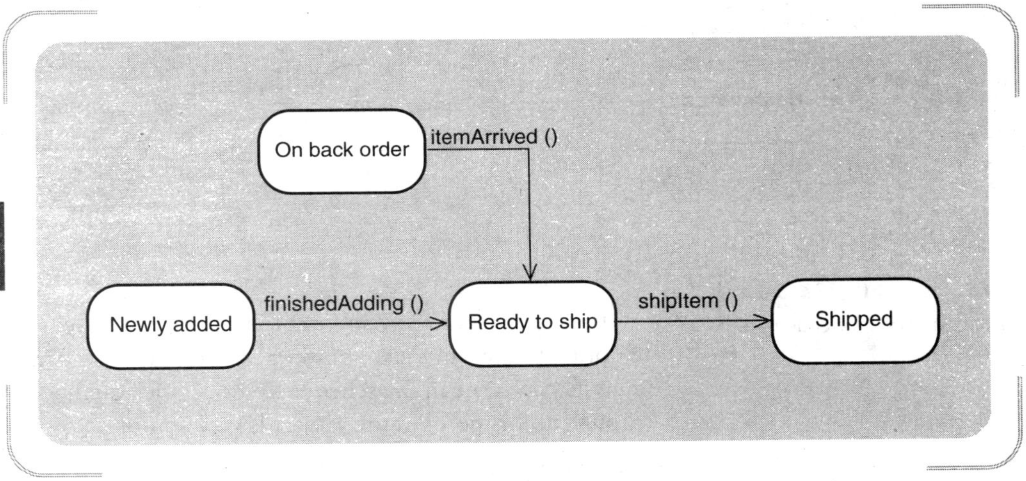

FIGURE 6-23
Partial statechart for OrderItem

The fifth step is to look for concurrent paths. In this case, it does not appear that an order item can be in any two of the identified states at the same time. Of course, since we chose to begin with a simple statechart, that is what was expected.

Step 6 is to look for additional transitions. This step is where we flesh out other necessary transitions. The first addition is to have a transition from *Newly added* to *On back order*. To continue, examine every pair of states to see whether there are other possible combinations. In particular, look for backward transitions. For example, can an order item go from *Ready to ship* to *On back order*? This would happen if the shipping clerk found that there were not enough items in the warehouse, even though the system indicated that there should have been. Other backward loops, such as from *Shipped* to *Ready to ship*, or from *On back order* to *Newly added*, do not make sense and are not included.

Step 7 is to complete all the transitions with correct names, guard-conditions, and action-expressions. Two new transition-names are added. The first is the transition from the beginning black dot to the *Newly added* state. That transition is the transition that causes the creation, or in system terms the instantiation, of a new OrderItem object. It is given the same name as the message into the system that adds it—addItem ( ). The final transition is the one that causes the order item to be removed from the system. This transition goes from the *Shipped* state to a final circled black dot, which is a final pseudostate. On the assumption that it is archived to a backup tape when it is deleted from the active system, that transition is named archive ( ).

Action-expressions are added to the transitions to indicate any special action that is initiated by the object or on the object. In this case, only one action needs to be done. When an item that was *Ready to ship* moves to *On back order*, the system should initiate a new purchase order to the supplier to buy more items. So, on the markBackordered ( ) transition, an action-expression is noted to place a purchase order. Figure 6-24 illustrates the final statechart for OrderItem.

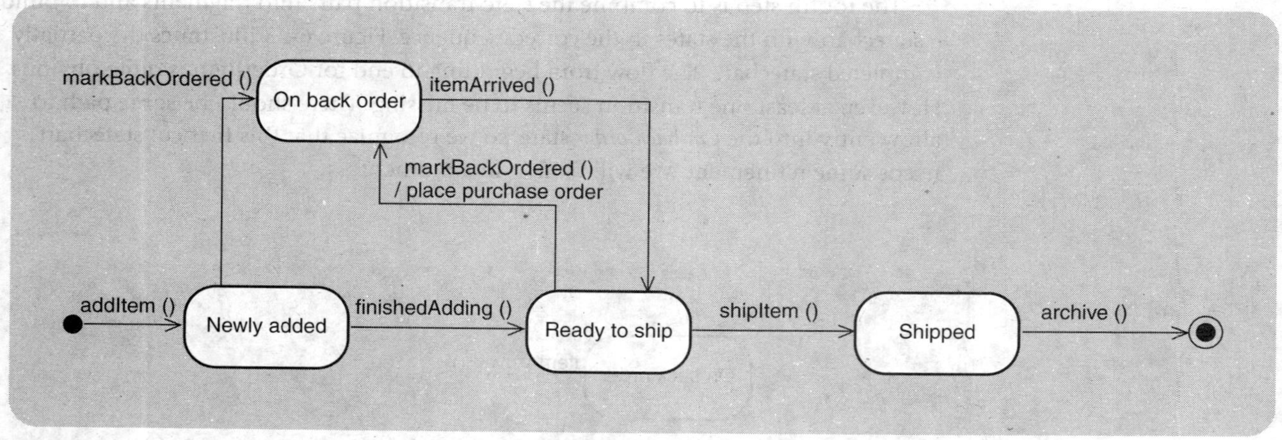

FIGURE 6-24
Final statechart for OrderItem

The final step, review and test the statechart, is the quality-review step. It is always tempting to omit this step; however, a good project manager ensures that the systems analysts have time in the schedule to do a quick quality check of their models. A walkthrough at this point in the project is very appropriate.

DEVELOPING THE ORDER STATECHART

An Order object is a little more complex than the OrderItem objects. In this example, you will see some additional features of statecharts that support more complex objects.

Figure 6-25 is a table of the defined states and exit transitions that, on first iteration, appear to be required. Reading from top to bottom, the states mirror the life cycle of an order. First, an order comes into existence and is ready to have items added to it—*Open for item adds*. The users in RMO indicated that they wanted an order to remain in this state for 24 hours in case the customer wanted to add more items. After all the items are added, the order is *Ready for shipping*. Next, it goes to shipping and is in the *In shipping* state. At this point, it is not quite clear how *In shipping* and *Waiting for back orders* relate to each other. That relationship will have to be sorted out as the statechart is being built. Finally, the order is *Shipped*, and after the payment clears, it is *Closed*.

FIGURE 6-25
States and exit transitions for Order

STATE	EXIT TRANSITION
Open for item adds	completeOrder
Ready for shipping	beginShipping
In shipping	shippingComplete
Waiting for back orders	backOrdersArrive
Shipped	paymentCleared
Closed	archive

In step 4, fragments are built and combined to yield the first-cut statechart. Figure 6-26 illustrates the first-cut statechart. The statechart built from the fragments appears to be correct for the most part. However, we note that there are some problems with the *Waiting for back orders* state.

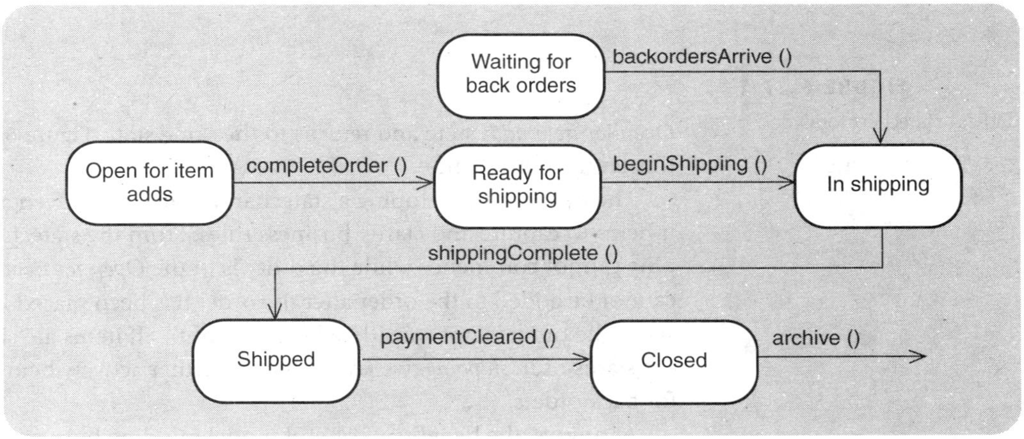

FIGURE 6-26
First-cut statechart for Order

After some analysis, we decide that being *In shipping* and *Waiting for back orders* are concurrent states. And another state is needed, called *Being shipped*, for the state in which the shipping clerk is actively shipping items. One way to show the life of an order is to put it in the *In shipping* state when shipping begins. It also enters the *Being shipped* state at that point. The order can cycle between *Being shipped* and *Waiting for back orders*. The exit out of the composite state only occurs from the *Being shipped* state, which is inside the *In shipping* state. Obviously, upon leaving the inside state, the order also leaves the composite *In shipping* state.

As we go through steps 5, 6, and 7, we note that new transitions must be added. The creation transition from the initial pseudostate is required. Also, transitions must be included to show when items are being added and when they are being shipped. Usually, we put these looping activities on transitions that leave a state and return to the same state. In this case, the transition is called addItem ( ). Note how it leaves the

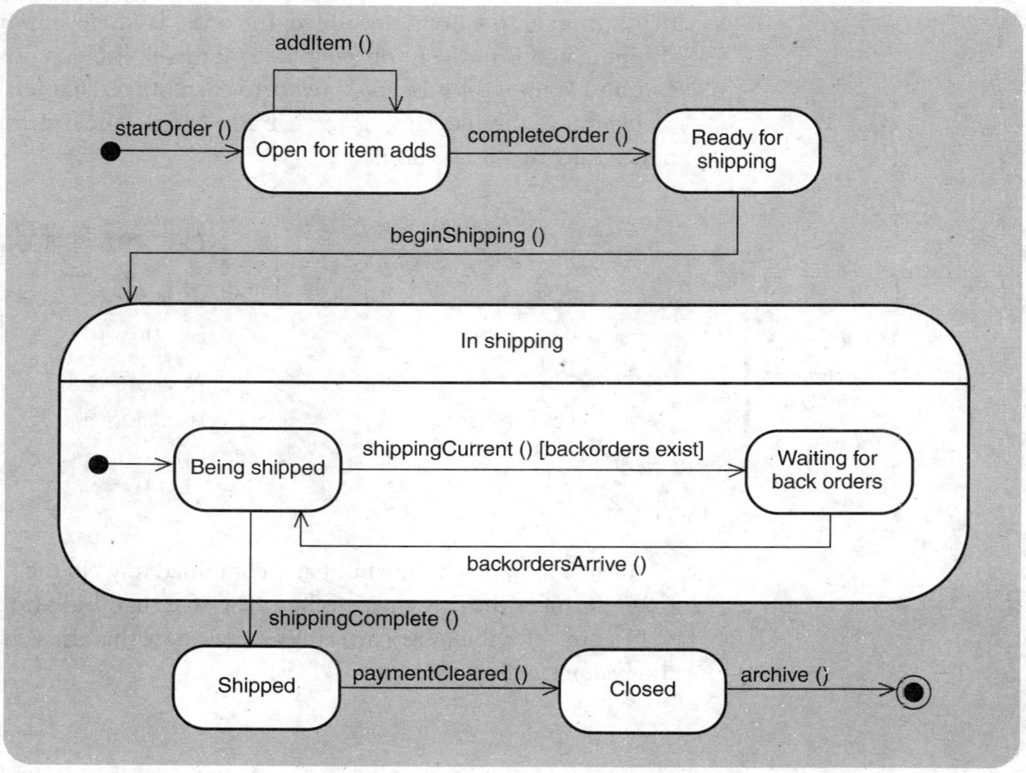

FIGURE 6-27
Second-cut statechart for Order

Open for item adds state and returns to the same state. Figure 6-27 takes the statechart to this level of completion.

The benefit of developing a statechart for an object, even a business object, is that it helps to capture and clarify business rules. From the statechart, we can see that shipping cannot commence while the order is in the *Open for item adds* state. New items cannot be added to the order after the order has been placed in the *Ready for shipping* state. The order is not considered shipped until all items are shipped. If the order has the status of *In shipping*, we know that it is either actively being worked on or waiting for back orders.

As always, the benefits of careful model building help us gain a true understanding of the system requirements. Let's now look at the big picture and pull the different models into a whole to see how they fit together.

INTEGRATING OBJECT-ORIENTED MODELS

The diagrams described in this chapter allow analysts to completely specify the system requirements. With the UP development approach, a set of requirements models for the work to be done during a given iteration is defined. During the inception phase, a complete use case diagram is used to define the complete scope of the new system. However, the detailed diagrams, which define the internal processing of a particular use case, are only necessary in the appropriate iteration.

In Chapter 5, you learned how to develop the domain class diagram. Although we did not repeat that discussion in this chapter, the domain class diagram is also begun and developed as far as possible during the inception phase. An important component of understanding the scope of the new system is to understand the overall information requirements. Since the domain model describes the data requirements, a first cut at a complete domain model is necessary. Refinement and actual implementation of many classes must wait for later iterations, but the domain model should be fairly complete. The domain model is necessary to help the analyst identify all of the domain classes that are required in the new system. Although we do not focus on database design in this chapter, you will learn in a later chapter how the domain model is used to design the database.

BEST PRACTICE: Developing and integrating models are critical to ensure that you understand the business requirements.

Throughout the chapter, you have seen how the construction of one diagram depends on information provided by another diagram. You have also seen that the development of a new diagram often helps refine and correct a previous diagram. You should also have noted that the development of detailed diagrams is critical to gaining a thorough understanding of the user requirements. Figure 6-28 illustrates the primary relationships among the requirements models for OO development. The use case diagram and other diagrams on the left are used to capture the processes of the new system. The class diagram box and its dependencies capture information about the classes for the new system. The solid arrows represent major dependencies, and the dashed arrows show a minor dependency. The dependencies generally flow from top to bottom, but some arrows have two heads to illustrate that influence goes in both directions.

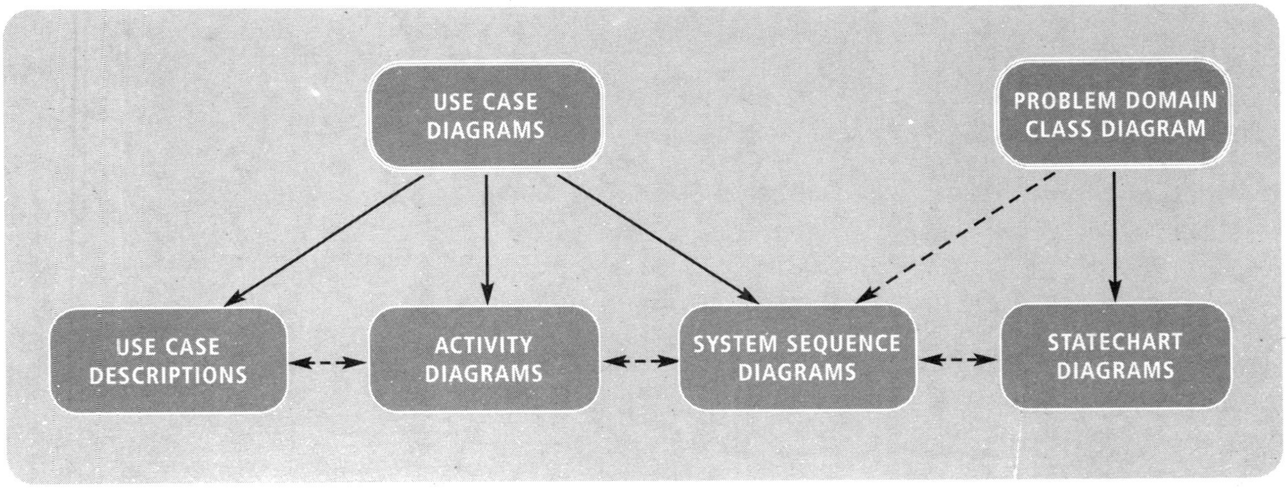

FIGURE 6-28
Relationships among OO requirements models

Note that the use case diagram and the problem domain class diagram are the primary models from which others draw information. You should develop those two diagrams as completely as possible. In earlier chapters, you learned how to do a CRUD analysis. In this chapter we noted that a CRUD analysis performed between the class diagram and use case diagram helps ensure that they are as complete as possible. The detailed descriptions, either in narrative format or in activity diagrams, are important internal documentation of the use cases and must completely support the use case diagram. Internal descriptions such as pre- and postconditions utilize information from the class diagram. These detailed descriptions are also important for development of system sequence diagrams. So, the detailed descriptions, activity diagrams, and system sequence diagrams must all be consistent with regard to the steps of a particular use case. As you progress in developing the system, and especially as you begin doing detailed system design, you will find that understanding the relationships among these models is an important element in the quality of your models.

Summary

The object-oriented approach has a complete set of diagrams that together document the users' needs and define the system requirements. These requirements are specified using the following models:

- Use case diagrams
- Use case detailed models, either descriptive format or activity diagram
- System sequence diagrams (SSDs)
- Domain model class diagrams—as discussed in Chapter 5
- Statechart diagrams

A use case diagram documents the various ways that the system can be used. It can be developed independently or in conjunction with the event table, in which one event triggers one use case. A use case consists of actors, use cases, and connecting lines. A use case identifies a single function that the system supports. An actor represents a role performed by someone or something that uses the system. The connecting lines indicate which actors invoke which use cases. Use cases can also invoke other use cases as a common subroutine. This type of connection between use cases is called the «includes» relationship.

The internal activities of a use case are first described by an internal flow of activities. It is possible to have several different internal flows, which represent different scenarios of the same use case. Thus, a use case may have several scenarios. These details are documented either in descriptive format or with activity diagrams to describe the workflows. Preconditions and postconditions can be defined for each use case to assist in understanding other effects on the system of executing a use case.

Another diagram that provides more details of the processing requirements of a use case is a system sequence diagram, or SSD. An SSD documents the inputs and outputs of the system. The scope of each SSD is usually a use case or a scenario within a use case. The components of an SSD are the actor—the same actor identified in the use case—and the system. The system is treated as a black box, in that the internal processing is not addressed. Messages, which represent the inputs, are sent from the actor to the system. Output messages are returned from the system to the actor. The sequence of messages is indicated by the top-to-bottom sequence of messages.

A statechart is an effective technique to describe the behavior, or life cycle, of an object or of the system. A statechart has two major components, states and transitions. A state is a condition of the object. For business objects, a state is often synonymous with a status condition of an object. For example, the state, or status condition, of a customer order might be "shipped." Transitions are the connectors between the states, and they permit an object to move from state to state. Hence, a statechart is a diagram that identifies all of the states of an object and the actions that cause it to change from state to state. Statecharts are useful during design for understanding the behavior of real-world objects, which must be captured within the system, and also for specifying precise behavior and constraints of the portions of the final solution system.

KEY TERMS

action-expression, p. 239
composite state, p. 239
concurrency, or concurrent states, p. 239
destination state, p. 238
guard-condition, p. 238
interaction diagram, p. 226
lifeline, or object lifeline, p. 228
message event, p. 238
origin state, p. 238
path, p. 239
postcondition, p. 225
precondition, p. 225
pseudostate, p. 237
scenario, or use case instance, p. 220
state, p. 238
statechart diagram, p. 214
system sequence diagram, p. 213
transition, p. 238
true/false condition, p. 230
use case diagram, p. 213

REVIEW QUESTIONS

1. What is UML? What type of modeling is it used for?
2. What are the two basic parts of a use case model? What is its purpose or objective?
3. What is the difference between a use case description and an activity diagram?
4. What is meant by a scenario? What is another term used to describe a scenario?
5. Why do actors have "hands"?
6. What is the «includes» relationship used for?
7. How does the focus on the boundary condition of a use case diagram differ from that of an event table?
8. With regard to a use case, what is an activity diagram used for?
9. What is a precondition? What is a postcondition? Why are they important in use case development?
10. What is the purpose of a system sequence diagram? What symbols are used in a system sequence diagram?
11. What steps are required to develop a system sequence diagram?
12. Identify the models explained in this chapter and their relationship to each other.
13. What is the purpose of a statechart?
14. List the primary steps for developing a statechart.
15. List the elements that make up a transition description. Which are optional?
16. What is a nested state? What is a composite state? What are they used for?

THINKING CRITICALLY

1. The following description identifies the business need for a simple university library system. Based on the description, develop the following diagrams:
   a. Develop a domain class diagram.
   b. Develop a use case diagram.
   c. Do a CRUD analysis to ensure that the identified classes and use cases are consistent. Update both your class diagram and use case diagram as necessary.

   Submit your class diagram, your use case diagram, and your CRUD matrix to your instructor.

   This case is a simplified (initial draft) description of a new system for the university library. Of course, the library system must keep track of books. Information is maintained about both book titles and the individual book copies. The book title class maintains information about title, author, publisher, and catalog number. The individual copy class maintains copy number, edition, publication year, ISBN, book status (whether it is on the shelf or on loan), and date due back in.

   The library also keeps track of patrons to the library. Since it is a university library, there are several types of patrons, each with different privileges. There are faculty patrons, graduate student patrons, and undergraduate student patrons. Basic information about all patrons is name, address, and telephone number. For faculty patrons, additional information is office address and telephone number. For graduate students, information such as graduate program and advisor is maintained. For undergraduate students, information on program and total credit hours is maintained.

   The library also keeps information about library loans. A library loan is a somewhat abstract object. A loan occurs when a patron approaches the circulation desk with a stack of books to check out. Over time a patron can have many loans. A loan can have many physical books associated with it. (And a physical book can be on many loans over a period of time. Information about past loans is kept in the database.) So, in this case, an association class should probably be created for loaned books.

   If a patron wants a book that is checked out, he/she can put that title on reserve. This is another class that does not represent a concrete object. Each reservation is for only one title and one patron. Information such as date reserved, priority, and date fulfilled is maintained. When the reservation is fulfilled, the system associates that reservation with the loan on which the book was checked out.

   Patrons have access to the library information to search for book titles and to see whether a book is available. A patron can also reserve a title if all copies are checked out. When patrons bring books to the circulation desk, a clerk checks the books out on a loan. Clerks also check books in. When books are dropped in the return slot, the clerks check them in. Stocking clerks keep track of the arrival of new books.

   The managers in the library have their own activities. They will print out reports of book titles by category. They also like to see (online) all overdue books. When books get damaged or destroyed, they will delete information about book copies. Managers also like to see what books are on reserve

The following description identifies the business need for a dental clinic system. Based on the description, develop the following diagrams:

a. Develop a domain class diagram.
b. Develop a use case diagram.
c. Do a CRUD analysis to ensure that the identified classes and use cases are consistent. Update both your class diagram and use case diagram as necessary.

Submit your class diagram, your use case diagram, and your CRUD matrix to your instructor.

A clinic with three dentists and several dental hygienists needed a system to help administer patient records. This system does not keep any medical records. It only processes patient administration.

Each patient has a record with his/her name, date of birth, gender, date of first visit, and date of last visit. Patient records are grouped together under a household. A household has attributes such as name of head of household, address, and telephone number. Each household is also associated with an insurance carrier record. The insurance carrier record contains name of insurance company, address, billing contact person, and telephone number.

In the clinic, each member of the staff also has a record that tracks who works with a patient (dentist, dental hygienist, x-ray technician). Since the system focuses on patient administration records, only minimal information is kept about staff personnel, such as name, address, and telephone number. Information is maintained about each office visit, such as date, insurance copay amount (amount paid by the patient), paid code, and amount actually paid. Each visit is for a single patient, but of course, a patient will have many office visits in the system. During each visit, more than one member of the staff may be involved in the patient's treatment. For example, the x-ray technician, dentist, and dental hygienist may all be involved on a single visit. In fact, it is even possible that more than one dentist may be involved with a patient, since some dentists are specialists in such things as crown work. For each *staff member does procedure in a visit* combination (many-to-many), detailed information is kept about the procedure. This information includes type of procedure, description, tooth involved, the copay amount, the total charge, the amount paid, and the amount the insurance company denied.

Finally, the system also keeps track of invoices. There are two types of invoices: invoices to insurance companies and invoices to heads of households. Both types of invoices are fairly similar, listing each visit, the procedures involved, the patient copay amount, and the total due. Obviously, the totals for the insurance company are different from the amounts owed by patients. Even though an invoice is a report (printed out), it also contains some information such as date sent, total amount, amount already paid, amount due and also the total received, date received, and total denied. (Insurance companies do not always pay the full amount they are billed for.)

The receptionist keeps track of patient and head-of-household information. He/she will enter information about the patient and head of household. He/she will also keep track of office visits by each patient. Patient information is also entered and maintained by the office business manager. In addition, the business manager maintains the information about the dental staff.

The business manager also prints the invoices. Patient invoices are printed monthly and sent to the head of household. Insurance invoices are printed weekly. When the invoices are printed, the business manager double-checks a few invoices against information in the system to make sure it is being aggregated correctly. The business manager also enters the payment information when it is received.

Each member of the dental staff is responsible for entering information about the dental procedures that he/she performs.

The business manager also prints an overdue invoice report showing heads of household who are behind on their payments. Sometimes dentists like to see a list of the procedures they performed during a week or month, and they can request that report.

3. Interpret and explain the use case diagram in Figure 6-29. Explain the various roles of those using the inventory system and the functions that each role requires. Explain the relationships and the ways the use cases are related to each other.
4. Given the following narrative, do the following:
   a. Develop an activity diagram for each scenario.
   b. Complete a fully developed use case description for each scenario.

   Quality Building Supply has two kinds of customers: contractors and the general public. Sales to each are slightly different.

   When a contractor buys materials, he/she takes them to the contractors' checkout desk. The clerk enters the contractor's name into the system. The system displays the contractor's information, including his/her current credit standing.

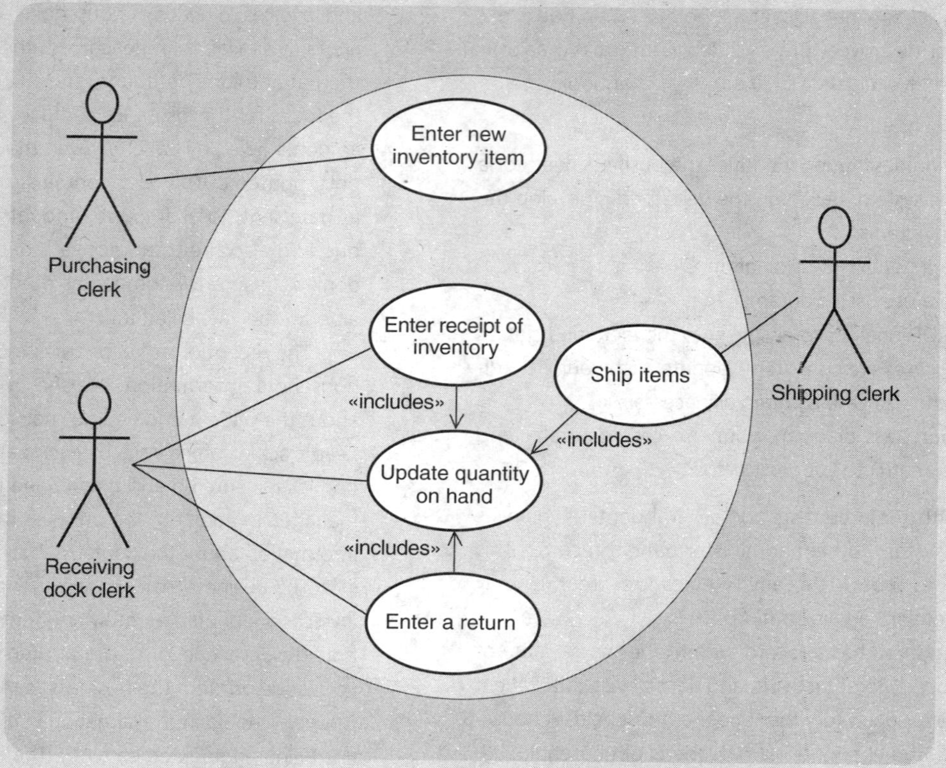

FIGURE 6-29
A use case diagram for the inventory system

The clerk then opens up a new ticket (sale) for the contractor. Next, the clerk scans in each item to be purchased. The system finds the price of the item and adds the item to the ticket. At the end of the purchase, the clerk indicates the end of the sale. The system compares the total amount against the contractor's current credit limit, and if the credit balance is adequate, finalizes the sale. The system creates an electronic ticket for the items, and the contractor's credit limit is reduced by the amount of the sale. Some contractors like to keep a record of their purchases, so they request that the ticket details be printed out. Others aren't interested in a printout.

A sale to the general public is simply entered into the cash register, and a paper receipt is printed as the items are identified. Payment can be by cash, check, or credit card. The clerk must enter the type of payment to ensure that the cash register balances at the end of the shift. For credit card payments, the system prints out a credit card voucher that the customer must sign.

5. Given the following narrative, develop either an activity diagram or a fully developed description for a use case of *Add a new vehicle to an existing policy* in a car insurance system.

A customer calls an insurance clerk at the insurance company and gives his/her policy number. The clerk enters this information, and the system displays the basic insurance policy. The clerk then checks the information to make sure that the premiums are current and the pol cy is in force.

The customer gives the make, model, year, and vehicle identification number (VIN) of the car to be added to the policy. The clerk enters this information, and the system confirms that the given data are valid. Next, the customer selects the types of coverage desired and the amount of each. The clerk enters the information, and the system records each and validates the requested amount against the policy limits. After all of the coverages have been entered, the system validates the total coverage against valid dollar ranges as well as the amounts for other cars on the policy.

Finally, the customer must identify all drivers and the percentage of time they drive the car. If a new driver is to be added, then another use case, *Add new driver*, is invoked.

At the end of the process, the system updates the policy, calculates a new premium amount, and prints the updated policy statement to be mailed out to the policy owner.

6. Given the following list of classes and relationships for the car insurance system in the preceding exercise, list the preconditions (i.e., the objects that need to exist in the system before the use case begins) and the postconditions (i.e., the objects and relationships that must exist after the use

case is completed). The use case you should consider is *Add a new vehicle to an existing policy.*

Classes in the system:

a. Policy
b. InsuredPerson
c. InsuredVehicle
d. Coverage
e. StandardCoverage (lists standard insurance coverages with prices by rating category)
f. StandardVehicle (lists all types of vehicles ever made)

Relationships in the system:

a. Policy has InsuredPersons (one to many)
b. Policy has InsuredVehicles (one to many)
c. Vehicle has Coverages (one to many)
d. Coverage is a type of StandardCoverage
e. Vehicle is a StandardVehicle

7. Develop a system sequence diagram based on the narrative and your activity diagram for Thinking Critically problem 4.
8. Develop a system sequence diagram based on the narrative or your activity diagram for Thinking Critically problem 5.
9. Review the cellular telephone statechart in Figure 6-30, then answer the following questions (note that this telephone has unique characteristics that are not found in ordinary telephones. Base your answers only on the statechart):
   a. What event turns on the telephone?
   b. What states does the telephone go into when it is turned on?
   c. What are the three ways that the telephone can be turned off? Identify what must be true for each case.
   d. Can the telephone turn off in the middle of the *Active* (*Talking*) state?
   e. How can the telephone get to the *Active* (*Talking*) state?

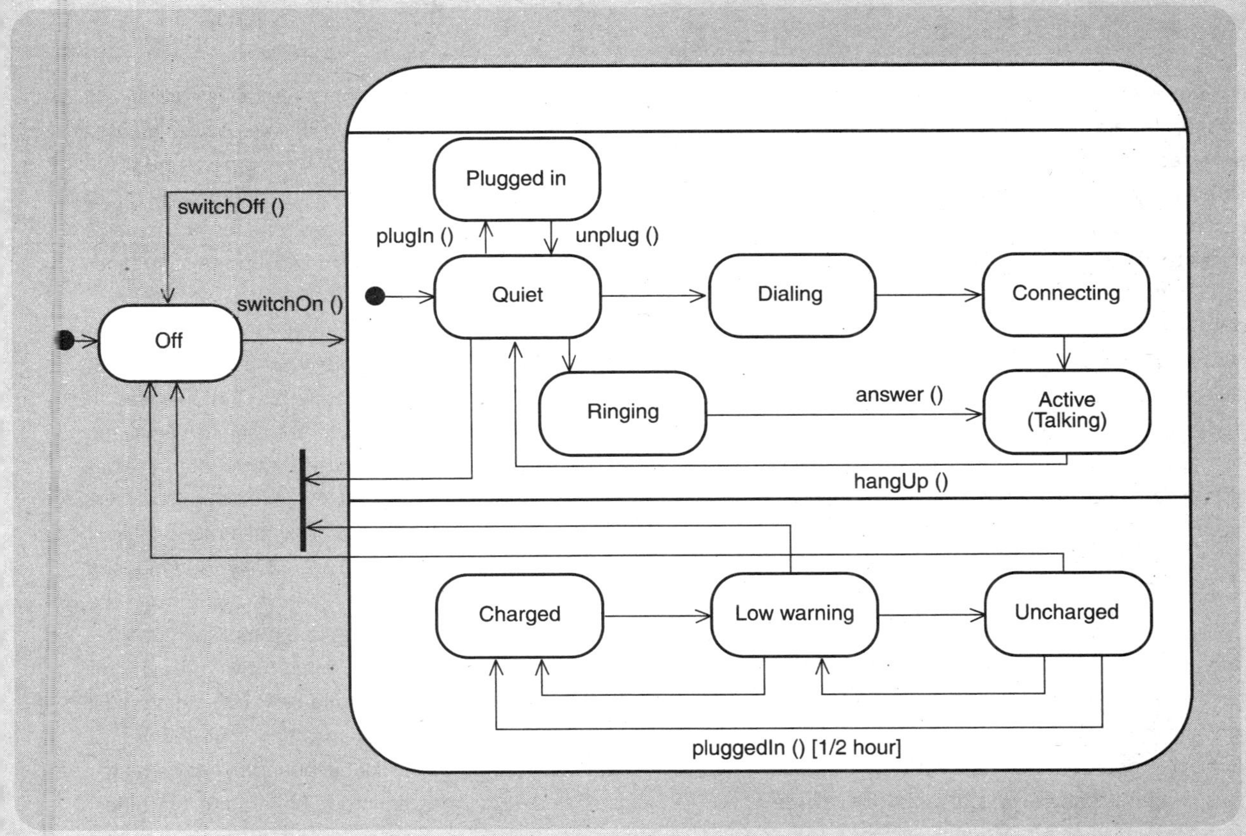

FIGURE 6-30
lular telephone statechart

f. Can the telephone be plugged in while someone is talking?

g. Can the telephone change battery states while someone is talking? Explain which transition is allowed, and which is not allowed.

h. What states are concurrent with what other states? Construct a two-column table showing states with concurrent states.

10. Given the following description of a Certified Parcel Shipments (CPS) shipment, first identify all of the states and exit transitions and then develop a statechart.

A shipment is first recognized after it has been picked up from a customer. Once it is in the system, it is considered to be active and in transit. Every time it goes through a checkpoint, such as arrival at an intermediate destination, it is scanned and a record is created indicating the time and place of the checkpoint scan. The status changes when it is placed on the delivery truck. It is still active, but now it is also considered to have a status of delivery pending. Of course, once it is delivered, the status changes again.

From time to time, a shipment has a destination that is outside the CPS service area. In those cases, CPS has working relationships with other couriers. Once a package is handed off to another courier, it is noted as being handed over. In those instances, a tracking number for the new courier is recorded (if it is provided). CPS also asks the new courier to provide a status change notice once the package has been delivered.

Unfortunately, from time to time a package gets lost. In those cases, it remains in an active state for two weeks but is also marked as misplaced. If after two weeks the package has not been found, it is considered lost. At that point the customer can initiate lost procedures to recover any damages.

EXPERIENTIAL EXERCISES

1. The functionality required by Rocky Mountain Outfitters' customer support system is also found in several real-world companies. Based on your experience with online shopping and shopping carts, build a use case diagram of functions that a Web customer can perform (similar to Figure 6-5). Web sites to which you might refer include L.L. Bean (www.llbean.com/), Lands' End (www.landsend.com/), Amazon.com (www.amazon.com/), and Barnes & Noble Booksellers (www.barnesandnoble.com/).
2. Develop fully developed use case descriptions for each of the use cases you defined in exercise 1.
3. Based on the flow of activities you developed in exercise 2, develop system sequence diagrams for those same use cases and scenarios. Add preconditions and postconditions to each use case.
4. Analyze the information requirements of the Web site from exercise 1. Doing a reverse CRUD analysis (going from the use case diagram to the domain model class diagram) will help you identify classes. As a review of domain modeling, develop a domain model class diagram.
5. Locate a company in your area that does software development. A consulting company or a company with a large staff of information systems professionals will tend to be more rigorous in its approach to software development. Set up an interview. Determine the development approaches that the company uses. Many companies still use traditional structured techniques combined with some object-oriented development. In other companies, some projects are structured, while other projects are object-oriented. Find out what kinds of modeling the company does for requirements specification. Compare your findings with the techniques taught in this chapter.
6. IBM Rational is a company that is a wholly owned subsidiary of IBM. The authors of UML were also executives of Rational Corporation. Consequently, IBM Rational was an early leader in developing CASE tools to support UML and object-oriented modeling. You can download an evaluation copy of IBM Rational's UML CASE (IBM Rational XDE Modeler) tool and use the tool to draw the RMO diagrams. This will give you experience with a widely used industry tool. Alternately, your college or university can enroll in the Seed program and provide copies of the tools in its laboratories. The URL is http://www-306.ibm.com/software/rational/. Statecharts are a variation of a basic computer model called a *finite state machine*, which has a rich theoretical body of knowledge. Using Google or another good search engine, find some articles about finite state machines. Identify and list several of the different names for this model, and describe some of the common uses for it.

Case Studies

THE REAL ESTATE MULTIPLE LISTING SERVICE SYSTEM

Refer to the description of the Real Estate Multiple Listing Service system in the Chapter 5 Case Studies. Using the event table and domain class diagram for that system as a starting point, develop the following object-oriented models:

[1] Develop a use case diagram.

[2] Develop a fully developed use case description or an activity diagram for each use case.

[3] Develop a system sequence diagram for each use case.

[4] Based on the information provided in the case, develop a statechart for a property listing.

THE STATE PATROL TICKET PROCESSING SYSTEM

Refer to the description of the State Patrol ticket processing system in the Chapter 5 Case Studies. Using the event table and domain class diagram for that system as a starting point, develop the following object-oriented models:

[1] Develop a use case diagram.

[2] Develop fully developed use case descriptions for two of the primary use cases, such as *Recording a traffic ticket* and *Scheduling a court date*.

[3] Develop system sequence diagrams for those same use cases.

[4] Develop a statechart for a ticket.

THE DOWNTOWN VIDEOS RENTAL SYSTEM

DownTown Videos is a chain of 11 video stores scattered throughout a major metropolitan area in the Midwest. The chain started with a single store several years ago and has grown to its present size. Paul Lowes, the owner of the chain, knows that competing with the national chains will require a state-of-the-art movie rental system. You have been asked to develop the system requirements for the new system.

Each store has a stock of movies and video games for rent. For this first iteration, just focus on the movies. It is important to keep track of each movie title: to know and to identify its category (classical, drama, comedy, and so on), its rental type (new release, standard), movie rating, and other general information such as movie producer, release date, and cost. In addition to tracking each title, the business must track individual copies to note their purchase date, their condition, their type (VHS or DVD), and their rental status. User functions must be provided to maintain this inventory information.

Customers, the lifeblood of the business, are also tracked. DownTown considers each household to be a customer, so special mailings and promotions are offered to each household. For any given customer, several people may be authorized to rent videos and games. The primary contact for each customer can also establish rental parameters for other members of the household. For example, if a parent wants to limit a child's rental authorization to only PG and PG-13 movies, the system will track that.

Each time a movie is rented, the system must keep track of which copies of which movies are rented, the rental date and time and the return date and time, and the household and person renting the movie. Each rental is considered to be open until all of the movies and games have been returned. Customers pay for rentals when checking out videos at the store.

For this case, develop the following diagrams:

[1] A use case.diagram. Analyze user functions. Also do a CRUD analysis based on the class diagram.

[2] An activity diagram for each of the use cases having to do with renting and checking in movies and for the use cases to maintain customer and family member information

[3] A system sequence diagram for each of the use cases from problem 2

[4] A statechart identifying the possible states (status conditions) for a physical copy of a movie, based on the case descriptions given previously and your knowledge of how a video store might work

THEEYESHAVEIT.COM BOOK EXCHANGE

TheEyesHaveIt.com Book Exchange is a type of e-business exchange that does business entirely on the Internet. The company acts as a clearinghouse for both buyers and sellers of used books.

For a person to offer books for sale, he/she must register with TheEyesHaveIt. The person must provide a current physical address and telephone number, as well as a current e-mail address. The system will then maintain an open account for this person. Access to the system as a seller is through a secure, authenticated portal.

A seller can list books on the system through a special Internet form. Information required includes all of the pertinent information about the book, its category, its general condition, and the asking price. A seller may list as many books as desired. The system maintains an index of all books in the system so that buyers can use the search engine to search for books. The search engine allows searches by title, author, category, and keyword.

People wanting to buy books come to the site and search for the books they want. When they decide to buy, they must open an account with a credit card to pay for the books. The system maintains all of this information on secure servers.

When a request to purchase is made, along with the payment, TheEyesHaveIt.com sends an e-mail notice to the seller of the book. It also marks the book as sold. The system maintains an open order until it receives notice that the book has been shipped. Once the seller receives notice that a listed book has been sold, he/she must notify the buyer via e-mail within 48 hours that the purchase is noted. Shipment of the order must be made within 24 hours after the seller sends the notification e-mail. The seller sends a notification to both the buyer and TheEyesHaveIt.com when the shipment is made.

After receiving notice of shipment, TheEyesHaveIt.com maintains the order in a shipped status. At the end of each month, a check is mailed to each seller for the book orders that have been in a shipped status for 30 days. The 30-day waiting period is to allow the buyer to notify TheEyesHaveIt.com if the shipment does not arrive for some reason, or if the book is not in the condition that was advertised.

The buyers can, if they desire, enter a service code for the seller. The service code is an indication of how well the seller is servicing book purchases. Some sellers are very active and use TheEyesHaveIt.com as a major outlet for selling books. So, a service code is an important indicator to potential buyers.

For this case, develop the following diagrams:

[1] A use case diagram

[2] A fully developed description of two use cases such as *Add a seller* and *Record a book order*

[3] A system sequence diagram for each of the two use cases in problem 2

RETHINKING ROCKY MOUNTAIN OUTFITTERS

ROCKY MOUNTAIN OUTFITTERS

The event table for RMO is given in Figure 5-11. Based on this event table and the domain model class diagram shown in Figure 5-31, the use case diagram in Figure 6-4 was developed. Chapter 6 illustrates detailed models (activity and system sequence diagrams) for *Create new order*.

Using the information provided in the RMO case descriptions and the figures in the book (Figure 5-11, 6-4, and 5-31), develop a fully developed use case description and system sequence diagram for each of the following Customer actor use cases: (1) *Update order* and (2) *Create order return*. Now do the same for both of the Shipping actor use cases.

FOCUSING ON RELIABLE PHARMACEUTICAL SERVICE

Reliable PHARMACEUTICALS

Previous chapters have described the activities and processes of Reliable Pharmaceutical Service. Use the previous descriptions, particularly the basic description in Chapter 1 and the detailed descriptions from Chapter 5, as well as the following, additional description of the case, to develop object-oriented requirements models.

Company processes (for use case development). There are several points in the order-fulfillment process where information must be recorded in the system. Obviously, new orders must be recorded. Case manifests must be printed at the start of each shift. In fact, since a prescription itself may take a fairly long time to be completely used, as in the case of long-standing prescriptions, each time a medication is sent out (prescription fulfillment), information must be entered into the system, noting the quantity of medication that was sent and which pharmacist filled the prescription for that shift.

As explained in Chapter 5, basic information about all of the patients, the nursing homes, the staff, the insurance companies, and so forth must also be recorded in the system.

Information requirements (for class diagram requirements). Reliable needs to know about the patients, the nursing home, and the nursing-home unit where each patient resides. Each nursing home has at least one but possibly many units. A patient is assigned to a specific unit.

Prescriptions are rather complex. They contain basic information, such as ID number, original date of order, drug, unit of dosage (pill, teaspoon, suppository), size of dosage (milligrams, number of teaspoons), frequency or period of dosage (daily, twice a day, every other day, every four hours), and special considerations (take with food, take before meals). In addition, there are several types of prescriptions, each with unique characteristics. Some orders are for a single, one-time-only prescription. Some orders are for a certain number of dosages (pills). Some orders are for a time period (start date, end date). Information about the prescription order must be maintained. An order occurs when the nursing home phones in the needed prescriptions. Since prescriptions may last for an extended period of time, a prescription is a separate entity from the order itself. The system records what employee accepted and entered the original order.

The system also has basic data about all drugs. Each drug has generic information, such as name, chemical, and manufacturer. However, more detailed information for each type of dosage, such as the size of each pill, is also kept. A single drug may have many different dosage sizes and types.

In addition, information about the fulfillment of orders must also be maintained. For example, on a prescription for a number of pills, each time a pill or a number of pills is dispensed, the system must keep a record of that fact. A record is also maintained of which pharmacist or assistant fulfilled the order. Assume all prescriptions are dispensed only as needed for a 12-hour shift.

Basic data are kept about prescription payers, such as name, address, and contact person. For this first iteration, do not worry about billing or payments. Those capabilities may be added in a later iteration.

Based on your previous work, the cases from prior chapters, and the description here, do the following:

[1] Refine and extend your domain class diagram developed in Chapter 5 as necessary.

[2] Develop a use case diagram. Base it directly on the event table you created for Chapter 5. Be sure to include a CRUD analysis with your class diagram from question 1 and discuss what additional use cases might be needed, based on your CRUD analysis.

[3] Develop an activity diagram for each use case related to entering new orders, creating case manifests, and fulfilling orders. You should have at least three activity diagrams. Write a fully developed use case description for each of these use cases.

[4] Develop a system sequence diagram for each use case you developed in question 3.

[5] Develop a statechart for an order.

FURTHER RESOURCES

Grady Booch, James Rumbaugh, and Ivar Jacobson, *The Unified Modeling Language User Guide*. Addison-Wesley, 1999.

E. Reed Doke, J. W. Satzinger, and S. R. Williams, *Object-Oriented Application Development Using Java*. Course Technology, 2002.

Hans-Erik Eriksson and Magnus Penker, *UML Toolkit*. John Wiley & Sons, 1998.

Martin Fowler, *UML Distilled: Applying the Standard Object Modeling Language*. Addison-Wesley, 1997.

Ivar Jacobson, Grady Booch, and James Rumbaugh, *The Unified Software Development Process*. Addison-Wesley, 1999.

Philippe Kruchten, *The Rational Unified Process, An Introduction.* Addison-Wesley, 2000.

Craig Larman, *Applying UML and Patterns: An Introduction to Object-oriented Analysis and Design and the Unified Process* (2nd ed.). Prentice-Hall, 2002.

James Rumbaugh, Ivar Jacobsen, and Grady Booch, *The Unified Modeling Language Reference Manual*. Addison-Wesley, 1999.

PART 3 THE DESIGN DISCIPLINE

CHAPTER 7
Design Activities and Environments

CHAPTER 8
Use Case Realization: The Design Discipline within UP Iterations

CHAPTER 9
Advanced Topics in Object-Oriented Design

CHAPTER 10
Designing the Data Access Layer

CHAPTER 11
Designing the User-Interface Layer

CHAPTER 12
Designing System Interfaces, Controls, and Security

chapter 7

DESIGN ACTIVITIES AND ENVIRONMENTS

LEARNING OBJECTIVES

After reading this chapter, you should be able to:

- Describe the differences between requirements activities and design activities
- Explain the purpose of design and the difference between architectural and detailed design activities
- Describe each design discipline activity
- Discuss the issues related to managing and coordinating design activities within the UP
- Describe common deployment environments and matching application architectures
- Develop a simple network diagram and estimate communication capacity requirements

CHAPTER OUTLINE

- Moving from Business Modeling to Requirements to Design
- Understanding the Elements of Design
- Design Discipline Activities
- Project Management—Coordinating the Project
- Deployment Environment
- Software Architecture
- Network Design

FAIRCHILD PHARMACEUTICALS: FINALIZING ARCHITECTURAL DESIGN FOR A PRODUCTION SYSTEM

James Schultz is a summer intern with Fairchild Pharmaceuticals. He has been assigned to a development project for a production scheduling and control system. The project was nearing the end of its first iteration when James joined the team two weeks ago.

James works for Carla Sanchez, the chief analyst and project manager. For the past two weeks, James has helped Carla prepare presentations to the project oversight committee and system users. He has absorbed a lot of information about the project in a very short time, but the details and overall project direction haven't yet formed a complete and coherent picture in his mind. Carla asked James to stop by her office first thing this morning to discuss his assignment for the next project iteration.

James knocked on Carla's open door and asked, "Is this a good time or should I come back later?"

"I have time now," she said. "Come in and have a seat. Let's start by reviewing the results of yesterday's meetings, and I'll answer any questions you have. Then we'll narrow down your tasks for the next project iteration."

James said, "I have two questions that I think are related. The first is, which design and implementation details have been decided and which haven't? The discussions with the users and oversight committee left me with the impression that the decision to go with a full-blown Web-based system had already been made. Yet none of the supporting infrastructure for a Web-based system currently exists, or does it?"

Carla replied, "A few elements are in place, but most of it will need to be designed and acquired. But let's hear your other question before we get into that."

James continued, "Well, you've sort of anticipated my next question, which is: What do we need to do next? There seem to be several important tasks that need to be started now, such as choosing system software to support Web services, determining what changes will be needed to the company network, and designing the database. But I suspect that I've left out a few important pieces. Also, the tasks and decisions are so interdependent that I don't know which should be tackled first or how we'll intertwine them with related requirements, construction, and deployment activities in the remaining iterations."

Carla smiled before she replied, "Well, you really were awake during all of the meetings! You should take some pride in knowing that you're confused about exactly the right things at this point in the project. Allocating requirements, design, construction, and deployment tasks across iterations is an important but uncertain issue in all projects, and this one is no exception. As you've correctly observed, there are many important decisions that need to be made very quickly, and they overlap. They're also heavily constrained by available time, budget, and existing systems, skills, and infrastructure."

Looking a bit relieved, James replied, "So what's up first, and where do I fit in?"

Carla replied, "In this iteration we'll finalize all of the big-picture design decisions, such as what hardware will support the new system, what operating systems we'll use, how we'll store and access data, and what languages and tools we'll use. Some of these issues were briefly addressed before the start of the project, and some decisions were implicit in the choice of deployment environment and automation scope approved by the oversight committee yesterday. What we need to do now is to lay all of them on the table, make sure they're compatible with one another and with existing systems and capabilities, and parcel out the detailed tasks associated with each."

Carla continued, "I spent yesterday afternoon dividing the work into major categories, including hardware and operating systems, Web support services, database design, application software design, and user interface design. I summarized the choices made so far and the remaining decisions we need to discuss. Key players will meet as a group for the rest of the week to discuss options in each area and develop the system architecture. For example, we'll decide whether to extend our existing database to support the new system or develop a new database with a new DBMS. By the end of the week, we'll have made all of the critical architectural decisions, ensured that the pieces all fit together, and developed an iteration plan that incorporates each area with personnel assignments and time lines. From that point forward, detailed design and deployment tasks can proceed in parallel for the next iteration or two. Professor Chen told me that you've done an independent study in Web services support software, right?"

"Yes," James replied. "I did a comparative study of infrastructure requirements and communication protocols for Web services using COM+, CORBA, and SOAP. I did an in-depth technology review of each and visited two sites using each technology to see how they worked in practice."

"Good," said Carla. "That knowledge will come in handy, since we need to decide whether to base the new system on SOAP and, if so, what supporting infrastructure and development tools to use. I think that you'll learn a lot by working with me for another week or two as we hammer out the architectural design. Once we get the detailed design tasks rolling, we'll choose one for you that suits your interests and abilities. There'll be plenty of interesting tasks from which to choose and more than enough work to keep you busy for the next month or two."

Overview

The last few chapters explained the requirements discipline activities and the models that describe system requirements. While the requirements discipline focuses on what the system should do—that is, the requirements—the design discipline is oriented toward how the system will be built—on defining structural components and dynamic interactions.

This chapter is the first of six chapters discussing design. In this chapter, we briefly describe all design discipline activities and discuss the first activity in more detail. Later chapters explore other design discipline activities in greater depth.

MOVING FROM BUSINESS MODELING TO REQUIREMENTS TO DESIGN

The primary purpose of the business modeling discipline is to understand business needs, key processes, and the business environment. Analysts develop or review business models such as organization charts, location diagrams, activity diagrams, and use cases to understand the business processes and develop a vision for the new system. In the requirements discipline, analysts build models to understand key business processes and data in greater detail. Analysts develop models such as domain model class diagrams, use case diagrams, and interaction diagrams. In some cases, models originally developed for business modeling are expanded with additional details or refined on the basis of new or corrected information.

The design discipline continues the modeling process by creating new models and expanding or refining business and requirements models. But both the purpose of modeling and the nature of the models change from the business modeling and requirements disciplines (see Figure 7-1).

FIGURE 7-1 Comparison of modeling during the business modeling, requirements, and design disciplines

DISCIPLINE	PURPOSE	MODELS DEVELOPED
Business modeling	Understand and communicate the nature of the business environment in which the system will be deployed	Organization chart Location diagram Activity diagram Use case
Requirements	Understand and document business needs and processing requirements	Activity diagram Use case Storyboard Domain model class diagram System sequence diagram
Design	Develop the architecture and details of hardware, networks, software, and the database	Design class diagram Network diagram Database schema Interaction diagram Package diagram

The nature of the change is best summarized by use of the words *what* and *how*. Business and requirements models are primarily concerned with *what* questions, which seek to uncover the reasons underlying business processes. For example:

- What are the business objectives of the system?
- What information must be collected and processed?
- What are the key processes for collecting and using that information?

In contrast, design models are primarily concerned with *how* questions, which specify the structure of a system:

- How will the key processes be performed?
- How will key data be collected and organized?
- How will the new system achieve business objectives?

Design models tend to be highly detailed and specific to implementation and deployment technology. They are, in essence, blueprints for a specific system that uses specific technologies within a specific deployment environment. Analysts may expand business or requirements models, such as domain class diagrams, to include design details such as specific methods of data access or low-level interactions with external systems and services. Analysts also develop many new models that are specific to design, including database models, network models, package diagrams, and interaction diagrams. Constructing and refining those models is the subject of the latter part of this chapter and the next several chapters.

UNDERSTANDING THE ELEMENTS OF DESIGN

Systems design is the discipline of describing, organizing, and structuring the components of a system at both the architectural level and a detailed level, for the purpose of constructing and deploying the proposed system. A system design is like a set of plans for a large building. Much of the design involves the low-level details of constructing the foundation, support structure, walls, roof, plumbing, electrical system, and heating and cooling systems. Blueprints model these design elements, with each page or set of pages describing particular features of the building at a particular level of detail with specific terminology and symbols. Other models are also used, such as load calculations for posts and beams and elevation drawings to show the building's external appearance. The entire set of models describes a complete plan of the building and the interaction of its various elements and systems. When the architect and contractor add a budget, schedule, and quality-control plan, they create a complete construction roadmap for the building.

For all but the smallest buildings and information systems, it is helpful to break down design discipline tasks into high and low levels, because there are simply too many design decisions and details to consider at one time. So architects, construction engineers, and systems analysts must decide which features of the building or system to design first—tackling the high-level elements first and the low-level elements later. High-level information system design tasks affect the entire system, such as designing the hardware, network, and system software infrastructure. Lower-level design discipline tasks encompass a relatively small part of the system with minimal impact on other parts of the system, such as software design for a single use case or the design of a related group of user interfaces.

architectural design
broad design of the overall system structure; also called *general design* or *conceptual design*

detail design
low-level design that includes the design of specific program details

As you begin working in the industry, you will find that various names are given to the design at the highest level, including architectural design, general design, and conceptual design. We will use the term **architectural design**. During architectural design, you first determine the overall structure and form of the solution, before trying to design the details. Designing the details is usually called **detail design**.

DESIGN DISCIPLINE ACTIVITIES

For the purpose of discussion and organization, we group design discipline activities into six high-level activities, as originally described in Chapter 2 and summarized in Figure 7-2. Each high-level activity contains many lower-level activities, develops and uses one or more models, and draws on one or more techniques. The detailed activities are described later in this chapter and in Chapters 8 through 12. For now, we'll begin with a brief overview of the high-level activities.

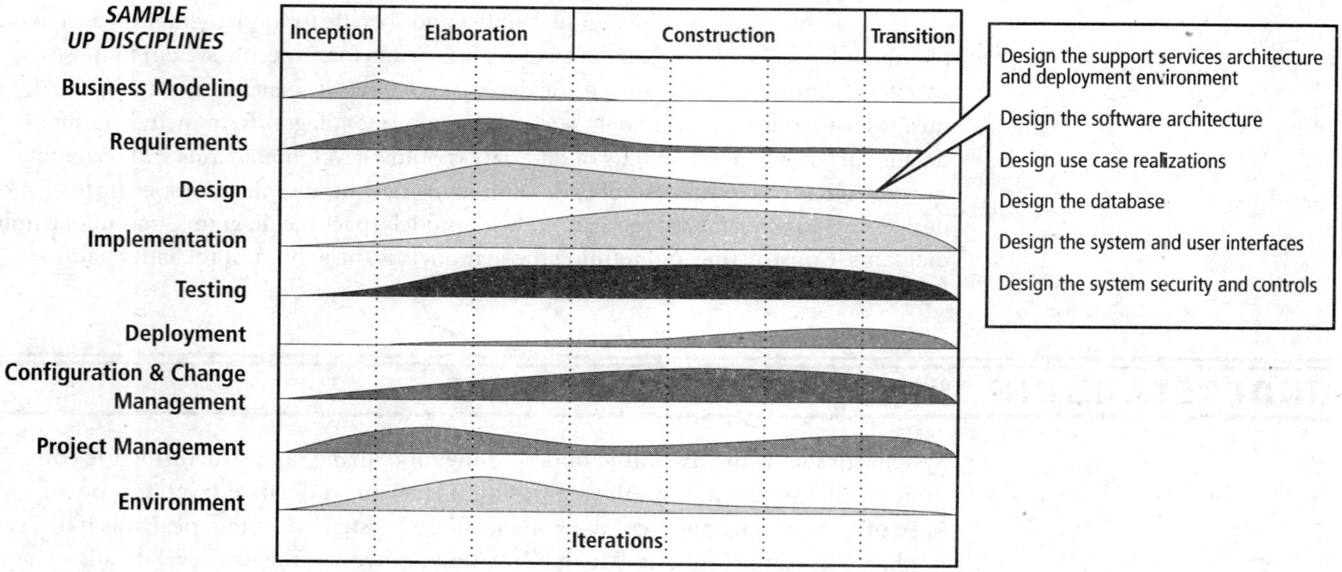

FIGURE 7-2
Design activities in the UP life cycle

DESIGN THE SUPPORT SERVICES ARCHITECTURE AND DEPLOYMENT ENVIRONMENT

Modern information systems operate within a complex collection of computer hardware, networks, and system software, which we collectively call the *support services architecture and deployment environment*. Computer hardware includes servers, client workstations, and related peripheral equipment such as storage arrays and printers. The network includes local area wiring, long-distance communication links, and related hardware such as switches, routers, and firewalls. System software includes operating systems, basic networking service software such as domain naming services (DNS), directory and security service software, component management software, and database management systems.

Most organizations already have a complex support services architecture for multiple information systems. When this is so, analysts must determine whether that architecture can support the new system and what changes, if any, are required. In essence, analysts must adapt the new system and the existing architecture to one another, while ensuring that existing systems continue to function. In rare cases, the organization may not have an existing architecture or may want to scrap its existing architecture. If so, analysts must design one to support the proposed system and anticipated future systems.

Analysts must address important technical issues, such as reliability, security, throughput, and synchronization, when designing and deploying a new system for existing support architecture. The knowledge required to address these issues is highly specialized. So, analysts typically work with specialists to design new support architecture or modify existing architecture. Later in this chapter, we highlight one of the most critical issues in designing the support services architecture—network design and planning.

DESIGN THE SOFTWARE ARCHITECTURE

The term *software architecture* refers to the "big picture" structural aspects of an information system. Two of the most important of these aspects are the division of software into classes and the distribution of those classes across processing locations and specific computers. Requirements definition activities result in a domain model class diagram that describes the data and objects manipulated by software. Architectural design extends the class diagram to produce a design class diagram that adds design details such as visibility of data attributes and required methods.

Design classes are blueprints for executable application software units. Those units can reside in many different locations and interact in various ways. For example, classes could execute on an application server in response to messages transmitted over a network using a protocol such as Simple Object Access Protocol (SOAP). Classes could also be installed on individual user workstations with traditional GUI interfaces and interact with a database management system via various database protocols. During architectural software design, analysts decide where classes and objects will execute, whether they will be distributed across multiple locations, how they will communicate, and what programming language(s) will be used to write them.

Software architecture is heavily constrained by the support services architecture and deployment environment. For example, the software architecture of a Web-based application operating within an environment based on UNIX, Common Object Request Broker Architecture (CORBA), and an Oracle DBMS will be very different from the software architecture of an application deployed within an environment based on Microsoft Windows, .NET, and SQL Server. The capacity and capabilities of the organization's local and wide area networks will also affect how application software is distributed across locations and what types of interactions are possible.

Software architecture is described in Chapters 8 and 9.

DESIGN USE CASE REALIZATIONS

Use case realization was defined in Chapter 3 as the design of software that implements each use case. The design of use case realizations differs from architectural design in several ways, including level of detail, number of iterations, and focus on the user interface and object interactions.

While application architecture is a high-level view of application software, use case realizations are a lower-level view. Architectural design defines a framework within which use cases are realized. That framework includes issues such as how software layers will be distributed across locations and computers and which software classes will support which use cases.

When designing use case realizations, the analyst focuses on the interactions among the classes required to support a particular use case and the interactions among software, users, and external systems. Interaction details that may have been ignored or glossed over during architectural design must be specified in detail during use case realization. In essence, the design focus shifts from big-picture structural issues to the dynamic interactions required to perform specific processing tasks. Design of use case realizations is typically spread over many iterations, with each iteration combining design and construction activities for one or more use cases. UML design class diagrams and interaction diagrams are used to document the design. Use case realization is covered in detail in Chapters 8 and 9.

DESIGN THE DATABASE

Designing the database for the system is another key design activity. The class diagram created in earlier iterations is used to create the physical model of the database. Usually, the physical model describes a relational database consisting of dozens or even hundreds of tables. Sometimes traditional computer files and relational databases are used in the same system. Sometimes object-oriented databases are used instead of relational databases.

Analysts must consider many important technical issues when designing the database. Many of the technical (as opposed to functional) requirements concern performance needs (such as response times). Much of the design work may involve performance tuning to make sure the system actually works fast enough. Another key aspect of designing the database is making sure that new databases are properly integrated with existing databases.

A detailed discussion of database design is presented in Chapter 10.

DESIGN THE SYSTEM AND USER INTERFACES

No system exists in a vacuum. A new information system affects many other existing information systems, and analysts must ensure that they all work together. Some system interfaces link internal organizational systems, so the analyst may have information about those other systems. In some cases, the new system needs to interface with a system outside the organization—for example, at a supplier's site or customer's home. In other cases, the new system needs to communicate with an application that the organization has purchased and installed.

Systems must also interact with users who are both inside and outside the organization. To most users, the interface is a graphical user interface with windows, dialog boxes, and mouse interaction. Increasingly, it can include sound, video, and voice commands. Users' capabilities and needs differ widely; each user interacts with the system in different ways. Additionally, different approaches to the interface may be needed for different parts of the system. Therefore, analysts need to consider many user interfaces. And as information systems become increasingly interactive and accessible, the user interface is becoming a larger part of the system.

The user interface is more than just the screens—it is everything the user comes into contact with while using the system, conceptually, perceptually, and physically. So, the user interface is not just an add-on to the system. It is something that needs to be considered throughout the development process. The nature of the user interface begins to emerge in early project iterations, when business models and requirements are being defined. The specification of the tasks the users complete begins to define the user interface. Then when alternatives are being defined, a key aspect of each alternative is its type of user interface. The activity of designing the user interface in detail, however, occurs during systems design.

User and system interface design are discussed in more detail in Chapters 11 and 12.

DESIGN THE SYSTEM SECURITY AND CONTROLS

A final design activity involves ensuring that the system has adequate safeguards to protect organizational assets. This activity is not listed last because it is less important than the others. On the contrary, it is a crucial activity. It is listed last because controls are an issue relevant to all other design activities.

User-interface controls limit access to the system to authorized users. System interface controls ensure that other systems cause no harm to this system. Application controls ensure that transactions recorded and other work the system does are done correctly. Database controls ensure that data are protected from unauthorized access and from accidental loss due to software or hardware failure. Finally, and of increasing importance, network controls ensure that communication through networks is protected. Specialists are often brought in to work on some controls, and all system controls need to be thoroughly tested.

Control issues are addressed in several chapters but more explicitly in Chapter 12.

DESIGN ACTIVITIES AND THE UP

In the UP, design activities can occur in any project phase or iteration. However, activities associated with architectural and detailed design tend to be distributed differently. Design activities concerned with system architecture and databases provide a foundation for detailed design and construction. Thus, they are typically concentrated in early iterations during the elaboration phase. Detailed design activities are typically spread more evenly throughout the project. For example, user interfaces are usually designed while their corresponding software components are being designed and constructed.

BEST PRACTICE: Complete architectural design activities in early iterations.

One of the more challenging aspects of UP systems design is determining which parts of a system need to be designed in which iterations. To do so, an analyst must have foresight—to "see down the road" to likely consequences of design decisions in early iterations. Decisions that affect many parts of the system and those that significantly constrain other design decisions and construction activities must be made early in the project. Analysts gain the knowledge and intuition needed to make that distinction primarily through experience in designing and developing a variety of systems.

PROJECT MANAGEMENT—COORDINATING THE PROJECT

Coordinating design activities is challenging for even the best project managers because myriad details and tasks must be handled to keep the project on track. Appendix A, which is on the book's Web site, identifies many project management tasks that are required during the design discipline activities. Most of these tasks involve monitoring the progress of the development project and coordinating the ongoing work.

Design activities also require substantial coordination. The project begins to fragment as an increasing number of design issues are addressed. Frequently, the system is divided into subsystems, and each subsystem has unique design requirements. The project team may also be divided into smaller teams to focus on the various subsystems and on other design issues, with multiple iterations proceeding in parallel. Some technical issues—such as network configuration, database design, distributed processing needs, and communications capability—are common to all subsystems. Other issues—such as response time and specialized input equipment—may be limited to specific subsystems. Coordinating and integrating all technical issues for all subsystems, along with any network communications software, are fundamental to the smooth functioning of the overall system. Ultimately, the success of a development project depends on how well all of the work of the design teams is coordinated.

Two other miniprojects may also be initiated at this point: a data conversion project and a test case development project. We will explain more about the details of these projects in Chapter 13. We mention them here simply to note that they add yet more complexity to the management of the project.

Finally, construction activities, such as programming, also begin around this time. In fact, design and programming for an iteration are usually conducted concurrently. Programming can begin as soon as design decisions are made. So, in addition to the various groups working on design issues, groups of programmers and programmer/analysts will probably be added to the project team.

Control and coordination of these various activities can be complicated further by the fact that people involved in the project may work at different locations. Project communications management, which is essential to successful coordination, becomes many times more complicated as people are added to the team.

Given these complexities, let's discuss several project management tools and techniques to help in the coordination of the project.

COORDINATING PROJECT TEAMS

The fundamental tool used to coordinate the various project teams' activities is the project schedule. As the activities of the design discipline begin, the project manager must update the schedule by identifying and estimating durations for all tasks associated with design and construction, as well as any outstanding tasks associated with ongoing requirements definition. The project schedule usually must be reworked substantially to ensure that the project remains organized.

In early iterations, the project manager and an assistant often do all project management tasks, but when the project expands and several teams are formed, management of the project becomes more complicated. Frequently, a committee composed of the leaders of the key design and construction teams assumes more responsibility for coordinating and controlling aspects of project management. Weekly, and sometimes daily, status meetings are held. If this group includes people at remote locations, teleconferencing support may be required.

BEST PRACTICE: Coordinate design activities with frequent meetings.

THE PROJECT TEAM AT RMO

As the RMO customer support system team begins design and construction activities, new team members have been added. RMO also initiated two new subprojects at this time, one for the database design and data conversion, and one for infrastructure upgrades. To integrate new people into the team, Barbara Halifax reorganized the structure of the project team. The accompanying RMO memo highlights some of the changes happening at this point.

COORDINATING INFORMATION

As design moves forward, the development teams begin to generate a tremendous amount of detailed information about the system. Classes, data fields, forms, reports, methods, and tables are all being defined in substantial detail. Tremendous coordination is needed to keep track of all of these pieces of information. But two kinds of tools can help in this process.

The most common and widespread technique to record and track project information is to use a CASE tool. Most CASE tools have a central repository to capture information. In Chapter 2, you learned about CASE tools, and Figure 2-24 illustrated the various component tools that make up a comprehensive CASE system. A major element in a CASE tool system is the central repository of information, which not only records all design information but also is normally configured so that all teams can view project information to facilitate communication among the teams of a project. Figure 7-3 illustrates the various information components that may exist within a CASE data repository.

Other electronic tools are also available to help with team communication and information coordination. These tools and techniques, often referred to as *computer*

February 18, 2006

To: John MacMurty

From: Barbara Halifax

Re: Customer Support System—Architectural Design

ROCKY MOUNTAIN OUTFITTERS

MEMO

John, this has been a very busy period! Here is a quick status report on completed and upcoming activities related to architectural design, infrastructure, and the first order-entry prototype.

Personnel assignments
We've added five more people to the project team: two users, one senior technical design person to act as chief architect, and two programmer/analysts. I assigned the users to our main team, which is now focusing on order-entry and related use cases. I also organized two small teams, one devoted to database design and data-conversion activities and another to bring new Web and application services online.

Plans for the next iteration
The database team will develop a relatively complete database schema and deploy a temporary database server to get us through the first round of order-entry software testing.

The infrastructure team will complete architectural design activities and deploy Web and application servers. The first round of order-entry software testing will also be a realistic test of the new servers, the software architecture, and the network.

The main team will work on requirements, design, implementation, and testing of all use cases related to order entry, including both telephone and online sales. We'll have a fairly complete prototype by the end of the iteration, which we'll refine in future iterations.

Problems, issues, and open items
The only major problem at this point is that there are several items on the open-items list that need to be finalized—both technical items that the infrastructure team needs to resolve and order-entry requirements definitions that need decisions. But we're making progress.

BH

cc: Steven Deerfield, Ming Lee

support for collaborative work, not only record final design information but also assist in team collaboration. Often during the development process, several people need to work together in the development of the design, so they need to discuss and dynamically update the working documents or diagrams. One collaborative tool that is frequently used is Lotus Notes. Other software programs allow figures and diagrams to be updated with tracking and version information so that the evolution of the result can be documented.

One especially difficult part of development projects is tracking open items and unresolved issues. We mention this issue here, not because it requires a new technique, but because the problem is pervasive and all good project managers develop techniques to track these items. One simple method is to have an open-items control log. We presented the idea of an open-items control list in Chapter 4 and provided an example in Figure 4-12. It is a sequential list of all open items, with information to track responsibilities and resolution of the open item, as shown by the column headings. Frequently,

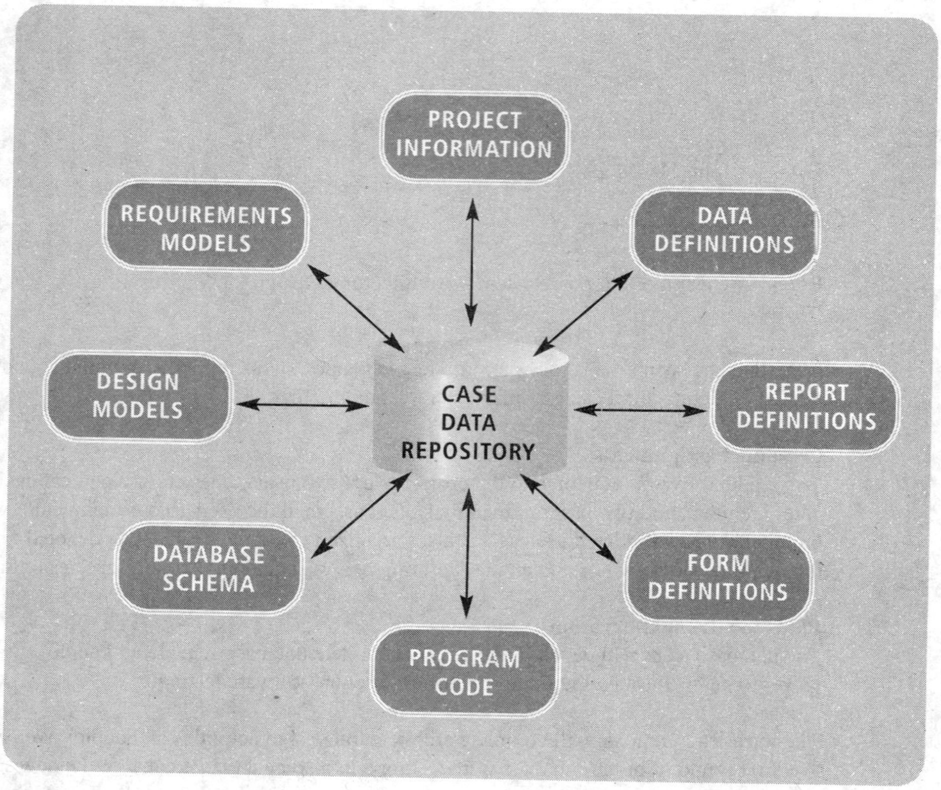

FIGURE 7-3
System development information stored in the CASE repository

closed items are shaded for easy identification. This technique is effective for requirements definition, design, and many other project activities.

BEST PRACTICE: Maintain an open-items list for unresolved problems and questions.

Now that you have an overview of the design discipline and major issues of project management, we turn to the tasks associated with architectural and network design. First, we discuss technical aspects of the deployment environment that directly affect architectural design. Then, we describe common approaches to architectural design and the software and network design issues associated with each approach.

DEPLOYMENT ENVIRONMENT

The deployment environment consists of the hardware, system software, and networking environment in which the system will operate. In this section, we describe common deployment environments in detail, and in the next section we'll explore related design patterns and architectures for application software.

single-computer architecture
architecture that employs a single computer system executing all application-related software

SINGLE-COMPUTER AND MULTITIER ARCHITECTURE

As its name implies, *single-computer architecture* employs a single computer system and its directly attached peripheral devices, as shown in Figure 7-4a. It can be a stand-alone

PC application, but in this context we are discussing large mainframe applications whose users interact with the system via input/output devices of limited functionality that are directly connected to the computer. Single-computer architecture often requires all system users to be located near the computer. The primary advantage of single-computer architecture is its simplicity. Information systems deployed on a single-computer system are relatively easy to design, build, operate, and maintain.

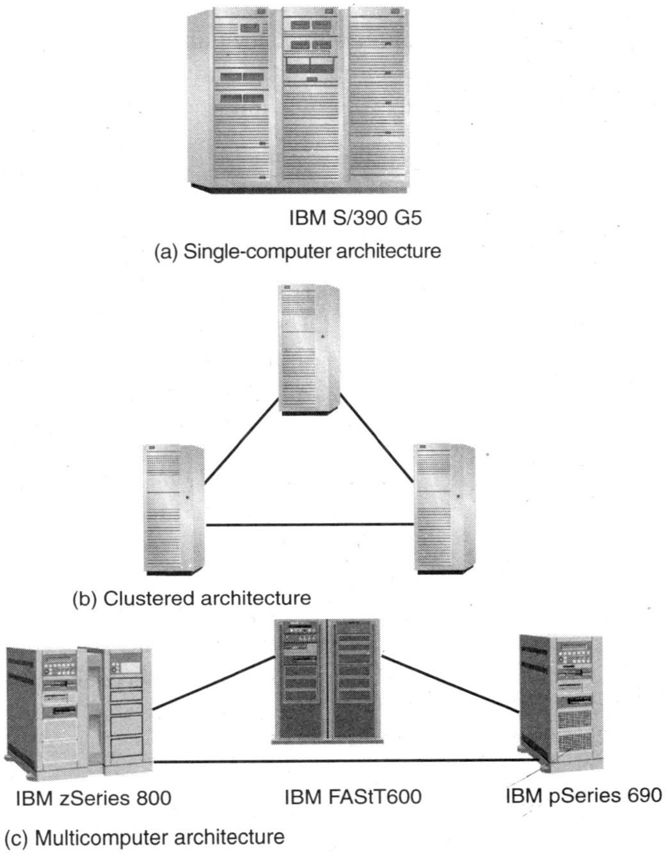

FIGURE 7-4
Single-computer, clustered, and multicomputer architectures

The capacity limits of a single computer may make single-computer architecture impractical or unusable for large information systems. Many systems are so large that even the largest mainframe computer cannot perform all the required processing, data storage, and data retrieval tasks. Such systems require another architectural approach.

Multitier architecture employs multiple computer systems in a cooperative effort to meet information-processing needs. Multitier architecture can be further subdivided into two types:

- *Clustered architecture*, shown in Figure 7-4b, employs a group (or cluster) of computers, usually from the same manufacturer and model family. Programs are allocated to the least-utilized computer when they execute, so that the processing load can be balanced across all machines. In effect, a cluster acts as a single large computer system. Clustered computer systems are normally located near one another so that they can be connected with short high-capacity communication links.
- *Multicomputer architecture*, shown in Figure 7-4c, also employs multiple computer systems. But hardware and operating systems are not as similar as in a clustered architecture. A suite of application or system programs and data

multitier architecture
architecture that distributes application-related software or processing load across multiple computer systems

clustered architecture
a group of computers of the same type that share processing load and act as a single large computer system

multicomputer architecture
a group of dissimilar computers that share processing load through specialization of function

resources is exclusively assigned to each computer system. Each computer system is optimized to the role that it will play in the combined system, such as database or application server.

CENTRALIZED AND DISTRIBUTED ARCHITECTURE

centralized architecture
architecture that locates all computing resources in a central location

The term *centralized architecture* describes deployment of all computer systems in a single location. Centralized architecture is generally used for large-scale processing applications, including both batch and real-time applications. Such applications are common in industries such as banking, insurance, and catalog sales. Information systems in such industries often have the following characteristics:

- Some input transactions do not need to be processed in real time (for example, time sheets processed by a payroll service).
- Online data-entry personnel can be centrally located (for example, a centrally located group of telephone order takers can serve geographically dispersed customers).
- The system produces a large amount of periodic outputs (for example, monthly credit card statements mailed to customers).
- A high volume of transactions occurs between high-speed computers (for example, business-to-business processing for supply chain management).

Any application that has two or three of these characteristics is a viable candidate for implementation on a centralized mainframe. Current trends in conducting e-business have instilled new life into centralized mainframe computing because of the transaction volumes of many business-to-business (B2B) processes.

Centralized computer systems are seldom used as the sole hardware platform for an information system. Most systems have some transaction inputs that must be accepted from geographically dispersed locations and processed in real time—for example, a cash withdrawal from an ATM. Most systems also have some outputs that are requested from and delivered to remote locations in real time—for example, an insurance policy inquiry by a state motor vehicle department. Thus, centralized computer systems are typically used to implement one or more subsystems within a larger information system that includes online, batch, and geographically dispersed components.

distributed architecture
architecture that deploys computing resources in multiple locations connected by a computer network

computer network
a set of transmission lines, equipment, and communication protocols that permits sharing of information and resources

local area network (LAN)
a computer network in which the distances are local, such as within the same building

wide area network (WAN)
a computer network spread across large distances, such as a city, state, or nation

A modern information system is typically distributed across many computer systems and geographic locations. For example, corporate financial data might be stored on a centralized mainframe computer. Smaller servers in regional offices might periodically generate accounting and other reports based on data stored on the mainframe. Workstations in many locations might be used to access and view periodic reports as well as to directly update the central database. Such an approach to distributing software and data across computer systems and locations is generically called *distributed architecture*. Distributed architecture relies on communication networks to connect geographically dispersed computer hardware components.

COMPUTER NETWORKS

A *computer network* is a set of transmission lines, specialized hardware, and communication protocols that enables communication among different users and computer systems. Computer networks are divided into two classes, depending on the distance they span. A *local area network (LAN)* is typically less than one kilometer long and connects computers within a single building or floor. The term *wide area network (WAN)* can describe any network over one kilometer, although the term typically implies much greater distances, spanning cities, countries, continents, or the entire globe.

Figure 7-5 shows a possible computer network for RMO. A single LAN serves each geographic location, and all LANs are connected by a WAN. Users and computers in a single location communicate via their LAN. Communication among geographically dispersed sites uses the LANs at both sites and the WAN. A *router* connects each LAN to the WAN. A router scans messages on the LAN and copies them to the WAN if they are addressed to a user or computer on another LAN. The router also scans messages on the WAN and copies them to the LAN if they are addressed to a local user or computer.

router
network equipment that directs information within the network

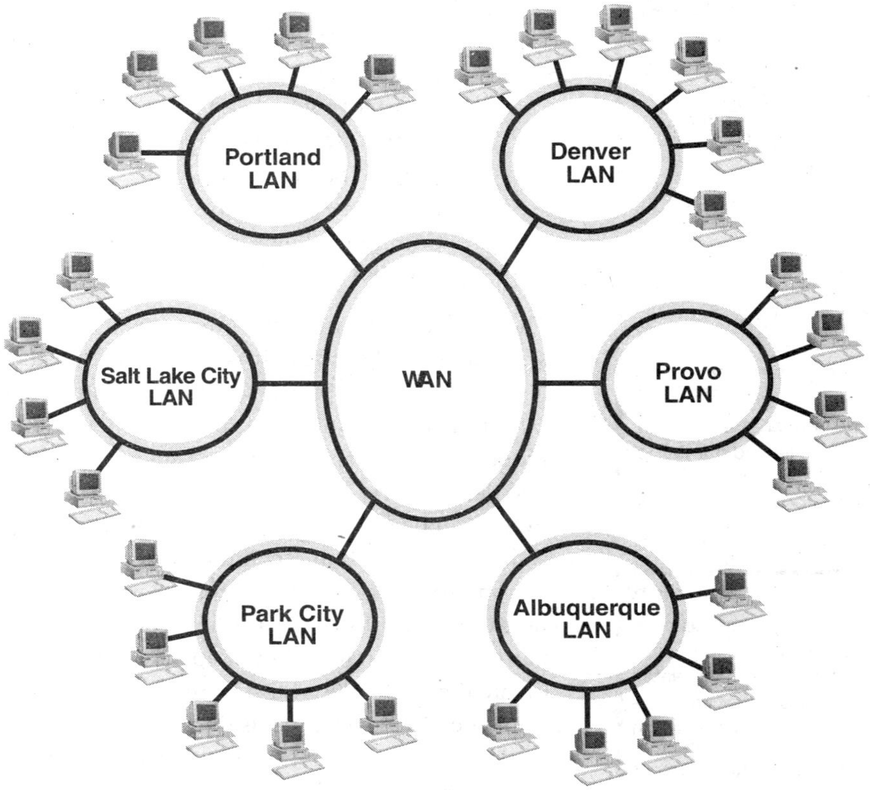

FIGURE 7-5
A possible network configuration for RMO

Technologies such as Ethernet are typically used to implement LANs. They provide low to moderate amounts of message-carrying capacity at a relatively low cost. WAN technologies such as Asynchronous Transfer Mode are more complex and expensive, although they typically provide higher message-carrying capacity and greater reliability. WANs may be constructed using purchased equipment and leased long-distance transmission lines. WAN setup and operation may also be subcontracted from a long-distance telecommunications vendor such as AT&T or Sprint.

Computer networks provide a generic communication capability among computer systems and users. This generic capability can support many services, including direct communications (such as telephone service and video conferencing), message-based communications (such as e-mail), and resource sharing (such as access to electronic documents, application programs, and databases). A single network can simultaneously support multiple services with appropriate hardware and sufficient transmission capacity.

There are many ways to distribute information system resources across a computer network. Users, application programs, and databases can be placed on the same computer system, on different computer systems on the same LAN, or on different computer systems on different LANs. Application software and databases can also be subdivided and each distributed separately.

THE INTERNET, INTRANETS, AND EXTRANETS

Internet
a global collection of networks that use the same networking protocol—TCP/IP

World Wide Web (WWW), or Web
a collection of resources such as files and programs that can be accessed over the Internet using standard protocols

The *Internet* is a global collection of networks that are interconnected using a common low-level networking standard—TCP/IP (Transmission Control Protocol/Internet Protocol). The *World Wide Web (WWW)*, also called simply the *Web*, is a collection of resources (programs, files, and services) that can be accessed over the Internet by a number of standard protocols, including the following:

- Formatted and linked document protocols, such as HyperText Markup Language (HTML), eXtensible Markup Language (XML), and HyperText Transfer Protocol (HTTP)
- Executable program standards, including Java, JavaScript, and Visual Basic Script (VBScript)
- Distributed software and Web-service standards, including Distributed Computing Environment (DCE), Common Object Request Broker Architecture (CORBA), and Simple Object Access Protocol (SOAP)

The Internet is the infrastructure on which the Web is based. In other words, the resources of the Web are delivered to users over the Internet.

intranet
a private network that is accessible to a limited number of users, but which uses the same TCP/IP protocol as the Internet

An *intranet* is a private network that uses Internet protocols but is accessible only by a limited set of internal users (usually members of the same organization or workgroup). The term also describes a set of privately accessible resources that are organized and delivered via one or more Web protocols over a network that supports TCP/IP. Access can be restricted in various ways, including unadvertised resource names, firewalls, and user/group account names and passwords.

extranet
an intranet that has been extended outside the organization, to directly related organizations, to facilitate the flow of information

virtual organization
a loosely coupled group of people and resources in different organizations that work together as though they were one organization

virtual private network (VPN)
a network with security and controlled access for a private group but built on top of a public network, such as the Internet

An *extranet* is an intranet that has been extended to include directly related business users outside the organization (such as suppliers, large customers, and strategic partners). An extranet allows separate organizations to exchange information and coordinate their activities, thus forming a *virtual organization*. One widely used method of implementing an extranet is through a *virtual private network (VPN)*. A private network is a network that is secure and accessible only to members of an organization (or virtual organization). Historically, implementing a private network required an organization to own and operate its own network lines or leased dedicated telephone lines. A VPN sends encrypted messages through public Internet service providers.

THE ENVIRONMENT AT ROCKY MOUNTAIN OUTFITTERS

The deployment environment at RMO had been built piecemeal over the life of the company to support the business functions at the various locations. Currently, there are two major manufacturing plants, which provide products for three warehouses. The warehouses also stock items from other manufacturers. RMO's manufacturing facilities, warehouses, retail stores, the mail-order center, the phone center, and the data center are currently networked.

THE CURRENT ENVIRONMENT

Figure 7-6 illustrates the current computer environment at RMO. Existing technology consists of a mainframe computer located at the home office in Park City, with dedicated lines connected to the three warehouse distribution sites in Salt Lake City, Portland, and Albuquerque. A dedicated line also connects the mainframe to the mail-order center in Provo, Utah. Both mail-order and distribution functions are linked directly to the mainframe to allow real-time connection of terminals. The communications technology is based on high-volume mainframe transaction technology. The merchandising and distribution system is a mainframe application written in COBOL and using a combination of IBM's DB2 database system and VSAM files. The system was written by RMO staff with assistance from outside technical consultants.

LOCATION AND FACILITY	EQUIPMENT	CONNECTION
Park City—Data Center	Mainframe	
Park City—Retail	Client/server	Daily dial-up
Salt Lake City—Manufacturing	Local LAN	Daily dial-up
Salt Lake City—Warehouse	Midrange computer	Dedicated line to Data Center
Salt Lake City—Phone Order	Client/server	Daily dial-up
Provo—Mail Order Center	Client/server	Dedicated line to Data Center
Portland—Warehouse	Midrange computer	Dedicated line to Data Center
Portland—Manufacturing	Local LAN	Daily dial-up
Denver—Retail	Client/server	Daily dial-up
Albuquerque—Warehouse	Midrange computer	Dedicated line to Data Center

FIGURE 7-6
The existing processing environment at RMO

Dial-up telephone lines are used to communicate with the manufacturing sites in Salt Lake City and Portland. Each manufacturing facility also has its own LAN to support specific manufacturing information. Updates to the central inventory system are done in a batch mode daily via the dial-up connection.

The retail stores have local client/server retail systems that collect sales and financial information through the cash registers. This information is also forwarded to the central accounting and financial systems residing on the mainframe. The transmittal is done in batch mode daily.

The phone-order system, in Salt Lake City, is a fairly small Windows application running in a client/server environment. It was built by RMO staff as an independent application and is not well integrated with the rest of the inventory and distribution systems. Information is forwarded daily in batches to the system in Park City.

Other applications, such as human resources and general accounting, are also mainframe systems running in Park City.

THE PROPOSED ENVIRONMENT

Many of the decisions associated with the target environment are made during strategic planning, which establishes long-term directions for an organization. In other situations, the strategic plan is modified as new systems are developed to use the latest technological advancements. In RMO's case, many technical decisions were made during the initial iterations of the supply chain management (SCM) project that is well under way. Since the new customer support system (CSS) must integrate seamlessly with the SCM, technical decisions must be consistent with prior decisions as well as the long-term technology plan.

Since environment decisions are corporate-wide strategic decisions, RMO convened a meeting to discuss the technology alternatives and to make decisions. Attendees consisted of Mac Preston, chief information officer; John MacMurty, director of system development; and Barbara Halifax, project manager. Additional technical staff members were also included in the meeting to provide details as needed.

To ensure that all participants were aware of potential alternatives, Barbara presented and reviewed the information shown in Figure 7-7. This figure identifies potential implementation alternatives and is similar to the one used to make decisions for the SCM project. The alternatives are listed by type of technology and degree of centralization. The first three alternatives considered are whether to:

- Move to Internet technology
- Use internal LAN/WAN technology
- Use a mix of the two options

The next two alternatives focus on the equipment—whether to:

- Use a mainframe central processor
- Use distributed client/server processors

FIGURE 7-7
Processing environment alternatives

ALTERNATIVE	DESCRIPTION
1. Move all functionality to be browser based (intranet/Internet)	Make both the internal and external applications Web-based with browser interface. This solution would provide a consistent interface and facilitate e-commerce growth.
2. Use internal LAN/WAN technology	Internal transactions can be faster. The database would not need an interface to the Web. Put only the catalog on the Web.
3. Use a mix of alternatives 1 and 2	Use the Web for customer interactions, but use internal LAN/WAN technology for back-end processing and an interface to SCM and other internal systems.
4. Use the mainframe as the central database server	Support for high-volume transactions. It will serve as a centralized database for all systems. It provides high security, control, and consistency.
5. Use a distributed database on multiple servers	Distributed data provides rapid response and load leveling. Growth can be done incrementally. Updating is more complex.
6. Use complete OO components such as Common Object Request Broker Architecture (CORBA) objects	This solution would make seamless interfaces between applications—SCM, CSS, and other systems—with object brokers. It would position RMO for future OO migration. This solution requires middleware integration software.
7. Use OO for the user interface with a back-end relational database	Use Visual Basic or Java to develop the applications. Use DB2 or relational Oracle for database processing This solution would be very efficient for high volumes.
8. Use OO for the user interface plus CORBA objects for communication between systems	This alternative would position RMO for a move to a complete OO environment. Middleware software is required for integration of systems.

Finally, the location and type of database are considered. The decision is whether to use more traditional relational database technology or to move to more advanced object-oriented databases. Any decisions made for the CSS would need to be consistent with prior decisions for the SCM.

RMO wants its system to be state of the art, but it also does not want to have a high-risk project and attempt new technology that is not yet proven. Figure 7-8 lists the major components of the strategic direction for RMO.

Current, well-tested technology can provide client/server processing on a rack of multiple processors to support high-volume Internet transactions. Microsoft's Internet Server will provide Internet support. The existing DB2 database on the mainframe is a very viable option to provide efficient back-end processing. The database will require redesign for the new system, but the fundamental processing environment is solid.

All of the COBOL applications will be replaced with new systems that will be written using Java, Visual Basic, VBScript, and PHP, as appropriate.

In this approach, the mainframe will remain as the central database server. The other two tiers will be application and Web servers. The users will have individual client personal computers that access the application and Web servers via a Web browser.

FIGURE 7-8
Strategic directions for the processing environment at RMO

ISSUE	DIRECTION(S)
Required interfaces to other systems	1. Automatic feed to SCM system 2. Interface to feed the accounting general ledger 3. Interface to provide automatic feed to external systems—credit card verification and package shipping 4. Potential move to XML for a common interface language
Equipment configuration	1. Servers with multiple CPU configuration for front-end applications 2. Database support provided with mainframe central processor
Operating system	1. Windows Server front-end servers 2. MVS for mainframe
Network configuration	1. Windows network 2. IIS for Web servers
Language environment	1. Visual Basic, Java, and PHP for application and Web development
Database environment	1. Maintain DB2 database on mainframe 2. Reevaluate long-term strategy for the OO database
CASE tools	1. Use only diagramming portions; various alternatives available

SOFTWARE ARCHITECTURE

Simple deployment environments, such as a single centralized computer with video display terminals, can be matched to relatively simple software architectures. More complex distributed and multitier hardware and network architectures require more complex software architectures. This section describes common examples of software architecture for distributed and multitier deployment environments and the design issues and decisions associated with each.

CLIENT/SERVER ARCHITECTURE

server
a process, module, object, or computer that provides services over a network

client
a process, module, object, or computer that requests services from one or more servers

Client/server architecture divides software into two types: client and server. A *server* manages one or more information system resources or provides a well-defined service. A *client* communicates with a server to request resources or services, and the server responds to those requests.

Client/server architecture is a general model of software organization and behavior that can be implemented in many different ways. A typical example is the interaction between a client application program executing on a workstation and a database management system (DBMS) executing on a larger computer system (see Figure 7-9). The application program sends database access requests to the database management system via a network. The DBMS accesses data on behalf of the application and returns a response such as the results of a search operation or the success or failure of an update operation.

The architectural issues to be addressed when designing client/server software are:

- Decomposing software into client and server programs or objects
- Determining which clients and servers will execute on which computer systems

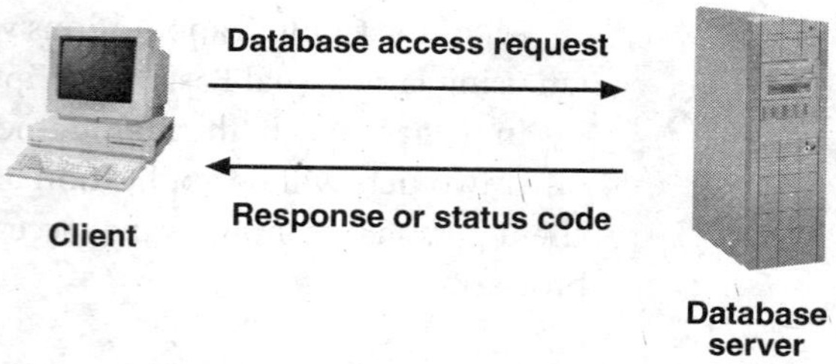

FIGURE 7-9
Client/server architecture with a shared database

- Describing the communication protocols and networks that connect clients and servers

The key to decomposing software into clients and servers is identifying resources or services that can be centrally managed by independent software units.

BEST PRACTICE: Identify resources or services that can be managed by independent software units.

Examples of centrally managed services include security authentication and authorization, credit verification, and scheduling. In each case, a service provides a set of well-defined processes such as retrieval, update, and approval based on a data store that is hidden from the client, as shown in Figure 7-10.

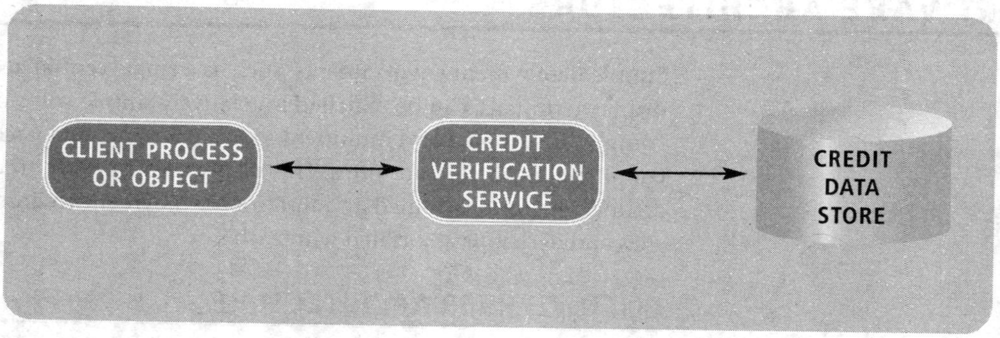

FIGURE 7-10
Interaction among client, server, and a service-related data store

Client and server software can execute on any computer system. But the most typical arrangement is to place server software on separate server computer systems and to distribute client software to computer systems "close" to end users, such as desktop workstations. Figure 7-11 shows a typical arrangement for an order-processing application. Credit verification, delivery scheduling, and database server processes execute on a centrally located minicomputer or mainframe, and users execute multiple copies of the client software on workstations.

Client and server communicate via well-defined communication protocols over a physical network. In Figure 7-11, the network is a LAN, and an appropriate low-level network protocol such as TCP/IP provides basic communication services. But the system designer must also specify higher-level protocols, or languages, by which client and server exchange service requests, responses, and data. In some cases, such as

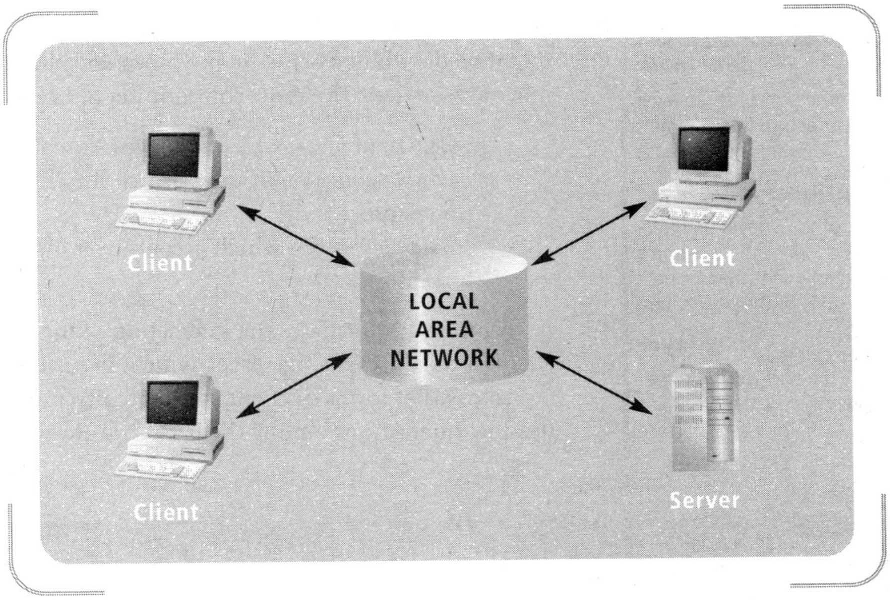

FIGURE 7-11
Interaction among multiple clients and a single server

communication with a DBMS, standard protocols and software may be employed, such as Structured Query Language (SQL) via an Open Database Connectivity (ODBC) database connection. But in other cases, the designer must define the exact format and content of valid messages and responses. If a service is provided by an external organization (for example, credit verification), then the external organization will have already designed an appropriate protocol, and the analyst must ensure that clients adhere to the protocol.

The primary advantage of client/server architecture is deployment flexibility. Client/server architecture arose as an approach to distributing software across networked computers. It provides the inherent advantages of a networked environment, including:

- **Location flexibility.** The ability to "move" system components without "disturbing" other system components, in response to changing organizational parameters such as size and physical location
- **Scalability.** The ability to increase system capacity by upgrading or changing the hardware on which key software components execute
- **Maintainability.** The ability to update the internal implementation of one part of a system without needing to change other parts (for example, the credit verification software can be rewritten or replaced as long as the new software uses the existing client/server protocol)

The primary disadvantages of client/server architecture are the additional complexity introduced by the client/server protocols and the potential performance, security, and reliability issues that arise from communication over networks. A single large program on a single computer needs no client/server protocols, and all communication occurs within the relatively secure, reliable, and efficient confines of a single machine.

For most organizations, the flexibility advantages of client/server far outweigh the disadvantages. As a result, client/server architecture and its newer variants have become the dominant architecture for the vast majority of modern software.

three-layer architecture
a client/server architecture that divides an application into the view layer, business logic layer, and data layer

THREE-LAYER CLIENT/SERVER ARCHITECTURE

A widely applied variant of client/server architecture, called *three-layer architecture*, divides application software into a set of client and server processes independent of

data layer
the part of three-layer architecture that interacts with the database

business logic layer
the part of three-layer architecture that contains the programs that implement the business rules of the application

view layer
the part of three-layer architecture that contains the user interface

hardware or locations. All layers might reside on one processor, or three or more layers might be distributed across many processors. In other words, the layers might reside on one or more tiers. The most common set of layers includes:

- The *data layer*, which manages stored data, usually in one or more databases
- The *business logic layer*, which implements the rules and procedures of business processing
- The *view layer*, which accepts user input and formats and displays processing results

Figure 7-12 illustrates the interaction of the three layers. The view layer acts as a client of the business logic layer, which, in turn, acts as a client of the data layer.

Like earlier forms of client/server architecture, three-layer architecture is inherently flexible. Interactions among the layers are always requests or responses, which makes

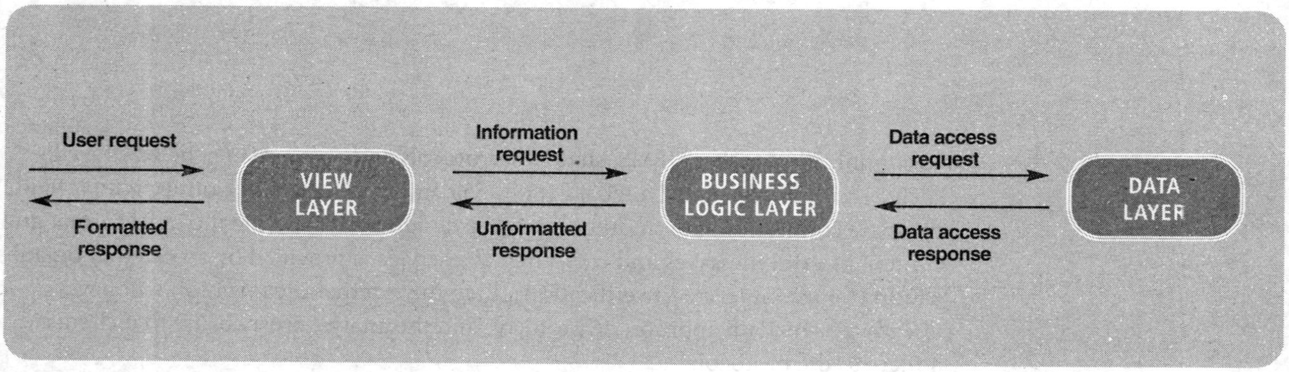

FIGURE 7-12
Three-layer architecture

the layers relatively independent of one another. It doesn't matter where other layers are implemented or on what type of computer or operating system they execute. The only interlayer dependencies are a common language for requests and responses and a reliable network with sufficient communication capacity.

BEST PRACTICE: Divide software into three or more layers to improve deployment flexibility.

Multiple layers can execute on the same computer, or each layer can operate on a separate computer. Complex layers can be split across two or more computers. System capacity can be increased by splitting layer functions across computers or by load sharing across redundant computers. In the event of a malfunction, redundancy improves system reliability if the server load can be shifted from one computer to another. In sum, three-layer architecture provides the flexibility needed by modern organizations to deploy and redeploy information-processing resources in response to rapidly changing conditions.

Three-layer architecture is a widely applied architectural design pattern for object-oriented software. As with other forms of client/server architecture, the key design tasks are decomposing the application software into layers, clients, and servers; distributing the "pieces" across hardware platforms; and defining the physical network and protocols.

The business logic layer is the core of the application software and is constructed according to the requirements. For example, the classes of objects in the RMO class diagram (see Figure 5-31) would be implemented within the business logic layer as classes of objects that interact to complete user tasks. In either case, the business logic layer is a server for the view layer and is a client of the data layer. However, the business logic layer may itself be decomposed into multiple clients and services. Chapter 8 describes three-layer design in greater detail.

MIDDLEWARE

middleware
computer software that implements communication protocols on the network and helps different systems communicate

Client/server and three-layer architecture rely on special programs to enable communication among layers. Software that implements this communication interface is usually called *middleware*. Middleware connects parts of an application and enables requests and data to pass among them. There are various methods to implement the middleware functions. Some common types of middleware include teleprocessing monitors, transaction processing monitors, and object request brokers (ORBs). Each type of middleware has its own set of protocols to facilitate communication among the various components of an information system.

When specifying the protocols to be used for client/server or interlayer communication, the designer usually relies on standard frameworks and protocols incorporated into middleware. For example, interactions with DBMSs usually employ standard protocols such as Open Database Connectivity (ODBC) and SQL with supporting software obtained from the DBMS vendor or a third party. Third-party service providers such as credit bureaus and electronic purchasing or bidding services usually employ a standard Web protocol such as HTTP or XML. Industry-specific protocols have been developed in many industries such as health care and banking.

Complex OO software distributed across multiple layers and hardware platforms relies on an ORB based on a distributed object interface standard such as CORBA. Distributed non-OO software relies on different middleware products based on standards such as DCE or Microsoft's COM+. Web-based applications rely on Web-oriented protocols such as Microsoft's .NET and Sun's J2EE and specific middleware products that implement and support those protocols.

INTERNET AND WEB-BASED SOFTWARE ARCHITECTURE

The Web is a complex example of client/server architecture. Web resources are managed by server processes that can execute on dedicated server computers or on multipurpose computer systems. Clients are programs that send requests to servers, using one or more of the standard Web resource request protocols. Web protocols define valid resource formats and a standard means of requesting resources and services. Any program (not just a Web browser) can use Web protocols. Thus, Weblike capabilities can be embedded in ordinary application programs.

service-oriented architecture (SOA)
architecture that packages application software into server software, which can be managed by and accessed via a Web server

Recent Web-service standards such as .NET and J2EE enable a Web-oriented client/server architecture commonly called a *service-oriented architecture (SOA)*. Under SOA, application software functions are packaged into server software, which can be managed by and accessed via a Web server. Service requests and responses are packaged in XML documents and transmitted over the Internet. SOA simplifies client and server interaction, particularly for business-to-business applications.

Internet and Web technologies present an attractive alternative for implementing information systems. For example, consider the problem of data entry and access by an RMO buyer when purchasing items from its suppliers. Buyers are typically on the road for several months a year, often for weeks at a time. A traveling buyer needs some means of remotely interacting with RMO's supply chain management (SCM) system to record purchasing agreements and query inventory status.

One way of providing these capabilities would be to design custom application software and a private network to connect to that software. The primary portion of the system could be installed on a server at RMO. The client portion of the application—for data entry—would then be installed on the buyers' laptop computers. A buyer would connect to the system from remote locations to gain access to the application server, make queries to the database, and enter data.

Another alternative for implementing remote access for buyers would be to construct an application that uses a Web browser interface. The application would execute on a Web server, communicate with a Web browser using HTML or XML, and be accessible from any computer with an Internet connection. Buyers could use a Web browser on their laptop computer and connect to the application via an Internet service provider wherever they are currently located. Buyers could also access the application from any other computer with Internet access (for example, a computer in a vendor's office, hotel business suite, or copy center such as Kinko's).

Flexibility is the key to the Internet alternative. Implementing the application via the Internet greatly expands the application's accessibility and also eliminates the need to install custom client software on buyers' laptop computers. With Internet technology, client software can be updated by simply updating the version stored on the Web server. The application is relatively cheap to develop and deploy because existing Web standards and networking resources are employed. Custom software and private access via modems require more complex development and maintenance of a greater number of customized resources.

Implementing an application via the Web, an intranet, or an extranet has a number of advantages over traditional client/server applications, including the following:

- **Accessibility.** Web browsers and Internet connections are nearly ubiquitous. Internet, intranet, and extranet applications are accessible to a large number of potential users (including customers, suppliers, and off-site employees).
- **Low-cost communication.** The high-capacity WANs that form the Internet backbone were funded primarily by governments. Traffic on the backbone networks travels free of charge to the user, at least for the present. Connections between private LANs and the Internet can be purchased from a variety of private Internet service providers at relatively low cost. In essence, a company can use the Internet as a low-cost WAN.
- **Widely implemented standards.** Web standards are well known, and many computing professionals are already trained in their use. Server, client, and application development software is widely available and relatively cheap.

Information resource delivery via an intranet or extranet enjoys all of the advantages of Web delivery, since intranets and extranets use Web standards. In many ways, intranets, extranets, and the Web represent the logical evolution of client/server computing into an off-the-shelf technology. Organizations that had shied away from client/server computing because of the costs and required learning curve can now enjoy client/server benefits at substantially reduced complexity and cost.

Of course, there are negative aspects of application delivery via the Internet and Web technologies, including the following:

- **Security.** Web servers are a well-defined target for security breaches because Web standards are open and widely known. Wide-scale interconnection of networks and the use of Internet and Web standards make servers accessible to a global pool of hackers.

- **Reliability.** Internet protocols do not guarantee a minimum level of network throughput or even that a message will ever be received by its intended recipient. Standards have been proposed to address these shortcomings, but they have yet to be widely adopted.
- **Throughput.** The data transfer capacity of many home users is limited by analog modems to less than 56 kilobits per second. Also, Internet service providers and backbone WANs can become overloaded during high-traffic periods, resulting in slow response time for all users and long delays when accessing large resources.
- **Volatile standards.** Web standards change rapidly. Client software is updated every few months. Developers of widely used applications are faced with a dilemma: whether to use the latest standards to increase functionality, or use older standards to ensure greater compatibility with older user software.

The primary disadvantages to RMO of implementing the customer order application via the Internet are in security, performance, and reliability. If a customer can access the system via the Web, then so can anyone else. Access to sensitive parts of the system can be restricted by a number of means, including user accounts and passwords. But the risk of a security breach will always be present. Performance and reliability are limited by the customer's Internet connection point and the available Internet capacity between that connection and the application server. Unreliable or overloaded local Internet connections can render the application unusable. RMO has no control over these factors.

The key architectural design issues for Web-based applications are similar to those for other client/server architectures: defining client and server processes or objects, distributing them across hardware platforms, and connecting them with appropriate networks, middleware, and protocols. However, for Web-based applications, the choices for middleware and protocols tend to be much more limited than for other forms of client/server architecture.

Now that we've discussed common patterns of application architecture, we'll turn our attention to designing the networking infrastructure that connects parts of a modern information system.

NETWORK DESIGN

Networks are used throughout organizations today. As a result, many new development projects involve network design. Network planning and design are critical issues for any multitiered system. The key design issues are:

- Integrating network needs of the new system with existing network infrastructure
- Describing the processing activity and network connectivity at each system location
- Describing the communication protocols and middleware that connect layers
- Ensuring that sufficient network capacity is available

NETWORK INTEGRATION

Modern organizations rely on networks to support many different applications. Thus, the majority of new systems must be integrated into existing networks without disrupting existing applications. Network design and management are highly technical tasks, and most organizations have permanent in-house staff, contractors, or consultants to handle network administration.

The analyst for a new project begins network design by consulting with the organization's network administrators to determine whether the existing network can accommodate the new system. In some cases, the existing network capacity is sufficient, and only minimal changes are required, such as adding connections for new servers or modifying routing and firewall configuration to enable new application layers to communicate.

> **BEST PRACTICE: Consult with in-house experts to determine whether the network can support the new system without disrupting existing services.**

Planning for more extensive changes—such as significant expansion of capacity, new communication protocols, or modified security protocols—is much more complex. Typically, the network administrator assumes the responsibility of acquiring new capacity and making any configuration changes to support the new system, since he or she understands the existing network and the way other network-dependent applications operate. The analyst's role for the new system in these cases is to provide the network administrator with sufficient information and time to enable system development, testing, and deployment.

NETWORK DESCRIPTION

Location-related requirements information may have been documented using location diagrams (such as Figure 5-32), use case–location matrices (such as Figure 5-33), and use case–problem domain class matrices (such as Figure 5-34). During network design, the analyst expands the information content of these documents to include processing locations, communication protocols, middleware, and communication capacity.

network diagram
a model that shows how application layers are distributed across locations and computer systems

There are many different ways to describe the network infrastructure for a specific application. Figure 7-13 shows a *network diagram* that describes how application layers are distributed across locations and computer systems for the RMO customer support system. The diagram summarizes key architectural decisions from Figure 7-8 and combines them with specific assumptions about where application software will execute, where servers and workstations will be located, and how network resources will be organized.

The diagram embodies specific assumptions about server locations, which would be decided in consultation with network administrators. The Web/application servers could have been distributed outside the Salt Lake City data center, which might have improved system response time and reduced data-communication capacity requirements on the private WAN. However, distributing the servers would also entail duplication of server administration at multiple locations, which would increase operational complexity and cost. Decisions such as server locations, communication routes, and network security options are determined both by application requirements and organization-wide policies.

COMMUNICATION PROTOCOLS AND MIDDLEWARE

The network diagram is also a starting point for specifying protocol and middleware requirements. For example, the private WAN connections must support protocols required to process Microsoft Active Directory logins and queries. If the WAN fails, messages are routed through encrypted (VPN) connections over the Internet, so those connections must support the same protocols as the private WAN. All clients must be able to send HTTP requests and receive active content such as HTML forms and

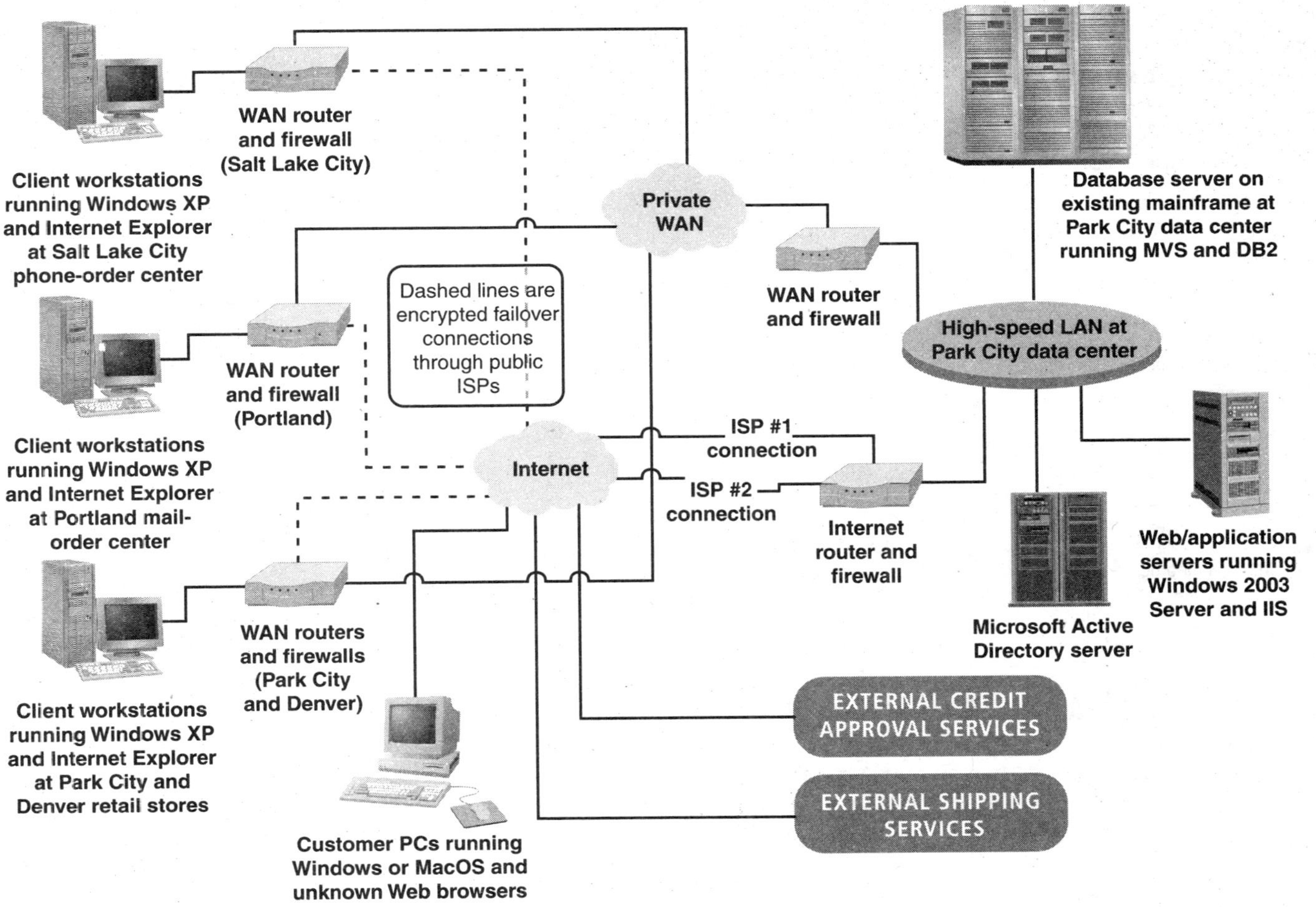

FIGURE 7-13
A network diagram for the RMO customer support system

embedded scripts. Application servers must be able to communicate with credit verification and shipping services via the Internet. Firewalls and routers must be configured to support all interactions among the workstations, customer PCs, Web/application servers, the Active Directory server, and external credit and shipping services. The Park City data center LAN must support at least one protocol for transmitting database queries and responses among the mainframe and Web/application servers.

NETWORK CAPACITY

Information from the use case–location and use case–problem domain class matrices is the starting point for estimating communication capacity requirements for the various LAN, WAN, and Internet connections. Figure 7-14 reproduces data from the RMO use case–problem domain class matrix (see Figure 5-34) covering two use cases (*Look up item availability* and *Create new order*) and three classes (Customer, Inventory Item, and Order). Similar tables would be required for all combinations of use case, class, and location. Figure 7-14 includes estimates of data size per access type and the average and peak number of accesses per minute or hour.

Data size per access type is an educated guess at this point in the system design, since none of the software layers, interlayer communication dialogs, or databases has yet been designed. Once those components have been designed in more detail or implemented, analysts can refine their estimates or actually sample and measure real data transmissions. Actual data transmission capacity will include communication protocol overhead in addition to raw data.

USE CASES AND LOCATIONS	PROBLEM DOMAIN CLASSES CUSTOMER	INVENTORYITEM	ORDER
Look up item availability (Salt Lake City phone-order center)		R (125 bytes, 25/min average, 250/min peak)	
Look up item availability (Park City retail store)		R (125 bytes, 5/hr average, 15/hr peak)	
Look up item availability (Denver retail store)		R (125 bytes, 5/hr average, 15/hr peak)	
Create new order (Salt Lake City phone-order center)	C (500 bytes, 2/min average, 10/min peak)	R (60 bytes, 30/min average, 300/min peak)	C (200 bytes, 10/min average, 100/min peak)
	R (500 bytes, 8/min average, 80/min peak)	U (60 bytes, 30/min average, 300/min peak)	
	U (500 bytes, 2/min average, 10/min peak)		
Create new order (Portland mail-order center)	C (500 bytes, 1/min average, 10/min peak)	R (60 bytes, 15/min average, 150/min peak)	C (200 bytes, 5/min average, 50/min peak)
	R (500 bytes, 4/min average, 40/min peak)	U (60 bytes, 15/min average, 150/min peak)	
	U (500 bytes, 1/min average, 10/min peak)		
Create new order (Park City retail store)	C (500 bytes, 1/hr average, 5/hr peak)	R (60 bytes, 15/hr average, 75/hr peak)	C (200 bytes, 5/hr average, 25/hr peak)
	R (500 bytes, 4/hr average, 20/hr peak)	U (60 bytes, 15/hr average, 75/hr peak)	
	U (500 bytes, 1/hr average, 5/hr peak)		
Create new order (Denver retail store)	C (500 bytes, 1/hr average, 5/hr peak)	R (60 bytes, 15/hr average, 75/hr peak)	C (200 bytes, 5/hr average, 25/hr peak)
	R (500 bytes, 4/hr average, 20/hr peak)	U (60 bytes, 15/hr average, 75/hr peak)	
	U (500 bytes, 1/hr average, 5/hr peak)		

C = Creates new data, R = Reads existing data, U = Updates existing data, D = Deletes existing data

FIGURE 7-14

Partial use case–problem domain class matrix for RMO customer support system, updated with data access size and volume

BEST PRACTICE: Refine network capacity estimates as detailed design activities are completed.

Summary

Systems design is the discipline of organizing and structuring the components of a system to enable construction and deployment. The design discipline consists of many detailed activities that relate to the various components of the new system. The detailed activities are grouped into high-level design activities, including designing the support services architecture and deployment environment, software architecture, use case realizations, user interfaces, system interfaces, database, network, and system controls and security.

The inputs to the design activities are business and requirements models. The outputs of the design are also a set of models that describe the architecture of the new system and the detailed structure of and interaction among its various components. Project management is critical when design activities are initiated. The tenor of the project changes at this point. During design, members of the technical staff are involved. The project manager has to pay particular attention to the schedule, staff, and design activities. Construction is usually intertwined with design, which requires the addition of programming staff. Other side projects for data conversion and test-data development are also begun at this time.

High-level design activities can be subdivided into architectural and detail design. Architectural design adapts the application to the deployment environment, including hardware, software, and networks. Modern application software is usually deployed in a distributed multicomputer environment and is organized according to client/server architecture or a variant such as three-layer architecture. Architectural design decisions include decomposing the application into clients, servers, or layers; distributing software across hardware platforms; and specifying required protocols, middleware, and networks.

Architectural design decisions can be documented in a network diagram. The network diagram describes the organization of computing and network resources and specifies details such as what the required protocols are and which application software and middleware executes on which computer systems. Required network capacity can be determined by expanding the use case–location and use case–problem domain class matrices to include estimates of message size and volume.

KEY TERMS

architectural design, p. 263
business logic layer, p. 280
centralized architecture, p. 272
client, p. 277
clustered architecture, p. 271
computer network, p. 272
data layer, p. 280
detail design, p. 263
distributed architecture, p. 272
extranet, p. 274
Internet, p. 274
intranet, p. 274
local area network (LAN), p. 272
middleware, p. 281
multicomputer architecture, p. 271
multitier architecture, p. 271
network diagram, p. 284
router, p. 273
server, p. 277
service-oriented architecture (SOA), p. 281
single-computer architecture, p. 270
three-layer architecture, p. 279
view layer, p. 280
virtual organization, p. 274
virtual private network (VPN), p. 274
wide area network (WAN), p. 272
World Wide Web (WWW), or Web, p. 274

REVIEW QUESTIONS

1. How do the models and activities of the requirements discipline differ from those of the design discipline?
2. What is the difference between architectural and detailed design?
3. List and briefly describe the high-level activities of the design discipline.
4. How does project management become more complex once design activities begin? What tools can a project manager use during design?
5. Explain the difference between centralized architecture and distributed architecture.
6. Explain the difference between clustered architecture and multicomputer architecture in a centralized system.
7. How are the Internet, intranets, and extranets similar? How are they different?
8. Describe client/server architecture and list the key architecture design issues that must be addressed when developing a client/server information system.
9. List and briefly describe the function of each layer in three-layer architecture.
10. What role does middleware play?
11. Describe the process of network design.
12. What roles do systems analysts and network administrators play in network design?
13. What is a network diagram? What information does it convey, and where does the analyst gather that information?
14. How does the analyst generate estimates of required communication capacity? What requirements models are used as input?

THINKING CRITICALLY

1. Review the definitions of architectural and detailed design and the brief descriptions of high-level design activities at the beginning of the chapter. Which activities are clearly architectural? Which are clearly detailed? Which can be architectural or detailed?
2. Discuss the evolution of client/server computing from file server to multilayer applications to Web-based applications. What has been the driving force causing this evolution? How do you think networks and distributed information systems will evolve over the next five years? Ten years?
3. Assume that the deployment environment for a high-volume payment-processing system consists of the following:
   - DB2 DBMS running under the OS/390 operating system on an IBM S/390 mainframe
   - WebSphere application server running under the Z/OS operating system on an IBM zSeries 900 mainframe
   - CORBA-compliant component-based application software written in Java that will be executed by other internal and external systems

   What are the key architectural design decisions that must be made for the system? When should the decisions be made, and who should make them? Outline the subsequent design tasks that should occur after the key architectural design decisions are made. To what extent can the subsequent steps be performed in parallel?
4. Develop a network diagram that supports the architectural design decisions in your answer to number 3.

EXPERIENTIAL EXERCISES

1. Assume the same application and deployment environment described in Thinking Critically exercise 3. Investigate possible development environments for this deployment environment. Describe their advantages and disadvantages and recommend a specific set of development tools.
2. Set up a meeting with the chief analysts of a medium- or large-scale development project, and discuss the transition from requirements to design for that project. Were requirements activities completed early in the project and design activities later, or were the activities intertwined throughout the project? How and when were key architectural decisions such as automation boundary, network design, and supporting infrastructure made? Who made the decisions? Were the early architectural decisions modified later in the project? If so, how and why?
3. Find an example of an application system that is browser-based and uses TCP/IP standards. Explain how it works, showing sample screens and reports. List each middleware component and describe its function. List each protocol employed and identify the standard family or families to which the protocol belongs.
4. Visit the Web site www.service-architecture.com. Investigate current service-oriented architectures and describe the differences between them and earlier standards and architectures that fill a similar role.
5. Examine the RMO network diagram in Figure 7-13 and note the connections to external service providers for credit verification and shipping services. Identify at least three companies that can provide each service. Investigate their online Web-based service capabilities and describe the protocols used by clients to interact with their services.

Case Studies

THE REAL ESTATE MULTIPLE LISTING SERVICE SYSTEM

Consider the requirements of the multiple listing service system developed in Chapters 5 and 6. Assume that you are the project manager and that you work for a consulting firm hired by the multiple listing service to perform requirements and architectural design activities. Assume that system users and owners have indicated a strong desire for a system that can be accessed "anytime, anywhere."

[1] Discuss the implications of the anytime, anywhere requirement for the application deployment environment. What type(s) of hardware, network, and software architecture will be required to fulfill that requirement?

[2] Develop a three-layer architecture using ordinary PCs running Web browsers to implement the view layer. Draw a network diagram to represent your solution.

[3] Today's computer-based real estate listings typically include graphical data, such as still and moving pictures in addition to text descriptions of properties. What is the impact of such data on data-communication requirements within your network design, assuming 10 listing accesses per hour? 100 listing accesses per hour? 1,000 listing accesses per hour?

RETHINKING ROCKY MOUNTAIN OUTFITTERS

ROCKY MOUNTAIN OUTFITTERS

Various application deployment environments can meet the requirements of RMO's strategic plan. The staff's current thinking is to move more toward a Microsoft solution, using the latest version of Microsoft Server with Microsoft's IIS as the Web server. However, Linux with Apache servers is a competing approach. Considering that RMO could also take that approach, do the following:

[1] Compare the relative market penetration of Microsoft and Apache/Linux (a good starting place is http://news.netcraft.com).

[2] Modify the network diagram in Figure 7-13 to describe a viable architecture using Apache/Linux. What changes, if any, are required for the client workstations and customer PCs? What changes, if any, are required in middleware and communication

protocols? Will there be any change in the estimates of required data-communication capacity among client workstations and servers located at the Park City data center? Why, or why not?

The database issue is another potential controversy for RMO. The current decision is to keep the mainframe and run DB2, a very efficient relational database. However, another alternative would be to implement an Oracle database. Oracle is also very strong in the marketplace. Given these two alternatives, do the following:

[3] Compare the relative market penetration of these two solutions.

[4] List the strengths and weaknesses of each approach, that of the DB2 mainframe approach, and that of Oracle running on some type of multiple processor server computer.

FOCUSING ON RELIABLE PHARMACEUTICAL SERVICE

Reliable PHARMACEUTICALS Reliable's management recently completed the task of choosing a system scope and implementation approach. As input to that process, you prepared the following table which divides the functional requirements into subsets; estimates the duration of requirements, design, implementation, and deployment activities for each function if software is custom-built; and categorizes the risk for each function based on software complexity, technology maturity, and certainty about requirements.

FUNCTION	PROJECT DURATION	RISK
Inventory and purchasing	9 months	moderate
Order fulfillment (manual data entry)	6 months	low
Web-based order entry	9 months	high
Prescription warning	12 months	high
Billing	18 months	high

Top executives evaluated the table content and determined that all of the functions were high-priority needs. Because they considered the combined project duration too long, they rejected the approach of developing custom software and instead chose to seek a strategic partner with an existing system that could be modified to match Reliable's needs. A request for proposals (RFP) was written and distributed, and a vendor was chosen after management had evaluated the responses.

Assume that you are the project manager for the selected vendor's development team. Your company, RxTechSys, develops and markets software to retail and hospital pharmacies and has decided to take on the Reliable project to expand potential market share. RxTechSys and Reliable will jointly develop the new software. RxTechSys will then market the finished product to other companies and pay a royalty to Reliable for each sale.

RxTechSys has been in the pharmacy software business for 20 years. The latest version of the software is a Web-based application built on the Microsoft .NET platform. Major functions such as inventory control, purchasing, billing, and prescription interaction warning are implemented as .NET Web services. As part of the team that prepared the response to Reliable's RFP, you determined that RxTechSys's current system can be adapted to Reliable's needs as follows:

- Existing browser-based prescription entry can be modified to handle data input from multiple customer locations over a VPN. This is a significant modification due to expanded data content and greater security requirements.
- Order fulfillment software will have to be written from scratch.
- Billing software will require significant modification, since your current system assumes that all patients have their health care managed by a single institution, with possible third-party reimbursements through Medicaid/Medicare.
- Other parts of your existing system can be used with little or no modification.

Reliable has provided you with a nearly complete set of object-oriented business and requirements models, the quality of which you approved during contract negotiations. Your task is to move the project forward through the remaining requirements, design, implementation, and deployment activities.

Reliable has assigned an operational manager with some computer experience to your team full time, and she is authorized to assign other Reliable personnel to your project as needed. You have been assigned a full-time staff of four developers, two of whom have substantial design experience and all of whom participated in developing the most recent version of RxPharmSys software.

Develop a plan and schedule covering the next four to six weeks (your expected project duration is 10 months). What design decisions must be made within the next two weeks? Who should make them? How will requirements, design, implementation, and deployment activities proceed thereafter—what tasks must be performed, and in what order? How will you manage and control the project?

FURTHER RESOURCES

Thomas Erl, *Service-Oriented Architecture: A Field Guide to Integrating XML and Web Services*. Prentice-Hall, 2004.

Luke Hohmann, *Beyond Software Architecture: Creating and Sustaining Winning Solutions*. Addison-Wesley, 2003.

Gregor Hohpe and Bobby Woolf, *Enterprise Integration Patterns: Designing, Building, and Deploying Messaging Solutions*. Pearson Education, 2003.

David S. Linthicum, *Next Generation Application Integration: From Simple Information to Web Services*. Addison-Wesley, 2003.

Robert Orfali, Dan Harkey, and Jeri Edwards, *Client/Server Survival Guide* (3rd ed.). Wiley, 1999.

Daniel J. Paulish, *Architecture-Centric Software Project Management: A Practical Guide*. Addison-Wesley, 2001.

Kathy Schwalbe, *Information Technology Project Management* (2nd ed.). Course Technology, 2002.

chapter 8

USE CASE REALIZATION: THE DESIGN DISCIPLINE WITHIN UP ITERATIONS

LEARNING OBJECTIVES

After reading this chapter, you should be able to:

- Explain the purpose and objectives of object-oriented design
- Develop design class diagrams
- Develop interaction diagrams based on the principles of object responsibility and use case controllers
- Develop detailed sequence diagrams as the core process in systems design
- Develop communication diagrams as part of systems design
- Document the architectural design using package diagrams

CHAPTER OUTLINE

- Object-Oriented Design—The Bridge between Requirements and Implementation
- Design Classes and Design Class Diagrams
- Interaction Diagrams—Realizing Use Cases and Defining Methods
- Designing with Sequence Diagrams
- Designing with Communication Diagrams
- Updating the Design Class Diagram
- Package Diagrams—Structuring the Major Components
- Implementation Issues for Three-Layer Design

NEW CAPITAL BANK: PART 1

Even though there had been some hiccups at the beginning of the project, things seemed to be under control now. Bill Santora, who was the project leader responsible for the development of an integrated customer account system at New Capital Bank, had just finished a technical review of the new system's first-cut design with the review committee. This first-cut design focused on six core use cases, which had been chosen as the most fundamental to the business and so would be implemented in the first iteration of the elaboration phase.

New Capital Bank had been using object-oriented languages for quite a while, but it had been slower to adopt object-oriented development techniques. Bill had been involved in some early pilot projects that had used the Unified Process (UP) and the Unified Modeling Language (UML) to develop systems. However, this development project was his first large-scale project that would be entirely object-oriented.

As Bill collected his presentation materials, his supervisor, Mary Garcia, spoke. "Your technical review went very well, Bill. The committee found only a few minor items that need to be fixed. Even though I am not completely current on the new object-oriented techniques, it was easy for me to understand what you presented and how these core functions will work. I still find it hard to believe that you will have these six pieces implemented in the next few weeks."

"Wait a minute," Bill laughed. "It won't be ready for the users then. Getting these six core functions coded and running doesn't mean that we are almost done. This project is still going to take a year to complete."

"Yes, I know. But it is nice that we will have something to show after only two months. Not only do I feel more confident about this project, but the users love to see things developing."

"I know. Remember how much grief I got when I originally laid out this plan based on the UP? Since the UP is an adaptive approach, it was more difficult to detail the project schedule for the later iterations. So I had a hard time convincing everybody that the project schedule was not too risky. The upside is that since each iteration is only six weeks long, we have something to show right at the beginning. You don't know how relieved I am that the design passed the review! The team has done a lot of work to make sure the design was solid, and we all felt confident. It is good to get confirmation, though. And we really will have some basic pieces of the new system working in two or three more weeks."

"Well, building it incrementally makes a lot of sense and certainly seems to be working. I especially liked the detailed sequence diagrams you showed for each use case. It was terrific how you showed that the three-layer design supported each use case. Even though I do not consider myself an advanced object-oriented technician, I could understand how each use case was implemented. I think you wowed everybody when you demonstrated how you could use the same basic design to support both our internal bank tellers and a Web portal for our customers. Congratulations."

Bill's response reflected Mary's enthusiasm. "How about the design class diagrams? Don't they give a nice overview of the classes and the methods? We use them extensively as a focus for discussion on the team. They really help the programmers write good, solid code."

"By the way, have you scheduled a review with the users?" Mary asked.

"No. We worked intimately with the users on developing the use cases and creating the fully developed use case descriptions. We also worked with the users to develop prototype screens for all of these use cases. So, rather than try to explain the details of the design models to the users, we are just going to code these use cases next. After all, we will have something to show them in a couple of weeks. Then we will have another round of meetings with users to let them verify our work and to begin work on the next iteration. We need their involvement as we develop the use case descriptions for the next set of use cases."

"I am anxious to see the first pieces run. It just makes so much sense to be able to test these core functions during the rest of the project. Let me congratulate you again," Mary said as she and Bill headed off to lunch together.

Overview

The primary focus of this chapter and the next is on how to develop detailed object-oriented design models, which the programmers then use to code the system. The two most important models that must be developed are design class diagrams and interaction diagrams (sequence diagrams and communication diagrams). You will learn how to develop design class diagrams for each layer of three-layer design: domain layer, view layer, and data access layer. Design class diagrams extend the domain model that was developed during the requirements activities. Interaction diagrams extend the system sequence diagrams, also developed during requirements activities. We also discuss how to associate classes into package diagrams to show relationships and dependencies. Finally, we discuss some principles of good design and ways to apply them.

OBJECT-ORIENTED DESIGN—THE BRIDGE BETWEEN REQUIREMENTS AND IMPLEMENTATION

If we compare the development of a new software system with building a house, we might say that business modeling and requirements are like the architect's initial sketches and conceptual drawings. Those drawings depict what the homeowner wants for rooms, floors, layout, location on the lot, and so forth. However, those drawings and sketches are inadequate for a contractor to build the house. The contractor needs much more detail. So, the architect takes the initial drawings and builds a set of detailed plans, called *blueprints*, which show exact measurements for walls, floors, and ceilings; specifications for plumbing and electrical wiring; and even the specific materials to be used. These detailed blueprints are similar to the design models that software developers build.

The analogy can be extended even further. While the sketches are being drawn, the homeowner is very involved in dictating his or her desires, but during development of the detailed blueprints, the homeowner is less involved. He or she does review and verify the specifications in the blueprints, but an expert, the architect, develops the wiring diagrams and plumbing layout in the walls to meet the buyer's desires and to direct the contractor later. Similarly, in system development, software design experts create the detailed design specifications, with occasional input by the users—primarily for verification of the design.

So what is object-oriented design? It is the process by which a set of detailed object-oriented design models is built, which the programmers will later use to write code and test the new system. Systems design is essentially a bridge between a user's requirements and programming for the new system. Just as a builder would never try to build anything larger than a doghouse or a shed without a set of blueprints, a system developer would never try to develop a large system without a set of design models. Sometimes students who are building personal Web pages or small systems for course assignments think that design models are unnecessary. Just remember that blueprints may not be necessary for a doghouse, but they are critical for something more complex, such as a home.

One of the tenets of the new adaptive approaches to development is to develop only models that have meaning and are necessary. Sometimes new developers interpret this guideline to mean that they do not need to develop design models at all. That is untrue. The design models may not be formalized into a comprehensive set of diagrams, but those that are developed are certainly necessary. Developing a system without doing design can be compared to writing a research paper without an outline. You could just sit down and start writing; however, if you want to write a paper that is cohesive, flows well, and is complete and comprehensive, then you should write an outline first. You could write a complex paper without an outline, but in all probability it would be disjointed, hard to follow, and missing important points—and only earn a C grade! The outline can be jotted down on note paper, but the process of thinking it through and writing it down allows the writer to ensure that it is cohesive. Systems design provides the same type of framework. It may not need to be a formal, finished product, but you must think it through and write it down to make sure you have a complete, comprehensive solution.

One point about adaptive approaches (including the UP) that is true, however, is that requirements and design are done incrementally within an iteration. So a complete set of design documents is not developed at one time. The requirements for a particular use case or several use cases may be developed, and then the design documents developed for that use case. Immediately following the design of the solution, the programming can be done. Usually there is no need to generate a formal set of documents since their purpose is simply to direct the programming.

Designing the application software, which is covered in this chapter, is just one part of OO design. As you learned in Chapter 7, user-interface design, network design, controls and security design, and database design also require design tasks and design models.

OVERVIEW OF OBJECT-ORIENTED PROGRAMS

Before going further, let's quickly review how an object-oriented program works. An object-oriented program consists of a set of objects that cooperate to accomplish a result. Each object contains program logic and any necessary attributes in a single unit. These objects work by sending each other messages and collaborating to support the functions of the main program.

Figure 8-1 depicts how an object-oriented program works. The program includes an Input window object that displays a form in which to enter student identification and other information. After the student ID is entered, the Input window object sends a message (message number 2) to the Student class to tell it to create a new Student object in the program and also to go to the database and get the student information and put it in the Student object (message 3). Once that is done, the new Student object also

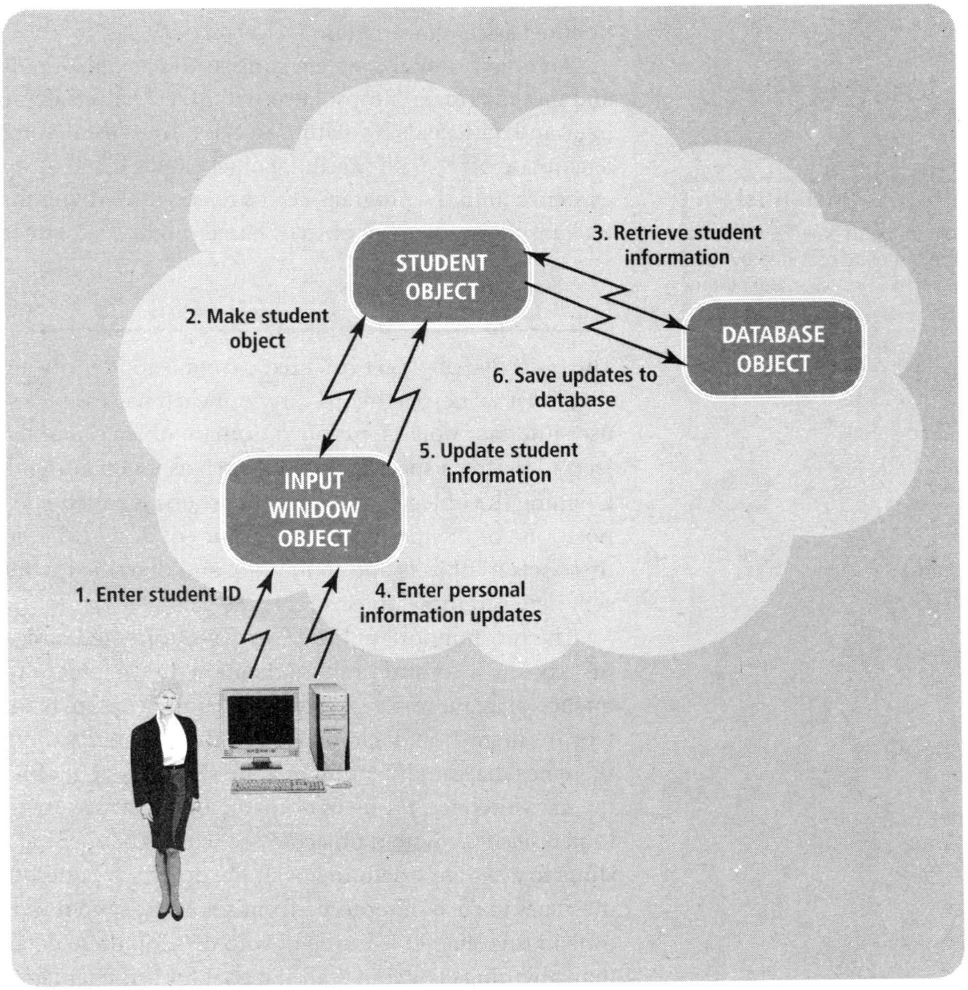

FIGURE 8-1
Object-oriented event-driven program flow

sends that information back to the Input window object to display it on the screen. The registration clerk then enters the personal information updates (message 4), and another sequence of messages is sent to update the Student object in the program and the student information in the database.

One common question about object-oriented programs is, Which program is in charge? Most object-oriented programs are event driven. Program execution is initiated by an actor wanting to carry out a use case, that is, a business event. A use case is executed by a set of collaborating and interacting objects. Thus, a single program or class does not need to be in charge. A particular object program is in charge of a single use case, not the entire executable program. The program simply must wait and listen for a message—an event—from an actor.

Let's use an analogy to clarify object-oriented programs further. A network of personal computers consists of many individual computers connected by network cables. Each computer has its own computing capability, but if you are working at one computer, you can communicate with another personal computer through a message and ask for assistance. For example, some of the individual computers on the network have large disk drives and special databases that you can access. They are called *file servers*. Other resources, such as printers, are also on the network. Typically, in most PC networks you have encountered, there is no single, coherent purpose for individual computers. But sometimes computers need to work together to accomplish a specific purpose. They do this by sending messages to each other to fulfill the overall computing objective. This networked system functions in much the same way that an object-oriented system or program is designed to.

An object-oriented system consists of sets of computing objects. Each object has data and program logic encapsulated within it. Analysts define the structure of the program logic and data fields by defining a class. The class definition describes the structure, or a template of what an executing object looks like. The object itself does not come into existence until the program begins to execute. We call that *instantiation* of the class, or making an instance (an object), based on the template provided by the class definition.

instantiation
creation of an object based on the template provided by the class definition

OBJECT-ORIENTED DESIGN MODELS

The objective of object-oriented design is to identify and specify all of the objects that must work together to carry out each use case. As seen in Figure 8-1, there are user-interface objects, problem domain objects, and database objects. Additional objects to perform specific services, such as logon authentication, may also be required. Dividing the objects into different groups is called *multilayer design*. As you may suppose, one of the major responsibilities of design is to identify and describe each of these sets of objects and to identify and describe the interactions or messages that are sent between these objects.

The most important model in object-oriented design is a sequence diagram—or its first cousin, a communication diagram. In Chapter 6, you learned that a system sequence diagram was a type of interaction diagram. A communication diagram is also a type of interaction diagram. During the design discipline, analysts extend the system sequence diagram by modifying the single :<u>System</u> object to include all of the interacting user-interface, problem domain, and database access objects. In other words, they look *inside* the :<u>System</u> object to see what is happening inside the system. Their focus shifts to accurately defining what the objects are and how they collaborate by sending messages to each other to perform a specific system function. We will spend lots of time in this chapter learning how to develop these detailed sequence diagrams. More than anything else, your learning goal for this chapter should be to learn how to develop sequence diagrams.

The other major design model, which you will also learn to develop in this chapter, is the design class diagram. Its main purpose is to document and describe the programming classes that will be built for the new system. Design class diagrams are the end result of the design process. They describe the set of object-oriented classes needed for programming, navigation between the classes, attribute names and properties, and method names and properties. A design class diagram is a summary of the final design that was developed using the detailed sequence diagrams. It summarizes the design and is used directly in the development of the programming code. Figure 8-2 is an example of one class from a design class diagram. Notice that it specifies the attributes and methods for a class.

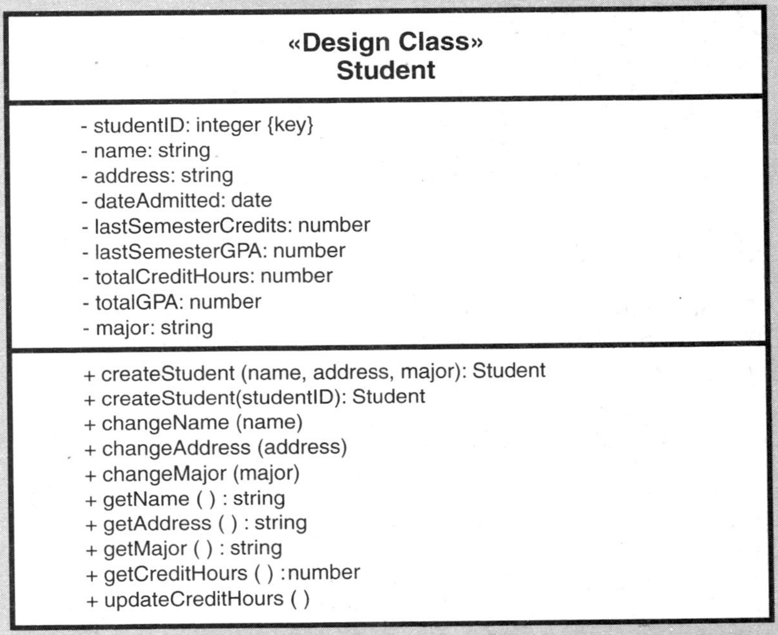

FIGURE 8-2
Design class for Student class

As an object-oriented system designer, you will need to provide enough detail so that a programmer can write the initial class definitions and then add considerable detail to the code. For example, a design class specification helps define the attributes and the methods. You will learn the detailed notation for design classes later in the chapter, but as a preliminary example, observe Figure 8-2 and compare that with Figure 8-3 (a) and (b). Figure 8-3 shows some detailed program code for class definitions. Part (a) illustrates the code in Java, and part (b) illustrates Visual Basic code. You should be able to see where the attributes and method signatures come from for the sample code shown in Figure 8-3. Notice that the class name, the attributes, and the method names are derived from the design class notation. Of course, in the design class we took some liberties by abbreviating first name and last name to simply *name* and by combining all the components of an address into one field called *address*. If there is any question whether a programmer will know that he or she should break these shortened names out into the detailed fields, then the designer should not take these shortcuts. Other

FIGURE 8-3
Class definition for the Student class (a) Java programming language (b) Visual Basic programming language

code that needs to be added to the class definition can be derived from the other design models. As we discuss design classes, be sure to refer back to the code snippets shown in Figure 8-3 to help you see the connection between design and programming.

Another model that we use in design is a detailed statechart diagram. As you learned in Chapter 6, statechart diagrams are useful in describing the life of an object.

(a)

```
public class Student
{
      //attributes
      private int studentID;
      private String firstName;
      private String lastName;
      private String street;
      private String city;
      private String state;
      private String zipcode;
      private Date dateAdmitted;
      private float numberCredits;
      private String lastActiveSemester;
      private float lastActiveSemesterGPA;
      private float gradePointAverage;
      private String major;

      //constructors
      public Student (String inFirstName, String inLastName, String inStreet,
            String inCity, String inState, String inZip, Date inDate)
      {
            firstName = inFirstName;
            lastName = inLastName;
            ...
      }
      public Student (int inStudentID)
      {
            //read database to get values
      }

      //get and set methods
      public String getFullName ( )
      {
            return firstName + " " + lastName;
      }
      public void setFirstName (String inFirstName)
      {
            firstName = inFirstName;
      }
      public float getGPA ( )
      {
            return gradePointAverage;
      }
      //and so on

      //processing methods
      public void updateGPA ( )
      {
            //access course records and update lastActiveSemester and
            //to-date credits and GPA
      }
}
```

(b)

```
Public Class Student

    'attributes
    Private studentID As Integer
    Private firstName As String
    Private lastName As String
    Private street As String
    Private city As String
    Private state As String
    Private zipcode As String
    Private dateAdmitted As Date
    Private numberCredits As Single
    Private lastActiveSemester As String
    Private lastActiveSemesterGPA As Single
    Private gradePointAverage As Single
    Private major As String

    'constructor methods
    Public Sub New(ByVal inFirstName As String, ByVal inLastName As String,
          ByVal inStreet As String, ByVal inCity As String, ByVal inState As String,
          ByVal inZip As String, ByVal inDate As Date)
        firstName = inFirstName
        lastName = inLastName
        ...
    End Sub

    Public Sub New(ByVal inStudentID)
        'read database to get values
    End Sub

    'get and set accessor methods
    Public Function GetFullName() As String
        Dim info As String
        info = firstName & " " & lastName
        Return info
    End Function

    Public Property firstName()
        Get
            Return firstName
        End Get
        Set (ByVal Value)
            firstName = Value
        End Set
    End Property

    Public ReadOnly Property GPA()
        Get
          Return gradePointAverage
        End Get
    End Property

    'Processing Methods
    Public Function UpdateGPA()
        'read the database and update last semester
        'and to date credits and GPA
    End Function

End Class
```

A statechart diagram captures information about the valid states and transitions of an object. Statecharts are an effective tool, but in designing business systems, they are only used for special situations. We will discuss how and when to use statecharts for design in the next chapter.

A final model that we use to document subsystems is called a *package diagram*. A package diagram is useful to denote which classes work together as a subsystem. You will learn more about how to use package diagrams later in this chapter.

Figure 8-4 illustrates which requirements models are directly used to develop which design models. The models on the left side—use case diagrams, use case descriptions and activity diagrams, domain model class diagrams, system sequence diagrams, and statechart diagrams—are those that were developed during requirements.

FIGURE 8-4
Design models with their respective input models

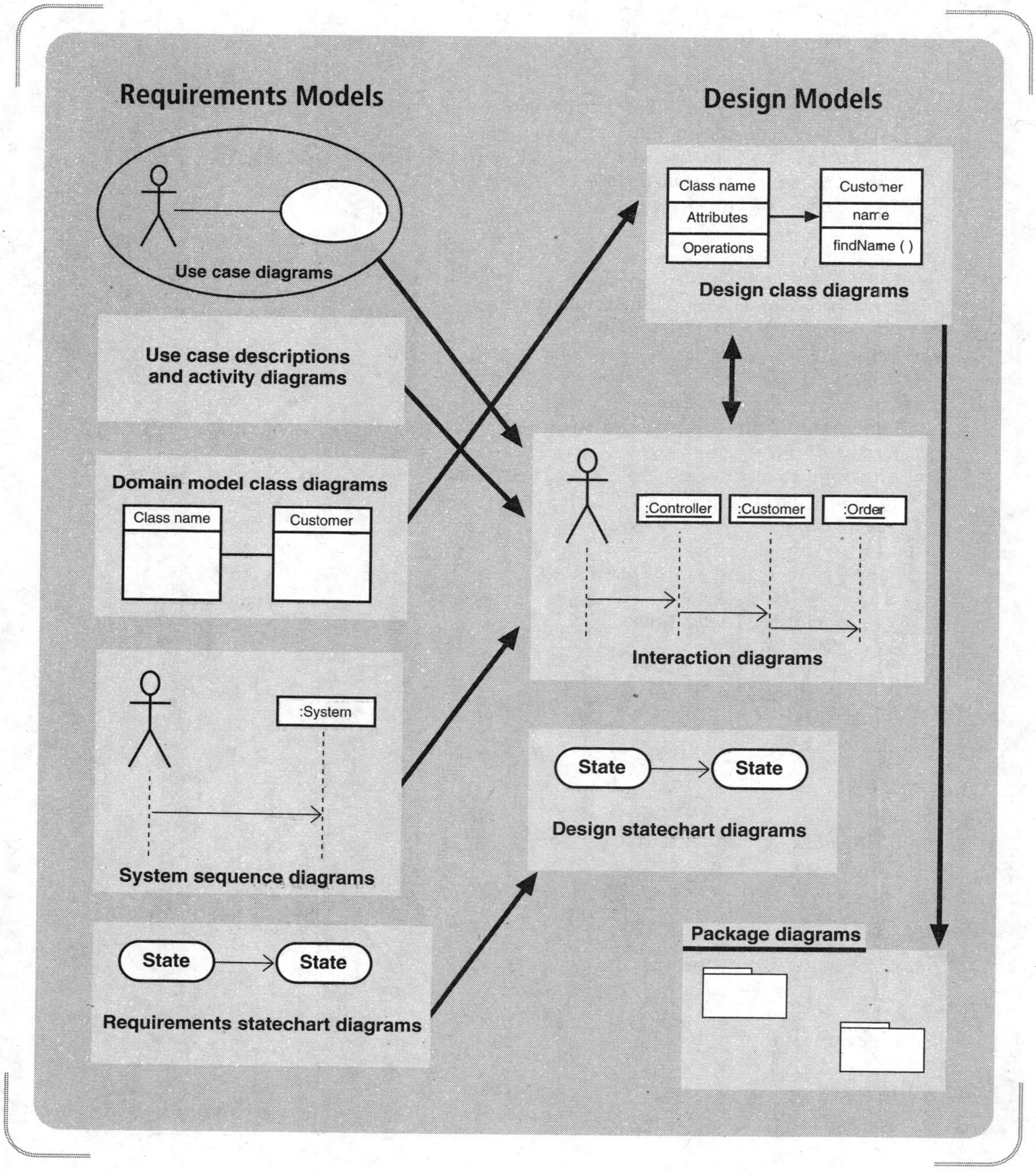

Those on the right side—design class diagrams, interaction diagrams, statechart diagrams, and package diagrams—will be developed during design. As you might infer from the number of arrows pointing to them in the figure, interaction diagrams are the core diagrams in design, and you will learn how to develop interaction diagrams in this chapter.

As shown in Figure 8-4, design information is derived from two sources: the domain model class diagram and the interaction diagrams. In fact, notice that the arrow between design class diagrams and interaction diagrams points two ways. The two-headed arrow indicates that some information in the design class diagram is needed to complete interaction diagrams and that information in the interaction diagrams is used to develop design class diagrams.

We will also describe other models and diagrams as part of OO design. These other models, such as package diagrams and deployment diagrams, are helpful as supporting documentation. Remember, however, that the primary OO design models are design class diagrams and interaction diagrams, with an occasional statechart diagram where necessary.

OBJECT-ORIENTED DESIGN PROCESS

Object-oriented design is use case driven, meaning that we develop a design with a sequence diagram use case by use case—one at a time. The process of designing requires several steps, or iterations. First, a preliminary version, or first-cut model, of the design class diagrams is created. Some basic information, such as attribute names, must be obtained from the first-cut model to develop the interaction diagrams.

The second step in design is to develop interaction diagrams—resulting in one sequence diagram for each use case or scenario. Developing an interaction diagram is a multistep process of determining which objects work together and how they work together. Development of the interaction diagrams is the heart of object-oriented systems design. As shown in Figure 8-4, input models for interactions diagrams are use case diagrams, use case descriptions, system sequence diagrams, and design class diagrams. The end result of the development of these design models is called *realization of use cases*. In this instance, the term *realization* is the specification of the detailed processing that the system must do to carry out the use case—in other words, making a set of software blueprints. Notice that just as object-oriented requirements activities were driven by use cases, so also are object-oriented design activities. That is, design is done on a use case–by–use case basis.

realization of use cases
specification of all detailed system processing for each use case

The third step in OO design is to return to the design class diagram and develop method names based on information developed during the design of the interaction diagrams. The navigation visibility and attribute information is also updated in this iteration of the design class diagram.

The final design step is to partition the design class diagram into related functions using package diagrams. There are several ways that a system might be partitioned. One way is by subsystem. Another is by layers. In Chapter 7, you learned about multilayer architectures and multiple tiers. In this chapter, you will learn how to partition design class diagrams into packages to represent the multiple layers in a multitier system. We focus on a basic multilayer design consisting of the view layer (user-interface classes), the domain layer (problem domain classes from the domain model class diagram), and the data layer (database access classes). Note that several terms are used to denote the domain layer. Synonymous terms include *domain layer*, *problem domain layer*, and *business logic layer*. Package diagrams provide an architectural, high-level view of the final system.

DESIGN CLASSES AND DESIGN CLASS DIAGRAMS

As shown in Figure 8-4, the design class diagrams and the detailed interaction diagrams use each other as inputs for design and are developed at the same time. A first iteration of the design class diagram is done based on the domain model and on engineering design principles. The preliminary design class diagram is then used to help develop interaction diagrams. As design decisions are made during development of the interaction diagrams, the results are used to refine the design class diagram.

As we mentioned previously, the design class diagram is an extension of the domain model class diagram developed during OO requirements. The domain model class diagram shows a set of problem domain classes and their association relationships. During specification of requirements, since it is a discovery process, analysts generally do not worry too much about the details of the class attributes or the methods. However, in object-oriented programming, the attributes of a class must be declared as public or private, and each attribute must also be defined by its type, such as character or numeric. During design, it is important to elaborate these details, as well as to define parameters that are passed to the methods and return values from methods. Sometimes analysts also define the internal logic of each method at this point. So, the design class diagram is a more detailed version of the domain model class diagram. We complete it by integrating information from interaction diagrams and other models.

As developers build the design class diagrams, they add many more classes than were originally defined in the domain model. Since the objective of requirements was to understand the business need, the focus was only on specifying the classes that defined the problem domain. However, to build a complete object-oriented system, we must identify and specify many other design classes. In Figure 8-1, the Input window objects and Database objects are examples of these additional classes that must be defined. As these classes are defined, we usually document them on various class diagrams. The classes in a system can be partitioned into various distinct class diagrams, such as user-interface classes. At times, we may also develop distinct class diagrams by subsystem. The point is that class diagramming is a tool that can be used in different ways. We now turn to design class diagram notation and the design principles used in the first iteration of developing the design class diagram.

DESIGN CLASS SYMBOLS

Unified Modeling Language (UML) does not specifically distinguish between design class notation and domain model notation. However, practical differences occur because of their objectives. Domain modeling shows things in the users' work environment and the naturally occurring associations among them. The classes are not specifically software classes. Once we start a design class diagram, though, we are specifically defining software classes. Since many different types of design classes will be identified during the design process, UML has a special notation, called a *stereotype*, that allows designers to designate a special type of class. A *stereotype* is simply a way to categorize a model element as a certain type. A stereotype extends the basic definition of a model element by indicating that it has some special characteristic that we want to highlight. The notation for a stereotype is the name of the type placed within printer's guillemets, like this: «control». You were first exposed to a stereotype when you were developing a use case diagram. You learned that connecting lines between actors and use cases indicated a relationship, and that a certain type of relationship existed between use cases, called the «includes» relationship. That was a stereotype because it categorized the relationship of one use case as including another use case.

stereotype
a way of categorizing a model element by its characteristics, indicated by guillemets (« »)

Four types of design classes are considered to be standard: an entity class, a control class, a boundary class, and a data access class. Figure 8-5 shows the notation used to identify these four stereotypes. Two types of notation can be used for design classes. The class rectangles on the left show the full symbols. Notice that the stereotypes are placed above the name in the name compartment. The circular symbols on the right are shorthand notation for these stereotypes, called *icons*. We will use the stereotype icons from time to time, but in most cases we prefer the full notation.

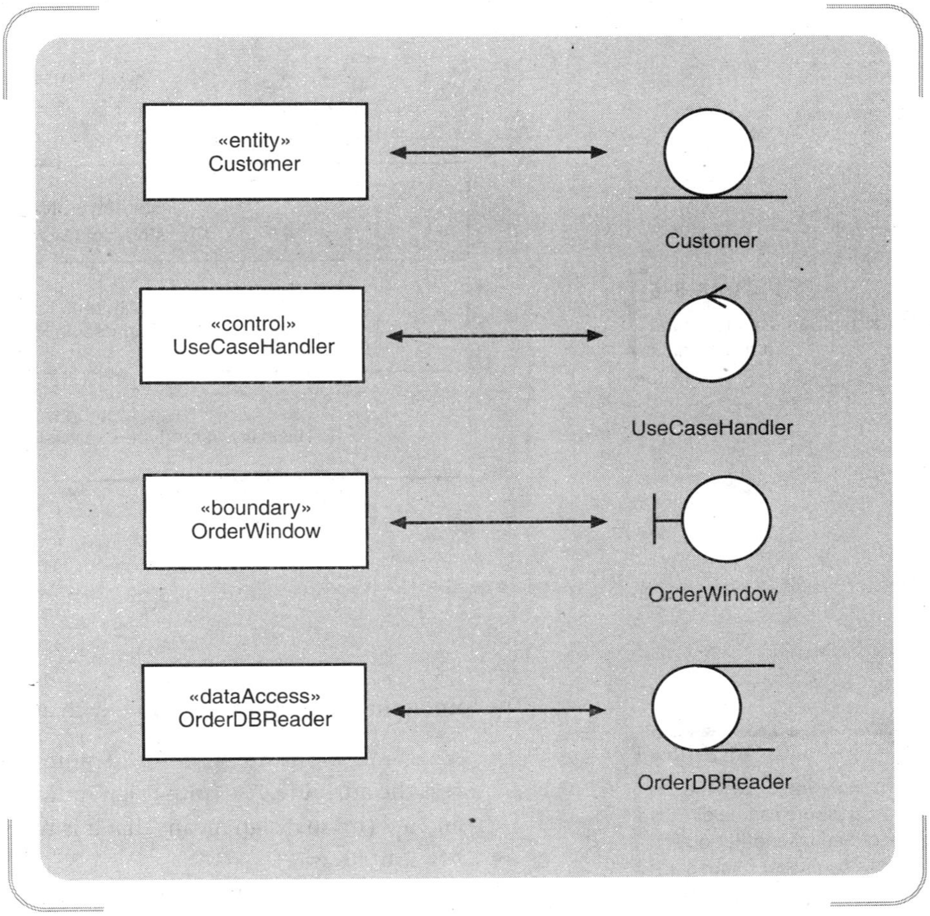

FIGURE 8-5
Standard stereotypes found in design models

entity class
design identifier for a problem domain class

persistent class
an entity class that exists after a system is shut down

boundary class
a class that exists on a system's automation boundary, such as an input window

control class
a class that mediates between boundary classes and entity classes, acting as a switchboard between the view layer and domain layer

data access class
a class that is used to retrieve data from and send data to a database

An *entity class* is the design identifier for a problem domain class. In other words, it comes from the domain model. These objects are normally passive, in that they wait for business events to occur before they do anything, and they are also usually persistent classes. A *persistent class* is one that exists after the program quits. In other words, the data must persist after the system is shut down. Obviously, the way to do that is to write it out to a file or database.

A *boundary class* is a class that is specifically designed to live on the system's automation boundary. In a desktop system, these classes would be the windows classes and all the other classes associated with the user interface.

A *control class* is a class that mediates between the boundary classes and the entity classes. In other words, its responsibility is to catch the messages from the boundary class objects and send them to the correct entity class objects. It acts as a switchboard, or controller, between the view layer and the domain layer.

A *data access class* is a class that is used to retrieve data from and send data to a database. Rather than insert database access logic, including Structured Query

Language (SQL) statements, into the entity class methods, a separate layer of classes to access the database is often included in the design.

DESIGN CLASS NOTATION

Figure 8-6 shows the details within a design class symbol. The name compartment includes the class name and the stereotype information. The lower two compartments contain more details about the attributes and the methods.

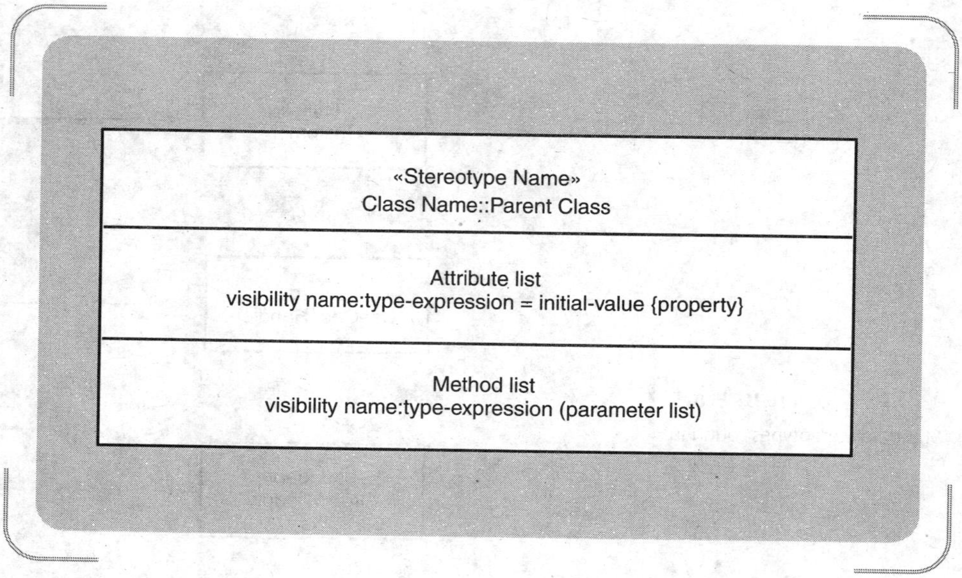

FIGURE 8-6
Internal symbols used to define a design class

visibility
notation of whether an attribute can be directly accessed by another object; indicated by plus or minus signs

method signature
notation that shows all of the information needed to invoke, or call, the method

The format that analysts use to define each attribute includes the following:

- **Attribute visibility.** *Visibility* denotes whether other objects can directly access the attribute. A + (plus) sign indicates an attribute is visible, or is public, and a – (minus) sign means that it is not visible, or is private.
- **Attribute name**
- **Type-expression.** A type-expression can be a character, string, integer, number, currency, or date.
- **Initial-value**
- **Property.** Properties are placed within curly braces, for example: {key}.

The third compartment contains the method signature information. A *method signature* shows all of the information needed to invoke (or call) the method. It shows the format of the message that must be sent, which consists of the following:

- Method visibility
- Method name
- Type-expression (the type of the return parameter from the method)
- Method parameter list (incoming arguments)

In object-oriented programming, analysts use the entire signature to identify a method. Some OO languages allow multiple methods to have the same name as long as they have different parameter lists or return types. In those languages, both the method name and the parameter list are used to invoke the correct method. For example, suppose that we want to be able to find a customer record either by the customer

ID number or by the customer name. We could identify two methods, each with the same name, such as getCustomer (customerID) and getCustomer (customerName). When a method such as getCustomer occurs more than once, with the same name but different parameter lists, we say that method is an *overloaded method*. To know which method to invoke, the run-time environment must also note what parameters are included—in this case, whether a number (customerID) or a text field (customerName) was entered.

overloaded method
a method that occurs more than once with the same name but with two or more different parameter lists

Chapter 6 illustrated several classes from the domain model for a student registration system. Figure 8-7 shows an enhanced domain model Student class and the design class diagram Student class for comparison.

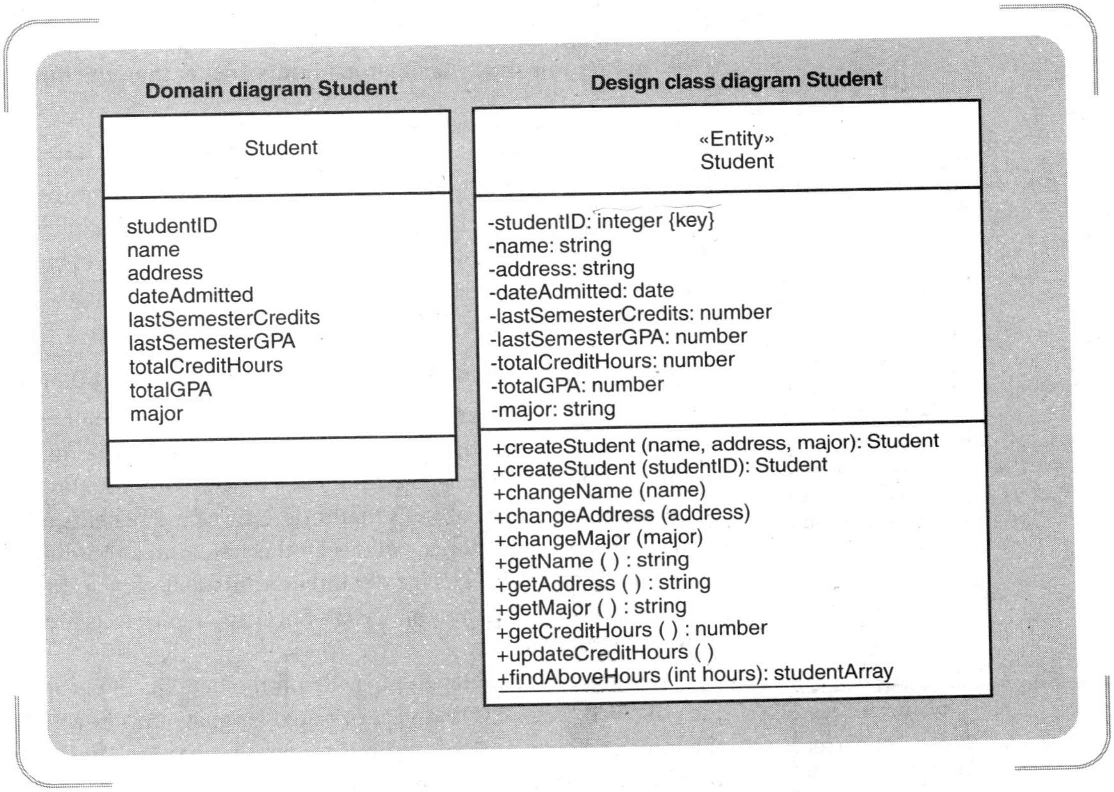

FIGURE 8-7
Student class examples for the domain diagram and the design class diagram

The domain model attribute list contains all attributes discovered during requirements activities. The design class diagram includes more information on attribute types, initial values, and properties. It can also include a stereotype for clarification, and the Student class is shown as an «entity» stereotype. In the design class diagram Student class, the third compartment contains the method signatures for the class. Most of the method signatures will be developed during the design of the interaction diagrams. Remember that UML is meant to be a general object-oriented notation technique and is not specific to any one language. So, the notation will not be exactly the same as programming method notation.

For example, for those of you who have programming experience, the constructor notation we use is *createStudent (name, address, major): Student*. Remember that the constructor is the method that makes a new object for that class. In many programming languages, the constructor is given the same name as the class. However, in this situation, we use a create statement to follow more closely the message names used in interaction diagrams. The figure also illustrates another constructor. In the second method line, only the student ID is passed in. This implies that a student with an ID exists, and the constructor itself must fill in the information about the student. This usually requires access to a database to get values for the fields.

The method called findAboveHours (int hours): studentArray, as denoted with an underlined name, is a special kind of method. Remember, in the object-oriented approach, a class is a template to create individual objects or instances. Most of the methods apply to each instance of the class. However, frequently analysts need to look through all of the instances at once. That type of method is called a *class-level method*, which is denoted by an underline. In VB .NET it is a *shared* method, and in Java it is a *static* method. This type of method is executed by the class instead of a specific object of the class. Because these methods are used at the class level, they do not depend on the existence of a particular object and, if necessary, can access data across all objects. In this example, the findAboveHours method looks through all the instances of this class and returns those having total hours greater than the input parameter.

class-level method
a method that is associated with a class instead of with objects of the class

SOME FUNDAMENTAL DESIGN PRINCIPLES

Now that you understand how an object-oriented program works and you know the notation for a design class, let's review several basic principles that will guide design decisions. We will mention these principles of good object-oriented design throughout the chapter as we discuss the steps of object-oriented design. The following basic principles are important to all parts of object-oriented design.

ENCAPSULATION AND INFORMATION HIDING

encapsulation
a design principle of objects in which both data and program logic are included within a single self-contained unit

Encapsulation is the design concept that each object is a self-contained unit including both data and program logic. Each object internally carries its own data and provides a set of methods that access the data. Each object also provides a set of services that are invoked by calling the object's methods. One of the benefits of this approach to design is that a software developer can design the system in a building-block fashion. Nearly all engineering disciplines have standard units that serve as building blocks and that can be combined into a final design. Encapsulated objects are the software equivalent of building blocks.

object reuse
a design principle in which a set of standard objects can be used over and over again within a system

Programmers also depend heavily on the benefits of encapsulation to support the idea of *object reuse*. Every object-oriented language comes with a set of standard objects that are used over and over again throughout a system. These standard sets of objects provide basic services that are used many times in the same system—and sometimes even in multiple systems. One frequent application of reuse is in the design of the user interface, either for desktop or Web applications. Designers often reuse the same classes for developing windows and window components such as buttons, menus, icons, and so forth. Problem domain classes can also be reused.

information hiding
a design principle in which data associated with an object are not visible to the outside world, but methods are provided to access or change the data

Related to encapsulation is the concept of *information hiding*. Information hiding dictates that the data associated with an object are not visible to the outside world. In other words, the object's attributes are private. A set of methods is provided to access the data and to modify or change them. Although this principle is primarily a programming concept and is most beneficial for programming and testing, several important design principles are based on it. The linkage or coupling between objects in a system is better if access to data attributes is done via a standard interface of method names, as explained in the next section.

NAVIGATION VISIBILITY

As stated earlier, an object-oriented system is a set of interacting objects. The interaction diagrams developed during design document what interactions occur between which objects. However, for one object to interact with another object by sending a

navigation visibility
a design principle in which one object is able to view and interact with another object

message, the first object must be visible to the second object. *Navigation visibility*, in this context, refers to the ability of one object to view and interact with another object. In programming jargon, invoking a method on an object frequently requires dot notation to invoke the correct method on the correct object. Sometimes developers refer to navigation visibility as just *navigation* or just *visibility*.

As a designer, you must always be aware of navigation visibility. Interactions between objects can only be accomplished with navigation visibility. One of the responsibilities of a design is to specify which classes have navigation visibility to other classes. Navigation visibility can be either one way or two way. For example, a Customer object may be able to view an Order object. That means that the Customer object knows which orders a customer has placed. In programming terms, the Customer class has a variable, or array of variables, that points to the Order object or objects for that customer. If navigation is two way, then each Order object will also have a variable that refers to the Customer object. If the navigation is not two way, then Order objects will not have a variable to point to the Customer object. In a design class diagram, navigation visibility is identified by an arrow between the classes, where the arrow points to the visible class.

Figure 8-8 shows one-way navigation visibility between the Customer class and the Order class. Notice that there is a variable called myOrder in the Customer class. This variable holds a value to refer to an order instance. Frequently, the reference variable myOrder is not explicitly shown in the design class. The navigation arrow indicates that visibility is required. We have included the variable in this example to emphasize the concept.

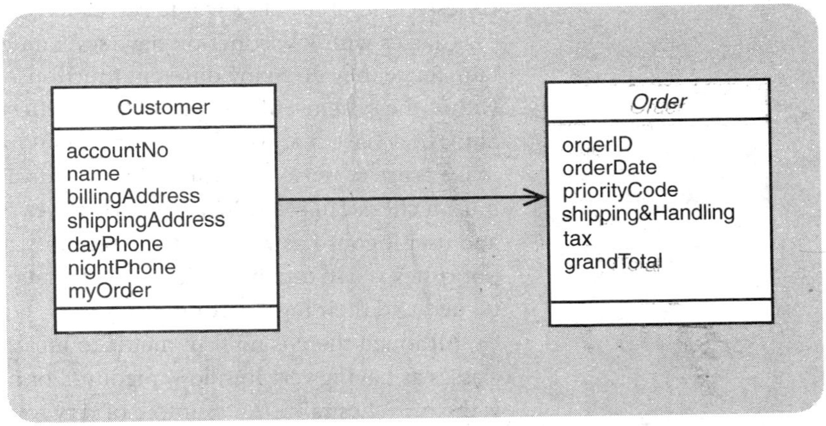

FIGURE 8-8
Navigation visibility between Customer and Order—coupling

coupling
a qualitative measure of how closely the classes in a design class diagram are linked

Coupling is a general term that is derived from navigation visibility. In the previous example, where Customer had navigation visibility to Order, one could also say that Customer and Order are coupled, or linked. Now, extend this same idea of visibility throughout all the classes in the entire system. *Coupling* is a qualitative measure of how closely the classes in a design class diagram are linked. A simple way to think about coupling is the number of navigation arrows on the design class diagram. Low coupling for the system is usually better than high coupling. In other words, fewer navigation visibility arrows indicate that a system is easier to understand and maintain.

We say that coupling is a qualitative measure because no specific number measures coupling in a system. A designer must develop a feel for coupling—to recognize when there is too much coupling or to know what is a reasonable amount of coupling.

Coupling is evaluated as a design progresses, use case by use case. Generally, if each use case design has a reasonable level of coupling, the entire system will, too.

Refer back to Figure 8-1 and observe the flow of messages between the objects. Obviously, objects that send messages to each other must have navigation visibility, and thus are coupled. For the Input window object to send a message to the Student object, it must have navigation visibility to it. So, the Input window object is coupled to the Student object. But notice that the Input window object is not connected to the Database object, so those objects are not coupled. If we designed the system so that the Input window object accessed the Database object, then the overall coupling for this use case would increase—that is, there would be more connections. Is that good or bad? In this simple example, it might not be a problem. But for a system with even 10 classes, undisciplined connections with navigation visibility can cause very high levels of coupling, making the system more complex.

So why is high coupling bad? It is bad primarily because it adds unnecessary complexity to a system, making it very hard to maintain. A change in one class ripples throughout the entire system. So, experienced analysts make every effort to simplify coupling and reduce ripple effects in the design of a new system.

COHESION AND SEPARATION OF RESPONSIBILITIES

cohesion
a qualitative measure of the consistency of functions within a single class

Cohesion refers to the consistency of the functions within a single class. *Cohesion* is a qualitative measure of the focus or unity of purpose within a single class. For example, in Figure 8-1, you would expect the Student class to have methods, that is, functions, to enter student information such as student identification number or name. That would represent a unity of purpose and a highly cohesive class. But what if that same object also had methods to make classroom assignments or assign professors to courses? The cohesiveness of the class would be reduced.

Classes with low cohesion have several negative effects. First, they are hard to maintain. Since they do many different functions, they tend to be overly sensitive to changes within the system, suffering from ripple effects. Second, it is hard to reuse such classes. Since they have many different—and often unrelated—functions, it usually does not make sense to reuse them in other contexts. For example, a button class that processes button clicks can easily be reused. However, a button class that processes button clicks and user logons has very limited reusability. A final drawback is that classes that are not cohesive are usually difficult to understand. Frequently, their functions are intertwined and their logic is complex.

Although there is no firm metric to measure cohesiveness, we can think about classes as having very low, low, medium, or high cohesion. Remember, high cohesion is the most desirable. An example of very low cohesion would be a class that has responsibility for services in different functional areas, such as a class that accesses both the Internet and a database. These two types of activities are very different and accomplish different purposes. To put them together in one class causes very low cohesion.

An example of low cohesion would be a class that has different responsibilities but in related functional areas, perhaps a class that does all database access for every table in the database. It would be better to have different classes to access customer information, order information, and inventory information. Although the functions are the same—that is, they access the database—the types of data passed and retrieved are very different. So, a class that is connected to the entire database is not as reusable as one that is only connected to the customer table.

An example of medium cohesion would be a class that has closely related responsibilities, such as a single class that maintains customer information and customer account information. Two highly cohesive classes could be defined, one for customer information, such as name and addresses, and another class or set of classes for customer accounts, such as balances, payments, credit information, and all financial activity. If the customer information and the account information are somewhat limited, then they could all be combined into a single class with medium cohesiveness. Either medium or highly cohesive classes are acceptable in system design.

The common solution to classes with low cohesion is to divide a class into several classes, each of which is highly cohesive. This concept, called separation of responsibilities, is another principle of good object-oriented design. *Separation of responsibilities* states that in most cases it is a better design to separate disparate tasks into distinct classes. Think of separation of responsibilities as another way to develop highly cohesive classes.

separation of responsibilities
design principle in which analysts divide a class into several highly cohesive classes

BEST PRACTICE: Good, experienced developers always think about how to keep coupling low and cohesion high. Always keep these concepts in mind when designing.

DEVELOPING THE FIRST-CUT DESIGN CLASS DIAGRAM

To start the design process, we develop a first-cut design class diagram based only on the domain model. Figure 8-9 repeats the domain model class diagram for RMO developed in Chapter 5. As you learned earlier, the focus during requirements was to identify the classes, their attributes, and the relationships between the classes.

The first-cut design class diagram is developed by extending the domain model class diagram. It requires two steps: (1) elaborating the attributes with type and initial value information and (2) adding navigation visibility arrows. Figure 8-10 is a design class diagram for RMO showing the results of these two steps.

The elaboration of the attributes is fairly straightforward. The type information is determined by the designer based on his or her expertise. Finally, in most instances, all attributes are kept invisible or private, as indicated by the minus signs preceding them in the diagram.

Navigation visibility is a little more difficult to design. Remember that we are designing just the first-cut class diagram, so we may need to add or delete navigation arrows as the design progresses. The basic question we ask when building navigation visibility is, Which classes need to have references to, or be able to access, which other classes? Here are a few guidelines—not hard-and-fast rules, but general guidelines.

- One-to-many relationships that indicate a superior/subordinate relationship are usually navigated from the superior to the subordinate, for example, from Order to OrderItem. Sometimes these relationships form hierarchies of navigation chains, for example, from Catalog to ProductItem to InventoryItem.
- Mandatory relationships, in which objects in one class cannot exist without objects of another class, are usually navigated from the more independent class to the dependent class, for example, from Customer to Order.
- When an object needs information from another object, then a navigation arrow may be required, pointing either to the object itself or to its parent in a hierarchy.
- Navigation arrows may also be bidirectional.

As indicated in the guidelines, Figure 8-10 shows that Customer has navigation visibility to Order. Order has navigation to OrderItem, to OrderTransaction, and to ReturnItem. Catalog, ProductItem, and InventoryItem form a hierarchy, with navigation

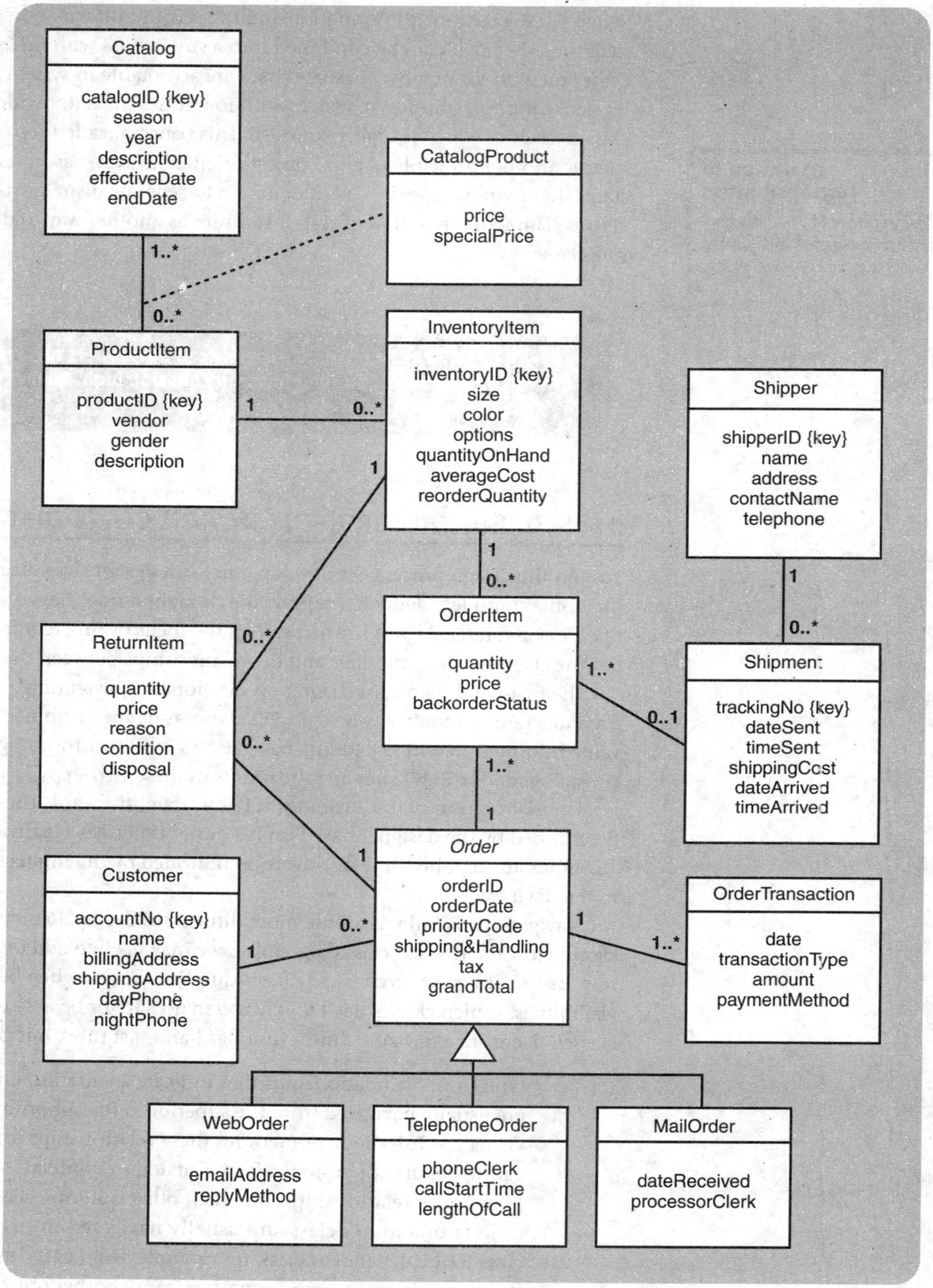

FIGURE 8-9
RMO domain model class diagram

going from top to bottom. CatalogProduct, as an association class, should also be visible from Catalog. Shipper has navigation visibility to Shipment.

There are still a couple of unresolved issues at this point concerning visibility between OrderItem and InventoryItem, and OrderItem and Shipment. It is not yet clear what is the best way to implement navigation between those classes. Those

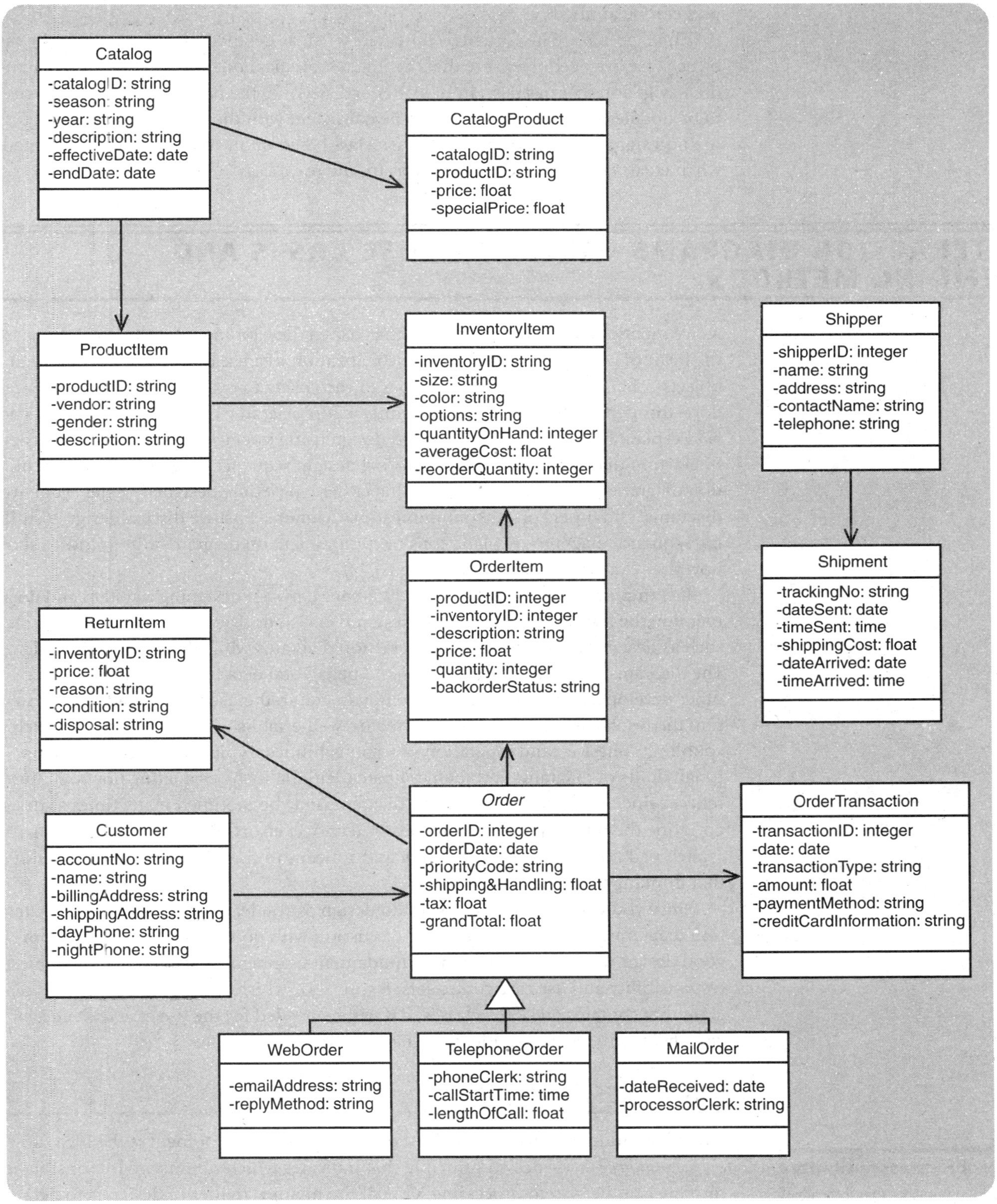

FIGURE 8-10
First-cut RMO design class diagram

questions may need to wait until additional design is done and other design principles can be applied.

Three points are important to note here. First, as detailed design proceeds, use case by use case, we need to ensure that the interaction diagrams support and implement the navigation that has been initially defined. Second, the navigation arrows will need to be updated as design progresses to be consistent with the design details. Finally, method signatures will be added to each class based on the design decisions we made when creating the interaction diagrams for the use cases.

INTERACTION DIAGRAMS—REALIZING USE CASES AND DEFINING METHODS

As we mentioned at the beginning of the chapter, developing interaction diagrams is at the heart of object-oriented design. The realization of a use case—determining what objects collaborate by sending messages to each other to carry out the use case—is done through the development of an interaction diagram. The objective of this section is to explain how to do object-oriented design using interaction diagrams. Two types of interaction diagrams are developed during design: sequence diagrams and communication diagrams. Design can be done using either type. Some designers prefer sequence diagrams, and others prefer communication diagrams. First we discuss design by utilizing sequence diagrams. Explanations of communication diagrams will follow to show how they can also be used to do design.

It is important to understand the difference between designing a system and documenting the results of the design process and decisions. Designers develop diagrams such as design class diagrams and interaction diagrams while doing software design. The diagrams communicate structural and behavioral details to programmers and other developers. But the diagrams are not an end in themselves. Instead, they represent the results of design decisions based on well-established design principles such as coupling, cohesion, and separation of responsibilities. Typically, designers develop rough drafts of diagrams and then evaluate their quality by evaluating how well they reflect principles of good design. The diagrams may be modified many times as designers refine them to improve their quality and correct errors. The diagrams are both a scratch pad for the designers' thinking and a means to communicate the final result of that thinking to developers.

Since you will be learning how to do design as you learn about the detailed interaction diagrams, we will intersperse the discussion with pointers on the principles of good design. We start with two more fundamental principles of good design—object responsibility and use case controllers. Figure 8-11, which is a partial design class diagram that contains all of the classes that will be needed for the use case *Look up item availability*, will be used to illustrate these two design principles.

OBJECT RESPONSIBILITY

object responsibility
design principle that indicates which objects are responsible for carrying out system processing

One of the fundamental principles of object-oriented development is the idea of *object responsibility*—design principle that indicates which objects are responsible for carrying out the system processing. One of the major activities of design is to define the responsibilities of classes of objects. These responsibilities are categorized in two major areas—knowing and doing. In other words, what is an object expected to know, and what is an object expected to do or to initiate?

Knowing includes such responsibilities as knowing about its own data and knowing about other classes with which it must collaborate to carry out use cases. Obviously,

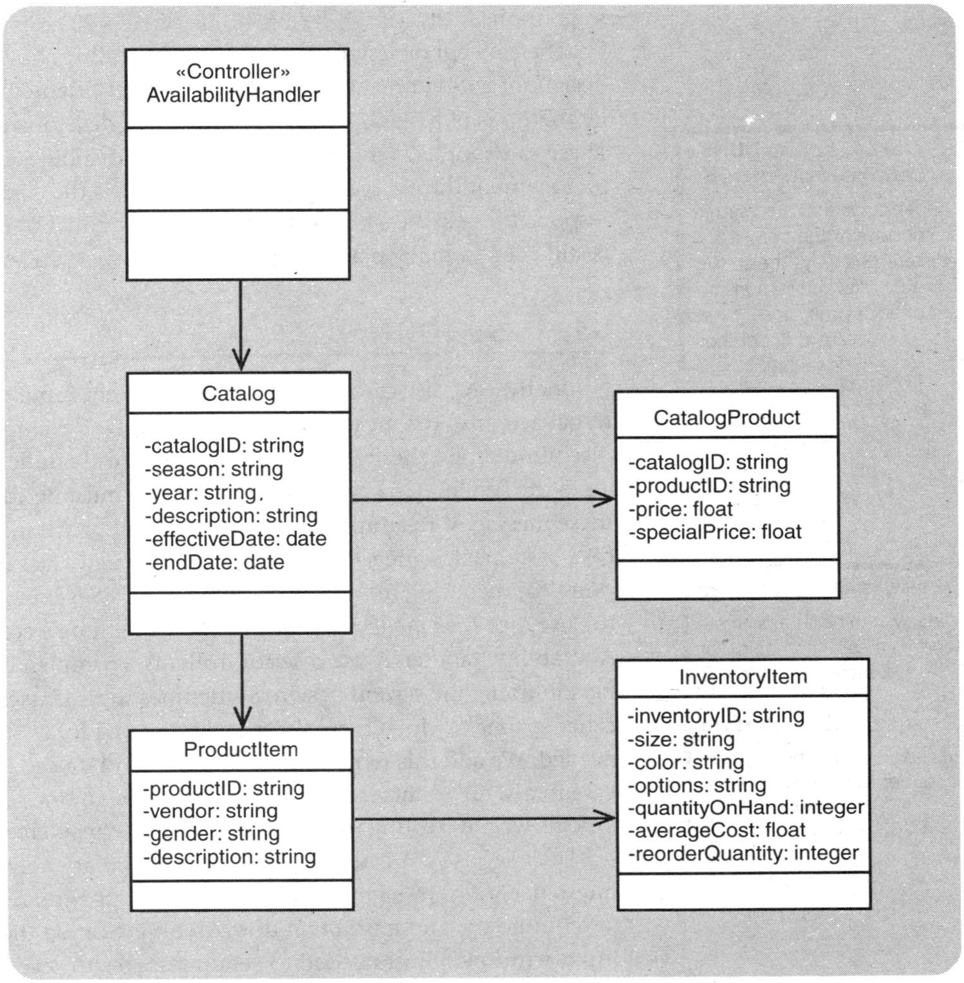

FIGURE 8-11

Partial design class diagram for the *Look up item availability* use case

a class should know about its own data, what attributes exist and how to maintain the information in those attributes. It should also know where to go get information when required. For example, during the initiation of an object, data for some attributes may be passed in as part of the constructor being invoked. However, other data that are not passed in may be required. An object should know about—that is, have navigation visibility to—other objects that can provide the required information. For example, in Figure 8-7, the constructor for the Student class does not receive a studentID value as a parameter. The Student class takes responsibility for creating a new studentID value based on some rules it knows.

Doing includes all the activities an object does to assist in the execution of a use case. Some of those activities will be to receive and process messages. Another doing responsibility will be to instantiate, or create, new objects that may be required for completion of a use case. Classes must collaborate to carry out a use case. Some classes are responsible for coordinating the collaboration. For example, for the use case *Look up item availability* in Figure 8-11, the Catalog class has primary responsibility to see that the use case is carried out. Another class, such as InventoryItem, is only responsible for providing information about itself.

One of the most important activities of a systems designer is to determine object responsibility and build the system based on those decisions. In the following sections, which discuss design, we provide more examples of object responsibility and of assigning responsibility.

The concept of assigning object responsibilities has been part of object-oriented design for a long time. In the history of object-oriented design, one of the most popular methods of assigning responsibilities was developed using 3″ × 5″ index cards. These cards, called *CRC cards*—for class-responsibility-collaboration cards—were used to document the classes in the system, the ways the classes collaborated, and the responsibilities of each class for each use case collaboration. The CRC card technique is still used in many places to assist in the design process.

CRC (class-responsibility-collaboration) cards
index cards that are used to document the classes in a system, the ways the classes collaborate, and the responsibilities of each class for each use case collaboration

USE CASE CONTROLLER

Normally, each use case can have many different input messages coming from the external actors. A system sequence diagram (SSD) developed as part of the requirements discipline shows these input messages, but it only indicates that all of these messages go to the system. However, during design we must decide which objects receive all of these messages. To simplify the collection and processing of all the messages for a use case, systems designers frequently make up a new class that can serve as a collection point for incoming messages. We call these classes *use case controllers*. For example, for the use case *Look up item availability*, there might be a controller class named AvailabilityHandler. A use case controller is a completely artificial class, created by the person doing the system design. Sometimes these classes that are just made up are called *artifacts*, which means something created for a specific purpose just because it is needed. We add this term because you will find it used frequently in industry. Essentially, an artifact is a person-made article. In one sense of the word, the design models we are creating in this chapter can be considered artifacts.

use case controllers
a class system designers create to serve as a collection point for incoming messages

artifact
a class invented by a system designer to handle a needed system function

The use case controller acts as an intermediary between the outside world and the internal system. In Figure 8-1, we saw an Input window object, which sits on the system boundary, and a problem domain object called the Student object. What if that Input window object needed to send messages to several objects? It would need references to all of the problem domain objects. The coupling between the Input window object and the system would be very high—there would be many connections. So, coupling between the user-interface objects and the problem domain objects could be reduced by making a single use case controller object to handle all of the input messages.

There are several ways to create use case controllers. A single use case controller could be defined for all use cases. The set of responsibilities assigned to such a use case would be very broad, and the cohesiveness of such a class would most likely be very low. So, a better design might result from defining several use case controllers, each with a specific set of responsibilities. It would also be possible to create a single use case controller for all the use cases in a single subsystem, such as the order-entry subsystem. Several use case controllers would raise the coupling between the user-interface classes and the internal classes, but it would result in highly cohesive classes with a defined set of responsibilities for each. A solution with one use case controller per use case is a viable option as well. Figure 8-11 illustrates a single use case controller for a single use case. The use case controller and the problem domain classes for the use case are included in one design class diagram. Note that in this design class diagram only the navigation visibility arrows are shown.

The thought process illustrated in the preceding paragraphs is precisely the process of systems design—to balance the design principles of coupling, cohesion, and class responsibility. We will elaborate on this process in the next sections.

DESIGNING WITH SEQUENCE DIAGRAMS

As mentioned previously, interaction diagrams form the heart of the OO design process, and sequence diagrams are used to explain object interactions and document design decisions. First let's review the mechanics and syntax of sequence diagrams and then follow with some principles and procedures to design the system. You first learned about sequence diagrams in Chapter 6 when you learned how to develop a system sequence diagram (SSD). By now you should feel comfortable not only reading and interpreting a system sequence diagram but also developing one. Remember that an SSD is used to document the inputs to and outputs from the system for a single use case or scenario. An SSD captures the interactions between the system and the external world as represented by the actors. The system itself is treated as a single object named :System. The inputs to the system are messages from the actor to the system, and the outputs are usually return messages showing the data being returned. Figure 8-12 is an elaborated version of Figure 6-14, which shows the basic components of a sequence diagram and gives explanations. Let us start with a simple RMO sample use case, *Look up item availability*. As seen in the figure, each message has a source and a destination.

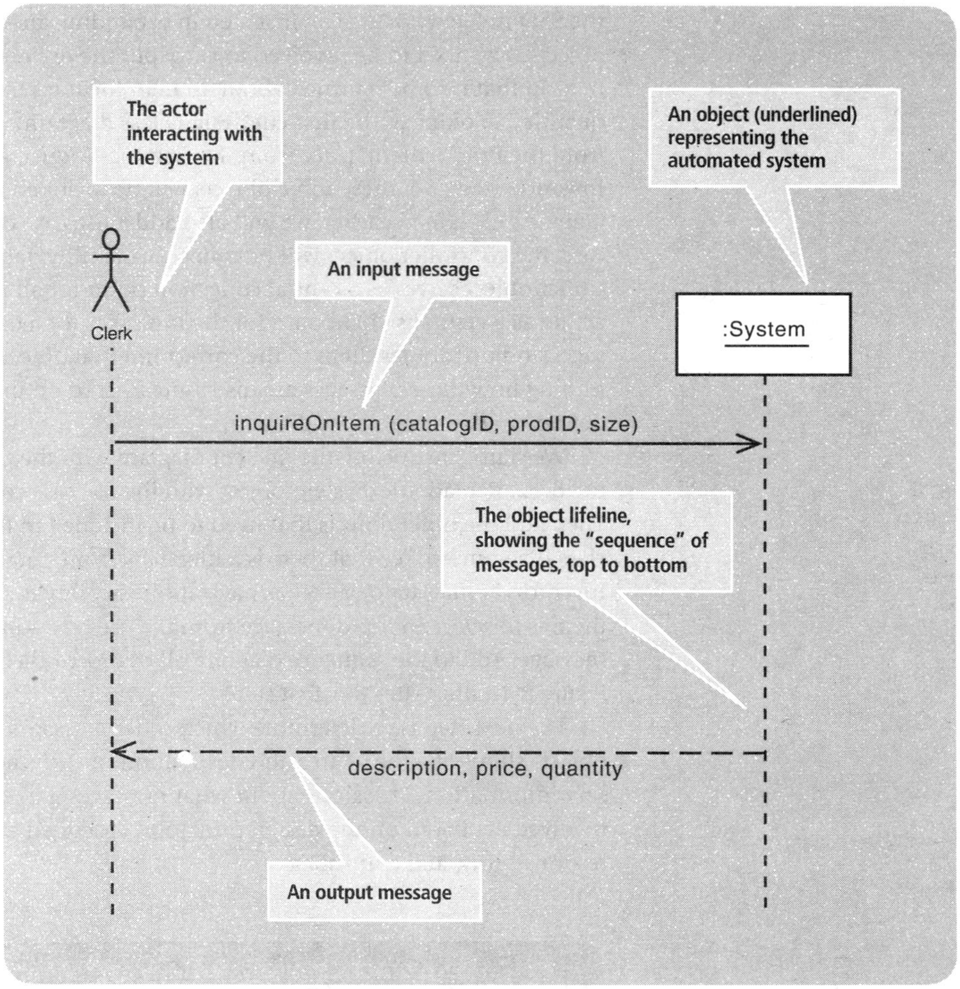

FIGURE 8-12
SSD for the *Look up item availability* use case

In an SSD, since there are only two objects with lifelines, the source and destination are constrained. When we get to detailed sequence diagrams, some of the most critical decisions to be made are the source and destination objects for the messages.

Remember that the syntax of an input message, discussed in Chapter 6, is

* *[true/false condition] return-value := message-name (parameter-list)*

For the output message, we normally only provide the parameter list without parentheses.

A detailed sequence diagram uses all the same elements as an SSD. The difference is that the :System object is replaced by all of the internal objects and messages within the system. In other words, for an SSD, the system was treated as a black box, and we could not see the internal processing. The objective of design is to open up the black box and determine the internal processing that must occur within the automated system. As explained earlier and shown in Figure 8-1, we need to identify the internal objects and messages that are involved in the realization of the use case or use case scenario. Notice that just as earlier requirements activities were centered around use cases, so is detailed design.

FIRST-CUT SEQUENCE DIAGRAM

Let's proceed with the detailed design for the *Look up item availability* use case based on the SSD in Figure 8-12. The first step in expanding an SSD is to determine which other objects may need to be involved to carry out the use case. The SSD indicates that information that is to be returned about an item includes the description, the price, and the quantity. Looking at the first-cut design class diagram, we see that description comes from the ProductItem, price from the CatalogProduct, and quantity from the InventoryItem. So, these three objects will be included in the first-cut sequence diagram. As explained earlier, we will also add a use case controller object. For this use case, the controller object will be called AvailabilityHandler. Remember that a controller object serves as a central collection point for all input messages for the use case, acting as a central switchboard for the messages for a use case. It accepts the input messages and distributes them to the correct internal objects. Part of the design is determining how these messages are distributed based on the navigation visibility you have defined in the design class diagram.

We start constructing the first-cut diagram with the elements from the SSD in Figure 8-12. Replace the :System object with the use case controller, :AvailabilityHandler. Then add the other objects that need to be included in the use case. From the design class diagram, we see that there is a hierarchy from Catalog to ProductItem and on to InventoryItem. Catalog also has navigation visibility to CatalogProduct. The first step, then, is to select an input message from the use case—in this example there is only one message. Add to the sequence diagram all of those objects that must collaborate. Figure 8-13 illustrates this first step.

The next step is to determine which other messages must be sent, including which objects should be the source and destination of each message, to collect all the necessary information. Decisions about what messages are required and which objects are involved are based on the design principles described earlier—coupling, cohesion, responsibility, and controller.

BEST PRACTICE: Always identify appropriate controller classes as entry points into the domain layer.

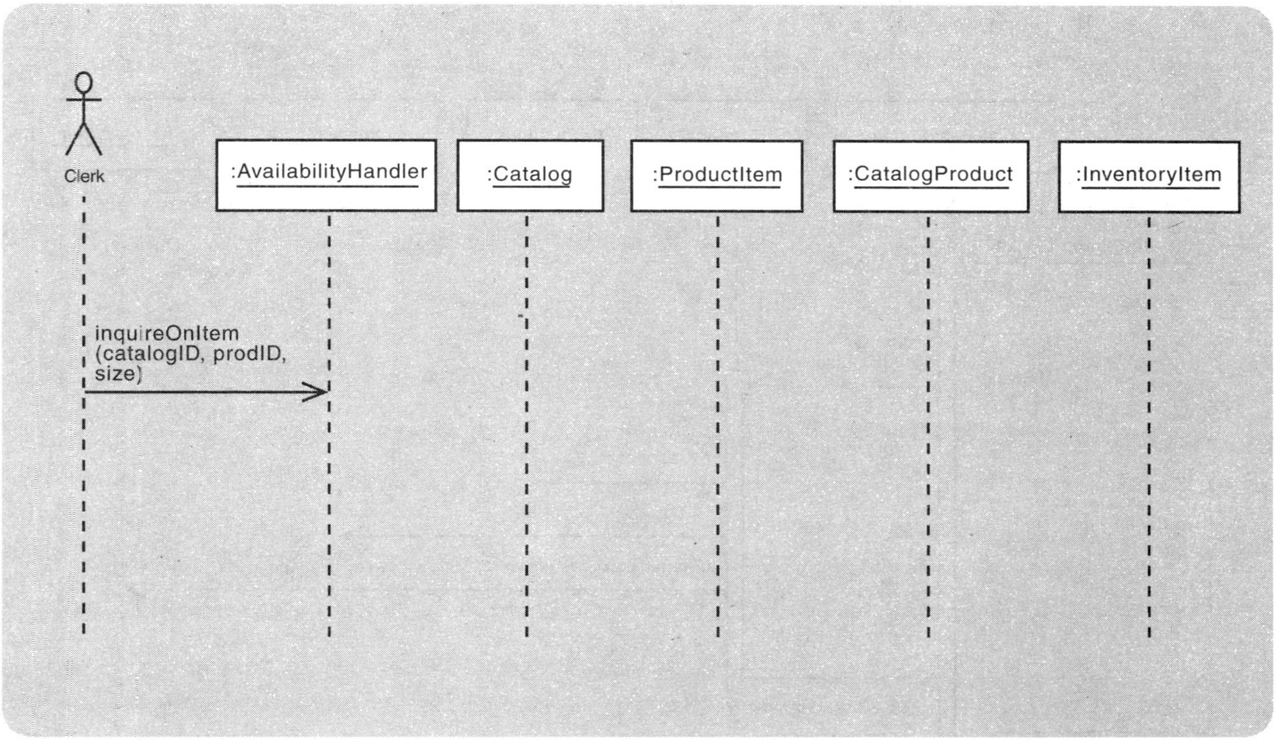

FIGURE 8-13
Objects included in *Look up item availability*

As noted earlier, the Catalog object is the top of a navigation hierarchy to other objects that have the required information. So, the :AvailabilityHandler forwards the input message to the :Catalog object. The :Catalog object sends messages to :ProductItem and :CatalogProduct to get the description and price. However, :Catalog does not have direct navigation visibility to :InventoryItem, so it sends another message to :ProductItem to ask for help getting the quantity. The :ProductItem object knows that :InventoryItem has quantity information, so it forwards the request and collects quantity information. :Catalog collects all the information and returns it to the :AvailabilityHandler, which sends it back to the Clerk. Figure 8-14 shows the completed first-cut sequence diagram for the *Look up item availability* use case.

Before moving on, let's analyze this solution based on some of the principles of good design that were previously discussed—coupling, cohesion, object responsibility, and use case controller.

The use case controller provides the link between the internal objects and the external environment. This limits the coupling to the external environment to that single object. The responsibilities assigned to :AvailabilityHandler are to catch incoming messages and distribute them to the correct internal domain objects and to return the required information to the external environment. Using a use case controller as the switchboard limits the overall coupling between the domain objects and the environment. The :AvailabilityHandler class also is highly cohesive, with only two primary responsibilities.

The responsibility assigned to :Catalog is to be in charge of collecting all product and inventory information in the product hierarchy. Since the catalog is at the top of the hierarchy, this appears to be a reasonable responsibility assignment. The :Catalog class is highly cohesive, at least for the messages seen in this use case. Coupling is straightforward, being basically vertical on the hierarchy. Thus, the assignment of responsibilities and corresponding messages seems to conform to good design principles.

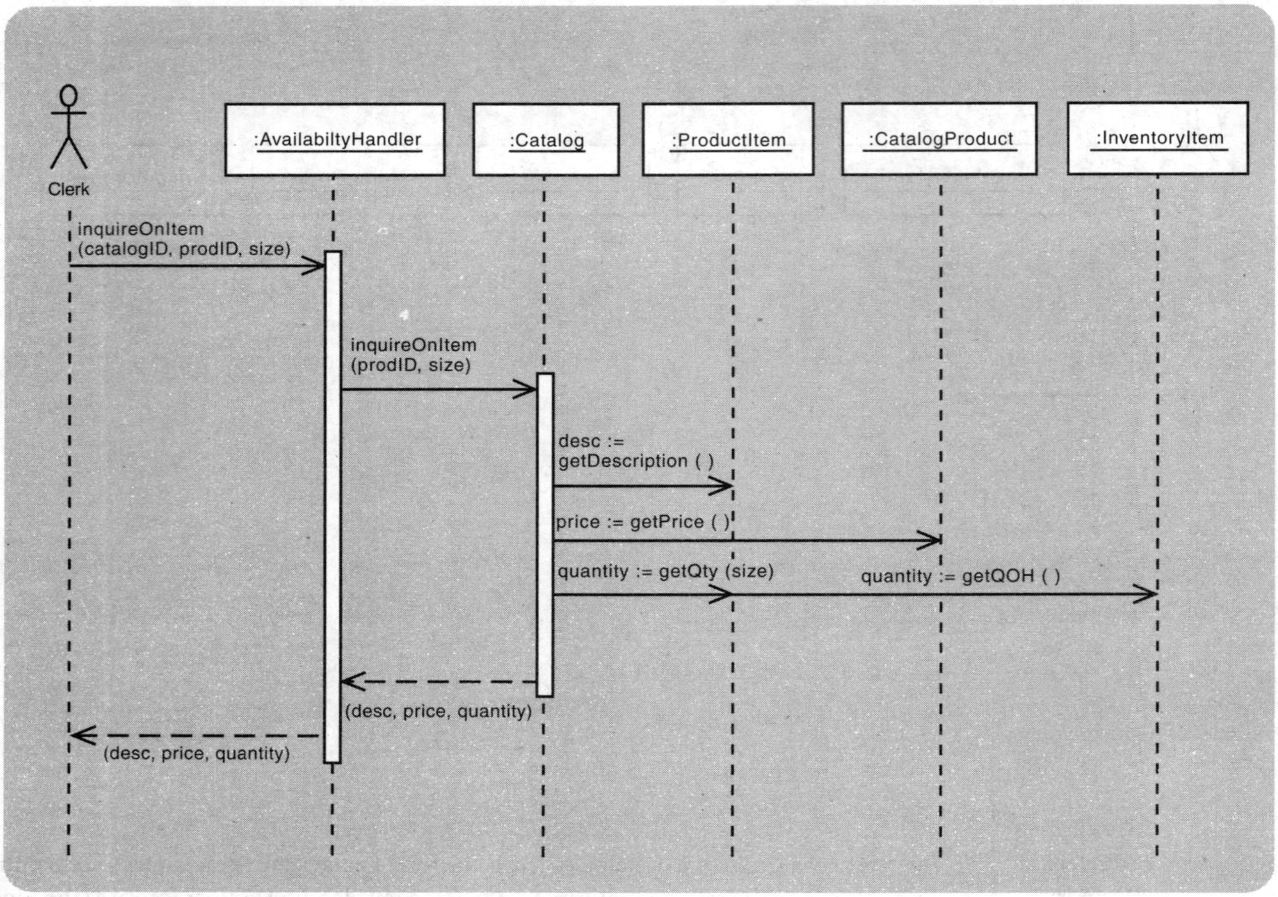

FIGURE 8-14
First-cut sequence diagram for the *Look up item availability* use case

One question we might ask is whether the request for the quantity should go from :ProductItem to :InventoryItem or come directly from :Catalog. As illustrated in Figure 8-14, it does follow the hierarchy, and since this hierarchy will probably be used in other use cases, the design as shown is a good choice. The more direct solution would result in fewer messages, but it would increase overall coupling. Both :Catalog and :ProductItem would require navigation visibility and hence increase coupling. So, the design as shown is the better solution.

activation lifelines
vertical rectangles in a sequence diagram that indicate when an object is executing a method

A new symbol is included within the diagram shown in Figure 8-14. The tall, narrow vertical rectangles on the :AvailabilityHandler and the :Catalog lifelines are called the *activation lifelines*. Remember from Chapter 6 that the lifeline of an object is represented by a vertical dashed line. An object can be in either an active or inactive state. An object is active while it is executing a method and inactive once that method terminates. An inactive object resides in memory awaiting further messages and remembers the values of its internal data attributes. The activation lifeline represents the period when the object is active and executing. In Figure 8-14, when :AvailabilityHandler receives the inquireOnItem message, it becomes active—begins executing a method—and it remains active until it sends a response back to the Clerk.

Obviously, with this preliminary design, we are focusing on problem domain classes and basic interactions. Many other details can be added to make the solution more complete. Such details as user-interface classes, indexes to find customers based on name, and maybe even a database to retrieve a customer could be added to the solution. That is the reason this is a preliminary solution.

GUIDELINES FOR PRELIMINARY SEQUENCE DIAGRAM DEVELOPMENT

Even though the example in Figure 8-14 was very simple, we can distill several tasks to help you learn to do design for a use case or scenario using sequence diagrams. Note that these tasks are not done sequentially, but they are done when necessary to build the sequence diagram. We only identify them as separate tasks to ensure that all three are completed.

- Take each input message and determine all of the internal messages that result from that input. For that message, determine its objective. Determine what information is needed, what class needs it—the destination—and what class provides it—the source. Determine whether any objects are created as a result of the input. This will help you to define internal messages, their origin objects, and their destination objects. In other words, you are trying to define which classes and which internal messages are needed to support the input message.
- As you work with each input message, be sure to identify the complete set of classes that will be affected by that message. In other words, select all the objects from the domain class diagram that need to be involved. In Chapter 6 you learned about use case preconditions and postconditions. Any classes that are listed in either the preconditions or postconditions are classes that should be included in the design. Other classes to be included, even though they might not be listed in the preconditions or postconditions, are classes that are created, that are the creators of objects for the use case, that are updated during the use case, or that provide information that is utilized in the use case.
- Additionally, flesh out the components for each message. Add iteration, true/false conditions, return values, and passed parameters. The passed parameters should be based on the attributes that are found in the domain class diagram. Return values and passed parameters can be attributes, but they may also be objects from classes.

This list of steps will produce the preliminary design. Refinements and modifications may be necessary, and again, we have only focused on the problem domain classes involved in the use case.

DEVELOPING A MULTILAYER DESIGN FOR *LOOK UP ITEM AVAILABILITY*

The development of the first-cut sequence diagram focuses only on the classes in the domain layer. However, as explained previously, in systems design we must also design the user-interface classes and, when appropriate, the data access classes. In this section, let's expand the design presented in Figure 8-14 and make it a multilayer design, including both a view layer and a data access layer.

In the early days of interactive systems and graphical user interfaces, tool developers invented languages and tools that made it easy to develop systems with graphical user interfaces, such as windows and buttons. Languages such as early versions of Visual Basic, Delphi, and PowerBuilder were designed to make it easy to build interactive, event-driven, graphical systems. However, in these languages, the program logic was attached to the windows and other graphical components. So, to move these systems to other environments, such as browser-based systems, designers had to completely rewrite the system. In fact, systems developed this way became good illustrations of the problems that follow when design principles such as highly cohesive classes and separating responsibilities are violated. When a class has both user-interface functions and business logic mixed together, upgrading and maintaining the system become more difficult.

BEST PRACTICE: Be sure the use case logic for the domain classes is solid before adding view and data layer classes.

As object-oriented programming became more prevalent and tools integrated both object-oriented programming and graphical interfaces, it became easier to build systems that could be partitioned and that allowed responsibilities to be separated. User-interface classes did not need to have business logic—other than edits on the input data. Designers could build multilayer systems that were more robust and easier to maintain, and they could apply the principles of good design. Tools such as Java and Visual Studio .NET provide the capability to easily build graphical user interfaces as well as sophisticated problem domain classes.

DESIGNING THE VIEW LAYER

The view layer involves human-computer interaction and requires designing the user interface for each use case. User-interface design is one of the key activities of the UP design discipline and is discussed in detail in Chapter 11. The interface designer takes the steps in a use case description and begins to develop a dialog design for the use case, usually defining one or more window forms or Web forms the user will use to interact with the system. Sometimes the forms are sketched out and shown as storyboards describing the dialog. Sometimes prototypes of the forms are created so that users can try out the interface design. Recall that the design activities are being completed at the same time, so some members of the project team are working on user-interface design while others are developing sequence diagrams. These two design activities must be coordinated so that the view layer classes defined in the sequence diagrams are consistent with the forms developed by the user-interface design team. Chapters 11 and 12 explain this process of designing the forms, reports, and even the dialogs used in the interface between the users and the system. Once the electronic forms are designed, an object-oriented window class can be defined for each form. Normally, the UML class definition for a form only specifies the data-entry attributes. Other class attributes, such as buttons and menu items, are specified in the form description and not in the class definition.

Based on the progress completed on the dialog design for a use case, forms are added as window classes to the sequence diagram—as the view layer. Typically, there is one input form for the messages entering the system for the use case. If the messages are unique, then each may require its own input form. In most instances, however, one form may be sufficient for all the related messages within a use case. Obviously, each message from an external actor must be entered into the system in some way, and output messages must be displayed. One logical way for this to happen is through a window form class that can accept input data and possibly display output data. Figure 8-15 illustrates the result of defining a window class for the input message named :ProductQuery from the Clerk.

Adding the user-interface classes to the sequence diagram is usually straightforward. As shown in Figure 8-14, we assumed that a message came directly from the external actor to the :AvailabilityHandler object. In reality, the data are entered into the electronic form via the keyboard, and the user-interface window object catches that information, formats a message, and transmits the message to the :AvailabilityHandler

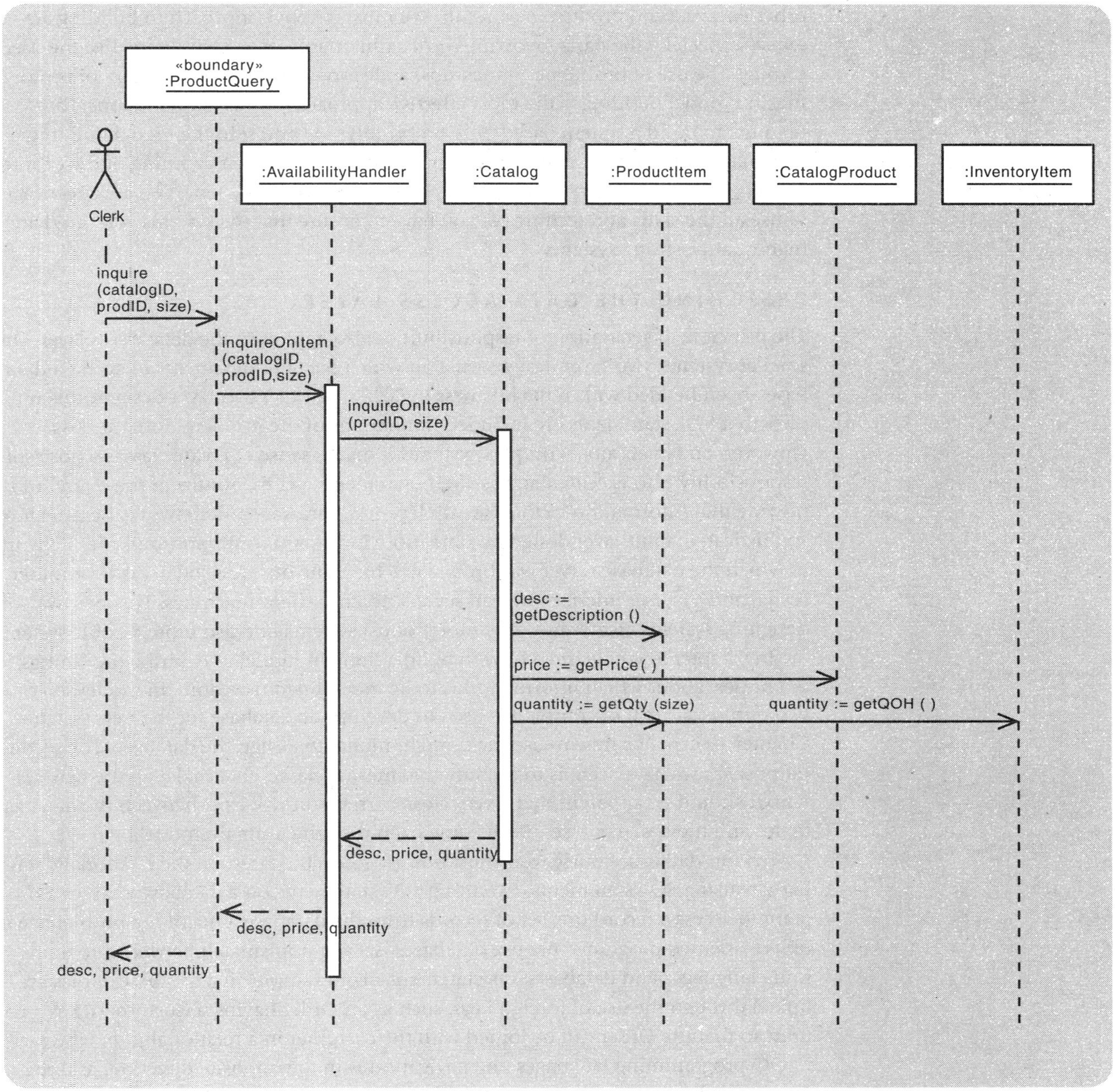

FIGURE 8-15
Look up item availability use case with view layer and user-interface object

object. Thus, adding the user-interface objects only requires us to place those objects between the actor—the Clerk—and the domain objects and to include the appropriate message. Figure 8-15 shows this process of adding a user-interface object to the sequence diagram.

It is critically important that you, as a system developer, understand how the work of the user-interface design team and their prototypes and dialog storyboards should affect the development of detailed sequence diagrams. In both Chapter 6 and this chapter, we have emphasized the benefits of capturing system requirements by building models. You should by now see the strengths of models and model building. However, building models based only on discussions with users has proven to be less than successful in constructing systems. The problem lies in the fact that users, like all human beings, may not understand exactly what they need unless they can see and experience the end product. As a result, the most effective approach to building systems—especially the parts involving the user interface—is to actively involve the users through the use of prototypes, mock-ups, and storyboards. A combination of prototyping and model building is the most effective approach. Sometimes developers are tempted to build a system based only on prototyping and skip the model building. This may work for very small systems, but as expressed at the beginning of the chapter, models are necessary to produce a truly robust and correct system. You are encouraged to use all the skills and techniques you have to ensure that the systems you build are high-quality, strong systems.

DESIGNING THE DATA ACCESS LAYER

The principle of separation of responsibilities also applies to the data access layer. On smaller systems, two-layer designs exist, in which the SQL statements to access a database are embedded within the business logic layer. In OO two-layer designs, this implies that SQL statements are included in methods of the problem domain classes. However, on larger, more complex systems, it makes sense to create classes whose sole responsibility is to execute database SQL statements, get the results of the query, and provide that information to the domain layer. As hardware and networks became more sophisticated, multilayer design became more important to support multitier networks in which the database server was on one machine, the business logic was on another server, and the user interface was on several desktop client machines. This new way of designing systems creates not only more robust systems but also more flexible systems.

In Chapter 5, you learned how to build a domain model to describe the "things," or entities, about which information is to be maintained. The domain model serves two purposes. First, of course, it is used to develop the database for the new system. Chapter 10 explains how to use the domain model to design the database. The second purpose, as we have seen, is to identify the internal classes that make up the new system. It should be apparent that a very close correlation will exist between the database tables and the design classes. Both come from the same domain model.

In your database course, you learn how to access the tables in the relational database by using SQL statements. Executing SQL statements on a database enables a program to access a record or a set of records from the database. One of the problems with object-oriented programs that use databases is a slight mismatch between programming languages and database SQL statements. For example, in a database, tables are linked through the use of foreign keys, such as an Order having a CustomerID as a column so that the Order can be joined with the customer in a relational join. However, in OO programming languages, the navigation is in the opposite direction, and the Customer class may have an array of references that point to the Order objects that are in the computer memory and are being processed by the system. In other words, design classes do not have foreign keys.

These differences between programming languages and database languages have partially driven the trend to a multilayer design. The design, programming, and maintenance of a system are easier if separate classes are defined to access the database and get the data in a form that is conducive to processing in the computer. Rather than mix the business logic with the data access logic, it is better to define separate classes and let each focus on its primary responsibility. This idea is an application of the good design principles of highly cohesive classes with appropriate responsibilities.

In this chapter, we take a somewhat simplified approach to design in order to teach the basic ideas without getting embroiled in the complexities of database access. Let us assume that every domain object will have a table in a relational database. Let's also assume that each domain object is responsible for initializing itself by going to the database, when necessary, to read the data. Given these assumptions, the modifications to the *Look up item availability* use case that are required to add the data access layer can be precisely defined. Before the use case can be executed, the domain objects have to be initialized with the necessary data from the database. Figure 8-16 illustrates this process.

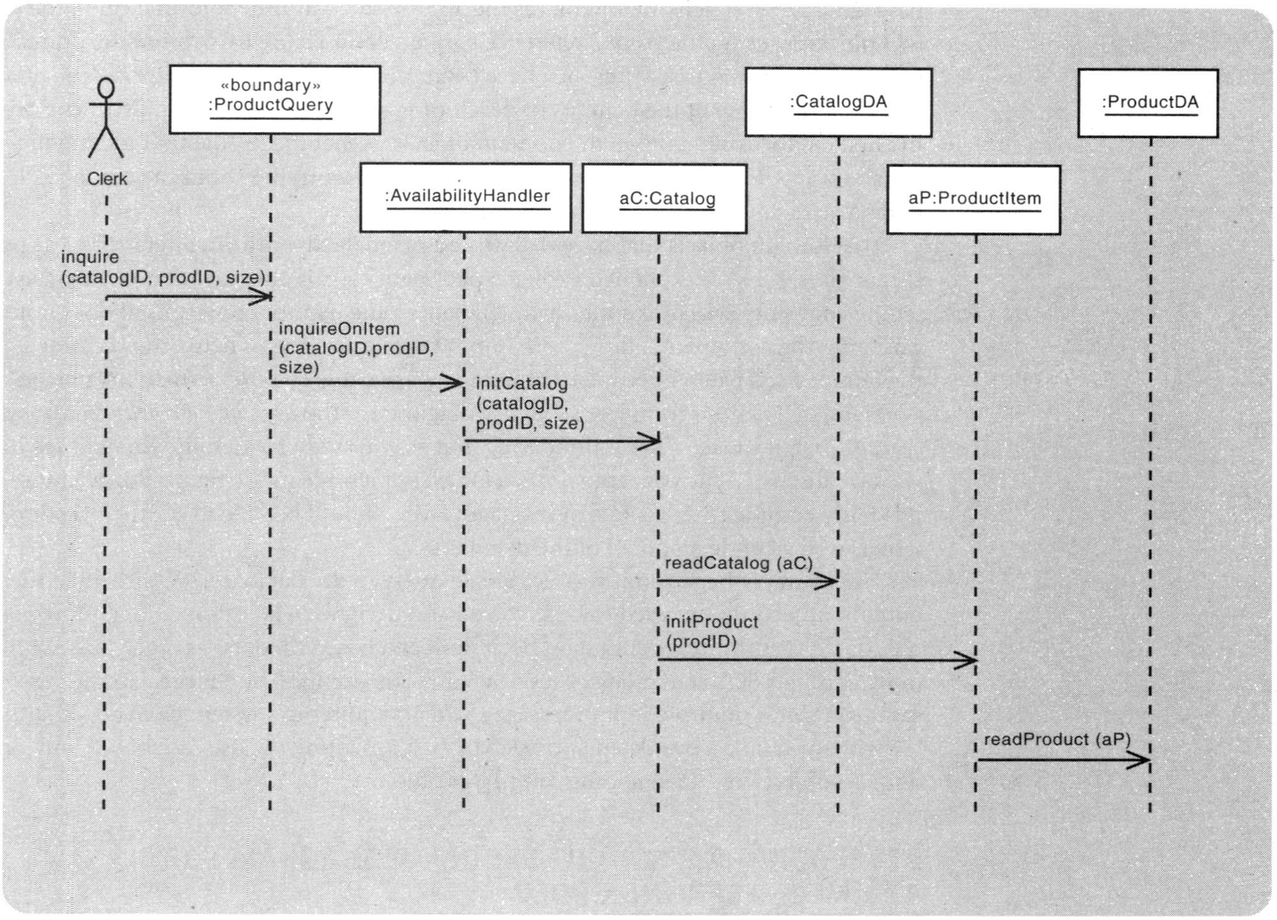

FIGURE 8-16
Partial three-layer design for *Look up item availability*

In Figure 8-16, we have only included the first few messages of the use case so that we can focus on the data access classes. Carefully note the changes between Figures 8-15 and 8-16. When the use case controller :AvailabilityHandler receives the initial request for an item inquiry, it first begins a process to initialize the necessary objects in memory. The set of "init" messages can either create new objects, if necessary, or simply verify that existing objects are in memory. The two classes CatalogDA and ProductDA are the data access classes. The incoming message to the catalog object simply identifies which catalog is needed. The catalog object reads the database, that is, accesses the CatalogDA object, to get all of the necessary data. The process to complete the product data fields is the same, as shown in the figure.

Remember that within sequence diagrams, the boxes refer to objects and not classes. The name within the box is underlined to indicate an object. In most cases, it is not important to specifically identify an object, so the notation would simply be Person or :Person. Sometimes, it is important to denote a specific object. In this case, the notation might be Mary:Person. When denoting a specific object, the colon serves as the divider between the object name and the specific object identifier. Specific identifiers are used when a reference to the object is required in another part of the diagram.

Note the description of each of the domain objects, for example, aC:Catalog. The "aC" is the identifier for a particular catalog object. When a new object is instantiated, such as a new catalog object, it recognizes that it needs to go to the database to retrieve its data. It sends a message to the :CatalogDA object with a reference to itself, that is, aC, to read and retrieve the data from the database. The data access class reads the database with a SQL statement and places the appropriate attribute information in the original object by using the passed reference parameter. In Figure 8-16, all of the domain objects are initiated first. After they have been initiated, the use case proceeds as previously defined. One of the benefits of developing sequence diagrams in two steps, with the first cut focusing only on the domain objects, is that the problem of identifying collaborating domain objects can be solved without worrying about the complexities of data access.

The domain objects that have data stored in a database are often referred to as persistent classes. As we explained earlier, a persistent class is an entity that must persist after the computer system is shut down. Of course, the memory object itself does not exist after the computer is turned off, but the data must persist between executions. So, the term is used when referring to objects or classes that require permanent storage.

Figure 8-17 is the complete sequence diagram for the *Look up item availability* use case. At first, it looks rather intimidating, but as you study it carefully, you will see that we have discussed the conceptual basis for every message in the figure. So, even though it is fairly complex—it has lots of messages—you should be able to see the overall pattern as well as understand all of the details.

This example began simply—as a single query to the database. We identified the domain objects that needed to be involved and designed a solution. Other, more complex database solutions could have been designed based on database joins and with more complex SQL statements. Let's now turn our attention to a more complex use case—one with multiple input messages, which requires the system to create objects. We will again take a multistep approach by first designing the use case based only on domain objects and then adding multilayer objects.

DEVELOPING A FIRST-CUT SEQUENCE DIAGRAM FOR AN RMO TELEPHONE ORDER

Figure 6-17 from Chapter 6 presented an SSD for a telephone order from RMO. Figure 8-18 is another version of the telephone order. This SSD is for the telephone scenario of the *Create new order* use case. As before, we will do a design for each input message in the SSD. The design components for all the messages are combined to provide a comprehensive sequence diagram for the entire use case. As in Figure 8-4, information from the SSD and the first-cut design class diagram will again be used to develop the sequence diagram, with one exception. We define a controller object for this use case with the name of :OrderHandler. We anticipate that this controller may serve both for creating new orders and for maintaining existing orders. Whether this is the best design will be decided after other use cases have been designed and the design has been reviewed for good design principles.

The first input message is startOrder (accountNo), which comes from the Order Clerk to the :System. What does the system need to do to start an order? The system needs to create a new Order object and connect that Order object to a Customer object. Thus, a message to create a new order is needed. The destination of the message will be the Order object itself. In fact, if you remember your programming class, the create message invokes a constructor method on the object, which will create a new object.

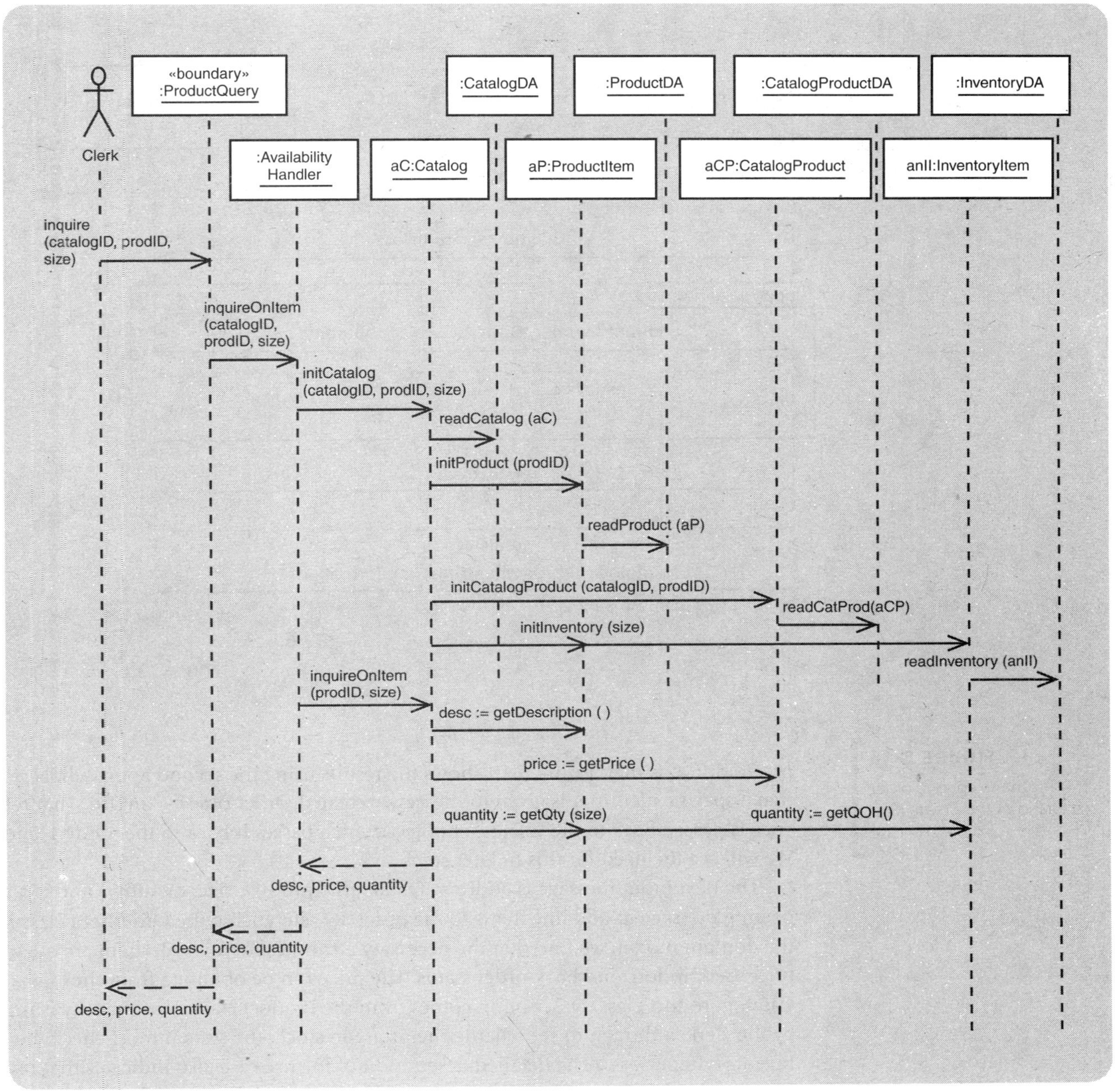

FIGURE 8-17
Completed three-layer design for *Look up item availability*

In UML when a create message is sent to an object, it is often drawn directly to the object's box and not to the lifeline. That is an optional diagramming technique used for convenience.

What object should be the source object for the create message? Should it be the <u>:OrderHandler</u> itself, or should it be some other object? Information included in the domain model indicates that the Order object has a relationship or link with the Customer object. There are several ways this link could be built. One would be to have the <u>:OrderHandler</u> object send the create message to the Order object, then send another message to the Customer object with a reference to the order. Another way is just to let the Customer object create the Order object. Since Order objects are not allowed unless a Customer object exists, this is one way to ensure that the customer existence

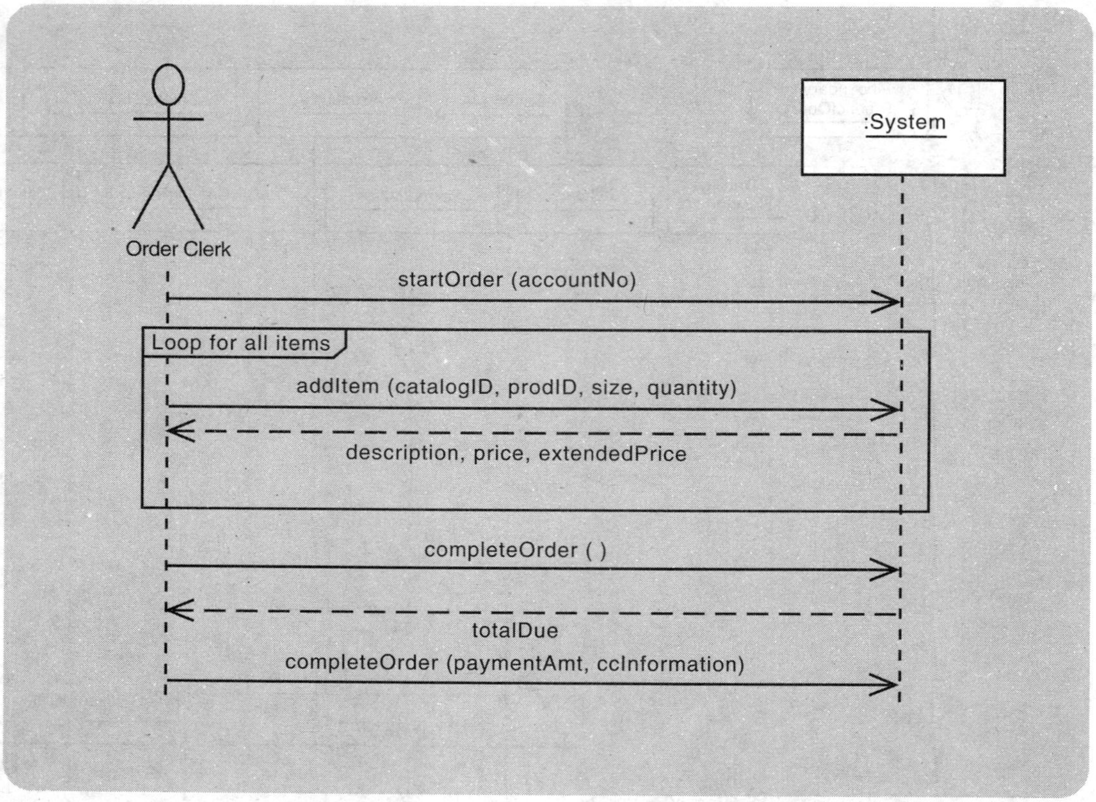

FIGURE 8-18
SSD for the telephone order scenario of the *Create new order* use case

precondition is met. Figure 8-19 shows the results using the second approach. Note that a specific identifier is given to the newly created Order object—anOrd. That reference is passed back to the Customer object, which passes it back to the :OrderHandler. We will see the need for this in later steps.

The next input message is addItem (catalogID, prodID, size, quantity) and is a repeating message to add line items to the order. By referencing the OrderItem class in the domain model, we find that the necessary attributes for an OrderItem are quantity, price, description, and back-order status. The price can be obtained from the CatalogProduct class. Description comes from the Product class. The quantity is input by the clerk, although to see whether items are in stock, the system must check the InventoryItem class. (The detailed description of the use case also indicates that inventory should be checked by the system.) So, the sequence diagram will also need objects for :OrderItem, :CatalogProduct, :Product, and :InventoryItem.

As we identify the specific messages, along with source and destination as well as the passed parameters, we need to consider some critical issues. As before, an important decision is, Which object is the source or initiator of a message? If the message is a query message, the source is the object that needs information. If the message is an update or create message, then the source is the object that controls the other object or that has the information necessary for its creation.

Another important consideration is navigation visibility—to send a message to the correct destination object, the source object must have visibility to the destination object. Remember that the purpose of doing design is to prepare for programming. As a designer, you will need to think about how the program will work and consider programming issues. Given these two considerations and the source considerations discussed in the previous paragraph, we have determined that the following internal

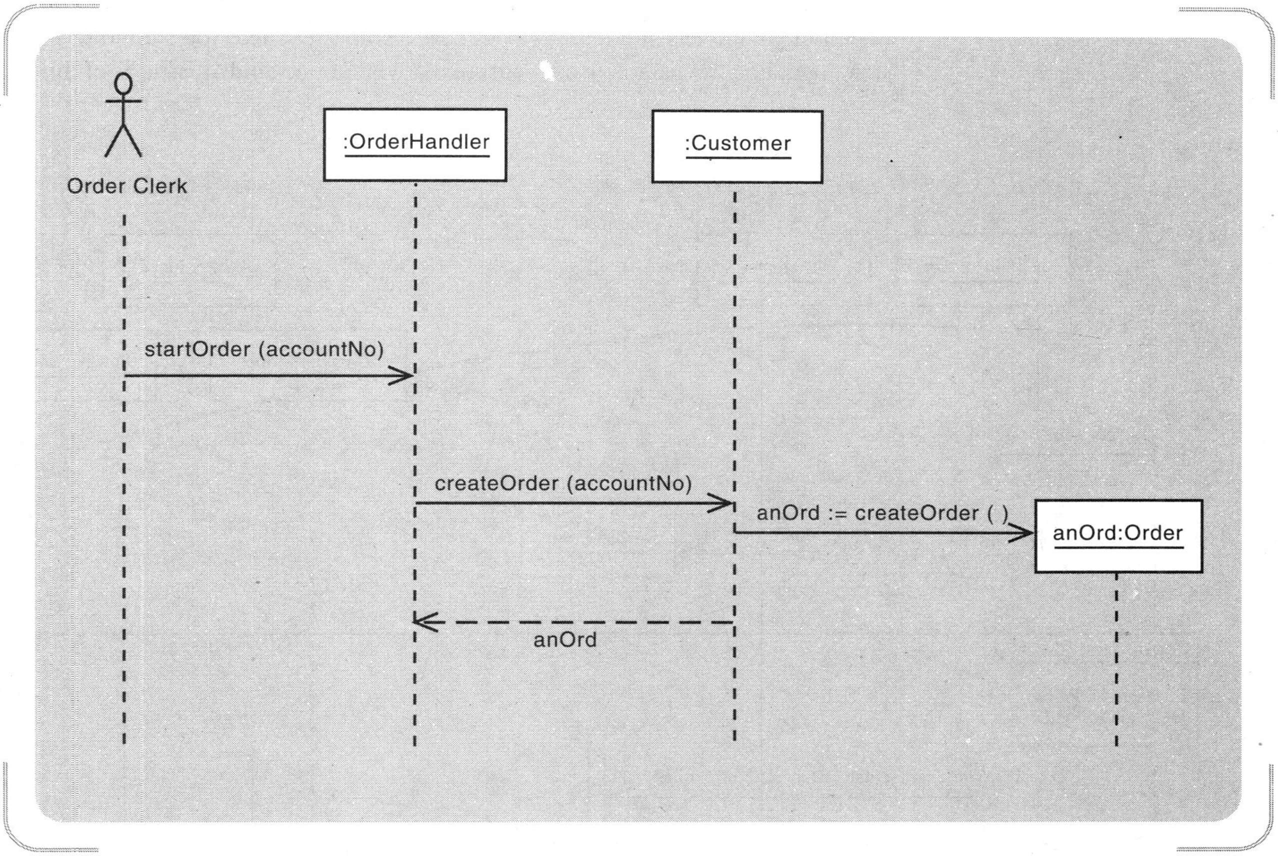

FIGURE 8-19
Partial sequence diagram for the telephone order scenario

messages will be required. For each message, a source object and a destination object have been identified.

- **addItem ( ).** Original message, from Clerk to :OrderHandler.
- **addItem ( ).** A forwarded version of the input message from :OrderHandler to :Order. Since OrderItem objects are dependent to Order, Order is the logical object to create OrderItems. System has visibility to the Order from the previous return message when anOrd was returned to the system.
- **createOrdItem ( ).** The internal message from :Order to :OrderItem. Since the OrderItem will be responsible for obtaining the data for its attributes, it needs visibility to :CatalogProduct, :Product, and :InventoryItem. As a result, those keys are sent as parameters. An alternate approach is to let :Order collect the required information, such as price and backOrderStatus, and send that to the :OrderItem as parameters. However, since the domain model indicates that there is a link between an OrderItem and an InventoryItem, the first approach is better.
- **getPrice ( ).** The message to get the price from the :CatalogProduct object. The :OrderItem initiates the message. It has visibility since it has the key values.
- **getDescription ( ).** The message, initiated by :OrderItem, to get the description from :Product.
- **updateQty ( ).** The message that checks to see that there is sufficient quantity on hand. This message also initiates the updating of the quantity on hand. The :OrderItem initiates the message. It does not have key visibility, but it does have enough information to search on an index of catalogID, productID, and size.

Figure 8-20 shows the results of the design for the addItem message. In the figure, the input parameters and return values have also been added. You should review the design, including the parameters, to ensure that you understand all aspects of this design.

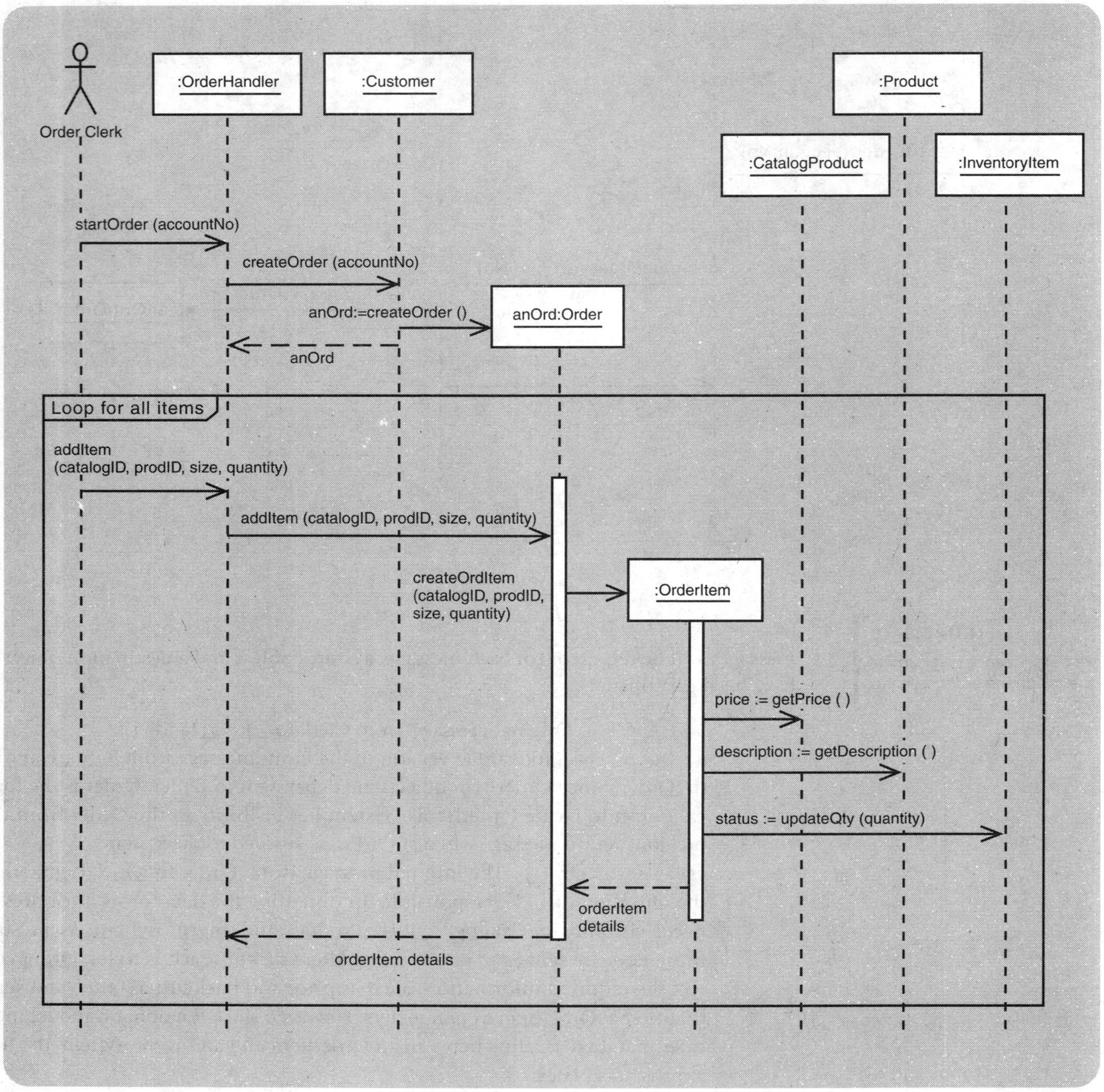

FIGURE 8-20
Another partial sequence diagram for the telephone order scenario

After each item is added to the order, control is returned to the Order Clerk. The clerk will add another item or, at the end of the order, will send a completeOrder( ) message. This message has no parameters. Its purpose is simply to tell the order to calculate the total amount due. If we assume, as designers, that the Order object keeps a running total of the individual line items that were added, then it simply calculates the appropriate tax and shipping and sends back a total amount. This is a valid and solid design. Another alternative is that the Order object does not keep a running total but must query each of the line items and accumulate a total. The second design requires additional detailed messages to be sent to the :OrderItem objects.

The final message on the SSD is the makePayment (ccInformation) message. We have made the simplifying assumption that it is always a credit card payment. As we review the domain model, we see that a new object must be created—the OrderTransaction object. Since transactions are connected to orders in the model, an Order object should create a transaction. Thus, the system forwards the completion message to the :Order, which in turn creates a payment for :OrderTransaction. These new messages are shown in Figure 8-21.

Figure 8-21 contains all of the internal messages for the final design. The figure contains the design of the domain model classes and the internal messages that are required to execute the use case. This section has focused only on the classes from the domain model, plus one additional object called :OrderHandler. By focusing only on the domain classes, we have been able to design the core processing for the use case without having to worry about the user interface or the database. Figure 8-21 is rather complex, even though it only contains domain objects. However, this design provides a very solid base for programming. Working with design models enables you—the designer—to think through all the requirements to process a use case without having to worry about code. More importantly, it enables the designer to modify and correct a design without having to throw away code and write new code. In the next section, we will add the view layer and the data access layer objects to the telephone order scenario.

DEVELOPING A MULTILAYER DESIGN FOR THE TELEPHONE ORDER SCENARIO

To reduce the complexity of the diagrams, we will extend this use case scenario one message at a time. The first message starts the order. As mentioned previously, if work has already been done on the user interface, then we will use that as the basis for the sequence diagram. Let's assume that enough preliminary work has been done so that we know there is a :MainWindow object with a menu item—or a button—that opens another window, which is the new :OrderWindow object. The new :OrderWindow contains some customer information, has the basic information about the order, and includes places to list the items that have been added to the order.

Figure 8-22 illustrates the additions to the first-cut sequence diagram to include the view layer for this first message. We add a message at the beginning to open up the :OrderWindow. Another message is initiated by :OrderHandler to retrieve a :Customer object and return that object to the :OrderWindow object so that customer information can be displayed.

To add the data layer for this first message, we simply need to allow the :Customer object to initialize itself. As with the previous use case, we will use a single data access class for Customer objects. The newly created :Order object is also saved to the database. Many database management systems automatically generate keys for records in a table. Saving the order early means that the key can be extracted and the data are backed up in case of computer failure. Figure 8-22 also includes the data access class.

The next message is a repeating message that adds items to the order. Let's assume that the :OrderWindow object has a button to allow a new item to be added. Clicking on the button pops up another window, :NewItemWin, that can be used to add the detailed items to the order. The Order Clerk enters the information about the new item to be ordered. At this point, the :NewItemWin window invokes the *Look up item availability* use case, which initializes the necessary :Product and :InventoryItem objects and verifies that the item is available. A note is added to the sequence diagram to indicate

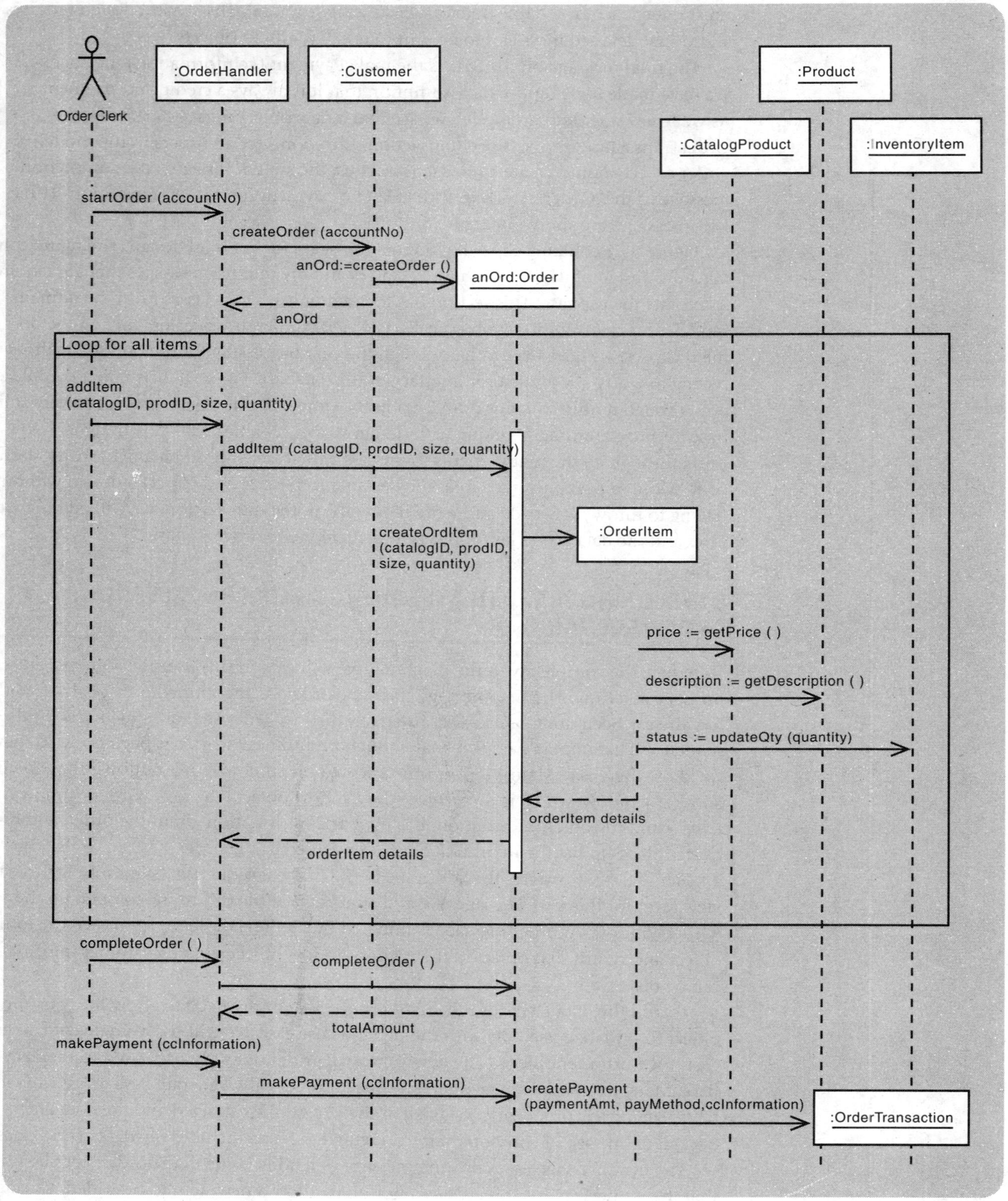

FIGURE 8-21
Sequence diagram for the telephone order scenario of the *Create new order* use case

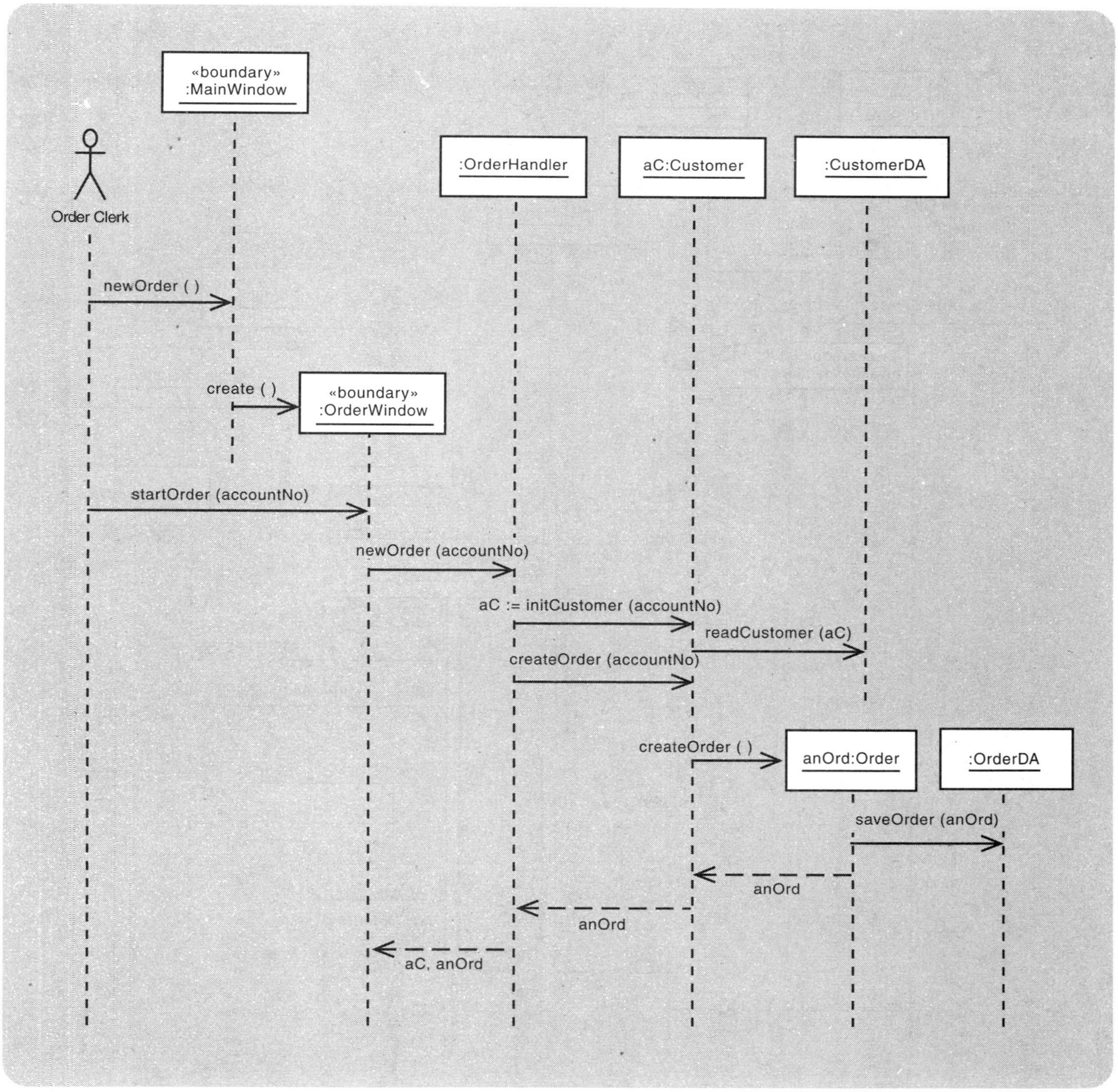

FIGURE 8-22
Telephone order sequence diagram for the startOrder message

this action. The :Order then creates the required :OrderItem. As discussed earlier, the :OrderItem is responsible for collecting all of the necessary data, so it sends the appropriate messages to collect data for its attributes. Finally, the :OrderItem sends a message to the :OrderItemDA data access object to save itself to the database. The :InventoryItem object also invokes its data access class to update its quantity-on-hand field. In this case, since the initializing of the product and inventory objects is done by the *Look up item availability* use case, the only data access required is to save the updated data. Figure 8-23 illustrates the addition of the view layer and the data access layer to this portion of the use case.

For the final two messages, completeOrder ( ) and makePayment ( ), no new window classes need to be defined. Let us assume that the :NewOrderWin window has

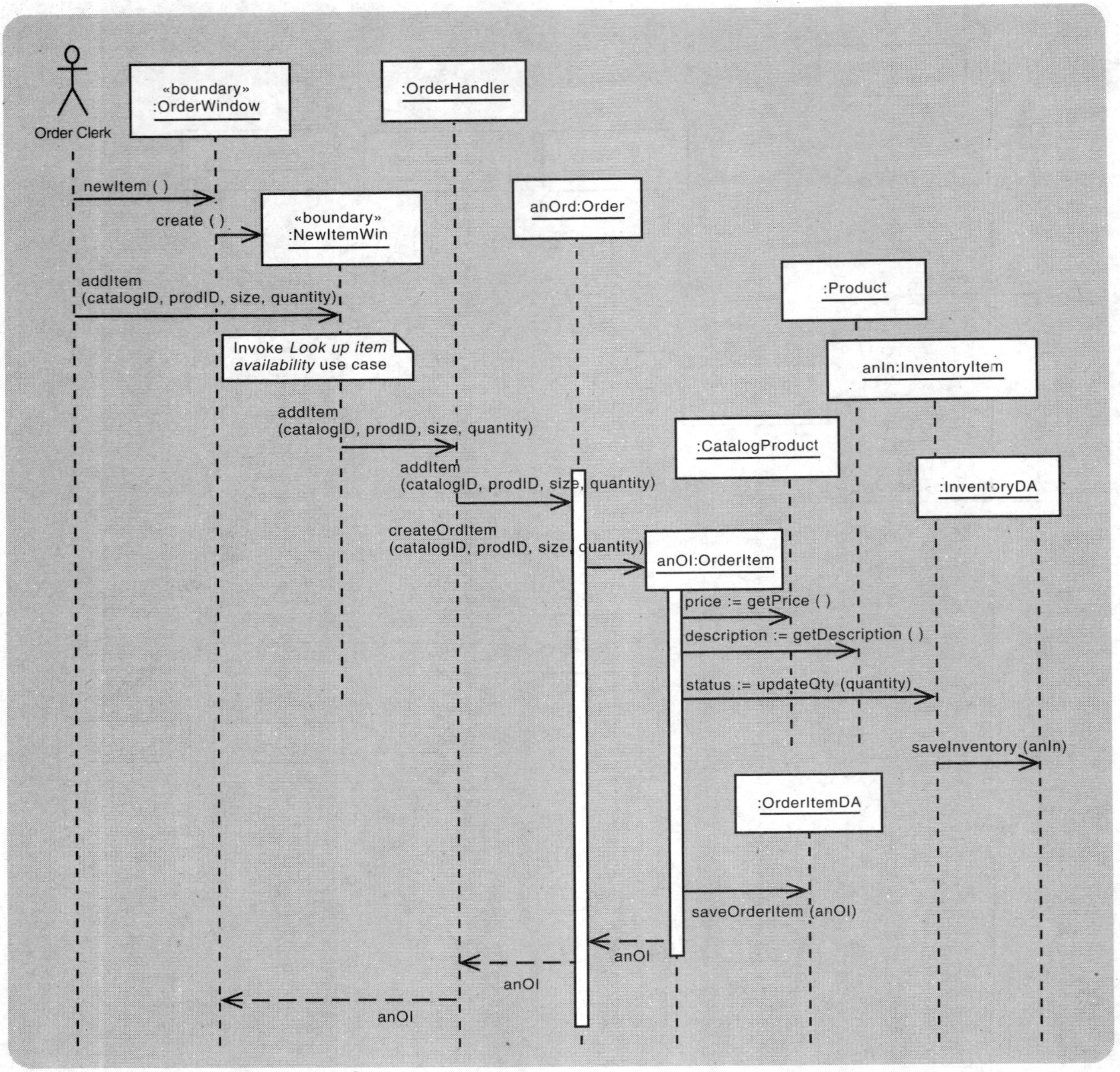

FIGURE 8-23

Telephone order sequence diagram for the addItem message

appropriate fields to indicate the completion of the order and to enter the payment amount. The order will need to be saved to the database using the <u>:OrderDA</u> data access class. One new data access class to save the <u>:OrderTransaction</u> object is needed. Figure 8-24 illustrates these final additions to the sequence diagram.

As you can see, these sequence diagrams do get somewhat busy and complicated. However, these diagrams provide an excellent foundation for programming the use case. By going through the process of detailed design, the designer can think through the complexities of each use case without programming complications. It should also be noted that no design elements have been added yet to cover error handling or failures in the use case. For example, what happens if a customer record is not found? Or what does the system do if the input edits fail? The sequence diagram could be

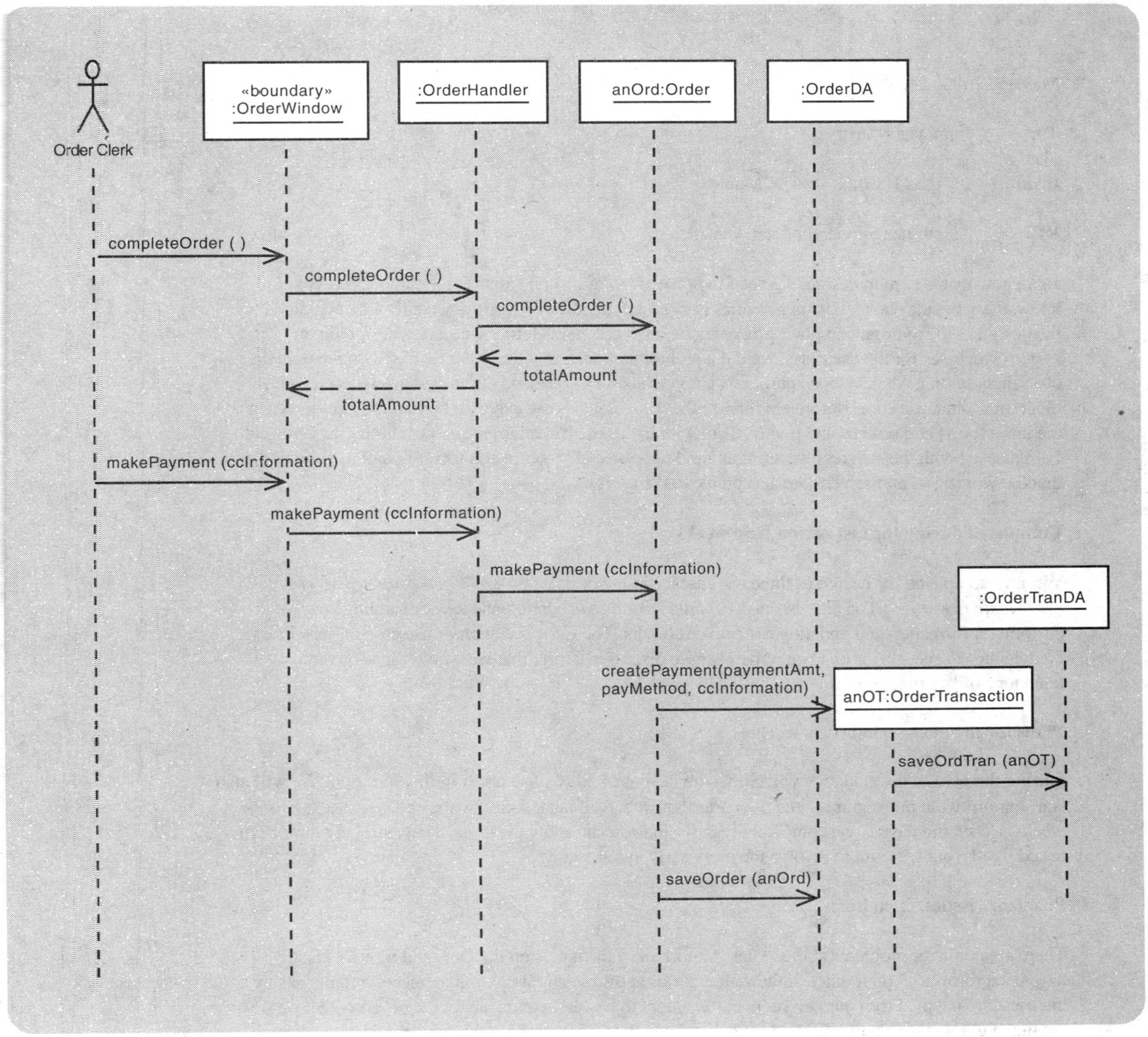

FIGURE 8-24
Telephone order sequence diagram for the final messages

extended to cover those situations. Another approach is simply to add narrative description to indicate how the system should handle those exception conditions and leave the details to the programmer.

BEST PRACTICE: Don't be tempted to put business logic in the view layer classes.

When developing a sequence diagram, it is often necessary to work on several tasks at the same time. For example, the database design and user-interface prototyping might be ongoing activities that are concurrent with detailed design. The RMO memo illustrates how this combination of design activities occurs.

May 15, 2006

To: John MacMurty

From: Barbara Halifax, Project Manager

RE: Customer Support System status

ROCKY MOUNTAIN OUTFITTERS
MEMO

John, now that we are in design, we need to proceed along several fronts at the same time. As you know, the schedule shows several activities going on in parallel. The primary controlling activity is the design of the internal computer processes for each use case. Before we started designing the system processes for the use cases, we did a preliminary design of the database based on the domain class diagram that we developed earlier. Next, we took a use case and developed a detailed sequence diagram for that use case. Before we finalize the design of any use case, we build a few prototypes of the input forms and screens and review them with the users. It is a fairly time-consuming process, but I am pleased with the progress we are making. I am especially confident that the design is solid and that the workflows and screens are acceptable to the users.

Completed during the last period (two weeks)

We have completed the design of three use cases, *Update customer account*, *Look up item availability*, and *Create new order*. The first use case, *Update customer account*, includes both adding new customer information and updating existing customers. The *Create new order* use case only includes the telephone order scenario. (You remember we discussed earlier that we would focus on the telephone orders first.)

Plans for the next period (two weeks)

During the next two weeks, we will finish the design of all the use cases in this iteration. We will also start tomorrow on programming the use cases that we have finished. So, by the end of the next two weeks, we should have some complete use cases that we can show the users. They will only have been tested lightly, but we want to involve the users early in our testing.

Problems, issues, open items

There are no major problems at this point. Almost all of the issues on the Outstanding Items Log have been resolved. You might test the waters for us at the oversight committee meeting to make sure the users are happy. From our perspective, they seem to be very excited about the progress that we are making. I would just like to make sure that the feeling is the same at the senior executive level.

BH

cc. Steven Deerfield, Ming Lee, Jack Garcia

DESIGNING WITH COMMUNICATION DIAGRAMS

Communication diagrams and sequence diagrams are both interaction diagrams, and they capture the same information. The process of designing is the same whether you are using communication diagrams or sequence diagrams. Which model is used for design is primarily a matter of a designer's personal preference. Many designers prefer to use sequence diagrams to develop the design because use case descriptions and dialog designs follow a sequence of steps. Communication diagrams are useful for showing a different view of the use case—one that emphasizes coupling.

For actors, objects, and messages, a communication diagram uses the same symbols as those found in a sequence diagram. The lifeline and activation lifeline symbols are not used. However, a different symbol, the link symbol, is used. Figure 8-25 illustrates the four symbols used in most communication diagrams.

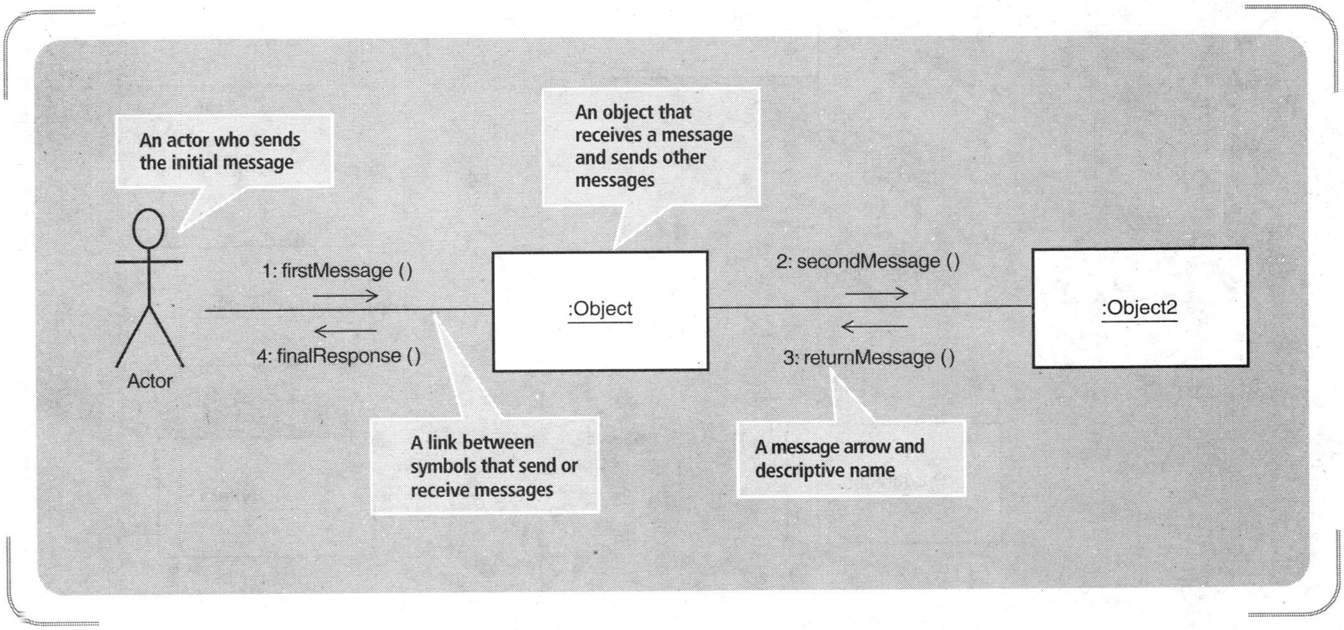

FIGURE 8-25
The symbols of a communication diagram

The format of the message descriptor for a communication diagram differs slightly from that for a sequence diagram. Since no lifeline shows the passage of time during a scenario, each message is numbered sequentially, to indicate the order of the messages. The syntax of the message descriptor in a communication diagram is the following:

[true/false condition] sequence-number: return-value := message-name (parameter−list)

As you can see in Figure 8-25, a colon always directly follows the sequence number.

The connecting lines between the objects or between actors and objects represent *links*. In a communication diagram, a link shows that two items share a message—that one sends a message and the other receives it. The connecting lines are essentially used only to carry the messages, so you can think of them as the wires used to transmit the messages.

links
notations in a communication diagram that carry messages between objects or between actors and objects

Figures 8-25 and 8-26 present communication diagrams for the same two RMO use cases shown earlier with the sequence diagrams in Figures 8-14 and 8-20, namely, *Look up item availability* and *Create new order*. These communication diagrams contain only domain model objects and not the view layer or data access layer. However, multilayer design can be done just as effectively with communication diagrams as with sequence diagrams.

The numbers on the messages indicate the sequence in which the messages are sent. Notice the messages numbered 5 and 5.1. The hierarchical dot numbering scheme is used when messages are dependent on other messages. In this instance, the primary message, 5: quantity := getQty (size), is sent to the :ProductItem, which then forwards a similar message, 5.1: quantity := getQOH ( ), to :InventoryItem. The second message is a direct result of the first, so it is numbered 5.1, as a subordinate to the primary message. Sometimes new designers struggle with figuring out when to number messages as subordinate and when to number them at the same level. For example, you could argue that the entire sequence of messages is dependent on the very first one

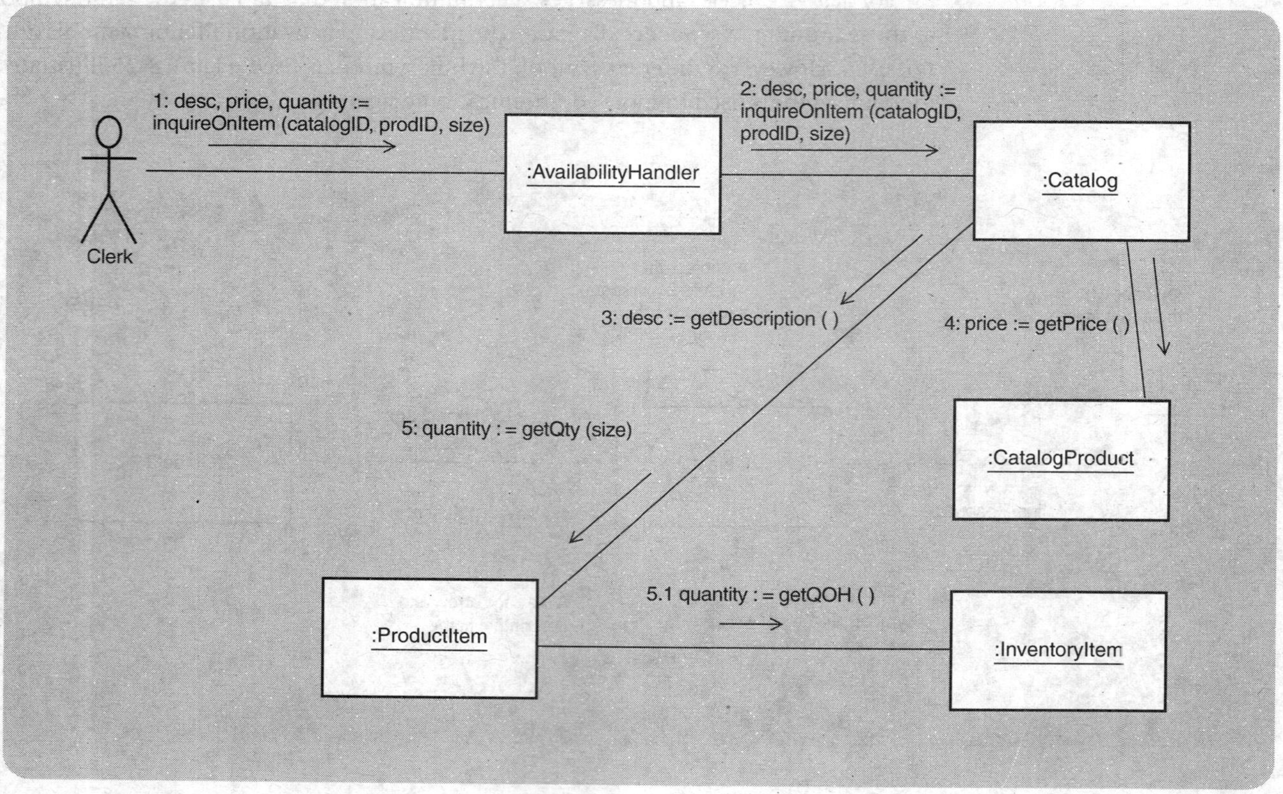

FIGURE 8-26
A communication diagram for *Look up item availability*

being sent and that the entire set should be subordinated to the initial message. One good way to think about when and how to number with subordinated numbers is to construct the set of messages in an outline format, as you would do with your material before writing a paper. The messages that are at the same level in an outline should all be numbered as primary messages. Lower-level messages are like dependent paragraphs and headings in a paper outline. The hierarchy of messages can go as deep as required to indicate dependency. In Figure 8-27, the numbering sequence goes down several levels. Since multiple input messages initiate a series of other messages, this diagram is very explicit in using the hierarchical numbering scheme.

When you compare the communication diagrams with the sequence diagrams, it should be evident that the focus of a communication diagram is on the objects themselves. Drawing a communication diagram is an effective way to get a quick overview of the objects that work together. However, as you look at the diagrams, you should observe that it is more difficult to visualize the sequence of the messages. You have to hunt to find the numbers to see the sequence of the messages. On the other hand, to get a quick overview of the collaborating objects, a communication diagram is very effective.

Many designers use communication diagrams to sketch out a solution. If the use case is small and not too complex, a simple communication diagram may suffice. However, for more complex situations, a sequence diagram may be required to allow you to visualize the flow and sequence of the messages. It is not unusual to find a mix within the same set of specifications: some use cases described by communication diagrams and others shown with sequence diagrams. As a system developer, you should be comfortable using both types of diagrams.

An even more abbreviated form of communication diagram can be used. Figure 8-5 showed two symbols that are used to specify objects. The iconic symbols show the object

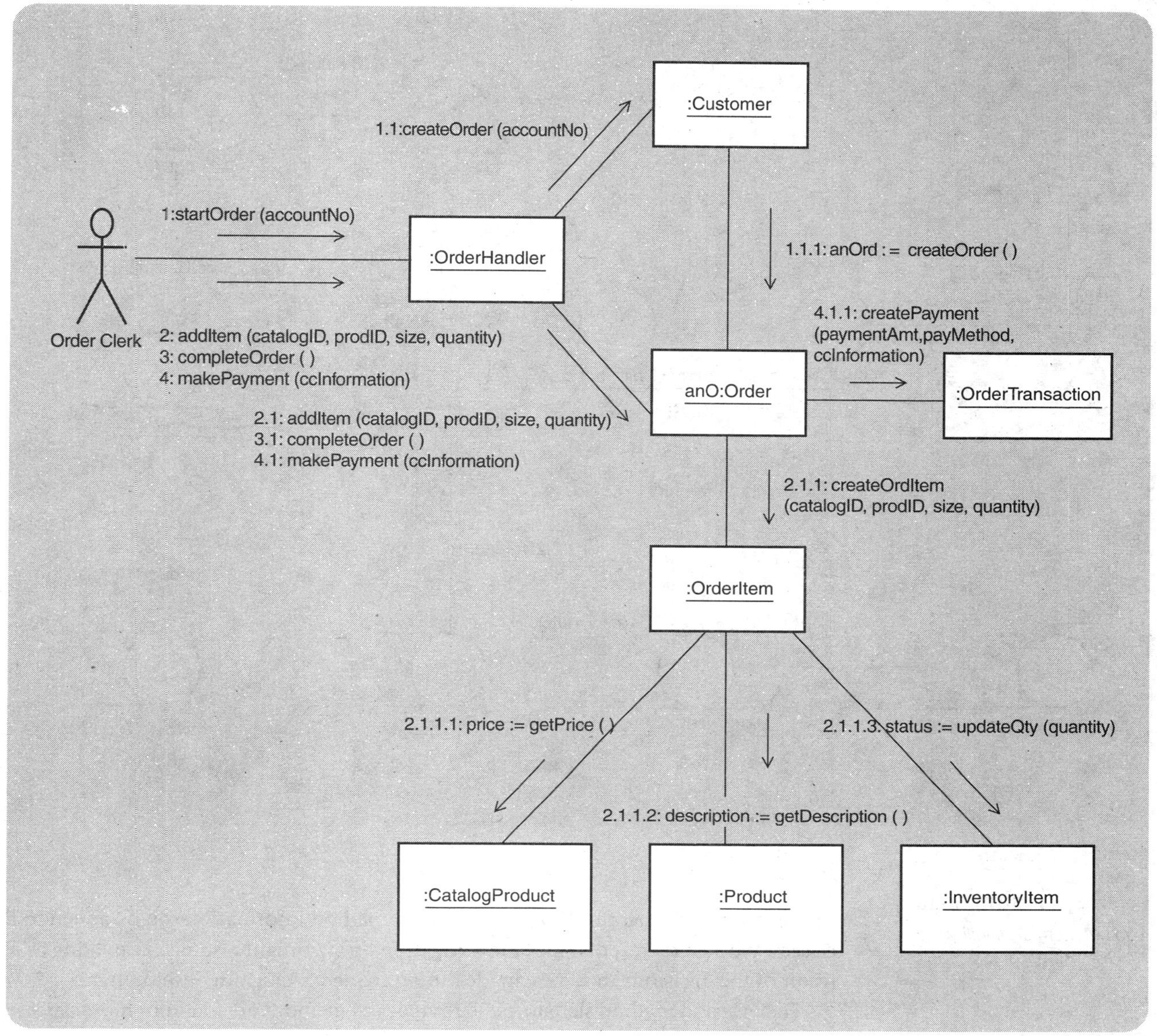

FIGURE 8-27
A communication diagram for *Create new order*

name, and the symbol itself indicates the stereotype that it is. Specific icons can be used to show the view layer, controller, domain layer, and data access layer. Figure 8-28 is an example of the multilayer design for the *Look up item availability* use case. This type of drawing can be used without messages to show collaborating objects or with messages to provide a shorthand notation for a complete communication diagram. The icons can also be used on sequence diagrams as shorthand notation for stereotypes.

UPDATING THE DESIGN CLASS DIAGRAM

Design class diagrams can now be developed for each layer. In the view layer and the data access layer, several new classes must be specified. The domain layer also has some new classes added for the use case controllers.

In Figure 8-10 we developed the first-cut design class diagram for the domain layer. At that point in the development, no method signatures had been developed. Now that

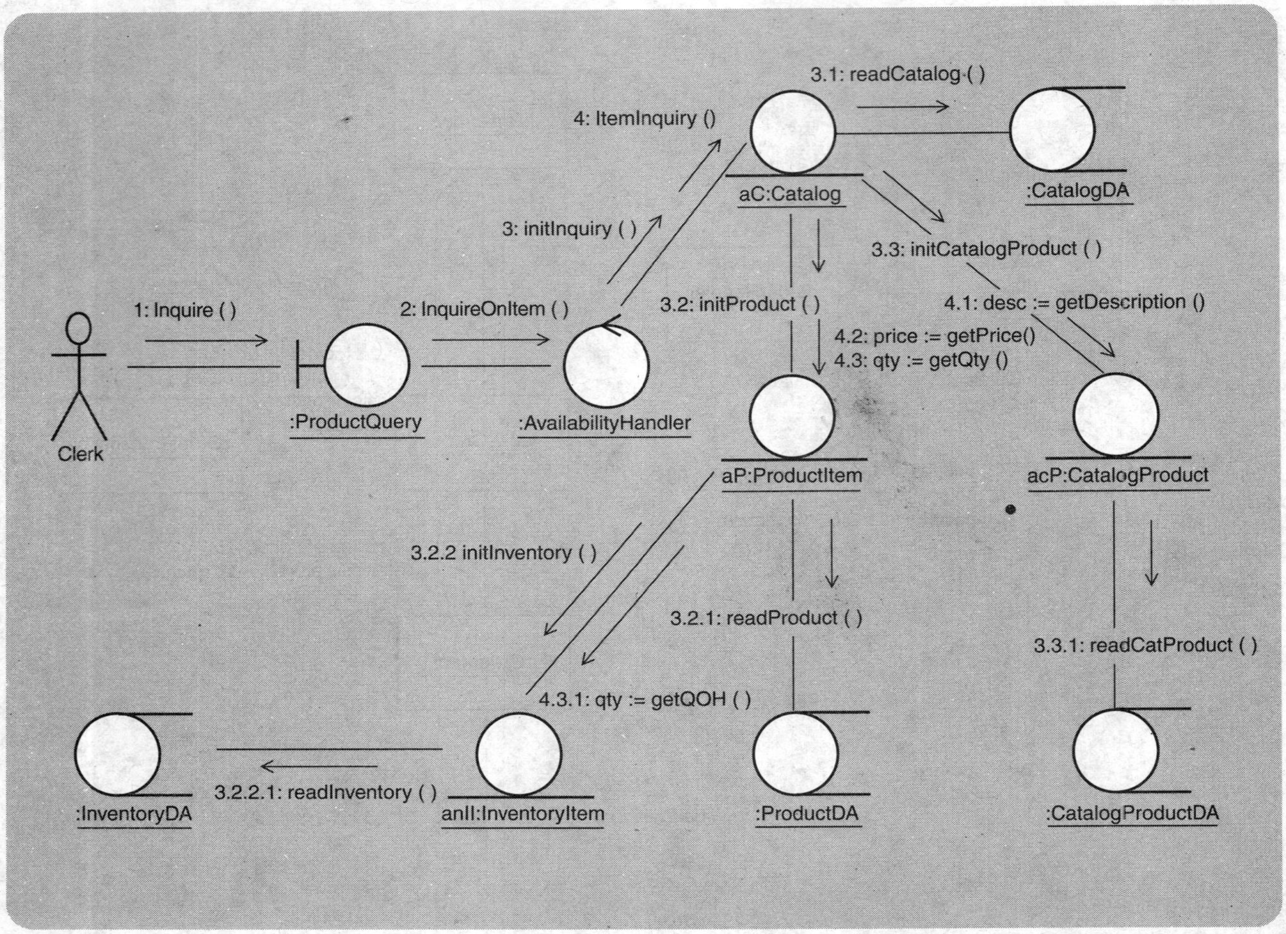

FIGURE 8-28

Look up item availability use case using iconic symbols

several sequence diagrams have been created, method information can be added to the classes. We also mentioned that the navigation arrows might also need updating as a result of the decisions that were made during sequence diagram development.

First, we add method signatures. Three types of methods are found in most classes: (1) constructor methods, (2) data get and set methods, and (3) use case specific methods. Remember that constructor methods are those that create new instances of the objects. Get and set methods retrieve and update attribute values. Since every class must have a constructor and most usually have get and set methods, it is optional to include those method signatures in the design class diagram. The third type of method must be included in the design class diagram. The following examples include all three types of method signatures as part of the process of finding and documenting method signatures.

As in sequence diagrams, every message has a source object and a destination object. When a message is sent to an object, the object must be prepared to accept that message and initiate some activity. This process is nothing more than invoking or calling a method on an object. In other words, every message that appears in a sequence diagram requires a method in the destination object. In fact, the syntax for a message looks very much like the syntax for a method. Thus, the process of adding method signatures to a design class is to go through every sequence diagram and find the messages sent to that class. Each message indicates a method.

Let's work through one example based on the Order class. The sequence diagrams that were completed during the examples in the chapter are shown in Figure 8-16 for the *Look up item availability* use case, and in Figure 8-21 for the *Create new order* use case. Since we are defining method signatures for domain model classes, we use the sequence diagrams prior to adding the multilayer design.

In Figure 8-16, no messages are sent to Order. In Figure 8-21, there are four messages to Order. The first message is createOrder ( ), with no parameters. The next message, addItem (catalogID, prodID, size, quantity), contains several parameters and has a return message with orderItem details. Finally, there are two messages, completeOrder ( ) and makePayment (ccInformation), one of which, completeOrder, initiates a return value of the totalAmount of the order. Given these messages and the return values, the design class notation for Order is shown in Figure 8-29.

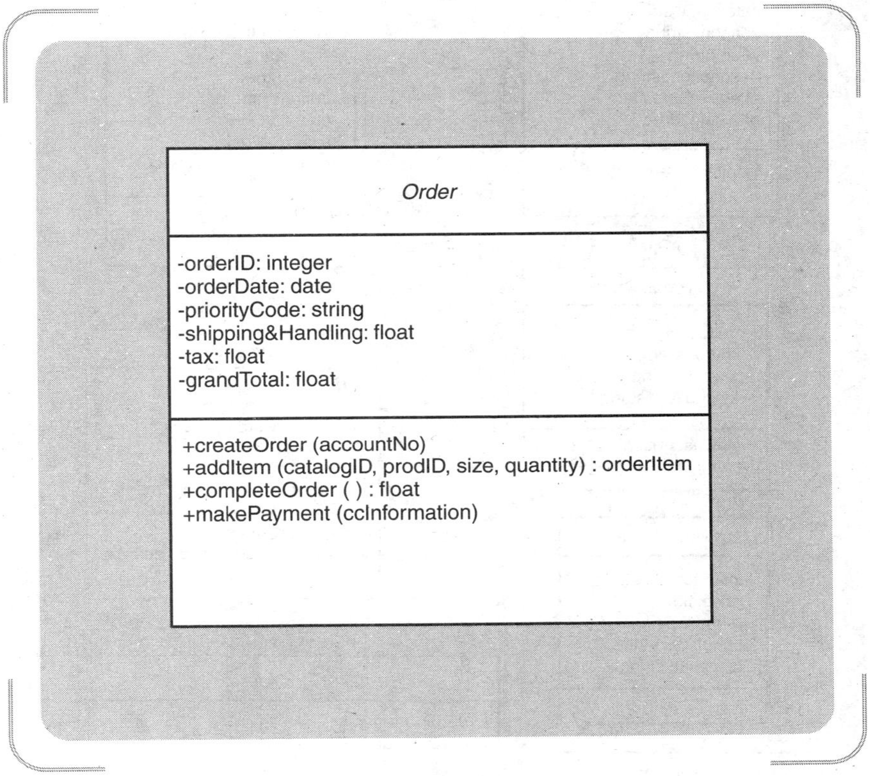

FIGURE 8-29
Design class, with method signatures, for the Order class

This process is continued for every class in the domain layer, including the added use case controller classes. Figure 8-30 contains the completed design class diagram for the domain layer classes. As you can see, this diagram provides excellent, thorough documentation of the design classes and serves as the blueprint for programming the system.

The two major additions to the domain layer classes are the two use case handlers. Additional navigation arrows have also been added to document which classes are visible from the controller classes. The other navigation arrows, which were defined during the first cut of the class diagram, have proved to be adequate for these two use cases. Additional use case development will enable us to add more navigation arrows, such as those to shipment and return items.

PACKAGE DIAGRAMS—STRUCTURING THE MAJOR COMPONENTS

A package diagram in UML is simply a high-level diagram that allows designers to associate classes of related groups. The preceding sections illustrated three-layer design, which

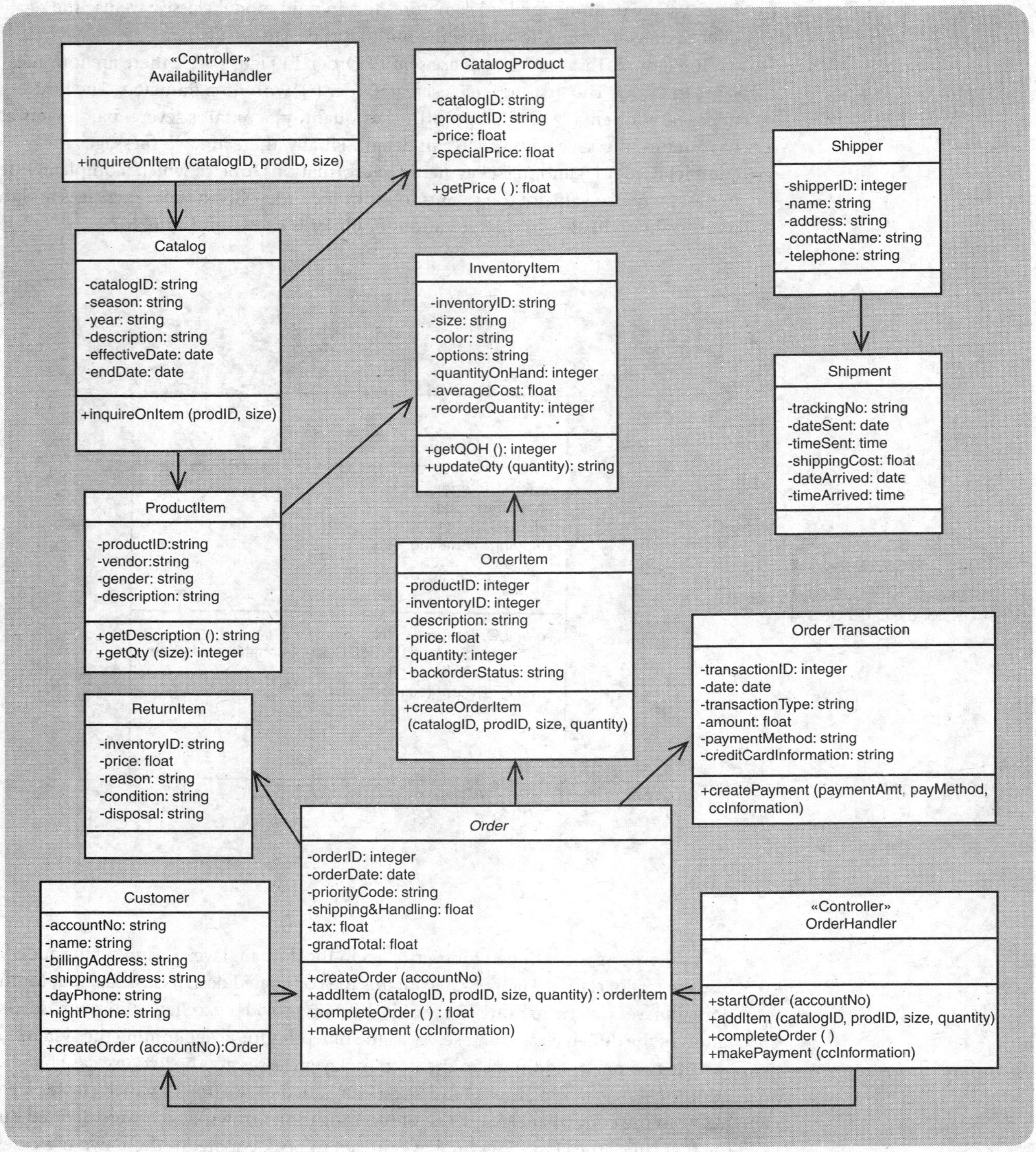

FIGURE 8-30
Updated design class diagram for the domain layer

includes the view layer, the domain layer, and the data access layer. In the interaction diagrams, the objects from each layer were shown together in the same diagram. However, at times designers need to document differences or similarities in the objects' relationships in these different layers—perhaps separating or grouping them based on a distributed processing environment. This information can be captured by showing each layer as a separate package. Figure 8-31 illustrates how these layers might be documented.

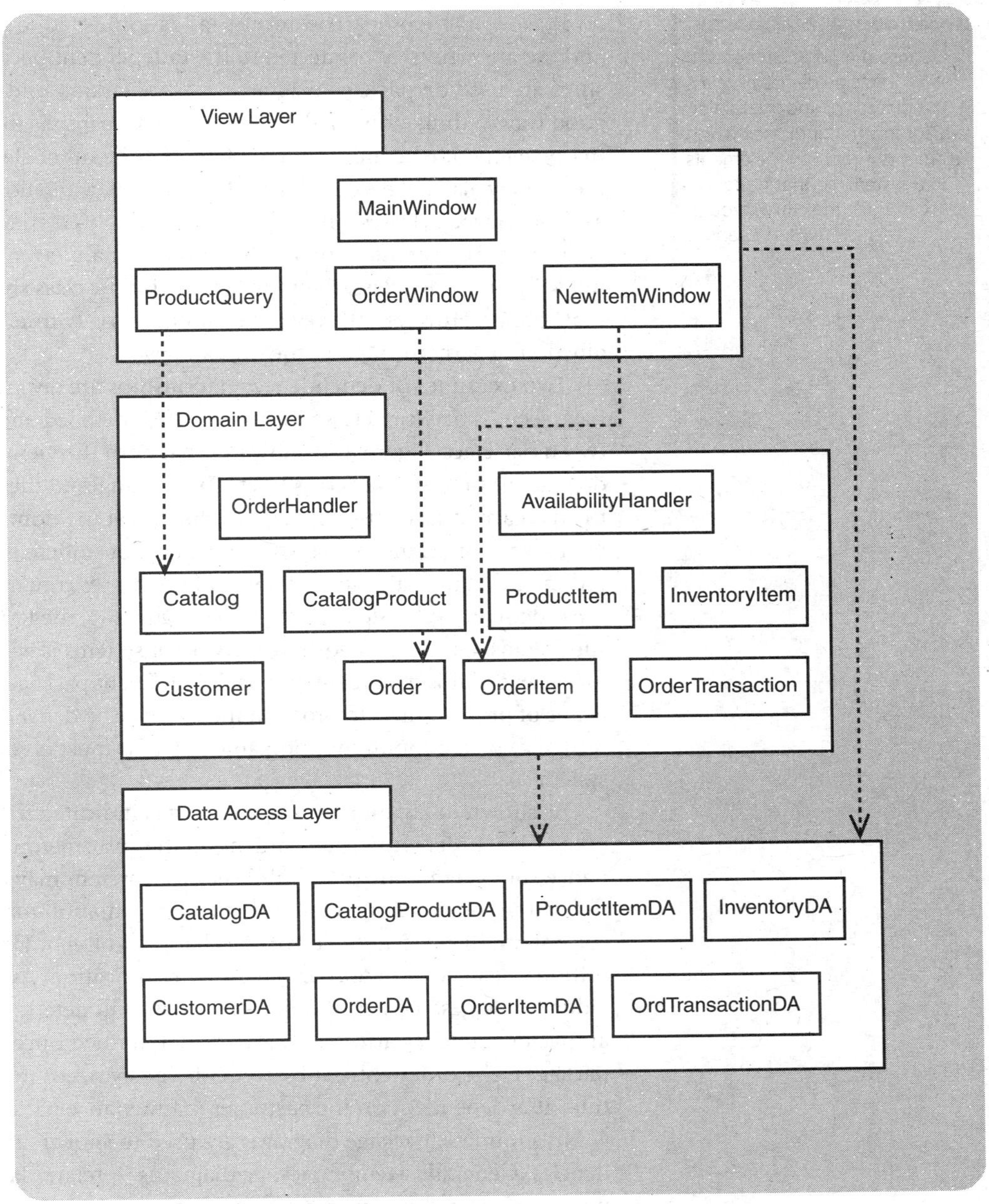

FIGURE 8-31
Partial design of a three-layer package diagram for RMO

The package notation is a tabbed rectangle. The package name is usually shown on the tab, although for a very high level view, if no details are shown inside the package, the name can also be placed inside the package rectangle. In this instance, the classes that belong to that package are placed inside the package rectangle.

The classes are placed inside the appropriate package based on the layer to which they belong. Classes are associated with different layers as they are developed in the interaction diagrams. To develop this package diagram, we simply extracted the information from design class diagrams and interaction diagrams for each use case. Figure 8-31 is only a partial package diagram because the packages contain only the classes from the use case interaction diagrams that were developed in this chapter.

dependency relationship relationship among elements in package diagrams, class diagrams, and interaction diagrams that indicates which elements affect other elements in a system, so that designers can track the carry-through effects of changes

The other symbol used on a package diagram is a dashed arrow, which represents a *dependency relationship*. The arrow's tail is connected to the package that is dependent, and the arrowhead is connected to the independent package. Dependency relationships are used on package diagrams, class diagrams, and even interaction diagrams. A good way to think about a dependency relationship is to note that if there is a change in one element (the independent element), the other element (the dependent element) may also have to be changed. Dependency relationships may be between packages or between classes within packages. Figure 8-31 indicates that two classes in the view layer are dependent on classes in the domain layer. So, for example, if a change is made in the Order class, then the OrderWindow class should be evaluated to capture that change. However, the reverse is not necessarily true. Changes to the view layer usually do not carry through to the domain layer.

Two examples of dependency relationships are given in Figure 8-31. The first, we have seen, is between classes. Another is less detailed and indicates a dependency between packages. Figure 8-31 indicates that both the view layer and the domain layer are dependent on the data access layer. Thus, changes to the data structures, as reflected in the data access layer, usually require changes at the domain layer and the view layer.

Package diagrams can also be nested to show different levels of packages. Figure 8-32 indicates that the packages and some of the classes contained within them are all part of the order-entry subsystem. As shown in Figure 6-4, the RMO system can be divided into subsystems. One way to document these subsystems is with package diagrams. One major benefit of this documentation is that different packages can be assigned to different teams of programmers to program the classes. The dependency arrows will help them recognize where communication among teams must occur to ensure a totally integrated system.

As shown in Figure 8-32, dependency is indicated from order fulfillment to order entry. Also, order entry is dependent on the customer maintenance and catalog maintenance subsystems. The order fulfillment subsystem may use the order classes that are defined in the order-entry subsystem, or information may be sent from the order-entry subsystem. In any event, if anything changes in the order-entry subsystem, the order fulfillment subsystem may also require modification. As the classes are added to individual packages, the use of objects in a class will determine the dependencies. For example, dependency arrows can also be determined once the classes are assigned to packages. The order-entry subsystem obviously needs to access the Customer class; thus, it is dependent on the customer maintenance package.

In summary, package diagrams are used to show related components and dependencies. Generally, we use package diagrams to relate classes or other system components such as network nodes. The preceding figures show two uses of package diagrams—to divide a system into subsystems and to show nesting within packages.

IMPLEMENTATION ISSUES FOR THREE-LAYER DESIGN

Using design class diagrams, interaction diagrams, and package diagrams, programmers can begin to build the components of a system. So, implementation in this sense means constructing the system by programming with a language such as Java or VB. NET. Over the last few years, very powerful integrated development environment (IDE) tools have been developed to help programmers construct systems. Such tools as Jbuilder and Eclipse for Java, Visual Studio for Visual Basic and C#, and C++Builder for C++ provide a very high level of programming support, especially in the construction of the view layer classes—the windows and window components of a system. Unfortunately, these same tools have also propagated some bad programming habits in some developers.

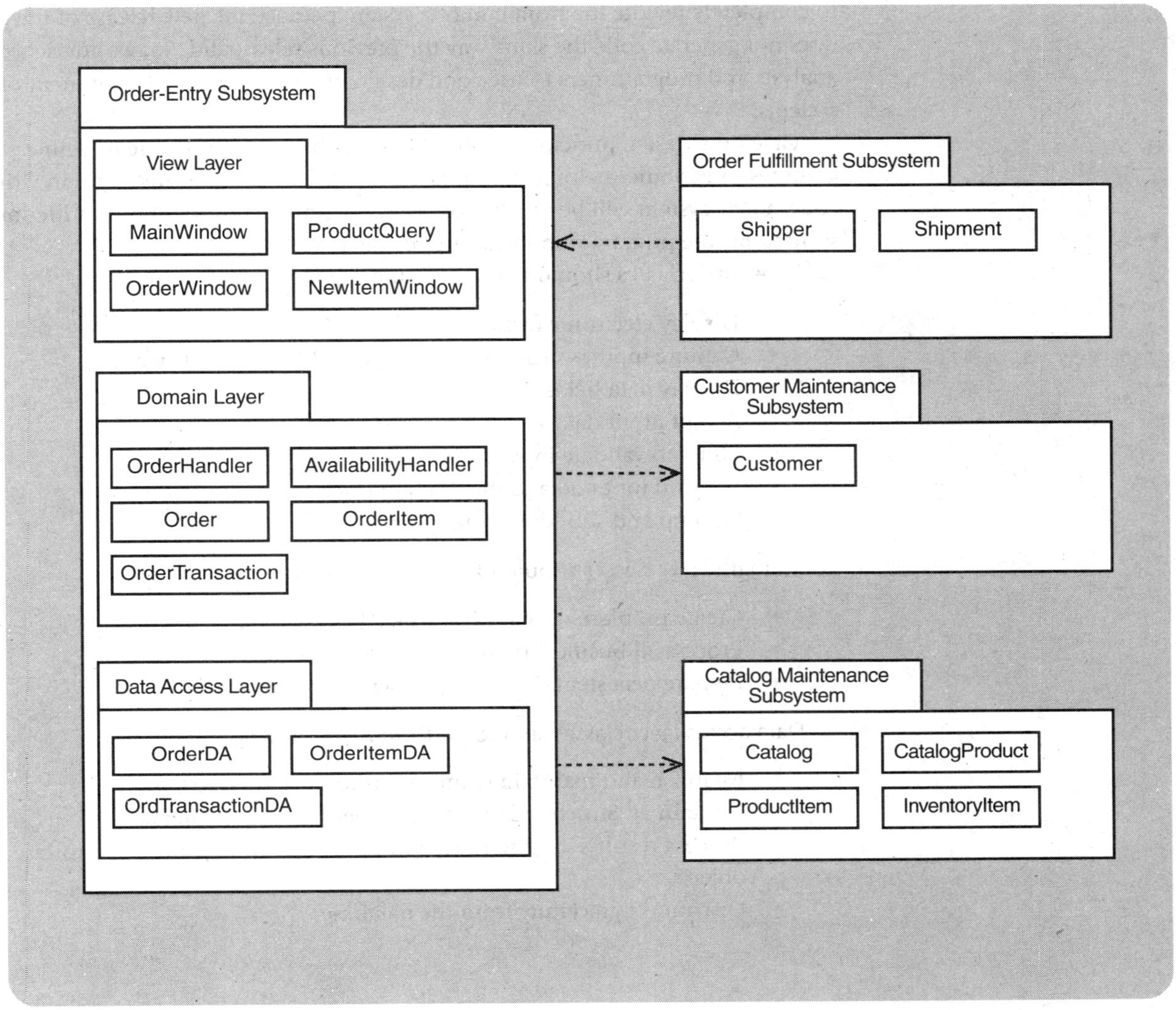

FIGURE 8-32
RMO subsystem packages

The ease with which programmers can build the graphical user interface windows and automatically insert programming code has allowed some programmers to put all of the code in the windows. Each windows component has several associated events where code can be inserted. So, some programmers find it easy to build a window with an IDE tool, let the tool automatically generate the class definition, and merely insert business logic code. No new classes need to be defined, and very little other coding is required. Many of these tools also have database engines, so the entire system can be built with only windows classes. Taking such shortcuts exacts a price later on, however.

The problem with this approach is the difficulty of maintaining the system. Code snippets scattered throughout the graphical user interface classes are very hard to find and maintain. Plus, when the user-interface classes need to be upgraded, the programmer must also find and update the business logic. If a network-based system needs to be enhanced to include a Web front end, then a programmer must rebuild nearly the entire system. Or, if two user interfaces are desired, then all of the business logic is programmed twice. Finally, without the tool that generates the code, it is almost impossible to keep the system current. This problem is exacerbated by new releases of the IDE tools, which may not be compatible with earlier versions. Many programmers have had to completely rewrite the front end of a system because the new release of the IDE tool does not generate code the same way the previous release did. So, we advise would-be analysts and programmers to use good design principles in the development of new systems.

Given the design principle of object responsibility, it is possible to define what program responsibilities belong to each layer. If you follow these guidelines in writing code, a new system will be much more easily maintained throughout its lifetime. Let's summarize the primary responsibilities of each layer.

View layer classes should have programming logic to:

- Display electronic forms and reports
- Capture input—such events as clicks, rollovers, and key entry
- Display data fields
- Accept input data
- Edit and validate input data
- Forward input data to the domain layer classes
- Start up and shut down the system

Domain layer classes should have the following responsibilities:

- Create problem domain (persistent) classes
- Process all business rules with appropriate logic
- Prepare persistent classes for storage to the database

Data access layer classes should perform the following:

- Establish and maintain connections to the database
- Contain all Structured Query Language (SQL) statements
- Process result sets (the results of SQL executions) into appropriate domain objects
- Disconnect gracefully from the database

Summary

Object-oriented design is the bridge between the requirements models and the final system, as constructed using a programming language. Systems design in the object-oriented approach is a highly technical activity that transforms the requirements models into a set of blueprints from which programmers can write code.

Design is driven by use cases. That is, design is done on a use case–by–use case basis. The two primary models that are developed during design are design class diagrams and sequence diagrams. Domain models—domain class diagrams—are transformed into design class diagrams by the addition of attribute type and visibility information and by the addition of method signatures. Sequence diagrams are extensions of system sequence diagrams and are developed by deriving the internal processing required to carry out a use case. A sequence diagram specifies the objects that collaborate and the way they collaborate, specifying the messages they send to each other to complete the processing for a use case.

To derive the correct set of messages and ensure a good design, analysts must apply certain object-oriented design principles. These principles include encapsulation, coupling, cohesion, navigation, and object responsibilities. Encapsulation is a standard OO principle that ensures that the data fields are placed in the correct classes and that there are sufficient methods to process the data. Coupling is a principle that applies to the entire set of classes and refers to the amount of connectivity between classes. Less connectivity is better when constructing a good design. Cohesion refers to the nature of an individual class. It is an expression of the focus of the class. If a class has methods that perform many disparate processes, it is said not to be cohesive. In other words, it is out of focus. Navigation refers to the access or visibility that certain classes have to other classes. A system with too many navigation links has too much coupling. Finally, object responsibility is a principle that helps analysts determine which classes should be receiving and sending certain messages. Objects should always be responsible for themselves, but they might also have other responsibilities. Analysts should carefully assign those responsibilities so that the system maintains low coupling and the classes are cohesive.

Three-layer design develops systems that are easily maintained. Multilayer designs partition classes into groups based on their primary focus or responsibility. You learned that three-layer design is made up of the view layer, consisting of those classes in the graphical user interface; the domain layer, consisting of business classes; and the data access layer, consisting of classes that access the database. A three-layer design is a very robust and flexible design for a system.

You also learned that designers can make use of communication diagrams to develop their systems. Communication diagrams are a viable alternative to sequence diagrams. Whether you use sequence diagrams or communication diagrams is primarily a matter of personal preference.

Finally, a new type of notation was introduced for grouping related components, particularly classes, of a system. Using a package diagram, which is denoted by a tabbed rectangle with the related classes inside, is analogous to placing items in a container. A package diagram can group classes by subsystem or by layer—by view layer, domain layer, and data access layer.

KEY TERMS

activation lifelines, p. 318
artifact, p. 314
boundary class, p. 303
class-level method, p. 306
cohesion, p. 308
control class, p. 303
coupling, p. 307
CRC (class-responsibility-collaboration) cards, p. 314
data access class, p. 303
dependency relationship, p. 342
encapsulation, p. 306
entity class, p. 303
information hiding, p. 306
instantiation, p. 296
links, p. 335
method signature, p. 304
navigation visibility, p. 307
object responsibility, p. 312
object reuse, p. 306
overloaded method, p. 305
persistent class, p. 303
realization of use cases, p. 301
separation of responsibilities, p. 309
stereotype, p. 302
use case controllers, p. 314
visibility, p. 304

REVIEW QUESTIONS

1. Which three models are most used to do object-oriented design?
2. Why do we say that design is "use case driven"?
3. Four icons, or shortcuts, can be used to depict different types of classes. List the four icons, tell what each means, and show the symbol for it.
4. List the elements included in a method signature. Give an example of a method signature with all elements listed correctly.
5. What notation is used to indicate a stereotype? Show an example of a stereotyped class.
6. What is meant by navigation visibility? How is it shown in UML? How is it implemented in programming code?
7. What does coupling mean? Why is too much coupling considered bad?
8. What are some of the problems that occur when classes have low cohesion?
9. What is meant by *object responsibility*? Why is it such an important concept in design?
10. What is the objective of a use case controller class? What design principles does it typify?
11. What is three-layer design? What are the most common layers found in three-layer design?
12. Why is three-layer design a good principle to follow?
13. What is the recommended way to carry out three-layer design? In other words, in what order are the layers designed?
14. To develop the first-cut sequence diagram, you should follow three steps. Briefly describe each of those three steps.
15. Briefly describe the major differences between a sequence diagram and a communication diagram.
16. Describe the message notation used on a communication diagram.
17. What is the purpose of a package diagram? What notation is used? Show an example.
18. How is dependency indicated on a package diagram? What does it mean?
19. List the primary responsibilities of classes in the view layer. Now do the same for the domain layer and the data access layer.
20. What is the difference between an Internet-based system and a network-based system?

THINKING CRITICALLY

Note: Exercises 1, 2, 3, and 4 build on the solutions you developed in Chapter 6 for "Thinking Critically" exercise 1, based on the university library system. Alternately, your teacher may provide you with a use case diagram and a class diagram.

1. Figure 8-33 is a system sequence diagram for the use case *Check out books* in the university library system. Do the following:
   a. Develop a first-cut sequence diagram, which only includes the actor and problem domain classes.
   b. Add the view layer classes and the data access classes to your diagram from part a.
   c. Develop a design class diagram based on the domain class diagram and the results of parts a and b.
   d. Develop a package diagram showing a three-layer solution with view layer, domain layer, and data access layer packages.

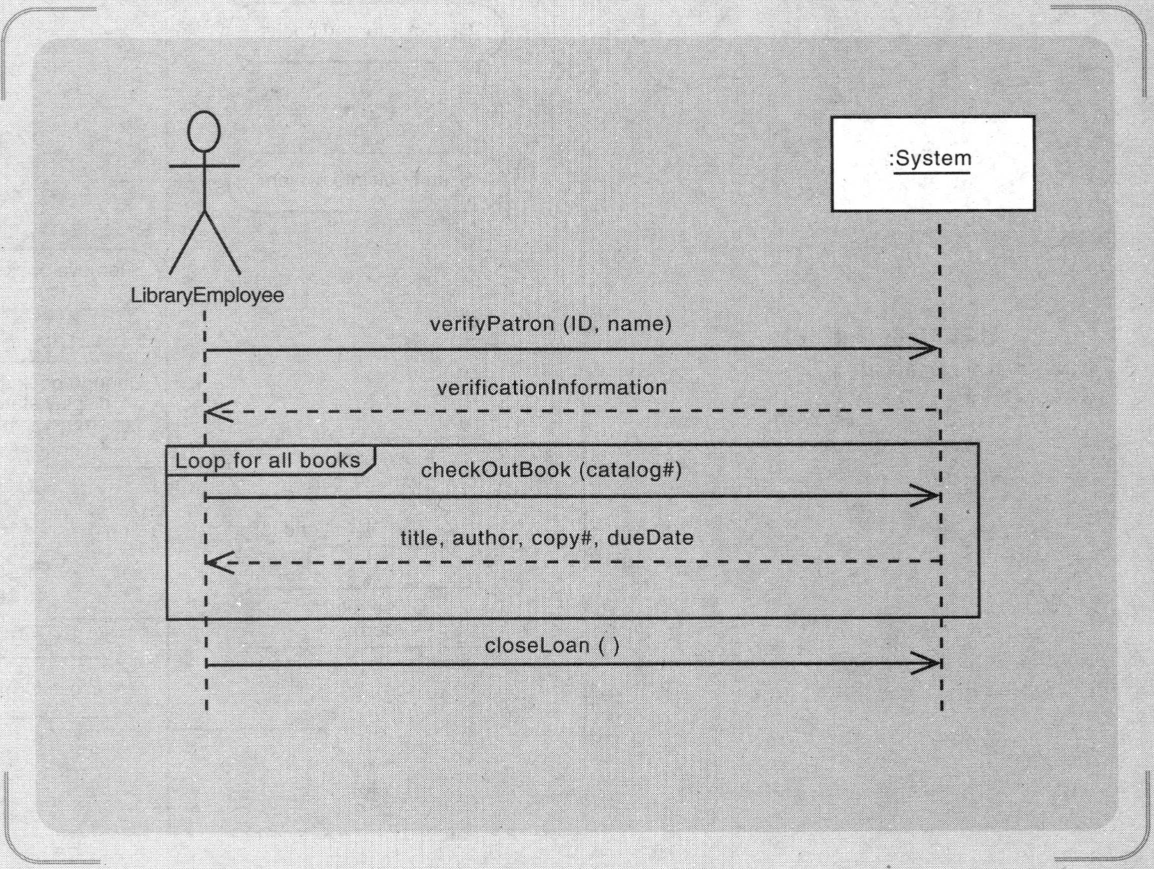

FIGURE 8-33
System sequence diagram for *Check out books*

2. Figure 8-34 is an activity diagram for the use case *Return books* for the university library system. Do the following:
   a. Develop a first-cut sequence diagram, which only includes the actor and problem domain classes.
   b. Add the view layer classes and the data access classes to your diagram from part a.
   c. Develop a design class diagram based on the domain class diagram and the results of parts a and b.
   d. Develop a package diagram showing a three-layer solution with view layer, domain layer, and data access layer packages.

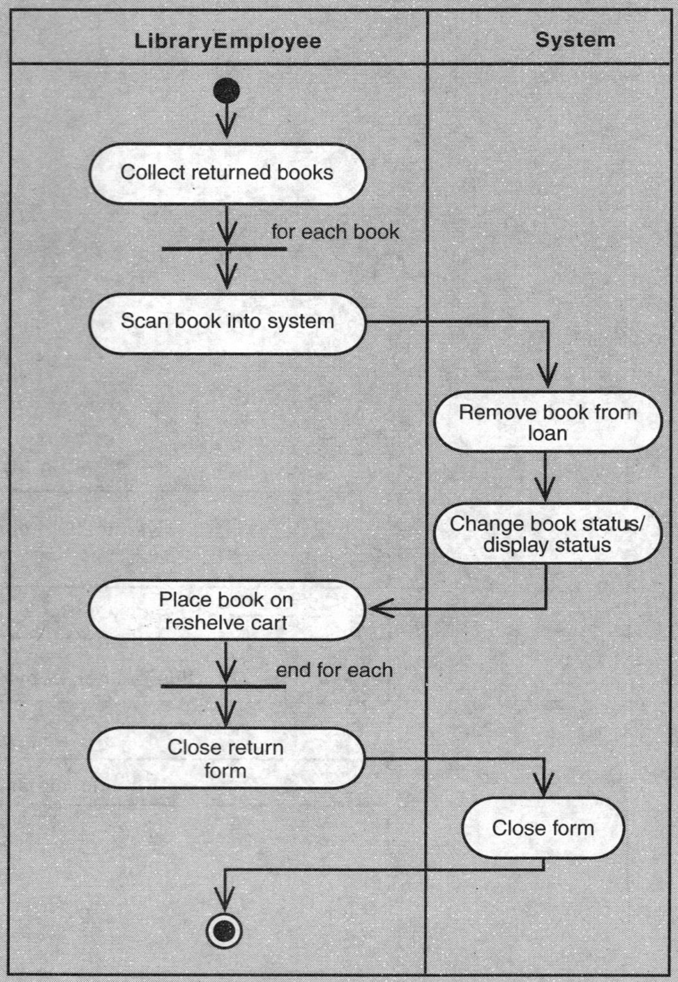

FIGURE 8-34
Activity diagram for *Return books*

3. Figure 8-35 is a fully developed use case description for the use case *Receive new book* for the university library system. Do the following:
   a. Develop a first-cut sequence diagram, which only includes the actor and problem domain classes.
   b. Add the view layer classes and the data access classes to your diagram from part a.
   c. Develop a design class diagram based on the domain class diagram and the results of parts a and b.
   d. Develop a package diagram showing a three-layer solution with view layer, domain layer, and data access layer packages.
4. Integrate the design class diagram solutions that you developed for exercises 1, 2, and 3 into a single design class diagram.

Use Case Name:	Receive new book	
Scenario:	Receive new book	
Triggering Event:	Book arrives for newly purchased book	
Brief Description:	The librarian decides on purchases of new books and places order (prior to this use case). Shipments of new books arrive. Each new book is assigned a library catalog number. Some books are simply additional copies of existing titles. Some books are new editions of existing titles. Some books are new titles and new physical books. The new book information is added to the system.	
Actors:	Library Employee	
Stakeholders:	Library Employee, Librarian	
Preconditions:	None	
Postconditions:	Book Title exists, Physical Book exists	
Flow of Events:	Actor	System
	1. Collect new books from receipt of shipment. 2. For each book, research book category and catalog numbers. Assign tentative number. 3a. If new copy of existing title, enter book information and catalog number into system. 3b. If new edition of existing title, enter book information, edition information, and catalog number. 3c. If new title, assign general catalog number. Assign book copy number. 4. Mark book with number. 5. Place book on shelving cart. 6. Repeat for each book (back to step 2).	3a.1 Update catalog with new number.Verify that not duplicate. 3b.1 Update catalog with new number. Verify that not duplicate. 3c.1 Verify that catalog number not duplicate.
Exception Conditions:	Duplicate numbers require further research and reassignment of catalog numbers.	

FIGURE 8-35
Fully developed use case description for *Receive new book*

Note: Exercises 5, 6, 7, and 8 are based on the solutions you developed for "Thinking Critically" exercises 2 and 3 in Chapter 6, on the dental clinic system. Alternately, your teacher may provide you with a use case diagram and class diagram.

5. Figure 8-36 is a system sequence diagram for the use case *Record dental procedure* in the dental clinic system. Do the following:
   a. Develop a first-cut sequence diagram, which only includes the actor and problem domain classes.
   b. Add the view layer classes and the data access classes to your diagram from part a.
   c. Develop a design class diagram based on the domain class diagram and the results of parts a and b.
   d. Develop a package diagram showing a three-layer solution with view layer, domain layer, and data access layer packages.

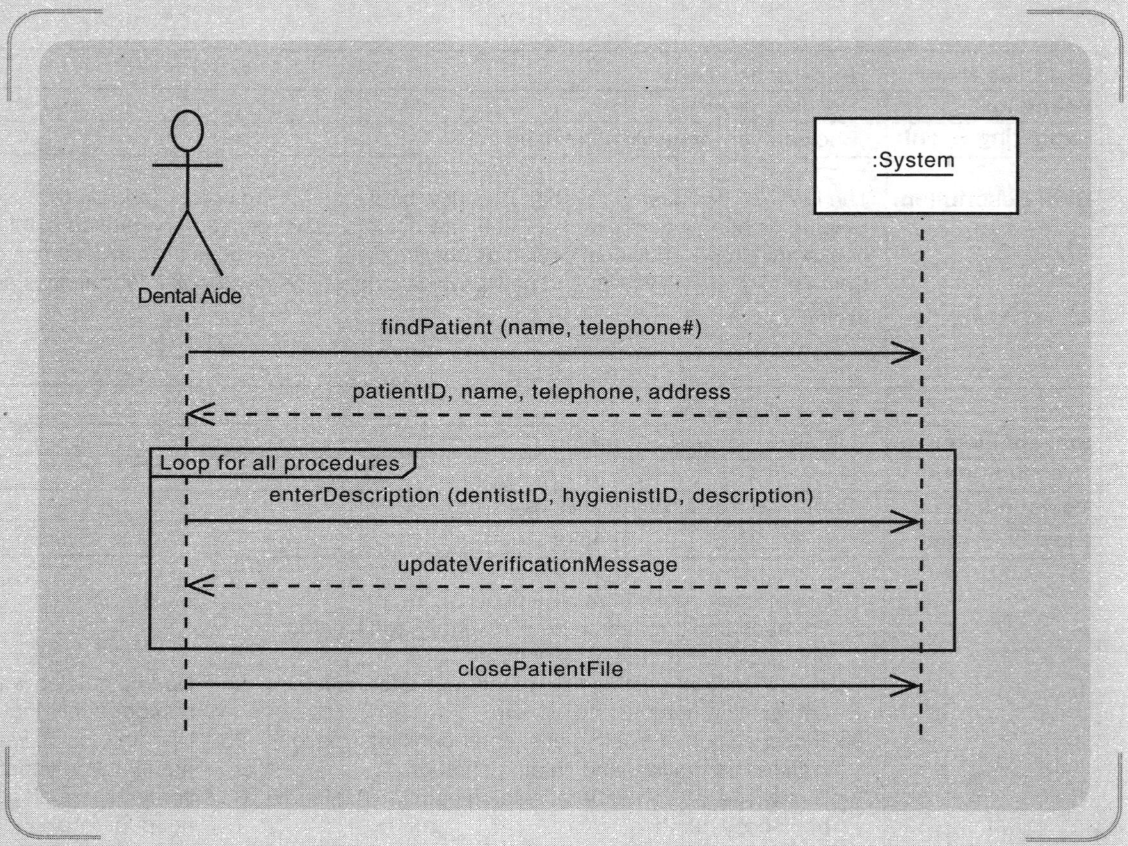

FIGURE 8-36
System sequence diagram for *Record dental procedure*

6. Figure 8-37 is an activity diagram for the use case *Enter new patient information* for the dental clinic system. Do the following:
   a. Develop a first-cut sequence diagram, which only includes the actor and problem domain classes.
   b. Add the view layer classes and the data access classes to your diagram from part a.
   c. Develop a design class diagram based on the domain class diagram and the results of parts a and b.
   d. Develop a package diagram showing a three-layer solution with view layer, domain layer, and data access layer packages.

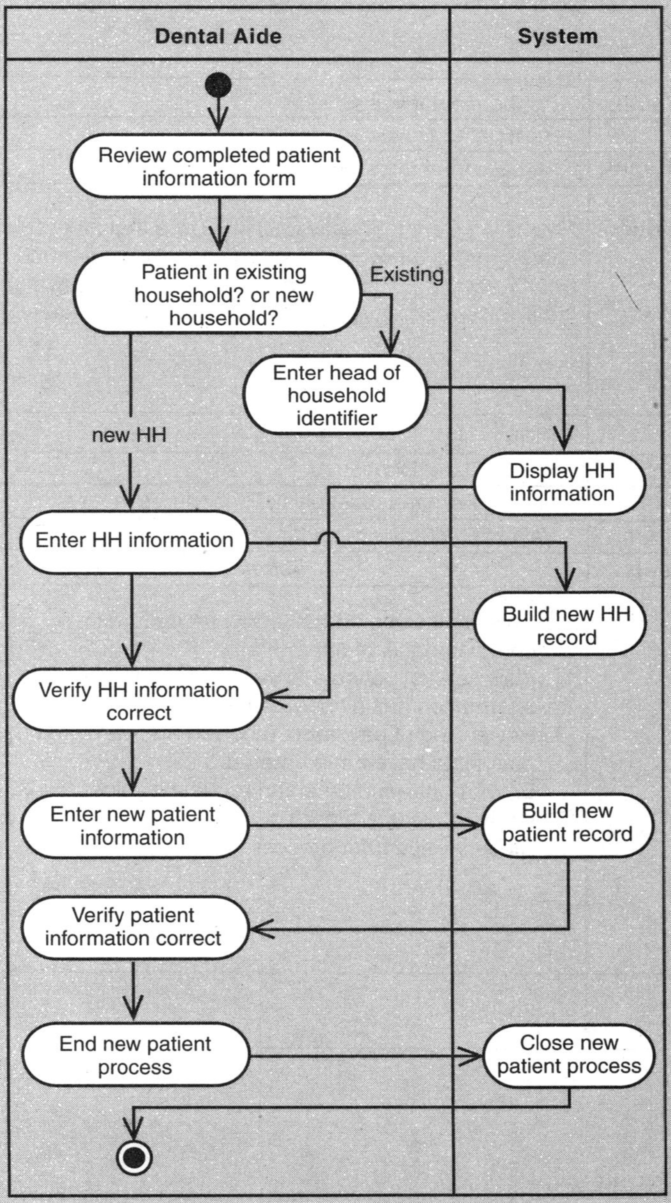

FIGURE 8-37
Activity diagram for *Enter new patient information*

7. Figure 8-38 is a fully developed use case description for the use case *Print patient invoices* for the dental clinic system. Do the following:
   a. Develop a first-cut sequence diagram, which only includes the actor and problem domain classes.
   b. Add the view layer classes and the data access classes to your diagram from part a.
   c. Develop a design class diagram based on the domain class diagram and the results of parts a and b.
   d. Develop a package diagram showing a three-layer solution with view layer, domain layer, and data access layer packages.
8. Integrate the design class diagram solutions that you developed for exercises 5, 6, and 7 into a single design class diagram.

Use Case Name:	Print patient invoices	
Scenario:	Print patient invoices	
Triggering Event:	At the end of the month, invoices are printed	
Brief Description:	The billing clerk manually checks to see that all procedures have been collected. The clerk spot-checks, using the written records to make sure procedures have been entered by viewing them with the system. The clerk also makes sure all payments have been entered. Finally, he/she prints the invoice reports. An invoice is sent to each patient.	
Actors:	Billing Clerk	
Stakeholders:	Billing Clerk, Dentist	
Preconditions:	Patient Records must exist, Procedures must exist	
Postconditions:	Patient Records are updated with last billing date	
Flow of Events:	Actor	System
	1. Collect all written notes about procedures completed this month. 2. View several patients to verify that procedure information has all been entered. 3. Review log of payments received and verify that payments have been entered. 4. Enter month-end date and request invoices. 5. Verify invoices are correct. 6. Close invoice print process.	2.1 Display patient information, including procedure records. 3.1 Display patient information including account balance and last payment transactions. 4.1 Review every patient record. Find unpaid procedures. List on report as aged or current. Calculate and break down by copay and insurance pay.
Exception Conditions:	None	

FIGURE 8-38
Fully developed use case description for *Print patient invoices*

9. In Chapter 6 "Thinking Critically" exercise 4, you developed an activity diagram for each of two scenarios for purchases at Quality Building Supply. In exercise 7, you developed a system sequence diagram. Based on either your activity diagram or your system sequence diagram and the following list of classes from the domain class diagram, develop a detailed communication diagram for each scenario. Include only problem domain classes.

   Classes to include: Contractor, ContractorAccount, Sale, SaleItem, ProductItem, InventoryItem, Payment

10. In Chapter 6 "Thinking Critically" exercises 5, 6, and 8, you developed a system sequence diagram for the *Add a new vehicle to an existing policy* use case. You were also provided with a list of classes. Based on the SSD you created, develop a detailed communication diagram. Include only problem domain classes.

EXPERIENTIAL EXERCISES

1. Find a local company that is using UML and object-oriented development. Set up an interview with a member of the IS staff. Find out how they use UML. Ask about using domain models to specify requirements. Find out whether they use sequence diagrams and how they actually carry out the design of new systems. Also ask about the development approach that they use. Is it an iterative approach? How closely does it follow the UP?
2. Find a system that was developed using Java. If possible, find one that has both an Internet user interface and a network-based user interface. Is it multilayer—three-layer or two-layer? Try to identify the view layer classes, the domain layer classes, and the data access layer classes.
3. Find a system that was developed using Visual Studio .NET (or Visual Basic). If possible, find one that has both an Internet user interface and a network-based user interface. Is it multilayer? Where is the business logic? Try to identify the view layer classes, the domain layer classes, and the data access layer classes.
4. Pick an object-oriented programming language with which you are familiar. Find a programming integrated development environment (IDE) tool that supports that language. Test out its reverse-engineering capabilities to generate UML class diagrams from existing code. Evaluate how well it does and how easy the models are to use. Does it have any capability to input UML diagrams and generate skeletal class definitions? Write a report on how it works and what UML models it can generate.

Case Studies

THE REAL ESTATE MULTIPLE LISTING SERVICE SYSTEM

In Chapter 6, you developed a use case diagram, a fully developed use case description or activity diagram, and a system sequence diagram for the real estate company's use cases. Based on those solutions, or others provided by your teacher, develop a first-cut sequence diagram for the problem domain classes. Next, add view layer and data access layer objects to the sequence diagram. Convert the domain class diagram to a design class diagram by typing the attributes and adding method signatures.

THE STATE PATROL TICKET PROCESSING SYSTEM

In Chapter 6 you developed a use case diagram, a fully developed use case description, a system sequence diagram, and a statechart for the use cases *Recording a traffic ticket* and *Scheduling a court date*. Based on those solutions, or others provided by your teacher, develop a first-cut sequence diagram for the problem domain classes. Next, add view layer and data access layer objects to the sequence diagram. Convert the domain class diagram you developed in Chapter 5 to a design class diagram by typing the attributes and adding method signatures.

THE DOWNTOWN VIDEOS RENTAL SYSTEM

In Chapter 6, you developed a use case diagram, an activity diagram, a system sequence diagram, and a statechart for the use cases *Check out movies* and *Return movies*. Based on those solutions, or others provided by your teacher, and the problem domain class diagram provided in Figure 8-39, develop a first-cut communication diagram for the problem domain classes. Next, add view layer and data access layer objects to the communication diagram. Convert the domain class diagram to a design class diagram by typing the attributes and adding method signatures.

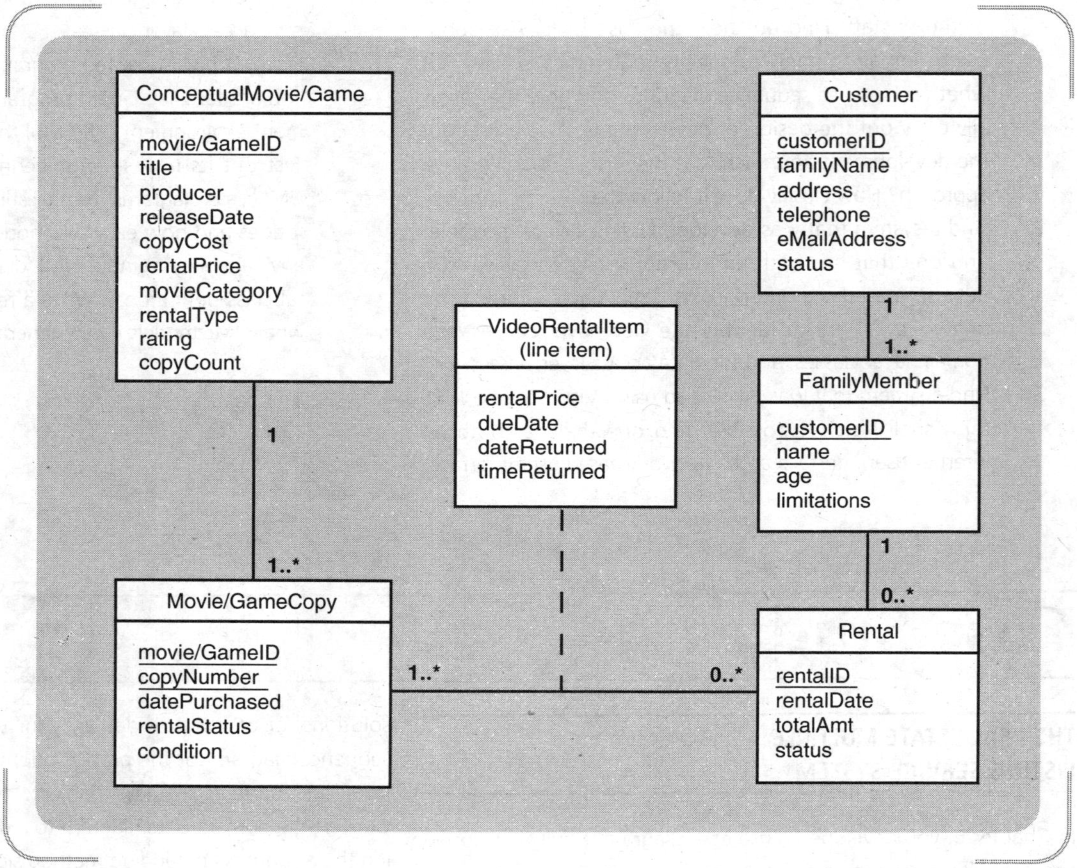

FIGURE 8-39
Domain class diagram for the DownTown Videos Rental System

THEEYESHAVEIT.COM BOOK EXCHANGE

In Chapter 6, you developed a use case diagram, a fully developed use case description, and a system sequence diagram for the use cases *Add a seller* and *Record a book order*. Based on those solutions, or others provided by your teacher, and the problem domain class diagram provided in Figure 8-40, develop a first-cut communication diagram for the problem domain classes. Next, add view layer and data access layer objects to the communication diagram. Convert the domain class diagram to a design class diagram by typing the attributes and adding method signatures.

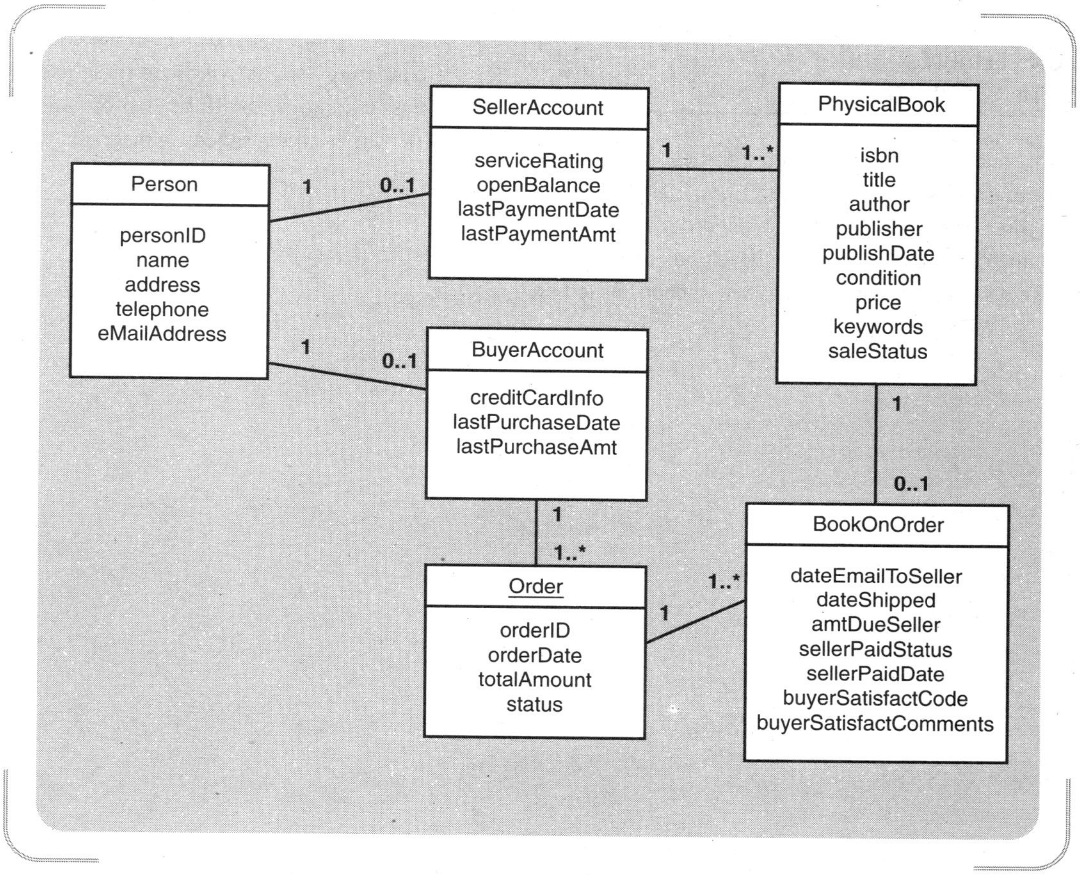

FIGURE 8-40
Domain class diagram for TheEyesHaveIt.com Book Exchange

RETHINKING ROCKY MOUNTAIN OUTFITTERS

This chapter presented the solutions for two use cases for RMO—*Look up item availability* and *Create new order* for the telephone order scenario. Design three-layer solutions for two more use cases, *Create order return* and *Record order fulfillment*. Update the design class diagram for the problem domain classes with method signatures from these use case designs. Often, the sequence diagram to produce a report can be quite interesting. Do a three-layer design for the use case *Produce order fulfillment report*. Since you do not have detailed user requirements for this use case, you will need to first lay out a sample fulfillment report.

FOCUSING ON RELIABLE PHARMACEUTICAL SERVICE

In Chapter 6, you developed a use case diagram, a domain model class diagram, and detailed documentation for three use cases. In your detailed documentation, you generated an activity diagram, a fully developed use case description, a system sequence diagram, and a statechart. Based on that information and the guidelines in this chapter, design a three-layer architecture for each of those three use cases. Update the design class diagram with attribute information and method signatures derived from the sequence diagrams.

FURTHER RESOURCES

Grady Booch, James Rumbaugh, and Ivar Jacobson, *The Unified Modeling Language User Guide*. Addison-Wesley, 1999.

Frank Buschmann, R. Meunier, H. Rohnert, P. Sommerlad, and M. Stal, *Pattern-Oriented Software Architecture: A System of Patterns*. John Wiley and Sons, 1996.

E. Reed Doke, J. W. Satzinger, and S. R. Williams, *Object-Oriented Application Development Using Java*. Course Technology, 2002.

E. Reed Doke, J. W. Satzinger, and S. R. Williams, *Object-Oriented Application Development Using Microsoft Visual Basic .NET*. Course Technology, 2003.

Ivar Jacobson, Grady Booch, and James Rumbaugh, *The Unified Software Development Process*. Addison-Wesley, 1999.

Philippe Kruchten, *The Rational Unified Process, An Introduction*. Addison-Wesley, 2000.

Craig Larman, *Applying UML and Patterns: An Introduction to Object-Oriented Analysis and Design and the Unified Process* (2nd ed.). Prentice-Hall, 2002.

James Rumbaugh, Ivar Jacobsen, and Grady Booch, *The Unified Modeling Language Reference Manual*. Addison-Wesley, 1999.

chapter 9

ADVANCED TOPICS IN OBJECT-ORIENTED DESIGN

LEARNING OBJECTIVES

After reading this chapter, you should be able to:

- Explain how statecharts can be used to describe system behaviors
- Use statecharts to model system behaviors and method logic
- Explain the importance of design patterns in object-oriented design
- Briefly describe and use the singleton, adapter, and observer design patterns
- Explain why enterprise-level systems require special design considerations
- Apply UML deployment architectural notation to Web-based systems
- Explain how Web services work to obtain information on the Internet

CHAPTER OUTLINE

- Modeling System Behavior and Method Logic with Design Statecharts
- Design Principles and Design Patterns
- Designing Enterprise-Level Systems

NEW CAPITAL BANK: PART 2

The integrated customer account system project for New Capital Bank was now several months old. The project was proceeding steadily; it was well past the elaboration iterations and into construction iterations. Most of the team's work now consisted of developing detailed designs and implementing many of the more advanced features of the new system. Bill Santora, the project leader, was discussing some of the system's technical details with one of his team leaders, Charlie Hensen.

"Are you sure you have covered all the security issues with the Web interface for the system?" Bill asked. "Senior managers, including our boss, want to be sure we don't have any holes where hackers can break in. Building an enterprise-level system with both a network front end and a Web interface magnifies the security issues—they just seem to multiply like rabbits."

Charlie nodded. "I agree completely. The team and I have spent hours brainstorming every possible security risk we could think of. We recognize the danger to the back end of the system if we miss anything."

"Well, I did feel better after we had those long review sessions with the system support staff. You did a good job of handling all the 'what if' questions they asked you. I especially liked your use of the statechart diagrams to show how the system would allow only certain transactions at certain times. Of course, the tricky part now is to write the code so that it conforms exactly to the diagrams, but the diagrams were a great piece of work."

"Thanks," said Charlie. "I have learned to appreciate the expressive power of statecharts. They really help you think about how the system should behave—what conditions should be allowed and what conditions shouldn't."

Bill continued, "Where did you learn about statecharts, and how did you learn to use them?"

"Remember that night course I took last fall on object-oriented development? We spent a couple of weeks learning how to do statecharts. At the time, I thought they were too complex for any of the stuff I was working on. But when the team got to the Web interface requirements for the system, they just fit the bill. It took a couple of days to get the rest of the team up to speed, but once they caught on, we were really able to look at a lot of different options quickly. The statecharts were invaluable to express the complexities we were facing."

"Well, I have to admit the systems programmers were impressed, not only with your solution but also with the elegance of how you had approached it. Congratulations on a job well done!"

Overview

In Chapter 8, you learned many fundamental principles of object-oriented design. However, designing, building, and deploying a complete system for an organization requires both broad and deep knowledge in many areas. In your other courses, such as programming, database management, and network administration, you extend your basic knowledge and develop many of those other necessary skills. But your learning does not end with formal schoolwork. You will need to pursue a path of lifelong learning to succeed as a system developer.

This chapter provides you with a broader understanding of some important issues of systems design. It elaborates on the fundamental principles presented in Chapter 8 and introduces the following new object-oriented design topics:

- Modeling system and object behavior
- Design principles and design patterns
- Designing enterprise-level systems, including Web-based systems

Many objects in a system—such as user-interface objects or network objects—have complex behavior. In Chapter 6, you learned how to use statecharts to capture status information. In this chapter, we extend the use of statecharts and show how they can be used to document design issues.

The basic principles of good design you learned in Chapter 8 included object responsibility, coupling, and cohesion. We build on those principles in this chapter, presenting two additional principles to enhance the flexibility of a new system and the ease with which it can be maintained. Systems designers should consider protection from variations to ensure that systems are stable and can be updated easily. Another principle of good design, indirection, helps stabilize and protect systems.

Every engineering discipline has a set of standard design rules and templates. For example, civil engineers learn about the strength of triangular support structures. Such design rules are sometimes called *patterns* or *templates* for good design. Even though software development is a young discipline, computer scientists and engineers have now begun to identify and categorize good design patterns. These patterns are an attempt to establish best practices in the construction of software systems. We introduce some basic design patterns and present some examples of the most important patterns.

Enterprise-level systems must support large distributed and networked organizations. Many pieces of an enterprise system can be purchased and must be considered part of the environment of design. We introduce various deployment environments and note what issues must be considered in designing systems for these environments, whether they are client/server systems run on a network or Internet-based systems. To design for Web-based systems, designers must consider a few additional design principles. We extend the design principles and diagrams from Chapter 8, modifying them to enable you to design for Web-based systems.

MODELING SYSTEM BEHAVIOR AND METHOD LOGIC WITH DESIGN STATECHARTS

The techniques and processes for system requirements presented in Chapter 6 and for systems design in Chapter 8 are sufficient to develop most business systems. Class diagrams are used to make program structure and database schemas easier to understand. Use case diagrams and interaction diagrams describe basic business and system processes. In Chapter 6 you were introduced to statechart diagrams as a technique to capture information about the various status conditions of business objects. You saw examples with two classes, Order and OrderItem, of how status information can be tracked by using a statechart. You also learned how to develop a statechart by defining states and exit transitions and then elaborating until you have a complete statechart.

During design, statecharts also play an important role. In fact, we use statecharts in two different ways during design. First, statecharts help analysts define and understand the behavior of the system and other utility and service classes. During requirements, analysts focus primarily on problem domain objects such as customers and orders. However, during design they need to understand the behavioral constraints of system classes—the additional classes that are identified and defined during design. Examples of system classes include windows menus, authentication and security classes, and error-handling classes.

The other major use of statecharts during design is to help define the method logic that will be placed in the various methods of a class. The action-expressions, which you have seen used in several statecharts, contain important information that can help define method logic.

SYSTEM-LEVEL STATECHARTS

You will find that statecharts are a very effective tool for describing all kinds of system behaviors and constraints. Recall from Chapter 6 that a statechart represents the life of the objects in a single class. However, since the system itself can be considered an object (everything is an object in OO development), then a statechart can also be developed for the system itself. This powerful tool allows a designer to designate the states of a system, including which menu items are enabled and disabled, which windows are modal (must be responded to and closed before the system will respond), and which tool bars and icons are active.

Figure 9-1 provides an example of how a statechart is used to describe the states and rules of a system that requires a user to log on before it allows processing. The statechart in the figure is not meant to be a complete statechart of the system. It is only a fragment used to illustrate a single control process in the system. In fact, as a designer, you will find yourself sketching out many statechart fragments to describe and document processing controls. You can probably imagine that if we tried to document an entire system in a single statechart, it would be massive. One of the strengths of models is that you can sketch out partial models containing only the immediately relevant points.

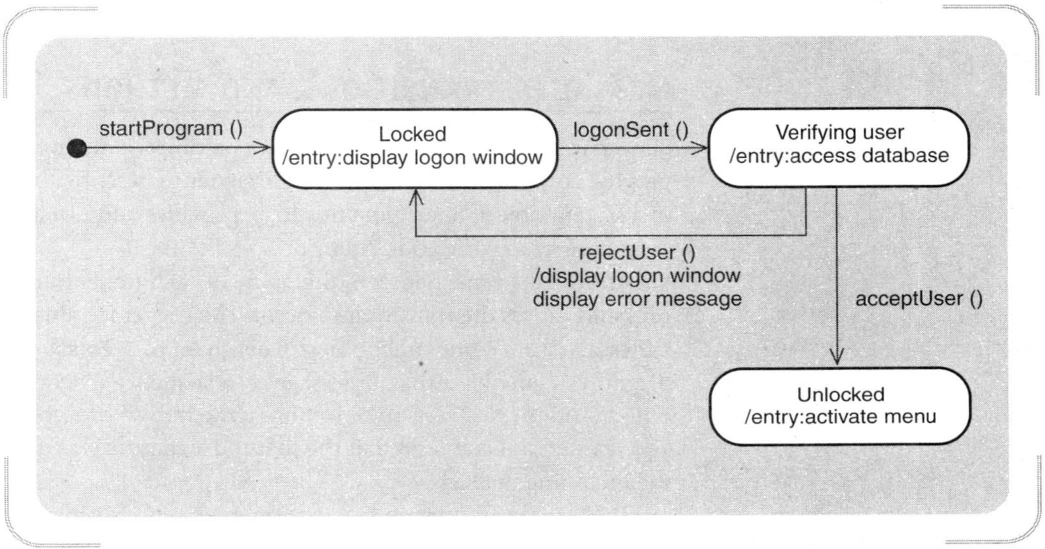

FIGURE 9-1
Logon statechart for a computer system

Let's review the statechart. The system opens with the transition startProgram ( ) and immediately enters the *Locked* state. An action-expression is attached to the entry into the state, which indicates that the system is to display the logon window. The system sits in that state until the logonSent ( ) transition occurs. Notice that this statechart indicates that nothing else can happen until the logon is sent. That is what the designer intends to happen. Once the logonSent ( ) transition occurs, then the system enters the *Verifying user* state. Again, an entry action-expression indicates that the system should access the database to verify the user. Exit transitions out of this state either return to the *Locked* state or move forward to the *Unlocked* state. Notice the associated action-expressions on each transition, indicating what the system must do before completing each transition. If the logon is rejected, the system displays the logon window again with appropriate error messages. Otherwise, the menu (and possibly other items) is activated for the user to continue using the system.

state variable
an attribute that records a value of a current state to inform a system which items to enable or disable and which messages to process or ignore

One other addition we would make to the design class that is controlling the logon is to define a new attribute to record a value of the current state. In programming jargon this is often called a *state variable*. In this instance, a variable called systemState can be created. It holds values such as *Locked*, *Verifying user*, and *Unlocked*. Based on the values in the state variable, the system can tell which menu items to enable and disable and which messages to process or to ignore.

In addition to logon status, analysts need to consider how interfaces should appear on screen and respond to users. When you are using your computer and you click your mouse on a drop-down menu, some menu items on the screen are enabled and others may be disabled—appearing faded on screen. For most computer systems, the behavior of the user interface is quite complex, so how does the designer know how and when to enable and disable menu items? Statecharts also fulfill this function, allowing designers to depict complex system behavior with nested states within other states and multiple parallel concurrent states.

During the final design of the menu items and Web user interface in RMO's customer support system, the design team depended heavily on statecharts to document the possible options that were to be presented to the users. When designing network-based systems, it is normal to enable and disable menu items to control what the user is allowed to do. The same controls can be done with a Web interface, but instead of enabling and disabling menu items, designers either include or exclude links from the Web page. Of course, removing links from a Web page must be done very carefully, or the user can become frustrated or even lost.

MESSAGES, TRANSITIONS, AND METHODS

Statecharts also help with the design of an object's method logic. In other words, they provide components that allow the designer to describe the internal activity, or logic, of a system object. Specifying this logic provides additional documentation to help the programmer to write code later.

As described in Chapter 6, the name of each transition represents a trigger that fires and causes the transition to occur. The trigger for a transition fires when it receives a message from some other object. This chain of events is reminiscent of sequence diagrams. Remember that a message on a sequence diagram goes to a destination object, and the destination object has a method to process that incoming message. You learned in Chapter 8 that the method signature was derived from the name of the incoming message.

These three entities—a message on a sequence diagram, a transition trigger in a statechart diagram, and a method signature in a design class—are very closely related. A message causes a transition trigger to fire. A message to a destination object is also the source for defining a method signature. So, a method and a transition must also be closely related. In fact, in most instances, you can think of a transition in a statechart as the execution of a method.

In a statechart, an action-expression describes the actions that must occur during the transition from one state to another. The action-expression is a procedural expression that executes when the transition fires. In other words, it describes the action to be performed. Given the close relationship between transitions and methods, it should be evident that these action-expressions can be used to help define the logic within a given method. Figure 9-2 summarizes the important elements in each of these three entities and shows how they are related. Each cell in the table identifies an element in the label of the entity for the column. The italicized entry in each cell is an example. You can see in rows three and four that the name and parameter list are found in all three components. Also, notice that row five indicates that the action-expression has a comparable component in the method logic.

ACTION-EXPRESSIONS AND METHOD LOGIC

In Chapter 8 you learned that a message in a sequence diagram indicates that a method is required in the message's destination object. Let's now see how the messages in a sequence diagram relate to a statechart. We will use examples from an Order object and an OrderItem object, just as we did in Chapter 8.

FIGURE 9-2
Comparison of messages, methods, and transitions

	MESSAGE (INTERACTION DIAGRAM)	METHOD (DESIGN CLASS)	TRANSITION (STATECHART)
1	[true/false condition]: *[existing customer]*	no comparable component	no comparable component
2	return-value: *custID*	return-value: *custID*	no comparable component
3	message-name: *updateCustomer*	method-name: *updateCustomer*	transition-name: *updateCustomer*
4	parameter-list: *(ID, name, ...)*	parameter-list: *(ID, name, ...)*	parameters: *(ID, name, ...)*
5	no comparable component	method logic: *if custUser = ID then ...*	action-expression: */authenticate user*
6	no comparable component	no comparable component	[guard-condition]: *[authenticated]*

Let's bring together information from multiple activities. Figure 9-3 is a simplified version of Figure 8-21, showing a sequence diagram for the *Create new order* use case. Figure 9-4 is the Order statechart that was developed from the states and exit transitions for Order in Figure 6-25. The sequence diagram only covers a single use case, which is just part of the life of an order. Consequently, the Order statechart is more comprehensive and will include information about an order that is not shown on the sequence diagram. However, all of the information relative to an order from the sequence diagram should be found in the statechart.

In the sequence diagram in Figure 9-3, four messages are sent to an Order object: createOrder ( ), addItem ( ), completeOrder ( ), and makePayment ( ). The statechart in Figure 9-4 contains a transition called createOrder ( ). This transition creates a new order and places it in the *Open for item adds* state. The addItem ( ) transition, corresponding to the message of the same name, causes an order object to add line items, but it also remains in the same state. Using a transition in this manner—to capture a message and perform an action but allow the object to remain in the same state—permits the object to handle multiple addItem messages. The next transition, completeOrder ( ), moves the object to a new state, *Ready for shipping*.

The final message, makePayment ( ), does not have a corresponding transition in the statechart. In this situation the statechart needs to be enhanced to ensure inter-model consistency. Given the description in the previous paragraph, if we wanted to allow multiple makePayment ( ) transitions, we could add a transition that leaves and returns to the same state, such as the *Ready for shipping* state. Another alternative is to add a new state—albeit a very short, temporary state—for the object to move to, after the payment is made. We choose the second option and add a new state called *Ready for payment* prior to the *Ready for shipping* state. The updated statechart is shown in Figure 9-5.

decision pseudostate
a diamond notation on a statechart indicating a decision point on a path

This figure also has two other important modifications to the original statechart. First, a diamond shape was added to the outbound makePayment transition. This shape is called a *decision pseudostate*. As the name implies, it is not a true state but serves one of the purposes of a state, which is to distinguish between transitions. Notice that there are two new transitions out of the decision pseudostate, allowing for different transition labels. In this case, neither transition has a trigger, meaning that the transition fires automatically. The guard conditions, however, will determine which transition can take place. In this case we have designed the guard conditions to be mutually exclusive so that the order object will take one path or the other, depending on the condition of the credit verification. The order object either arrives at the *Ready for shipping* state if the credit is approved, or it is deleted if the credit is rejected.

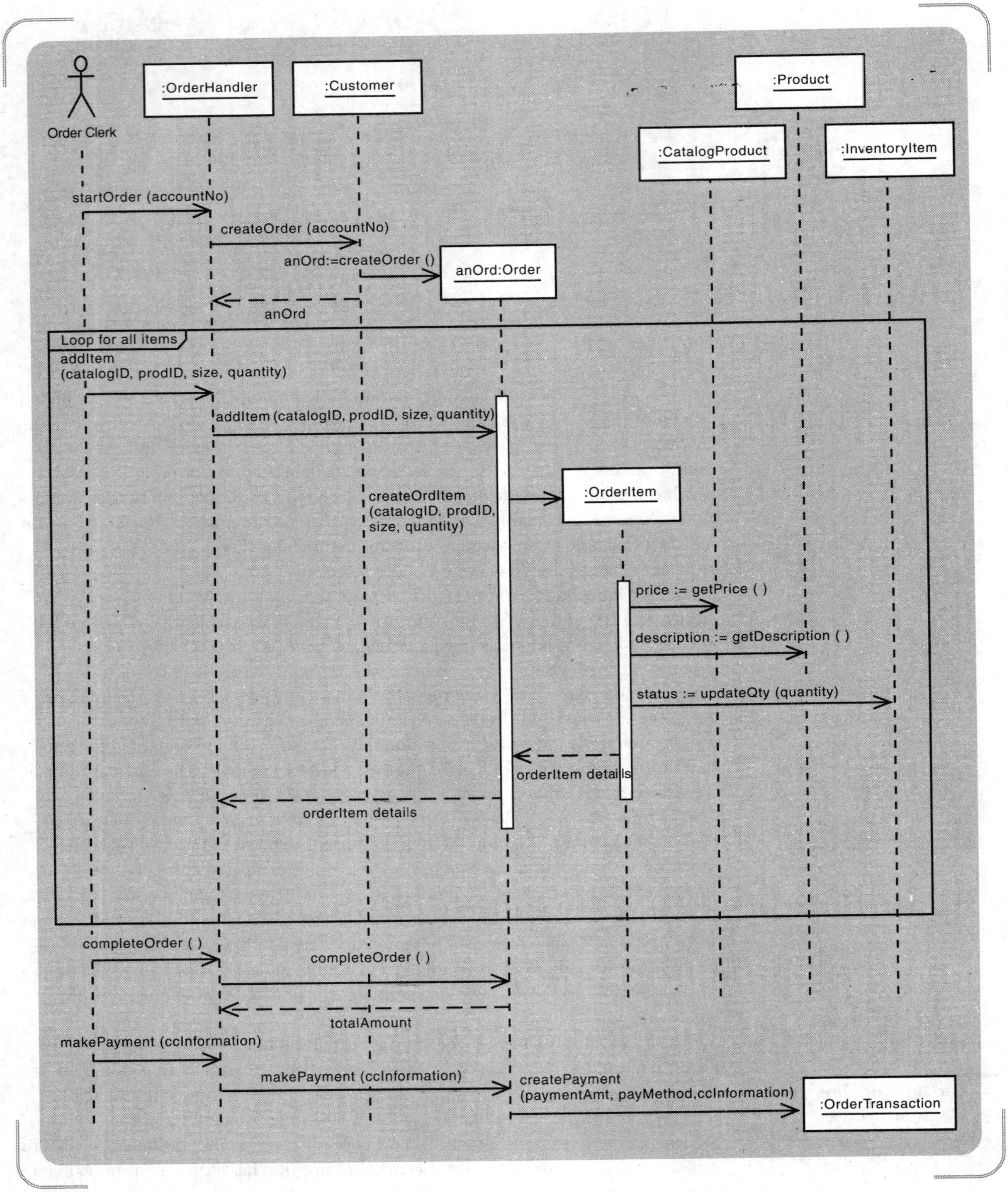

FIGURE 9-3
Sequence diagram for
Create new order

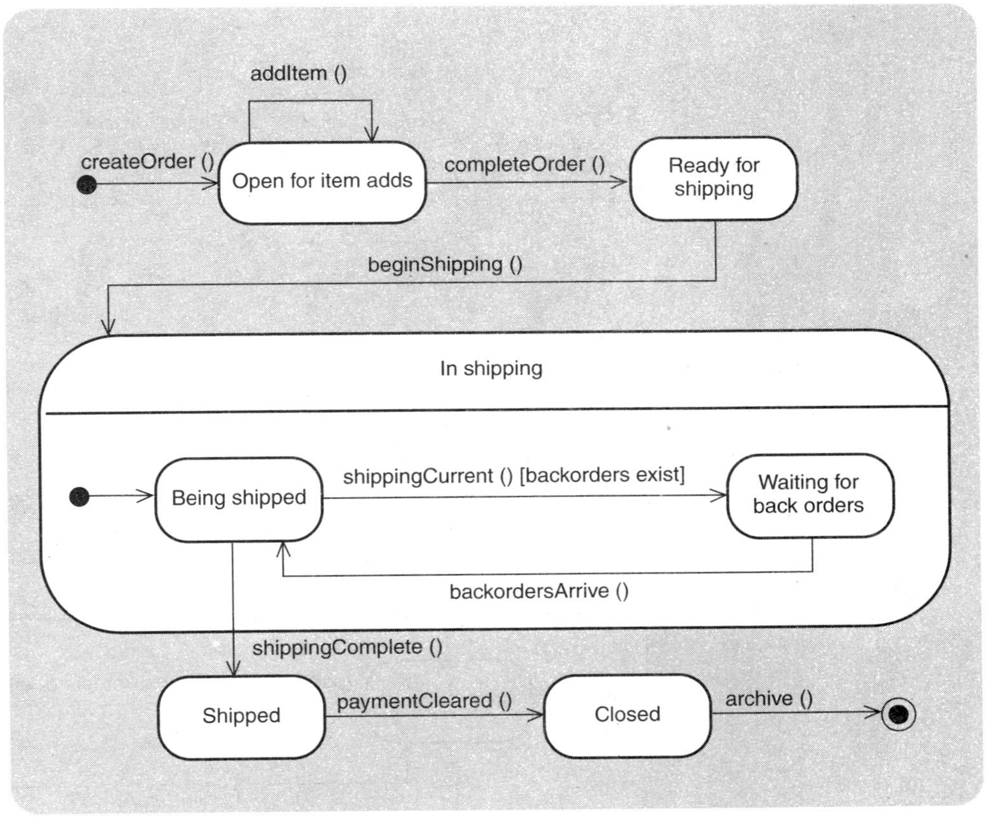

FIGURE 9-4
Statechart for Order

We have kept this case simple to illustrate the concepts. In reality, the order would probably enter some type of pending credit state, which would allow the customer to use another card or pay with another method. If the credit is approved, the order also sends a message to each item and marks it as ready to ship.

The other important concept illustrated in this statechart is the use of action-expressions on the transitions. As you learned in Chapter 6, an action-expression is a statement of some activity that the object performs before the transition is completed. The action-expression on the makePayment ( ) transition is rather involved. If the credit is approved, then the order object changes status to *Ready for shipping*. Messages are also sent to each item so that it is also marked as *Ready To Ship*. In this case, the statechart adds messages that were not identified on the sequence diagram. Normally, we would go back and update the sequence diagram based on the additional understanding that came from developing the action-expression.

Another example of an action-expression is on the completeOrder ( ) transition. In this instance the order object will calculate the dollar fields associated with tax amount, shipping and handling, and the order total. The benefit of these action-expressions is that they document what method logic will be required during programming. Admittedly, this example is very simple, so it may be obvious to the programmer what needs to be done. However, looking back at Figure 9-3, the Order object has an activation lifeline indicated by the vertical rectangle on the anOrd:Order lifeline that indicates that the object is active. Another way to think about the vertical box is that the addItem ( ) method is executing. The important point to notice is that a sequence diagram often does not provide enough information about the internal details of a method, but a statechart can provide those details through the use of action-expressions.

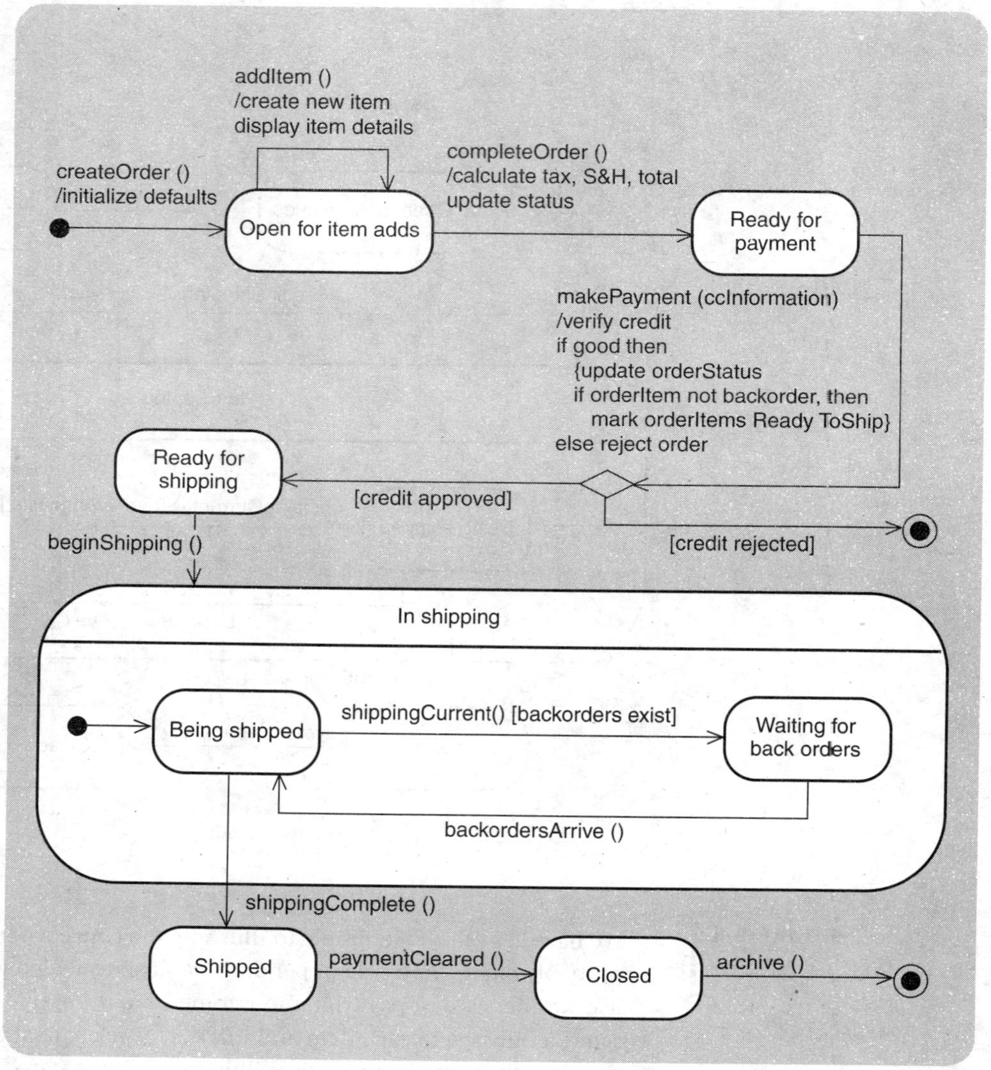

FIGURE 9-5
Design statechart for Order

In Chapter 6 you learned how to develop a statechart to track the status conditions for a problem domain object. In this section, you learned how to extend a requirements statechart to include action-expressions, which can be used by a programmer to help develop the method logic. Although for many business systems this level of detail may not be necessary, you now understand a powerful modeling technique that you can use for complex situations that do require this level of detail.

DESIGN PRINCIPLES AND DESIGN PATTERNS

In Chapter 8, as you learned the fundamental concepts of design, you were introduced to several principles of good design. One principle was the idea of object responsibility. As a designer, you must identify what the responsibilities of each class are. One basic object responsibility is that an object is responsible for maintaining its own attributes, including getting information from other objects, when needed, to fill in values. Another general object responsibility is to create objects that depend on it. Yet another general responsibility may be for an object to be an expert on certain sets of information. An object can be an expert either by having the needed information itself or by having navigation visibility and access to the other objects that do have the information. Among the concepts that will help you to design logical, easily maintained systems, the principle of object responsibility is one of the most important.

Two other related principles that you learned were coupling and cohesion. A cohesive class is one whose set of responsibilities—and methods—are all closely related. The functions that are assigned to the class and that are executed through the methods are focused. Coupling, on the other hand, relates to the idea of links between classes. Coupling must always be considered from the perspective of an entire system. The objective of this principle is to couple the classes that need to work together, but not to have excessive links between classes. You will see the reason for this in the next section, when you learn about a principle called *protection from variations*.

ADDITIONAL DESIGN PRINCIPLES

We have stated many times that developing software systems is difficult and complex. Historically, developers have not routinely been able to develop systems that work correctly and solve the right business problem. In addition, every system requires constant modification and upgrading. Perhaps functions that were not added in the first version need to be added later or errors need to be fixed. Or maybe the business requirements have changed, and the system needs to be upgraded. The cost of maintaining a system over its lifetime can be many times the cost of the original development. However, systems that are based on good design principles are not only easier to develop and put into operation the first time but also much easier to maintain. The following principles enhance the flexibility, ease of maintenance, and extensibility of a new system.

PROTECTION FROM VARIATIONS

protection from variations
a principle of design whereby parts of a system that are unlikely to change are segregated from those that will

One of the underlying principles of good design is protection from variations. *Protection from variations* is a principle that says that parts of a system that are unlikely to change should be segregated (or protected) from those that will need to be changed. In other words, as you design systems, you should try to isolate the parts of the system that are likely to change from those that are more stable. You will notice in following sections that many design patterns are solutions to problems of changes in a system.

Protection from variations is one of the principles that drive the multilayer design pattern. Designers could mix all of the user-interface logic and business logic together in the same classes. In fact, in early user-oriented, event-driven systems, the business logic was put right in the view layer classes, often in the windows input forms. For example, early versions of Visual Basic and PowerBuilder were very good at building graphical user interfaces, but they did place all of the business logic in the view layer classes. The problem with this design is that when an interface needed to be updated, all of the business logic also had to be rewritten. A better approach is to decouple the user-interface logic from the business logic. Then, the user interface can be rewritten without affecting the business logic. In other words, the business logic, being more stable, is protected from variations in the user interface.

Also, what if the updates to the business required the addition of new classes and new methods? If the user-interface classes were tightly coupled to the business classes, then there could be a ripple effect of changes throughout the user-interface classes. However, since the user interface can simply send all of its input messages to the use case controller class, as discussed in Chapter 8, changes to the methods or classes in the business logic and domain layer are isolated to the controller class. As we describe design patterns in a later section, you will find that this principle affects almost every design decision. You should watch for and recognize the application of this principle in all design activities.

INDIRECTION

indirection
a principle of design whereby two classes or other system components are decoupled by inserting an intermediate class between them

Indirection is a frequently used object-oriented design principle that is used to protect stable components from variations and to reduce coupling. *Indirection* is the principle of decoupling two classes or other system components by placing an intermediate class between them to serve as a link. In other words, instructions don't go directly from A to B; they are sent through C first. Or in message terminology, don't send a message from A to B. Let A send the message to C, and then let C forward it to B.

Although there are many ways to implement protection from variations, indirection is one method that is frequently used. Inserting an intermediate object allows any variations in one system to be isolated in that intermediate object. Indirection is also a principle that applies to many corporate security systems. Many companies have firewalls and proxy servers that receive and send messages between an internal network and the Internet. A proxy server appears as a real server, ready to receive messages such as e-mail and HTML page requests. However, it is a fake server, which catches all of the messages and redistributes them to the recipients. This step of indirection allows security controls to be put in place to protect the system.

BEST PRACTICE: Continually think about protection from variations as you design—during user-interface design, program logic design, and database design.

IMPORTANCE OF DESIGN PATTERNS

Templates and patterns are used repeatedly in everyday life. A chef uses a recipe, which is just another word for a pattern, to combine ingredients into a flavorful dish. A tailor uses a pattern to cut fabric for a great-fitting suit. Engineers take standard components and combine them into established configurations or set patterns to build buildings, sound systems, and thousands of other products. Patterns are created to solve problems. Over time and with many attempts, those working on a particular problem develop a set solution to the problem. The solution is general enough so that it can be applied over and over again. As time passes, the solution is documented and published and eventually becomes accepted as the standard.

design patterns
templates used to speed OO design

In Chapter 8 we briefly introduced you to two standard design templates—use case controller and three-layer design. The use of standard design templates has become very popular among software developers because they can speed OO design work. The formal name for these templates is *design patterns*. Design patterns became a widely accepted object-oriented design technique in 1996 with the publication of the book *Elements of Reusable Object-Oriented Software* by Eric Gamma, Richard Helm, Ralph Johnson, and John Vlissides. The four authors of this book are now referred to as the Gang of Four (GoF). As you become better informed about design patterns, you will often see references to a particular design pattern as a GoF pattern. In the original book, the authors identified 23 basic design patterns. Today, scores of patterns have been defined—from low-level programming patterns, to mid-level architectural patterns, to high-level enterprise patterns. The two primary enterprise platforms, Java and .NET, have sets of enterprise patterns, which are described in various books and publications.

Patterns exist at various levels of abstraction. At a concrete level, a pattern may be a class definition that is written in code to be used by any developer. At the most abstract level, a pattern might only be an approach to solving a problem. For example, the multilayer design pattern tends to be more abstract, stating that it is better to separate system functions into three layers of classes: the graphical user interface logic is placed in a set of view-layer classes that are separate and distinct from the domain layer and data access layer. So, multilayer design is an approach to building a system rather than a specific solution.

The use case controller pattern is more concrete. That pattern defines a specific class or classes that act as the switchboard for all incoming messages from the environment. As with all patterns, there are multiple ways to implement the controller pattern. A single controller class can be defined to handle all messages from the view layer to the domain layer. Alternately, a class can be defined for each use case. Or some combination of the two can be used. Regardless of the specific approach, the controller pattern does require a separate, specified class.

The specification for a pattern should contain at least five main elements:

[1] The pattern name
[2] The problem that requires a solution
[3] The solution, or explanation of the pattern
[4] Examples of the pattern
[5] The benefits and consequences of the pattern

We show these five elements for the controller pattern in Figure 9-6.

BASIC DESIGN PATTERNS

The study of design patterns is an ongoing effort. Numerous books list hundreds of design patterns. The objective of this section is to introduce you to a few of the more basic patterns so that you will have a foundation from which to become more knowledgeable about design patterns as you mature in your career.

In their pioneering work, the GoF developed a basic classification scheme for patterns. Figure 9-7 lists most of the original patterns, showing their classifications. The rows of the table identify the scope of the pattern—whether the design is a class-level or object-level pattern. Class-level patterns define solutions such as abstract classes that apply to static methods—that do not actually instantiate objects. Object-level patterns apply when the implementation of the pattern results in specific objects being instantiated from classes. The columns of the table classify the patterns as creational, structural, or behavioral. Creational patterns are patterns that help assign responsibilities to classes to instantiate new objects. Structural patterns provide solutions to meet the architectural needs of the system—that is, the set of classes and the ways they are related. Structural patterns help solve problems associated with indirection. Behavioral patterns provide solutions to problems related to the way internal system processes execute. For example, the iterator pattern provides a solution to the problem of how to process arrays and lists effectively.

Even though the GoF patterns are some of the most fundamental and important patterns, many other patterns are also frequently used. We will limit our discussion to GoF patterns. To help you get started learning about design patterns, we present one pattern from each category. The following sections explain the singleton, adaptor, and observer patterns.

SINGLETON

Some classes must have exactly one instance—for example, a class that starts up the system or the main window class. These classes have only one instance, but since they are instantiated from only one place, it is a simple matter to limit the logic to create only one object.

Other classes must have exactly one instance but cannot be easily controlled by having only one place to invoke the constructor. Usually, these classes are service

Name:	Controller
Problem:	Domain classes have the responsibility of processing use cases. However, since there can be many domain classes, which one(s) should be responsible for receiving the input messages? User-interface classes become very complex if they have visibility to all of the domain classes. How can the coupling between the user-interface classes and the domain classes be reduced?
Solution:	Assign the responsibility for receiving input messages to a class that receives all input messages and acts as a switchboard to forward them to the correct domain class. There are several ways to implement this solution: (a) Have a single class that represents the entire system, or (b) Have a class for each use case or related group of use cases to act as a use case handler.
Example:	The RMO order-entry subsystem accepts inputs from an OrderWindow. These input messages are passed to an OrderHandler, which acts as the switchboard to forward the message to the correct problem domain class.

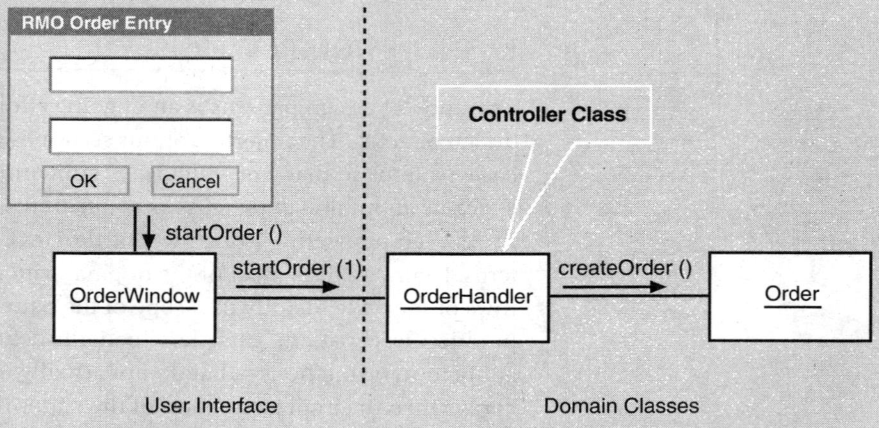

	Other examples of the controller can be found for each RMO subsystem.
Benefits and Consequences:	Coupling between the view layer and the domain layer is reduced. The controller provides a layer of indirection. The controller is closely coupled to many domain classes. If care is not taken, controller classes can become incoherent, with too many unrelated functions. If care is not taken, business logic will be inserted into the controller class.

FIGURE 9-6
Pattern description for the controller pattern

classes that manage a system resource, such as a database connection. They are usually invoked by many other classes and from many locations throughout the system. This common problem has a standard solution: the singleton pattern.

Figure 9-8 presents the template of the pattern description for the singleton pattern. You should carefully read the contents of Figure 9-8, especially the example section, to ensure that you understand how it works. The singleton pattern provides a solution in which the class itself controls the creation of only one instance.

The approach of the singleton solution is that the class has a static variable that refers to the object that is created. A method, such as getInstance, is defined that is used to get the reference to the object. The first time the getInstance method is called, it

SCOPE OF PATTERN	TYPE OF PATTERN		
	CREATIONAL	STRUCTURAL	BEHAVIORAL
Class-level patterns	Factory Method	Adapter	Interpreter Template Method
Object-level patterns	Abstract Factory Builder Prototype Singleton	Adapter Bridge Composite Decorator Façade Proxy	Chain of Responsibility Command Iterator Mediator Memento Flyweight Observer State Strategy Visitor

FIGURE 9-7 Classification of design patterns

instantiates an object and returns a reference to it. On later calls to the method, it simply returns a reference to the already instantiated object. As shown in the figure, the code is simple and elegant. The example does not show the constructor; however, to ensure that only one instance is created, all constructors are specified as private—not accessible—so that no other class can accidentally invoke one.

In the singleton template, the pattern is represented by code. To specify this in your design, you should stereotype the class as a «singleton». Good programmers will recognize the stereotype and know exactly how to code that class.

ADAPTER

The basic idea behind the adapter pattern is the same as that of an electrical adapter used for international travel. Say that you are traveling to the United Kingdom, and you want to take your hair dryer with you. Your hair dryer has a switch for either 110 volts or 220 volts, so you think you can run it on either voltage. However, the plug on the end of the power cord has two flat prongs. Unfortunately, in the United Kingdom, the wall sockets have slots for three large prongs set at angles. What you need is an adapter. You need something that can adapt the power cord's two prongs to the wall's three angled slots. Figure 9-9 shows a typical electrical adapter you might use.

The adapter design pattern works just like the electrical adapter; it plugs an external class into an existing system. The method signatures on the external class are different from the method names that are being called from within the system, so the adapter class is inserted to convert the method calls from within the system to the method names in the external class.

This pattern is a standard solution for protection from variations. The external class could be a variable class—that is, it could be replaced at any time by an upgrade or an entirely different class. This situation often occurs when commercial software libraries are purchased to provide special services. For example, in an organization's internal payroll system, designers might purchase a set of classes to calculate all of the complex income tax deductions. Since tax deductions are a very specialized area, and since most companies do not have tax specialists on their IT staff, an easy solution is simply to purchase those classes. However, knowing that those classes could be replaced at a later time if the tax law changes, a designer would be wise to create an adapter class between the system and the tax calculation classes.

Figure 9-10 describes the details of the adapter design pattern. Be sure to read it carefully. In the sample diagram, there are four UML classes. The one labeled System represents the entire system. The classes within the system use method names such as getSTax ( ) and getUTax ( ) to access the tax routines. The tax calculator class has method names of findTax1 ( ) and findTax2 ( ). The two UML classes in the middle represent the adapter. The top class symbol is an interface class. An interface is useful to specify the names of the methods. Although not absolutely necessary, it is a simple way to specify and enforce the use of the correct method names. The adapter class then

FIGURE 9-8
Singleton pattern template

Name:	Singleton
Problem:	Only one instantiation of a class is allowed. The instantiation (new) can be called from several places in the system. The first reference should make a new instance, and later attempts should return a reference to the already instantiated object. How do you define a class so that only one instance is ever created?
Solution:	A singleton class has a static variable that refers to the one instance of itself. All constructors to the class are private and are accessed through a method or methods, such as getInstance(). The getInstance() method checks the variable; if it is null, the constructor is called. If it is not null, then only the reference to the object is returned.

Example:	In RMO's system, the connection to the database is made through a class called Connection. However, for efficiency, we want each desktop system to open and connect to the database only once, and to do so as late as possible. Only one instance of Connection, that is, only one connection to the database, is desired. The Connection class is coded as a singleton. The following coding example is similar to C# and Java.
	
	`Class Connection`
	`{`
	`private static Connection conn = null;`
	`public synchronized static getConnection ( )`
	`    {`
	`      if (conn = = null) {`
	`     conn = new Connection ( ) ;}`
	`      return conn;`
	`    }`
	`}`
	
	Another example of a singleton pattern is a utilities class that provides services for the system, such as a factory pattern. Since the services are for the entire system, it causes confusion if multiple classes provide the same services.
	
	An additional example might be a class that plays audio clips. Since only one audio clip should be played at one time, the audio clip manager will control that. However, for this to work, there must be only one instance of the audio clip manager.

Benefits and Consequences:	There are other times when only one instance of an object is needed, but if it is instantiated from only one place, then a singleton may not be required. The singleton object controls itself and ensures that only one instance is created—no matter how many times it is called and wherever the call occurs in the system. The code to implement the singleton is very simple, which is one of the desirable characteristics of a good design pattern.

FIGURE 9-9
Electrical adapter

Name:	Adapter
Problem:	A class must be replaced, or is subject to being replaced, by another standard or purchased class. The replacing class already has a predefined set of method signatures that are different from the method signatures of the original class. How do you link in the new class with a minimum of impact so that you don't have to change the names throughout the system to the method names in the new class?
Solution:	Write a new class, the adapter class, which serves as a link between the original system and the class to be replaced. This class has method signatures that are the same as those of the original class (and the same as those expected by the system). Each method then calls the correct desired method in the replacement class with the method signature. In essence, it "adapts" the replacement class so that it looks like the original class.
Example:	There are several places in the RMO system where class libraries were purchased to provide special processing. These purchased libraries provide specialized services such as tax calculations and shipping and postage rates. From time to time, these service libraries are updated with new versions. Sometimes a service library is even replaced with one from an entirely different vendor. The RMO systems staff applies protection from variations and indirection design principles by placing an adapter in front of each replaceable class. 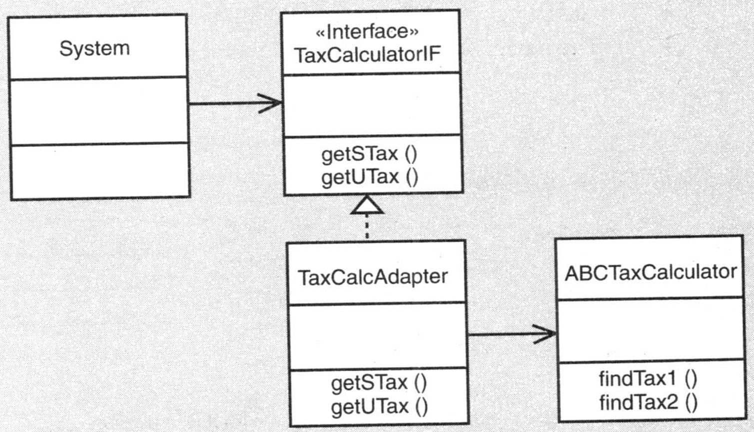
Benefits and Consequences:	The adaptee class can be replaced as desired. Changes are confined to the adapter class and do not ripple through the system. Two classes are defined, an inte:face class and the adapter class. Passed parameters may add more complexity, and it is difficult to limit changes to the adapter class.

FIGURE 9-10
Adapter pattern template

inherits those method names and provides the method logic for those methods. The body of each method simply extends a call to the final method name of findTax1 ( ) or findTax2 ( ). In other words, it "adapts," or translates, the method names from one to the other.

As you become familiar with this design pattern, you will find a multitude of uses for it. It is a very powerful and elegant solution to making a system more maintainable. Experienced developers use this pattern frequently, not only for foreign classes but also for classes that are written internally that may need to be upgraded often. It is an excellent way to insulate the system from frequently changing classes.

OBSERVER

The observer pattern is a powerful approach to solving an interesting system problem. In fact, this solution is more than just a pattern. It is an entire approach to a particular problem and has been around for a long time. The observer pattern has been used with all types of system development, even before object-oriented techniques were used. It has several names—observer, listener, publish/subscribe. Sometimes you may even hear developers refer to it as the callback technique.

Let's first describe a scenario to illustrate the problem. As discussed in Chapter 8, generally the view layer classes have navigation visibility to the problem domain layer classes. In other words, the windows classes know about the domain layer classes, such as Customer and Order, and can send messages to those internal classes. However, when the design is being developed, it is better if the domain layer classes are not coupled to the view layer classes. So, even though a Customer window can send a message to a Customer object, the Customer object should not have navigation visibility to the Customer window and should not be able to send a message to it.

In this hypothetical example, let's use three classes: a Customer window, an Order window, and an Order class. The first two are windows classes and part of the view layer. The Order class is a domain layer class. The use case is *Create new order*, which you learned about in Chapter 8. When the order was first created, navigation visibility was provided from both the Customer window and the Order window to the Order class. Figure 9-11 illustrates the three classes with two windows and the Order class. The navigation arrows show how messages can be sent.

FIGURE 9-11
Three classes in the *Create new order* use case

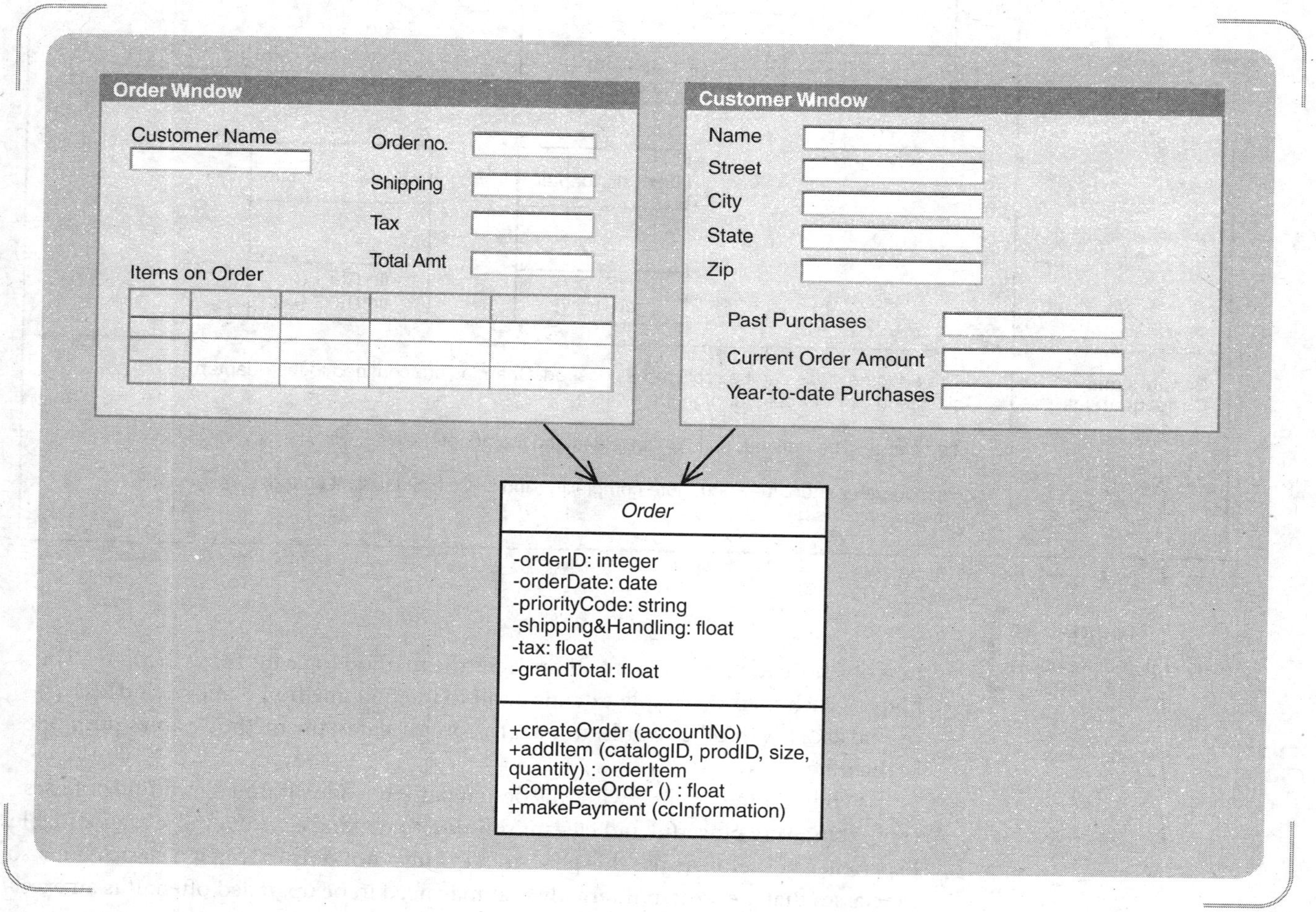

Notice on the Customer window that there are fields called Past Purchases, Current Order Amount, and Year-to-date Purchases. Since Rocky Mountain Outfitters (RMO) provides special discounts to customers when their year-to-date purchases exceed a certain amount, the telephone clerk watches these amounts as the order is being taken to see whether he or she can suggest additional purchases to take advantage of the discounts. As items are added to the order, the Current Order Amount and Year-to-date Purchases fields need to be updated. The data to update these fields are contained in the Order class. But since Order does not have navigation visibility to the Customer window, how can it send information to that window? A novice designer would probably say, "Well, let's just put a reference to the Customer window in the Order object." But that violates the coupling principle. Instead, the observer pattern has been developed to handle this problem. Let's see how that solution works.

The concept of the observer, or listener, pattern is to have the Customer window "listen" for any changes to the Order object. When it "hears" of a change in an order, it updates the appropriate fields. For the listening to work, the Order class must contain mechanisms that (1) allow other classes to "subscribe" as listeners and (2) "publish" the changes to the listeners when they occur.

The Order class must have the following components. First, the Order class must have an array of object references that holds the list of all objects that have subscribed as listeners. The type of the array is an object array. Second, the Order class must have a method, usually something like addOrderListener, which can be called by potential listeners to subscribe. When a class wants to subscribe as a listener, it just calls the addOrderListener method and sends a reference to itself as a parameter. The logic of addOrderListener is simply to add the passed reference parameter to the array. Third, the Order class has a method named *notify*, which iterates through the array and sends a message to each object referenced in the array. Normally, along with the Order class, a designer develops an interface class, which we call OrderEvents, to provide the method signature that will be called by the Order object—often this interface class is called the *publisher*. The listener class, that is, the CustomerWindow, can then inherit from the OrderEvents interface to define the method signatures.

Figure 9-12 illustrates the changes required to implement the observer pattern. The changes have been added in bold. The Order class has a new array variable called orderListeners to hold the subscriber objects. Order has three new methods—one each to add and remove listeners and one to notify OrderListener of any changes. The third method is private or invoked internally. The interface class OrderListener is used to specify the name of the method that will be called when the listener is called back. This callback approach is why the pattern is sometimes called the *callback pattern*.

The CustomerWindow class has navigation visibility to the Order object—it is needed to be able to subscribe to it. The CustomerWindow also inherits from the OrderListener interface so that it knows which method to implement. The OrderListener interface is dependent on the Order class. So, if the Order class changes, the OrderListener might need to change, too. The figure also includes some snippets of code to illustrate how the methods are invoked between the classes. You should carefully read the code to ensure that you understand how this works.

Since the link from the Order to the CustomerWindow is dynamic and temporary, it has no negative side effects on the code. In other words, if the CustomerWindow were no longer there, it would not affect the Order class. Or, if multiple windows wanted to listen to the order amount changing, no changes would be required in the Order class. This type of dynamic linking is a powerful and effective technique to avoid permanent coupling in places where it could cause problems.

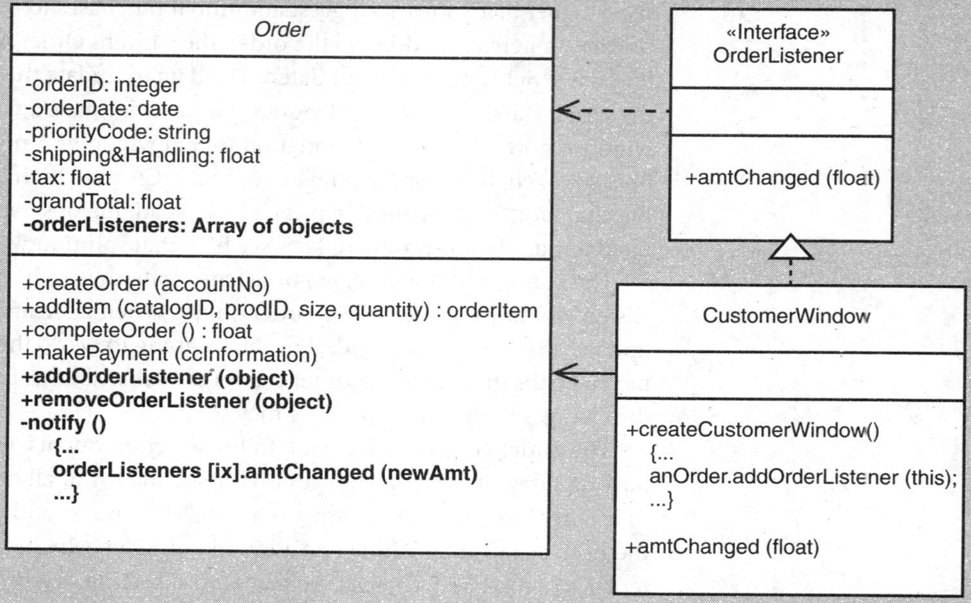

FIGURE 9-12
Implementation for the observer pattern

Figure 9-13 is the pattern template for the observer pattern. The listener design pattern is used extensively as the technique to handle event processing by window objects. The class windows libraries for Java and .NET are all implemented using the listener pattern as the fundamental event-handling technique. The explanation in Figure 9-13 illustrates the names used in the window's events. For example, the method on a windows button to add a listener is addListener ( ). The method that is invoked on the subscriber is actionPerformed ( ). By using these standard names, the window's graphical user interface classes become standard classes that can be reused in any application.

BEST PRACTICE: Begin building your own list or journal of design techniques and patterns. You could even build your own "class library" of reusable components.

DESIGNING ENTERPRISE-LEVEL SYSTEMS

In Chapter 8 and so far in Chapter 9, you have learned the principles, techniques, and patterns of object-oriented design. The general principles apply to all types of systems—whether they are desktop, client/server, or Web-based systems. But systems that are developed to serve an entire organization deserve special consideration, so we cover those topics here.

enterprise-level system
a system that has shared components among multiple people or groups in an organization

First, what is an enterprise-level system? The term can mean many different things. We define an *enterprise-level system* as a system that has shared components among

<table>
<tr><td>Name:</td><td>Observer</td></tr>
<tr><td>Problem:</td><td>One class has attributes that change or events that other classes need to know about. However, the original class does not know which other classes are interested in its internal activity. How do you allow classes to observe this behavior without coupling them?</td></tr>
<tr><td>Solution:</td><td>The original class has methods to allow other classes to dynamically register themselves for particular events. Then when the event occurs, it notifies all those classes that have registered.

This pattern is also called the listener pattern, and the observer class is sometimes referred to as the listener class.</td></tr>
<tr><td>Example:</td><td>The entire windows event-handling system is based on this pattern. Windows components, such as text boxes and buttons, should not be directly coupled to classes and methods that process events, such as text entry or button clicks. Each component will have a method such as addListener () to allow other objects to register themselves. In windows, the listener method that notifies the listeners when an event occurs is often called actionPerformed ().

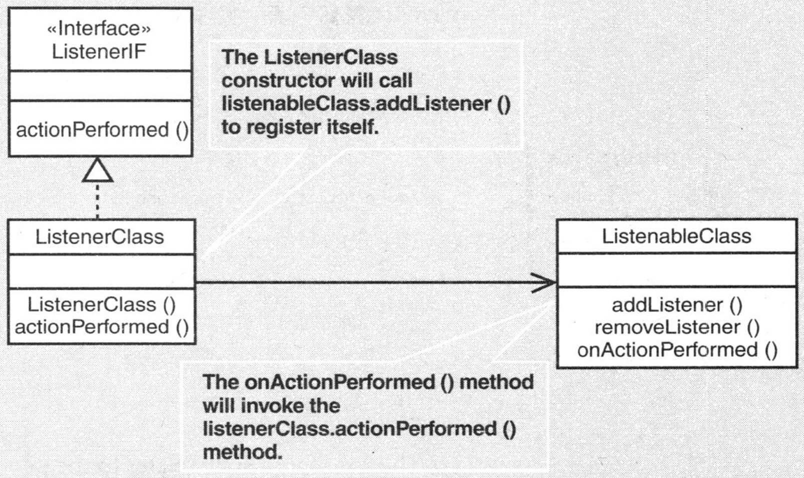
</td></tr>
<tr><td>Benefits and Consequences:</td><td>This pattern is a variation of the publish/subscribe pattern.

This pattern keeps coupling low because dynamic coupling does not cause maintenance problems.

If a class has many observers, there can be a delay in notifying all of them.</td></tr>
</table>

FIGURE 9-13
Observer pattern template

multiple people or groups in an organization. In Chapter 8 you learned about two- and three-layer design as a good approach for designing maintainable systems. A multilayer design, however, does not necessarily imply an enterprise-level system. It is just as applicable to a single desktop system.

Enterprise-level systems almost always use multiple tiers of computers. You learned about *n*-layer or *n*-tiered architectures in Chapter 7. A typical example of this architecture is a client/server environment, where the client computers contain the view and domain layer programs, and the data access layer is on a central server. This configuration is a three-layer, two-tiered system. Because the central database is shared across the enterprise, it is placed on a central server that everyone using the application program can share. Since local client computers are often very powerful Macintosh or personal computers, both the view layer and domain logic can be executed locally.

Our definition of an enterprise-level system is a broad one. Two major categories of systems fit this definition in relation to systems design: client/server network-based systems and Internet-based systems. You may find that many people only think of the second category when they talk about enterprise-level systems because so much new development is being done for the Web. Remember, however, that the broader definition is equally valid.

These two methods of implementing enterprise-level systems have many similar properties. Both require a network. Both have central servers. Both have the view layer on the client machines. However, some fundamental differences also exist in the design and implementation of these two approaches. The primary difference is in how the view layer interacts with the domain and data access layers. It is important for us, as developers, to be able to distinguish between these two types of systems because we must consider important design issues. Figure 9-14 identifies three fundamental differences that affect the architectural design of the system.

DESIGN ISSUE	CLIENT/SERVER NETWORK SYSTEM	INTERNET SYSTEM
State	"Stateful" or state-based system, e.g., client/server connection is long term.	Stateless system, e.g., client/server connection is not long term and has no inherent memory.
Client Configuration	Screens and forms that are programmed are displayed directly. Domain layer is often on the client or split between client and server machines.	Screens and forms are displayed only through a browser. They must conform to browser technology.
Server Configuration	Application or data server directly connects to client tier.	Client tier connects indirectly to the application server through a Web server.

FIGURE 9-14
Differences between client/server and Internet systems

The concept of state relates to the permanence of the connection between the client view layer and the server domain layer. If the connection is permanent, as in a client/server system, values in variables can be passed back and forth and are remembered by each component in the system. The view layer has direct access to the data fields in the domain layer. For example, data in an order, such as all of the line items and their prices, are displayed in the forms.

In a stateless system such as the Internet, the client view layer does not have a permanent connection to the server domain layer. The Internet was designed so that when a client requests a screen via a URL address typed in the browser, the server sends the appropriate document, and then the two disconnect. In other words, the client does not know the state of the server, and the server does not remember the state of the client. This transient connection makes it difficult to implement such things as an order in a shopping cart. To add more permanence to the stateless environment, Web designers have developed other techniques, such as cookies and session variables. As a systems designer, you must consider these additional components when designing an Internet enterprise-level system.

Concerning client configuration, the client side of a network-based system contains the view layer classes and often the domain layer classes. Formatting, displaying, and event processing within the screens are all directly controlled by the view layer and domain layer program logic. There is great flexibility in the design and programming of these electronic screens. The view layer classes and domain layer classes can communicate directly with each other. Even if the domain layer is split across tiers, a permanent communication link can be established—all under the program's control.

In an Internet-based system, all electronic screens are displayed by a browser. The formatting, displaying, and event processing all must conform to the capabilities of the browser being used. Special techniques and tools, such as scripting languages and applets, have been developed to simulate the network-based capability. However, as a designer, you will need to design for the environment.

The server configuration in a network-based system consists of data access layer classes and sometimes domain layer classes. These classes collaborate through direct communication and access to each other's public methods. In an Internet-based system, all communications from the client tier must go through the HTTP server. Communication is not direct, and methods and program logic are invoked indirectly through passed parameters. This indirect technique of accessing domain layer logic is more complex and requires additional care in designing the system.

As you can see at the enterprise level of design, we have started to become concerned about the physical components of the system—how the system is partitioned into executable components. Earlier design discussions focused on identifying logical components. But as we begin identifying physical components, we move toward a system's physical implementation. Diagrams that depict physical components are called *implementation diagrams*. There are several types of implementation diagrams; however, we will use a specific implementation diagram that shows how the components are deployed across the various tiers. This type of diagram is called a *deployment diagram*. So, a deployment diagram is a type of implementation diagram whose purpose is to show the deployment of various physical components across different locations.

implementation diagram
a diagram that depicts physical components of a system

deployment diagram
a type of implementation diagram that shows the physical components across different locations

UML has specific notations for implementation diagrams. In the next section, we explain that UML notation. UML does not currently have specific notations for Internet elements such as Web pages. It does, however, allow for extensions to the existing notation. Therefore, in the last two sections, we introduce an extension to UML that has been developed for depicting physical elements of Internet-based systems.

UML NOTATION FOR DEPLOYMENT DIAGRAMS

The two symbols we use for deployment architectural design as shown in deployment diagrams are the component symbol and the node symbol. A component is an executable module or program, and it consists of all the classes that are compiled into a single entity. It has well-defined interfaces, or public methods, that can be accessed by other programs or external devices. The set of all of these public methods that are available to the outside world is called the *application program interface*, or *API*. Figure 9-15 illustrates the UML notation for a component and its interfaces. It consists of a rectangle with two smaller rectangles protruding from one side. It is not necessary to list all of the interfaces on a single component. Only those that are pertinent to the context of the diagram are listed. The name of the component is written inside. Sometimes designers want to emphasize a single instance of a component rather than a classification. In that situation, the name of the component is underlined.

application program interface (API)
the set of public methods that are available to the outside world

A node can be thought of as a computer or a bank of computers representing a single computing resource. A node is a physical entity at a specific location. Figure 9-16 illustrates the symbol that is used for a node—a shaded rectangle. The shading is added to represent a real object that can cast a shadow. The name of the node is listed inside, either as a type or classification of node or as a single instance with the name underlined.

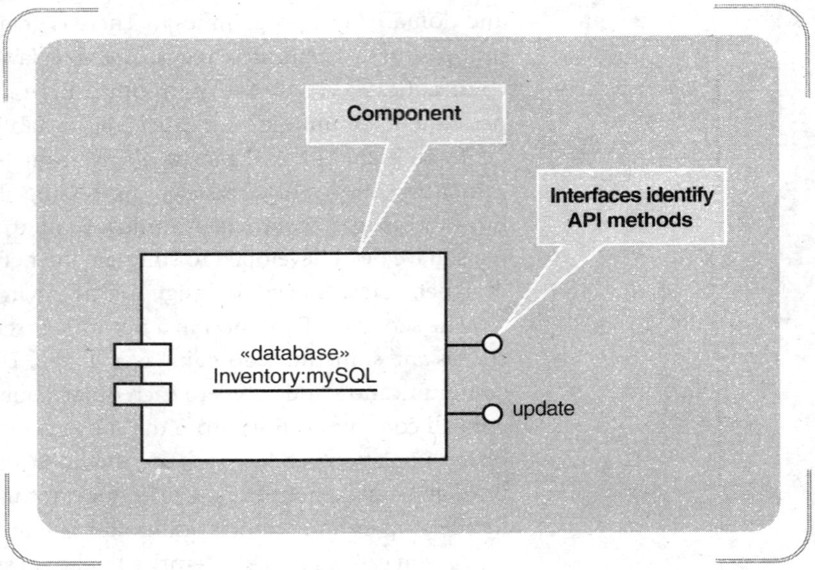

FIGURE 9-15
UML component notation

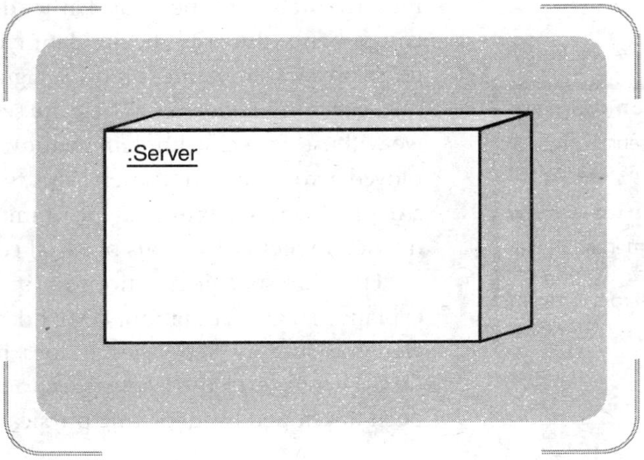

FIGURE 9-16
UML node notation

frameset
a high-level object that holds items to be displayed by a browser

The other notation needed for implementation components is a symbol to represent a Web page or frameset. A *frameset* is a high-level object that can hold items to be displayed by a browser. We will use a frameset notation and stereotype to indicate a Web page. You can think of a frameset as the window in a browser that can display frames or a set of frames. Figure 9-17 shows the notation for a frameset.

We now apply these implementation notations within deployment diagrams to show various configurations that are applicable for Internet-based systems.

INTERNET-BASED SYSTEMS

Many colleges have courses in Web development. Most of those courses fall into two categories: Web site design or Web programming languages. Both classes are important and beneficial for your education as a system developer.

The Web site design courses usually focus on usability. You learn how to design a set of attractive and effective Web pages to support a business application. Some of the critical issues addressed are graphical design, Web page layout, and navigation among pages. You might also learn how to program in HTML and how to use special development tools such as FrontPage or Dreamweaver. Knowing how to use these tools is vital if you plan to do Web site design.

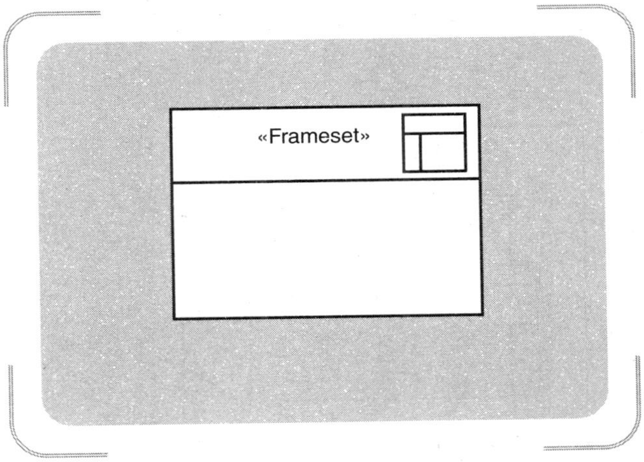

FIGURE 9-17
UML extension for frameset

Web programming courses teach you various programming languages and the ways to insert program logic into Web pages. You learn JavaScript, VBScript, PHP, and ASP (Active Server Pages). You may learn how to use advanced database tools, such as Cold Fusion, to access databases from your pages. You also learn how the browser and server work together to serve up pages that have sufficient programming logic to support the business application. Advanced versions of this course even teach you the Java or .NET environments so that you can configure an entire application.

We do not intend this short section to replace those courses. Instead, we introduce the architecture of these Web-based systems and provide a few principles of good design that you can apply as you develop skills in those other courses. In Chapter 8, we explained three-layer design as one effective approach to developing robust, easily maintainable systems. But how can designers implement a three-layer design in a Web-based architecture? This question is particularly important if an organization wants to use the same domain logic for both types of enterprise systems, a client/server system and an Internet-based system. We start the discussion with an example of Internet-based system architecture.

SIMPLE INTERNET ARCHITECTURE

Figure 9-18 illustrates a very simple Internet architecture. The two nodes represent two separate computers. On the client computer, the browser component is executing. On the server computer, the Internet server component is executing. The browser requests a page. The server sends the page. The pages, indicated by the framesets, reside permanently on the server but are transported for display to the client. Within the page, program logic can be inserted through the use of JavaScript, VBScript, Java Applets, or ActiveX controls.

This simple architecture allows users to view static information on the Web or other Internet locations. The scripting languages, JavaScript and VBScript, and other program elements are useful for making the page more attractive with animation, rollovers, and so forth. However, users only interact with the system by clicking on links to other URLs and viewing other Web pages.

This set of components is used only for viewing information and is insufficient for creating a business application. Note, however, that this framework is the architecture within which Internet business systems must operate. The browser and server are key elements that transport all information between the client computer and the server computer.

As noted in Chapters 1 and 2, RMO's new customer support system needed to support both a Web user interface and an internal desktop interface. It is critically important

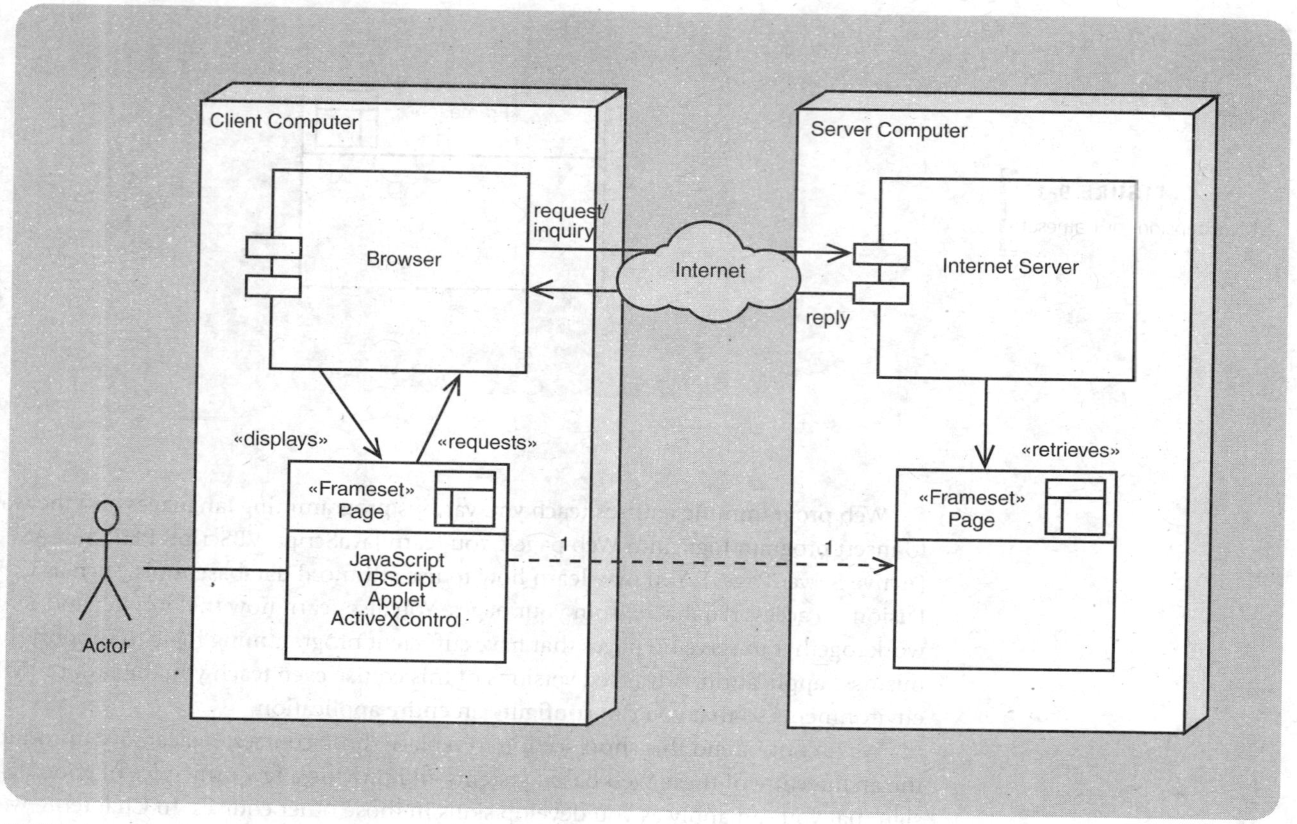

FIGURE 9-18
Simple Internet architecture

for the same back end—business logic and database access—to link with either user interface. Consequently, the design team must specify the architectural design in enough detail to ensure that the programmers implement the system so that it supports both user interfaces. Barbara Halifax has updated John MacMurty on her team's progress in creating the system's Web interface (see the memo).

TWO-LAYER ARCHITECTURE FOR USER INTERACTION

To support a business application, the system must be able to respond to other user requests—to accept inputs and events from the user, process those inputs, and respond with a meaningful output. The interaction diagrams developed in Chapter 8 also were designed to handle all such use cases—to accept inputs and requests from users; process those requests, including updating the database; and display the results. So, the structure for Internet-based systems should be similar.

As indicated in Chapter 8, many simple business systems can be designed as two-layer systems. These systems primarily capture information from the user and update a database. No complex domain layer logic is required. In those instances, the domain layer and data access layer are usually combined. The business logic in the domain layer frequently relates only to the formatting of the data and to deciding which database table to update. Many business applications fall in this category. A system such as a customer sales system could be easily designed as a two-layer system.

Let's expand the simple Internet architecture diagram to illustrate a two-layer design. Figure 9-19 shows a more complex Internet architecture to support user interaction. The original frameset includes a form, which allows the user to enter information. When the form is sent, the browser forwards it back to the server. Embedded in the form is information about where the input data should be sent. In the figure, there are

July 15, 2006

To: John MacMurty

From: Barbara Halifax, Project Manager

RE: Customer Support System status

ROCKY MOUNTAIN OUTFITTERS

MEMO

John, during the last several weeks we have been working on the design of the Web interface for the system. This task has been very challenging. I knew it would be complex, but I had no idea of the level of detail that we needed to address. This has been a joint activity, involving my technical staff, the systems analysts, and the user-interface people. We have been identifying which functions are allowed from which Web pages and at the same time trying to keep the system very user-friendly and intuitive. As I mentioned to you, we have developed a statechart for every Web page to ensure that we know exactly what services we want to provide for that page. It has been a lot of work, but the team is very confident that the solution is solid.

Completed during the last period (two weeks)

We completed the design of the Web interface for the order shopping cart. This took us longer than expected, since Bill McDougal and JoAnn White were both very concerned that we make sure that the Web pages and underlying system did not have any security holes. Consequently, we are about a week behind schedule on this part of the design, but we are confident that the solution is correct and has good security.

Plans for the next period (two weeks)

During the next period, we are going to begin implementing the Web interface. With the iterative approach we are using with the UP, we will be programming the Web interface and inserting it into the portions that are already coded and running.

Problems, issues, open items

Nothing major at this point. There is just a lot of work to do. However, we are moving ahead rapidly and making good progress.

BH

cc: Steven Deerfield, Ming Lee, Jack Garcia

two paths, one to a common gateway interface (CGI) component and the other to an application component. In reality, these two components are very similar. We divide them in the figure to emphasize their differences.

The CGI was the original way to process input data. The CGI directory contains compiled programs that are available to receive input data from the server. The programs in the CGI directory can be written in any compiled language, such as C++. This technique is very effective and usually has very quick response and processing times. The only downside is that these programs can be quite complex and difficult to write. They process the input data, access any required database, and format a response page in HTML, as indicated by the Response Page in the diagram.

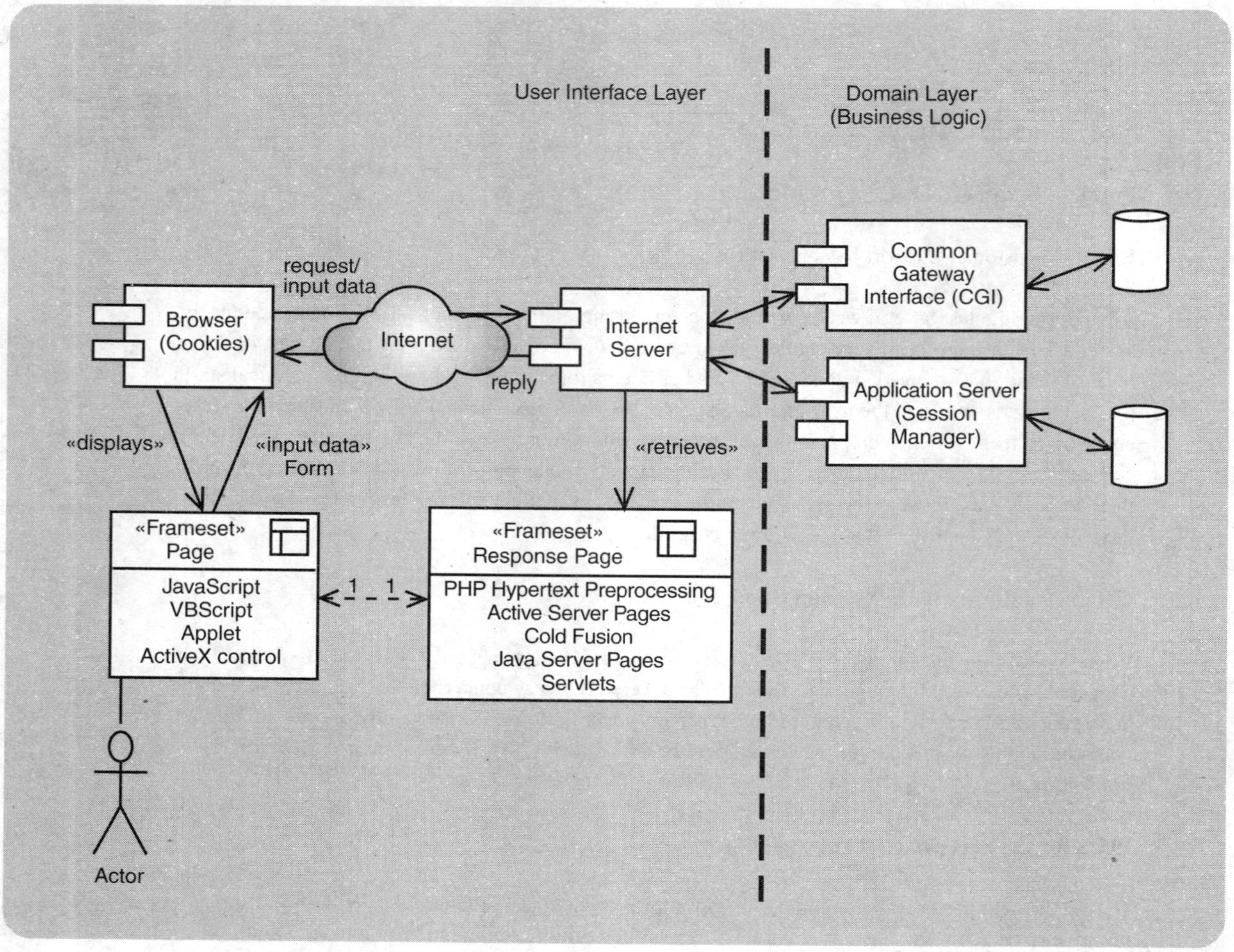

FIGURE 9-19
Two-layer Internet architecture

The other potential direction for input data is directly to a URL for a Web page with embedded program code. The extension shown on the Response Page indicates what type of program code is embedded in the page—ASP for Active Server Pages, PHP for PHP Hypertext Preprocessor, JSP for Java Server Pages, CFM for Cold Fusion Pages, and so forth. Depending on the type of extension, an application server—which is the language processor—is invoked to process the embedded code. The embedded code, via the application server, can process the code, including reading and writing to a database. The application server working with cookies on the browser can manage sessions with the user. Session variables are set up to maintain information about the user across multiple page requests and forms. The application server also formats the response page based on the HTML statements and the code and forwards it back to the Internet server.

Even though we have referred to this design as a two-layer architecture, the user interface classes often contain the business logic and data access. Due to the structure of Web servers, the program (defined as object-oriented classes) that processes the input forms also outputs the HTML code that is sent back to the client browser. For example, in Java-based systems, Java servlets receive the data from input on a Web form, process the data, and format the output HTML page. To process the data, the servlets usually include any required business logic and data access logic. The .NET environment is very similar. For every Web form, there is a *code behind* class written in Visual Basic, C#, J#, or some similar language. The code behind object receives the data from the Web form, processes the data, and formats the output HTML page. So, it is often not clear whether the architecture is one layer or two layer. However, we refer to this architecture as two layer to emphasize the fact that it is dynamic and that the HTML response pages are built dynamically.

This architecture works well for two-layer applications that are not too complex—for example, when the response pages already have most of the HTML written. The embedded code performs functions such as validating the data and storing them in the database. Note that the business logic is minimal, so mixing it with the data access logic still provides a maintainable solution.

However, some inherent complexities exist with this Internet system. The processing and data access code is embedded within the HTML pages, which are also user-interface pages. Since these response pages may also contain additional forms, they may also have other client-side code such as JavaScript and VBScript. So, a single entity—the HTML page—could potentially contain user-interface controls, user-interface logic, problem domain logic, and data access logic. All three layers are mixed together. Many Internet systems have been built with this architecture. As you might guess, if any of the three pieces of logic gets complex, testing and maintaining the system becomes very difficult.

THREE-LAYER ARCHITECTURE FOR USER INTERACTION

For systems that require more complex business logic, it is better to add a domain layer with separate classes for both the domain logic and data access. Three-layer architecture is also more appropriate for systems that need to support multiple user interfaces, both Internet-based and network-based. Figure 9-20 expands the diagram in Figure 9-19 to show how a three-layer approach can be implemented.

On the CGI leg, the three-layer approach is implemented by defining separate domain layer and data access layer classes. These classes are designed the same way that was shown in Chapter 8. A use case controller is identified for each input form. The use case controller then distributes messages to the individual objects of the system. The design follows the three-layer structure that was developed in Chapter 8.

On the application server side, the programmer has less direct control. However, tools make development faster and easier. Let's address two approaches—the Java approach and the .NET approach.

For Java server pages, which have the .jsp extension, the application server invokes a Java servlet when the input form is received. A Java servlet is a Java program that executes like any other program. The Java servlet identified for the input form can be the use case controller, which can then distribute the input message to other domain classes to process the request. After the request is processed, including any database access, the servlet takes control and formats the output response page. The sequence of messages flows exactly as indicated by the design sequence diagrams in Chapter 8. The difference, of course, is that the output is in HTML statements and must flow through the server and browser before it is displayed back to the user.

For the .NET environment, the process is very similar. The input data form is sent to the ASP.NET application server, which invokes the code behind object (written in Visual Basic, C#, or J#) for the particular Web form. The code behind object will then call appropriate methods in other objects. In the new .NET environment, the program modules are compiled into a common language called *Common Language Runtime*. Common Language Runtime is a mid-level language that allows programs to be partially compiled and managed for faster, more efficient execution. As with Java, the program structure can use a three-layer design based on the principles from

Common Language Runtime
a mid-level language that allows programs to be partially compiled and managed for faster execution

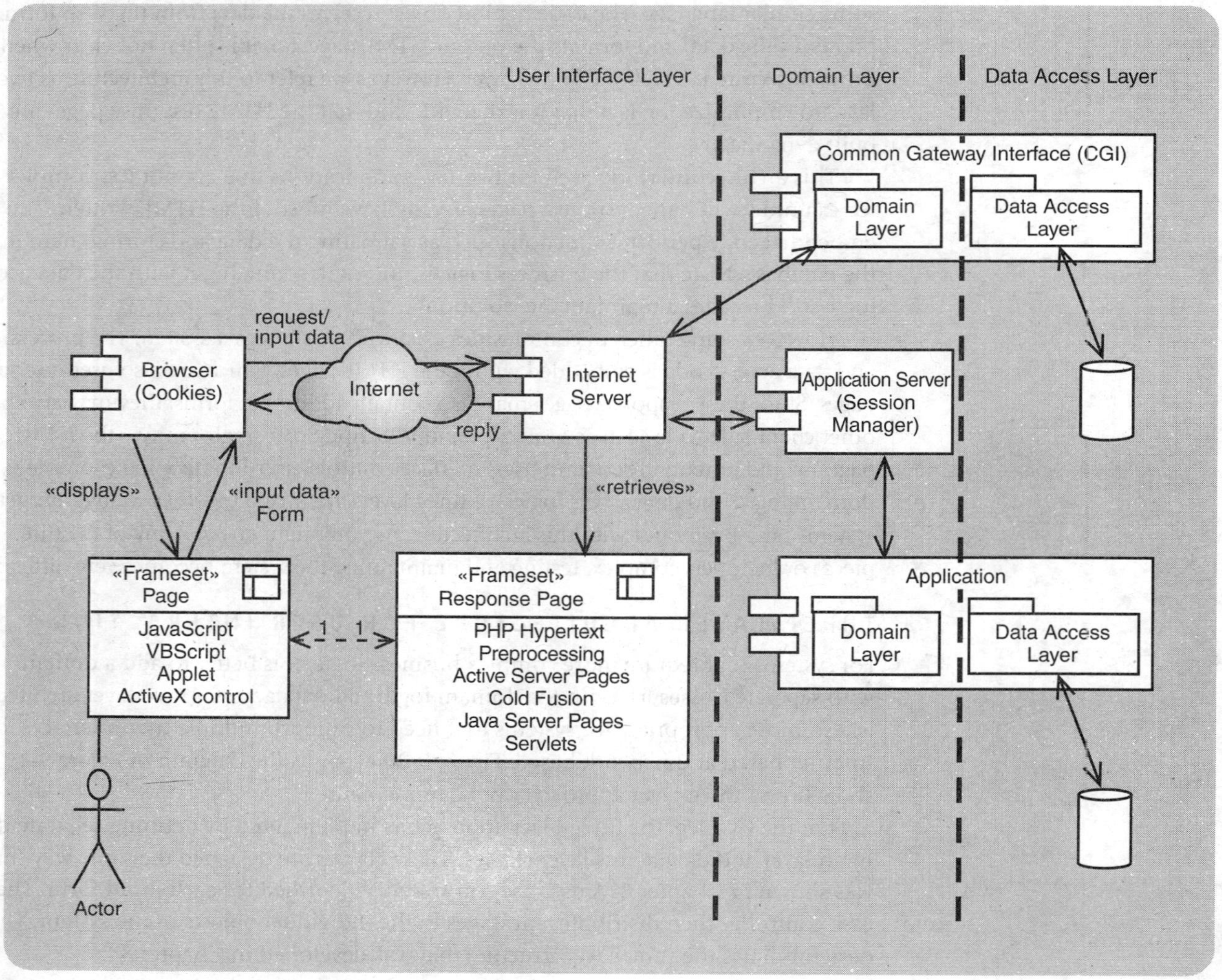

FIGURE 9-20
Three-layer Internet architecture

Chapter 8. One of the major differences in the .NET environment is that the .NET framework has a very extensive library of standard components that does everything from automatically authenticating users to accessing data and populating forms. But this feature can be both an advantage and disadvantage. The advantage is that the high-level components provided by .NET make it easy to program and build forms. However, the disadvantage is that it is also easy to mix the layers, scattering business logic in with user-interface processes and data access logic.

BEST PRACTICE: Be sure the problem domain classes are well defined first, before defining the Web forms and user-interface pages.

WEB SERVICES

One of the new techniques being used in the development of Internet-based systems is the use of Web services. We expect to hear and see much more about Web services in the near future. So what are Web services? A Web service is simply a computer

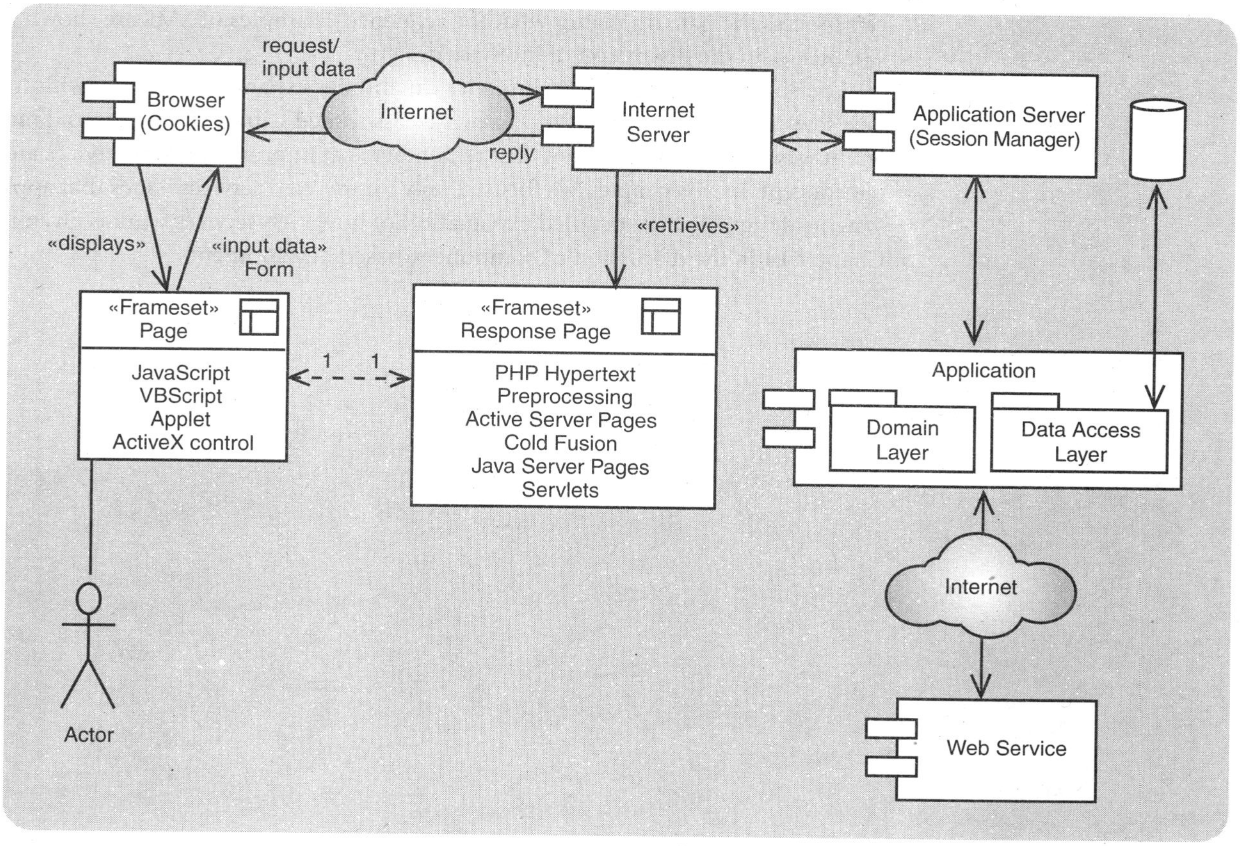

FIGURE 9-21
Invoking a Web service

program that provides a service to other systems via the Internet and is posted in a directory so that other systems can find it and use it. Figure 9-21 shows how a Web service might be used.

Suppose in processing an input form the application requires some data from an external database. Perhaps the application is a financial services system, and it needs the latest financial information about a particular company. Instead of trying to maintain these data itself and keep them current, the system developers decide to access them from some other service on the Internet. So, as the program is executing, it determines that it needs current financial data. It does not care where it gets these data, just that they be current. First, the program sends out a request for information. This request will go to a services directory called *Universal Discovery, Description, and Integration (UDDI)*, which is an indexing service to help locate Web services. The request will be based on certain keywords that describe exactly what is desired. The UDDI will provide an Internet address of a program that will provide that service. The application then requests the desired information over the Internet.

This process sounds very easy, but it has never been possible before, for various reasons. One of the major obstacles was that the requestor and the provider both had to use exactly the same format of data exchange. Defining the same format is easy if only two programs are involved. But to have a general-purpose format that any program could use has been a major problem. In Web services, however, all communication is based on XML. XML (eXtensible Markup Language) is a text-based language much like HTML. The difference is that HTML has standard tags, whereas XML can include self-defining tags to describe any data desired. In other words, the sequence and format of the data are defined within the transmitted file itself. Thus, the recipient of the data can process the data no matter what the sequence. Examples of XML are shown in Chapter 11 in the discussion of interface design.

You should expect to see Web service capabilities expand very rapidly within the next few years. There are a lot of buzzwords associated with Web services and many different ways to implement them. Just remember that in principle Web services are a simple concept. In this chapter, we focused only on the Web services issues that apply to systems design. A more detailed explanation of how Web services work is given in Chapter 14 in the discussion of component-based development.

Summary

Statecharts are useful during design to specify precise behavior of and constraints on the various portions of the final system. They are also useful to describe the method logic within an object.

Systems that are based on good design principles are not only easier to develop but are also more maintainable. As object-oriented development becomes more mature, the principles that drive good design are becoming better understood. Good design is based on two factors: good principles and standard design patterns.

Two new design principles that were introduced in the chapter are protection from variations and indirection. Protection from variations is applied to a system by separating components or design elements that do not change from those that are more apt to change. The purpose is to make the system more maintainable by isolating the changes to well-identified and easily replaceable components. The other principle, indirection, is one way to implement protection from variations. Indirection is a technique for inserting an intermediate object between two objects that need to be linked but that do not have a natural interface to each other. The intermediate object provides an interface between the other two elements. The advantages of this technique are that (1) neither of the two elements must be changed to interface with the other, and (2) if one needs to be replaced, then the impact on the other is minimized.

In addition to design principles, the use of design patterns is becoming more popular to ensure that the design of a new system follows accepted approaches. A design pattern is like a template or a standard solution to a common problem. Patterns are used frequently in all engineering fields because many engineering problems are very similar. In software development, a set of commonly accepted design patterns is now providing standard solutions to speed design.

Three design patterns were presented as an introduction to this approach to design: singleton, adapter, and observer. The singleton pattern is a standard solution to the problem of ensuring that only one object of a given class is created. In some software situations, an object may have to maintain control over various system processes. To ensure that control is maintained, all processing is forced to go through one control point. To make sure that another object is not inadvertently subverting this control, only one control object is allowed. The singleton pattern is one way to implement this requirement.

The adapter pattern is an example of the indirection design principle. As with an electrical adapter, which adapts one set of plugs to the socket for another set, the adapter pattern converts one application program interface (API) into another API. Thus, an object that normally would not be compatible with a system can be "plugged into" the system through the use of an adapter object.

The observer pattern is a fairly complex pattern, but it is widely used and critically important. All of the windows GUI event-processing capability is built around the observer pattern. The observer pattern allows two objects to be linked dynamically. This pattern is important for keeping coupling low in a system, while still providing communication capability between objects that should not be permanently linked.

KEY TERMS

application program interface (API), p. 379
Common Language Runtime, p. 385
decision pseudostate, p. 363
deployment diagram, p. 379
design patterns, p. 368
enterprise-level system, p. 376
frameset, p. 380
implementation diagram, p. 379
indirection, p. 368
protection from variations, p. 367
state variable, p. 361

REVIEW QUESTIONS

1. What are the two primary purposes of a design statechart? How is it different from a statechart used for requirements?
2. What is the purpose of a state variable?
3. Describe the relationship between a message and a transition. Also, describe the relationship between a message and a method.
4. What is an action-expression? How is it used in design and programming?
5. Why is a decision pseudostate inserted in a statechart? How is it represented in a statechart?
6. What is meant by *protection from variations*? Why is it an important design principle?
7. What is meant by *indirection*? Why is it important in systems design?
8. What is a design pattern? How are design patterns used in the design discipline?
9. What problem does the singleton design pattern address?
10. Briefly explain how the singleton pattern works.
11. What problem does the adapter pattern solve? Briefly explain how it is implemented.
12. What are the basic elements of the observer pattern?
13. Give an example or two of situations in which the observer pattern might be used.
14. What is meant by an enterprise-level system? Why is it an important consideration in design?
15. What is a deployment diagram used for?
16. Describe the two primary symbols used for deployment diagrams. What do they mean?
17. What are some of the differences between a network-based system and a Web-based system?
18. What are Web services? How are they implemented?

THINKING CRITICALLY

1. In Figure 9-22, the package on the left contains the classes in a payroll system. The package on the right is a payroll tax subsystem. What technique would you use to integrate the tax subsystem into the payroll system? Show how you would solve the problem by modifying the existing classes (in either figure). What new classes would you add? Use UML notation.

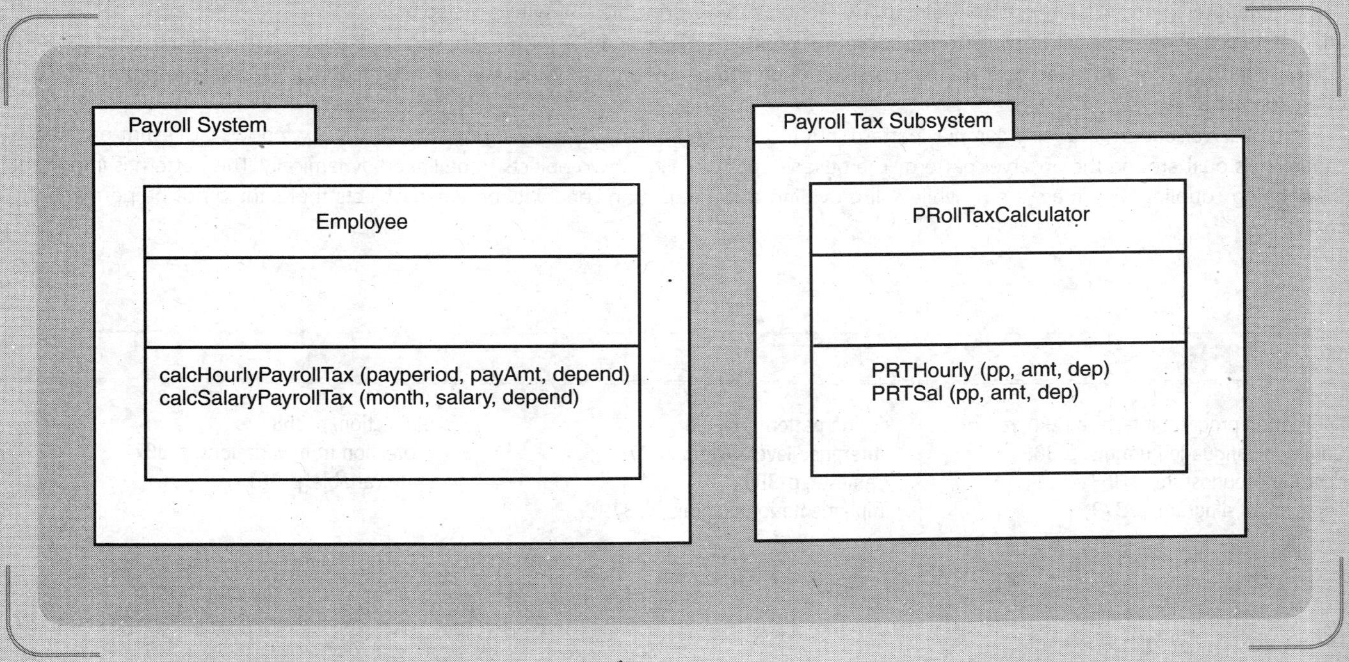

FIGURE 9-22
Payroll system packages and classes

2. The right side of Figure 9-23 shows a system that is simulating the manufacture of computer chips. The equations in the simulation system are based on statistical probabilities of failures in the manufacturing process. The package on the left illustrates a window (and its associated class definition) that will display these results dynamically. The values in the top five fields are obtained when the window is opened. However, the bottom three fields should be updated after every iteration, which takes about one second. From a design standpoint, the simulation system on the right should not be coupled to the user-interface system on the left. Show how you would solve this problem, including any class methods for existing classes, new classes, and new definitions that you would use. Use UML notation.

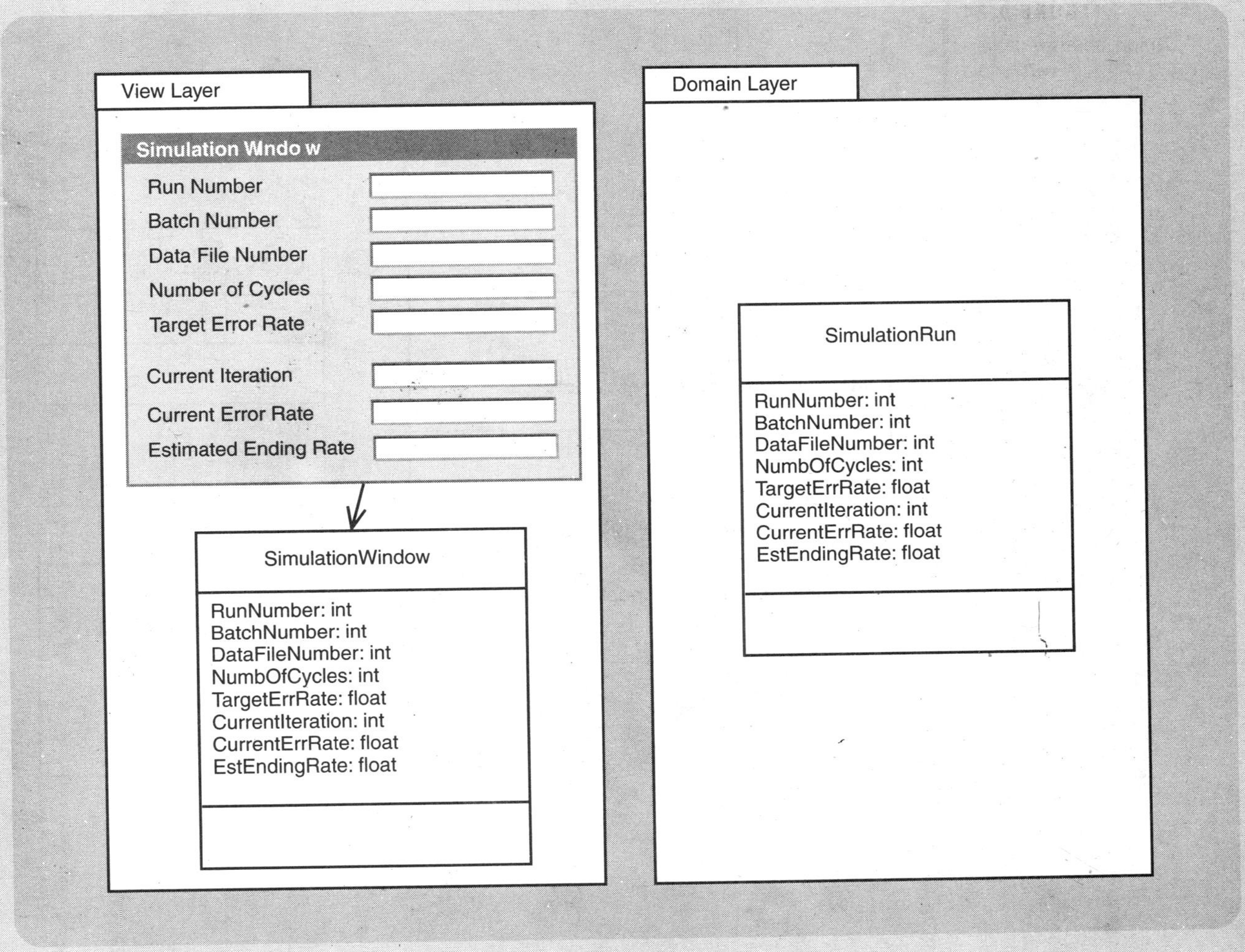

FIGURE 9-23
Simulation system classes

3. Review the observer pattern description in Figure 9-24. Find the errors in the diagram. After you have identified the errors, state what you would do to fix them.
4. In Thinking Critically problem 2 of Chapter 8, you developed a three-layer design for the use case *Returnbooks*. Assume that the library has a main office and branch locations. The library staff would like to make this use case available with a Web interface so that various locations can access it. Take your three-layer design and superimpose it on the deployment diagram in Figure 9-20 for an enterprise-level solution. In which package would you put the domain classes and data access classes? Modify the diagram. Replace the «Boundary» with the «Frameset» classes that are appropriate for a Web solution.

FIGURE 9-24
Sample observer pattern with errors

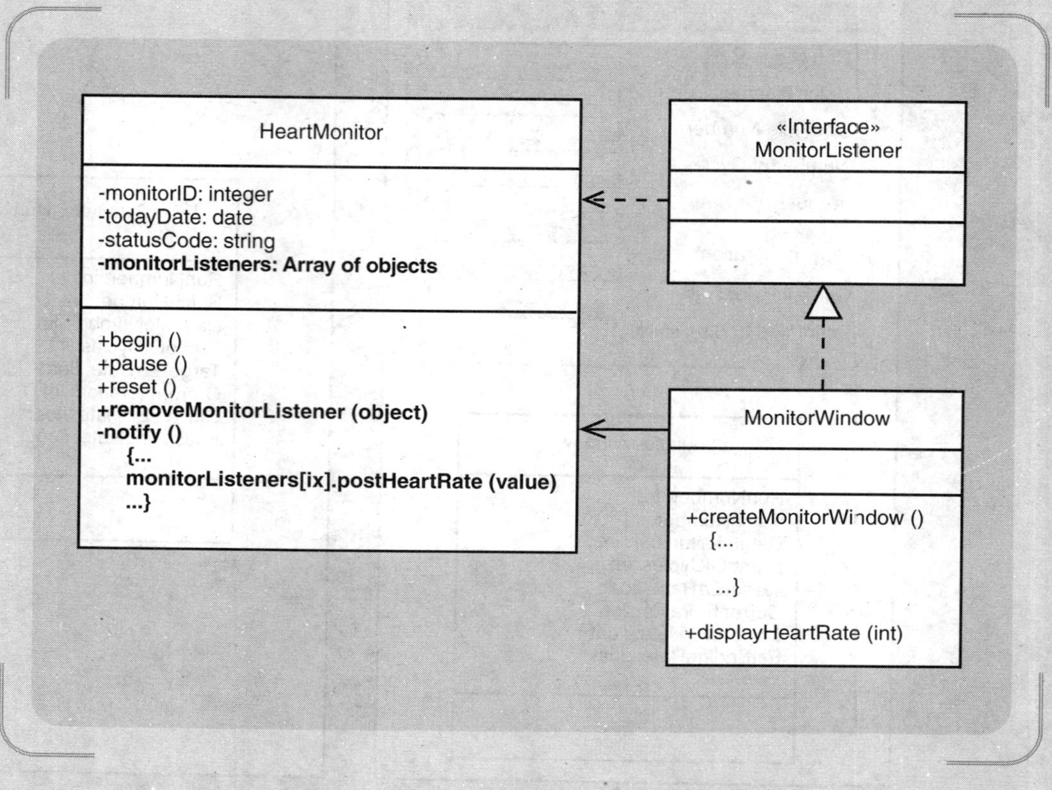

5. In Thinking Critically problem 3 of Chapter 8, you developed a three-layer design for the use case *Receive new book*. Assume that the library has a main office and branch locations. The library staff would like to make this use case available with a Web interface so that various locations can access it. Take your three-layer design and superimpose it on the deployment diagram of Figure 9-20 for an enterprise-level solution. In which packages would you put the domain classes and data access classes? Modify the diagram. Replace the «Boundary» classes with the «Frameset» classes that are appropriate for a Web solution.
6. The International Hospital Service (IHS) is building a new scheduling system to help track occupancy of beds and rooms in its hospital. The following narrative explains how rooms are scheduled. Develop a statechart based on the narrative description.

    A hospital room is either occupied or vacant. However, scheduling a room is a little more complicated. A room can be scheduled or unscheduled, independently of whether it is occupied or not. When a room is vacant, it becomes occupied when a patient is assigned to the room. If the patient is admitted as an emergency (unscheduled), then nothing else needs to happen. However, if admittance is a scheduled arrival, the room-scheduling system must note that fact and update the schedule to show it as being fulfilled.

    Immediately after a room is vacated, it goes into a temporary state of dirty. That simply means that it must be cleaned before another patient can be moved in. So, even though it is in reality vacant, it is not considered vacant until it has been cleaned.

    When a scheduled patient arrives, the room changes to an occupied state. Since it is impossible to ascertain exactly how long a patient will be in a room, the hospital does not allow a room to be scheduled by more than one patient at a time.

EXPERIENTIAL EXERCISES

1. Design patterns are a young, but rich, field of research and study. Locate the original GoF book on design patterns and give a brief summary of two or three patterns discussed in that text. This exercise will begin your lifelong learning process of reading and understanding technical design material.
2. Find another book on design patterns (see the "Further Resources" list for suggestions) and report on two or three of the patterns listed in that book. Some patterns are for network designs. Books on enterprise-level designs frequently discuss Internet design.
3. Do more research into the basics of Web services. Chapter 14 will also add to your understanding. Find some articles on the Internet that explain how Web services are implemented. Then find an example of a company that provides Web services and document what it provides and how it does so.
4. Find a system that was developed using Visual Studio .NET (or Visual Basic). Find one that has both an Internet user interface and a network-based user interface. Is it multilayer? Where is the business logic? Can you identify the view layer (user interface) classes, the domain layer classes, and the data access layer classes?
5. Find some examples of system behavior that have been documented through the use of statecharts. Discuss the various ways that statecharts are used.

Case Studies

THEEYESHAVEIT.COM BOOK EXCHANGE

In Chapter 8 you built a network-based solution for TheEyes HaveIt.com Book Exchange. Of course, the real intent of this system is to provide access via the Internet. Using Figure 9-20 and your solution in Chapter 8 as the starting point, show which classes and framesets you would add to Figure 9-20 to provide an enterprise-level solution. Place your classes in package diagrams, as appropriate, to group them according to layers.

RETHINKING ROCKY MOUNTAIN OUTFITTERS

Chapter 8 provided detailed three-layer sequence diagrams for *Look up item availability* and the telephone order scenario of *Create new order*. Chapter 6 provided a system sequence diagram for the Web scenario of *Create new order*. Starting from Figure 9-20, add the appropriate classes and framesets to the diagram for each of the use cases. Create two separate drawings, one for *Look up item availability* and one for the Web scenario of *Create new order*. Add your classes to the appropriate packages depicted inside the components. Delete any components or packages that are not necessary. You will need to replace the windows boundary classes with Web framesets based on the design and the system sequence diagram.

FOCUSING ON RELIABLE PHARMACEUTICAL SERVICE

In Chapter 8, you developed a three-layer design for three use cases that you had documented in Chapter 6. Based on the Web design principles given in this chapter, show how a Web solution would be structured. Begin with Figure 9-20 and place the classes you identified in your Chapter 8 solution in the appropriate packages. You will need to replace your windows classes with frameset classes as required for the Web interface.

FURTHER RESOURCES

Grady Booch, James Rumbaugh, and Ivar Jacobson, *The Unified Modeling Language User Guide*. Addison-Wesley, 1999.

Frank Buschmann, R. Meunier, H. Rohnert, P. Sommerlad, and M. Stal, *Pattern-Oriented Software Architecture: A System of Patterns*. John Wiley and Sons, 1996.

Alur Deepak, J. Crupi, and D. Malks, *Core J2EE Patterns: Best Practices and Design Strategies*. Sun Microsystems Press, 2001.

Erich Gamma, R. Helm, R. Johnson, and J. Vlissides, *Elements of Reusable Object-Oriented Software*. Addison-Wesley, 1995.

Mark Grand, *Patterns in Java*, Volumes I and II. John Wiley and Sons, 1999.

Craig Larman, *Applying UML and Patterns: An Introduction to Object-Oriented Analysis and Design and the Unified Process* (2nd ed.). Prentice-Hall, 2002.

David S. Linthicum, *Next Generation Application Integration: From Simple Information to Web Services*. Addison-Wesley, 2004.

James Rumbaugh, Ivar Jacobsen, and Grady Booch, *The Unified Modeling Language Reference Manual*. Addison-Wesley, 1999.

chapter 10

DESIGNING THE DATA ACCESS LAYER

LEARNING OBJECTIVES

After reading this chapter, you should be able to:

- Describe the differences and similarities between relational and object-oriented database management systems
- Design an object database schema based on a class diagram
- Design a relational database schema based on a class diagram
- Describe object-relational design issues, including data access classes and data types
- Describe the different architectural models for distributed databases
- Determine when and how to design the database

CHAPTER OUTLINE

- Databases and Database Management Systems
- Object-Oriented Databases
- Relational Databases
- Object-Relational Interaction
- Distributed Databases
- Database Design within the UP

NATIONWIDE BOOKS: DESIGNING A NEW DATABASE

The project leaders for Nationwide Books' (NB) new Web-based ordering system were meeting with NB's database administrator to discuss how they were going to tackle the database design. Present at the meeting were Sharon Thomas (who had led the project since its inception), Vince Pirelli (a contractor who had completed most of the requirements activities), and Bill Anderson (NB's database administrator, who hadn't directly participated in earlier phases of the project). Sharon started the meeting by saying, "When the project began, we planned to use the existing DB2 database. Maria Peña [the chief information officer] also wanted us to use this project to try out newer development methods and tools that we knew we'd need in the coming years. So we hired Vince to define the system requirements using object-oriented [OO] methods. We also purchased a Java development tool and sent two of our programmers to a three-week training course."

Vince added, "I developed a domain model class diagram and checked it against the current database schema. Most of the information needed by the new system is already there, although we'll need to add some new attributes. But now that we're looking at design and implementation, I'm concerned that we may be handicapping our new system with an outdated database management system."

Sharon added, "We decided to use this project as a pilot for OO development and implementation to speed up development. But I'm not sure that we'll actually achieve that if we use the existing DB2 database."

Bill said, "I understand your concerns about interfacing OO programs with a relational database. It sounds like trying to mix oil and water, but it's really not that difficult. We just hired Anna Jorgensen, a database developer who has experience writing Java programs that interface with relational databases. I had her look over the class diagrams and use cases for the new system, and she assures me that the interfaces to DB2 will be straightforward and simple. I can assign her to your project for a few months if you need the help."

Vince responded, "There's no question that an interface can be written, but it may not be as easy as Anna thinks. There are also problems with basic elements of an OO program such as inheritance and class methods. Those things simply can't be represented in a relational database. That'll force us to make some ugly compromises when designing and implementing our OO code. I'm afraid that it'll lengthen our design and implementation activities and make future system upgrades much more difficult."

"I've done some research, and there are quite a few commercial OO data packages available," said Sharon. "None of them has the track record of DB2, but then the technology is fairly new. An OO database management system would be the best fit with Java, and it would open the door to other new technologies."

Vince added, "It would also shorten the time we need to complete design, since an OO database is directly based on the class diagram."

Sharon continued, "I think that this project presents a good opportunity for us to make the leap to the next generation of database software."

Bill was taken aback by the suggestion but quickly replied, "Are you asking me to support two redundant databases based on two completely different database technologies? Management is already breathing down my neck about my budget. I've managed to save some money by switching to cheaper server hardware, but it's only a marginal improvement. Supporting another database management system will be a major effort. And we'd need new hardware to isolate the new DBMS from our existing database. I can't risk having a buggy new piece of software crash our operational databases. I'd also need to train my people to bring them up to speed on the new software. And how will we get data back and forth between the two databases?"

Sharon let the air clear for a bit before replying. "There's no question that it'll be a major undertaking. I'm not trying to downplay that fact or stretch your people and equipment to the breaking point. But there comes a time when we need to move on to newer technologies, and I think that time has arrived. I've already discussed the idea with Maria, and she thinks it deserves serious consideration."

Vince added, "I can do the database design either way. But we won't be building a base for the future if we use a relational database. I could design it to interface with indexed files on an old IBM mainframe if I had to. But why would we want to go backward instead of forward?"

Overview

Databases and database management systems are important components of a modern information system. Databases provide a common repository for data so that it can be shared by the entire organization. Database management systems provide designers, programmers, and end users with sophisticated capabilities to store, retrieve, and manage data. Sharing and managing the vast amounts of data needed by a modern organization simply would not be possible without a database management system.

In Chapter 5, you learned to construct a domain model class diagram, which is a conceptual model of the information manipulated and stored by an information system. To design and build the system, developers must transform conceptual models into more detailed design models. In Chapter 8, you created detailed design models based on use case diagrams, use case descriptions and activity diagrams, domain model class diagrams, system sequence diagrams, and statechart diagrams. In this chapter we'll transform the domain model class diagram into a detailed database model and implement that model using a database management system.

The process of developing a database model depends on the type of database management software that will be used to implement the system. This chapter will describe the design of relational and OO data models and their implementation using database management systems. We will use examples from Rocky Mountain Outfitters to show how requirements models are used in database design.

DATABASES AND DATABASE MANAGEMENT SYSTEMS

database (DB)
an integrated collection of stored data that is centrally managed and controlled

A *database (DB)* is an integrated collection of stored data that is centrally managed and controlled. A database typically stores information about dozens or hundreds of classes. The information stored includes class attributes (for example, names, prices, and account balances) as well as associations among the classes (for example, which orders belong to which customers). A database also stores descriptive information about data such as attribute names, restrictions on allowed values, and access controls to sensitive data items.

database management system (DBMS)
system software that manages and controls access to a database

A database is managed and controlled by a *database management system (DBMS)*. A DBMS is a system software component that is generally purchased and installed separately from other system software components (for example, operating systems). Examples of modern database management systems include Microsoft Access, Oracle, DB2, ObjectStore, and GemStone.

DBMS COMPONENTS

physical data store
the storage area used by a database management system to store the raw bits and bytes of a database

schema
a description of the structure, content, and access controls of a physical data store or database

Figure 10-1 illustrates the components of a typical database and its interaction with a DBMS, application programs, users, and administrators. The database consists of two related information stores: the physical data store and the schema. The *physical data store* contains the raw bits and bytes of data that are created and used by the information system. The *schema* contains descriptive information about the data stored in the physical data store, including the following:

- Access and content controls, including allowable values for specific data elements, value dependencies among multiple data elements, and lists of users allowed to read or update data element contents
- Associations among data attributes and groups of data attributes (for example, a pointer from a set of customer data attributes to orders made by that customer)
- Details of physical data store organization, including type and length of data elements, the locations of data elements, indexing of key data elements, and sorting of related groups of data attributes

A DBMS has four key components: an application program interface (API), a query interface, an administrative interface, and an underlying set of data access programs and subroutines. Application programs, users, and administrators never access the physical data store directly. Instead, they tell an appropriate DBMS interface what data they need to read or write, using names defined in the schema. The DBMS accesses the schema to verify that the requested data exist and that the requesting user has appropriate access privileges. If the request is valid, the DBMS extracts information about the physical

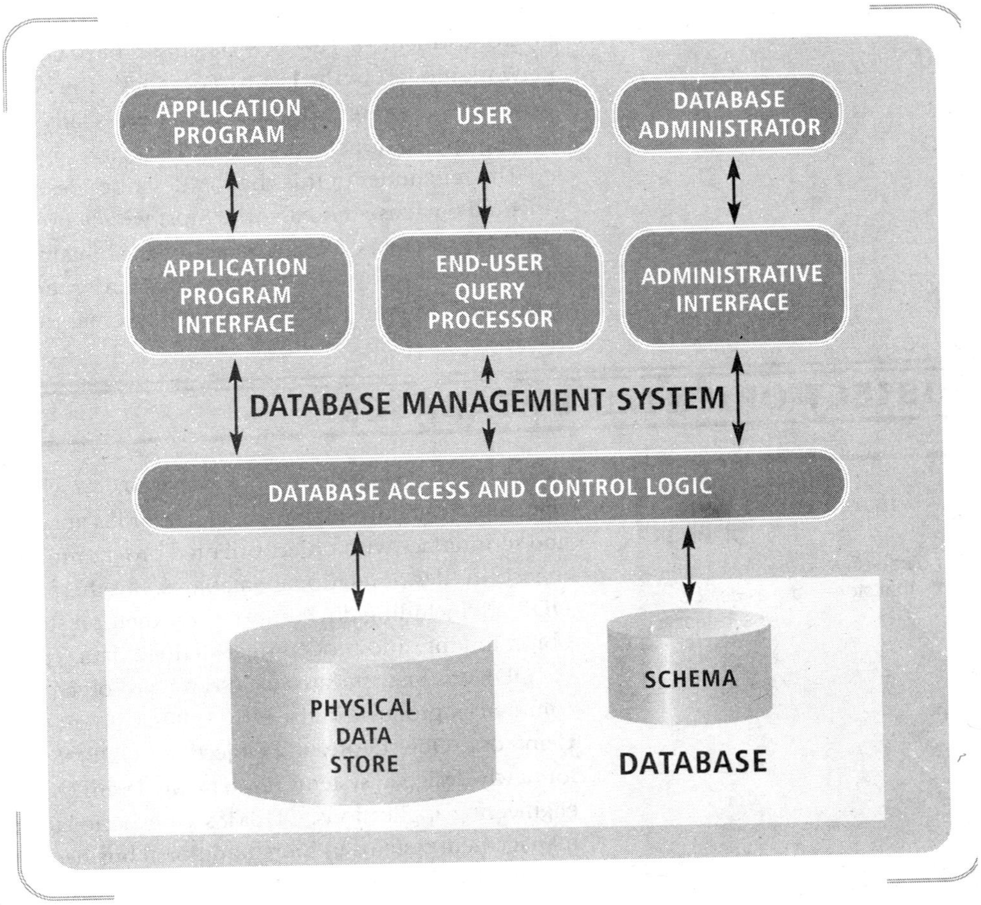

FIGURE 10-1

The components of a database and database management system and their interaction with application programs, users, and database administrators

organization of the requested data from the schema and uses that information to access the physical data store on behalf of the requesting program or user.

Databases and database management systems provide several important data access and management capabilities, including the following:

- Simultaneous access by many users and application programs
- Access to data without writing application programs (that is, via a query language)
- Application of uniform and consistent access and content controls

For these and other reasons, databases and DBMSs are widely used in modern information systems.

DATABASE MODELS

DBMSs have evolved through a number of technology stages since their introduction in the 1960s. The most significant change has been the type of model used to represent and access the content of the physical data store. Four such model types have been widely used:

- Hierarchical
- Network
- Relational
- Object-oriented

The hierarchical model was developed in the 1960s. It represented data using sets of records organized into a hierarchy. The network model also grouped data elements into sets of records, but it allowed those records to be organized into more flexible network structures. Few new databases have been developed with the hierarchical and network models in the last two decades. However, a few older hierarchical and network databases are still in use today, especially in large-scale batch transaction processing applications.

The remainder of this chapter describes design issues for the relational and object-oriented database models—the most widely used models for both existing and newly developed systems. Design issues for the hierarchical and network models are not described, since few students of information systems are likely to encounter DBMSs based on these models by the time they enter the workforce.

OBJECT-ORIENTED DATABASES

object database management system (ODBMS)
a database management system that stores data as objects or class instances

Object database management systems (ODBMSs) are a direct extension of the OO design and programming paradigm. ODBMSs are designed specifically to store objects and to interface with object-oriented programming languages. It is possible to store objects in files or relational databases. But there are many advantages to using an ODBMS, including direct support for method storage, inheritance, nested objects, object linking, and programmer-defined data types.

ODBMSs first appeared as research prototypes in the 1980s and later as fledgling commercial products in the early 1990s. Current commercial ODBMSs include GemStone, ObjectStore, and Objectivity. ODBMSs are the database technology of choice for newly designed systems implemented with OO tools, especially for scientific and engineering applications. ODBMSs are expected to gradually supplant relational database management systems in more traditional business applications over the next decade.

Object Definition Language (ODL)
a standard object database description language promulgated by the Object Database Management Group

Java Data Objects (JDO)
A Java-specific object database standard based on standards developed by the Object Database Management Group

Because ODBMSs are relatively new, there are few widely accepted standards for specifying an object database schema. In the late 1990s and early 2000s, the Object Database Management Group (ODMG) developed and refined a standard called the *Object Definition Language (ODL)*, a language for describing the structure and content of an object database. ODMG standards became the basis of the *Java Data Objects (JDO)* standard, which was adopted in 2003. ODMG standards are also the basis of some interfaces between ODBMSs and the C++ and SmallTalk programming languages. The schema examples in the sections that follow use ODL.

DESIGNING OBJECT DATABASES

To create an object database schema from a class diagram, follow these steps:

[1] Determine which classes require persistent storage.
[2] Represent persistent classes.
[3] Represent associations among persistent classes.
[4] Choose appropriate data types and value restrictions (if necessary) for each field.

Each of these steps is discussed in detail in the following sections.

transient class
a class that doesn't need to store object attribute values between instantiations or method invocations

REPRESENTING CLASSES

Classes can be classified into two broad types for purposes of data management. Objects of a *transient class* exist only during the lifetime of a program or process. Several transient object types were defined in Chapter 8, including boundary, control, and data access classes. Transient objects are created each time a program or process is executed and then destroyed when a program or process terminates.

persistent class
a class that must store one or more object attribute values between instantiations or method invocations

An object of a *persistent class* is not destroyed when the program or process that creates it ceases execution. Instead, the object continues to exist independently of any program or process. Domain or business classes from the domain model class diagram are usually persistent. Storing the object state to persistent memory (such as a magnetic disk or optical disc) ensures that the object exists between process executions. Objects can be persistently stored within a file or database management system.

An object database schema includes a definition for each class that requires persistent storage. ODL class definitions derive from the corresponding UML domain model class diagram. Thus, classes already defined in UML are simply reused for the database schema definition.

For example, an ODL description of the RMO Customer class in Figure 10-2 is:

```
class Customer {
  attribute string accountNo
  attribute string name
  attribute string billingAddress
  attribute string shippingAddress
  attribute string dayTelephoneNumber
  attribute string nightTelephoneNumber
}
```

A similar ODL class definition would be created for each class shown in Figure 10-2. After defining each class, the analyst must define associations among classes.

REPRESENTING ASSOCIATIONS

object identifier
a physical storage address or a reference that can be converted to a physical storage address at run time

An ODBMS automatically assigns a unique object identifier to each stored object. An *object identifier* may be a physical storage address or a reference that can be converted to a physical storage address at run time.

An ODBMS represents associations by storing the identifier of one object within related objects. Object identifiers provide navigation visibility among objects, as described in Chapter 8. For example, consider a one-to-one association between the classes Employee and Workstation, as shown in Figure 10-3. Each Employee object has an attribute called *computer* that contains the object identifier of the Workstation object assigned to that employee. Each Workstation object has a matching attribute called *user* that contains the object identifier of the Employee who uses that workstation.

navigation
the process of accessing an object by extracting its object identifier from another (related) object

An ODBMS uses attributes containing object identifiers to find objects that are associated with other objects. The process of extracting an object identifier from one object and using it to access another object is sometimes called *navigation*. For example, consider the following query posed by a user:

List the manufacturer of the workstation assigned to employee Joe Smith.

An ODBMS query processor can find the requested Employee object by searching all Employee objects for the name attribute Joe Smith. The query processor can then find Joe Smith's Workstation object by using the object identifier stored in the *computer* attribute. The query processor can also answer the opposite query (list the employee name assigned to a specific workstation) by using the object identifier stored in *user*. A matched pair of attributes enables navigation in both directions.

Attributes that represent associations are not usually specified directly by an object database schema designer. Instead, designers specify them indirectly by

FIGURE 10-2
The RMO domain model class diagram

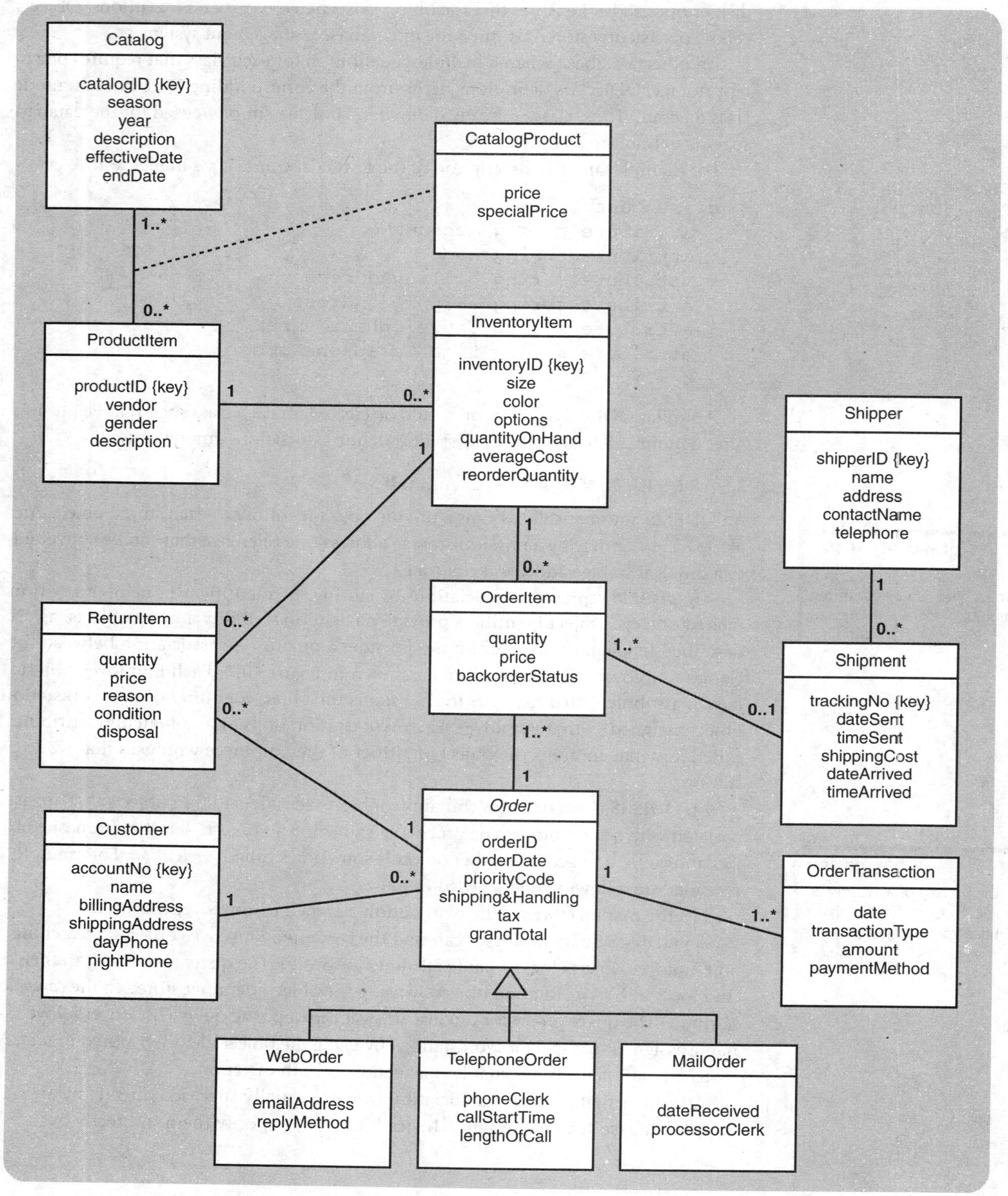

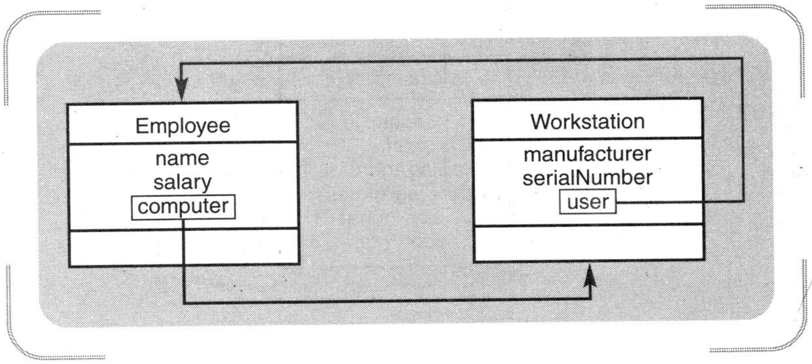

FIGURE 10-3
A one-to-many association represented with attributes (shown in color) containing object identifiers

declaring associations between objects. For example, consider the following ODL class declarations:

```
class Employee {
  attribute string name
  attribute integer salary
  relationship Workstation Uses
   inverse Workstation::AssignedTo
}
class Workstation {
  attribute string manufacturer
  attribute string serialNumber
  relationship Employee AssignedTo
   inverse Employee::Uses
}
```

The ODL keyword *relationship* declares an association between one class and another. The class Employee has an association called Uses with the class Workstation. The class Workstation has a matching association called AssignedTo with the class Employee. Each association includes a declaration of the matching association in the other class using the keyword *inverse*, which tells the ODBMS that the two relationships are actually mirror images of one another.

Declaring an association as shown here, instead of creating an attribute containing an object identifier, has two advantages:

- The ODBMS assumes responsibility for determining how to implement the connection among objects. In essence, the schema designer has declared an attribute of type *relationship* and left it up to the ODBMS to determine how to represent that attribute.
- The ODBMS assumes responsibility for maintaining referential integrity. For example, deleting a workstation will cause the Uses link of the related Employee object to be set to NULL or undefined.

The ODBMS automatically creates attributes containing object identifiers to implement declared associations. But the user and programmer are shielded from all details of how those identifiers are actually implemented and manipulated.

One-to-Many Associations Figure 10-4 shows the one-to-many association between the RMO classes Customer and Order. A Customer can make many different Orders, but a single Order can be made by only one Customer. A single object identifier represents the association of an Order to a Customer. Multiple object identifiers represent the association between one Customer and many different Orders, as shown in Figure 10-5.

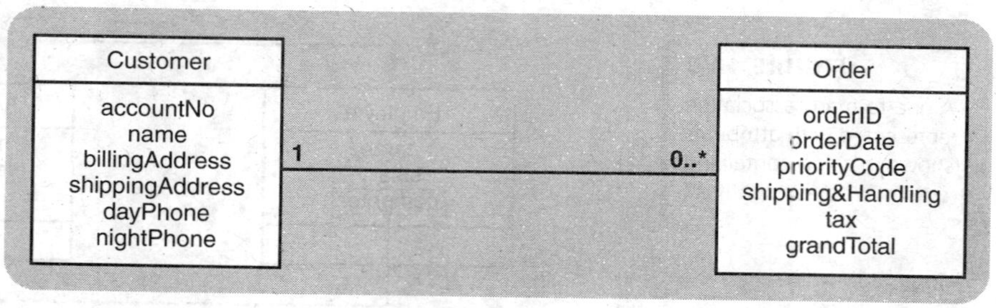

FIGURE 10-4 The one-to-many association between Customer and Order

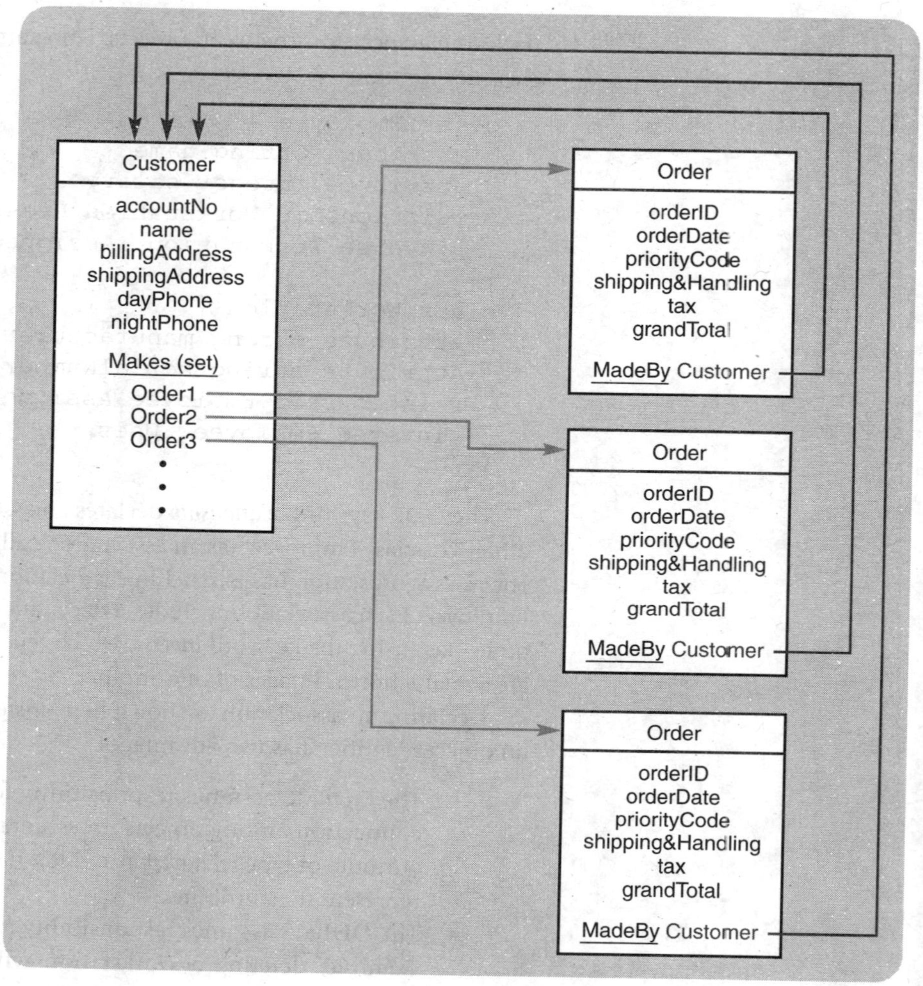

FIGURE 10-5 A one-to-many association represented with attributes containing object identifiers

Partial ODL class declarations for the classes Customer and Order are as follows:

```
class Customer {
  attribute string accountNo
  attribute string name
  attribute string billingAddress
  attribute string shippingAddress
  attribute string dayPhone
  attribute string nightPhone
  relationship set<Order> Makes
    inverse Order::MadeBy
}
```

```
class Order {
  attribute string orderID
  attribute string orderDate
  attribute string priorityCode
  attribute real shipping&Handling
  attribute real tax
  attribute real grandTotal
  relationship Order MadeBy
   inverse Customer::Makes
}
```

The association Makes connects a single Customer object to a set of Order objects. By declaring the association as a set, you instruct the ODBMS to allocate as many Order object identifier attributes to each Customer object as are needed to represent association instances. The ODBMS dynamically adds or deletes object identifier attributes to the set as instances of the association are created or deleted.

multivalued attribute
an attribute that contains zero or more instances of the same data type

Many-to-Many Associations How a many-to-many association is represented depends on whether the association has any attributes. Many-to-many associations without attributes are represented as a set of object attributes in both associated classes. Both classes have a *multivalued attribute* containing object pointers to related objects of the other class. For example, the many-to-many association between Employee and Project shown in Figure 10-6 is represented as follows:

```
class Employee {
  attribute string name
  attribute string salary
  relationship set<Project> WorksOn
   inverse Project::Assigned
}
class Project {
  attribute string projectID
  attribute string description
  attribute string startDate
  attribute string endDate
  relationship set<Employee> Assigned
   inverse Employee::WorksOn
}
```

Representing a many-to-many association with attributes requires a more complex approach. The RMO class diagram has a many-to-many association between Catalog and ProductItem with an association class named CatalogProduct (see Figure 10-2). Recall from Chapter 5 that an *association class* is a class that stores the attributes of a many-to-many association.

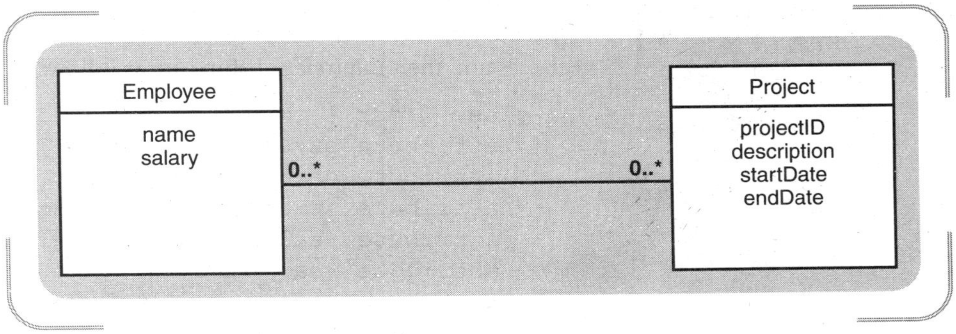

FIGURE 10-6
A many-to-many association between Employee and Project

To represent a many-to-many association with an association class, we must reorganize the association as shown in Figure 10-7. The many-to-many association between Catalog and ProductItem has been decomposed into a pair of one-to-many associations between the original classes and the association class. The ODL schema descriptions are as follows:

```
class Catalog {
  attribute string catalogID
  attribute string season
  attribute integer year
  attribute string description
  attribute string effectiveDate
  attribute string endDate
  relationship set<CatalogProduct> Contains1
   inverse CatalogProduct::AppearsIn1
}
class ProductItem {
  attribute string productID
  attribute string vendor
  attribute string gender
  attribute string description
  relationship set<CatalogProduct> AppearsIn2
   inverse CatalogProduct::Contains2
}
class CatalogProduct {
  attribute real price
  attribute real specialPrice
  relationship Catalog AppearsIn1
  inverse Catalog::Contains1
  relationship ProductItem AppearsIn2
   inverse ProductItem::Contains2
}
```

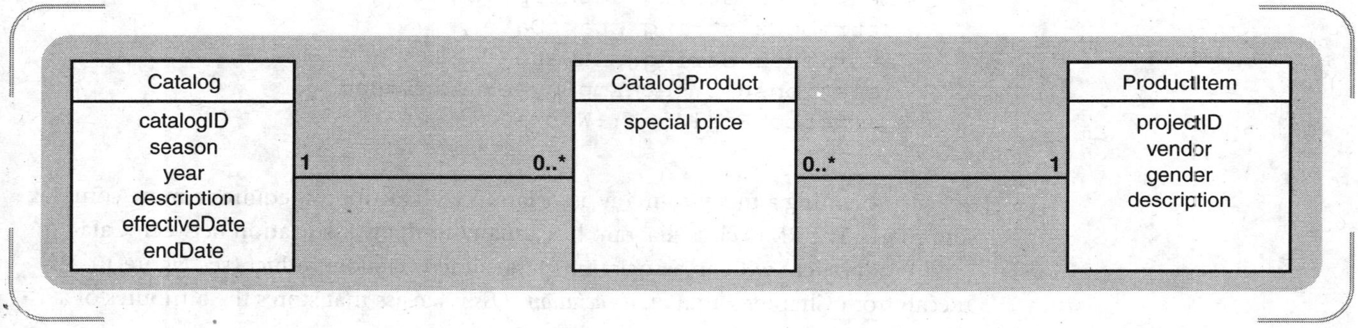

FIGURE 10-7
A many-to-many association represented with two one-to-many associations

Generalization Associations Figure 10-8 shows the order generalization hierarchy from the RMO class diagram. WebOrder, TelephoneOrder, and MailOrder are more specific versions of the class Order. The ODL class definitions that represent these classes and their interrelationships are as follows:

```
class Order {
  attribute string orderID
  attribute string orderDate
  attribute string priorityCode
  attribute real shipping&Handling
  attribute real tax
  attribute real grandTotal
}
```

```
class WebOrder extends Order {
  attribute string emailAddress
  attribute string replyMethod
}
class TelephoneOrder extends Order {
  attribute string phoneClerk
  attribute string callStartTime
  attribute integer lengthOfCall
}
class MailOrder extends Order {
  attribute string dateReceived
  attribute string processorClerk
}
```

FIGURE 10-8
A generalization hierarchy within the RMO class diagram

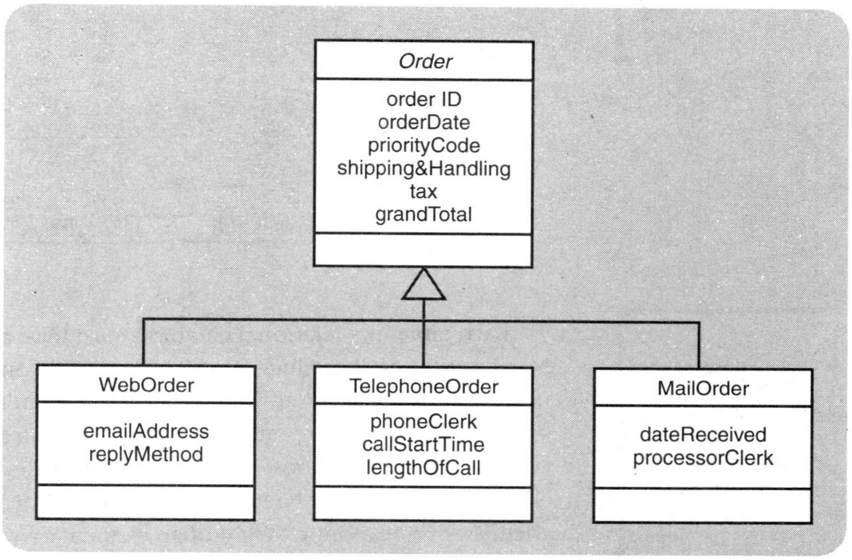

The keyword *extends* indicates that WebOrder, TelephoneOrder, and MailOrder derive from Order. When stored in an object database, objects of the three derived classes will inherit all of the attributes and relationships defined for the Order class.

RELATIONAL DATABASES

relational database management system (RDBMS)
a database management system that stores data in tables

table
a two-dimensional data structure containing rows and columns; also called a *relation*

row
the portion of a table containing data that describes one class, association, or object; also called *tuple* or *record*

The relational database model was first developed in the early 1970s. Relational databases were slow to be adopted because of the difficulties inherent in converting systems implemented with hierarchical and network DBMSs and because of the amount of computing resources required to implement them successfully. As with other theoretical advances in computer science, it took many years for the cost-performance characteristics of data storage and processing hardware to catch up to the new theory. Relational DBMSs now account for the vast majority of DBMSs currently in use.

A *relational database management system (RDBMS)* is a DBMS that organizes stored data into structures called *tables*, or *relations*. Relational database tables are similar to conventional tables—that is, they are two-dimensional data structures of columns and rows. However, relational database terminology is somewhat different from conventional table and file terminology. A single row of a table is called a *row*, *tuple*, or *record*, and a column of a table is called an *attribute* or *field*. A single cell in a table is called an *attribute value*, *field value*, or *data element*.

attribute
a column of a relational database table; also called a *field*

attribute value
the data value stored in a single cell of a relational database table; also called a *field value* or *data element*

Figure 10-9 shows the content of a table as displayed by the Microsoft Access relational DBMS. Note that the first row of the table contains a list of attribute names (column headings) and that the remaining rows contain a collection of attribute values, each of which describes a specific product. Each row contains the same attributes in the same order.

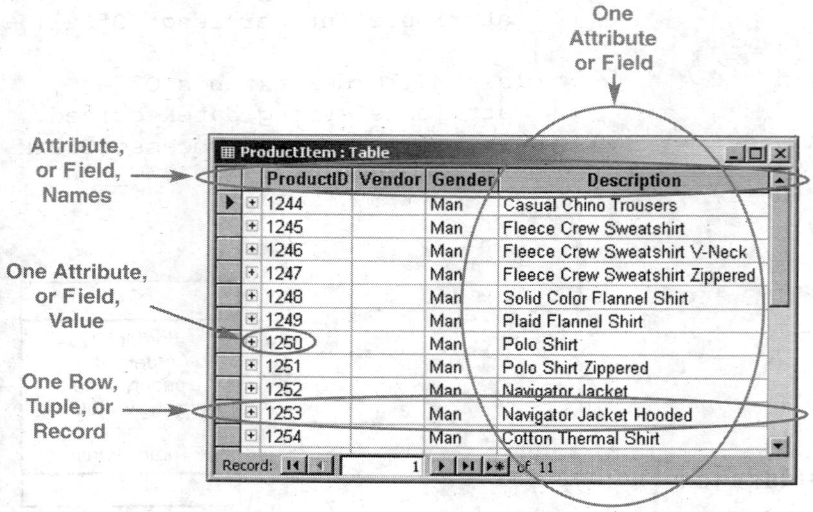

ProductID	Vendor	Gender	Description
1244		Man	Casual Chino Trousers
1245		Man	Fleece Crew Sweatshirt
1246		Man	Fleece Crew Sweatshirt V-Neck
1247		Man	Fleece Crew Sweatshirt Zippered
1248		Man	Solid Color Flannel Shirt
1249		Man	Plaid Flannel Shirt
1250		Man	Polo Shirt
1251		Man	Polo Shirt Zippered
1252		Man	Navigator Jacket
1253		Man	Navigator Jacket Hooded
1254		Man	Cotton Thermal Shirt

FIGURE 10-9
A partial display of a relational database table

key
an attribute that contains a value that is unique within each row of a relational database table

primary key
a key used to uniquely identify a row of a relational database table

Each table in a relational database must have a unique *key*. A key is an attribute or set of attributes, the values of which occur only once in all the rows of the table. If only one attribute (or set of attributes) is unique, then that key is also called the table's *primary key*. If there are multiple unique attributes (or sets of attributes), then the data base designer must choose one of the possible keys as the primary key.

Key attributes may be natural or invented. An example of a natural key attribute in chemistry is the atomic weight of an element in a table containing descriptive data about elements. Unfortunately, in business, few natural key attributes are useful for information processing, so most key attributes in a relational database are invented. Your wallet or purse probably contains many examples of invented keys, including your Social Security number, driver's license number, credit card numbers, and ATM card number. Some invented keys are externally assigned (for example, a shipping company's tracking number) and some are internally assigned (for example, ProductID in Figure 10-9). Invented keys are guaranteed to be unique because unique values are assigned by a user, application program, or the DBMS as new rows are added to the table.

Keys are a critical element of relational database design because they are the basis for representing relationships among tables. Keys are the "glue" that binds rows of one table to rows of another table—in other words, keys relate tables to each other. For example, consider the class diagram fragment from the Rocky Mountain Outfitters example shown in Figure 10-10 and the tables shown in Figure 10-11. The class diagram fragment shows an optional one-to-many association between the classes ProductItem and InventoryItem. The upper table in Figure 10-11 contains data representing the ProductItem class. The lower table contains data representing the InventoryItem class.

foreign key
an attribute value stored in one relational database table that also exists as a primary key value in another relational database table

The association between the ProductItem and InventoryItem classes is represented by a common attribute value within their respective tables. The ProductID attribute (the primary key of the ProductItem table) is also stored within the InventoryItem table, where it is called a foreign key. A *foreign key* is an attribute that duplicates the primary key of a different (or foreign) table. In Figure 10-10, the existence of the value 1244 as a foreign key within the InventoryItem table indicates that the values of

FIGURE 10-10
A portion of the RMO class diagram

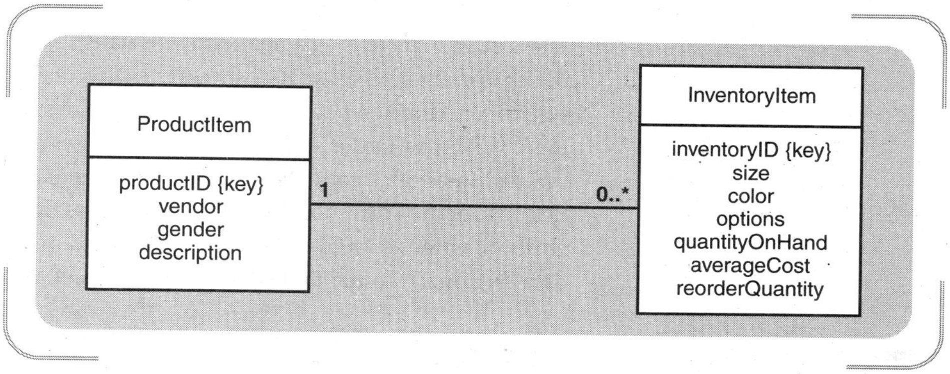

FIGURE 10-11
An association between data in two tables; the foreign key ProductID in the InventoryItem table refers to the primary key ProductID in the ProductItem table

ProductItem : Table

ProductID	Vendor	Gender	Description
1244		Man	Casual Chino Trousers
1245		Man	Fleece Crew Sweatshirt
1246		Man	Fleece Crew Sweatshirt V-Neck
1247		Man	Fleece Crew Sweatshirt Zippered
1248		Man	Solid Color Flannel Shirt
1249		Man	Plaid Flannel Shirt
1250		Man	Polo Shirt
1251		Man	Polo Shirt Zippered
1252		Man	Navigator Jacket
1253		Man	Navigator Jacket Hooded
1254		Man	Cotton Thermal Shirt

Record: 1 of 11

InventoryItem : Table

InventoryID	ProductID	Size	Color	Options	QuantityOnHand	Average Cost	RecorderQuantity
86779	1244	30/30	Khaki		45	$12.75	100
86780	1244	30/30	Slate		10	$12.75	100
86781	1244	30/30	LightTan		17	$12.75	100
86782	1244	30/31	Khaki		22	$12.75	100
86783	1244	30/31	Slate		6	$12.75	100
86784	1244	30/31	LightTan		31	$12.75	100
86785	1244	30/32	Khaki		120	$12.75	100
86786	1244	30/32	Slate		28	$12.75	100
86787	1244	30/32	LightTan		21	$12.75	100
86788	1244	30/33	Khaki		7	$12.75	100
86789	1244	30/33	Slate		41	$12.75	100
86790	1244	30/34	LightTan		35	$12.75	50

Record: 1 of 12

Vendor, Gender, and Description in the first row of the ProductItem table also describe inventory items 86779 through 86790.

DESIGNING RELATIONAL DATABASES

To create a relational database schema from a class diagram, follow these steps:

[1] Create a table for each class.
[2] Choose a primary key for each table (invent one, if necessary).
[3] Add foreign keys to represent one-to-many associations.
[4] Create new tables to represent many-to-many associations.
[5] Represent classification hierarchies.
[6] Define referential integrity constraints.
[7] Evaluate schema quality and make necessary improvements.
[8] Choose appropriate data types and value restrictions (if necessary) for each field.

The following subsections discuss each of these steps in detail

REPRESENTING CLASSES

The first step in creating a relational DB schema is to create a table for each class on the class diagram. Figure 10-2 shows the class diagram for the RMO customer support system with fourteen classes, three of which are specialized classes of Order. For the moment we'll treat Order and its specialized classes as if they were a single class containing the attributes of all four classes. The attributes of each table will be the same as those defined for the corresponding class in the class diagram. To avoid confusion, table and attribute names should match the names used in the class diagram and in the project data dictionary. Initial table definitions for the RMO case are shown in Figure 10-12.

TABLE	ATTRIBUTES
Catalog	Season, Year, Description, EffectiveDate, EndDate
CatalogProduct	Price, SpecialPrice
Customer	AccountNo, Name, BillingAddress, ShippingAddress, DayTelephoneNumber, NightTelephoneNumber
InventoryItem	InventoryID, Size, Color, Options, QuantityOnHand, AverageCost, ReorderQuantity
Order	OrderID, OrderDate, PriorityCode, ShippingAndHandling, Tax, GrandTotal, EmailAddress, ReplyMethod, PhoneClerk, CallStartTime, LengthOfCall, DateReceived, ProcessorClerk
OrderItem	Quantity, Price, BackorderStatus
OrderTransaction	Date, TransactionType, Amount, PaymentMethod
ProductItem	ProductID, Vendor, Gender, Description
ReturnItem	Quantity, Price, Reason, Condition, Disposal
Shipment	TrackingNo, DateSent, TimeSent, ShippingCost, DateArrived, TimeArrived
Shipper	ShipperID, Name, Address, ContactName, Telephone

FIGURE 10-12
An initial set of tables representing RMO classes

After creating tables for each class, the designer selects a primary key for each table. If a table already has an attribute or set of attributes that are guaranteed to be unique, then the designer can choose that attribute or set of attributes as the primary key (for example, TrackingNo in the Shipment table). If the table contains no primary keys, then the designer must invent a new key attribute. Any name can be chosen for an invented key field, but the name should indicate that the attribute contains unique values. Typical names include Code, Number, and ID, possibly combined with the table name (for example, ProductCode and OrderID). Figure 10-13 shows the class tables and identifies the primary key of each.

REPRESENTING ASSOCIATIONS

Associations are represented within a relational database by foreign keys. Which foreign keys should be placed in which tables depends on the type of association being represented. The RMO class diagram in Figure 10-2 contains nine one-to-many associations. There is a many-to-many association between Catalog and ProductItem, which is represented by two one-to-many associations and the association class CatalogProduct. The rules for representing one-to-many and many-to-many associations are as follows:

- **One-to-many association.** Add the primary key attribute(s) of the "one" class to the table that represents the "many" class.
- **Many-to-many association.** If no association class exists, create a new table to represent the association. If an association class does exist, use its table to represent the association. Use the primary key attribute(s) of the associated classes as the primary key of the table that represents the association.

TABLE	ATTRIBUTES
Catalog	**CatalogID**, Season, Year, Description, EffectiveDate, EndDate
CatalogProduct	**CatalogProductID**, Price, SpecialPrice
Customer	**AccountNo**, Name, BillingAddress, ShippingAddress, DayTelephoneNumber, NightTelephoneNumber
InventoryItem	**InventoryID**, Size, Color, Options, QuantityOnHand, AverageCost, ReorderQuantity
Order	**OrderID**, OrderDate, PriorityCode, ShippingAndHandling, Tax, GrandTotal, EmailAddress, ReplyMethod, PhoneClerk, CallStartTime, LengthOfCall, DateReceived, ProcessorClerk
OrderItem	**OrderItemID**, Quantity, Price, BackorderStatus
OrderTransaction	**OrderTransactionID**, Date, TransactionType, Amount, PaymentMethod
ProductItem	**ProductID**, Vendor, Gender, Description
ReturnItem	**ReturnItemID**, Quantity, Price, Reason, Condition, Disposal
Shipment	**TrackingNo**, DateSent, TimeSent, ShippingCost, DateArrived, TimeArrived
Shipper	**ShipperID**, Name, Address, ContactName, Telephone

FIGURE 10-13
Class tables with primary keys identified in bold

One-to-Many Associations Figure 10-14 shows the results of representing the nine one-to-many associations within the tables from Figure 10-13. Each foreign key represents a single association between the table containing the foreign key and the table that uses that same key as its primary key. For example, the attribute AccountNo was added to the Order table as a foreign key representing the one-to-many association between the Customer and Order classes. The foreign key ShipperID was added to the Shipment table to represent the one-to-many association between Shipper and Shipment. When representing one-to-many associations, foreign keys do not become part of the primary key of the table to which they are added.

TABLE	ATTRIBUTES
Catalog	**CatalogID**, Season, Year, Description, EffectiveDate, EndDate
CatalogProduct	**CatalogProductID**, Price, SpecialPrice
Customer	**AccountNo**, Name, BillingAddress, ShippingAddress, DayTelephoneNumber, NightTelephoneNumber
InventoryItem	**InventoryID**, *ProductID*, Size, Color, Options, QuantityOnHand, AverageCost, ReorderQuantity
Order	**OrderID**, *AccountNo*, OrderDate, PriorityCode, ShippingAndHandling, Tax, GrandTotal, EmailAddress, ReplyMethod, PhoneClerk, CallStartTime, LengthOfCall, DateReceived, ProcessorClerk
OrderItem	**OrderItemID**, *OrderID*, *InventoryID*, *TrackingNo*, Quantity, Price, BackorderStatus
OrderTransaction	**OrderTransactionID**, *OrderID*, Date, TransactionType, Amount, PaymentMethod
ProductItem	**ProductID**, Vendor, Gender, Description
ReturnItem	**ReturnItemID**, *OrderID*, *InventoryID*, Quantity, Price, Reason, Condition, Disposal
Shipment	**TrackingNo**, *ShipperID*, DateSent, TimeSent, ShippingCost, DateArrived, TimeArrived
Shipper	**ShipperID**, Name, Address, ContactName, Telephone

FIGURE 10-14
Represent one-to-many associations by adding foreign key attributes (shown in italics)

Many-to-Many Associations Figure 10-15 expands the table definitions in Figure 10-14 by updating the CatalogProduct table to represent the many-to-many association between Catalog and ProductItem. The primary key of the CatalogProduct becomes the combination of CatalogID and ProductID. The old primary key CatalogProductID is discarded. The two fields that make up the primary key are also foreign keys. CatalogID is a foreign key from the Catalog table, and ProductID is a foreign key from the ProductItem table.

TABLE	ATTRIBUTES
Catalog	**CatalogID**, Season, Year, Description, EffectiveDate, EndDate
CatalogProduct	***CatalogID, ProductID***, Price, SpecialPrice
Customer	**AccountNo**, Name, BillingAddress, ShippingAddress, DayTelephoneNumber, NightTelephoneNumber
InventoryItem	**InventoryID**, *ProductID*, Size, Color, Options, QuantityOnHand, AverageCost, ReorderQuantity
Order	**OrderID**, *AccountNo*, OrderDate, PriorityCode, ShippingAndHandling, Tax, GrandTotal, EmailAddress, ReplyMethod, PhoneClerk, CallStartTime, LengthOfCall, DateReceived, ProcessorClerk
OrderItem	**OrderItemID**, *OrderID, InventoryID, TrackingNo*, Quantity, Price, BackorderStatus
OrderTransaction	**OrderTransactionID**, *OrderID*, Date, TransactionType, Amount, PaymentMethod
ProductItem	**ProductID**, Vendor, Gender, Description
ReturnItem	**ReturnItemID**, *OrderID, InventoryID*, Quantity, Price, Reason, Condition, Disposal
Shipment	**TrackingNo**, *ShipperID*, DateSent, TimeSent, ShippingCost, DateArrived, TimeArrived
Shipper	**ShipperID**, Name, Address, ContactName, Telephone

FIGURE 10-15
The table CatalogProduct is modified to represent the many-to-many association between Catalog and ProductItem

CLASSIFICATION HIERARCHIES

Classification hierarchies such as the association among Order, MailOrder, TelephoneOrder, and WebOrder are a special case in relational database design. Just as a child class inherits the data and methods of a parent class, a table representing a child class inherits some or all of its data from the table representing its parent class. This inheritance can be represented in two ways:

- Combine all the tables into a single table containing the superset of all class attributes but excluding any invented key fields of the child classes.
- Use separate tables to represent the child classes, and use the primary key of the parent class table as the primary key of the child class tables.

Either method is an acceptable approach to representing a classification hierarchy.

Figure 10-15 shows the definition of the Order table under the first method. All of the non-key attributes from MailOrder, TelephoneOrder, and WebOrder are stored in the Order table. For any particular order, some of the attribute values in each row will be NULL. For example, a row representing a telephone order would have no values for the attributes EmailAddress, ReplyMethod, DateReceived, and ProcessorClerk.

Figure 10-16 shows the table definitions for the RMO case using the second method for representing inheritance. The relationship among the three child order types and the parent Order table is represented by the foreign key OrderID in all three child class tables. In each case, the foreign key representing the inheritance association also serves as the primary key of the table representing the child class.

ENFORCING REFERENTIAL INTEGRITY

referential integrity
a consistent relational database state in which every foreign key value also exists as a primary key value

Now that we've described how foreign keys are used to represent relationships, we need to describe how to enforce restrictions on the values of those foreign key fields. The term *referential integrity* describes a consistent state among foreign key and primary key values. Each foreign key is a reference to the primary key of another table. In most cases, a database designer wants to ensure that these references are consistent. That is, foreign key values that appear in one table must also appear as the primary key value of the related table. A referential integrity constraint is a constraint on database content—for example, "an order must be from a customer" and "an order item must be something that we normally stock in inventory."

TABLE	ATTRIBUTES
Catalog	**CatalogID**, Season, Year, Description, EffectiveDate, EndDate
CatalogProduct	***CatalogID, ProductID***, Price, SpecialPrice
Customer	**AccountNo**, Name, BillingAddress, ShippingAddress, DayTelephoneNumber, NightTelephoneNumber
InventoryItem	**InventoryID**, *ProductID*, Size, Color, Options, QuantityOnHand, AverageCost, ReorderQuantity
MailOrder	***OrderID***, DateReceived, ProcessorClerk
Order	**OrderID**, *AccountNo*, OrderDate, PriorityCode, ShippingAndHandling, Tax, GrandTotal
OrderItem	**OrderItemID**, *OrderID*, *InventoryID*, *TrackingNo*, Quantity, Price, BackorderStatus
OrderTransaction	**OrderTransactionID**, *OrderID*, Date, TransactionType, Amount, PaymentMethod
ProductItem	**ProductID**, Vendor, Gender, Description
ReturnItem	**ReturnItemID**, *OrderID*, *InventoryID*, Quantity, Price, Reason, Condition, Disposal
Shipment	**TrackingNo**, *ShipperID*, DateSent, TimeSent, ShippingCost, DateArrived, TimeArrived
Shipper	**ShipperID**, Name, Address, ContactName, Telephone
TelephoneOrder	***OrderID***, PhoneClerk, CallStartTime, LengthOfCall
WebOrder	***OrderID***, EmailAddress, ReplyMethod

FIGURE 10-16
Specialized classes of Order are represented as separate tables with OrderID as both primary and foreign key

The DBMS usually enforces referential integrity automatically once the schema designer identifies primary and foreign keys. Automatic enforcement is implemented as follows:

- When a row containing a foreign key value is created, the DBMS ensures that the value also exists as a primary key value in the related table.
- When a row is deleted, the DBMS ensures that no foreign keys in related tables have the same value as the primary key of the deleted row.
- When a primary key value is changed, the DBMS ensures that no foreign key values in related tables contain the same value.

In the first case, the DBMS will simply reject any new row containing an unknown foreign key value. In the latter two cases, a database designer usually has some control over how referential integrity is enforced. When a row containing a primary key is deleted, the DBMS can be instructed to delete all rows in other tables with corresponding keys. Or, the designer can instruct the DBMS to set all corresponding foreign keys to NULL. A similar choice is available when a primary key value is changed. The DBMS can be instructed to change all corresponding foreign key values to the same value or to set foreign key values to NULL.

EVALUATING SCHEMA QUALITY

After creating a complete set of tables, the designer should check the entire schema for quality. Ironing out any schema problems at this point ensures that none of the later design effort will be wasted. A high-quality data model has the following features:

- Uniqueness of table rows and primary keys
- Lack of redundant data
- Ease of implementing future data model changes

Unfortunately, there are few objective or quantitative measures of database schema quality. Database design is the final step in a modeling process, and as such, it depends on the analyst's experience and judgment. Various formal and informal techniques for schema evaluation are described in the following sections. No one technique is sufficient by itself, but a combination of techniques can ensure a high-quality database design.

Row and Key Uniqueness A fundamental requirement of all relational data models is that primary keys and table rows be unique. Since each table must have a primary key, uniqueness of rows within a table is guaranteed if the primary key is unique. Data access logic within programs usually assumes that keys are unique. For example, a programmer writing a program to view customer records will generally assume that a database query for a specific customer number will return one and only one row (or none if the customer doesn't exist in the database). The program will be designed around this assumption and will probably fail if the DBMS returns multiple rows.

A designer evaluates primary key uniqueness by examining assumptions about key content, the set of possible key values, and the methods by which key values are assigned. Internally invented keys are relatively simple to evaluate in this regard because the system itself creates them. That is, an information system that uses invented keys can guarantee uniqueness by implementing appropriate procedures to assign key values to newly created rows.

It is common for several different programs in an information system to be capable of creating new database rows. Each program needs to be able to assign keys to newly created database rows. However, the importance of key uniqueness requires key-creation procedures to be consistently applied throughout the information system.

Because key creation and management are such pervasive problems in information systems, many relational DBMSs automate key creation. Such systems typically provide a special data type for invented keys (for example, the AutoNumber type in Microsoft Access). The DBMS automatically assigns a key value to newly created rows and communicates that value to the application program for use in subsequent database operations. Embedding this capability in the DBMS frees the IS developer from designing and implementing customized key-creation software modules.

Invented keys that aren't assigned by the information system or DBMS must be given careful scrutiny to ascertain their uniqueness and usefulness over time. For example, employee databases in the United States commonly use Social Security numbers as keys. Since the U.S. government has a strong interest in guaranteeing the uniqueness of Social Security numbers, the assumption that they will always be unique seems safe. But other assumptions concerning their use deserve closer examination. For example, will all employees who are stored in the database have a Social Security number? What if the company opens a manufacturing facility in Europe or South America?

Invented keys assigned by nongovernmental agencies deserve even more careful scrutiny. For example, Federal Express, UPS, and most shipping companies assign a tracking number to each shipment they process. Tracking numbers are guaranteed to be unique at any given point in time, but are they guaranteed to be unique forever (that is, are they ever reused)? Could reuse of a tracking number cause a primary key duplication in the RMO database? And what would happen if two different shippers assigned the same tracking number to two different shipments?

Uncertainties such as these make internally invented keys the safest long-term strategy in most cases. Although internally invented keys may initially entail additional design and development, they prevent one possible source of upheaval once the database is installed. Few changes have the pervasive and disruptive impact of a database key change in a large information system with terabytes of stored data and thousands of application programs and stored queries.

Data Model Flexibility Database flexibility and maintainability were primary goals in the original specification of the relational database model. A database model is considered flexible and maintainable if changes to the database schema can be made with minimal disruption to existing data content and structure. For example, adding a new class to the schema should not require redefining existing tables. Adding a new one-to-many association should only require adding a new foreign key to an existing table. Adding a new many-to-many association should only require adding a single new table to the schema.

Data redundancy plays a key role in determining the flexibility and maintainability of any database or data model. A truism of database processing is that "redundant storage requires redundant maintenance." That is, if data are stored in multiple places, then each of those places must be found and manipulated when data are added, changed, or deleted. Of course, performing any of those actions on multiple data storage locations is more complex (and less efficient) than performing them on a single location. Failure to update, modify, or delete multiple copies of the same information creates a condition called *inconsistency*. By definition, inconsistency cannot occur if every data item is stored only once.

The relational data model deliberately stores key attributes multiple times (that is, redundantly) and non-key attributes only once. Key values are stored once as a primary key and again each time they are used as a foreign key. The relational model requires such redundancy because correspondence between the primary and foreign key is the only way to represent relationships among tables, but using redundant key values adds complexity to processes that manipulate key fields.

Relational DBMSs ensure consistency among primary and foreign keys by enforcing referential integrity constraints, but there are no automatic mechanisms for ensuring consistency among other redundant data items. Thus, the best way to avoid inconsistency in a relational database is to avoid redundancy in non-key fields. Database designers can avoid such redundancy by never introducing it into a schema—but it is all too easy to let redundancy slip in. If data redundancy is somehow introduced into the schema, then it must be identified and removed. The most commonly used process to detect and eliminate redundancy is database normalization.

DATABASE NORMALIZATION

Normalization is a formal technique for evaluating the quality of a relational database schema. It determines whether a database schema contains any of the "wrong" kinds of redundancy and defines specific methods to eliminate them. Normalization is based on a concept called *functional dependency* and on a series of normal forms:

- **First normal form (1NF).** A table is in *first normal form* if it contains no repeating attributes or groups of attributes.
- **Functional dependency.** A *functional dependency* is a one-to-one association between the values of two attributes. The association is formally stated as follows: *Attribute A is functionally dependent on attribute B if for each value of B there is only one corresponding value of A.*
- **Second normal form (2NF).** A table is in *second normal form* if it is in first normal form and if each non-key attribute is functionally dependent on the entire primary key.
- **Third normal form (3NF).** A table is in *third normal form* if it is in second normal form and if no non-key attribute is functionally dependent on any other non-key attribute.

Let's explain these concepts further.

First Normal Form First normal form defines a structural constraint on table rows. Repeating fields such as Dependent in Figure 10-17 are not allowed within any table in a relational database. Repeating groups of fields are also prohibited. In practice, this constraint is not difficult to enforce since relational DBMSs do not allow a designer to define a table containing repeating fields.

normalization
a technique that ensures relational database schema quality by minimizing data redundancy

first normal form (1NF)
a relational database table structure that has no repeating attributes or groups of attributes

functional dependency
a one-to-one correspondence between two attribute values

second normal form (2NF)
a relational database table structure in which every non-key attribute is functionally dependent on the primary key

third normal form (3NF)
a relational database table structure in which no non-key attribute is functionally dependent on any other non-key attribute(s)

SSN	Name	Department	Salary	Dependent1	Dependent2	Dependent3 ...	DependentN
111-22-3333	Mary Smith	Accounting	40,000	John	Alice	Dave	
222-33-4444	Jose Pena	Marketing	50,000				
333-44-5555	Frank Collins	Production	35,000	Jan	Julia		

FIGURE 10-17
An employee table with a repeating attribute

Functional Dependency Functional dependency is a difficult concept to describe and apply. The most precise way to determine whether functional dependency exists is to pick two attributes in a table and insert their names in the italicized portion of the definition shown previously. For example, consider the attributes ProductID and Description in the ProductItem table (see Figure 10-11). ProductID is an internally invented primary key that is guaranteed to be unique within the table. To determine whether Description is functionally dependent on ProductID, substitute Description for attribute A and ProductID for attribute B in the italicized portion of the functional dependency definition:

> Description is functionally dependent on ProductID if for each value of ProductID there is only one corresponding value of Description.

Now ask whether the statement is true for all rows that could possibly exist in the ProductItem table. If the statement is true, then Description is functionally dependent on ProductID. As long as the invented key ProductID is guaranteed to be unique within the ProductItem table, then the preceding statement is true. Therefore, Description is functionally dependent on ProductID.

A less formal way to analyze functional dependency of Description on ProductID is to remember that the ProductItem table represents a specific product sold by RMO. If that product can have only a single description in the database, then Description is functionally dependent on the key of the table that represents products (ProductID). If it is possible for any product to have multiple descriptions, then the attribute Description is not functionally dependent on ProductID.

Second Normal Form To evaluate whether the ProductItem table is in second normal form, we must first determine whether it is in first normal form. Since it contains no repeating attributes, it is in first normal form. Then we must determine whether every non-key attribute is functionally dependent on ProductID (that is, consider each attribute in turn by substituting it for A in the functional dependency definition). If all the non-key attributes are functionally dependent on ProductID, the ProductItem table is in 2NF. If one or more non-key attributes are not functionally dependent on ProductID, then the table is not in 2NF.

Verifying that a table is in 2NF is more complicated when the primary key consists of two or more attributes. For example, consider the RMO table CatalogProduct shown in Figure 10-18. Recall that this table represents a many-to-many association between Catalog and ProductItem. Thus, the table representing this association has a primary key consisting of the primary keys of Catalog (CatalogID) and ProductItem (ProductID). The table also contains two non-key attributes called Price and SpecialPrice.

If this table is in 2NF, then each non-key attribute must be functionally dependent on the *combination* of CatalogID and ProductID. We can verify the first functional dependency by substituting terms in the functional dependency definition and determining the truth or falsity of the resulting statement:

> Price is functionally dependent on the combination of CatalogID and ProductID if for each combination of values for CatalogID and ProductID there is only one corresponding value of Price.

FIGURE 10-18
A simplified RMO CatalogProduct table

CatalogProduct : Table

CatalogID	ProductID	Price	SpecialPrice
23	1244	$15.00	$12.00
23	1245	$15.00	$12.00
23	1246	$15.00	$13.00
23	1247	$15.00	$13.00
23	1248	$14.00	$11.20
23	1249	$14.00	$11.20
23	1252	$21.00	$16.80
23	1253	$21.00	$16.40
23	1254	$24.00	$19.20
23	1257	$19.00	$15.20

Record: 11 of 11

Analyzing the truth of the preceding statement is tricky because you must consider all the possible combinations of key values that might occur in the CatalogProduct file. A simpler way to approach the question is to think about the underlying classes represented in the table. A product can appear in many different catalogs, and multiple catalogs can be current at the same time. If Price can be different in different current catalogs, then the preceding statement is true. If a product's Price is always the same, regardless of the catalog in which it appears, then the preceding statement is false and the table is not in 2NF. The correct answer doesn't depend on any universal sense of truth. Instead, it depends on RMO's normal conventions for setting product prices in different catalogs.

If a non-key attribute is functionally dependent on only part of the primary key, then you must remove the non-key attribute from its present table and place it in another table. For example, consider a modified version of the CatalogProduct table, as shown in the upper half of Figure 10-19. The non-key attribute CatalogIssueDate is

CatalogProduct1NF : Table

CatalogID	ProductID	Price	SpecialPrice	CatalogIssueDate
23	1244	$15.00	$12.00	8/1/2006
23	1245	$15.00	$12.00	8/1/2006
23	1246	$15.00	$13.00	8/1/2006
23	1247	$15.00	$13.00	8/1/2006
23	1248	$14.00	$11.20	8/1/2006
23	1249	$14.00	$11.20	8/1/2006
23	1252	$21.00	$16.80	8/1/2006
23	1253	$21.00	$16.40	8/1/2006
23	1254	$24.00	$19.20	8/1/2006
23	1257	$19.00	$15.20	8/1/2006

Record: 11 of 11

CONVERT TO SECOND NORMAL FORM

FIGURE 10-19
Decomposition of a first normal form table into two second normal form tables

CatalogProduct : Table

CatalogID	ProductID	Price	SpecialPrice
23	1244	$15.00	$12.00
23	1245	$15.00	$12.00
23	1246	$15.00	$13.00
23	1247	$15.00	$13.00
23	1248	$14.00	$11.20
23	1249	$14.00	$11.20
23	1252	$21.00	$16.80
23	1253	$21.00	$16.40
23	1254	$24.00	$19.20
23	1257	$19.00	$15.20

Record: 11 of 11

Catalog : Table

CatalogID	IssueDate
19	11/1/2005
20	2/1/2006
21	4/1/2006
22	6/1/2006
23	8/1/2006
24	9/15/2006

Record: 7

functionally dependent only on CatalogID, not on the combination of CatalogID and ProductID. Thus, the table is not in 2NF.

To correct the problem, you must remove CatalogIssueDate from the CatalogProduct table and place it in a table that uses CatalogID alone as the primary key. Since the Catalog table in Figure 10-16 uses CatalogID alone as its primary key, you should add CatalogIssueDate to that table. If a Catalog table did not already exist, then you would need to create a new table to hold CatalogIssueDate, as shown in Figure 10-19.

Third Normal Form To verify that a table is in 3NF, we must check the functional dependency of each non-key attribute on every other non-key attribute. This can be cumbersome for a large table since the number of pairs that must be checked grows quickly as the number of non-key attributes grows. The number of functional dependencies to be checked is $N \times (N - 1)$, where N is the number of non-key attributes. Note that functional dependency must be checked in both directions (that is, A dependent on B, and B dependent on A).

In practice, you can simplify finding 3NF violations by concentrating on two common types of problems:

- Tables that store attributes describing two or more classes
- Computable attributes

Consider the simple table shown in the upper half of Figure 10-20. Assume that AccountNo is the primary key and that all customers live in the United States. Since there are three non-key attributes, you must check six functional dependencies:

- Is State functionally dependent on StreetAddress?
- Is StreetAddress functionally dependent on State?
- Is ZipCode functionally dependent on StreetAddress?
- Is StreetAddress functionally dependent on ZipCode?
- Is ZipCode functionally dependent on State?
- Is State functionally dependent on ZipCode?

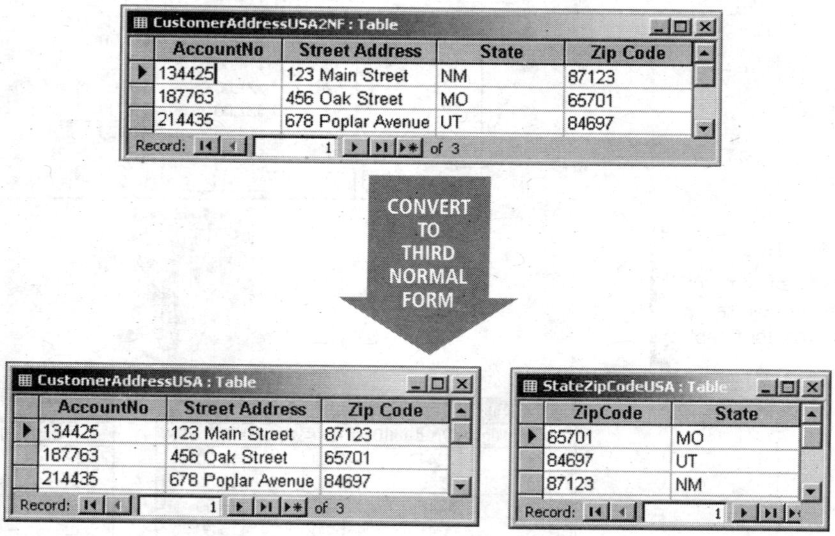

AccountNo	Street Address	State	Zip Code
134425	123 Main Street	NM	87123
187763	456 Oak Street	MO	65701
214435	678 Poplar Avenue	UT	84697

AccountNo	Street Address	Zip Code
134425	123 Main Street	87123
187763	456 Oak Street	65701
214435	678 Poplar Avenue	84697

ZipCode	State
65701	MO
84697	UT
87123	NM

FIGURE 10-20
Converting a second normal form table into two third normal form tables

The answer to the first five statements is no, but the answer to the last is yes. In the United States, all zip codes are wholly contained within a single state. Thus, for each value of ZipCode there is only one corresponding value of State (for example, 87123 is always in New Mexico). Including both fields in this table is a form of redundancy. For example, if the addresses of 100 customers who live in the 87123 zip code are stored in the table, the fact that 87123 is located in New Mexico is redundantly stored 100 times.

In essence, the table combines information about two classes—Customer and Postal Delivery Area. Each class has its own primary key (AccountNo for Customer and ZipCode for Postal Delivery Area) and its own non-key attributes (StreetAddress and ZipCode for Customer, and State for Postal Delivery Area).

Because State is functionally dependent on ZipCode, the table is not in 3NF. To correct this problem, you must remove State from the table. However, the association between states and zip codes must be stored somewhere in the database or the information system can't generate complete mailing labels. The solution is to create a new table containing only ZipCode and State (see Figure 10-20) and remove State from the Customer table. ZipCode is the primary key of the new table, and State is its only non-key attribute. Programs or methods that print or display a complete mailing address must now use the value of ZipCode in the CustomerAddress table to look up the corresponding value of State in the newly created table.

A computable attribute stores a value that can be computed by a formula or algorithm that uses other database attributes as inputs. Common examples of computable attributes include subtotals, totals, and taxes. For example, consider the attribute GrandTotal in the Order table in Figure 10-16 and the formula:

$$GrandTotal = (\Sigma\ Quantity \times Price) + Shipping + Tax$$

Note that all of the inputs to the formula are not stored in the same table (see Figure 10-21). Violations of third normal form involving computable attributes can be localized to a single table or spread across multiple tables. In this case, Shipping and Tax are stored in the Order table, and Quantity and Price are stored in related rows of the OrderItem table. An algorithm that computes GrandTotal for a particular invoice needs to extract all matching rows in the OrderItem table using the OrderID foreign key.

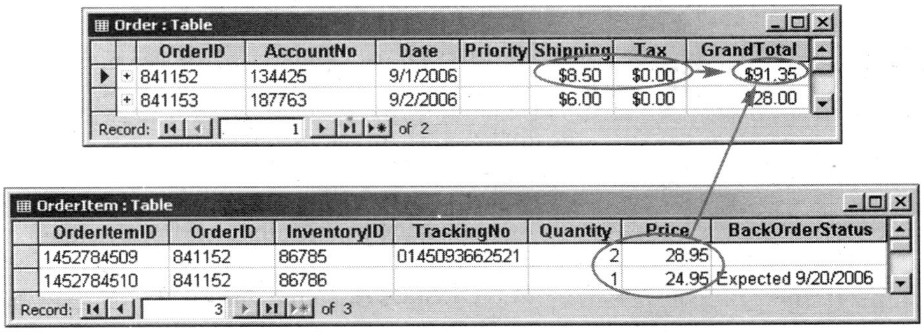

Order : Table

OrderID	AccountNo	Date	Priority	Shipping	Tax	GrandTotal
841152	134425	9/1/2006		$8.50	$0.00	$91.35
841153	187763	9/2/2006		$6.00	$0.00	$28.00

Record: 1 of 2

OrderItem : Table

OrderItemID	OrderID	InventoryID	TrackingNo	Quantity	Price	BackOrderStatus
1452784509	841152	86785	0145093662521	2	28.95	
1452784510	841152	86786		1	24.95	Expected 9/20/2006

Record: 3 of 3

FIGURE 10-21
GrandTotal is computed from attributes in two tables

GrandTotal is functionally dependent on the combination of the other four attributes. Computational dependencies are a form of redundancy because a change to the value of any input variable in the computation (for example, Shipping) also changes the result of the computation (in other words, GrandTotal).

The way to correct this type of 3NF violation is simple: Remove the computed attribute from the database. Eliminating the computed attribute from the database doesn't mean that its value is lost. For example, any program or method that needs GrandTotal can query the OrderItem table for matching values of Quantity and Price, sum the result of multiplying each Quantity and Price, and add Shipping and Tax.

DOMAIN CLASS MODELING AND NORMALIZATION

Domain class modeling and normalization are complementary techniques for relational database design. Note that the tables generated from the RMO domain model class diagram (see Figure 10-16) do not contain any violations of first, second, or third normal form. This is not a chance occurrence. Attributes of a class are functionally dependent on any unique identifier (primary key) of that class. Attributes of a many-to-many association are functionally dependent on unique identifiers of both participating classes. Thus, while creating a class diagram, an analyst must directly or indirectly consider issues of functional dependency when deciding which attributes belong with which classes or associations.

OBJECT-RELATIONAL INTERACTION

OO programming languages and related development tools were first widely employed in the mid- to late 1980s. During this same time period, RDBMSs were mature and widely used, while ODBMSs were in their infancy. Many OO tool developers exploited the existing base of RDBMS tools and knowledge by using an RDBMS to store persistent object states. This made sense both because it was economical (there was one less OO tool to develop) and because many newer OO systems needed to manipulate data stored in existing relational databases. Despite the current availability of commercial ODBMSs, the hybrid DBMS approach is still the most widely employed approach for persistent object storage, probably due to the large number of relational databases still in existence. The dominance of RDBMSs, especially in business information systems, is likely to persist for many more years.

hybrid object-relational DBMS
a relational database management system used to store object attributes and relationships; also called *hybrid DBMS*

There is no widely accepted name to describe object storage using an RDBMS, so we will invent one to use for the remainder of the text: *hybrid object-relational DBMS* (or simply hybrid DBMS). Designing a hybrid database is essentially three design problems in one:

- Designing OO application software, as described in Chapters 7 through 9
- Designing a relational database schema that can store persistent object states, as described earlier in this chapter
- Designing an interface between persistent classes and the RDBMS

The third design problem is particularly complex because the designer must bridge the differences between the object-oriented and relational views of stored data, which include:

- Class methods cannot be directly stored or automatically executed within an RDBMS.
- ODBMSs can represent a wider range of data types than RDBMSs. New classes can be defined to store application-specific data.

Because RDBMSs were developed prior to the OO paradigm, they have no features to represent methods or inheritance. OO programs that access the database must implement methods internally. Inheritance cannot be directly represented in an RDBMS because a classification hierarchy cannot be directly represented.

Although the relational and OO views of stored data have significant differences, they also have significant overlaps. The process of developing a domain model class diagram, as described in Chapter 5, is based on many of the same principles as relational database design, including:

- Grouping of data items into tables or classes based on one-to-one associations among attributes
- Defining one-to-many and many-to-many associations among tables or classes

These similarities were exploited earlier in this chapter as we described the steps to develop a relational database schema based on a domain model class diagram. The remaining steps to developing a complete relational database schema deal with aspects of OO and relational database design that are most different—data access classes and complex data types.

DATA ACCESS CLASSES

In Chapter 9 you learned how to develop an OO design based on three-layer architecture. Under that architecture, data access classes implement the bridge between data stored in program objects and in a relational database.

Figure 10-22 illustrates the interaction among the RMO problem domain class ProductItem, the data access class ProductItemDA, and the relational database. The data access class has methods that add, update, find, and delete fields and rows in the table or tables that represent the class. Data access class methods encapsulate the logic needed to copy values from the problem domain class to the database, and vice versa. Typically, that logic is a combination of program code in a language such as C++ or Java and embedded relational database commands in Structured Query Language (SQL).

FIGURE 10-22
Interaction among a problem domain class, a data access class, and the DBMS

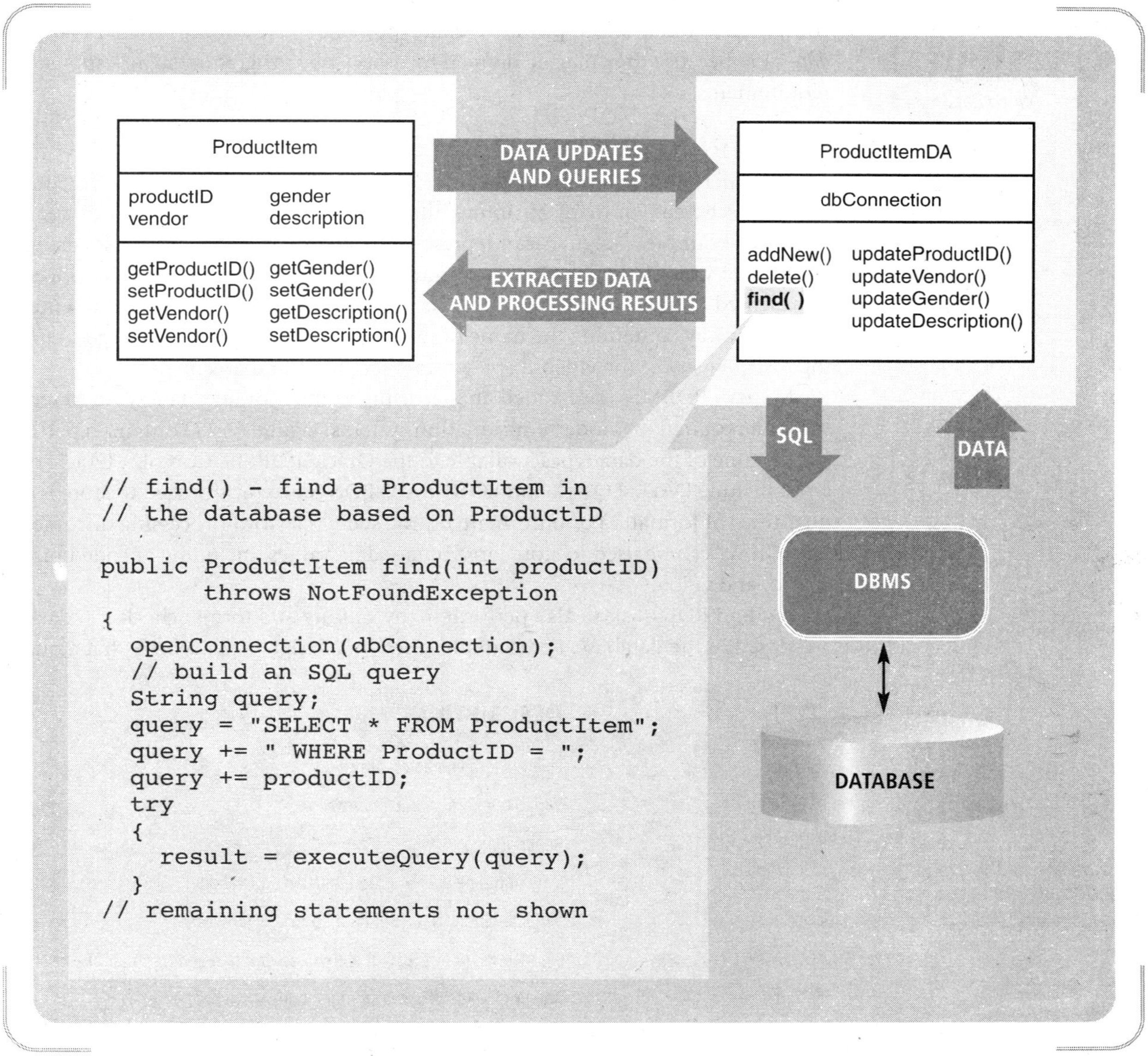


```
// find() - find a ProductItem in
// the database based on ProductID

public ProductItem find(int productID)
      throws NotFoundException
{
  openConnection(dbConnection);
  // build an SQL query
  String query;
  query = "SELECT * FROM ProductItem";
  query += " WHERE ProductID = ";
  query += productID;
  try
  {
    result = executeQuery(query);
  }
// remaining statements not shown
```

The lower-left part of Figure 10-22 shows a fragment of Java code with an embedded SQL statement that implements the find ( ) method of ProductItemDA. Similar code is needed for all other methods in the data access class.

DATA TYPES

data type
the storage format and allowable content of a program variable or database attribute

primitive data type
a storage format directly implemented by computer hardware or a programming language

A *data type* defines the storage format and allowable content of a program variable, class attribute, or relational database attribute or column. *Primitive data types* are data types that are supported directly by computer hardware and programming languages. Examples include memory address (a pointer), Boolean, integer, unsigned integer, short integer (one byte), long integer (multiple bytes), single characters, real numbers (floating-point numbers), and double-precision (double-length) integers and real numbers. In some procedural programming languages (such as C) and most OO languages, programmers can define additional data types using the primitive data types as building blocks.

As information systems have become more complex, the number of required data types has increased to include dates, times, currency (money), audio streams, still images, motion video streams, and uniform resource locators (URLs or Web links). Such data types are sometimes called *complex data types* because they are usually defined as complex combinations of primitive data types. They may also be called *user-defined data types* because they may be defined by users or by programmers in response to user requirements.

complex data type
a data type not directly supported by computer hardware or a programming language; also called *user-defined data type*

RELATIONAL DBMS DATA TYPES

The designer must choose an appropriate data type for each attribute in a relational database schema. For many attributes, the choice of a data type is relatively straightforward. For example, designers can represent customer names and addresses using a set of fixed- or variable-length character arrays. Inventory quantities and item prices can be represented as integers and real numbers, respectively. A color can be represented by a character array containing the name of the color or by a set of three integers representing the intensity of the video-display colors red, blue, and green.

Modern RDBMSs have added an increasing number of new data types to represent the data required by modern information systems. Figure 10-23 contains a partial listing of some of the data types available in the Oracle RDBMS. Complex Oracle data types include DATE, LONG, and LONGRAW. LONG is typically used to store large quantities of formatted or unformatted text (such as a word-processing document). LONGRAW can be used to store large binary data values, including encoded pictures, sound, and video.

Modern RDBMSs can also perform many validity and format checks on data as they are stored in the database. For example, a schema designer can specify that a quantity

TYPE	DESCRIPTION
CHAR	Fixed-length character array
VARCHAR	Variable-length character array
NUMBER	Real number
DATE	Date and time with appropriate checks of validity
LONG	Variable-length character data up to 2 gigabytes
LONGRAW	Binary large object (BLOB) with no assumption about format or content
ROWID	Unique six-byte physical storage address

FIGURE 10-23
A subset of the data types available in the Oracle relational DBMS

on hand cannot be negative, that a U.S. zip code must be five or nine digits long, and that a string containing a URL must begin with *http://*. All application programs that use the database then automatically share the validity and format constraints. Each program is simpler, and the possibility for errors from mismatches in data validation logic is eliminated. Application programs still have to provide program logic to recover from attempts to add "bad" data, but they are freed from actually performing validity checks.

OBJECT DBMS DATA TYPES

ODBMSs typically provide a set of primitive and complex data types comparable to those of an RDBMS. ODBMSs also allow a schema designer to define format and value constraints. But ODBMSs provide an even more powerful way to define useful data types and constraints. A schema designer can define a new data type and its associated constraints as a new class.

A class is a complex user-defined data type that combines the traditional concept of data with methods that manipulate that data. In most OO programming languages, programmers are free to design new data types (classes) that extend those already defined by the programming language. Incompatibility between system requirements and available data types is not an issue, since the designer can design classes specifically to meet the requirements. To the ODBMS, instances of the new data type are simply objects to be stored in the database.

Class methods can perform many of the type- and error-checking functions previously performed by application program code and/or by the DBMS itself. In essence, the programmer constructs a "custom-designed" data type and all of the programming logic required to use it correctly. The DBMS is freed from direct responsibility for managing complex data types and the values stored therein. It indirectly performs validity checking and format conversion by extracting and executing programmer-defined methods stored in the database.

The flexibility to define new data types is one reason that OO tools are so widely employed in nonbusiness information systems. In fields such as engineering, biology, and physics, stored data is considerably more complex than simple strings, numbers, and dates. OO tools enable database designers and programmers to design custom data types that are specific to a problem domain.

Another issue that must be considered during database design is the locations where data are stored and accessed. In today's networked information systems, organizations often use distributed databases.

DISTRIBUTED DATABASES

Rarely does an organization store all of its data in a single database. Instead, organizations typically store data in many different databases, often under the control of many different DBMSs. Reasons for employing a variety of databases and DBMSs include the following:

- Information systems may have been developed at different times using different DBMSs.
- Parts of an organization's data may be owned and managed by different organizational units.
- System performance improves when data are physically close to the applications that use them.

DISTRIBUTED DATABASE ARCHITECTURES

Chapter 7 described various approaches to organizing computers and other information-processing resources in a networked environment. Several architectures for distributing database services are possible, including the following:

- Single database server
- Replicated database servers
- Partitioned database servers
- Federated database servers

Combinations of these architectures are also possible.

SINGLE DATABASE SERVER

Figure 10-24 shows a typical single database server architecture. Clients on one or more LANs share a single database located on a single computer system. The database server may be connected to one of the LANs or directly to the WAN backbone (as shown in the figure). Connection directly to the WAN ensures that no one LAN is overloaded by all of the network traffic to and from the database server.

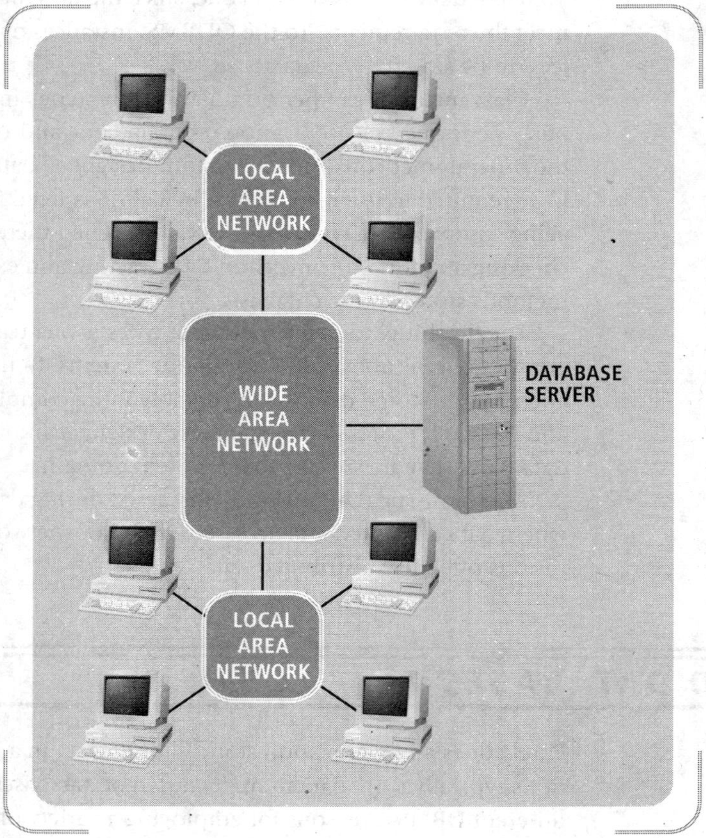

FIGURE 10-24
A single database server architecture

The primary advantage of single database server architecture is its simplicity. There is only one server to manage, and all clients send requests to that server. Disadvantages of the single database server architecture include susceptibility to server failure and possible overload of the network or server. A single server provides no backup capabilities in the event of server failure. All application programs that depend on the server are disabled whenever the server is unavailable (such as during a crash or during hardware maintenance). Thus, single database server architecture is poorly suited to applications that must be available on a 7-day, 24-hour basis.

Performance bottlenecks can occur within a single database server or in the network segment to which the server is attached. As transaction volumes grow, the capabilities of a single database server may be insufficient to respond quickly to all of the service requests it receives. In an attempt to improve performance, a designer may employ a more powerful computer system as the database server. But in an era of multi-terabyte databases, it is not unusual for the size and transaction volume of larger databases to exceed the capabilities of any single computer system. Employing the largest mainframes may also be impractical due to cost, system management, or network performance considerations.

Requests to and responses from a database server may traverse large distances across local and wide area networks. Database transactions must also compete with other types of network traffic (such as voice, video, and Web site access) for available transmission capacity. Thus, delays in accessing a remote database server may result from network congestion or propagation delay from client to server.

One way to reduce network congestion is to increase the capacity of the entire network. But this approach is expensive and often impractical. Another approach specifically geared to improving database access speed is to locate database servers physically close to their clients (for example, on the same LAN segment). This approach minimizes the distance-related delay for requests and responses and removes a large amount of traffic from the WAN.

Moving a database server closer to its clients is a relatively simple matter when all of the clients are located close to one another. But what happens when clients are widely dispersed, as in a multinational corporation? In this case, no single location for the database server can possibly improve database access performance for all clients at the same time. Thus, the "distant" clients must pay a greater performance penalty for database access.

REPLICATED DATABASE SERVERS

Designers can eliminate delay in accessing distant database servers by using a replicated database server architecture (see Figure 10-25). Each server stores a separate copy of the needed data. Clients interact with the database server on their own LAN. Such an architecture eliminates database accesses from the WAN and minimizes propagation delay. Local network and database server capacity can be independently optimized to local needs.

Replicated database servers also make an information system more fault tolerant. Applications can direct access requests to any available server, with preference to the nearest server. When a particular server is unavailable, clients can redirect their requests across the WAN to another available server. Designers can also achieve load balancing by interposing a transaction server between clients and replicated database servers. The transaction server monitors loads on all database servers and automatically directs client requests to the server with the lowest load.

In spite of their advantages, replicated database servers do have some drawbacks. Data inconsistency is a problem whenever multiple database copies are in use. When data are updated on one database copy, clients accessing that same data from another database copy receive an outdated response. To counteract this problem, each database copy must periodically be updated with changes from other database servers. This process is called *database synchronization*.

database synchronization
the process of ensuring consistency between two or more database copies

Designers can implement synchronization by developing customized synchronization programs or by using synchronization utilities built into the DBMS. Custom application programs are seldom employed because they are difficult to develop and because they would need to be modified each time the database schema or number and location of database copies change. DBMS synchronization utilities are generally

FIGURE 10-25

A replicated database server architecture

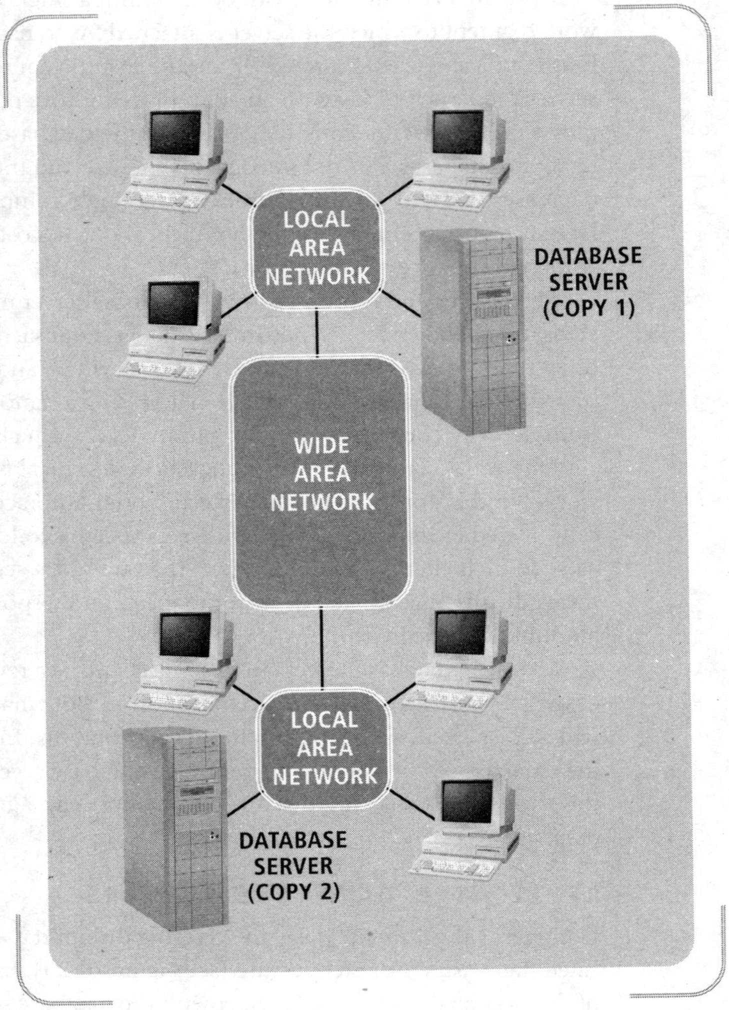

powerful and flexible but also expensive. Incompatibilities among synchronization methods make using DBMSs from different vendors impractical.

The time delay between an update to a database copy and the propagation of that update to other database copies is an important database design decision. During the time between the original update and the update of database copies, application programs that access outdated copies aren't receiving responses that reflect current reality. Designers can address this problem by reducing the synchronization delay. But shorter delays imply more frequent (or possibly continuous) database synchronization. Synchronization then consumes a substantial amount of database server capacity, and a large amount of network capacity among the related database servers must be provided. The proper synchronization strategy is a complex trade-off among cost, hardware and network capacity, and the need of application programs and users for current data.

PARTITIONED DATABASE SERVERS

Designers can minimize the need for database synchronization by partitioning database contents among multiple database servers. Figure 10-26 shows the division of a hypothetical database schema into two partitions. A different group of clients accesses each partition. Figure 10-27 shows a partitioned database server architecture that maintains each partition on a separate database server. Traffic among clients and the database server in each group is restricted to a local area network.

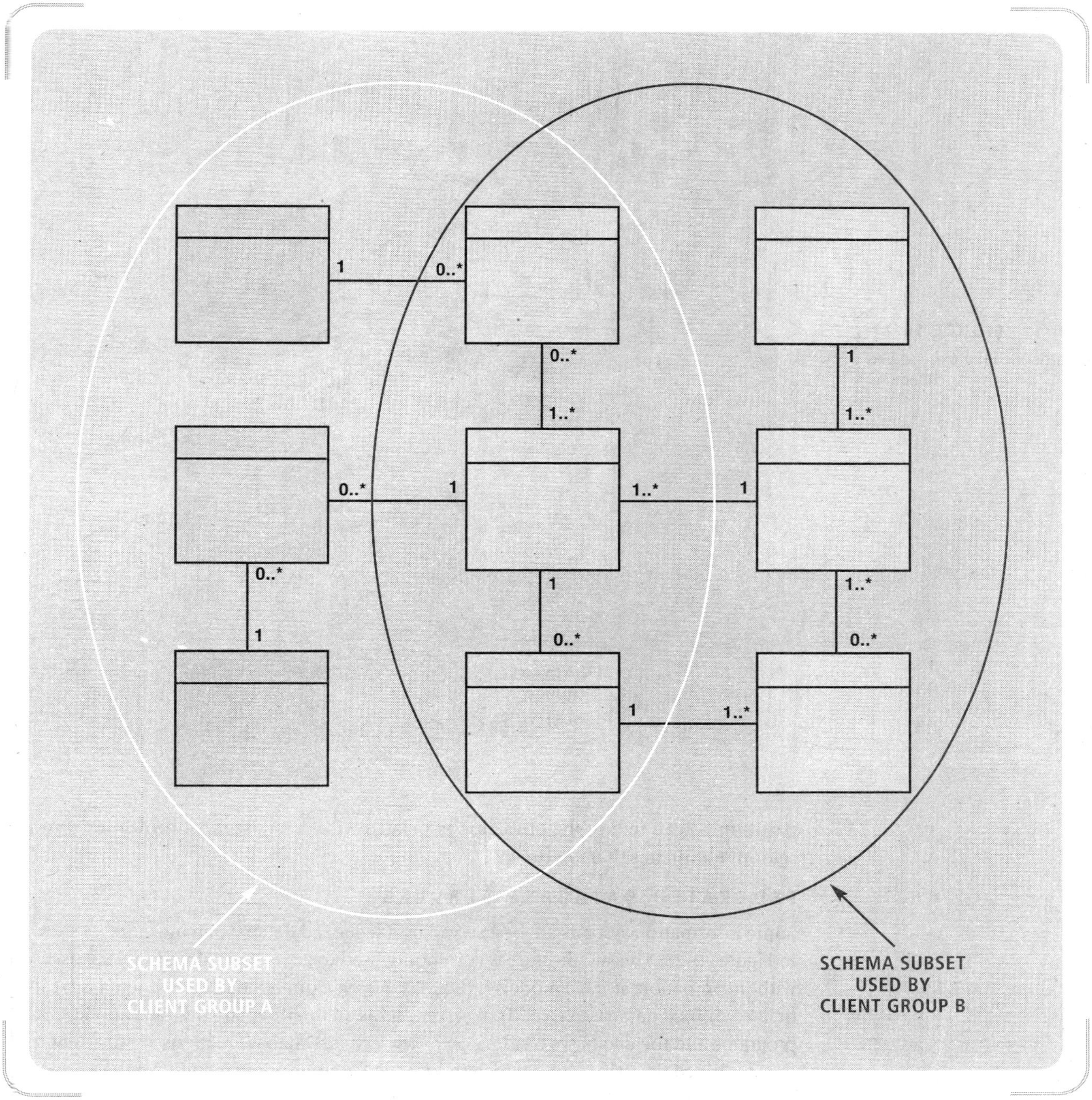

FIGURE 10-26
Partitioning a database schema into client access subsets

Partitioned database server architecture is feasible only when a schema can be cleanly partitioned among client access groups. Client groups must require access to well-defined subsets of a database (for example, marketing data rather than production data). In addition, members of a client access group must be located in small geographic regions. When a single access group is spread among multiple geographic sites (for example, order processing at three regional centers), then a combination of replicated and partitioned database server architecture is usually required.

It is seldom possible to partition a database schema into mutually exclusive subsets. Some portions of a database are typically needed by most or all users, and those portions must exist in each partition. For example, data in the region of overlap in Figure 10-26 should be stored on each server with periodic synchronization. Thus,

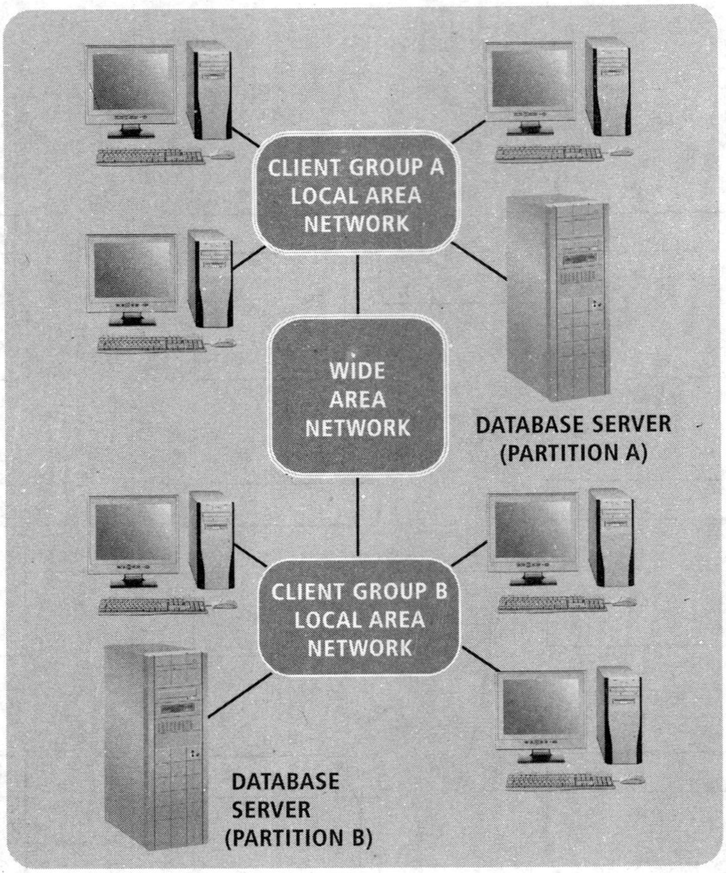

FIGURE 10-27
A partitioned database server architecture

partitioning can reduce the problems associated with database synchronization, but it seldom eliminates them entirely.

FEDERATED DATABASE SERVERS

Some information systems are best served by a federated database architecture, as shown in Figure 10-28. This architecture is commonly used to access data stored in databases with incompatible storage models or DBMSs. A single unified database schema is created on a combined database server. That server acts as an intermediary between application programs and the databases residing on other servers. Database requests are first sent to the combined database server, which in turn makes appropriate requests of the underlying database servers. Results from multiple servers are combined and reformatted to fit the unified schema before the system returns a response to the client.

Federated database server architecture can be extremely complex. A number of DBMS products are available to implement such systems, but they are typically expensive and difficult to implement and maintain. Federated database architectures also tend to demand considerable computer hardware and network capacity, but their expense and management complexity are generally less than would be required to implement and maintain application programs that interact directly with all of the underlying databases.

data warehouse
a collection of data used to support structured and unstructured managerial decisions

A common use of federated database server architecture is to implement a data warehouse. A *data warehouse* is a collection of data used to support structured and unstructured managerial decisions. Data warehouses typically draw their content from operational databases within an organization and from multiple external databases

FIGURE 10-28
A federated database server architecture

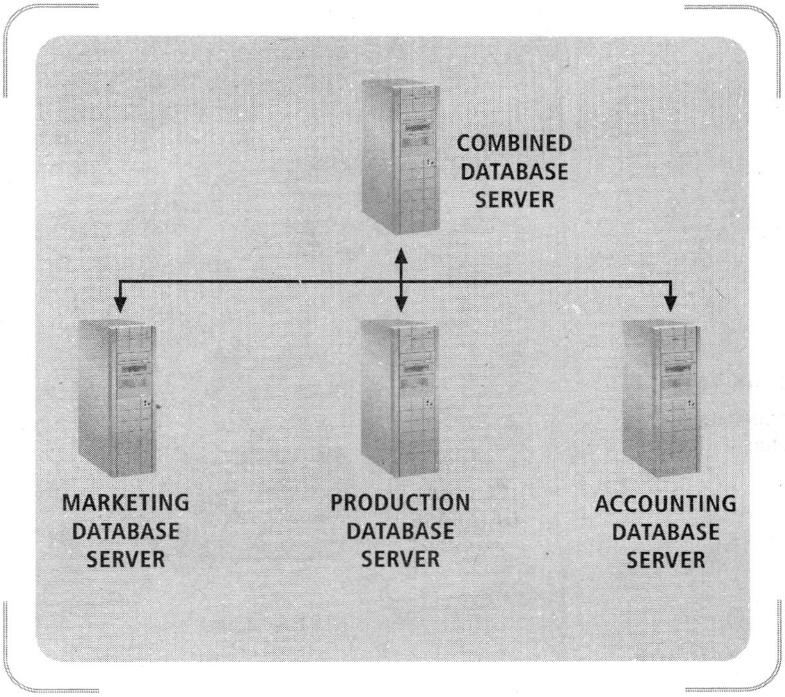

(for example, economic and trade data from databases maintained by governments, trade industry associations, and private research organizations). Because data originate from a large number of incompatible databases, a federated architecture is typically the only feasible approach for implementing a data warehouse.

Now that we've discussed the basic issues underlying distributed database design, we will show how they come into play when making decisions for Rocky Mountain Outfitters' new customer support system.

RMO DISTRIBUTED DATABASE ARCHITECTURE

The starting point for designing a distributed database architecture is information about the data needs of geographically dispersed users. Some of this information for RMO was gathered during requirements activities (see Figures 5-32, 5-33, and 5-34) and is summarized here:

- Warehouse staff (Portland, Salt Lake City, and Albuquerque) need to check inventory levels, query orders, record back orders and order fulfillment, and record order returns.
- The phone-order staff (Salt Lake City) need to check inventory levels; create, query, update, and delete orders; query customer account information; and query catalogs.
- The mail-order staff (Provo) need to check inventory levels, query orders, query catalog information, and update customer accounts.
- Customers (location not yet determined) need the same access capabilities as phone-order staff.
- Headquarters staff (Park City) need to query and adjust orders, query and adjust customer accounts, and create and query catalogs and promotions.

RMO has already decided to manage its database using the existing mainframe computer in the Park City data center. Thus, a WAN will be required to connect the server to LANs in the warehouses, phone-order center, mail-order center, headquarters, and data center. A connection will eventually be required for the Web servers used for

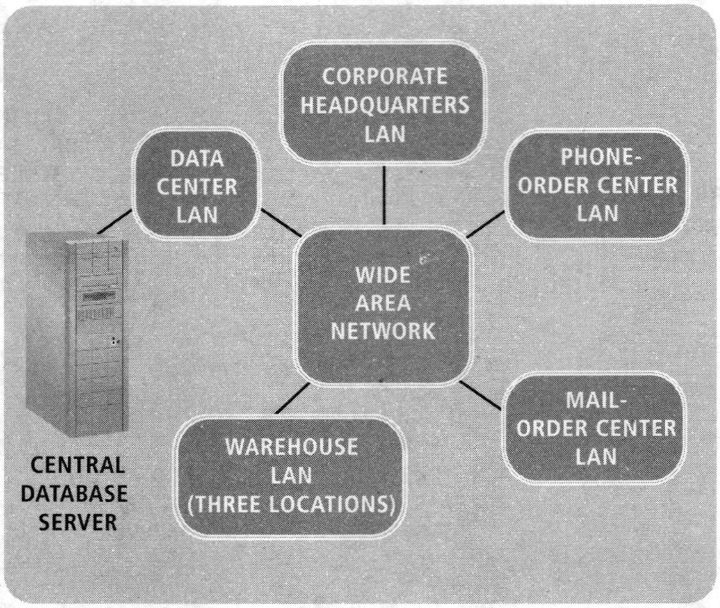

FIGURE 10-29
A single-server database architecture for RMO

direct customer ordering, although they probably will be located at an existing site (such as the data center).

A single-server architecture for RMO is shown in Figure 10-29. This architecture requires sufficient WAN capacity to carry database (and other) traffic from all locations. The primary advantage of this architecture is its simplicity. There are no partitions or database copies to manage, and only a single server must be maintained. The primary disadvantages are relatively high WAN capacity requirements and the susceptibility of the entire system to failure of the single server.

A more complex alternative is shown in Figure 10-30. Each remote location employs a combination of database partitioning and replication. A server at each warehouse stores a local copy of the order and inventory portions of the database. Servers in the phone- and mail-order centers store local copies of a larger subset of the database. Corporate headquarters relies on the central database server in the data center.

The primary advantages of this architecture are fault tolerance and reduced WAN capacity requirements. Each location could continue to operate if the central database server failed. However, as the remote locations continued to operate, their data would gradually drift out of synchronization. A synchronization strategy must be implemented to address both regular database updates and recovery from server failure. The strategy could vary by location.

The primary disadvantages to the distributed architecture are cost and complexity. The architecture saves WAN costs through reduced capacity requirements but adds costs for additional database servers. The cost of acquiring, operating, and maintaining the additional servers would probably be much higher than the cost of adding greater WAN capacity.

So which alternative makes the most sense for RMO? The answer depends on some additional data and on answers to some questions about desired system performance. RMO management must determine its goals for system performance and reliability. The distributed architecture would provide higher performance and reliability but at substantially increased cost. Management must determine whether the extra cost is worth the expected benefits.

Additional data about network traffic are needed to precisely determine LAN and WAN communication requirements between clients and database servers. Estimates of

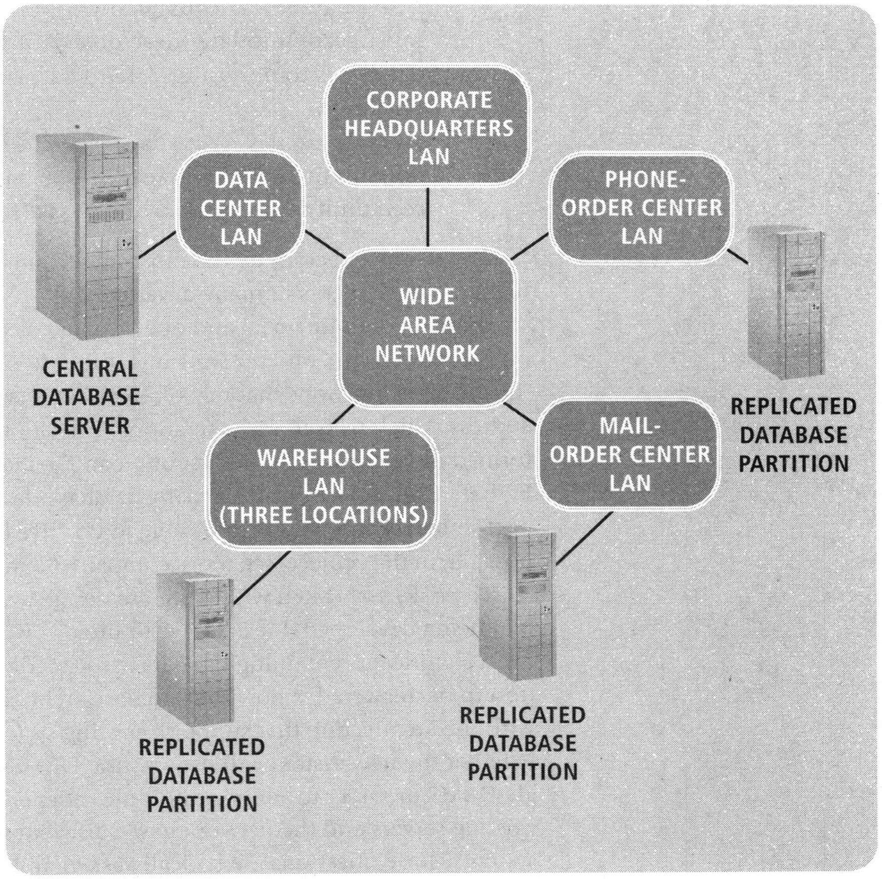

FIGURE 10-30
A replicated and partitioned database server architecture for RMO

transaction and query volume, including normal and peak demand, are required for each location. Such estimates are often made as a business modeling activity when the current network and architecture are being evaluated (see Figure 7-14). The estimates are required to determine an optimal configuration of LAN, WAN, and database server capacity. Analysis of the estimates and the actual design of the networks and database architecture are complex endeavors that require highly specialized knowledge and experience.

DATABASE DESIGN WITHIN THE UP

Database design has profound impacts on other development activities. Key questions that many analysts raise are when to design the database and whether to design and build the entire database at once or spread those activities across multiple project iterations. Unfortunately, there are no simple answers to those questions. We now discuss the complicating factors of designing databases.

The primary factors that complicate the decision of when and how to perform database design are the following:

- **Architecture.** Decisions about DBMSs, database servers, and database distribution are key architectural decisions for the entire system. They are tightly integrated with other architectural decisions, including network design, Web and component services, and security.

- **Existing databases.** Most new or upgraded systems must interact with existing databases. Thus, many aspects of database design and architecture must accommodate these preexisting constraints. While adapting existing databases to new or updated systems, analysts must ensure their continued operation.
- **Domain model class diagram.** The starting point for database design is the domain model class diagram. Database design in whole or part cannot proceed until related parts of the class diagram have been developed.

The first two factors are the most significant—they make database design one of the highest-risk elements in many development projects. The risk is multidimensional, encompassing both financial and operational risks through high costs, pervasive impacts on the new system, and possible disruption to or modification of existing systems and the business functions that rely on them. As described in Chapter 2, the UP purposely addresses high risks in early iterations. Thus, in many projects, database design is performed in its entirety in the first or second iteration. Concern about such risks led Barbara Halifax to front-load many database design tasks for the RMO customer support system. The goal was to be able to do "live load" performance testing as early as possible in the project (see the accompanying memo).

The risks associated with database design are substantially reduced when the system being developed doesn't have to interact with existing databases. In that case, the most significant remaining risks are associated with architecture. The primary question to be answered is how the database architecture of the new system will interact with the architecture that supports existing systems. More specific questions include whether the new system will use existing DBMSs and servers—it is possible for a single DBMS or server to support multiple independent databases—and whether the existing servers and the network have sufficient unused capacity to support the new system. Those questions are typically asked and answered in an early project iteration or before the project is even approved. If the answer to both questions is yes, then the database-related risks of the new project are relatively low and the need to front-load database design in the project is substantially reduced.

When database-related risks are low, database design and deployment tasks can be spread across multiple iterations. Typically, the database schema is developed incrementally as related portions of the domain model class diagram are developed. As portions of the schema are developed, corresponding portions of the database are created and populated with test data. This enables development and testing of software in general and data access classes in particular. As the database and application software move closer to completion, performance and stress testing can proceed in earnest.

March 24, 2006

To: John MacMurty

From: Barbara Halifax

RE: Customer support system update—database issues

ROCKY MOUNTAIN OUTFITTERS

MEMO

John, we're nearing the end of the second project iteration, and I wanted to give you some additional details concerning database design and testing. As you may recall, for the second iteration, we created a test database on a small IBM server running MVS and DB2. Although the server is too small to be used in production, it enabled us to develop and debug most of the data access logic for the order-entry functions. We expect some functional changes in the next iteration, but we don't expect significant changes to the schema design or access logic.

We've reached a critical juncture in the project with respect to testing and deployment. When the supply chain management (SCM) system was designed, the team provided extra network and database server capacity in anticipation of the later addition of the customer support system (CSS). But we need to subject our core database architecture to some realistic performance tests to see whether our estimates were accurate. The detailed plan is as follows:

Week	Tasks
April 3–7	Create a copy of the current production database for use in combined testing of the SCM and CSS. Migrate three months of SCM data from the production database to the test database.
April 10–14	Modify the test database schema to include all of the rows developed during the last iteration. Migrate data for approximately 10,000 customers and their orders during the last three months from the old customer database to the test database.
April 17–21	Modify the CSS application and Web servers to interact with the test database on the mainframe. Do a "live load" performance test early on Friday. Evaluate the results before lunch. If no problems are encountered, do another test that afternoon, when system load and network load is generally near its peak.
April 24–28	Evaluate the results of both tests in detail. If any serious problems are found, make adjustments to the database or network and test again on Friday.

Of course, we hope that all will go well on April 21 and that we won't need a second round of testing on April 28. But we do plan to do live load testing as additional software is deployed on the Web and application servers and as corresponding changes are made to the test database on the mainframe. We expect database testing to occur approximately every three weeks for the next few project iterations.

Thanks and take care.

BH

cc: Steven Deerfield, Ming Lee, Jack Garcia, Ann Hamilton

Summary

Most modern information systems store data in a database and access and manage the data using a DBMS. Relational databases and DBMSs are most commonly used today, but object databases and DBMSs are increasing in popularity. One of the key activities of systems design is developing a relational or object database schema.

An object database stores data as a collection of related objects. The design class diagram is the starting point for developing an object database schema. The database schema defines each class, and the ODBMS stores each object as an instance of a particular class. Each object is assigned a unique object identifier. Associations among objects are represented by storing the object identifier of an object within related objects.

A relational database is a collection of data stored in tables. A relational database schema is normally developed from a class diagram. Each class is represented as a separate table. One-to-many associations are represented by embedding foreign keys in class tables. Many-to-many associations are represented by creating additional tables containing foreign keys of the related classes.

Medium- and large-scale information systems typically use multiple databases or database servers in various geographic locations. Replicated database architecture employs multiple database copies on different servers, usually in different geographic locations. Partitioned database architecture employs partial database copies stored on different servers in proximity to a distinct user subset. Federated database architecture employs multiple databases (possibly of different types) and a special-purpose DBMS that provides a unified view of the databases and a single point of access.

Database design is usually performed in an early iteration of a development project, to minimize project risk. Many new systems interact with existing databases, and the architectural decisions associated with databases are intertwined with other architectural issues. The combination of these factors increases the risk associated with database design tasks. When the risks are low, the database can be designed and implemented incrementally across multiple project iterations.

KEY TERMS

attribute, p. 408
attribute value, p. 408
complex data type, p. 422
database (DB), p. 398
database management system (DBMS), p. 398
database synchronization, p. 425
data type, p. 422
data warehouse, p. 428
first normal form (1NF), p. 415
foreign key, p. 408
functional dependency, p. 415
hybrid object-relational DBMS, p. 420
Java Data Objects (JDO), p. 400
key, p. 408
multivalued attribute, p. 405
navigation, p. 401
normalization, p. 415
object database management system (ODBMS), p. 400
Object Definition Language (ODL), p. 400
object identifier, p. 401
persistent class, p. 401
physical data store, p. 398
primary key, p. 408
primitive data type, p. 422
referential integrity, p. 412
relational database management system (RDBMS), p. 407
row, p. 407
schema, p. 398
second normal form (2NF), p. 415
table, p. 407
third normal form (3NF), p. 415
transient class, p. 400

REVIEW QUESTIONS

1. List the components of a DBMS and describe the function of each.
2. What is a database schema? What information does it contain?
3. Why have databases become the preferred method of storing data used by an information system?
4. List four different types of database models and DBMSs. Which are in common use today?
5. Describe the steps used to transform a class diagram into an object database schema.
6. What is the difference between a persistent class and a transient class? Provide at least one example of each class type.
7. What is an object identifier? Why are object identifiers required in an object database?
8. How is a class on a class diagram represented in an object database?
9. How is a one-to-many association on a class diagram represented in an object database?
10. How is a many-to-many association without attributes represented in an object database?
11. Does an object database require key attributes? Why or why not?
12. With respect to relational databases, briefly define the terms *row* and *attribute*.
13. What is a primary key? Are duplicate primary key values allowed? Why or why not?
14. What is the difference between a natural key and an invented key? Which type is most commonly used in business information processing?
15. What is a foreign key? Why are foreign keys used or required in a relational database? Are duplicate foreign key values allowed? Why or why not?
16. Describe the steps used to transform a class diagram into a relational database schema.
17. How is a class on a class diagram represented in a relational database?
18. How is a one-to-many association on a class diagram represented in a relational database?
19. How is a many-to-many association on a class diagram represented in a relational database?
20. What is an association class? How are association classes used to represent many-to-many associations in an object database?
21. Describe the two ways in which a generalization association can be represented in an object database.
22. What is referential integrity? Describe how it is enforced when a new foreign key value is created, when a row containing a primary key is deleted, and when a primary key value is changed.
23. What types of data (or attributes) should never be stored more than once in a relational database? What types of data (or attributes) usually must be stored more than once in a relational database?
24. What is relational database normalization? Why is a database schema in third normal form considered to be of higher quality than an unnormalized database schema?
25. Describe the process of relational database normalization. Which normal forms rely on the definition of functional dependency?
26. What is the difference between a primitive data type and a complex data type?
27. What are the advantages of having an RDBMS provide complex data types?
28. Does an ODBMS need to provide predefined complex data types? Why or why not?
29. Why might all or part of a database need to be replicated in multiple locations?
30. Briefly describe the following distributed database architectures: replicated database servers, partitioned database servers, and federated database servers. What are the comparative advantages of each?
31. What additional database management complexities are introduced when database contents are replicated in multiple locations?
32. Describe the risk factors associated with database design.
33. When should database design be performed? Can the database be designed iteratively, or must the entire database be designed at once?

THINKING CRITICALLY

1. The Universal Product Code (UPC) is a bar-coded number that uniquely identifies many products sold in the United States. For example, all copies of this textbook sold in the United States have the same UPC bar code on the back cover. Now consider how the design of the RMO database might change if all items sold by RMO were required by law to carry a permanently attached UPC (for example, on a label sewn into a garment or on a radio frequency ID tag attached to a product). How might the RMO relational database schema change under this requirement?
2. Assume that RMO plans to change its pricing policy. If two or more catalogs are in circulation at the same time, then all item prices in the catalogs must be the same. Prices can still rise or fall over time, and those changes will be recorded in the database and printed in newly issued catalogs. Any customer who places an order will always be given the lower of the current price or the price in the current catalog. What changes to the tables shown in Figure 10-15 will be required to ensure that the RMO database is in 3NF after the pricing policy change?
3. Assume that RMO will begin asking a random sample of customers who order by telephone about purchases made from competitors. RMO will give customers a 15 percent discount on their current order in exchange for answering a few questions. To store and use this information, RMO will add two new classes and three new associations to the class diagram. The new classes are Competitor and Product Category. Competitor has a one-to-many association with ProductCategory, and the existing Customer class also has a one-to-many association with ProductCategory. Competitor has a single attribute called Name. ProductCategory has four attributes: Description, DollarAmountPurchased, Month Purchased, and YearPurchased. Revise the relational database schema shown in Figure 10-15 to include the new classes and associations. All tables must be in 3NF.
4. Assume that RMO is developing its database using object-oriented methods. Assume further that the database designers want to make some changes to the class diagram in Figure 10-2. Specifically, they want to make ProductItem an abstract parent class from which more specific product classes are specialized. Three specialized classes will be added: ClothingItem, EquipmentItem, and OtherItem. ClothingItem will add the attribute *color*, and that same attribute will be removed from the InventoryItem class. EquipmentItem will also add an attribute called *color* but will not have an attribute called *gender*. OtherItem will have both the *color* and *gender* attributes. Revise the relational database schema in Figure 10-16 to store the new ProductItem generalization hierarchy. Use a separate table for each of the specialized classes.
5. Assume that RMO will use a relational database as shown in Figure 10-15. Assume further that a new catalog group located in Milan, Italy, will now create and maintain the catalog. To minimize networking costs, the catalog group will have a dedicated database server attached to its LAN. Develop a plan to partition the RMO database. Which tables should be replicated on the catalog group's local database server? Update Figure 10-30 to show the new distributed database architecture.
6. Revisit the issues raised in the Nationwide Books (NB) case at the beginning of the chapter. Should NB adopt an ODBMS for the new Web-based ordering system? Why or why not?
7. Revisit the issue of risk associated with database design for the customer support system as described in the RMO memo in this chapter. Assume that the customer support and supply chain management systems will use completely separate databases running on separate DBMSs and servers. Under those assumptions, how much risk is involved in the customer support system database design? Should the database design and testing plan be modified? If so, how?

EXPERIENTIAL EXERCISES

1. This chapter did not discuss network databases in detail, but some database textbooks discuss them. Investigate the network database model and its use of pointers to represent associations among record types. In what ways is the use of pointers in a network database similar to the use of object identifiers in an object database? Does the similarity imply that object databases are little more than a renamed version of an older DBMS technology?
2. Access the Object Database Management Group Web site (www.odmg.org) and gather information on the current status of the ODMG standard. Follow the links to the JDO standards page and investigate the standard. Does the JDO standard define a complete ODBMS?
3. Investigate the student records management system at your school to determine what database management system is used. What database model is used by the DBMS? If the DBMS isn't object oriented, find out what plans, if any, are in place to migrate to an ODBMS. Why is the migration being planned (or not being planned)?
4. Visit the Web site of an online catalog vendor similar to RMO (such as www.llbean.com) or an online vendor of computers and related merchandise (such as www.cdw.com). Browse the online catalog and note the various types of information contained there. Construct a list of complex data types that would be needed to store all of the online catalog information.

Case Studies

REAL ESTATE MULTIPLE LISTING SERVICE SYSTEM

Refer to the description of the Real Estate Multiple Listing Service system in the Chapter 5 case studies. Using the class diagram for that system as a starting point:

[1] Develop a relational database schema in 3NF.

[2] Develop an ODL database schema.

STATE PATROL TICKET PROCESSING SYSTEM

Refer to the description of the State Patrol ticket processing system in the Chapter 5 case studies. Using the class diagram for that system as a starting point:

[1] Develop a relational database schema in 3NF.

[2] Develop an ODL database schema.

COMPUTER PUBLISHING, INCORPORATED

In only a decade, Computer Publishing, Incorporated (CPI) grew from a small textbook publishing house into a large international company with significant market share in traditional textbooks, electronic books, and distance education courseware. CPI's processes for developing books and courseware were similar to those used by most other publishers, but those processes had proven cumbersome and slow in an era of rapid product cycles and multiple product formats.

Text and art were developed in a wide variety of electronic formats, and conversions among those formats were difficult and error-prone. Many editing steps were performed with traditional paper-and-pencil methods. Consistency errors within books and among books and related products were common. Developing or revising a book and all its related products typically took a year or more.

CPI's president initiated a strategic project to reengineer the way that CPI developed books and related products. CPI formed a strategic partnership with Davis Systems (DS) to develop software that would support the reengineered processes. DS had significant experience developing software to support product development in the chemical and pharmaceutical industries using the latest development tools and techniques, including object-oriented software and databases. CPI expected the new processes and software to reduce development time and cost. Both companies expected to license the software to other publishers within a few years.

A joint team specified the workflows and high-level requirements for the software. The team developed plans for a large database that would hold all book and courseware content through all stages of production. Authors, editors, and other production staff would interact with the database in a variety of ways, including traditional word-processing programs and Web-based interfaces. When required, format conversions would be handled seamlessly and without error. All content creation and modification would be electronic—no text or art would ever be created or edited on paper, except as a printed book ready for sale.

Software would track and manage content through every stage of production. Content common to multiple products would be stored in the database only once. Dependencies within and across products would be tracked in the database. Software would ensure that any content addition or change would be reflected in all dependent content and products, regardless of the final product form. For example, a sentence in Chapter 2 that refers to a figure in Chapter 1 would be updated automatically if the figure were renumbered. If a new figure were added to a book, it would be added automatically to the related courseware presentation slides. Related courseware and study material on the Web site would automatically reflect changes, such as a new answer to an end-of-chapter question.

[1] Consider the contents of this textbook as a template for CPI's database content. Draw a class diagram that represents the book and its key content elements. Expand your diagram to include related product content such as a set of PowerPoint slides, an electronic book formatted as a Web site, and a Web-based test bank.

[2] Develop a list of data types required to store the content of the book, slides, and Web sites. Are the relational DBMS data types listed in Figure 10-23 sufficient?

[3] What features of an ODBMS, beyond or different from RDBMS features, might be useful when implementing CPI's database? Give examples of how they might be used.

RETHINKING ROCKY MOUNTAIN OUTFITTERS

The "Rethinking RMO" case in Chapter 5 asked you to consider additional things and associations among things that would need to be modeled if RMO were to implement its own customer charge accounts. If you have not already done so, complete that exercise and update the class diagram accordingly, then complete the following tasks:

[1] Update the RMO relational database design in Figure 10-15 based on the changes that you made to the class diagram. Be sure that all your database tables are in 3NF.

[2] Write ODL schema specifications for all new classes and associations that you added to the class diagram.

[3] Verify that the new classes and associations are accurately represented in the updated relational database design that you developed for question 1.

FOCUSING ON RELIABLE PHARMACEUTICAL SERVICE

Use the class diagram that you developed in Chapter 5 and the design class diagram that you developed in Chapter 6 to complete the following tasks:

[1] Develop a relational database schema in 3NF.

[2] Develop an ODL database schema.

[3] Discuss the pros and cons of distributed database architecture. Which architectural approach (or combination of approaches) should Reliable employ in their new system once it is fully implemented?

FURTHER RESOURCES

Dirk Bartels and Greg Chase, "A Comparison Between Relational and Object-oriented Database Systems for Object-oriented Application Development," http://www.fastobjects.com/us/pdf/ODBMSvsRDBMS.pdf, 2001.

Robert Orfali, Dan Harkey, and Jeri Edwards, *The Essential Client/Server Survival Guide* (3rd ed.). John Wiley & Sons, 1999.

The Object Database Management Group Web site, http://www.odmg.org.

Peter Rob and Carlos Coronel, *Database Systems: Design Implementation and Management* (6th ed.). Course Technology, 2004.

chapter 11

DESIGNING THE USER-INTERFACE LAYER

LEARNING OBJECTIVES

After reading this chapter, you should be able to:

- Understand the difference between user interfaces and system interfaces
- Explain why the user interface *is* the system to the users
- Discuss the importance of the three principles of user-centered design
- Describe the historical development of the field of human-computer interaction (HCI)
- Describe the three metaphors of human-computer interaction
- Discuss how visibility and affordance affect usability
- Apply the eight golden rules of dialog design when designing the user interface
- List the key principles used in Web design
- Define the overall system structure as a menu hierarchy
- Write user-computer interaction scenarios as dialogs
- Create storyboards to show the sequence of forms used in a dialog
- Use UML class diagrams and sequence diagrams to document dialog designs
- Design windows forms and browser forms that are used to implement a dialog

CHAPTER OUTLINE

- Identifying and Classifying Inputs and Outputs
- Understanding the User Interface
- Guidelines for Designing User Interfaces
- Documenting Dialog Designs
- Guidelines for Designing Windows and Browser Forms
- Guidelines for Designing Web Sites
- Designing Dialogs for Rocky Mountain Outfitters

INTERFACE DESIGN AT AVIATION ELECTRONICS

Bob Crain was admiring the user interface for the new object-oriented manufacturing support system recently installed at Aviation Electronics (AE). Bob is the plant manager for AE's Midwest manufacturing facility, which is responsible for producing aviation devices used in commercial aircraft. These aviation devices provide guidance and control functions for flight crews, and they provide the latest safety and security features that pilots need when flying commercial aircraft.

The manufacturing support system is used for all facets of the manufacturing process, including product planning, purchasing, parts inventory, quality control, finished goods inventory, and distribution. Bob was involved extensively in the development of the system over a period of several years, including initial planning and development. The system reflected almost everything he knew about manufacturing. The information systems team that developed the system relied extensively on Bob's expertise. That was the easy part for Bob.

What particularly pleased Bob was the final user interface. Bob had insisted that the development team think "outside the box." He did not want just another cookie-cutter transaction processing system. He wanted a system that acted as a partner in the manufacturing process—with a look and feel that really fit the work the users were doing. After all, the facility produced devices whose major design goal was usability. Shouldn't the manufacturing support system be designed that way, too?

The first manager assigned to the project didn't want to discuss usability at all. "We'll add the user-interface later, after we work out the accounting controls and master these OO development tools" was a typical comment. When Bob insisted that the project manager be replaced, the information systems department sent Sara Robinson to lead the project.

Sara had a completely different attitude; she started out asking about events affecting the manufacturing process and about use cases where users need support from the system. Although she had a team of analysts working on the accounting transaction details right from the beginning, she always focused on how the user would interact with the system. Sara explained that the Unified Process suggests defining the user interaction and usability requirements early in the project, when analysts are first discussing requirements—an approach that made perfect sense to Bob. So Bob and Sara conducted meetings to involve users in discussions about how they might use the system, even asking users to act out the roles of the user and the system carrying on a conversation. That approach seemed outside the box.

Meetings with users continued during each iteration. Sara presented sketches of screens and asked users to draw on them, placing right on the sketches information they wanted to see and options they wanted to be able to select. These sessions produced many ideas. For example, many users did not sit at their desks all day—they needed larger and more graphic displays they could see from across the room. Many users needed to refer to several displays, and they needed to be able to read them simultaneously. Several functions were best performed using graphical simulations of the manufacturing process. Users made sketches showing how the manufacturing process actually worked, and the team used these sketches later to define much of the interface. Sara and her team kept coming back every month or so with more examples to show, asking for more suggestions.

When the system was finally completed and installed, most users already knew how to use it, since they had been so involved in its design. Bob knew everything the system could do, but he had his own uses for it. He sat at his desk and clicked the *review ongoing processes* button on the screen, and the manufacturing support system gave him his morning briefing.

Overview

Information systems capture inputs and produce outputs, and inputs and outputs occur where there are *interfaces* between the system and its environments. System interfaces handle inputs and outputs that require minimal human intervention. User interfaces handle inputs and outputs that involve a system user directly. This chapter differentiates between the two types of interfaces and then focuses on the design of user interfaces. Then Chapter 12 focuses on system interfaces, system outputs, and systems controls.

One of the key requirements discipline activities is to develop the user-interface dialogs for the system. Similarly, a key design discipline activity is to design the user and system interfaces in more detail. Designing the user interface means designing the inputs and outputs involved for each use case when the user interacts with the computer to carry out a task. This chapter emphasizes the interaction between the user and the computer—called *human-computer interaction*, or HCI. For every use case with an input, a developer must consider the interaction between user and computer and design an interface to process the input. Similarly, for every use case with an output produced at the request of a user (an online report, for example), the developer must design the interaction. Because the interaction is much like a dialog between the user and the computer, user-interface design is often referred to as *dialog design*.

This chapter begins with discussion of the user interface by providing background on user-centered design, the development of the field of human-computer interaction, and several metaphors used to describe the user interface. Many guidelines are available to help ensure the usability of the system, and some of the most important guidelines are discussed, including guidelines for Web-based development. Next, approaches to documenting dialog designs are presented, including the use of UML diagrams. Examples are given throughout the chapter, including some dialog design examples for Rocky Mountain Outfitters that show windows forms and Web pages. Remember, user-interface design is completed during each iteration, addressing only a few use cases at a time. But it is important to establish an overall user-interface design concept early in the project so the design of each dialog is coordinated.

IDENTIFYING AND CLASSIFYING INPUTS AND OUTPUTS

Inputs and outputs of the system are an early concern of any system development project. The project vision and business case document lists key inputs and outputs that the analysts identified when defining the scope of the system. During the inception phase and early elaboration phase iterations, analysts discuss inputs and outputs early and often with system stakeholders to identify actors that interact with the system and that depend on information it produces. For example, the event table includes a trigger for each external event, and the triggers represent inputs. Outputs are shown as responses to external, state, and temporal events. Use case diagrams identify the system boundary and the actors. Use case descriptions and system sequence diagrams also emphasize the details of inputs and outputs. As shown in Chapter 8, the user-interface (view) layer in a three-layer design involves inputs and outputs. In the object-oriented approach, inputs and outputs are defined by messages entering or leaving the system. The messages exchanged during a use case realization define these inputs and outputs in more detail, and as the design of each scenario becomes more detailed, so does the specification of messages.

USER VERSUS SYSTEM INTERFACES

system interfaces
the parts of an information system involving inputs and outputs that require minimal human intervention

user interfaces
the parts of an information system requiring user interaction to create inputs and outputs

A key step in the requirements discipline is to classify the inputs and outputs for each event as either a system interface or a user interface. *System interfaces* involve inputs and outputs that require minimal human intervention. They might be inputs captured automatically by special input devices such as scanners, electronic messages from another system, or batch processing transactions compiled by another system. Many outputs are considered system interfaces if they primarily send messages or information to other systems or if they produce reports, statements, or documents for external agents or actors without much human intervention.

User interfaces involve inputs and outputs that more directly involve a system user. A user interface enables a user to interact with the computer to record a transaction—for example, when a customer service representative records a phone order for an RMO customer. Sometimes outputs are produced after user interaction, such as the information displayed after a user query about the status of an order. In Web-based systems, a customer can interact directly with a system to request information, place an order, or look up the status of an order.

In most system development projects, analysts separate design of system interfaces from design of user interfaces because the two types require different expertise and technology. But as with the design of any system component, considerable coordination is required. This chapter discusses user interfaces. The next chapter deals with system interfaces and system controls. At Rocky Mountain Outfitters, Barbara Halifax's regular status memo updates John MacMurty on some of the activities of user-interface design for the customer support system.

ROCKY MOUNTAIN OUTFITTERS

MEMO

May 12, 2006

To: John MacMurty

From: Barbara Halifax

RE: User-interface design for the Customer Support System

John, we have been working on the user interface almost from the beginning of the project as we worked with various end-user groups. The Web-based components of the system have also been given a lot of attention, starting really when we were prototyping to prove technical feasibility in the inception phase. I have one team working on the user-interface design and another team assigned to developing the detailed design of system interfaces and controls in a later iteration (including the printed forms and reports). I'll have more on the system interfaces later.

I just wanted to report briefly that we are on track to finalize the design of most interactive dialogs. I know you have seen the storyboards of key dialogs and have tried out many of the user interface designs from early iterations of the project. Many of the models we created when designing the software were useful for dialog design, particularly the detailed sequence diagrams showing the view layer interactions. These diagrams are helping us work through the technical issues for implementation, and they serve as templates to make sure we provide a consistent look and feel from one dialog to another.

We have conducted usability tests on the designs and have held focus group meetings with users, particularly the phone-order representatives and customer groups recruited to help with the design of the Web components. The gift certificates we offered the customer focus group are really paying off.

Thanks for your input on the interface designs. I'll check in later before our next status meeting.

BH

cc: Steven Deerfield, Ming Lee

UNDERSTANDING THE USER INTERFACE

Many people think the user interface is developed and added to the system near the end of the development process. But the user interface of an interactive system is much more than that. The user interface is everything the end user comes into contact with while using the system—physically, perceptually, and conceptually (see Figure 11-1). To the end user of a system, the user interface *is* the system itself.

FIGURE 11-1
Physical, perceptual, and conceptual aspects of the user interface

Many system developers, particularly those who work on highly interactive systems, echo this point of view in claiming that to design the user interface is to design the system. Therefore, consideration of the user interface should come very early in the development process. The term *human-computer interaction (HCI)* is generally used to refer to the study of end users and their interaction with computers.

human-computer interaction (HCI)
the study of end users and their interactions with computers

PHYSICAL ASPECTS OF THE USER INTERFACE

Physical aspects of the user interface include the devices the user actually touches, including the keyboard, mouse, touch screen, or keypad. But other physical parts of the interface include reference manuals, printed documents, data-entry forms, and so forth that the end user works with while completing tasks at the computer. For example, a mail-order data-entry clerk at Rocky Mountain Outfitters works at a computer terminal but uses printed catalogs and hand-written order forms when entering orders into the system. The desk space, the documents, the available light, and the computer terminal hardware all make up the physical interface for this end user.

PERCEPTUAL ASPECTS OF THE USER INTERFACE

Perceptual aspects of the user interface include everything the end user sees, hears, or touches (beyond the physical devices). What the user sees includes all data and instructions displayed on the screen, including shapes, lines, numbers, and words. The user might rely on the sounds made by the system, even a simple beep or click that tells the user that the system recognizes a keystroke or selection. More recently, computer-generated speech makes it seem that the system is actually talking to the user, and with speech recognition software, the user can talk to the computer. The user "touches" objects such as menus, dialog boxes, and buttons on the screen using a mouse, but the user also touches objects such as documents, drawings, or records of transactions with a mouse when completing tasks.

CONCEPTUAL ASPECTS OF THE USER INTERFACE

user's model

what the user knows about using the system, including the problem domain "things" the user is manipulating, the operations that can be performed, and the procedures followed when carrying out tasks

Conceptual aspects of the user interface include everything the user knows about using the system, including all of the problem domain "things" in the system the user is manipulating, the operations that can be performed, and the procedures followed to carry out the operations. To use the system, the end user must know all about these details—not how the system is implemented internally, but what the system does and how to use it to complete tasks. This knowledge is referred to as the *user's model* of the system. Much of the user's model is based on the requirements model of the system, as you learned in Chapters 5. A requirements model of the system can be quite detailed, so the user must know quite a few details to operate the system. Recall also that a systems analyst relies on the end users to help define the requirements that the analyst captures in various models. The user's knowledge of the requirements for the system becomes the fundamental determinant of what the system is, and if the user's knowledge of the system is part of the interface, then the user interface must be much more than a component added near the end of the project.

BEST PRACTICE: Remember that to the user, the user interface is the system itself.

USER-CENTERED DESIGN

user-centered design

a collection of techniques that place the user at the center of the development process

Many researchers focus their attention on creating analysis and design techniques that place the user interface at the center of the development process because they recognize the importance of the user interface to system developers and system users. These techniques are often referred to collectively as *user-centered design*. The Unified Process embraces the ideas of user-centered design. User-centered design techniques emphasize three important principles:

- Focus early on the users and their work.
- Evaluate designs to ensure usability.
- Use iterative development.

The object-oriented approach focuses on users and their work by identifying actors, use cases, and scenarios followed when using the system. As discussed in Chapter 6, the automation boundary between the user and the computer is defined very early during requirements modeling.

User-centered design goes much further in attempting to understand the users, however. What do they know? How do they learn? How do they prefer to work? What motivates them? The amount of focus on users and their work varies with the type of system being developed. If the system is a shrink-wrapped desktop application marketed directly to end users, the focus on users and their preferences is intense.

usability

the degree to which a system is easy to learn and use

The second principle of user-centered design is to evaluate designs to ensure usability. *Usability* refers to the degree to which a system is easy to learn and use. Ensuring usability is not easy; there are many different types of users, with differing preferences and skills to accommodate. Features that are easy for one person to use might be difficult for another. If the system has a variety of end users, how can the designer be sure that the interface will work well for all of them? If it is too flexible, for example, some end users may feel lost. On the other hand, if the interface is too rigid, some users will be frustrated.

But there is more to consider for ease of learning and ease of use. These concepts often conflict, because an interface that is easy to learn is not always easy to use. For example, menu-based applications with multiple forms, many dialog boxes, and extensive prompts and instructions are easy to learn—indeed, they are self-explanatory. Easy-to-learn interfaces are appropriate for systems that end users use infrequently. But if office workers use the system all day, it is important to make the interface fast and flexible, with shortcuts, hot keys, and information-intensive screens. This second interface might be harder to learn, but it will be easier to use once it is learned. Office workers (with the support of their management) are willing to invest more time learning the system to become efficient users.

Developers employ many techniques to evaluate interface designs to ensure usability. User-centered design requires testing all aspects of the user interface. Some usability testing techniques collect objective data that can be statistically analyzed to compare designs. Some techniques collect subjective data about user perceptions and attitudes. To assess user attitudes, developers conduct formal surveys, focus group meetings, design walkthroughs, paper and pencil evaluations, expert evaluations, formal laboratory experiments, and informal observation.

The third principle of user-centered design is to use iterative development—doing some requirements modeling, then some design, then some implementation and testing, and then repeating the processes. After each iteration, the project team evaluates the work on the system to date. Iterative development keeps the focus on the user by continually returning to the user requirements during each iteration and by evaluating the system after each iteration.

HUMAN-COMPUTER INTERACTION AS A FIELD OF STUDY

human factors engineering (ergonomics)
the study of human interaction with machines in general

User-interface design techniques and HCI as a field of study evolved from studies of human interaction with machines in general, referred to as *human factors engineering* or *ergonomics*. The formal study of human factors began during World War II, when aerospace engineers studied the effects on airplane pilots of rearranging controls in the cockpit. Pilots are responsible for controlling many devices as they fly, and the effectiveness of the interaction between the pilot and the devices is critical. If the pilot makes a mistake (that is, if he or she can't correctly use a device), the plane may crash. What the pilot does is the "human factor" that engineers realized was often beyond their control.

One story about the importance of the human factor involved a minor change to the design of the cockpit of a plane. The designers switched the locations of the throttle and the release handle for the ejection seat. The result was a dramatic increase in the number of unexplained pilot ejections. When under pressure, the pilots grabbed what they thought was the throttle and ejected themselves from the plane. Initially, designers dismissed the problem as the need for better training. But even with training, pilots under pressure continued to grab the wrong handle. It became apparent that the key to the "human factor" was to change the machine to accommodate the human rather than trying to change the human to accommodate the machine.

The field of human factors was first associated with engineering, since engineers designed machines. But engineers, who are generally used to precise specifications and predictable behavior, often find the human factor frustrating. Gradually, specialists emerged who began to draw on many disciplines to understand people and their behavior. These disciplines include cognitive psychology, social psychology, linguistics, sociology, anthropology, and others, as shown in Figure 11-2. Information systems specialists with an interest in human-computer interaction study computers plus all of these disciplines.

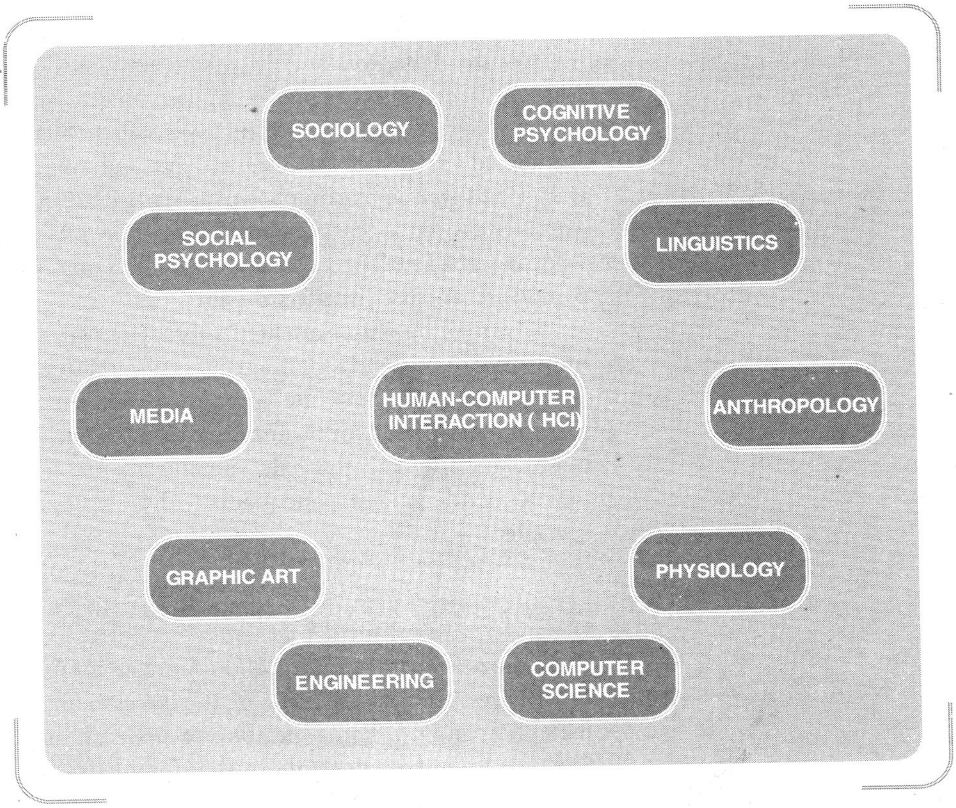

FIGURE 11-2
The fields contributing to the study of HCI

An important contribution to the development of the field of human-computer interaction began with the Xerox Corporation in the 1970s. Xerox produced high-speed photocopying machines that provided an increasing number of special options and capabilities that the human operator could specify. The designers of the photocopying machines recognized the importance of making the complex machines easy for the operators to learn and use. Xerox customers wanted minimal training time for their operators, and operator errors could be costly. For example, if a clerk began a large photocopying job but made a mistake in specifying details, the error would cause waste and delay the distribution of important documents. Therefore, Xerox emphasized the usability of its machines.

Xerox established a research and development laboratory, called the Xerox Palo Alto Research Center (Xerox PARC), to study issues that affect how humans operate machines. As a result of this investment, Xerox eventually offered photocopying machines with touch-screen, menu-driven interfaces that displayed icons representing objects such as documents, stacks of paper, staples, and sorting bins.

Research and development at Xerox PARC also involved work on computers and object-oriented programming. The first pure object-oriented programming language, called Smalltalk, was created at Xerox PARC by Alan Kay and associates to facilitate the development of interactive user interfaces. In the early 1970s, Kay envisioned an advanced, portable personal computing platform (similar to today's ultralight notebook computers) called the Dynabook. Many researchers thought such a machine could not be built for three or four decades because the hardware required for the Dynabook was not available. Kay decided to work on the software that would run the machine in anticipation of the hardware, which led to Smalltalk.

Smalltalk includes classes that make up the key parts of window interfaces today—windows, menus, buttons, labels, text fields, and so forth. The design and programming philosophy used to describe and build these interfaces was developed along with the language—all 100 percent object oriented.

Because of the work at PARC, Xerox eventually developed and marketed one of the first general-purpose personal computers with a graphical user interface—the Xerox Star—in the late 1970s. Although it was ahead of its time and far too expensive, it is considered a landmark development in computing. Its key features were exploited in the early 1980s by a small company near Xerox PARC named Apple Computers. Apple first exploited the Xerox Star's features as the Apple Lisa and then as the Apple Macintosh. The work at Xerox PARC had a substantial impact on object-oriented programming, personal computers, and user-interface design.

Now that the object-oriented approach to system development is becoming more influential, user-interface design concepts and development techniques pioneered at labs such as Xerox PARC are becoming better integrated into system development methodologies used for business systems. The field of HCI has grown and now supports many academic journals, conferences, and book series devoted to research and practice. Undergraduate and graduate degree programs are also available to train HCI specialists.

METAPHORS FOR HUMAN-COMPUTER INTERACTION

There are many ways to think about human-computer interaction, including *metaphors* or *analogies*. Three alternatives are the direct manipulation metaphor, the document metaphor, and the dialog metaphor. Since each metaphor provides an analogy to a different concept, each has implications for the design of the user interface.

THE DIRECT MANIPULATION METAPHOR

direct manipulation
a metaphor of HCI in which the user interacts directly with objects on the display screen

Direct manipulation assumes that the user interacts with objects on the screen instead of typing commands on a command line. Objects that the user can interact with are made visible on the screen so the user can point at them and manipulate them with the mouse or arrow keys. The earliest direct manipulation interfaces were word processors that allowed users to type in words directly where desired in a document. By the early 1980s, electronic spreadsheet applications (first VisiCalc, then Lotus 1-2-3) became available for IBM DOS PCs. These applications used a direct manipulation approach—the user typed numbers, formulas, or text directly into cells on a spreadsheet. The spreadsheet on the screen was conceptually similar to a paper spreadsheet, a format that was familiar to people working in accounting and finance. The familiarity and direct manipulation features made these applications easy to understand and natural to use, and end users could speed their work by including formulas to do the calculations on the spreadsheets automatically. These early direct manipulation DOS applications were an important reason for the success of the personal computer. Even though they did not have graphical user interfaces, they were very popular because they made interacting with a computer straightforward, natural, and productive.

The Smalltalk language developed at Xerox PARC extended direct manipulation to all objects on the screen. Some of these objects are interface objects such as buttons, check boxes, scroll bars, and slider controls, but other problem domain objects such as documents, schedules, file folders, and business records are also displayed as objects that the user can directly manipulate. For example, an interface might include a trash can object; to delete a document file, the user clicks on the document with the mouse and drags the document to the trash can. By directly manipulating the objects in this way, the user tells the computer to delete the document file.

desktop metaphor
a direct manipulation approach in which the display screen includes an arrangement of objects commonly found on a desk

Direct manipulation coupled with object-oriented programming eventually evolved into the *desktop metaphor*, in which the display screen includes an arrangement of common desktop objects—a notepad, a calendar, a calculator, and folders containing documents. Many desktops now also include a telephone, an answering machine, a CD player, and even a video monitor. Interacting with any of these objects is similar to interacting with the real-world objects they represent (see Figure 11-3). End users now expect all applications, including business information systems, to be as natural to work with as objects on the desktop.

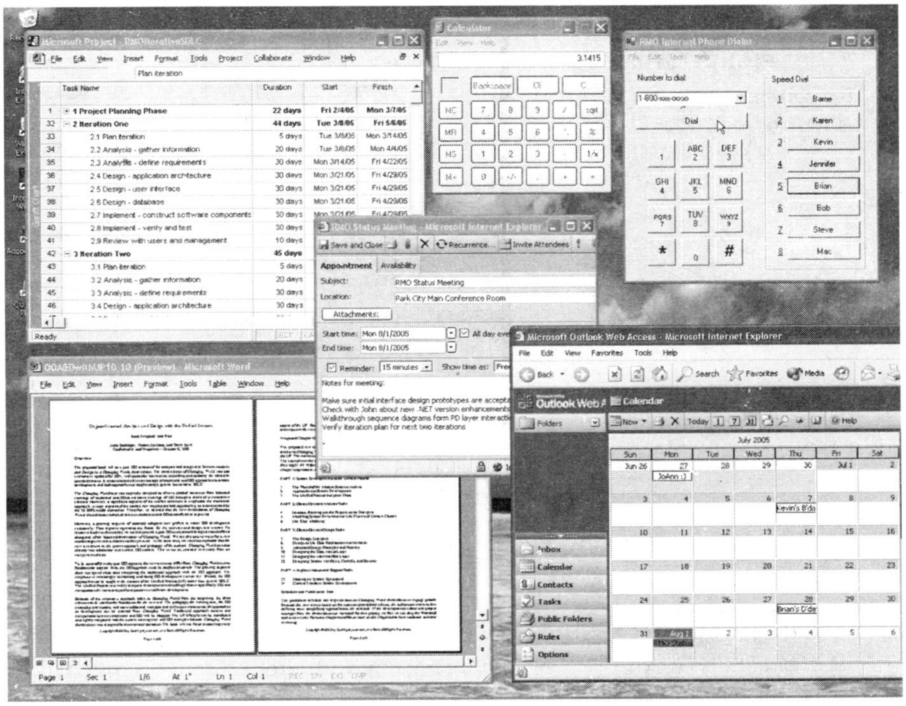

FIGURE 11-3
The desktop metaphor based on direct manipulation, shown on a display screen

THE DOCUMENT METAPHOR

document metaphor
a metaphor of HCI in which interaction with the computer involves browsing and entering data on electronic documents

hypertext
documents that allow the user to click on a link and jump to a different part of the document or to another document

Another view of the interface is the *document metaphor*, in which interaction with the computer involves browsing and entering data on electronic documents. These documents are much like printed documents, but because the documents are electronic, they are more interactive. Electronic versions of documents can be organized differently from paper versions because the reader can jump around from place to place. *Hypertext* documents allow the user to click on a link and jump to a different part of the document or to another document entirely.

hypermedia
technology that extends the hypertext concepts to include multimedia content such as graphics, video, and audio

Most common desktop applications create and edit electronic documents, which are not limited to text and usually include word processing, spreadsheets, presentations, and graphics. All of these applications produce documents, but any one document can contain words, numbers, and graphics produced by any of these appiications, making documents into collections of all sorts of interrelated media. *Hypermedia* extends the hypertext concept to include multimedia content such as graphics, video, and audio in a document, all of which can be linked for navigation by a user.

The World Wide Web is based on the document metaphor, because everything at a Web site is organized as pages that are linked as hypermedia (note that HTML means *Hypertext* Markup Language). A Web site processes transactions by selecting information on a Web page document. The document metaphor and the browser interface function as useful ways of describing and designing interactive systems, and they will continue to affect user-interface designs (see Figure 11-4).

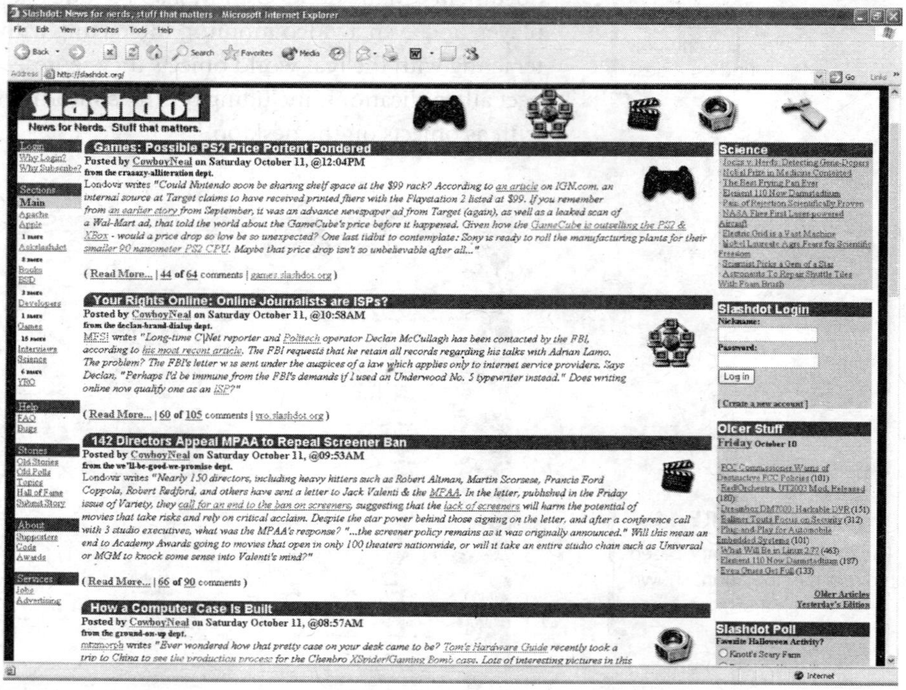

FIGURE 11-4
The document metaphor shown as hypermedia in a Web browser

THE DIALOG METAPHOR

dialog metaphor
a metaphor of HCI in which interacting with the computer is much like carrying on a conversation or dialog

The direct manipulation and document metaphors emphasize objects in the computer with which the user interacts. Another view of the interface is the *dialog metaphor*, in which interacting with the computer is much like carrying on a conversation or dialog. In fact, user-interface design is often referred to as *dialog design*. Carrying on a dialog, or conversation, requires each participant to listen to and respond to questions and comments from the other, exchanging information in a sequence. The dialog metaphor is another way of thinking about human-computer interaction because the computer "listens to" and responds to user questions or comments, and the user "listens to" and responds to the computer's questions and comments. Like the direct manipulation metaphor, the dialog metaphor is based on an object-oriented view of the system because communication involves messages from one "object" to another. Figure 11-5 shows how the user and the computer communicate by sending messages to each other.

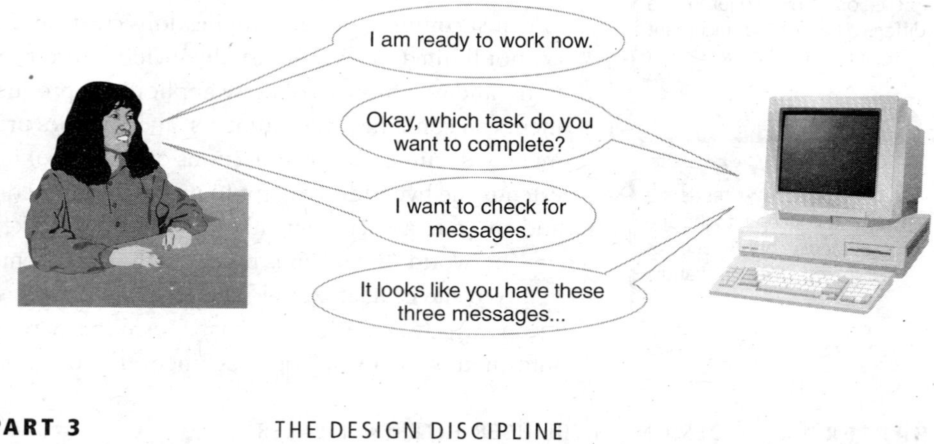

FIGURE 11-5
The dialog metaphor expresses the concept that the user and computer interact by sending messages

Consider the following dialog between a manager and an assistant:

Manager:	Did I get any messages while I was out?
Assistant:	Yes, you have three messages—from Bob, Mary, and Lim.
Manager:	What did Lim have to say?
Assistant:	Lim left a message at 8:15 P.M. last night regarding the meeting next Monday about the inventory management system. The message is, "Can we change the time for the meeting to 10:30? I'll be delayed by the testing session."
Manager:	I better respond. Say that the change is not a problem.
Assistant:	Okay, I'll leave him that message. Do you want the next message?
Manager:	What did Mary have to say?
Assistant:	She left a message at 8:15 this morning regarding lunch. She said, "Lunch is still on, but Joe will not be able to join us."
Manager:	Okay, no response. And that's all for now. Thanks.
Assistant:	Okay, you still have one message from Bob. I'll remind you later.

This dialog involves the manager and the assistant carrying on a conversation about messages. The questions asked by the manager and the responses and follow-up questions from the assistant seem clear and natural. Would the basic dialog be any different if this were an automated phone-answering service that responded to voice commands and replied in a computer-generated voice? Probably not. Would it be any different if this were a computer application simulating an intelligent "assistant"? Probably not. The basic dialog followed would be the same: a question, a response, another question, a response that might include a request for clarification, a response to the request for clarification, and a final response.

The basic dialog is also the same for a typical e-mail application, even though the user and computer send messages in different ways. The user selects a menu item for *read new mail*. The computer lists the new mail messages for the user to choose, the user chooses one message, then the computer displays the message. It might seem odd to think of interaction with an e-mail application as being similar to the dialog just presented, but the basic information exchanged and the sequence of actions are the same.

The user and the computer both send messages, but each is forced to use a different language because of the limitations of both the user and the computer. The user cannot understand cryptic binary codes or plug in directly to the computer to interpret the electrical impulses the computer uses to represent the binary codes. The natural language of the computer just won't work for people. The computer has to adapt to the user and provide its messages in a form that is natural for the user—text and graphics that the user can see and read.

Similarly, the computer cannot understand complex voice messages, facial expressions, and body language that are the natural communication cues of the user, so the user has to adapt to the computer and provide messages by clicking the mouse, dragging objects, and typing words on the keyboard. Advances in computer technology are making it possible for the user to communicate in more natural ways, but the typical user interfaces today still rely on the mouse and keyboard. One reason is the need for silence and also privacy in the office, so it is not clear whether voice commands will become common in computer applications.

The challenge of user-interface design is to construct a natural dialog sequence that allows the user and computer to exchange the messages required to carry out a task. Then the designer needs to develop the details of the language required for the user to send the messages to the computer (the user's language), plus the language needed for the computer to send messages to the user (the computer's language).

FIGURE 11-6
The user's language and the computer's language used to implement an e-mail application based on the natural dialog between manager and assistant

Figure 11-6 shows the earlier dialog between manager and assistant translated into the languages used by the user and the computer. Interface designers use a variety of informal diagrams and written narratives to model human-computer interaction. This is just one way the dialog design details can be modeled; you'll learn about additional techniques later in this chapter.

	MESSAGE	USER'S LANGUAGE	COMPUTER'S LANGUAGE
Manager	Did I get any messages while I was out?	Click the *read messages* menu item on the main menu.	
Assistant	Yes, you have three messages—from Bob, Mary, and Lim.		Look up new messages for the user and display a new message form with message headers listed in a list box.
Manager	What did Lim have to say?	Double-click the message from Lim in the list box.	
Assistant	Lim left a message at 8:15 P.M. last night regarding the meeting next Monday about the inventory management system. The message is, "Can we change the time for the meeting to 10:30? I'll be delayed by the testing session."		Look up the message body for the selected message and display it in message detail form.
Manager	I better respond. Say that the change is not a problem.	Click the Reply button on the message detail form. Type in the message, "Okay, that is not a problem." Click the Send Button.	Display the new message form addressed to the sender.
Assistant	Okay, I'll leave him that message. Do you want the next message?		Display the Message Sent dialog box and redisplay the new messages form with message headers listed in the list box.
Manager	What did Mary have to say?	Double-click the message from Mary in the list box.	
Assistant	She left a message at 8:15 this morning regarding lunch. She said, "Lunch is still on, but Joe will not be able to join us."		Look up the message body for the selected message and display it in message detail form.
Manager	Okay, no response. And that's all for now. Thanks.	Click the *close message* button. Click the *close new message form* button.	Redisplay a new message form with message headers listed in the list box.
Assistant	Okay, you still have one message from Bob. I'll remind you later.		Display the Closing Read New Mail dialog box, showing one unread message remaining.

GUIDELINES FOR DESIGNING USER INTERFACES

There are many published interface design guidelines to guide system developers. User-interface design guidelines range from general principles to very specific rules. This section describes some well-known guidelines for designing the user interface. Later, this chapter presents some of the guidelines and rules for designing windows forms and browser forms used with Web-based development. Some system development organizations adopt *interface design standards*—general principles and rules that an organization must follow when developing any system. Design standards help ensure that all user interfaces function well and that all systems developed by the organization have a similar look and feel.

interface design standards
general principles and rules that must be followed for the interface of any system developed by the organization

VISIBILITY AND AFFORDANCE

Donald Norman is a leading researcher in HCI who proposes two key principles to ensure good interaction between a person and a machine: visibility and affordance. These two principles apply to human-computer interaction just as they do for any other device.

visibility
a key principle of HCI that states that all controls should be visible and provide feedback to indicate that the control is responding to the user's action

Visibility means that a control should be visible so users know it is available and that the control should provide immediate feedback to indicate it is responding. For example, a steering wheel is visible to a driver, and when the driver turns it to the left, it is obvious that the wheel is responding to the driver's action. Similarly, a button that can be clicked by a user is visible, and when it is clicked, it changes to look as though it has been pressed, to indicate it is responding. Some buttons make a clicking sound to provide feedback.

affordance
a key principle of HCI that states that the appearance of any control should suggest its functionality

Affordance means that the appearance of any control should suggest its functionality—that is, the purpose for which the control is used. For example, a control that looks like a steering wheel suggests that the control is used for turning. On the computer, a button affords (provides the means for) clicking, a scroll bar affords scrolling, and an item in a list affords selecting. Norman's principles apply to any objects on the desktop, such as those shown previously in the examples in Figures 11-3 and 11-4.

If user-interface designers make sure that all controls are visible and that their appearance suggests what they do, the interface will be usable. Most users are familiar with the Windows interface and the common Windows controls. However, designers should be careful to apply these principles of visibility and affordance when designing Web pages. Many new types of controls are now possible at Web sites, but these controls are not always as visible and their effects are not always as obvious as they are in a standard Windows interface. More objects are clickable, but it is not always clear what is clickable, when a control has recognized the click, and what the click will accomplish. For example, sometimes you click on an image and a new page opens in the browser. Other times you click on an image and nothing happens.

FIGURE 11-7
The eight golden rules for designing interactive interfaces

1. Strive for Consistency
2. Enable Frequent Users to Use Shortcuts
3. Offer Informative Feedback
4. Design Dialogs to Yield Closure
5. Offer Simple Error Handling
6. Permit Easy Reversal of Actions
7. Support Internal Locus of Control
8. Reduce Short-Term Memory Load

EIGHT GOLDEN RULES

Ben Shneiderman, another leading researcher in HCI, proposes eight underlying principles that are applicable in most interactive systems (see "Further Resources" at the end of the chapter for Shneiderman's text). Although they are general guidelines rather than specific rules, he names them "golden rules" to indicate that they are the key to usability (see Figure 11-7).

STRIVE FOR CONSISTENCY

Designing a consistent-looking interface that functions consistently is one of the most important design goals. The way that information is arranged on forms, the names and arrangement of menu items, the size and shape of icons, and the sequence followed to carry out tasks should be consistent throughout the system. Why? People are creatures of habit. Once we learn one way of doing things, it is difficult for us to change. When we operate a computer application, many of our actions become automatic—we do not think about what we are doing. People who can touch-type do not have to think about each key press—their fingers just respond automatically. Consider what would happen to touch-typists if rows two and three on the keyboard were reversed. They would not be able to use the keyboard (and certainly wouldn't like it). If a new application comes along that has a different way of functioning, productivity suffers and users are not happy.

The Apple Macintosh first emphasized the benefits of consistency in the 1980s. Apple provided applications for the Macintosh that set the standard for developers to follow when creating new applications. If new applications were consistent with these applications, Apple claimed, learning them would be easy. Apple also published a standards document to explain how to be consistent with the Macintosh interface. Similar examples and standards documents followed for the Microsoft Windows interface.

Business information systems are different from desktop applications originally produced for the Macintosh. Sometimes an application needs to be inconsistent with the original guidelines. For example, the original standards specified that every application include menus on the menu bar for File, Edit, and Format. All document-oriented applications—such as word processors, spreadsheets, and graphics—need those menus. But many business systems do not have file, edit, and format functions. Most other guidelines and standards do apply, however.

Research has also shown that inconsistent interfaces sometimes are beneficial. If the user is interacting with multiple applications in separate windows, a different visual appearance may help the user differentiate them. Additionally, when the user is learning several applications in one session, some differences in the interfaces may help the user remember which application is which. Inconsistencies introduced for these reasons should be subtle and superficial. The basic operation of the applications should be the same.

ENABLE FREQUENT USERS TO USE SHORTCUTS

Users who work with one application all day long are willing to invest the time to learn shortcuts. They rapidly lose patience with long menu sequences and multiple dialog boxes when they know exactly what they want to do. Therefore, designers provide shortcut keys that reduce the number of interactions for a given task. Also, designers should provide macro facilities for users to create their own shortcuts.

Sometimes the entire interface should be designed for frequent users who do not need much flexibility. Consider the mail-order data-entry clerks for Rocky Mountain Outfitters. They enter orders into the system all day long from paper forms mailed by customers. These users need an interface that is simple, fast, and accurate. Long dialogs, multiple menus, and multiple forms would slow these users down.

OFFER INFORMATIVE FEEDBACK

Every action a user takes should result in some type of feedback from the computer so that the user knows the action has been recognized. Even keyboard clicks help the user, so an electronic "click" is included deliberately by the operating system. If the user clicks a button, the button should visually change and perhaps make a sound.

Feedback of information to the user is also important. If the Rocky Mountain Outfitters mail-order clerk enters a customer ID number in an order screen, the system should look up the customer to validate the ID number, but it should also display the name and address to the clerk so that the clerk is confident the number is correct. Similarly, when the clerk enters a product ID for the order, the system should display a description of the product. As the clerk's attention shifts back and forth from the mail-order form to the computer screen, he or she compares the name and product description from the system with the information on the form to confirm that everything is correct. This sense of confirmation and the resulting confidence in the system are very important to users, particularly when they work with a system all day. But the system should not slow the user down by displaying too many dialog boxes to which the user must respond.

Sometimes feedback is provided to help the user in other ways. The phone-order representative at Rocky Mountain Outfitters needs information from the system, just as the mail-order clerk does, but he or she also needs additional information. Phone customers may ask questions, so the information provided as feedback for the phone-order representative is more detailed and flexible. We discuss some designs for the system used by the phone-order representative at RMO later in this chapter.

DESIGN DIALOGS TO YIELD CLOSURE

Each dialog with the system should be organized with a clear sequence—a beginning, middle, and end. Any well-defined task has a beginning, middle, and end, so user's tasks on the computer should also feel this way. If the user is thinking, "I want to check my messages," as in the earlier manager and assistant dialog example, the dialog begins with a request, exchanges information, and then ends. The user can get lost if it is not clear when a task starts and ends. Additionally, the user often focuses intently on a task, so when it is confirmed that the task is complete, the user can clear his or her mind and get ready to focus on the next task.

If the system requirements are defined initially as events to which the system responds, each event leads to processing of one specific, well-defined use case. Each use case might be further defined as multiple scenarios, each with a flow of steps. Each scenario is a well-defined interaction; therefore, event decomposition sets the stage for dialogs with closure.

OFFER SIMPLE ERROR HANDLING

User errors are costly, both in the time needed to correct them and in the resulting mistakes. If Rocky Mountain Outfitters sends the wrong items to a customer, it is a costly error. So, the systems designer must prevent the user from making errors whenever possible. A chief way to do this is to limit available options and allow the user to choose only from valid options at any point in the dialog. Adequate feedback, as discussed previously, also helps reduce errors.

If an error does occur, the system needs mechanisms for handling it. The validation techniques discussed in Chapter 12 are useful for catching errors, but the system must also help the user correct the error. When the system does find an error, the error message should state specifically what is wrong and explain how to correct it. Error messages should not be judgmental. It is not appropriate to blame the user or make the user feel inadequate.

The system also should make it easy to correct the error. For example, if the user typed in an invalid customer ID, the system should tell the user that and then place the cursor in the customer ID text box with the previously typed number displayed and ready to edit. This way, the user can see the mistake and edit it rather than having to retype the entire ID. Consider the following error message, which occurs after a user has typed in a full screen of information about a new customer:

```
The customer information entered is not valid. Try again.
```

This message does not explain what is wrong or what to do next. Further, what if the system cleared the data-entry form and redisplayed it after this message appeared? The user would have to reenter everything previously typed yet would still have no idea what is wrong. The error message did not explain it, and now that the typed data have been cleared, the user cannot tell what might have been wrong. A better error message would say:

```
The date of birth entered is not valid. Check to be sure
only numeric characters in appropriate ranges are entered
in the date of birth field...
```

The input form should be redisplayed with all fields still filled in, and the cursor should be placed at the field with invalid data, ready for the user to edit the field.

PERMIT EASY REVERSAL OF ACTIONS

Users need to feel that they can explore options and take actions that can be canceled or reversed without difficulty. This is one way that users learn about the system—by experimenting. It is also a way to prevent errors; as users recognize they have made a mistake, they cancel the action. In the game of checkers, a move is not final until the player takes his or her fingers off the game piece; it should be the same when a user drags an object on the screen. Additionally, designers should be sure to include Cancel buttons on all dialog boxes and allow users to go back one step at any time. Finally, when the user deletes something substantial—a file, a record, or a transaction—the system should ask the user to confirm the action.

SUPPORT INTERNAL LOCUS OF CONTROL

Experienced users want to feel that they are in charge of the system and that the system responds to their commands. They should not be forced to do anything or made to feel as if the system is controlling them. Systems should make users feel that they are deciding what to do. Designers can provide much of this comfort and control through the wording of prompts and messages. Writing out a dialog like the manager and assistant message dialog given previously will lead to a design that conveys the feeling of control.

REDUCE SHORT-TERM MEMORY LOAD

People have many limitations, and short-term memory is one of the biggest. People can remember only about seven chunks of information at a time. The interface designer cannot assume that the user will remember anything from form to form, or dialog box to dialog box, during an interaction with the system. If the user has to stop and ask, "Now what was the filename? the customer ID? the product description?" then the design places too much of a burden on the user's memory.

With these eight golden rules in mind, an interface designer can help ensure that user interactions are efficient and effective. We now turn to some basic techniques for documenting the design of the dialog.

DOCUMENTING DIALOG DESIGNS

Many techniques are available to help the designer think through and document dialog designs. The dialogs that must be designed are based on use cases with inputs and outputs requiring user interaction, as discussed earlier. They are used to define a menu hierarchy that allows the user to navigate to each dialog. Storyboards, prototypes, and UML diagrams can be used to complete the designs.

USE CASES, SUBSYSTEMS, AND THE MENU HIERARCHY

Inputs and outputs are obtained from use cases and scenarios. Generally, each use case with an input *obtained interactively from a user* requires a dialog design. Additionally, each use case with an output produced *at the request of a user* requires a dialog design. So, each dialog is based on a use case documented early during the inception phase that is classified as requiring a user interface rather than a system interface.

The available menus reflect the overall system structure from the standpoint of the user. Each menu contains a hierarchy of options, and they are often arranged by subsystem or by actions on objects. Rocky Mountain Outfitters' customer support system includes the order-entry subsystem, order fulfillment subsystem, customer maintenance subsystem, and catalog maintenance subsystem, as well as a reporting subsystem. Each subsystem might be represented as a menu, with each menu option representing a use case. Menus might also be arranged according to objects—customers, orders, inventory, and shipments—with each menu option representing an operation on an object. Each menu hierarchy might include duplicate menu options, such as *Look up past orders*, under customers and under inventory.

Sometimes several versions of the menus are needed based on the type of user. For example, mail-order clerks at RMO do not need many of the options available—they process new orders only. The phone-order sales representatives need many more options, but they still do not need all system functions. And some options should be available only to managers, such as management reports and price adjustments.

Menus should also include options that are *not* use cases based on the event list—most important are options related to the system controls, which are discussed in Chapter 12. These include backup and recovery of databases in some cases, plus user account maintenance. Additionally, user preferences are usually provided to allow the user to tailor the interface. Finally, menus should always include help facilities.

All use cases that lead to dialogs in the RMO customer support system are listed and grouped by subsystem in Figure 11-8. These groupings form one set of menu hierarchies. In addition, there are menu hierarchies for utilities, preferences, and help. The list in the figure is only one of many possible menu hierarchy designs—a starting place.

FIGURE 11-8

One overall menu hierarchy design for the RMO customer support system (not all users will have all of these options available)

Five menu hierarchies grouped by subsystem and based on use cases

- Order Entry
  - Check Availability
  - Create New Order
  - Update Order
- Order Fulfillment
  - Check Order Status
  - Record Fulfillment
  - Record Back Order
  - Create Return
- Customer Account Maintenance
  - Provide Catalog
  - Update Customer Account
  - Adjust Customer Charges
  - Distribute Promotional Package
- Catalog Maintenance
  - Update Catalog
  - Create Special Promotion
  - Create New Catalog
- Reporting and Queries
  - Order Summary Report
  - Transaction Summary Reports
  - Fulfillment Summary Reports
  - Prospective Customer Lists
  - Customer Adjustment Reports
  - Catalog Activity Reports
  - Ad Hoc Query Facility

Three menu hierachies added during design for controls, preferences, and help

- System Utilities
  - Printers and Devices
  - Backup and Recovery
  - User Accounts
    - Maintain Accounts
    - Change Current User Password
- User Preferences
  - Dialog Style
  - Color and Font
  - Shortcuts
  - Macro Facility
- Help
  - Contents and Index
  - Search for Help
  - Task List
  - About the RMO System

A dialog design is created for each of these menu options. After completing the dialog designs for all options, the designer can redefine the structure of the menus for different types of users. Menu hierarchies can be rearranged easily as the design evolves.

DIALOGS AND STORYBOARDS

After identifying all required dialogs, the designers must document the dialogs. Many options exist; there are no de facto standards. One approach is to list the key steps followed for the dialog with a written description of what the user and computer do at each step. The format for writing these steps can follow the activity diagram described in Chapter 4 or the use case description format in Chapter 6, or they can be more free-form.

Designers can also document dialog designs by writing out a human and computer "dialog" such as the one presented earlier in this chapter (for the manager and assistant), then documenting how the user and computer express themselves, as shown previously in Figure 11-6. They do this only if there are complicated or uncertain aspects to the requirements. Often the designer can go right from the use case description to sketching a series of screens that make the design more visible. Consider the DownTown Videos rental system described in a case study at the end of Chapter 6. One use case is *Rent videos*, and the dialog for renting videos to a customer that goes on between the clerk and the system would follow this pattern:

System:	What DownTown Videos option do you want?
User:	I need to rent some videos.
System:	Okay, what is the customer's ID number for this rental?
User:	It is 201564.
System:	Fine, your customer is Nancy Wells at 1122 Silicon Avenue. Note that she has two kids, Bob and Sally, who can only rent PG-13 videos. Correct?
User:	Yes.
System:	What's the ID number of the first video she wants to rent?
User:	It is 5312.
System:	Fine, that is *Titanic* (the 1953 version with Barbara Stanwyck) with a rental charge of \$1.00 for three days, rated PG. What's the ID number of the next video, or is that all?
User:	It is 8645.
System:	Fine, that is *Titanic* (the 2006 reissue version) with a rental charge of \$3.00 for three days, rated PG-13. What's the ID number of the next video, or is that all?
User:	That's all.
System:	Okay, collect \$4.00 plus \$.24 tax, for a total of \$4.24, and let me know when you are done.
User:	Yes, I'm done.
System:	Remind Nancy Wells that these videos are due back Wednesday, the ninth, before 11 P.M. closing.
User:	Okay. Thanks.

The designer thinks through the sequence of screens the user would need to carry on this dialog with the computer. The user needs to enter a customer ID and several video IDs. The computer has to look up and display information on the customer and each video rented. Then the computer calculates the total due and reminds the user of the due date so the user can pass that information on to the customer.

storyboarding
a technique used to document dialog designs by showing a sequence of sketches of the display screen

One technique used to show the screens is called *storyboarding*—showing a sequence of sketches of the display screen during a dialog. The sketches do not have to be very detailed to show the basic design concept. Designers can implement a storyboard with a visual programming tool such as Visual Basic, but using simple sketches drawn with a graphics package can help keep the focus on the fundamental design ideas.

BEST PRACTICE: The UP considers user-interface storyboarding to be a requirements discipline activity, completed early, when defining the requirements for each use case.

Figure 11-9 shows the storyboard for the *rent videos* dialog. The system has a menu hierarchy based on the use cases plus needed system controls, preferences, and help. The dialog uses one form and a few dialog boxes and adds more information to the form as the dialog progresses. Note that the prompt area at the bottom of the form displays the questions the computer asks, which match the phrases used in the written dialog almost identically. The user has a choice of either scanning or typing the few IDs that must be entered. Information provided to the user is shown in labels on the form. The information provided allows the user to confirm the identity of the customer, to see any restrictions that might apply, and to pass on to the customer any information about cost and return dates. In other words, the system helps the user do a better job of interacting with the customer by confirming information, providing feedback, and providing closure.

These approaches to dialog design provide only a framework to work from, and the resulting design remains fairly general. As working prototypes are produced, many details still have to be worked out. As the design progresses, reviewing the golden rules and other guidelines will help you keep the focus on usability.

DIALOG DOCUMENTATION WITH UML DIAGRAMS

Many UML diagrams are useful for modeling user-computer dialogs. Use case descriptions, shown in Chapter 6, include a list of steps followed as the user and system interact. Activity diagrams, shown in Chapters 4 and 6, also document the dialog between user and computer for a use case. Both can be used to provide models of the user-computer interaction required in each dialog. In the object-oriented approach, objects send messages back and forth, listening to and responding to each other in sequence. People also send messages to objects and receive messages back from them. The system sequence diagram (SSD) described in Chapter 6 includes an actor (a user) sending messages to the system and the system returning information in the form of messages, shown in sequence. It basically shows a dialog between the user and the system. The SSD is based on the sequence of steps included in the use case description, so the dialog design for the use case begins very early and is refined continually.

FIGURE 11-9
Storyboard for the DownTown Videos *rent videos* dialog

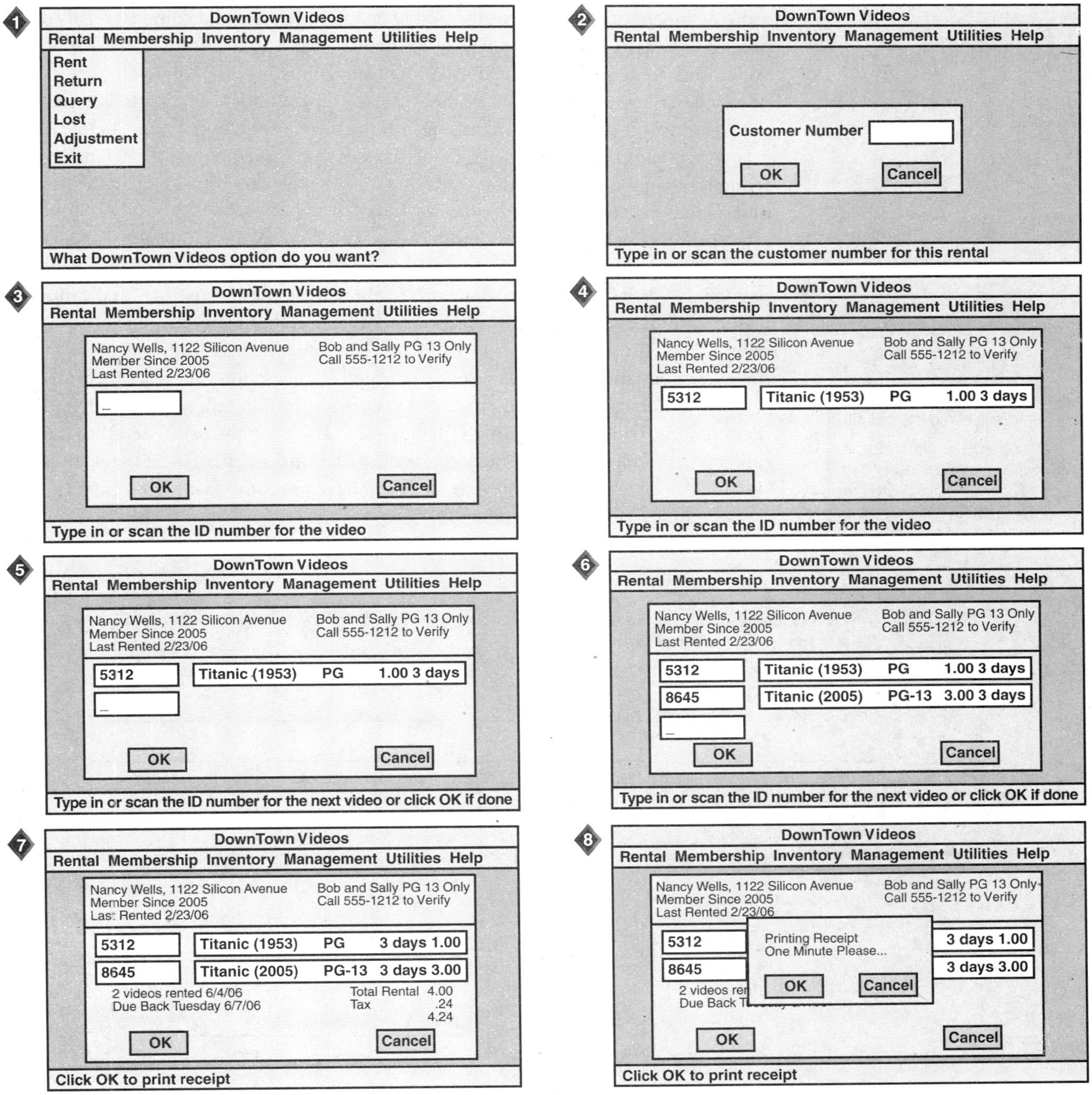

The object-oriented approach involves adding more types of objects to class diagrams and interaction diagrams as the project moves from requirements to design, as discussed in Chapters 8 and 9. The additional classes of objects are packaged into three layers that contain user-interface classes, problem domain classes, and data access classes. Designers add user-interface classes and objects to these diagrams to show more detail about the design of the dialog between the user and computer. This design process was demonstrated in Chapter 8. The first step is to determine what window or Web forms are required for the dialog, by means of the informal dialog design techniques described previously. Next, the sequence diagram for the scenario is expanded to show the user (an actor) interacting with the forms. The designer can then use a class diagram to model the user-interface classes that make up the forms. Finally, the sequence diagram can be further expanded to show the user interacting with specific objects that make up the form.

Recall the Rocky Mountain Outfitters use case *Look up item availability*. A system sequence diagram was shown for this use case in Chapter 8 (Figure 8-12), and it was expanded in a series of sequence diagrams to show the complete use case realization. Figure 11-10 shows a version of the sequence diagram that includes a form (or window) named ProductQueryForm. The form represents the user-interface layer of the three-layer design. The form is inserted between the actor and the use case controller. The actor interacts with the interface objects on the form to talk to the problem domain objects, which reply through the interface objects on the form. Recall that the requirements model of the interaction just shows the messages between the actor and the system. The design model inserts the user-interface layer to create a physical model of how the interaction is implemented.

FIGURE 11-10
A sequence diagram for the RMO *Look up item availability* dialog with the ProductQueryForm added

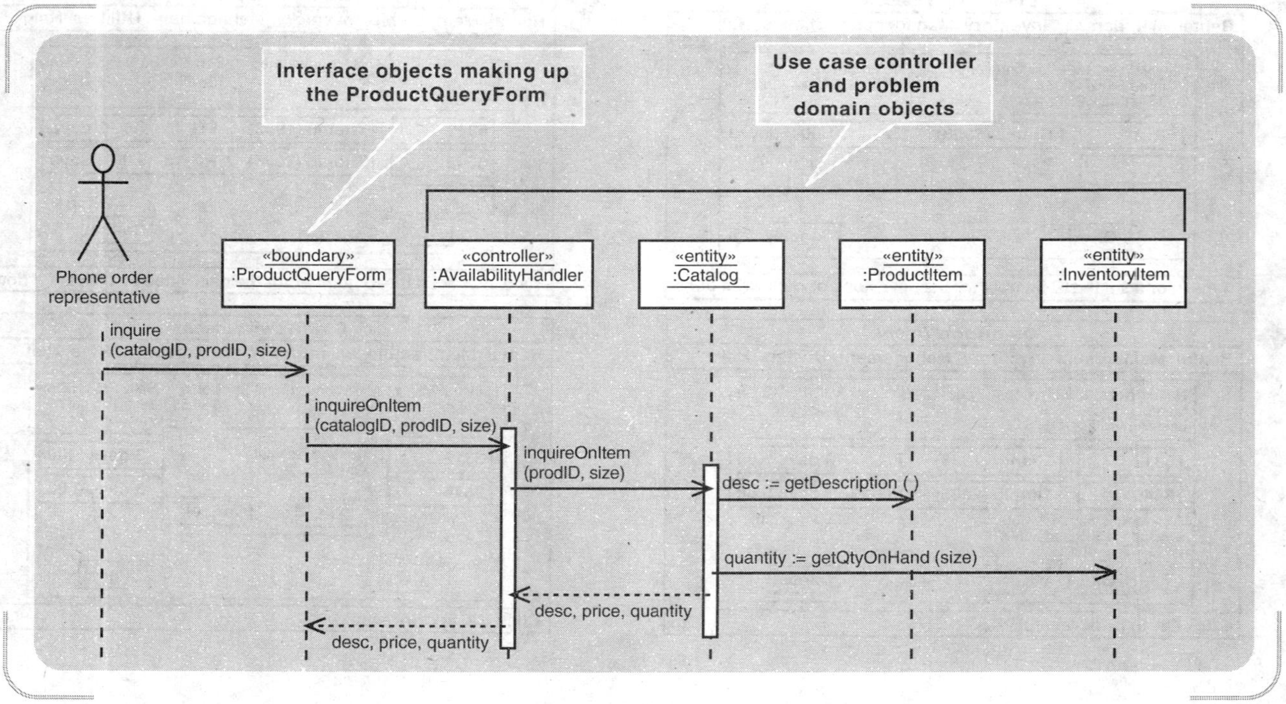

The form shown on the sequence diagram includes specific interface objects. Figure 11-11 shows a class diagram with the interface classes used to make up the form. The Frame class in Figure 11-11 represents the basic structure that contains other interface objects. A MenuBar is attached to the frame, a menu bar contains Menus, and a menu contains MenuItems. The associations between these classes are aggregations shown with the diamond symbol on the class diagram (aggregation relationships are discussed in Chapter 5). Other classes shown are List, Button, and Label, which also are parts of the frame. This example, based loosely on Java, enables the frame to "listen" for events that occur to interface objects, such as clicking a menu item or a button. The frame's actionListener( ) method is invoked when the frame "hears" that an event has occurred.

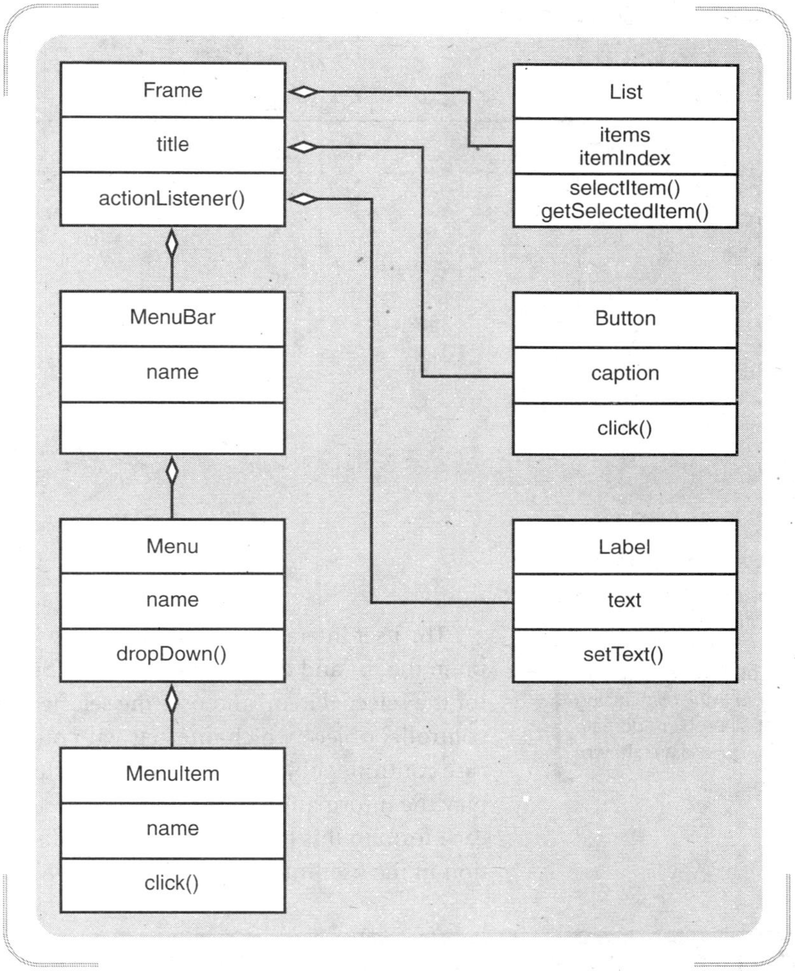

FIGURE 11-11
A class diagram showing interface classes making up the ProductQueryForm

A sequence diagram can be used to model the messages between the user and the specific objects making up the form, including the messages that the interface objects send to each other. Figure 11-12 shows the further expanded sequence diagram. This model emphasizes the details of the form's design, so the problem domain details can be omitted. Nothing has changed for the part of the sequence diagram where the controller and problem domain objects interact among themselves. The interface objects simply have been plugged in between them and the actor.

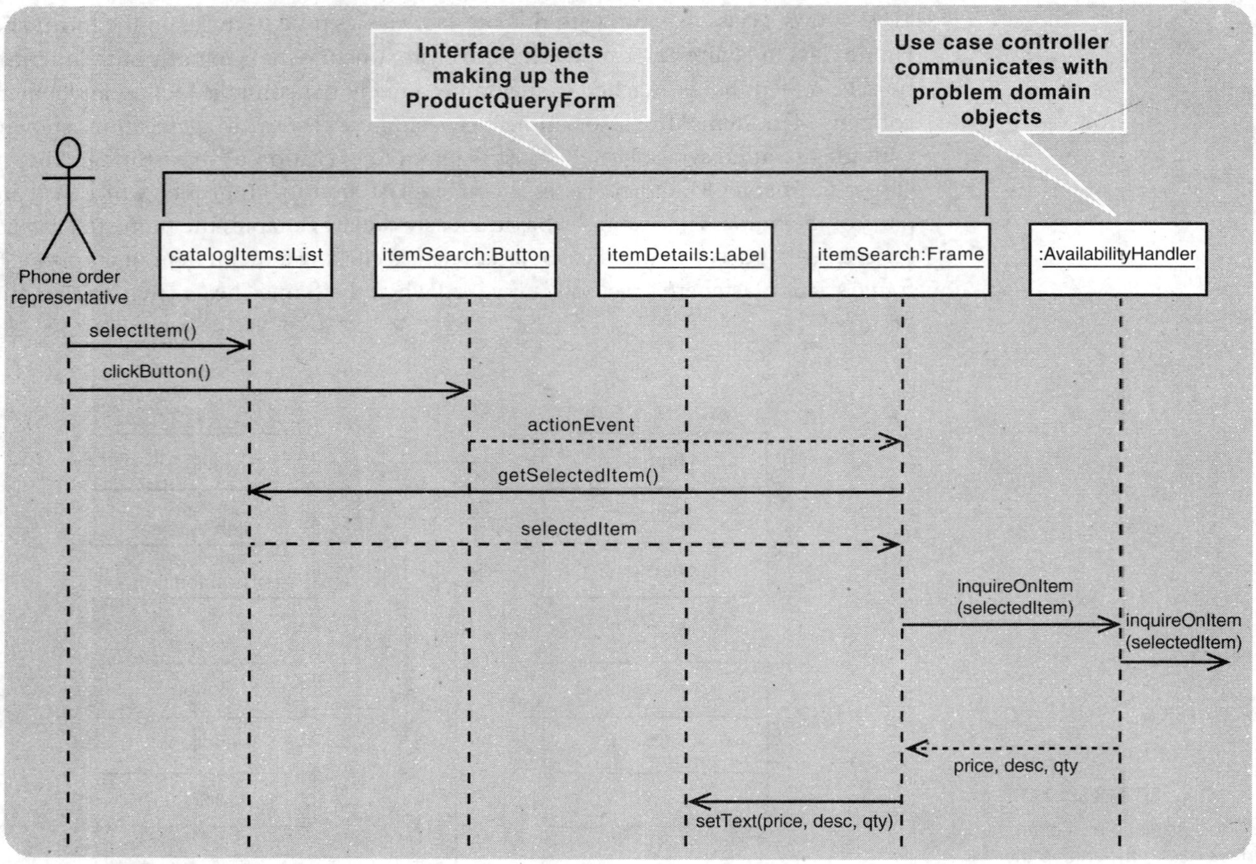

FIGURE 11-12
A sequence diagram showing specific interface objects making up the ProductQuery Form for the *Look up item availability* dialog (not all problem domain objects are shown)

The user interacting with the *Look up item availability* form selects an item to look up in the list and then clicks the search button. The frame "hears" the click, asks the list for the selected item, and uses the selected item in the message to query the use case controller object, which interacts with other problem domain objects. When the use case controller object returns the requested information, the frame tells the label to display the information to the user. The designer would probably not specify the design of each form to this level of detail; the example is intended to illustrate how the interaction in the user-interface layer occurs.

GUIDELINES FOR DESIGNING WINDOWS AND BROWSER FORMS

As with the previous activities of user-interface design, analysts must take care in designing the forms that users see on the screen. Each dialog might require several windows forms, and each form must be designed for usability. Almost all of the new business systems today are developed for an interactive Microsoft Windows, X-Windows (UNIX), or Macintosh environment. The underlying principles are the same for forms in any of these environments. In this section, when we refer to forms or windows, we mean any of these three environments. Within each windows environment, however, we need to consider two types of forms: windows and browsers.

Windows forms are programmed in a full-featured programming language, such as Visual Basic, C++, or Java. Because of this, windows forms have the advantage of being extremely flexible and capable of accessing data directly on a workstation. **Browser forms**, on the other hand, are programmed using HTML and script languages such as VBScript or JavaScript. Browser forms can be displayed using any Internet browser, which makes them accessible on a variety of platforms. Browser forms produced by Visual Studio .NET are now called *Web forms*, and they now provide the same design flexibility as windows forms. Additionally, server-side processing using Active Server Pages (ASP) or Java servlets can add functionality. The advantage of browser forms is that the same forms can be used for both internal staff on company intranets and customers and suppliers on the Internet. As a result, many firms are designing user interfaces for their new systems as browser forms.

> **browser forms**
> forms programmed using HTML and script languages that follow Internet conventions

After identifying the objective of a form and its associated data fields, the system developer can construct the form using one of the many prototyping tools available. Earlier, developers spent tremendous amounts of time laying out a form on paper diagrams before beginning programming. Today, however, the process is streamlined with prototyping tools. Not only can developers design the content of the form, but they can also design the look and feel of the form at the same time. Prototyping tools also permit users to be heavily involved in the development, and such involvement ensures that the user interface is in fact the *user's* interface, providing a strong sense of ownership and acceptance.

Categories of forms include input forms, input/output forms, and output forms. Input forms are used to record a transaction or enter data, although some portions of the form may display information from the system. The form used in the DownTown Videos storyboard in Figure 11-9 is an example of an input form. Input/output forms are generally used to update existing data. These forms display information about a single entity, such as a customer, and enable users to type over existing information to update it. Output forms are primarily for displaying information. The design of output forms is based on the same principles as report design, discussed later in Chapter 12. Input and input/output forms are closely related and are designed using similar principles. Before developing a form, the designer should carefully analyze the integrity controls required for data input, which are discussed in Chapter 12.

There are four major issues to consider in the design of these forms:

- Form layout and formatting
- Data keying and entry
- Navigation and support controls
- Help support

FORM LAYOUT AND FORMATTING

Form layout and formatting are concerned with the general look and feel of the form. You may have encountered systems with hard-to-use input forms—the font was too small, the labels were hard to understand, the colors were abrasive, the navigation buttons were not obvious, and so forth. These deficiencies can occur on both windows forms and browser forms. In contrast, forms that are easy to use are well laid out, with the fields easily identified and understood. One of the best methods to ensure that forms are well laid out is to prototype various alternatives and let users test them. Users will let you know which characteristics are helpful and which are distracting. As you design your input forms, you should think about the following:

- Consistency
- Headings, labels, and logos
- Distribution and order of data-entry fields and buttons
- Font sizes, highlighting, and colors

Consistency belongs at the top of the list because of its importance for ease of learning and use, as discussed previously. Some large systems require multiple input forms and several teams of programmers and analysts to develop them. Sometimes those teams don't coordinate their efforts, resulting in inconsistencies, and a system that is not consistent across all forms can be error prone and difficult to use. To avoid these problems, all of the forms within a system need to have the same look and feel. A consistent use of function keys, shortcuts, control buttons, and even color and layout makes a system much more useful and professional looking. Cascading style sheets help designers control the consistency of Web forms. Design templates help designers control the consistency of windows forms. For example, with Microsoft Visual Studio .NET, a template form can be designed that is used as the superclass of all forms in the project.

The headings, labels, and logos on the form help to convey the purpose and use of the form. A clear, descriptive title at the top of the form helps to minimize confusion about a form's use. Labels should also be easy to identify and read.

The designer should also carefully position the data-entry fields around the form. Related fields are usually placed next to each other and can even be isolated with a fine-lined box. The designer should carefully consider the tab order also. If input is coming from a paper form, then the tab order should follow the order of the paper form—left to right, top to bottom. Blank space should be used throughout the form so that the fields do not appear crammed together and are easy to distinguish and read. Normally, navigation buttons are at the bottom of the window. De facto traditions for the placement of buttons are developing based on the standards of the large development firms such as Apple, Microsoft, Sun, Oracle, and others. It is a good idea to be sensitive to these traditions as they change with technology upgrades.

The purpose of font size, highlighting, and color is to make the form easy to read. A careful mix of large and small fonts, bold and normal type, and fonts with different colors or backgrounds can help a user find important or critical information on the form. Too much variation makes the form cluttered and difficult to use. However, judicious use of these techniques will make the form more easily understood. Column headings and totals can be made slightly larger or boldfaced. The form can highlight negative or credit balances by changing font color. However, font color and background color should be used in concert to ensure that the field is readable. For example, neither red type on green or black backgrounds nor a dark color on a dark background is a good choice—some people with color blindness cannot distinguish red from green or black.

Figure 11-13 is an example of a windows form designed for the Rocky Mountain Outfitters customer support system. This form is used to look up information about a product and to add it to an order. Notice how the title and labels make the form easy to read. The natural flow of the form is top to bottom, with related fields placed together. Navigation and Close buttons are easily found but are not in the way of data-entry activity.

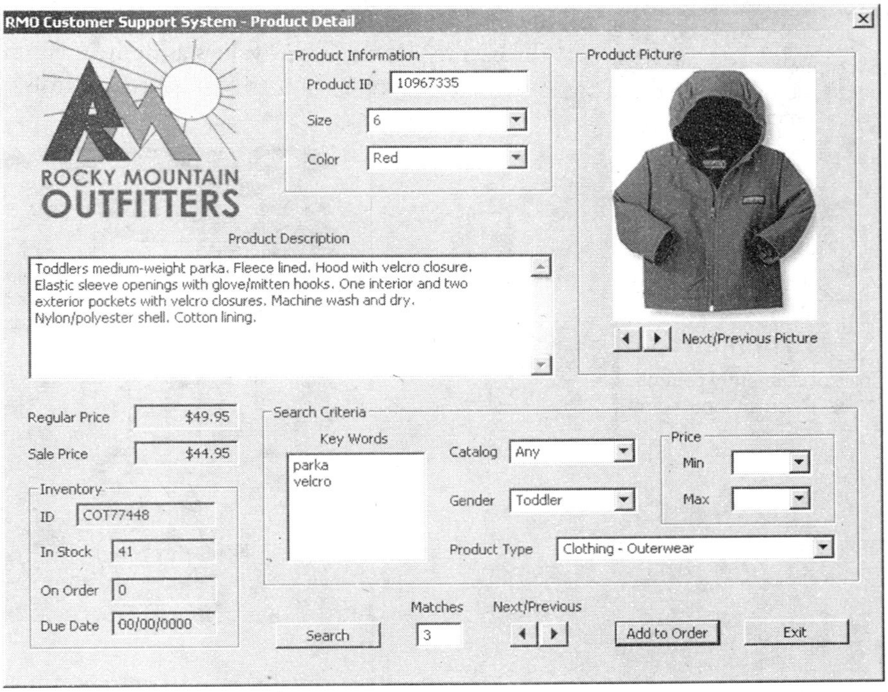

FIGURE 11-13

The RMO Product Detail form used to look up information about a product, select size and color, and then add the product to an order

DATA KEYING AND DATA ENTRY

The heart of any input form is the entry of the new data. Even here, however, a primary objective is to require as little data entry as possible. Any information that is already in the computer, or that can be generated by the computer, should not be reentered. A generous use of selection lists, check boxes, automatic retrieval of descriptive fields, and so forth will speed up data entry and reduce errors. The Product Detail form for RMO (Figure 11-13) shows many examples of input controls that reduce the need to enter data.

text box
an input control that accepts keyboard data entry

list box
an input control that contains a list of acceptable entries the user can select

spin box
a variation of the list box that presents multiple entries in a text box from which the user can select

combo box
another variation of the list box that permits the user to enter a new value or select from the entries

radio buttons (option buttons)
input controls that enable the user to select one option from a group

Several types of data-entry controls are widely used in windows systems today. A *text box* is the most common element used for data entry. A text box consists of a rectangular box that accepts keyboard data. In most cases, it is a good idea to add a descriptive label to identify what should be typed in the text box. Text boxes can be designed to limit the entry to a specified length on a single line or to permit scrolling with multiple lines of data.

Variations of a text box include a list box, a spin box, and a combo box. A *list box* contains a list of the acceptable entries for the box. The list usually consists of a predefined list of data values from which the user selects the desired entry. The list can be presented either within a rectangular box or as a drop-down list. A variation of a list box is a spin box. A *spin box* presents the possible values within the text box itself. Two spinner arrows let the user scroll through all the values. A *combo box* also contains a predefined list of acceptable entries, but it permits the user to enter a new value when the list does not contain the desired value. Both a list box and combo box facilitate data entry by minimizing keystrokes and the corresponding possibility of errors.

Two types of input controls are used in groups: radio buttons (sometimes called *option buttons*) and check boxes. *Radio buttons* are associated as a group, and the user selects one and only one of the group. The system automatically turns off all other buttons in the group when one is selected. Since all of the possible values appear on the form, this control is used only when the list of alternatives is small and the values

check boxes
input controls that enable the user to select more than one option from a group

never change. *Check boxes* also work together as a group. However, check boxes permit the user to select as many values as desired within the group. Figure 11-14 shows a form with examples of these data-entry controls.

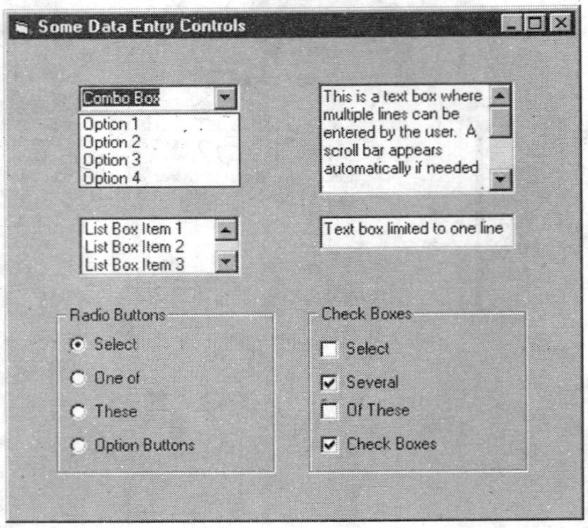

FIGURE 11-14
Examples of data-entry controls on an input form

Browser forms contain similar controls. A major difference between a standard windows input form and a browser input form is that the windows form can easily perform edits field by field as the data are entered. In a basic browser input form, the edits are not performed until the entire form is transmitted to the server computer. However, as browser programs become increasingly sophisticated, more and more capabilities are being provided for data entry. Windows input forms and browser input forms now have very similar capabilities.

NAVIGATION AND SUPPORT CONTROLS

Standard window interfaces provide several controls for navigation and window manipulation. For Microsoft applications, these controls consist of Minimize, Maximize, and Close buttons in the top-right corner, horizontal and vertical scroll bars, the record selection bar on the left panel, record navigation arrows at the bottom of the window, and so forth. To maintain consistency across systems, it is generally a good idea to utilize these navigation controls when possible. However, a well-designed user interface should also include other controls or buttons. You can place buttons on the form to enable users to move to other relevant screens, to search and find data, and to close the open window. Browser forms also provide navigation and support controls. The browser contains navigation buttons and controls that the application should support using browser forms. Each page might include its own navigation buttons also.

HELP SUPPORT

A primary objective in the design of each input form is for it to be intuitive so that users will not need help. However, even well-designed forms will be misunderstood, and access to online help is always recommended. Three types of help are common in today's systems: a tutorial that walks the user through the use of the form, an indexed list of help topics, and context-sensitive help.

Most systems provide tutorial help to assist in training new users. Tutorials can be organized by task, in which case the tutorial generally includes one dialog with a set of related forms. Every new system also should have an indexed list of help topics. This list can be invoked either through a keyword search or, as with many Microsoft systems, with a help wizard. The help wizard is simply a program that does an automatic keyword search based on words found in a question or sentence. The wizard will return several alternative help topics based on the results of the keyword searches.

Context-sensitive help can be based on the indexed list of help topics, but it is invoked differently. Context-sensitive help automatically displays the appropriate help topic based on the location of the cursor. In other words, if the cursor is within a certain text field on a form, and the user invokes context-sensitive help, then the system displays the help for that text field.

GUIDELINES FOR DESIGNING WEB SITES

Web-site design draws from the guidelines and rules for designing the windows forms and browser forms just presented. Many business systems today, including the RMO customer support system, make use of both technologies. Yet a business system such as the order-processing function for RMO is just part of the RMO Web site. Web sites also are used for corporate communication, customer information and service, online sales and distribution, and marketing. Because they are available 24 hours a day, 7 days a week, they need to interact seamlessly with customers. This section introduces some guidelines and lessons for Web design. A complete discussion of Web-site design principles is beyond the scope of this book. Many excellent books are available, and we list some of them in the "Further Resources" at the end of this chapter.

TEN GOOD DEEDS IN WEB DESIGN

Jacob Nielsen is an HCI researcher who now focuses specifically on Web design. Like many useful guidelines, Nielsen's guidelines focus on general issues, including these "Ten Good Deeds in Web Design":

[1] Place the organization's *name and logo* on every page and make the logo a link to the home page.
[2] Provide a *search* function if the site has more than 100 pages.
[3] Write straightforward and simple *headlines and page titles* that clearly explain what the page is about and that will make sense when read out of context in a search engine listing.
[4] Structure the page to *facilitate reader scanning* and help users get the gist of the information at a glance while ignoring large chunks of the page. For example, use grouping and subheadings to break a long list into several smaller units.
[5] Instead of cramming everything about a product or topic into a single, huge page, use *hypertext to structure the content space* into a starting page that provides an overview and several secondary pages that each focus on a specific topic.
[6] Use *product photos*, but avoid cluttered and bloated product family pages with lots of photos. The primary product page must load quickly and function fast, so it should be limited to a thumbnail product shot.
[7] Use *relevance-enhanced image reduction* when preparing small photos and images. Instead of simply reducing the original image to a tiny and unreadable thumbnail, zoom in on its most relevant detail by cropping and resizing the image.

[8] Use *link titles* to provide users with a preview of where each link will take them, *before* they have clicked on it.

[9] Ensure that all important pages are *accessible for users with disabilities*, especially visually impaired users.

[10] *Do the same as everybody else*, because if most big Web sites do something in a certain way, users will expect other sites to work similarly.

WEB SITE DESIGN PRINCIPLES

Because Web sites include so many facets, many designers take a broader view of Web-site design principles. A Web-design book by Joel Sklar suggests that the designer should focus on three broad aspects of Web design: (1) designing for the computer medium, (2) designing the whole site, and (3) designing for the user.

DESIGNING FOR THE COMPUTER MEDIUM

It is important to remember that the Web site will be displayed on a computer screen and not on paper. Designers can select from a wide array of video display fonts, colors, and layouts, but the look of the site should flow from its function and the organization's goals. Hypermedia allows the user to navigate through the site in nonlinear ways, so the designer should take advantage of new ways to organize information. Five guidelines to consider include:

- Craft the look and feel of the pages to take advantage of the medium.
- Make the design portable, since it will be accessed with a wide range of technology.
- Design for low bandwidth, since users will not want to wait for a page to load.
- Plan for clear presentation and easy access to information to ease users' navigation through the site.
- Reformat information for online presentation when it comes from other sources.

DESIGNING THE WHOLE SITE

The entire site must have unifying themes and an overall structure, and the theme should reflect the impression the organization wants to convey. For example, a site for adult, business-oriented users should use subdued colors, familiar business-oriented fonts, and structured linear columns. A site for children should combine bright colors, an open and friendly dynamic structure, and simple, appealing graphics. Four guidelines to consider include:

- Craft the look and feel of the pages to match the impression desired by the organization.
- Create smooth transitions between Web pages so that users are clear about where they have been and where they are going.
- Lay out each page using a grid pattern to provide visual structure for related groups of information.
- Leave a reasonable amount of white space on each page between groups of information.

DESIGNING FOR THE USER

We discussed user-centered design earlier in this chapter, and it is important to focus Web-design efforts on the users and their needs. If a feature will annoy or distract users, do not include it. It is sometimes difficult to know who the Web users will be, but if the purpose and objectives of the whole site are defined carefully, the designer can make better judgments. Some guidelines to consider include:

- Design for interaction because Web users expect sites to be interactive and dynamic.
- Guide the user's eye to information on the page that is the most important.
- Keep a flat hierarchy so that the user does not have to drill down too deeply to find detailed information.
- Use the power of hypertext linking to help users move around and through the site.
- Decide how much content per page is enough based on the characteristics of the typical user; don't clutter the pages.
- Design for accessibility for a diverse group of users, including those with disabilities.

DESIGNING DIALOGS FOR ROCKY MOUNTAIN OUTFITTERS

Now that dialog design concepts and techniques have been discussed, we can demonstrate the process of designing one specific dialog for Rocky Mountain Outfitters, as well as part of the RMO Web site.

DIALOG DESIGN FOR THE RMO PHONE-ORDER REPRESENTATIVES

The Rocky Mountain Outfitters customer support system includes support for the phone-order sales representatives who process orders for customers. The dialog corresponds to the use case *Create new order* and more specifically to the scenario *Phone-order representative creates new order*. The target environment for this part of the system is the phone-order representative's desktop PC on a Windows platform.

The designer starts by referring to the models produced as requirements: the use case description, activity diagram, or system sequence diagram. The four basic steps followed in these models are as follows:

[1] Record customer information.
[2] Create a new order.
[3] Record transaction details.
[4] Produce order confirmation.

The system sequence diagram for this scenario would be expanded to include forms the user will need for interaction, as shown in Chapter 8 for the user-interface (view) layer. The dialog design activity coordinates the user-interface design with the processing design for the use case realization.

Based on the sequence of processing required, a basic dialog can be written to convey in more detail how the dialog will flow from the user's perspective. The details of the interface objects needed on each form should wait until this dialog is refined. The process of a new customer placing an order with a phone sales representative (the user) might resemble the following dialog:

Computer:	What customer support system option do you want?
User:	I need to create a new order.
Computer:	Okay, is it a new or existing customer?
User:	It's a new customer.
Computer:	Fine, give me the customer's name, address, phone, and so on.

User:	The customer is Ginny Decker, 11980 Visual Blvd. . . .
Computer:	Okay, what is the first item she wants to order?
User:	Boots, Women's, Hiking Supreme Line in the Spring Fling catalog.
Computer:	They come in these sizes and colors, and we have all in stock except size 9.
User:	Okay, one pair of size 8 in tan.
Computer:	That comes to $65.50 plus tax, shipping, and handling. Anything else?
User:	Yes, Raincoat, Women's, On the Run Line in the Spring Fling catalog.
Computer:	They come in these sizes and colors, and we have all in stock except medium and large blue.
User:	Okay, one coat size small in brown.
Computer:	That comes to $87.95 plus tax, shipping, and handling. Anything else?
User:	That's it.
Computer:	How does the customer want the order shipped?
User:	UPS two-day air.
Computer:	Does the customer want to use a credit card, or is there another payment approach for this order?
User:	Use the MasterCard number *xx*674-22-xxxx expiring January 06.
Computer:	Okay, the order is recorded. To summarize, for customer Ginny Decker, ship by UPS two-day mail Boots, Women's, Hiking Supreme Line, size 8, tan, at $65.50, and Raincoat, Women's, On the Run Line, size small, brown, at $87.95. Total cost, $153.45 plus $9.20 tax and $13.40 shipping and handling—$176.05 charged to MasterCard *xx*674-22-xxxx.
User:	Thanks.

While working on this dialog, the designer can begin to refine the forms that will be required for the user and the computer. A list of required forms might include the following:

- Main menu form
- Customer form
- Item search form
- Product detail form
- Order summary form
- Shipping and payment options form
- Order confirmation form

The designer can use the list of forms to define a design concept for the flow of interaction from form to form. One approach is to show potential forms in sequence, as shown in Figure 11-15. After the main menu form, the customer form appears first; the user fills it in or updates it, and then the item search form is displayed, to let the user search for an item. Product details are shown for the item, and then the item search form is shown again. When all items are selected, the order summary form is shown, and so on. The designer should concentrate on highlighting parts of the dialog that occur through each form rather than worrying about the physical design of each form. After considering what information is needed on each form, the designer can create a more detailed storyboard or implement prototype forms using a tool such as Visual Basic.

This initial design is very sequential but reasonable for a first iteration. Phone sales representatives at RMO evaluated the storyboard and the prototype, and they suggested that the sequence was too rigid. It assumes that the dialog always follows the same

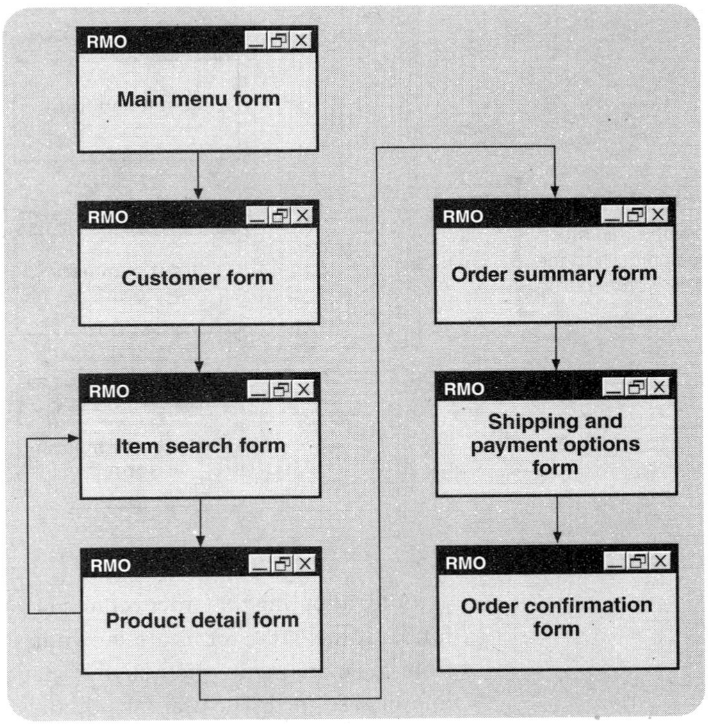

FIGURE 11-15
A design concept for the sequential approach to the *Create new order* dialog

sequence, but phone-order representatives are on the phone with customers, and they have to follow the customers' lead. Sometimes customers do not want to give out information about themselves until the order is processed and confirmed, for example. Sometimes customers want to know the totals for the order or want to review details about something already included in the order. But the sequential design assumes that the customer information always comes first. Although the sequential approach might work well for mail-order clerks, more flexibility is required for the phone-order representatives.

To address the flexibility and information needs of the users, the project team developed a second design concept. This design concept makes the order form the center of the dialog, with options to switch to other forms at will. After each action, the order form is redisplayed to the phone-order representative with the current order details. The order-centered design concept is shown in Figure 11-16. It allows the same sequence to be followed as the basic dialog, but it also allows flexibility when needed. It also shows the user more information about the order throughout the dialog in case the user needs the information.

BEST PRACTICE: When storyboarding the user interface for each use case, you will find that you can reuse forms from one use case to another. Begin a list of shared forms early in the project. Reusing forms saves design and implementation effort, and it provides an additional benefit of consistency.

FIGURE 11-16
A design concept for an order-centered approach to the *Create new order* dialog

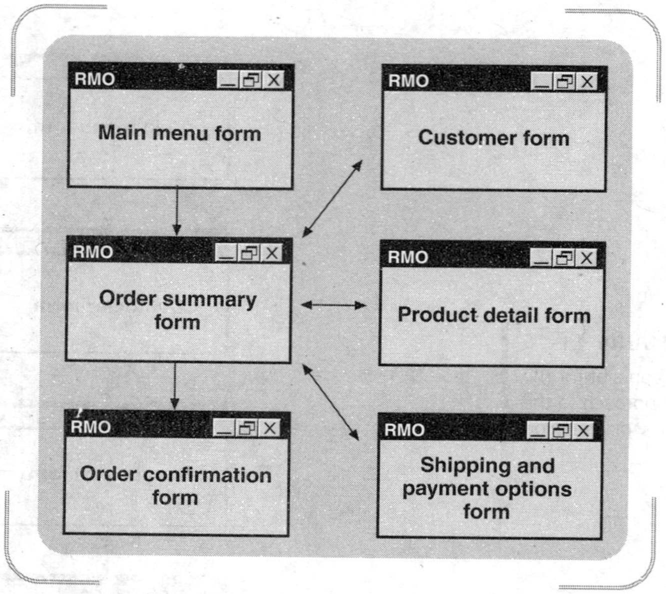

After adopting the order-centered concept, the project team designed the detailed forms. Some of the forms are shown in Figure 11-17. After the user selects *Place an order* from the main menu, the system displays the Order Summary form with a new order number assigned. The user can add the customer information immediately (either by searching for a previous customer, based on customer number or name, or by adding new customer information). The user can then search for a requested item and look up more details about the item on the Product Detail form. If the customer wants to order the item, the user adds it to the order, and the Order Summary form is redisplayed. The user can add another item to the order, make changes to the first item ordered, or select shipping and payment options. This flexibility and information display are what the phone-order representatives wanted. It took quite a few iterations and user evaluations to begin to achieve the best design.

FIGURE 11-17
Prototype forms for an order-centered approach to the dialog

(a) The Main Menu form for an order-centered approach to the dialog

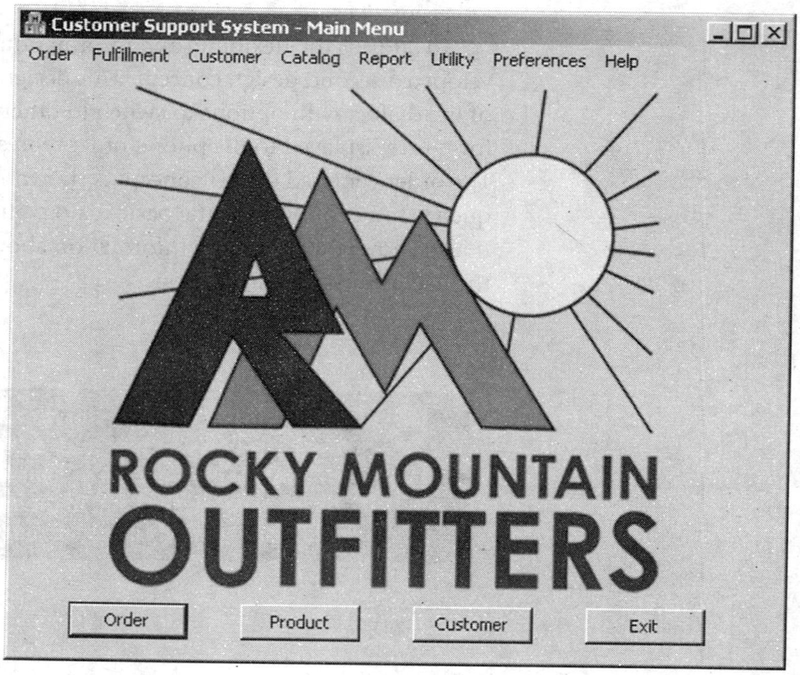

(b) The Order Summary form for an order-centered approach to the dialog beginning a new order

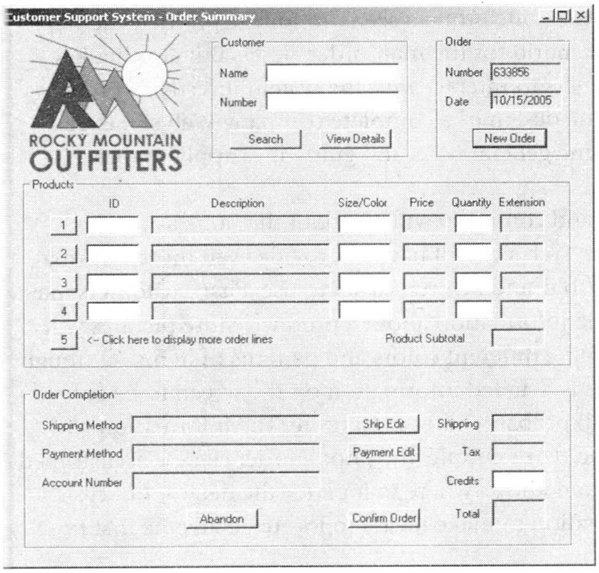

(c) The Product Detail form after the user decides to add a product

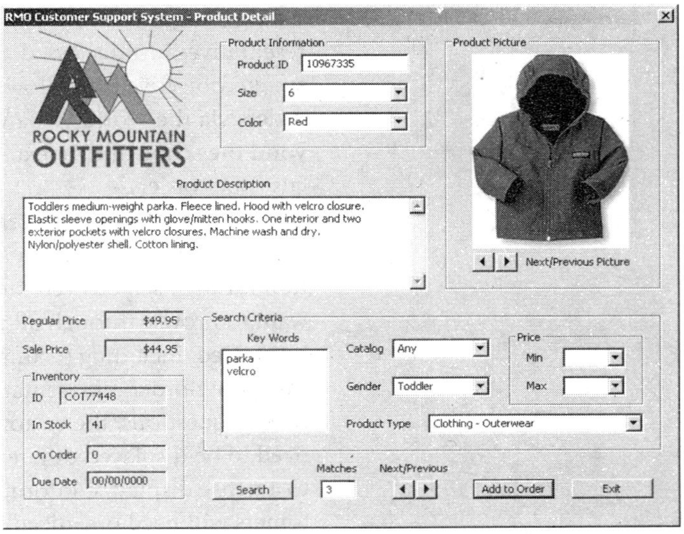

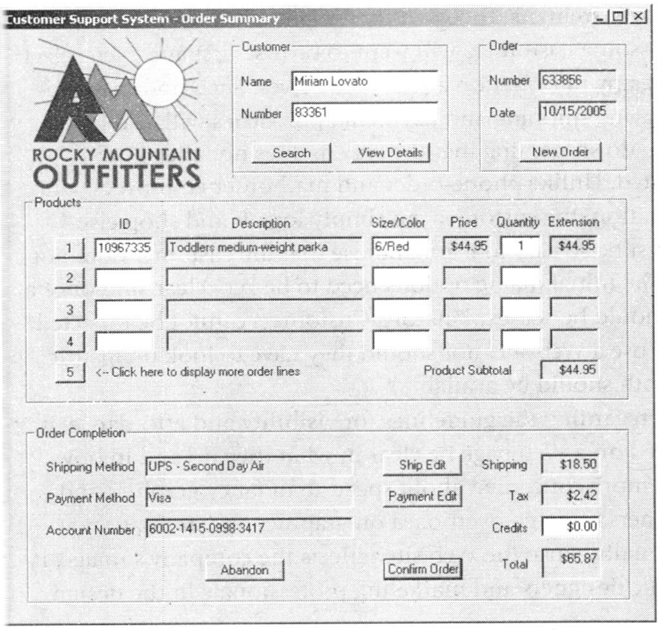

(d) The Order Summary form after the user adds the product

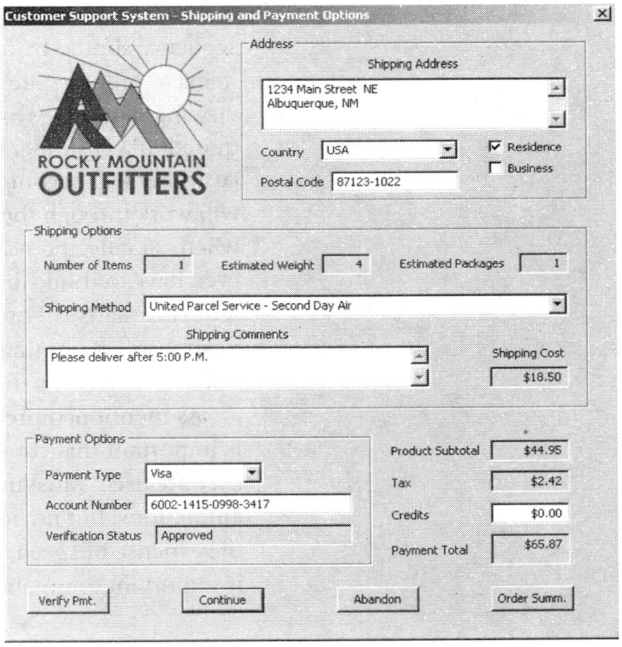

(e) The Shipping and Payment Option form for the completed order

DIALOG DESIGN FOR THE RMO WEB SITE

The RMO customer support system use case *Create new order* requires several different dialog designs (one for each scenario), including a scenario for the phone-order representatives just discussed and a scenario for the mail-order clerks. But another key system objective is to allow customers to interact with the system directly to place orders via the World Wide Web. The design of a complete company Web site is beyond the scope of this text, but some general rules and guidelines apply to direct customer orders.

The basic dialog between user and computer will be about the same as for the phone-order representative, but the Web site will have to provide even more information for the user, be even more flexible, and be even easier to use. First, customers may want to browse through all possible information about a product. More pictures will be needed, including pictures showing different colors and patterns of items. Although the phone-order representative needs detailed information on the screen to be able to answer questions, the customer will probably want even more. The information will need to be displayed differently, too. For example, the phone-order clerk is accustomed to a dense display of information and knows where to look for the details, but customers will need organized information to make it easy to locate details the first time they use the system.

The system will need to be very flexible because customers will have different preferences for interacting with the system. As discussed for the phone-order scenario, the sequence should be flexible—some customers will want to browse first and even select items to order before entering any information about themselves. Such options as reviewing past orders and reviewing shipping and payment approaches will also be required. If a customer wants to do something that the system does not allow, the customer will become frustrated. Unlike phone-order and mail-order employees, who will work through their frustration, the customer can simply log off and shop elsewhere. Finally, the system must be so easy to learn and use that the customer does not even have to think about it. The initial dialog options need to be very clear, and once a sequence starts, all options should be self-explanatory. Customers cannot be expected to sit through training just to use a Web site, nor should they have to look up instructions or help (even though both should be available).

As mentioned previously regarding the guidelines for visibility and affordance, it is important that controls used on a Web page be clear in what they do and in how they are used. Most users are more concerned about speed than fancy graphics and animations, but novice designers often go overboard on graphics and animation at the expense of speed. Additionally, since the Web site reflects the company's image, it is important to involve graphic designers and marketing professionals in the design.

A well-thought-out visual theme is important. Focus groups and other feedback techniques should be used in generating the design.

The Rocky Mountain Outfitters' home page is shown in Figure 11-18. The main emphasis is direct customer interaction. The user can choose to learn more about RMO, contact RMO with an e-mail message, or request a catalog. There is no main menu option to place an order. Instead, the Web site offers the opportunity to browse through pages of RMO products. The customer can search for products by keyword or product ID number, or the customer can select a category of product from a list. Weekly specials are also offered. When customers find something they want, they can create an order. They can also change their minds at any time.

FIGURE 11-18
Rocky Mountain Outfitters' home page

The RMO Web site uses the shopping cart analogy for orders. Once customers find a product they want, they select the quantity, size, and other options, and then they add the item to their shopping cart. They can view the shopping cart at any time and then continue browsing and adding items. When they are done, they check out, and the system confirms the order. Figure 11-19 shows a Product Detail page reached after a user navigates through the women's clothing option. Figure 11-20 shows the shopping cart with a summary of an order.

FIGURE 11-19
The Product Detail page from the Rocky Mountain Outfitters Web site

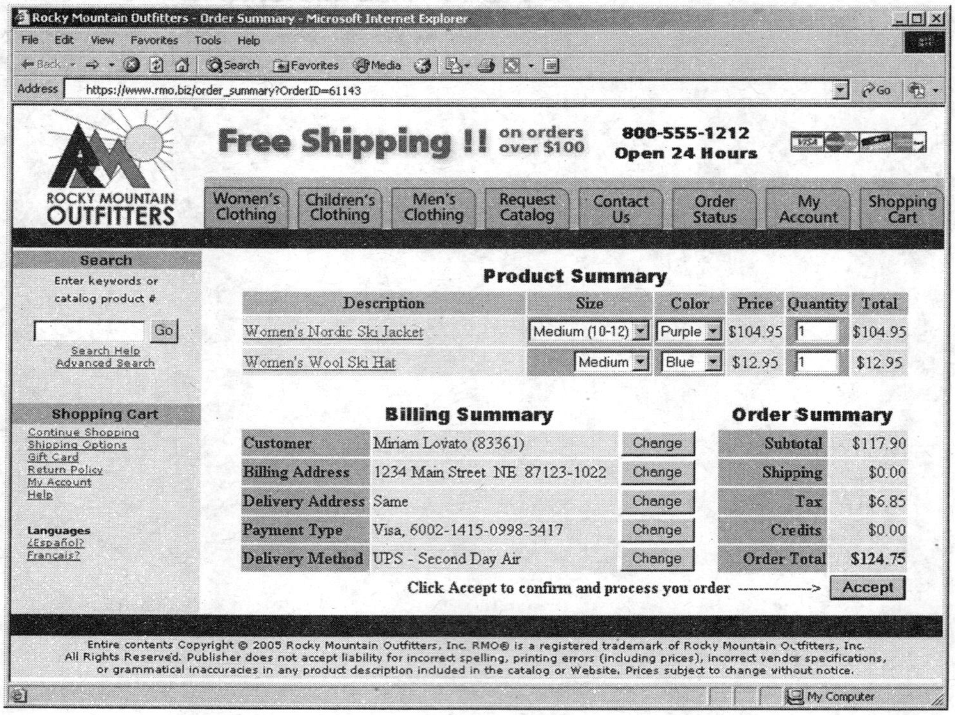

FIGURE 11-20
The shopping cart page from the Rocky Mountain Outfitters Web site

Summary

Inputs and outputs can be classified as system interfaces or user interfaces. This chapter focuses on user interfaces and describes concepts and techniques for designing the interaction between the user and the computer—human-computer interaction (HCI). Chapter 12 describes system interfaces, including system outputs and system controls. Each iteration involves user-interface design for the use cases addressed in the iteration, but it is important to define an overall user-interface concept for the system early in the project.

The user interface is everything the user comes into contact with while using the system—physically, perceptually, and conceptually. To the user, the user interface *is* the system. The knowledge the user must have to use the system (the user's model) includes information about objects and functions available in the system—the kind of information that defines the requirements model the analyst works hard to uncover during early iterations.

User-centered design refers collectively to techniques that focus early on users and their work, evaluate designs to ensure usability, and apply iterative development. The Unified Process (UP) embraces the ideas of user-centered design. Usability refers to the degree to which a system is easy to learn and use. Ensuring usability is a complex task because design choices that promote ease of learning often conflict with those that promote ease of use. Additionally, there are many different types of users to consider for any system. Human-computer interaction as a field of research grew out of human factors engineering (ergonomics) research, which studies human interaction with machines in general.

There are many different ways to describe the user interface, including the desktop metaphor, the document metaphor, and the dialog metaphor. The dialog metaphor emphasizes the interaction between user and computer, and interface design is often called *dialog design* for that reason. Interface design guidelines and interface design standards are available from many sources. Norman's visibility and affordance guidelines state that controls should be visible, provide feedback indicating that they are working, and be obvious in their function. Shneiderman's eight golden rules are to strive for consistency, provide shortcuts, offer informative feedback, design dialogs to yield closure, offer simple error handling, permit easy reversal of actions, support internal locus of control, and reduce short-term memory load.

Dialog design starts with identifying dialogs based on use cases. Additional dialogs are needed for integrity controls added during design, for user preferences, and for help. Menu hierarchies can be designed for different types of users, and once the dialogs are designed, menu hierarchies can be rearranged easily. Writing a dialog sequence much like a script can help a developer work out the key information that needs to be exchanged during the dialog. A storyboard showing sketches of screens in sequence can be drawn to convey the design for review with users, or prototypes can be created using a tool such as Visual Basic. The object-oriented approach provides UML models that can document dialog designs, including sequence diagrams, collaboration diagrams, and class diagrams.

Each form used in a dialog needs to be designed, and there are guidelines for the layout, selection of input controls, navigation, and help. These guidelines apply to windows forms and to browser forms used in Web-based systems. Designing a dialog for a Web site is similar to creating any other dialog, except that users need more information and more flexibility. Additional Web-design guidelines apply to designing for the computer medium, designing the whole site, and designing for the user. Additionally, because a Web site reflects the company's image to customers, graphic designers and marketing professionals should be involved.

KEY TERMS

affordance, p. 453
browser forms, p. 465
check boxes, p. 468
combo box, p. 467
desktop metaphor, p. 449
dialog metaphor, p. 450
direct manipulation, p. 448
document metaphor, p. 449
human-computer interaction (HCI), p. 444
human factors engineering (ergonomics), p. 446
hypermedia, p. 449
hypertext, p. 449
interface design standards, p. 453
list box, p. 467
radio buttons (option buttons), p. 467
spin box, p. 467
storyboarding, p. 460
system interfaces, p. 442
text box, p. 467
usability, p. 445
user-centered design, p. 445
user interfaces, p. 442
user's model, p. 445
visibility, p. 453

REVIEW QUESTIONS

1. Why is interface design often referred to as *dialog design*?
2. What are the three aspects of the system that make up the user interface?
3. What term is generally used to describe the study of end users and their interaction with computers?
4. What are some examples of physical aspects of the user interface?
5. What are some examples of perceptual aspects of the user interface?
6. What are some examples of conceptual aspects of the user interface?
7. What collection of techniques places the user interface at the center of the development process?
8. What are the three important principles emphasized by user-centered design?
9. What term refers to the degree to which a system is easy to learn and use?
10. What is it about the "human factor" that engineers find difficult? What is the solution to human factor problems?
11. What are some of the fields that contribute to the field of human-computer interaction?
12. What research center significantly influenced the nature of the computers we use today?
13. What are the three metaphors used to describe human-computer interaction?
14. A desktop on the screen is an example of which of the three metaphors used to describe human-computer interaction?
15. What type of document allows the user to click on a link and jump to another part of the document?
16. What type of document allows the user to click on links to text, graphics, video, and audio in a document?
17. What is the name for general principles and specific rules that developers must always follow when designing the interface of a system?
18. What two key principles are proposed by Norman to ensure good interaction between a person and a computer?
19. List the eight golden rules proposed by Shneiderman.
20. What is the technique that shows a sequence of sketches of the display screen during a dialog?
21. What UML diagram can be used to show how the interface objects are plugged in between the actor and the problem domain classes during a dialog?
22. What UML diagram can be used to show the interface objects that are contained in a window or form?
23. What are the three basic types of windows and browser forms used in business systems?
24. What is the input control (interface object) used for typing in text?
25. What are some of the input controls that can be used to select an item from a list?
26. What two types of input controls are included in groups?
27. What are three requirements for usability of a direct customer access Web site, beyond those of a windows interface used by employees?
28. What popular analogy is used for direct customer interaction with a Web site when customers shop online?
29. What are three principles of Web design that guide designers?
30. What are 4 of the 10 good deeds of Web design?

THINKING CRITICALLY

1. Think of all of the software you have used. What are some examples of the conflict between ease of learning and ease of use?
2. Visit some Web sites and identify all of the controls used for navigation and input. Are they all obvious? Discuss some differences in visibility and affordance of the controls.
3. Consider the human factor solution that states that it is better to change the machine than to try to change the human to accommodate the machine. Are there machines (or systems) that you use in your daily life that still have room for improvement? Are the current generations of Windows PC and Apple Mac as usable as they might be? If not, what improvements can you suggest? Is the World Wide Web as usable as it might be? If not, what improvements would help? Are we just beginning to see some breakthroughs in usability, or have most of the big improvements already been made?
4. Review the dialog between user and computer shown for DownTown Videos. Create a table like Figure 11-6 that shows how the dialog can be converted to the user's language and the computer's language. Discuss how moving

from the dialog to the table starts with a logical model and then creates a physical model.

5. Refer again to the table shown in Figure 11-6. Create a storyboard for the e-mail system based on the information in the table.
6. Read through the following dialog, which shows a user trying to place an order with the system. Critique the dialog in terms of ease of learning and ease of use.

User:	I want to order a product.
System:	Okay. Enter your name and address.
User:	My name is Timothy Mudd, 5139 North Center Street, Los Angeles, CA 98210.
System:	Oh, we have all of that information on file, but thank you for entering it again.
User:	I want to order the Acme Drill Press with ad–justable belt drive.
System:	Sure, continue with your request.
User:	I want the blue color and rubber feet but not the foot brake.
System:	Sure, anything else?
User:	I want it shipped priority with the special discount you offer.
System:	We hear you.
User:	Okay, that's all.
System:	We are sorry, but your transaction violated transaction code 312 and we must terminate the session.

7. Refer to the form shown in Figure 11-14, showing data-entry controls. Draw a UML class diagram that represents the objects that make up the form.
8. Review all of the controls that come with Visual Basic that are visible when added to a form. Discuss how well each satisfies the visibility and affordance requirements.
9. Discuss how the Unified Process addresses human factors and HCI very early in the development process. What are some of the features of the UP that support the objectives of user-centered design?

EXPERIENTIAL EXERCISES

1. Review the sequential design concept and the order-centered design concept for the Rocky Mountain Outfitters *Create new order* dialog. Consider what information and navigation options are not needed by the mail-order clerks. Then design the forms that would be appropriate for clerks to use when entering mail orders for RMO. Either sketch the forms or implement the forms using a tool such as Visual Basic. Use input controls that minimize data entry.
2. Evaluate the course registration system at your university. List the basic steps followed through a dialog with the system. What are some of the problems with the system from the perspective of ease of learning and ease of use? In what ways is the system inflexible? In what ways is needed information not available? Is too much information provided that distracts from the task at hand?
3. Evaluate the online catalog system at your university library (see some of the questions and issues in exercise 2). Write a dialog that shows the interaction between the user and the system. Rewrite the dialog to improve it. Create a storyboard to show how your design would look and feel.
4. Locate a system that users work with all day. Ask some of the users of the system what they like and dislike about it. Ask how they learned the system. Ask them what typical errors they make when using the system and how these errors are prevented or corrected. Observe the users working with the system. Does it appear that any of the interaction is "automatic"?
5. Find a Web site with direct customer ordering. Browse through some product descriptions and note the design of the dialog and the Web pages. What do you like and dislike about the design? Evaluate the Web site based on visibility and affordance and on the eight golden rules. Evaluate the design based on the 10 good deeds and three principles of Web design.

Case Studies

THE 21ST CENTURY UNIVERSITY SYSTEM

Consider the following dialog for a user interacting with the course registration system at 21st Century University. The user is a student registering for classes at the university.

System: What course registration function do you want to perform?

User: *Preregistration.*

System: Okay, what is your account ID and password?

User: *My account ID is SATZ791, and my password is xxxxxxxx.*

System: Okay, welcome back, Kevin. You last adjusted your schedule on 7/7. What preregistration function do you want to perform?

User: *To add courses.*

System: These are the courses you are preregistered for now:

(The system displays a list of course information for three courses.)

Since you are a CIS major, these are all of the CIS courses you might add that have no time conflicts with your present schedule (note, though, that prerequisites have not been checked for these courses).

(The system displays a list of CIS courses available.)
Your options are:

- Switch to a list of courses in another department
- List these courses again but ignore time conflicts
- List these courses again after checking prerequisites
- Provide details of the indicated course
- Add the indicated course to your schedule
- Cancel

User: *I want to switch to courses in another department.*

System: Fine. To what department do you want to switch?

User: *Art.*

System: These are the courses for which you are registered now:

(The system displays a list of course information for three courses.)

As requested, these are the art courses you might add that have no time conflicts with your present schedule (note, though, that prerequisites have not been checked for these courses).

(The system displays a list of art courses available.)
Your options are:

- Switch to a list of courses in another department
- List these courses again, but ignore time conflicts
- List these courses again after checking prerequisites
- Provide details of the indicated course
- Add the indicated course to your schedule
- Cancel

User: *Add the second course in the list.*

System: (The system continues the dialog.)

[1] How much design detail is implied by the dialog? Could it be a phone registration system? Could a clerk at a desk handle the dialog manually? Is it Internet-based? Discuss.

[2] Discuss how well this dialog follows the eight golden rules.

[3] Complete the dialog by adding likely exchanges between the student and the system as the student adds one more course. The student should request more details about a course, and then decide to add the course. Include a request from the student to see final schedule details.

[4] Design and implement either a storyboard or prototype for this dialog, using a tool such as Visual Basic and being as faithful to the dialog as possible. Make up some sample data to show in your design as needed.

THE DOWNTOWN VIDEOS RENTAL SYSTEM

This chapter includes an example of a storyboard for DownTown Videos, a case study first introduced in Chapter 6. The storyboard showed the *Rent out videos* dialog. Revisit the DownTown Videos case and complete the following:

[1] Implement the storyboard in this chapter as a prototype using a tool such as Visual Basic.

[2] Write a dialog, and then create a storyboard for the use case *Return rented videos*. Consider that one or more videos might be returned and that one or more of them might be late, requiring a late charge.

[3] Using a tool such as Visual Basic, implement the storyboard as a prototype, and then ask several people to evaluate it. Discuss the suggestions made.

THE WAITERS ON CALL SYSTEM

Review the Chapter 5 opening case study that describes Waiters on Call, the restaurant meal-delivery service. The analyst found at least 14 events that trigger use cases, which are listed in the case.

[1] Create a set of menu hierarchies for the system based on the use cases. Then add more menu hierarchies for system utilities based on controls, user preferences, and help.

[2] The most important event listed in the case is *Customer calls in to place an order*, and the use case might be named *Process food order*. Write out a dialog between the user and the computer with a natural sequence and appropriate exchange of information.

[3] Sketch a storyboard of the forms needed to implement the dialog.

[4] Ask several people to evaluate the design and discuss any suggested changes.

[5] Implement a prototype of the final dialog design using a tool such as Visual Basic.

THE STATE PATROL TICKET PROCESSING SYSTEM

Review the State Patrol ticket processing system introduced as a case study at the end of Chapter 5.

[1] Create a set of menu hierarchies for the system based on the use cases in the case study. Then add more menu hierarchies for system utilities based on controls, user preferences, and help.

[2] For the event *Officer sends in new ticket*, write out a dialog between the user and the computer for the use case *Record new ticket* with a natural sequence and appropriate exchange of information.

[3] Sketch a storyboard of the forms needed to implement the dialog. Be sure to use input controls that minimize data entry, such as list boxes, radio buttons, and check boxes.

[4] Ask several people to evaluate the design and discuss any suggested changes.

[5] Implement a prototype of the final dialog design using a tool such as Visual Basic.

RETHINKING ROCKY MOUNTAIN OUTFITTERS

A few of the phone-order representatives at Rocky Mountain Outfitters were not completely satisfied with the order-centered dialog design presented in this chapter. They suggested that the design could be streamlined if only one form were displayed throughout the dialog—the order summary form. They thought the order summary form could expand to show additional information instead of switching to separate forms for customer information, product information, or shipping information. When the additional information is not needed, the form could contract. They thought this approach would be easier on the eyes, requiring less effort to focus and refocus on multiple forms that pop up. They requested that a prototype of the one-form design concept be created for their review. The interface might include both options, allowing users to choose the one they prefer.

[1] Draw a storyboard to show how the one-form design concept might look as customer information, product information, and shipping information are added to the expanded form.

[2] Implement a prototype of the storyboard using a tool such as Visual Basic.

[3] Ask several people to evaluate the design, specifically comparing it with the order-centered design in the text, and discuss the results.

[4] Can you describe or implement yet another alternative?

FOCUSING ON RELIABLE PHARMACEUTICAL SERVICE

The Reliable Pharmaceutical Service system has users who process orders in the Reliable offices and users who place orders and monitor order information in the nursing homes. Consider the use cases that apply to Reliable employees versus nursing-home employees.

[1] Design two separate menu hierarchies, one for Reliable employees and one for nursing-home employees.

[2] Write out the steps of the dialog between the user and the system for the use case *place new order* for nursing-home employees.

[3] Create a storyboard for the dialog for *place new order* by making a sketch of the sequence of interaction with Web pages. Implement a prototype for the Web pages using a Web development tool such as Dreamweaver or FrontPage.

FURTHER RESOURCES

Merlyn Holmes, *Web Usability and Navigation*, McGraw-Hill Osborn, 2002.

Patrick J. Lynch and Sarah Horton, *Web Style Guide: Basic Design Principles for Creating Web Sites*. Yale University Press, 1999.

Deborah J. Mayhew, *Principles and Guidelines in Software User Interface Design*. Prentice Hall, 1992.

Jakob Nielsen, *Designing Web Usability: The Practice of Simplicity.* New Riders Publishing, 2000.

Donald Norman, *The Design of Everyday Things*. Doubleday, 1990.

Jenny Preece, Yvonne Rogers, David Benyon, Simon Holland, and Tom Carey, *Human Computer Interaction*. Addison Wesley, 1994.

Ben Shneiderman, *Designing the User Interface* (3rd ed.). Addison Wesley, 1998.

Joel Sklar, *Principles of Web Design* (2nd ed.). Course Technology, 2003.

chapter 12

DESIGNING SYSTEM INTERFACES, CONTROLS, AND SECURITY

LEARNING OBJECTIVES

After reading this chapter, you should be able to:

- Discuss examples of system interfaces found in information systems
- Define system inputs and outputs based on the requirements models of the system
- Design printed and on-screen reports appropriate for recipients
- Explain the importance of integrity controls
- Identify required integrity controls for inputs, outputs, data, and processing
- Discuss issues related to security that affect the design and operation of information systems

CHAPTER OUTLINE

- Identifying System Interfaces
- Designing System Inputs
- Designing System Outputs
- Designing Integrity Controls
- Designing Security Controls

DOWNSLOPE SKI COMPANY: DESIGNING A SECURE SUPPLIER SYSTEM INTERFACE

Downslope Ski Company is a medium-sized manufacturer of skis and snowboards. The company started with the manufacture of downhill snow skis, hence its name. But a few years ago, it expanded into the production of snowboards and then into water skis. In the company's early years, ski manufacturing was fairly straightforward. However, with the introduction of advanced materials such as carbon-laced resins and other sophisticated compounds, manufacturing has become quite complicated, requiring exacting controls for the precise mixture of ingredients and temperature tolerances in baking furnaces. To maintain consistency in snowboard production, Downslope has been very demanding in the quality of the raw materials that it buys. Several times over the last few years, it has had to change suppliers to ensure an adequate supply of high-quality raw materials.

In addition to controlling the quality of materials for manufacturing, Downslope instituted a modified just-in-time (JIT) manufacturing process, which means that it does not stockpile a large quantity of raw materials. Generally, it keeps about a five-day supply on hand and depends on its suppliers to restock materials at least weekly. To facilitate quick ordering and delivery of its many raw materials, senior management at Downslope decided to permit its suppliers to access its inventory database. Depending on which types of boards were being produced, the various raw materials would be depleted at different rates. So, Downslope began developing and installing a complex inventory management system that was integral to the manufacturing process.

Nathan Lopez, Downslope's system development project manager, was fast recognizing that providing a system interface for suppliers to access the database was more complex than he had originally thought. He reported to Downslope management the results of a two-month study to determine the feasibility of various alternatives for this electronic approach to supply chain management.

"I have met with each of our suppliers and determined what information they need and the formats they would like it in. As expected, there was little consistency in the desired formats. I have been able to consolidate some of their needs to narrow them down to three basic formats. Originally, we thought we could convince our suppliers to accept our output design—in other words, to make them conform to our output. However, that does not seem to be such a good idea anymore. If we do not build flexibility into our system, it will be more difficult for us to add or change suppliers. Instead, if we build the interface correctly, with several versions, it should be much easier for suppliers to gain access to the data that we allow them to see.

"Another critical issue that has surfaced is the integrity and security of our data and our systems. For example, our production process is unique and one of our competitive advantages. If the wrong company got access to our data, it could potentially analyze our usage patterns and not only discover what materials we use but perhaps even reverse-engineer our processes. To protect our data, we need to ensure that our computers allow only secure access. We also need to ensure that data are secure while being transmitted to our suppliers and are protected after arrival there. These security issues relate to both our systems and our suppliers."

The meeting lasted a long time, with considerable discussion about the opportunities and dangers of opening company systems to an outside system interface. The oversight committee finally decided that Nathan should study the situation for a couple of weeks more and develop a list of every possible breach of security with potential solutions for each one. Only after these issues were addressed would the project move forward. Nathan knew that the development of this new type of system interface would be a very sticky problem. He hoped he would be able to find solutions for all of the issues that had been raised.

Overview

Most object-oriented information systems involve extensive input and output (I/O), and many people and organizations require access to the data stored by a system. In Chapter 11, you read about human-computer interaction (HCI) and user interfaces, whose inputs and outputs are the result of user interaction with the computer. But many system inputs and outputs do not involve much human interaction. Many of these system interfaces are not as obvious to end users. But systems analysts need a deep understanding of existing systems, databases, and network technologies involving I/O to design an information system that incorporates all I/O needs. We therefore discuss system interfaces separately from user interfaces in this chapter.

Many system interfaces are electronic transmissions or paper outputs to external agents, including reports, statements, and bills. They need to be identified and designed to suit their intended purpose. Frequently, the quality of the system outputs is a mark of the quality of the entire system and of the company that uses it. This chapter discusses the design of these outputs.

Because of the many and varied inputs and outputs, system developers need to design and implement integrity controls and security controls to protect the system and its data. Today more than ever, designing system controls is crucial because computer systems increasingly exist in an open environment. They are part of networks that provide broad access to many different people both within and outside an organization. So, one of the major considerations in systems design is how to ensure that errors or fraudulent transactions are not entered into a system. Integrity controls validate data when they are input and processed. Internal checks and cross-checks help ensure that data integrity is maintained. This chapter discusses techniques to provide the integrity controls to reduce errors, fraud, and misuse of system components.

Finally, outside threats to systems, business organizations, and individuals continue to be a major concern of companies that are connected to the Internet. Many companies use the Internet as a marketing and sales channel, so they need to let customers and prospective customers into their systems, yet keep intruders and malicious hackers out. In addition, e-commerce also entails transmission of private information, such as credit card numbers and financial transactions. The last section of the chapter discusses security controls and explains the basic concepts of data protection, digital certificates, and secure transactions.

Recall that with the Unified Process, early iterations address functional and nonfunctional requirements with the greatest risk. Sometimes system interfaces have technical requirements that pose a high risk. Sometimes security is high risk. Therefore, the design discipline activities described in this chapter could come up in early elaboration phase iterations. Sometimes system interfaces are more routine, such as the design of reports and other system outputs. These less risky features are often addressed in construction phase iterations. Integrity controls are typically added during the construction phase iterations to complete the detailed design of use case realizations started in earlier iterations.

IDENTIFYING SYSTEM INTERFACES

The user interface, as described in the previous chapter, includes inputs and outputs that directly involve system users. But there are many other system interfaces. We define *system interfaces* broadly as any inputs or outputs with minimal or no human intervention. Included in this definition are standard outputs such as billing notices, reports, printed forms, and electronic outputs to other automated systems. Inputs that are automated or come from nonuser interface devices are also included. For example, inputs from automated scanners, bar-code readers, optical character recognition devices, and other computer systems are included as part of a system interface.

It often seems that user interfaces are the most common—and thus most important—interfaces to consider when analyzing and designing an information system. In fact, considerable progress has been made in understanding human-computer interaction and applying user-centered design principles to user-interface design. However, today's highly integrated and interconnected information systems increasingly go beyond user needs, requiring system interfaces to handle inputs and outputs faster, more efficiently, more accurately, and at any hour of the day or night.

System interfaces can process inputs, interact with other systems in real time, and distribute outputs with minimal human intervention. When researching and modeling the requirements for a system, analysts must look carefully for system interfaces that might not appear obvious at first. When designing the system, they should consider alternatives to HCI to automate the capture of inputs and the distribution of outputs. The full range of inputs and outputs in an information system is shown in Figure 12-1.

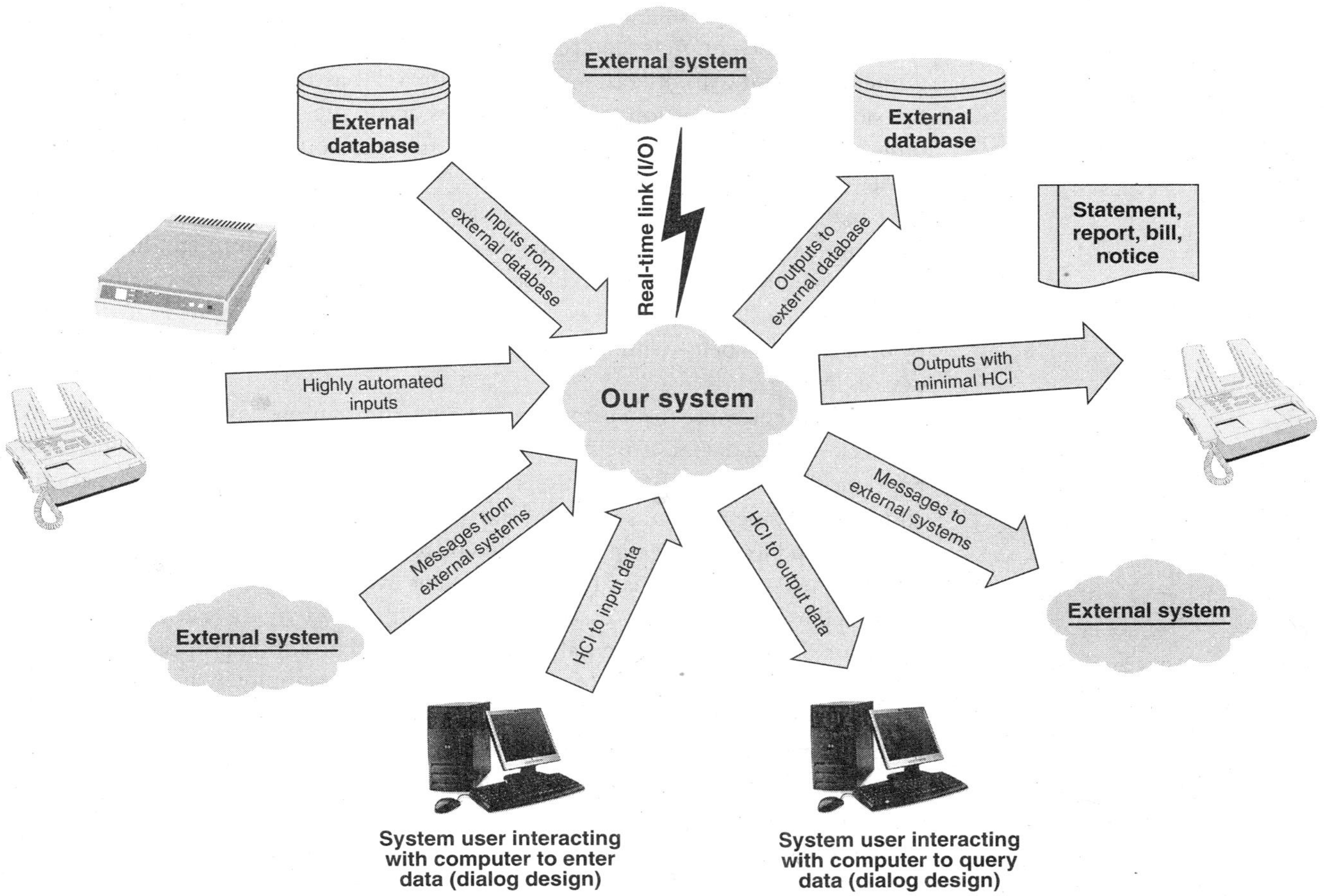

FIGURE 12-1
The full range of inputs and outputs in an information system

BEST PRACTICE: System interfaces are becoming more and more important as information systems become integrated and function in real time. Be sure to identify opportunities to automate system interfaces whenever possible because they have a large impact on system performance and ROI.

The following list provides some categories of system interfaces to aid in identifying I/O requirements and design possibilities:

- Inputs from other systems
- Highly automated inputs
- Inputs that are from data in external databases
- Outputs that are to external databases
- Outputs with minimal HCI
- Outputs to other systems
- Real-time connections (both input and output)

Inputs can arrive directly from other information systems as network messages. Electronic data interchange (EDI) and many Web-based systems are integrated with other systems through direct messaging. The message received triggers system processing in much the same way that user interaction does. For example, in RMO's integrated supply chain management and customer support systems, the arrival of inventory items from a supplier might trigger the shipment of a back-ordered item to a customer. No human intervention is required, and as a result, the transaction can be processed immediately and with little chance of error. In Web-based systems, a separate shopping cart order-entry application might send a message to the order fulfillment system to process a new order. Analysts decide what is an input and what is an internal message by determining the scope of the system.

Highly automated input devices such as scanners can capture many system inputs. An item in a warehouse that is picked for shipment, for example, might have a machine-readable label that an attendant can scan. This highly automated process represents an input to a system. In some cases, a scanner might record the input as an item moves by on a conveyor belt—with no human interaction at all. We discuss specialized input devices later.

Many inputs come from external databases. For example, one system might record transactions in a database, perhaps as a batch of transactions. Another system might periodically search those transactions and process one or more of them. For example, consider a charge-account system in which charges are stored in a database throughout the billing period. A separate billing and collection system might later process those transactions. As with inputs from other systems, whether these inputs come from an external database or are processed within one billing system is a question of scope.

Some inputs from an external database might occur during processing of another input—for example, verifying credit history or verifying employment prior to extending credit. When a credit application is received, the user processing the application may have to rely on information from an external database before the application can be approved. Within the use case *Process credit application* is a requirement for a system input from an external database.

The output side of system interfaces mirrors the input side. Outputs to external databases might be required when the system produces large amounts of detailed data. Many system outputs are produced with minimal human intervention. Reports are produced and e-mailed to recipients or printed and distributed, but the user is not interacting with the system directly to obtain the output. Bills, notices, statements, form letters, and so on are similarly produced with minimal human intervention. They might be sent electronically or be printed. Messages sent to external systems, triggering processing, are also system outputs.

Sometimes system inputs and outputs must be real-time connections. RMO's real-time credit card authorization is an example. Rather than accessing an external database, RMO's system establishes a real-time connection with another system that accepts inputs and provides outputs. A real-time connection is therefore both a system output and a system input, much like a system-to-system dialog. In this aspect, real-time connections parallel user-interface functions, which use a dialog to enter data and look up data in the system (as shown in Figure 12-1).

Another mechanism for correct system input is to have a direct interface with another system. EDI reduces the need for user input. Purchase orders, invoices, inventory updates, and payment all are generated by one system sending transactions to another. With EDI, these transactions normally occur between systems in separate organizations. However, the same principle can be applied to systems within an organization.

One of the main challenges of EDI is defining the format of the transactions. It is easy enough to design the format for a single type of transaction, but it becomes more complex when many different types of transactions are going to many different systems. The complexity and difficulty multiply when many different companies are trying to work together. For example, General Motors, which was one of the early users of EDI, has literally thousands of suppliers with thousands of different transactions, each in a different format. To complicate the situation further, each of these suppliers may also be linked via EDI with tens or hundreds of customers, many of whom may also use EDI. So, a single type of transaction may have a dozen or more defined formats. It is easy to see why it is so costly to set up and maintain EDI systems. Even so, EDI is much more efficient and effective than paper transactions, which must be printed and reentered.

In recent years there has been a move to develop a standard communication method between systems based on Hypertext Markup Language (HTML) concepts. As you know, HTML embeds beginning and ending markup codes within a text-based document to define the characteristics, such as formatting, of text or of a figure. HTML embeds formatting information within the document itself. Thus, a program that can read HTML reads a text document and then, using the embedded markup codes, can format the document correctly. Although this system is not extremely efficient from a computational point of view, it has many advantages due to its simplicity and readability by human beings.

This new system-to-system interface that is gaining popularity is called *eXtensible Markup Language* (*XML*). XML is an extension of HTML that embeds self-defining data structures within textual messages. So, a transaction that contains data fields can be sent with XML codes to define the meaning of the data fields. Many newer systems are using XML to provide a common system-to-system interface. Figure 12-2 illustrates a simple XML transaction that can be used to transfer customer information between systems.

```
<customer record>
        <accountNumber>RMO10989</accountNumber>
        <name>William Jones</name>
        <billingAddress>
                <street>120 Roundabout Road</street>
                <city>Los Angeles</city>
                <state>CA</state>
                <zip>98115</zip></billingAddress>
        <shippingAddress>
                <street>120 Roundabout Road</street>
                <city>Los Angeles</city>
                <state>CA</state>
                <zip>98115</zip></shippingAddress>
             dayPhone>215.767.2334</dayPhone
        <nightPhone>215.899.8763</nightPhone>
</customer record>
```

FIGURE 12-2
A system-to-system interface based on XML

Just like HTML, XML is simple and readable by human beings. For it to work, both systems must recognize the markup codes, but once a complete set of codes is established, transactions can include many different formats and still be recognized and processed. The receiving system merely has to parse the incoming data stream and extract the values from the markup codes. XML is extremely scalable—it does not matter how many different companies or different transaction types there are. Every transaction can have its own format as long as it uses the standard markup codes.

Markup codes for XML are defined in a separate file called a *document type definition* (*DTD*) file or *XML schema*. Many industries and specialty groups have now formed standards committees, which are defining sets of markup codes. Standard codes already exist for general business, retailing, railroad, news media. and medical transactions. The list of groups forming and defining standard codes is extensive.

Chapter 9 introduced the idea of Web services. Web services are based on XML, so these business transactions can be sent over the Internet. In fact, XML was designed to take advantage of the Internet.

DESIGNING SYSTEM INPUTS

When designing inputs for a system, the system developer must focus on three areas:

- Identifying the devices and mechanisms that will be used to enter input
- Identifying all system inputs and developing a list with the data content of each
- Determining what kinds of controls are necessary for each system input

The first task, identifying devices and mechanisms, is a high-level review of the most up-to-date method of entering information into a system. In nearly all business systems, end users perform some input through electronic forms. However, in today's high-technology world, there are numerous ways to enter information into a system—among them are scanning, reading, and transmitting devices that are faster, more efficient, and less error-prone than user input.

The second task, developing the list of required inputs, provides the link between the use case descriptions and the design of the user and system interfaces. As described earlier, the design of the system inputs and interfaces must be integrated with the design of the software. This task accomplishes that purpose.

The third task is to identify the control points and the level of security required for the system being developed. The project team should develop a statement of policy and control requirements before beginning the detailed design of the electronic forms making up the system interface. These concepts are discussed in the last two sections of the chapter.

INPUT DEVICES AND MECHANISMS

Often when analysts begin developing a system, they assume that all input will be entered via electronic, graphical forms because they are now so common on personal computers and workstations. However, as the design of the user inputs commences, one of the first tasks is to evaluate and assess the various alternatives for entering information into the system.

The primary objective of any form of data input is to enter or update error-free data into the system. The key word here is *error-free*. Several good practices can help reduce input errors:

- Capture the data as close to the originating source as possible.
- Use electronic devices and automatic entry whenever possible.
- Avoid human involvement as much as possible.
- If the information is available in electronic form anywhere, use it instead of reentering the information.
- Validate and correct information at the time and location it is entered.

Today, many systems enable the data to be captured electronically at the point at which they are generated. For example, the old way of selling a life insurance policy is to have the applicant or the insurance agent fill out a paper policy application. Then the agent sends the application to a central office to be entered into the system. With this method, numerous errors can occur from indecipherable writing, key-entry errors, missing fields, and so forth. Currently, agents often carry laptop computers with easy-to-use electronic forms, so applicants can fill in the data themselves. Or the agent can enter the data while the applicant looks over the agent's shoulder and verifies that the information is accurate and complete. A portable printer can even be attached to the laptop to print out the completed form for the applicant to review immediately. This new approach dramatically reduces the error rate and speeds the business process of new policy data entry.

The second and third practices, automating data entry and avoiding human involvement, are very closely related and often are essentially different sides of the same coin, although using electronic devices does not automatically avoid human involvement. When system developers think carefully about minimizing human input and using electronic input media, they can design a system with fewer electronic input forms and avoid some common data-entry problems. One of the most pervasive sources of erroneous data is users' typing mistakes in fields and numbers. A few of the more prevalent devices used to avoid human keystroking are:

- Magnetic card strip readers
- Bar-code readers
- Radio frequency identification tags
- Optical character recognition readers and scanners
- Touch screens and devices
- Electronic pens and writing surfaces
- Digitizers, such as digital cameras and digital audio devices

We have all seen new electronic input devices. At the grocery store, electronic scanners identify and price each item from the printed UPC codes. Machines weigh and price the produce automatically at the checkout. Cash registers now read your check, including the amount and customer and bank information. New self-service checkout stations depend almost entirely on automated data-entry devices.

Historically, paper contracts and ink signatures were necessary for legally binding contracts. Today, new laws and regulations allow paper documents and signatures to be digitized. Credit card purchases now also record digitized signatures to eliminate the need for paper vouchers. This technique conforms to the good practices stated previously—the information is captured at its source in electronic form, which eliminates many of the sources of errors.

The next principle of error reduction is to reuse the information already in the computer whenever possible. Some outdated systems require reentry of the same information multiple times. This practice not only generates errors but also creates multiple copies of the same information, which require more checks and balances—as well as computer resources—to synchronize the various copies. And when an error is discovered, it is very difficult to know which copy is correct. Also, when a change is required, it must be made to all copies of the data. One current high-tech example of using existing information is found in car rental systems. When a customer rents a car, the rental agency's system captures the customer's name and credit card, car mileage, and fuel information. Then when the customer returns the car, an agent in the parking lot simply scans the contract ID and enters the return mileage and fuel-gauge level. The system calculates the charges and prints a credit card receipt for the customer right in the parking lot. This solution was designed primarily to provide a higher level of customer service, but it also eliminates many problems and errors in data entry.

Eliminating input errors through various techniques, one of which is using electronic devices for data input, is critical, but another potential source of problems is the input of fraudulent information. Two problems with fraudulent data need to be addressed: access control and input control. First, access to the system must be controlled so that only authorized persons or systems can gain access. Today, devices such as fingerprint readers, body temperature sensors, and iris scanners are used more and more often to provide additional security to standard password access. Second, input controls must be built into the system so that fraudulent data cannot easily be entered. Although it is impossible to completely eliminate the potential for fraud, the careful design of input controls will help minimize the risk. More discussion on security devices and input controls is provided later in the chapter.

DEFINING THE DETAILS OF SYSTEM INPUTS

The objective of this task is to ensure that the designer has identified all of the required inputs to the system and specified them correctly. In the previous chapter, you learned various methods of defining user inputs based on use case descriptions. Those techniques defined the user interface through user-centered design. In this chapter, we focus on defining the system inputs. The fundamental approach that analysts use to identify user and system inputs is to identify all information that crosses the system boundary for each use case.

Identifying user and system inputs with the object-oriented approach requires the use of system sequence diagrams and design class diagrams. The system sequence diagrams identify the incoming messages, and the design class diagrams are used to identify and describe the input parameters.

Figure 12-3 is a simplified system sequence diagram for a payroll system. In this system sequence diagram, snippets from various use cases have been combined to illustrate the major inputs. The messages that cross the system boundary identify inputs, both system inputs and user-interface inputs. The identification of these inputs on the sequence diagram provides a cross-check with the user-interface forms defined with the user-centered design as described in Chapter 11. The three system inputs that cross the system boundary are:

- updateEmployee (empID, empInformation)
- updateTaxRate (taxTableID, rateID, rateInformation)
- inputTimeCard (empID, date, hours)

BEST PRACTICE: Consider and plan for system interfaces for inputs and outputs very early—when defining requirements with use case descriptions and system sequence diagrams.

The first input is part of the user-interface design. The other two inputs, however, are from external systems and do not require user involvement. The information from the tax bureau may be sent as a set of real-time messages or in the form of an input file on a CD or some other electronic device. The time card information could come into the system in various formats. Perhaps paper time cards are entered via an electronic card reader. Or an input from a subsystem, such as an electronic employee ID card reader, may send time card information at the end of every workday. These last two input messages need to be precisely defined, including transmission method, content, and format.

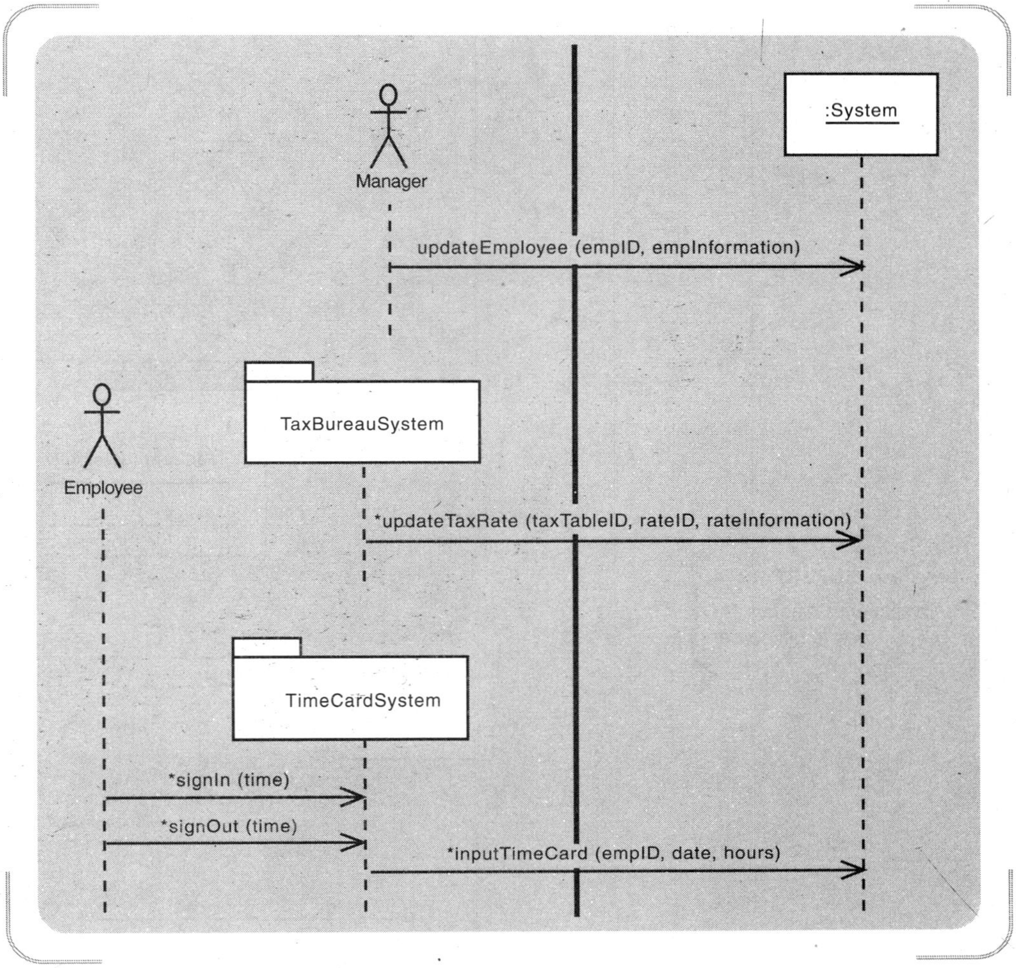

FIGURE 12-3
Partial system sequence diagram for the payroll system use cases

Figure 12-4 is a variation of the system sequence diagram for the telephone order scenario of the *Create new order* use case, as originally given in Figure 6-17. In the figure, the Order Clerk actor and the BankSystem package are external to the system. The messages that go from the Order Clerk to the system are part of the user interface. The messages that go between the external BankSystem package and the system are system inputs. In the object-oriented models, the boundary between actors and external packages with the internal objects is explicit. In Figure 12-4, four messages go from the Order Clerk actor to the system, and one input message enters the system boundary from the BankSystem package. The input messages, along with the actual message signatures as shown in the figure, are:

- startOrder (accountNo)
- addItem (catalogID, prodID, size, quantity)
- completeOrder ( )
- makePayment (paymentAmt, ccInformation)
- returnVerification (creditCard#, verificationCode, amount)

The system sequence diagram developed to define the requirements identifies the series of steps that occur in the overall process to create a new order from a telephone call. Along with a sequence diagram, a detailed dialog might be developed to highlight the communications between the user and computer, as explained in Chapter 11. The point to note here is that a sequence diagram provides a detailed perspective of the user and system inputs to support the use case and the corresponding business event,

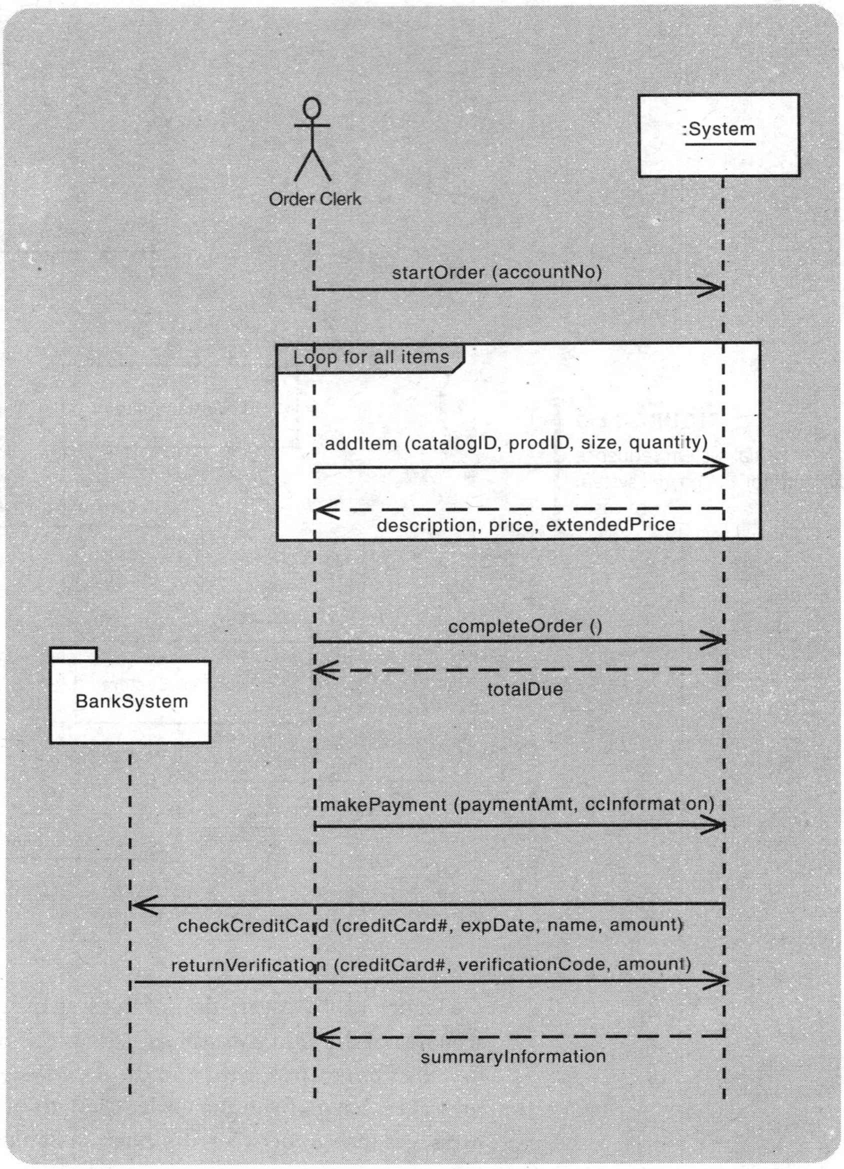

FIGURE 12-4
System sequence diagram for *Create new order*

Additional analysis of the messages themselves also supplies information about the data fields on the message. To obtain a more thorough analysis of the messages, the developer may need to consult the design class diagram. The actual parameters that are passed in on the messages need to be consistent with the attributes that are found in the design classes. Since the design class attributes are typed, the input parameters can also be typed to be consistent with the design class attributes.

Figure 12-5 lists each input message and the data fields that must be passed with the message. In the example, we show the data associated with every input message. However, the messages associated with the user interface may have already been precisely specified during the design of the user interface. In that case, only the system inputs need to be placed in the table. Not only is this analysis necessary to develop the details of system inputs, but it also provides a good check. Notice that the table is more detailed to define the input parameters more precisely. Often this detail will be transferred back to the sequence diagram to make it more complete also.

MESSAGE	DATA PARAMETERS
startOrder	accountNo
addItem	catalogID, prodID, size, quantity
completeOrder	—
makePayment	paymentAmt, creditCard#, expDate, name
returnVerification	creditCard#, verificationCode, amount

FIGURE 12-5
Input messages and data parameters from an RMO system sequence diagram

DESIGNING SYSTEM OUTPUTS

The primary objective of system outputs is to present information in the right place at the right time to the right people. Historically, the most common form of output information has been printed textual reports. Although straight text and tables are still used extensively, new formats, such as charts and diagrams, provide many more options for presenting, emphasizing, and summarizing information.

As with input design, the tasks accomplish four objectives:

- Determine the type of each system output.
- Make a list of specific system outputs required based on application design.
- Specify any necessary controls to protect the information provided in the output.
- Design and prototype the output layout.

The purpose of the first two tasks is to evaluate the various alternatives and to design the most appropriate approach for each needed output. The list of required output reports is normally specified during early iterations as part of modeling system requirements. During design, the task is to coordinate the production of those outputs with the methods that are identified during the design of each use case realization.

The third task ensures that the designer evaluates the value of the information to the organization and protects it. Frequently, organizations implement controls on the inputs and system access but forget that output reports often have sensitive information. The upcoming section "Designing Integrity Controls" identifies several important controls that all outputs should include.

ad hoc reports
reports that are not predefined by a programmer but designed as needed by a user

Today users can develop their own reports using tools and preformatted templates. These reports, called *ad hoc reports*, have not been designed by programmer/analysts. Instead, an ad hoc report is the result of a new user query to a database in response to a specific question or need. In Chapter 10, you learned about relational databases and Structured Query Language (SQL). Many systems provide a simplified graphical tool to permit users to formulate queries in SQL to produce ad hoc reports. Obviously, analysts do not design those reports during system development. However, the tools and capability to support user requests do need to be built into the system. When designing reports, however, analysts should ask whether the system requires an ad hoc reporting capability and, if so, add such a capability.

DEFINING THE DETAILS OF SYSTEM OUTPUTS

The objective of this task is to ensure that the designer has identified and specified all of the outputs for the new system. The technique is the same as that used for the definition of the system inputs. This model-based approach utilizes the information in the event table and other models to identify and define the detailed specifications of the outputs. Although many system inputs may be defined as part of the user-interface design, many outputs do not require dynamic human-computer interaction—for example, printed reports, turnaround documents, or simple screen displays. So, analysts must look to the requirements models they developed for many more system outputs. For object-oriented techniques, messages that originate on internal classes and whose destination is an actor or another external system are the outputs.

In the object-oriented approach, outputs are indicated by messages in sequence diagrams that originate from an internal system object and are sent to an external actor. In Figure 12-5, the output message with the parameters of description, price, extendedPrice is an example of an output message. This message is generated as a result of the input message addItem(catalogID, prodID, size, quantity) to the internal order object. A review of all the output messages generated across all sequence diagrams provides the consistency check against the required outputs identified in the requirements models.

Output messages that are based on an individual object (or record) are usually part of the methods of that object class. To report on all objects within a class, a class-level method is used. A class-level method is a method that works on the entire class of objects, not a single object. For example, a customer confirmation of an order is an output message that contains information for a single order object. However, to produce a summary report of all orders for the week, a class-level method looks at all the orders in the Order class and sends output information for each one with an order date within the week's time period.

The system sequence diagram in Figure 12-4 shows four output messages—three from the system to the Order Clerk actor, shown as returned data with a dashed line, and one to the BankSystem package, shown as the message checkCreditCard (creditCard#, expDate, name, amount). Note that returned data named summaryInformation remains too general. Output design is a good time for analysts to elaborate the messages to include all of the required details. Figure 12-6 shows a table listing the output messages, data parameters, database files or tables involved, and the number of records (a single object or a set of objects) to be included in the output.

OUTPUT MESSAGE	DATA PARAMETERS	CLASSES OR DATABASE TABLES	SINGLE RECORD/ MULTIPLE RECORDS
Response to addItem ( )	description, price, extendedPrice	CatalogProduct, ProductItem, InventoryItem, OrderItem	Single
Response to completeOrder ( )	totalDue	Order, OrderItem	Single
checkCreditCard ( )	creditCard#, expDate, name, amount	Customer, OrderTransaction	Single
summary Information—response to makePayment ( )	customerName, billingAddress, shippingAddress, orderNumber, date, s&h, tax, totalAmount	Order, OrderItem, Customer	Single

FIGURE 12-6
A table of system outputs based on object-oriented messages

DESIGNING REPORTS, STATEMENTS, AND TURNAROUND DOCUMENTS

With the advent of office automation and other business systems, businesspeople originally thought that paper reports would no longer be needed. In fact, just the opposite has happened. Business systems have made information much more widely available, resulting in a proliferation of all types of reports, both paper and electronic. In fact, one of the major challenges to organizations and the designers of their information systems today is to organize the overwhelming amount of information so that it is meaningful. One of the most difficult aspects of output design is to decide what information to provide and how to present it to avoid a confusing mass of complex data.

TYPE OF OUTPUT

Before looking at the different formats that analysts use in designing reports, let's discuss four types of output reports that users require: detailed reports, summary reports, exception reports, and executive reports.

> **detailed report**
> a report containing detailed transactions or records

Detailed reports are used to carry out the day-to-day processing of the business. They contain specific information on business transactions. Sometimes a report may be for a single transaction, such as an order confirmation sheet with details of a particular customer order. Other detailed reports may list a set of transactions—for example, a list of all overdue accounts, with each line of the report presenting information about a particular account. A clerk could use this report to research overdue accounts and determine actions to collect past-due amounts. The purpose of detailed reports is to provide working documents for people in the company.

> **summary report**
> a report that recaps or summarizes detailed information over a period of time or belonging to some category
>
> **exception report**
> a report that contains only information about nonstandard, or exception, conditions

Summary reports are often used to recap periodic activity. An example of this type of report is a daily or weekly summary of all sales transactions, with a total dollar amount of sales. Middle managers often use summary reports to track departmental or division performance. Exception reports are also used to monitor performance. An *exception report* is produced only when a normal range of values is exceeded. When business is progressing normally, then no report is needed. But when something exceeds an expected range, a report is produced to alert staff. An example is a report from a production line that lists rejected parts. If the reject rate is above a set threshold, then a report is generated. Sometimes exception reports are produced regularly. The rejected parts report might be produced every day if the production line usually has some rejected parts. An aged accounts receivable report might be produced each month showing the accounts that are past due. Unfortunately, the organization may always have some accounts to list in such reports, so they are produced regularly.

> **executive report**
> a summary report from various information sources that is normally used for strategic decisions

Top management uses *executive reports* to assess overall organizational health and performance. These reports thus contain summary information from activities within the company. They may also contain comparative performance with industry-wide averages. Using these reports, executives can assess competitive strengths or weaknesses of their company.

Chapter 1 discussed the various types of information systems that systems analysts develop. You will note that some types of information systems focus on producing a particular type of report. Although there is no strict requirement for a system to produce only one type of report, we often categorize a system according to the type of report it produces. The next section looks at some examples of printed reports.

INTERNAL VERSUS EXTERNAL OUTPUTS

> **internal output**
> a printed report or document produced for use inside an organization
>
> **external output**
> printed documents—such as statements, notices, form letters, and legal documents—produced for use outside an organization

Printed outputs are classified as either internal outputs or external outputs. *Internal outputs* are produced for use within the organization. The types of reports just discussed belong to this category. *External outputs* include statements, notices, and other documents that are produced for people outside the organization. Because they are official business documents for an outside audience, they need to be produced with the highest-quality graphics and color. Some examples include monthly bank statements, late notices, order confirmation and packing slips (such as those provided to Rocky Mountain Outfitters' customers), and legal documents such as insurance

turnaround document
an external output that includes a portion that is returned to the system as an input

policies. Some external outputs are referred to as *turnaround documents* because they are sent to a customer but include a tear-off portion that is returned for input later—for example, a bill that contains a payment stub to be returned with a check. All of these printed outputs must be designed with care, but organizations have many more options for printed output. Today's high-speed color laser printers enable all types of reports and other outputs to be produced.

An example of a detailed report for an external output is shown in Figure 12-7. This report is produced from a Web order similar to that shown in Figure 11-20. Good user-interface design specifies that when a customer places an order over the Web, the system will be able to print the order information as a confirmation. Of course, a user can always print the Web screen display using the browser's print capability, but doing so is time-consuming since it includes all of the graphics and index links on the page. It is much more user-friendly to provide shoppers with a formatted order confirmation only. Figure 12-7 illustrates such a report. This type of report is based on the information of a single order. The data required to print this order is a customer record, an order record, and all of the line-item records for ordered items. Notice that it is nicely formatted for easy reading. Different pieces of information are grouped together and placed within boundaries. The report is comprehensive; it contains complete and current information about the transaction, including today's date, items on the order, payment details, and shipping details.

In contrast to the Web shopping cart order report, Figure 12-8 is an example of an internal output. This report is different in several ways. First, it is based on an entire set of records from the inventory database, whereas the shopping cart order is for a single

FIGURE 12-7
RMO shopping cart order report

ROCKY MOUNTAIN OUTFITTERS

Rocky Mountain Outfitters—Shopping Cart Order

Customer Name: Fred Westing
Customer Number: 6747222

Order Number: 4673064
Today's Date: May 18, 2006

Shipping Address:
936 N Swivel Street
Hillville, Ohio 59222

Billing Address:
936 N Swivel Street
Hillville, Ohio 59222

Qty	Product ID	Description	Size	Color	Price	Extended Price
1	458238WL	Jordan Men's Jumpman Team J	12	White/ Light Blue	$119.99	$119.99
1	347827OP	Woolrich Men's Backpacker Shirt	XL	Oatmeal Plaid	$41.99	$41.99
2	8759425SH	Nike D.R.I. – Fit Shirt	M	Black	$30.00	$60.00
1	5858642OR	Puma Hiking Shorts	L	Tan	$15.00	$15.00
					Subtotal	$236.98
					Shipping	$8.50
					Tax	$11.25
					Total	$256.73

Shipping Information:

Shipping Method:	Normal 7-10 day
Shipping Company:	UPS
Tracking Number:	To be sent via email
Email Address:	FredW253@aol.com

Payment Information:
American Express ☐ MasterCard ☐ VISA ☒ Discover ☐
Account Number
X X X X – X X X X – X X X X – 5 7 8 4
MO YR
Expiration Date 05 /07

Thank you for your order. It is a pleasure to serve you.
Check back next week for new weekly specials!!

control break report
a report that includes detailed and summary information

order. The report includes both a detailed and summary section, sometimes called a *control break report*. A control break is the data item that divides the report into groups. In this example, the control break is on the product item number—called ID on the report. Whenever a new value of the ID is encountered on the input records, the report begins a new control break section. The detailed section lists the transactions of records from the database, and the summary section provides totals and recaps of the information. The report is sorted and presented by product. However, within each product is a list of each inventory item showing the quantity currently on hand.

FIGURE 12-8
RMO inventory report

ROCKY MOUNTAIN OUTFITTERS

Rocky Mountain Outfitters — Products and Items

ID	*Season*	*Category*	*Supplier*	*Unit Price*	*Special Price*	*Discontinued*
RMO12587	*Spr/Fall*	*Mens C*	*8201*	*$39.00*	*$34.95*	*No*

Description *Outdoor Nylon Jacket with Lining*

Size	*Color*	*Style*	*Units in Stock*	*Reorder Level*	*Units on Order*
Small	Blue		1500	150	
	Green		1500	150	
	Red		1500	150	
	Yellow		1500	150	
Medium	Blue		1500	150	
	Green		1500	150	
	Red		1500	150	
	Yellow		1500	150	
Large	Blue		1500	150	
	Green		1500	150	
	Red		1500	150	
	Yellow		1500	150	
Xlarge	Blue		1500	150	
	Green		1500	150	
	Red		1500	150	
	Yellow		1500	150	

ID	*Season*	*Category*	*Supplier*	*Unit Price*	*Special Price*	*Discontinued*
RMO28497	*All*	*Footwe*	*7993*	*$49.95*	*$44.89*	*No*

Description *Hiking Walkers with Patterned Tread Durable Uppers*

Size	*Color*	*Style*	*Units in Stock*	*Reorder Level*	*Units on Order*
7	Brown		1000	100	
	Tan		1000	100	
8	Brown		1000	100	
	Tan		1000	100	
9	Brown		1000	100	
	Tan		1000	100	
10	Brown		1000	100	
	Tan		1000	100	
11	Brown		1000	100	
	Tan		1000	100	
12	Brown		1000	100	
	Tan		1000	100	
13	Brown		1000	100	
	Tan		1000	100	

External outputs can consist of complex, multiple-page documents. A well-known example is the set of reports and statements that you receive with your car insurance statement. This statement is usually a multipage document consisting of detailed automobile insurance information and rates, summary pages, turnaround premium payment cards, and insurance cards for each automobile. Another example is a report of employment benefits with multiple pages of information customized to the individual employee. Sometimes the documents are printed in color with special highlighting or logos. Figure 12-9 is one page of a sample report for survivor protection from an employee benefit booklet. The text is standard wording, and the numbers are customized to the individual employee.

Survivor Protection

In the event of your death while working for a participating employer, your designated beneficiaries could receive:

Lump Sum Benefits

$50,000	Basic Life Insurance
$230,000	Supplemental Life Insurance
$148,677	Thrift Plan
$31,686	Tax Sheltered Annuity (TSA) Plan
$255	Social Security for your eligible dependents
$460,618	Total*

You have not elected Universal Life Insurance. If you would like more information on this plan, please call 1-800-555-7772.

*Refer to page 7 for additional information on the amount of coverage needed to provide ongoing replacement income.

Accidental Death Benefits

If your death is due to an accident, your designated beneficiaries will receive the above benefits plus:

$100,000	24-Hour Accidental Death and Dismemberment Insurance
$100,000	Occupational Accidental Death and Dismemberment Insurance, if the accident is work related

Monthly Death Benefits

If you die before receiving the Master Retirement Plan benefits and you are vested and have a surviving spouse, your spouse may be eligible for a Qualified Pre-Retirement Survivor Annuity.

In addition, your family may be eligible for the following estimated monthly benefits from Social Security, not to exceed a maximum of $2,591 based on:

$1,110	for each child under age 18
$1,110	for a spouse with children under age 16; or
$1,058	for a spouse age 60 or older

FIGURE 12-9
A sample employee benefit report

ELECTRONIC REPORTS

Organizations use various types of electronic reports, each serving a different purpose, and each with its respective strengths and weaknesses. Electronic reports provide great flexibility in the organization and presentation of information. In some instances, screen output is formatted like a printed report but displayed electronically. However, electronic reports can also present information in many other formats: Some have detailed and summary sections, some show data and graphics together, others contain boldface type and highlighting, others can dynamically change their organization and summaries, and still others contain hotlinks to related information. An important benefit of electronic reporting is that it is dynamic—it can change to meet the specific needs of a user in a particular situation. In fact, many systems provide powerful ad hoc reporting capabilities so that users can design their own reports on the fly. For example, an electronic report can provide links to further information. One technique, called *drill down*, allows the user to activate a "hot spot hyperlink" on the report, which tells the system to display a lower-level report, providing more detailed information. For example, Figure 12-10 contains a summary valuation report of inventory on hand. The report provides a summary valuation for each product item. However, if the user clicks on the hotlink for any product, a detailed report pops up with the list of inventory items, the quantities on hand, and the valuation for each inventory item.

drill down
to link a summary field to its supporting detail and enable users to view the detail dynamically

Monthly Sales Summary

Year **2006** *Month* **January**

Category	*Season Code*	*Web Sales*	*Telephone Sales*	*Mail Sales*	*Total Sales*
Footwear	All	$ 289,323	$ 1,347,878	$ 540,883	$ 2,178,084
Men's Clothing	Spring	$ 1,768,454	$ 2,879,243	$ 437,874	$ 4,691,484
	Summer	213,938	387,121	123,590	724,649
	Fall	142,823	129,873	112,234	384,930
	Winter	2,980,489	6,453,896	675,290	10,109,675
	All	1,839,729	4,897,235	349,234	7,086,198
Totals		[illegible]	[illegible]747,368	$ 1,698,222	$ 23,391,023
Women's Clothing	Spring				965,610
	Summer				
	Fall				
	Winter				
	All				
Totals					

Monthly Sales Detail

Year **2006** *Month* **January** *Category* **Men's Clothing** *Season* **Winter**

Product ID	*Product Description*	*Web Sales*	*Telephone Sales*	*Mail Sales*	*Total Sales*
RMO12987	Winter Parka	$ 1,490,245	$ 3,226,948	$ 337,640	$ 5,054,833
RMO13788	Fur-Lined Gloves	149,022	322,695	33,765	505,482
RMO23788	Wool Sweater	596,097	1,290,775	135,058	2,021,930
RMO12980	Long Underwear	298,050	645,339	68,556	1,003,005
RMO32998	Fleece-Lined Jacket	447,075	1,258,079	100,271	1,805,425
Total		$ 2,980,489	$ 6,743,836	$ 675,290	$ 10,394,615

FIGURE 12-10
An RMO summary report with drill down to the detailed report

Another variation of this hotlink capability lets the user correlate information from one report to related information in another report. Most people are familiar with hotlinks from using their Internet browsers. In an electronic report, hotlinks can refer to other information that correlates or extends the primary information. This same capability can be very useful in a business report, which, for example, links the annual statements of key companies in a certain industry.

Another dynamic aspect of electronic reports is the capability to view the data from different perspectives. For example, it might be beneficial to view sales commission data by region, by sales manager, by product line, or by time period or to compare the data with last season's data. Instead of printing all these reports, you can use an electronic format to generate the different views only as needed. Sometimes long or complex reports include a table of contents with hotlinks to the various sections of the report. Some report-generating programs provide electronic reporting capability that includes all of the functionality that is found on pages on the Internet, including frames, hotlinks, graphics, and even animation.

GRAPHICAL AND MULTIMEDIA PRESENTATION

The graphical presentation of data is one of the greatest benefits of the information age. Tools that permit data to be presented in charts and graphs have made information reporting much more user-friendly for printed and electronic formats. Information is being used more and more for strategic decision making as businesspeople examine their data for trends and changes. In addition, today's systems frequently maintain massive amounts of data—much more than people can review. The only effective way to use much of these data is by summarizing them and presenting them in graphical form. Figure 12-11 illustrates a bar chart and a pie chart, which are two common ways to present summary data.

FIGURE 12-11
Sample bar chart and pie chart reports

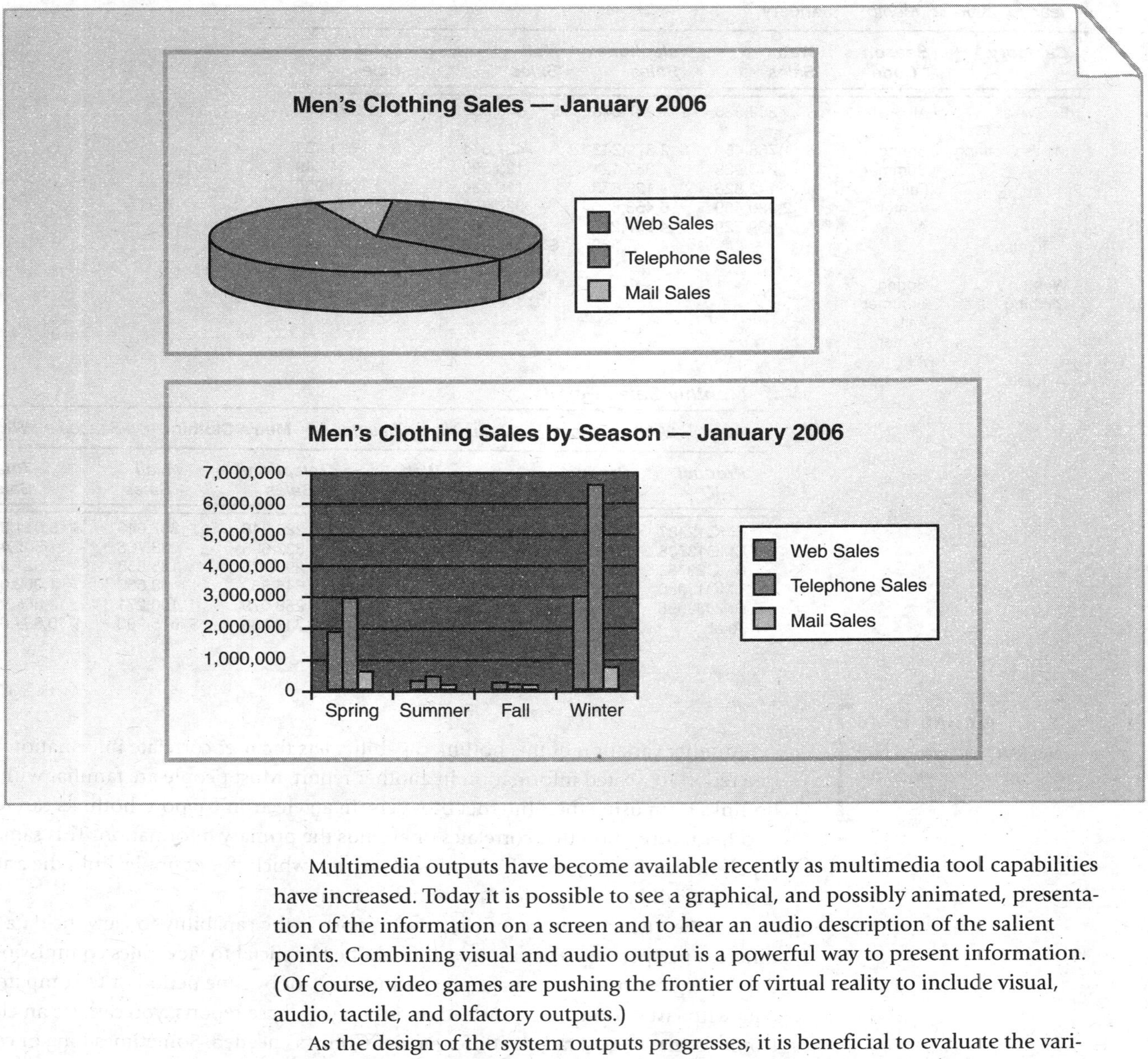

Multimedia outputs have become available recently as multimedia tool capabilities have increased. Today it is possible to see a graphical, and possibly animated, presentation of the information on a screen and to hear an audio description of the salient points. Combining visual and audio output is a powerful way to present information. (Of course, video games are pushing the frontier of virtual reality to include visual, audio, tactile, and olfactory outputs.)

As the design of the system outputs progresses, it is beneficial to evaluate the various presentation alternatives. Reporting packages can be designed into the system to provide a full range of reporting alternatives. Developers should carefully analyze each output report to determine the objective of the output and to select the form of the output that is most appropriate for the information and its use.

The previous examples illustrated some reports for RMO's customer support system. RMO has many options for presenting data to satisfy the needs of the different users. In Chapter 3, the RMO organization chart showed that many upper and middle managers had an interest in the new system. Each of the departments represented needs information from the system, and in most cases, each will want the information to be presented in a format unique to its needs. Barbara Halifax emphasized to her team the importance of this flexibility at various times during the development of the outputs (see the accompanying memo).

ROCKY MOUNTAIN OUTFITTERS
MEMO

To: John MacMurty
From: Barbara Halifax
Date: May 19, 2006
RE: Customer Support System Project Status

John, as you requested, I am writing this memo to update you on the information reports that the various departments throughout the company wanted. One of your concerns was that the definition of the reports could potentially uncover information requirements that we had not anticipated. In other words, there is a risk that the definition of the reports will cause substantial scope creep.

At this point,we have defined essentially all of the reports. I am happy to report that none of the report definitions has caused changes to the database structure or to the system architecture. We have had several requests for new reports, as well as more dynamic updating of the reports. For example, marketing wants not only printed reports but also online reports that are linked to provide drill-down capability. However, the basic information is all in the database, and we have been able to define the reports without major problems.

Would you please indicate in the next oversight committee meeting that we are still on schedule? Please thank all the members of the committee for the instructions they gave to their departments of the need to keep the project on schedule and to work within the boundaries of the previously defined functions and data structures. I think every department's information requirements have been satisfied.

BH

cc: Steven Deerfield, Ming Lee

FORMATTING REPORTS

With all of the choices available today for output format, system designers have great flexibility in what they can offer users. But sifting through those options to provide workable reports can be challenging. Analysts must keep three principles in mind during the design of output reports:

- What is the objective of the report?
- Who is the intended audience?
- What is the medium for presentation?

The importance of these principles cannot be overemphasized for designing reports. In some instances users only need the reports to monitor progress. In others, however, the report may be a critical element in a strategic decision. As a systems designer, you should be sure you understand who is going to use the report and how he or she is going to use it. Decisions about both the content and the format should be based on the audience and the use of the report. Without considering these factors, you could easily omit critical information or present it in an unwieldy format.

Often designers must decide on the level of detail for the format of the report. It can be tempting to produce reports that mirror the structure and format of the data in the database. Newer systems, however, maintain a tremendous amount of detail in the database. Without careful consideration, designers can easily produce reports that suffer from information overload. Information overload occurs when such large quantities of data are provided that it becomes difficult for the user to find and focus on the information that is important. Many people have this problem when searching the Internet—the search engine often returns an overwhelming number of results for the search. Careful design and presentation are required to prevent the same problem with output reports.

The format of the report is also important. Every report should have a meaningful title to indicate the data content. The heading should also list both the date the report was produced and a separate date indicating the effective date of the underlying information; sometimes the two dates may be different. Reports should also be paginated. In earlier systems, when reports were printed on continuous forms, page numbers were not as critical. With today's sheet-fed printers, however, it is easy for pages to be misplaced, and results can then be misinterpreted.

Labels and headings should be used to ensure the correct interpretation of the report data. Charts should be clearly labeled with the identification of the axes and units of measure, and a legend should be provided. In Figure 12-8, showing an RMO inventory report, notice the headings and labels on the report, which help to ensure that the reader does not misinterpret the data. Control breaks are used to divide the data into meaningful pieces that can be easily referenced. Use of lines, boldfacing, and different font sizes makes the report easy to read. Generally, report design is not difficult if you remember that the objective of any report is to provide meaningful information, not just data, and to provide it in a format that is easy to read.

Designers often assume that reports will be printed on standard stock paper. However, that assumption may not be correct. As we just saw, electronic reports are also a very powerful method of producing output information, and the forms of electronic presentation are becoming more and more diverse, ranging from standard computer screens to wireless portable devices. Designers need to carefully consider whether output information will be accessed from nonstandard devices and transmitted via limited bandwidth channels.

DESIGNING INTEGRITY CONTROLS

Information system controls are mechanisms and procedures that are built into a system to safeguard both the system and the information within it. Let's describe a few scenarios to illustrate the need for controls.

- A furniture store sells merchandise on credit with internal financing. An error was made to a customer balance. How do we ensure that only a manager, someone with authority to make adjustments to credit balances, can make the correction?

- A person in accounts payable uses the system to write checks to suppliers. How does the system ensure that the check is correct and that it is made out to a valid supplier? How does the system ensure that no one can commit fraud by writing checks to a bogus supplier? How does the system know that a given payment has been authorized?
- Many companies now have internal LANs or intranets. How does a company protect its sensitive data from being accessed by outsiders or even by disgruntled employees?
- Electronic commerce is expanding exponentially, and many companies are now providing e-commerce sites. How does a company ensure that the financial transactions of its customers are protected and secure? How does a company make sure that its systems and databases are protected from hackers who use the Internet access paths to break in?
- Many companies are now connected to the Internet to provide online access to external employees, such as salespeople, or to customers and suppliers. How does a company safeguard its systems from viruses, worms, and other malicious attacks?

All of these situations involve common business and system activities. Since a company's information is one of its most valuable assets, developers of a new system must consider how to protect and maintain information integrity. As illustrated in Figure 12-12, various locations must be protected with security measures and controls. Some of the controls must be integrated into the application programs that are being developed and the database that supports them. Other controls are part of the operating system and the network. Generally, controls that are integrated into the application and database are called *integrity controls*. The controls in the operating system and network are often referred to as *security controls*. This section explains integrity controls. Later sections discuss security controls.

integrity control
mechanisms and procedures that are built into an application system to safeguard information contained within it

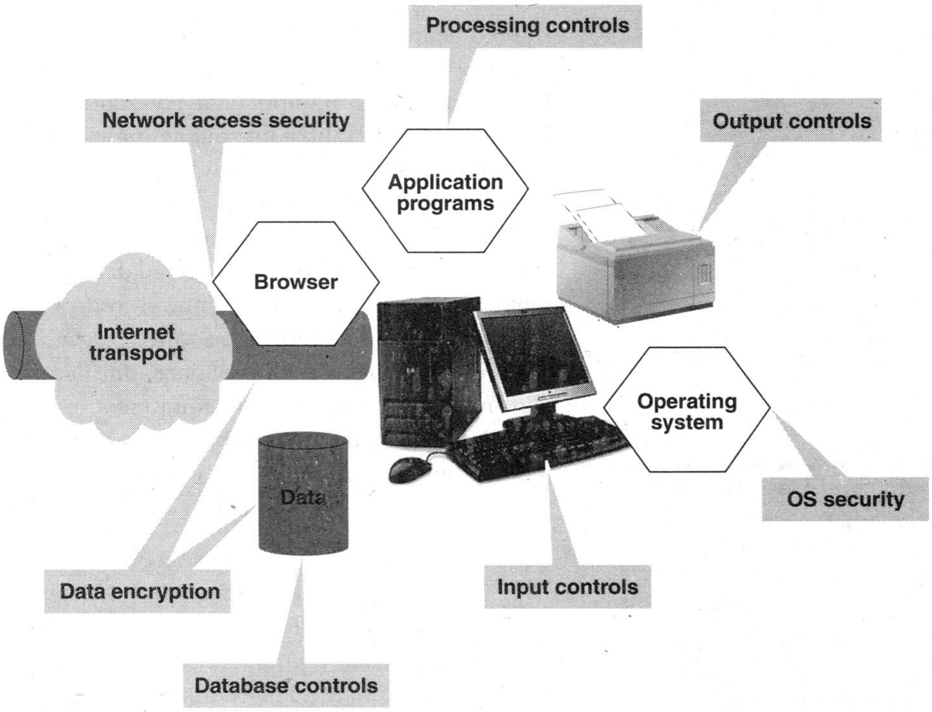

FIGURE 12-12
Points of security and integrity controls

Usually when considering integrity controls, system developers focus on avoiding problems with the application systems and the employees who rightly have access to those systems. Thus, the primary focus is internal—inside the organization. The primary objectives of integrity controls are to:

- Ensure that only appropriate and correct business transactions occur
- Ensure that the transactions are recorded and processed correctly
- Protect and safeguard the assets of the organization (including hardware, software, and information)

The first objective, to ensure that only appropriate and correct business transactions occur, focuses on the identification and capture of input transactions. Integrity controls must make sure that all important business transactions are included—that is, that none is lost or missing and that no fraudulent or erroneous transactions are entered.

The second objective, to ensure that the transactions are recorded and processed correctly, also relates to errors and fraudulent activities. Controls need to detect and alert users to data-entry errors and system bugs that cause problems in processing and recording data. An example of a fraudulent activity is a change in the dollar amount on an otherwise valid transaction.

The third objective, to protect and safeguard the assets of the organization, addresses loss of information from computer crashes or catastrophes. It also includes protection of important information on computer files that could be destroyed by a disgruntled employee or possibly even a hacker.

Frequently, system developers are so focused on designing the system software itself that they forget to develop the necessary controls. Because computer systems are so pervasive and companies depend on information systems so heavily, a development project that does not specifically include integrity controls is inviting disaster. The system will be subject to errors, fraud, and deceptive practices, making it unusable. One of the primary control points for ensuring correct data is at the points of data input.

INPUT INTEGRITY CONTROLS

Input integrity controls are used with all input mechanisms, from electronic devices to standard keyboard inputs. Input controls are an additional level of verification that helps reduce errors in input data. For example, a system may need a certain amount of information for a valid entry, but an input device cannot ensure that all the necessary fields have been entered. An additional level of verification, a *control,* is necessary to check for completeness.

The old computer systems adage of "garbage in, garbage out" relates to input controls, whose objective is to reduce bad data within the system by limiting erroneous input. Historically, the most common control method to ensure correct input was to enter data twice. This technique, called *keypunch and verify*, was first developed for batch entry of large amounts of data. One person would enter the data, and a second person would reenter them on equipment that would then verify that the two inputs were the same. Today, that technique is not used as much because many high-volume transactions are scanned for data. Online systems also validate input as it is being entered. Here are the more common control techniques in use today:

field combination control
an integrity control that verifies the data in one field by checking them against data in another field or fields

value limit control
an integrity control that identifies when a value in a field is too large or too small

- *Field combination controls* review various combinations of fields to ensure that the correct data are entered. For example, on an insurance policy, the application date must be prior to the date the policy is placed in force.
- *Value limit controls* check numeric fields to make sure that the amount entered is reasonable. For example, the amount of a sale or the amount of a commission usually falls within a certain range of values.

completeness control
an integrity control to ensure that all necessary fields on an input form have been entered

data validation control
an integrity control to validate the input data for correctness and appropriateness

- *Completeness controls* ensure that all the necessary fields are completed. This check can be executed as input occurs so that, when certain fields are entered, additional required fields must also be entered. For example, if a dependent is entered on an insurance form, then that person's birthday must also be entered.
- *Data validation controls* ensure that numeric fields that contain codes are correct. For example, bank account numbers might be created with a seven-digit field and a trailing check digit to make an eight-digit account number. The calculation of the check digit is based on the previous seven digits, and the system recalculates it as the data-entry person enters the account number with the check digit. If results do not match, then an input error has occurred. Other data validation can be done online against internal tables or files. For example, a customer number can be validated against the customer file at the time a new order is entered. The systems designer can reduce the need for this type of control by designing a system to obtain the data for a particular field from other information already in the system.

DATABASE INTEGRITY CONTROLS

Most database management systems include integrity controls and security features providing an additional layer of control. Five major areas of security and control can be implemented at the database level:

- Access control
- Data encryption
- Transaction control
- Update control
- Backup and recovery protection

ACCESS CONTROLS

access control
an integrity control that determines who has access to a system and its data

Access controls refer to the ability of a user to get access to the data. An operating system typically applies security and access controls on a file-by-file basis. A DBMS can apply these controls at a much finer level of detail. Controls can be defined on schema subsets such as groups of related tables or objects, single tables or objects, or single attributes. For example, different controls might be applied to the name, Social Security number, and salary fields of an employee table. Also, controls on a single field might differ for read and write access.

A DBMS stores security access information within the schema and applies controls each time data are read or written. When the DBMS enforces security controls, it automatically enforces them for application programs that access the database. Some DBMSs rely on the operating system to identify the user who is attempting to access data, which relieves the user from having to identify himself or herself multiple times. Other DBMSs implement security controls independently of the operating system.

ENCRYPTION

Encryption is used both for data within a database and the transmission of data, especially over public carriers. Data within a database are normally encrypted with a single-key encryption method. More details on the various types of encryption are explained in the section on security controls.

TRANSACTION CONTROLS

transaction logging
a technique whereby all updates to a database are recorded with the information on who performed the update, when, and how

Transaction logging is a technique by which any update to the database is logged with audit information such as user ID, date, time, input data, and type of update. The fundamental idea is to create an audit trail of all updates to the database that can trace any errors or problems that occur. The more advanced database systems—such as those that run on servers, workstations, and mainframes—include transaction logging as part of the DBMS software. However, several smaller DBMSs, particularly those that run on personal computers, do not include this capability, so design teams must add it directly to those applications.

Transaction logging achieves two objectives. First, it helps discourage fraudulent transactions. If a person knows that every transaction is logged, then that person is less apt to attempt a fraudulent transaction. For example, if a person knows that his or her ID will be associated with every check request, then that person is not likely to request a bogus payment.

The second objective of a logging system is to provide a recovery mechanism for erroneous transactions. A mid-level logging system maintains the set of all updates. The system can then recover from errors by "unapplying" the erroneous transactions. More sophisticated logging systems can provide a "before" and "after" image of the fields that are changed by the transaction, as well as the audit trail of all transactions. These sophisticated systems are typically used only for highly sensitive or critical data files, but they do represent an important control mechanism that is available when necessary.

UPDATE CONTROLS

Database management systems are designed to support many application programs simultaneously. Thus, several programs may want to access and update a record or field at the same time. Update controls within a DBMS provide record locking to protect against multiple updates that might conflict with or overwrite each other.

In addition, some transactions that are applied to the database have multiple parts, such as a financial transaction that must credit one account and debit a different account. Delaying commitment of the update until all updates have been verified is a technique used to protect the data from partial updates of these complex transactions.

BACKUP AND RECOVERY

Backup and recovery procedures are designed to protect the database from all other types of catastrophes. Many database management systems provide various levels of backup and recovery. Partial or incremental backups are used to capture changes to the database during the time periods between total backups. A total backup is used only periodically to archive a complete copy of all the data. Frequently, this archive is placed in a secure off-site location to protect it against catastrophic threats such as fire, earthquake, or terrorist attacks.

Another popular security measure used for systems that rely on up-to-the-minute data is a mirror database or mirror site. This technique completely duplicates the database and all transactions as they occur. Obviously, this approach can be expensive, but it is becoming more important as information becomes more and more critical to the daily operations of organizations.

OUTPUT INTEGRITY CONTROLS

As already discussed, output from a system comes in various forms, such as output that is used by other systems, printed reports, and data output on computer screens. The purpose of output controls is to ensure that output arrives at the proper destination and is accurate, current, and complete. It is especially important that reports with sensitive information arrive at the proper destination and that they not be accessed by unauthorized persons.

DESTINATION CONTROLS

In the past, when most output was in printed form, a distribution control desk collected all the printed reports from the nightly processing and distributed them to the correct departments and people. This control desk was important because some of the reports had sensitive, confidential information, and it was important to keep those reports secure. Systems with good controls printed destination and routing information on a report cover page along with the report. Today, businesses accomplish the same function of a control desk by placing printers in each of the locations that need printed reports. It is still a good idea to print a cover sheet with destination and report heading information. Destination codes and routing capabilities are included during the design process to handle the distribution of reports to separate printing facilities. Controlling access to these reports then becomes an issue of physical access. These types of controls are called *destination controls*.

destination controls
integrity controls to ensure that output information is channeled to the correct persons

Electronic output to other systems is usually provided in one of two forms: either an online transaction-by-transaction output or a single data file with a batch of output transactions. Each form has its own type of controls. If the system produces online transactions, then it must ensure that each transaction includes the routing codes identifying the correct destination. Both systems need to work together to ensure that each transaction is sent and received correctly. The output transaction will have verification codes and bits to permit the receiving system to verify the accuracy of the transaction. The receiving system also responds with an acknowledgment of a successful receipt of the transaction. Many of these controls are now built into the network transmission protocols. However, during the design activities, the systems designers need to be aware of the network and operating system capability and supplement it where necessary to ensure that the data are received successfully.

Controls for output data files carefully identify the contents, version, date, and time of the file. Normally, a system produces a data file, either on magnetic tape or disk, and another system must find that data file and use it. The major control issue is how to ensure that the second system uses the correct data file. For example, to avoid serious problems, we want to make sure that Friday's transactions aren't run twice. Or, if by some processing quirk, two data files are produced for the same day—one for the first half of the day and another for the second—the system must use both data files. Or, if the second system had processing errors and needs to be rerun, it must be able to find the correct file to use on its rerun. Controls for this situation generally have special beginning and ending records that contain date, time, version, record counts, dollar control totals, processing period, and so forth. During systems design, provision must be made to accumulate the appropriate totals and to produce the necessary control records.

Destination controls for computer screen output are not as widely used as those for printed reports. Normally, the previously discussed user access controls manage the availability of information on computer screens. In some instances, however, destination controls limit what information can be displayed on which terminal. This extra safeguard is used primarily for military or other systems that house computer terminals in secure areas and provide access to the system's information to anyone who has access to the area. The design of these systems requires close coordination between the application program and the network security control system.

COMPLETENESS, ACCURACY, AND CORRECTNESS CONTROLS

The completeness, accuracy, and correctness of output information are a function primarily of the internal processing of the system rather than any set of controls. System developers ensure completeness and accuracy by printing control fields on the output report. For example, every report should have a date and time stamp, both for the time the report was printed and for the date of the underlying data. Frequently, they are the same, but not always, especially when a report is reprinted because of a previous error. The following items are controls that should be printed on reports:

- Date and time of report printing
- Date and time of data on the report
- Time period covered by the report
- Beginning header with report identification and description
- Destination or routing information
- Pagination in the form "page __ of __"
- Control totals and crossfootings
- An "End of Report" trailer
- The report version number and version date (such as those for special printed forms)

INTEGRITY CONTROLS TO PREVENT FRAUD

The preceding sections have identified several types of integrity controls that support the three control objectives. Many of those techniques are focused on preventing errors and protecting the system from foreign intrusion. However, an equally serious problem is the use of the system by authorized people to commit fraud against an organization.

Fraud is a problem that is reaching epidemic proportions in the United States and around the world. Almost every week we see newspaper articles describing fraud and other white-collar crime. The economic losses caused by fraudulent activity around the world are staggering. These losses reach into the billions of dollars and far exceed those from violent and personal crimes. In the last few years, several major corporations have been forced into bankruptcy or closure due to the fraudulent behavior of key executives. Obviously, software and system controls will not completely eliminate fraud. However, system developers should be aware of the fundamental elements that make fraud possible and incorporate system controls to combat it. The controls that we discussed previously—input controls, database controls, and output controls—are critical components in the battle against fraud, but several additional techniques should be considered in system design to further increase protection.

Research into the perpetration of fraud indicates that three conditions are present in almost all fraud cases:

- Personal pressure, such as the desire to maintain an extravagant lifestyle
- Rationalization, such as the thought "I will repay this money."
- Opportunity, such as unverified cash receipts

The objective of integrity controls is to reduce or eliminate the opportunity for fraud by having adequate manual controls and automated records of money and assets. Control of fraud requires both manual procedures and computer integrity controls. Neither component is sufficient by itself to reduce the opportunities for fraud. System developers need to work closely with business users who are knowledgeable about accounting principles to prevent fraud.

Sometimes system developers may think that integrity controls are not necessary, since the system in development is not a financial or accounting system. However, an opportunity for fraud exists in almost every business system. Since most business systems track an organization's assets, someone could manipulate those assets, writing checks for incorrect amounts or to fictitious parties. Hence, almost every system requires some type of integrity controls.

Figure 12-13 contains several of the more important factors that increase the risk of fraud. This list is not comprehensive, but it does provide a foundation on which developers can design a computer system that reduces the opportunity for fraud. As a system developer, you should include discussions both with your users and within the project teams to ensure that adequate controls have been included to reduce fraud.

FACTORS AFFECTING FRAUD RISK	TECHNIQUES TO REDUCE RISK
Separation of duties	Design separate electronic forms, with separate access controls, for request, approval, and generation of expenditures.
Inadequate audit trails	Include transaction logging. Avoid, or very tightly control, manual override capability that circumvents logs.
Inadequate records	Implement a comprehensive database with sufficient detail and logs.
Inadequate monitoring	Include manual procedures and automated routines to monitor patterns and out-of-bound conditions. Include exception reports. Implement third-person audit capability.
Easily removable assets	Include an easy-to-use capability to cross-check physical counts with automated records.
Inadequate security system	Supplement operating system security features with additional program and data level security. Include automatic shutdown and lockup features. Include routines to analyze access patterns.

FIGURE 12-13
Fraud risks and prevention techniques

Source: Information in the table was provided by Dr. Marshall Romney of the School of Accountancy and Information Systems at Brigham Young University.

Now that we have an overview of input and output integrity controls, we turn our attention to security controls.

DESIGNING SECURITY CONTROLS

security controls
mechanisms usually provided by the operating system or environment to protect the data and processing systems from malicious attack

Although the objective of *security controls* is to protect the assets of an organization from all threats, as indicated earlier, the primary focus is generally on external threats. In addition to the objectives enumerated earlier for integrity controls, security controls also have the following two objectives:

- Maintain a stable, functioning operating environment for users and application systems (usually 24 hours a day, 7 days a week)
- Protect information and transactions during transmission outside the organization (public carriers)

BEST PRACTICE: Be prepared to answer this question every time your system project is discussed with management: "Are you sure the company will be protected from all threats when this system is operational?"

The first objective, to maintain a stable operating environment, focuses on security measures to protect the organization's systems from external attacks such as from hackers, viruses, worms, and message overloads. Most organizations today have gateways between their internal systems and the Internet. Every time someone in an organization sends a communication to or receives one from the Internet, there is the potential for a security violation and for undesirable access that could disrupt the internal systems. So, eliminating and controlling any undesirable access helps avoid disruption of the system.

The second objective, to protect transactions during transmission, focuses on the information that is sent or received via the Internet. More and more organizations utilize the Internet as a portal to their customers and to their suppliers. Once a transaction is sent outside the organization, it could be intercepted, destroyed, or modified. So, security controls use techniques to protect data while they are in transit from the source to the destination.

Security controls can be implemented within different types of software, including the network and computer operating system, the database management system, or the application programs. The most common security control points are network and computer operating systems because they exercise direct control over assets such as files, application programs, and disk drives. All modern operating systems contain extensive security features that can identify users, restrict access to files and programs, and secure data transmission among distributed software components. Operating system security is the foundation of security for most information systems.

On some occasions, developers may implement security controls directly within application software. Developers may define their own security controls over individual data items or records when data are stored in files instead of a database. Developers may also implement security controls to prevent unauthorized users from performing certain functions such as deleting existing data or creating backup copies on removable storage media.

Most developers avoid implementing security controls within application software because of the complexity and importance of security functions. Most operating system and DBMS developers have a large programming staff dedicated exclusively to developing and maintaining security software. It is difficult for application developers to dedicate sufficient resources to implement system security controls correctly and fully. Thus, security-related implementation tasks in a typical information system development project are usually limited to configuring security software in the underlying operating system or DBMS.

SECURITY FOR ACCESS TO SYSTEMS

Modern operating systems, networking software, and Internet access all need to implement control mechanisms. These mechanisms can be used to control access to any resource managed by the operating system or network—including hardware, application programs, and data files.

System access controls are mechanisms that are established to restrict what portions of the computer system a person can use. This category includes controls to limit access to certain applications or functions within an application, restrict access to the computer system itself, and limit access to certain pieces of data.

With proper design and implementation, an information system can use access control functions embedded in system software. The advantage to this approach is that a consistent set of access controls is then applied to every resource on a hardware platform or network. Thus, the systems designer can implement a single access control scheme and apply it to every resource or information system.

The systems designer can also add controls over and above those already provided by system software. However, designing and implementing effective application-based access controls require technical expertise. Operating system and network software developers expend considerable energy and resources to develop reliable and efficient access controls, and it is difficult and expensive for a typical organization to duplicate these efforts. For these reasons, most information systems build on the access control already within system software.

TYPES OF USERS

System developers must consider different types of users when designing access controls. Figure 12-14 illustrates various types of users and the access that is appropriate for each. The following paragraphs explain the types of system access available to users.

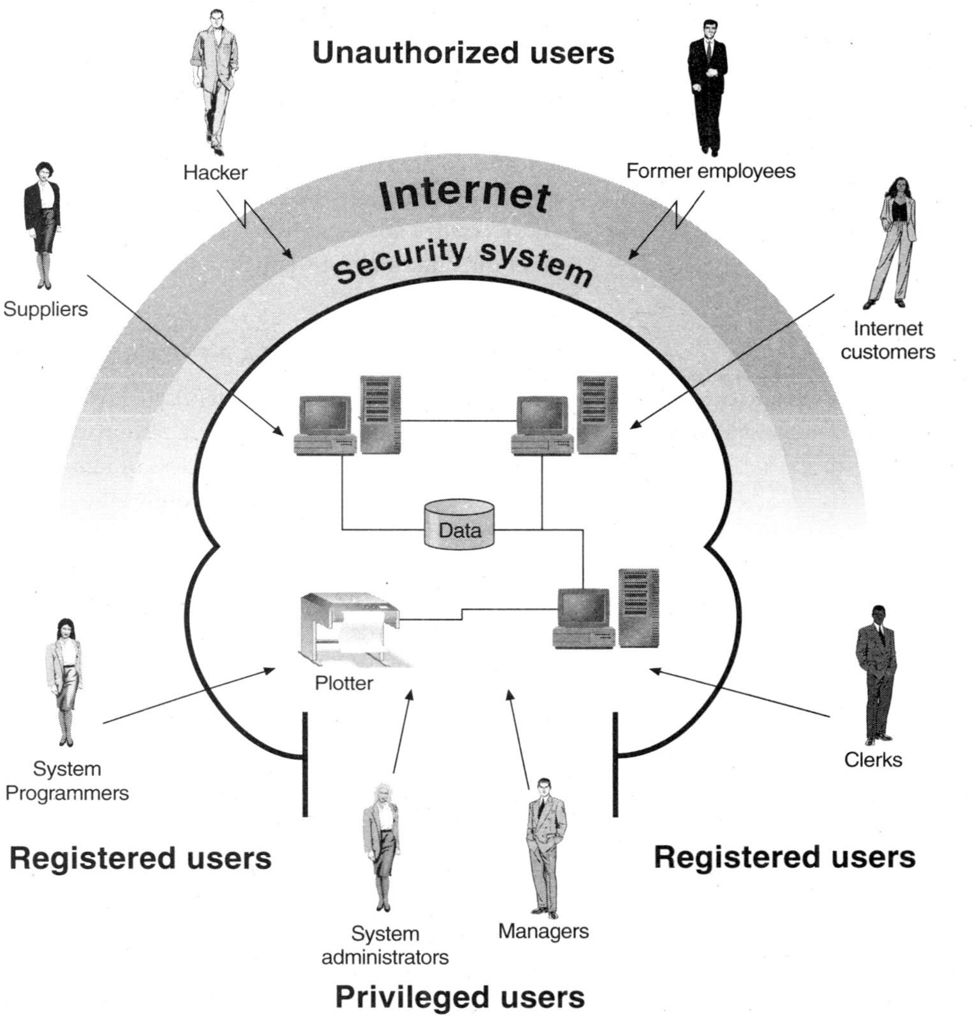

FIGURE 12-14
Users and their access to computer systems

unauthorized user
a person who does not have authorized access to a system

registered user
a user who is registered or known to the system and is authorized to access some part of it

To begin development of access controls, designers first must identify and consider all three of these user categories: unauthorized users, registered users, and privileged users. *Unauthorized users* are people who are not allowed access to any part or functions of the system. Such users include employees who are prohibited from accessing the system, former employees who no longer are permitted to access the system, and outsiders such as hackers and intruders. Controls must be able to identify and exclude access by these people.

Registered users are those who are authorized to access the system. Normally, various levels of registered users are set up depending on what they are authorized to view and update. The different levels of access are defined during the design of the new system. For example, some users may be allowed to view data but not update them, and other users can update only certain data fields. Some screens and functions of the new system may be hidden from other levels of registered users. The important point for systems designers to recognize is that there may be multiple levels of registered users. *Authorization* is the process of determining whether a user is permitted to access a specific resource for a particular purpose. In other words, it is the process of deciding whether a user should be a registered user. The security system stores an access control list for each protected resource. An *access control list* is a list of users or user groups that can access a resource and the permitted access type(s).

authorization
the process of determining whether a user is permitted to have access to the system and data

access control list
the list of users who have rights to access the system and data

privileged user
a user who has special security access privileges to a system

Privileged users include people who have access to the source code, executable program, and database structure of the system. These people include system programmers, application programmers, operators, and system administrators, and they may also have differing levels of security access. Usually system programmers have full access to all components of the systems and data. Application programmers have access to the applications themselves but often not to the secure libraries and data files used for the systems in production. System administrators have access to all functions of the system and can control and establish the various levels of registration and register users. A system administrator also usually has software programs to help control access and to monitor access attempts.

PASSWORDS AND SMART CARDS

authentication
the process of identifying a user to verify that he or she can have access to the system

Authentication is the process of identifying users (that is, the authorized or registered users) who request access to sensitive resources. Authentication is the basis of all security because security controls are useless unless the user is correctly identified. In many operating systems, authentication requires the user to enter a username and password. The user is authenticated if the password he or she enters matches the password stored in the security database.

Two techniques are used to define passwords. The computer can randomly generate and assign passwords, or each user can define his or her own password. There are advantages to both techniques. The first creates passwords that are usually longer and more random, but they tend to be hard for users to remember. Most users would have a hard time trying to remember a password such as a3x7869bts21. User-developed passwords are easier to remember, but they are usually not as complex and therefore not quite as secure. Some restrictions can be placed on the syntax of the password to ensure at least a minimum level of security.

Of course, one of the problems with passwords is remembering what they are. It is not uncommon for heavy computer users to have 5 or even 10 different passwords for different systems that they access. One alternative is to use the same password for all systems, but then if someone determines the password, all the systems are compromised. Most often, the security system should be organized so that all resources can be accessed with the same unique identifier and password combination. In other words, only one user ID/password combination should be required for access to the different systems throughout the organization. When users have to remember different IDs and passwords to access different systems, they often write them down and post them near the computer. Obviously, this practice defeats the purpose of user verification security.

smart card
a computer-readable plastic card with security information embedded within it

A *smart card* is a computer-readable plastic card with a small amount of stored security data that can be read by a card scanner in much the same way a credit or debit card can be read at a supermarket checkout counter. The smart card stores an encrypted version of the user's password, fingerprint, retinal scan, or voice characteristics. To authenticate himself or herself, the user scans the card and then enters the password or submits to a fingerprint, retinal, or voice scan. Such a system enhances security because the user must possess both the card and the appropriate identifying information to be authenticated. Only the security subsystem knows the key, which prevents potential intruders from using cards with altered data.

A final security step is to make sure the system keeps a record of attempted logons, especially unsuccessful ones. An unsuccessful logon may simply indicate that the user mistyped or forgot a password, but it may also indicate an attempted breach of security, which should be investigated.

BIOMETRIC DEVICES

Authentication can also be based on other forms of personal identification, including keystroke patterns, fingerprints, retinal scans, and voice characteristics. When a user enters a password or other keystroke sequence, the timing and force of each keystroke are unique. Some security systems use both the password and the keystroke pattern to authenticate the user, which prevents someone with a stolen password from accessing system resources.

Many companies are now experimenting with a new form of security based on biometric devices. The principle behind use of a biometric device is that the individual becomes the password or gateway into a secure system. These more sophisticated security systems can scan fingerprints, retinal blood vessels, or voices, which are unique for every person. With the advent of very small computer chips with very high memory densities and logic circuitry, biometric devices can be built into almost any of the normal hardware components of a computer. In addition, the complex logic necessary to do sophisticated pattern matching of fingerprints, hand vein patterns, retinas, iris patterns, or complete facial patterns can be located right in the micro-sized biometric device itself.

Biometric fingerprint devices are now being embedded in such components as a computer mouse, computer keyboard, and small touch pads. Other biometric scanners, such as very small cameras, can be embedded in the computer monitor. Such a device might do an iris or facial scan of the person looking at the monitor. Figure 12-15 illustrates a computer mouse with an embedded touch pad to test fingerprints. Other types of mouse devices have the sensor on the side so that the thumb must be placed on it and authorization can be performed before every mouse action.

FIGURE 12-15
Biometric mouse

Source: Used with permission of onClick Corporation, Houston, Texas.

Security based on biometric devices can also be multilevel. Security verification can be done when the user first tries to log on. Higher levels of security can later be activated within a given program to obtain additional authorization to access specific forms or database records. Obviously, each individual must be authorized and appropriate information stored for the level of security allowed.

DATA SECURITY

In addition to the need for controlling access to an organization's systems and internal network, it is frequently important to make the data themselves secure. For example, user IDs and passwords are important information that must be secret. Frequently, the password information is even kept secret from the system administrators. They can assign a new password to a user, but they cannot read or access the current password. So, if a user forgets his or her password, the administrator assigns a new one.

Many other types of files are also kept confidential. Some examples include files that contain the following:

- Financial information
- Credit card numbers, bank account numbers, payroll information, and other personal data
- Strategies and plans for products and other mission-critical data
- Government and sensitive military information

Some operating systems, especially UNIX and its derivations, have built-in security for each file in the system. Each UNIX file has security corresponding to three types of users: the owner of the file, other members of the owner's workgroup, and all other users. The security for each user is also further divided into three levels: read access, update (create, update, and delete) access, and execute access. Execute access determines whether the file is executable (for example, an .exe file in Windows), and the security level determines who is allowed to execute the file.

Data that reside on an internal system need to be protected, but data that are being transmitted outside the organization are especially subject to snooping and even modification. With the increasing acceptance of electronic communications, more and more organizations are transmitting and receiving transactions via the Internet. On the sales and distribution side of business, customers are viewing catalogs, ordering products, making payments, and tracking shipments all via the Internet. On the supply side, organizations are ordering inventory, monitoring receivables, sending purchase orders, and making financial transactions through the Internet. Since this information is being transmitted via the public Internet, the raw data are available to anybody who has tools to listen and intercept information packets.

encryption
the process of altering data so that they are unreadable by unauthorized users

decryption
the process of converting encrypted data back into a readable format

encryption algorithm
a complex mathematical formula and process that encrypts or decrypts data

encryption key
a binary field that the encryption algorithm uses to transform the data

symmetric key encryption
an encryption process that uses the same key to encrypt and to decrypt the data

The primary method of maintaining the security of data, both on internal systems and transmitted data, is by encrypting the data. *Encryption* is the process of altering data so that unauthorized users cannot view them. *Decryption* is the process of converting encrypted data back to their original state. Data stored in files or a database on hard drives or other storage devices can be encrypted to protect them against theft. Data sent across a network can be encrypted to prevent eavesdropping or theft during transmission. A thief or eavesdropper who steals or intercepts encrypted data receives a meaningless group of bits that are difficult or impossible to convert back into the original data.

An *encryption algorithm* is a complex mathematical transformation that encrypts or decrypts binary data. An *encryption key* is a binary input to the encryption algorithm—typically a long string of bits. The encryption algorithm varies the data transformation based on the encryption key so that data can be decrypted only with the same key or a compatible decryption key. Many encryption algorithms are available, and a few, including Data Encryption Standard (DES) and several algorithms developed by RSA Security, are widely deployed governmental or Internet standards. An encryption algorithm must generate encrypted data that are difficult or impossible to decrypt without the encryption key. Decryption without the key becomes more difficult as key length is increased. Both sender and receiver must use the same or compatible algorithms.

Figure 12-16 is an example of *symmetric key encryption*, in which the same key encrypts and decrypts the data. A significant problem with symmetric key encryption is that both sender and receiver use the same key, which must be created and shared in a secure manner. Security is compromised if the key is transmitted over the same channel as messages encrypted with the key. Also, sharing a key among many users increases the possibility of key theft.

FIGURE 12-16
Symmetric key encryption

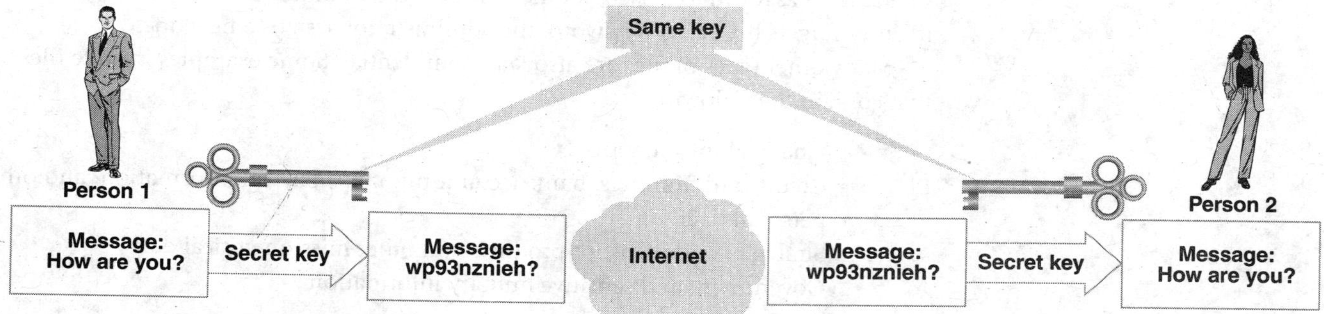

asymmetric key encryption
an encryption process that uses one key to encrypt and a different key to decrypt the data

public key encryption
an asymmetric key method in which one key is publicized and the other key is kept private

Asymmetric key encryption uses different but compatible keys to encrypt and decrypt data. *Public key encryption* is a form of asymmetric key encryption that uses a public key for encryption and a private key for decryption. The two keys are like a matched pair. Once information is encrypted with the public key, it can be decrypted only with the private key. It cannot be decrypted with the same public key that encrypted it. Organizations that use this technique broadcast their public key so that it is freely available to anybody who wants it. Then when some entity—for example, someone who wants to order something from the vendor—wishes to transmit a secure message to a vendor, that customer reads the vendor's public key from a public source such as a Web site. The customer encrypts the message with the public key and sends the message to the vendor. The vendor then decrypts the message with the private key. Since no one else has the private key, no one else can decrypt the message.

Some asymmetric encryption methods can encrypt and decrypt messages in both directions. That is, in addition to using the public key to encrypt a message that can be decrypted with the private key, an organization can also encrypt a message with the private key and decrypt it with the public key. Notice that both keys must still work as a pair, but the message can go forward or backward through the encryption/decryption pair. This second technique is the basis for digital signatures and certificates, which are explained in the next section. Figure 12-17 illustrates an asymmetric key encryption transmittal.

FIGURE 12-17
Asymmetric key encryption

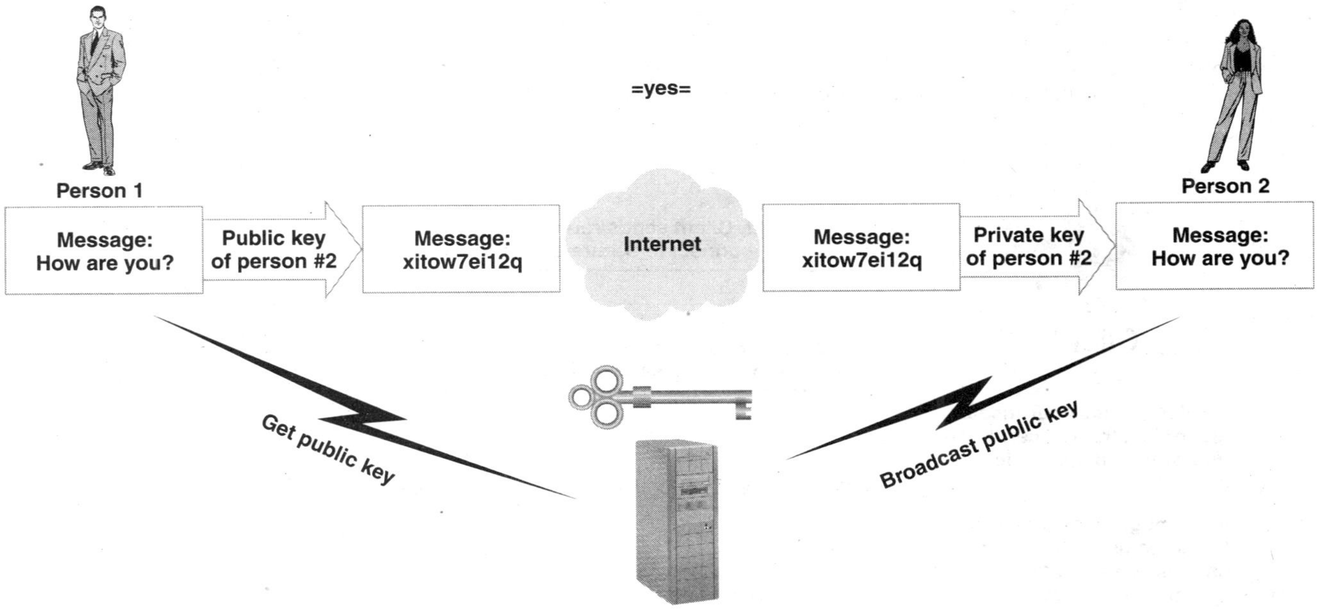

You may ask, "How can an encryption algorithm go one direction (with one key) and not be able to come back the same way (be decrypted with the same key)?" The mathematics of this type of algorithm is beyond the scope of this text. However, you should be able to understand a simple example: multiplication and factoring. If someone gives you two or three numbers, even big numbers, and asks you to multiply them, you can do that fairly easily. However, if someone gives you one very big number and asks you to factor it (that is, find the numbers that were originally multiplied to get that number), you would not be able to do that easily. It would take you a long time. Algorithms based on this one-directional mathematical characteristic form the basis of many asymmetric key encryption routines.

DIGITAL SIGNATURES AND CERTIFICATES

The encryption of messages is an effective technique to enable a secure exchange of information between two entities who have appropriate keys. However, how do you know that the entity on the other end of the communication is really who you think it is? A *digital signature* is a technique in which a document is encrypted using a private key to verify who wrote the document. If you have the public key of an entity, and that entity sends you a message with its private key, you can decode it with the public key. You know that the party is the one you want to communicate with because that entity is the only one who can encode a message with that private key. The encoding of a message with a private key is called *digital signing*.

digital signature
a technique in which a document is encrypted using a private key to verify who wrote the document

Taking the example one step further, you can ask the question, "How do I know that the public key I have is the correct public key and not some counterfeit key?" In other words, maybe someone is impersonating another entity and is passing out false public keys to be able to intercept encoded messages (such as financial transactions) and steal information. In essence, the problem is ensuring that the key that is purported to be the public key of some institution is in fact that institution's public key. The solution to that problem is a certificate.

certificate, or digital certificate
a text message that is encrypted by a verifying authority and used to broadcast an organization's name and public key

certifying authority
a well-known third party that sells digital certificates to organizations

A *certificate*, or *digital certificate*, is an institution's name and public key (plus other information such as address, Web site URL, and validity date of the certificate), encrypted and certified by a third party. Many third parties, such VeriSign and Equifax, are very well known and widely accepted *certifying authorities*. In fact, they are so well known that their public keys are built right into Netscape and Internet Explorer. As shown in Figure 12-18, you can know that the entities with whom you are communicating are in fact who they say they are and that you do have their correct public key.

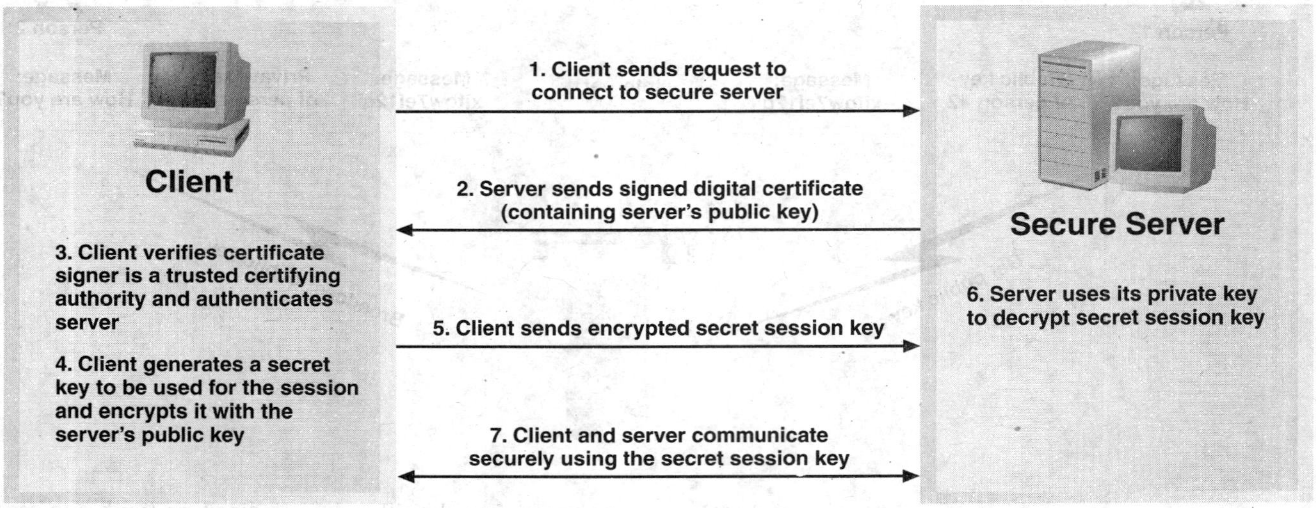

FIGURE 12-18
Using a digital certificate

An entity that wants a certificate with its name and public key goes to a certifying authority and buys a certificate. The certifying authority encrypts the data with its own private key (signs the data) and gives the data back to the original entity. Now when someone, such as a customer, asks the entity for its public key, it sends the certificate. The customer receives the certificate and opens it with the certifying authority's public key. Again, the certifying authority is so well known that its public key is built into everyone's browser and is essentially impossible to counterfeit. Now the customer can be sure that he or she is communicating with the original entity and can do so with encrypted messages using the entity's public key.

A variation of this scenario occurs when the buyer and seller transmit their certificates to one another. Each participant can decrypt the certificate using the certifying authority's public key to extract information such as name and address. However, to ensure that the public key contained within the certificate is valid, the certificates are transmitted to the certifying authority for verification. The authority stores certificate data, including public keys, within its database and verifies transmitted certificates by matching their content against the database.

SECURE TRANSACTIONS

Secure Sockets Layer (SSL)
a standard protocol to connect and transmit encrypted data

Transport Layer Security (TLS)
an updated version of SSL

Secure electronic transactions require a standard set of methods and protocols that address authentication, authorization, privacy, and integrity. Netscape originally developed the *Secure Sockets Layer (SSL)* to support secure transactions. SSL was later adopted as an Internet standard and renamed *Transport Layer Security (TLS)*, though the original name, SSL, is still widely used.

TLS is a protocol for a secure channel to send messages over the Internet. Sender and receiver first establish a connection using ordinary Internet protocols and then ask each other to create a TLS connection. Sender and receiver then verify each other's identity by exchanging and verifying identity certificates as explained previously. At this point, either or both have exchanged public keys, so they can send secure messages. Since asymmetric encryption is quite slow and difficult, the two entities agree on a protocol and encryption method, usually a single-key encryption method. Of course, all of the messages to establish a secure connection are sent using the public key/private key combination. Once the encryption technique has been determined and the secret, single key has been transmitted, all subsequent transmission is done using the secret, single key.

IP Security (IPSec) is a newer Internet standard for secure message transmission. IPSec is implemented at a lower layer of the network protocol stack, which enables it to operate with greater speed. IPSec can replace or complement SSL. Both protocols can be used at the same time to provide an extra measure of security. IPSec supports more secure encryption methods than SSL, but these methods are not yet fully deployed on the Internet.

Secure Hypertext Transport Protocol (HTTPS or HTTP-S)
an Internet standard for transmitting Web pages securely

Secure Hypertext Transport Protocol (HTTPS or *HTTP-S)* is an Internet standard for securely transmitting Web pages. HTTPS supports several types of encryption, digital signing, and certificate exchange and verification. All modern Web browsers and servers support HTTPS. It is a complete approach to Web-based security, although security is enhanced when HTTPS documents are sent over secure TLS or IPSec channels.

Security is an important consideration in the development and deployment of information systems in today's networked environment. Fortunately, many tools and programs are available and can be integrated into new systems as part of the total solution. System developers need to be aware of the need to include security measures and to be familiar with the latest tools and techniques.

Summary

The chapter began with a discussion of identifying and then designing system interfaces. System interfaces include all inputs and outputs except those that are part of the interactive user interface.

Designing the inputs to the system is a three-step process:

- Identify the devices and mechanisms that will be used to enter input.
- Identify all system inputs and develop a list with data content of each.
- Determine what kinds of controls are necessary for each system input.

To develop a list of the inputs to the system, designers use requirements models and design models that were developed when completing each use case realization. Sequence diagrams are the primary source of information, but the design class diagram is used to ensure that the correct data fields and the correct methods that produce the outputs are provided.

The process to design the outputs from the system consists of the same steps as for input design. For output design, sequence diagrams are used to identify messages that exit the system. New technology provides numerous ways to present output with charts, graphs, and multimedia. Before deciding on an output medium, the designer should carefully consider the intended audience and the purpose of the output.

This chapter next discussed the concepts of integrity controls in systems. The objectives of integrity controls are to:

- Ensure that only appropriate and correct business transactions occur
- Ensure that the transactions are recorded and processed correctly
- Protect and safeguard the assets (including information) of the organization

Integrity controls are concerned with defining who has access to the various components of the system and the database. Access controls identify various classifications of users—such as unauthorized users, registered users, and privileged users—to ensure that systems are safeguarded. Additional integrity controls are concerned with reducing errors, preventing fraud, and maintaining the correctness of the data in the system.

The last section of the chapter introduced the basic concepts of security for systems that have access to public networks (primarily the Internet). Security is becoming more and more important, and various techniques should be considered when developing new information systems. The underlying technology in many of the security approaches is based on public key systems that have public and private key components. Encryption and public key systems are the basis for digital signatures, digital certificates, secure connection, and secure transaction implementations.

KEY TERMS

access control, p. 509
access control list, p. 516
ad hoc reports, p. 497
asymmetric key encryption, p. 519
authentication, p. 516
authorization, p. 516
certificate, or digital certificate, p. 520
certifying authority, p. 520
completeness control, p. 509
control break report, p. 501
data validation control, p. 509
decryption, p. 518
destination controls, p. 511
detailed report, p. 499
digital signature, p. 520
drill down, p. 503
encryption, p. 518
encryption algorithm, p. 518
encryption key, p. 518
exception report, p. 499
executive report, p. 499
external output, p. 499
field combination control, p. 508
integrity control, p. 507
internal output, p. 499
privileged user, p. 516
public key encryption, p. 519
registered user, p. 515
Secure Hypertext Transport Protocol (HTTPS or HTTP-S), p. 521
Secure Sockets Layer (SSL), p. 521
security control, p. 513
smart card, p. 516
summary report, p. 499
symmetric key encryption, p. 518
transaction logging, p. 509
Transport Layer Security (TLS), p. 521
turnaround document, p. 500
unauthorized user, p. 515
value limit control, p. 508

REVIEW QUESTIONS

1. What does XML stand for? Explain how XML is similar to HTML. Also discuss the differences between XML and HTML.
2. Compare the strengths and weaknesses of using a system sequence diagram to define inputs.
3. Which requirements model shows most clearly the messages that cross the system boundary?
4. Why is it important to review the event table to make sure all outputs are identified?
5. If a report is produced when a user selects a menu item on a form, is the event that triggers the use case still described as temporal? If the system automatically produces the report, is this still a use case? Explain.
6. How are the data fields on an input or an output identified using UML with the object-oriented approach?
7. Explain four types of integrity controls for input forms. Which have you seen most frequently? Why are they important?
8. What protection does transaction logging provide? Should it be included in every system?
9. What are the different considerations for output screen design and output report design?
10. What is meant by *drill down*? Give an example of how you might use it in a report design.
11. What is the danger from information overload? What solutions can you think of to avoid it?
12. Describe what kinds of integrity controls you would recommend to place on all output reports. Why?
13. What are the objectives of integrity controls in information systems? In your own words, explain what each of the three objectives means. Give an example of each.
14. What are the four types of input controls used to reduce input errors? Describe how each works.
15. Explain what is meant by update controls for a database management system.
16. What is the basic purpose of transaction logging? Microsoft Access does not have automatic transaction logging. Is this a deficiency, or is it not really an important consideration in database integrity?
17. On a printed output report, what is the difference between the date the report was printed and the date of the data?
18. What are the two primary objectives of security controls?
19. Explain the three categories of user access privileges. Is three the right number, or should there be more or fewer than three? Why or why not?
20. How does single-key (symmetric) encryption work? What are its strengths? What are its weaknesses?
21. How does public key (asymmetric) encryption work? What are its strengths? What are its weaknesses?
22. What is a digital certificate? What role do certifying authorities play in security systems?
23. What is a digital signature? What does it tell a user?

THINKING CRITICALLY

1. The chapter described various situations that emphasized the need for controls. In the first scenario presented, a furniture store sells merchandise on credit. Based on the descriptions of controls given in the chapter, identify the various controls that should be implemented in the system to ensure that corrections to customer balances are made only by someone with the correct authorization.
2. In the second scenario illustrating the need for controls, an accounts payable clerk uses the system to write checks to suppliers. Based on the information in the chapter, what kinds of controls would you implement to ensure that checks are written only to valid suppliers, that checks are written for the correct amount, and that all payouts have the required authorization? How would you design the controls if different payment amounts required different levels of authorization?
3. The executives of a company have asked for a special decision support system report on corporate financials. They want this report to be based on actual financial data for the past several years. The report is to have several input parameters so that the executives can do "what-if" analysis of future sales based on past performance. They would like the report to be viewable online and in printed form. What kinds of controls would you implement to ensure that (1) only authorized executives can request the report, (2) the executives understand the basis (past and projected data) for a given report, and (3) executives are aware of the sensitive nature of the information and treat it as confidential?
4. A payroll system has a data-entry subsystem that is used to enter time card information for hourly employees. What kinds of controls would you implement to ensure that the data are correct and error-free? What other controls would

you include to ensure that a data-entry clerk (who may be a friend of an employee) cannot inflate the hours on the time card (after it was approved by a supervisor)?

5. A university library system is depicted in Figure 12-19, with partial system sequence diagrams for two use cases, *Check out a book* and *Return a book*. Based on the figure, construct four tables showing inputs and outputs as shown in Figures 12-5 and 12-6: (1) Inputs for the Library System, (2) Outputs for the Library System, (3) Inputs for the Student Record System, and (4) Outputs for the Student Record System.

6. You work for a grocery chain that always has many customers in the stores. To facilitate and speed checkout, the company would like to develop self-service checkout stands. Customers can check their own groceries and pay by credit card or cash. How would you design the checkout register and equipment? What kinds of equipment would you use to make it easy and intuitive for the customers, make sure that prices are entered correctly, and ensure that cash or credit card payments are done correctly? In other words, what equipment would you have at the checkout station? In your solution, you may use existing state-of-the-art solutions or invent new devices.

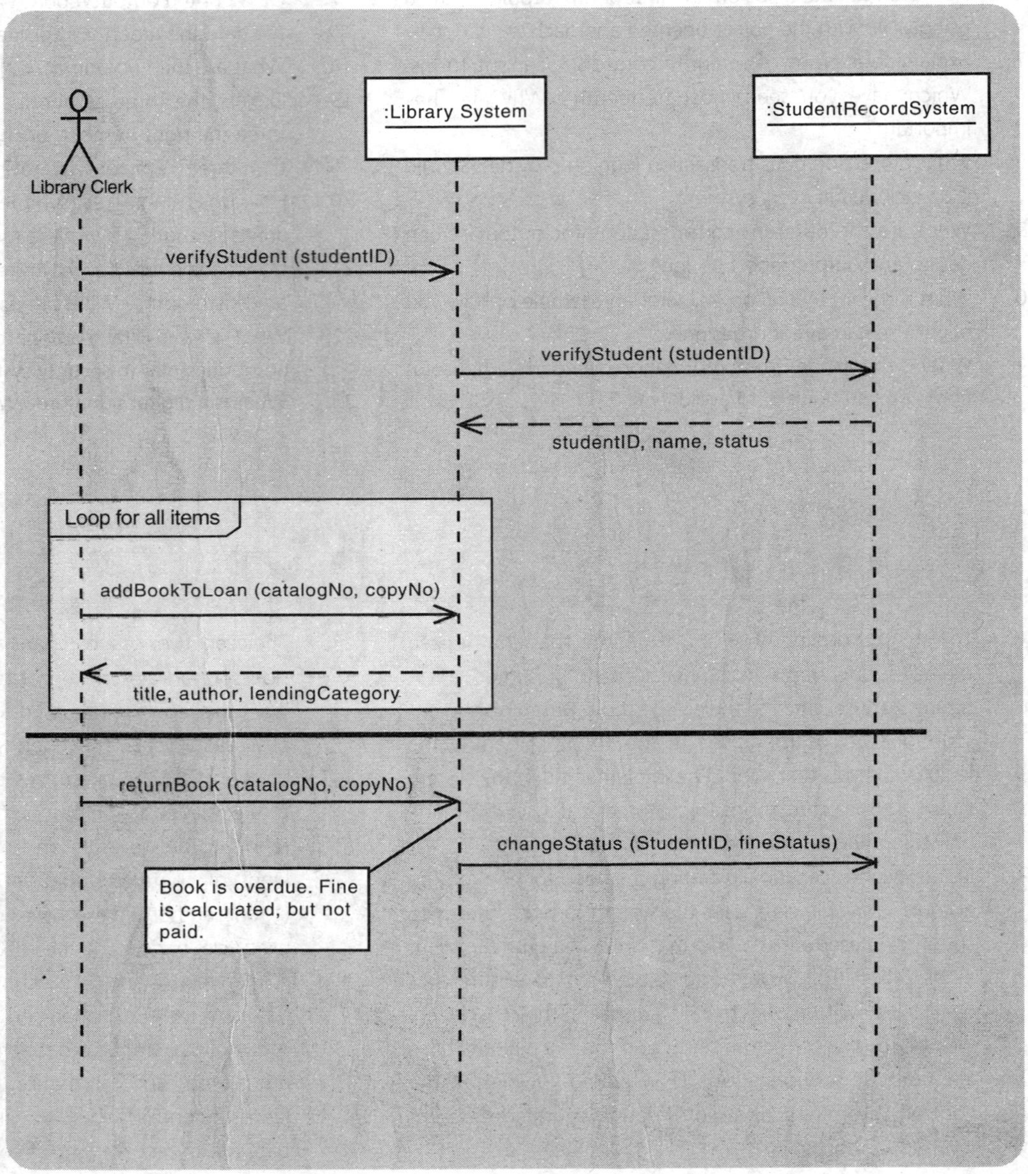

FIGURE 12-19

Partial system sequence diagram for the university library system

EXPERIENTIAL EXERCISES

1. Look on the Web for an e-commerce site (for example, Amazon.com or eBay). Evaluate the effectiveness of the Web pages. What kind of security and controls are integrated into the system? Do you see potential problems with the integrity controls? How effective are they in minimizing data-entry errors?
2. Examine the information system of a local business (a fast-food restaurant, doctor's office, video store, grocery store, and so forth). Evaluate the screens (and reports, if possible) for ease of use and effectiveness. What kinds of integrity controls are in place?
3. Find and research a system that is being constructed or has recently been constructed. You may work for a company that has a development project in progress or have a friend who works for such a company. Another source of development projects is your university or college itself. Interview one of the developers. Ask about integrity controls, methodology for screen design, and guidelines to ensure consistency across the user interface. Ask about the number and scope of the input and output design tasks (for example, how many screens or hours required) and the method used to lay out the screens and reports (such as prototyping, CASE tools, and so forth).
4. Go to the Internet and find out what you can about Pretty Good Privacy. What is it? How does it work? Research what you can about a passphrase. What does it mean? Here are two sites that you can use to start your research: www.pgpi.org/ and http://web.mit.edu/network/pgp.html.

Case Studies

ALL-SHOP SUPERSTORES

All-Shop Superstores is a regional chain of superstores in the Boston, New York, and Washington, DC, corridor. These stores compete with other giants, such as Wal-Mart, Kmart, Target, and other budget retailers. The stores contain large grocery stores as well as departments for domestics, clothing, automotive merchandise, and home improvement products. Overall, the margins in this portion of the retail industry are very small. Grocery profits have always been small, in the range of 5 to 10 percent. The margin for domestics, clothing, and other goods is a little higher, but to compete with Wal-Mart, All-Shop must keep all margins low.

To reduce operating costs as much as possible, All-Shop has decided to move very heavily into electronic data interchange (EDI) with its suppliers. All-Shop is aware that several of its more advanced competitors allow their suppliers to manage inventory levels in the stores themselves. For example, paper hygiene products such as disposable diapers and toilet paper are high-volume products that require very close monitoring of inventory levels. All-Shop has already installed sophisticated sales and inventory systems that track the activity of each item (using the UPC code) daily. These systems not only capture daily activity but also maintain histories in a data warehouse to support online data analysis.

The first step for All-Shop was to enable its major suppliers to have access to its daily sales and inventory database. That way, the suppliers could monitor sales activities and check inventory to ensure that deliveries are made on time to maintain optimal inventory levels. The system should also permit each supplier to access and check the status of its individual accounts and a history of past payment activity. Obviously, All-Shop must control all of this information so that suppliers cannot observe each other's information.

[1] Given what you have learned in this and previous chapters, develop a use case diagram identifying the use cases that apply to the supplier as an actor. Even though it is really a system-to-system interface, the supplier system can be considered an actor. Identify two lists of controls that you consider necessary for this interface. On the first list, identify overall controls for the entire EDI interface. Then, for the second list, for each identified use case, develop a specific set of controls that will be necessary. Base your analysis on the types of controls discussed in the chapter as well as the three primary objectives of integrity controls. In other words, your assignment is to develop a statement of required controls that the system developers can use to ensure that the system adequately protects the assets and information of All-Shop.

[2] All-Shop is considering a plan to provide supplier access to its data warehouse to enable executives to analyze past trends

and help design promotions to increase overall sales and those of individual products. In other words, All-Shop is building partnerships with its suppliers to maximize its presence in the retail marketplace. One major concern of All-Shop executives is how to ensure that the suppliers treat this information with maximum security and do not damage All-Shop. How can they ensure that the suppliers do not use this information to benefit All-Shop's competitors inadvertently, since suppliers also work with these competitors?

[3] Do you think this second step is a wise move for All-Shop? If not, why not? If so, what kinds of controls and contractual arrangements should be made to protect All-Shop? You may see how a narrow focus on integrity controls may be inadequate to protect proprietary information. A broader view and understanding of controls and their objectives are required in this instance.

THEEYESHAVEIT.COM BOOK EXCHANGE SYSTEM

Based on the system sequence diagrams you developed in Chapter 6, develop a list of inputs and outputs required for this system. Also, identify any specific controls that may be necessary to ensure that information is entered accurately.

DOWNTOWN VIDEOS RENTAL SYSTEM

Using the system sequence diagrams you developed in Chapter 6, develop a list of inputs and outputs, along with the necessary data fields, for the system.

RETHINKING ROCKY MOUNTAIN OUTFITTERS

The RMO event table lists six system reports that are part of the new system:

- Order summary
- Transaction summary
- Fulfillment summary
- Prospective customer activity
- Customer adjustments
- Catalog activity

For each of these six reports, answer the following questions:

[1] What data fields should each report include?

[2] What questions will users want each report to answer?

[3] What type of report is it: detailed, summary, or exception?

[4] How might graphics be used? What about drill-down capabilities?

[5] How would you prepare a mock-up of each report, assuming a printed output and also an online output?

[6] What output controls should be associated with each report?

FOCUSING ON RELIABLE PHARMACEUTICAL SERVICE

Reliable PHARMACEUTICALS One of the challenges of a pharmaceutical company is keeping current with new drugs and changes to existing drugs. New drugs are continually being developed and approved. In addition, generic drugs are often available to compete with brand-name drugs. One of the services that Reliable provides is to try to find the least expensive alternative to fulfill a prescription. This cost-saving service is one of the marketing advantages that the nursing homes can use to promote their services. Obviously, this service builds tremendous loyalty between Reliable and its customers.

To keep current with these changes, Reliable subscribes to an online drug-update service. The service provides updates in several formats, one of which is an XML file.

[1] Based on the content of the design class diagram that you developed in Chapter 8, illustrate a sample XML input file that could be used to update drug information in the Reliable database.

[2] In earlier chapters, the case description indicated that a case manifest was produced for each patient whenever prescriptions needed to be filled and delivered. Based on the data found in your class diagrams, design a case manifest. Consider that a patient may have multiple prescriptions that are being filled on the same delivery.

[3] Each month, Reliable produces a statement for each nursing home. The statement lists each patient who received prescriptions during the month. All the filled prescriptions are listed. For each prescription, the following information is listed: the price, the amount billed to the patient's insurance provider, the amount paid by the insurance provider, and the co-pay amounts due from the patients. Design this monthly statement. Also, identify and highlight output controls that you believe are appropriate for this type of report.

[4] In the preceding chapter, you defined an input form to be used to collect orders from the nursing homes. Go back and analyze that input form and identify all of the input controls that you think are necessary to ensure that the prescriptions are correct. What other procedures or controls would you recommend to make sure that there are no mistakes in the prescriptions?

FURTHER RESOURCES

David Benyon, Diana Bental, and Thomas Green, *Conceptual Modeling for User Interface Development*. Springer-Verlag, 1999.

Elfriede Dustin, Jeff Rashka, Douglas McDiarmid, and Jakob Nielson, *Quality Web Systems: Performance, Security, and Usability*. Addison-Wesley, 2001.

Simson Garfinkel, Gene Spafford, and Debby Russell, *Web Security, Privacy, & Commerce*. O'Reilly Publishing, 2001.

Anup K. Ghosh, *E-Commerce Security: Weak Links, Best Defenses*. John Wiley & Sons, 1997.

IS Audit and Control Association, *IS Audit and Control Journal*, Volume I, 1995.

Brenda Laurel, *The Art of Human-Computer Interface Design*. Addison-Wesley, 1990.

Ben Shneiderman, *Designing the User Interface: Strategies for Effective Human-Computer Interaction*. Addison-Wesley-Longman, 1998.

Donald Warren Jr. and J. Donald Warren, *The Handbook of IT Auditing*. Warren Gorham & Lamont, 1998.

Donald A. Wayne and Peter B. B. Turney, *Auditing EDP Systems*. Prentice Hall, 1990.

PART 4 IMPLEMENTATION, TESTING, AND DEPLOYMENT DISCIPLINES

CHAPTER 13
Making the System Operational

CHAPTER 14
Current Trends in System Development

chapter 13

MAKING THE SYSTEM OPERATIONAL

LEARNING OBJECTIVES

After reading this chapter, you should be able to:

- Describe implementation activities
- Describe various types of software tests and explain how and why each is used
- Explain the importance of the configuration and change management discipline to the implementation, testing, and deployment of a system.
- List various approaches to data conversion and system deployment and describe the advantages and disadvantages of each
- Describe training and user support requirements for new and operational systems

CHAPTER OUTLINE

- Implementation
- Testing
- Configuration and Change Management
- Deployment
- Planning and Managing Implementation, Testing, and Deployment
- Putting It All Together—RMO Revisited

TRI-STATE HEATING OIL: JUGGLING PRIORITIES TO BEGIN OPERATION

It was 8:30 A.M. on Monday morning, and Maria Grasso, Kim Song, Dave Williams, and Rajiv Gupta were just about to begin the weekly project status meeting. Tri-State Heating Oil had started developing a new scheduling system for customer orders and service calls five months earlier. The target completion date was 10 weeks away, but the project was behind schedule. Early project iterations had accomplished far less than anticipated because key users had disagreed on what new system requirements to include and the system scope was larger than expected.

Maria began the meeting by saying, "We've gained a day or two since our last meeting due to better-than-expected unit testing results. All of the methods developed last week sailed through unit testing, so we won't need any time this week to fix errors in that code."

Kim spoke, "I wouldn't get too cocky just yet. All of the nasty surprises in my last object-oriented project came during integration testing. We're completing the user-interface classes this week, so we should be able to start integration testing with the business classes sometime next week."

Dave nodded enthusiastically and said, "That's good! We have to finish testing those user-interface classes as quickly as possible because we're scheduled to start user training in three weeks. I need that time to develop the training materials and work out the final training schedule with the users."

Rajiv replied, "I'm not sure that we should be trying to meet our original training schedule with so much of the system still under development. What if integration testing shows major bugs that require more time to fix? And what about the unfinished business and database classes? Can we realistically start training with a system that's little more than a user interface with half a system behind it?"

Dave replied, "But we have to start training in three weeks. We contracted for a dozen temporary workers so that we could train our staff on the new system. Half of them are scheduled to start in two weeks and the rest two weeks after that. It's too late to renegotiate their start dates. We can extend the time they'll be here, but delaying their starting date means we'll be paying for people we aren't using."

Maria spoke up. "I think that Rajiv's concerns are valid. It's not realistic to start training in three weeks with so little of the system completed and tested. We're at least five weeks behind schedule, and there's no way we'll recapture more than four or five days of that during the next few weeks. I've already looked into rearranging some of the remaining coding to give priority to the work most critical to user training. There are a few batch processes that can be back-burnered for a while. Kim, can you rearrange your testing plans to handle all of the interactive applications first?"

Kim replied, "I'll have to go back to my office and take another look at the dependencies among those programs. Offhand, I'd say yes, but I need a few hours to make sure."

Maria replied, "Okay, let's proceed under the assumption that we can rearrange coding and testing to complete a usable system for training in five weeks. I'll confirm that by e-mail later today, as soon as Kim gets back to me. I'll also schedule a meeting with the CIO to deliver the bad news about temporary staffing costs."

After a few moments of silence, Rajiv asked, "So what else do we need to be thinking about?"

Maria replied, "Well, let's see. . . . There's user documentation, hardware delivery and setup, operating system and DBMS installation, importing data from the old database, the network upgrade, and stress testing for the distributed database accesses."

Rajiv smiled and said to Maria, "You must have been a juggler in your youth, and it was good practice for keeping all of these project pieces up in the air. Does management pay you by the ball?"

Maria chuckled. "I do think of myself as a juggler sometimes. And if management paid me by the ball, I could retire as soon as this project is finished!"

Overview

We've spent many chapters describing the activities of the business modeling, requirements, design, and project management UP disciplines. They are important and complex disciplines and are the primary focus of this text, but activities from additional UP disciplines are needed to bring a system into being. Those disciplines—including implementation, testing, deployment, and configuration and change management—are the subject of this chapter.

The fact that we are covering several disciplines in a single chapter does not mean that they are simple or unimportant. Rather, they are complex disciplines that you will learn in detail in other courses and by reading textbooks. Our purpose in covering them in this chapter is to round out our discussion of the UP and to show how all of the disciplines relate to each other.

We'll begin by discussing each discipline and its activities in isolation. We'll then discuss the interrelationships among the disciplines and describe how those interrelationships affect project and iteration planning and management.

IMPLEMENTATION

Developing any complex system is inherently difficult. For example, consider the complexity of manufacturing automobiles. Tens of thousands of parts must be fabricated or purchased. Laborers and machines assemble parts into small subcomponents such as dashboard instruments, wiring harnesses, and brake assemblies, which are in turn assembled into larger subcomponents such as instrument clusters, engines, and transmissions, and eventually into a complete automobile. Parts and subcomponents must be constructed, tested, and passed on to subsequent assembly steps. There are tens or hundreds of thousands of individual production steps. The effort, timeliness, cost, and output quality of each step depend on all of the preceding steps.

Software construction is similar in many ways to automobile manufacturing—it is a complex production and assembly process that must use resources efficiently, minimize construction time, and maximize product quality. But unlike automobile manufacturing, the process is not designed once and then used to build thousands of similar units. Instead, software construction is unique to each new project because it must match that project's characteristics.

component
a software module that is fully assembled, is ready to use, and has well-defined interfaces for connection to clients or other parts of the system

Figure 13-1 shows the activities of the implementation discipline. The activities are all concerned with software components, which may be built or acquired, depending on the specific project. In the generic sense, a *component* is a software module that is fully assembled, is ready to use, and has well-defined interfaces for connection to clients or other parts of the system.

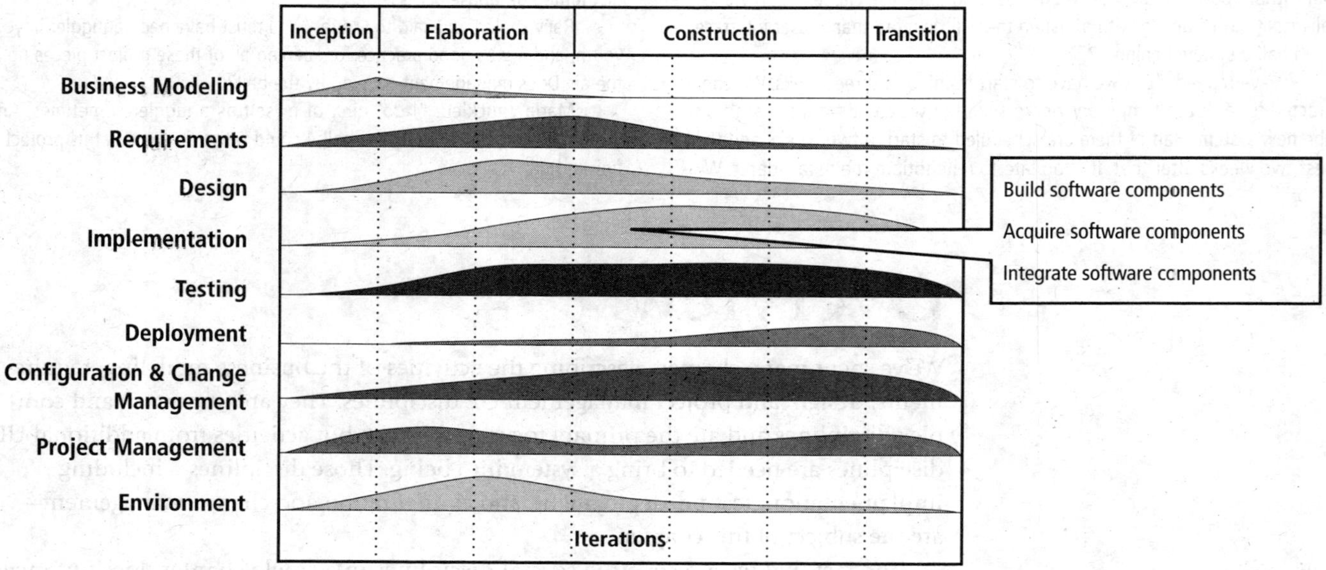

FIGURE 13-1
Implementation discipline activities

Any system of interchangeable components requires standards that describe how the components interact. Unfortunately, there are several current component interaction standards, including:

- Common Object Request Broker Architecture (CORBA)
- Java 2 Enterprise Edition (J2EE)
- Common Object Model (COM)
- Simple Object Access Protocol (SOAP)

The standards embody different but overlapping approaches to distributing object-oriented software across processing locations and enabling message passing among the objects and locations. Later standards, such as SOAP and J2EE, employ Web-oriented protocols such as eXtensible Markup Language (XML) to encode messages and responses and transport the messages with ordinary Internet protocols. A Web server provides the "front line" interface to application components—an approach sometimes referred to as *service-oriented architecture*.

Building and deploying modern application software is essentially a process of choosing a component interaction standard, implementing the classes of an object-oriented design, packaging those classes into executable units compatible with the chosen standard, and installing the application software within the supporting hardware and system software infrastructure.

TESTING

Figure 13-2 shows the activities of the testing discipline. Testing is the process of examining a product to determine what defects it contains. To conduct a test, developers must have already constructed or acquired the software and have well-defined standards for what constitutes a defect. The developers can test software by reviewing its construction and composition or by designing and building the software, exercising its function, and examining the results. If the results indicate an error, developers cycle through design, construction, exercise, and evaluation until no errors are found.

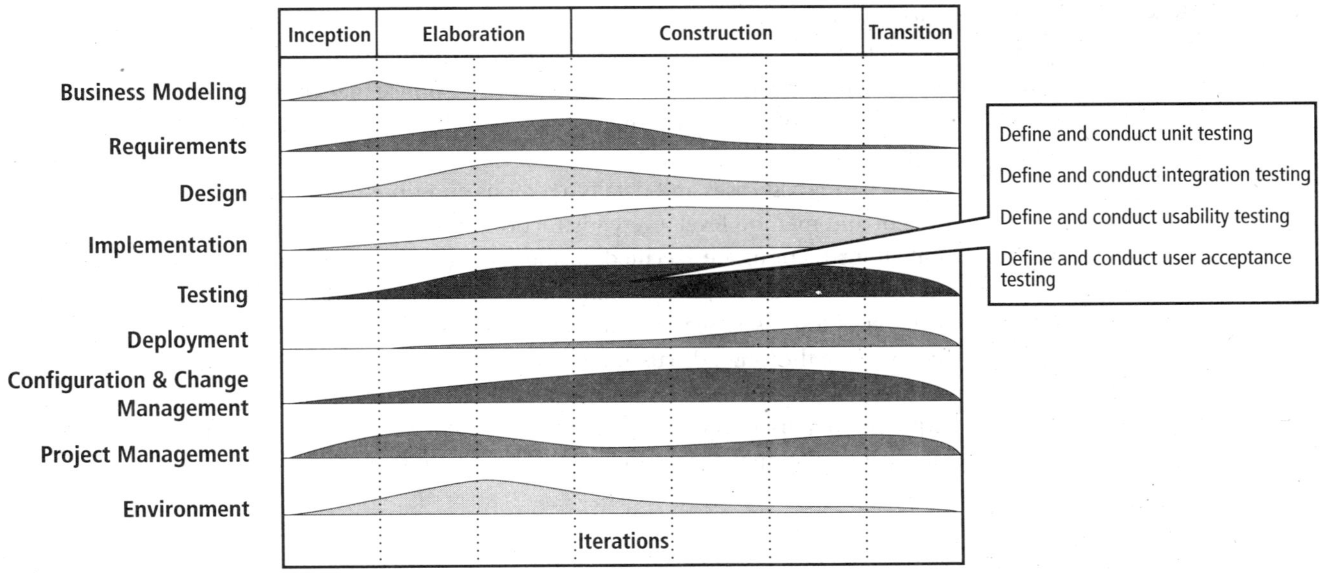

FIGURE 13-2
Testing discipline activities

Testing is a process of identifying defects. The defect types and corresponding tests are summarized in Figure 13-3. Each type of testing is described in detail later in this section.

FIGURE 13-3
Test types and detected defects

TEST TYPE	DEFECT(S) DETECTED
Ubit testing	Software component that doesn't correctly perform its function when tested in isolation Example: A component for calculating sales tax that consistently computes sales tax incorrectly for one or more localities
Integration testing	Software component that doesn't correctly perform its function or fails to meet a nonfunctional requirement when operated with other components Example: An order retrieval function that displays a result in 2 seconds when tested with a dummy database but requires 30 seconds when using a live database
Usability testing	Software that works but fails to satisfy one or more user requirements related to function or ease of use Example: A user-interface component that forces a user to follow a needlessly complex procedure to complete a common and simple task
User acceptance testing	All defect types

test case
a formal description of a starting state, one or more events to which the software must respond, and the expected response or ending state

test data
a set of starting states and events used to test a module, group of modules, or entire system

An important part of developing tests is specifying test cases and data. A *test case* is a formal description of the following:

- A starting state
- One or more events to which the software must respond
- The expected response or ending state

The starting and ending states and the events are represented by a set of *test data*. For example, the starting state of a system may represent a particular set of data, such as the existence of a particular customer and order for that customer. The event may be represented by a set of input data items, such as a customer account number and order number used to query order status. The expected response may be a described behavior, such as the display of certain information, or a specific state of stored data, such as a canceled order.

Preparing test cases and data is a tedious and time-consuming process. At the component and method level, every instruction must be executed at least once. Ensuring that all instructions are executed during testing is a complex problem. Fortunately, automated tools based on proven mathematical techniques are available to generate a complete set of test cases. See the Watson and McCabe article in the "Further Resources" section for a thorough discussion of this topic.

Developers and users typically prepare test cases for each use case and scenario as requirements discipline activities are completed. Many test cases representing both normal and exceptional processing situations should be prepared for each scenario.

UNIT TESTING

unit testing
testing of individual methods, classes, or components before they are integrated with other software

Unit testing is the process of testing individual methods, classes, or components before they are integrated with other software. The goal of unit testing is to identify and fix as many errors as possible before modules are combined into larger software units, such as programs, classes, and subsystems. Errors become much more difficult and expensive to locate and fix when many units are combined.

Few units are designed to operate in isolation. Instead, groups of units are designed to execute as an integrated whole. If a method is considered a unit, that method may be called by messages sent from methods in one or more classes and may, in turn, send messages to other methods in its own or other classes. These relationships are easily seen in a sequence diagram such as Figure 13-4, which duplicates Figure 9-3. For example, when the class OrderItem receives a createOrdItem( ) message, it performs internal processing and sends messages to three other methods—getPrice( ), getDescription( ), and updateQty( )—in three other classes—CatalogProduct, Product, and InventoryItem.

driver
a method or class, developed for unit testing, that simulates the behavior of a method that sends a message to the method being tested

If the createOrdItem( ) method of OrderItem is being tested in isolation, then two types of testing methods are required. The first method type is called a *driver*. A *driver* simulates the behavior of a method that sends a message to the method being tested—the createOrdItem( ) method of Order in this example. A driver module implements the following functions:

- Sets the value of input parameters
- Calls the tested unit, passing it the input parameters
- Accepts return parameters from the tested unit and prints them, displays them, or tests their values against expected results and then prints or displays the results

Figure 13-5 shows a simple driver module for testing createOrdItem( ). A more complex driver module might use test data consisting of hundreds or thousands of test inputs and correct outputs stored in a file or database. The driver would loop through the test inputs and repeatedly call createOrdItem( ), check the return parameter against the expected value, and print or display warnings of any discrepancy. Using a driver allows a subordinate method to be tested before methods that call it have been written.

stub
a method or class, developed for unit testing, that simulates the behavior of a method that hasn't yet been written

The second type of testing method used to perform unit tests is called a *stub*. A *stub* simulates the behavior of a method that hasn't yet been written. A unit test of createOrdItem( ) would require three stub methods—getPrice( ), getDescription( ), and updateQty( ). Stubs are relatively simple methods that usually have only a few executable statements. Each of the stubs used to test createOrdItem( ) can be implemented as a statement that simply returns a constant, regardless of the parameters passed as input. Figure 13-6 shows sample code for each of the three stub modules.

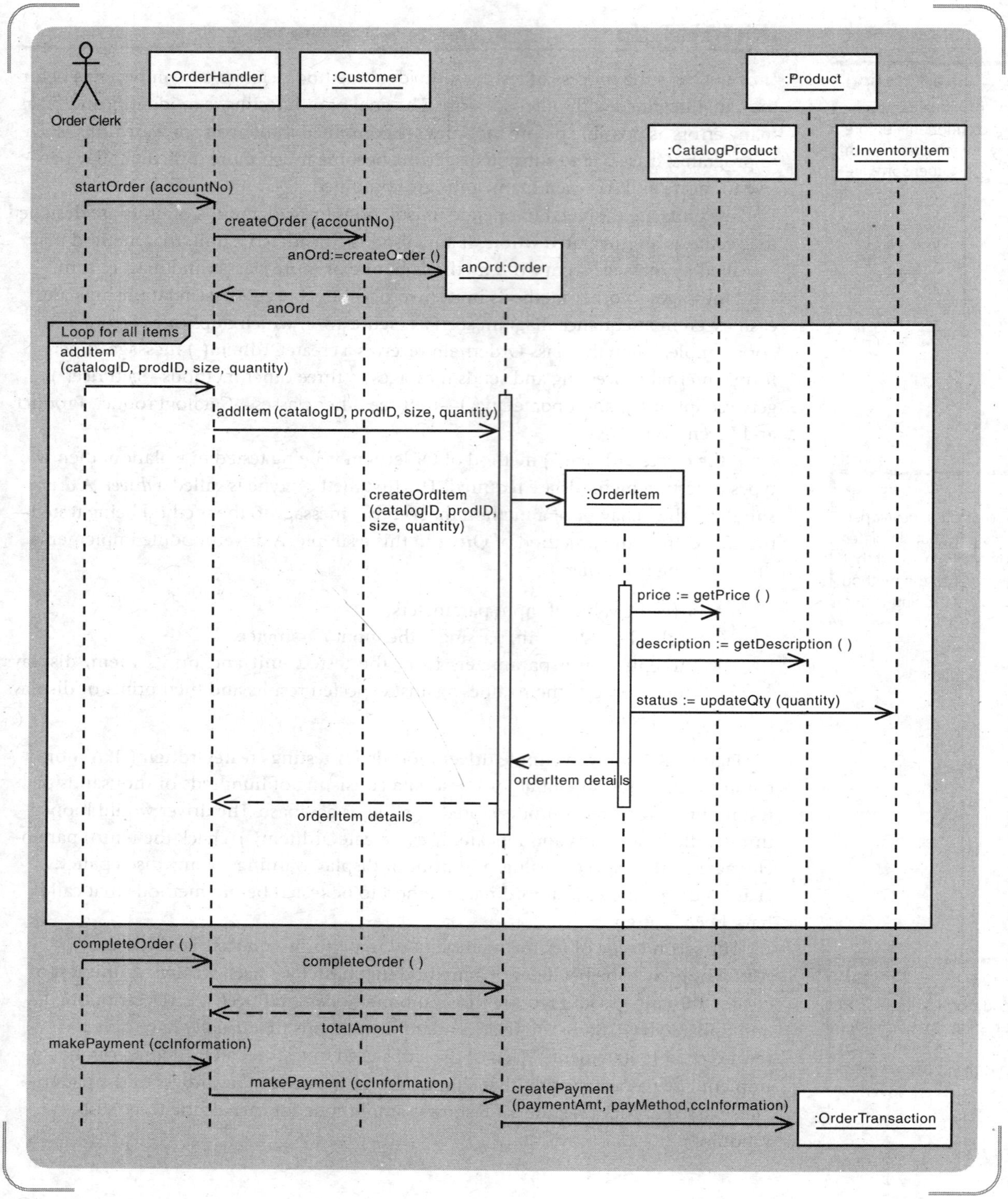

FIGURE 13-4

Sequence diagram for *Create new order*

INTEGRATION TESTING

integration test

a test of the behavior of a group of methods or classes

An *integration test* evaluates the behavior of a group of methods or classes. The purpose of an integration test is to identify errors that were not or could not be detected by unit testing. Such errors may result from a number of problems, including:

```
main()
{
  // driver method to test OrderItem::createOrdItem()

  // declare input parameters and values

  int catalogID = 23;
  int prodID = 1244;
  String size = "large";
  int quantity = 1;

  // perform test

  orderItem orderItem = new OrderItem();
  orderItem.createOrdItem(catalogID,prodID,size,quantity);

  // display results

  System.out.println("price=" + orderItem.getPrice());
  System.out.println("description=" + orderItem.getDescription();
  System.out.println("status=" + orderItem.getStatus());
} // end main()
```

FIGURE 13-5

A driver module to test createOrdItem( )

```
float getPrice()
{
  // stub method for CatalogProduct::getPrice()

  return(24.95);
} // end getPrice()

String getDescription()
{
  // stub method for Product::getDescription()

  return("men's khaki slacks");
} // end getDescription()

String updateQty(int decrement)
{
  // stub method for InventoryItem::updateQty()

  return("OK");
} // end updateQty()
```

FIGURE 13-6

Stub modules used by createOrdItem( )

- **Interface incompatibility.** For example, one method passes a parameter of the wrong data type to another method.
- **Parameter values.** A method is passed or returns a value that was unexpected, such as a negative number for a price.
- **Run-time exceptions.** A method generates an error such as "out of memory" or "file already in use" due to conflicting resource needs.
- **Unexpected state interactions.** The states of two or more objects interact to cause complex failures, as when an Order class method operates correctly for all possible Customer object states except one.

These problems are some of the most common integration testing errors, but there are many other possible errors and causes.

Once an integration error has been detected, the responsibility for incorrect behavior must be traced to a specific method or methods. The person responsible for performing the integration test is generally also responsible for identifying the cause of the error. Once the error has been traced to a particular method, the programmer who wrote the method is asked to rewrite it to correct the error.

Integration testing of OO software is very complex. Because an OO program consists of a set of interacting objects that can be created or destroyed during execution, there is no clear hierarchical structure. Object interactions and control flow, as a result, are dynamic and complex.

Additional factors that complicate OO integration testing include the following:

- Methods can (and usually are) called by many other methods, and the calling methods may be distributed across many classes.
- Classes may inherit methods and state variables from other classes.
- The specific method to be called is dynamically determined at run time based on the number and type of message parameters.
- Objects can retain internal variable values (that is, the object state) between calls. The response to two identical calls may be different due to state changes that result from the first call or occur between calls.

This combination of factors makes it difficult to determine an optimal testing order. The factors also make it difficult to predict the behavior of a group of interacting methods and objects. Thus, developing and executing an integration testing plan for OO software are extremely complex. Specific methods and techniques for dealing with that complexity are well beyond the scope of this textbook. See the "Further Resources" for OO software testing references.

system test
an integration test of the behavior of an entire system or independent subsystem

A *system test* is an integration test of the behavior of an entire system or independent subsystem. System testing is normally first performed by developers or test personnel to ensure that the overall system does not malfunction and that the system fulfills the developers' understanding of user requirements. Later testing by users confirms whether the system does indeed fulfill their requirements. System testing is usually performed at the end of each iteration to identify significant issues such as performance problems that will need to be dealt with in the next iteration.

build and smoke test
a system test that is performed daily or several times a week

System testing may also be performed more frequently. A *build and smoke test* is a system test that is typically performed daily or several times per week. The system is completely compiled and linked (built), and a battery of tests is executed to see whether anything malfunctions in an obvious way ("smokes").

Build and smoke tests are valuable because they provide rapid feedback on significant problems. Any problem that occurs during a build and smoke test must result from software modified or added since the previous test. Daily testing ensures that errors are found quickly and that they can be easily tracked to their source. Less frequent testing provides rapidly diminishing benefits because more software has changed and errors are more difficult to track to their source.

USABILITY TESTING

usability test
a test to determine whether a method, class, subsystem, or system meets user requirements

A *usability test* is a test to determine whether a method, class, subsystem, or system meets user requirements. Because there are many types of requirements, both functional and nonfunctional, many types of usability tests are performed at many different times.

The most common type of usability test evaluates functional requirements and the quality of a user interface. Users interact with a portion of the system to determine whether it functions as expected and whether the user interface makes the system easy to use. Such tests are conducted frequently as user interfaces are developed to provide rapid feedback to developers for improving the interface and correcting any errors in the underlying software components.

performance test
an integration and usability test that determines whether a system or subsystem can meet time-based performance criteria

response time
the desired or maximum allowable time limit for software response to a query or update

throughput
the desired or minimum number of queries and transactions that must be processed per minute or hour

A *performance test* is an integration and usability test that determines whether a system or subsystem can meet time-based performance criteria such as response time or throughput. *Response time* requirements specify desired or maximum allowable time limits for software responses to queries and updates. *Throughput* requirements specify the desired or minimum number of queries and transactions that must be processed per minute or hour.

Performance tests are complex because they can involve multiple programs, subsystems, computer systems, and network infrastructure. They require a large suite of test data to simulate system operation under normal or maximum load. Diagnosing and correcting performance test failures are also complex. Bottlenecks and underperforming components must first be identified. Corrective actions may include application software tuning or reimplementation, hardware or system software reconfiguration, and upgrade or replacement of underperforming components.

USER ACCEPTANCE TESTING

user acceptance test
a system test performed to determine whether the system fulfills user requirements

A fourth type of testing involves the end users of a system. A *user acceptance test* is a system test performed to determine whether the system fulfills user requirements. In some projects, acceptance testing may be the last round of testing before a system is handed over to its users. Under the UP, acceptance testing is usually broken down into a series of tests that are conducted as parts of the system are completed. Acceptance testing is a very formal activity in most development projects. Details of acceptance tests are sometimes included in the request for proposal (RFP) and procurement contract when a new system is built by or purchased from an external party.

WHO TESTS SOFTWARE?

Many people participate in the testing process, and their exact number and role depend on the size of the project and other project characteristics. Participants are drawn from both technical and nontechnical backgrounds:

- Programmers
- Users
- Quality assurance personnel

testing buddy
a programmer assigned to test code written by another programmer

Programmers are generally responsible for unit testing their own code prior to integrating it with modules written by other programmers. In some organizations, programmers are assigned a *testing buddy* to help them test their own code. The name refers to programmers who are assigned the specific responsibility for testing another programmer's (their "buddy's") code prior to integration testing. Having a different programmer test the code usually finds more errors.

Users are primarily responsible for usability and acceptance testing. In some projects, software is developed in a series of versions, and the earlier versions are called *beta versions* (this topic is discussed in more detail later in this chapter). When beta versions are developed, they are distributed to a group of users for testing over a period of days, weeks, or months. Volunteers are frequently used, although they are not always desirable since they tend to be more computer literate and have a higher tolerance for malfunctions than ordinary users. These characteristics may result in higher-quality feedback for some problems but a lack of feedback for other problems.

Acceptance testing is normally conducted by users with assistance from IS development or operations personnel. The rigor and importance of acceptance tests require participation by a large number of users across a wide range of user levels (for example, data-entry clerks and the managers who will "own" the system). Although IS personnel may perform system setup and troubleshooting functions, it is ultimately up to the users to accept or reject the system.

In a large system development project, a separate quality assurance (QA) group or organization may be formed. The QA group is responsible for all aspects of testing except unit testing and acceptance testing. The QA group's responsibilities and activities typically include the following:

- Developing a testing plan
- Performing integration and system testing
- Gathering and organizing user feedback on beta software versions and identifying needed changes to the system design or implementation

To maintain objectivity and independence, the QA group normally reports directly to the project manager or to a permanent IS manager.

CONFIGURATION AND CHANGE MANAGEMENT

Medium- and large-scale systems are complex and constantly changing. Changes occur rapidly during implementation and more slowly afterward. System complexity and rapid change create a host of management problems—particularly for testing and post-deployment support. As already mentioned, testing is problematic in such an environment because the system is a moving target. By the time an error is discovered, the code that caused it may already have been moved, altered, or deleted. Support is complex for similar reasons. To respond properly to a bug report or request for help, support personnel need to know the state of the system as it is installed on a user's computer system or application server.

The configuration and change management discipline comes into play especially during implementation, testing, and postdeployment support activities. Configuration and change management encompass activities that help control the complexity associated with testing and supporting a system through multiple development and operational versions. Figure 13-7 shows the activities of the configuration and change

FIGURE 13-7
Configuration and change management discipline activities

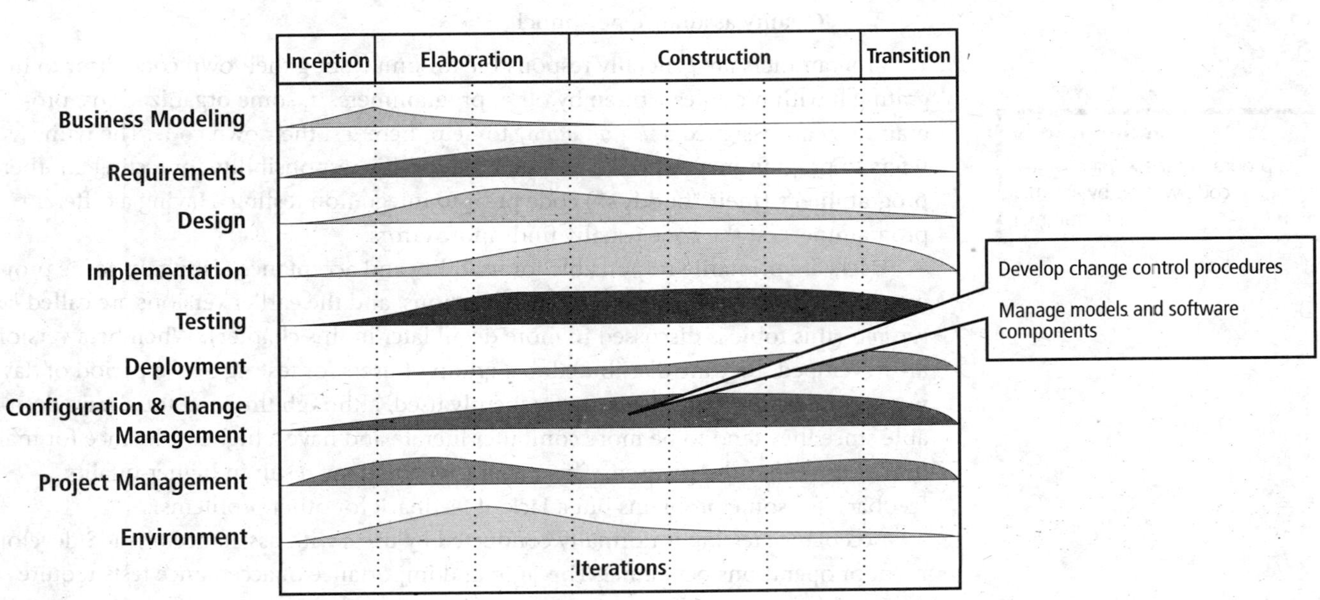

management discipline. The goal of these activities is to define a system of controls that ensures that implementation, testing, deployment, and support activities proceed smoothly. Although the figure shows only two activities, a considerable amount of complexity lies within those activities.

Configuration and change management activities are integrally related to project management, implementation, testing, and deployment discipline activities. Change control procedures are typically developed in the first iteration before any significant software development is undertaken. Once the change control procedures are defined, all other development activities occur within the context of these procedures.

The need for and formality of configuration and change management procedures depend primarily on the size of the development project and the cohesiveness of the development staff. Change management procedures for a small project with a cohesive development staff may be informal or nonexistent. Larger projects and projects with development staff separated by time or geography usually require formal change management procedures for requirements and design models, source code, and components.

VERSIONING

Complex systems are developed, installed, and maintained in a series of versions to simplify testing, deployment, and support. It is not unusual to have multiple versions of a system deployed to end users and yet more versions in different stages of development. A system version created during development is called a *test version*. A test version contains a well-defined set of features and represents a concrete step toward final completion of the system. Test versions provide a static system snapshot and a checkpoint to evaluate the project's progress.

alpha version
a test version that is incomplete but ready for some level of rigorous integration or usability testing

beta version
a test version that is stable enough to be tested by end users over an extended period

An *alpha version* is a test version that is incomplete but ready for some level of rigorous integration or usability testing. Multiple alpha versions may be built, depending on the size and complexity of the system. The lifetime of an alpha version is typically short—days or weeks.

A *beta version* is a test version that is stable enough to be tested by end users over an extended period. A beta version is produced after one or more alpha versions have been tested and known problems have been corrected. End users test beta versions by using them to do real work. Thus, beta versions must be more complete and less prone to disastrous failures than alpha versions. Beta versions are typically tested over a period of weeks or months.

production version, release version, or **production release**
a system version that is formally distributed to users or made operational for long-term use

maintenance release
a system update that provides bug fixes and small changes to existing features

A system version created for long-term release to users is called a *production version*, *release version*, or *production release*. A production version is considered a final product, although software systems are rarely "finished" in the usual sense of that term. Minor production releases (sometimes called *maintenance releases*) provide bug fixes and small changes to existing features. Major production releases add significant new functionality and may be the result of rewriting an older release from the ground up.

Figure 13-8 shows a series of possible test and production versions for the RMO customer support system (CSS). Each version is described in Figure 13-9. The system is delivered in two major production releases—versions 1.0 and 2.0. Each initial production release is preceded by one or more alpha and beta test versions. Each version adds or updates functionality and includes bug fixes for the previous version. Version 1.1 is a maintenance or minor production release of version 1.0. Note that the time line for developing version 2.0 overlaps maintenance changes to version 1.0. Overlapping older production versions with test versions of future production releases is typical.

Keeping track of versions is complex. Each version needs to be uniquely identified for users and testers. In applications designed to run under Windows, users typically view the

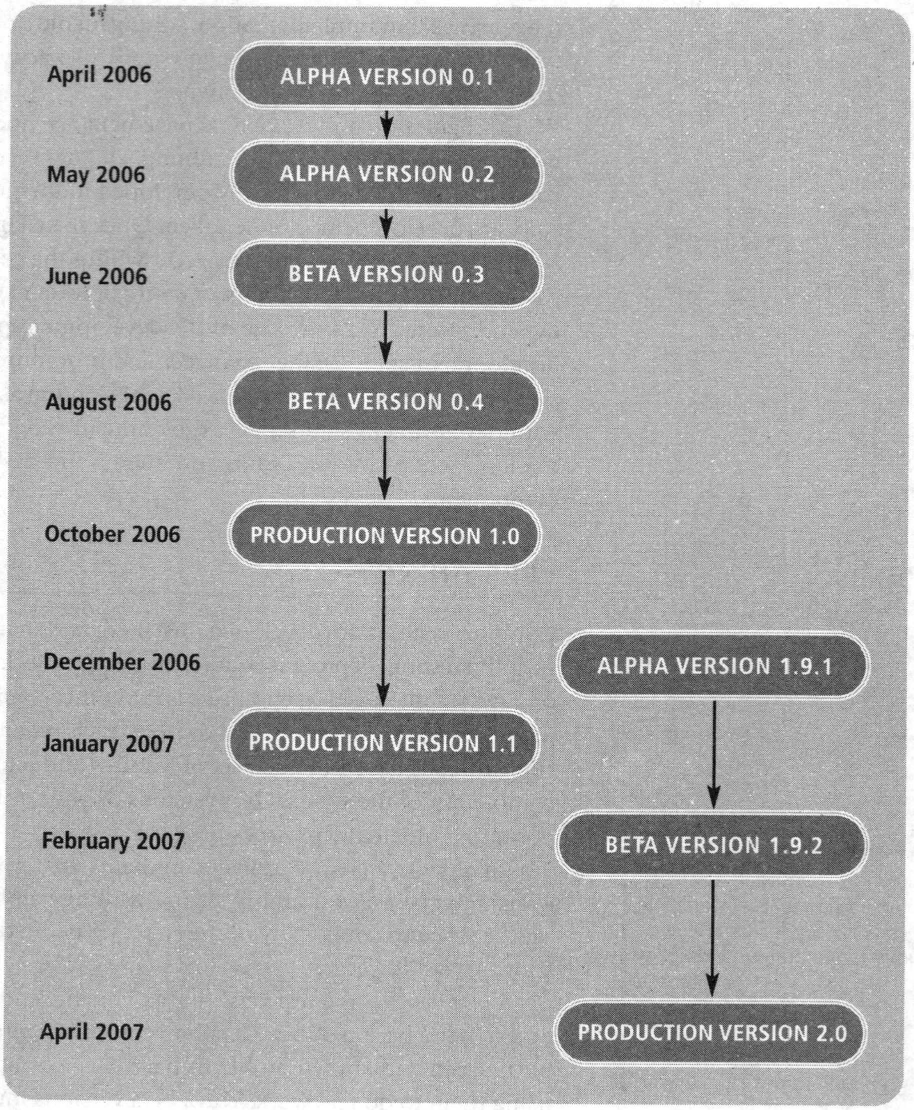

FIGURE 13-8
A time line of test and production versions for the RMO customer support system (CSS)

version information by choosing the About item from the standard Help menu, as shown in Figure 13-10. Users seeking support or reporting errors in a beta or production version use this feature to report the system version to testers or support personnel.

BEST PRACTICE: Assign version numbers and enable users to display them.

Controlling multiple versions of the same system requires sophisticated version control software. Version control capabilities are normally built into sophisticated development tools or can be obtained through a separate source code and version control system, as described later in this chapter. Programmers and support personnel can extract the current version or any previous version for execution, testing, or modification. Modifications are saved under a new version number to protect the accuracy of the historical snapshot.

Alpha 0.1—First version of software; implements order-related use cases using test database server. Handles simple order entry and lookup for existing customers.

Alpha 0.2—Adds full customer maintenance, order update, and order deletion. Incorporates bug fixes and usability enhancements to version 0.1.

Beta 0.3—Adds printing and simple online help. Incorporates bug fixes and usability enhancements to version 0.2.

Beta 0.4—Incorporates bug fixes and usability refinements to version 0.3. Adds support for catalog and product maintenance use cases.

Production 1.0—Incorporates bug fixes, usability refinements, and performance enhancements to version 0.4. Adds full context-sensitive help and online user manual.

Production 1.1—Refines version 1.0 user interface to improve usability for high-volume transaction processing. Refines help system and online user manual.

Alpha 1.9.1—Adds simple capability to version 1.0 to extract data using SQL queries for custom report generation and decision support analysis.

Beta 1.9.2—Updates base system to version 1.1. Refines database extraction utility with GUI. Incorporates bug fixes and other usability enhancements to version 1.9.1.

Production 2.0—Incorporates bug fixes and usability enhancements to version 1.9.2.

FIGURE 13-9
Description of RMO CSS versions

Beta and production versions must be stored as long as they are installed on any user machines. Stored versions are used to evaluate future bug reports. For example, when a user reports a bug in version 1.0, support personnel extract that release from the archive, install it, and attempt to replicate the user's error. Feedback provided to the user is specific to version 1.0, even if the most recent production release is a higher-numbered version.

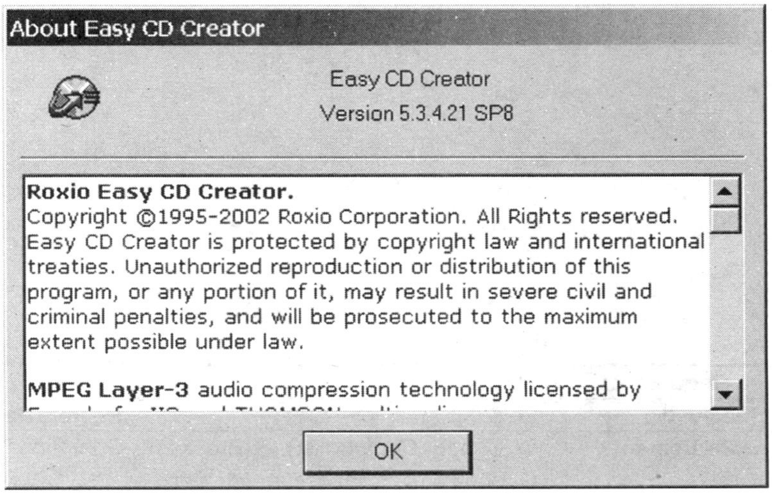

FIGURE 13-10
The About box of a typical Windows application

SUBMITTING CHANGE REQUESTS AND ERROR REPORTS

To manage the risks associated with change, most organizations adopt formal control procedures for all operational systems. Formal controls are designed to ensure that potential changes are adequately described, considered, and planned before being implemented. Typical change control procedures include the following:

- Standard change request forms
- Review of requests by a change control committee
- Extensive planning for design and implementation

Figure 13-11 shows a sample change request form that has been completed by a user or system owner and submitted to the change control committee for consideration. The change control committee reviews the change request to assess the impact on existing computer hardware and software, system performance and availability, security, and operating budget. The recommendation of the change control committee is formally recorded in a format such as the sample shown in Figure 13-12. Approved changes are added to the list of pending changes for budgeting, scheduling, planning, and implementation.

FIGURE 13-11
A sample change request form

Change Request

Request Date	2/1/2006	**Change Type**	☐	**Error Correction**
Requested By	Wen-Hsu Chang, Comptroller		☒	**Modification**
Target System	Customer Accounts - Refunds		☐	**New Function**

Change (or Error) Description

U.S. check formats will soon change due to a recently enacted federal law. The new format reserves an area to the right of the current routing number to be used for a security bar-code checksum.

The law requires the new checksum to be printed on checks dated on or after January 1, 2007.

We currently use a portion of the area in question to print a multicolored security symbol. The security symbol will need to be moved or eliminated, and the security bar-code checksum will have to be added.

Change Request ID	2006-11		
Date Received	2/2/2006	**Review Date**	2/7/2006, 0930-1100
Review Participants	W. Chang (Comptroller), R. Brooks (IS Operations), J. Hernandez (IS Security), G. Weeks (IS Change Coordinator)		

Change Review			
Change Request ID	2006-11	Date Reviewed	2/7/2006
Priority	☐ **Critical**	☒ **Necessary**	☐ **Optional**
Hardware Implications need to verify ability of current printers to write a security bar code in mandated area			
Software Implications database will need to be modified to store the security bar code with other check information check-writing program must be modified to generate and print the security bar code			
Performance Implications none			
Operating Budget Implications none			
Other Implications none			
Disposition	☒ **Approved**	☐ **Rejected**	☐ **Suspended**
Reason			
Latest Implementation Date	12/31/2006		
Reevaluation Date	n/a	**Signature**	

FIGURE 13-12
A sample change review form

Bugs can be reported using a standard change request form, but many computing organizations use a different form and procedure because they need to fix such bugs immediately. Bug reports can come from many sources, including end users, computer operators, or IS support staff. Bug reports are typically routed to a single person or organization for logging and follow-up.

IMPLEMENTING A CHANGE

Change implementation follows a miniature version of the UP life cycle. Most of the UP activities are performed, although they may be reduced in scope or sometimes completely eliminated. In essence, a change for a maintenance release is an incremental development project in which the user and technical requirements are fully known in advance. Business modeling and requirements discipline activities are typically skimmed or skipped, design activities are substantially reduced in scope, and the entire project is typically completed in one or two iterations.

Planning for a change includes the following activities:

- Identify what parts of the system must be changed.
- Secure resources (such as personnel) to implement the change.
- Schedule design and implementation activities.
- Develop test criteria and a testing plan for the changed system.

Design, implementation, and testing staff review the system documentation to determine the scope of the change. Test criteria and plans for the existing system are the starting point for evaluating the new system. The testing plan is simply updated to account for changed or added functions, then the modified plan and test data are archived for use in future change projects. The existing system design is evaluated and modified as necessary to implement the proposed changes. As with test plans and data, the revised design is archived for use in future change projects.

Whenever possible, changes are implemented and tested on a copy of the operational system. The *production system* is the version of the system used day to day. The *test system* is a copy of the production system that is modified to test changes. The test system may be developed and tested on separate hardware or on a redundant system. The test system becomes the operational system only after complete and successful testing.

production system
the version of the system used from day to day

test system
a copy of the production system that is modified to test changes

BEST PRACTICE: Test all changes on a test system before deploying them to the production system.

UPGRADING COMPUTING INFRASTRUCTURE

Computer hardware, system software, and networks must be periodically upgraded for many reasons, including:

- Software maintenance releases
- Software version upgrades
- Declining system performance

Like application software, system software such as operating and database management systems must periodically be changed to correct errors and add new functions. System software developers typically distribute maintenance releases several times per year. The frequency of maintenance updates has increased in recent years in part because of the convenience of Internet-based software distribution. In some cases, such as virus checkers and operating system security subsystems, updates may be released weekly or even more frequently.

As with internally generated changes, system software updates are risky. Application software that worked well with an older software version may fail when that software is updated. For this reason, system software updates are extensively tested before they are applied to operational systems. In many cases, maintenance and version updates are simply ignored to reduce risk. Unless errors related to system software have already been encountered, there is little immediate benefit to an upgrade. Operational system maintenance usually follows the old engineering maxim, "If it isn't broken, don't fix it!"

BEST PRACTICE: If an operational system isn't broken, don't fix it!

Over time, hardware and network performance may decrease to unacceptable levels due to increases in transaction volume or the deployment of new software. So, an infrastructure upgrade to add capacity or address a performance-related problem may be required. Infrastructure upgrades are implemented just as any other change is. The primary difference is in how a performance upgrade is initiated.

Input from user or IS staff may indicate the need for a performance upgrade. But a final determination of whether an upgrade is needed and what exactly should be upgraded requires thorough investigation and research. Computer and network performance is complex and highly technical, so what appears to be a performance problem may have little to do with hardware or network capacity. If the problem is ultimately traced to hardware or networks, then the specific cause must be identified and a suitable upgrade chosen.

Performance problems require careful diagnosis to determine the best approach to address the problem. Staff with solid technical backgrounds who can understand all of the relevant trade-offs should diagnose the problem. Larger IS organizations may have permanent staff with such skills, but many organizations must rely on contract personnel or consultants to diagnose performance problems, recommend corrective measures, and install or configure those measures. The skills come at a high price, but they can prevent an organization from wasting larger amounts of money buying hardware or network capacity that isn't really needed.

DEPLOYMENT

Once a new system has been developed and tested, it must be deployed and placed into operation. The deployment discipline is the set of activities required to make a new system operational (see Figure 13-13). Deployment activities involve many conflicting constraints, including cost, the need to maintain positive customer relations, the need to support employees, logistical complexity, and overall risk to the organization. The following sections provide additional details about deployment activities. Deployment planning activities that overlap activities from other disciplines are discussed later in this chapter.

FIGURE 13-13
Deployment discipline activities

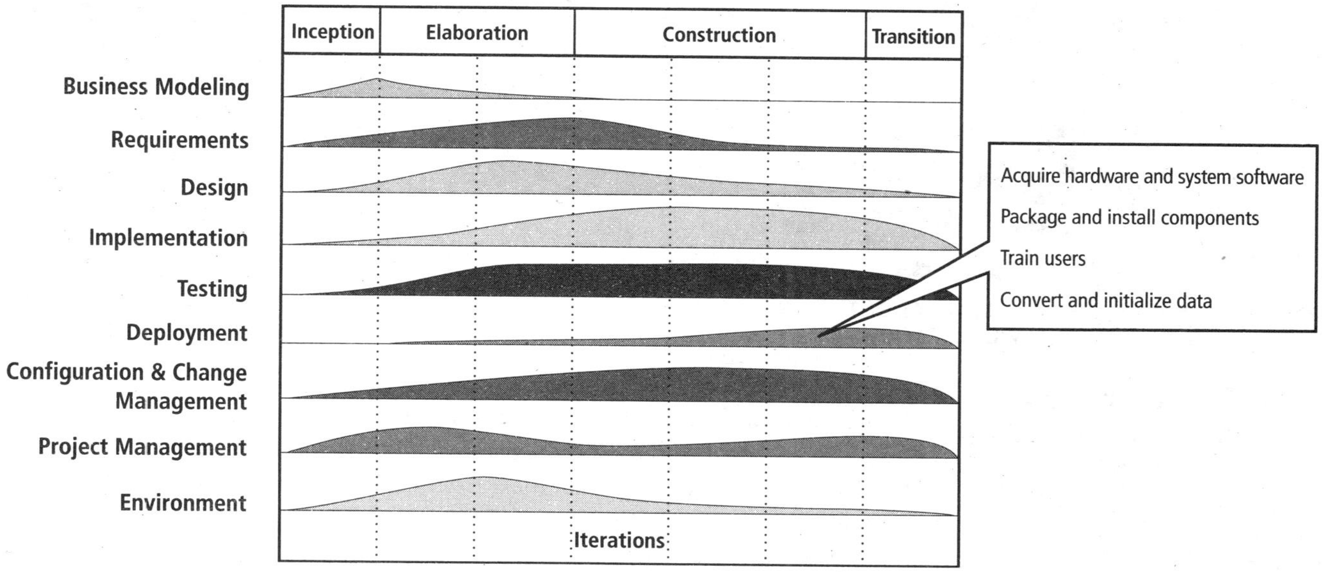

ACQUIRING HARDWARE AND SYSTEM SOFTWARE

As described earlier in the chapter, modern applications are built from components based on interaction standards. Each standard defines specific ways in which components locate and communicate with one another. Each standard also defines a set of supporting system software to provide needed services, such as maintaining software directories, enforcing security requirements, and encoding and decoding messages across networks and other transport protocols. The exact system software, its hardware, and its configuration requirements vary substantially among the component interaction standards.

Figure 13-14 shows a typical support infrastructure for an application deployed using Microsoft .NET, a variant of SOAP. Application software components written in programming languages such as Visual Basic and C# are stored on one or more application servers. Other required services include a Web server for browser-based interfaces, a database server to manage the database, an Active Directory server to authenticate users and authorize access to information and software resources, a router and firewall, and a server to operate low-level Internet services such as domain naming (DNS) and Internet address allocation (DHCP).

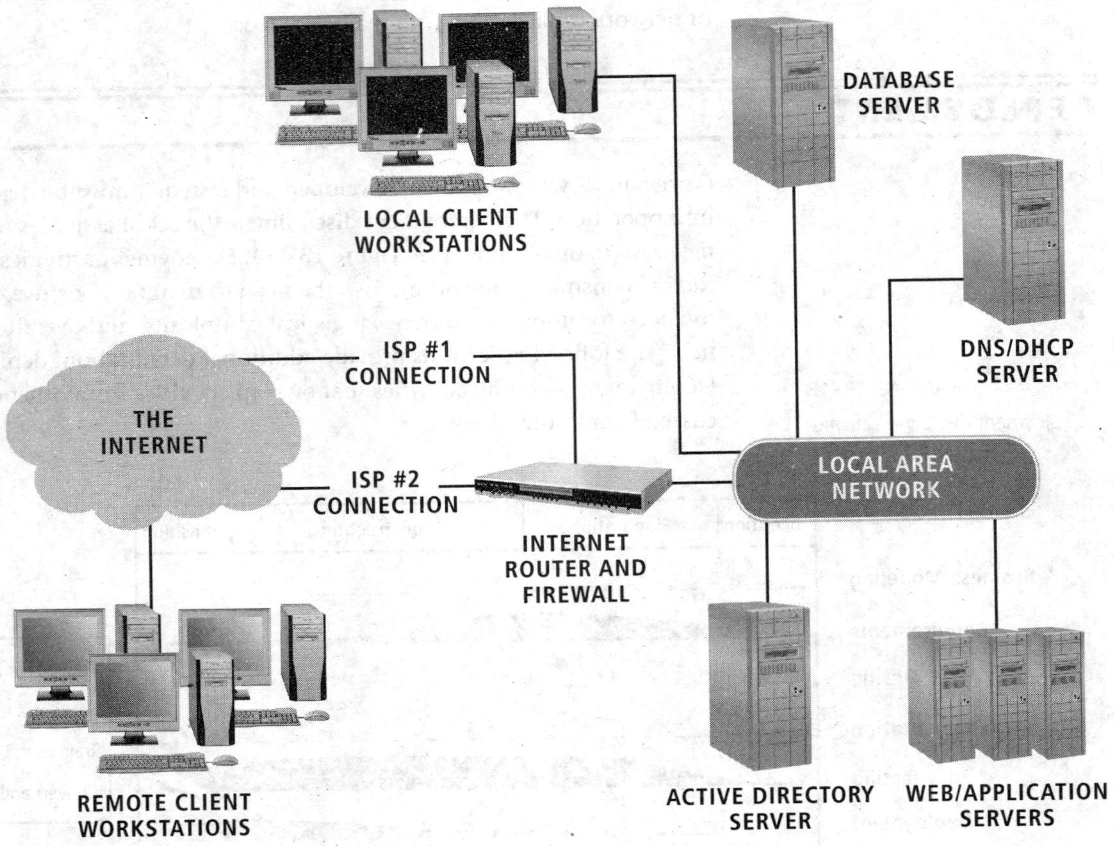

FIGURE 13-14
Infrastructure and clients of a typical .NET application

Unless it already exists, all of this hardware and system software infrastructure must be acquired, installed, and configured before application software can be installed and tested. In most cases, some or all of the infrastructure will already exist—to support existing information systems. In that case, developers work closely with personnel who administer the existing infrastructure to plan the support for the new system. Developers estimate requirements for the new system, and the infrastructure administrators determine how best to satisfy those requirements by configuring existing infrastructure, acquiring new infrastructure, or both.

If an entirely new infrastructure must be acquired, then developers work with IS staff to choose and acquire it. Acquisition includes these steps:

- Planning
- Developing a request for proposal
- Evaluating results
- Choosing one or more vendors
- Installing and configuring new hardware and system software

Perhaps the most important and difficult task is choosing an appropriate component interaction standard and supporting system software. The chosen standard and software will likely support the system under development and many future systems. Thus, staff must choose a standard to satisfy both present and future requirements. Because of its importance to the organization and its future, the choice is typically made as a part of a comprehensive strategic plan for information technology and resources.

PACKAGING AND INSTALLING COMPONENTS

As with hardware and software infrastructure, the specifics of application software installation and configuration vary depending on the component interaction standard. Components must be physically installed on a host server, added to a component registry, and assigned one or more network addresses to enable client access. Newer component interaction standards contain formatted XML files to store registration and access information. Developers normally deploy components to a test or production server as they are developed and tested.

Developers can usually package and install components using utilities provided with the application development software. Figure 13-15 shows one step in component deployment under J2EE using Oracle JDeveloper. Other development tools provide similar utilities.

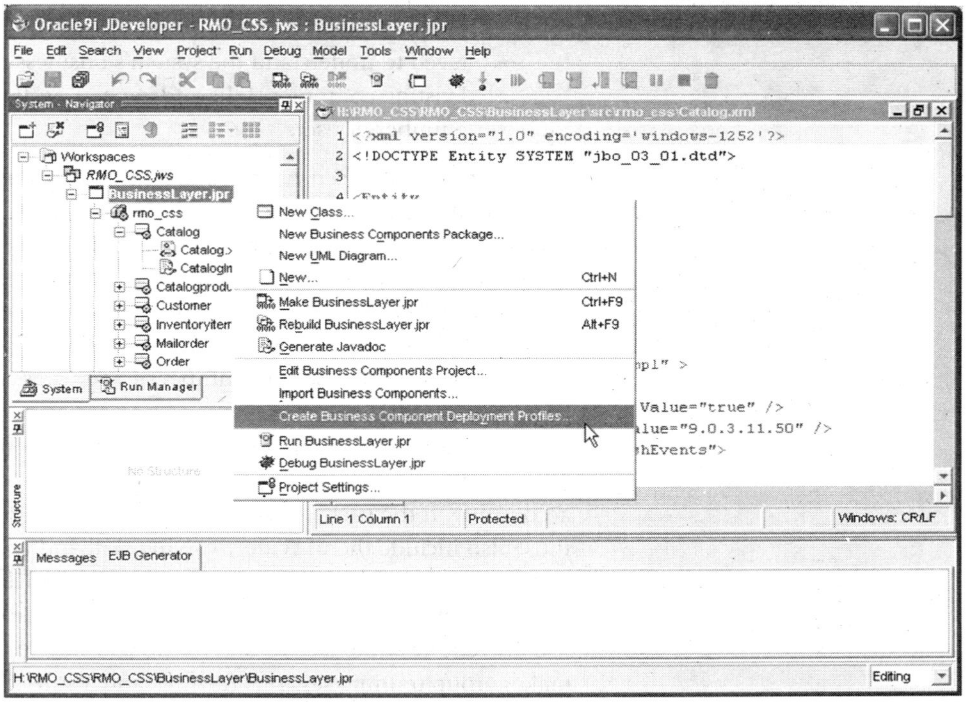

FIGURE 13-15
Automated component deployment with Oracle JDeveloper

BEST PRACTICE: Automate component deployment with appropriate development tools and utilities.

TRAINING USERS

Training is an essential part of any system deployment. Remember, users are part of the system, too! Without training, users would slowly work their own way up the learning curve, error rates would be high, and the system would operate well below peak efficiency. Training allows users to be productive as soon as the system becomes operational.

Two classes of users—end users and system operators—must be trained. End users are people who use the system from day to day to achieve the system's business purpose. System operators are people who perform administrative functions and routine maintenance to keep the system operating. Figure 13-16 shows representative activities for each role. In smaller systems, a single person may fill both roles.

FIGURE 13-16
Typical activities of end users and system operators

END-USER ACTIVITIES	SYSTEM OPERATOR ACTIVITIES
Creating records or transactions	Starting or stopping the system
Modifying database contents	Querying system status
Generating reports	Backing up data to archive
Querying database	Recovering data from archive
Importing or exporting data	Installing or upgrading software

The nature of training varies with the target audience. Audience characteristics that affect training include the following:

- Frequency and duration of system use
- Need to understand the system's business context
- Existing computer skills and general proficiency
- Number of users

In general, end users use the system frequently and for extended periods of time, and system operators interact with the system infrequently and usually for short periods. End users solve a particular business problem with the system or implement specific business procedures. System operators are usually computer professionals with limited knowledge of the business processes that the system supports. End-user computer skill levels vary widely, while system operators typically have higher and more uniform skill levels. Also, the number of end users is generally much larger than the number of system operators.

Training for end users must emphasize hands-on use and application of the system for a specific business process or function, such as order entry, inventory control, or accounting. If the users are not already familiar with those procedures, then training must also include them. Widely varying skill and experience levels call for at least some hands-on training, including practice exercises, questions and answers, and one-on-one tutorials. Self-paced training materials can fill some of this need, but complex systems usually require some face-to-face training also. The relatively large number of end users makes group training sessions feasible, and a subset of well-qualified end users can be trained and then pass their knowledge on to other users.

System operator training can be much less formal when the operators are not end users. Experienced computer operators and administrators can learn most or all they need to know by self-study. Thus, formal training sessions may not be required. Also, the relatively small number of system operators makes one-on-one training feasible, if it is necessary.

Determining the best time to begin formal training can be difficult. On one hand, users can be trained as parts of the system are developed and tested, which ensures that they hit the ground running. On the other hand, starting early can be frustrating to both users and trainers because the system may not be stable or complete. End users can quickly become upset when trying to learn on a buggy, crash-prone system with features and interfaces that are constantly changing.

In an ideal world, training doesn't begin until the interfaces are finalized and a test version has been installed and fully debugged. But the typical end-of-project crunch makes that approach a luxury that is often sacrificed. Instead, training materials are normally developed as soon as the interfaces are reasonably stable, and end-user training begins as soon as possible thereafter. It is much easier to provide training if system interfaces are completed in early project iterations.

CONVERTING AND INITIALIZING DATA

An operational system requires a fully populated database to support ongoing processing. For example, the RMO order-entry subsystem relies on stored information about catalogs, products, customers, and previous orders. Developers must ensure that such information is present in the database at the moment the subsystem becomes operational.

Data needed at system startup can be obtained from the following sources:

- Files or databases of a system being replaced
- Manual records
- Files or databases of other systems in the organization
- User feedback during normal system operation

REUSING EXISTING DATABASES

Most new information systems replace or augment an existing manual or automated system. In the simplest form of data conversion, the old system's database is used directly by the new system with little or no change to the database structure. Reusing an existing database is fairly common because of the difficulty and expense of creating new databases from scratch, especially when a single database often supports multiple information systems, as in today's enterprise resource planning (ERP) systems.

Although old databases are commonly reused in new or upgraded systems, some changes to database content are usually required. Typical changes include adding new classes, adding new attributes, and modifying existing attributes. Modern database management systems (DBMSs) usually allow database administrators to modify the structure of a fully populated database. Simple changes such as adding new attributes or changing attribute types can be performed entirely by the DBMS.

RELOADING DATABASES

More complex changes to database structure may require reloading data after the change. In that case, implementation staff must develop programs to alter data after the database has been modified. Figure 13-17 shows two possible approaches to reloading data. The first approach initializes a new database and copies the contents of the old database to it. The conversion program translates data stored within the former database structure into the newly modified database structure.

The second approach uses a program or DBMS utility to extract and delete data from an existing database and store it in a temporary data store. The database structure is then modified, and a second DBMS utility or program is used to reload the modified database. The first approach is simpler than the second, but it requires sufficient data storage to hold both databases temporarily. The second approach is required if there is insufficient data storage to hold two complete sets of data.

Many DBMSs provide a rich set of import utilities to extract and load data from existing databases, files, or scanned documents. DBMS developers provide such utilities

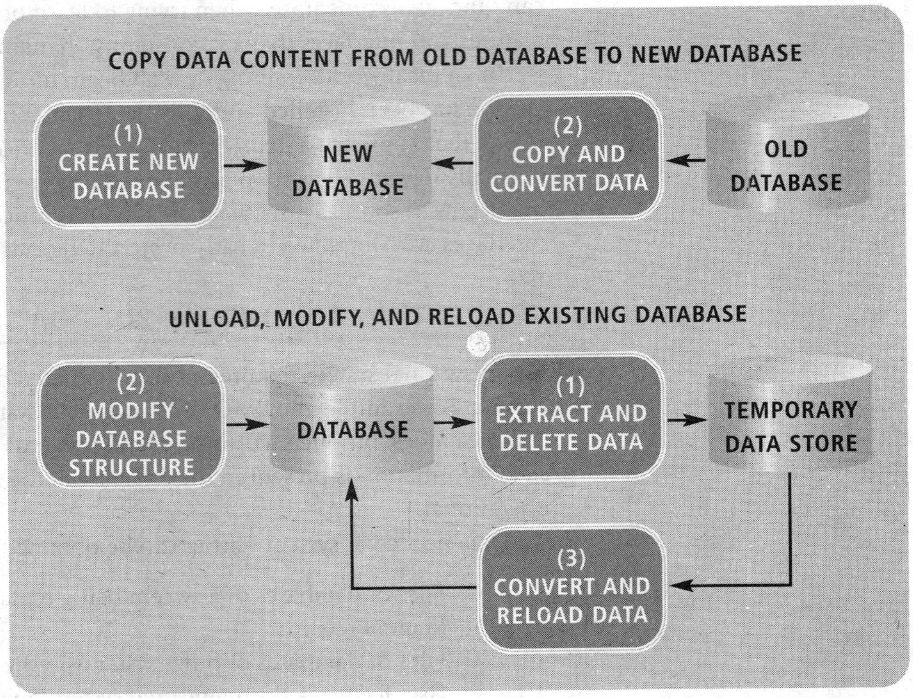

FIGURE 13-17
Two approaches to reloading database content after a structural modification

because system developers are more likely to adopt a DBMS that eases the process of importing data from other sources. If DBMS import and export utilities are inadequate for data conversion, then developers must construct conversion programs that will be used only once. Although conversion programs are not part of the operational system, they must be constructed and tested in the same manner as operational software.

CREATING NEW DATABASES

If the system being developed is entirely new or if it replaces a manual system, then initial data must be obtained from manual records or from other automated systems in the organization. Data from manual records can be entered using the same programs being developed for the operational system. In that case, data-entry programs are usually developed and tested as early as possible. Initial data entry can be structured as a user training exercise. In addition, data from manual records can also be scanned into an optical character recognition program and then entered into the database using custom-developed conversion programs or a DBMS import utility.

Some data may already be stored in other automated systems within the organization. For example, when team members are implementing a new order-entry system, they may find some product data in a manufacturing planning and control system and some customer data in an existing billing system. Copying such data to a new database is similar to reloading a modified database from an old database or backup data store.

Figure 13-18 shows a complex data-conversion process that draws input from a variety of sources. Data are input using a mix of manual data entry, optical character recognition, conversion programs, and DBMS import and export utilities. Data-conversion processes of this complexity are common in large system development projects.

In some cases it may be possible to begin system operation with a partially or completely empty database. For example, a customer order-entry system need not have existing customer information loaded into the database. Customer information could be added the first time a customer places an order, based on a dialog between

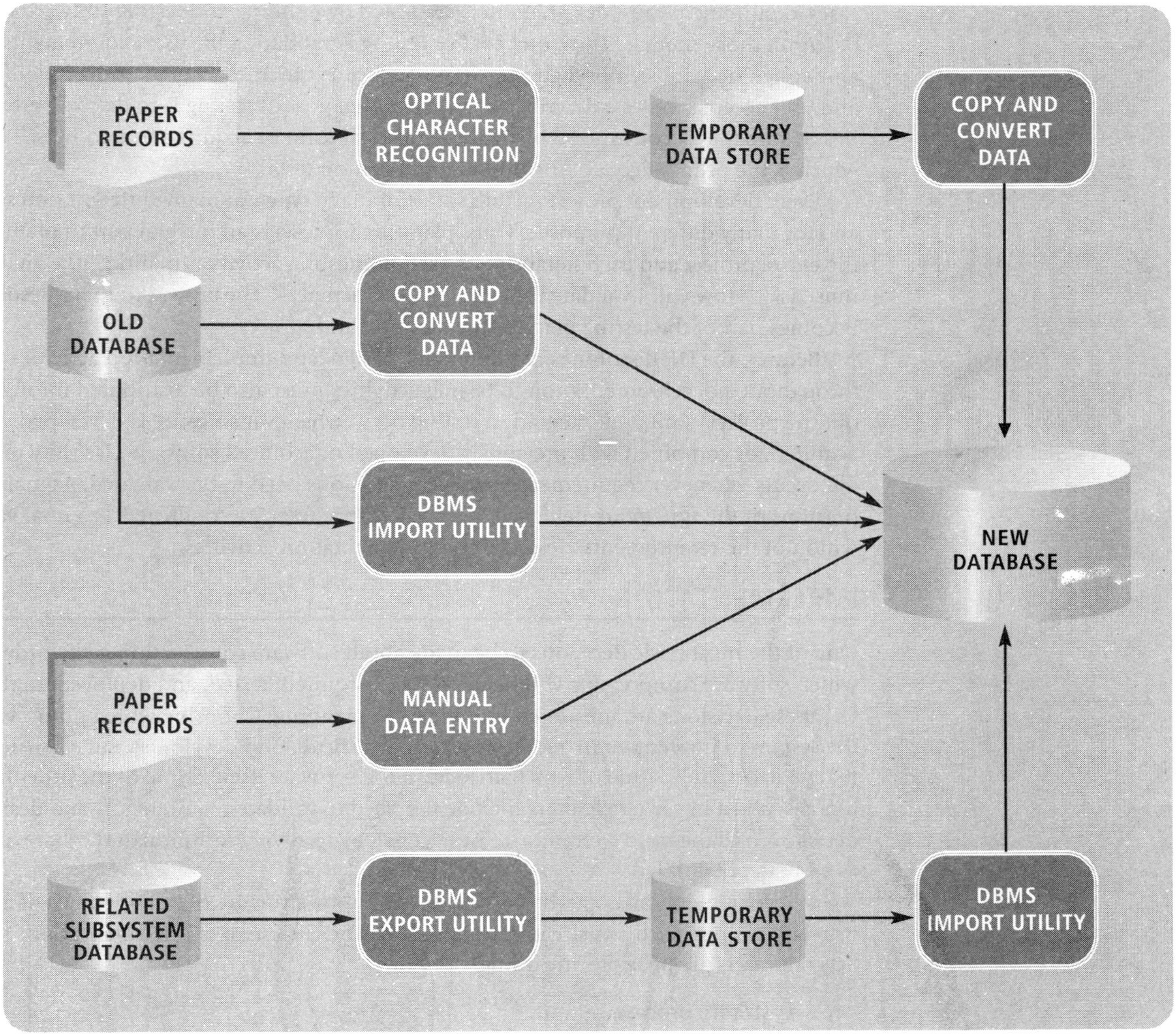

FIGURE 13-18
A complex data-conversion example

a telephone order-entry clerk and the customer. Adding data as they are encountered reduces the complexity of data conversion but at the expense of slower processing of initial transactions.

PLANNING AND MANAGING IMPLEMENTATION, TESTING, AND DEPLOYMENT

The previous sections have discussed the implementation, testing, deployment, and configuration and change management disciplines in isolation. In this section we concentrate on their interrelationships and describe how developers create an iteration plan and manage the activities of all four disciplines.

TESTING

Chapter 2 described the UP as a form of adaptive development in which a system is incrementally described, built, and tested. Other chapters have briefly described the role of testing as a validation technique for requirements and design models. In most cases, requirements and design models are tested by building and testing software based on those models. Thus, one goal of testing is validating the user requirements and design decisions embodied in software, which is the primary goal of the usability and user acceptance tests described earlier. Another goal of testing is to discover errors in software that is constructed by the development team or acquired from others, which is the primary goal of the unit and integration tests.

Every development project includes tests of many types, at many different times, and for many different purposes. Thus, planning for tests is an integral part of planning the entire project and each iteration. As each nontesting activity is planned, the analyst must ask, "How will I validate the results of this activity?" The answer to that question becomes part of the testing plan for the iteration and project.

Because the UP distributes requirements, design, and implementation activities throughout a development project, testing activities must also be distributed throughout the project. Unit and integration testing occur whenever software is developed, acquired, or combined with previously developed or acquired software. Usability testing occurs whenever requirements or design decisions need to be evaluated. As major portions of the system are deployed, user acceptance tests are conducted as a final validation of the requirements, design, and implementation activities.

IMPLEMENTATION

One of the most basic decisions to be made about software construction is the order in which software components will be developed, acquired, tested, and deployed. In the UP, these decisions are subsumed into iteration planning. Choosing which portions of the system to implement in which iterations is difficult, and developers must consider many factors, only some of which arise from the software itself. Some of the other factors discussed in earlier chapters include the need to validate requirements and design decisions and the need to minimize project risk by resolving technical and other risks as early as possible.

A development order can be based directly on the structure of the system itself and its related issues, such as use cases, testing, and efficient use of development staff. Several orders are possible, including:

- Input, process, output
- Top down
- Bottom up

Each project must adapt one or a combination of these approaches to specific project requirements and constraints.

INPUT, PROCESS, OUTPUT DEVELOPMENT ORDER

input, process, output (IPO) development
a development order that implements input modules first, process modules next, and output modules last

The *input, process, output (IPO) development* order is based on data flow through a system or program. Programs or modules that obtain external input are developed first. Programs or modules that process the input (that is, transform it into output) are developed next. Programs or modules that produce output are developed last. The key issue to analyze is dependency—that is, which classes and methods capture or generate data that are needed by other classes or methods? Dependency information is documented in package diagrams and may also be documented in a class diagram. Thus, either or both diagram types can guide implementation order decisions.

For example, the package diagram in Figure 13-19 shows that the customer and catalog maintenance subsystems are not dependent on each other or on either of the other two subsystems. The order-entry subsystem is dependent on both the customer

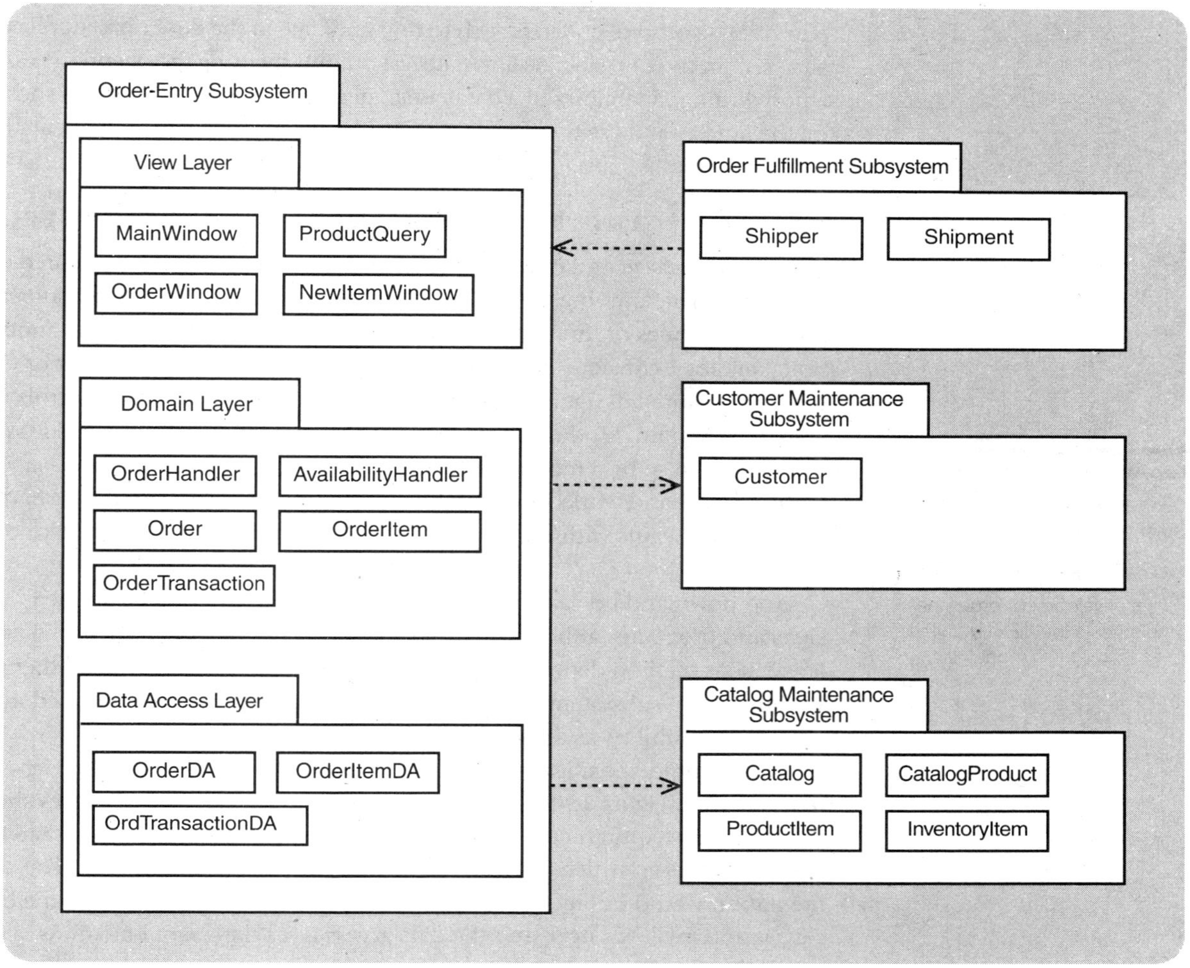

FIGURE 13-19
A package diagram for the four RMO subsystems

and catalog maintenance subsystems, and the order fulfillment subsystem is dependent on the order-entry subsystem.

Data dependency among the packages (subsystems) implies data dependency among their embedded classes. Thus, the classes Customer, Catalog, and Shipper have no data dependency on the remaining RMO classes. Under IPO development order, those three classes are implemented first.

The chief advantage of the IPO development order is that it simplifies testing. Because input programs and modules are developed first, they can be used to enter test data for process and output programs and modules. The need to write special-purpose programs to generate or create test data is reduced, thus speeding the development process.

IPO development order is also advantageous because important user interfaces (for example, data-entry routines) are developed early. User interfaces are more likely to require change during development than other portions of the system, so early development allows for early testing and user evaluation. If changes are needed, there is still plenty of time to make them. Early development of user interfaces also provides a head start for related activities such as training users and writing documentation.

A disadvantage of IPO development order is the late implementation of outputs. Output programs are useful for testing process-oriented modules and programs; analysts can find errors in processing by manually examining printed reports or displayed outputs. IPO development defers such testing until late in the development phase. However, analysts can usually generate alternate test outputs by using the query-processing or report-writing capabilities of a database management system (DBMS). If such outputs can be quickly and easily defined, then the disadvantage of late implementation of output routines is substantially mitigated.

TOP-DOWN AND BOTTOM-UP DEVELOPMENT ORDER

The terms *top-down* and *bottom-up* have their roots in traditional structured design and structured programming. A traditional structured design decomposes software into a series of modules or functions, which are hierarchically related to one another. As a visual analogy, consider a typical organization chart with the president or CEO at the top. In structured design, a single module (the president or CEO) controls the entire software program. Modules at the bottom perform low-level specialized tasks when directed to do so by a module at the next higher level. ***Top-down development*** begins with the CEO and works down to those providing finer levels of detail. ***Bottom-up development*** begins with the detailed modules at the lowest level and works upward to the CEO.

top-down development
a development order that implements top-level modules first

bottom-up development
a development order that implements low-level detailed modules first

Top-down and bottom-up program development can also be applied to OO designs and programs, although a visual analogy is not obvious with OO diagrams. The key issue is method dependency—that is, which methods call which other methods. Within an OO subsystem or class, method dependency can be examined in terms of navigation visibility, as discussed in Chapters 9 and 11.

For example, consider the three-layer design of part of the RMO order-entry subsystem shown in Figure 13-20. The arrows connecting packages and classes show navigation visibility requirements. Methods in the view (user-interface) layer call methods in the domain layer, which in turn call methods in the data access layer. Top-down implementation would implement the view layer classes and methods first, the domain layer classes and methods next, and the data access layer classes and methods last. Bottom-up implementation would reverse the top-down implementation order.

Method dependency is also documented in a sequence diagram. For example, in Figure 13-4, method dependency is documented in the left-to-right flow of messages among objects. Rotating the figure 90 degrees to the right creates a top-down and bottom-up visual analogy similar to an organizational chart. Top-down development would proceed through OrderHandler, Customer, Order, OrderItem, and the set of classes CatalogProduct, Product, and InventoryItem. Bottom-up development would reverse this order, starting with Catalog, Product, and InventoryItem and ending with OrderHandler.

The primary advantage of top-down development is that there is always a working version of a program. For example, top-down development in Figure 13-4 would begin with a partial or complete version of the OrderHandler class and dummy (or stub) versions of the Customer and Order classes. This set of classes forms a complete program that can be compiled, linked, and executed, although at this point it wouldn't do very much when executed.

Once the topmost classes and methods are complete, development proceeds downward to the next level. As each method or class is implemented, stubs for the methods or classes on the next lower level are added. At every stage of development, the program should be complete (that is, it should be able to be compiled, linked, and executed). Its behavior becomes more complex and realistic as development proceeds.

The primary disadvantage of top-down development order is that it doesn't use programming personnel very efficiently at the beginning of software development. Development has to proceed through two or three levels before a significant number of

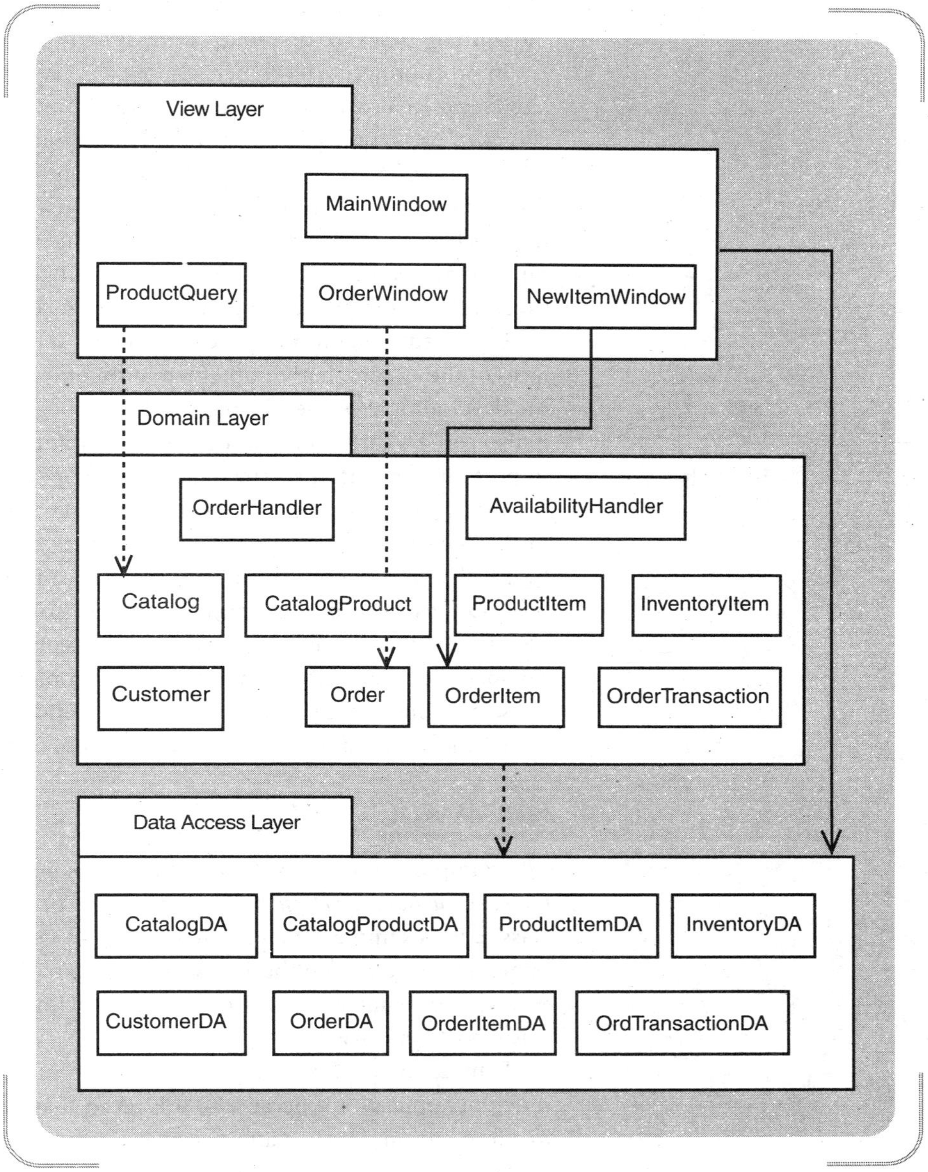

FIGURE 13-20
A package diagram for a three-layer OO design

classes and methods can be developed simultaneously. However, if the first few iterations of the program can be completed quickly, then the disadvantage is minimal.

The primary advantage of bottom-up development is that many programmers can be put to work immediately on classes that support a wide variety of use cases. In addition, those classes and methods are often the most difficult to write, so early development of those classes allows more time for development and testing. Unfortunately, bottom-up development also requires writing a large number of driver methods to test bottom-level classes and methods, which adds additional complexity to the implementation and testing process. Also, the entire system isn't assembled until the topmost classes are written. Thus, integration testing and testing for individual use cases are delayed.

OTHER DEVELOPMENT ORDER CONSIDERATIONS

IPO, top-down, and bottom-up development are only a starting point for creating a software development plan. Other factors that must be considered include use case driven development, user feedback, training, documentation, and testing. Use cases deserve special attention in determining development order because they are one of the primary bases for dividing a development project into iterations.

In most projects, developers choose a set of related use cases for a single iteration and complete those requirements, design, implementation, and testing activities. The choice of use cases to focus on in an iteration may be based on many factors, including minimizing project risk, efficiently using nontechnical staff, or deploying some parts of the system earlier than others. For example, use cases with uncertain requirements or high technical risks are typically addressed in early iterations. Addressing uncertain requirements requires usability and other testing by nontechnical development staff, and those staff members may only be available at certain times in the project.

User feedback, training, and documentation all depend heavily on the user interfaces of the system. Early implementation of user interfaces enables user training and the development of user documentation to begin early in the development process. It also gathers early feedback on the quality and usability of the interface. Note the important role that this issue played in the opening case of this chapter.

Testing is also an important consideration when determining development order. As individual software components are constructed, they must be tested. Programmers must find and correct errors as soon as possible because they become much harder to find and more expensive to fix as the implementation process proceeds. It's important both to identify portions of the software that are susceptible to errors and to identify portions of the software where errors can pose serious problems that affect the system as a whole. These portions of the software must be built and tested early, regardless of where they fit within the basic approaches of IPO, top-down, or bottom-up development.

FRAMEWORK DEVELOPMENT

When implementing a large OO system, it is not unusual to build an object framework (or set of *foundation classes*) that covers most or all of the domain and data access layer classes. For example, when implementing an OO account maintenance system for a bank, developers might build a set of classes to represent and store customers and various types of bank accounts (for example, savings accounts, checking accounts, and certificates of deposit).

Foundation classes are typically reused in many parts of the system and across many different applications. Because of this reuse, they are a critical system component. Errors in a foundation class can affect every program in the system. In addition, later changes to foundation classes may require significant changes throughout the system.

Whenever possible, developers choose use cases for early iterations that rely on many foundation classes. By front-loading the project with development of many foundation classes, developers can test those classes early and frequently as subsequent parts of the system are developed. Early and thorough testing guarantees that bugs or other problems will be discovered before other code that depends on the foundation classes has been written.

TEAM-BASED SOFTWARE DEVELOPMENT

A team of programmers normally works on software development. Using multiple programmers compresses the development schedule by allowing many portions of the system to be developed simultaneously. However, team-based program development introduces its own set of management issues, including:

- Organization of programming teams
- Task assignment to specific teams or members
- Member and team communication and coordination

There are many different ways of organizing an implementation team. Some commonly used organizational models include the following:

- Cooperating peer
- Chief developer
- Collaborative specialist

Figure 13-21 summarizes the characteristics of each team type and the types of projects and tasks best suited to each.

FIGURE 13-21
A comparison and summary of development team types

TEAM TYPE	TEAM CHARACTERISTICS	TASK AND PROJECT TYPES
Cooperating peer	Equal skill levels Overlapping specialties Consensus-based decision making	Experimentation Creative problem solving
Chief developer	Organized like a military platoon or squad One leader makes all important decisions	Well-defined objectives Well-defined path to completion
Collaborative specialist	Wide variation in skill and experience Minimal overlap in technical specialties Leader is primarily an administrator Consensus-based decision making	Diagnosis or experimentation Creative and integrative problem solving Wide range of technology

cooperating peer team
a team with members of roughly equal skill and experience with overlapping areas of specialization

chief developer team
a team with a single leader who makes all important decisions

collaborative specialist team
a team with members who have wide variation in and minimal overlap of skills and experience

A *cooperating peer team* includes members of roughly equal skill and experience with overlapping areas of specialization. Members are considered equals, although they may be assigned tasks of varying importance or complexity. Decisions are primarily made by consensus, and the team frequently meets to exchange information and build consensus.

A *chief developer team* is similar to a small military unit. An assigned leader performs a number of functions, including technical consulting, team coordination, and task assignment. In this type of team, there is much less communication than with a cooperating peer team. The chief developer makes most of the important decisions, although he or she may seek input from members individually or collectively.

A *collaborative specialist team* is similar to a cooperating peer team, but its members have wide variation in and minimal overlap of skills and experience. Such teams are often composed of members from different organizational subunits. The team may have an appointed leader, but his or her leadership covers only administrative functions such as scheduling, coordinating, and interacting with external constituencies. Technical decisions are generally made by consensus, although member opinions usually carry extra weight within the member's own area of expertise. In large projects, a collaborative specialist team may be formed to "float" among other teams to deal with complex problems as they arise.

Some common principles of team organization underlie all development projects and organizational structures. One is that team size should be kept relatively small (no more than 10 members). Larger teams tend to be inefficient because of the inherent complexity of communication and coordination in large groups. When more than 10 developers are assigned to a project, it is best to break them into small teams (approximately five members each). Each team should be assigned a relatively independent portion of the project. One member of each team should be designated to handle coordination and communication with other teams. Having a single point of contact simplifies communication and provides for some specialization of functions within each team.

Another common principle of team organization is that team structure should be matched to the task and project characteristics. Teams with a well-defined implementation task that does not push the limits of member knowledge or technical feasibility are usually best organized as chief programmer teams. A chief programmer team operates very efficiently in such an environment.

Teams assigned to tasks that require experimentation or a high level of creativity are better served by a cooperating peer or collaborative specialist model. Because of their more open communication, cooperating peer teams are especially well suited to tackling tasks that require generating and evaluating a large number of ideas. Overlap in skill, specialty, and experience allows thorough evaluation of each idea.

Collaborative specialist teams are well suited to projects that span a wide range of cutting-edge technology. They are also well suited to tackling projects that require integrated problem solving (for example, diagnosing and fixing bugs in an existing complex system). However, success depends on a true collaborative process, which is sometimes difficult to achieve among members with wide variation in skill and experience.

Member skills must be matched to the tasks at hand. Skill matching is fairly easy with respect to technical skills such as database management, user interfaces, and numeric algorithms. Skill matching is harder but no less important for nontechnical skills. Teams need a mix of nontechnical skills and traits, including the ability to generate new ideas, build consensus, manage details, and communicate with external constituencies. The project manager should perform a skills inventory early in the project so that gaps can be filled to avoid project delays and inappropriate personnel assignments.

SOURCE CODE CONTROL

source code control system (SCCS)
an automated tool for tracking source code files and controlling changes to those files

Development teams need tools to help coordinate their programming tasks. A *source code control system (SCCS)* is an automated tool for tracking source code files and controlling changes to those files. An SCCS stores project source code files in a repository. The SCCS acts the way a librarian would—it implements check-in and checkout procedures, tracks which programmer has which files, and ensures that only authorized users have access to the repository.

Programmers can manipulate files in the repository as follows:

- Check out a file in read-only mode
- Check out a file in read/write mode
- Check in a modified file

A programmer checks out a file in read-only mode when he or she wants to examine the code without making changes (for example, to examine a module's interfaces to other modules). When a programmer needs to make changes to a file, he or she checks out the file in read/write mode. The SCCS allows only one programmer to check out a file in read/write mode. The file must be checked back in before another programmer can check it out in read/write mode.

Figure 13-22 shows the main display of Microsoft Visual SourceSafe. Various source code files from the RMO CSS are shown in the display. Some files are currently checked out by programmers. For each file checked out in read/write mode, the program lists the programmer who checked it out, the date and time of checkout, and the current location of the file. The icon for each checked-out file is displayed with a red border and check mark.

An SCCS prevents multiple programmers from updating the same file at the same time, thus preventing inconsistent changes to the source code. Source code control is an absolute necessity when programs are developed by multiple programmers. It prevents inconsistent changes and automates coordination among programmers and teams. The repository also serves as a common facility for backup and recovery operations.

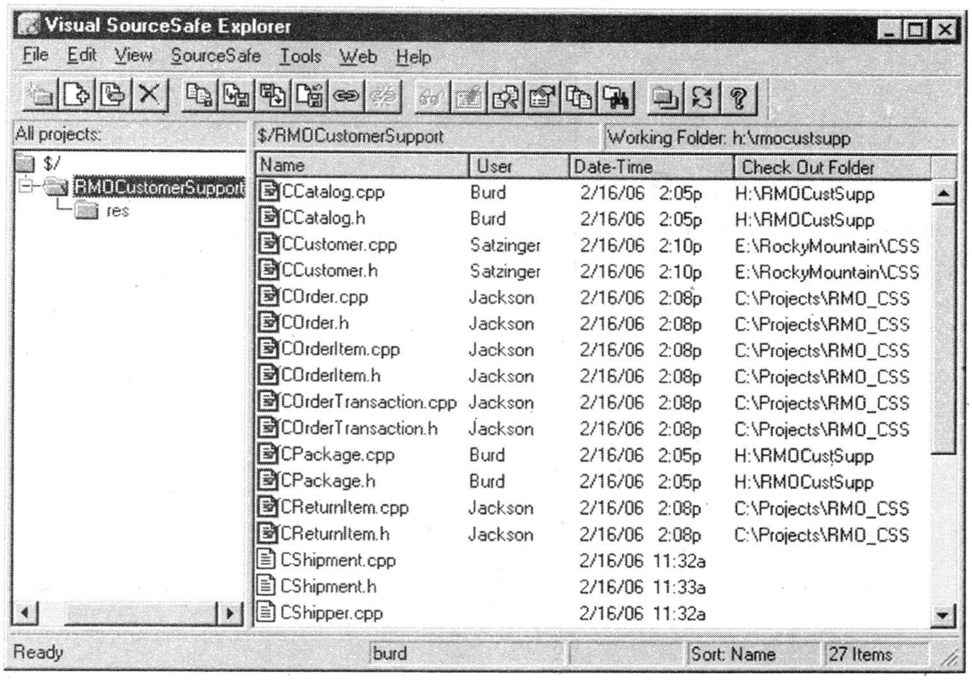

FIGURE 13-22
Project files managed by a source code control system

DEPLOYMENT

As with the other disciplines discussed in this chapter, deployment activities are highly interdependent with activities of the other disciplines. In short, a system or subsystem can't be deployed until it has been implemented and tested. If a system or subsystem is large and complex, it is typically deployed in multiple stages or versions, thus necessitating some formal method of configuration and change management.

Some of the more important issues to consider when planning deployment include the following:

- Incurring costs of operating both systems in parallel
- Detecting and correcting errors in the new system
- Potentially disrupting the company and its IS operations
- Training personnel and familiarizing customers with new procedures

Different approaches to deployment represent different trade-offs among cost, complexity, and risk. The most commonly used deployment approaches are:

- Direct deployment
- Parallel deployment
- Phased deployment

Each approach has different strengths and weaknesses, and no one approach is best for all systems. Each approach is discussed in detail here.

DIRECT DEPLOYMENT

direct deployment, or **immediate cutover**
a deployment method that installs a new system, quickly makes it operational, and immediately turns off any overlapping systems

In a *direct deployment*, the new system is installed and quickly made operational, and any overlapping systems are then turned off. Direct deployment is also sometimes called *immediate cutover*. Both systems are concurrently operated for only a brief time (typically a few days or weeks) while the new system is being installed and tested. Figure 13-23 shows a time line for direct deployment.

The primary advantage of direct deployment is its simplicity. Since the old and new systems aren't operated in parallel, there are fewer logistical issues to manage and fewer

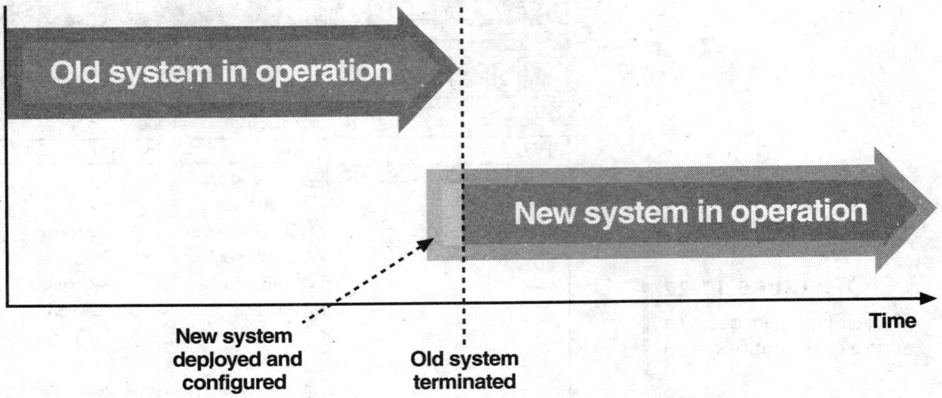

FIGURE 13-23
Direct deployment and cutover

resources required. The primary disadvantage of direct deployment is its risk. Because older systems are not operated in parallel, there is no backup in the event that the new system fails. The magnitude of the risk depends on the nature of the system, the cost of workarounds in the event of a system failure, and the cost of system unavailability or less-than-optimal system function.

Direct deployment is typically used under one or both of the following conditions:

- The new system is not replacing an older system (automated or manual).
- Downtime of days or weeks can be tolerated.

If neither condition applies, then parallel or phased deployment is usually preferable to minimize the risk of system unavailability.

PARALLEL DEPLOYMENT

parallel deployment
a deployment method that operates both the old and new systems for an extended time period

In a *parallel deployment*, the old and new systems are both operated for an extended period of time (typically weeks or months). Figure 13-24 illustrates the time line for parallel deployment. Ideally, the old system continues to operate until the new system has been thoroughly tested and determined to be error-free and ready to operate independently. As a practical matter, the time allocated for parallel operation is often determined in advance and limited to minimize the cost of dual operation.

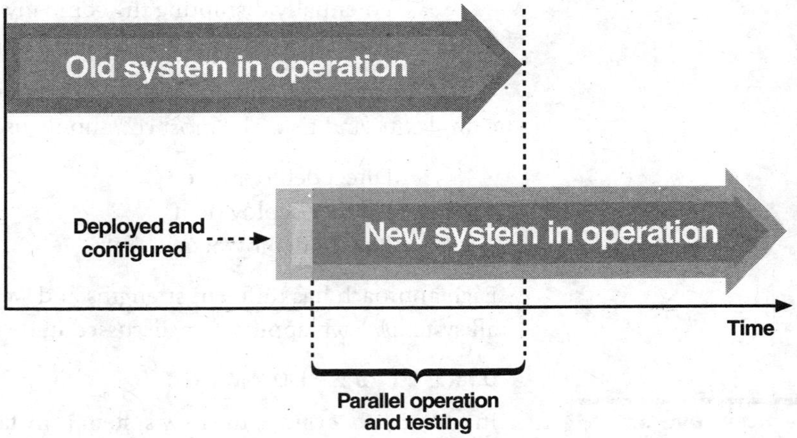

FIGURE 13-24
Parallel deployment and operation

The primary advantage of parallel deployment is a relatively low risk of system failure and the negative consequences that might result from that failure. If both systems are operated completely (that is, using all data and exercising all functions), then the old system functions as a backup for the new system. Any failure in the new system can be mitigated by relying on the old system.

The primary disadvantage of parallel deployment is cost. During the period of parallel operation, the organization pays to operate both systems. Extra costs associated with operating two systems in parallel include:

- Hiring temporary personnel or temporarily reassigning existing personnel
- Acquiring extra space for computer equipment and personnel
- Increasing managerial and logistical complexity

Unless the operational costs of the new system are substantially less than those of the old system, the combined operating cost is typically 2.5 to 3 times the cost of operating the old system alone.

Parallel operation is generally best when the consequences of a system failure are severe. Parallel operation substantially reduces the risk of a system failure through redundant operation. The risk reduction is especially important for "mission-critical" applications such as customer service, production control, basic accounting functions, and most forms of online transaction processing. Few organizations can afford any significant downtime in such important systems.

Full parallel operation may be impractical for any number of reasons, including the following:

- Inputs to one system may be unusable by the other, and it may not be possible to use both types of inputs.
- The new system may use the same equipment as the old system (for example, computers, I/O devices, and networks), and there may not be sufficient capacity to operate both systems.
- Staffing levels may be insufficient to operate or manage both systems at the same time.

When full parallel operation is not possible or feasible, a partial parallel operation may be employed instead. Possible modes of partial parallel operation include the following:

- Processing only a subset of input data in one of the two systems. The subset could be determined by transaction type, geography, or sampling (for example, every 10th transaction).
- Performing only a subset of processing functions (for example, updating account history but not printing monthly bills).
- Performing a combination of data and processing function subsets.

Partial parallel operation always entails the risk that significant errors or problems will go undetected. For example, parallel operation with partial input increases the risk that errors associated with untested inputs will not be discovered.

PHASED DEPLOYMENT

phased deployment
a deployment method that installs a new system and makes it operational in a series of steps or phases

In a *phased deployment*, the system is deployed in a series of steps or phases. Each phase adds components or functions to the operational system. During each phase, the system is tested to ensure that it is ready for the next phase. Phased deployment can be combined with parallel deployment, particularly when the new system will take over the operation of multiple existing systems.

Figure 13-25 shows a phased deployment with both direct and parallel deployment of individual phases. The new system replaces two existing systems. The deployment is divided into three phases. The first phase is a direct replacement of one of the existing systems. The second and third phases are different parts of a parallel deployment that replace the other existing system.

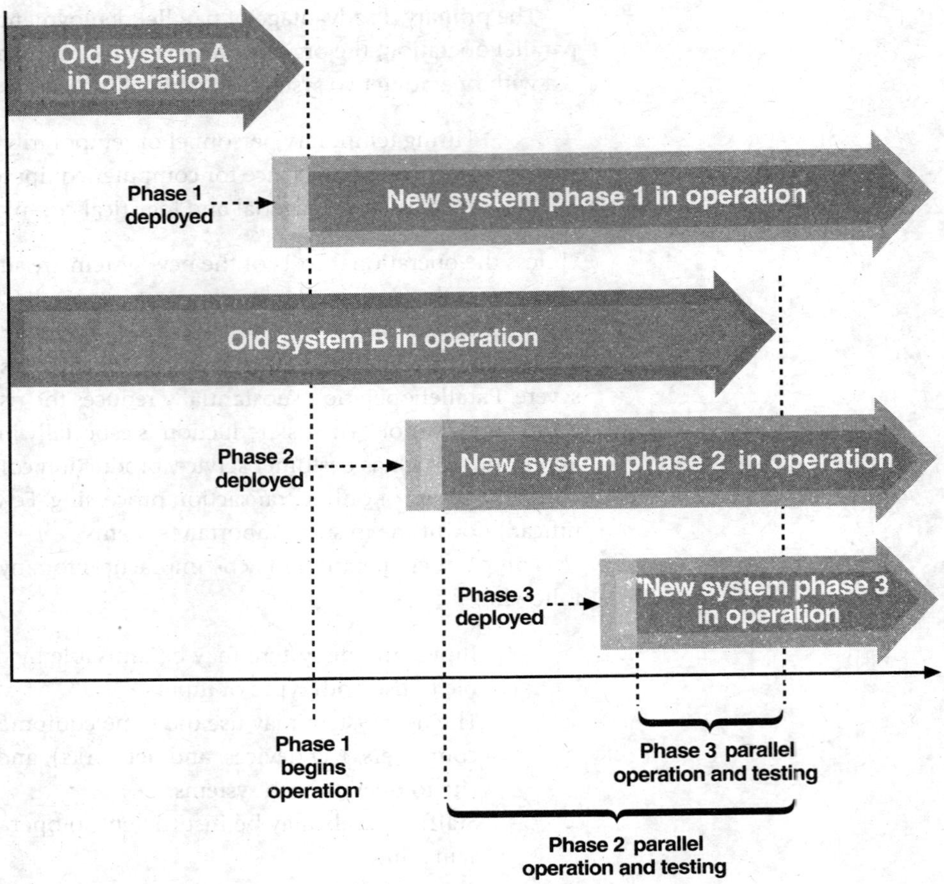

FIGURE 13-25
Phased deployment with direct cutover and parallel operation

There is no single method for performing phased deployment. Deployment details such as the composition of specific phases and their order of deployment vary widely from one system to another. These specifics determine the number of deployment phases, the order of deployment, and the parts of the new system that are operated in parallel with existing systems.

The primary advantage of phased deployment is reduced risk. Risk is reduced because failure of a single phase is less problematic than failure of an entire system. The primary disadvantage of phased deployment is increased complexity. Dividing the deployment into phases creates more activities and milestones, thus making the entire process more complex. However, each phase contains a smaller and more manageable set of activities. If the entire system is simply too big or complex to install at one time, then the reduced risks of phased deployment outweigh the increased complexity inherent in managing and coordinating multiple phases.

Phased deployment is most useful when a system is large, complex, and composed of relatively independent subsystems. If the subsystems are not substantially independent, then it is difficult or impossible to define separate deployment phases. System size and complexity may also be too great for an "all at once" deployment to be feasible. In that case, there is really no choice but to use phased deployment.

PERSONNEL ISSUES

Deploying a new system places significant demands on personnel throughout an organization. Deployment typically involves demanding schedules, rapid learning and adaptation, and high stress. Planning should anticipate these problems and take appropriate measures to mitigate their effects.

New system deployment usually stretches IS personnel to their limits. Many tasks must be performed in little time. The problem is most acute in parallel deployment, where personnel must operate both the old and new systems. Often, development and customer support personnel must be temporarily reassigned to provide sufficient manpower to operate both systems. Reassignment may reduce progress on other ongoing projects and also reduce support and maintenance activities for other systems.

Temporary and contract personnel may be hired to increase available manpower during a deployment. Two types are particularly useful:

- Personnel with experience in hardware and software deployment and configuration
- Personnel with experience operating (or who can be trained to operate) the old system

Deployment may require technical skills that are in short supply within the organization. In that case, hiring contractors to assist in hardware and system software deployment is a necessity. Hardware and system software specialists can be contracted directly from vendors or from IS consulting firms.

Hiring temporary employees to operate the old system during a parallel deployment has several benefits. First, it provides the extra manpower needed to operate both systems. Second, it frees permanent employees for training and new system operations. Temporary personnel are often hired several months in advance, trained to operate the old system, and employed for the duration of parallel operation. If problems occur with the new system, then employment contracts can be extended until the old system can be safely phased out.

Another personnel issue that must be considered is employee productivity. All new systems have a learning curve for users and system operators. Both groups require training before operation begins, but no matter how good the training, users and operators require some time (typically a few months) to reach their peak efficiency with a new system. Manpower requirements are higher during that time, as is the general level of employee stress.

PUTTING IT ALL TOGETHER—RMO REVISITED

In any medium-sized or large-scale development project, managers usually feel overwhelmed by the sheer number of activities to be performed, their interdependencies, and the risks involved. In this section, we give you a glimpse of the interplay among those issues by showing how Barbara Halifax's team developed an iteration plan for RMO's customer support system (CSS). But keep in mind that no single example can adequately prepare you to tackle iteration planning for a complex project. That's why iteration planning and other project planning tasks are typically performed by developers with years of experience.

To start, Barbara established some basic parameters for the project, including its total length and number of iterations. Projects that follow the UP typically use iterations ranging in length from four to six weeks. Barbara chose six-week iterations for this project and seven iterations overall. Figure 13-26 shows an initial iteration plan under these assumptions.

Barbara developed the plan for the first iteration at the project's inception. She developed plans for subsequent iterations near the end of the first iteration and modified and expanded them as the project proceeded. The initial plan was developed based on the scope of the work documented during the first iteration and the available budget and schedule. During the first iteration, Barbara met with key stakeholders to negotiate

FIGURE 13-26
RMO CSS iteration plan

ITERATION	DATES	DESCRIPTION
1	01/9/2006 02/17/2006	Define business models and development/deployment environment. Define essential use cases and rough class diagram. Storyboard customer order processing. Review deployment environment and required changes/updates to existing infrastructure. Select and acquire network components, system software, hardware, and development tools. Construct a simple prototype for adding a customer order (no database updates), and perform usability testing.
2	02/20/2006 03/31/2006	Define class, use case, and sequence diagrams, concentrating on the key use cases (*Look up item availability, Create new order, Update order, and Create new customer*). Develop a prototype covering the four key use cases. Run Web site and telephone sales portions in parallel as different user interfaces that interact with the same back-end business and data layers. Deploy infrastructure services, including Web, application, and DBMS. Develop DBMS schema, and deploy new database to a spare DBMS server. Perform usability, unit, and integration testing to validate database design, technical feasibility, customer/order function set, and user interfaces.
3	04/03/2006 05/12/2006	Expand requirements and design to cover additional use cases (*Ship an order, Return an item, Backorder an item*). Loop through iteration 2 essential use cases again, and make all changes determined at end of previous iteration. Once that's done, do additional performance testing with close to live transaction loads and database size. Make a copy of the SCM database structure on the mainframe, and add rows defined in previous iteration for order entry—this is now a stand-alone test database running on the production server. Migrate a sizable portion of existing data into the test database to support testing efforts (not the final migration since data won't be maintained, but it can be considered a dry run for final migration or individual migration steps in later iterations).
4	05/15/2006 06/23/2006	Expand requirements and design to cover additional use cases (*Create new customer and Maintain customer account*). Loop through iteration 3 essential use cases again, and make all changes determined at end of previous iteration. Develop training materials for order entry and begin user and operator training. Monitor training exercises for effects on system performance, and make any needed changes.
5	06/26/2006 08/04/2006	Expand requirements and design to cover additional use cases (*Create a new catalog and Update a catalog*). Loop through iteration 4 essential use cases again, and make all changes determined at end of previous iteration. Continue training with additional software deployed in previous iteration. Migrate all order, shipment, and customer data from old system. Deploy first CSS production version.
6	08/07/2006 09/15/2006	Expand requirements and design to cover additional use cases (*Create special promotion and Send promotion materials*). Loop through iteration 5 essential use cases again, and make all changes determined at end of previous iteration. Continue training with additional software deployed in previous iteration. Operate first production version in parallel with existing system. If no problems are encountered, discontinue old system operation at the end of this iteration.
7	09/18/2006 10/27/2006	Loop through iteration 6 essential use cases again, and make all changes determined at end of previous iteration. Deploy and begin using second CSS production version, which covers bug fixes to first version and adds functions for catalog creation/maintenance and promotional materials. Continue training with additional software deployed in previous and current iterations.

January 30, 2006

To: John MacMurty

From: Barbara Halifax

RE: Customer support system update – iteration plan

ROCKY MOUNTAIN OUTFITTERS

MEMO

John, we're about halfway through the first iteration of the project, and it's time for some concrete plans for the remainder of the project. I met with all the key stakeholders last week and nailed down initial estimates of the project's scope, budget, and schedule. The scope ended up smaller than many people wanted, but it's the best we can do with the available time and money.

A detailed iteration plan is attached. We'll divide the project into seven 6-week iterations, which will complete the system a month ahead of the holiday rush. In developing the plan, my main concerns were the risks involved in new technology, our lack of existing infrastructure to support that technology, and uncertainty about how we'll address our key use cases with that technology. To address those risks, I front-loaded the plan with work on infrastructure and requirements for key use cases. That'll give us ample time to work up the learning curve, find any technology- or tool-related problems, and ensure that the users are happy with the order-entry interfaces and functions.

We should meet ASAP to go over the details and address any of your questions or concerns. Let me know when you're available.

Thanks and take care.

BH

cc: Steven Deerfield, Ming Lee, Jack Garcia, Ann Hamilton

a project scope that was feasible, given the project's time and budget constraints as described in the accompanying memo.

Allocating activities and use cases among the iterations was one of Barbara's chief concerns in developing the iteration plan. There is no checklist of universal "most important" factors in creating an iteration plan because each project is unique. But three factors that are commonly included are risk, infrastructure, and use cases. Barbara realized that RMO faced two significant risks that permeated the CSS project. The first was technology—specifically, RMO's lack of familiarity with the technologies that would support the new system. That risk manifested itself in several ways, including:

- Lack of existing infrastructure to support the new system
- Lack of experience with the required development tools
- Unfamiliarity with the capabilities of Web-based systems, resulting in uncertainty about exact requirements

To minimize the overall project risk, Barbara structured the iteration plan to deal with the highest risks in early iterations. Thus, she planned to acquire and install all new infrastructure in the first two iterations. Early infrastructure installation enabled developers to develop "live" application software starting in iteration 2. Developing, deploying, and testing that software provided early feedback about possible technical shortcomings, such as inadequate performance or security.

BEST PRACTICE: Schedule high-risk activities in early iterations.

Figure 13-27 lists the essential use cases addressed by the CSS. The highest-risk use cases involve Web-based interfaces and those associated with order entry. The risks arise from new technology, uncertainty about requirements, and the operational importance of order processing to RMO. By tackling those use cases first, Barbara allowed her development staff plenty of time to resolve uncertainties and to test related software. Note that significant testing of these functions began in iteration 2 and continued through most of the project.

Look up item availability
Create new order
Update order
Ship an order
Return an item
Backorder an item
Create new customer
Maintain customer account
Create a new catalog
Update a catalog
Create special promotion
Send promotion materials

FIGURE 13-27
Essential use case list for RMO

The CSS was too large and operationally important to be deployed all at once. Thus, the iteration plan called for a phased deployment in two versions, starting at the end of iteration 5. Again, the highest-risk portion of the system, order processing, was deployed first to provide ample testing opportunities. The new system was operated in parallel with the old throughout iteration 6. If the team encountered problems, they could continue parallel operation through iteration 7.

Training activities were spread throughout later project iterations, beginning in iteration 4. Initial training exercises covered the highest-risk portion of the system prior to deployment. They also enabled developers to do integration and performance testing on the order-entry subsystem before it was deployed at the end of the next iteration. Additional training continued as new functions were added to the system, providing a gradual ramp up of both user skills and system load.

Summary

Implementation is complex because it consists of many interdependent activities, including building software components, acquiring software components, and integrating software components. Implementation is difficult to manage because activities must be properly sequenced and progress must be continually monitored. Implementation is risky because it requires significant time and resources and because it often affects systems vital to the daily operation of an organization.

Implementation and testing are two of the most interdependent UP disciplines. Software components must be constructed in an order that minimizes the use of development resources and maximizes the ability to test the system and correct errors. Unfortunately, those two goals often conflict. Thus, a program development plan is a trade-off among available resources, available time, and the desire to detect and correct errors prior to system deployment.

Activities of the UP configuration and change management discipline are most applicable to projects that are too large to deploy in a single version. Activities of the discipline track changes to models and software through multiple system versions, which enables developers to test and deploy a system in stages. Versioning also improves postdeployment support by enabling developers to track problem support to specific system versions.

Deployment activities consist of acquiring hardware and system software, packaging and installing components, training users, and converting and initializing data. They are highly interdependent activities, since a deployed and documented system is a prerequisite for complete training and a fully populated database is needed to begin operation. Manpower utilization and the number of directly affected personnel generally peak during these activities.

KEY TERMS

alpha version, p. 541
beta version, p. 541
bottom-up development, p. 556
build and smoke test, p. 538
chief developer team, p. 559
collaborative specialist team, p. 559
component, p. 532
cooperating peer team, p. 559
direct deployment, or immediate cutover, p. 561
driver, p. 535
input, process, output (IPO) development, p. 554
integration test, p. 536
maintenance release, p. 541
parallel deployment, p. 562
performance test, p. 539
phased deployment, p. 563
production system, p. 546
production version, release version, or production release, p. 541
response time, p. 539
source code control system (SCCS), p. 560
stub, p. 535
system test, p. 538
test case, p. 534
test data, p. 534
test system, p. 546
testing buddy, p. 539
throughput, p. 539
top-down development, p. 556
unit testing, p. 535
usability test, p. 538
user acceptance test, p. 539

REVIEW QUESTIONS

1. What are the characteristics of good test cases?
2. Define the terms *unit test*, *integration test*, *system test*, and *user acceptance test*. When is each test type normally performed? Who performs (or evaluates the results of) each type of test?
3. What is a driver? What is a stub? With what type of test is each most closely associated?
4. Define the terms *alpha version*, *beta version*, and *production version*. Are there well-defined criteria for deciding when an alpha version becomes a beta version or a beta version becomes a production version?
5. Why might system software upgrades not be deployed? What are the costs of not deploying them?
6. How do training activities differ between end users and system operators?
7. List possible sources of data used to initialize a new system database. Briefly describe the tools and methods used to load initial data into the database.
8. List and briefly describe the three basic approaches to program development order. What are the advantages and disadvantages of each?
9. How can the concepts of top-down and bottom-up development order be applied to object-oriented software?
10. Describe three approaches to organizing programming teams. For what types of projects or development activities is each approach best suited?
11. What is a source code control system? Why is such a system necessary when multiple programmers build a program or system?
12. Briefly describe direct, parallel, and phased deployment. What are the advantages and disadvantages of each deployment approach?
13. Why are additional personnel generally required during the later stages of deployment?

THINKING CRITICALLY

1. Describe the process of testing software developed with input-process-output, top-down, and bottom-up development order. Which development order results in the fewest resources required for testing? What types of errors are likely to be discovered earliest under each development order? Which development order is best, as measured by the combination of required testing resources and ability to capture important errors early in the testing process?
2. Assume that Rocky Mountain Outfitters' customer support system will be developed as described at the end of the chapter. What sizes and types of teams are best suited to the major tasks in each iteration?
3. Assume that the RMO customer support system project is beginning in late May rather than early January. Because of the relatively short time available, only a portion of the system can be completed and deployed before the holiday shopping season. Assume further that anticipated sales volume increases are too great for the existing system to handle. Develop a plan to partition the development project into two or more production versions, with the first version released before the holiday shopping season and subsequent versions released the next year. Describe each alpha, beta, and production version and specify how production versions will be deployed.

EXPERIENTIAL EXERCISES

1. Assume that you and three of your classmates are charged with developing the first prototype to implement the RMO use case *Create new order* (see Figure 13-4). Create a development and testing plan to write and test the classes and methods. Assume that you have three weeks to complete all tasks.
2. Implement a buddy system for testing in a program or project class (be sure to first obtain permission from your instructor). Evaluate the results in terms of time required for code development and quality of the final product.
3. Talk with a computer center or IS manager about the testing process used with a recently deployed system or subsystem. What types of tests were performed? How were test cases and test data generated? What types of teams developed and implemented the tests?
4. Talk with an end user at your school or work about the training provided with a recently installed or distributed business application. What types of training were provided? Did the user consider the training to be sufficient?

Case Studies

HUDSONBANC BILLING SYSTEM UPGRADE

Two regional banks with similar geographic territories merged to form HudsonBanc. Both banks had credit card operations and operated billing systems that had been internally developed and upgraded over three decades. The systems performed similar functions, and both operated primarily in batch mode on IBM mainframes. Merging the two billing systems was identified as a high-priority cost-saving measure.

HudsonBanc initiated a project to investigate how to merge the two billing systems. Upgrading either system was quickly ruled out because the existing technology was considered old, and the costs of upgrading the system were estimated to be too high. HudsonBanc decided that a new component-based Web-oriented system should be built or purchased. Management preferred the purchase option since it was assumed that a purchased system could be brought online more quickly and cheaply. An RFP (request for proposal) was prepared, many responses were received, and after months of business modeling and requirements activities, a vendor was chosen.

Hardware for the new system was installed in early January. Software was installed the following week, and a random sample of 10 percent of the customer accounts was copied to the new system. The new system was operated in parallel with the old systems for two months. To save costs involved with complete duplication, the new system computed but did not actually print billing statements. Payments were entered into both systems and used to update parallel customer account databases. Duplicate account records were checked manually to ensure that they were the same.

After the second test billing cycle, the new system was declared ready for operation. All customer accounts were migrated to the new system in mid-April. The old systems were turned off on May 1, and the new system took over operation. Problems occurred almost immediately. The system was unable to handle the greatly increased volume of transactions. Data entry slowed to a crawl, and payments were soon backed up by several weeks. The system was not handling certain types of transactions correctly (for example, charge corrections and credits for overpayment). Manual inspection of the recently migrated account records showed errors in approximately 50,000 accounts.

It took almost six weeks to adjust the incorrect accounts manually and to update functions to handle all transaction types correctly. On June 20, the company attempted to print billing statements for the 50,000 corrected customer accounts. The system refused to print any information for transactions more than 30 days old. A panicked consultation with the vendor concluded that fixing the 30-day restriction would require more than a month of work and testing. It was also concluded that manual entry of account adjustments followed by billing within 30 days was the fastest and least risky way to solve the immediate problem.

Clearing the backlog took two months. During that time, many incorrect bills were mailed. Customer support telephone lines were continually overloaded. Twenty-five people were reassigned from other operational areas, and additional phone lines were added to provide sufficient customer support capacity. System development personnel were reassigned to IS operations for up to three months to assist in clearing the billing backlog. Federal and state regulatory authorities stepped in to investigate the problems. HudsonBanc agreed to allow customers to spread payments for late bills over three months without interest charges. Setting up the payment arrangements further aggravated the backlog and staffing problems.

[1] What type of installation did HudsonBanc use for its new system? Was it an appropriate choice?

[2] How could the operational problems have been avoided?

RETHINKING ROCKY MOUNTAIN OUTFITTERS

ROCKY MOUNTAIN OUTFITTERS

Revisit the iteration plan developed at the end of the chapter under the following revised assumptions:

- RMO has previous experience developing and deploying .NET Web-based applications.
- RMO has existing infrastructure to support .NET applications and Web services.
- The CSS system will be developed and deployed using .NET technologies.

What changes, if any, should be made to adapt the iteration plan to these assumptions?

FOCUSING ON RELIABLE PHARMACEUTICAL SERVICE

Reliable PHARMACEUTICALS Using the package diagrams and other design models that you developed in Chapter 9 for Reliable Pharmaceutical Service, develop an implementation and testing plan. Specify the order in which modules will be implemented and the groups of modules that will be tested during integration testing.

FURTHER RESOURCES

Robert V. Binder, *Testing Object-Oriented Systems: Models, Patterns, and Tools*. Addison-Wesley, 2000.

Barry Boehm, *Software Engineering Economics*. Prentice Hall, 1981.

Mark Fewster and Dorothy Graham, *Software Test Automation*. Addison-Wesley, 1999.

William Horton, *Designing and Writing Online Documentation: Hypermedia for Self-Supporting Products* (2nd ed.).John Wiley & Sons, 1994.

William Horton, *Designing Web-Based Training: How to Teach Anyone Anything Anywhere Anytime*. John Wiley & Sons, 2000.

William Horton, *Illustrating Computer Documentation: The Art of Presenting Information Graphically on Paper and Online*. John Wiley & Sons, 1991.

International Association of Information Technology Trainers (ITrain) Web site, http://itrain.org/.

David Kung, Jerry Gao, Pei Hsia, Yasufumi Toyoshima, Chris Chen, Young-Si Kim, and Young-Kee Song, "Developing an Object-Oriented Software Testing and Maintenance Environment." *Communications of the ACM*, volume 38:10 (October, 1995), pp. 75–87.

Steve McConnell, *Code Complete*. Microsoft Press, 1995.

David Yardley, *Successful IT Project Delivery*. Addison-Wesley, 2003.

chapter 14

CURRENT TRENDS IN SYSTEM DEVELOPMENT

LEARNING OBJECTIVES

After reading this chapter, you should be able to:

- Explain the Agile Development philosophy
- List and describe the features of Agile Modeling
- Compare and contrast the features of Extreme Programming and Scrum development
- Explain the importance of Model-Driven Architecture on enterprise-level development
- Describe frameworks and components, the process by which they are developed, and their impact on system development

CHAPTER OUTLINE

- Software Principles and Practices
- Adaptive Approaches to Development
- Model-Driven Architecture—Generalizing Solutions
- Frameworks and Components

VALLEY REGIONAL HOSPITAL: MEASURING A PROJECT'S PROGRESS

Claire Haskell, the vice-president of technology at Valley Regional Hospital (VRH), listened quietly to Henry Williams's progress report on the new patient records system. Henry was the project leader for a team that was developing the patient records system for VRH. Also in the meeting were the project's sponsor, Charlie Montgomery, who was the director of patient information and records, and Jason Smith, the director of software development. Months before, Jason and Henry had approached Claire and asked her to try a new development approach called *Agile Development* for this recently approved project. They had already spoken with Charlie, and he had agreed to try Agile Development. Claire had approved the project and their request to try the new approach, even though she knew very little about it.

During his presentation, Henry kept talking about how wonderfully the team worked together and how much fun they were having. Although she was glad that the team was functioning well, Claire wanted more specifics. She wanted to know whether the new system was on schedule and within budget. After about 20 minutes of patient listening, she couldn't wait any longer; she asked Henry directly to show her the schedule and to report on the team's progress. He flipped up a schedule, but that did little to help—the schedule had no familiar milestones such as analysis, design, and programming. Instead, she saw other terms: *iteration*, *user stories*, and *refactoring*.

At this point Claire really became worried. So she turned to Charlie and said pointedly, "Exactly how is the project progressing from your viewpoint?" His answer surprised her.

Charlie said, "The records administrators and I are extremely pleased with the demos we are seeing. We are also satisfied with the quality of the system we saw during our acceptance testing. From what we have seen so far, the system seems to be exactly what we need. But as far as the schedule is concerned, I'm not certain whether the entire system will be delivered on time. I think so, but I'm not involved in the day-to-day development."

Claire felt a little better. At least the system was doing what it needed to do so far. But she still wanted reassurance from the project leader. "Henry, are we going to hit the completion date? The system needs to be ready on time."

Henry responded, "We are progressing on schedule so far and everything looks fine. But no, I can't show you a traditional schedule—one with major milestones. But here is a short-term schedule for the next two months of work."

Claire wasn't satisfied. She asked Henry to stay and talk with her privately after the meeting ended. She became agitated and said, "Henry, we need more accountability for this project. The only solution I can see is to meet with you frequently to monitor its progress. I want a rough schedule for the rest of the project on my desk on Monday morning. That gives you three days to develop one. Then I want you to meet with me every Monday from here out so that we can be sure we are on track and hit the delivery date."

Although he was not pleased with Claire's suggestion, Henry reluctantly agreed.

Overview

In previous chapters, you have been introduced to many concepts and skills that are necessary to develop robust information systems to solve real business needs. You have learned so-called "soft" skills associated with managing projects, interacting in teams, gathering information, and making presentations. You have also learned "hard" skills—those associated with problem solving, building requirements models, and designing new systems. And you have learned many important concepts about projects, the Unified Process, and implementation alternatives. In short, you have developed a solid working knowledge of system development and obtained a bag of tools to get you started developing information systems for businesses and other organizations.

As you have learned through your exposure to information systems, the IS discipline is dynamic and ever changing. Many of the tools and techniques that were commonly used just a few years ago have disappeared, replaced by newer approaches. In addition, the reach of today's systems has broadened, encompassing systems that are enterprise-wide, distributed, interactive, and interconnected; that support both desktop and Internet-based computing; and that run on all types of computers and mobile devices.

These more complex system requirements have necessitated a whole new set of programming languages and tools. As part of this continual reinvention of the discipline, IS professionals are also creating and developing new techniques for building systems, that is, new methodologies to support system development.

In Chapter 2 you were introduced to predictive and adaptive development methodologies. Historically, predictive approaches have dominated the field. Today, however, many developers are inventing different, more adaptive approaches to system development. In this chapter, we introduce you to some of the newest approaches to organizing and running a system development project, both predictive and adaptive:

- We explain several radical approaches that are very adaptive in nature, including Agile Development, Extreme Programming, and Scrum. These three approaches share many ideas but also have some distinct features.
- We introduce Model-Driven Architecture (MDA), which consists of ideas for enterprise-level integration of systems. MDA is applicable to predictive approaches and the Unified Process. (Recall that we classified the Unified Process as being somewhat adaptive.)
- We present basic ideas associated with object frameworks and components. These two technologies provide additional support to increase developer productivity, speed the rate of development, and improve the quality of the final system.

But the material in this chapter is only introductory. Your interest may be piqued, and you may want to investigate one or more of these approaches in more detail. If so, you will be contributing both to your own professional development and to the advancement of the field of system development.

SOFTWARE PRINCIPLES AND PRACTICES

The last 50 years have seen tremendous advances in all areas of computing. Moore's law, which states that hardware computing power doubles approximately every 18 months, has yet to be disproved. Computing capability still continues to advance at an astounding rate. In addition, all sorts of new uses and devices for computing have been created, including cell phones with digital cameras, handheld PCs, Internet-enabled telephones, appliances with embedded computer chips, and radio frequency ID chips on products in retail stores. Large-scale systems, although not as obvious to consumers, drive many of the basic activities on which our society is based. Such activities as money transactions between banks and other financial institutions support our banking and credit card industries. Behind the scenes, supply chain management systems trigger instant production of new products based on sales and inventory levels halfway around the world. Transportation scheduling and information sharing between carriers and shippers enable people and goods to travel worldwide with minimal disruptions. Today we speak of *ubiquitous computing*, meaning that computer technology is everywhere and affects almost every aspect of our lives. Just as one set of computing and system problems is solved, an entirely new need or desire is uncovered. The quest for improved business and consumer computing solutions continues unabated. Because of these trends, the long-term outlook for information systems specialists is incredibly positive. The downside for the industry is that the effort to keep current is extremely demanding.

ubiquitous computing
the current trend of using computer technology in every aspect of our lives

So how are we able to address the multifaceted computing needs of industry and society? Obviously, no single solution or technology can satisfy all needs. Solutions come about because thousands of people are working on and solving individual problems. However, some principles and practices can advance the industry. Many come from the field of computer science, which focuses on the theories and principles of computing. Others develop from the discipline of information systems, which applies the principles of computing to everyday business problems. Of course, there is substantial overlap between these two disciplines, which can be compared to the relationship between scientists and engineers—for example, the chemists who do research and the chemical engineers who apply that research. Collaboration between people in all of the disciplines of computer science, information systems, decision sciences, and mathematics provides the fuel to propel the technology of our society forward.

Before we discuss the current trends, let's look back at this textbook for a moment. If you were asked to summarize the contents of this textbook in one or two sentences, what would you say? What are the main ideas you learned from the previous chapters in this book? We hope you would include these two points:

[1] You learned how to build models—models to capture and explain needs, requirements, and solutions. In a broad definition of a model, we would also include writing the code, which is a model of a real-world process.

[2] You learned the processes or steps necessary to build a solution—processes to both manage and conduct a system development project.

In this chapter, we also focus on those two primary areas, by describing current trends in modeling and in processes. In addition, we discuss some current tools and techniques that support these trends.

To begin, we should review five important software principles and practices before discussing the details of current trends:

- Abstraction
- Models and modeling
- Patterns
- Reuse
- Methodologies

ABSTRACTION

Abstraction is the process by which we extract and distill core principles from a set of facts or statements. You learned about this principle when you learned to identify an abstract class—one that has no instances. An abstract class serves as a repository of generalized attributes and methods from which other classes inherit. You also learned to think abstractly when you built models to define user requirements. Thinking abstractly is a difficult skill to learn. Most people learn new concepts by seeing examples—that is, concrete instances. However, as you become more sophisticated in your thinking ability, you learn to think in abstract terms.

Abstraction is important in the field of computing. Many advances in computing have been developed because computer scientists were able to think abstractly and in fact to raise the level of abstraction. For example, in the early days of computing, developers wrote systems using assembly language, which is essentially machine language. Then they thought more abstractly and invented programming languages, such as Fortran, COBOL, C, Java, and Visual Basic. To do so, they had to think in the abstract about the characteristics of computer languages and language compilers. Then, thinking about user requirements led to the invention of models and diagrams to represent those requirements. Again, the process required thinking in the abstract about the characteristics of a good model and inventing class diagrams and sequence diagrams and

metamodel
a model that describes the characteristics of another model

their properties. Today, we think more abstractly by defining metamodels. A *metamodel* is a model that describes another model. For example, could you define a class diagram that would generalize and describe the components of any class diagram? As you will see when we discuss Model-Driven Architecture, abstraction is an important idea in advancing the body of knowledge for computing and system development.

MODELS AND MODELING

The second important software principle is models and modeling. You learned what a model is early in the book, and you practiced building models throughout the course. A model is an abstraction of something in the real world, representing a particular set of properties. There are two primary reasons developers build models. First, we must understand a process or thing by identifying and explaining its key characteristics. Modeling helps us crystallize our thinking so that we are more precise. In many instances, we cannot truly understand something until we try to model it. Second, we use models to document ideas that we need to remember and to communicate those ideas to other people. You will see later in this chapter that some of the current trends focus on how to better use models in software development—by doing either more or less modeling.

PATTERNS

The third software principle—patterns—is closely associated with abstraction and modeling. A pattern is a standard solution to a given problem or a template that can be applied to a problem. As we begin to think more abstractly and build models, we recognize that problems or issues that at first seemed very different in fact have similar characteristics when viewed at a generalized level. Patterns begin to form, both in the problems and in the solutions. In Chapter 9 we presented some ideas about design patterns. We noted that different industries have standard patterns to solve recurring problems. For example, banking systems serve the fundamental purpose of recording and processing financial transactions. So, design patterns exist not only for system structure but also for entire systems. Standard design patterns are becoming widely accepted as they are identified and refined to solve problems. We will not revisit the discussion of patterns in this chapter, but you should recognize that they are a driving force in improving the quality of systems and speeding system development.

REUSE

The fourth software principle—reuse—is an outgrowth of the previous principles. Because developers have discovered patterns, they are building standard solutions and components that can be used over and over again. Through the principle of reuse, today's developers have become more productive. For example, to develop a graphical user interface for the Windows platform, nearly all developers use standard class libraries of forms, buttons, menus, drop-down boxes, text boxes, and radio buttons. If we instead had to write the code to display a button every time we put one on a screen, it would take a very long time to create a graphical system. Windows components are examples of reuse at the code level. Developers also like to think more abstractly and invent higher-level components that can be reused. Industry experts now indicate that many new systems are built primarily by integrating operating systems, communication systems, and applications into a single system. So, system developers today often work to integrate components into a complete solution. Reuse is a driving force in technologies such as Web services, CORBA, .NET, and ERP systems. We will discuss the idea of reuse in more detail when we discuss component libraries and frameworks.

METHODOLOGIES

The fifth and final principle, methodologies, was also introduced earlier in the book. By methodology, we mean a process—including the rules, guidelines, and techniques—that defines how systems are built. A methodology describes the process of developing a system. Over the years, system developers have experimented with many different methodologies. In Chapter 2, we explained that those methodologies can be categorized as either predictive or adaptive. We now discuss three adaptive approaches to systems development:

- Agile Development
- Extreme Programming
- Scrum

In her routine report to John Blankens concerning Rocky Mountain Outfitters' customer support system, Barbara Halifax recapped her team's basic approach to system development—one based on the adaptive Unified Process—and its progress (see Barbara's memo).

ROCKY MOUNTAIN OUTFITTERS
MEMO

August 4, 2006

To: John Blankens

From: Barbara Halifax

RE: Update on programming and testing

I wanted to give you an update on our programming and testing efforts and the effectiveness of the rapid application development techniques we're using. We're currently a bit ahead of schedule on our programming and testing. Approximately 40% of the code has been developed and unit tested. Integration testing on the first major system is in progress, and the problems we've discovered thus far are all minor.

As you remember, before starting the CSS project, we decided to utilize the Unified Process but also incorporate some techniques from the Agile Development and Extreme Programming methodologies. We developed a project schedule, but we have adapted it several times between iterations based on what we learned during an iteration. Pair programming, in particular, has been a boon to productivity. Everyone on the project is amazed at how quickly code is being developed and how few errors are being discovered during integration testing.

Purchasing components for credit authorization and shipment preparation has also saved us considerable time. Searching for those components, designing around their infrastructure needs, and testing them did add a few weeks. But that investment has been repaid severalfold by not having to write code to perform those functions. We shortened the entire project by a month or more, and I expect similar benefits during future upgrades of the system.

I know it's a bit early to talk about life after this project, but I think that we should consider conducting a postmortem analysis as soon as the project is completed. Perhaps we could start right after the New Year holiday. We could learn a lot by examining the successes and failures of this project and deciding what tools and techniques should be incorporated into future projects.

BH

ADAPTIVE APPROACHES TO DEVELOPMENT

Adaptive approaches to system development allow for uncertainty. In development projects that focus on entirely new applications, many times the user's requirements are not well understood and cannot be described in detail. Since the scope of a new system may not be well defined, it is difficult, if not impossible, for analysts to create a detailed project plan. The best way to carry out a system development project in this situation is to identify core objectives early and to develop detailed work plans as the project progresses.

Two forces drive the increased interest in adaptive development. First, as you learned in Chapter 3, the low success rate of system development projects has always been troubling. Developing software is difficult, and success has always been elusive. In Chapter 3 we discussed the importance of good project management skills to improve processes and increase the chance of success. In addition, industry experts and developers have been inventing various adaptive development approaches to improve success rates.

The other force behind adaptive approaches is the volatility of today's business climate. Yesterday's more stable environment relied mainly on controlling costs and on tight management of internal procedures. In contrast, business success today depends on flexibility and rapid response to changes in the marketplace. Hence, a rigid system development process that defines system requirements 12, 24, or more months in advance is not necessarily flexible enough to meet the accelerated pace of change. But the newer, adaptive approaches allow for critical changes in business needs.

From a theoretical viewpoint, the development of any item, either a physical item or a software item, is completed by following a process. Every process needs controls to ensure that it stays on track. Process controls can be categorized into two types: predictive and empirical. Predictive controls define the steps to monitor a process in great detail. If a process gets off track, then more detailed steps (for example, a work breakdown structure) and descriptions are required to control it. Predictive control works well when more planning can provide more detail. However, for processes that are unpredictable, adding more detail and more controls only exacerbates the problem; trying to control the uncontrollable results in further loss of money and time.

Empirical controls, in contrast, describe processes that are variable and unpredictable. These processes are best controlled by handling each variation as it occurs and determining the best way to correct the deviation. In other words, empirical controls monitor progress and then make corrections on the fly, based on the specific situation. Since many software development projects contain a high amount of uncertainty, an empirical process may be a better choice.

Adaptive or empirical approaches all have their own set of rules and guidelines. However, they do share a few characteristics:

- Less emphasis on up-front analysis, design, and documentation
- More focus on incremental development
- More user involvement in project teams
- Reduced detailed planning, which is used for near-term work phases only; downstream phases may have high-level plans
- Tightly controlling schedules by fitting work into discrete time boxes
- More use of small work teams that are self-organizing

First, the team does not spend a lot of time analyzing, designing, and documenting because these activities are means to an end; they are simply tools for writing executable code. Second, the only way to develop code quickly is to do it in small chunks and to develop the system incrementally. Third, developing code quickly requires the user to be completely involved with the project team—to become part of the project team and work side by side with the developers in creating the solution so that it fits the business needs.

Reducing detailed planning and scheduling the work to fit in time boxes help control the team's progress. Each iteration defines a specific function that will be added to the system, and the function is small enough so that a meaningful detailed schedule can be developed. Then the team completes the work in the time allotted. As developers become more experienced, they become proficient at knowing what can be done in a small time box of three or four weeks.

Consistent with time boxing, under adaptive approaches, each team develops its own schedule for each iteration and organizes itself and its work productively. The only external schedules that are imposed on the work are those that require coordination with other projects or deliverables.

Let's look now at one specific approach that provides a foundation for adaptive software development: Agile Development. Later we explore Extreme Programming and Scrum, two specific methodologies that implement an agile philosophy.

THE AGILE DEVELOPMENT PHILOSOPHY AND AGILE MODELING

The high volatility of the marketplace has forced businesses to respond rapidly to new opportunities. Sometimes new opportunities appear in the middle of implementing another business initiative. To survive, businesses must be agile. Agility—being able to change directions rapidly, even in the middle of a project—is the keystone of Agile Development. Agile Development is a philosophy and set of guidelines for developing software in an unknown, rapidly changing environment. It provides an overarching philosophy for specific development approaches such as the Unified Process. The amount of agility in each approach can vary. For example, we identified the UP as being somewhat adaptive. Some UP projects may adopt many agile philosophies, and others may use them less.

Related to Agile Development, Agile Modeling is a philosophy about how to build models, some of which are formal and detailed and others sketchy and minimal. Figure 14-1 illustrates the relationships among an Agile Development philosophy, specific adaptive approaches, and Agile Modeling.

FIGURE 14-1
Adaptive methodologies using Agile Modeling

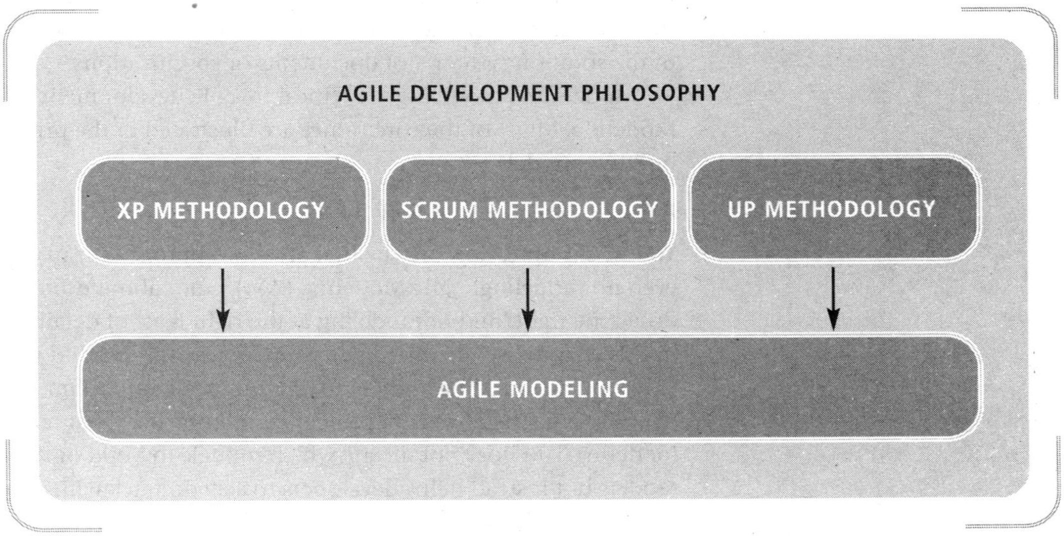

AGILE DEVELOPMENT PHILOSOPHY AND VALUES

The "Manifesto for Agile Software Development" (see the "Further Resources" section) identifies four basic values, which represent the core philosophy of the agile movement. The four values emphasize

- Responding to change over following a plan
- Individuals and interactions over processes and tools
- Working software over comprehensive documentation
- Customer collaboration over contract negotiation

Each of the phrases in the list prioritizes the value on the left over the value on the right. The people involved in system development, whether as team members, users, or other stakeholders, all need to accept these priorities for a project to be truly agile. Adopting an agile approach is not always easy.

chaordic
a term used to describe adaptive projects, which are both chaotic and ordered

Some industry leaders in the agile movement coined the term *chaordic* to describe an agile project. *Chaordic* comes from two words, *chaos* and *order*. The first two values in our list—responding to change over following a plan and individuals and interactions over processes and tools—do seem to be a recipe for chaos. But they recognize that software projects inherently have many unknowns and unpredictable elements, and hence a certain amount of chaos. Developers need to accept the chaos but also need to use the specific methodologies discussed later to organize and impose order on this chaos to move the project ahead.

Managers and executive stakeholders frequently struggle to accept this point of view, often wanting to impose more controls on development teams and to enforce detailed plans and schedules. However, the agile philosophy takes the opposite approach, providing more flexibility in project schedules and letting the project teams plan and execute their work as the project progresses.

Another important value is that customers must continually be involved with the project team. They do not sit down with the project team for a few sessions to develop the specifications and then go their separate ways. Instead, customers collaborate with and become part of the technical team. Since working software is being developed throughout the project, customers are continually involved in defining requirements and testing components.

Contracts also take on an entirely different flavor. Fixed prices and fixed deliverables do not make sense. Contracts take more of a collaborative tack but include options for the customer to cancel if the project is not progressing, as measured by the incremental deliverables. Incremental deliverables in agile projects are working pieces of the solution system, not documents or specifications.

Models and modeling are critical to agile development, so we look next at Agile Modeling. Many of the core values are illustrated in the principles and practices of building models.

AGILE MODELING PRINCIPLES

Your first impression may be that an agile approach means less modeling, or maybe even no modeling. Agile Modeling (AM) is not about doing less modeling but about doing the right kind of modeling at the right level of detail for the right purposes. Early in this chapter we identified two primary reasons to build models: (1) to understand what you are building and (2) to communicate important aspects of the solution system. AM consists of a set of principles and practices that reinforce these two reasons for modeling. AM does not dictate which models to build or how formal to make those models but instead helps developers to stay on track with their models—by using them as a means to an end instead of building models as end deliverables. AM's basic principles express the attitude that developers should have as they develop software. Figure 14-2 summarizes Agile Modeling principles. We discuss those principles next.

FIGURE 14-2
Agile Modeling principles

Agile Modeling Principles

- Develop software as your primary goal.
- Enable the next effort as your secondary goal.
- Minimize your modeling activity—few and simple.
- Embrace change, and change incrementally.
- Model with a purpose.
- Build multiple models.
- Build high-quality models and get feedback rapidly.
- Focus on content rather than representation.
- Learn from each other with open communication.
- Know your models and how to use them.
- Adapt to specific project needs.

Develop software as your primary goal The primary goal of a software development project is always to produce high-quality software. The primary measurement of progress is working software, not intermediate models of system requirements or specifications. Modeling is always a means to an end, not the end itself. Any activity that does not directly contribute to the end goal of producing software should be questioned and avoided if it cannot be justified.

Enable the next effort as your secondary goal Focusing only on working software can also be self-defeating, so developers must consider two important objectives. First, requirements models may be necessary to develop design models. So do not think that if the model cannot be used to write code it is unnecessary. Sometimes several intermediate steps are needed before the final code can be written. Second, although high-quality software is the primary goal, long-term use of that code is also important. So, some models may be necessary to support maintenance and enhancement of the system. Yes, the code is the best documentation, but some architectural design decisions may not be easily identified from the code. Look carefully at what other artifacts may be necessary to produce high-quality systems in the long term.

Minimize your modeling activity—few and simple Create only the models that are necessary. Do just enough to get by. This principle is not a justification for sloppy work or inadequate analysis. The models you create should be clear, correct, and complete. But do not create unnecessary models. Also, keep each model as simple as possible. Normally the simplest solution is the best solution. Elaborate solutions tend to be difficult to understand and maintain. However, we emphasize again that simplicity is not justification for being incomplete.

Embrace change and change incrementally Since the underlying philosophy of Agile Modeling is that developers must be flexible and respond quickly to change, a good agile developer willingly accepts—and even embraces—change. Change is seen as the norm, not the exception. Watch for change and have procedures ready to integrate changes into the models. The best way to accept change is to develop incrementally. Take small steps and address problems in small bites. Change your model incrementally, and then validate it to make sure it is correct. Do not try to accomplish everything in one big release.

Model with a purpose We indicated earlier that the two reasons to build models are to understand what you are building and to communicate important aspects of the solution system. Make sure that your modeling efforts support those reasons. Sometimes developers try to justify building certain models by claiming that (1) the development methodology mandates the development of the model, (2) someone wants a model, even though the person does not know why it is important, or (3) a model can replace a face-to-face discussion of issues. Always identify a reason and an audience for each model you develop. Then develop the model in sufficient detail to satisfy the reason and the audience. Incidentally, the audience may be you.

Build multiple models UML, along with other modeling methodologies, has several models to represent different aspects of the problem at hand. To be successful—in understanding or communication—you will need to model various aspects of the required solution. Don't develop all of them; be sure to minimize your modeling, but develop enough models to make sure you have addressed all the issues.

Build high-quality models and get feedback rapidly Nobody likes sloppy work. It is based on faulty thinking and introduces errors. One way to avoid error in models is to get feedback rapidly, while the work is still fresh. Feedback comes from users as well as technical team members.

Focus on content rather than representation Sometimes a project team has access to a sophisticated CASE tool. CASE tools can be helpful, but at times they are distracting because developers spend time making the diagrams pretty. Be judicious in the use of tools. Some models need to be well drawn for communication or contracts or even to handle expected changes and updates. In other cases, a hand-drawn diagram may suffice.

Learn from each other with open communication All of the adaptive approaches emphasize working in teams. Do not be defensive about your models. Other team members have good suggestions. You can never truly master every aspect of a problem or its models. Others will have helpful insights and different ways to view a problem and identify a solution.

Know your models and how to use them Being an agile modeler does not mean that you are not skilled. If anything, you must be *more* skilled to know the strengths and weaknesses of the models, including how and when to use them. An expert modeler applies the previous principles of simplicity, quality, and development of multiple models.

Adapt to specific project needs Every project is different because it exists in a unique environment; involves different users, stakeholders, and team members; and requires a different development environment and deployment platform. Adapt your models and modeling techniques to fit the needs of the business and the project. Sometimes models can be informal and simple. For other projects, more formal, complicated models may be required. An agile modeler is able to adapt to each project.

AGILE MODELING PRACTICES

The following practices support the AM principles just expressed. The heart of AM is in its practices, which give the practitioner specific modeling techniques. Figure 14-3 summarizes the Agile Modeling practices. We discuss each of the practices next.

Iterative and incremental modeling Remember that modeling is a support activity, not the end result of software development. As a developer, you should develop small models frequently to help you understand or solve a problem. New developers sometimes have difficulty deciding which models to select. You should continue to learn about models and expand your repertoire. UML has a large set of models that cover a lot of analysis and design territory. However, they are not the only models you might find useful. Many developers still use data flow diagrams and decomposition

Agile Modeling Practices

- Iterative and incremental modeling
  - Use the right models.
  - Create several models in parallel.
  - Iterate frequently.
  - Model in small increments.
- Teamwork
  - Model with others.
  - Involve users and other stakeholders.
  - Share ownership of the models.
  - Display the models publicly.
- Simplicity
  - Create simple content.
  - Depict the models simply.
  - Use simple tools.
- Validation
  - Prove it with code.
- Documentation
  - Discard temporary models.
  - Formalize contract models.
  - Update only when it hurts.
- Motivation
  - Model to communicate.
  - Model to understand.

FIGURE 14-3
Agile Modeling practices

diagrams from the traditional structured approach. The point is that models are a tool, and as a professional, you should have a large set of tools.

Teamwork As shown in Figure 14-1, AM supports various development methodologies. One of the tenets in all of these methodologies is that developers work together in small teams of two to four members. In addition, users should be integrally involved in modeling exercises. For example, say the task at hand is to understand how a purchase order is created and processed. Good AM practice says to get the right players together, including team members and users, and develop a detailed model of the process, possibly on a whiteboard. Other teams could then take a digital photograph of the whiteboard and post it in a repository on the project's network server. The model then becomes public; no one owns it, and all can access it. If it later needs to be corrected, it can be annotated with software and reposted. An alternative method, especially if the model will become a permanent document, is to develop the model using a drawing tool such as Visio with a laptop and a projector. This process is not quite as flexible as a whiteboard, but it yields a more permanent figure. In any case, the model is again posted for all to use, review, and update.

Simplicity The previous purchase order example illustrated an approach that is simple and easy to support. Also, developers should create a set of models to help them understand or solve a narrow problem. In the purchase order example, the model focused on one business process or use case. In the first iteration, developers should only focus on the typical process, one without all of the possible variations. Then later iterations can add exception conditions, security and control requirements, and other details.

Validation Between modeling sessions, the team can begin to write code for the solutions already conceived so that they can validate the models. Simplicity supports frequent validation. Do not create too many or complex models until the simple ones have been validated with code.

Documentation Many models are temporary working documents that are developed to solve a particular problem. These models quickly become obsolete as the code evolves and improves. Do not try to keep them up to date. Discard them. If they were posted to a repository, date them so that everyone knows they show a history of decisions and progress but are not now in sync with the code. Updating only when it hurts is a guideline that tells us not to waste time trying to keep temporary models synchronized. During the first iteration, when many models are developed concurrently, they should be consistent. However, as development progresses, some models will become working documents that no longer relate well to other models. Remember that the objective of the project is to develop software, not to have a set of pretty models. Only update when it hurts—that is, when the project team can't work effectively without the information.

Motivation Remember the basic objectives of modeling. Only build a model if it helps you understand a process or solve a problem, or if you need to record and communicate something. For example, the team members in a design session may make some design decisions. To communicate these decisions, the team posts a simple model to make it public. The model can be a very effective tool to document the decisions and ensure that all have a common understanding and reference point. Again, a model is simply used as a tool for communication, not as an end in itself.

Now that we have explored the basic philosophy, principles, and practices underlying Agile Development, we turn to two methodologies that employ agile concepts: Extreme Programming and Scrum.

EXTREME PROGRAMMING

Extreme Programming (XP) is an adaptive, agile development methodology that was created in the mid-1990s. The word *extreme* sometimes makes people think that it is completely new and that developers who embrace XP are radicals. However, XP is really an attempt to take the best practices of software development and extend them "to the extreme." Extreme programming—

- Takes proven industry best practices and focuses on them intensely
- Combines those best practices (in their intense form) in a new way to produce a result that is greater than the sum of the parts

Figure 14-4 lists the core values and practices of XP. In the following sections we first present the four core values of XP. Then we explain its 12 primary practices. Finally, we describe the basic structure of an XP project and the way XP is used to develop software.

XP CORE VALUES

The four core values of XP—communication, simplicity, feedback, and courage—drive its practices and project activities. You will recognize the first three as best practices for any development project. With a little thought, you should also see that the fourth is a desired value for any project, even though it may not be stated explicitly.

Communication One of the major causes of project failure has been a lack of open communication with the right players at the right time and at the right level. Effective communication involves not only documentation but also open verbal discussion. The practices and methods of XP are designed to ensure that open, frequent communication occurs.

FIGURE 14-4
XP core values and practices

XP Core Values	XP Practices
• Communication • Simplicity • Feedback • Courage	• Planning • Testing • Pair programming • Simple designs • Refactoring the code • Owning the code collectively • Continuous integration • On-site customer • System metaphor • Small releases • Forty-hour week • Coding standards

Simplicity Even though developers have always advocated keeping solutions simple, they do not always follow their own advice. XP includes techniques to reinforce this principle and make it a standard way of developing systems.

Feedback As with simplicity, getting frequent, meaningful feedback is recognized as a best practice of software development. Feedback on functionality and requirements should come from the users, feedback on designs and code should come from other developers, and feedback on satisfying a business need should come from the client. XP integrates feedback into every aspect of development.

Courage Developers always need courage to face the harsh choice of doing things right or throwing away bad code and starting over. But all too frequently they have not had the courage to stand up to a too-tight schedule, resulting in bad mistakes. XP practices are designed to make it easier to give developers the courage to "do it right."

XP PRACTICES

XP's 12 practices embody the basic values just presented. These practices are consistent with the agile principles explained earlier in the chapter.

Planning Some people describe XP as glorified hacking or as the old "code and fix" methodology that was used in the 1960s. That is not true; XP does include planning. However, XP is an adaptive technique that recognizes that you cannot know everything at the start. As indicated earlier, XP embraces change. XP planning focuses on making a rough plan quickly and then refining it as things become clearer. This reflects the Agile Development philosophy that change is more important than detailed plans. It is also consistent with the idea that individuals—and their abilities—are more important than an elaborate process.

The basis of an XP plan is a set of stories that users develop. A story simply describes what the system needs to do. XP does not use the term *use case*, but a user story and a use case express a similar idea. Planning involves two aspects, business issues and technical issues. In XP the business issues are decided by the users and clients, while technical issues are decided by the development team. The plan, especially in the early stages of the project, consists of the list of stories—from the users—and the estimates of effort, risk, and work dependencies for each story—from the development team. As in Agile Development, the idea is to involve the users heavily in the project, rather than requiring them simply to sign off on specifications.

Testing Every new piece of software requires testing, and every methodology includes testing. XP intensifies testing by requiring that the tests for each story be written first—before the solution is programmed. There are two major types of tests: unit tests, which test the correctness of a small piece of code, and acceptance tests, which test the business function. The developers write the unit tests, and the users write the acceptance tests. Before any code can be integrated into the library of the growing system, it must pass the tests. By having the tests written first, XP automates their use and executes them frequently. Over time, a library of required tests is created, so when requirements change and the code needs to be updated, the tests can be rerun quickly and automatically.

Pair programming This practice, more than any other, is one for which XP is famous. Instead of simply requiring one programmer to watch another's work, *pair programming* divides up the coding work. First, one programmer may focus more on design and double-checking the algorithms while the other writes the code. Then they switch roles so that both think about design, coding, and testing. XP relies on comprehensive and continual code reviews. Interestingly, research has shown that pair programming is actually more efficient than programming alone. It takes longer to write the initial code, but the long-term quality is higher. Errors are caught quickly and early, two people become familiar with every part of the system, all design decisions are developed by two brains, and fewer "quick and dirty" shortcuts are taken. The quality of the code is always higher in a pair-programming environment.

pair programming
XP practice in which two programmers work together on designing, coding, and testing

Simple designs Opponents say that XP neglects design, but that is not true. XP conforms to the principles of Agile Modeling expressed earlier by eschewing the "Big Design Up Front" approach. Design is so important that it should be done continually, but in small chunks. As with everything else, the design must be verified immediately by reviewing it along with coding and testing.

So what is a simple design? It is one that accomplishes the desired result with as few classes and methods as possible and that does not duplicate code. Accomplishing all that is often a major challenge.

Refactoring the code *Refactoring* is the technique of improving the code without changing what it does. XP programmers continually refactor their code. Before and after adding any new functions, XP programmers review their code to see whether there is a simpler design or a simpler method of achieving the same result. Refactoring produces high-quality, robust code.

refactoring
revising, reorganizing, and rebuilding part of a system so that it is of higher quality

Owning the code collectively This practice requires all team members to have a new mindset. In XP, everyone is responsible for the code. No one person can say, "This is my code." Someone can say, "I wrote it," but everyone owns it. Collective ownership allows anyone to modify any piece of code. However, since unit tests are run before and after every change, if programmers see something that needs fixing, they can run the unit tests to make sure that the change did not break something. This practice embodies the team concept that developers are building a system together.

Continuous integration This practice embodies XP's idea of "growing" the software. Small pieces of code—which have passed the unit tests—are integrated into the system daily or even more often. Continuous integration highlights errors rapidly and keeps the project moving ahead. The traditional approach of integrating large chunks of code late in the project often resulted in tremendous amounts of rework and time lost while developers tried to determine just what went wrong. XP's practice of continuous integration prevents that.

On-site customer As with all adaptive approaches, XP projects require continual involvement of users who can make business decisions about functionality and scope. Based on the core value of communication, this practice keeps the project moving ahead rapidly. If the customer is not ready to commit resources to the project, then the project will not be very successful.

System metaphor This practice is XP's unique and interesting approach to defining an architectural vision. It answers the questions, "How does the system work? What are its major components?" To answer those questions, developers identify a metaphor for the system. For example, Big Three automaker Chrysler's payroll system was built as a production-line metaphor, with its system components using production-line terms. Everyone at Chrysler understands a production line, so a payroll transaction was treated the same way—developers started with a basic transaction and then applied various processes to complete it. Of course, the metaphor should be easily understood or well known to the members of the development team. A system metaphor can guide members toward a vision and help them understand the system.

Small releases A release is a point at which the new system can be turned over to users for acceptance testing, and sometimes even for productive use. Consistent with the entire philosophy of growing the software, small and frequent releases provide upgraded solutions to the users and keep them involved in the project. They also facilitate other practices, such as immediate feedback and continual integration.

Forty-hour week and coding standards These final two practices set the tone for how the developers should work. The exact number of hours a developer works is not the issue. The issue is that the project should not be a death march that burns out every member of the team. Neither is the project a haphazard coding exercise. Developers should follow standards for coding and documentation. XP uses just the engineering principles that are appropriate for an adaptive process based on empirical controls.

XP PROJECT ACTIVITIES

Figure 14-5 shows an overview of the XP system development approach. The XP development approach is divided into three levels—system (the outer ring), release (the middle ring), and iteration (the inner ring). System-level activities occur once during each development project. A system is delivered to users in multiple stages called *releases*. Each release is a fully functional system that performs a subset of the full system requirements. A release is developed and tested within a period of no more than a few weeks or months. The next level (middle) cycles multiple times—once for each release. Releases are divided into multiple iterations. During each iteration, developers code and test a specific functional subset of a release. Iterations are coded and tested in a few days or weeks. There are multiple iterations within each release, so the iteration ring (inner) cycles multiple times.

The first XP development activity is creating user stories, which are similar to use cases in OO analysis. A team of developers and users quickly documents all of the user stories that the system will support. Developers then create a class diagram to represent objects of interest within the user stories.

Developers and users then create a set of acceptance tests for each user story. Releases that pass the acceptance tests are considered finished. The final system-level activity is to create a development plan for a series of releases. The first release supports a subset of the user stories, and subsequent releases add support for additional stories. Each release is delivered to users and performs real work, thus providing an additional level of testing and feedback.

The first release-level activity is planning a series of iterations. Each iteration focuses on a small (possibly just one) system function or user story. The iterations' small size allows developers to code and test them within a few days. A typical release is developed using a few to a few dozen iterations.

Once the iteration plan is complete, work begins on the first iteration-level activity. Code units are divided among multiple programming teams, and each team develops

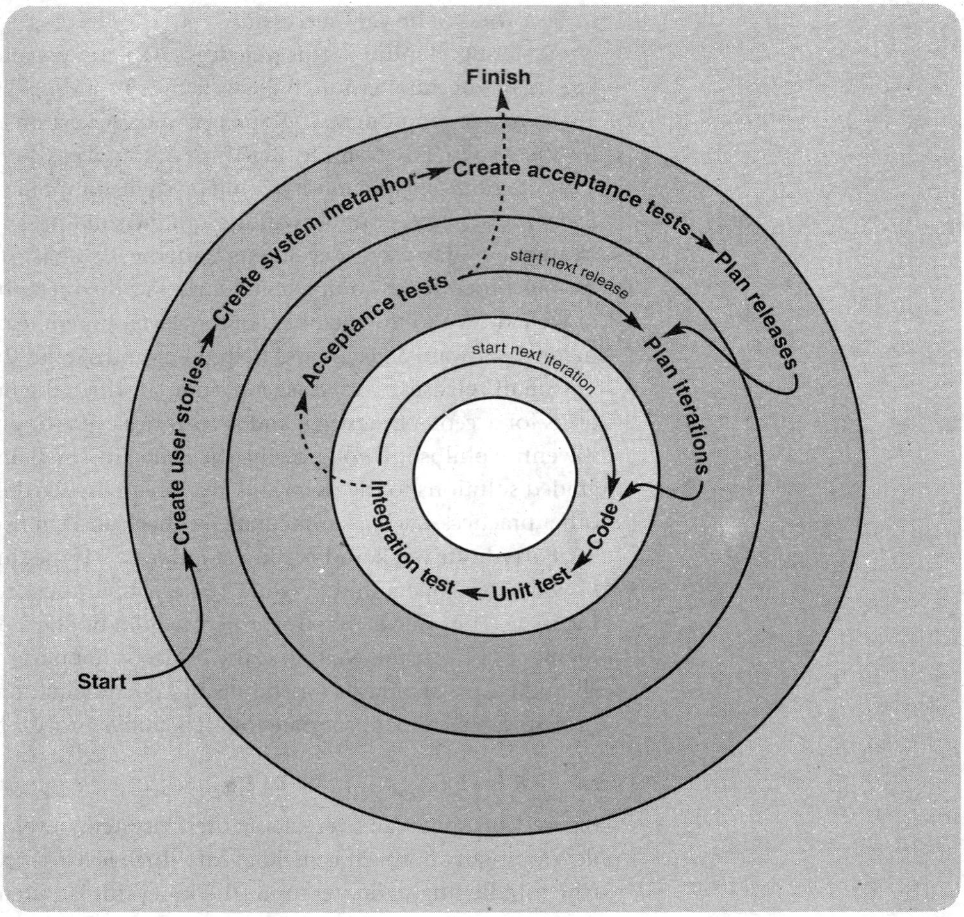

FIGURE 14-5
The XP development approach

and tests its own code. XP recommends a test-first approach to coding. Test code is written before system code. As code modules pass unit testing, they are combined into larger units for integration testing. When an iteration passes integration testing, work begins on the next iteration.

When all iterations of a release have been completed, the release undergoes acceptance testing. If a release fails acceptance testing, the team returns it to the iteration level for repair. Releases that pass acceptance testing are delivered to end users, and work begins on the next release. When acceptance testing of the final release is completed, the development project is finished.

SCRUM

Scrum is another adaptive development methodology. The term refers to rugby's system for getting an out-of-play ball back into play. Rugby players get together in a big mass, the referee drops the ball, and then the scrum participants pass the ball backward through their legs to a waiting runner. The name stuck due to many similarities between the sport and the system development approach: both are quick, adaptive, and self-organizing. The basic idea behind Scrum is to respond to a current situation as rapidly and positively as possible. Scrum can be described as a truly empirical process control approach to developing software. The Scrum software development process is shown in Figure 14-6. There are three important concepts that describe Scrum: (1) its philosophy, (2) its organization, and (3) its practices.

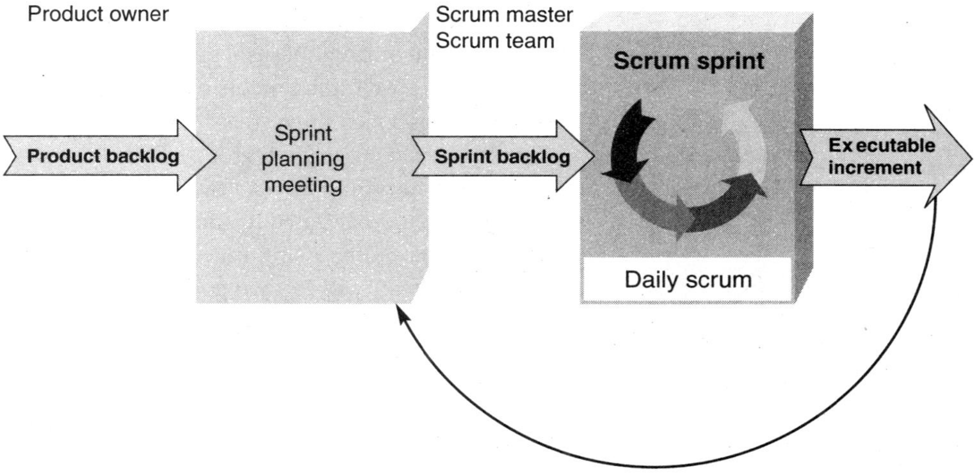

FIGURE 14-6
Scrum software development process

SCRUM PHILOSOPHY

The Scrum philosophy is based on the Agile Development principles described earlier. Scrum is responsive to a highly changing, dynamic environment in which users may not know exactly what is needed and may also change priorities frequently. In this type of environment, changes are so numerous that projects can bog down and never reach completion. Scrum excels in this type of situation.

Scrum focuses primarily on the team level. It is a type of social engineering that emphasizes individuals more than processes and describes how teams of developers can work together to build software in a series of short miniprojects. Key to this philosophy is the complete control a team exerts over its own organization and its work processes. Software is developed incrementally, and controls are imposed empirically—by focusing on the things that can be accomplished.

product backlog
a prioritized list of user requirements used to choose work to be done during a Scrum project

The basic control mechanism for a Scrum project is a list of all the things the system should include and address. This list, called the *product backlog*, includes user functions (such as use cases), features (such as security), and technology (such as platforms). The product backlog list is continually being prioritized, and only a few of the high-priority items are worked on at a time, according to the current needs of the project and its sponsor.

SCRUM ORGANIZATION

The three main organizational elements that affect a Scrum project are the product owner, the Scrum master, and the Scrum team or teams.

product owner
the client stakeholder for whom a system is being built

The *product owner* is the client, that is, the one who is buying the result, but the product owner has additional responsibilities. Remember that in Agile Development the user and client are closely involved in the project. In Scrum, the product owner maintains the product backlog list. For any function to be included in the final system, it must first be placed on the product backlog. Since the product owner maintains that list, any request must first be approved and agreed to by the product owner. In traditional development projects, the project team initiates the interviews and other activities to identify and define requirements. In a Scrum project, the primary client controls the requirements. This forces the client and user to be intimately involved in the project. Nothing can be accomplished until the product owner creates the backlog.

Scrum master
the person in charge of a Scrum project, similar to a project manager

The *Scrum master* enforces Scrum practices and helps the team complete its work. A Scrum master is comparable to a project manager in other approaches. However, since the team is self-organizing and there is no overall project schedule, the Scrum master's duties are slightly different. He or she is the focal point for communication and progress reporting, just as in a traditional project. But the Scrum master does not set the schedule or assign tasks. The team does. One of the primary duties of the Scrum master is to remove impediments so that the team can do its work. In other words, the Scrum master is a facilitator.

Scrum team
the team members working on a Scrum project

The *Scrum team* is a small group of developers, typically five to nine people, who work together to produce the software. For projects that are very large, the work should be partitioned and delegated to smaller teams. If necessary, the Scrum masters from all the teams can coordinate multiple team activities.

The Scrum team sets its own goal for what it can accomplish in a specific period of time. It then organizes itself and parcels out the work to members. In a small team it is much easier to sit around a table, decide what needs to be done, and have members of the team volunteer or accept pieces of work.

SCRUM PRACTICES

The Scrum practices are the mechanics of how a project progresses. Of course, the practices are based on the Scrum philosophy and organization. The basic work process is called a *sprint*, and all other practices are focused on supporting a sprint.

sprint
a time-controlled miniproject that implements a specific portion of a system

A Scrum *sprint* is a firm 30-day time box, with a specific goal or deliverable. At the beginning of a sprint, the team gathers for a one-day planning session. In this session, the team decides on the major goal for the sprint. The goal draws from several items on the prioritized product backlog list. The team decides how many of the highest-priority items it can accomplish within the 30-day sprint. Sometimes lower-priority items can be included for very little additional effort and may be added to the deliverables for the sprint.

Once the team has agreed on a goal and has selected items from the backlog list, it begins work. The scope of that sprint is then frozen, and no one may change it—neither the product owner nor any other users. If users do find new functions they want to add, they put them on the product backlog list for the next sprint. If team members determine that they cannot accomplish everything in their goal, they can reduce the scope for that sprint. However, the 30-day period is kept constant.

Every day during the sprint, the Scrum master holds a daily Scrum, which is a meeting of all members of the team. The objective is to report progress. The meeting is limited to 15 minutes or some other short time period. Members of the team answer only three questions:

- What have you done since the last daily Scrum (last 24 hours)?
- What will you do by the next daily Scrum?
- What got in your way, or is in your way, preventing you from completing your work?

The purpose of this meeting is simply to report issues, not to solve them. Individual team members collaborate and resolve problems after the meeting as part of the normal workday. One of the major responsibilities of the Scrum master is to note the impediments and see that they are removed. A good Scrum master clears impediments rapidly. The Scrum master also protects the team from any intrusions. The team members are then free to accomplish their work. Team members do talk with users to obtain requirements, and users are involved in the sprint's work. However, users cannot change the items being worked on from the backlog list or change the intended scope of any item without putting it on the backlog list.

At the end of each sprint, the agreed-upon deliverable is produced. A final half-day review meeting is scheduled to recap progress and identify changes that need to be made for following sprints. By time boxing these activities—the planning, the sprint, the daily Scrum, and the Scrum review—the process becomes a well-defined template to which the team easily conforms, which contributes to the success of Scrum projects.

PROJECT MANAGEMENT AND ADAPTIVE METHODOLOGIES

As indicated in the Valley Regional Hospital case at the beginning of the chapter, the adaptive approach to system development can sometimes frustrate executives who are accustomed to having a complete schedule at the start of a project and tracking the progress against this schedule. But in the adaptive approach, developers create the schedule as the project progresses. This can seem chaotic and uncontrolled to those who are not used to it. In fact, some may think that advocates of adaptive development are throwing project management out the window. Project management is an integral part of adaptive approaches, however. Those methodologies face the same scrutiny as any other traditional software development approach.

In Chapter 3 we identified several criteria of successful projects. Included on the list were the following:

- Clear system requirement definitions
- Substantial user involvement
- Support from upper management
- Thorough and detailed project plans
- Realistic work schedules and milestones

Let's review the eight primary areas in the project management body of knowledge to see how project management changes for adaptive projects.

Project time management is radically changed in the adaptive approach. Since projects operate under uncertain conditions, the project team does not attempt to make a complete, detailed project schedule. However, as we saw, time and the schedule are managed in different ways. First, in some approaches such as Scrum, each cycle must conform to a firm time box. In other approaches such as XP or the UP, the length of iterations is more flexible, but each has its own schedule. In fact, the schedule can be very detailed and is usually more accurate because of the smaller scope and focused nature of each iteration. So, time management is still an important skill for a project manager using adaptive approaches. One key success element, that of realistic work schedules, is much more evident in adaptive projects than in purely predictive approaches.

Project scope management is also radically altered. With predictive development, one of the project manager's primary responsibilities is to control the project scope. The most difficult tasks of the project manager are ensuring that the requirements are correct, seeing that the users are involved, and preventing the scope from growing uncontrollably. In contrast to this control-from-the-top viewpoint, adaptive development makes the users or clients part of the team and gives them responsibility for the scope. The backlog list in Scrum is the responsibility of the client. The scope of an iteration, or sprint, is not allowed to change. The scope of the project can only change through a very controlled mechanism, which includes the approval of the client. One potential problem with this approach, however, is that project iterations could just go on forever. So, scope control for adaptive projects consists of controlling the iterations. For a UP project, the elaboration iterations would be stopped, and the team would move on to implementation, testing, and deployment. Scope control is still necessary; it just takes a different form.

Time and scope are always interdependent. Changes in scope influence the schedule and time required to complete project deliverables. Monitoring and control are still critical to a successful project. Within an XP iteration or a Scrum sprint, monitoring and control techniques are still needed to keep the project on schedule. If the team is self-organizing, as in the Scrum approach, then the members need to establish project management tasks. Deliverables and time frames are still required. So, the project can still include metrics to measure progress and predict completion dates.

Project cost management is still important in adaptive approaches. Total project costs may be harder to predict, since the complete project schedule is unknown. Executives will feel uneasy about the lack of both an overall project schedule and a total budget, so the team will need to reassure them by emphasizing iteration control and scope control.

Project communication management is critical in adaptive approaches because users are heavily involved in all aspects of the project. Since requirements are identified, defined, implemented, and tested in short iterations, the success factors associated with defining requirements and eliciting user support are emphasized. Open verbal communication and collaborative work are the primary tools for defining the business need. Communication throughout the entire team is a must for adaptive projects.

Project quality management is a continual focus of adaptive projects, and in fact, more tools are provided to the project manager and the team to ensure a high-quality system. Two major techniques are available. First, testing is conducted throughout the project—from writing test plans first to continual checks and integration. Second, time is allocated to refactor the system as it is built, so the resulting code is simple and solid. The project manager needs to ensure that adequate time is scheduled in each iteration for these important activities.

Project risk management is also enhanced in adaptive approaches. Early iterations should address the high-risk aspects of the system. As a result, the project team and client find out early in the project whether there are insurmountable obstacles that could seriously undermine the project's success.

Project human resource management is as challenging in adaptive approaches as in any project. Good project management in both predictive and adaptive approaches emphasizes small teams that are self-managed. The major difference is that the adaptive techniques have a built-in mechanism for teams to organize themselves for each iteration or sprint. So project managers are less tempted to take control in adaptive approaches.

Project procurement management must address the same issues for all projects. Issues such as integrating purchased elements into the overall project, verifying the quality of the purchased components, and satisfying contractual commitments must be completed in both approaches.

We next turn to new ideas for integrating all system development work across a large organization or enterprise. The adaptive and agile concepts that were just discussed focus on individual projects within an organization. Rather than focus on individual efforts, Model-Driven Architecture focuses on enterprise-level activities. It describes a use of models and modeling that is different from that of Agile Modeling.

MODEL-DRIVEN ARCHITECTURE—GENERALIZING SOLUTIONS

One of the primary problems medium-sized and large organizations face is how to build enterprise-level systems that work together seamlessly or that are at least able to communicate. Organizations frequently have legacy mainframe systems, coupled with UNIX-based systems, coupled with Windows platform systems. Each of these systems has its own operating systems, middleware systems, and specific business application systems. The question facing many organizations today is how to make all of these systems work together.

Middleware includes such services as messaging and e-mail, HTML servers, directory and data name servers (DNS), database and data servers, and transaction and event processing handlers. It is very difficult for a large organization to establish a single middleware platform because different groups and divisions often have unique needs, which led them to settle on various platforms and environments. Some of the most widely used environments today include CORBA, Enterprise JavaBeans, message-oriented programs, XML/SOAP, COM+, and .NET. These environments are explained later in the chapter.

The question system developers must answer is how to capture and extract the information from all of these different enterprise-level middleware environments and use it independently of the middleware systems themselves. In other words, how can a company understand its architectural needs independently of any vendor or platform?

One solution proposed by the Object Management Group (OMG) is Model-Driven Architecture. The OMG, which is a consortium of more than 800 companies and organizations, sets standards for interoperability that are independent of language, platform, and vendor. Some of these standards are developed and established by the OMG itself. One such example is Common Object Request Broker Architecture (CORBA), which describes a standard communication architecture for enterprise-level interfaces. Other standards are developed in conjunction with outside groups. UML, which we have been discussing throughout the course, was first proposed as a standard by Grady Booch, Ivar Jacobson, and James Rumbaugh. It has since been adopted as a standard and incorporated into the OMG procedures for updating and approval.

Model-Driven Architecture (MDA) is an OMG initiative that is built on the principles of abstraction, modeling, reuse, and patterns to provide companies with an additional tool to help them understand and extend their enterprise-level systems. MDA provides a framework to identify and classify all the system development work being done in an enterprise. As we look at the details of the MDA, you will recognize many of its concepts. MDA helps describe the concepts that you have been learning throughout this course.

Figure 14-7 is a diagram that depicts the typical process for software development. This model applies to both predictive processes and adaptive, iterative processes. In predictive processes, the development team gathers all the requirements, does a comprehensive design, and then codes the entire system. In the adaptive approaches, the flow is repeated many times in several iterations. But note the rectangles on the right side of the diagram. The top rectangle, showing descriptive text, represents the documents that describe the users' needs. These documents are usually notes, rough sketches, outlines, and other unorganized descriptions of the business processes and user activities.

platform-independent model (PIM)
a model describing system characteristics that are not specific to any deployment platform

The second rectangle in the diagram, called the *platform-independent model (PIM)*, models information about the business that is independent of how it will be built. One example of PIM that you will recognize is a UML class diagram. A UML class diagram describes the information requirements of a system, regardless of whether it is implemented using a relational database system such as SQL Server or a hierarchical database system such as IBM's DB2.

platform-specific model (PSM)
a model describing system characteristics that include deployment platform requirements

The third rectangle, called the *platform-specific model (PSM)*, provides detailed information that includes computer platform and implementation specifics. So, for example, a PSM would contain a relational data model showing the data tables, the keys, the foreign keys, and the type information of individual fields for a SQL Server database. It provides the details about how to implement the PIM.

The other rectangles are the specific implementations of the models in programming code and routines. At this point, you may be asking, "What is so great about the

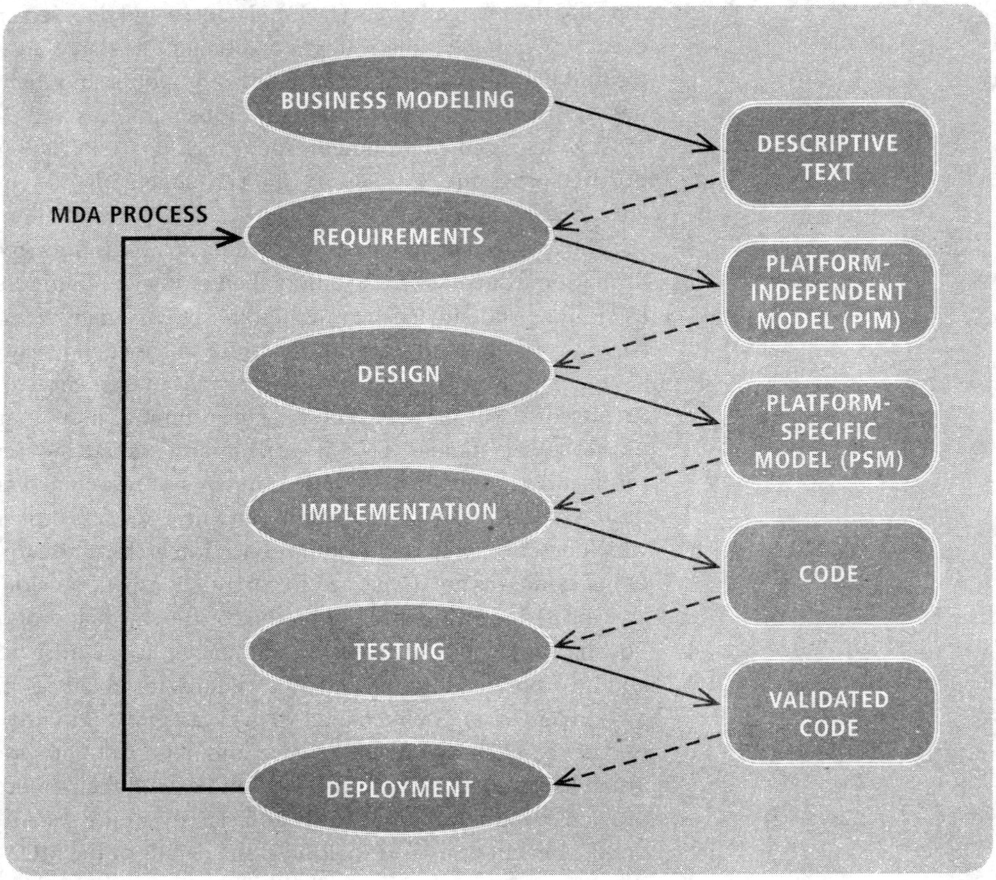

FIGURE 14-7
Software development and MDA

MDA? So far, it just seems to be putting fancy names on activities that we already know how to do." What the MDA does is provide a mechanism by which organizations can extract critical features and information about each of their current systems and combine them into a PIM. As we indicated earlier, most organizations have multiple systems running in many different platforms and programming languages. To describe those systems, individual PSMs are used, all of which are different. So, extracting that information into a PIM allows an organization to analyze the combined PIM to determine where duplication, inconsistencies, and conflicts in technologies exist. In addition, new systems can be designed to conform to existing systems.

For an organization to use an MDA strategy, it must first have a common modeling system and language to describe the PIMs. A key component of the PIM modeling language is the UML, which you have learned in this textbook.

The other required component is a set of standard transformations to move from the code to a PSM and from a PSM to a PIM. In fact, it would be ideal if the transformations could be automated. Then a company could use the automated tools to read existing code, generate PSMs, analyze the PSMs, and generate PIMs. Once those tools were in place, they could also assist in the transformation in the other direction—from PIM to PSM to code.

The role of the OMG is to help define these standard transformations. The creation of specific tools to support this activity is usually done by commercial companies, which create the tools and sell them.

Figure 14-8 illustrates how this process occurs. A new concept that is introduced in this figure is the idea of a metamodel. To build tools that automatically convert one

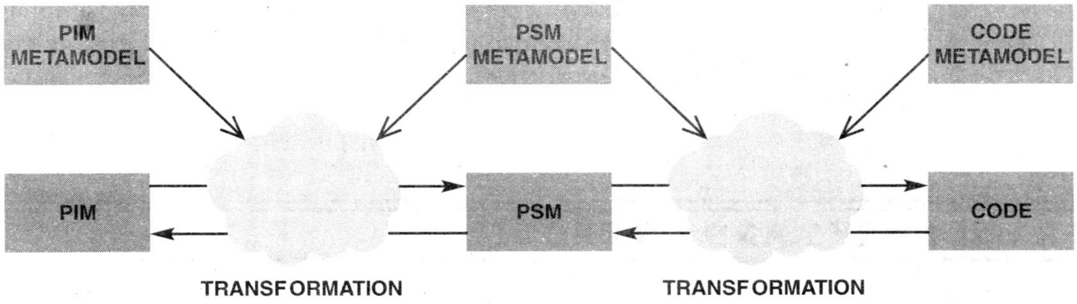

FIGURE 14-8
Metamodels and transitions between PIM, PSM, and code

model into another model, developers need to describe each of those models in precise mathematical terms. That mathematical description is a special type of model called a *metamodel*—a model that describes the characteristics of another model.

For example, if we were to describe a UML design class diagram, we would say that it is made up of boxes and lines. A box represents a class. The boxes have three compartments, with the top being a class name, the middle a list of attributes, and the bottom a list of methods. The lines represent relationships. Each line is connected to a box. Each connection has a numeric text field that describes the multiplicity of the connection. Figure 14-9 shows a partial class diagram metamodel that describes a UML design class diagram.

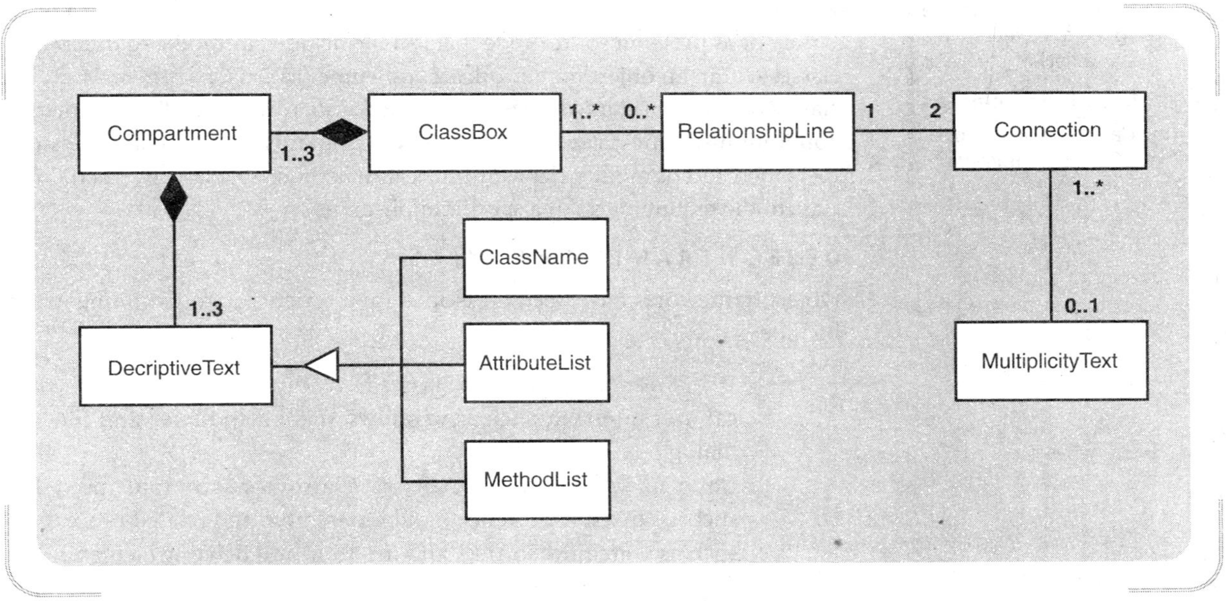

FIGURE 14-9
Partial metamodel of UML class diagram

With a metamodel for each model and a defined set of transformations, organizations can automatically transform the models. The OMG is currently finalizing the first release of the MDA standards to define these models and the transformations. This initiative is ongoing, with many organizations contributing to the standard and with commercial companies beginning to build automated tools.

The MDA was originally defined to fit into a more predictive development approach. The adaptive approaches minimize documentation and model building. So, are the two ideas incompatible or contradictory?

The primary benefit of MDA is to give a big-picture view of the architecture of the entire enterprise. Any new system should fit into the existing data and platform configuration. Hence, it makes sense during system development, even with adaptive approaches, to maintain consistency with the existing infrastructure. So, adaptive development approaches can benefit from utilizing principles of MDA. The important point is to use each technique in its appropriate situation to maximize productivity and organizational benefits.

FRAMEWORKS AND COMPONENTS

Similar functions are embedded in many different types of systems. For example, the graphical user interface (GUI) is nearly ubiquitous in modern software. Many features of a GUI—such as drop-down menus, help screens, and drag-and-drop manipulation of on-screen objects—are used in many or most GUI applications. Other functions—such as searching, sorting, and simple text editing—are also common to many applications. Reusing software to implement such common functions is a decades-old development practice. But such reuse was awkward and cumbersome with older programming languages. Object-oriented programming languages provide a simpler method of software reuse. Object-orientation includes two powerful techniques, frameworks and components, that support software reuse.

OBJECT FRAMEWORKS

object framework
a set of classes that are designed to be reused in a variety of programs

foundation classes
the classes within an object framework

An *object framework* is a set of classes that are specifically designed to be reused in a wide variety of programs. The object framework is supplied to a developer as a precompiled library or as program source code that can be included or modified in new programs. The classes within an object framework are sometimes called *foundation classes*. Foundation classes are organized into one or more inheritance hierarchies. Programmers develop application-specific classes by deriving them from existing foundation classes. Programmers then add or modify class attributes and methods to adapt a "generic" foundation class to the requirements of a specific application.

OBJECT FRAMEWORK TYPES

Object frameworks have been developed for a variety of programming needs. Examples include:

- **User-interface classes.** Classes for commonly used objects within a graphical user interface, such as windows, menus, toolbars, and file open and save dialog boxes.
- **Generic data structure classes.** Classes for commonly used data structures such as linked lists, indices, and binary trees and related processing operations such as searching, sorting, and inserting and deleting elements.
- **Relational database interface classes.** Classes that allow OO programs to create database tables, add data to a table, delete data from a table, or query the data content of one or more tables.
- **Classes specific to an application area.** Classes specifically designed for use in application areas such as banking, payroll, inventory control, and shipping.

General-purpose object frameworks typically contain classes from the first three categories. Classes in these categories can be reused in a wide variety of application areas. Application-specific object frameworks provide a set of classes for use in a specific industry or type of application. Third parties usually design application-specific frameworks as extensions to a general-purpose object framework. Many large organizations have moved aggressively to develop their own application frameworks. Smaller firms usually do not do so because the resource requirements are substantial. An application- or company-specific framework requires a significant development effort typically lasting several years. The effort is repaid over time through continuing reuse of the framework in newly developed systems. The effort is also repaid through simplified maintenance of existing systems. But the payoffs occur far in the future, often making them less valuable than the current funds required to build the frameworks.

THE IMPACT OF OBJECT FRAMEWORKS ON DESIGN AND IMPLEMENTATION TASKS

Developers need to consider several issues when determining whether to use object frameworks. Object frameworks affect the process of systems design and development in several different ways:

- Frameworks must be chosen early in the project—within the first development iteration.
- Systems design must conform to specific assumptions about application program structure and operation that the framework imposes.
- Design and development personnel must be trained to use a framework effectively.
- Multiple frameworks may be required, necessitating early compatibility and integration testing.

The process of developing a system using one or more object frameworks is essentially one of adaptation. The frameworks supply a template for program construction and a set of classes that provide generic capabilities. Systems designers adapt the generic classes to the specific requirements of the new system. Frameworks must be chosen early so that designers know the application structure imposed by the frameworks, the extent to which needed classes can be adapted from generic foundation classes, and the classes that cannot be adapted from foundation classes and thus must be built from scratch.

Of the three object layers typically used in OO system development (view, business logic, and data access), the view and data layers most commonly derive from foundation classes. User interfaces and database access tend to be the areas of greatest strength in object frameworks, and they are typically the most tedious classes to develop from scratch. It is not unusual for 80 percent of a system's code to be devoted to view and data classes. Thus, constructing view and data classes from foundation classes provides significant and easily obtainable code reuse benefits. Adapting view classes from foundation classes has the additional benefit of ensuring a similar look and feel of the user interface across systems and across application programs within systems.

Successful use of an object framework requires a great deal of up-front knowledge about its class hierarchies and program structure. That is, designers and programmers must be familiar with a framework before they can successfully use it. Thus, a framework should be selected as early as possible in the project, and developers must be trained in use of the framework before they begin to implement the new system.

COMPONENTS

In addition to using object frameworks, developers often use components to speed system development. A *component* is a software module that is fully assembled and tested, is ready to use, and has well-defined interfaces to connect it to clients or other components. Components may be single executable objects or groups of interacting objects. A component may also be a non-OO program or system "wrapped" in an OO interface. Components implemented with non-OO technologies must still implement objectlike behavior. In other words, they must implement a public interface, respond to messages, and hide their implementation details.

component
a standardized and interchangeable software module that is fully assembled and ready to use and that has well-defined interfaces to connect it to clients or other components

Components are standardized and interchangeable software parts. They differ from objects or classes because they are binary (executable) programs, not symbolic (source code) programs. This distinction is important because it makes components much easier to reuse and reimplement than source code programs.

For example, consider the grammar-checking function in most word processing programs. A grammar-checking function can be developed as an object or as a subroutine. Other parts of the word processing program can call the subroutine or object methods via appropriate source code constructs (for example, a C++ method invocation or a BASIC subroutine call). The grammar-checking function's source code is integrated with the rest of the word processor's source code during program compilation and linking. The executable program is then delivered to users.

Now consider two possible changes to the original grammar-checking function:

- The developers of another word processing program want to incorporate the existing grammar-checking function into their product.
- The developers of the grammar-checking function discover new ways to implement the function that result in greater accuracy and faster execution.

To integrate the existing function into a new word processor, the word processor developers must be provided with the source code of the grammar-checking function. They then code appropriate calls to the grammar checker into their word processor source code. The combined program is then compiled, linked, and distributed to users. When the developers of the grammar checker revise their source code to implement the faster and more accurate function, they deliver the source code to the developers of both word processors. Both development teams integrate the new grammar-checking source code into their word processors, recompile and relink the programs, and deliver a revised word processor to their users.

So what's wrong with this scenario? Nothing in theory, but a great deal in practice. The grammar-checker developers can provide their function to other developers only as source code, which opens up a host of potential problems concerning intellectual property rights and software piracy. Of greater importance, the word processor developers must recompile and relink their entire word processing programs to update the embedded grammar checker. The revised binary program must then be delivered to users and installed on their computers. This is an expensive and time-consuming process. Delivering the grammar-checking program in binary form would eliminate or minimize most of these problems.

A component-based approach to software design and construction solves both of these problems. Component developers, such as the developers of the grammar checker, can deliver their product as a ready-to-use binary component. Users, such as the developers of the word processing programs, can then simply plug in the component. Updating a single component doesn't require recompiling, relinking, and redistributing the entire application. Perhaps applications already installed on user machines could query an update site via the Internet each time they started and automatically download and install updated components.

At this point, you may be thinking that component-based development is just another form of code reuse. But systems design, object frameworks, and client/server architecture all address code reuse in different ways. The following points are what makes component-based design and construction different:

- Components are reusable packages of executable code. Systems design and object frameworks are methods of reusing source code.
- Components are executable objects that advertise a public interface (that is, a set of methods and messages) and hide (encapsulate) the implementation of

their methods from other components. Client/server architecture is not necessarily based on OO principles. Component-based design and construction are an evolution of client/server architecture into a purely OO form.

Components provide an inherently flexible approach to systems design and construction. Developers can design and construct many parts of a new system simply by acquiring and plugging in an appropriate set of components. They can also make newly developed functions, programs, and systems more flexible by designing and implementing them as collections of components. Component-based design and construction have been the norm in the manufacturing of physical goods (such as cars, televisions, and computer hardware) for decades. However, it has only recently become a viable approach to designing and implementing information systems.

COMPONENT STANDARDS AND INFRASTRUCTURE

Interoperability of components requires standards to be developed and readily available. For example, consider the video display of a typical IBM-compatible personal computer. The plug on the end of the video signal cable follows an interface standard. The plug has a specific form, and each connector in the plug carries a well-defined electrical signal. Years ago, a group of computer and video display manufacturers defined a standard that describes the physical form of the plug and the type of signals carried through each connector. Adherence to this standard guarantees that any video display unit will work with any compatible personal computer and vice versa.

Components may also require standard support infrastructure. For example, video display units are not internally powered. Thus, they require not only a standard power plug but also an infrastructure to supply power to the plug. A component may also require specific services from an infrastructure. For example, a cellular telephone requires the service provider to assign a transmission frequency with the nearest cellular radio tower, to transfer the connection from one tower to another as the user moves among telephone cells, to establish a connection to another person's telephone, and to relay all voice data to and from the other person's telephone via the public telephone grid. All cellular telephones require these services.

Software components have a similar need for standards. Components could be hard-wired together, but this reduces their flexibility. Flexibility is enhanced when components can rely on standard infrastructure services to find other components and establish connections with them.

In the simplest systems, all components execute on a single computer under the control of a single operating system. Connection is more complex when components are located on different machines running different operating systems and when components can be moved from one location to another. In this case, a network protocol independent of the hardware platform and operating system is required. In fact, a network protocol is desirable even when components all execute on the same machine because such a protocol guarantees that systems can be used in different environments—from a single machine to a network of computers.

Modern networking standards have largely addressed the issue of common hardware and communication software to connect distributed software components. Internet protocols are a nearly universal standard and thus provide a ready means of transmitting messages among components. Internet standards can also be used to exchange information between two processes executing on the same machine. However, Internet standards alone do not fully supply a component connection standard. The missing pieces are:

- Definition of the format and content of valid messages and responses
- A means of uniquely identifying each component on the Internet and routing messages to and from that component

To address these issues, some organizations have developed and continue to modify standards for component development and reuse.

CORBA

Common Object Request Broker Architecture (CORBA)
a standard for software component connection and interaction developed by the Object Management Group (OMG)

object request broker (ORB)
a CORBA service that provides component directory and communication services

Internet Inter-ORB Protocol (IIOP)
a CORBA protocol for communication among objects and object request brokers

Component Object Model Plus (COM+)
a standard for software component connection and interaction developed by Microsoft

The *Common Object Request Broker Architecture (CORBA)* was developed by the OMG, a consortium of computer software and hardware vendors. CORBA was designed as a platform- and language-independent standard. The standard is currently in its third revision and is widely used.

The core elements of the CORBA standard are the *object request broker (ORB)* service and the *Internet Inter-ORB Protocol (IIOP)* for component communication. A component user contacts an ORB server to locate a component and determine its capabilities and interface requirements. Messages sent between a component and its user are routed through the ORB, which performs any necessary translation services.

COM+

The *Component Object Model Plus (COM+)* is a Microsoft-developed standard for component interoperability. It is widely implemented in Windows-based application software, and it is often used in three-tier distributed applications based on Microsoft Internet Information Server and Transaction Server. Most Windows office suites, such as Microsoft Office, are constructed as a cooperating set of COM+ components.

COM+ components are registered by individual computer systems within the Windows Registry, which limits COM+ components to computer systems running Windows operating systems. Once components locate one another through the Registry, they communicate directly using a network protocol or Windows interprocess communication facilities.

ENTERPRISE JAVABEANS

Java is an OO programming language developed by Sun Microsystems. Most people have heard of Java in connection with applets that execute on Web pages. Java differs from other OO programming languages in several important ways, including the following:

- Java programs are compiled into object code files that can execute on many hardware platforms under many operating systems.
- The Java language standard includes an extensive object framework, called the Java Development Kit (JDK), which includes classes for GUIs, database manipulation, and internetworking.

The JDK defines a number of classes and naming conventions that support component development. One class enables a Java object to convert its internal state into a sequence of bytes that can be stored or transmitted across a network. Other classes allow components to enumerate a Java object's internal variables. Naming conventions allow components to deduce the names of methods that manipulate those variables. An object of a class that implements all of the required component methods and follows the required naming conventions is called a *JavaBean*.

JavaBean
an object that implements the required component methods and follows the required naming conventions of the JavaBean standard

Enterprise JavaBean (EJB)
a JavaBean that can execute on a server and communicate with clients and other components using CORBA

An *Enterprise JavaBean (EJB)* is a JavaBean that can execute on a server and communicate with clients and other components using CORBA. EJBs provide additional capabilities beyond JavaBeans, including:

- Multicomponent transaction management
- Packaging of multiple components into larger run-time units
- Sophisticated object storage and retrieval in relational or object DBMSs
- Component and object access controls

The JavaBean and EJB standards have created new opportunities for software developers to use component-based technologies. Applications built on these standards can be easily deployed across a wide range of software and hardware platforms. The platform independence of JavaBean components makes them more portable and scalable.

SOAP AND .NET

Both CORBA and COM+ have some significant disadvantages for building distributed component-based software. For CORBA, the primary problem is the complexity of the standard and the need for ORB servers. For COM+, the primary problem is dependence on proprietary technology and limited support outside Microsoft products.

Simple Object Access Protocol (SOAP)
a standard for component communication over the Internet using HTTP and XML

Simple Object Access Protocol (SOAP) is a standard for distributed object interaction that attempts to address the shortcomings of both CORBA and COM+. Unlike CORBA, SOAP has few infrastructure requirements, and its programming interface is relatively simple. SOAP is an open standard developed by the World Wide Web Consortium (W3C). Perhaps the best evidence of SOAP's long-term potential for success is that Microsoft has adopted it as the basis of its .NET distributed software platform.

SOAP is based on existing Internet protocols, including Hypertext Transport Protocol (HTTP) and eXtensible Markup Language (XML). Messages between objects are encoded in XML and transmitted using HTTP, which enables the objects to be located anywhere on the Internet. Figure 14-10 shows two components communicating with SOAP messages. The same transmission method supports server-to-client and component-to-component communication. The SOAP encoder/decoder and HTTP connection manager are standard components of a SOAP programmer's toolkit. Applications can also be embedded scripts that use a Web server to provide SOAP message-passing services.

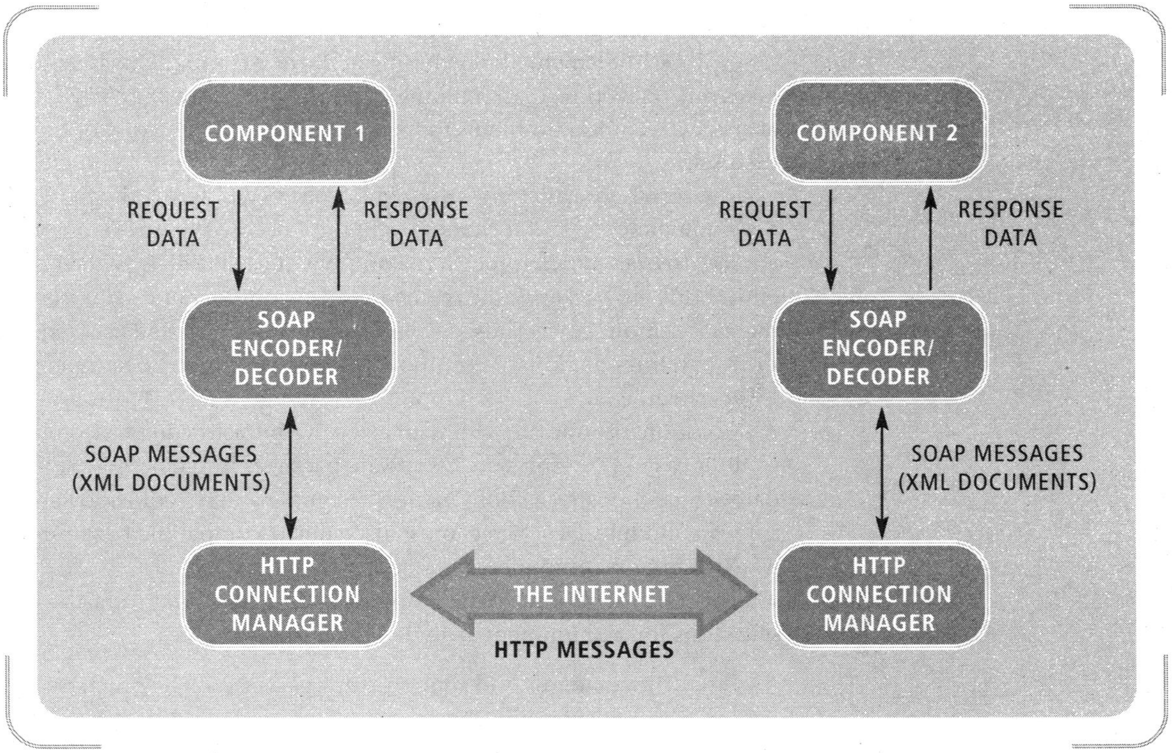

FIGURE 14-10
Component communication using SOAP

Although SOAP is a promising component-communication standard, it is still in its formative period. Current standard-development activity is addressing many missing or underdeveloped parts of the initial standard, including security, message delivery guarantees, and specific conversion rules between programming language and CPU data types and XML. SOAP is often considered a "lighter-weight" version of CORBA because it is simpler and requires little supporting infrastructure to enable component communication. However, the standard may "gain weight" as it evolves to include capabilities needed by high-availability, mission-critical applications.

SOAP and XML have enabled a new era of component-based applications, commonly described by the phrase *Web services*. Simply put, a Web service is a component or entire application that communicates using SOAP. Because SOAP components communicate using XML, they can be easily incorporated into applications that use a Web-browser interface. Complex applications can be constructed using multiple SOAP components that communicate via the Internet. We are only now beginning to see the potential of such applications.

COMPONENTS AND THE DEVELOPMENT LIFE CYCLE

Component purchase and reuse is a viable approach to speeding completion of a system. Two development scenarios involve components:

- Purchased components can form all or part of a newly developed or reimplemented system.
- Components can be designed in-house and deployed in a newly developed or reimplemented system.

Each scenario has different implications for system development, as explored in the following sections.

PURCHASED COMPONENTS

Components change the project inception activities because they affect the way the system will be implemented. Purchasing and using components is generally cheaper and takes much less time than building equivalent software. Purchased components may also solve technical problems that developers could not easily or inexpensively solve themselves.

The search for suitable components must begin during the first iteration of the UP development cycle, but it cannot begin until user requirements are understood well enough to evaluate their match to component capabilities. When developers purchase entire software packages, the match between component capabilities and user requirements is seldom exact. Thus, developers may need to refine user requirements based on the capabilities of available components, particularly if the development project has a short schedule.

Components operate within an extensive infrastructure based on standards such as CORBA or SOAP. Many system software packages implement key parts of each standard. Thus, choosing a component isn't simply a matter of choosing an application software module. Developers must also choose compatible hardware and system software to support components.

The reliance of purchased components on a particular infrastructure has several implications for development activities, including:

- The standards and support software required by purchased components must become part of technical requirements definition.
- A component's technical support requirements restrict the options considered during software architectural design.
- Hardware and system software that provide component services must be acquired, installed, and configured before testing begins.
- The components and their support infrastructure must be maintained after system deployment.

Many development projects, particularly large ones, may use components from many different vendors, which raises compatibility issues. The component search and selection process must carefully consider compatibility—often eliminating some choices and altering the desirability of others. Preliminary testing may have to be conducted early to verify component performance and compatibility before the architectural design is structured around those components and their support infrastructure. Maintenance is also more complicated because significant portions of the system are not under the direct control of the system owner or the in-house IS staff.

SYSTEM PERFORMANCE

Component-based software is usually deployed in a distributed environment. Components typically are scattered among client and server machines and among local area network (LAN) and wide area network (WAN) locations. Distributing components across machines and networks raises the issue of performance. System performance depends on the location of the components (that is, component topology), the hardware capacity of the computers on which they reside, and the communications capacity of the networks that connect the computers. Performance also depends on the demands on network and server capacity made by other applications and communication traffic, such as telephone, video, and interactions among traditional clients and servers.

The details of analyzing and fine-tuning computer and network performance are well beyond the scope of this text. But anyone planning to deploy a distributed component-based system should be aware of the performance issues. These issues must be carefully considered during systems design, implementation, and deployment.

Steps developers should take to ensure adequate performance include the following:

- Examine component-based designs to estimate network traffic patterns and demands on computer hardware.
- Examine existing server capacity and network infrastructure to determine their ability to accommodate communication among components.
- Upgrade network and server capacity prior to development and testing.
- Test system performance during development and make any necessary adjustments.
- Continuously monitor system performance after deployment to detect emerging problems.
- Redeploy components, upgrade server capacity, and upgrade network capacity to reflect changing conditions.

Implementing these steps requires a thorough understanding of computer and network technology, as well as detailed knowledge of existing applications, communications needs, and infrastructure capability and configuration. Applying this knowledge to real-world problems is a complex task typically performed by highly trained specialists.

Summary

The focus of this chapter is on new techniques that are advancing the way systems are being developed. The chapter begins by reviewing five important principles in software development: abstraction, models and modeling, patterns, reuse, and methodologies. Together, these principles form the foundation on which object-oriented development is based. System developers are using these principles to devise new, unique approaches to developing systems.

One of the most active trends in software development is adaptive development methodologies. The idea behind adaptive methodologies is that software projects need to be agile, or flexible, since the business world is so unpredictable and changes so rapidly. The "Manifesto for Agile Software Development" describes four philosophical principles for software projects. These principles emphasize:

- Responding to change over following a plan
- Individuals and interactions over processes and tools
- Working software over comprehensive documentation
- Customer collaboration over contract negotiation

Agile Modeling, another core concept in Agile Development, proposes several guidelines on how models and modeling should be done within a development project. The essence of this approach is to remember that models are a means to an end and not the end. Hence, the Agile Modeling philosophy views models as a tool—for example, for understanding a user requirement or for designing a specific function—rather than as elaborate, formal diagrams that are important by themselves.

Specific development approaches, such as Extreme Programming and Scrum, are unique methodologies that embody adaptive principles. Core elements of XP are that the system tests are written first and that programmers work in pairs to design, code, and test the software. So, when a function is completed, it has not only been designed and coded but has also been reviewed and tested.

The Scrum approach defines a specific goal that can be completed within four weeks. During the four-week sprint, the project team is protected from all outside distractions so that they can complete the defined goal. A product backlog of all outstanding requests is maintained by the client, and changes to the work the team is doing are only allowed between sprints.

Model-Driven Architecture is an initiative of the OMG to provide techniques for large organizations to integrate all software and all software development across the entire enterprise. At this point, the Model-Driven Architecture is primarily a set of principles and ideas. For the MDA initiative to be used, specific tools need to be developed by tool vendors. The MDA defines models at various levels, including a platform-independent model (PIM) and a platform-specific model (PSM), which can provide a comprehensive view of all enterprise-level systems. The MDA is a framework in which all new development can be done so that the organization is able to maintain an integrated, consistent operating environment.

Software reuse is a fundamental approach to rapid development. It has a long history, although it has been applied with greater success since the advent of object-oriented programming, object frameworks, and component-based design and development. Object frameworks provide a means of reusing existing software through inheritance. They provide a library of reusable source code, and inheritance provides a means of quickly adapting that code to new application requirements and operating environments.

Components are units of reusable executable code that behave as distributed objects. They are plugged into existing applications or combined to make new applications. Like the concept of software reuse, component-based design and implementation are not new, but the standards and infrastructure required to support component-based applications have only recently emerged. Thus, components are only now entering the mainstream of software development techniques.

KEY TERMS

chaordic, p. 582
Common Object Request Broker Architecture (CORBA), p. 602
component, p. 599
Component Object Model Plus (COM+), p. 602
Enterprise JavaBean, p. 602
foundation classes, p. 598
Internet Inter-ORB Protocol (IIOP), p. 602
JavaBean, p. 602
metamodel, p. 578
object framework, p. 598
object request broker (ORB), p. 602
pair programming, p. 588
platform-independent model (PIM), p. 595
platform-specific model (PSM), p. 595
product backlog, p. 591
product owner, p. 591
refactoring, p. 588
Scrum master, p. 591
Scrum team, p. 592
Simple Object Access Protocol (SOAP), p. 603
sprint, p. 592
ubiquitous computing, p. 576

REVIEW QUESTIONS

1. Identify the five important principles and practices that are driving many of the current trends in software development. Briefly explain each.
2. What are the driving forces that are moving many companies to adopt more adaptive approaches to system development?
3. Explain the difference between a predictive control process and an empirical control process.
4. List the six fundamental characteristics of adaptive projects.
5. What are the elements of the "Manifesto for Agile Software Development"? Explain what each means.
6. What does *chaordic* mean? What implications does it have for development projects?
7. List the basic principles of Agile Modeling.
8. Why is the word *extreme* included as part of Extreme Programming?
9. List the core values of XP.
10. List the XP practices.
11. What is the product backlog used for in a Scrum project?
12. Explain how a Scrum sprint works.
13. Explain the difference in project time management and project scope management for projects using agile methods.
14. What is a PIM? What is a PSM? How are they related?
15. What are the potential benefits of Model-Driven Architecture?
16. What is a metamodel? How is a metamodel used?
17. What is an object framework? How is it different from a library of components?
18. For which layers of an OO program are off-the-shelf components most likely to be available?
19. What is a software component?
20. Why have software components only recently come into widespread use?
21. In what ways do components make software development faster?

THINKING CRITICALLY

1. Consider the capabilities of the programming language and development tools used in your most recent programming or software development class. Are they powerful enough to implement developmental prototypes for single-user software on a personal computer? Are they sufficiently powerful to implement developmental prototypes in a multiuser, distributed, database-oriented, and high-security operating environment? If they were used with a tool-based development approach, what types of user requirements might be sacrificed because they didn't fit language or tool capabilities?
2. Consider XP's team-based programming approach in general and its principle of allowing any programmer to modify any code at any time in particular. No other development approach or programming management technique follows this particular principle. Why not? In other words, what are the possible negative implications of this principle? How does XP minimize these negative implications?
3. Visit the Web sites of the Agile Alliance (www. agilealliance. com/home) and Agile Modeling (www.agilemodeling.com/). Find some articles on project management in an agile environment. Summarize key points that you think make

project management more difficult in this environment than in a traditional, predictive project. Do the same for key points that make project management easier for an agile project.

4. The chapter discussed the benefits of using Agile Development techniques. List and explain the conditions under which it would be unwise to use an Agile Development methodology such as XP or Scrum.
5. Read the article by Scott Lewandowski listed in the "Further Resources" section. Compare and contrast the CORBA and Microsoft COM+ approaches to component-based development. (Note: COM+ is called *DCOM* in the article.) Which approach appears better positioned to deliver on the promises of component-based design and development? Which approach is a true implementation of distributed objects? Which approach is likely to dominate the market in the near future?
6. Visit the Web site of the World Wide Web Consortium (www.w3.org) and review recent developments related to the SOAP standard. What new capabilities have been added, and what is the effect of those capabilities on the standard's complexity and infrastructure requirements?
7. Compare and contrast object frameworks and components in terms of ease of modification before system deployment, ease of modification after system deployment, and overall cost savings from code reuse. Which approach is likely to yield greater benefits for a unique application system (such as a distribution management system that is highly specialized to a particular company)? Which approach is likely to yield greater benefits for general-purpose application software (such as a spreadsheet or virus protection program)?
8. Consider the similarities and differences between component-based design and construction of computer hardware (such as personal computers) and design and construction of computer software. Can the "plug-compatible" nature of computer hardware ever be achieved with computer software? Does your answer depend on the type of software (for example, system or application software)? Do differences in the expected lifetime of computer hardware and software affect the applicability or desirability of component-based techniques?

EXPERIENTIAL EXERCISES

1. Talk with someone at your school or place of employment about a recent development project that was canceled because of slow development. What development approach was employed for the project? Would a different development approach have resulted in faster development?
2. Find someone in your community who is working on a software development project that is using agile principles. How was the team trained to use Agile Development? How was this approach adopted in the organization? What is the general feeling about its success? What aspects does this developer like? What aspects does he/she find frustrating or difficult to use?
3. Consider a project to replace the student advisement system at your school with one that employs modern features (for example, Web-based interfaces, instant reports of degree program progress, and automatic course registration based on a long-term degree plan). Now consider how such a project would be implemented using tool-based development. Investigate alternative tools, such as Visual Studio, PowerBuilder, and Oracle Forms, and determine (for each tool) what requirements would need to be compromised for the sake of development speed if the tool were chosen.
4. Examine the capabilities of a modern programming environment such as Microsoft Visual Studio .NET, IBM WebSphere Studio, or Borland Enterprise Studio. Is an object framework or component library provided? Does successful use of the programming environment require a specific development approach? Does successful use require a specific development methodology?
5. Examine the technical description of a complex end-user software package such as Microsoft Office. In what ways was component-based software development used to build the software?

Case Studies

MIDWESTERN POWER SERVICES

Midwestern Power Services (MPS) provides natural gas and electricity to customers in four Midwestern states. Like most power utilities, over the last several years, MPS has seen significant changes in federal and state regulations. Several years ago, federal deregulation opened the floodgates of change but provided little guidance or restriction on the future shape of the industry. State legislatures also changed their laws and regulations significantly. The industry went through tremendous upheaval, with significant problems created by power shortages at several California power companies and the Enron debacle. Now regulations such as the Sarbanes-Oxley Act are changing the scenario again. These new regulations seriously affect all areas of business, including accounting, record keeping, power purchases, distribution agreements, and customer consumption and billing.

New and proposed regulations seek to increase controls and expand competition for electricity and natural gas. The final form these regulations will take is unknown, and the exact details will probably vary from state to state.

MPS needed to prepare its systems rapidly for these new regulations. Three systems are most directly affected—one for purchasing wholesale natural gas, one for purchasing wholesale electricity, and one for billing customers for combined gas and electric services. The billing system is not currently structured to separate supply and distribution charges, and it has no direct ties to the natural gas and electricity purchasing systems. MPS's general ledger accounting system is also affected because it is used to account for MPS's own electricity-generating operations.

MPS plans to restructure its accounting, purchasing, and billing systems to match the proposed regulation framework:

- Customer billing statements will clearly distinguish between charges for supply and distribution of both gas and electricity. The wholesale suppliers of each power commodity will determine prices for supply. Revenues will be allocated to appropriate companies (for example, distribution charges to MPS and supply charges to wholesale providers).
- MPS will create a new payment system for wholesale suppliers to capture per-customer revenues and to generate payments from MPS to wholesale suppliers. Daily payments will be made electronically based on actual payments by customers.
- MPS will restructure its own electricity-generating operations into a separate profit center, similar to other wholesale power providers. Revenues from customers who choose MPS as their electricity supplier will be matched to generation costs.

MPS's current systems were all developed internally. The general ledger accounting and natural gas purchasing systems are mainframe-based. They were developed in the mid-1990s, and incremental changes have been made ever since. All programs are written in COBOL, and DB2 (a relational DBMS) is used for data storage and management. There are approximately 50,000 lines of COBOL code.

The billing system was also rewritten from the ground up in the mid-1990s and has been slightly modified since that time. The system runs on a cluster of servers using the UNIX operating system. The latest version of Oracle (a relational DBMS) is used for data storage and management. Most of the programs are written in C++, although some are written in C and others use Oracle Forms. There are approximately 80,000 lines of C and C++ code.

MPS has a network that is used primarily to support terminal-to-host communications, Internet access, and printer and file sharing for personal computers. The billing system relies on the network for communication among servers in the cluster. The mainframe that supports the accounting and purchasing systems is connected to the network, although that connection is primarily used to back up data files and software to a remote location. The company has experimented with Web-browser interfaces for telephone customer support and online statements. However, no functioning Web-based systems have been completed or installed.

MPS is currently in the early stages of planning the system upgrades. It has not yet committed to specific technologies or development approaches. MPS has also not yet decided whether to upgrade individual systems or replace them entirely. The target date for completing all system modifications is three years from now, but the company is actively seeking ways to shorten that schedule.

[1] Describe the pros and cons of the UP approach versus XP and Scrum development approaches to upgrading the existing systems or developing new ones. Do the pros and cons change if the systems are replaced instead of upgraded? Do the pros and cons vary by system? If so, should different development approaches be used for each system?

[2] Is component-based development a viable development approach for any of the systems? If so, identify the system(s) and suggest tools that might be appropriate. For each tool suggested, identify the types of requirements likely to be sacrificed because of a poor match to tool capabilities.

[3] Assume that all systems will be replaced with custom-developed software. Will an object framework be valuable for implementing the replacements? Is an application-specific framework likely to be available from a third party? Why or why not?

[4] Assume that all systems will be replaced with custom-developed software. Should MPS actively pursue component-based design and development? Why or why not? Does MPS have sufficient skills and infrastructure to implement a component-based system? If not, what skills and infrastructure are lacking?

RETHINKING ROCKY MOUNTAIN OUTFITTERS

Now that you have studied the material in this textbook, you'll be able to make more informed and in-depth choices regarding development approach and techniques for the RMO customer support system (CSS). Review the CSS system capabilities in Figure 3-6, and the "Rethinking RMO" cases at the end of Chapters 2 and 3. You may also need to look at other RMO material from Chapters 2 and 3 to answer the following questions:

[1] Consider the criteria discussed in this chapter for choosing among the adaptive approaches to system development. Which CSS project characteristics favor a predictive approach? Which favor the UP? What characteristics might indicate use of a more agile approach? Which approach is best suited to the CSS development project?

[2] Should RMO consider using purchased components within the new CSS? If so, when should it begin looking for components? How will a decision to use components affect the requirements, design, and implementation phases? If purchased components are used, should the portions of the system developed in-house also be structured as components? Will a decision to pursue component-based design and development make it necessary to adopt OO analysis and design methods?

FOCUSING ON RELIABLE PHARMACEUTICAL SERVICE

Reread the Reliable Pharmaceutical Service cases in Chapters 2 and 3. Armed with the new knowledge that you've gained from reading this chapter, answer the following questions:

[1] Which of the development approaches described in this chapter seem best suited to the project? Why? Plan the first six weeks of the project under your chosen development approach.

[2] What role will components play in the system being developed for Reliable? Does it matter on which component-related standards they're based? Why or why not?

FURTHER RESOURCES

Agile Alliance Web site, www.agilealliance.com/home.

Scott W. Ambler, *Agile Modeling: Effective Practices for Extreme Programming and the Unified Process*. John Wiley and Sons Publishing, 2002.

Ken Auer and Roy Miller, *Extreme Programming Applied: Playing to Win*. Addison-Wesley Publishing Company, 2002.

Kent Beck, *Extreme Programming Explained: Embrace Change*. Addison-Wesley Publishing Company, 1999.

Anneke Kleppe, Jos Warmer, and Wim Bast, *MDA Explained: The Model Driven Architecture: Practice and Promise*. Addison-Wesley Publishing Company, 2003.

Craig Larman, *Agile and Iterative Development: A Manager's Guide*. Addison-Wesley Publishing Company, 2004.

Scott M. Lewandowski, "Frameworks for Component-Based Client/Server Computing." *ACM Computing Surveys*, volume 30:1 (March 1998), pp. 3–27.

"Manifesto for Agile Software Development," the Agile Alliance, http://agilemanifesto.org.

Pete McBreen, *Questioning Extreme Programming*. Addison-Wesley Publishing Company, 2003.

Stephen Mellor, Kendall Scott, Axel Uhl, and Dirk Weise, *MDA Distilled: Principles of Model-Driven Architecture*. Addison-Wesley Publishing Company, 2004.

Ken Schwaber and Mike Beedle, *Agile Software Development with Scrum*. Prentice-Hall, 2002.

Steve Sparks, Kevin Benner, and Chris Faris, "Managing Object-Oriented Framework Reuse." *Computer*, volume 29:9 (September 1996), pp. 53–61.

INDEX

A
About box, 543
abstract classes, 193. *See also* abstraction
abstraction, 47, 577–578. *See also* abstract classes; models
acceptance testing
  described, 539–540
  XP (Extreme Programming) and, 589
Access (Microsoft), 398, 408
access control. *See also* security
  described, 509
  lists, 516
accuracy controls, 511–512
action-expressions
  described, 239
  method logic and, 362–366
actions, easy retrieval of, 456–457
activation lifelines, 318
Active Directory (Microsoft), 284, 548
Active Server Pages. *See* ASP (Microsoft Active Server Pages)
activity diagram(s)
  concurrent paths and, 147
  described, 144–145, 226–228
  documenting with, 144–148
  requirements discipline and, 144–148
  SSDs based on, 232–236
  symbols, 145
actors
  described, 214–215
  identifying, 219–220
ad hoc reports, 497. *See also* reports
adapter pattern, 371–373
adaptive development. *See also* ASD (adaptive systems development)
  Agile Development and, 581–586
  described, 580–594
  project management and, 593–594
  requirements discipline and, 154
  Scrum and, 590–593
  XP (Extreme Programming) and, 586–590
adaptive systems development. *See* adaptive development; ASD (adaptive systems development)
affordance, 453–454, 476
aggregation
  described, 191
  domain classes and, 191
Agile Development
  described, 51, 581–586
  inception phase and, 95
  philosophy 582
  practices, 584–586
  principles, 582–584
  values, 582
Agile Modeling. *See* AM (Agile Modeling)
algorithms, 518
alpha versions, 541, 543
AM (Agile Modeling), 581–586. *See also* Agile Development
Amazon.com Web site, 16
American Telephone & Telegraph. AT&T (American Telephone & Telegraph)
analogies, 98
analysis
  activities, described, 40
  iterations and, 44
  "paralysis," 127
  phase (SDLC), 40–42
  spiral model and, 43
APIs (application program interfaces)
  DBMSs and, 398
  described, 379–380
Apple Computer, 448, 454–455
Apple Lisa, 448
Apple Macintosh, 448, 454–455, 465
applets, 381. *See also* Java
application architecture plans
  described, 16–17
  sample, 24–26
application program interfaces. *See* API (application program interfaces)
application service provider. *See* ASP (application service provider)
architectural design, described, 263
artifacts, 54–55, 314
ASD (adaptive systems development), 95, 96. *See also* adaptive development
ASP (Microsoft Active Server Pages), 381, 384
ASP (application service provider), 15
ASP.NET (Microsoft), 385
assignment operator, 231
association(s). *See also* association classes
  attributes and, 401, 410
  classification hierarchies and, 412
  data access layer and, 401–407
  described, 66, 181–182
  design classes and, 192
  domain classes and, 186
  many-to-many, 405–406, 410, 411–412
  one-to-many, 402, 403–405, 410, 411, 415
  relational databases and, 410–412
  relationships, 66
  representing, 401–407, 410–412
association classes. *See also* associations
  described, 187–189, 405–406
  domain classes and, 187–189
asymmetric key encryption, 519. *See also* encryption
AT&T (American Telephone & Telegraph), 273
attribute(s)
  associations and, 401, 410
  compound, 183
  described, 61–63, 183, 408
  design classes and, 193–194
  domain classes and, 183, 186
  functional dependency and, 416
  relational databases and, 407, 408
  static, 194
  values, 407, 408
authentication
  described, 516
  passwords and, 516–517
authorization, 516
automation
  boundaries, 8, 215–216
  organization, 215–216

B

B2B (business-to-business)
  e-commerce, 9
B2C (business-to-commerce)
  e-commerce
  strategic planning and, 20
  TPS and, 9
backup and recovery controls, 510
bar charts, 504
best practices
  actors and, 214
  described, 49
  design discipline and, 267, 268, 280, 284, 286
  domain classes and, 184, 386
  event tables and, 174
  high-risk activities and, 568
  JAD sessions and, 149
  postconditions and, 225
  preconditions and, 225
  project success factors and, 81
  protection from variations and, 368
  requirements discipline and, 142, 149, 154
  SDLC and, 46
  security controls and, 513
  system interface design and, 494
  techniques and, 49
  test systems and, 546
  tools and, 68
  upgrading knowledge and, 14
  use cases and, 52, 167, 316, 320, 333
  user-interface design and, 445, 460, 473
  versioning and, 539, 542
  walkthroughs and, 157
beta versions, 541, 543
binary associations, 182
biometric devices, 517
blueprints, 293
Booch, Grady, 48, 50
Borland, 71
bottlenecks, performance, 425
bottom-up development techniques
  implementation discipline and, 556–557
  WBS and, 98–99
boundary
  automation, 8, 215–216
  classes, 303
  system, 8
breakeven points, 113
broadband Internet access, 10
browser forms, designing, 464–467. *See also* forms
bug reports, 543
build and smoke tests, 538
business. *See also* business logic; business modeling; business processes
  analysts, 14
  consultants, 14
business logic, 367, 382
  layer, 280–281, 301
  protection from variations and, 367
  use cases and, 301, 343, 344
  view layer classes and, 333
business modeling
  creating models, 93–94
  described, 28, 55–56, 86–87
  design discipline and, 262–264
  inception phase and, 86–94
  project management and, 85
  UP life cycle and, 53–54
business process(es). *See also* processes
  identifying, 136–138
  observing/documenting, 142–148
  reengineering, 15–16
  requirements discipline and, 142–148
button(s). *See also* objects
  attributes, 62
  Cancel button, 456
  methods, 62
  object interactions and, 64

C

C (high-level language)
  abstraction and, 577
  data types and, 422
C++ (high-level language), 342, 383
  classification of, as an object-oriented language, 60
  data access classes and, 421
  forms and, 465
C++ Builder, 342
C# (high-level language), 342, 385
  classification of, as an object-oriented language, 60
  deployment discipline and, 548
caculateInterest message, 67–68
callback pattern, 375
Cancel button, 456
cardinality, described, 66
CASE (computer-aided system engineering), 49. *See also* CASE tools
CASE tools. *See also* CASE (computer-aided system engineering)
  Agile Development and, 584
  characteristics of, 68–69
  coordinating information and, 268–270
  described, 49
  design discipline and, 268–270
  inception phase and, 94–95
  JAD and, 151
  prototypes and, 148
  repositories, 68–69
  requirements discipline and, 129
centralized architecture, 272
CEOs (chief executive officers), 22
certifying authority, 520
CFM (Cold Fusion Pages), 384
CGI (common gateway interface), 383, 385
change
  embracing, 583
  implementing, 545–546
  requests, 544–545
chaordic, use of the term, 582
CHAR data type, 422
check boxes, described, 468
chief developer team, 559
CIOs (chief information officers), 22
class(es). *See also* class diagrams
  abstract, 193
  association, 187–189, 405–406
  boundary, 303
  classification hierarchies and, 412
  concrete, 193
  definitions, 298
  described, 63
  entity, 303
  foundation, 598–599
  implementation testing and, 538
  indirection and, 368
  -level methods, 306
  libraries, 61
  problem domain, 183–184
  relational databases and, 410
  representing, 400–401, 410
  reuse of, 61
  sub-, 67, 189–190
  super-, 67, 189–190
class diagram(s)
  developing, 309–312
  dialog design and, 463
  domain classes and, 184–197
  hierarchies in, 189–191
  notation, 185–194
  object-oriented databases and, 400–407
  Together tool and, 71
classification hierarchies, 412
class-responsible collaboration cards. *See* CRC (class-responsible collaboration) cards
client(s). *See also* client/server architecture
  described, 89, 277
  yielding, 455–456

client/server architecture. *See also* clients
described, 277
design discipline and, 276–281
enterprise-level systems and, comparison of, 378
three-layer, 279–281
clustered architecture, 271
Coad, Peter, 71
COBOL, 22, 577
code
classification of, as an artifact, 55
collective ownership of, 587
control systems, 560–561
standards, 589
cohesion, 308–309
Cold Fusion, 381
Cold Fusion Pages. *See* CFM (Cold Fusion Pages)
collaborative specialist team, 559
colon (:), 335
COM (Common Object Model), 533. *See also* COM+ (Component Object Model Plus)
COM+ (Common Object Model Plus). *See also* COM (Common Object Model)
components, 602
described, 602
model-driven architecture and, 595
SOAP and, 603
combo boxes, 467
common gateway interface. *See* CGI (common gateway interface)
Common Language Runtime, 385–386
Common Object Model. *See* COM (Common Object Model)
Common Object Model Plus. *See* COM+ (Common Object Model Plus)
Common Object Request Broker Architecture. *See* CORBA (Common Object Request Broker Architecture)
communication. *See also* feedback
Agile Development and, 584
diagrams, 334–337
managing/controlling, 114
skills, overview of, 12–13
support systems, 10
XP (Extreme Programming) and, 586–587
competency, computer, 107
completeness control, 509, 511–512
complex data types, 422
component(s)
architectures, 52
deployment discipline and, 549–551
described, 530, 599–601
development life cycle and, 604–605
implementation and, 530
infrastructure, 601–604
installing, 549–551
packaging, 549–551
purchased, 604–605
standards, 601–604
composite state, 239
composition
described, 191
domain classes and, 191
compound attributes, 183
computer
competency, 107
medium, designing for, 470
concrete classes, 193
concurrency (concurrency states)
described, 239
nested states and, 239–240
conditions
post-, 225, 235–236
pre-, 224–225, 235–236
Configuration and Change management
described, 59, 540–547
project management and, 85
UP life cycle and, 53–55
versioning and, 541–543
consistency, striving for, 454–455
construction phase, 45, 46–47
contracts, 582
control
break reports, 501
changes, 52
classes, 303
internal locus of, 457
controller classes, 369
cooperating peer team, 559
CORBA (Common Object Request Broker Architecture), 265, 274, 275, 277
described, 602
EJBs and, 603
implementation and, 533
model-driven architecture and, 595
reuse and, 578
SOAP and, 603, 604
correctness controls, 511–512
cost/benefit analysis
annual operating costs and, 111–112
described, 109
detailed estimates, 111
developing, 110–113
feasibility assessment and, 109–113
NPV and, 112–113
coupling, described, 307–308
courage, importance of, 588
CRC (class-responsible collaboration) cards, 314
create, read, update, and delete matrix. *See* CRUD (create, read, update, and delete) matrix
critical path, 103
CRM (customer relationship management), 20, 24, 26
CRUD (create, update, read, and delete) matrix
described, 197–200
integrating models and, 247–248
requirements and, 212
CSS (customer support system)
application architecture plans and, 24, 25, 26
design discipline and, 275–277
inception phase and, 89, 91–93, 99
sample document for, 92–93
SCCS (source code control system) and, 560–561
schedules and, 108
system capabilities and, 92–93
versioning and, 541–543
WBS and, 99
curly braces ({}), 193
Customer class, 61, 66–67, 229, 307, 322
customer support system. *See* CSS (customer support system)
customer relationship management. *See* CRM (customer relationship management)
customers, on-site, 587–588

D

data. *See also* data access layer; data types
access classes, 303, 421–422
converting, 551–553
elements, 407, 408
initializing, 551–553
validation controls, 509
warehouses, 428–429
data access layer
classes, 344
designing, 322–324, 396–439
object-relational interaction and, 420–423
relational databases and, 407–423
Data Encryption Standard. *See* DES (Data Encryption Standard)
data types
complex, 422
described, 422
ODBMSs and, 423
primitive, 422
relational DBMSs and, 422–423

Data Sources, 152–153
database(s). *See also* DBMSs (database management systems); tables
architecture, 431–432
complications related to, 431–433
creating new, 552–553
data access layer and, 398–400
data types and, 422–423
described, 398
design discipline and, 57–58, 265–266, 275
distributed, 423–431
flexibility of, 414–415
integrity controls and, 509–510
maintainability of, 414–415
models, 399–400
normalization, 415–220
object-oriented, 400–407
relational, 407–423
reloading, 551–552
reusing existing, 551
schema quality, evaluating, 413–420
servers, 424–425
synchronization, 425–428, 430
system interface design and, 490
use cases and, 344
DATE data type, 422
DB2 relational databases (IBM), 22, 275, 276, 398, 595
DBMSs (database management systems). *See also* databases
components of, 398–399
data access layer and, 398–400
data types and, 422–423
described, 398
design discipline and, 265, 277–279
export utilities and, 552
hybrid object-relational, 420
import utilities and, 551, 552
integrity controls and, 509–510
referential integrity and, 413
relational, 407–423
reloading databases and, 551–552
synchronization and, 425–428, 430
deadlines, 109. *See also* schedules
decision pseudostate, 363
decision support systems. *See* DSS (decision support systems)
decryption. *See also* encryption
asymmetric encryption and, 519
described, 518
Delphi, 319
dependency relationships, described, 342
deployment discipline
acquiring hardware and system software, 547–549
described, 29, 55, 59, 547–553
design discipline and, 264, 270–277
diagrams, 379–380
direct (immediate cutover), 561–562
inception phase and, 94
managing, 553–565
packaging and installing components, 549–551
parallel, 562–563
personal issues and, 564–565
phased, 563–564
planning, 553–565
project management and, 85
training users and, 549–551
UP life cycle and, 53–54
DES (Data Encryption Standard), 518. *See also* encryption
descriptions
activity diagram, 226–228
brief, 220–221
detailed, 220–226
fully-developed, 221–225
intermediate, 221
descriptive models, described, 133
design. *See also* design classes; design discipline
activities, 260–291
class diagrams and, 191–194
deployment and, 264
described, 55, 57–58
elements of, understanding, 263
environments, 260–291
iterations and, 44
models and, 134–135
object frameworks and, 599
patterns, 366–376
phase (SDLC), 40–42
principles, 306–309, 366–376
project management and, 85
statecharts and, 360–366
support services and, 264
three-layer, 342–344
UP life cycle and, 53–54
use cases and, 57, 292–357
design class(es)
described, 302–312
diagrams, 302–312, 337–339
notation, 304–306
symbols, 302–304
design discipline. *See also* design; design classes
activities, 263–267
client/server architecture and, 276, 277–281
databases and, 265–266
deployment environments and, 264, 270–277
described, 29, 259–291
HTTP and, 274, 281, 284–285
the Internet and, 274, 276, 281–283
LANs and, 272–274, 276, 278, 282, 285–286
middleware and, 281, 284–285
moving from business modeling to, 262–263
networks and, 272–274, 283–286
project management and, 267–270
security and, 266, 282
software architecture and, 264–265, 277–283
system interfaces and, 266
system security and, 266
UP and, 266–267
use cases and, 265, 286
user interfaces and, 266
XML and, 274, 281, 282
desktop metaphor, 449
destination(s)
controls, 511
described, 175
state, 238
detailed reports, 499
dialog design
described, 128–129, 450
documenting, 457–464
HCP and, 450–452
help support and, 468–469
navigation controls and, 468
requirements discipline and, 128–129
samples, 476–478
storyboards and, 459–460
support controls and, 468
use cases and, 457–459
user-centric, 470–471
yielding closure and, 455–456
dialog metaphor, 450–452
digital
certificates, 520–521
signatures, 520–521
direct manipulation metaphor, 448–449
disciplines. *See also specific disciplines*
described, 52–53, 55–60
project management and, 85
discovery
described, 56–57
prototypes, 148
distributed
architecture, 272, 424–431
databases, 424–431
DNS (domain naming services)
deployment discipline and, 548

design discipline and, 264
model-driven architecture and, 595
DOBMS (object database management system), 400
document metaphor, 449–450
document type definitions. *See* DTDs (document type definitions)
documentation. *See also* reports
Agile Development and, 586
classification of, as artifacts, 55
system interface design and, 498–499
turnaround documents, 498–499, 500
domain class(es)
associations and, 181–182
attributes and, 183
class diagrams and, 184–197
described, 178–185
developing "lists of things" for, 179–183
diagrams, 57–58, 194–197
iteration planning and, 201
normalization and, 419–420
objects and, 183–184
problem, 178–185
domain layer
classes, 344, 374–375
described, 301, 382
domain model(s)
class diagrams, 432
integrating, 246–247
object-relational interaction and, 420–423
domain naming services. *See* DNS (domain naming services)
Dreamweaver (Macromedia), 380
drill-down techniques, 503
driver(s)
described, 535
modules, 535
DSS (decision support systems), 9–10
DTDs (document type definitions), 492
duration
resource requirements and, 105
use of the term, 102
Dynabook, 447

E

eBay, 16
EBPs (elementary business processes), 167
Eclipse, 342
economic feasibility, determining, 109–113
EDI (electronic data interface), 490–491
effort, use of the term, 102
EIS (executive information systems), 9
elaboration phase, 45, 46, 54
elementary business processes. *See* EBPs (elementary business processes)
electronic data interface. *See* EDI (electronic data interface)
electronic reports, 502–504
Elements of Reusable Object-Oriented Software (Gamma, Helm, Johnson, and Vlissides), 368
e-mail
communications support and, 10
indirection and, 368
Embarcadero Describe, 72
Embarcadero Technologies, 72
emphasis, of project teams, 45
empirical controls, 580
encapsulation
described, 66, 306
domain classes and, 184–185
encryption. *See also* security
algorithms, 518
asymmetric key, 519
described, 509, 518
digital certificates and, 520–521
public key, 519
symmetric key, 518
end user(s). *See also* users
analysts, 14
training, 550–551
enterprise(s). *See also* enterprise-level systems; ERP (enterprise resource planning)
three-layer architecture, 385–386
two-layer architecture, 382–384
Enterprise JavaBeans (EJBs)
described, 602–603
model-driven architecture and, 595
enterprise-level systems. *See also* enterprises
described, 376
designing, 376–388
entity classes, 303
environment discipline
business modeling and, 56
described, 28, 60
inception phase and, 94–95
project management and, 85
UP life cycle and, 53–54
ergonomics, 446–448
ERP (enterprise resource planning). *See also* enterprises
described, 17
reuse and, 578
error(s). *See also* exceptions
handling, described, 456
reports, submitting, 544–545
system input and, 492–494
essential use case model
described, 97
inception phase and, 97
Ethernet, 273
ethics, personal, 13
event(s)
decomposition, 166, 167–168
described, 167
examining, 174–177
external, 169
identifying, 170–173
prior conditions and, 170–171
responses and, 170–171
sequence of, 172
state, 170
system controls and, 172–173
tables, 174–177
technology-dependent, 172–173
temporal, 169–170
types of, 168–170
evolving prototypes, 148. *See also* prototypes
exception(s). *See also* errors
conditions, 241
reports, 499
executables, classification of, as artifacts, 55
executive reports, 499
eXtensible Markup Language (XML), 387–388, 595
design discipline and, 274, 281, 282
implementation and, 533
middleware and, 281
schema, 492
SOAP and, 603, 604
system interface design and, 491–492
external
output, 499–502
users, described, 88
extranets
described, 274
design discipline and, 274
Extreme Programming (XP), 95, 586–590
core values, 586–587
practices, 587–588
project activities, 589–590
project management and, 593

F

fault tolerance, 430
feasibility
assessment, 96, 106–113
confirming, 106–113

cultural, 107–108
economic, 109–113
organizational, 107–108
resource, 109
schedule, 108–109
technological, 108
Federal Express, 414
federated database servers, 428–429
feedback. *See also* communication
Agile Development and, 584
offering informative, importance of, 455
user-interface design and, 455
XP (Extreme Programming) and, 587
field(s)
combination control, 508
relational databases and, 407
values, 407, 408
finish
-finish relationships, 100
-start relationships, 100
first normal form (1NF), 415
float (slack time), described, 104
fonts, 465, 466
foreign keys. *See also* keys
associations and, 411
classification hierarchies and, 412
described, 408–409
referential integrity and, 413
form(s). *See also* objects
attributes, 62
data entry and, 467–468
described, 465
design, 464–469
formatting, 465–467
layout, 465–467
methods, 62
prototypes, 474
requirements discipline and, 138–139
reusing, 473
types of, 465
Fortune 500 companies, 14
foundation classes, 598–599
frameset(s)
described, 380
extensions, 381
frameworks
development, 558
impact of, 599
object, 598–599
types, 598–599
fraud, preventing, 512–513
FrontPage (Microsoft), 380
functional decomposition, 7
functional dependency
data access layer and, 415, 416
described, 415
functional requirements
described, 129
models and, 133, 134–135
functionality, 58–59

G
Gamma, Eric, 368
Gantt charts
described, 48, 101
Microsoft Project and, 101–103
updating, 103
GemStone, 398, 400
generalization associations, 406–407. *See also* associations
generalization/specialization hierarchy
described, 67
domain classes and, 189–191, 193, 195–197
generic data structure classes, 598
GoF (Gang of Four) pattern, 368, 369
grammar checking, 600
graphical
models, described, 133
presentations, 504–505
GSSs (group support sessions), 151–152
guard-conditions
described, 238
true/false conditions and, 239
guillemets («»), 302

H
hardware
acquiring, 547–549
deployment discipline and, 547–549
HCI (human-computer interface)
affordance and, 453–454
as a field of study, 446–448
described, 444
direct manipulation and, 448–449
fields contributing to the study of, 447
metaphors for, 448–452
system interface design and, 489
visibility and, 453–454
Web design and, 469
Helm, Richard, 368
help systems, 468–469
HTML (HyperText Markup Language), 284–285, 380, 383–385
XML and, 387
described, 449
design discipline and, 274, 282
document metaphor and, 449–450
forms and, 465
indirection and, 368
model-driven architecture and, 595
servers, 595
system interface design and, 491
XML and, relationship of, 491
HTTP (HyperText Transfer Protocol)
design discipline and, 281, 274, 284–285
middleware and, 281
servers, 379
SOAP and, 603
HTTPS (Secure HyperText Transfer Protocol), 521
human factors engineering (ergonomics), 446–448
human-computer interface
affordance and, 453–454
as a field of study, 446–448
described, 444
direct manipulation and, 448–449
fields contributing to the study of, 447
metaphors for, 448–452
system interface design and, 489
visibility and, 453–454
Web design and, 469
hybrid DBMSs, 420. *See also* DBMSs (database management systems)
hypermedia. *See also* HTML (HyperText Markup Language); hypertext
described, 449–450
design principles and, 470
document metaphor and, 449–450
hypertext. *See also* HTML (HyperText Markup Language); hypermedia
described, 449–450
document metaphor and, 449
HyperText Markup Language. *See* HTML (HyperText Markup Language)
HyperText Transfer Protocol. *See* HTTP (HyperText Transfer Protocol)

I
IBM (International Business Machines), 15, 50
DB2 relational databases, 22, 275, 276, 398, 595
PCs (personal computers), 448, 601
UML and, 48
identifiers (keys), 183
identity, described, 66
IDEs (integrated development environments)
inception phase and, 94
Rational Rose and, 70
Rational XDE Professional, 73
tools included with, 49
use cases and, 342, 343, 344

IIOP (Internet Inter-ORB Protocol), 603
IIS (Microsoft Internet Information Server), 602
immediate cutover (direct deployment), 561–562
implementation discipline
activities, described, 40
bottom-up development order and, 556–557
described, 29, 40–42, 55, 58, 532–533
diagrams, 379
IPO (input, process, output) development and, 554–556
iterations and, 44
managing, 553–565
object frameworks and, 599
planning, 553–565
project management and, 85
three-layer design and, 342–344
top-down development order and, 556–557
UP life cycle and, 53–54
use cases and, 342–344
inception phase, 45, 46
ASD and, 95, 96
business benefits and, 91–92
business modeling and, 86–94
completing, 113–114
described, 28, 78–121
environment discipline and, 94–95
finalizing system and project scope, 96–97
objectives, 86
project feasibility and, 106–113
project risks and, 106–113
resource requirements and, 104–106
sponsors and, 89
staffing plans and, 104–106
system capabilities and, 92
system vision and, 91–93
inconsistency, described, 415
incremental
development, 45
modeling, 584–585
independent contractors, 15
indirection, described, 368
information. *See also* data; information systems
coordinating, 268–270
hiding, 66, 306
information gathering. *See also* information; information systems
requirements and, 56–57, 127–128, 135–153
techniques, 135–153
information system(s). *See also* information; information gathering
component parts of, 8
departments, 22–23
described, 6–7
role of, in problem solving, 6–8
strategic planning and, 16–26
subsystems and, 7
types of, 8–10
infrastructure upgrades, 546–547
inheritance
described, 66–68
design classes and, 192
domain classes and, 190
hierarchy, 67, 190, 412
implementation testing and, 538
subclasses and, 190
input(s). *See also* IPO (input, process, output) development
details of, 494–497
devices, 492–494
forms, described, 467–468
integrity controls, 508–509
mechanisms, 492–494
system, designing, 492–497
instances, described, 63, 64
instantiation, 63, 296
integrated application development tools, 69. *See also* tools
integrated development environments (IDEs)
inception phase and, 94
Rational Rose and, 70
Rational XDE Professional, 73
tools included with, 49
use cases and, 342, 343, 344
integration testing
described, 58–59, 534, 536–538
errors, 537–538
integrity, personal, 13
integrity controls
database, 509–510
described, 507
designing, 506–513
input, 508–509
output, 510–512
preventing fraud with, 512–513
interaction diagrams, 226, 312–314. *See also* SSDs (system sequence diagrams)
internal
outputs, 499–502
users, described, 88
International Business Machines. *See* IBM (International Business Machines)
Internet
architecture, simple, 381–382
-based enterprise-level systems, 378, 380–386
broadband access to, 10
described, 274
design discipline and, 274, 276, 281–283
indirection and, 368
stateless systems and, 378
Internet Inter-ORB Protocol. *See* IIOP (Internet Inter-ORB Protocol)
Internet Service Providers. *See* ISPs (Internet Service Providers)
interpersonal skills, 12–13
interviews
conducting, 141–142
follow-up after, 142
preparing for, 140–141
requirements discipline and, 139–142
intranets
described, 274
design discipline and, 274
integrity controls and, 507
inventory reports, 501
inverse keyword, 403
IPO (input, process, output) development, 554–556
IPSec (IP Security), 521
ISPs (Internet Service Providers), 22
issues logs, 115
iteration(s). *See also* iteration planning
described, 43, 52
disciplines and, 52–53, 292–357
high-risk activities and, 568
project management and, 85
schedules, 97–98
spiral model approach and, 43–44
UP disciplines and, 53–54
iteration planning. *See also* iteration
described, 565–566
domain classes and, 201
use cases and, 201
XP (Extreme Programming) and, 589–590

J

J2EE (Java 2 Enterprise Edition)
deployment discipline and, 549
design discipline and, 281
implementation and, 533
technology architecture plans and, 24
Jacobson, Ivar, 48, 50
JAD (joint application design)
described, 150

requirements discipline and, 138, 149–152
session leaders, 150–151
Java, 381, 385. *See also* J2EE (Sun Java 2 Enterprise Edition)
abstraction and, 577
attributes and, 194
class definitions and, 298–299
classification of, as an object-oriented language, 60
data access classes and, 421
Data Objects (JDO), 400
design discipline and, 277
design patterns and, 368
Development Kit (JDK), 603
forms and, 465
inception phase and, 87
patterns and, 376
Server Pages (JSK), 384
SDK (Software Development Kit), 61
Together tool and, 71
UP disciplines and, 54
use cases and, 342, 298–299
Javabeans, 603
JavaScript, 465, 381, 385
Jbuilder, 342
JDeveloper (Oracle), 549
JDK (Java Development Kit), 603
JDO (Java Data Objects), 400
job titles, 14–15
Johnson, Ralph, 368
joint application design. *See* JAD (joint application design)
JSP (Java Server Pages), 384

K
Kay, Alan, 447
key(s). *See also* identifiers (keys)
creation, automatic, 414
described, 408
foreign, 408–409, 411–413
invented, 414
primary, 408, 410, 413, 414
uniqueness of, 414
keypunch and verify technique, 508
knowledge
areas, project management and, 83–84
business, 11–12
interpersonal skills and, 12–13
upgrading, 14

L
label(s). *See also* objects
attributes, 62
methods, 62
labor costs, 110–111
LANs (local area networks). *See also* networks
components and, 604
databases and, 424–425, 430–431
described, 272
design discipline and, 272–274, 276, 278, 282, 285–286
integrity controls and, 507
life cycle (Unified Process). *See also* UP (Unified Process)
components and, 604–605
described, 38–39, 45–47, 52
disciplines and, 52–54
sequence of events in, 172
tracing, 172
lifelines, object, 228–229
links, described, 335. *See also* URLs (Uniform Resource Locators)
list boxes, 467
local area networks. *See* LANs (local area networks)
location
diagrams, 197–200
flexibility, 279
logical models, 134
logon statecharts, 361
LONG data type, 422
LONGRAW data type, 422
"look and feel," of Web sites, 470
Lotus 1-2-3, 448

M
Macintosh (Apple Computer), 448, 454–455, 465
mainframe applications, 22
maintainability, 279
maintenance releases, 541
many-to-many
associations, 405–406, 410, 411–412
relationships, 187–188
mathematical models, 133
maxtrix (CRUD)
described, 197–200
integrating models and, 247–248
requirements and, 212
MDA (Model-Driven Architecture), 594–598
memory, short-term, 457
menu(s)
hierarchy, 457–459
user-interface design and, 457–459
message(s)
described, 63
events, 238
indirection and, 368
polymorphism and, 67–68
metamodels
described, 578
model-driven architecture and, 597
method(s)
class-level, 306
defining, 312–314
dependency, 556
described, 61–63
domain classes and, 184
implementation testing and, 538
overloaded, 305
shared, 306
signatures, 304, 338
method logic
action-expressions and, 362–366
modeling, 360–366
methodologies
described, 47–55, 579
techniques and, relationship of, 50
Microsoft Access, 398, 408
Microsoft Active Directory, 284, 548
Microsoft ASP (Active Server Pages), 381, 384
Microsoft ASP.NET, 385
Microsoft Corporation, software developers hired by, 15
Microsoft FrontPage, 380
Microsoft IIS (Internet Information Server), 602
Microsoft .NET Framework, 381, 384–386
deployment discipline and, 548
described, 603–604
design discipline and, 281, 368
model-driven architecture and, 595
patterns and, 368, 376
reuse and, 61, 578
SOAP and, 603
technology architecture plans and, 24
Microsoft Office, 15
Microsoft Project, 100–106, 110–111
Microsoft SQL Server, 595
Microsoft Transaction Server, 602
Microsoft VBScript, 274, 277, 381, 385, 465
Microsoft Visio, 69–70
Microsoft Visual Basic, 277, 385, 577
class definitions and, 298–299
deployment discipline and, 548
forms and, 465
protection from variations and, 367
use cases and, 298–299, 319, 342
Microsoft Visual Basic .NET
class diagrams and, 194

classification of, as an object-oriented language, 60
shared methods and, 306
UP disciplines and, 54
use cases and, 306, 342
Microsoft Visual SourceSafe, 560
Microsoft Visual Studio, 342
Microsoft Visual Studio .NET
forms and, 465, 466
Rational XDE Professional, 70, 73
templates and, 466
Microsoft Windows
forms, designing, 464–467
inception phase and, 87
model-driven architecture and, 594
middleware
described, 281, 595
design discipline and, 281, 284–285
model-driven architecture and, 595
protocols and, 284–285
milestones
described, 104
inception phase and, 95
Microsoft Project and, 104
project success factors and, 81
MIS (management information systems), 9, 12, 13
mock-ups, described, 148
model(s). *See also* modeling
building multiple, 584
classification of, as artifacts, 55
described, 47–48, 133–135, 578
-driven architecture, 594–598
integrating, 246–248
list of, 48
meta-, 578, 597
purpose of, 131–133
requirements discipline and, 131–135
techniques and, relationship of, 50
types of, 133–134
modeling. *See also* models
activity, minimizing, 583
agile (AM), 581–586
described, 578
multicomputer architecture, 271–272
multilayer design
described, 296
use cases and, 319–324, 329–334
multimedia presentations, 504–505
multiplicity, 66
multitier architecture
described, 271
design discipline and, 270–272
multivalued attribute, 405

N
n-ary associations, 183
naturalness, use of the term, 61
navigation
described, 401
dialog design and, 469
visibility, 306–309
.NET Framework (Microsoft), 381, 384–386
deployment discipline and, 548
described, 603–604
design discipline and, 281, 368
model-driven architecture and, 595
patterns and, 368, 376
reuse and, 61, 578
SOAP and, 603
technology architecture plans and, 24
net present value. *See* NPV (net present value)
network(s). *See also* intranets; LANs (local area networks); WANs (wide area networks)
capacity, 285–286
components and, 601–602, 604
described, 272–273
design discipline and, 272–274, 283–286
diagrams, 104, 284
integration, 283–284
Nielsen, Jacob, 469
n-layer architectures, 377
nonfunctional requirements, 130–131
normalization, 415–220
Norway, 60
notify method, 375
Novell, 87
NPV (net present value), 112–113
n-tier architectures, 377
NUMBER data type, 422

O
object(s)
behavior, identifying, 237–246
described, 60, 61–63
frameworks, 598–599
identifiers, 401
implementation testing and, 538
interactions, 63–65
lifelines, 228–229
naturalness of, 61
problem domain, 63, 184
responsibility, 312–314
reuse, 61, 306
Object Definition Language. *See* ODL (Object Definition Language)
Object Management Group. *See* OMG (Object Management Group)
objectives
of the inception phase, 86
project success factors and, 81
of project teams, 45
ObjectStore, 398, 400
observer pattern, 374–375, 377
ODBC (Open Database Connectivity), 279, 281
ODBMSs (object database management systems)
associations and, 401, 403, 405
data types and, 423
ODL (Object Definition Language)
associations and, 403–405
class definitions, 401
described, 400
ODMG (Object Database Management Group), 400
office support systems, 10
Office (Microsoft), 15
OLTP (online transaction processing systems), 9
OMG (Object Management Group), 48, 595–597
one-to-many associations, 402, 403–405, 410, 411, 415
online transaction processing systems. *See* OLTP (online transaction processing systems)
OOA (object-oriented analysis)
described, 28, 60
naturalness of, 61
OOP (object-oriented programming)
described, 60
naturalness of, 61
reuse and, 61
Open Database Connectivity. *See* ODBC (Open Database Connectivity)
operational, making systems, 530–573
Oracle databases, 398, 422
ORB (object request broker)
described, 602
design discipline and, 281
middleware and, 281
SOAP and, 603
Order class, 64–65, 244–246
OrderItem class, 242–244
OrderTransaction class, 233–234, 237
organizational structure, 20–22
origin state, described, 238
output(s)
details, 497–498
integrity controls, 510–512
internal versus external, 499–502

system, designing, 497–506
types of, 499

P
package diagrams
described, 300, 339–342
notation, 341
pair programming, 588
parallel deployment, 562–563
parameter values, 537
partitioned database servers, 426–428
path(s)
concurrent, 241–242
described, 239
reviewing, 241–242
pattern(s)
adapter, 371–373
basic, 369–376
callback, 375
classification of, 271
class-level, 369, 271
described, 578
design, 366–376
importance of, 368–369
object-level, 369, 271
observer, 374–375, 377
singleton, 369–371
specifications, 369
payback periods, 113
PeopleSoft, 17
perfect technology assumption, 173
performance
requirements, 130
testing, 539
persistent
classes, 303, 401
objects, 66
Personal Home Page. *See* PHP (Personal Home Page)
PERT/CPM charts
described, 48, 101
network diagrams as, 104
phases
described, 40–42
phased deployment and, 563–564
PHP (Personal Home Page), 277, 381, 384
physical data store, 398
pie charts, 504
PIM (platform-independent model), 595–597
planning
activities, described, 40
project success factors and, 81
spiral model and, 43
XP (Extreme Programming) and, 587
PMI (Project Management Institute), 83
polymorphism
close message and, 67
described, 66–68
postconditions, 225, 235–236
PowerBuilder, 319, 367
preconditions, 224–225, 235–236
predecessor tasks
described, 100
inception phase, 100
predictive development, 154
presentations
formatting, 505–506
graphical, 504–505
multimedia, 504–505
primary keys
associations and, 410
described, 408
referential integrity and, 413
schema quality and, 413, 414
uniqueness of, 414
primitive data types, 422
privileged users, 516
problem domain, 63, 301
classes, 29, 421
data access classes and, 421
described, 56
requirements and, 56
problem solving
role of systems analysts in, 4–6
stages of, 5
systems, 6–10
procedure descriptions, 138–139
processes. *See also* business processes
described, 47, 51
identifying, 136–138
inception phase and, 94
requirements discipline and, 136–138
production
releases, 541
system, 546
versions, 541, 543
product(s)
backlogs, 591
owners, 591
programmer analysts, 14, 15
project(s). *See also* project management
adaptive approach to, 39
charters, 93
controls, 95, 114–115
creating new, 101
described, 80
leaders, 14
monitoring, 114–115
planning phase (SDLC), 40–42
predictive approach to, 39
scope, 96–97, 593
success factors for, 80–81, 82, 91
system development, 38
time management, 593
Project (Microsoft), 100–106, 110–111
project management. *See also* project managers
adaptive methodologies and, 593–594
described, 55, 59, 78–121
design discipline and, 267–270
inception phase, 95–113
as a integral part of the Unified Process, 85–86
knowledge areas, 83–84
lead engineer approach to, 83
project plans and, 114
role of, 82–83
UP life cycle and, 53–54
Project Management Institute. *See* PMI (Project Management Institute)
project managers. *See also* project management
cost/benefit analysis and, 110
role of, 14, 82–83
project team(s)
Agile Development and, 585
-based software development, 558–560
coordinating, 268
design discipline and, 268
JAD sessions and, 151
organization of, common principles of, 559–560
Scrum, 592
UP life cycle and, 45
protection from variations, principle of, 367, 368
protocols, 284–285
prototypes, 42–43, 333
discovery, 148
effective, characteristics of, 148
forms and, 474
proxy servers, 368
pseudostate
decision, 363
described, 237–238
statechart diagrams and, 237
PSM (platform-specific model), 595–597
public key encryption, 519. *See also* encryption
publisher, use of the term, 375

Q

quality
  assurance (QA) groups, 540
  verification of, 52
questionnaires
  distributing/collecting, 148–149
  requirements discipline and, 148–149
questions
  close-ended, 141, 149
  open-ended, 141, 149

R

radio (option) buttons, 467
Rational Rose, 69–70
Rational Software, 48, 50, 69–70
Rational XDE Professional, 73
RDBMSs (relational database management systems). *See also* relational databases
  described, 407
  object-relational interaction and, 420–423
read-only modes, 560
read/write mode, 560
realization(s)
  described, 301
  design discipline and, 292–357
  interaction diagrams and, 312–314
refactoring, 587
referential integrity
  constraints, 412
  described, 412
  enforcing, 412–413
registered users, 515–516
Registry (Windows), 602
relational databases. *See also* RDBMSs (relational database management systems)
  classes and, 598
  classification hierarchies and, 412
  data access layer and, 407–423
  data types and, 422–423
  described, 407
  designing, 409–413
  normalization, 415–220
relations, described, 407
relationship keyword, 403
release(s)
  described, 589
  small, 589
  versions, 541
reliability
  Internet protocols and, 283
  requirements, 130
replicated database servers, 425–426
report(s). *See also* documentation
  bar chart, 504
  control break, 501
  designing, 498–499
  detailed, 499
  drill-down technique and, 503
  electronic, 502–504
  exception, 499
  executive, 499
  formatting, 505–506
  inventory, 501
  pie chart, 504
  requirements discipline and, 138–139
  summary, 499, 503
  system interface design and, 498–499
repositories, 68–69, 560–561
requirements
  activities, list of, 127
  activity diagrams and, 144–148
  conducting interviews and, 139–142
  defining, 128, 212–214
  design discipline and, 262–264
  detailed, 126–129, 210–258
  developing user interface dialogs and, 128–129
  evaluating, with users, 129
  forms and, 138–139
  inception phase and, 89
  information gathering and, 56–57, 127–128, 135–153
  models and, 131–135
  object-oriented, 212–214
  overview of, 28–29, 55–57, 124–163
  prioritizing, 128
  procedure descriptions and, 138–139
  project management and, 85–113
  prototypes and, 148
  question themes, 136–138
  questionnaires and, 148–149
  reports and, 138–139
  resource, 104–106
  UP life cycle and, 53–54
  use case modeling and, 210–258
  validating, 153–156
resource(s)
  feasibility assessment and, 109
  requirements, developing, 104–106
response
  time, 539
  use of the term, 175
responsibilities, separation of, 308–309
reuse
  components and, 600–601
  described, 61, 578
  principle of, 578
risk
  adaptive approaches and, 594
  analysis, 106–107
  association of, with database design, 432
  descriptions, 107
  identifying, 106–113
  integrity controls and, 513
  iterations and, 44
  management, 106–107, 114–115, 594
  parallel deployment and, 563
  schedules and, 108
  spiral model approach and, 43
round-trip engineering
  described, 71
  tools, 69
routers, described, 273
row(s)
  described, 407
  referential integrity and, 413
  schema quality and, 413, 414
  uniqueness of, 414
ROWID data type, 422
RSA Security, 518
Rumbaugh, James, 48, 50

S

salaries, 110
scalability, 279
SCCS (source code control system), 560–561
scenarios, described, 220
schedules
  developing, 97–98, 100
  feasibility, determining, 108–109
  inception phase and, 95, 96, 97–98, 100
  managing/controlling, 114–115
  project success factors and, 81
schema
  described, 398
  partitioning, 427
  quality, evaluating, 413–420
  XML, 492
SCM (supply chain management), 20, 199–199
  application architecture plans and, 24, 25, 26
  design discipline and, 282
Scrum
  backlog, 593
  described, 590–593
  inception phase and, 95
  masters, 591–592
  organization, 591–592

philosophy, 591
practices, 592–593
project management and, 593
teams, 592
SDLC (software development life cycle)
adaptive approaches to, 39, 42–51
described, 37–47, 45–51
phases, 40–42
predictive approach to, 39–42
waterfall approach to, 40–42
second normal form (2NF), 415, 416–418
Secure Sockets Layer. *See* SSL (Secure Sockets Layer)
Secure HyperText Transfer Protocol. *See* HTTPS (Secure HyperText Transfer Protocol)
security. *See also* security controls
access control, 509, 516
authentication and, 516–517
data, 517–518
design discipline and, 266, 282
digital certificates and, 520–521
digital signatures and, 520–521
encryption and, 509, 518–521
requirements, 130
servers and, 282
system, 266
Web servers and, 282
security controls. *See also* security
for access to systems, 514–517
data security and, 517–518
described, 513, 507
designing, 513–524
sequence diagrams. *See also* SSDs (system sequence diagrams)
action-expressions and, 363–264
described, 315–334
dialog design and, 464
first-cut, 316–318, 324–329
guidelines for, 319
server(s)
databases and, 424–429
described, 277
federated, 428–429
inception phase, 87
partitioned, 426–428
replicated, 425–426
security and, 282
service-oriented architecture, 281, 533
shortcuts, enabling users to use, 455
Simple Object Access Protocol. *See* SOAP (Simple Object Access Protocol)
simplicity
importance of, 585, 587
XP (Extreme Programming) and, 587
SIMS (strategic information management system), 24, 25
Simula, 60
single-computer architecture
described, 270
design discipline and, 270–272
singleton pattern, 369–371
Sklar, Joel, 470
slack time (float), described, 104
Smalltalk, 60, 447–448
smart cards, 516–517
SOA (service-oriented architecture), 281, 533
SOAP (Simple Object Access Protocol), 265, 548
described, 603–604
design discipline and, 274
encoder/decoder, 603
implementation and, 533
model-driven architecture and, 595
software. *See also* software architecture
acquiring, 547–549
deployment discipline and, 547–549
engineers, 14
maintenance releases, 546
principles/practices, 576–579
system, 547–549
version upgrades, 546
software architecture
design discipline and, 264–265, 277–273, 281–283
Web-based, 281–283
source code
classification of, as an artifact, 55
collective ownership of, 587
control systems, 560–561
standards, 589
sources, described, 175
spin boxes, described, 467
spiral life cycle model approach, to the SDLC, 42–43
split windows, 102
sponsors
described, 89
examples of, 90
sprints
described, 592
project management and, 593
SQL (Structured Query Language)
data access classes and, 421–422
design discipline and, 279, 281
middleware and, 281
system interface design and, 497
use cases and, 303–304, 322, 344
SQL Server (Microsoft), 595
square brackets ([]), 231
SSDs (system sequence diagrams). *See also* sequence diagrams
classification of, as interaction diagrams, 226
controllers and, 314
described, 213, 314–335
developing, 231–236
dialog design and, 460–464
first-cut, 316–318, 324–329
guidelines for, 319
notation for, 226–231
object lifelines and, 228–229
system interface design and, 494–497
true/false conditions and, 230–231, 233
user-interface design and, 460–464
SSL (Secure Sockets Layer), 521
staffing
requirements, 110
plans, developing, 104–106
stakeholder(s)
analysis, 88, 90–91
described, 88, 89–91
examples of, 89–91
standards, user interface design, 453–457
Standish Group, 81
starting state, 534
start-start relationships, 100
state(s)
concept of, 378
described, 238
interactions, unexpected, 537
-less systems, 378
nested, 239–240
pseudo-, 237–238, 363
variables, 361
statechart(s)
described, 214, 237–246, 300
logon, 361
rules for, 241–242
system-level, 360–362
testing, 242–246
statements, designing, 498–499
stereotypes
described, 302
standard, 303
storyboards
best practices for, 473
described, 57–58, 460
dialog design and, 459–461
strategic information management system. *See* SIMS (strategic information management system)
strategic planning
information systems and, 16–26

organizational structure and, 20–22
role of systems analysts in, 15–17
strategic issues and, 19–20
structured walkthroughs, 155–158
Structured Query Language. *See* SQL (Structured Query Language)
stub(s)
described, 535
modules, 535–536
subclasses
described, 67
domain classes and, 189–190
subsystems
use of the term, 7
user-interface design and, 457–459
success factors, for projects, 80–81, 82, 91
successor tasks, described, 100
summary reports, 499, 503
superclasses, described, 67, 189–190
supersystem, use of the term, 7
supply chain management. *See* SCM (supply chain management)
support. *See also* CSS (customer support system)
phase (SDLC), 40–42
services, 264
swimlanes, described, 145
symbols
* (asterisk), 231–232
: (colon), 335
{} (curly braces), 193
«» (guillemets), 302
[] (square brackets), 231
symmetric key encryption, 518. *See also* encryption
synchronization bar, 145
system. *See also* system development; system interfaces; system requirements
architect, 14
behavior, modeling, 360–366
boundary, 8
capabilities, 92–93
controls, 172–173
design, described, 4
developers, systems analysts as, 27–30
-level statecharts, 360–362
liaison, 14
metaphor, 589
operators, training, 550–551
processes, use case/scenario view of, 214–226
scope, finalizing, 96–97
support analyst, 14
tests, described, 538
use of the term, 6
vision, 56, 91–93
system development
adaptive approaches to, 580–594
components and, 599–601
current trends in, 574–611
model-driven architecture and, 594–598
software principles/practices and, 576–579
system interfaces
ad hoc reports and, 497
identifying, 488–492
described, 442
designing, 266, 486–488
user interfaces versus, 442–443
system requirements. *See also* requirements
defining/managing, 52
described, 129–131, 212–213
project success factors and, 81
system sequence diagrams. *See* SSDs (system sequence diagrams)
systems analysis. *See also* system analysts
described, 4
requirements and, 56
systems analyst(s). *See also* systems analysis
business knowledge of, 11–12
described, 2–35
environment surrounding, 13–15
ERP and, 17
job titles, 14–15
people knowledge of, 12–13
as problem solvers, 4–6
required skills of, 10–13
role of, in strategic planning, 15–17
special projects and, 15–16
as system developers, 27–30
technical knowledge of, 10–11
systems consultant, 14
systems designer, 14
systemState variable, 361

T
table(s). *See also* databases
classification hierarchies and, 412
creating, 410
described, 407
referential integrity and, 413
schema quality and, 413
tasks
assigning resources to, 105
critical path and, 103
TCP/IP (Transmission Control Protocol/Internet Protocol), 274, 278
teams, project
Agile Development and, 585
-based software development, 558–560
coordinating, 268
design discipline and, 268
JAD sessions and, 151
organization of, common principles of, 559–560
Scrum, 592
UP life cycle and, 45
technical
knowledge, importance of, 10–11
requirements, 130, 133
support, 81
techniques
UP, 47–51
use of the term, 11
technology architecture plan, 17, 24
templates, 98, 368–369, 466. *See also* patterns
ternary associations, 182
test. *See also* testing
cases, 534
data, 534
discipline, 29
system, 546
testing. *See also* test
buddies, 539–540
described, 55, 58–59
discipline, 533–540
managing, 85, 553–565
planning, 553–565
requirements and, 154
role of, 553–554
spiral model and, 43
types of, 58–59
UP life cycle and, 53–54
XP (Extreme Programming) and, 588
text boxes, 467
third normal form (3NF), 415, 418–419
three-layer architecture, 279–281
throughput, 283, 539
time boxing, 581
timetables, for strategic plans, 25. *See also* schedules
TLS (Transport Layer Security), 521
Together (tool), 71
TogetherSoft, 71
tool(s)
inception phase and, 94–95
repositories, 68–69
techniques and, relationship of, 50
types of, 68–73
UP (Unified Process), 47–51
use of the term, 11, 49

top-down techniques
implementation discipline and, 556–557
WBS and, 98–99
TPS (transaction processing systems), 9
training
materials, 550
project iterations and, 568
users, 549–551
transaction(s). *See also* TPS (transaction processing systems)
controls, 509–510
logging, 509–510
Transaction Server (Microsoft), 602
transient classes, 400
transition(s)
described, 238
exit, identifying, 243
phase, 45, 46, 47
triggers, 362
Transport Layer Security. *See* TLS (Transport Layer Security)
triggers
described, 175
guard-conditions and, 238
transition, 362
true/false conditions, 230–231, 233, 239
turnaround documents, 498–499, 500
two-layer architecture, 382–384

U

ubiquitous computing, 576
UDDI (Universal Discovery, Description, and Integration), 387
UI (user interface) objects, 62
UML (Unified Modeling Language)
advent of, 50
Agile Development and, 584–585
data access layer and, 401
described, 48
design class symbols and, 302–304
dialog design and, 460–464
domain classes and, 184–185
Embarcadero Describe and, 72
implementation diagrams and, 379
model-driven architecture and, 596
multiplicity and, 66
patterns and, 371–373
Rational Rose and, 69–70
requirements and, 135, 212–214
Together tool and, 71
Visio and, 69–70
unary (recursive) associations, 182
unauthorized users, 515
Unified Process. *See* UP (Unified Process)
unique keys, 408
unit testing, 58–59, 534, 535–537
Universal Discovery, Description, and Integration. *See* UDDI (Universal Discovery, Description, and Integration)
UNIX, 265, 517–518, 594
UP (Unified Process). *See also* UP (Unified Process) life cycle
Agile Development and, 581
change requests and, 545–546
described, 28–29, 36–77, 50
design discipline and, 266–267, 292–357
inception phase and, 78–121
iterations and, 292–357
methodologies and, 47–55
models and, 47–48
project management and, 78–121, 593
requirements discipline and, 127, 129
techniques, 47–51
tools, 47–51
user-interface design and, 445–446
UP life cycle. *See also* UP (Unified Process)
described, 45–47, 52
development, components and, 604–605
disciplines and, 52–54
sequences of events in, 172
of systems, described, 38–39
tracing, 172
update controls, 510
UPS (United Parcel Service), 414
URLs (Uniform Resource Locators), 378, 384. *See also* links
usability
requirements, 130
testing, 58–59, 534, 538–539
use of the term, 445–446
use case(s). *See also* use case diagrams
actors and, 214–215
communication diagrams and, 334–337
controllers, 314, 317
CRUD matrix and, 197–200
described, 29, 52, 164–209
design discipline and, 265, 286, 292–357
detailed descriptions of, 220–226
detailed requirements and, 210–258
dialog design and, 457–459
-driven development, 52
events and, 166–177
identifying, 166–167
instances, 220
interaction diagrams and, 312–314
iteration planning and, 201
location diagrams and, 197–200
modeling, 210–258
multilayer design and, 319–324, 329–334
object responsibility and, 312–314
objected-oriented design and, 294–301
package diagrams and, 339–342
patterns and, 374–375
realization, 57, 265, 292–357
scope of, 225
sequence diagrams and, 315–334
system processes and, 214–226
XP (Extreme Programming) and, 587
use case diagrams
automation boundaries and, 215–216
described, 213
developing, 218–220
system processes and, 215–218
user(s). *See also* end users; user interfaces
acceptance testing, 58–59, 534, 539
-centered design, 445–446
goals, 166–167
interaction, architectures for, 382–386
interviews with, 139–142
JAD sessions and, 151
model, described, 445
privileged, 516
registered, 515–516
security controls and, 514–517
types of, 515–516
unauthorized, 515
user interface(s). *See also* user interface layer
classes, 598
conceptual parts of, 445
described, 442–443
design discipline and, 58, 266
dialogs, developing, 128–129
perceptual aspects of, 444–445
physical aspects of, 444
storyboards, 58
understanding, 444–445
user interface layer. *See also* user interfaces
affordance and, 453–454, 476
classifying inputs/outputs and, 442–452
conceptual parts of, 445
consistency and, 454–455
designing, 440–485
eight golden rules for, 454–457
ergonomics and, 446–448

error handling and, 456
form design and, 464–469
guidelines/standards, 453–457
locus of control and, 457
perceptual aspects of, 444–445
physical aspects of, 444
retrieval of actions and, 456–457
short-term memory load and, 457
system interfaces and, comparison of, 442–443
understanding, 444–445
user-centered design and, 445–446
visibility and, 453–454, 476
Web design and, 469–471

V
validation
Agile Development and, 585–586
requirements discipline and, 153–156
value limit control, 508
VARCHAR data type, 422
variations, protection from, 367, 368, 371
VBScript (Microsoft), 274, 277, 381, 385, 465
vendors
requirements discipline and, 152–153
researching, 152–153
view layer
classes, 333, 344, 367
described, 280, 320
developing, 320–322
virtual organizations, 274
virtual private networks. *See* VPNs (virtual private networks)
visibility, 304, 453–454, 476
VisiCalc, 448
Visio (Microsoft), 69–70
Visual Basic (Microsoft), 277, 385, 577
class definitions and, 298–299
deployment discipline and, 548
forms and, 465
protection from variations and, 367
use cases and, 298–299, 319, 342
Visual Basic .NET (Microsoft)
class diagrams and, 194
classification of, as an object-oriented language, 60
shared methods and, 306
UP disciplines and, 54
use cases and, 306, 342
visual modeling tools, 69. *See also* tools
Visual SourceSafe (Microsoft), 560
Visual Studio (Microsoft), 342
Visual Studio .NET (Microsoft)
forms and, 465, 466
Rational XDE Professional, 70, 73
templates and, 466
Vlissides, John, 368
VPNs (virtual private networks)
described, 274
design discipline and, 274, 284–285
VSAM files, 22

W
W3C (World Wide Web Consortium), 603
walkthrough(s)
control sheets, 158
execution of, 156–157
follow-up after, 157–158
preparation for, 156
structured, 155–158
WANs (wide area networks). *See also* networks
components and, 604
databases and, 424–425, 429–431
described, 272
design discipline and, 272–274, 276, 282–286
warehouses, data, 428–429
waterfall approach, to the SDLC, 40–42
WBS (work breakdown structure)
described, 98
developing, 96, 97–100, 114
entering, in Microsoft Project, 100–104
guidelines, 100
inception phase, 96, 97–100
resource requirements and 104
staffing plans and, 104
Web developers, 14
Web forms, 464–467. *See also* forms
Web servers, 548. *See also* servers
Web services
described, 386–387, 603
invoking, 387
Web site(s). *See also* World Wide Web
design guidelines, 469–471
strategic planning and, 22, 23, 24, 26
technology architecture plans and, 24
Webmasters, 14
whole-part hierarchy notation, 190–191, 192
wide area networks. *See* WANs (wide area networks)
Windows (Microsoft)
forms, designing, 464–467
inception phase and, 87
model-driven architecture and, 594
work breakdown structure. *See* WBS (work breakdown structure)
workflows
described, 144
requirements discipline and, 144–148
World Wide Web. *See also* Web sites
-based software architecture, 281–283
described, 274
design discipline and, 274

X
Xerox PARC (Palo Alto Research Center), 447–448
Xerox Star, 448
XML (eXtensible Markup Language), 387–388, 595
design discipline and, 274, 281, 282
implementation and, 533
middleware and, 281
schema, 492
SOAP and, 603, 604
system interface design and, 491–492
XP (Extreme Programming), 95, 586–590
core values, 586–587
practices, 587–588
project activities, 589–590
project management and, 593
X-Windows (UNIX), 464